Readings in African American Church Music and Worship

Volume 2

Readings in African American Church Music and Worship

Volume 2

Compiled and Edited by
James Abbington

GIA Publications, Inc.
Chicago

G-8462
Copyright © 2014
GIA Publications, Inc.
7404 S. Mason Ave., Chicago, IL 60638
www.giamusic.com
ISBN: 978-1-62277-100-4
Book layout and design: Martha Chlipala
Printed in the United States of America

Dedicated to
The Reverend Dr. Wyatt Tee Walker
and
The Reverend Dr. Jeremiah A. Wright Jr.

Table of Contents

III. Proclamation of the Word

IV. Hymnody: Sound and Sense

V. Perspectives on Praise and Worship

VI. Hip Hop and/in the Church

VII. Perspectives on Women and Gender

Foreword

John D. Witvliet

The volume you are holding is a vivid testimony to the dynamic, richly variegated practices of worship music in several African American traditions. One of the joys of learning about church life is that of discovering the stunning diversity of practices and dispositions that often emerge within a particular tradition and ethnic or cultural group. African American church music is no exception. There is a wide divergence of both practice and opinion about spirituals, gospel music, hip hop, and praise and worship; about pipe organs and drums, praise bands and choirs; dance, prayer, and prophetic proclamation. A volume of this size only begins to scratch the surface of this dynamism and variety!

Second, the volume you are holding is a vivid testimony to the value of examining this variety and dynamism from multiple, overlapping points of view. There is great value in understanding contemporary practices from a historical perspective, a socio- logical perspective, a theological perspective, and a practical perspective, and each of these from both an "insider's" and "outsider's" point of view. No one methodology or point of view captures the whole. A host of academic disciplines—theology, history, sociology, cultural anthropology, music theory, dance studies, cultural studies—have something to contribute.

Third, the volume you are holding is a vivid testimony to the value of both realist and idealist voices. Most of us as individuals tend to be either pessimists or optimists, and we tend to read people who agree with our point of view. True wisdom and poise comes from a blending of realist and idealist perspectives, of seeing both problems and possibilities. As you read these essays, there is so much to celebrate: the outpouring of creative, faithful music, in a stunning variety of forms by musicians in every generation. There is also much to pray about: barriers, dilemmas, temptations, and obstacles that come in many forms—spiritual, societal, financial. The value of reading multiple authors, side by side in a volume like this, is that we can test our own assumptions, and learn from people with a variety of temperaments and assessments.

Further, the volume you are holding is a vivid testimony to the value of articulating wisdom. These essays are not gathered to simply describe and analyze, but to articulate wisdom that can deepen ongoing practice of vital and faithful worship. They share a common desire to "discern what is best," which as Paul says to the Philippians happens best when "love overflows with knowledge and depth of insight" (Philippians 1:9). As you study these essays, look for the kinds of enduring wisdom they articulate, the kind of the wisdom that can shape worship in any time and place, in any tradition or ethnic or cultural group.

Importantly, the wisdom offered here is not only offered for African American communities, but for the wider church. Music that has emerged from African American contexts has been nourishing the church all over the world. Spirituals have become hallmarks of choral singing in Asia, South America, and Europe. Gospel choirs can be found in Korea, Kenya and Croatia. These essays call all of us, within and beyond African American communities, to give thanks for the many ways that the worship music of African American Christian traditions has blessed the wider church—its capacity to express pathos and celebration, its passionate commitment to singing songs of liberation and redemption, of eschatological longing and cruciform hope. These essays make it possible not only to glean songs and stylistic idioms, but also to grasp more fully in the internal dynamics and implicit wisdom inherent in these idioms which can shape practices in quite different contexts.

In the fall of 2012, it was our privilege at the Calvin Institute of Christian Worship to host a consultation of 20 leading teachers, scholars, pastors, musicians and community leaders who gathered to propose and review several of the selections included in this volume. What was so striking about that gathering was the sheer joy of learning (and laughing!) together as part of the body of Christ—the sheer joy of learning from people representing so many different denominations, temperaments, styles, methods and disciplines. It was a 2 Peter 3:18 experience, a "grow in the grace and knowledge of our Lord and Savior" kind of experience. May this volume by used by God's Spirit to further that kind of joy of discovery in individual readers, small groups who read this volume together, and courses of study in both congregation and academic institutions that use these materials to further common learning and growth.

Calvin Institute of Christian Worship
Calvin College and Calvin Theological Seminary
Grand Rapids, Michigan

Preface

James Abbington

More than a decade has passed since the first volume of *Readings in African American Church Music and Worship* was published. It succeeded in bringing into a single compilation the collective wisdom, research and writings of authors who provided invaluable insight on the topic through the end of the twentieth century. Since that time, public and academic interest in the music and worship in black churches has significantly increased, for which I am extremely grateful and delighted. For such readers, this second volume is intended to make available the most recent, twenty-first-century developments and trends in the worship and music of black Americans. A representative number of articles, essays, and chapters have been written in recent years by some of the most brilliant scholars, authors, and theologians of our time; their significant contributions to this second volume greatly broaden the field of study.

Both volumes may be used as independent anthologies and/or as supplements to the various topics covered therein. One aim of this collection is to present the music and worship of the black church from a variety of perspectives, research, and insight, through an interdisciplinary engagement that includes worship and liturgical studies, ethnomusicology, theology, homiletics, cultural anthropology, gender studies, and popular culture.

The list of contributors includes some of the finest emerging scholars in their fields, whose voices we will be hearing for years to come: Lisa M. Weaver, Kathleen S. Turner, Leo H. Davis Jr., Stephanie Y. Mitchem, Kenyatta R. Gilbert, Luke A. Powery, Michael Fox, Braxton D. Shelley, Teresa L. Reed, Birgitta J. Johnson, Melinda E. Weekes, Sandra L. Barnes, Tamura Lomax, Josef Sorett, Monica R. Miller, Christina Zanfagna, Daniel White Hodge, Alisha Jones, Gayle Wald, Melvin L. Butler, and Tammy L. Kernodle.

This volume is divided into seven sections or categories that I like to think of as "clusters" of knowledge on the topic:

> Section One: Worship and Liturgical Practices
> Section Two: Liturgical Theologies

Volume 2 is the culmination of a difficult five-year process of reading, researching, interviewing, discerning, and searching for the most valuable contributions to scholarship on the topic. Inevitably, there were choices to be made among sources that represented the same subjects with similar points of view. I must assume full responsibility, therefore, for errors of judgment in this edition.

This publication could never have come to fruition without the unfailing support and encouragement of Dr. John D. Witvliet and the Calvin Institute of Christian Worship for hosting a consultation at Calvin College in Grand Rapids in September of 2012; this event provided feedback and helped shape the final list of contents. The collective professional wisdom and innovative thinking present at this consultation significantly enlightened, revised and enhanced this volume. The attendees were:

Daniel Camacho, Calvin College, Grand Rapids
Mark Charles, Calvin Institute of Christian Worship, Grand Rapids
Todd Cioffi, Calvin College, Grand Rapids
Robert Darden, Baylor University, Waco (Texas)
Betty Grit, Calvin Institute of Christian Worship, Grand Rapids
Birgitta Johnson, University of South Carolina School of Music, Columbia
Kimberleigh Jordan, The Riverside Church of New York City
Michelle Loyd-Paige, Calvin College, Grand Rapids
Andrew McCoy, Hope College, Holland (Michigan)
Mwenda Ntarangwi, International Association for the Promotion of
    Christian Higher Education, Grand Rapids
Emmett Price, Northeastern University, Boston
Charsie Sawyer, Calvin College, Grand Rapids
Kathy Smith, Calvin Institute of Christian Worship, Grand Rapids
Frank Thomas, Christian Theological Seminary, Indianapolis
Kristen Verhulst, Calvin Institute of Christian Worship, Grand Rapids
Ralph Watkins, Columbia Theological Seminary, Decatur (Georgia)
Lisa Weaver, Catholic University of America, Washington (DC)
John D. Witvliet, Calvin Institute of Christian Worship, Grand Rapids

My deepest appreciation extends to all the contributors, who answered countless queries, returned numerous calls and emails, and willingly reviewed many drafts of their essays; and Dr. Pamela Green, my research and administrative assistant, without whom this task would have been much greater and almost impossible.

I should also like to express my indebtedness to my amazing and supportive colleagues at GIA Publications, particularly Alec Harris, President of GIA Publications, Inc.; Michael Boschert, Permissions Editor, who provided editorial support and secured all necessary licensing; and Martha Chlipala, Graphic Designer, responsible for the layout and cover design. I am grateful for the permission granted by the authors, publishers, and copyright holders who understood the value of having their articles included with other contributors of note to this volume.

There are many whose telephone calls, e-mails, texts and constant thoughts, prayers, and encouragement I must acknowledge with deep gratitude and affection: my mother, Daisy Ann Abbington, whose love and prayers have sustained me from birth; Jan Love, Dean of the Candler School of Theology; my Emory University colleagues; Dr. Uzee Brown Jr., Chair of the Department of Music and Professor of Voice at Morehouse College; The Reverend Dr. Ralph Douglas West, Pastor and Founder of The Church Without Walls in Houston; the wonderful members of my church, Friendship Baptist Church, Atlanta; my dear protégé and colleague, Nathaniel Gumbs, Director of Music and Arts at Friendship Missionary Baptist Church in Charlotte, North Carolina; and so many others that space will not permit me to list.

With great love, fondness, respect, admiration and gratitude, I dedicate this volume to two of the giants in the field of black sacred music: The Reverend Dr. Wyatt Tee Walker, Pastor Emeritus of the Canaan Baptist Church of Christ in Harlem, and The Reverend Dr. Jeremiah A. Wright Jr., Pastor Emeritus of the Trinity United Church of Christ in Chicago. Your inspiration, encouragement and support have helped to shape who I am today!

Foreword to Volume One

James Abbington

As a student at Morehouse College in Atlanta between the years 1980 and 1983, I was privileged to take two courses—Readings in Music History and Introduction to Church Music—with my teacher, mentor, and musical idol, the late Dr. Wendell P. Whalum. I was so fascinated and captivated by his ability to accurately recall sources right off the top of his head. He could tell you the title of the book, author, chapter, place of publication, publisher, and year it was published. It was in that course that I was introduced to two books that have influenced my musical studies until this very day as a professor of Western Music History, Introduction to Church Music, and African American Music History.

The first book was *Source Readings in Music History*, compiled and edited by Oliver Strunk. This compilation made available for the first time in its history a representative selection from all of the great writings on music from the times of ancient Greece through the Romantic era. The reader can acquire a comprehensive knowledge of the history of musical thought and of the changing ideas and interpretations of music throughout the ages.

It was in this single work that I read the philosophical theories of Plato and Aristotle that embody the Greek view of music, the writings of the Church Fathers from Clement of Alexandria to St. Augustine, the elaborate theories of the medieval scholars, the first stirrings of modern concepts among Renaissance musicians, and the psychological attitudes of the Baroque writers. The eighteenth and nineteenth centuries are represented by significant selections from Jean Paul, E. T. A. Hoffman, Weber, Schumann, Berlioz, Liszt, and Wagner. This book opened up a whole world of musical insight and permitted me to discover the intellectual and aesthetic foundations of western musical development.

The second book was entitled *Readings in Black American Music*, edited by Eileen Southern. She is also the author of *The Music of Black Americans*, now in its third edition, published by W. W. Norton & Company (New York). Eileen Southern is not only one of the finest musicologists to be found anywhere in the world (who happens to be African American), but she has consistently pioneered the most critical and scholarly research in African American music. Her years at Harvard University were fruitful, productive, and bountiful. There she founded and edited the journal, *The Black Perspective in Music,* from 1973–1990.

The purpose of her collection was to make available to persons interested in the history of Black Americans a representative number of authentic, contemporary documents illustrating that history from the seventeenth century to the present time. The main criterion used in selecting the readings was their relevance to the history of music, and although the readings follow in chronological order, they are grouped under topics that derive from the history. To my knowledge, *Readings in Black American Music* represents the first publication of a documentary history of African American music that not only covers the full three and a half centuries of the sojourn of African Americans, but their African heritage as well.

It was in this volume that I read the statements of Black music makers to the accounts of eyewitnesses to musical events, and to the writings of persons deeply involved with the music of Black folk in one way or another. Thus, I was acquainted with the writings of Frederick Douglass, W. E. B. Du Bois, Richard Allen, Daniel A. Payne, William C. Handy, Will Marion Cook, "Dizzy" Gillespie, Hall Johnson, John W. Work, Mahalia Jackson, William Grant Still, and T. J. Anderson, to name a few.

I recall in the Introduction to Church Music class Dr. Whalum's frustration and impatience with not having a source that contained significant writings about music in the African American church. He would place articles on reserve in the library from his personal collection and assign readings from journals, books, and periodicals to complement the textbook. What a journey we encountered!

Several years ago, I was privileged to meet a lifelong friend and colleague of Dr. Whalum's, Professor Evelyn Davidson White, a retired professor of music and director of the Howard University Choir in Washington, DC. She told me the story of her book, *Choral Music by Afro-American Composers: A Selected, Annotated Bibliography*, published by The Scarecrow Press (Metuchen, NJ). An assignment to a class at Catholic University in Washington, DC yielded insufficient sources for her students. A nun replied to a correction on her assignment, "Professor White, how would I know that Blacks did not write some of these spirituals?" She could not refer her to a source, and that question became the impetus to her book.

Much like Professor White, I have discovered that I cannot refer students, scholars, and colleagues to a source that appropriately covers the topic of music and worship in the African American church without sending them on the same journey that I encountered at Morehouse.

I have compiled chapters, essays, articles, and unpublished papers on music and worship in the African American church during the twentieth century by pastors, scholars, theologians, historians, ethnomusicologists, organists, professors, and conductors. I feel that their writings represent some of the greatest writings, musical comment and discourse, histories, perspectives, and concepts on the subjects. I have not sought to give this book a spurious unity by imposing upon it a particular point of view. At the same time, the book has of itself a natural unity and continuity of another sort. I have divided the readings into seven categories: (1) Historical Perspectives; (2) Surveys of Hymnals and Hymnody; (3) Liturgical Hymnody; (4) Worship; (5) Composers; (6) The Organ; and (7) Contemporary Perspectives, with a selected bibliography.

Of the items included in this volume, only eight essays (as notated in the Acknowledgments) have not been previously published. In determining what and how to annotate, I have simply given the title of the article, the author's name, and the book or journal in which it appeared. The writings speak for themselves!

When I shared my vision and desire with Edward J. Harris, President, and Robert J. Batastini, Vice President and Senior Editor of GIA Publications in Chicago, they were enthusiastic, supportive, and offered me a contract. I am eternally grateful and indebted to GIA for their commitment to music in the African American church. In 1987, GIA published *Lead Me, Guide Me: An African American Catholic Hymnal*, and in 2001, they published the *African American Heritage Hymnal*, the first non-denominational African American Protestant hymnal. The African American Church Music Series by GIA is another component of that commitment to the music of the African American church worship experience by African American composers.

The debt that I have incurred from the giant contributors to this volume is beyond verbal and monetary gratitude. A biographical statement for each contributor is provided in the back of this book. I am most appreciative of the quiet, meticulous competence of Vicki Krstansky, who typeset the entire book, and for my editor, Linda Vickers, with her painstaking efficiency and patience, Denise Wheatley, editorial assistant, Robert Sacha, graphic designer, Yolanda Durán, graphic designer for the cover illustration, and the entire GIA family for making this book a reality.

There are those whose telephone calls, e-mails, prayers, and constant encouragement I must acknowledge with deep gratitude and affection: Daisy Ann Barlow, my mother; Wilbur J. Abbington, Sr., my father; Walter Barlow, my stepfather; William and Christine Anderson, my godparents; Pam and Ted Jones, my adopted sister and brother; Reverend Dwight M. Jackson, Pastor of the Amity Baptist Church; my godsent brother and eternal friend; Dr. Calvin B. Grimes, my former professor and Dean of the Division of Humanities and Social Sciences at Morehouse College; Dr. Gale Isaacs and Dr. Charles Tita, my colleagues at Shaw University; Mrs. Mildred Hooker, my secretary; Antwan Lofton, my student assistant and choir business manager; my students at Shaw University, and so many that space will not permit me to list.

Section One

Worship and Liturgical Practices

1
Twenty-One Questions Revisited

Valerie Bridgeman Davis

In the first *Africana Worship* volume, I listed twenty-one questions I believe worship leaders and planners might consider when preparing liturgy. Since the volume appeared, we have received feedback that the questions were helpful and used over and over by groups discussing and planning worship. I first drafted the list during a writing consultation as we tried to figure out what we meant by "Africana worship." It seemed to me that there were compelling concerns that needed to be addressed, regardless of the worship setting.

1. Is the worship biblically resonated?
2. Is the worship theologically sound?
3. Is it ritually profound?
4. Is worship invitational?
5. Is this worship contextually relevant? Does worship reflect the culture(s), lands, and peoples gathered for worship?
6. Does the worship open an aperture to the presence of God? Have we created space for God to work and speak and encounter us, and us God?
7. Is the worship participatory? Or, are there simply "talking heads" up front that we may "tune out"?
8. Does worship pull people from the outer edges into the center?
9. Does worship incorporate gifts from the larger church (worldwide) into our local context?
10. Does this worship challenge our local context to be a witness of God through the holy, catholic (universal) church? Does the worship "prophesy" a more inclusive reality than the one the congregation currently knows?
11. Did we leave appropriate space for stillness and silence?
12. Does worship incarnate God in Christ, begging participants to be reconciled to God?

13. Do the words of the liturgy bog down and drown out the rhythm and mystery of the liturgy? Or, are litanies and prayers easy to enter, with refrains and rhythms that hold the central message in place? Is there a "heartbeat" (rhythm) worshipers can carry beyond this "thin line" moment?

14. Is worship hermetically sealed? Does it have one way in and one way out, and is it over when it's over, not carrying worshipers into the world to continue to praise, worship, repent, grow, and work?

15. Is worship permeable? Are there several entry points into divine mystery and is it portable into the rest of the worshiper's life?

16. Is worship democratic? Does it allow voices from the center and the margin to commingle in such a way that there is no clear dominant voice? Have we invited the communion of saints from the beginning of the church's existence to the present day to speak? Do we have a word from the Old Testament, the New Testament, and the Now Testament? Do we believe God continues to speak?

17. Does the music we sing, pray, and dance reflect the reality of more than a "village" God? Are we creating theology by our worship that says God is truly the God of all universes, places, and times?

18. Did we use technology wisely and economically? Did we allow the "bells and whistles" to get in the way of the simplicity of grace?

19. Is worship visionary and prophetic? Does this worship service point us to God of the whole creation, God who loves diversity in color and sunsets, in temperature and foliage? In mountains and valleys, in rushing waterfall and gentle, flowing brooks?

20. Is worship sensory-rich? Does worship use art in ways that God is danced back into the consciousness of people? Do we sing God into the room? Do we vision God into the room with banners and clips? Do we act God into the room?

21. Does this worship return us to the miracle of hearing on the day of Pentecost, and to the great celebration around the throne of God when the reign of God is fully and completely realized and we out of every tongue, language, tribe, nation, gender, and age, lift our voices in awesome wonder of God who is majestic, powerful, holy, generous, friend, glorious, wonderful, and worthy of all this worship?

Revisiting these questions, I now see that they can be grouped into some general categories, that they might be reduced to five or expanded to fifty, depending on how in-depth one wants to be. The goal, of course, is to get congregations and worship planners to think deeply, to consider seriously, and to pray about the "pause" that gathered worship represents.

In this essay, I do not list the questions one by one, but rather reconsider the concerns I intended to address in them. Those concerns, as I see them now, include biblical content in worship, theological integrity, pastoral concerns, prophetic energy, authenticity, ecumenism, intercessory passion, spiritual openness, and ritual richness.

The first question (*Is the worship biblically resonated?*) did not mean—and still does not mean—whether the litany or call uses actual Scripture. Instead, I tried to impress upon writers (and, by extension, planners) that the biblical story and words are located in the bones of Bible-believing people. As such, phrases like "God of widows and orphans" or "Seeking God" sound like the Bible to people. That is, people recognize the God these words reflect, and remember they have heard them somewhere. Having "biblically resonating" words allows the writer or planner to also use words native to the context in which they live, so people will recognize the extra-canonical words of popular culture married to biblical phrases. The dialogue between the biblical world and the worshipers' world provides the space for theological inquiry.

Theological integrity means worship pushes worshipers to go beyond merely mouthing liturgical words; the worship design drives people to consider issues of justice: Are we creating theology that says God is truly God of all universes, places, and times (#17; also #2, #5)? Does worship reflect the God of Pentecost and a vision of a world reconciled to God? This concern, in fact, permeated all the questions in my mind.

When people gather, they come weary, battered, hopeful, needy, and in so many other human states of being. Worship must discern, in its shape, how to meet the pastoral needs of those gathered, while provoking worshipers beyond themselves. Meditations, prayers, and litanies, for example, express very real human conditions, authentically and unapologetically describing pain, hopelessness, anger, and sadness while declaring God's good news. Pastoral concerns acknowledge that worshipers gather to be "leaning posts" for one another, in black church vernacular. When people receive a benediction and leave the confines of the worship space, they should believe that those who led them cared deeply about their lives and that they wanted for them what God wants.

Whatever pastoral means, it does not mean that people are not challenged to "heal the world." Worship may be shaped to reflect concerns for all creation, for people in other lands, and for the whole church. These concerns are prophetic. Worship should call people with power to accountability; comfort those who are oppressed; and empower oppressed people to revolutionize their own lives, with the help of God. In order to get everyone present to participate in the prophetic ministry of the church, worship, of necessity, must be participatory. Participation in worship allows people to practice in the gathered community that which is the people's worship in the world. So, I asked whether worship was hermetically sealed, "over when it's over, not carrying worshipers into the world to continue to praise, worship, repent, grow, and work" (#14).

For me, ecumenism is one dimension of prophetic energy. Jesus prayed that his disciples would live in unity. A glance around the globe shows us a fractured church. One way that worship can help reflect our prayer for unity as we work for it is to sing and pray as we "incorporate gifts from the larger church (worldwide) into our local context" (#9), and "challenge our local context to be a witness of God through the holy, catholic (universal) church. . . [and] 'prophesy' a more inclusive reality than the one the congregation currently knows" (#10). Churches still may be mono-cultural, but our singing, our litanies, etc., may borrow from the larger church as testimony to our relationship and our commitment to unity and solidarity. Ecumenism and prophetic witness go hand in hand.

Intercessory passion is another dimension of ecumenism and prophetic witness. We pray with deep concern and fervor for the church, the world, and all creation when we believe God is at work. Prayer is the church's primary work, even when those prayers are with our feet and hands. The church is Christ's intercessory presence in the world. On some level, each question begs worshipers to pray.

The bulk of the questions reflect my concern for the "twins," *spiritual openness* and *ritual richness*, because I believe all the aforementioned issues can find their voice when these two ideas are addressed. These concerns demand: that simplicity not get drowned in bells and whistles; that worship is sensory-rich; that worship is profound, rather than mundane or profane; that worship must "open an aperture to the presence of God" where we create "space for God to work and speak and encounter us, and us God" (#6).

When we consider these categories, worship then becomes authentic and fully embodied by a local congregation. As such, local congregations will find their prophetic voice, own their theology contextualized by the realities of the lives they lead and the lives they touch, and be aware of their relationship with the global church. Whether the questions contract or expand for planners, when taken seriously, they lead us into an abiding relationship with God who so loves the world. Liturgies that prayerfully lead us to the world-loving God are sound—biblically, theologically, pastorally, and prophetically.

2

Lectio Divina:
A Transforming Engagement
with Sacred Scripture

Lisa M. Weaver

From its nascent beginning, the church has understood that the sacred scripture is central to its life and Christian faith. It is the record of God's salvific work in human history. It is the record of the earthly life and ministry of Jesus Christ. It is the record of the birth, development, and ministry of the early church and the apostles. It contains the prayers and hymns of the people of faith, and the eschatological vision of their future. As such, its placement as a centrally constitutive element in liturgical celebrations in the history of Christian liturgy is no surprise. The church has understood the power of sacred scripture to evoke response, effect conversion, and transform the lives of those who read it and hear it. However, and regrettably, while churches, both Catholic and Protestant, seek, in the words of Charles Wesley, "to serve this present age," in either continuing the work of implementing the reforms of Vatican II or changing the church's "worship format," it does so to the chagrin of many who contend that "the church looks too much like the world" and that "the church is conforming to the world rather than the world conforming to the church." One arena in which these changes are being experienced concerns our engagement with the sacred scripture.

It is indeed possible to go to church on a Sunday morning and the only sacred scripture we might hear is the one on which the sermon is based (that is, if the sermon is based on sacred scripture at all). And while the reading and proclamation of sacred scripture within the liturgy is the corporate setting in which Christians encounter and experience God, it is not the only setting. The ancient tradition of *lectio divina* provides us with an opportunity to encounter and experience God through the sacred scripture.

However, lectio divina is more than a vehicle through which we encounter and experience God. Different from the study of sacred scripture in familiar formats of either individual or group Bible study or more formal tasks of biblical exegesis, I contend that the act of lectio divina leads to our conversion and our transformation more into the image and likeness of Christ, and I am convinced it must be a lifelong practice of the Christian life.

This chapter examines the meaning, practice, and effects of lectio divina. In the first section the meaning of lectio divina is examined along with approaches and methods in the reading of sacred scripture. The second section examines the practice of lectio divina as a medium of conversion and transformation and discusses some obstacles that can impede the process. The final section offers a pedagogical method for lectio divina and some effects and eschatological implications of its practice.

Lectio Divina: Background, Approaches, and Methods

Lectio divina, or divine reading, is also known as *lectio sacra,* holy reading. Deriving from the monastic tradition, lectio divina traditionally has a four-part movement of *lectio* (reading), *meditatio* (meditation), *oratio* (prayer), and *contemplatio* (contemplation). It is a spiritual practice that is attested to as early as the third century. For both Jerome and Benedict, lectio divina meant the actual text itself, which was prayerfully read. It was simply a lesson or passage from sacred scripture. Later, it most often referred to the page itself, so the text was viewed in an objective manner: "Scripture was studied for its own sake."[1] We see below how this shift has enormous consequences for not only the practice of lectio divina but also for its effects on the person practicing it.

The most significant exposition of lectio divina is found in the Rule of St. Benedict, in which Benedict writes that the during the course of a day, a monk should have specific periods of time for work and specific periods of time for prayerful reading. In lectio a person reads the text aloud (the first movement). In contrast to how we read today, silently and with our eyes, the monastic practice of lectio demands more of our senses and of ourselves, for we read the text with the eyes, speak the words of the text with the mouth, then listen to the text with the ears. Reading is not simply an activity; it is a prayer experience. Similarly, meditatio is to consider, to reflect, to think, but not simply as a cognitive activity; rather, as a prayer experience.

In meditatio (the second movement), a person speaks the words of the text aloud and while so doing, meditates (reflects) on their meaning. It is often described as "rumination" (from the Latin *ruminatio,* a chewing the cud, based on the word *rumina).* In meditatio, a person "chews over" the text. A person is ruminating to the end of answering the questions, "What is the text saying to me in this moment? What is God saying to me through this text?" Third, meditatio leads to oratio (prayer), the reader's response to what is heard and experienced. The language of the prayer is informed by the words read and meditated upon in lectio and meditatio and what the person "hears" from God through the text. This leads to the fourth and final movement, contemplatio (contemplation), which is communion with God. Lectio is a way of reading that reorients a person's view of God, others, self, and the world. It is oriented towards communion with God, wisdom, and appreciation, and its goal is heaven. In the monastic context, the accent during lectio is on meditatio and oratio (meditation and prayer).

However, during the Middle Ages the meaning of the term lectio shifted to refer more to the act of reading itself, specifically reading the sacred scripture. It focused on grammatical analyses of texts, which led to a literal interpretation of the text. Lectio in this period was informative, rather than formative. It was oriented towards knowledge and science.[2] So, in contrast to the monastic period's accent on meditatio and oratio, during the scholastic period the accent on the activity is placed on *quaestio* and *disputatio*, questioning and disputation. However, in spite of the different places of accentuation, in both the monastic and scholastic periods, lectio divina is understood as a holy, sacred activity. However, it is the monastic approach to lectio divina that lends itself to ongoing conversion and transformation of the Christian life.[3]

One Approach and One Perspective: Abbot Smaragdus and Walter Wink

In his ninth-century commentary on the Rule of St. Benedict, Smaragdus of Saint-Mihiel, monk of Castellio,[4] writes about those who practice lectio divina. He writes:

> The knowledge of sacred reading provides those who cultivate it with keenness of perception, increases their understanding, shakes off sluggishness, does away with idleness, shapes their life, corrects their behavior, causes wholesome groaning and produces tears from a heart pierced by compunction; it bestows eloquence in speaking and promises eternal rewards to those who toil; it increases spiritual riches, curbs vain speech and vanities, and enkindles the desire for Christ and our heavenly homeland. It is always associated with prayer, and must always be joined to prayer. For prayer cleanses us, while reading instructs us. And therefore he who wishes to be always with God must frequently pray and frequently read. For when we pray, we speak with God; but when we read, God speaks with us. All progress, then, proceeds from reading, prayer and meditation. What we do not know we learn by reading; what we have learned we retain by meditations; and by prayer we reach the fulfillment of what we have retained. Therefore the reading of the sacred scriptures confers a twofold gift: it instructs the mind's understanding, and it brings the one who is withdrawn from the world's vanities to the love of God.[5]

Smaragdus provides a rich description of the experience and benefits of lectio divina. Some translations render the word "knowledge" in the first sentence as "experience." Using the word experience, it is noteworthy that Smaragdus writes that it is the "experience" of lectio divina, not the exercise of it, that confers certain benefits.[6] There is a distinction between an experience versus an exercise, between engaging something within the realm of interiority versus simply rotely and routinely performing a sequence of steps or tasks. What Smaragdus' comment underscores is that the performance of lectio, absent the presence of God and posture of those who attend it being inclined toward or attentive to God, is not the same as other kinds of experience. Walter Wink would agree that antiseptic, disengaged methods are ineffective.

In 1973, biblical scholar Walter Wink asserted that biblical criticism did not offer a way of engaging the sacred scripture that was transformative. He remarked that biblical criticism was bankrupt because at that time it was incapable of achieving its goal: to interpret the scripture in a way "that the past becomes alive and illumines our present with new possibilities for personal and social transformation."[7] Speaking specifically of the New Testament, he writes that "The writers of the New Testament bore witness to events which had led them to faith. They wrote 'from faith to faith,' to evoke or augment faith in their readers."[8] Wink's point is that historical-critical methodology requires that one remain interiorly disconnected from the text in order to engage and work with the text in an objective way. Wink asserts that the scholar is required to remove him/ herself from the text. What Wink says is the problem is that the subject and the object became distanced rather than in communion with one another.

Wink's point is well taken. The historical-critical methodology was at odds with its stated goal. Wink's critique does not reveal a flaw in the methodology; his critique more reveals his disappointment in historical-critical methodology's failure to produce its goal of interpreting scriptures in a way that is personally and socially transformative. The distance between the subject and the text that the historical-critical method requires is necessary for good biblical exegesis, and this methodology has served the field well. However, for the goal that Wink desired, his point needs to be furthered in this way: the subject does not need to be in communion with the sacred scripture proper; the subject needs to be in communion with God, and the text (the sacred scripture) is the mediator of that communion.

The Power of the Sacred Scripture: The Medium of Transformation

The transcendent, personal, and transformative power of the gospel is evidenced in the liturgical rites of the Christian tradition. In some Christian traditions, during the liturgy the gospel book is brought into the midst of the people and the people turn towards it. In some other Christian traditions, while the book is not brought in the midst of the people, the people do stand for the reading of the gospel. The performance of these rites evidences the way the Good News of God in Christ Jesus has come to humanity and has the power to change humanity's posture and turn it to God. Thus, in the context of the liturgy in many Christian traditions, the centrality and power of the gospel is clear. In his book *Shaped by the Word: The Power of Scripture in Spiritual Transformation*,

M. Robert Mulholland asserts that that same centrality and power is true of the entire corpus of sacred scripture and not just the gospel. He writes, ". . . scripture stands close to the center of this whole process of being conformed to the image of Christ. . . the scripture is one of the primary channels through which God encounters us in our grasping, controlling, manipulative mode of existence. The scripture is one of the focal means whereby God awakens us to the dynamics and possibilities of a new way of being."[9] That is because God has inspirited the text with God's own Spirit and encounters individuals through God's own text. Origen of Alexandria, who is the first to provide "a detailed Christian approach to reading sacred texts,"[10] testifies to this. In his book *On First Principles* (Book IV, chapter I, section 1) he attests to the inspiration of scripture. He writes that "it seems necessary first of all to show that the scriptures themselves are divine, that is, are inspired by the Spirit of God."[11]

In *Shaped by the Word*, Mulholland presents a method of reading sacred scripture as praxis for spiritual formation. He suggests that there are three stages to the reading of sacred scripture (spiritual reading, as he calls it): approach, encounter, and response.[12] I would like to refer back to the subtitle of Mulholland's book, *The Power of Scripture in Spiritual Formation*, and suggest that all the elements of his model do not serve the act of spiritual reading as much as they are part of the process of spiritual formation. Both lectio divina and Mulholland's spiritual reading create the context for the amendment of a person's life, for the opportunity for a person to be more conformed to the image of Christ. However, it should be noted that Mulholland's spiritual reading is a process for spiritual formation that can, in turn, lead to prayer, while lectio divina is itself prayer, specifically, praying the sacred scriptures. It is Mulholland's first stage, approach, that illumines our understanding of lectio divina. I hold that the first element, approach, is a method of lectio divina and that encounter and response are the results of a person's reading and a course of action that a person chooses as a result of encounter, respectively. Thus, it is helpful for us to continue with an examination of Mulholland's notion of approach as a method of lectio divina.

For Mulholland, "approach" involves two constitutive elements: attitudes and structures. Mulholland describes structures as "the framework within which our spiritual reading takes place"[13] and suggests that there are two essential structures for spiritual reading, spiritual discipline and practical guidelines. While structures include (1) coming to the reading with the purpose of knowing the entire will of God; and (2) engaging the entire process with prayer, they largely concern elements of praxis like making sure the time is most optimal (i.e., no distractions, environmentally conducive for our concentration and engagement). The element of attitude more concerns our interior disposition and the activities that impact transformation and as such will be our focus for consideration.

According to Mulholland, approach concerns "the posture of being we bring to the reading of scripture" and includes "our views of self, the Bible, and Christian existence, as well as the formational and relational dynamics we employ in our reading."[14] Approach is a matter of interiority. Approach involves (1) our attitudes about God (reverence, awe, etc.); (2) our attitudes about the process (how we come, whether with expectancy, joy, drudgery, etc.); and (3) our perspective and beliefs about the process. Mulholland asserts that a person's view of self involves having an understanding of self as integrally connected to God as an object of God's creation and as the audience of God's Word. We must understand God as not only being involved in the entire scope of salvation history, but also involved in our personal history. Mulholland describes this as "being a word spoken forth by God. . . that God is seeking to conform to the image of Christ through the nurture of God's living word. We must come to the scripture, therefore, as a word of God seeking to be addressed by the Word of God."[15] We must view the sacred scripture as the lens through which our view of the world is ordered.

Sacred scripture provides an alternate world that Mulholland describes as iconographic. It provides us with a lens through which to view an alternative reality, a reality radically different from the one that we currently occupy which clarifies and enhances what God has intended us to be.[16] Our view of Christian existence changes in that the sacred scripture involves an understanding that the profound value system and values communicated in it far exceed those in the world and that its order is so profound that it reorders our existence and breathes life into death.[17] Finally, Mulholland offers that our approach to sacred scripture can set us up for being transformed by the experience and for relational involvement with God.[18] The two are not mutually exclusive. If we are actively engaged in our relationship with God, transformation is an inevitable consequence of that relationship.

Approach leads to and sets us up for encounter with God. However, as was stated earlier, encounter and response are the results of our reading and a course of action we choose as a result of our encounter with God. Lectio divina is prayer, and as an ongoing method of conversion, it requires that we continue to approach God in the ways outlined by Mulholland, with each encounter more deeply pulling us into the mystery of God and more deeply transforming us into the image and likeness of Christ. However, being pulled more deeply into the mystery of divine Being and the transforming of ourselves that occurs *as a result of* our encounter requires our volitional response to that graced, privileged moment of encounter we have with God. And our response is predicated on what Bernard Lonergan calls an "insight."

Lectio Divina and the Process of Conversion

Lonergan and Insight: The Turning Point of Conversion

Conversion as a process of transformation is central to Canadian-born theologian and philosopher Bernard Lonergan's notion of conversion. Lonergan describes conversion in this way:

> By conversion is understood a transformation of the subject and his [sic] world. Normally it is a prolonged process though its explicit acknowledgment may be concentrated in a few momentous judgments and decisions. Still it is not just a development or even a series of developments. Rather it is a resultant change of course and direction. It is *as* if one's eyes were opened and one's former world faded and fell away. There emerges something new that fructifies in interlocking, cumulative sequences of developments on all levels and in all departments of human living.[19]
>
> Conversion, as lived, affects all of a man's conscious and intentional operations. It directs his gaze, pervades his imagination, releases the symbols that penetrate to the depths of his psyche. It enriches his understanding, guides his judgments, reinforces his decisions.[20]

Lonergan's understanding of conversion accords with much of Mulholland's notion of approach. Like Mulholland, Lonergan recognizes transformation *as* a process. It is not something that happens to us once, and it is completed. Rather, conversion is an ongoing process of our spiritual development. Additionally, Lonergan describes conversion *as* a "change of course and direction." He uses the motif of seeing to describe the way our worldview is reoriented. It accords with the way Mulholland asserts that our view of ourselves, the sacred scripture and Christian existence changes in light of lectio divina. Lonergan contends that in conversion something new emerges that affects every level of human living.

Lonergan continues by describing the effect of conversion on our interiority. What Lonergan refers to as "conscious and intentional" operations is basically all that we human beings do when we are awake. The operations are "seeing, hearing, touching, smelling, tasting, inquiring, imagining, understanding, conceiving, formulating, reflecting, marshalling and weighing the evidence, judging, deliberating, evaluating, deciding, speaking, writing,"[21] organized into four levels of what he calls consciousness and intentionality. Essentially, these conscious and intentional operations orient us in the world and shape the lens through which we view the world, experience the world, understand the world, evaluate the world, make judgments about the world, and then decide how to live in the world.[22] As a method of ongoing conversion and transformation, then, lectio divina serves as the medium through which we are not only continually transformed, but the place where our views are continually sharpened to see clearly ourselves and the world in the light of God's will. However, conversion for Lonergan is predicated on an insight.

An insight is a "eureka" moment. It is an "aha" moment. It is a moment when we come to a point of clarity of understanding about something which has heretofore been unanswered, unresolved, or simply nebulous. For Lonergan, an insight has five characteristics. It "(1) comes as a release to the tension of inquiry; (2) comes suddenly and unexpectedly; (3) is a function not of outer circumstances but inner conditions; (4) pivots between the concrete and the abstract; and (5) passes into the habitual texture of one's mind."[23] Insights are also part of a learning process in which an insight leads to questions that in turn leads to more insights, which Lonergan calls "complimentary insights."[24]

Learning occurs through the accumulation of insights, and information is acquired through the accumulation of insights. If we were to amass all the learning we have accomplished and information we have acquired, we would soon discover that there are still areas of deficit, areas in which our learning and information are still incomplete. Those areas of incompleteness give rise to questions. So, as valuable and illuminating as insights are, they are not discrete entities in and of themselves; they lead to more questions, which in turn lead to further insights. Lonergan identifies this continuous cycle of insights and questions as a "spontaneous process of learning." He writes,

> Just as there is spontaneous inquiry, so too there is a spontaneous accumulation of related insights. For questions are not an aggregate of isolated monads. In so far as any question is followed by an insight, one has only to act, or to talk, or perhaps merely to think on the basis of that insight, for its incompleteness to come to light and thereby generate a further question. In so far as the further question is in turn met by the gratifying response of a further insight, once more the same process will reveal another aspect of incompleteness to give rise to still further questions and still further insights. Such is the spontaneous process of learning. It is an accumulation of insights in which each successive act complements the accuracy and covers over the deficiency of those that went before.[25]

Insights and questions form a continuous process, each a catalyst for the other. Insights lead to more questions, and new questions lead to new insights. Lonergan asserts that insights answer inquiries, resolve deficiencies, and raise new questions with a greater end than is seen in its immediate view. "The whole point to the process of cumulative insight is that each insight regards the concrete while the cumulative process heads towards an ever fuller and more adequate view."[26] The implications of this for lectio divina are significant.

Lectio divina provides us with a privileged encounter with God through God's word. We read, pray, meditate, and contemplate to "hear" God, to hear and discern what God is saying to us about us. We listen to discern the will of God for our lives. At least two notions implicit in this understanding of lectio divina invite the practice to be an ongoing activity of the Christian life. First, God's infinite nature suggests that a lifetime of practicing lectio divina will never plumb the depths of all of who God is. Our knowledge of God cannot ever be exhausted. Since knowledge of God is inexhaustible, so then is the knowledge of God's will also inexhaustible. Second, though graced with being the *imago Dei*, humanity's imperfection continues to demand the work of ongoing conversion and sanctification. There continue to be areas of growth and development for human beings. God continually wants to conform us more and more into the image and likeness of Christ. Hence, lectio divina provides a context for both our discerning and our transformation.

What then is the relationship of insight to conversion, and how is all of this connected to the practice of lectio divina? Through lectio divina, God speaks to us. As we read prayerfully, thoughtfully, intentionally, and expectantly, we read *listening* for God. When we hear God speak, *that* is a moment of insight. That is a moment of revelation. It is an "aha" moment. However, hearing is not conversion. It is our response to the insight that initiates the process of conversion. Thus, lectio divina is a method for ongoing conversion and transformation because, through it, the infinite God makes self-disclosures, and the insights we receive provide opportunities for our response, in Mulholland's language. And, it is our response that sets in motion our ongoing conversion and transformation.

Conversion's Goal: The Continuously Transformed Life

If we are Christians, transformation is not an option. Mulholland is essentially asserting the same when he speaks of spiritual formation. He writes:

> Spiritual formation is not an option. Spiritual formation is not a discipline just for "dedicated disciples." It is not a pursuit only for the pious. Spiritual formation is not an activity for the deeply committed alone. It is not a spiritual frill for those with the time and inclination. *Spiritual formation is the primal reality of human existence.* Every event of life is an experience of spiritual formation. . . We are being shaped either toward the wholeness of the image of Christ or toward a horribly destructive caricature of that image.[27]

Mulholland asserts four things about spiritual formation. He writes that it is not (1) a discipline just for "dedicated disciples"; (2) a pursuit exclusively for the pious; (3) an activity solely for the deeply committed; and (4) a pastime activity. First, with respect to the type of activity spiritual formation is, Mulholland understands it as an existential experience. It is neither a "discipline" nor a "pursuit" nor an "activity." This echoes and accords with Smaragdus' assertion of lectio sacra being an experience, not an exercise. Spiritual formation, transformation, is not something that is accomplished through a prescription of steps and exercises that will yield a holy result and a pious person. It is not formulaic.

Second, spiritual formation is not the exclusive domain of individuals who are perceived (by others or themselves) as dedicated, pious, and holy. Many individuals often think that they are not "holy enough" to engage certain spiritual practices and disciplines. The truth is that spiritual formation is the existential reality of every human being, the end being that we are either more or less conformed to the *imago Dei* (to Christ). To reiterate, conversion is the process through which God works to conform people to the image and likeness of Christ.

Third, spiritual formation is not limited to those who are deeply committed, either by vocational orders or those who in themselves feel deeply committed to spiritual formation. In actuality, spiritual formation is the ground in which those individuals whose commitments are weak and lackluster become strong and robust. Spiritual formation is not just for those in ordained ministry or religious life. Spiritual formation is the existential reality of every Christian continuously because God continuously pours out God's love to us and never ceases to desire our growth and transformation, i.e., ongoing conversion.

Fourth, spiritual formation is not a fad, and it is not something to do when we have "nothing better to do." Neither of these approaches honors God. Spiritual formation is the "primal reality of human existence" that "moves against the grain of acculturation."[28] Walter Schöpsdau writes that because ". . . conversion always means both the act of faith and the outward expression of its implications, it can never be rid of this tension. It contains both the reorientation of conviction and the ethical and social implications of this reorientation."[29] What both Mulholland and Schöpsdau refer to is the consequences of the lived reality of our spiritual formation. When we begin to reorient our lives and behavior in accord with the reorientation of our worldview, we often find ourselves at odds with or excluded from some of the community or communities to which we formerly belonged. This is because we no longer share the views of some of these communities. Our views have been reoriented. Our views have been transformed. Finally, Mulholland recognizes a fundamental truth. In our daily lives, every interaction, every encounter is one that spiritually forms us, for good or for ill. Every event shapes us. When we are authentically engaged in ongoing transformation, it reverses the ways in which we have been negatively formed by culture.[30] Mulholland writes that, "It reverses our role from being the subject who controls the objects of the world, to being the object of the loving purposes of God who seeks to 'control' us for our perfect wholeness."[31]

Obstacles to Ongoing Conversion and Transformation

In a perfect world, Christians would be perfect. We would all hear God clearly and exercise perfect obedience. This is not a perfect world, and we are not perfect Christians. It is precisely because of our imperfections that God continues to call us to the process of ongoing conversion and transformation. However, we are often less than swift to respond to God's call to conversion and transformation. Why? If we are honest, most of us would acknowledge that submission to the will of God does not always accord with our "will" at any given moment. In other words, submitting to conversion and transformation is unpleasant, either because it is difficult, it is painful, it causes us to have to give up something or change something about ourselves or it causes us to acknowledge something about ourselves that is not always so pleasant to acknowledge. We return again to Lonergan's notion of insight.

In my earlier treatment of insight, I noted that Lonergan describes an insight as a eureka moment, an "aha" moment. He described an insight as a revelation in which we learn something. Lonergan asserted that insights lead to more questions and provide new insights that he called "complimentary insights." However, what happens when those moments of revelation do not affirm who we are, confirm our point of view, help us to move forward on a project or task, or tell us how wonderful we are? What happens when insights tell us something unpleasant about ourselves, tell us that our point of view is incorrect, tell us that we need to redirect our course of direction, or tell us we are not so wonderful? This is when insights are not so wanted. Lonergan expresses it in this way: "Insights are [sometimes] unwanted, not because they confirm our current viewpoints and behavior, but because they lead to their correction and revision."[32] One obstacle to conversion is an unwillingness to receive the insights, or revelations, that God gives us during our time of lectio divina. In these moments, we can suffer from spiritually arrested development, choosing not to continue the course of spiritual development because the path is difficult and the information is unpleasant.

This somewhat accords with an obstacle Mulholland lists as a person's self-image. If we fail to see ourselves as a word spoken forth by God, we will continue to have reinforced in us the negative self-images that currently exist within us. What I do not see in Mulholland's writing (though I am not suggesting he is not aware of it) is a balance of what healthy self-image and awareness is. Another obstacle to the ongoing conversion and transformation that comes through lectio divina is the refusal to receive what God speaks in that moment. Referring back to Mulholland's paradigm of spiritual formation as approach, encounter, and response, this is where the response stage of the equation is operating. I want to note here that the response aspect of the equation is always operating, for we can choose to respond "yes" or "no." When we respond "no," some would argue that transformation has become halted. I disagree. I strongly believe that even when we wrestle against what we have heard God speak to us, in the divine economy God is transforming us even in our moments of wrestling. If transformation were not taking place, we would not be conscious of or express discontent with insights received through lectio divina.

A second obstacle to ongoing conversion and transformation that Mulholland notes is our perception of reading. Mulholland discusses and makes distinctions between informational reading and formational reading. As the name suggests, informational reading is reading for that purpose: acquiring information. It is linear, quantitatively oriented (i.e., attempts to cover as much information as possible as quickly), has mastery of the text as its goal, is analytical, is characterized by a problem-solving orientation to the text, and the text is the object of the activity while the reader is the subject.[33] Informational reading is cognitively oriented. It is the way we have been socialized to process information. Our educational system is based on an informational model of learning.

On the other hand, formational reading is reading where quantity is not the goal of the reading; it is quality. While it is also linear like informational reading, we are reading for depth of information, not amount of information. In formational reading, the text is the subject and the reader is the object; subsequently, the reader is to be mastered by the text and not the text by the reader. So with regard to an obstacle to conversion, if we come to lectio divina with an informational reading agenda, we have still not surrendered to the process and trusted the process enough to let the text (i.e., the sacred scripture) master us rather than our trying to master the text.[34]

A third obstacle Mulholland cites concerns our view of the sacred scripture. If we do not see and believe that in the sacred scripture God presents us with a new worldview and reality (an iconographic view in Mulholland's words), then we will relapse into an old, historical, traditional, or even familiar reading of the text that is not life giving or transformative. If the sacred scriptures are not viewed as the resource for the transformation of values, then a privileged, graced moment of lectio divina will be missed.[35]

Mulholland's fourth obstacle to ongoing conversion and transformation is the inability to see in the world the radically new order that God is actively effecting in the world, one that brings life through Christ in the midst of death. If we cannot see this new world order, then we not only get stuck, but Mulholland says imprisoned in what he refers to as the "garbled, debased, and distorted" word of the world.[36]

These were Mulholland's perceptual obstacles. He also has a list of four experiential obstacles that impede ongoing conversion and transformation which lectio divina overcomes. He writes that if we operate out of a functional dynamics mode, we approach lectio divina as an activity for which we have our own agenda to be accomplished in the doing of the activity. There are two problems with this obstacle. One is the activity orientation to *lectio,* and the other problem is the personal agenda. I have discussed the activity-oriented approach earlier; thus, I will not revisit it here. However, the notion of personal agenda bears repeating because of the insidious nature of how our own agenda can be hidden even from us. Being a mature Christian is a privilege. And at the same time, we must be vigilant in our own self-critique because familiarity, especially of self, can allow us to ignore or rationalize truths that should be dealt with. It is easy for us to say that we know what God wants of us because it is in the sacred scriptures (a way of literalizing scripture as a kind of "proof text" for our lives). God has revealed God's will for humanity in God's word. However, one of the objectives of lectio divina is to discern the will of God for our own personal lives. If we come with the agenda (presumption!) of already knowing what God wants, then we have already positioned ourselves to miss the voice of the Spirit and miss what God has to say.[37]

The second experiential obstacle is what Mulholland calls "doing" dynamics. This is the mistaken notion that we can by our own sheer strength of volition become what God wants us to become.[38] This posture tends to be oriented around the view of the sacred scripture as the concordance of "thou shall" and "thou shall not" activities. There are two significant and dangerous consequences for this kind of approach to lectio divina. The first is this: if we believe that by our own sheer will we can become what God wants us to become, this is tantamount to idolatry. It is to suggest that we are equal in ability to God in being able to accomplish God's will and plan for our lives apart from God. We are on dangerous spiritual ground when have set ourselves up as an as idol. However, the insidious element here is that we often do not know we have done it.

The second significant and dangerous consequence of this kind of approach to lectio divina is this: to operate out of a "thou shall" and "thou shall not" place leads us to tend to live with a notion of a retributive God who is punitive when we fail to live up to an expectation and rewarding or kind when we do well. It completely obliterates God's grace in our lives as we seek to be conformed to the image and likeness of Christ. In a related way, in their book *Seasons of Strength: New Visions of Adult Christian Maturing,* Evelyn Eaton Whitehead and James D. Whitehead discuss the ways in which the imagination can be rendered impotent and thus impede our ability to be and live wholly and holy. They discuss how the other side of impotence can manifest itself as compulsion and lead us to think that we are solely responsible for our own being and for our own product. They write, "When we describe an imagination as 'possessed' we suggest that ancient demons can appear in contemporary guise. In my compulsions and obsessions a part of me becomes demonic, consuming my attention and energy. I 'have to' achieve that goal, no matter what! I 'must' do better than that person, that last time, than ever before."[39] Becoming so consumed is another form of idolatry in which we (1) set ourselves up as equal to God in ability; (2) obliterate the grace that exists in the journey of our ongoing conversion and transformation; and (3) completely misses the privileged, graced opportunity that God provided in lectio moments and thereafter.

Mulholland's third experiential obstacle is a lack of attention. I would add to that the surrender to the lack of attention. I treat Mulholland first. Mulholland acknowledges a fundamental reality of life: everybody's mind wanders every now and then. I think related to the way in which we have been socialized as informational readers, we have been given messages (at home, school, in the media) that a little "mental roaming" is not a good thing. Or, in this age where diagnoses like ADD, ADHD, Adult ADD, and Adult ADHD have become familiar diagnostic parlance, some of us have become (more) concerned (afraid?) that we may have one of these conditions. Or, we may be ADD-affective. So when we sit down to read the sacred scripture, and all of a sudden we want to do something that we may not have thought about in weeks, we immediately surrender to the distraction, do something else, self-diagnose, and then psychologically self-flagellate. There are two things that we need to be mindful of when this type of obstacle occurs. First, a little mind wandering is absolutely normal. We have to remind ourselves that lectio divina is more than simply a spiritual discipline. It is also an experience. Again, as externally oriented as human beings have been socialized to be, we often think of discipline as stilling and organizing everything around us, but we are not often reminded to be still and organize things *within* us. When I teach, I often say to students, "I want everyone to be quiet. Now, I want everyone to become quiet." Then I proceed to explain the difference. The difference for me is one of interiority. Becoming quiet means to still our spirit, our mind, to internally organize and put things in their mental compartments or closets for the moment, and to make a clear space (as much as possible) to receive and hear God afresh and anew. So, when the obstacle of lack of attention arises, we all need to be reminded that even the most seasoned saints encounter times of struggle, distraction, and inattentiveness.

We have discussed lectio divina as a spiritual *discipline*. We must now recognize lectio divina as a *spiritual* discipline. We must remember that whenever we seek to engage any spiritual discipline, all distractions are not earthly. Some distractions are Satan's way of keeping us from engaging disciplines that would bring us closer to God. So we must be encouraged to push through the distraction.

Finally, Mulholland's fourth experiential obstacle is approaching the text from our own perceived need. This is similar to approaching the text with an agenda when we come to the text because we need or "want" something from God, whether it be comfort for a painful situation, an answer to a situation, or affirmation of our feelings or position, even if they are wrong. From this position, we sometimes read what we know, what is familiar, what soothes us and not necessarily what God wants us to read in that moment. This is not a trusting position from which to engage the process of lectio divina. Ongoing conversion and transformation means that we grow in our development and allows God to grow us even when it does not feel good. However, our surrender to the process is a statement of our surrender to God and a statement of our trust in God and the process.

Lectio Divina: Towards Praxis and Promise

The disciples asked Jesus to teach them how to pray, and the gospel records the beginning of that prayer as "Our Father." The disciples' request of Jesus underscores a fundamental human reality: everyone needs to be taught something.

A Pedagogical Model

John H. Westerhoff wrote an article entitled "Fashioning Christians in Our Day" in which he discusses the catechetical process of the church. He quotes Tertullian's famous dictum "Christians are made, not born" to underscore the necessity for catechesis. Westerhoff asserts that "Catechesis necessitates three deliberate or intentional, systemic or interrelated, sustained or lifelong processes essential to Christian faith and life: formation, education, and instruction."[40] Westerhoff provides a model of catechetical instruction that is quite useful in helping people engage the discipline of lectio divina and advance in their own spiritual development.

The first task of a catechetical process is to offer *instruction*. The purpose of instruction is to help "persons to acquire knowledge and those abilities useful for responsible personal and communal Christian life in church and society."[41] As the next step, the goal of *education* is to help individuals "reflect critically on their behavior and experiences in light of the gospel so that they might discern if they are being faithful and when they might need to change their behavior."[42] Finally, *formation* is a process which "aids persons to acquire Christian faith (understood as a particular perception of life and our lives), Christian character (understood as identity and appropriate behavioral dispositions), and Christian consciousness (understood as that interior subjective awareness or temperament that predisposes persons to particular experiences)."[43]

This three-pronged model of catechesis is a method of forming and nurturing people in the Christian faith that I think is useful, with modification, as a model for helping people in their engagement of lectio divina as a discipline. This is fairly standard pedagogical progression of skills, not unlike what we would find in Bloom's taxonomy of learning domains. The first domain is instruction. The goal would be to help people understand the terms lectio, meditatio, oratio, and contemplatio. It would also be to lead them in the exercise of those terms and to have discussions about the experience. The goal of this first phase would be to provide people with an opportunity to learn the language of lectio divina, begin engaging the discipline of lectio divina, and have a place of reflection to process their learning and experiences in order to reinforce and affirm them.

In the second domain of education, the discussions would move beyond a discussion of how the experiences of lectio divina went to the content of the experiences. The person leading would function somewhat in the role of a spiritual director in that people would not necessarily be asked to share what they heard God saying to them but be led in a series of questions and discussion to understand how to discern what God is saying and the ways in which God speaks. Individuals would be led to pay attention to insights, their responses to insights, and the motivations of their responses. Overall, the second phase would be to lead people more deeply into the practice of lectio divina and to help them become more self-critiquing of their own process and journey with God.

The formation phase is the lifetime phase. People are no longer in an instructional environment per se. There would be a closing session to provide a type of transition. However, it would be explained that formation is the lifetime work of lectio divina. It is the constant dynamic of God constantly calling God's people into communion so that they may be conformed more closely to the image of Christ. Participants would be reminded to expect lulls in the tenor of their devotion. Expect times of feeling like we are in a dry place. Expect times of distraction. Expect times of the Spirit's effusive outpouring. If there would be the articulation of a goal, it would be to remain consistent and persistent.

The Eschatological Dimension of Lectio Divina

We stated above that God is infinite, and humanity is imperfect. And that dynamic means that just as knowledge and relationship about God cannot be exhausted, neither can our complete perfection be attained while still on this earth. There are at least three visions that are given in lectio divina: God's vision for the individual, God's vision for the individual's life, and God's vision of the eschaton.

We have seen that one thing that individuals should seek in lectio divina is to discern the will of God for their lives. The will of God can concern us personally, and the will of God can concern our lives. The first is a call to character correction. This goes back to the unwanted insights. Again, ordinarily, insights are wanted because they affirm who we are, confirm our point of view, help us to move forward on a project or task, or tell us how wonderful we are. When they cease to do these, we generally do not want them. However, it is usually what we find distasteful that is the area in which God is trying to conform us to the image and likeness of Christ. It should be noted that character correction is not always about what is often considered "poor" behavior. Sometimes character correction is a challenge to correct good behavior wrongly motivated. So it is as much an inventory of behavior as it is of motivation.

Secondly, in lectio divina God expresses God's will for the context of our lives. It may or may not be something in our control, and it may or may not be something that has a connection to character correction. In either event, what a vision concerning the will of God for our lives does is challenge us to journey with God as God's plan for our lives unfolds. God's vision for our lives challenges us to surrender our plans and what we think is best, prudent, safe, wise, or even desirable and accept and embrace God's plans for us. In doing so, we become stewards of the vision and co-journeyers with God in a pilgrimage to the fruition of a given vision. There are myriad reasons for visions, and it would be imprudent to begin to list possible reasons. However, the challenge for Christians is to discern what the will of God is for their behavior and their lives.

Finally, in lectio divina God orients our vision towards the eschaton. We do not literally see the events of salvation history unfold exactly as they will occur; rather, as we spend more and more time with God and allow God to conform us more perfectly to the image and likeness of Christ, we will soon find our vision oriented less to the things of this world and more oriented toward heavenly things. As Smaragdus put it, "The knowledge of sacred reading. . . enkindles the desire for Christ and our heavenly homeland."[44] The sacred scripture informs us that our lives in eternity will be spent with the triune God in the abode of God, a place that we call heaven. However, we before we can go *there*, we have the work of finishing our living *here*. And even as we live in hope, expectancy, and wonder about eternal life with God, lectio divina does not orient us towards the eschaton in such a way as to render us so heavenly minded that we are of no earthly good. Rather, it turns our worldview into an other-worldly view. It puts this world and the things and concerns we have of this world in their proper perspective and allows us to wear this world, as my Pastor would often say, "like a loose garment." It reminds us that as Christians who are passing through this life on our way to the next, we have the privilege and responsibility of reflecting Christ in our lives as we live in expectant hope of God's promise of life beyond this earthly realm. So while lectio divina conforms us more to the image and likeness of Christ *here*, it simultaneously prepares us for and pulls us *there*.

All of this is the work of the Holy Spirit. The surrender that each new experience of lectio divina demands positions us to be breathed upon, breathed *into* anew by and with the Holy Spirit. The Holy Spirit is not only active in the revelation of God's plans for our lives *to* us; the Holy Spirit is also the One who prepares the way for God's will to be born *in* us. The breath of the Holy Spirit clears the landscape of our hearts, minds, and spirits so that we can hear, vision, and receive God's will for us and for our lives. These divine revelations help us in living with expectancy in God's promise to give us, like Jeremiah, "a future and a hope."[45]

Conclusion

The ancient practice lectio divina, with the four movements of lectio, oratio, meditatio, and contemplatio, is a moment of privilege and graced encounter with God through the sacred scripture, through our *praying* the sacred scripture. Informed by the monastic rather than scholastic orientation to lectio, when we read, praying the sacred scripture, God speaks to us, and in our reading, we "hear" God speaking to us. God's speaking unctions us to pray. The consequence of our conversion is a new, other-worldly view and a disposition towards an amendment of life to be lived in greater conformity to the image and likeness of Christ. However, our reading and our listening is not the activity wherein our conversion lies. Our transformation consists in our approach, encounter, and response. Conversion is not possible without our response to God's initiating of God's self-gift to us, which is God's love. However, our response and subsequent conversion is predicated on insights. They can be wanted or unwanted, but insights gained from God through lectio divina tell us the truth about who God is, the truth about who we are, the truth about our lives, and the true will of God for our lives, whether we like it or not. What we do as a result of those insights does not determine if we will be converted and transformed; it determines the measure and direction of our conversion and transformation. Thus, conversion and transformation require our participation. It is by volition and not by force.

Our ongoing conversion is the partnership of our surrender and God's shaping. God does not work where we have neither invited nor submitted, and we do not invite God where we are not ready to do the work of conversion. The locus for all of this activity is the sacred scripture, the record of God's salvific work in human history. However, the fruitfulness of our time spent in lectio divina is determined in part by our approach to and perspective on sacred scripture. It requires that we take certain views and perspectives on the sacred scripture and read in a way that balances formation and information. It requires that we abandon our agendas and listen for God's agenda.

We are not born knowing how to do lectio divina. Like all children, we must be tutored in the ways of the things of God, including how to hear God's voice. Westerhoff's description of the three-pronged model of catechesis provides a good paradigm for a possible pedagogical model for lectio divina. The catechesis is important because we need to be tutored in how to hear God's voice and see God's vision. Discernment is a mode of seeing. In discerning the will of God for our lives through lectio divina, God provides the vision for who God wants us to become. The more time we spend in lectio, the more we see beyond ourselves, beyond our lives, beyond our circumstances, and even beyond the affairs of this world, for in lectio God orients us towards the eschaton and breaths in us the desire for our heavenly home.

Notes

1. Jean Leclercq, *The Love of Learning and the Desire for God: A Study of Monastic Culture* (New York: Fordham University Press, 1988), 8.
2. Ibid.
3. For further discussion, see Kevin W. Irwin, "Lectio Divina" in *Encyclopedia of Monasticism*, Vol. 1 (Chicago: Fitzroy Dearborn, 2000), 750–52; Raymond Studzinski, O.S.B., *Reading to Live: The Evolving Practice of Lectio Divina* (Collegeville: Cistercian Publications, 2009), 12–17, 125–26, 169–70); see also Joyce Ann Zimmerman, C.PP.S., *Silence: Everyday Living and Praying* (Chicago: Liturgy Training Publications, 2010), 64–67.
4. Smaragdus of Saint-Mihiel, *Commentary on the Rule of Saint Benedict*, trans. David Barry (Kalamazoo: Cistercian Publications, 2007), 1.
5. Ibid., 227.
6. For purposes of this paragraph, either the word "experience" or "knowledge" could be used because my point is the interiority implied in Smaragdus' word choice vis-à-vis the exercise of lectio divina. A basic distinction between knowledge as a body of facts or information and experience as a by-product of a person's encounter with a person or thing is duly noted. Substantive differences will not be treated at length here. For further reading on experience, see Dermot A. Lane, *The Experience of God: An Invitation to Do Theology* (New York: Paulist, 1981), 4–9.
7. Walter Wink, *The Bible in Human Transformation: Toward a New Paradigm for Biblical Study* (Philadelphia: Fortress, 1973), 2.
8. Ibid.
9. M. Robert Mulholland Jr., *Shaped by the Word: The Power of Scripture in Spiritual Formation* (Nashville: Upper Room, 1985), 30.
10. Raymond Studzinski, *Reading to Live: The Evolving Practice of Lectio Divina* (Collegeville: Liturgical Press, 2009), 28.
11. Origen, *On First Principles. Being Koetschau's Text of* the De Principiis *Translated into English, Together with an Introduction and Notes*, trans. G. W. Butterworth (Gloucester, MA: Peter Smith, 1973), 256.
12. Mulholland, *Shaped by the Word*, 139.
13. Ibid., 142.
14. Ibid., 140.
15. Ibid.
16. Ibid., 141.
17. Ibid.
18. Ibid., 141–42.

19. Bernard J. F. Lonergan, *Method in Theology* (New York: Herder and Herder, 1972), 130.
20. Ibid., 131.
21. Ibid., 6.
22. Ibid., 238.
23. Bernard J. F. Lonergan, *Insight: A Study of Human Understanding* (New York: Longmans, Green and Co. Ltd, 1968), 3–4.
24. Ibid.
25. Ibid., 174.
26. Bernard J. F. Lonergan, "Healing and Creating in History" in *A Third Collection: Papers by Bernard J. F. Lonergan,* ed. Frederick E. Crowe (New York: Paulist, 1985), 104.
27. Mulholland, *Shaped by the Word*, 25–26.
28. Ibid., 26.
29. Walter Schöpsdau, "Conversion" in *The Encyclopedia of Christianity. Vol. 1:A–D.* (Grand Rapids: Eerdmans, 1999), 684.
30. Mulholland, *Shaped by the Word*, 26.
31. Ibid., 27.
32. Lonergan, "Healing and Creating in History," 193.
33. Mulholland, *Shaped by the Word*, 49–50.
34. Ibid., 130.
35. Ibid., 130.
36. Ibid., 131.
37. Ibid., 133.
38. Ibid., 133.
39. Evelyn Eaton Whitehead and James D. Whitehead, *Seasons of Strength: New Visions of Adult Christian Maturing* (Garden City, NY: Doubleday & Company, Inc., 1984), 98.
40. John H. Westerhoff, "Fashioning Christians in Our Day" in *Schooling Christians: "Holy Experiments" in American Education* (Grand Rapids: Eerdmans, 1992), 266.
41. Ibid., 266.
42. Ibid., 267.
43. Ibid., 267.
44. Smaragdus, *Commentary on the* Rule, 227.
45. Jeremiah 29:11.

3
Differences in Similarity: An Examination of the Baptismal Rite in the Apostolic Tradition and the African Methodist Episcopal Church

Lisa M. Weaver

Introduction

Liturgy is an enterprise that is historically, geographically, culturally, and experientially conditioned. It derives from the shared theological understandings and experiences of a group of individuals located in a particular historical time, in a particular geographical place, in a particular cultural context, with a particular and shared worldview and experience of life in the world. Thus, from an examination of liturgical practices and worship forms from different periods and regions, one should discover foundational elements reflective of the shared Christian tradition as well as particularities that are unique to each respective worshipping community. With the development of the Christian church, the emergence of episcopal systems of governance led to the standardization of liturgical forms and worship practices in increasingly larger territories and regions. Even within this standardization, there still existed liturgical variances among regions. The outcomes of the Reformation effected another significant diversification of liturgical forms and worship practices. Even in the midst of these changes, historical study and textual analysis helps to detect and analyze the many evolutions, developments, and divergences in liturgical forms and worship practices. However, in the post-Reformation context, this type of liturgical analysis presents formidable challenges in the study of traditions that have congregational polity and cooperative fellowship among ecclesial bodies. Often times, these traditions do not have "service books" (missals, sacramentaries, or books of prayer, order, or discipline) in which the liturgy is prescribed and preserved. Regardless of whether a Christian tradition is episcopal or congregational and regardless of where a particular Christian tradition falls on the continuum of liturgy that is formal or informal, the one liturgical element that is common to all is that which provides entrance into the community of the faithful, and that is baptism.

In spite of the aforementioned difficulties, it is still illuminating and useful to examine a current liturgical tradition in the light of the Christian liturgical tradition. Liturgical study provides a context for analyzing current liturgical practices and worship forms in the light of the gospel and the Christian tradition and guarding against uncritical and ineffective appropriation of liturgical practices and worship forms for purposes other than the glorification of God and the continued spiritual formation of the people of God to become more perfectly conformed to the image and likeness of Christ.

For this study, I have chosen to examine the baptismal rite in two documents, one ancient and one contemporary. The *Apostolic Tradition of Hippolytus* is used because it provides one of the earliest and robust descriptions of the baptismal rite. The African Methodist Episcopal baptismal rite was chosen as a point of contemporary comparison because they are an African American Christian community who has preserved its liturgical rites in print with revised editions that facilitate the analysis of changes and trajectories in practice over time.

This study begins with a presentation of different biblical paradigms of baptismal practice as recorded in the New Testament. It moves to an examination of the baptismal rite as witnessed to in *The Apostolic Tradition of Hippolytus*, with other contemporary sources cited in tandem with particular elements of the baptismal rite. It is followed by a brief summary of the emergence of the African Methodist Episcopal Church and an examination of its baptismal rite from 19th, 20th, and 21st century sources. The final section compares the two baptismal rites and explores the places of divergence from historical and cultural perspectives.

Some Early Models of Baptismal Practice

As evidenced by the New Testament Acts of the Apostles, the preaching and spread of the gospel by the early church leaders led to the development of the Christian church in the world at various times and in different places. There are several ways in which these phenomena can be understood and studied. If the primary operating determinant is geography, for example, the development of Christian churches could be examined in one particular region over a specified period of time. Alternatively, if the primary operating determinant is chronology, churches in several regions could be examined within one particular period of time. Inasmuch as a theory of homogeneity would be at once comforting and simple, the truth is that, in either approach of study, one thing will quickly become evident: the practices of the early church were as ritually diverse as the places in which they were practiced.

One of the earliest examples of ritual heterogeneity is provided in the Acts of the Apostles. Three different baptismal practices are evidenced. In Acts 8, Philip goes down to the city of Samaria and preaches to crowds of people who believe and are baptized, including Simon who until his conversion and baptism practiced magic and amazed the crowds. Once the other apostles hear of the conversion in Samaria, Peter and John are sent there to pray for the newly converted that they might receive the Holy Spirit. When the two arrive, they lay hands on those baptized, and they receive the Holy Spirit.[1] Acts 10 provides a different paradigm; the order of baptismal elements is reversed. People receive the Holy Spirit, then they are baptized. While Peter is speaking at the house of Cornelius in Caesarea, the Holy Spirit descends upon all who are listening to his message, which was accompanied by the manifestation of speaking in tongues. Peter asks the Jewish believers in their midst, "Can anyone withhold the water for baptizing these people who have received the Holy Spirit just as we have?" He subsequently orders that the Gentiles who have just received the Holy Spirit be baptized. The final witness to a different practice is found in Acts 19.[2] A group of believers in Christ, most likely followers of John, are asked by Paul if they have received the gift of the Holy Spirit, to which they reply that they have not even heard that the Holy Spirit existed but that they have received John's baptism of repentance. After listening to a succinct statement by Paul explaining John's position as forerunner to Jesus, that group of believers receives Christian baptism (after having already received John's baptism), had hands laid on them by Paul, and then they received the Holy Spirit. Thus, in the development of the nascent Christian community, the biblical witness evidences three different paradigms of baptismal practice.

In a similar way, an examination of the extant writings of the early church will also evidence a diversity of baptismal practices, now beginning to be formulated as rituals. However, in spite of these divergences, one aspect remains central: the water bath. Among the various elements of the pre-baptismal rites, post-baptismal rites, euchology, rubrics, participation and participants, a comparative analysis of any two or more rites could very well yield variances in any of the above elements, a different constellation of elements, a difference in the ordering of the elements, even omissions or additions of elements from one rite to another. In other words, in the early church, all liturgy was local and as a result was not necessarily identical from church to church or from region to region. Thus, no single document can be touted as the first or original or paradigm from which all other liturgies spring. All the aforementioned qualification notwithstanding, there is one document that is quite valued in liturgical studies for the wealth of fairly explicit information that is gleaned about liturgical practices in the early church. It is called *The Apostolic Tradition of*

Hippolytus,[3] and for the above-mentioned reasons, it will be the primary source of ancient liturgical information for the purpose of this article.

The *Apostolic Tradition* (hereinafter referred to as "*ApTrad*") is erroneously attributed to Hippolytus. Categorically a church order, it came to be known as the Egyptian Church Order and was written between c. 200–250 A.D. Extant manuscripts are in Bohairic, Sahidic, Arabic, Ethiopic, and Latin.[4] *ApTrad* contains liturgical information regarding ordinations, the catechumenate, various other subject matter pertaining to Christian life (fasting, prayer, offerings), and a short epilogue. Chapters 15–21 contain the information pertinent to this study. In chapter 15, the catechumens are brought to teachers. According to chapter 19, the teachers can be either clergy or laity. The catechumens are examined regarding their reason for coming to faith. In addition, the sponsors of those catechumens testify to their fitness for hearing the Word and are questioned about the catechumens' status in life. All of this takes place before the liturgy (i.e., theoretically, it takes place before the people arrive). In chapter 16, the criteria of the catechumenate are specified. The expectation was that in order for one to be considered for the catechumenate, it was required that one have a particular moral character and certain professions were understood to be in conflict with good moral character.[5] In chapter 17, the time and activity for participation in the catechumenate is specified. Catechumens shall hear the Word for a period of three years, with some exception.[6] In chapter 21, the priest hands the catechumen over to the bishop, who then baptizes the catechumen using the creedal formula. After the third time the catechumen is dipped into the water, she or he is anointed with the oil of thanksgiving (now known as chrism) by the presbyter, dries her/himself, dresses, and enters the church. Then the bishop lays hands on the newly baptized person, now known as a neophyte, and prays for her/him. The bishop then pours the oil of thanksgiving on the neophyte, places his hand on the neophyte's head, prays, and then signs[7] the neophyte on the head. This is the only time in the rites analyzed in this study that there is a signing of any individual. After the bishop signs the neophyte's forehead, he kisses neophyte and says to neophyte, "The Lord be with you," and the neophyte responds, "And with your spirit." After this is done for each neophyte, they (the now illumined ones) pray with the faithful and then exchange the kiss of peace. This is followed by the Eucharist.[8]

Prelude to Entrance into the Christian Community

Early Christian documents provide us with great witnesses to the early church's sense of one's personal accountability in Christian living and understanding of the very communal nature of the church. *ApTrad* provides us with insight into these two aspects of church understanding and communal life. Paragraph 15 of *ApTrad* reads, in part,

> Those who come forward the first time to hear the word shall first be brought to the teachers before all the people arrive, and shall be questioned about their reason for coming to the faith. And those who have brought them shall bear witness about them, *whether they are capable of hearing the word. They shall be questioned about the state of their life. . .*

We live in an age which values, even extols, rugged individualism, fierce self-reliance, and complete autonomy. In other words, we are socialized and seduced, erroneously, into believing that we can do anything we want to do by ourselves. Said differently, we can do anything and everything by ourselves, and we do not need anyone's help. In stark contrast to these 21st century sensibilities, in the early church, if one desired to become a member of the church, it was required that a member of the Christian community, sometimes referred to as a sponsor, present that individual to the church for consideration to become a member of the community. Individuals could not come on their own and alone; one had to be brought to the community by a member of the community, and that member had to bear witness about you. The church relied on the sponsor's witness to attest to the individual's ability to hear and receive the gospel of Christ, the individual's disposition and desire to live the Christian life, and evidence of an amendment of life consistent with conversion to Christ. Thus, the church understood the Christian life as a way of life that was undertaken by each member of the community and that each member of the community had a responsibility for presenting to the church those persons whose disposition and manner of life were consistent with the community into which they were seeking entrance. Uniting with the church was not only about one's personal relationship to God; it was also about one's relationship to the people of God in the local Christian community called the church.

Once a person's ability, desire, disposition, and evidence of learning and growth in Christ and gospel living were attested to positively, she or he was admitted to a preparatory program for full admittance to the church known as the catechumenate. For the community of the *Apostolic Tradition*, the catechumenal period was generally three years. ("Catechumens shall continue to hear the word for three years.")[9] It should be noted, however, that three years was not the standard catechumenal period for every community. While three years may seem incredibly long to modern sensibilities, the length of time informs us of how important Christian formation was to the early church. Three years was the average time that conversion to living the life of the gospel required, and this community evidences no short cuts or short-circuiting of the process. The process was neither short nor rushed; one's commitment to the length of time was one indication that the new life of Christian faith was taken seriously, but it was not taken for granted. Simply because one remained in the catechumenate for the entire three years was not a guarantee that she or he would be baptized. It was not only the quantity of the time spent in the program that mattered; the quality of one's life and conversion process mattered as well. The church also required evidence of a commitment made with the right motive and intention. The life one lived while in the catechumenate had to bear witness that the message and life of the gospel of Jesus Christ has been embodied in such a way that one's lifestyle—one's words and deeds—were the testimony of one who had accepted Christ and the message of the gospel. *ApTrad* 20 reads:

> And when those who are to receive baptism are chosen, let their life be examined: have they lived good lives when they were catechumens? Have they honoured the widows? Have they visited the sick? Have they done every kind of good work? And when those who brought them bear witness to each: "He has," let them hear the gospel.

Just as one's fitness to hear the word of God had to be attested to prior to entering the catechumenate, so also the life the catechumen lived while progressing along the catechumenate journey had to be attested to as well. There was an expectation by the Christian community that in the course of three years, there would be evidence of Christian growth and maturity in the life of one seeking baptism and communion with the church, evidence of a turning away from one's old life and a taking on, embracing, and living out of this new Christian life. The witness to one's conversion was offered by one who was already part of the Christian community. It is one vivid witness to us today that in the ancient Christian church, the community was integrally involved in the process of individuals being brought into the Christian community.

Sign Me Up: The Election/Enrollment. . .

Again, prior to enrollment, individuals were questioned regarding the candidate's spiritual life and witness.[10] Once a person's lifestyle was attested to, that person had to be officially and solemnly received by the church to be baptized. As Easter was the time established to be the most appropriate time to perform baptism,[11] the names of those desiring baptism were received prior to the preparatory season for Easter, which is Lent.[12] While the catechumenate is understood as preparing catechumens for baptism, Lent is known as the "proximate period of preparation." It is the intense preparatory period immediately preceding baptism at the Easter vigil. Prior to the start of Lent, the names of those who wished to be baptized were submitted to the church. This action was understood as the catechumen petitioning the church for baptism.[13] The process of the church receiving the names of persons who were "requesting" baptism was called "election" or "enrollment." After the "election" or "enrollment," persons were no longer called catechumens. They were now called "applicants" or "co-applicants" (*competentes*) since they petition the church for baptism along with members of the community, "chosen" or "elect" (*electi*) or "those destined for illumination" (*photizomenoi*).[14] A pilgrim traveler to Jerusalem named Egeria, most noted for her late fourth century account of Holy Week in Jerusalem, provides us a witness to this practice.

I must also describe how those who are baptized at Easter are instructed. Whoever gives his name does so the day before Lent, and the priest notes down all their names; and this is before those eight weeks during which, as I have said, Lent is observed here.[15]

Strength to Resist, Strength to Stand: The Exorcisms

One thing that individuals who are uniting with the church need to remember is that they are uniting with *the church*, that is, with a body of faithful believers gathered in one place.[16] They are joining a community, and early church history informs us that the church, the local body of believers in any given church, had a role and responsibility in the entrance of those joining the community, and part of the community's responsibility was to participate in the exorcisms of those who would be joining the church.

Regrettably, Hollywood filmmakers do not have a history of treating the subject of the church, the church's life, and the church's purpose completely, accurately, or well. In the context of preparing individuals for baptism, the early church used the term "exorcism" to refer to the church's prayer for those who are about to receive baptism that they be protected against the power and influences of Satan. These prayers were accompanied by the laying on of hands. In other words, after the election (enrollment), the church began to pray that those who would soon make their public declaration (baptism) of their allegiance to God, Christ, the Holy Spirit, and the church would be protected from Satan, would be strengthened to withstand temptation and evil, and would be no longer vulnerable to the ways and wiles of evil. This is a powerful testimony to the church's understanding that one's profession of faith immediately positions one, spiritually, to be open and vulnerable to evil and that the church, as the body of believers mature in the faith, was responsible to cover in prayer those who would be soon joining them. Once again, *ApTrad* provides a witness to this practice.

> And when those to receive baptism are chosen, let their life be examined: have they lived good lives when they were catechumens? Have they honoured the widows? Have they visited the sick? Have they done every kind of good work? And when those who brought them bear witness to each: "He has," let them hear the gospel. From the time that they are set apart, let hands be laid on them daily while they are exorcized. And when the day of their baptism approaches, the bishop shall exorcize each one of them. . . (*ApTrad* 20)

That's What I Believe: The Baptismal Creed

During the Lenten period, the creed was one of the major instructional texts for those who were going to be baptized. The creed was also known as the "symbol" because it was a concrete compendium (in language form) of the Christian faith. The creed was an instructional tool *par excellence* because it contained, in a few relatively short stanzas, the complete foundation of the Christian faith. It is a succinct statement about the identity and work of God, Jesus, the Holy Spirit, and the church and provided a brief eschatological declaration ("Christ Jesus. . . will come to judge the living and the dead"). In the context of baptismal preparation, the baptismal creed[17] served several purposes. First, to reiterate, it served as the primary text for baptismal preparation. Second, within the services leading up to baptism, the creed appeared in two places. In the *traditio symboli* (the "handing over of the creed"), those to be baptized were "handed over" the creed. In this ritual action, the church was *handing over*, sharing with, and entrusting the Christian faith to those who desired to join them. It was an act of sharing the church's faith with those who would soon become part of the family of the faithful. It was the responsibility of those to be baptized to memorize the creed and be able to recite it by heart at their baptism, in this way demonstrating that they had received, internalized, and fully embraced the faith of the church. They were given time to memorize the creed, and at an appointed time, they were to "return it," that is, to recite it from memory. This is the third place in which the creed appears. This is called the *redditio symboli* (the "giving back of the creed"). Those to be baptized were brought back to the church and stood before the church and recited the creed from memory. However, it was not the last time that they would recite the creed. It will appear again during the baptism itself.

Turning One's Back on the Past to Walk in the Light: The Apotaxis, the Syntaxis, and the Water Bath

The *apotaxis* and *syntaxis* are treated together because of the content and ritual counterpoints of these two actions, and these two actions lead directly to what was known in the early church as the water bath, baptism. As discussed earlier, the early church understood coming to Christ and becoming a member of the church as a spiritual enterprise ritually enacted and that within the spiritual realm, there were two sides—God's and Satan's. Baptism marked the movement of those to be baptized from the dominion of Satan's influence and power to the protection and safety of God. And because adult baptism was the norm for baptism in the early church, part of the ritual required that the one to be baptized not only make a public profession and declaration of trust in God but also make a public rejection and renunciation of Satan. The renunciation and rejection of Satan and Satan's influences is known as the *apotaxis*, and the profession and declaration of trust in God is known as the *syntaxis*. One of the earliest witnesses to these practices is found in *ApTrad*.

> And when the priest takes each one of those who are to receive baptism, he shall bid him renounce, saying: I renounce you, Satan, and all your service and all your works. (*ApTrad* 21)

Fourth century bishop Ambrose of Milan provides a more detailed and elaborate (dramatic?) account of the *apotaxis* (renunciations). This could be due, in part, to the time between *ApTrad* and Ambrose and could suggest a development in the practice.[18] In his mystagogical catechesis, Ambrose provides a witness to questions that are presented individually and accompanied by embodied ritual action on the part of the person to be baptized. He writes,

> (2) First, ye entered into the outer hall of the Baptistery, and there facing towards the West, ye heard the command to stretch forth your hand, and as in the presence of Satan ye renounced him. . . (4) However, thou art bidden with arm outstretched to say to him as though actually present, I RENOUNCE THEE, SATAN. . . (5) Then in the second sentence thou art told to say, AND ALL THY WORKS. . . (6) Then thou sayest, AND ALL HIS POMP. . . (8) And after this thou sayest, and ALL THY SERVICE. (*Mystagogical Catechesis* I, 2, 4–6, 8)

Ambrose's exposition on the *apotaxis* suggests a dialogue between the bishop and the one to be baptized. It is an interrogation of the person to be baptized in order that his or her heart and intentions are made known. African church father Tertullian (born Quintus Septimius Florens Tertullianus) attests to this practice also. Tertullian's description provides the counterpoint relationship of the *apotaxis* and *syntaxis*. In *De Corona*, he writes,

> In short, to begin with baptism, when on the point of coming to the water we then and there. . . affirm that we renounce the devil and his pomp and his angels. After this we are three times immersed, while we answer interrogations rather more extensive than our Lord has prescribed in the gospel. (*De Corona*, c. 3)

The individuals to be baptized were questioned (once or three times, depending on the provenance of the source; here we cannot definitively determine) as to whether they renounced Satan. The *apotaxis* is followed by a two-fold act of interrogation and immersion in the baptismal waters. This second interrogation is the *syntaxis*, and after each question is asked and answered, the candidate is immersed in the water. Tertullian is a witness for triple immersion baptism. Our faithful witness *ApTrad* depicts this more clearly.

> And in this way he shall hand him over naked to the bishop or the priest who stand by the water to baptize. In the same way a deacon shall descend with him into the water and say, helping him to say: I believe in one God, the Father almighty. . . And he who receives shall say according to all this: "I believe in this way." And the giver, having his hand placed on his head, shall baptize him once.
>
> And then he shall say, Do you believe in Christ Jesus, the Son of God, who was born from the Holy Spirit from the Virgin Mary, and was crucified under Pontius Pilate, and died, and rose again on the third day alive from the dead, and ascended into heaven, and sits at the right hand of the Father, and will come again to judge the living and the dead? And when he has said, "I believe," he shall be baptized again.
>
> And he shall say again: Do you believe in the Holy Spirit and the holy Church and the resurrection of the flesh? Then he who is being baptized shall say, "I believe," and thus he shall be baptized a third time. (*ApTrad* 21)

The *apotaxis* and *syntaxis* serve as counterpoints. Those to be baptized are asked (in some instances) three questions in the *apotaxis*; three questions are presented in which they are asked if they renounce Satan, Satan's works, and some other element of Satan's realm or activity (e.g., his pomp, his service). That complete rejection is followed by the *syntaxis*, which takes the form of a triple interrogation of their belief in and commitment to the complete Godhead. Here is where the creed appears for the fourth time (the first time was in Lenten instruction, the second time was the *traditio symboli*, and the third time was the *redditio symboli*). Each tripartite unit of the creed is employed as the question presented to those being baptized. We learn from *ApTrad* that, for this particular community, the interrogation questions are derived from the creed that is commonly known as the Apostles' Creed ("I believe in one God, the Father almighty... Do you believe in Jesus Christ, the son of God, who was born from the Holy Spirit from the Virgin Mary... do you believe in the Holy Spirit and the holy church and the resurrection of the flesh?"), and the response from the one being baptized after *each* question is "I believe." *ApTrad* also witnesses to the practice of triple immersion, an immersion followed by each declaration of faith in each of the persons of the Godhead. Today, many churches have some form of this tripartite structure in their baptismal practice.

Signed and Sealed: The Anointing(s)

Depending on one's faith tradition, when speaking in the context of baptism, if someone were to say the word "anointing," most people immediately think of either "baptism" or "confirmation." Hopefully, with the brief number of sources cited in this article, it should be clear that very little is clear or clear cut when it comes to the practices of the early church, and the practice of anointing in the early church in the context of baptism is also complex and varied. In her article "The Original Meaning of the Pre-baptismal Anointing and Its Implications," Gabriele Winkler provides a detailed analysis of the various terms used for "oil," when candidates were anointed with oil (whether before or after baptism), and the meaning of those anointings. Therefore, it is important to understand that in the early church there were different anointing practices with different meanings. In *ApTrad*, we find that the practice of that community was to anoint the newly baptized with oil after the water bath *two* times. Chapter 21 reads, in part:

> And then, when he has come up, he shall be anointed from the oil of thanksgiving by the presbyter who says: I anoint you with holy oil in the name of Jesus Christ. And the bishop shall lay hands on them... Then, pouring the oil of thanksgiving from his hand and placing it on his head, he shall say: I anoint you with holy oil in God the Father almighty and Christ Jesus and the Holy Spirit. And having signed him on the forehead, he shall give him a kiss and say: The Lord be with you. And he who has been signed shall say: And with your spirit. (*ApTrad* 21)

Thus, in *ApTrad*, we have two post-baptismal anointings, using the same oil (the "oil of thanksgiving"), administered by two different individuals using similar euchology, which may or may not have been administered in the same way. The second anointing was followed by the bishop signing (making the sign of the cross) the forehead of the newly baptized and then imparting a kiss.[19]

On the other hand, Cyril of Jerusalem provides a different example of an anointing associated with baptism, a pre-baptismal anointing. In *Mystagogical Catechesis II*, Cyril writes, in part:

(3) Then, when ye were stripped, ye were anointed with exorcized oil, from the very hairs of your head, to your feet, and were made partakers of the good olive-tree, Jesus Christ. . . The exorcized oil therefore was a symbol of the participation of the fatness of Christ, the charm to drive away every trace of hostile influence. . . so also this exorcized oil receives. . . not only to burn and cleanse away the traces of sin, but also to chase away all the invisible powers of the evil one. (4) After these things, ye were led to the holy pool of Divine Baptism. . . [20]

In Jerusalem during Cyril's time, *prior to* baptism, candidates were stripped of their clothing (yes, candidates were baptized naked!) and were given a full body anointing (as opposed to just on the head and forehead as in *ApTrad*) with an "exorcized" oil (called the oil of the catechumens). In some parts of the ancient world, athletes were bathed with oil in preparation for competition. In Cyril's context, the pre-baptismal anointing was understood in a similar way. This pre-baptismal anointing symbolized the candidate's preparation for the spiritual battle against evil, given ritual expression in the *apotaxis*, the candidate's renunciation of the devil and everything associated with his realm. As such, it was part of the prelude to the candidate's *syntaxis* and being grafted into the body of Christ through the baptismal waters. It is *after* this pre-baptismal anointing that the candidates are led to the pool and baptized. There are several other sources that can be cited that provide a witness to different anointing practices and different meanings attached to those anointings. These two are given to provide one category of distinction between baptismal anointings—pre-baptismal and post-baptismal.

It is important to remember that all of the elements of baptismal practice discussed in this section were ritualized activity. In other words, they were acted out, enacted, embodied behaviors. The church not only understood that it was the responsibility of believers to pray for those who would be baptized, but the church made it part of the baptismal process. Not only was it understood that giving one's life to Christ meant rejection of Satan and all satanic ways, that understanding was given ritual expression in baptism, as individuals stretched their hand out, renounced Satan, and professed Christ. The church understood that the gift of the Holy Spirit and the gifts of the Holy Spirit were given to those who confess and belong to Christ, and when the newly baptized are anointed after baptism that understanding is given visible, ritual expression. The robust and multifaceted theological understandings and implications of what it meant to be baptized into Christ were all reflected in the baptismal liturgy of the early church.

From *ApTrad*, we gain the following outline of the baptismal rite.

Apostolic Tradition

Prayer over the water
Candidates undress
Prayer of thanksgiving over the oil
Exorcism a of different oil

Apotaxis (renunciation)

Pre-baptismal anointing with oil of exorcism

Syntaxis (adherence) and water bath (triple interrogation with triple immersion)

Post-baptismal anointing with oil of thanksgiving (chrism)

Neophytes dress and enter the church (joining the faithful)

Post-baptismal laying on of hands and prayer

Second post-baptismal anointing with oil and laying on of hands of neophytes with Trinitarian formula

Kiss of Peace from bishop

Prayer of the Faithful

Exchange of Kiss of Peace

The African Methodist Episcopal (AME) Church[21]

At the end of the 18th century and the beginning of the 19th in the United States, the relationship between the white and black Christians of the Methodist Episcopal (M.E.) tradition was fraught with great and escalating tensions. One critical turning point in the separation of black Methodists from white Methodists occurred in 1787. During a worship service at St. George's Methodist Episcopal Church, a group of black worshippers were on their knees praying. In the midst of their praying, they were pulled up from their knees for being in an area that was off limits to blacks. During that same year, although it is a subject of debate whether it was before or after the St. George incident, Richard Allen and Absalom Jones organized the Free African Society.[22] The Free African Society served both spiritual and secular interests. However, it was not a remedy for the situation encountered by blacks at church. Blacks continued to experience harsh and inequitable treatment in matters of worship. As a result of what Daniel Payne recounts of the experiences of blacks "suffering from the unkind treatment of their white brethren, who considered them [black Christians] a nuisance in the house of worship,"[23] a group of black Christians met in an effort to organize "colored Methodists into a society separate and apart from the control of the white Methodists."[24] After many meetings and in spite of great opposition, in 1816, delegates representing five churches from New Jersey, Pennsylvania, Delaware, and Maryland formally organized the African Methodist Episcopal Church,[25] with Richard Allen serving as its first bishop.

Worship in the African Methodist Episcopal Tradition

In 1817, one year after the formal organization of the African Methodist Episcopal Church, Richard Allen along with one other person published the first denominational resource entitled *The Doctrines and Disciplines of the African Methodist Episcopal Church*. It is organized into two parts. The first part is organized into three chapters, each addressing specific topics under section headings. It is the third chapter entitled "Sacramental Services, &c." that contains the rite for adult baptism ("The Ministration of BAPTISM to such as are of Riper Years"). The African Methodist Episcopal

Church also publishes a smaller book entitled *AME Church Liturgy (Revised)*, which contains only the liturgy of the AME church along with the consecration and ordination rituals.

In order to discern any ritual variations from the African Methodist Episcopal Church's inception as a denomination, an examination of the adult baptismal rite in three different books was conducted, the first book of discipline published in 1817, the second entitled *The Doctrine and Discipline of the African Methodist Episcopal Church* (32nd revised edition, published in 1940), and the most recent one, *The Book of Discipline of the African Methodist Episcopal Church—2008* (48th edition, published in 2009). The same ritual structure was found in each edition of the book. The order of the adult baptismal rite in the African Methodist Episcopal Church is as follows:

The Order for the Baptism of Adults (in The Book of Doctrine and Discipline of the African Methodist Episcopal Church, 1817, 1940, and 2008)

Exhortation (minister)
Prayer for Remission of Sins of Candidates
Prayer for Bestowal of Holy Spirit to the candidates
Gospel Reading (John 3:1–8)
Minister addresses candidates
Apotaxis (renunciation)
Syntaxis (adherence)
Question of Desire to be Baptized
Question of Intent to Live the Christian Faith
The Collects
Prayer Over the Water and for Candidates
Water bath with Trinitarian formula (single immersion)
Lord's Prayer
Concluding Prayer

In all three books, regarding the *apotaxis*, only one question is asked that addresses the evil one and his domain ("... [1] the devil and [2] all his works, [3] the vain pomp and glory of the world, with [4] all covetous desires of the flesh; so that thou wilt not follow, nor be led by them?"). The candidate responds by saying, "I renounce them all." It is immediately followed by the *syntaxis*, presented in the same style. The entire tripartite baptismal creed (the Apostles' Creed) is presented in the form of a single question, to which the candidate answers, "All this I steadfastly believe." While there is no difference in the ritual structure, there is one difference in the euchology in the 2008 edition in contrast to the 1817 and 1940 versions. In the 1817 and 1940 collects, there are four collects. They are as follows:

1. "O merciful God, grant that the old Adam in these persons may be so buried, that the new man may be raised in them. Amen."

2. "Grant that all carnal affections may die in them and that all things belonging to the Spirit may live and grow in them. Amen."

3. "Grant that they may have power and strength to have victory, and triumph against the devil, the world, and the flesh. Amen."

4. "Grant that they being here dedicated to thee by our office and ministry, may also be endued with heavenly virtues, an everlastingly rewarded, through thy mercy, O blessed Lord God, who dost live, and govern all things, world without end. Amen."

The second collect is omitted from the 2008 version of the rite.[26] Other textual differences between the 2008 Book of Discipline and the earlier two is the use of an updated version of the sacred scriptures, the use of contemporary pronouns in place of archaic ones, and the use of gender-inclusive pronouns.

Differences in Similarity:
Comparison of the Baptismal Rite in Apostolic Tradition
and the Baptismal Rite in the African Methodist Episcopal Church

A comparative examination of rites over time can yield some fruitful insights; it can also raise as many or more questions. In addition, while answers to the divergences may not (and are often not) answerable, they do often provide a window into the theology, significant themes and understandings of communities being studied. In comparing the baptismal rite in *ApTrad* to the baptismal rite of the African Methodist Episcopal Church, there are some significant things to note. *(See table at the end of this chapter.)*

Of elements common to both rites, there is a difference in the placement of the blessing over the baptismal waters. In *ApTrad*, the baptismal rite begins with the blessing of the water, followed by a description of the type of water it should be ("flowing") and a description of a suitable alternative of flowing water not unavailable. This description echoes similar stipulations regarding the baptismal waters found in the *Didache*.[27] However, in the African Methodist Episcopal Church, the prayer over the water occurs immediately before the water bath and is part of a larger prayer that petitions God for the candidates "to receive the fullness of thy grace and ever remain in the number of the faithful and elect children." The second petition of the prayer in the African Methodist Episcopal Church rite is found in the post-baptismal position in *ApTrad* and is offered along with the post-baptismal laying on of hands by the bishop. While the petition for grace in the African Methodist Episcopal Church ritual is for grace to remain in the body of the faithful, in *ApTrad*, the petition is made so that the candidates may serve God according to God's will.

Also in common is the *apotaxis* and *syntaxis*, but, again, with slight variation between the two rites. Both rites appropriately place these two ritual elements in close proximity to the water bath. The formula for the *apotaxis* is different between the two rites, and the African Methodist Episcopal rite provides a slightly fuller description of the breadth of the domain of the evil one. In *ApTrad*, candidates are instructed to renounce using the words, "I renounce you, Satan, and all your service and all your works." In the African Methodist Episcopal rite, the *apotaxis* element is introduced in a four-fold interrogatory form to the candidate. "Dost thou renounce the devil and all his works, the vain pomp and glory of the world, with all covetous desires of the flesh; so that thou wilt not follow, nor be led by them?" After which the candidate responds, "I will renounce them all." With regard to the *syntaxis*, however, there is greater similarity in euchology but structurally presented in slightly different ways. In both rites, the *syntaxis* is introduced in interrogatory form, and the content of the question is the language of the baptismal creed presented in question form. However, where the *ApTrad* divides the interrogation at the Trinitarian divisions of the baptismal creed, the African Methodist Episcopal Church asks candidates one question, the content of which is the entire creed. In *ApTrad*, the *syntaxis* is administered in the form of three questions. "Do you believe in one God, the Father almighty. . . ?" "Do you believe in Christ Jesus, the Son of God. . . and will come to judge the living and the dead?" "Do you believe in the Holy Spirit. . . ?" After each question, the candidate responds, "I believe." In the African Methodist Episcopal rite, the entire baptismal creed is put in the form of one question ("Dost thou believe in God the Father Almighty. . . and everlasting life?"), to which the candidates respond, "All this I steadfastly believe."

The places of divergence are greater in number. However, before proceeding to a discussion of the divergences, a discussion regarding incorporation and interpretation of liturgical practices is warranted. Many individuals who serve in liturgical leadership in the church are often guilty of an uncritical appropriation of liturgical forms and worship practices. Some liturgical elements are incorporated because they draw attention to an aspect or a particular area of the church. Others liturgical elements are incorporated because they showcase a particular person and/or that person's talents or abilities. Sometimes, the impulse behind a new liturgical form or worship practice is simply the notion that it is "the new, cool thing to do," it is trendy and feeds leadership's desire to do what it popular, or it will increase church attendance and subsequently (hopefully) revenue. In these and other instances, it is often the case that liturgical elements are introduced and incorporated into a congregation's liturgy without regard for historical or theological context or current and contemporary relevance. Revising the liturgy of any church requires significant historical, theological, and cultural and prayerful consideration.

The history of the early church is of great value to liturgical study because it provides a window into early church baptismal theology and practice, and it is studied in order to inform and expand current understandings and practice. However, one is cautioned of the need to always to be mindful to avoid the trap of making an idol out of what is ancient and making tradition an inviolable law. Traditions are meant to be revisited and revised in light of a community's current context and theological understanding. So as ancient liturgical documents are read and studied to in order to enhance our current theological understanding and practice, Laurence Hull Stookey provides sage cautionary advice. He writes, "A crucial question to ask when contemplating the restoration of an ancient practice is, 'What sense does it make in our age?'"[28] With this in mind, we continue with our examination and discussion of the divergences.

The first difference between the adult baptismal rite in *ApTrad* as compared to the adult baptismal rite in the African Methodist Episcopal Church is that candidates were baptized naked in the third century community of *ApTrad* and not in the African Methodist Episcopal rite. It should be noted that the rise of infant baptism around the sixth century with a corresponding decline in adult baptism accounts for the disappearance of some liturgical elements that were present in the earlier centuries of the church (among them, the stripping of adult baptism candidates). This historical fact notwithstanding, had the stripping of adult baptism candidates endured in the liturgical practice of the church to the time of the inception of the African Methodist Episcopal Church in 1816, its absence from the African Methodist Episcopal Church's rite would be historically and contextually understood.

First, a different sense of propriety may have existed in the third century in contrast to the nineteenth and twentieth centuries. Even in the third and fourth century, propriety was an issue that the church was intentional about trying to manage in order to guard the dignity of the candidates, separating and attending to female baptismal candidates apart from male ones. For example, female candidates were anointed by deaconesses, and male candidates were anointed by deacons. Second, differing architectural contexts in the third century as compared to the later centuries in the context of the African Methodist Episcopal Church may have made the propriety of naked candidates easier to guard. In some ancient churches, baptisteries were located *outside* the church, so baptisms were administered in a more secluded and private context. Third, the cultural context has an even greater bearing on this distinction. Within the baptismal rite in the early church, the stripping of the garments before baptism represented the stripping of one's former self with all of its worldly and evil influences coupled with the sense of returning to the edenic "pre-Fall" innocence of Adam and Eve, and after one was baptized, a white garment was given because now one was "clothed in Christ." However, the emergence and growth of the African Methodist Episcopal Church took place in a United States that was still embroiled in the evils of slavery and racism. It was not uncommon for the degradation of blacks to include the humiliating public display of their unrobed bodies. Even if the practice of candidates being baptized naked was operant in United States churches at this time, that the practice would be abandoned by the African Methodist Episcopal Church is certainly plausible, understandable, and defensible.

Second, conspicuously absent from the African Methodist Episcopal Church rite is the lack of mention and use of oil and of hand laying. Conversely, in *ApTrad*, there are two different oils used at three different times in the rite, once pre-baptism and twice post-baptism. We cannot reach any valid conclusions regarding the divergences in the African Methodist Episcopal rite versus the rite as presented in *ApTrad* because a more in-depth study would be required that would examine the possible recensions in Methodist tradition, the possible recensions in the Episcopal tradition, the time and context of those recensions and where those recensions occurred in the development of the liturgical tradition of the African Methodist Episcopal Church. Even mindful of the aforementioned considerations, one possibility for the absence of oil in this context could be an issue of access. The founders and members of this new, young, *black* denomination were met with great opposition from their white counterparts, and punitive and retributive actions were not uncommon. Is it possible that one of the ways in which that animosity was expressed was to deny or make access to the materials for liturgy difficult if not impossible to obtain by this new black Methodist Episcopal community of Christians? As history attests, venues for blacks to worship were denied and destroyed, so it is not infeasible to conceive of the elements needed to conduct worship be denied or made difficult to obtain. This is a consideration for further investigation.

The third element absent from the African Methodist Episcopal Church rite is the kiss of peace, both by the bishop and among the faithful. The ritual kiss in the early Christian church was the symbol of kindred relationship. A kiss was an act that was exchanged among members of the same family. The ritual kiss is a symbol of the belonging to the family of God. Thus, those who were in the process of becoming members of the church were not permitted to participate in the kiss of peace until they received the sacraments of initiation, which made them full members of the family of God. In 19th century America, in the context of slavery and racism, blacks were not considered part of the community of humanity in law and society, and they were regarded and treated with equal and even more egregious inequity in the church because it was done in the name of God. Blacks had a sense of kinship and family by virtue of their shared experience as an oppressed people in a society hostile to their existence. The kiss did not make them family. They were already family by virtue of their shared past and their common struggle in a brutally unkind world. They understood that they were family also because they, too, were blood-bought and water washed children of God as much as anyone else. However, as mentioned in the divergence with regard to the oil, a more in-depth study would be required that would examine the recensions in the Methodist tradition, the Episcopal tradition, and the time and context of those recensions and where those recensions occurred in the development of the liturgical tradition of the African Methodist Episcopal Church with regard to the kiss of peace.

One interesting additional element exists in the African Methodist Episcopal rite that is absent from the ancient *ApTrad* rite. After the *syntaxis*, two questions are asked of the candidate. First, candidates are asked, "Wilt thou be baptized in this faith?" They are required to state their desire to be baptized in the Christian faith. The second question candidates are asked is, "Wilt thou then obediently keep God's holy will and commandments, and walk in the same all the days of thy life?" Candidates respond, "I will endeavor to do so, God being my helper." This seemingly small insertion is significant in its meaning, particularly given its historical context. The second question provides an understanding of the implications of baptism for Christian living and praxis. The African Methodist Episcopal Church understood that among the gospel commandments, Jesus stated that the greatest commandment was to "love your neighbor as yourself,"[29] and it knew that what it experienced in church was not the gospel being lived out as Jesus required. This question is a testimony to the theological understanding of the African Methodist Episcopal Church that Christian identity demanded Christian praxis, and it embedded that understanding in its liturgical rite.

The common ground on which both rites stand and in which they are anchored is evident and simple: the rejection of evil, the profession of Christian faith, and the water bath. These three elements are the *common* tradition of the *Christian* Church, and they reorient all individuals, whosoever will, positionally into being children of God and joint heirs with Christ. The other ritual elements provide a theological robustness and depth to understanding the implications of this movement from the realm of the evil one to the realm of God, Christ, and the Holy Spirit. However, it is the articulation of the volition of the spirit and the submission to the ritual water bath that ontologically moves us from dimension of existence to another holy and divine realm. These are the gateway into the kingdom of God.

Conclusion

Any study of liturgical texts reminds us that liturgical rites emerge within a particular *Sitz im Leben*. While ancient extant history provides a relatively varied and robust array of rites, an examination of the differences, particularly over time, requires that recensions, lacunae, and embolisms be treated with a critical analysis of the variables to determine the extent to which a given community may have had some influence or control over them. Any community's time, geographical location, social and political context, along with worldview, shapes its theology and its praxis. The difference between the baptismal rite found in the *Apostolic Tradition* and the African Methodist Episcopal baptismal rite is not based solely on the roughly 1500 years of difference between them. Those differences speak to and challenge contexts and worldviews that are historically, geographically, culturally, and experientially conditioned. Any uncritical importation of liturgical rites and worship practices from one context to another, without the appropriate investigative and prayerful due diligence, courts liturgical failure and exposes poor pastoral stewardship and leadership. At the same time, interpretations and conclusions regarding the presence or absence of any liturgical element should not be too quickly or too severely drawn Within this study, some of the absences within the African Methodist Episcopal rite are easily historically explained *and* the reasons for their importation being a bad idea are obvious. Where the common liturgical elements are found is the ontological ground of being in the common Christian tradition, that place that makes all who participate in them part of the family of God. Regardless of what comes before and what comes after, one's entrance into the Christian community and communion requires a yes, a yes to the rejection of all forms and manifestations of evil in word and in deed *and* a yes to a unified submission of one's will and one's being to the Christian faith and Christian life. And, in that promised life eternal beyond this earthly realm, our yes will be all that truly matters.

Notes

1. Acts 8:5–17.
2. Acts 19:1–7.
3. Geoffrey J. Cumming, ed., *Hippolytus: A Text for Students with Introduction, Translation, Commentary and Notes* (Bramcote, England: Grove Books, 1976).
4. Cumming, *Hippolytus*, 3.
5. Cumming, *Hippolytus*, 15–16. Hippolytus sets forth criteria for those who are to be admitted into the catechumenate. It reads, in part, that "If a man is brothel-keeper, let him cease or be rejected. If anyone is a sculptor or a painter, let them be instructed not to make idols; let them cease or be rejected." Similar admonitions are given for actors, teachers (with an exception), "a charioteer who competes in the games, or goes to them. . . one who is a gladiator, or teaches gladiator," "one who fights with beasts in the games," "a public official employed on gladiatorial business," priests of idols, keepers of idols, soldiers who kill, "a magistrate of a city who wears purple," a catechumen who wants to be a soldier, "a prostitute, a profligate, a eunuch, or anyone else who does things which it is a shame to speak. . . a magician, a charmer, an astrologer, a diviner, an interpreter of dreams, a mountebank, a cutter of fringes of clothes, or a maker of phylacteries, a man's concubine" (in certain circumstances).
6. Cumming, *Hippolytus*, 16. ". . . but if a man is keen, and perseveres well in the matter, the time shall not be judged, but only his conduct."
7. In liturgical contexts, to "sign" an individual means to make the sign of the cross on some part of the body (e.g., the forehead).
8. Cumming, *Hippolytus*, 18–21.
9. Cumming, *Hippolytus*, 16.
10. Edward Yarnold, *The Awe-Inspiring Rites of Initiation: The Origins of the R.C.I.A.* (Collegeville: Liturgical Press, 1994), 8.
11. While Easter was held as the *most* appropriate day, baptisms were also held on other days of the year (e.g., Pentecost).
12. It should be noted that the 40 day Lenten season that we currently observe did not have the same shape in the earliest days of the Christian church. It has been traditionally held that Lent has its origins in a one- to two-day fast in preparation for Easter, and over time, the preparation period evolved to one week to three weeks to the length currently observed by most Christian churches. This belief has been seriously questioned by some and explicitly refuted by others. The development of the season of Lent has a far more complex developmental history. See Maxwell E. Johnson, "Baptismal Preparation and the Origins of Lent" in *The Rites of Christian Initiation: Revised and Expanded* (Collegeville: Liturgical Press, 2007), 201–218.
13. Yarnold, *AIRI*, 7.
14. Yarnold, *AIRI*, 8.
15. George E. Gingras, *Egeria: Diary of a Pilgrimage* (New York: Newman, 1970), 122.
16. Individuals are also grafted into the universal Body of Christ, but this ecclesiological discussion is beyond the scope of this study.
17. The baptismal creeds used in the rites of Christian initiation are but one of many creeds. Church councils issued many creeds during the course of church history (e.g., Nicene-Constantinopolitan Creed). For English translations of early creeds, see J.N.D. Kelly, *Early Christian Creeds* (London: Longmans, Green and Co. Ltd, first edition 1950, second edition 1960).
18. *ApTrad* was written in approximately the first half of the third century. Ambrose was bishop of Milan in the latter half of the fourth century.

19. The kiss from the bishop and the exchange ("The Lord be with you. . . and with your spirit") are significant at this point. Prior to baptism, while these individuals were going through the catechumenate and the Lenten preparation for baptism, they were dismissed from the liturgy before the kiss of peace was exchanged in the assembly. It was only after they were officially part of the family of God (as a result of their baptism) that they were allowed to participate in the kiss. The kiss, like the Eucharist, is reserved for those who are part of the Body of Christ.

20. F. L. Cross, *St. Cyril of Jerusalem's Lectures on the Christian Sacraments: the Procatechesis and the Five Mystagogical Catechesis* (Crestwood, NY: St. Vladimir's Seminary, 1977), 60.

21. Detailed historical accounts of the events leading up to emergence and growth of the African Methodist Episcopal denomination can be found in Daniel A. Payne's *History of the African Methodist Episcopal Church* (New York: Arno, 1969) and from Charles Smith's *A History of the African Methodist Episcopal Church being A Volume Supplemental to the The African Methodist Episcopal Church, by Daniel Alexander Payne* (Philadelphia: Book Concern of the AME Church, 1922).

22. C. E. Lincoln and Lawrence H. Mamiya, *The Black Church in the African American Experience* (Durham: Duke University Press, 1990), 50–51.

23. Payne, *History*, 4.

24. Smith, *History*, 13.

25. Smith, *History*, 13–14.

26. The second collect is also missing from the 1956 Book of Doctrine and Discipline (36th revised edition) and 1980 Book of Discipline (42nd revised edition).

27. *Didache*, VII.

28. Laurence Hull Stookey, *Baptism: Christ's Act in the Church* (Nashville: Abingdon), 154.

29. Matthew 22:39, Mark 12:31, Luke 10:27.

Apostolic Tradition	_The Order for the Baptism of Adults (in The Book of Doctrine and Discipline of the African Methodist Episcopal Church, 1817, 1940, and 2008)_
	Exhortation (minister)
	Prayer for remission of sins of candidates
	Prayer for Bestowal of Holy Spirit to the candidates
	Gospel Reading (John 3:1-8)
	Minister addresses candidates
Prayer over the water	
Candidates undress	
Prayer of thanksgiving over the oil	
Exorcism of different oil	
Apotaxis (renunciation)	_Apotaxis_ (renunciation)
Pre-baptismal anointing with oil of exorcism	
Syntaxis (adherence) and water bath (triple interrogation with triple immersion)	_Syntaxis_ (adherence) (Apostles' Creed asked in the form of a single question)
	Question of Desire to be Baptized
	Question of Intent to Live the Christian Faith
Post-baptismal anointing with oil of thanksgiving (chrism)	
Neophytes dress and enter the church (joining the faithful)	
Post-baptismal laying on of hands and prayer	
Second post-baptismal anointing with oil and laying on of hands on head of neophyte with Trinitarian formula	
Kiss of Peace from bishop	
Prayer of the Faithful	
Exchange Kiss of Peace	
	The Collects
	Prayer over the Water and for Candidates
	Water bath with Trinitarian formula (single immersion)
	Lord's Prayer
	Concluding Prayer

4

Introduction to Conversations with God: Two Centuries of Prayers by African Americans

James Melvin Washington

A strange irony haunts this book. I did not believe that it could or should be done. Others believed in it before I did. I am unsure of the mixture of motivations for their efforts to encourage me to edit this book, but my reasons for resisting their entreaties are now clearer to me. They constituted a threefold ensemble of fears. Rather than see this book as a presentation of acts of faith, profiles of spiritual intimacy and courage among an often despised people, and insights into the oratory and rhetoric of personal prayer, I feared unwittingly making a contribution to the grotesque profiteering, profanation, and cultural voyeurism that stalk our times.

I felt that such a book might be seen as another attempt to maraud the African American past for the sake of profit and curiosity. My disdain for profiteers is matched only by my repugnance for eavesdroppers who have spawned what Stephen Carter rightly calls "the culture of disbelief." I did not want to participate in parading the spiritual healing processes of my wounded people before unempathetic consumers.

As a historian of African American religion, I was quite aware of the cynicism that has often made the spiritual life of my people part of a cultural menagerie. This indecency callously subjects genuine spiritual struggles to ridicule, dismissing them as superstitious and escapist, or reducing them to various doctrinaire theories of group frustration.

The intellectual hegemony of the social sciences for most of the twentieth century accounts for how some descriptions profane African American spirituality. Even

William E. B. Du Bois, the great African American social scientist and historian, was a captive of the objectivist language of his academic disciplines. On the one hand, he admonished those who observe "the frenzy of a Negro revival in the untouched backwoods of the South" to remember the limitations of the art of description. "As described," he opined, "such scenes appear grotesque and funny," but, on the other hand, "as seen they are awful."[1] Portrayals of the sublime usually defy the rationalistic assumptions of modernists. The sometimes-violent churnings of religious experience strike its bourgeois analysts as vile precisely because such sacred wrenchings labor for rebirth oblivious to the canons of correct behavior.

The tools of intellectual analyses are actually a double-edged sword. They allow us to see into the entrails of human expressions of the divine. But they are rarely able to explain the meaning of what is seen, or how to recreate the corpora of divinity. The sublime, with its mixture of beauty and ugliness, is best acknowledged in its extremities. After his close documentation of the various macrocosms of religious experience, William James felt the necessity to explain why he chose the most graphic examples to illustrate his theories. He wrote, "I took these extreme examples as yielding the profounder information. To learn the secrets of any science, we go to expert specialists, even though they may be eccentric persons, and not to commonplace pupils. We combine what they tell us with the rest of our wisdom, and form our final judgment independently. Even so with religion."

From the standpoint of many believers, however, such procedures are fraught with sacrilege. Even some describers of black religious experience admit their feelings of embarrassment in reveling details of spiritual intimacy. Those who report on their visits to black prayer meetings often feel compelled to apologize for their fascination. Eli N. Evans, a southern-born Jew, highlighted this ambivalence in how he remembered his attendance at black prayer meetings:

> We white boys went to black prayer meetings of the holy rollers just to watch them move, and clap hands, and sing out "Hallelujahs" and "Amen, brother." We bathed in the "Oh tell it...tell it" magic of hypnotic stimulation between preacher and congregation, each driving the other on to mounting excess of singsong sermonizing and jump-up conversions and twitching moments of "cain't-stand-it-no-more" spiritual release and liberation.

He went on to describe the cultural chasm separating the observer and the believer: "For us white boys clustered way back where we had to stand to see anything, it was more like going to a performance than to a religious service."

The necessity for such distancing is entirely understandable for a Jew who finds Christianity oppressive. Indeed, Evans quickly asserted that African American religion posed no threat to his sense of Jewish identity. He reasoned that no black preacher would invite Jewish white boys to convert to Christianity. Moreover, "afterwards, all of us [white boys] together would imitate the Negro preacher, moaning and crying out the 'praise the Lawd' accents of the panting sermons." The problems and pains of African Americans as evident in their religious expressions have been too often a source of humor, black or white.[2] Why I take religion so seriously can best be explained autobiographically.

If I do not add this parenthetical comment, what follows might be viewed as unwarranted vanity, if not spiritual arrogance. I must speak in this way, however, even though it makes me uneasy. Self-disclosure is fraught with pretension and unwitting, if not intentional, caricature. Nonetheless, an editor has an obligation to disclose the criteria, assumptions, and worldview that influenced the content and structure of his or her book. The ethics of authorship demand at least that modicum of respect for one's readers. Yet, encroachments of self-deception, those fleeting shadows of the unconscious, often disguise the layered masks of years of carefully crafted repressions. This of course cannot lead to the presentation of the real person. That is too ugly to see and too painful to share. Nevertheless, the servanthood of authorship, especially of a text that is so shamelessly about the spirituality of a despised people, must attempt to draw from the encrusted conventicles of the author's persona precisely because what the author sees is inevitably the hidden sinew of the book itself. And only the author is situated behind those eyes. An author must therefore choose an appropriate camera for the self-examination of his soul lest the enterprise fall prey to an embarrassing sentimentality.[3] With this confessional excursus out of the way, I can now explain why I strongly dislike caricatures of any people's or person's spirituality.

Unlike Evans', my first experience in observing the prayers and rituals of another faith tradition and race struck me as poignant and holy. Like most kids, I definitely could be silly and frivolous—but not about religion. According to my mother, and many other adults in my neighborhood and at the Mount Olive Baptist Church, I had the mark of divine anointment on me. In fact, my mother often told me that Mr. Warren, our next-door neighbor in the Austin Homes Project, looked over in my crib when she and my father brought me home from the old Colored General Hospital in Knoxville, Tennessee, and yelled, "Annie! Will! That little rascal will either be a preacher or go crazy!" He told them that he saw the light of God's countenance shine upon my little face. Later, I indeed felt that some strange sunshine was beaming excruciatingly hot rays upon my soul. A crass materialist reading of my experience might conclude that it was the churning of hormones, or the whirlwinds of the Civil Rights Movement. I was in a state of profound angst, but I did not have the intellectual or social maturity to speculate about the source of my experience of God's presence. I only knew I felt the numinous clearly and powerfully.

The year was 1962, and I was 15 years old and in the tenth grade. The tumultuous public anxiety surrounding the student sit-ins beckoned me to join the fray. I tried. But Willie, one of my older brothers threatened to beat me if he saw me embarrassing us by joining in with "those crazy students." I always took his threats seriously—perhaps because he made good on them with what I felt was rather malevolent precision. In order to keep me out of trouble and encourage me to help ease our poor family's enormous financial burdens, he secured a job for me as his helper. He was the custodian of the Heska Amuna Synagogue, which belongs to the Orthodox branch of American Judaism.

After sundown on Fridays, the men of this congregation, usually led by Rabbi Max Zucker and the cantor, would have their prayer services. I found it enthralling and enchanting to hear the descendants of Jesus sing praises and utter prayers to the God of Abraham and Sarah in the Hebrew tongue. As I listened to their services, I thought about the lessons I was learning from Mr. Lorenzo Grant, my black world history teacher, about the evils of Christendom's pogroms against the Jews, and especially about what Hannah Arendt called "the banality of evil" that was shamelessly fomented by the Nazi Holocaust. I heard and felt the pain and suffering of the Jewish people remembered and surrendered to Yahweh.

I was not sure even then, however, that these affluent people understood and appreciated the terrors and pains of my people's history. I sensed that they were more sensitive than most other white people. But I felt their sensitivity was based more on pity than on personal knowledge or affection. Too many of them did not even see me. I was invisible until they needed a light switch turned on, a meat dish rather than a dairy dish, and so on. I did not feel the need to hold this against them. After all, they were white. I had been taught to expect to be treated like a "'whatnot" by white people. But these Jews were a different sort of white people. They seemed to have real religion. I felt the presence of God as they prayed and sang. For me, no one's religion is a laughing matter, most certainly not my own.

In the summer of 1961, I had already arisen from my seat at a youth convocation sponsored by the National Baptist Young People's Union (BYPU) declaring that God had called me to be a preacher while the great Lucie Eddie Campbell Williams sang "It Pays to Serve Jesus." She died the following year. But my commitment did not wane.

I began my ministry as a teenage pastor in east Tennessee after I was ordained in 1967 by the Mount Olive Baptist Church at the request of the Riverview Missionary Baptist (Lenoir City, Tennessee). In the midst of the Black Power Revolt, I became my 126-member congregation's nineteen-year-old pastor. I underwent the traumas of confronting the need to change from a Negro to a black man. Then from black to Afro-American, and now to African American. These demands for identity changes bespoke a deep yearning for roots and continuity on the part of many baby boomers like myself. Those of my generation who were saved from the altars of infanticide in the service of the American war against Vietnam often found ourselves seeking messianic hope wherever we could find it. The American Dream, John Winthrop's City upon a Hill, collapsed under the weight of the shameful and macabre spectacle of the wanton destruction of Vietnamese villages, body bags containing our dead friends and neighbors, as well as pompous and unrepentant nationalism paraded daily on national television. That theater of the Cold War shattered the youthful idealism that was spawned by the Civil Rights Movement as well as the collapse of colonialism and the repressive comatose shadows of Victorian culture.

I escaped military experience because of severely fallen arches, conscientious objection to war, and a fervent call to ordained Christian ministry. My contemporary religious hero was Martin Luther King Jr. When he was martyred on 4 April 1968, I reexamined my vocational commitments. Inspired partly by James Baldwin's *The Fire Next Time* (1962) and James H. Cone's *Black Theology and Black Power* (1969), I discovered in existentialism a certain secular celebration of the inevitability of marginality. I now have recovered what I repressed then: These intellectually respectable endorsements of black self-respect and disciplined alienation salvaged crucial dimensions of the black church that were being severely challenged by my superb training in the Department of Religious Studies at the University of Tennessee at Knoxville.

As my professors at Tennessee introduced me to the ideas and history of modern European thought between 1600 and the 1960s, I resonated best with those thinkers—like Kierkegaard, Nietzsche, Barth, and Sartre—who grappled with the problem of the absurd. Thanks to my later exposure to the thought of Professor Charles Long of the University of California at Riverside, I now understand why Professor Long, one of the seminal African American religious scholars of this century, argues in his book *Signification: Signs, Symbols, and Images in the Interpretation of Religion* (1986), and elsewhere, that if the problem of meaninglessness, or the absurd, is the root metaphor of modernity, then the African American experience of slavery and racism must be counted as a major embodiment of the modern problem of alienation. My own extensive research and writing in African American religious history has confirmed the significance and veracity of this rich insight.

The absurdities of racism insinuate themselves in conscious and unconscious ways in the lives of black people. Religion has been a central way for us to maintain our sanity. But we live in a time when too many African Americans are being infected with the ensemble of societal viruses that Cornel West calls "nihilism." This undisciplined and callous anger grieves me deeply. And it offers a fundamental challenge to my own faith commitment in ways that my struggles with intellectual secularism have never succeeded in doing.

My experience in the pastorate caught me that spiritual malaise is the root cause of the social callousness that has befallen too many segments of African America. Given this belief, I have been asking myself several questions: Can I really prove that spiritual malaise is the cause and not the consequence of nihilism? And if I could succeed in proving this point, what difference would this make? How could I as a middle-aged black religious scholar address this crisis? Should I return to the pastorate and share in the valiant struggle to combat this evil that *Emerge* magazine has rightly called "the worst crisis since slavery"? Over the years several friends of mine, especially those who are pastors, have urged me to return to that most primary form of ministry. But when I recall the intellectual and social experiences that led me to leave the pastorate, my urge is tempered. I have been trying to recover the history of the spiritual disciplines that sustained my people through slavery, Jim and Jane Crowism, and the Civil Rights Movement. Some of those disciplines are still nurtured by institutional African American religion. But many of them have been either deemed irrelevant or have been forgotten. Most have simply died with an older generation whose insights and practices were dismissed by well-meaning advocates of Black Power who saw such people as obstructions on their self-proclaimed "progressive" road to African American nationalism.

As we have come to expect from him, Cornel West, in his brilliant manifesto *Prophesy Deliverance! An Afro-American Revolutionary Christianity* (1982), has telescoped the significance of the problem of both human and divine evil in the history of Christian thought. Indeed he examines the possibilities and contradictions of the major streams of progressive African American religious history. Those who now regularly assess his work often fail to mention this book. They seem unaware of its emerging landmark status in the history of Christian thought in the United States precisely because he succeeds in making the connection between the crisis of modernity and religious responses to the terrors of African American history.

When West and I began teaching at Union Theological Seminary in the late 1970s, we spent seven unforgettable years discussing problems and issues that still command the foci of our intellectual concerns. Among those issues were these questions he raised in his first book: "Why did large numbers of American black people become Christians? What features of Protestant Christianity persuaded them to become Christians?" He framed these questions in a way that demanded the largely philosophical and historical responses that he offers. But, as West would readily agree, far more historical and theological work is needed.

More than a decade later, I am still asking those kinds of questions. But I have also been asking the question of faith. That is, why do people who suffer continue to believe in a God who supposedly has the power to prevent and alleviate suffering? This question bedevils the history of Western monotheism. Indeed, some walk away from such questions because they no longer believe in the existence of God. I must confess that for the sake of my own peace of mind I sometimes wish that I could do the same. But I have been burdened with the assumptions and responsibilities of an intellectual monotheist who still believes in the God that I first came to acknowledge through the Hebrew and Christian scriptures.

The denial of the reality of God has become fashionable among the affluent. Such secularity often belittles folk thought as if learning how to read and write in the halls of academe is a guarantor of our supposedly greater wisdom. But one need only observe the stars on a clear evening to register the unimaginativeness of such cynicism. Indeed, stargazing, a favorite pastime of those, such as unmolested children, who still cherish wonder and curiosity, offers awesome, transporting access to the utter beauty and terrifying grandeur of the universe.[4] Such stargazing is pleasurable precisely because it defies the banal interests of our utilitarian age.

Prayer is an attempt to count the stars of our souls. Under its sacred canopy, an oratory of hope echoes the vast but immediate distances between who we are and who we want to be. This peculiar trek sentences its devotees to an arduous discipline. Prayer demands focus and obedience, as well as intimacy and faithful nurture. A certain civility is inherent in this transaction. Its requirements are both communal and individual. I accept Ludwig Wittgenstein's tightly reasoned convictions that language itself is social.[5] I guess that is why I believe that the oratory of prayer is deeply shaped by one's upbringing.

Those of us who cherish the fading art of counting the stars above, and the stars within, should not become despondent. Every minute of each fleeting day documents how human forgetfulness ends with someone's death, or is diminished by someone's birth. Children who have not been captured by the cynicisms of adulthood replenish the imagination of the human community. My personal experience and historical research have taught me that the children of God, when at their best, also inspire the best in us. My mother, Annie Beatrice Moore Washington, whose fifth-grade education could assist her in getting no further than a career as an honest domestic worker, has taught me more about prayer in the African American community than anyone else I know. I wish I could remember the exact day, my age, the circumstance of what follows, but I cannot.

It was during the early morning hours, while the gladiatorial snores of my sleeping family rebuked silence, that two of us were actually awake. The window of the crowded children's bedroom framed the East Tennessee sky as I lay communing with the stars. A whisper from my parents' bedroom forced me to cease my transporting enterprise. I strained to hear what I would now call a divine soliloquy. It was Mama's voice. She was speaking in piteous hush. I yearn to recapture her exact words. I cannot. I do know that the drama of the moment demanded that I should stop counting stars. I could not resist the temptation to eavesdrop on a most unusual conversation. Mama said a few words about her burdens, anxieties, children. Then an awesome silence would punctuate her lamentation to. . . God? Who was her conversation partner? Daddy was working on the night shift. "Please, Jesus!" she cried. I felt she was hurt, maybe even dying. I ran to be with her. I rubbed her back while she sobbed.

In many ways I have been in spiritual solidarity with my mother since that moment. She taught me to pray. Her silence and her action taught me that I must pray. The distinction between necessity and instructions is paramount. There is a vast difference between giving directions and believing that those directions are either helpful or vital. As I watched her for most of my young life, I noticed that for her prayer is a way of life. At any moment, pray. I learned many things from that strange moment when my mother and I were on our knees in prayer. Indeed, more than any other, through precept and example, she taught me that prayer is a conversation with God. That was the reigning assumption of the African American Christian community that nurtured me. God is a living, personal presence that is insinuated at all times and in all circumstances.

When I was eight years old, it was the custom in our small community to assign to youngsters responsibilities that would teach them "to respect their elders." There was a proud and severely crippled elderly black woman whose name was Mrs. Helen Grady. Because she was a good friend of both my mother and my grandmother, it gradually became my duty and privilege to perform errands for this strange woman. She had the dubious reputation among my playmates of being "an old grouch." But she had her reasons for being temperamental.

Her very physical presence would startle any "normal" person. A dark hue in a racist society was not an asset—even among her own people. Her face bore the imprimatur of deep pain, and I discovered later that she was indeed in constant agony. Polio, that dreaded disease, had dealt its greatest blow to her right side. Her shriveled right hand was permanently cupped. She often joked about this by saying it was always ready for work. It could only assist her left hand, however, since all its muscles were totally useless. She used a strong cane to help her left side drag her right side along. But Helen Grady's handicap did not define or fully describe the rich complexity of her personality.

I learned that her gruff manner was actually a protective facade developed to ward off busybodies. But she really loved children. I sensed this and learned to love her back. I eagerly looked forward to my daily visits to her home. She became a generous teacher, and I became an eager student. She taught me how to hoe a garden with only "one good arm," how to get eggs out of the chicken coop without getting pecked, how to light a fire in an old iron stove which burned coal and wood, and countless other practicalities of poor folk existence. But most important, she took time to introduce a small-town boy to black agrarian culture. She told me countless stories and interpreted the Bible to me after I read passages to her. Even though, I discovered later, she could read, she indulged my passion to display my ability.

She even became my confessor. She confronted the awful monsters of my childhood dreams with the tough realism of folk wisdom and Christian charity. She often ended our little dialogues by saying, "Now, honey, let's talk to the Lord." I cannot recall her exact words. But I can still relive, even now, the sense of God's presence her words invoked. I did not mistake her words for magical incantations. God was there. I could feel a third presence. When she finished what she had to say to God, she invited me to join the conversation. Sometimes we even prayed at the same time. After all, we believed that God is supralingual and omnipresent. As she appealed to "the Throne of Grace," she sobbed with tears of protest against the human condition; and, with tears of faith and thanksgiving, she told the Lord how grateful she was that the Lord God could care about "worms" like us. She asked the Lord to have mercy on my soul and lead me in "the paths of righteousness." These numinous moments captured my attention, affections, and faith. If God could make a crippled bulwark like Mrs. Grady break down in tears and shout with joy, how could I possibly escape this awesome power? I came to believe that such escape was both impossible and exceedingly undesirable.

Mrs. Grady taught me that I should not feel like a prisoner or a slave. She taught me that I am a free spiritual being. She taught me that true spirituality is the ability to see beyond my own prejudices and shortsightedness. Mrs. Grady introduced me to the reality of the spiritual world. She, along with numerous other saints, convinced me that there is a spiritual realm that is available to all who find its many entrances.

In the Mount Olive Baptist Church, where I belonged and was later ordained, I often watched oppressed black women, and sometimes even men, offer shouts of joy embellished with fierce, holy gesticulations. The first enduring sounds of black worship I saw and heard included the strangely warm and often intense cadence of black preachers like Dearing E. King and Charles Dinkins. I also witnessed the prayers of Deacons C. L. Bell, Robert Minter, and George Thorton; the testimonies of Mothers Eliza Dunlap and Lizzie Bates, as well as the angelic singing of Sister Mary Usher and Brother Murphy Strong. Their praise still rings with delight within my memory.

Mrs. Grady revealed to me that these "friends of Jesus" actually slipped into a different time zone, a different realm of existence. I saw these glorious excursions most intensely in her local church. She was a member of the Mothers' Board of the Victory Baptist Church, a tiny congregation endeavoring to maintain the "Ole-Time Religion." The residuals of African American Slave Religion were quite evident here, where they moaned and groaned before God. Her pastor whooped, and her church relied on common meter hymn singing more than my home church.

Mrs. Grady, my beloved friend and spiritual counselor, is dead now. Perhaps the only recognizable living form of the religious culture she loved so dearly exists in black congregations like Mount Olive and Victory. When I attend black worship services of numerous denominations as either a guest preacher or fellow worshiper, I often see Mrs. Grady's face, and feel her presence among my sisters and brothers in the faith as they pray, sing, testify, and shout about what the Lord has done for them. But where I experience her companionship the most is in my own peculiar prayer life. For me prayer is not a ritual. It is a mode of being. I agree with John Macquarrie in his *Paths to Spirituality* that prayer is "a way of thinking." I also like the way my colleagues Ann and Barry Ulanov define and describe prayer as "primary speech." These assessments of the meaning of prayer only ratified what I first learned in the African American religious community. I was taught that we muse know how to talk and think with God.

One need only look at the prayers in this book to see that African Americans have believed fervently that prayer is a necessity in time of crisis. Those who have been the victims of what Orlando Patterson has called "natal alienation" understand this. Prayer in the midst of the abortion of one's human, political, and social rights is an act of justice education insofar as it reminds the one who prays, and the one who overhears it, that the one praying is a child of God. The Reverend Horace J. Bailey, pastor of the Payne Avenue Baptist Church (Knoxville, Tennessee), reminded me of this in 1970.

That year I learned from him that prayer is more than ordering from the menu of divinity, as if God is some cosmic waiter who serves us at our convenience. I found myself undergoing the humiliations of the sacrament of imprisonment, in jail for a righteous cause. I carried a sign amidst a small group of antiwar demonstrators who were protesting the presence of the president of the United States, Richard M. Nixon, at a Billy Graham Crusade that was being held at the University of Tennessee at Knoxville's Neyland Stadium. The authorities issued John Doe warrants with the cooperation of the university administration and the local media.[6] For the first time in my life, I discovered that righteousness and "good" citizenship are often incompatible. This was a painful lesson in its own right. But an even more profound lesson awaited me when I visited the pastor's study of the very pious Reverend Bailey. I recounted the experience of being arrested in the middle of campus, carted in a paddy wagon, fingerprinted, photographed and slammed behind bars for several hours until the Reverend Robert Parrott, director of the Wesley Foundation at the university, secured a bail bond. A sense of rejection, alienation, humiliation, and defeat impeded my spirit from rallying.

The good pastor interrupted my self-pitying litany of woes when he said, "Wait a minute, James." He was an old minister of the gospel. The arthritis that had taken residence in his body made his movements slow and agonized. He kneeled in front of his desk chair. "Let's talk to God about this," he said. He prayed for my soul and my ministry, and against the demons of bitterness. He asked God to give me strength to look beyond the faults of others. "Keep James in your care, O Lord! He will be a mighty strong weapon in your warfare against evil!" My Black Power outlook disliked his tolerance for human evil. But I have come to see that he was more concerned about what human evil was doing to my soul than about what human evil was doing to my body. This might be a false dichotomy. But it is a real distinction in many African American prayers.

A satisfactory comparative history and anthropology of prayer has yet to be written. But whenever such a study appears, surely Theodore Parker Ferris' apt description of the transaction called prayer will be uncontested. According to Ferris, "People who pray feel that they are in some communication with God." Millions believe in the power of this mysterious transaction. Yet few can translate the spiritual content of this peculiar form of communication. In fact many believe that it is impossible.

The prayers in this book were all uttered within the last 230 years under various circumstances, which will be described whenever possible in the Contributors section. A common mood of resistance to racial oppression informs the authors' petitioning for divine affirmation, yearning for divine presence, protesting the seeming absence thereof, and finally feelings and manifestations of divine grace. Sometimes these varied moods and purposes appear so rapidly that they are indistinguishable. This prayerful thought of David Walker illustrates this point:

> I aver, that when I look over these United States of America, and the world, and see the
> ignorant deceptions and consequent wretchedness of my brethren, I am brought ofttimes
> solemnly to stand, and in the midst of my reflections I exclaim to my God, "Lord didst thou
> make us to be slaves to our brethren, the whites?" But when I reflect that God is just, and
> that millions of my wretched brethren would meet death with glory—yea, more, would
> plunge into the very mouths of cannons and be torn into particles as minute as the atoms
> which compose the elements of the earth, in preference to a mean submission to the lash
> of tyrants, I am with streaming eyes, compelled to shrink back into nothingness before my
> Maker, and exclaim again, "thy will be done, O Lord Almighty."[7]

Without his saying it explicitly, Walker's moment of liberation came when he recalled that
God had nurtured a community of resisters. Walker assumed that a community of what Karl
Rahner called "anonymous Christians" constitute a corporation committed to the sanctity of
freedom and the liberation of the oppressed.[8] Many African Americans believe that this sanctified
corporation exists both within and beyond the Christian churches. For them prayer is not the
possession either of white folk or of the churches. Prayer is something that all human beings have
a right to do. But they believe that "the prayers of the righteous prevaileth much." If one has a right
relationship with God, certain activities are inexcusable. They believe that the truly righteous do
not pull black preachers like Richard Allen and Absalom Jones from their knees while they are
praying. The truly righteous do not deny slaves the right to pray and worship.

Greenburg W. Offley, a black Methodist minister, expressed the social nature of this tradition
in the following story. He was careful to assert that a theology of resistance was imbued in the
relative privacy of the slave cabin.

> Our family theology teaches that God is no respecter of persons, but gave his Son to die for
> all, bond or free, black or white, rich or poor. If we keep his commandments, we will be
> happy after death. It also teaches that if God calls and sanctifies a person to do some great
> work, that person is immortal until his work is done; that God is able and will protect him
> from all danger or accident in life if he is faithful to his calling or charge committed by the
> Lord. This is a borrowed idea from circumstances too numerous to mention. Here is one
> man we present as a proof of the immortality of man, while in the flesh: Praying Jacob. This
> man was a slave in the State of Maryland. His master was very cruel to his slaves. Jacob's
> rule was to pray three times a day, at just such an hour of the day; no matter what his work
> was or where he might be, he would stop and go and pray. His master had been to him and
> pointed his gun at him, and told him if he did not cease praying he would blow out his
> brains. Jacob would finish his prayer and then tell his master to shoot in welcome—your
> loss will be my gain—I have two masters, one on earth and one in heaven—master Jesus in
> heaven, and master Saunders on earth. I have a soul and a body; the body belongs to you,
> master Saunders, and the soul to master Jesus. Jesus says men ought always to pray, but you
> will not pray, neither do you want to have me pray. This man said in private conversation
> that several times he went home and drank an unusual quantity of brandy to harden his
> heart that he might kill him; but he never had power to strike or shoot him, and he would
> freely give the world, if he had it in his possession for what he believed his Jacob to possess.

He also thought that Jacob was as assured of Heaven as the apostle Paul or Peter. Sometimes Mr. S. would be in the field about half drunk, raging like a madman, whipping the other slaves; and when Jacob's hour would come for prayer, he would stop his horses and plough and kneel down and pray; but he could not strike the man of God.

Hardly any slaves or slave masters are still living, thus we are dependent on their competing historical tracings. Each oftentimes made quite different claims about the nature of that social order. If an interpreter sides with the beneficiaries of the system, it is usually because he or she is in sympathy with that kind of social philosophy. I am not. Therefore, I find the reports of the slaves to have more moral cogency. We are living in a period when our social memories are constantly being dislocated by too much information and not enough insight. Russell Jacoby calls this phenomenon "social amnesia." I believe there are grave consequences when we cannot locate and integrate the memories of our forebears. Perhaps the most ominous consequence is what I call soul murder.[9]

I believe that somewhere in the infrastructure of the human soul there dwells a dormant anger poised to register its complaint about the unfairness of life. The public and collective expression of this rage oftentimes comes in the form of perverse and harmful civic arrangements that lead to what I call social murder. Every social murder is the consequence of public expressions of this perversion of the human soul. If we look only at the consequence and not at the genesis of social murder, however, we will never be in a position to develop an antidote.

Therefore, we need to understand how social homicides germinate. This requires an examination of the sequence of psychic events that precedes collective demonic deeds. I call my analytical procedure "historical demonology." This strategy assumes that demons are intelligible. And all intelligent beings have a history that yearns for exposure and analysis. Demons thrive best in the dark intervals of human history, and the parentage of real power lies in the sinister womb of negativity. Plato tried to express this in his *Republic* by characterizing humanity as cave dwellers who define reality as a reflection of a reflection of a beam of light forced through a shaft of light. Hegel defined this negativity as "the unhappy conscious." Freud called it "the psyche." Jean-Paul Sartre said in his *Being and Nothingness* that all of reality is like looking through a keyhole. Carl Jung called it "the shadow." But Jesus called it "sin." Whatever we call it, it does exist. All it requires is our cooperation. Unfortunately, the dynamics of demonology are propelled by our tendency to deny its existence. We repress it into the regions of our unconscious where it becomes powerful because it is in the dark, seamy recesses of our soul where it constantly vies for attention and control. We need a historical analysis of these mysterious intervals in order to develop a spiritual practice capable of fortifying our souls against the inevitable assaults of the wiles of the devil.

Let me illustrate what I mean by historical demonology by examining this struggle within the soul as it has manifested itself in an old African American bread-and-water forgiveness festival. On Sunday, 4 January 1884, the first Sunday of the new year, Charles Edwardes attended a black worship service in Jacksonville, Florida. Edwardes described the elderly black pastor's homily that opened this special 11 a.m. service.

> It was the old lesson and story which clergymen have to teach and tell while they have breath for speech—the old lesson, new dressed. The first Sunday in the new year! He told them that they were, one and all, at a crisis in their lives; they might have been, as be hoped they had been, good men and women in the past; but now they were facing the future, they were beginning a new year. How could they best start afresh? he asked them. How? Why, by clearing all the naughty weeds out of the garden of their souls, to be sure; and the way to do that was by prayer and asking forgiveness of friends and neighbors for the injuries they had done them last year. Some might say they had done no wrong to nobody. But they made a mistake if they said that—for they *must* do no wrong, whether they mean it or not. It's human nature to do it, and they can't help themselves. This, then, was what they were here for this first Sunday in the new year. There was bread and there was water by his side—a good quantity of both—and he hoped they would all be so hungry and thirsty for the forgiveness of each other that they would use them both up very soon; for if they didn't he should have to finish them, and it was too cold to drink much cold water, in his opinion.

The pastor then invited his assistants to distribute bread from the table below the dais. This was not a communion service, nor was the table an altar. The bread was passed to members of the congregation who desired to forgive their neighbors for any offense. The aggrieved sister or brother in the faith would then use his or her right hand to pinch a morsel of bread that was held in the left hand of the one willing to forgive. Everyone who so desired sought those willing to forgive. Apparently the water was used to wash down the bread of those who required much forgiveness.

They then followed this practice with prayers and testimonies of faith. In the midst of this segment of the service, one of the most graphic illustrations of the pastoral problem faced by African American spirituality can be found.

> Then a yellow girl, shapely and well-dressed, with tears coursing down her cheeks, cried out and besought that she too might be prayed for. This said, she moved rapidly from her seat, and walked towards the clergyman, with a strange look in her eyes. The worthy man encountered her gaze with his old smile, though it froze somewhat when the girl stopped and continued staring at him—face to his face, with only a few inches between them—in the presence of the whole congregation. "Well!" he said, "what's the matter with you?" and by now his smile had lost all its cordiality; the spirit of it had, as it were, departed.
>
> The question arose the girl from her trance. Shaking her head from side to side madly, and stamping with her feet, she cried—
>
> "Brothers and sisters, pity me. Oh, how I hates myself! I don't know why such a young girl as me was sent into this 'ere earth, 'cept to be made miserable, which don't seem as if it ought to be. I'm all bad, every part of me, and the devil, he's got a finger in everything I do. Yet I hates him, friends, as much as I hates myself. I hate him more than I can say—I'd like to tear his nasty black eyes out of his lying head, that I would! Nor I don't think it a wrong passion to go into! But, dear brothers and sisters, I don't know what to do to be made happy—I don't know what to do. Oh, pray for me, dear brothers and all, pray for me!"

And sobbing aloud, with her hands to her face, the poor girl retraced her steps, and sat down.

This young woman's experience of radical alienation, as well as her willingness to embrace hatred to cure her own self-hatred illustrates the rampant plague of nihilism that infests parts of black America.

In his best-selling book, *Race Matters,* Cornel West offers a powerful analysis of the reasons for the moral collapse of large segments of the African American communities in America's cities. Why all the murders, drug addiction, teen pregnancy, broken homes, and other various forms of violence? Here, West argues more explicitly than ever before that a pervasive nihilism is at fault. This sense that life is useless and worthless, and that values, beliefs, and tradition are for chumps, describes the psychic and spiritual impoverishment of a forgotten people, often odiously referred to as "the underclass." West rightly places these developments at the feet of the general deterioration of values and justice in a racist and classist society that has minimized its commitments to democracy. I agree with him. But I want to examine some of the religious dimensions of these developments.

I could focus on institutional religion's failure to respond adequately to the challenge of nihilism. I do not feel, however, that institutional religion can respond to this challenge. Its own infighting over theological and ethical issues since the 1890s has spent its energies, and driven away much-needed talent. Moreover, its often uncritical acceptance of the excesses of industrial capitalism, anti-communism, racism, and sexism has severely weakened its moral credibility. Whether Protestant, Catholic, Jewish, or African American, institutional religion has had its potentially sharp prophetic edge dulled by its overt or silent complicity in maintaining the status quo. If the powerful, affluent machineries of institutional religion have been so disabled, who then can respond? I believe that this is the wrong question. I believe we need to ask, what is there about the nature of the present cultural crisis that makes it almost impervious to religion? The answer is both simple and complex.

Nathan Hatch recently captivated devotees of American religious history with the obvious but powerful argument that the United States is responsible for the democratization of Christianity. Yet at this crucial moment, the role of religion with regard to racism is unclear. There are many possible explanations, but perhaps some psychological insights would be most helpful in conveying my viewpoint about this subject.

I begin with the hypothesis that the roots and rationale for systemic racism have become an unconscious social creed, with all the traits of a folk religion. I invoke the notion of "folk" here not as a trivializing gesture but as an attempt to suggest how thoroughly unconscious the processes of racism can be. Racism is the perversion of the primeval impulse to protect, advance, and enhance one's tribe. Although we need not pursue interesting questions about the degree to which biology determines this noble phenomenon, this set of impulses undoubtedly underwrites the self-justifying fears that fuel racist attitudes and practices.

Fears become a clinical issue when they can no longer be influenced by the legislative, judicial, or executive inquiries of communal forms of reason. Much hinges here on the breadth of our notions of community. But what is clear is that the narrower our conception of community, the narrower our conception of what is reasonable. Racists believe that the reasoning of their own particular tribe is exclusively correct. Erik Erikson has called this modern phenomenon "pseudospeciation" because racism makes the absurd assumption that one race is the quintessential embodiment of the entire species. Thus other racial groups are seen as expendable. If those who hold this assumption acquire the awesome destructive power that nuclear weapons provide, such racism is not a matter of merely mean social practices. Whole segments of the human race find their existence threatened.

Racism is therefore a more dangerous social practice than tribalism and nationalism. Its modern history crosses all these boundaries. It constitutes a conglomerate of cultural and social forces that sanction political and economic privileges as a natural or divine right. Such cultural enclaves become a set of religious practices and beliefs when they are placed beyond the critical borders of discussion. That was one of the central problems with racism in the South between 1865 and 1965. Everyone with a minimal amount of common sense knew that racism existed, but southern moderates did not want to speak about it lest they disrupt delicate local political coalitions. And religious leaders did not want to talk about it because many considered lynchings, and mean political tactics, such as gerrymandering and voting tests, to belong to the domain of "politics as usual."

Such popular political cynicism bas become a degenerative tradition in this country. It is a form of hoodwinking, a set of unprincipled rituals that foster false appearances in the service of disguising where real power lies. This is why during the 1960s white thugs eagerly accepted the dubious "honor" of "eliminating" black civic "irritants" like Medgar Evers or northern white righteous "invaders" such as the Reverend James Reeb.[10] The state could not summon enough moral courage to be true to its own principles of justice because it had no desire to disclose or expose the white male power structure. Few in that power structure were as vociferous in their defense of this sinful arrangement as were right-wing ministers such as the Reverends Billy Hargis and Jerry Falwell.[11] They condemned Martin Luther King Jr. and his cohorts for daring to challenge the racist privileges exercised by the white community with brazen impunity. And they insisted that politics and religion should have nothing to do with each other. Once political "problems" lie beyond the precincts of public discussion, however, they themselves become religious artifacts.

A religion without theological discussion is a religion that has no room for negotiation, no room for change. White people utter constant refrains such as "I am not a racist. I am not responsible for creating oppression. That's the way the world is!" Carl Jung once said that unconsciousness is the greatest sin that bedevils humanity. At the root of racist unconsciousness is a social anemia that prevents the oxygen of cultural knowledge from circulating throughout the body politic. Something akin to a religion of social fears sanctifies the tribalism that keeps us apart. This peculiar faith in genetic superiority, however, receives more unwarranted solace from the plagues of forgetfulness than from a sinister plot to bolster the privileges of the privileged.

I recall an important comment by Herbert Marcuse in his book *Eros and Civilization*. Marcuse argued that it is practically impossible to remember what you never knew. Several thoughtful analysts of the national soul, such as Frances FitzGerald, have been warning us for more than two decades that our country places itself at serious intellectual risk when it does not have public history textbooks that recount the rich diversity of this nation's history.

But what if the problem is not mere ignorance but forgetfulness understood in an immediate as well as a primeval sense? Is it possible, as Freud suggested in *The Psychopathology of Everyday Life*, that the phenomenon of forgetfulness represents incursions of a repressed unconscious into the realm of consciousness?

When my book *A Testament of Hope: The Essential Writings of Martin Luther King Jr.* appeared in January 1986, my publisher arranged for me to be on several radio "talk shows" to promote it. I was astonished at how many white people literally hate Martin Luther King Jr. Some of the calls were from individuals who identified themselves as religious who felt that King was more of an agitator than a reconciler. I have a nagging feeling that there is more to the hatred against King's ministry within white America than meets the eye. After much reflection, I have concluded that King's determination to insist that America be conscious about its history of mistreating black Americans is a rather perverse example of the classic transference syndrome.[12] As a therapeutic prophet, Dr. King insisted that his nation of patients (white and black) confront their repressed social history not with tribalistic bloodshed but with forgiving love baptized in the caldrons of racial justice.

My own experience of growing up in Knoxville, Tennessee, introduced me quite early to the absurdities of segregation. I attended totally black schools from kindergarten to high school, and was forbidden by law from using the magisterial Lawson McGhee Library. From a youngster's perspective, it was a huge, Romanesque building with big marble columns and a seemingly endless supply of books. I, however, had to use the old, dingy, poorly equipped and staffed Andrew Carnegie Library on Vine Avenue. Finally, though, after the local newspapers announced that the library had agreed to desegregate, I entered the portals of the white people's library, a white building that seemed to me bigger than a whale.

And like Captain Ahab I resolved immediately to pursue my white whale. I walked into its jaws, approached the frowning commander at its mouth, the person behind the circulation desk, and asked, "May I use the library?" She glared at me with an air of stark incredulity. "Listen, little nigger," she whispered with righteous indignation, "colored people are not allowed to use this library! I must ask you to leave immediately!" My bruised ego retorted, "But I read in the newspaper that—" She interrupted my pending recitation with a humiliating interjection delivered with whispered ferocity, "Out!" The acoustics of this temple of learning seized her malevolent whisper and transformed it into a jolting crescendo. The eyes of the white users quickly executed my already bruised ego with glares that sought to incinerate my soul. I wanted to join this anonymous fraternity of learners. Unfortunately, however, I became a victim of social fratricide.

I grew up in a family that could not afford to buy books for me. I worked at odd jobs to amass about twenty books by age fifteen. Books were my extended family, especially philosophical and historical ones. Why would anyone want to keep me from my family? I left not only dejected but with a deficit in my reservoir of unused tears. This self-pity quickly turned to anger, however. I felt like many black youngsters in the 1960s. I wanted to burn that "damn" building down. I reasoned, if I don't have the right to use the public library, then why should I obey a system that deceives, belittles, and degrades me for trying to cultivate my intellectual gifts? Should I torch the white library like some Black Power anarchists advised, or should I continue to emulate the model of gentle strength I cherished in my pastor, the Reverend Dr. William T. Crutcher, who was the leader of the Civil Rights Movement in Knoxville, Tennessee?[13]

I found myself caught between the powerful sway of the religions of tribalism and racism, and the prophetic interpretation of the Bible that I had learned at the Mount Olive Baptist Church under the guidance of Dr. Crutcher. As I reflected on what to do, I realized that I also needed to analyze what had happened at that circulation desk. I concluded that a righteous sense of racial and intellectual pride had emboldened me to go to the white library in the first place. Perhaps I was the one in the wrong. I recall wondering whether or not such a conclusion was an instance of what Black Power advocates called "Uncle Tomism." I thought, Am I blaming myself for offending white sacred space? Who designated this space, "For White People Only"? I wondered why white people needed to exclude people who looked like me from *public* space. From a practical standpoint, I decided not to either burn the building or "cast my pearls before swine." I decided to retreat to the safety of the black communal womb.

The black congregation, when at its best, is a cultural system that teaches self-respect as well as advocates and promotes initiative. My decision to do nothing, however, was an affirmation of my tribal religion's long-standing teaching that self-respect demands that you not go where you are not wanted. I decided to continue building my own personal library. But civil rights integrationism was challenging the separatist social doctrine prevalent in the black church as well as in the African American community at large. The universalist assumptions of the Civil Rights Movement strongly objected to decisions not to confront systemic racial evil. Movement apologists, such as Professor

George Kelsey in his *Racism and the Christian Understanding of Man*, argued that the spiritual and intellectual problems such compromises engender are an offense to our common humanity and to God because they make an idol of white claims for genetic superiority. In fact the more I retreated, the more I realized that the system invades the precincts of conscience most effectively at the primal level of culture and religion.

I began to ask questions that I later pursued more systematically in my undergraduate work in religious studies. I have learned much since I began in 1967, but one of the most enduring lessons is that religion does as much to divide humanity as it does to help us grasp meaning. For proof of this, we have only to recall that religious doctrines sanctioned white supremacy among the Mormons, many Southern Baptists, Methodists, and Presbyterians, as well as within the Dutch Reformed Church in South Africa.

The sin is to do nothing to resist and change the conditions that encourage us to remain either ignorant or forgetful. Resistance, however, requires the prophetic insight and guts to examine the infrastructure of our own souls in search of the contours of the social malignancy of racism. As Abraham Heschel reminds those who still read him, God is a God of "pathos." God feels and responds to the oppressed. Can we religious people possibly do any less? Past betrayals of the best in our religious cultures do not give us license to continue the same degenerative habits. We must respond to the sins of exploitation, injustice, violence, hatred, and war with something more than bureaucratic finesse.[14] We need to respond also as individuals who, to quote Howard Thurman, the great African American Christian mystic, have yielded "the nerve center of our consent" to God, and consequently to the noblest impulses of the human spirit.[15]

The disease of social amnesia plagues the African American community. Large segments of our community have lost the discipline of humanity bestowed upon us by our foreparents. As Ralph Ellison once said in response to a white critique of his work, "He seems never to have considered that American Negro life (and here he is encouraged by certain Negro 'spokesman') is, for the Negro who must live it, not only a burden (and not always that) but also a *discipline*—just as any human life which has endured so long is a discipline teaching its own insights into the human condition, its own strategies of survival." This discipline is at risk because we have sacrificed virginity of our cultural woman on the altar of integration.

The myth of integration—historically conceived—assumed that racism was caused by the difference of black people as evidenced in their physiognomy. The doctrine of integration argued that African Americans needed to become as close to perfect copies of white people as possible. This required the emasculation of their culture and history. In order to do this, one had to infantilize African American history by placing black people on the lower scale of historical development

A close examination of the genealogy of this argument would reveal that some African American leaders, such as Alexander Crummell, prepared the way for this historical condescension in their arguments for supporting home missions and African missions.[16] Both liberated slaves and the colonialized Africans became examples of historical progress. Proponents of racial reform saw cultural homogeneity as the necessary condition for black "uplift." African culture in any form was viewed as animistic, deformed, indeed, pathological.

This concession to white supremacy oftentimes unwittingly or tacitly endorsed what James William Charles Pennington called that "stupid theory" that "nature has done nothing but fit us for slaves, and that art cannot unfit us for slavery!" This has led to what Carter G. Woodson has called "the miseducation of the Negro." Prayer becomes the primal way of conducting "justice education."

African American prayers as a literary genre, and religious social practice, assume that God is just and loving, and that the human dilemma is that we cannot always experience and see God's justice and love. We pray for faith to trust God's ultimate disclosure. Thus prayer as act and utterance teaches the believer to exercise what Adrienne Rich calls "revolutionary patience." But the literary history of African American prayers suggests that, besides anticipating God's ultimate self-disclosure in the history of the oppressed, we are the trustees of the spiritual legacy paid for with the blood, sweat, tears, and dreams of a noble, even if not triumphant, people. The culture, grammar, and promise of the African American prayer tradition is in our hands. Only time will tell whether or not their faith in us was worth the price they paid.

Thus, in editing this book, my first urge was to protect the preciousness of the spiritual womb that birthed and now continuously nourishes my soul. Fortunately, the critical historian in me vetoed that paternalistic impulse. I felt a professional responsibility and personal urge to share my knowledge of the history of African American spirituality in order to combat misunderstandings of its value and culture. Before I could do this, however, I had to ponder where I had seen prayers in the course of more than two decades of arduous research. The prayers in this book are the by-product. When I really put my mind the task, I began to find prayers seemingly everywhere.

I have organized these prayers chronologically. In order to give a sense of the general circumstance that framed these prayers in particular periods, I have subdivided them into six parts: Part I. Slavery and the Eclipse of the African Gods, 1760–1860; Part II. The Crucible of the Anglo-African Conscience, 1861–1893; Part III. The Vale of Tears, 1894–1919; Part IV. The New Negro, 1920–1955; Part V. The Civil Rights Ethos, 1956–1980; Part VI. Postmodern African American Worlds, 1981–1994. The names I have given for these periods reflect the central crisis out of which and to which these prayers come. It is a mistake to see these prayers *only* as the personal conversations that each of these African Americans has had with God. They are certainly this. But from a cultural and social standpoint, as Benjamin Mays tried to argue in his *The Negro's God As Reflected in His Literature*, these prayers represent major moods in the complex spiritual history of a people who have obvious reasons to be angry with God.

Each division represents the invasions of a new form of the absurd: Part I, the experience of being chattel with the failure of the African gods to prevent enslavement, as well as the various forms of racism in the antebellum period; Part II, the struggle to divine what kind of community could be crated in the face of the nation's unwillingness to compensate ex-slaves justly; Part III, the moral dilemma of what to do in the face of the murders and lynching of black people especially in the period between 1889 and 1919; Part IV, the place of African American Christianity in the face of a nascent agnosticism and atheism that was sometimes evident as a young generation emerged in the Harlem Renaissance; Part V, facing the flaws in the myth of the American Dream as evident in the successes and failures of the Civil Rights Movement; and Part VI, the increasing decline of the moral influence of African American Christianity.

The prayers in this anthology are attempts to converse with God about the joys, burdens, and hopes of being African people in a racist society. All these prayers trusted that the Lord would make a way somehow.

Notes

1. From the standpoint of late-twentieth-century American usage, Du Bois' use of "awful" is somewhat archaic. If he were writing today, he would probably use "awesome."
2. Studies of African American humor have been written by William Schechter, Lawrence Levine, and Mel Watkins. Langston Hughes also edited a very useful anthology on the subject.
3. The complexity of the notion of the soul is reflected in recent religious scholarship on this subject contained in the nine articles on the concept of soul in primitive, Ancient Near Eastern, Greek and Hellenistic, Indian, Buddhist, Chinese, Jewish, Christian, and Islamic religions in Eliade's *The Encyclopedia of Religion.*
4. I use "stargazing" as a metaphor for the experience of the numinous conveyed through sight—with an acute awareness of the experiential limitations and intellectual difficulties of the use of ocular metaphors. Taking the metaphor at its face value, sightless people like John M. Hull remind us that listening and touching can have the same effect as seeing. On a deeper level, I use this metaphor despite my understanding of the intellectual hegemony of the assumptions and metaphors about sight in modern thought as reflected in recent discussions about "representation." This subject has been explored with much vigor and brilliance by students of modern and postmodern culture. Martin Jay calls it the problem of ocularcentrism. Jay rightly identifies Jacques Ellul as having an important influence on his understanding of ocularcentrism's evolution. Major religious historians, theologians, and biblical scholars have explored ocularcentrism under the rubric of the idolatry of culture that is oftentimes called "henotheism." But even though H. Richard Niebuhr appealed to the transcendent regime of radical monotheism as an antidote to henotheism, he did not reduce the problem of idolatry to its ideational plenipotentiary, ideology, nor to the distortion of vision or language. A very helpful attempt to relate this problem to African American cultural studies can be found in a recent study by W. T. J. Mitchell.
5. The primal role of nurture in what Wittgenstein calls "the language game" is accented in his pregnant exegesis of how a language is acquired by a child. According to Wittgenstein, especially in his *Brown Book*, "The child learns this language from grown-ups by being trained to its use." Language is acquired through "demonstrative teaching of words." I am suggesting that prayer is an acquired ontology often of a religious cultus that offers a grammar whose objective is to proffer a "cure of disease based on dogma set forth by its promulgator." The role of metaphors and assertions of contamination in religious language and practice has been explored by several scholars, including Mary Douglass and Paul Ricoeur, whose works have influenced me the most. I am acutely aware of the complexity of using metaphors to express religious ideas and describe religious practices despite my rather shameless deploy-

ments in this introduction. Nonetheless, I have been helped most recently by the quite engaging study work of Janet Martin Soskice.

6. Peace demonstrators at the Billy Graham Crusade were particularly offended that President Nixon's visit was his first to a college campus after the United States invaded Cambodia. For a somewhat fuller description of this event, see some of the contemporary local newspaper accounts in the *Knoxville News-Sentinel* (1–4 November 1971) and the *Knoxville Journal* (1–4, 11, and 17 November 1971), as well as books by Michael J. McDonald, Judith Isenhour, and Marshall Frady.

7. David Walker's *Appeal* is a jeremiad that has a secure place in American history. Like most jeremiads, *Walker's Appeal* uses righteous indignation both to lament and condemn American slavery and racism. The broader literary and ideological context of the jeremiad has been studied by Sacvan Bercovitch and David Howard-Pitney.

8. Karl Rahner, S.J. (1904–1984), a famous and distinguished Roman Catholic theologian, used this term to grapple with the proposition that there are those who are seemingly predisposed to be theists and Christians without formally being so. He included ethical agnostics and even atheists as possible members of this righteous conventicle. Several theologians have strongly objected to Rahner's imaginative idea. I invoke it even though Rahner believed that this is "first and foremost a controversy internal to Catholic theology," because I believe that the African American community, agnostics and atheists included, have often seen themselves as morally superior to white America. Some even believed that the so-called "Invisible Institution" of free and enslaved Christians were the true church. Among Abolitionist Christians who practiced "comeouterism," true Christians had to break all ties with slave-holding Christians. The best study on comeouterism was written by John R. McKivigan. Other studies by Albert J. Raboteau and James M. Washington offer useful information about this subject as it relates to slave religion and African American Baptists.

9. I am using the concept of soul murder to suggest that the deformation of the character and human worth of African Americans has historically been used to belittle the collective ego of African Americans. Scholarly studies and literary depictions of this phenomenon are vast. Of course this is not a new idea. The prevalence of racial stigmas and systematic discrimination were cited in the famous case *Brown v. Board of Education* (1954). Major studies on the effects of racism on African American children informed the Supreme Court's decision, which mandated the desegregation of American public education. Perhaps the best-known psychological studies were those of Kenneth and Mamie Clark. Beyond the Clarks, the most helpful and critical influence upon my thinking about this was written by William E. Cross Jr. I have also learned much from other general studies on the spirituality of children by Robert Coles and Dorothy W. Martyn.

10. The Reverend James Joseph Reeb (1927–1965), assassinated while participating in the famous Civil Rights demonstrations in Selma, Alabama. He was the Associate Minister of All Souls Unitarian Universalist Church in Washington DC.

11. John Redekop has written a very reliable analysis of the opposition of Billy James Hargis' Christian Crusade to the Civil Rights Movement, as well as other progressive movements. One of the sermons in which Falwell attacks Martin Luther King Jr. can be found in the appendix to a recent book by Perry Deane Young.

12. I use the term *transference* to describe the human proclivity to predict and project one's own desires and interests, as well as the desires and interests of others. My views on this psychological and philosophical concept have been deeply influenced by the work of psychoanalysts Nelson Goodman and Paul Ricoeur. Indeed, Ricoeur's work has especially enabled me to see how it is possible to recast Freud's psychological theory of transference to mesh with various hermeneutical phenomenological theories. Much work lies ahead for those like myself who believe that these ideas would greatly assist students of racism, race relations, cultural studies, and the history of spirituality. Some very important suggestions along these lines can be found in the work of Richard Wright, Ralph Ellison, Franz Fanon, James Baldwin, and Toni Morrison. Getting psychologists and historians to appreciate the importance of the history of African American spirituality is a somewhat more difficult task.

13. Crutcher is one of the major subjects of a recently reprinted book by Merrill Proudfoot on the Civil Rights Movement in Knoxville, Tennessee.

14. Like many other scholars, my view that violence is an archetypal form of sin has been influenced by Rene Girard, the most well-known and influential student of the relationship between violence and religion. His work is having a profound effect on the study of religion.

15. Thurman offered a deeply affective explication of his frequently used phrase, "the nerve center of consent," in the chapter titled "Commitment" in his *Disciplines of the Spirit*. He said, "The yielding of the deep inner nerve center of consent is not a solitary action, unrelated to the total structure or context of the life." Indeed, he continued to explain, "It is a saturation of the self with the mood and the integrity of assent."
16. Wilson Jeremiah Moses has written excellent studies of Crummell's life and thought that focus on this irony.

5

And We Shall Learn through the Dance: Exploring the Instructional Relationship between Liturgical Dance and Religious Education

Kathleen S. Turner

Introduction

This chapter analyzes the relationship liturgical dance has with religious education in the life of the church as a community place of learning. This affiliation is viewed through the imaginative imagery of two partners dancing together in a choreographed dance. In dance as in the circus arts, partnering happens between two people or within a group of dancers. In some dance styles, the two people can be of the same gender, as in a duet, where they represent two voices dancing different choreography simultaneously, or dancing the same movement in unison. However there are other dance styles where they are to support each other's weight in a variety of wonderful and imaginative lifts. In addition, each partner complements and highlights the other partner as in a ballet's *pas de deux*[1] (Anderson 1979) or they dance as one, as in ballroom dances like the waltz. In both of these cases the partners are made up of one male dancer and one female dancer. Whether the correlation between the partners is seen through unison choreographed movement, improvisational movement, solo moments when each partner is featured separate from the other, or during the acrobatics of real partnering where one partner lifts the other, all of these images place the two partners in the position of being collaborators who are dancing toward a finished end. So, too with liturgical dance and religious education. The aim of this chapter is to suggest that liturgical dance has a valid role in the instructional life of the church, and that this role is witnessed through its ongoing relationship with religious education.

In identifying the variety of partnering formations that can take place within a choreographed dance, this chapter identifies four partnering positions that represent four instructional formats which place liturgical dance and religious education together as teaching partners operating in activities both inside and outside the walls of the church. These four arrangements are derived and crafted from the accumulated research found in chapters 3, 4 and 5 [of *And We Shall Learn through the Dance*]. First, these four designs reflect the meaning and purpose of liturgical dance as defined in the conclusion of chapter 5. Second, they reflect the research gleaned from Maxine Greene (2000), John Dewey ([1938] 1997, 1944, 1974, [1934] 1980), Jennifer Zakkai (1997), Charles Foster (1994), Norma Cook Everist (2002), Anne Streaty Wimberly (2004), and Carla De Sola (1977, 1979, 1990). As in chapter 5, the use of the ten samples from the conducted interviews will complete the information needed to support the four instructional strategies. One principle that undergirds each of the four teaching strategies is the principle of listening and why listening is imperative for the teaching success of Christian education in congregational life. The work of Margaret Crain (1997) on the sensitivity of listening sets the foundation for this final chapter.

The Importance of Listening

Margaret Crain (1997) makes a strong case in describing what the Christian educator needs to address the educational needs of the members of the congregation. What Crain stresses is the need for the Christian educator to know how to listen in order to ask the pertinent questions in matters pertaining to religious education for the life of the congregation. Such an act requires that religious educators learn and practice patience, quietness and endurance when waiting for the questions to materialize. Crain contends that such questions "emerge out of the life events and communal identity of the congregation" (101). She affirms that the theological questions that arise out of the lives of the congregation tend to be unique, and they are shaped by specific personalities, diversity and culture, and detailed experiences of the lives of those who make up the congregation. Hence, such an action requires careful and vigilant listening.

The ability to hear the deep seated questions will always be limited by the religious educator's own experiences and needs. Since it is impossible to fully understand the needs or questions of another, Crain poses the following question, "How do educators look for these glimpses of God's transformative power within a congregation?" (1997: 101). Her answer is simple; she explains that it is looked upon with eyes of love:

I believe that eyes of love are eyes that do not begin with judgment, but instead seek to see lives and groups as whole and complex, living within a web of forces. . . Educators must begin by taking seriously the whole of those lives. The issues of that reality should be a foundation of the curriculum for religious education. (101)

According to Crain (1997), the Christian educator cannot see the glimpses of the reign of God that are already present in a congregation until he or she sees the people who are a part of the congregation in the complexity of the lives they lead, recognizing that each one seeks to be faithful, and that each one is a child of God touched by grace. Judgment is not the place to begin but listening is. This means that the Christian educator must listen to every facet of the educational life that comprises the church, whether it is the Sunday school class, the weekly bible study class, the assembled members of the choir, or the Sunday school staff. A Christian educator is to listen with the assumption that the people are speaking from their own lives, which are touched by grace. Crain contends that each one has spiritual needs, shaped by all the experiences of his or her life, and the questions that each one is asking are slightly different because of those unique experiences.

Crain submits that the skills of an ethnographer, specifically the skills to look, to listen, and to reflect on moments where God's grace is present, are the tools the religious educator should use in seeking the answers to the question, "How do I guide the congregation into focusing on one or another of the approaches to Christian education," (1997: 102). It is here that the ethnographic methods will help an educator identify what approaches are already present and are a part of the life of the congregation. Once these approaches are identified and honored, the educator can build and strengthen them. If they are not identified, the educator is too often working at cross-purposes to the presuppositions and comforts of the congregation. However, if the educator honors, utilizes and encourages those identified practices of the congregation that are already present, they can build and expand the repertoire of learning opportunities in an easier and more successful fashion.

Crain (1997) also addresses how an educator can begin to understand the complex webs of interaction and meaning that are part of his or her congregation. Questions asked by the educational ethnographer would be specific to the congregational setting with which they are interacting. The questions should focus on three primary issues, namely, the people and their lives, the dynamics of the congregation, and the environment of the community in which the people reside. In terms of the people, the questioning goal is to discern the issues that command the attention of the people, how their faith affects the ways they engage with these issues, and how the church either assists or inhibits their addressing these issues (Crain 1997: 105). In terms of the congregation she suggests that the educator seeks to discern the places where the congregation honestly engages the issues of the people's lives, where the congregation is particularly effective in helping people integrate faith and life, and how truth-telling and honest reflection can be enhanced. Regarding the community, Crain (1997) suggests that the Christian educator needs to reflect on the forces that are affecting the lives of the people; how culture, class, and values focus people's attention, and how the congregation can impact the forces that affect, and even define, the meanings with which people live.

Crain (1997) proposes three qualities that are essential, effective and mutual for Christian education. They are:

> (1) The educator must see herself or himself as an interpreter among interpreters; (2) the contexts for learning must create hospitable and just space; and (3) the congregation must practice the presence of God. (105–106)

For the first, she explains that in a congregation of interpreters, the Christian educator seeks to bring possibilities and resources to any question, but does not seek to control the outcome. This can happen if the teacher takes on the role of a co-learner, one who must listen carefully to the questions and answers of all participants, helping each to offer "answers" in an atmosphere of shared vulnerability and mutual search for truth (106). She suggests that when the interpreters who are evaluating and planning for education discover contexts within the life of the congregation where mutuality is not occurring, interventions may be necessary.

In addressing the contexts for which learning can create both a hospitable and just space, Crain suggests that listening and shared vulnerability is the starting point. She explains this further:

> A hospitable context is one in which the individual feels the security of "home." One feels welcomed. . . It is dependent upon both seeking relationships and honoring differences. To hold ourselves in relationship and yet to honor difference is difficult at times, yet it promotes growth. (1997: 107)

As an aid in creating a hospitable and just space, Crain cites to the work of Brother Lawrence2 and his notion that the route to faithfulness is to practice the presence God. This notion has caught the imagination of many Christians because it is so simple and yet so profound. Practicing the presence of God is the final criterion for evaluating the contexts for learning in a congregation. Lawrence explains, "When we practice God's presence, we seek to live in 'an habitual, silent and secret conversation of the soul with God,'" (quoted in Crain 1997: 107). Crain explains that as we enter into relationship with one another we risk knowing that we are also in relationship with God, and we are to pay attention to one another as we pay attention to God. Practicing presence also raises one's awareness of how God's graceful presence undergirds one's learning (107). Another dimension in practicing the presence of God is honoring the whole of the Christian tradition. Such awareness brings to the educator the rich and diverse fund of images, stories, songs, movement gestures and concepts from the Christian tradition that can prompt questions of faith while supplying guidelines that can be followed. Crain explains this further:

> This means that the interpreter must be steeped in her or his faith tradition. But it also means that the educator must attempt to provide opportunities for everyone in the congregation to acquire a rich fund from the religious tradition. . . In practicing the presence

of God we ask, "What is God's call to us in this situation?" We seek answers in the Bible, in the Christian tradition, in our own experiences and in those of our fellow interpreters, and through the gift of reason. Through it all, we listen for God's answers. God empowers us with moments when we live justly and lovingly. Those moments provide hope and possibilities. We seek to join with God in working toward the reign of God. (1997: 108)

Crain provides a landscape of suggestions in aiding the listening ear and heart of the Christian educator when it comes to matters of faith learning and development. These recommendations are particularly useful for the implementation of the four formats that merge liturgical dance and religious education as working and supportive partners in a dance that highlights faith development and Christian love. In proposing these four formats, Crain provides a foundation for how such suggestions can be visualized and implemented.

Format One: Dancing In Unison

Format One displays liturgical dance and religious education as partners dancing in simultaneous unison, while being spatially arranged side by side. This setting presents both partners as equals, and when viewed side by side, each dancer presents not only themselves but they also present the uniqueness of the relationship they share with the other. Such a partnership presents the strength and the creative capabilities found within each one, while both dance simultaneously together.

The format setting for this side by side partnership is situated at the beginning of congregational worship, where praise and worship music are utilized to gather the congregation together.[3] By way of song and simple liturgical dance movement[4] this gathering identifies the congregation as Christian and confirms the relationship they have with the Godhead. Within this praise and worship setting, liturgical dance and the praise and worship music work hand in hand to support the educational message that Christians come together in time and space to learn more about the Trinity through praise, worship, prayer and communing with God. Dance is a bridge from the world of intellect to the world of the imagination, according to De Sola and Easton (1979), and through dance, one can grasp in deeper ways the meaning of religious concepts. In this partnership both liturgical dance and religious education are supporting one another in united movement by helping to identify the essence, meaning and the scriptural text that undergirds each praise and worship song.

Both partners contribute to the instructional setting of the moment, where the religious themes are uplifted in the words that are sung and in the movement gestures that are danced. Both partners give visualization and comprehension to the meaning of the words. An example of a praise and worship song that is accompanied by liturgical dance movement is the song "Welcome into this Place," that was used as a teaching example on the subject of grace for the entire congregation found in chapter 4 [of *And We Shall Learn through the Dance*].[5] As explained, this example focused on the entire congregation with the assistance of the Praise and Worship leader, the singing worship team and liturgical dancers. The primary goal of such a partnership is the internalization of the song's meaning and the congregation's critical reflection upon that meaning for themselves and for the "grace" actions that they are encouraged to display toward others in Jesus' name. This type of learning integration exemplifies the portion of the definition of liturgical dance found in chapter 5, which emphasized that it be expressive and imaginative movement used inside the worship experience which creatively educates and instructs in the matters of the Bible and faith in the Trinity through the elements of space, time, and design, and that it has a relationship with music.

Wimberly (2004) introduced one aspect of the nurturing components of music within black worship through the spontaneous and improvisational style of expression known as "spiritual free play." In "spiritual free play," its essence is centered in the response of the heart and the body to the movement of the Holy Spirit, and the mind's connection with the message or content of the music. In "spiritual free play," the whole self is released to delight in the personal experience of seeing and hearing God, and it is through this experience that one creates, and adds new sounds, rhythms, movement accompaniment and thoughts that respond to and add further meaning to a truth or belief disclosed in a song. Wimberly declares "'spiritual free play' creates a climate of imaginative experience and artistry that builds creative musical capacities from which life outside the congregation is embellished" (2004: 152).

This creative response to the movement of the Holy Spirit is what takes place during praise and worship, where the understanding of God's love for every congregational member is witnessed through the songs that are sung and the movements that accompany the words. The movements are usually choreographed, however there can also be moments where spontaneous movement occurs. The dancer's creativity is nurtured through the work of improvisation, which is the creation of unplanned movement on the spot, (Penrod and Plastino 2005). Dance improvisation aids the dancer in finding new ways to move, develop technical skills, and provides another means to develop as an artist (81). "Spiritual free play," creates enriching moments where new movement gestures through improvisation enriches the educational underpinnings of the spur-of-the-moment change of praise and worship music that is in response to the movement of the Holy Spirit.

During such times the entire congregation is welcomed to join in, and, as explained earlier, all who gather are termed *differently abled* according to Norma Cook Everist (2002). As previously described, differently abled is a term that allows people to see how they view one another regardless of their physical, mental and/or emotional well-being. Everist explains that each person in some way is able and each is disabled, regardless if the disability is hidden as in heart disease or lupus, or the disability is revealed as in cerebral palsy or deafness. The goal is not to change, or even to "cure" certain "disabilities," but to care in a way which gives attention to each person individually (Everist

2002: 36). It is during times of praise and worship that all differently abled members of the congregation can freely join in and sing and dance the songs of praise and worship and genuinely feel the love of the Lord inside the sanctuary space. Doreen Holland[6] shares a memory of seeing the love of God through the dancing of her differently abled son during a time of praise and worship.

> My middle son is 18 years old and was diagnosed with autism since he was sixteen months old and he has been with us in the church setting. He feels the beat of the music and he marches, he claps his hands and marches to the beat of the music. If I am in the congregation and I am doing my personal praise and worship as an observer, he mirrors me, if I wave my hands, he is waving his hands, if I am clapping my hands, he is clapping his hands. I would have my oldest son clap his hands and the 18 year old will clap his hands also. He doesn't do this at home, but he knows that this is what we do at church and he does it solely at church. People have gotten used to him doing this.
>
> There was a period where he wasn't doing this, there were a few challenges that he was facing and caused him not to dance in his seat for a few months. There were those in the congregation who asked what was wrong because he wasn't dancing and they had missed him moving. Now that he is up and doing it again, then those in the congregation were excited that he was back and he was dancing to the church music. Again the movement of liturgical, dance whether small or great, is a bridge for those who watch it. In this case liturgical dance was the bridge for my middle son and for the congregational members who were used to seeing him move near his seat. (Holland interview)

Yvonne Peters[7] shares the importance of the use of liturgical dance as a facilitating tool that can lead others to worship God through the dance.

> David selected those musicians who were skilled and excellent in their craft to minister before the Lord and to instruct others. They were literally to prophecy on their instruments and release the expression of their intimate communion with God through the sound of their instruments. Liturgical dancers seek the same. With excellence comes skill, with skill responsibility to impart and teach others. We are called to lift up others into a higher level of worship. Liturgical dancers cannot be just demonstrators in front of congregations but we are to be facilitators, we do not just craft but we instruct and lead others to worship through the dance with their entire selves. (Peters interview)

This praise and worship setting reveals just how stable a partner both liturgical dance and religious education are as they function equally through the vehicle of praise and worship music. Both partners are unified in their responsibilities to teach what it means to be Christian in a congregational setting that fosters such instruction through creative and spontaneous expression. The ability to listen deeply to the needs of God's people who assemble in the sanctuary space can bring about the revelation that all of God's people can respond to God in ways that are expressive yet undergirded with opportunities to learn just how good God is. One partner does not upstage the other, but they dance together side by side revealing the educational value that undergirds such a partnership.

Format Two:
The Dance of Balance and Harmony

Format Two highlights the balancing capabilities of liturgical dance and religious education in a movement relationship that supports each other's total weight equally and harmoniously. This type of movement allows one partner to hold onto the other by the pulling of the hands and arms, or the pushing toward one another through bodily contact of the back, or sides of the body. In each scenario the body weight of one is totally supported by the body weight of the other. To explain this position using the hands, each partner's body is pulled away from the other, and the tension felt between the two through the connection of both hands and arms allows for both to be in total balance with the other. This type of partnership requires a total and complete trust on behalf of each partner, and, if achieved, such interaction produces complete harmony and complete balance. However, if one partner stops supporting the weight of the other, one partner if not both partners lose balance and can possibly fall. This dancing relationship signifies that the contributions of one partner are totally supported by the contributions of the other partner and vice versa. Therefore, in this dancing partnership liturgical dance and religious education are not seen as equals in their individual contributions, but they are equals *because* of the contributions of the other.

Penrod and Plastino (2005) present two improvisational exercises that deal with partner awareness through the use of body weight. One exercise has each partner face the other, standing with the feet comfortably balanced and three feet apart, with the arms forward and slightly bent and with the palms of one partner resting against the palms of the other. Each partner is to take turns leaning passively forward into the palms of the other allowing one to support the weight of the other. The overall aim of this exercise is the development of trust (88). The second exercise highlights the exact positioning which liturgical dance and religious education occupy *informal two*. This exercise is explained as follows:

> With feet comfortably together and knees bent, hold hands at the wrist and lean back away from each other. Experiment with sensitively using each other's weight to oppositionally shift the weight forward, backward, and sideward, eventually cooperatively moving downward with control, to sit on the floor. (89)

These are typical partnering exercises that are explored in improvisational classes when the themes of trust and partnership are highlighted.

For Christian education, the setting of this balancing partnership is during worship where the actual teaching of a song or movement to a song takes place. There are many types of worship services within Christian traditions where teaching is a welcomed way to learn and develop faith. This type of setting exists during the various chapel services held on college, seminarian and even on military campuses as well as in churches that are moderate in size. Charles Foster (1994) explores how the church can participate in the "formative and transformative events of Christian tradition and witness" (8). His work mirrors Dewey's (1944) understanding of community as communication, where the participation of people within the learning process is assured because of a common understanding.

Foster (1994) sets forth suggestions on how to nurture meaning making within a church that considers itself to be a disciple community. One suggestion is to implement disciplined reflection which promotes a better comprehension of an event and the implications of an event upon the lives of the congregation (102–103). The ability to honestly reflect on the struggles and the new understandings requires theological and educational perspective. Dewey (1944) presses this point in his understanding of experiential learning. Learning does not take place when a routine action is done in which the action is automatic. Learning is only achieved because after the act is performed; there are results which were not noted previously.

Patrick Evans[8] is a proponent of the teaching and learning act within the worship service, and of how it highlights the notion of Christians being imitators of Christ. However he does have two principles as to how the teaching and learning act should transpire. He explains this further:

> Two principles: #1 knowing that people will be invited to do something that they are not use to doing. #2 creating a place where it is safe to do that and it is okay to make a mistake. To try it and "fail" because you don't ever risk anything if you never do. It is such a different experience in seminary from the classroom where there is such pressure to *never* fail, to get the prefect grade point average, to get Latin honors; so the concept of doing something and learning from the not immediate brilliance success of it is really important. Those principles over a long period of time create a situation or help foster a situation in which people are willing to risk. In which even though this is not the way I worship, and I feel uncomfortable doing it, I know that this is important to you and you have found God *in it*, that makes me willing to risk, feeling foolish, or doing something that may not be perfect, because I am an expert and I only want to do things in public that I am expert at. (Evans interview)

Deconstructing personal opinions of failure or vulnerability while building up love and transparency can promote an individual's healing and faith nurturing within a worship service. It is here that Crain's earlier question and answer is situated, "how do educators look for these glimpses of God's transformative power within a congregation?" (Crain 1997: 101) Once again her answer is simple; the glimpses of God's transformative power are looked upon with eyes of love. It is here where the mutual trust in the partnering and balancing dance between liturgical dance and religious education can be witnessed.

To bring the concepts of meaning making, experiential learning, active and alive teaching in worship, and the viewing of God's transformative power within the congregation through the eyes of love in context, the following example of a chapel service shows the mutual trust, balance and harmony found between liturgical dance and religious education. The chapel service would take place on the campus grounds of a boarding school, college, seminary or military base, where there is a collective body of people who attend daily or weekly chapel service. The religious nature of this particular faith community is ecumenical, where the knowledge of Christ is upheld, although religious backgrounds can stem from Catholicism to a wide variety of Protestant denominations. The chapel service is entitled, "You Have Turned My Mourning Into...,"[9] based on Jeremiah 31: 13 which states,

> Then shall the young women rejoice in the dance, and the young men and the old shall be merry. I will turn their mourning into joy. I will comfort them, and give them gladness for sorrow.

During the opening welcome it will be explained that this service will be interactive in nature. This means that there will be an element of teaching throughout the thirty minute service including in the singing of song, the dancing of liturgical movement, and the moving throughout the space to prayer stations. The opening welcome serves as an official invitation for those attending the chapel service to feel free to participate in order to experience the many ways God has turned ones' mourning into song, praise, peace, prayer, hope and dancing.

This type of service highlights the aesthetic as the driving force behind the learning experiences that will be attained. As explained earlier, Dewey ([1934] 1980) claims that "the [a]esthetic is no intruder in experience from without, whether by way of idle luxury or transcendent ideality, but that it is the clarified and intensified development of traits that belong to every normally complete experience," (46). Artistic expression unites the same relation of doing and undergoing, outgoing and incoming energy that makes an experience to be an experience. Artistic expression can be seen in an instructional tool as in this present example, or in the creation of a work of art to be observed. Whichever the case, the attitude of the perceiver is embodied within the work being created. This incorporation allows the art to be an aesthetic work. For Dewey ([1934] 1980), the perceiver must create one's own experience. In the partnership suggested here, the artistic expressions of music, word and dance lend themselves to formulate both artistic and educational experiences for those who created and for those who attend the chapel service.

The opening song, "You've Turned My Mourning into Dancing,"[10] is the theme song and serves as the opening and closing song of the service. This song is also the first teaching moment that transpires in the chapel service. The song exemplifies the 11th and 12th verses of Psalm 30 which states:

> You have turned my mourning into dancing; you have taken off my sackcloth and clothed me with joy, so that my soul may praise you and not be silent. O LORD my God, I will give thanks to you forever.

The song by John Tirro (2008)[11] has only two lines which repeat. The first line is repeated four times before moving on to the chorus which is repeated twice before repeating the entire song again. The first line is, "You've turned my mourning, my mourning, my mourning into dancing." The second line is, "You've turned my sorrow into song, you've turned my singing into praise, you've turned my praise, to peace, my peace to joy and dancing!" Once the song is taught, everyone will be asked to stand and then sing the song a few times, so as to begin comprehending the deeper meaning of the song text in relation to the scripture. Once this has been done, the accompanying movement will be taught to complete this portion of the interactive cycle.

In applying liturgical movement as a teaching tool, it will be explained that the gestures help to bring light to the fullness of both the Psalm 30 text and the song text that was inspired by the scripture, and a demonstration of the mourning movement will be done. The members of the congregation will be encouraged to join in and follow the movements of the leader. The initial movement of the body is a rocking motion from side to side since the musical accompaniment is upbeat and in common time.[12] The mourning position will be explained by having the arms slowly cross each other, while they are being folded inward toward the chest with the head slightly lowered in the forward direction. The movement to accompany the words, "into dancing," will have the arms release slowly from the chest as they are raised gradually upward above the head, one arm at a time (right, left, right, left) in the four count rhythm. The releasing of the arms and their motioning upward resembles the joyous motions of happiness and emancipation, especially the feeling one has once a weight has been lifted off of one's shoulders. This gesture is repeated four times as the song verse is repeated four times.

The second line, which begins with the words, "You've turned my sorrow into song," will continue with the rocking motion of the body since this is the constant full body motion that accompanies the entire song. The arms will fold into the chest, resembling sorrow, but will open and release upward in almost a V shape, once "song" is sung and then the hands will clap five times as the body is rocking side to side, resembling the change of temperament, which is captured in the words, "singing, praise, peace, and joy." The arms push upward two times on the last word of the song, "dancing," while the body continues to rock from side to side. This movement gesture signifies the desire to be in a state of joy, merriment, praise, comfort, and divine peace. This combined song and movement opening will be repeated at least twice so that everyone can get familiar with the accompaniment and they begin internalizing the educational meanings of both scripture and song text through the use of movement.

Patrick Evans gives dutiful caution when using liturgical dance as a teaching tool within congregational worship. He states,

> There are cautions in doing liturgical dance in congregational settings. You are inviting people to do things with their bodies and they have issues with their bodies. Age and bodies have changed, been physically abused, or sexually abused, and they may not realize until they are touched by someone else that there are deep wounds and deep scars there, but liturgical dance can be healing in these situations. We just have to be mindful when we use it and teach it in congregational worship. (Evans interview)

Throughout the service when the congregation sings, hears readings, watches others do liturgical dance,[13] and prays the members of the community are given the space to reflect upon themselves and where they are and how they are responding to what they are doing, seeing, and praying. It is during these moments that the Holy Spirit is welcomed into the service to relieve the congregation of their sorrows, hurts, and concerns through the modalities of song, movement and prayer. When the opening song is sung again at the conclusion of the service, it is anticipated that those who attended the service will be changed in some way and will be moving from a state of mourning to a state of wondrous dancing in Jesus' name. *Format Two* supports the portion of the liturgical dance definition that identifies the church as community though individual and mutual movements and dance explorations that cultivate love, prayer, healing and reconciliation, while deepening Christian identity. The balance and harmony found between liturgical dance and religious education in this supportive and trusting partnership is one that points to the continual theme of God's desire to transform the state of God's children from that of mourning to a state of peace, song, praise, joy and dancing.

Format Three: To Be Lifted Up

In the first two examples liturgical dance was utilized in a setting that addressed predominately non-dancers. Both settings took place inside the sanctuary during worship, where the congregation is made up of an assortment of people, ranging in age, gender, and capabilities. However *format three* looks at liturgical dance as the primary subject to be taught while religious education is the secondary underlining subject that gives credence and stability to it. This example also addresses the teaching audience composed of liturgical dancers or those who are interested in learning more about the subject. Here the dancing partnership between liturgical dance and religious education favors that of a *pas de deux* where the male and female dancers are doing a meaningful adagio, which encompasses slow, continuous and sustained movement with an incorporation of wonderful and effortless lifts with the male dancer lifting up the female dancer. Thus this format will show liturgical dance is the subject being taught and religious education is the subject that gives it its foundation.

Wimberly (2004) explained in chapter 4 that evocative nurture "builds on the view that worshipers desire and are ready for nurture and have the wherewithal to receive nurture and discern its meaning for their lives," (xv). She pointed out that black worshipers come into the worshiping congregation seeking nourishment that affirms and responds to their capacity to receive it, struggle with it, and to discover, build on, and act on what is enormously important to their lives as Christians. God is the evocator who reaches out and invites the people of God to reach back and to vow that they will not look backwards but will move forward, "to see what the end will be," (Wimberly xix).

Evocative nurture is the type of teaching the liturgical dancer needs. This type of nurture is what Carla De Sola (1979) describes as "the corresponding spirituality for the dancer as a total union of body, spirit, music, and space forgetting the self in actualizing the dance," (73). For her liturgical dance is assumed to be the result of a personal, meditative experience of God; the movement's sources come from the heart's response, in an overflowing of gratitude or speech to God. As explained earlier, Christ is the partner in an ever-new dance which is inspired by the Holy Spirit and is offered to God. However, there should be a teaching approach that guides the liturgical dancer to comprehend exactly what liturgical dance is and how it affects both those who watch it, and the dancers of faith who participate in it.

Eyesha Marable[14] shares some of the problems the liturgical dancer could face if proper and meaningful instruction is not created, established or implemented. She states:

> There are those who are studying the Word of God and there are those who are not studying and speaking from Word, but they are dancing in God's name. The real precaution are those who are studying on line and getting these online degrees and giving themselves titles of reverend, apostle, and prophet and they are going into churches and sabotaging God's pure praise. When pastors experience them and there is a profane spirit moving though the worship and arts movement, the pastor and congregation say that we do not want this. We have to be mindful that the body speaks such strong languages and the enemy (Satan) is angry. So we have dancers who dance with exposed bodies, and that either offends members of the congregation or it entices pedophiles who may be present, or the rate of teenage pregnancies escalate because of the lack of teaching and learning concerning liturgical dance and the worship and the arts. A profanity can enter into the church and we have to make sure to study and study correctly. (Marable interview)

From another perspective De Sola and Easton (1979) warns against the overwhelming attention given towards the dancer's technique which can be based on imitation or copying the style of present or former teachers (75). Since much of a dancer's life is spent doing repetitive exercises that train the body to perform actions with as little strain as possible, the dancer is seldom guided through those maturing steps from technique to performance level of interpretation and, ultimately, to spiritual understanding and freedom (75). De Sola and Easton explain this further:

> We are not saying that technique is wrong, but the emphasis is misplaced when the goal of the dancer becomes glamorized, when the only objective is to dazzle and to prove one's worth as a performer.

> The church can offer opportunities to both dancers and non-dancers by helping them
> to share selflessly in services and festive events; such participation lifts individuals from
> personality preoccupation to holistic experience. (1979: 75)

Crain's (1997) principle of listening can assist in the area of instructing liturgical dancers particularly addressing the concerns of both. Marable and De Sola and Easton (1979). The questions asked by the educational ethnographer are appropriate for this instructional setting to gain a deeper awareness of the individuals who call themselves liturgical dancers or who are interested in learning more about the subject. The three issues Crain (1997) suggests specifically target the dancers and their lives, the dynamics of the congregations they serve, and the environment of the community in which the people reside. In terms of the liturgical dancer, the questioning goal is to discern the issues that command the attention of the dancers, how their faith affects the ways they engage with these issues, and how the church either assists or inhibits the way they address these issues. With this type of questioning, De Sola and Easton's (1979) suggestion of the church giving opportunities for the liturgical dancer to selflessly give to the church and its liturgical and festive events would help in this area. Regarding the liturgical dance ministry of the church, Crain's (1997) suggestion that the educator seeks to discern the places where the dancers honestly engages the issues of both their lives and the lives of the congregation, is essential for helping the dancers integrate faith and life. Concerning the community, she suggests that the Christian educator reflect on the forces that are affecting the lives of the dancers; how culture, class, and values focus people's attention, and how the liturgical dancers can impact the forces that affect, and even define, the meanings with which they and those in the congregation live.

Marable, De Sola and Easton's (1979) Crain's (1997) observations highlight the need for liturgical dancers to gain strength by learning a variety of subjects that are related to the field whether the subject is dance technique that can span a variety of disciplines, or that of biblical studies, or the use of liturgical dance in liturgy. In addition there is a discernment process that liturgical dancers must engage in as it relates to faith building, and the use of movement in liturgical choreography. Discernment sustains a knowing about movement, movement choices and the movements that are or are not appropriate to use under the rubrics of liturgical dance. As Marable and De Sola and Easton (1979) have indicated, movements that place a heavier emphasis on the personal self and on the physicality of the body are primarily movements that highlight the dancer and not the Trinity. The use of such movements causes confusion and division among the dancers and the congregations they serve. As a parent of daughters who do liturgical dance, Lori Dekie [15] emphasizes how important it is to teach liturgical dance in such a way that its intent is clearly godly. She states:

> It could be an instructional tool, it needs to be taught and understood in such a way so that
> the movement and its intent are clearly godly. We have to watch out for the secular

influence of movement not to have a place within liturgical dance. It must be taught in such a way that the biblical understanding and association of the word of God coincides with the movement. There should not be a certain musical language and movements, like gyrations inside liturgical dance. There is a difference between understanding how it is done and the manifestation of the actual movement being done. There is a difference in teaching older people what to do and the teaching of teens. There is such a difference and the teacher must be aware enough so to correct if the movement interpretation is more worldly than it is supposed to be. The meaning of the movements and the meaning of the dance must be explained and taught. Secular dance has an emphasis on the self and liturgical dance highlights God and our worship of God. If the congregation is not taught correctly about liturgical dance, then their understanding will be off. (Dekie interview)

Therefore, the type of teaching and evocative nurturing the liturgical dancer needs should be developed from a foundation that is undergirded by religious education. Such a foundation promotes a curriculum of learning, investigation, deep inquiry and exploration, while promoting a need to seek God through tools, instruments and available subject material. Some of the subjects that could be included in such a curriculum are as follows:

- Bible study—exegetical investigations that bring comprehension and light to the biblical text;
- History—learning the history of liturgical dance starting with the earliest of cultures, to the Old Testament, to the early church, to present day Christian faith traditions and organizations that have implemented dance and worship.
- Prayer—both verbal and embodied that develops the inner soul and spirit of the dancer to learn how to pray both verbally and physically through movement;
- Movement technique including strengthening and stretching;
- Composition—learning the craft of choreography and movement development through improvisation and compositional forms, using biblical themes;
- Liturgy—Understanding what liturgy is, what it does, and how formational it is when it includes the use of dance and the arts within the worship setting.
- Collaboration—how to work successfully and creatively with other ministries within the church under the guidance of religious education and liturgical studies.
- Evangelism—exploring ways to take the ministry of dance outside the walls of the church and out to the streets.

In addressing the implementation of liturgical dance within the church, suggestions surfaced during the interviews that addressed this issue. Yvonne Peters makes several suggestions to the religious educator and the liturgist on how to utilize liturgical dance within the worship setting that will help educate the liturgical dancer, the pastoral leadership and the congregation. She states:

1. Keep the roots of dance as an active expression to God not as a spectacle before Him.
2. Worship is active not passive. One enters into worship to the degree one is willing to invest themselves in the worship experience. To lead worship, to teach worship, one must remain and be an active worshipper. Unlike other disciplines, there is no end to exploring the realms of worship. In this respect, student and teacher are ever pursuing.

3. Liturgical dance must be fitted into the entire context of the liturgy. There is grave danger of adding it on as a new flavor or spice to the liturgical service. To do this may cause the dance expression to become entertainment instead of a tool of facilitating corporate worship. (Peters interview)

Eyesha Marable explains one technique she uses in teaching liturgical dancers how to approach choreographing liturgical dance that is based on a particular scripture:

> The preacher is required to exegete the biblical text in bringing forth the Word of God in the sermon, by studying the Greek and the Hebrew significance of the word, read commentaries and read other authors and challenge the ideas and interpretations of other authors. So should the dancer. Choreographically I challenge the physical language of others, what does this text mean to you? In choreographing, "My Help," I used Psalm 121:1, "I will lift up mine eyes unto the hills, from whence cometh my help." I am bringing in their language in the study of the text. I am then going to find out what God meant by "help" and how help was used in other parts of the bible. Was it a help where we prostrate before him, or the type of help where we have to reach toward him? I am exegeting the text in a theological perspective and in a social context, what does that help look like socially. Who needs help in our community? We may need to bring in characters in the dance who are homeless, hungry, pregnant, or that they are bearing a cross because they need that type of help. It is a very instructional tool, because it is trying to preach a sermon through movement. (Marable interview)

Setting up such a curriculum is not necessarily new, however, there were past efforts to do such a work and these efforts took on a variety of forms and shapes. For example, Mary Jones[16] (1987) and fifteen other people met and formed the Christian Dance Fellowship of Austria in 1978. Jones explains the aims of the organization.

> The aim of the new organization was to join over the huge distances those scattered people who were already involved in trying to use dance in worship and provide training, encouragement and resources for them. The Fellowship would also aim to increase people's understanding and experience of sacred dance through literature, workshops and demonstrations, encouraging it as prayer, worship, teaching and evangelism, coming from a personal faith commitment. (35)

As the fellowship developed, Jones expanded the aims to include the following:

a. Stimulate interest in and exchange information about using movement to celebrate and explore our life and worship together in Christian community;
b. Increase people's understanding of the history and theology of dance in the church;
c. Reach those outside the church with the message of the gospel presented through dance, mime, and drama;
d. Encourage and train both individuals and groups in dance ministry;
e. Encourage the formation of branches of the Fellowship around Australia;
f. Promote performances, conferences and other functions in furtherance of these objectives (40)

Marable describes the beginnings of the National Liturgical Dance Network,[17] which was created in 1998 after the first Liturgical Dance Conference sponsored by The Allen Liturgical Dance Ministry of the Greater Allen AME Cathedral of New York as follows:

> During the final morning worship of the first conference (1998), one of the directors asked how do we stay in touch? God gave me the mandate to create a national liturgical dance network to keep us all together so that when we come together in another eleven months instruction would have been given to these churches on how to maintain and feed your liturgical dance ministry. Dance not only out of their flesh and out of their feelings but to learn how to dance the Word of God. We created a curriculum a pedagogy that worked at Allen and is being replicated around the world on how to feed, teach and maintain dance ministries. Ministries throughout the world are sitting down to be feed spiritually, educationally, and scripturally to learn how to dance the word. (Marable interview)

Recently accredited college and graduate programs are offering dance and theology, or liturgical dance as regular courses in the curriculum. Mary Jones (1987) cites the International Institute for Creative Ministries,[18] an accredited theological college, which is an interdenominational college associated with Christian Life Centre in Sydney, offering courses in dance, drama, music, art and theology. The creation of the college was the result of a joint vision of director David Johnston, who is a native of California, U.S. and Frank Houston, New Zealand-born pastor of the Christian Life Centre. Jones explains that the college has a uniquely conceived curriculum that ensures that each student has general experience in all areas of theology and the arts offered by the college, while specializing in one or two specific areas.

Also Marable describes the newly established graduate program at Drew seminary where there is a concentration in liturgical dance.

> At Drew Seminary, it is fascinating to mix the pedagogy of worship and the arts there. There are believers and nonbelievers, agnostics, Mennonites, Methodists, confused people and pastors. It is amazing that at that instructional place they do not just hear the word, study different theologians but they have a space to dance it out. At Drew, they created the first ATS accredited curriculum on liturgical dance, where people can get a Masters of Arts in Liturgical Dance, where people are studying all the dynamics of theology, but we are given space to embody our theology. What does it look like to believe God, to preach the word? This semester I am teaching a class on Preaching the Word through the Body, Performing Arts and Preaching. We are teaching people how to preach from the pulpit but how to use their bodies, how to use other people's bodies from the congregation. To actualize and to visualize what the word looks like. Using the story of Lazarus being raised from the dead, you can have someone wrapped in toilet tissue and then they are released. They do not have to dance, but dance is a visual in the learning. (Marable interview)

The partnering of liturgical dance with religious education allows it to be considered as a course of study not only for the liturgical dancer, as in the example displayed in *Format Three*, but also as a course of study for clergy, congregations, religious educators and liturgists. Such a partnership reveals its validity as both a topic of study for collegiate and seminarian study, and as a viable method of study by which other religious topics can be investigated. In either example, both the instructor and learner can fulfill and reflect Psalm 150:6 which states, "Let everything that breathes praise the LORD! Praise the LORD!"

Format Four: The Partnership of One

Format Four is the final format, and it makes use of the imagination to such a degree as to visualize the extreme uniqueness found in the partnership between liturgical dance and religious education. In this duet, the many relational opportunities found between both partners are viewed though the different choreographic movements and lifts displayed. From collaborative and unison movements, to postures that solely rely on the element of trust, to distinctive and extraordinary lifts that display both liturgical dance and religious education, this last format includes evangelism and outreach found both outside and inside the walls of the church. What evangelism looks like is immeasurable to imagine, however when it is creatively devised it can help surface components of restoration and healing that are underscored by the agape love of Christ. In this last format, both liturgical dance and religious education are joint partners whose choreographic and performing endeavors seek to uplift and share the name of Christ to a world that at times appears to be unlovable and immensely broken.

Evangelism in the Christian context can help form and create community. Evangelism in this regard typifies the Marcan scripture which heralds the great commission. In Mark 16:15 Jesus told the disciples to, "Go into all the world and proclaim the good news to the whole creation." The imagination is helpful in establishing a setting where the good news of evangelism can formulate community. For example Maxine Greene's (2000) notion of the imagination is important for forming community. In describing community, Greene emphasizes process words such as making, creating, weaving, saying, and the like. Community is achieved by persons who offer the space to discover what they recognize together and to appreciate in common with one another; they have to find ways to make intersubjective sense (Greene 2000: 39). She states, ". . . it ought to be a space infused by the kind of imaginative awareness that enables those involved to imagine alternative possibilities for their own becoming and their group's becoming," (39). For Greene community is not the encountering social contracts that are the most reasonable to enter, but it is the question of what might contribute to the pursuit of shared goods: what ways of being together, of attaining mutuality, of reaching toward some common world (39). Community, such as the one described by Greene, can be easily established within a church and within an evangelistic event where the sharing of the good news can be experienced by all especially if it is shared with the use of the imagination through the partnership of liturgical dance and religious education.

One example of an evangelistic outreach is described by Lori Dekie concerning her youngest daughter who was fulfilling her Girl Scout "Silver Award" requirements and used liturgical dance to do so. Lori shares the memory:

> Our youngest daughter is a Girl Scout and there is a second to last step, the Silver Award and her project had her bring liturgical dance to the girls in all of the Girl Scout troops across Suffolk County and she taught them liturgical dance and they performed it in nursing homes which was part of her project. The community has been influenced by liturgical dance, something that she has learned and taken out of the church and into the surrounding community. (Dekie interview)

Such an example not only influenced Lori's daughter, but also she found it appealing to build a community through the use of religious education and liturgical dance with the members of her Girl Scout troop. They learned the movements, they learned what the movements signified, they learned the various meanings that undergirded the movements—meanings such as hearing the good news of Jesus Christ, living life more abundantly, living with hope and living to love and to be loved. However the building of community did not stop at that evangelistic setting between the Girl Scout members themselves, but it expanded to the nursing homes where he shared through liturgical dance the love of God, the love of neighbor, and the sharing of the good news to those residing in nursing homes. Such a partnership allows one's imagination to be energized and to expand to create numerous ways of sharing the gospel that are inspirational, inventive and educational.

Robert Evans[19] described how important it was to imagine both cognitively and artistically how the structure of the *Nativity*[20] was going to transpire. He asked God,

> How do we develop character; how do we move from one conversation to another; what dance movement language does this character need? Those things became the framework that I can then put walls onto. What songs help describe the characters within the *Nativity?* The question was not which Christmas songs should I use? (Evans interview)

Evans understood that in order to clearly craft the *Nativity* so it tells the story accurately, an artistic and a religious educational approach had to be intertwined within the choreographic process.

Evans' use of outreach and community formation initially took place within the casting of *Nativity*. He believes that dance ministry is not solely for children, as in an activity to keep their attention, or solely for women, because of its gracefulness. But it is also for males from the youngest to the oldest. He explains:

> Dance ministry is ministry and anybody who has ever been ministered to knows that it is, regardless of gender, age, ethnic group. In some circles when you talk about males in dance ministry, typically the only dance form that is acceptable is African or manly stuff with fists and stomping. And yes, God is all of that, but sometimes what we are really dealing with is people's image of what manhood is or their image of what a man is. God is a God of love and of strength and if you can convey that to your children, to be a father of both strength and love then why can we not be both strong and soothing in and through dance?

I used to have these conversations with God, you give me this stuff that has more male leads than female leads and in the *Nativity,* there are only two female leads, so what is this, a joke? And I am not desperate enough to strap females down to make them shepherds. So the males have to come from some place. And it is a walk by faith. . . We did not have our shepherds until three weeks to tech, and the shepherd's scene, those guys should have been rehearsed long before that. But we kept plowing though, plowing through, plowing through. But we then began to get phone calls, and I said "yes, tell them to get over here, right now!" One of the things that bring me a great deal of joy is that one of my students from this classroom was a shepherd. He heard me talking about it on the phone and I was going through some of the photos and he said, "What is that?" And I began to tap out some stuff and he began to repeat it and so he would take the trip up to Westchester, Metro North, every Saturday for rehearsal. . . We had a lot of men in the production and not all were dancers, but they wanted to be apart. My son is also in it and he grew up in DMI starting off as a sheep and assumed lead roles this 2011 production and also choreographed for the *Nativity* as well. (Evans interview)

As with the *Nativity,* when doing liturgical dance for evangelistic purposes, during the initial stages the teaching must always begin with the cast and those who are directly related to the production. This gives space for those who are involved to learn the deeper biblical lessons and principles that give foundation to the production. From this educational perspective, those involved in the production can perform and minister the movement and characters with clarity, understanding and honest conviction so the message transcends outward to the audience. The movements speak but they also teach, give witness and transform the community.

Another example of creating community through evangelism occurred during the initial years after the 9/11 tragedy. The September 11, 2011 attacks were the most deadly international terrorist attack in history and the largest attack on United States territory since the Japanese attack on Pearl Harbor on December 7, 1941 (Lee 2004). Lee captures the untiring rescuing efforts of those lost in the remains of the collapsed twin towers of the World Trade Center buildings by the firefighters, rescue workers, police officers and countless others. He states:

Rescue efforts started immediately as surviving police, firefighters, engineers, construction workers, and other arriving emergency personnel began a determined search for colleagues and civilian survivors. Although intense rescue efforts continued for more than a week, the tremendous force of the collapsing buildings spared few of those trapped inside. The tremendous volume of falling material compacted into a tight and dense mass, providing few spaces that held the possibility of finding survivors. Death for thousands had been swift, and beyond a handful of survivors found in the first hours, no one survived the full fury of the collapse. Despite a 24-hour operation throughout the winter by large and dedicated crews, a full excavation of the site and forensic determinations of human remains would take more than half a year. (Learner, 4)

There were many organizations that provided a variety of services and spiritual counseling programs to help bring healing to the people of the United States and to the world community. In addition, numerous benefit concerts emerged to help raise funding for the victims and families of the 9/11 tragedy. One organization that participated was the New York City inspirational radio station, KISS Inspirations,[21] which presented a benefit gospel concert annually entitled, "A Night of Healing,"[22] held at the Theatre at Madison Square Gardens. The Allen Liturgical Dance Ministry[23] was invited to participate as the only dance ministry on the program which included noted gospel artists. It was accompanied by an inspirational message given by a notable preacher. The use of dance in this particular venue represented a huge shift from inspirational and gospel music alone. With the combination of music, word and dance the concert provided healing for many. One website source records reactions from the 2003 benefit concert:

> The kind of response the event gathered was rather surprising. People went crazy after watching the show. While some of them felt awesome and blessed, the others felt that the spirituality was healed by the various artists. . . The audiences could not forget each and every scene from their memory and the scenes progressed in their minds in full sequence even after watching the show a few days back. (OnlineSeats.com)

The dancers' preparation for this two-year event was standard, as it required bible study, prayer and numerous rehearsals. However, within any evangelism project the love of God permeates not only through the body's movements, but also in the dancers facial expressions and demeanor as they entered on and off stage. During the 2003 concert, one of the gospel artists, Bryon Cage, who knew of the dance ministry's work, asked if ALDM could accompany one of his songs. Although this was not a planned component of the concert, the reasons behind this spontaneous change revealed the rich partnership between liturgical dance and religious education. Cage indicated that he wanted the words of the song to jump out and reach the people in the audience, and since he knew of ALDM's movement version, it was allowed to take place. For both the dancer and audience member the words and movements to the song, "The Presence of the Lord Is Here," rang true.

Lastly, an example of evangelism that is highlighted by the partnership of liturgical dance and religious education is found inside the walls of the church. The illustrated sermons of Bishop Charles Ellis[24] are moments in the seasonal work of Greater Grace Temple that invite not only the members of the congregation, but it ultimately invites people from the community including groups from a variety of non-religious agencies as well as church groups who travel from out of state. The first two, "Whip, Hammer and Cross" and "From Hell and Back" were given to him from Pastor Tommy Burnett, the originator of the illustrated sermon[25] Ellis explains the creative license he utilizes in presenting these sermons.

> These two, "From Hell and Back" and "Whip, Hammer and Cross," are Tommy Barnett's illustrations and he gave us free reign to use them. Whip, Hammer and Cross is Jesus from his triumphant entry into Jerusalem to his ascension up from the grave. It is the story of Christ, but Barnett put it in a dramatized form, and he has given us the access and permission to use the title and to take it and adjust it for our audience and local. Phoenix,

> AZ is a predominant Caucasian, Hispanic, Native American audience and culture. So a lot
> of his music, dance, and choreography would not work here in Detroit. So you would have
> to adapt it to your audience. So if you would watch Barnett's "Whip, Hammer and Cross,"
> and then mine, well the story is the same, nothing in the story changes, but when you look
> at the dramatization of it and the music you will see a vast difference between Barnett's and
> Bishop Ellis. If you see "From Hell and Back," you will see a big difference between
> Barnett's and Bishop Ellis, but the concepts were given from Barnett for those two and
> those two are staples that we do every year. I went to Barnett's conference in February of
> 1997 and then Good Friday of that same year I did "Whip, Hammer, and Cross." That
> New Year's Eve, 97–98, we did "From Hell and Back," and we were off and running, we
> baptized 100 people that Good Friday and baptized 238 people that New Year's Eve. So
> we were off and running then. . . (Ellis interview)

Ellis explains that the illustrated sermon topics come from him, and he shares the assignment of getting it into dramatic form with the director, choreographer, set designer, and musical director. From his perspective, the people who come and witness the illustrated sermons are made up of two types of audiences. The first are Christians, whether they are from Greater Grace or from churches located either near or far away. For those who travel from afar, there are designated seats throughout the sanctuary reserved for these groups, so they will have the best viewing, since they have traveled great distances to see the production. However, goof seats are also reserved for those groups from social service agencies who make it an outing to come out and view the multi-dimensional productions.

Ellis' use of the illustrated sermon is another form of witness. However it is one that "pushes the pastoral envelope" since the entire sanctuary is transformed for the setting of the production. He explains the yearly format for the use of the illustrated sermon as follows:

> Now I do a minimal of four illustrations per year. I always do "Whip, Hammer and Cross,"
> Good Friday, and "From Hell and Back," the Friday before Halloween, and they are
> predetermined illustrated sermons. Then I do one on Easter Sunday and I do one on New
> Year's Eve. I usually title them after a popular movie title. That title for Easter will always
> tie in to the resurrection. *Ransom*, *The Blind Side*, and *Tomb Raiders* are movie titles that tie
> in to the resurrection message. On New Year's Eve, those are movie titles but they go along
> with what is going on at the time, there are movie titles and it will get that person who may
> not go to church interested in coming to see what these titles are all about. (Ellis interview)

The description of the opening scene of the *Whip, Hammer and Cross* reveals the magnitude of the production and how Bishop Ellis employs professionalism and creativity in presenting the educational underpinnings of the gospel account. In the production the dancers play the followers of Jesus as well as the Jews who despise him. At the beginning of the production, the dancers, both adults and children, use the double level of both the pulpit and sanctuary floor, to open the triumphant entry theme with movement and streamers. This is being done while a group of Roman soldiers are lined up on the back of the pulpit stage on a variety of levels. After the dancers are finished dancing on the stage, they exit as one Roman soldier comes in on a horse and rides on the pulpit stage to see who is coming and what the commotion is all about. As the opening song continues, the dancers return coming from the back of the sanctuary, and they dance down three isles of the sanctuary, while Jesus and the disciples are coming down the main aisle. The disciples are dancing as well as the entire cast with the exception of Jesus who is on a donkey. Jesus, the donkey and the disciples are led onto a huge ramp that connects the lower level of the sanctuary floor to the upper level of the pulpit platform.

This opening scene tells the entire story of the triumphant entry into Jerusalem as found in the gospel accounts,[26] as it utilizes dance, both animal and pageantry props, dramatic interpretations, and music. Movements are varied as the dancers perform more full bodied movement combinations while the disciples do more movement gestures that signify the celebration of Jesus as the "one who comes in the name of the Lord!" Whether the movement is full bodied or is gestural, the significance of the movement is key for it helps to bring animation to the events of the triumphant entry. As well, it gives religious education foundation to the biblical event. Such a production brings life to the biblical accounts while affording the audience moments to contemplate and question their relationship to the text.

Bishop Ellis' work is both commended as well as questioned by those inside and outside of his denomination. He shares teachings on the subject of illustrated sermons yearly so present day pastors understand the importance of the visual in today's 21st century postmodern church. Pastor Tommy Barnett, Bishop Charles Ellis, Rev. Dr. Floyd H. Flake and other pastors have been at the forefront of progressive ministry especially as it relates to the use of the arts, liturgical dance and religious education. True innovation has the ability to change and transform life. As a pastor who has welcomed the use of liturgical dance inside the walls of the church for the past thirty-five years, Rev. Flake[27] shares some advice to those pastors venturing into the pastorate, especially on the subject of innovation. He states:

> Rather than spending time talking about the successful churches and what they have, look at them in terms of being models, where innovative ideas were birthed, then speak with them and see how you can produce the innovative ideas that God has placed within you. Pastors have been limited by the definition of what ministry is supposed to do. What is the business of the ministry? It is to meet the needs of the people daily. (Flake interview)

Conclusion

All four formats in this chapter explain the unique partnership between liturgical dance and religious education. As in a dance, whether it is a well-crafted piece of choreography or it is an improvisational exercise of movement exploration, the two partners learn how to exist one with the other, while also learning how to support one another unselfishly. The work of both learning modalities exposes the uniqueness found within each, while revealing just how effective they can be once paired together to relay the messages of hope and restoration. As the four examples illustrate, whether the format is found within the worship service, a teaching chapel service, a liturgical dance curriculum or a curriculum for those in ministry, or within the work of evangelism, each of them display the meaning of corporation and imaginative creativity.

The correlation between the newly formed definition of liturgical dance and the four formats highlight four basic principles. The *first basic principle* captures liturgical dance as expressive and imaginative movement that is used both inside and outside of worship that creatively educates and instructs Christians to comprehend the Bible and their faith in the Trinity through the elements of space, time and design. Whether the space is inside the walls of the sanctuary, in a nursing home, on a stage, or in a classroom, religious education takes place through time and through innumerable and imaginative choreographic shapes that edify the mind, body and spirit.

The *second basic principle* describes the creative and educational relationship liturgical dance has with music, whether the music is instrumental, a newly composed inspirational song, a praise and worship song or a traditional sacred hymn. Its relationship with the spoken word gives vision and depth to the whole text regardless if is extracted from the Bible, a sermon, a poem, or words from a sacred play. Its relationship with silence truly gives space for the movement itself to speak, to teach, and to be reflective on themes of faith and faith development.

The *third basic principle* promotes the formation of community through individual and mutual movement and dance explorations. Community is formed wherever two or three are gathered in the name of Christ and it is formed through the listening eyes of love. Therefore, genuine community is formed out of the need to extend love in Jesus' name. So whether the community is formed by the congregational members waving their arms in a worship service, by the audience that views a liturgical dance or liturgical dance play, or inside the classroom walls where liturgical dancers are being instructed, a teachable witness of this partnership is enough to form community. Regardless of the setting, the themes of love, prayer, healing and reconciliation are cultivated.

The *fourth basic principle* gives attention to the experiential natural of liturgical dance, and because of this attribute anyone, regardless of religious affiliation, can be exposed to liturgical dance in the Christian context and be influenced by it. From the smallest gesture to the largest of movements, liturgical dance grounded in partnership with religious education can help exemplify a way of knowing that transcends the ordinary in church worship, but more importantly in life itself. It opens the heart through bodily expression, to learn the meaning of a love that is non-negotiable and never-ending. To this end, this type of love is in partnership with God and with neighbor and it fuels liturgical dance to be a dance that is transforming.

Appendix A

You've Turned My Mourning into Dancing
Written and Composed by John Tirro,[28] 2008

You've turned my mourning, my mourning, my mourning into dancing.
You've turned my mourning, my mourning, my mourning into dancing.
You've turned my mourning, my mourning, my mourning into dancing.
You've turned my mourning, my mourning, my mourning into dancing.

Chorus
You've turned my sorrow into song, you've turned my singing into praise,
you've turned my praise, to peace, my peace to joy and dancing!
You've turned my sorrow into song, you've turned my singing into praise,
you've turned my praise to peace, my peace to joy and dancing!

Notes

1. The *pas de deux* originated in ballet choreography and appears throughout the ballet, but it is also known to end the ballet, with a spectacular *pas de deux*. It is comprised of the ballerina and her partner. This *pas de deux* usually developed according to a strict form: first came a stately section (the adagio) for both performers, emphasizing lyrical and sustained movements. Then came two solos (called "variations"), the first for the man and the second for the ballerina. Finally, in the coda, the stars appeared together again, the choreography emphasizing quick, flashy steps. If the *pas de deux* form could degenerate into a formula, it nonetheless permitted adroit displays of male and female movement. (Anderson 1979: 66)
2. The work of Brother Lawrence of the Resurrection can be found in the following text: Delaney, John J. 1977. *The Practice of the Presence of God.* New York: Doubleday Image Book.
3. A Praise-and-Worship approach to corporate liturgy sequences the order of worship, using contemporary Christian music to lead participants through a series of affective states. . . The name itself, "Praise-and-Worship," parallels the logic of this typology. Proponents make a distinction between praise—usually defined as extolling God by remembering or proclaiming God's character and activity—and worship—usually defined in more relational terms of direct communion with God. The basic movement from praise to worship is achieved by adjusting certain characteristics of the music. At least three are standard. The first is a move in the types of personal pronouns used for God, from third person to second person. As participants progress into worship, they begin to address God with the more intimate "you." The second common adjustment is in the tempo, tone and key of the music. Frequently, Praise-and-Worship services begin upbeat, utilizing songs in major keys to proclaim the goodness of God's character and activity. Somewhere in the progression, the tempo slows and repetition is more frequent and extended. The volume is diminished as worshippers enjoy communion with the living God. The third shift is in the songs' content. Frequently, the Praise-and-Worship progression moves from more objective remembrance of God to songs reflecting upon God's person and our relationship with God. (Bradshaw 2002: 379–380) Within certain Protestant denominations, Praise and Worship songs are led by a praise and worship leader, and a praise and worship team help supply singing support. During the opening of The Greater Allen Cathedral's worship service, a prayer is spoken and then the praise and worship singing begins with the praise leader, praise team and the congregation.
4. Numerous Christian churches have liturgical dancers active during the praise and worship segment of the worship service. The dancers demonstrate simple movement that the congregation can follow, if they choose to do so. In most cases there is a moving atmosphere found within this portion of the service where the congregation is given the opportunity to either follow fully or in part the liturgical dance movement gestures that are presented by the liturgical dancers. These movement gestures accompany the words of the praise and worship songs that are sung. Both song and dance should work together to support and translate the scriptural meanings that undergird the songs.

5. See chapter 4 [of *"And We Shall Learn through the Dance": Liturgical Dance as Religious Education*], Teach Me and Give Me Understanding: Experiential Learning and the Church Community, pages 30–32, for the song, movement, and educational underpinnings of the teaching on grace.
6. Doreen Holland, a sixteen-year member of the Allen Liturgical Dance Ministry, in an interview with the researcher in November 2011.
7. Yvonne Peters, an international liturgical dancer, teacher, and choreographer located in Lutz, Florida who was the director of the International Celebration of the Feasts of Tabernacles in Jerusalem for the past 22 years, in an interview with the researcher in January 2012.
8. Dr. Patrick Evans, an Associate Professor of the Practice of Sacred Music at the Institute of Sacred Music at Yale Divinity School (YDS) and was the former director of music for the Marquand Chapel, which supplied daily ecumenical worship at YDS, in an interview with the researcher in January 2012.
9. "You Have Turned My Mourning into. . ." was an actual title of a chapel service held on the grounds of Yale Divinity School on April 21, 2008 which the researcher attended 2005–2009.
10. "You've Turned My Mourning into Dancing," was written and composed by John Tirro, a 2009 MDIV graduate from Yale Divinity School (YDS) who was attending YDS during the same time as the researcher. During the 2007–2009 academic years, both individuals had the opportunity to work on numerous chapel services together that featured both music and liturgical dance as worship and teaching tools for the YDS community. "You Have Turned My Mourning into. . ." was one such collaboration that was featured in Marquand Chapel.
11. See Appendix A [in *And We Shall Learn through the Dance*] for the "You've Turned My Mourning into Dancing" song text.
12. Common time—4/4 time.
13. During this particular service and services like these, one or two dances can be presented by individuals or groups of liturgical dancers that reflect the theme of the service, along with scriptural readings, and reflective songs. The times of prayer are moments that will afford individuals the opportunity to pray at their seats or travel to designated prayer stations to write down their mourning prayers for themselves or to intercede in prayer for others. The entire service is a teaching service utilizing the interactions of the congregation to gather together in order to lift each other up from a state of mourning to a state of joyful dancing.
14. The Reverend Eyesha Katurah Marable, an Itinerant elder in the AME church as well as the founding director of the National Liturgical Dance Network, [NLDN] an international liturgical dance organization, in an interview with the researcher in January 2012.
15. Jay and Lori Dekie, members of The Greater Allen AME Cathedral of New York and parents of three children, in an interview with the researcher in December 2011.
16. Mary Jones, an international liturgical dancer, teacher, and choreographer in Sidney, Australia is the founder of the Christian Dance Fellowship of Australia in 1978 and the International Christian Dance Fellowship in 1988, in an interview with the researcher in January 2012.
17. The Network was developed to provide organizational development and leadership training to Christians who participate in, lead or have a vision to begin liturgical dance ministries at their respective churches. It is designed:
   —To help dance ministries best witness to the unsaved through dance, and to edify God's kingdom by enhancing the praise and worship experience for the church universal
   —To promote the development of an intimate relationship with God through praise and worship
   —To share, encourage, edify, and lift up dance ministers functioning in the body of Christ
   —Provide ongoing training, support and resources for dance ministers that will help them continually mature as leaders over their respective ministries
   —To transform people into leaders that can submit, support and complement the authority of their church; direct a group with authority, compassion, confidence, and commitment (accessed on March 10, 2012 from www.natldancenetwork.com)
18. Mary Jones points out that the IICM became Wesley Institute when it changed ownership from an AOG church to Wesley Mission (Methodist/Uniting). David Johnston continues currently as principal. The course of study at Wesley once was for Christians and included Dance Ministry as well as all the regular dance courses, but now there is a majority of non-Christians in the courses and the person in charge of the department has a different vision for it. Plus there is always the economic factor. However they will have to take biblical studies and theology (Jones interview)

19. Robert Evans, Founding Director of the Dance Ministry Institute in Westchester, NY, in an interview with the researcher in January 2012.

20. The *Nativity* is the liturgical dance presentation choreographed and directed by Robert Evans and referred to in chapter 5 [in *And We Shall Learn through the Dance*] during his interview.

21. http://www.98.7kissfm.com.

22. OnlineSeats.com, 98.7 Kiss FM A Night of Healing. The station presented A Night of Healing, a show that changed the parameters of all other shows owing to its exceptional presentation that went straight through the heart. They were emotionally attached with the stage sequence of the show. . . The talent line of the show includes Donnie McClurkin, Fred Hammond, The Clark Sisters, Andraé Crouch, Richard Smallwood, Kelly Price, Tie Tribbett, J Moss and other special guests. . . The others who extended significant roles in making the show a major hit were Kim Burrell, Natalie Wilson, Smokie Norful, Byron Cage, Hezekiah Walker, The Allen Liturgical Dance Ministry, Martha Munizzi, Israel & New Breed and Donnie McClurkin. Article portion (accessed March 11, 2012, http://www.OnlineSeats.com/a-night-of-healing-tickets/index.asp).

23. The Allen Liturgical Dance Ministry (ALDM) was invited to participate during the 2003 and 2004 productions of, "A Night of Healing." Under the direction of the researcher, ALDM ministered a ten-minute segment of liturgical dance for each benefit concert. For 2003, ALDM presented two liturgical dances, "Receive Our Praise, Oh, God," an original score by Stanley Brown and "We Speak to Nations," by Lakewood Church. The first was ministered by the men and teen boys (8) and the second by a 50-member representation of ALDM (this representation included girls, boys, teen girls and boys and women and men). For 2004 ALDM (a 50-member representation) presented three dances in a form of a choreo-drama that was accompanied by the Greater Allen Cathedral Praise and Worship singers and musicians. Two songs were originals, the first by Benjamin Love entitled, "If My People. . . ," and the repeat of Stanley Brown's "Receive Our Praise Oh God, and the traditional song "Holy, Holy, Holy," text by Reginald Heber and tune by John Dykes (Carpenter and Williams 2001: 329–331).

24. Bishop Charles Ellis, Senior Pastor of The Greater Grace Temple Church of the Apostolic Faith in Detroit, MI and the presiding bishop of the Apostolic Faith, a division of the Pentecostal Denomination, in an interview with researcher in October, 2011. Bishop Ellis is one of the forerunners of the "illustrated sermon," a sermon that is illustrated through drama, music, dance, set design and props, and stage lighting with the preacher as the conduit that links the entire dramatic ministry together.

25. See footnote on page 46 of chapter 5 [in *And We Shall Learn through the Dance*].

26. Jesus' Triumphal entry into Jerusalem is found in Matthew 21:1–11; Mark 11:1–11, and Luke 19:28–40.

27. Rev. Dr. Floyd H. Flake, senior pastor of The Greater Allen AME Cathedral of New York, in an interview with the researcher, December 2011. Rev. Flake is one of the first AME pastors who allowed liturgical dance to take place at Allen through the creation of the Allen Liturgical Dance Ministry in 1978 to the present.

28. John Tirro's contact information: johntirro@mac.com.

References

Anderson, Jack. *Dance.* New York: Newsweek Books, 1979.

Carpenter, Delores, and Nolan Williams Jr., eds. *African American Heritage Hymnal.* Chicago: GIA, 2001.

Crain, Margaret Ann. "Listening to Churches: Christian Education in the Congregational Life." In *Mapping Christian Education: Approaches to Congregational Learning.* Edited by Jack L. Seymour, 93–109. Nashville: Abingdon, 1997.

De Sola, Carla. ". . . And the Word Became Dance: A Theory and Practice of Liturgical Dance." In *Dance as Religious Studies.* Edited by Doug Adams and Diane Apostolos-Cappadona, 153–166. Chestnut Ridge, NY: Crossroad, 1990.

———. *The Spirit Moves, Handbook of Dance and Prayer.* Austin: Sharing Company, 1977.

———, and A. Easton. "Awakening the Right Lobe through Dance." In *Aesthetic Dimensions of Religious Education.* Edited by Gloria Durka and Joanmarie Smith, 69–81. New York: Paulist, 1979.

Dewey, John. *Art as Experience*. New York: Minton, Balch & Company, 1934. Reprint, New York: Perigee Books, 1980. Citations refer to Perigee edition.

———. *Experience and Education*. New York: Kappa Delta Pi, 1938. Reprint, New York: Touchstone, 1997. Citations refer to Touchstone edition.

———. *Democracy and Education*. New York: Free Press, 1944.

———. "Psychology, Pedagogy and Religion." *Religious Education* 69 (1974): 6–11.

Everist, Norma Cook. *The Church as Learning Community*. Nashville: Abingdon, 2002.

Foster, Charles R. *Educating Congregations*. Nashville: Abingdon, 1994.

Greene, Maxine. *Releasing the Imagination*. San Francisco: Jossey-Bass, 1995b. Paperback reprint, San Francisco: Jossey-Bass, 2000. Citations refer to paperback edition.

Jones, Mary. *Growth of a Dance Movement*. Melbourne, Australia: Christian Dance Fellowship, 1987.

Juarez, Orlando. "Welcome into this Place." In *African American Heritage Hymnal*. Edited by Delores Carpenter and Nolan E. Williams Jr., 114. Chicago: GIA, 2001. The song text and tune is written by Orlando Juarez and arranged by Jimmie Abbington. 1991, CMI-HP Publishing, admin. by Word Music, Inc. / Life Spring Music.

Lerner, Lee K. "September 11 Terrorist Attacks on the United States." *Encyclopedia of Espionage, Intelligence, and Security* (2004). http://www.encyclopedia.com.

National Liturgical Dance Network. "Statement and Purpose." Accessed March 10, 2012. http://www.natldancenetwork.com.

OnlineSeats.com. "A Night of Healing." Article portion accessed March 11, 2012. http://www.OnlineSeats.com/a-night-of-healing-tickets/index.asp.

Penrod, James, and Janice Plastino. *The Dancer Prepares*. 5th ed. New York: McGraw Hill, 2005.

Tirro, John. "You Have Turned My Mourning into Dancing." Mondo Zen Music, 2008.

Wimberly, Anne E. Streaty. *Nurturing Faith & Hope*. Cleveland: Pilgrim, 2004.

Zakkai, Jennifer Donohue. *Dance as a Way of Knowing*. Los Angeles: Stenhouse Publishers, 1997.

6

The Spiritual Arrangement Since 1999 and Its Use in Contemporary Worship

Leo H. Davis Jr.

The spiritual originated as a vital part of the African American worship experience in the eighteenth century. This provocative form of singing was/is embraced by some and adamantly rejected by others, yet continues to be a practice found in twenty-first-century worship. This chapter seeks to explore the spiritual arrangement since 1999 and its use in contemporary worship by discussing five key areas:

- The origin and development of the spiritual
- The importance of preserving spirituals in our liturgical expression
- Contemporary arrangers of spirituals
- Examples of spirituals in contemporary worship through a survey of 23 churches
- Strategies for the sustained use of spirituals in contemporary worship

The spiritual originated in the 1740s as a result of slaves being forced to conform their beliefs to Christianity. In the eighteenth and nineteenth centuries, missionaries sought to proselytize the slaves and refused any allegiances to the African heritage. As the slaves converted to Christianity, some chose to worship in a manner that reflected the practices of their European counterparts while others chose to worship in a manner that coincided with their African heritage. The latter resulted in what is known as the Negro spiritual. As a result of the demonstrative behavior that characterized this new form of worship, style, and song, whites and other blacks were adamantly opposed to the spiritual. For instance in 1819, a white Methodist minister, John F. Watson, published a book entitled *Methodist Error or Friendly Christian Advice to Those Methodists Who Indulge in Extravagant Religious Emotions and Bodily Exercises,* in which he stated, "We have too, a growing evil, in the practice of singing in our places of public and society worship, merry airs, adapted from old songs, to hymns of our composing: often miserable as poetry, and senseless as matter."[1] Bishop Daniel Alexander Payne of the African Methodist Episcopal Church and college president of Wilberforce University in 1888 published a text entitled "Recollections of Seventy Years," which states:

> The strange delusion that many ignorant but well-meaning people labor under leads me to speak particularly of them. About this time I attended a "bush meeting," where I went to please the pastor whose circuit I was visiting. After the sermon they formed a ring, and with coats off, sung, clapped their hands and stamped their feet in a most ridiculous and heathenish way. I requested the pastor to go and stop their dancing. At his request they stopped their dancing and clapping of hands, but remained singing and rocking their bodies to and fro.[2]

These two examples illustrate the resistance to the characteristics of the Negro spiritual.

There are two types of Negro spirituals, the first being the folk spiritual. The folk spiritual is characterized by hand clapping, foot-stomping, call-and-response, demonstrative behavior, and heterophonic singing.[3] The folk spiritual was usually performed in autonomous environments such as the praise houses and the invisible church.

The second type of spiritual is called concert or arranged spiritual. This type of spiritual was popularized in October of 1871 by the Fisk Jubilee Singers. Mr. George White, treasurer of the school had gained interest in the songs that were sung by the students. Mr. White organized a tour of twelve premiere singers selected from the student body. Dr. John Work asserts:

> ... while their repertoire consisted of various pieces from the Western European tradition, it was Mr. White's intent on a style of singing the spiritual which eliminated every element that detracted from the pure emotion of the song. Harmony was diatonic and limited very largely to the primary triads and the dominant seventh. Dialect was not stressed but was used only where it was vital to the spirit of the song. Finish, precision, and sincerity were demanded by this leader. While the program featured the spirituals, variety was given it by the use of numbers of classical standard. Mr. White strove for an art presentation, not a caricature of atmosphere.[4]

The arranged spiritual is characterized by homophonic singing,[5] European vocal technique, and call-and-response. However the demonstrative characteristics of the folk spiritual such as hand clapping, foot stomping and shouting were non-existent in the arranged spiritual. The performance context of the arranged spiritual shifted from the autonomous environment of the folk spiritual to the concert stage.

The spirituals affirm our Africanized sociocultural and spiritual dimensions. It not only talks about our God, but our social circumstances. It is one of the earliest documented illustrations of an approach to negotiating within a Europeanized environment. Without the spiritual we lose our sense of historical self. For instance, many of us today look at the spiritual as a solely religious artistic expression, however as John Work put forth over sixty years ago, the spiritual functions outside of its spiritual context as work and social song. We must conceptualize the spiritual not only as it functions in our religious environments, but also as a manifestation of our ideas and values within a secular context. As the slaves moved about the plantations they sang the work and social songs that gave commentary on their daily conditions. Put succinctly the Negro spiritual chronicles the sacred and secular aspects of African American life worlds.

A list of prominent early arrangers of the "concert" or "anthemized" spiritual includes, but is not limited to, Hall Johnson, Harry T. Burleigh, Nathaniel Dett, William Dawson, Undine Smith Moore, and Eva Jessye. The general characteristics of their compositions include:

- Homophonic textures
- Triadic voicing, or harmony
- Simple to complex rhythms
- Terse dynamics

Arrangements of the spiritual in particular since 1999 have broadened the musical parameters of the genre. Contemporary arranger's compositional techniques consist of:

- Virtuosic vocal technique
- Homophonic and polyphonic textures
- Extended sonorities
- More complex rhythms
- More percussive attack of consonants, along with other musical techniques

Some of the contemporary arrangers include Damon Dandridge, Courtney Carey, Stacey Gibbs, Rosephanye Powell, Roland Carter, and Uzee Brown Jr.

Arranged Negro spirituals by the aforementioned composers and arrangers are still being presented in the African American worship experience today, but tragically, they are few and far between. To further illustrate this point, I devised a random survey of 23 African American churches in the United States across various denominations to ascertain the use of spirituals within the worship experience of various congregations from January 1 through April 31, 2008. Table 1 shows the distribution of the 23 denominations surveyed.

Table 1.

Denomination	#
African Methodist Episcopal	1
Apostolic	1
Baptist	12
Catholic	1
Disciples of Christ	1
Episcopal (AME)	3
Non-Denominational	1
United Church of Christ	1
United Methodist Church	2
Total	**23**

The average attendance of congregations surveyed ranged from 150 to 8000. The choral classification ranged from adult mixed, youth, male, treble, children, and solo voice with piano accompaniment. The majority of the choral arrangements listed are to be performed a cappella, along with two that include piano accompaniment.* Table 2 displays the findings of the survey.

Table 2.

First African Methodist Episcopal: Bethel New York, New York Rev. Henry Belin III, Pastor Courtney Carey, Musical Leadership **Average Attendance** Sunday 7:00 a.m. – 150 Sunday 11:00 a.m. – 250	African Methodist Episcopal	*Adult Mixed Choir (SATB)* Lily of the Valley – arr. Wendell P. Whalum Ride On, King Jesus – arr. Roland Carter What You Gonna Call the Pretty Little Baby – arr. Ronald Stevens Don't You Let Nobody Turn Me 'Roun – arr. Phillip McIntyre My Soul's Been Anchored in the Lord – arr. Glenn Jones *Solo Voice and Piano* Set Down Servant – arr. Phillip McIntyre You Can Tell the World – arr. Courtney Carey Let's Have a Union – arr. Hall Johnson
The African Episcopal Church of St. Thomas Philadelphia, Pennsylvania Father Martini Shaw, Rector Dr. Jay Fluellen, Musical Leadership **Average Attendance** Sunday 10:00 a.m. – 300	African Episcopal	*Adult Mixed Choir (SATB)* Ride On, King Jesus – arr. Clayton White

Fifteenth Avenue Baptist Church
Nashville, Tennessee
Dr. William F. Buchanan,
    Senior Pastor
Diana K. Poe, Musical Leadership
	Baptist	*Adult Mixed Choir (SATB)*
		I'll Stand – arr. Raymond Wise
		I Got a Robe – arr. Raymond Wise
		My Soul's Been Anchored in the Lord
		    – arr. Glenn Jones
		Guide My Feet – arr. Avis Graves

Average Attendance Sunday 7:30 a.m. – 100 Sunday 10:00 a.m. – 500		
St. Augustine Catholic Church Memphis, Tennessee Father John Geaney, Rector Albert Langston, Musical Leadership	Catholic	*Adult Mixed Choir (SATB)* Ain't Got Time to Die – arr. Hall Johnson Elijah Rock – arr. Jester Hairston King of Kings – arr. Glenn Burleigh
Average Attendance Saturday 5:30 p.m. – 100 Sunday 8:00 a.m. – 125 Sunday 11:00 a.m. – 250		

Second Baptist Church
Evanston, Illinois
Rev. Mark A. Dennis Jr.,
    Senior Pastor
Dr. C. Charles Clency,
    Musical Leadership
	Baptist	*Adult Mixed Choir (SATB)*
		I've Been 'Buked – arr. Hall Johnson
		Keep Your Lamp – arr. André Thomas
		Do, Lord, Remember Me – arr. Moses G. Hogan
		Guide My Feet – arr. Avis Graves

Average Attendance Sunday 8:00 a.m. – 100 Sunday 11:00 a.m. – 400		
St. Paul Episcopal Church Atlanta, Georgia Rev. Robert C. Wright, Pastor Trey Clegg, Musical Leadership	Episcopal	*Adult Mixed Choir (SATB)* Cert'nly, Lord – arr. Moses G. Hogan Every Time I Feel the Spirit – arr. Moses G. Hogan Ain't Got Time to Die – arr. Hall Johnson I Want Jesus to Walk with Me – arr. Moses G. Hogan *Treble Chorus (SSAA)* Ride the Chariot – arr. Beatrice and Max T. Krone
Average Attendance Sunday 9:15 a.m. – 200 Sunday 11:15 a.m. – 200		

Bethel Institutional Baptist Church
Jacksonville, Florida
Drs. Rudolph McKissick Sr. &
    Rudolph McKissick Jr., Pastors
Omar Dickenson,
    Musical Leadership
	Baptist	*Adult Mixed Choir (SATB)*
		Give Me Jesus – arr. Roland Carter
		Ride Up in de Chariot – arr. H. Alvin Green
		You Must Have True Religion – arr. Roland Carter
		Every Time I Feel the Spirit – arr. Moses G. Hogan

Average Attendance Sunday 7:45 a.m. – 2500 Sunday 10:45 a.m. – 3500		

Brentwood Baptist Church Houston, Texas Dr. Joe Samuel Ratliff, Senior Pastor Lydia Alston, Musical Leadership	Baptist	*Adult Mixed Choir (SATB)* Ain't Got Time to Die – arr. Hall Johnson *Young Adult Choir (SATB)* King of Kings – arr. Glenn Burleigh
Average Attendance Sunday 7:45 a.m. – 1000 Sunday 10:45 a.m. – 1300		
Greater Mt. Olive Baptist Church Oklahoma City, Oklahoma Dr. A. G. Woodberry, Senior Pastor Brenda S. Johnson, Musical Leadership	Baptist	*Adult Mixed Choir (SATB)* He Is tuh Keeper – arr. William Barksdale (modern-day spiritual) *Youth/Children's Choir (SA)* King Jesus Is a-Listening – arr. William Dawson Ride On, King Jesus – arr. Glenn Burleigh
Average Attendance Sunday 8:00 a.m. – 200 Sunday 11:00 a.m. – 1000		
Metropolitan Baptist Church Washington DC Dr. H. Beecher Hicks, Senior Pastor Rev. Nolan Williams Jr., Musical Leadership	Baptist	*Adult Mixed Choir (SATB)* Done Made My Vow to the Lord – arr. Rev. Nolan Williams Jr. Been in the Storm – arr. Wendell P. Whalum Rock-a My Soul – arr. Moses G. Hogan Wade in the Water – arr. Moses G. Hogan
Average Attendance Sunday 7:30 a.m. – 1200 Sunday 11:00 a.m. – 1200		

**Mississippi Boulevard
  Christian Church**
Memphis, Tennessee
Dr. Frank A. Thomas, Senior Pastor
Dr. Leo H. Davis Jr.,
  Musical Leadership
	Disciples
	of Christ
		Adult Mixed Choir (SATB)
		My Soul's Been Anchored in the Lord
		– arr. Moses G. Hogan
		His Light Still Shines – arr. Moses G. Hogan
		Rockin Jerusalem – arr. Damon Dandridge
		Glory Hallelujah to the New Born King
		– arr. Mark Butler
		Daniel, Servant of the Lord – arr. Undine Smith
		Moore Lord, If I Got My Ticket
		– arr. Stacey Gibbs
		Great God A'mighty – arr. Jester Hairston
		Youth Choir (SATB)
		I'm Gonna Sing till the Spirit
		– arr. Moses G. Hogan
		Children's Choir (SA)
		*Jordan's Angels – arr. Rollo Dilworth
		Solo Voice and Piano
		Is There Anybody Here – arr. Roland Carter
		Keep Your Lamps Trimmed and Burning!
		– arr. Uzee Brown Jr.
		I'll Stand – arr. Raymond Wise

Average Attendance Sunday 10:00 a.m. – 1400		

Shalom Church St. Louis, Missouri Dr. F. James Clark, Senior Pastor Dello Thedford, Musical Leadership **Average Attendance** Sunday 7:45 a.m. – 900 Sunday 10:00 a.m. – 1200 Sunday 12:00 p.m. – 500	Baptist	*Adult Mixed Choir (SATB)* Every Time I Feel the Spirit – arr. William Dawson Ezekiel Saw de Wheel – arr. William Dawson Ride the Chariot – arr. Henry Smith The Battle of Jericho – arr. Moses G. Hogan *I Want Jesus to Walk with Me – arr. Mark Hayes I'll Never Turn Back – arr. Nathaniel Dett

Shiloh Baptist Church
Washington DC
Dr. Wallace Charles Smith,
    Senior Pastor
Thomas Dixon Tyler,
    Musical Leadership
 	
Average Attendance
Sunday 7:45 a.m. – 1000
Sunday 10:45 a.m. – 1400
	Baptist	*Adult Mixed Choir (SATB)*
		Elijah Rock – arr. Moses G. Hogan
		My Soul's Been Anchored in the Lord
		    – arr. Moses G. Hogan
		I'll Stand – arr. Raymond Wise
		Ride the Chariot – arr. Harry T. Burleigh
		Every Time I Feel the Spirit – arr. William Dawson
		I'm Gonna Sing till the Spirit
		    – arr. Moses G. Hogan
		Oh, Glory – arr. Evelyn Simpson Currenton
		I Wanna Be Ready – arr. James Miller
		Done Made My Vow to the Lord
		    – arr. Rev. Nolan Williams Jr.
		Soon I Will Be Done – arr. William Dawson

Shiloh Metropolitan Baptist Church Jacksonville, Florida Dr. H. B. Charles Jr., Senior Pastor Roger Sears & Antonia Hunt, Musical Leadership **Average Attendance** Sunday 8:00 a.m. – 1300 Sunday 10:00 a.m. – 3000	Baptist	*Adult Mixed Choir (SATB)* I Believe This Is Jesus – arr. Undine Smith Moore

**St. Andrew African Methodist
    Episcopal Church**
Memphis, Tennessee
Dr. Kenneth S. Robinson, Pastor
Linda Herring, Musical Leadership
 	
Average Attendance
Sunday 7:45 a.m. – 300
Sunday 11:00 a.m. – 1000
	African
	Methodist
	Episcopal
		Adult Mixed Choir (SATB)
		Guide My Feet – arr. Avis Graves
		Shut de Door – arr. Randy Stonehill
		Treble Chorus (SSA)
		Every Time I Feel the Spirit
		    – arr. Rosephanye Powell
		Male Chorus (TTBB)
		I'm Building Me a Home – arr. Uzee Brown

Apostolic Church of God Chicago, Illinois Bishop Arthur M. Brazier, Senior Pastor Mark Jordan, Musical Leadership **Average Attendance** Sunday 9:10 a.m. – 4500 Sunday 11:40 a.m. – 4500	Pentecostal	*Adult Mixed Choir (SATB)* In Bright Mansions – arr. Roland Carter Mighty Long Way – arr. Bradley Knight I've Been 'Buked – arr. Hall Johnson

Friendship Missionary Baptist Church Charlotte, North Carolina Dr. Clifford A. Jones, Senior Pastor Tony McNeill, Musical Leadership **Average Attendance** Sunday 7:30 a.m. – 900 Sunday 9:30 a.m. – 2500 Sunday 11:30 a.m. – 1500	Baptist	*Male Chorus (TTBB)* Go Down, Moses – arr. Moses G. Hogan Heaven – arr. André Thomas Hush, Somebody's Calling My Name – arr. Brazeal Dennard *Adult Mixed Choir (SATB)* Oh, Freedom – arr. Brazeal Dennard Fanfare and Processional – arr. Undine Smith Moore My Soul's Been Anchored in the Lord – arr. Glenn Jones I'm Gonna Sing till the Spirit – arr. Moses G. Hogan Great Day – arr. Marvin Curtis
New Psalmist Baptist Church Baltimore, Maryland Bishop Water S. Thomas, Senior Pastor J. D. Alston, Musical Leadership **Average Attendance** Sunday 7:30 a.m. – 1800 Sunday 9:30 a.m. – 1800 Sunday 11:30 a.m. – 1800	Baptist	*Male Chorus (TTBB)* You Must Have That True Religion – arr. Roland Carter My Soul's Been Anchored in the Lord – arr. Glenn Jones Ain't Got Time to Die – arr. Hall Johnson Every Time I Feel the Spirit – arr. William Dawson
Salem Baptist Church Chicago, Illinois Rev. Senator James T. Meeks, Senior Pastor Walter M. Owens Sr., Musical Leadership **Average Attendance** Sunday 10:00 a.m. – 8000	Baptist	*Adult Mixed Choir (SATB)* The Battle of Jericho – arr. Moses G. Hogan Elijah Rock – arr. Moses G. Hogan
Trinity United Church of Christ Chicago, Illinois Dr. Otis Moss, Senior Pastor Robert E. Wooten Jr., Musical Leadership **Average Attendance** Sunday 7:15 a.m. – 2500 Sunday 11:00 a.m. – 2500 Sunday 6:00 p.m. – 2500	United Church of Christ	*Adult Mixed Choir (SATB)* I've Been 'Buked – arr. Hall Johnson Free at Last – arr. Robert Mayes
University Park Baptist Church Charlotte, North Carolina Bishop Claude Alexander Jr., Senior Pastor Avis Graves, Musical Leadership **Average Attendance** Sunday 7:00 a.m. – 500 Sunday 8:30 a.m. – 1100 Sunday 9:30 a.m. – 2700 Sunday 11:30 a.m. – 2700	Baptist	*Adult Mixed Choir (SATB)* Guide My Feet – arr. Avis Graves I'm Determined to Walk with Jesus – arr. Avis Graves I've Been 'Buked – arr. Hall Johnson

The spirituals hold a critical place in the history of the African American experience as historical testament, survival mechanism, and cultural identity. This heritage must be sustained as they continue to serve a similar function today. Therefore, some strategies for sustaining the spirituals within our current worship experience are offered which I have developed within my nineteen-year career as Minister of Music at Mississippi Boulevard Christian Church.

1. **Congregational spirituals.** The congregational spiritual requires a leader and a congregation, which can be found in every church in some form or another. Dr. James Abbington so eloquently states in his text *Let Mount Zion Rejoice*, "The early black church never had or needed a choir. The entire congregation sang. If a member of the congregation could not sing, he or she could pat a foot. If one could not pat a foot, one could clap hands. If people could not clap their hands, they could sway their heads. If they could not sway their heads, they could wave their hands. And if they could not do this, they could testify. Everyone was expected to participate, and they did."[6]

2. **Adjust the instrumentation.** There are several arrangements of spirituals that provide varied accompaniment for solo voice, mixed chorus, unison voices, etc. For congregation accessibility, I would suggest offering a long-meter, rubato-style spiritual, with free accompaniment (either piano or percussion instrument); for example, "Is There Anybody Here Who Loves My Jesus," arranged by Roland Carter with solo voice and acoustic guitar/piano.

3. **The use of interdisciplinary artistic expressions.** The combination of liturgical dance, media, and spoken-word/poetry. This not only presents a broad sense of the black aesthetic as all of the art forms exist in an organic manner, but the synergy of which enhances the worship experience for the congregation.

4. **It is incumbent upon the musical leadership to consistently offer the presentation of spirituals.** If there is not an ample vocal resource within the congregation, take the time to become acquainted with the talent within the congregation and/or community, such as the high school chorus, professional ensemble, or vocal soloist.

Within the ever evolving trends of the twenty-first-century African American church liturgy, there is yet and still a clarion call from the congregation to the pulpit, to be reminded historically of our journey, within a blended context. The spiritual may not be integrated into the weekly worship service of many of our congregations today, due to numerous services, sermon themes, and even pastoral preference. However, there are unique and clever ways that we, as leaders of congregational worship, must seek out to continue to educate and edify our congregations through this valuable genre of repertoire and heritage. I strongly sense the need to have more dialogue at our worship tables with pastoral leads, and lay leaders in the planning and synchronizing of the worship experience. So often, we have "shoot from the hip" experiences, without prayerful and thoughtful planning of the worship regarding the message we want the congregation to experience. Within today's culture, even with the educational prowess of pastoral leadership, there is still a dearth of expertise and willingness to gather information for the good of the body. At the table, we can begin to educate team members of the importance and value, not only of this genre, but the variety of musical settings, vocalists, instrumental solos, intertwined within the worship experience, to further heighten the blended style. There are many ways to make use of the arranged spiritual within the context of the worship experience. Most recently within the Memphis community we experienced the loss of a significant civil rights leader. We have two locations that have completely different worship styles, and we were able to pay homage to the work and life of this abolitionist by video montages, under-padded by Negro spirituals, and the live performance of phenomenal arrangements that not only brought the congregation to its feet, but helped connect the sermon topic "Building a Solid Foundation" Ephesians 2 to an unmatched plateau.

I am a strong proponent of the WIDE variety of blended worship and genre mixtures within the worship experience. I am also committed to the spiritual remaining a part of the rich legacy of the African American worship experience, especially given its historical role in supporting our life journeys and faith formation. It appears that the spiritual continues to hold a valuable place in our lives and liturgy, while simultaneously losing its prominence as an expression of worship. Therefore, further research is needed in this area to expand our knowledge base and enable us to make well-informed recommendations to resuscitate this part of our cultural heritage.

Notes

1. Eileen Southern, *Readings in Black American Music* (New York: W. W. Norton, 1983), 62.
2. Ibid., 65.
3. Heterophonic: The simultaneous playing or singing of two or more versions of a melody.
4. John W. Work, *American Negro Songs: 230 Folk Songs and Spirituals, Religious and Secular* (Mineola, NY: Dover, 1998), 15.
5. Homophonic: Having one part or melody predominating.
6. James Abbington, *Let Mt. Zion Rejoice! Music in the African American Church* (Valley Forge: Judson), 83.

For additional references for locating new, arranged, or traditional spirituals see:
- www.theafricanamericanlectionary.org
  This web site contains lectionary commentaries specially designed to address the liturgical moments of significance to most African American Christians. Pastors, musicians, and laity are invited to read them online or print readings to review at your leisure. Please be aware that each reading is intended to be accompanied by corresponding cultural resource material and worship resources.
- www.giamusic.com
- *Waiting to Go! African American Worship Resources: Advent through Pentecost*, ed. James Abbington and Linda H. Hollies (Chicago: GIA, 2002).
- *Going to Wait! African American Worship Resources: Pentecost and Advent* ed. James Abbington and Linda H. Hollies (Chicago: GIA, 2003).

7

If It Had Not Been for the Lord on My Side: Hymnody in African American Churches

James Abbington

In his enduring classic *The Souls of Black Folk*, published in 1903, W. E. B. Du Bois (1868–1963) declared, "Three things characterized this religion of the slave—the Preacher, the Music, and the Frenzy. The Preacher is the most unique personality developed by the Negro on American soil." He continued,

> The Music of Negro religion is that plaintive, rhythmic melody, with its touching minor cadences, which, despite caricature and defilement, still remain the most original and beautiful expression of human life and longing yet born on American soil. . . Finally, "the Frenzy" or "Shouting," when the Spirit of the Lord passed by, and seizing the devotee, made him mad with supernatural joy, was the last essential of Negro religion and the more devoutly believed in than all the rest.[1]

In a work published in 1984, titled *Soul of Black Worship*, Wyatt Tee Walker (b. 1929) set forth three primary support systems that are always operative in the African American religious experience: *Preaching, Praying,* and *Singing*.[2] One need only to visit an African American church worship experience to witness the significance and reality of Du Bois' and Walker's assertions in the twenty-first century.

For certain, the sermon, or more accurately, the *preaching*, and the music, or more precisely, the *singing*, are the focal points of worship in the black church as magnets of attraction and primary vehicles for spiritual transport and formation. All other activities find their place in some subsidiary relationship. C. Eric Lincoln (1924–2000) and

Lawrence Mamiya concluded in their critical study *The Black Church in the African American Experience*:

> [I]n the Black Church, good preaching and good singing are almost invariably the minimum conditions of a successful ministry. Both activities trace their roots back to Africa where music and religion and life itself were all one holistic enterprise... First of all, music served the important function of convoking the cultus, that is, assembling the faithful to a common place and a common experience of worship. Once this was accomplished it functioned to transcend or to reduce to insignificance those social, cultural, or economic barriers [that] separated individuals in their secular interests in order that genuine corporate worship might take place.[3]

A balanced study of African American church history must keep in full perspective two unquestionable elements. One, African Americans felt the need to be converted, to "get religion," and to know God for themselves—that is, on their own terms. This strong, consistent pattern of religious involvement has long been criticized as being pious, otherworldly, a flight from reality. The second element has been the struggle for survival and eventual liberation. It is this position that critics of the former emphasis declare ought to be the church's full agendum. Gayraud Wilmore's study, *Black Religion and Black Radicalism* (third ed., 1998), remains the best historical overview of the involvement of black religious groups and individuals in black-oriented efforts in political and social change in the United States. As Wilmore, C. Eric Lincoln, and others have pointed out, the mere fact of black survival in a total system of dehumanization and exclusion is by itself a significant political act.

Before the enslaved Africans in the United States learned to read or write, they sang songs, told stories, listened and responded to sermons, and expressed their hopes, fears, trials, tribulations, and sorrows through the medium of an oral tradition that had characterized the West African culture from which their ancestors had come. As the enslaved heard sermons of the slave preacher based upon the Bible, they created songs in response to them. Spirituals grew out of the experiences of slavery and the covert religious practices of enslaved Africans, and were referred to as the invisible institution. Gospel music is a post-emancipation development and a product of the early twentieth century and the concerns of the Great Migration. The musical genres of African American congregations have developed from folk spirituals, to black-meter music, to prayer and praise hymns, improvised Euro-American hymns, hymns by African American hymn writers, traditional and contemporary gospel music, and today to praise and worship music and Holy Hip Hop.

Political and Economic Influences on African American Congregational Song

Since the Second Vatican Council (1962–1965), a number of social, political, and economic reforms significantly influenced and shaped congregational singing in African American churches.

During this time the Civil Rights Movement, led by the Reverend Dr. Martin Luther King Jr. was at its peak, having experienced the Montgomery, Alabama, bus protest (1955–1956), the Sit-In Movement (1960) in Greensboro, North Carolina, the Freedom Ride (1961), demonstrations in Albany, Georgia, (1961–1962) and Birmingham, Alabama, (1963), the march from Selma to Montgomery (1965), Chicago race riots (1966), anti-Vietnam protests (1967), the Poor People's Campaign (1968), and the assassination of Dr. King on April 4, 1968, in Memphis, Tennessee. The Reverend Dr. Wyatt Tee Walker's article, "The Soulful Journey of the Negro Spiritual; Freedom Songs" (1963) demonstrated the direct transference of the Negro Spiritual form to the then developing "freedom song." Walker's example "The Birth of the Freedom Song" included in *Negro Digest* provides a clear insight into this phenomenon:

The Birth of the Freedom Song[4]

Refrain: I want Jesus to walk with me, Yes, I want Jesus to walk with me; All along my pilgrim journey, Lord, I want Jesus to walk with me. *Stanza:* When I'm in trouble, Lord, walk with me; When I'm in trouble, Lord, walk with me. All along my pilgrim journey, Lord, I want Jesus to walk with me.	I want Jesus to walk with me, Yes, I want Jesus to walk with me; All along *this Freedom* journey, Lord, I want Jesus to walk with me. *Down in the jailhouse,* Lord, walk with me; *Down in the jailhouse,* Lord, walk with me. All along *this Freedom* journey, Lord, I want Jesus to walk with me.

Woke up this mornin' with my mind
    Stayed on Jesus;
Woke up this mornin' with my mind
    Stayed on Jesus;
Woke up this mornin' with my mind
    Stayed on Jesus;
Hal-le-lu, Hal-le-lu, Hal-le-lu-jah!
	Woke up this mornin' with my mind
	    Stayed on *Freedom*;
	Woke up this mornin' with my mind
	    Stayed on *Freedom*;
	Woke up this mornin' with my mind
	    Stayed on *Freedom*;
	Hal-le-lu (Hal-le-lu), Hal-le-lu (Hal-le-lu),
	Hal-le-lu-jah!

Oh, Freedom! Oh, Freedom! Oh, Freedom over me; And befo'ah I'd be a slave I'd be buried in my grave And go home to my Lord and be free.	(This spiritual hymn's refrain is sung in its exact original form.)
No more weeping, etc. No more moaning (mourning), etc. No more dyin', etc.	No more segregation, etc. No more Jim Crow, etc.

These songs were not only sung in freedom marches and rallies but also were regularly sung as congregational songs in worship, especially in churches throughout the South.

In the late 1930s, the term *gospel* eventually came to identify contemporary religious music that was being performed in Chicago. Thomas A. Dorsey (1899–1993) is considered the "Father of Gospel Music," and it was he who gave it its name—*gospel* music—in contradistinction to the gospel hymns used in the crusades of Dwight L. Moody and Ira D. Sankey. In his essay on Dorsey, Horace C. Boyer (1935–2009) is explicit about this distinction:

> A cursory glance at these songs will show that they are in fact "gospel hymns": strictly organized, standard Protestant hymns of eight bars to the stanza and eight bars to the chorus, with no provisions for the improvisation so much a part of Prof. Dorsey's song, nor the textual attention given to such matters as blessings, sorrows, woes, and the joys of the "after-life," nor the Africanisms, which really constitute gospel music—the altered scale degrees and the intricate rhythm [that] separates this music from all others.[5]

Although many African American churches did not readily embrace gospel music, it began to find its way into churches throughout the United States and first introduced by choirs, ensembles, and soloists, and later embraced by the congregation as its song. Wyatt Tee Walker offers a critical insight:

> Gospel music, at bottom, is religious folk music that is clearly identifiable with the social circumstances of the Black community in America. The authenticity of folkways and folk expressions (including music) can be gauged by how closely they mirror the experience of the group. Gospel music, then, is an individual expression of a collective predicament within a religious context.[6]

Gospel music has been generally accepted by most African American churches, but there are still some prominent segments within elite African American Baptists, Methodists, and other main-line majority denominations who customarily express annoyance with, or outright rejection of gospel music, both in terms of its often problematic theology and because of its alleged secularity. Lincoln and Mamiya observed:

> The problem begins with the fact that gospel choirs often select their repertoires based on what is popular on the radio or television, despite the fact that not all gospel packaged commercially is ideal for worship. Because commercialization presupposes secularization, it is inevitable that many metaphors and musical embellishments acceptable for secular performances are considered unacceptable in a worship setting.[7]

Other concerns about gospel music and its influence upon congregational song include the perception that gospel songwriters compose their songs based upon their personal theology and experiences, or without consideration of broader theological implications rather than with any offi-cial theological canon in mind. However, in William B. McClain's (b. 1938) preface to *Songs of Zion*, he asserts:

The gospel song expresses theology. Not the theology of the academy or the university, not formalistic theology or the theology of the seminary, but a *theology of experience*—the theology of a God who sends the sunshine and the rain, the theology of a God who is very much alive and active and who has not forsaken those who are poor and oppressed and unemployed. It is a *theology of imagination*—it grew out of the fire shut up in the bones, of words painted on the canvas of the mind. Fear is turned into hope in the sanctuary and storefronts, and burst forth in songs of celebration. It is a *theology of grace* that allows the faithful to see the sunshine of His face—even through their tears. Even the words of an ex-slave trader became a song of liberation and an expression of God's amazing grace. It is a *theology of survival* that allows a people to celebrate the ability to continue the journey in spite of the insidious tentacles of racism and oppression and to sing, "It's another day's journey, and I'm glad about it!"[8]

It was in the context of the Civil Rights and Black-Power Movement that Black Theology was born. According to James H. Cone (b. 1939),

Black Theology is an attempt to show liberation as the central message of the Christian gospel and thereby bring the contemporary black church back to its liberating heritage. Our worship service must be free and liberating, because we believe "the Lord will make a way somehow." Therefore, we must fight until freedom comes.[9]

[T]he certainty about God's immediate presence with the weak is the heart of black worship service. Black worship is a series of recitals of what God has done to bring the people out of "hurt, harm, and danger." Through sermon, song, prayer, and testimony, the people tell their story of "how they got over." God is that divine miracle who enables the people to survive amid wretched conditions. God is holy, personal, and all-powerful. God is everything the people need in order to triumph over terrible circumstances.[10]

Black Theology strongly influenced the worship and congregational song of many African American congregations throughout the late 1960s and 1970s. In his vintage book, *The Spiritual and the Blues*, James Cone is emphatic when he declares:

Black music is unity music. It unites the joy and the sorrow, the love and the hate, the hope and the despair of black people; and it moves the people toward the direction of total liberation. It shapes and defines black existence and creates cultural structures for black expression. Black music is unifying because it confronts the individual with the truth of black existence and affirms that black being is possible only in a communal context. . .

Black music is functional. Its purposes and aims are directly related to the consciousness of the black community. To be functional is to be useful in community definition, style, and movement. . . Black music is a living reality. And to understand it, it is necessary to grasp the contradictions inherent in black experience. . .

Black music is also social and political. It is social because it is *black* and thus articulates the separateness of the black community. It is an artistic rebellion against the humiliating deadness of western culture. Black music is political because in its rejection of white cultural values, it affirms the political "otherness" of black people. Through song, new political consciousness is continuously created, one antithetical to the values of white society. . .

Black music is also theological. That is, it tells us about the divine Spirit that moves the people toward unity and self-determination. It is not possible to be black and encounter the Spirit of black emotion and not be moved.[11]

Wyatt Tee Walker is convinced that Black Theology is more clearly ensconced in the music of the African American religious experience than attempting to fit the theology of African American Christians into European theological systems. Another quotation by Walker might be helpful in understanding his posture on this point:

> Afro-centric Christian theology proceeds from a different center than does traditional Eurocentric theology. The theology of African American Christians issues from our pain-predicament (which has been pervasive) and thereby, is more experiential than reflective. Ours is a learned and lived theology. This is not to suggest that the religious faith of African Americans is impervious to Continental musings but only that Afro-centricity is dominant.[12]

Walker maintains that the sacred music of African American Christians reveals the answers to the questions of any Christian theological inquiry: (1) What is the view of God (Jesus)? (2) What is the view of humankind? (3) What is the view of [the] Judgment? (4) What is the view of salvation? and (5) What is the view of justice?[13] The thesis of his major work, *Somebody's Calling My Name: Black Sacred Music and Social Change* is that a survey of the musical content of the black religious tradition can serve as a commentary of what was happening to the black community and its response to those conditions. Simply put, what black people are singing religiously will provide a clue to what is happening to them sociologically.

However, that major body of congregational song sung in most main-line African American churches is almost exclusively Euro-American with the exception of a few hymns by Charles A. Tindley (1851–1933), Charles P. Jones (1865–1949), Thomas A. Dorsey (1899–1993), Lucie E. Campbell (1885–1963), Kenneth Morris (1917–1988), Andraé Crouch (b. 1942), Doris Akers (1923–1995), and Margaret Douroux (b. 1941).

Table 1 provides a list of the most commonly sung hymns in African American churches by Anglo-Americans and British text writers taken from numerous surveys across the country from music directors and church musicians, denominational conferences, the annual Hampton University Ministers' Conference & Choir Directors' and Organists' Guild Workshop, the Jackson State University Church Music Workshop, to name a few.

Table 1
Anglo-American and British Hymns
Commonly Sung in African American Churches
Songs that have titles different from their first lines are listed in italics.

"Amazing Grace"	John Newton (1725–1807)
At the Cross	Isaac Watts (1674–1748)
"Blessed Assurance"	Fanny J. Crosby (1820–1915)
Blessed Be the Name	William H. Clark (1854–1925)
Blessed Quietness	Manie P. Ferguson (1850–1932)
Count Your Blessings	Johnson Oatman Jr. (1856–1922)

"Down at the Cross" (*Glory to His Name*)	Elisha A. Hoffman (1839–1929)
Farther Along	W. B. Stevens (1862–1940)
God Will Take Care of You	Civilla D. Martin (1869–1948)
"Guide Me, O Thou Great Jehovah"	William Williams (1717–1791)
Higher Ground	Johnson Oatman Jr. (1856–1922)
"Holy, Holy, Holy"	Reginald Heber (1783–1826)
"How Firm a Foundation"	"K" in Rippon's *Selection of Hymns* (1787)
"I Am Thine, O Lord"	Fanny J. Crosby (1820–1915)
"I Must Tell Jesus"	Elisha A. Hoffman (1839–1929)
"I Need Thee Every Hour"	Annie S. Hawks (1835–1918)
I'll Fly Away	Albert E. Brumley (1905–1977)
In the Garden	C. Austin Miles (1868–1946)
Is Your All on the Altar?	Elisha A. Hoffman (1839–1929)
It Is Well with My Soul	Horatio G. Spafford (1828–1888)
"Jesus Is All the World to Me"	Will L. Thompson (1847–1909)
"Jesus, Keep Me Near the Cross"	Fanny J. Crosby (1820–1915)
Keep Me Every Day	F. L. Eiland (1860–1909)
Lead Me to Calvary	Jennie E. Hussey (1874–1958)
Lift Him Up	Johnson Oatman Jr. (1856–1922)
"Must Jesus Bear the Cross Alone"	Thomas Shepherd (1665–1739)
"My Faith Looks Up to Thee"	Ray Palmer (1808–1887)
"My Hope Is Built On Nothing Less"	Edward Mote (1797–1874)
"Nearer My God to Thee"	Sarah F. Adams (1805–1848)
No, Not One	Johnson Oatman Jr. (1856–1922)
O How I Love Jesus	Frederick Whitfield (1829–1904)
"Pass Me Not, O Gentle Savior"	Fanny J. Crosby (1820–1915)
"Praise Him, Praise Him"	Fanny J. Crosby (1820–1915)
"Savior, More Than Life to Me"	Fanny J. Crosby (1820–1915)
"Softly and Tenderly Jesus Is Calling"	Will L. Thompson (1847–1909)
"Standing on the Promises"	R. Kelso Carter (1849–1926)
"There Is a Fountain Filled with Blood"	William Cowper (1731–1800)
"'Tis So Sweet to Trust in Jesus"	Louisa M. R. Stead (1850–1917)
Trust and Obey	John H. Sammis (1846–1919)
We're Marching to Zion	Isaac Watts (1674–1748)
"What a Fellowship"	Elisha A. Hoffman (1839–1929)
"What a Friend We Have in Jesus"	Joseph M. Scriven (1819–1886)
When We All Get to Heaven	Eliza E. Hewitt (1851–1920)
"Yield Not to Temptation"	Horatio R. Palmer (1834–1907)

These hymns, and others, have been maintained, preserved in, and perpetuated by the canon of the African American religious experience, primarily because of their texts and musical accessibility. The texts and music were relevant, applicable, conforming, and unimpeachable with their expressions of praise, adoration, thanksgiving, struggle, pain, hope, joy, aspirations, faith, admonition, pilgrimage, salvation, tribulations; in short, the total religious journey. Referring to an extensive list of "Hymns of Improvisation" in *Somebody's Calling My Name*, Walker offers an excellent analysis of many of these hymns.

> About one-half of the hymns listed have "Jesus themes," mirroring the centrality of Jesus in the Black religious experience... Admittedly, the Jesus umbrella includes such topics as "Trust and Confidence," "Cross and Resurrection," "Praise and Adoration," but the fixation on the Black religious community on Jesus is widely known. As in the music of spirituals, the Jesus emphasis transmits a quality of intimacy and companionship that leaps the barrier of God's transcendence. The commonality of this theme—Jesus emphasis—runs throughout Black hymnody. One-fourth of the hymns thematically expresses "Dependence on God" one-tenth "Praise and Adoration" and one-tenth "Death and Immortality." The remaining five percent is variously divided among other religious themes.[14]

It is interesting to observe that the influences of the Civil Rights Movement, Black Theology, Black Nationalism, and Afro-centrism—all post-Vatican II movements—critically contributed to the increase and urgency of African American hymnals published by various denominations. At the same time, the rapid development of gospel choirs and smaller ensembles tended to dominate the worship services and congregational singing was significantly reduced to accommodate these special selections. Table 2 provides a chronological listing of African American denominational hymnals and African American hymnals and supplements published by Anglo-majority denominations since Vatican II.

Table 2
African American Hymnals and Hymnal Supplements
Published Since Vatican II[15]

1977: *The New National Baptist Hymnal*. Chair, Editorial Committee: Ruth Lomax Davis (Nashville: National Baptist Publishing Board).	According to the Foreword, this hymnal "was conceived and published to serve a two-fold purpose; that of enhancing all aspects of [their] worship services, and for the preservation of [their] great religious heritage and musical taste for generations to come."
1977: *His Fullness Songs*, (Jackson, Mississippi: National Publishing Board of the Church of Christ [Holiness] USA).	A large number of the hymns in this hymnal (the first edition was published in 1906) were composed by the founder and bishop of this church, Charles P. Jones Sr.

1981: *Songs of Zion*. Eds. Verolga Nix and J. Jefferson Cleveland (Nashville: Discipleship Resources).	This collection was published by The United Methodist Church as a supplemental worship resource for African American congregations. *Come Sunday: The Liturgy of Zion* by William B. McClain is a companion to *Songs of Zion*.
1981: *Lift Every Voice and Sing: A Collection of Afro-American Spirituals and Other Songs*. Chair, Ed., Irene V. Jackson. (New York: The Church Hymnal Corp).	This hymnal was published by the Episcopal Church (USA) in conjunction with the Episcopal Commission for Black Ministries.
1982: *Yes, Lord!* Chair, Editorial Committee, Norman N. Quick (Memphis: Church of God in Christ Publishing Board).	This hymnal was the first official hymnal of the COGIC.
1982: *The New Progressive National Baptist Hymnal*, Ed. D. F. King (Washington DC: Progressive National Baptist Convention, Inc.).	This hymnal was a special edition of *The New National Baptist Convention* with adaptations and approximately thirty-five new hymns.
1984: *AMEC Bicentennial Hymnal*, Ed. Robert O. Hoffelt (Nashville: The African Methodist Episcopal Church).	This is a completely revised edition of the 1954 hymnal which included African-American spirituals for the first time and songs from the AME Church in Africa.
1987: *Lead Me, Guide Me: The African American Catholic Hymnal*, Project Coordinator, James P. Lyke, O.F.M. (Chicago: GIA).	According to the Foreword, this hymnal was "born of the needs and aspirations of Black Catholics for music that reflected both [an] African American heritage and [their] Catholic faith." Contains a ten-page introduction to the history of African American song.
1987: *The Hymnal of the Christian Methodist Episcopal Church*, Chairperson, Othal Hawthorne Lakey (Memphis: CME Publishing).	The CME Church was founded in 1870. This hymnal is a duplication of *The New National Baptist Hymnal* (1977) with adaptations and additions by the Commission for the Hymnal.
1993: *Lift Every Voice and Sing II: An African American Hymnal*, Ed., Horace Clarence Boyer (New York: Church Pension Fund).	This hymnal was prepared by the Episcopal Commission for Black Ministries in collaboration with the Standing Committee on Church Music under the aegis of the Church Hymnal Corporation. The hymnal contains eleven pages of performance notes at the beginning.
1996: *The AME Zion. Bicentennial Hymnal*, (New York: The African American Episcopal Church).	This hymnal was published by the African Methodist Episcopal Zion Church.
1999: *This Far By Faith: An African American Resource for Worship*, Project Managers, Bryant Clancy and Karen M. Ward (Minneapolis: Augsburg Fortress).	This resource was developed by a cooperative inter-church process involving the Evangelical Lutheran Church in America and the Lutheran Church—Missouri Synod.
2000: *The Hymnal of The Christian Methodist Episcopal Church Discipleship 2000 Edition*, Volume IV, William E. George, General Secretary (CME Publishing).	This hymnal is a revised and edited version of the 1987 hymnal.
2001: *The African American Heritage Hymnal*, Eds. Delores Carpenter and Nolan B. Williams (Chicago: GIA).	Prompted in part by the success of *Lead Me, Guide Me*, a hymnal intended primarily for African American Catholics, GIA created a similar edition for African American Protestant congregations.

2001: *The New National Baptist Hymnal 21st Century Edition*, (National: National Baptist Convention of America, Inc.).	This hymnal was a revision of the 1977 that includes additional hymns and "Glossary of Musical Terms."
2006: *Beams of Heaven: Hymns of Charles Albert Tindley*, Eds. S T Kimbrough, Jr. and Carlton R. Young (New York: General Board of Global Ministries, GBGMusik).	This collection of forty-six hymns by Charles A. Tindley was published by the General Board of Global Ministries of The United Methodist Church.
2007: *Zion Still Sings! For Every Generation*, Eds. Myron F. McCoy and Marilyn E. Thornton (Nashville: Abingdon).	This supplement is a complete revision and updating of *Songs of Zion* with a separate and extensive accompaniment edition.
2007: *New Wine in Old Wineskins*, Volume 1, Ed. James Abbington (Chicago: GIA).	This contemporary congregational supplement reflects the marriage of new hymn texts by modern writers to time-honored tunes from many different traditions. It also contains twenty-three lesser-known hymns by African American hymn writers Charles P. Jones, Charles A. Tindley, G. T. Haywood, Margaret Pleasant Douroux, Charles Watkins, Laymon T. Hunter, Eli Wilson Jr. and others.
2010: *New Wine in Old Wineskins*, Volume 2, Ed. James Abbington (Chicago: GIA).	A second compilation of contemporary congregational hymnody reflects the marriage of new texts by modern writers to time-honored tunes from many traditions. It contains eighteen lesser-known hymns by African American hymn writers Glenn Burleigh, Charles H. Nicks Jr., Stephen Key, V. Michael McKay, Jimmy Dowell, Oliver J. Owens, David Frazier, and others.
2011: *Total Praise: Songs and Other Worship Resources for Every Generation.* (Chicago: GIA. Nashville: Sunday School Publishing Board).	This hymnal was co-published by the Sunday School Publishing Board of the National Baptist Convention, USA and GIA Publication and is an expanded and revised edition of the *African American Heritage Hymnal*.
2012: *Lead Me, Guide Me* Second Edition. (Chicago: GIA).	This hymnal includes the full breadth of African American church music that is suitable for Catholic worship, along with a broader mix of common Catholic repertoire. It includes a comprehensive array of ritual music, Mass settings, and Lectionary psalms written by some of today's finest African American composers.

In spite of the plethora of hymnals available today, the repertoire of hymns sung by main-line African American church congregations consists of fewer than fifty hymns, including Christmas carols and Easter hymns. In some cases, it is fewer than twenty-five and in others, no hymns are sung at all and no hymnal is used.[16]

Given the extensive list of hymns in Table 1 Anglo-American and British text writers sung in African American churches, it is even more astonishing and bewildering that the representation of hymns by African American hymn writers such as Charles A. Tindley (1851–1933), Charles P. Jones (1865–1949), James Weldon Randolph (1842–unknown), Thomas A. Dorsey (1899–1993), Lucie E. Campbell (1885–1963), Doris Akers (1922–1995), Garfield T. Haywood (1880–1931), Robert C. Lawson (1883–1961), Roberta Martin (1907–1969), Kenneth Morris (1917–1988), Margaret Douroux (b. 1941), Andraé Crouch (b. 1942), Albert A. Goodson (b. 1933) and others, are very few. The theological themes of the African American church focus on tribulation, comfort, holding on, consolation, assurance, judgment, and eschatology. Furthermore, many of the hymns listed in Table 1 articulate these themes, indicating that African Americans took their primary theology from any place they could find it. Until more recently, hymns of praise are not as common in the African American tradition and, consequently, have been borrowed and adapted from Anglo-American and British authors.[17]

Table 3 is a list of some of the most commonly sung hymns in African American churches by African American hymn writers provided by respondents in national surveys found in many of the aforementioned hymnals.

Table 3
African American Hymns Most Commonly Sung in African American Churches

Songs that have titles different from their first lines are listed in italics.

A Praying Spirit (1980)	Elbernita "Twinkie" Clark (b. 1955)
Bless His Holy Name (1973)	Andraé Crouch (b. 1942)
Can't Nobody Do Me Like Jesus (1982)	Andraé Crouch (b. 1942)
"Deeper, Deeper" (1900)	Charles P. Jones (1865–1949)
"Give Me a Clean Heart" (1970)	Margaret Douroux (b. 1941)
"God Has Smiled on Me" (1973)	Isaiah Jones Jr. (1940–2008)
He'll Understand and Say "Well Done"	Lucie E. Campbell (1885–1963)
"I Don't Feel No Ways Tired" (1978)	Curtis Burrell (20th c.)
"If It Had Not Been for the Lord" (1980)	Margaret Douroux (b. 1941)
"Jesus, You're the Center of My Joy" (1987)	Richard Smallwood (b. 1948) (in collaboration with William and Gloria Gaither)
Just a Little Talk with Jesus (1937)	Cleavant Derricks (1910–1977)
"Lead Me, Guide Me" (1953)	Doris Akers (1923–1995)
Leave It There (c. 1906)	Charles A. Tindley (1851–1933)
"Lord, Help Me to Hold Out" (1974)	James Cleveland (1932–1991)
My Tribute ("How Can I Give Thanks") (1971)	Andraé Crouch (b. 1942)
"Oh, To Be Kept By Jesus" (1966)	Thurston Frazier (20th c.)

Praise Him ("From the Rising of the Sun") (1986)	Donnie Harper (20th c.)
"Precious Lord, Take My Hand" (1932)	Thomas A. Dorsey (1899–1993)
"Sign Me Up for the Christian Jubilee" (1979)	Kevin Yancy/Jerome Metcalfe (20th c.)
"Something Within" (1919)	Lucie E. Campbell (1885–1963)
"Soon and Very Soon" (1978)	Andraé Crouch (b. 1942)
Sweet, Sweet Spirit (1962)	Doris Akers (1923–1995)
"The Lord Is My Light" (1980)	Lillian Bouknight (20th cent.)
This Day	Edwin Hawkins (b. 1943)
Total Praise (1996)	Richard Smallwood (b. 1948)
"Touch Me, Lord Jesus"	Lucie E. Campbell (1922–1995)
Walking Up the King's Highway (1940)	Mary Gardner and Thomas A. Dorsey (1899–1993)
We'll Understand It Better By and By (c. 1906)	Charles A. Tindley (1851–1933)
"We've Come This Far by Faith" (1956)	Albert A. Goodson (b. 1933)
Where Shall I Be?	Charles P. Jones (1865–1949)
Yes, God Is Real (1944)	Kenneth Morris (1917–1988)
"You Can't Beat God's Giving"	Doris Akers (1923–1993)

In her essay, "Hymnals of the Black Church," Eileen Southern (1920–2002) declared:

> The year 1921 brought a milestone in the history of Black church hymnody. In my opinion, *Gospel Pearls*, published that year by the Sunday School Publishing Board of The National Baptist Convention, USA, ranks with Richard Allen's hymnal [*A Collection of Spiritual Songs and Hymns, Selected from Various Authors*] of 1801 in terms of its historical importance. Like the Allen hymnal, it is an anthology of the most popular Black church music of its time. The Music Committee that compiled the hymnal, under the direction of Willa Townsend, included some of the nation's outstanding composers and performers of religious music—among them, John W. Work [Jr., 1871–1925], Frederick J. Work [1879–1942], Lucie Campbell [1885–1963] and W. M. Nix—and the resulting product was truly a "soul-stirring, message-bearing" songbook.[18]

Recent Significant African American Hymnals

Since the Second Vatican Council, there have been, in my opinion, seven hymnals and supplemental worship resources in particular that continue that rich legacy and historical importance. They are *His Fullness Songs* (1977), *Songs of Zion* (1981), *Yes, Lord!* (1982), *African American Heritage Hymnal* (2001), and *Zion Still Sings! For Every Generation* (2007), *Total Praise: Songs and Other Worship Resources for Every Generation* (2011), *and Lead Me, Guide Me, Second Edition: An African American Catholic Hymnal* (2012).

His Fullness Songs (1977) is the official hymnal of the Church of Christ (Holiness) USA, and is a revision of earlier hymnals from the turn of the twentieth century (1899—*Jesus Only, No.1;*

1901—*Jesus Only, No.1* revised and *No. 2*; and 1906—*His Fullness Songs*). Over 350 of the 512 songs in the hymnal were written or co-written by the founder and Bishop Charles Price Jones.

Yes, Lord! (1982), Bishop Charles H. Mason in Memphis, Tennessee, founded the first official hymnal of the Church of God in Christ, in 1897. The title "Yes, Lord" is taken from a praise chant that was often sung by Bishop Mason to gather the congregation in spiritual unity during an out-pouring of the Holy Spirit in worship. It is significant. According to Eileen Southern, "*Yes, Lord!* makes a sharp break with the past. In its collection of fifty songs, the handling of accompaniment, in particular, reflects the importance given to instruments and polyphonic textures in the Pentecostal tradition."[19] It contains a wide variety of standard hymns, gospel hymns, spirituals, gospel songs, and songs by some of the denominations most outstanding hymn writers such as Mattie Moss Clark, Andraé Crouch, and Iris Stevenson, among others.

Songs of Zion grew out of the Consultation on the Black Church in Atlanta, Georgia, in 1973, sponsored by the Board of Discipleship to develop a songbook from the black religious tradition to be made available to United Methodist churches. This supplemental worship resource edited by J. Jefferson Cleveland (1937–1988) and Verolga Nix [-Allen] (b. 1933), chaired by William B. McClain (b. 1938) contained the largest number of Negro spirituals and black gospel songs with "Keys to Musical Interpretation, Performance, and Meaningful Worship," "A Historical Account of the Hymn in the Black Worship Experience," "A Historical Account of the Negro Spiritual," "A Historical Account of the Black Gospel" and "Songs for Special Occasions." This was an anthology of the most popular black church music of that time.

Come Sunday: The Liturgy of Zion: A Companion to Songs of Zion by William B. McClain was published by Abingdon Press in 1990. It begins with a discussion of the importance of Sunday in the black experience that explores the meaning and rich tradition of Sunday within the black community from the time of slavery to the present day. It is divided into two parts. The first part helps readers to understand the spiritual response of black people, the singular nature of worship in the black experience, and the importance of fellowship and community. The second part includes a survey of the different types of songs contained in *Songs of Zion*. It also includes chapters devoted to Negro spirituals, hymns, and gospel songs, in addition to a discussion of liturgy and a topical/scriptural index.

The *African American Heritage Hymnal* published by GIA Publications, Inc. in 2001 was a much-needed and long-awaited worship resource and practical anthology of the rich musical diversity of the African American church. It is the most inclusive compilation of musical and liturgical significance for African American Protestant churches in the twenty-first century. Wyatt Walker said of the hymnal that it "is probably the most important addition to Protestant hymnody within the past century."[20] It contains 582 hymns, spirituals, meter hymns, African music, and Gospel songs. In addition it has fifty-two Litany Prayers for the Black Church Year and fifty-two Biblical Responsive Readings from the Old and New Testaments based upon a large array of topics. The most significant feature of the hymnal is that the musical notations follow very closely the performance practices and idiomatic treatments of the unique African Americans genres.

Zion Still Sings! For Every Generation published by Abingdon Press was a revision of *Songs of Zion*. The work of this project began during the 2000–2004 quadrennial with the positing of such as idea to Neil Alexander, President and Publisher of The United Methodist Publishing House. Following the widespread acceptance across ecumenical lines and continuing sales of *Songs of Zion* more than twenty years after its first printing, the project to contemporize and expand musical offerings in a new songbook was met with a great degree of interest and support.

In the spirit of honoring and preserving the richness and inclusiveness of the African American musical heritage in worship, *Zion Still Sings*: (1) celebrates the diversity of styles, genres, and performance practices that are rendered in praise to God; (2) offers up new music that will inspire and challenge persons to see God with new eyes; (3) seeks to motivate those outside the church to come to know God; (4) does not compromise the theological and biblical integrity of the church; and (5) in the spirit of Matthew 28:19, serves as a motivating force for persons to "do" the gospel.

The songbook has two editions, Pew and Accompaniment. The Pew Edition has all vocals needed for congregational participation with specific instructions concerning songs that may be linked in medleys. The Accompaniment Edition includes piano accompaniment, synthesizer, and percussion parts. Some songs are exactly the same in both editions, usually four-part hymn style.

Total Praise: Songs and Other Worship Resources for Every Generation (2011) is a co-publication of GIA Publications and the Sunday School Publishing Board of the National Baptist Convention, USA, Inc. The predecessor to this long awaited hymnal was *The Baptist Standard Hymnal with Responsive Readings* published in 1961, an updated edition of the hymnal of 1924 with responsive readings and "A New Book for All Services." *Total Praise* is a multi-faceted worship tool that contains 569 traditional and contemporary songs, fifty-two Responsive Readings, one for every Sunday of the year, forty-six Litanies designed for special days through the year such as Church Anniversaries, Advent, Singles Ministry, Martin Luther King Jr. Day, Rites of Passage for Youth, Health and Wellness, Racial Reconciliation, and Elder Saints, to name a few.

This hymnal is substantive in content, containing hymnody of all styles, including praise and worship music from the first decade of the twenty-first century by composers such as Kurt Carr, Deon Kipping, Israel and Meleasa Houghton, Martha Munizzi, Kirk Franklin, Steven Hurd, Joseph Pace II, and others. In addition, it includes contemporary writers such as Mary Louise Bringle, Adam Tice, Brian Wren, Herman G. Stuempfle Jr., Ruth Duck, Shirley Erena Murray, Delores Dufner, and others. It also includes traditional Black gospel hymnody not found in other hymnals and worship resources by hymn writers such as Charles H. Nicks Jr., Glenn Burleigh, Norris O. Garner, Walter Hawkins, Robert J. Fryson, Eddie Robinson, Stephen Key, Gale Jones Murphy, Harrison Johnson, Leonard Burks, and others. It also has selections from two historic publications of the Sunday School Publishing Board, *Gospel Pearls* (1921) and *Spirituals Triumphant Old and New* (1927) edited and arranged by Edward Boatner and Willa A. Townsend.

Finally, eight years in the making, the second edition of *Lead Me, Guide Me: An African American Catholic Hymnal* (2012), is an expanded and enhanced version of its predecessor. The hymnal includes the full breadth of African American church music that is suitable for Catholic worship, along with a broader mix of common Catholic repertoire. There are an extensive variety of music styles, including a representative selection of music from Africa and the Caribbean. Following the success of GIA Publication's, Inc. *African American Heritage Hymnal* and *Total Praise*, the music notation attempts to reflect the performance practices in the African American church communities. Also included is a comprehensive array of ritual music, mass settings, and Lectionary psalms written by some of today's finest African American composers such as M. Roger Holland II, Kenneth W. Louis, Norah Duncan IV, Rawn Harbor, Richard Cheri, and others. The Most Reverend Wilton D. Gregory, SLD, Archbishop of Atlanta summarizes it best in his Foreword to the hymnal:

> *Lead Me, Guide Me* is a compilation of a generous selection of that music arranged for use within the celebration of the Roman Catholic liturgy. As Catholics now prepare to receive the third edition of the *Roman Missal* for the English-speaking world, it is most appropriate for a new edition of *Lead Me, Guide Me* to be issued to accompany that new book of Catholic prayer. Those blessed original collaborators have today been joined by a new generation of very capable colleagues in preparing this new text. They build on a solid foundation for faith and now present a worthy successor to that first effort. While *Lead Me, Guide Me* was specifically developed with the particular liturgical needs of the African American Catholic community in mind, it was never envisioned to be used exclusively in those parish communities. Other Catholics throughout our nation and beyond have made very effective use of this liturgical resource, and we anticipate that they, too, will welcome this newest edition. Music has a unique capacity to transcend cultures and races and provide a bridge to understanding other people through the vehicle of its combined words and melodies...[21]

Current Trends in African American Congregational Song

A discussion of congregational song in the late twentieth and early twenty-first century African American churches would not be complete without examining the new trends in music and worship, which now includes Holy, or Christian Hip Hop. As previously mentioned, rapid development of gospel choirs and ensembles reduced congregational song between the mid-1960s and 1980s.

Congregational singing in the 1990s and early twenty-first century is dominated by praise and worship. This period of time, usually at the beginning of worship services, which varies in length from fifteen minutes to one hour, is now essential to the worship of most African American churches in the United States.

Holiness-Pentecostal, or Sanctified Worship has been historically characterized by hand capping, holy dancing, and the distinctive sound of musical instruments such as the Hammond organ, piano, keyboard synthesizers, drums, tambourines, electric bass and lead guitars, and saxophones. Most main-line and non-denominational African American congregations adopted and adapted these instruments into their regular worship services.

Cheryl Sanders' *Saints in Exile: The Holiness-Pentecostal Experience in African American Religion and Culture*, a ground-breaking book written from an insider's perspective, studies the worship practices and social ethics of the African American family of Holiness, Pentecostal, and Apostolic churches known collectively as the Sanctified Church. After reviewing four, written descriptive narratives of black Pentecostal worship based upon participant observation, Sanders identifies at least eight basic elements in common, with some variation in order: (1) call to worship, (2) songs and hymns, (3) prayer, (4) offering, (5) Scripture reading, (6) preaching, (7) altar call, and (8) benediction.[22] Additionally, Sanders detects that:

> The singing of some combination of songs, hymns, choruses, and Negro spirituals is a vital part of all these worship services. It is difficult to denote the role music plays in worship with any degree of precision because music tends to undergird everything else that is done. Unlike some of the other elements of worship, music is interspersed throughout the service and not at just one or two points in the order of worship. In the composite outline, however, the singing of songs and hymns represents a major component of congregational involvement in the worship experience. The sacred repertoire is inclusive of hymns of the mainline evangelical Protestant church, gospel songs, praise choruses, and Negro spirituals.[23]

The Church of God in Christ, commonly referred to by its acronym, COGIC, was formed in 1897 by a group of excommunicated Baptists most notably, Charles Price Jones (1865–1949) and Charles Harrison Mason (1866–1961). It has long been held as the birthplace of leading gospel recording artists such as Andraé Crouch, The Winans, the Clark sisters, and many others. Known for their vibrant and fervent music in worship, The West Angeles Church of God in Christ in Los Angeles, CA, Bishop Charles E. Blake, senior pastor, began a series of recordings that captured the congregational music of the COGIC. The first, and probably most popular was *Saints in Praise: Volume 1* released in 1989 by The West Angeles Church of God in Christ Mass Choir, which became the model for African American church praise and worship music across denominations. *The Celebration Medley* which contained "This Is the Day" / "I Will Enter His Gates" / *He Has Made Me Glad* / *We Come to Glorify His Name* / and *Victory Is Mine* remains one of the most sung selections in Praise and Worship services.[24] Recordings helped to make these songs popular. In 1990, *Saints in Praise:*

Volume 2 was released and *Saints in Praise: Volume 3* in 1992. *Yes, Lord! Saints in Praise* with Judy McAllister was released in 2002 and *Bishop Charles E. Blake and The West Angeles COGIC Mass Choir* in 2007.

Another significant recording project began in 1995 entitled *Carlton Pearson Live at Azusa. Live at Azusa, Volume 2: Precious Memories [Live]* was released in 1997 and *Carlton Pearson Live at Azusa 3* followed in 1999. *Carlton Pearson: Azusa Praise Jubilee* released in 2000 was the last in that series of the historic and contemporary praise and worship music of The Church of God in Christ.

In 2005, another CD/DVD project of congregational singing from the Church of God in Christ tradition was released. The late presiding bishop of the Church of God in Christ was Bishop G. E. Patterson of Memphis, Tennessee. He produced and led his congregation, Temple of Deliverance Church of God in Christ Cathedral of Bountiful Blessings, in an award-winning recording project titled *Bishop G. E. Patterson & Congregation Singing the Old Time Way*, Volume 1 in 2005 and Volume 2 in 2006. When Bishop Patterson passed away in March 2007, he left behind another monumental recording *Having Church with the Saints* which also captures the best of congregational song in The Church of God in Christ. These records not only chronicled the gems of that denomination, but also provided helpful insight and direction for the performance practices of that repertoire.

In her book, *When the Church Becomes Your Party: Contemporary Gospel Music*, Deborah Smith Pollard notes during the 1970s, the youth of many black churches were not active participants in "traditional devotional services; a similar level of disengagement was running through the white Protestant church. For many on each side of the Christian church's racial divide, the praise and worship movement would be the sound that drew them back."[25] Pollard points out that praise and worship music arose within the white Evangelical church because of a remarkable set of circumstances.[26]

Since 1970, seeker services and praise and worship services are becoming increasingly influential among main-line churches. They attract mainliners with their potential to stimulate evangelism and spiritual growth. The seeker-service strategy raises important questions about the relationship of worship and evangelism and the place of popular culture, multimedia technology, and the arts in worship. In addition, Praise and Worship services challenge mainliners to rethink the range of physical and emotional expression in worship and to think differently about the role of music in worship. Certainly, in African American churches we can already see the convergence of elements from these two approaches and from historic liturgies that are custom-fitted to meet the needs of individual congregations.

According to Robb Redman, two major influences shaped what he calls the "sweeping changes in Christian worship" during the latter part of the twentieth century. The first, the evangelical seeker-service movement, was launched by those who, after reviewing research on the habits of the baby boomer generation, "set to create a 'non-religious' environment for services, an alternative setting for connotations." The second is the charismatic praise and worship movement. He outlines this worship experience stating, "a typical service begins with twenty- to thirty-minutes or more of congregational singing, led by a worship leader, a band with a small ensemble of singers, and often a choir as well, modeling on the gospel choir in African American churches. Leaders encourage a wide range of physical expressions through clapping, raising hands, swaying, and even dancing."[27]

From these seeker services and praise and worship service movements emerged the popular praise and worship musical genre that not only reflects these influences but also mirrors the fact that a generation that defines its youth by music—rock and roll and Motown—seeks to do so during its religious life as well. As a result, Michael S. Hamilton states, "thousands of individuals select their churches, or at least the services they attend within a given church, not on the doctrine preached, but on the music that is performed."[28]

Some of the leading African American composers of praise and worship music most widely sung in churches today include: Stephen Hurd, Byron Cage, Israel Houghton, Chester Baldwin, Donald Lawrence, Fred Hammond, Hezekiah Walker, Jean Eggleston, Joe Pace, John P. Kee, Joshua's Troop, Judith McAllister, Kurt Carr, Norman Hutchins, Norris Garner, Smokie Norful, Terrance Daye, Tony Griffin, and many others. Fortunately, music scores, as well as DVDs and CDs of their compositions can be found today in many religious music stores and bookstores.[29]

In his book *The Black Church in the Post-Civil Rights Era*, Anthony Pinn makes this observation:

> [C]omplaints by black churches point to contemporary gospel's attempt to reach the unchurched, to draw them in by avoiding a message of repentance and salvation that is too confrontational. Christians interested in the music have come to terms with a more subtle message of Jesus Christ and merits of salvation, a form of the Christian message with a new set of influences ranging from post-Civil Rights politics to the aesthetics of R&B and hip hop culture.[30]

Alan Light has noted that:

> [H]istorically most R&B singers have grown up singing in the church; still today, artist from Cordozar Calvin Broadus (known as "Snoop") to Kimberly Denise Jones (known as "Lil' Kim") have sung in the choir as kids. And the two genres have met in the middle any number of times, from the Teddy Riley who produced "Return" by the Winans (1990), to L. L. Cool J's track "The Power of God."

Light continues by pointing out:

> The Edwin Hawkins Singers' "Oh Happy Day" was a chart smash in 1972, and the Clark Sisters' "You Brought the Sunshine" lit up discos in 1982. And, who could forget M. C. Hammer's 1990 "Pray."[31]

Historically, the black community's most celebrated secular artists have deep roots in the black church such as James Brown, Ruth Brown, Sam Cooke, DeBarge, Roberta Flack, Aretha Franklin, Marvin Gaye, Whitney Houston, Louis Jordan, B. B. King, Gladys Knight, Jackie Wilson, Tina Turner, Dinah Washington, and Stevie Wonder. They represent but a fraction of the list of major artists who grew up in the black church singing, praising, preaching, praying, and shouting long before they took to the secular stage and commercial industry.

The most widely discussed and debated artist, yet probably the most popular of the late twentieth century, is probably Kirk Franklin (b. 1970), founder of Kirk Franklin and the Family as well as God's Property. As with Andraé Crouch during the 1970s and 1980s, Franklin developed an exceptional musical form that combines current musical trends—both sacred and secular—and blends them with the message of the gospel worded in slang. His most popular selections, "(The Reason) Why We Sing" and "Now Behold the Lamb" now appear in hymnals and congregational song supplements across denominations. Presently, Franklin reportedly sold ten to twelve million recordings, making him the most successful gospel artist to date.[32] The most famous example of Franklin's style for many years was his 1997 recording of "Stomp" with the group God's Property. According to Horace C. Boyer, "his excursion into rap, hip hop, and rhythm and blues, and the success that his adventures brought to gospel music brought millions of new listeners to gospel, created a record-buying frenzy for gospel music, and even helped other gospel singers gain attention."[33]

The historical struggle of the black church with the appropriation of the sacred and the secular, the culture, and the integrity of God's church began with Thomas A. Dorsey and his leadership in the development of gospel music when he took the feel of the blues and blended it into church music. The black church also faced this struggle and challenge with the advent of James Cleveland, Edwin Hawkins, and Andraé Crouch as it had to deal with the next wave of gospel music. There was the great upheaval and uproar regarding the song "Oh Happy Day" by Edwin Hawkins and then came Kirk Franklin with "Stomp," and yet another struggle emerged. The conflict over the influence and use of new music styles and popular culture is not new to the black church.

Deborah Smith Pollard asserts, "Given the importance of speech throughout the African diaspora in general and within African American culture in particular, gospel and rap were bound to converge. Holy hip hop, then, can be seen as a logical continuation of Black Church speech patterns."[34] "Indeed," writes Horace C. Boyer, "many gospel music lovers insist that African American preachers were the first rappers and that gospel rappers have been long overdue."[35]

In their book, *The Hip Hop Church: Connecting with the Movement Shaping Our Culture*, Efrem Smith and Phil Jackson declare:

Holy Hip Hop is rap music created specifically to glorify Jesus Christ and bring the good news of Jesus Christ to those who are living in and influenced by the hip hop culture. Now this is just a definition that I am offering; you may hear others as you venture further into this music genre, subculture, and ministry opportunity. Some involved in Holy Hip Hop probably have yet to define what it is that they are doing. Many likely started out loving hip hop, became Christian, and now are simply putting Jesus lyrics with their artistic gift and passion. In any case, the existence of Holy Hip Hop is a great opportunity for the church to embrace the emerging generation and create new ministry methods for advancing the church's Mission. . .

This style of rap music ought to be embraced by the church for a couple of reasons. One, Holy Hip Hop can be used as an evangelism and outreach tool. Second, young people who are gifted in the arts, especially those with gifts of dance, spoken word or art with the spray can, ought to be nurtured within the church so that they realize how to use their God-given gifts to glorify the Gift Giver.[36]

In *Zion Still Sings: For Every Generation*, four rap selections appear with complete texts and are rhythmically notated by Frederick Burchwell, Craig Watkins, and Kyle Lovett: "God Made Me," "I Remember," "He's My Foundation," and "Never Been Scared."[37] To the knowledge of this writer, this is a first for Holy Hip Hop being included in a major denominational congregational song supplement.

Conclusion

In *The Black Church in the African American Experience*, C. Eric Lincoln and Lawrence Mamiya declare that,

Congregational singing is a well-known device for the temporary reduction of social alienation and for the accomplishment of an *ad interim* sense of community. In the Black church, singing together is not so much as effort to find, or to establish, a transitory community as it is the reaffirmation of a common bond that, while inviolate, has suffered the pain of separation since the last occasion of togetherness.[38]

In a published conversation about music between David Day and my former professor, the late Dr. Wendell P. Whalum Sr. (1931–1987), entitled "Why Sing?" conducted by The National Humanities Faculty Series in 1972, Day asked Dr. Whalum "[I]n what ways are children going to be better off, and society better off, if they do have opportunities to express themselves creatively, musically, to make music, to learn to enjoy music making, to learn to appreciate the music that other people make?" Dr. Whalum responded:

[I] think music helps to order a person's life. It brings him to participation with art. That's unity. If it's singing, group singing, it brings the principle of organization and strength even closer. I think, though, it has another dimension. A human being is better off in recognizing the joy associating with other human beings and realizing the worth of such exposure. If he's properly taught, properly encouraged, he may not know all the history, but he will know that music just isn't something that's out there; it's part of "in there" and it comes out of him as he participates. That's it. That may be the greater value. He's better because he's able to recognize the beauty, the aesthetics. He's able to recognize the subjectivity and the creativity of his existence.[39]

This interview dealt with singing in general, but there are some most appropriate applications and admonishments for the future of congregational singing in church in general and in African American congregations specifically. Regardless of the style or genre of congregational music, the Christian church must sing in order to be the Christian church. It must be a purposeful act, never merely a time filler or matter of routine. It must be done enthusiastically, not with tentative sighs and spasmodic mumbling, shamefacedly with an ill grace. If it is contemporary, and one fears the obvious root in the word "temporary," it should be biblically based, theologically based, and relevant to the culture of the congregation. And, most important, each member should depart the sanctuary worship vowed to say and mean, in the words of Thomas A Dorsey, "I'm Going to Live the Life I Sing about in My Song," as the African American church continues to "Lift Every Voice and Sing!" remembering and affirming that "If It Had Not Been for the Lord on My Side, Where Would I Be?"

Notes

1. W. E. B. Du Bois, *The Souls of Black Folk* (New York: Dover, 1903, 1994), 116.
2. Wyatt Tee Walker, *The Soul of Black Worship: A Trilogy—Preaching, Praying, Singing* (New York: Martin Luther King Fellows Press, 1984).
3. C. Eric Lincoln and Lawrence H. Mamiya, *The Black Church in the African American Experience* (Durham: Duke University Press, 1990), 346–347.
4. Wyatt Tee Walker, "The Soulful Journey of the Negro Spiritual," *Negro Digest* (July, 1963), 93.
5. Horace C. Boyer, "An Analysis of His Contributions: Thomas A Dorsey: 'Father of Gospel Music,'" *Black World* 23:9 (July, 1974), 21–22.
6. Wyatt Tee Walker, *Somebody's Calling My Name: Black Sacred Music and Social Change* (Valley Forge: Judson, 1979), 128.
7. C. Eric Lincoln and Lawrence H. Mamiya, *The Black Church in the African American Experience*, 377.
8. William B. McClain, "Preface," *The Songs of Zion*, eds. J. Jefferson Cleveland and Verolga Nix (Nashville: Abingdon, 1981), x.
9. James H. Cone, *Speaking the Truth: Ecumenism, Liberation, and Black Theology* (Grand Rapids: Eerdmans, 1986), 137.
10. James H. Cone, *Speaking the Truth*, 139–140.
11. James H. Cone, *The Spiritual and the Blues* (Maryknoll: Orbis, 1972), 5–6.
12. Wyatt Tee Walker, *Spirits That Dwell in Deep Woods III* (New York: Martin Luther King Fellows Press, 1991), 37.
13. Walker, *Somebody's Calling My Name*, 15–17.
14. Wyatt Tee Walker, *Somebody's Calling My Name*, chapter 6, "What a Friend We Have in Jesus: Hymns of Improvisation," 110–119.
15. For a list of African American hymnals before 1977, see Melva Wilson Costen, "Published Hymnals in the Afro-American Tradition," *The Hymn* 40:1 (January 1989), 7–13. Also published in *Readings in African American Church Music and Worship*, ed. James Abbington Jr. (Chicago: GIA, 2001), 153–165.
16. James Abbington, *Let Mt. Zion Rejoice! Music in the African American Church* (Valley Forge: Judson, 2001), 58–63.

17. Until the publication of the *African American Heritage Hymnal* (Chicago: GIA, 2001), the ethnicity of a hymn writer has not always been apparent. See the "Black History Index," 692–693.
18. Eileen Southern, "Hymnals of the Black Church" in *Readings in African American Church Music and Worship*, ed. James Abbington (Chicago: GIA, 2001), 146.
19. Eileen Southern, "Hymnals of the Black Church," 149.
20. "Introduction" to *African American Heritage Hymnal*, no page number given.
21. "Preface," *Lead Me, Guide Me, Second Edition: An African American Catholic Hymnal* (Chicago: GIA, 2012), no page number given.
22. Cheryl J. Sanders, *Saints in Exile: The Holiness-Pentecostal Experience in African-American Religion and Culture* (New York: Oxford University Press, 1996), 53.
23. Sanders, 54.
24. While the initial songs are usually the same, there are a number of variations to *The Celebration Medley*.
25. Deborah Smith Pollard, *When the Church Becomes Your Party: Contemporary Gospel Music* (Detroit: Wayne State University Press, 2008), 24.
26. This is confirmed by Robb Redman who most convincingly examines this claim in his book *The Great Worship Awakening: Singing a New Song in the Postmodern Church* (San Francisco: Jossey-Bass, 2002), 3–92.
27. Robert L. Redman. "Welcoming to the Worship Awakening," *Theology Today* 58:3 (October 2001), 369–383.
28. Michael S. Hamilton. "The Triumph of the Praise Songs," *Christianity Today* 43, no. 8 (July 12, 1999), 29.
29. I highly recommend NTIMEMUSIC.COM in Charlotte, NC for the most up-to-date and comprehensive collection of this music. The address is NTIMEMUSIC.COM, 4913 Albemarle Road, Charlotte, NC 28205, telephone: (704) 531.8961. Visit their website at www.ntimemusic.com, accessed March 18, 2013.
30. Anthony B. Pinn, *The Black Church in the Post-Civil Rights Era* (Maryknoll: Orbis, 2002), 55.
31. Alan Light, "Say Amen, Somebody!" *Vibe Magazine* (October 1997), 92.
32. This designation does not include artists such as Aretha Franklin and Amy Grant who sing both secular and gospel. In an e-mail to Deborah Smith Pollard dated December 24, 2004, Vice President Tracey Artis of GospoCentric Records explains that Franklin sold twelve million units as of February 2005.
33. Horace C. Boyer. "African American Gospel Music" in *African Americans and The Bible: Sacred Texts and Social Textures*, ed. Vincent L. Wimbush (New York: Continuum, 2000), 484.
34. Pollard, *When the Church Becomes Your Party*, 140.
35. Horace C. Boyer. "African American Gospel Music," 486.
36. Efrem Smith and Phil Jackson, *The Hip Hop Church: Connecting with the Movement Shaping Our Culture* (Downers Grove: InterVarsity, 2005), 131–132.
37. See *Zion Still Sings: For Every Generation* (Nashville: Abingdon, 2007), 17, 126, 181, 185.
38. C. Eric Lincoln and Lawrence Mamiya, *The Black Church in the African American Experience* (Durham: Duke University Press, 1990), 347.
39. *Why Sing? A Conversation about Music with Wendell Whalum conducted by David Day* **(San Francisco: Chandler & Sharp Publishers, 1975), 22.**

Section Two

Liturgical Theologies

8
Black Worship: A Historical Theological Interpretation

James H. Cone

Black worship is connected with black life, and it is characterized by a religious sense inseparable from the suffering that determined it. Whether Catholic or Protestant—Methodist, Baptist, or Pentecostal—black worship is not derived primarily from these theological and historical traditions. To be sure, there are elements of Catholic and Protestant doctrine and rituals (mostly Protestant) in black worship. In black congregations of the Methodist and Presbyterian churches, one is likely to find an order of worship that reflects the content and style of those traditions. But to use John Wesley's theology or the Westminster Confession as the hermeneutical key to explain why a black congregation has adopted the Methodist or Presbyterian denominational structure is to misunderstand black worship and thus to distort its theological meaning. When black people gather together for worship and praise to God, it is not because they have made a decision about the theological merits of Luther's Ninety-Five Theses or of Calvin's *Institutes of the Christian Religion*. These are not our ecclesiastical and theological traditions. At most, they are secondary structures in which God has placed us so that we might "work out our salvation in fear and trembling."

Since we did not create the various Catholic and Protestant structures, we cannot use these labels as the primary definition of our religious experience. Indeed, these white religious structures are the reason for the black necessity to create a style of worship that does not deny our essential humanity. A black congregation may be Methodist, Baptist, or even Catholic, but always with a difference. And this difference is far more important in the assessment of the meaning of black worship than are the white traditions from which the black church often derives its name.

Black worship has been wrought out of the experience of slavery and lynching, ghettos and police brutality. We have "been 'buked and scorned" and "talked about sho's you borned." In worship, we try to say something about ourselves other than what has been said about us in the white church and the society it justifies. Through sermon, prayer, and song, we transcend societal humiliation and degradation and explore heavenly mysteries about starry crowns and gospel shoes. Our church is the only place we can go with tears in our eyes without anyone asking, "what are you crying about?" We can preach, shout, and sing the songs of Zion according to the rhythm of the pain and joy of life, without being subjected to the dehumanizing observations of white intellectuals—sociologists, psychologists, and theologians. In worship we can be who we are as defined by our struggle to be something other than what the society says we are. Accordingly, our gathering for worship is dictated by a *historical* and *theological* necessity that is related to the dialectic of oppression and liberation. Apart from the historical reality of oppression and our attempt to liberate ourselves from it, we would have no reason to sing, "My soul looks back and wonders how I got over." To understand the interplay of the past, present, and future as these are expressed in black worship, it is necessary to examine first the historical context that created its unique style and then the theological content that defined its meaning.

The Historical Context of Black Worship

Black worship was born in slavery. What else could the word "black" mean in relation to worship except a description of the historical origin of those assembled. Most black worshipers do not know the details of our historical beginnings. What they know and feel is that they are *black* and therefore connected with Africa, slavery, and the struggle of freedom. Black worship was born on the slave ships and nurtured in the cotton fields of Alabama, Arkansas, and Mississippi. What we believe and how we express it in worship cannot be separated from our African heritage on the one hand and American slavery and Christianity on the other. African life and culture was the bedrock of the African personality. It was that element in the black slaves' being that structured their response to American slavery and the Christian gospel. Black worship was born in the meeting of the West African High God with the God of Moses and Jesus. Black worship was created and formed in the context of American slavery as African slaves sought to create meaning in a completely alien and oppressive environment. In order to keep a measure of sanity in a completely alien and oppressive environment, slaves had to fashion a theological system of beliefs and create a worship style that did not destroy them physically and mentally.

Initially black worship was determined largely by our African heritage, with an emphasis on the rhythm of our dance and music. There was no separation of the secular and sacred. Reality was viewed as a single system. In some sense, everything one did should be service to the divine, whether directed to the High God, to lesser divinities, or to ancestors. These beliefs and ideas gave structure and meaning to the African world and served as the theological starting point for African captives in the Americas.

In Latin America and the Caribbean, African theology and rituals remained visibly present in black religious structures, including worship. In North America, however, white slaveholders did not permit Africans to practice their religion openly. The intensity and success with which whites destroyed African life and culture has led many scholars to conclude that Africanisms were completely eliminated in the life of the American slaves. It was the studies of Melville Herkovits that changed the course of scholarly debate on this issue. With the publication of his *Myth of the Negro Past*, it was no longer possible to take for granted that everything black slaves did was derived from their oppressors. Although Herkovits was seriously challenged by E. Franklin Frazier and others, it is safe to say that he showed that Africans in North America did preserve some African cultural forms. Beliefs and customs were transmitted by slaves to their descendants, and they are found in our music, speech, and thought patterns. Africanisms are also found in the rhythm of our dance and the emotional structure of our being. When Christianity was introduced to slaves, Africans converted it to their religious heritage, refusing to accept any version of the gospel that did not harmonize with the African spirit of freedom.

This conversion of Christianity by Africans to their life-situation accounts for the fact that white slaveholders had radically different views of the gospel than those held by African slaves. Initially, white masters did not permit their slaves to be Christianized. Some understood that Christian baptism implied manumission, and there were too many biblical references to freedom. But white missionaries and preachers convinced many slave masters that Christianity made blacks better slaves—that is, obedient and docile. As one slaveholder put it, "The deeper the piety of the slave, the more valuable he is in every respect." However, it is important to point out that before the First and Second Great Awakening and the emergence of the Methodists and Baptists, most African slaves remained outside the belief systems of Christianity. Later, when Africans did "convert" to it, their conversion was not identical with the religious conversion of the whites who held them as slaves. That was why the independent black churches were founded in the North and the so-called invisible institution flourished in the South.

The affirmation of some people that there is no difference between black worship and white worship is clearly problematic in light of both historical and contemporary evidence. If worship is inseparably connected with life, then we must assume that the worship services of slaves could not have had the same meaning as the worship services of slaveholders, because they did not share the same life. They may have used the same words in prayer, songs, and testimony, or even preached similar sermons. But slaves and slaveholders could not mean the same thing in their verbal and rhythmic expressions, because their social and political realities were radically different. That was why black slaves organized the first Baptist church in Silver Bluff, South Carolina, between 1773 and 1775 and also why Richard Allen and Absalom Jones walked out of St. George Methodist Church of Philadelphia in 1787. Similar events took place in New York, Baltimore, and other places among black Methodists and Baptists. This same black version of the gospel produced such prophetic persons as Henry Highland Garnet, David Walker, and Nathaniel Paul—all of whom recognized the radical incompatibility of Christianity and slavery. No one expressed this point any clearer than Walker, in his "Appeal" of 1829:

> I ask every [person] who has a heart and is blessed with the privilege of believing—Is not God a God of justice to all his creatures?. . . Then if he gives peace and tranquility to tyrants, and permits them to keep our fathers, our mothers, ourselves and our children in eternal ignorance and wretchedness to support them and their families, would he be to us a God of *justice?*[1]

However even before Walker wrote his famous "Appeal," and prior to the rise of the independent black Baptist and Methodist churches, there was already present an "invisible institution" in the South that emphasized the "overturned pot," the "prayin' ground," and the "hush harbor." An ex-slave preacher described those secret meetings in this manner:

> Meetings back there meant more than they do now. Then everybody's heart was in tune and when they called on God they made heaven ring. It was more than just Sunday meeting and then no more Godliness for a week. They would steal off to the fields and in the thickets and there, with heads together around a kettle to deaden the sound, they called on God out of heavy hearts.[2]

The slaves were searching for a private place where they could sing and shout and there would be nobody there to turn them out. In these secret meetings were born not only the major slave insurrections but also a black version of Christianity that was consistent with their search for freedom.

African slaves refused to accept Christianity as a given datum or as a deposit of fixed doctrines from white missionaries and preachers. Christianity as a rigidly defined system of beliefs about God, Jesus, and the Holy Spirit was inconsistent with the African personality, in which rhythm, passion, and feeling defined the structure of one's being in the world. Therefore, when white Baptists and Methodists arrived on the North American scene in a significant manner during the late eighteenth and early nineteenth centuries, Africans, for the first time during their presence, responded with enthusiasm. This response, contrary to popular opinion, was not to the system of beliefs in either denomination or to a religious consciousness traceable merely to white evangelical Protestantism. African slaves' response to Baptists and Methodists was complex and cannot be reduced to a single factor. The appeal of Methodists and Baptists was partly due to their antislavery reputation, the opportunities for black leadership provided by camp meetings, a tolerance for somatic and ecstatic worship, and an encouragement of the conversion experience. Among the Methodists and Baptists, blacks were permitted some freedom in worship, reminiscent of their African heritage and related to their fight against slavery.

Black worship is not white worship, no matter how close the similarities might be in appearance. Black people have always known that. It does not matter that white people sometimes copy our preaching style. Whites may pray, sing, or clap their hands with a rhythm that makes it difficult for even blacks to make the distinction. Conversely, no one can deny that white evangelical Protestantism of the Second Great Awakening, particularly the revival hymns, did influence the content and style of black worship. One need only point to the popularity of the hymns of Isaac Watts among black congregations in order to demonstrate that point. Nevertheless there is a radical difference between black and white worship services. Both whites and blacks know this, and that is why even today one seldom finds them worshiping together.

The source of the difference between black and white worship services is found at the point of a difference in life. Even when slaves worshiped with their masters, it was usually out of necessity to put on a "good front" so that the masters would think of them as pious and religious. The "real meetin'" and the "real preachin'" were held in the swamp, out of the reach of the patrols. An ex-slave, Litt Young, tells of a black preacher who preached, "obey your master," as long as her mistress was present. When the mistress was absent, she said, "He came out with straight preachin' from the Bible."[3]

The need for secret meetings was created by the legal restrictions against African slaves assembling without the presence of whites and also black people's dissatisfaction with the worship and preaching of white churches. Although slaves knew they were risking a terrible beating or perhaps even death, they nonetheless found it necessary to "steal away" into the woods at night in order to sing, preach, and pray for their liberation from slavery. Adeline Cunningham, an ex-slave from Texas, reported,

> No suh, we never goes to church. Times we sneaks in de woods and prays de Lawd to make us free and times one of de slaves got happy and made a noise dat dey heard at de big house and den de overseer come and whip us 'cause we prayed de Lawd to set us free.[4]

Black slaves had to create their own style of worship. They shouted and prayed for the time they would "most be done toilin' here."

Because black people were victims, they could not accept white people's interpretation of the gospel. The apostle Paul's "slave be obedient to your master" was a favorite text of white missionaries and preachers. Hannah Scott of Arkansas expressed her reaction to one such preacher in this way: "But all he say is 'bedience to the white folks, and we hears 'nough of dat without him tellin' us."[5]

In order to hear another word and to sing another song, they held secret worship services in the slave cabin or in the woods at night. As one ex-slave put it, "Dey law us out of church, but dey couldn't law 'way Christ."[6] These worship services included singing, preaching, shouting, and conversion. Black slaves used the "overturned pot" in order to keep from being heard by their masters or the patrollers. Carey Davenport, a former slave, remembered those meetings: "Sometimes the cullud folks go down in dugouts and hollows and hold they own service and they used to sing songs what come a-gushing up from the heart."[7] In this worship context was born their encounter with God, the One they believed would bring them through. The preacher often spoke about "dark clouds hanging over their heads" and of the "rocky roads they have to travel." At other times, he told them about "deep valleys" and "high mountains," but he assured them that they had a future not made with human hands. The element of faith in the righteousness of God prevented black slaves from accepting despair as the logical consequence of their servitude.

Immediately following the legal abolition of slavery, the "invisible institution" became visible as newly freed blacks joined independent black churches. What was once done in secret could now be done in the open. Like the secret meetings during the slavery era, black worship after the Civil War was defined by the sermon, song, shout, and the experience of conversion. Each of these elements in black worship was defined by the freedom of the Spirit who moved into the lives of the people, giving them hope and the courage to defend their dignity in an extreme situation of oppression.

An important moment in the history of black worship came during World War I, when many blacks migrated to the cities in search of a measure of freedom in employment and other aspects of black life. Needless to say, most did not find what they had hoped for, and once again they found it necessary to "take their burdens to the Lord and to leave them there." This they did by creating storefront churches and other praise houses of the Lord. This was also the period of the rise of black sects and cults with such figures as Father Divine and Daddy Grace. But more important for black Christian churches was the rise of gospel music with Thomas Dorsey and Mahalia Jackson as dominant personalities. This music put life into the churches by emphasizing the presence of the Spirit.

It was the presence of God's Spirit as defined by gospel music which empowered civil rights activists to fight for justice even though the odds were against them. Because they believed that God was in the black struggle for freedom, they refused to allow George Wallace and Mississippi Klansmen to destroy their faith that "we shall overcome." In Alabama, Mississippi, and Georgia, facing constant terror and death, poor blacks and their supporters kept on marching, singing "woke up this morning with my mind stayed on freedom" and "I ain't gonna let nobody turn me around."

Black worship today is very similar to what it was in the past. The names of the denominations may be new, but the style and content of our worship is very much like that of our grandparents. Instead of singing and preaching in those small southern church houses, we are now proclaiming God's word in storefront churches in New York, Detroit, Philadelphia, and Chicago. We sometimes call the places the "United House of Prayer for All People" or the "Church of What's Happening Now."

From the time of slavery to the present, the black church has been that place where African Americans could go in order to get some release from the harsh, oppressive realities of the white world. Black people go to church in order to be renewed by God's liberating Spirit. In prayer, sermon, and song, they tell God about "rollin' through an unfriendly world" as a "pilgrim of sorrow" and "motherless child."

> Sometimes I'm up, sometimes I'm down,
> Oh, yes, Lord!
> Sometimes I'm almost to the ground,
> Oh, yes, Lord!

Living in a "troublesome world," "tossed and driven," blacks have been enabled by the felt presence of the Spirit to acknowledge their suffering without being determined by it.

> Oh, nobody knows the trouble I've seen,
> Nobody knows my sorrow.
> Nobody knows the trouble I've seen,
> Glory, Hallelujah!

During the late 1960s, some expressions of black worship began to take on a more "secular" form with no obvious reference to the God of Christian theism. Theater and poetry workshops began to replace the church. An example is the National Black Theatre in Harlem founded by Barbara Ann Teer. Others like Haki R. Madhubuti, Nikki Giovanni, and Gwendolyn Brooks articulated a black spiritual and political message that affirmed the dignity and worth of blacks in their struggle for justice. Some black churches had become too middle-class to accommodate the spirit and aspiration of the Black Power movement. A new form of black ritual was developed wherein the poet became the preacher with a message for the people.

It was in the context of the civil rights and Black Power movements that black theology was born. Black theology is an attempt to show liberation as the central message of the Christian gospel and thereby bring the contemporary black church to its liberating heritage. Our worship service must be free and liberating, because we believe "the Lord will make a way somehow." Therefore, we must fight until freedom comes.

The Theological Meaning of Black Worship

Black worship is more than an expression of our historical struggle to be free. Because it is more than what we do, a mere historical analysis of the context of its origin is simply not adequate. We can talk about certain sociological conditions and how they affected the style and content of our songs and sermons. We can mention slavery, the great migrations, the Civil Rights Movement, and their effect on black worship. But we have not really touched the heart of black worship from the perspective of the people until we deal with the *theological* claim affirmed in prayer, song, and story.

In the struggle of black slaves to define their humanity according to freedom and not slavery there was present the divine Power who was greater than the white structures that enslaved them. When black slaves were tempted to give up in despair, this Power gave them hope that slavery would soon come to an end.

The source which black people used for explaining this Power was scripture as interpreted by their African heritage and their desire for freedom. Black worship is biblical. One of the most amazing facts of history is that many African American slaves did not accept the white interpretation of the gospel, even though they could not read or write. Although whites contended that scripture endorsed slavery, black slaves argued differently. They contended that God willed their freedom and not their slavery. Their hermeneutics was not derived from an intellectual encounter with the text but from a gift of the Spirit. A white preacher in 1832 noted, "Many of the blacks look upon white people as merely taught by the Book; they consider themselves instructed by inspiration of the Spirit."[8]

Because slaves were able to make a radical epistemological distinction between the gospel of Jesus and the religion of whites, they also came to different theological conclusions about God. When African slaves heard the Old Testament story of Israel in Egypt, they identified themselves with the Hebrew slaves and identified white slaveholders with the Egyptians, and no amount of clever white exegesis could change their thinking on this matter. As Israel was in Egyptland, oppressed so hard they could not stand, so blacks were in American slavery, working under the whip and pistol. As Israel was liberated from Egypt across the Red Sea, so blacks would also be set free. It is this theological certainty that characterizes black worship, enabling blacks to sing with assurance:

> Oh, Mary, don't you weep, don't you moan,
> Oh, Mary, don't you weep, don't you moan,
> Pharaoh's army got drownded,
> Oh, Mary, don't you weep.

The theme of God as the Liberator is found throughout the history of black religion. It is found among black Protestants and Catholics. Black Christians have always known that the God of the biblical tradition and of their African heritage is the One whose righteousness is identical with the liberation of the weak and helpless.

The theological conviction that the God of the Bible is the liberator of the poor and the downtrodden has been and is the important distinction between black and white religion. White Christianity may refer to liberation in limited times and places as shown by the abolitionists, the social gospel preachers, and the recent appearance of political and liberation theologians in Europe and America. But liberation is not and has never been the dominant theme in white church songs, prayers, and sermons. The reason is obvious: white people live in and identify with a social, economic, and political situation which blinds them to the biblical truth of liberation. Expecting white oppressors to recognize black liberation as central to the gospel is like expecting Pharaoh in Egypt to respond affirmatively to God's plea to "let my people go." To hear that plea is to recognize the limitations of one's power, a recognition oppressors seldom if ever make. Even when oppressors express the liberation theme in words, as found in Lyndon Johnson's affirmation that "we shall overcome" and white theologians' endorsement of liberation theology, that expression remains at a theoretical level and is seldom put into practice. White oppressors merely want to co-opt the language of the oppressed so they will not have to change societal structures of oppression.

In black religion and worship, God is known primarily as the liberator of the poor and the downtrodden. God is the Almighty Sovereign One who is sometimes called a "heartfixer" and a "mind regulator." During the worship service, God is known by the immediate presence of the divine Spirit with the people, giving them not only the vision that the society must be transformed but also the power and courage to participate in its transformation.

The certainty about God's immediate presence with the weak is the heart of the black worship service. Black worship is a series of recitals of what God has done to bring the people out of "hurt, harm, and danger." Through sermon, song, prayer, and testimony, the people tell their story of "how they got over." God is that divine miracle who enables the people to survive amid wretched conditions. God is holy, personal, and all-powerful. God is everything the people need in order to triumph over terrible circumstances.

It is important to note that there are no metaphysical distinctions between God and Jesus in black worship. The distinction between the Father and the Son is defined according to the rhythm of the people's language as they seek to communicate with the divine. Jesus is their constant companion, the one who walks with the people and tells them he is their own. He is the Oppressed One who experiences the brokenness of humanity. He is God's child who was born of "Sister Mary" in Bethlehem, and "every time the baby cried, she'd a-rocked him in the weary land."

In the black church, Jesus is also known for his identification with the poor, his suffering and death on the cross, and his resurrection from the dead. When the people get tired of struggling for survival and liberation and their "road gets rocky and rugged," they go to church in order to hear the preacher talk about Jesus. Sensing their impending despair, the preacher offers them hope by reminding them of the liberating power of Jesus' cross and resurrection:

> Have you considered the one who died on Calvary and was resurrected on the third day? Have you considered Jesus, the lily of the valley and the bright and morning star? He is able to smooth out the rough places in your life. He can place your feet on the solid rock of salvation.

It is not unusual for the preacher to call the name of Jesus repeatedly, according to the mood and spirit of the congregation. He may call Jesus' name as many as twenty-five or thirty times if the Spirit warrants it. If the people "get happy," as is so often the case, they may call Jesus' name for ten or fifteen minutes. In sermon, testimony, and prayer, the people invite Jesus to come and be with them and to "throw his strong arm of protection around them." To understand the theological significance of Jesus in black worship, the interpreter needs to experience Jesus' presence with the people and hear them call on his holy name as disclosed in this black deacon's prayer:

> Uh Jesus, we know all power is in thy hands. Uh Jesus! Uh Jesus! We need you right now. Uh Jesus, I know you heard me pray in days that's past and gone. Don't turn a deaf ear to thy servant's prayer right now. Uh Jesus, Uh Jesus![9]

The importance of Jesus and God in the black church service is perhaps best explained when one considers the preponderance of suffering in black life. When we consider slavery, lynching, and ghettos, how can we explain black people's mental and physical survival? How was it possible for black slaves to hope for freedom when a mere empirical analysis of their situation of oppression would elicit despair? How is it possible for poor blacks today to keep their sanity in the struggle for freedom when one considers the continued worsening of their economic exploitation? The answer is found in Jesus and God. Jesus heals wounded spirits and broken hearts. No matter what trials and tribulations the people encounter, they refuse to let despair define their humanity. They simply believe that "God can make a way out of no way." Blacks do not deny that trouble is present in their life; they merely contend that trouble does not have the last word and that "we'll understand it better by and by." In the words of Charles Tindley,

> Trials dark on every hand, and we cannot understand
> All the ways that God would lead us to that Blessed Promise Land.
> But God guides us with God's eye and we'll follow till we die,
> For we'll understand it better by and by.
>
> By and by, when the morning comes,
> All the saints of God are gathered home.
> We'll tell the story how we overcome,
> For we'll understand it better by and by.

Notes

1. Walker, in *Walker's "Appeal" and Garnet's "Address to the Slaves of the United States of America,"* American Negro: His History and Literature Series (New York: Arno, 1969), p. 16.
2. Cited by George P. Rawick in *From Sundown to Sunup* (Westport, CT: Greenwood, 1972), p. 40.
3. Young, cited by Norman R. Yetman in *Life under the "Peculiar Institution": Selections from the Slave Narrative Collection* (New York: Holt, Rinehart & Winston 1970), p. 337.
4. Cunningham, cited by Rawick in *From Sundown to Sunup,* p. 35.
5. Scott, cited by Eugene Genovese in *Roll, Jordan, Roll* (New York: Pantheon Books, 1972), p. 207.
6. Cited by Genovese in *Roll, Jordan, Roll,* p. 213.
7. Davenport, cited by Rawick in *From Sundown to Sunup,* p. 34.
8. Cited by Genovese in *Roll Jordan Roll,* p. 214.
9. Cited by Harold A. Carter in *The Prayer Tradition of Black People* (Valley Forge: Judson, 1976), p. 49.

9
The Theological Validation of Black Worship

Samuel D. Proctor

The sheer breadth of this topic invites the widest possible consideration and the most esoteric and subjective treatment. It cries out for narrowing, and for the setting of some limits that will not obfuscate the principal inquiry itself. The writer himself feels the impulse to "sound off" before allowing sufficient reflection and the patient analysis that the topic deserves. What a temptation it is to unload all of one's prejudices and stored up complaints about a matter that is so fraught with emotion!

First, there is indeed an urgent need to address the issue of black worship, for the spiritual needs of blacks, compounded by their historical and endemic economic deprivation, social insularity, civil injustices and cultural isolation, somehow are reliably and honestly reflected in the varieties and styles of black worship, including those common and seductive forms of idolatry that have crept into most worship experiences. Religion is highly vulnerable to the anthropomorphisms that are indigenous to the culture and to the easy identification of God with the "dearest idols" we have known. Black worship is likewise vulnerable to such idolatry, the "worship" of order, size, personalities, affluence, class distinctions, power and prestige. It is also vulnerable to the emotional responses, to extreme quietness, rhythm, crowds, loudness, organ sounds, vocal perambulations, glossolalia, dancing and moaning. Blacks are as capable as any others of giving the praise that belongs to an infinite and eternal God to finite and temporal objects and giving the focus to ancillary religious expressions and practices that should be given only to a high and holy God.

Any persons who have made the circuit among black churches, from the high Anglican, with acolytes, incense and the Evensong, to the shouting, whooping, whining and breathless ecstasy of a charismatic Baptist or Pentecostal church, will know that some thought should be given to the whole question of valid worship for *any* people; and with our uniqueness, it is especially relevant for black people. It is not a trivial pursuit. It has to do with the whole matter of what is happening to the most important aspects of our total being, our quest for communion with the good, the true, the ultimate, the beautiful, the abiding and the eternal.

The topic deserves attention not only because of the distortions and the misrepresentations that some worship experiences project, but also because of the helplessness and the abuse of so many trusting souls who look upon church and clergy with respect. Further, it deserves attention because of the possibility of the denial of opportunity for authentic and sincere worship, and communication with God, on the part of a people who have been compelled to look beyond history and culture for the affirmation of their personhood, for life's true meaning, and for a hope and a faith that transcend the evil, the racism and the rejection of the world. Blacks have never been able to take their faith lightly. They have been driven to stay close to the radical and culturally transcendent message of the gospel, as Robert McAfee Brown has described it:

> The institutional church has done a pretty good job for 2000 years of keeping the radical message of the gospel under wraps, and we may accept it as axiomatic that it will continue to do so. . . The radical message, nevertheless, is there, and it is not going to go away—one of the advantages of possessing canonical writings that cannot indefinitely be bent to the hermeneutical desires of those with power. Indeed, one thing that ties together Christians otherwise divided by race, class, skin color and geographical location, is that despite all those differences, they share common scriptures, out of which a common faith is always escaping ecclesiastical and cultural control, and rising up to challenge and ultimately defeat the pretensions of those who try to control it for their own ends.[1]

Black worship deserves discussion also because of our marginal social experience that is fragmented, disintegrated, lacunal and debilitating. Our need for a pillow of a cloud by day, and a ball of fire by night, to guide us to our Canaan, across the desert of our pain and travail, is an urgent matter. We have had to look to religion with an earnestness and a zeal that could easily be exploited and misdirected. And when this God hunger is treated with vulgar profaneness, it is a matter of life and death for us. It is surely the case for others as well, but most others in our society have a repository of social experience replete with positive references. Our social experiences have been negative, destructive and self-denying. This is especially true of our need to find in the scriptures those evidences of God's deliverance. This is why the Exodus has always meant so much to blacks, as J. Deotis Roberts explains:

> The Exodus is the exegetical thread which runs through black religious history from its inception to contemporary black theology and which has provided the perspective for preaching, music and thought. The remembrance of things past in reference to bondage and freedom is a sacred thread that provides continuity for the faith of black Christians. It follows that the call to remember the providential purpose of God in the liberation of Israel

of old has profound meaning for black people no less than for the Jewish people. Blacks participate in this event indirectly through the revelation of faith, rather than through their direct participation in the Exodus or the holocaust. Also, it is slavery in the United States that provides the paradigmatic connection to the Exodus in the history of black faith.[2]

The task is, first of all, to ascertain the criteria for valid worship for *any* people in the Christian context. What is theologically valid worship for any group? The limitations are that the question is addressed in the context of the black experience in the United States and from a Christian, Protestant perspective. The writer readily disclaims any competency to deal with the topic focusing on African or Caribbean black worship, or the Moslem, the Roman Catholic, or Coptic experience. There is no apology for this limitation, for the issue is so pressing for the black Protestant community in the United States that the broader, more global considerations could detract from an urgent, simple and forthright approach. However, scarcely could anything be said about blacks in the United States with authenticity that did not tacitly or explicitly acknowledge the residuals of our African past, despite the unsettled debates on what that quotient may be.

We are searching here for some understanding of this kaleidoscopic array of black people in our family of Protestant communions, with our great variety, in our approach to the experience commonly called the worship of God. Given these limitations, we must begin with an understanding of the criteria of theologically valid worship for persons generally, black or otherwise. What makes worship theologically valid?

Theological validity requires, first, that one step forward and declare without equivocation where he or she stands theologically, or this question will stay in the air somewhere like a helium balloon and never touch ground. Unless one asserts a position on "theological validity," there is no basis for discussion. And, oddly enough, the emphasis here is on "validity," and "theological" is the modifier. Therefore, one has some liberty in signing off on his or her understanding of the "theological" quality of the "validity" in honestly and faithfully describing "theological" as a given and by being held accountable as it is applied with the term "validity." In other words, in order to speak of the theological validity of black worship we are not about the business of inventing "theological." We are indeed about a closer look at black worship and how it squares with what we acknowledge to be valid worship, theologically.

One should welcome an opportunity, anywhere, anytime, to confess what it means to himself/herself to do "God-talk," for that is theology—"God-talk." And, this discussion calls for us to settle on what we mean when we do "God-talk"; and then we must hold that in mind while we lift up black worship beside it. And, then the question must be answered: "If this is black worship; and if this is our understanding of "God-talk," can this black worship be judged valid in the light of our understanding of "God-talk"? Does what we know about God square with what we find in black worship? If not, where is the problem? What must give?

Next, of course, we must set some limits on the term "black worship." This is troublesome because often, on the one hand, when black persons are at worship they are following exercises invented outside of the black spiritual sojourn altogether. And, often, on the other hand, when they are allegedly at worship, something else entirely is actually happening, frequently nothing more than a pagan, sensuous klan-gathering where God is mentioned incidentally. Despite the risks involved, therefore, for the sake of clarity, some perimeters must be placed on the term "black worship."

Obviously, black worship will bear its own *imprimatur*, it need not look like other forms of worship. It was born out of different conditions, and it has had its own symbiosis with the changing conditions in America and the black response. Any attempt to ignore this uniqueness, this "folk" aspect is an error. Gayraud S. Wilmore reminds us:

> To the extent that these groups and others continue to draw their main strength from the masses, they will foster the rationalization of certain elements of black religion toward the pursuit of freedom and social justice. Their ideological roots, however, must go down into the soil of the folk community if they are to maintain their credibility. That is why the lower-class black community must be considered one of the primary sources for the development of a black Christian theology.
>
> Folk religion is a constituent factor in every significant crisis in the black community. We ignore it only at the risk of being cut off from the real springs of action. When the black community is relatively integrated with white society, the folk religious elements recede from black institutions to form a hard core of unassimilable nationalism in the interstices of the social system—biding its time. When the black community is hard-pressed by poverty and oppression, when hopes are crushed under the heels of resurgent racism, then essential folk elements exhibit themselves and begin once again to infiltrate the power centers that ignored or neglected them.[3]

C. Eric Lincoln makes the same point regarding the emergence of an adaptive, accommodated black expression of Christianity that will not go away:

> Often, when the white man's worship service was over, the black man's might truly begin, for neither his heart nor his private membership was in the white church, where he was scorned and demeaned. There was that other church, that invisible institution which met in the swamps and the bayous, and which joined all black believers in a common' experience at a single level of human and spiritual recognition. Deep in the woods and safely out of sight of the critical, disapproving eyes of the master and the overseer, the shouts rolled up—and out. The agony so long suppressed burdened the air with sobs and screams and rhythmic moans. God's praises were sung. His mercy enjoined. His justice invoked. There in the Invisible Church the black Christian met God on his own terms and in his own way without the white intermediary. That invisible communion was the beginning of the black church, the seminal institution that spans most of the history of the black experience. It offers the most accessible key to the complexity and the genius of the black subculture, and it reflects both a vision of the tragedy and an aspect of hope of the continuing American dilemma.[4]

Nevertheless, with the criteria for Christian worship before us, along with an understanding of black worship, the answer to our question lies in applying our criteria for theologically valid worship to what we characterize as "black worship."

When Is Worship Theologically Valid?

Christian worship is the adoration and praise of God and the exercise of seeking communion with God, privately or corporately, in a cathedral or in a tent, in a temple or an open field, at home or in a store-front.

This writer is a practitioner in black worship. He serves a black congregation in Harlem with a long history of identification with black people at the vortex of their struggle for meaning and liberation in America. Each week he is engaged in *praxis* that interplays with theory. Each week he must ask himself if what happens at worship has validity. Therefore, he lives and struggles with this issue week in and week out. What, then, are the criteria in use, in his experience? As he selects the hymns, the anthems, hires the musicians, selects a text, chooses a sermon theme, orders the service, selects the words and phrases of his prayers, decides on the hour and length of the service and the color of his gown and hood, what on earth lies in the back of his mind? What gives coherence to his effort?

Admittedly, this is only one way of getting at the question, looking at the private experience of an average or prototypical black practitioner. One could turn to classical theology and look for criteria there or to the scriptures. Nevertheless, as we look at it from the perspective of a prototypical practitioner, with a case study methodology, what do we find?

Christian worship may be judged in many ways, but if one judges it in the light of the ideas, the practices, the outlook and attitude of Jesus Christ, the burden of proof is on all others who choose other approaches. In other words, in judging or assessing black worship, or any form of Christian worship, we should ask, fundamentally, how closely it corresponds to the attitude and ideas of Jesus. And this is where this writer takes his position. The centrality of Jesus was the principal affirmation of black religion, and black worship is anchored in this affirmation. Despite the myriad ways in which their treatment differed at the hands of Christian slave-masters, they emerged with their Jesus-faith intact. Cone summarizes this matter as follows:

> It is this affirmation of transcendence that prevents black theology from being reduced merely to the cultural history of black people. For black people the transcendent reality is none other than Jesus Christ, of whom scripture speaks. The Bible is the witness to God's self-disclosure in Jesus Christ. Thus the black experience requires that scripture be a source of black theology. For it was scripture that enabled slaves to affirm a view of God that differed radically from that of the slave masters. The slave masters' intention was to present a "Jesus" who would make the slave obedient and docile. Jesus was supposed to make black people better slaves, that is, faithful servants of white masters. But many blacks rejected that view of Jesus not only because it contradicted their African heritage, but also because it contradicted the witness of scripture.[5]

Following Jesus, we find that worship was at first simple and unpretentious. He criticized those who were carried away with tithes of "mint, anise and cummin" and who "neglected the weightier matters of the law." He taught that one ought not to pray with ostentation, or parade one's religious loyalties. He taught simplicity in our relation to God. He taught that the true worshipper worshipped in spirit and in truth; and that it did not matter where that worship took place, in the mountains of Samaria or beside a quiet, shallow stream.

He taught simplicity and he taught sincerity; he taught trust and openness with God. His own practice was to be quiet every now and then and to lay his own life bare before God. His temptation experience was precisely a moment of such candor, when he acknowledged the lures that tugged on his heartstrings. Likewise, in Gethsemane he underwent a long period of confession and affirmation with God.

The centrality of Jesus in black religion has particular significance because blacks identified so closely with Jesus as Liberator. Cone writes:

> In the final analysis we must admit that there is no way to "prove objectively" that we are telling the truth about ourselves or about the One who has called us into being. There is no place we can stand that will remove us from the limitations of history and thus enable us to tell the whole truth without the risk of ideological distortion. As long as we live and have our being in time and space, absolute truth is impossible. But this concession is not an affirmation of unrestricted relativity. We can and must say something about the world that is not reducible to our own subjectivity. That trans-subjective "something" is expressed in story, indeed is embodied in story.
>
> Story is the history of individuals coming together in the struggle to shape life according to commonly held values. The Jewish story is found in the Hebrew Bible and the rabbinic traditions. The early Christian story is told in the Old and New Testaments, with the emphasis on the latter as the fulfillment of the former. The white American story is found in the history of European settlements struggling against dark forests and savage people to found a new nation. The black American story is recorded in the songs, tales, and narratives of African slaves and their descendants, as they attempted to survive with dignity in a land inimical to their existence. Every people has a story to tell, something to say to themselves, their children, and to the world about how they think and live, as they determine and affirm their reason for being. The story both expresses and participates in the miracle of moving from nothing to something, from nonbeing to being.[6]

For Jesus, worship and communion with God were far from exclusively a Sabbath session of formal worship. Had he remained present in body with the newly emerged church we cannot tell what he might have preferred, but at best we can only infer that our traditions and styles of worship are a far departure from the practice of Jesus.

However, the New Testament is *germinative* into rather than *normative*. The teachings and practices of Jesus were not a new legalism. He forbade such. When asked, "Who is my neighbor?" he replied that anybody who is hurt, bruised, alone, left to die in the street is our neighbor. "How many times must I forgive my brother?" Any number of times. Seventy times seven. Let your spirit be a forgiving spirit. His was not a "cookbook" religion of proscribed recipes.

He did not give us a roadmap but a direction. He did not give rules but principles. And they are binding, even in their broad and general application. There are no soldiers to compel us to carry their backpacks. We are not under an occupation army. But we still have opportunity to demonstrate how to rise above legal demands and lived by a higher law. It is impractical to continue to give away our second coat, but it is still a sin to be stingy, callous and indifferent toward the poor.

So, if we were to regard to his teachings and practice on the matter of worship as germinative, the starting point, the first principles, then anything in worship that was showy or ostentatious, anything exhibitionistic or pretentious, anything for our glory rather than the glory of God would be prohibited. These would violate the principle of simplicity.

Anything in worship that was misleading, deceptive, fraudulent, or a misrepresentation of truth would violate the principle of sincerity. Pretending to be spirit-filled in order to appeal to the emotions of naïve and unsuspecting people is *ipso facto* invalid. Dressing in such a manner as to focus attention on oneself rather than on God is invalid. Gathering people for the worship of God and "shaking them down for money" is a fraud and is invalid worship. Inducing worshipers to direct attention away from God to sensuous topics and feelings, to exploit their gullibility, innocence, naïveté and emotional vulnerability for private gain is invalid. These all fly in the face of the sincerity that Jesus taught and practiced.

Indeed, there are those whose sanctuaries are adorned to glorify God, whose services are highly emotional, and who really believe in the efficacy of such practices as faith, healing, and who are coherently, consistently and faithfully in consonance with the teachings and practices of Jesus: simplicity, sincerity and trust. Wyatt T. Walker addresses the issue of variety in black worship, all of which may be consistent with the criteria of simplicity, sincerity and trust:

> Jesus is the central figure in the theology of the contemporary black church. In fact, the form of Christianity practiced by the folk community in black America is appropriately called the Jesus faith. It is an evidence of the nonacceptance of traditional European theological systems. The Jesus faith of blacks reveals an Africanization of Christianity rather than the Christianizing of Africans. It stands counterposed to western Christianity whose trinitarian formula is capitalism, racism and militarism. The Jesus faith is covered by its cultural antecedent, traditional West African religion, and is thereby "wholistic" in its theological posture. It is an everyday religion that sings "Amazing Grace" over dishwater and invokes God's help for a good number to play in the number-game. It is not devoid of the traditional accoutrements of western-style Christianity, but it is more than ceremony and form. It explores the world of faith healing and ecstatic joy in religion. The presence of speaking in tongues and holy dancing are frequent. The realm of the supraphysical is just a prayer away. God can do anything but fail![7]

Unfortunately, however, in cathedrals, in storefronts on Harlem's 131st Street, in ornate Texas tabernacles and glass temples in California, the scenes, the motivation, the practices, the sermons and the music may all be designed and presented without the confidence of the mind of Christ. Indeed, medieval cathedrals, often built to assuage the vanity of dukes and the barons, lords and ladies, bedecked in precious jewels to compete with other cathedrals, were dedicated to the most high God in pomp and ceremony, with long processions, with dignitaries clad in silks and satins, carrying gold chalices and silver crosses; but the lonely Galilean still rode into Jerusalem sitting sideways on the back of a donkey, and he was the Son of God.

Assuming that valid worship of God, in the Christian context, is worship that follows the spirit, the style, the motivation and the attitude of Jesus, such worship will conform to the simplicity, the sincerity and the trust Jesus taught and practiced.

Theology is empty verbosity without the element of trust. Nothing could be more meaningless than words about God without the risk of trust. "God-talk" is sounding brass without commitment. This is true of any "ology," but theology, with God as the topic, is nothing but noise without the investment of trust. Worship in the name of God lacks the tangible, material, empirical evidence that an activity in physics, pharmacology or even astronomy may have. Yet, even without such empirical tests the most important issues of life must be decided, and in place of the empirical lies the intuitive reach of faith and trust. So, as was the case with Jesus, we worship when we exercise our trust in God's existence, in his accessibility, in his love and power. And, any trifling, casual or superficial act or gesture that deals with trust likely or not at all such as prayers "prayed" to the congregation, songs sung for applause, sermons preached to amuse or to entertain are far from the mark and failed to engage the attitude of trust in God.

Worship that is theologically valid is worship marked by simplicity, sincerity and trust. Of course, these all include other basic elements such as confession, intercession, adoration, edification, commitment and challenge.

What Is Black Worship?

Black worship can only mean worship that takes place in the black community and which relates to the peculiar black experience. Surely, worship is worship, and it would violate all that we understand about Christ if we concluded that persons went to God closed primarily in ethnocentricity. In Christ there is neither male nor female, bond or free, Jew or Greek or black!

Notwithstanding, blacks do worship separately because of the existence of two societies in America, and to behave as though there were nothing that could be called black worship would be deceitful. Charles H. Long has written of unique black experience out of which the deep spiritual needs of blacks derive:

Through the contingencies of history and biology, blackness has been preeminently revealed in the lives and histories of those souls who possess black skins and who have had to undergo the opaque meanings in the modern period. This blackness is both natural and holy. It is in fact the natural biological fact that destiny has chosen some of human kind to bear this color. For us this is natural, but destiny has also chosen that the last four hundred years have been in fact what they have been and during this time it seemed often as if blackness had opposed itself even to us. Blackness in its own seasons forced itself upon us in innumerable ways and many of us cried out in amazement and even hate, that we were in fact, black. And so blackness caught us people of color in its own convolutions; it forced upon us "a highly exceptional and extremely impressive Other." The otherness of blackness hit us so hard that we hated that life could be this way. This black reality took us down, down, way down younder where we saw only another deeper blackness, down where prayer is hardly more than a moan, down there where life and death seem equitable. We descended into hell, into the deepest bowels of despair, and we were becoming blacker all the time.[8]

Black worship originated in the slave experience as blacks blended their African heritage with the Anglo-Saxon Protestant ethos in the plantation South. The conditions and the expressions of this worship are widely known and discussed. Suffice to say here that it was an adaptation, a welding of the evangelical Protestant forms, with African rhythms and corporate feelings, and the longing for transcendence, for relief now and in life everlasting. Again, Wyatt Tee Walker, along with many others, holds to the view that West African religions, as well as the total reservoir of West African art, music, etc., became the source of black religion in the West, and the fertile soil for Christianity among the slaves. Walker wrote:

The Jesus-faith, new to the transplanted African, had fertile ground in which to grow and develop because we possessed a religious heritage founded on the one-God principle. Christianity might not have taken hold as it did, had we not had a theological orientation of the High God and the concomitant worldview of nature and man. It was that part of our African heritage which was most difficult to destroy. The oral tradition preserved our spirituality and nurtured our newly found Jesus-faith. Any superficial study of traditional West African religions will quickly reveal that there is no such thing as a non-religious African. The great reservoir of West African culture; art, music, dance, folk wisdom, is traditional African religion. And that religion has been preserved, not in writing, but in the oral tradition, passing from one generation to another.[9]

Therefore, the deliverance and liberation themes have always accompanied black worship. And, when these are absent, it is because blacks have turned away from their true and basic spiritual need and taken on the worldview, the *Zeitgeist*, of others, chanting their themes and following their patterns of worship. Granted, there are common spiritual needs that all persons must address in worship, but the uniqueness of the black experience, and the pervasiveness of the liberation theme in black worship cause black worship to be distinctive. God, to the black worshipper is not some unknown "id," some *Agnosto Theos*, the resolution of a riddle about creation, or the end of a syllogism in logic, or the Prime Mover and the First Cause in physics and astronomy. Indeed, he is at least all of the above but much more. Ronald C. Potter, an I.T.C. student, wrote:

> God, in black theology, is first and foremost the liberative One. God is not the originator and sanctifier of the status quo. Rather, God is the One who continually calls into question the status quo and subsequently transforms it. Fundamentally, the liberation and humanization of the oppressed attest to the presence of God in human history. One recognizes the divine presence in the world by witnessing the liberation of the oppressed, the elimination of injustice and dehumanization, and by the social transformation of the world.[10]

Black worship is characterized by a simple and trusting approach to God in the vernacular available. It is spirit-filled, marking the feeling of release and asylum, defense and protection, dependence and thanksgiving, abandonment of fear and insecurity and "holding to God's unchanging hand."

Because of this trusting aspect of black worship, it is highly vulnerable to vulgar exploitation and easily deflected from the simplicity, the sincerity; the true trust that Jesus calls us to practice in worship and communion with God, and the true trust in the hearts of the people. Every charismatic leader becomes aware of the proneness of desperate people to anoint their own messiahs and to project into their favorite personalities the answers to all of the frustrations and inhibitions that have been generated in their own struggles for survival.

Dr. Lillian Webb, in her report on the ministry of Elder Lightfoot Solomon Michaux, wrote:

> When he and Mrs. Michaux entered one of the several churches, the congregation rose quickly to honor them. The Elder realized that he could be idolized and implicitly cautioned members to temper their esteem by saying to them, "When you rise to honor me, I kneel to honor God." Members often referred to Michaux in testimonies as "a prophet in the last days," "the Man of God," "The last prophet."[11]

As we examine the positive and inspiring aspects of black worship, we need to be mindful of the excesses that come to mind as we hold up the criteria of theologically valid worship.

However, there is one further imperative that we must face regarding this question of the validity of black worship. Our families are disappearing fast; the discipline and commitment on which the marriage relationship rests are eroded; our youth are carelessly bearing children and leaving this burden on family members and the begrudging and contemptible taxpayers; too many males are wasting in our prisons, in the drug world and forsaking marriage for homosexuality and its psychotic abyss. The loyalty we need for economic and political cohesion is sadly sporadic.

The benefits and blessings that worship and faithfulness caused to inure to our fathers, and that—with so much less—caused them to have so much more, and that brought them through deep waters like crossing dry land, and that caused them to scale high mountains like walking on a level place—these blessings are withheld from us. Prophetic utterance cried out against idolatry more than against anything, giving the praise and the adoration that the heart should hold for the Lord to other idols. And I risk the notion that the wells that our fathers dug must now be dug again with the junk and debris cleaned out, that the pure waters might flow again.

We must cease this childish exaltation and applause of anything that anybody wants to do and call it worship of the most high God! All of this cheap exhibitionism, this pretentious yelling and screaming, these profane and self-serving prayers, and these minstrel shows that some dare to call sermons ought not to be encouraged. Our wells are dry! And we need to tap fresh springs of living water, to bring strength and nurture to our lives and to cause our efforts to bear a richer fruitfulness.

In all of our big city ghettos there is more yelling and hollering and wiggling and rocking per square acre than there is corn in Nebraska; alongside this wasted exercise a quality of life that must be improved, and that will require the best of our efforts to overcome the consequences of oppression and exclusion. We do indeed need to look at our worship and separate the circuses from those who seek the Lord while he may be found and call upon him while he is near.

Conclusion

Black worship is valid insofar as God is approached without "form and fashion" but in simplicity and sincerity. It is valid insofar as it avoids superficiality and idolatry and embraces the attitude of trust in God. It loses its validity when the pastor insists on being the object of worship, when the music is presented to glorify the performers, and when the prayers are not prayed to God at all but to the people present. None of the above is said without regard to the peculiar and characteristic modes of black worship that honestly—and without sham and pretense—arise out of the black experience. None of the above is a denial of the basic authenticity and sincerity of black worship that is free, uninhibited, and very overt. The criteria of simplicity and sincerity are not at all in jeopardy in genuine black worship, no matter how emotional. James H. Cone has made this very clear:

> As with the sermon and prayer, the spirituals and gospel songs reveal that the truth of black religion is not limited to the literal meaning of the words. Truth is also disclosed in the movement of the language and the passion created when a song is sung in the right pitch and tonal quality. Truth is found in shout, hum, and moan as these expressions move the people closer to the source of their being. The moan, the shout, and the rhythmic bodily responses to prayer, song, and sermon are artistic projections of the pain and joy experienced in the struggle of freedom. It is the ability of black people to express the tragic side of social existence but also their refusal to be imprisoned by its limitations.[12]

Television and religious "marketing" are awfully tempting. It is time now for someone to say that too many black churches are copying the worst elements of "commercial" religion. The music gets sensuous, the preaching becomes entertaining primarily, and the costumes, "props," and decor are for fund raising and "marketing" rather than obedience in discipleship.

Therefore, the rich experience with God, that brought us such a "mighty long way," as he fed us in our deserts of despair and brought water for us out of the rock of persecution and oppression, is about to be forfeited as we dance around the golden calf of commercial, "marketed" religion rather than worshipping in spirit and in truth.

Several years ago, from the agony of his South African experience, Desmond M. Tutu wrote about the spiritual opportunity that the black experience opened before us, and it is this tone, this expression, this level of love, this Christian dynamic that redefines black worship:

> Our blackness is an intractable ontological surd. You cannot will it away. It is a brute fact of existence and it conditions that existence as surely as being male or female, only more so. But would we have it otherwise? For it is not a lamentable fact. No, far from it. It is not a lamentable fact because I believe that it affords us the glorious privilege and opportunity to further the gospel of love, forgiveness and reconciliation,—the gospel of Jesus Christ in a way that is possible to no other group.[13]

In the end, black worship, as is the case for all true worship, lifts us toward God, from whatever our condition may be, and provides for us the wisdom and the power, the courage and the fortitude to endure, and to run without getting weary, and to walk without fainting.

Notes

1. Robert McAfee Brown, "Perspectives from the Alternative Theology Project," *Doing Theology in the United States* I (Spring/Summer 1985): 21.
2. J. Deotis Roberts, "Perspective from the Alternative Theology Project," *Doing Theology in the United States* I (Spring/Summer 1985): 24.
3. Gayraud S. Wilmore, *Black Religion and Black Radicalism* (Maryknoll: Orbis, 1984), p. 235.
4. C. Eric Lincoln, *Race, Religion and the Continuing American Dilemma* (New York: Hill and Wang, 1984), p. 33.
5. James H. Cone, *God of the Oppressed* (New York: Seabury, 1975), p. 30.
6. James H. Cone, "The Content and Method of Black Theology," *The Journal of Religious Thought* XXXII (Fall-Winter 1975): 102.
7. Wyatt T. Walker, Harold A. Carter, and William A. Jones Jr., *The Black Church Looks at the Bicentennial* (Elgin: Progressive Baptist, 1976), p. 61.
8. Charles H. Long, "Structural Similarities and Dissimilarities in Black and African Theologies," *The Journal of Religious Thought* XXXII (Fall-Winter 1975): 21.
9. Wyatt T. Walker, *The Soul of Black Worship* (New York: Martin Luther King Fellows Press, 1984), p. 11.
10. Ronald C. Potter, "A Comparison of the Conceptions of God in Process and Black Theology," *The Journal of the Interdenominational Theological Center* XII (Fall 1984): 51.
11. Lillian Webb, "Michaux as Prophet," *The Journal of the Interdenominational Theological Center* VIII (Fall 1980): 10.
12. Cone, "The Content and Method of Black Theology," p. 22.
13. Desmond M. Tutu, "Black Theology/African Theology—Soul Mates or Antagonists," *The Journal of Religious Thought XXXII* (Fall-Winter 1975): 25.

10
Transformational Worship in the Life of a Church

Kenneth C. Ulmer

We have been called "to the kingdom for such a time as this" (Esther 4:14 RSV). Bob Dylan was right when he sang, "The times they are a-changin'." There was a time when people "went" to church. Now we "have" church. There was a time when we came to praise the Lord. Now we come to get our praise on!" However, while it may be *practice* that's changing, principles do not. Forms may change, but function is more rigid. On the other hand, we practice within a certain context. We respond to the Lord and affirm our relationship with our Lord through worship; but we worship in a context. We practice our praise in a *place*.

The powerful and deliberate chord progressions of "A Mighty Fortress Is Our God" often struggle for survival when sandwiched between the toe-tapping improvisation in the gospel melodies of a James Cleveland and the emerging prominence of the exuberant, contrapuntal holy hip hop of a Kirk Franklin. It is in this postmodern world, this hip hop, secularized, humanistic, technological information age, that you and I become the object of the divine quest of the omnipotent God. As Jesus said, "The hour is coming, and is now here, when the true worshipers will worship the Father in spirit and truth, for the Father seeks such as these to worship him" (John 4:23). Even during such a time as this, God is seeking *worshipers*. Not church members. Not preachers. Not choir members or ushers or greeters or musicians or deacons or elders. God is on a search mission for *worshipers!*

Aside from the weekly worship services at the Faithful Central Bible (where I have served since 1982), I have joined the ranks of passionate scribes exhorting the saints of God to make the worship of God a priority. By divine order in the heavenlies, yet out of the clear blue in the earth realm, I received a call from my dear friend Buddy Owens, asking me to serve as a contributor to the first Bible devoted exclusively to worship. Buddy wrote that the *NIV Worship Bible* "is neither a study Bible, nor is it a devotional Bible. The unique aspect of this Bible is that the notes do not interact with you, the reader. Instead, they interact with God."[1] A significant revelation comes forth from description of a worship Bible: worship is interaction with God. This revelation provides the framework for our examination of the practice of worship.

Our concern is beyond information about worship or the study of worship, and even beyond an exegetical and hermeneutical investigation of worship. As Robert Webber suggests in both the title and emphasis of his work of the same name, "Worship is a verb." "It is not something done to us or for us, but by us," Webber states.[2] Worship is an action, not an observation. My colleagues have sufficiently covered the technical, theological, and biblical dynamics of worship. Ryan Bolger (in chapter 9 of *Worship That Changes Lives: Multidisciplinary and Congregational Perspectives on Spiritual Transformation*, ed. Alexis D. Abernethy) has detailed an active, participatory approach to worship. Similarly, our interest at this juncture is on "doing worship." I pray that you will become a worshiper and move beyond one who merely knows about worship. The context for my reflections herein is the church that I have been blessed and honored to pastor for some twenty-five years. Over the years, I have noticed a significant transition and transformation in the worship of this congregation.

Historically, worship in the African American tradition might well be viewed as a series of blocks stacked one on top of the other. The first block was most often the "devotion." That is when the deacons and/or trustees of the church (or sometimes it was performed by women who served as deaconesses) would gather across the front of the church in a line. They would often start a song by "lining" a hymn. This refers to the call-and-response genre of African American hymnody: one person sings the first line of a song, and the congregation "answers" with the next line or a repetition of the initial line. This song style was characterized by what often sounded like humming and/or moaning on the part of the congregation's response. Words, phrases, and melodies were stretched and extended beyond meter and beyond the more structured European methods of precision timing. Without a conductor or director, it seems that everyone "sensed" when it was time to move to the next line or stanza. There was always a verse of moans, oohs, and aahs. Often the would start with the congregation sitting, and then, as if responding to some invisible cue, everyone would stand and sing their way through the song, concluding with a sit-down verse of humming and moaning of the repeated melody.

The next block would consist of the entrance of the choir. Most often they came in from the back of the church, in a kind of holy two-step, rocking from side to side in rhythm with the strains of the processional song. Many times the first song performed as the choir stepped its way to the choir stand was "The Lord's Prayer," with the choir and congregation performing this ethnic version of the prayer. This weekly performance was again sung *ad lib* and without rhythm, with both choir and worshipers singing, pausing, and breathing in concert, with or without the leadership of the choir director.

Following the "Amen" of "The Lord's Prayer," there was often the welcoming of the visitors and the morning announcements by the announcement clerk. This often-extensive overview of both past and future parish events set the stage for the choir's performance of an "A and B" selection. These two songs often lifted the congregation in praise while the choir was pushed higher and higher by the shouts of "Sing choir! Sing it!"

The third block would often consist of pastoral reflections, which was an extended emphasis and repetition of many or most of the announcements given by the clerk before the choir's songs. The pastor would close his remarks by preparing the congregation for the offering. The offering would almost invariably include a missions offering and a building fund offering. The choir would sing again during the offering, often leading the congregation in the lines of the standard offering song, "You can't beat God giving, no matter how you try."

Following the offering, the choir would sing another song or two. After the choir's song, it would sometimes be said (and often implied), "We will now move it on up a little higher." I always felt that everything up until that point was merely warm-up for the sermon. No doubt the high point of this worship experience was the preaching of the gospel. The sermon would end with the singsong style of preaching colloquially referred to as "whooping." This musical style of ending the sermon set the stage for yet another song, sung by the preacher and/or the choir.

The final block was always the invitation. The preacher would say something like this: "You can come as a candidate for baptism [implying salvation for the first time], by letter [from a previous church], or by Christian experience [already saved but not coming with a referral from a previous church]." The service would then end with the benediction, and there might be yet one more song while the worshipers exited the sanctuary.

This structure was typical of the African American baptistic tradition. There were variations on this block-upon-block style of worship in many other denominations, but the experience always seemed to be punctuated with pauses between one block or section and the next. There was a feeling that the service had vertical movement, block upon block, from one section up to another, from glory to glory, climaxing with the proclamation of the Word and the extension of salvation to the lost and/or unchurched.

Then a new and fresh style was introduced into African American worship through the ministry of the West Angeles Church of God in Christ, led by their minister of music, Patrick Henderson. Henderson received the label "Godfather of Praise and Worship" and is credited with bringing this new music style to the forefront of African American worship.[3]

The power and excitement of a live worship service was captured on a musical recording titled *Saints in Praise*. However, history will record that this project is so much more than a collection of songs on tape, an electronic masterpiece, or even the capturing for the future of the spiritual experience of thousands of worshipers. "Saints in Praise" launched a revolution within the black church. The musical ministry that characterized the worship at West Angeles in Los Angeles became a model not only of musical excellence but also of a new paradigm in worship structure: music moved to the forefront of worship. As opposed to being viewed as blocks upon which the sermonic highlight of the gathering was built, music in general (and praise music in particular) became part of a more linear structure of worship, preparing and leading the people into worship and enhancing the entire worship setting. "Praise *and* worship" not only became inseparable elements of a total worship experience but also launched a new and different music organization: the praise team.

Worship was now significantly reordered. Instead of the block upon disconnected block style of the tradition, there was now a "flow." In this reordering, worship is intended to be a continuum— rather than climbing higher and higher from one segment to the next—with worship flowing as seamlessly as possible from glory to glory. The deacons' devotion is replaced by the praise team, which now stands before the congregation singing choruses (rather than hymns), which are easily and quickly picked up by the congregation. The choirs' opening song(s) are often replaced by an extended time of music ministry by the praise team.

This change has caused much conflict in some churches because it has left many a deacon board with nothing to do at the beginning of the service. When the choir does sing, it does not perform an "A and B" selection, but ministers in song. This music ministry often includes monologues by the choir director or soloists who set up the song or serve as bridges between multiple songs tied together in some sort of thematic continuity. Ideally, the praise team becomes "ushers," leading the congregation into the presence of God.

The atmosphere is set for worship, not so much as in one segment and then the other, but as a continuum on a spiritual journey into the holy of holies and beyond the veil to the very glory of God. It is there in the presence of the glory of God that true worship takes place.

There are several practical challenges that must be faced when the people of God gather to worship. These challenges include *transformation, presentation, revelation,* and *participation.*

Transformation

In Romans 8:29, Paul tells the Roman believers they have been' predestined to be conformed to the image of Christ. Conformation is a concept synonymous with the sanctification process and involves the divine creation of a heart like that of the Lord Jesus, manifested in our relationships and our walk in and before the world. This conformation results in believers taking on the outward expression of the inward essence or nature of Christ.

Later, in Romans 12:2, Paul warns believers not to be conformed to the world. In these two passages he uses two different words for *conform*. In Romans 8:29, he uses the word *symmorphos*, "to be fashioned in the likeness of something."[4] The same word in verb form is *symmorphoō*, "to bring to the same form with" some other person or thing, "to render like." The root is the noun *morphē*, which refers to the outward expression of an inward essence or nature.[5] However, in Romans 12:2, Paul uses a different word: *syschēmatizō*.

Spiros Zodhiates comments on Romans 12:2 in this way: "Do not fall in with the external and fleeting fashions of this age nor be yourselves fashioned to them, but undergo a deep inner change. . . by the qualitative renewing. . . of your mind as the Spirit of God alone can work in you."[6] Paul exhorts us not to allow the world to fashion or shape or squeeze us into its mind-set of values, priorities, and lifestyle. Instead of being conformed to the world, we are to be transformed by the renewing of our minds.

Transformation involves change. It is the word from which we obtain our English word *metamorphosis*. It is the idea of a visible and outwardly expressive change of heart. It refers to living a life divinely changed by the power of God, and living it in the world. This change is cooperative and involves our submission to the word, will, and way of God. Dallas Willard says about change, "Projects of personal transformation rarely if ever succeed by accident, drift, or imposition. Indeed, where these dominate very little of any human value transpires. Effective action has to involve intention."[7] This change is at the heart level, but it is demonstrated kinetically in our daily lives. It is an invisible process that is visibly and observationally manifested in our lives. It is a process of passing and becoming (2 Cor. 5:17), becoming more and more like our Savior on a practical, daily basis. Most of all, this process of transformation is possible. Transformation therefore is a journey into Christlikeness. It is sometimes an exciting journey, sometimes a painful journey, sometimes a challenging journey. But it is always a God-ordained journey that fulfills God's purpose, which is to conform us and transform us into the likeness of his Son, Jesus the Christ.

We are transformed in a spiritual process that is in fact a progression. We progress in the process. One of the methods God has given us to facilitate this process is worship. Hull writes, "Worship does not train and develop people for ministry; it expresses the heart-felt awe of those trained and developed as disciples. Worship is the *result* of God's working in us, not the *cause*."[8] The value and legitimacy of worship therefore is not so much what is done and even accomplished "in" the worship assembly, but rather what that gathering produces and demonstrates after the benediction. Part of church outreach is what the church is before the watching world. Thus, effective worship produces disciples who leave the worship experience and re-enter the world with the likeness of the Christ they worship. Christ working in us produces worship that works out of us.

Presentation

One of the pictures of the people of God gathering for worship is seen in such phrases as "presented themselves before God" (Josh. 24:1) and "come into his presence" (Pss. 95:2; 100:2). These ideas suggest that coming to worship is like taking a journey. There are no fewer than fifteen psalms with the title "A Song of Degrees" or "A Song of Ascents" or "Pilgrim Song." The section of Israel's hymnbook from Psalm 120 to 134 was sung by pilgrims going up to the temple in Jerusalem.[9]

To enter the temple area, which is on a hill, the traveler from the east would have come around the Mount of Olives, dip through the Kidron Valley, and climb the road up to the temple. The arriving worshipers could be heard singing their way around the mountain, through the valley, and up the hill. They may have been singing one of the fifteen songs of ascents or degrees, or they may have been singing one of the Zion hymns scattered throughout the Psalms (Pss. 46; 48; 76; 84; 87; 122), which speak of Zion as the city of God,[10] the place of residence for the God of Israel. The focal point of the city is the temple. The focal point of the temple is the holy of holies. The focal point of the holy of holies is the ark, symbolizing the glory and presence of God.

Coming into God's presence was a journey. Worshipers came from all over the then-known world (Acts 2), making the journey through many paths, trails, and roads. They came into God's presence to worship God, and they made a *journey* to get there. Worship was the culmination of that journey—often a journey with baggage and with many mixed emotions. Some came with rejoicing. Some came with thanksgiving. Some came with burdens. Some came to repent. Some came with tears. But they came!

We strain to make worship a journey into the presence of God. It is a programmatic movement from celebration to revelation and adoration. Although the term *megachurch* has been overused (and often abused), a church of even several hundred—and certainly any that approach one thousand—will be hard-pressed to find a worship model in the New Testament.

First-century worshipers transitioned from a temple-based setting to much more intimate gatherings, meeting from house to house (Acts 2:46; 5:42; Rom. 16:5; Col. 4:15). Both by circumstance and choice, the New Testament pattern of worship seems to be that worshipers met most often in homes and in small gatherings (Acts 2:46). Although the principles of Christ-centered worship obviously prevailed, the pragmatism of doing worship with a larger congregation finds minimal assistance and few examples in the New Testament. However, there is much to learn and follow when we look at the Old Testament pattern of worship. There we see the paradigm of worship as a journey, and there we find much help in serving the people of God and the corporate worship of our Lord.

The goal of the pastor or worship leader must be to lead the people of God into the presence of God. There must be an atmosphere created by music and message, by attitude and actions that accentuate acceptance and welcome to pilgrims. It must be an atmosphere of joy an celebration that offers help and healing for the baggage of pain and grief brought on the journey, but that allows worshipers to check their baggage at the foot of the throne of a loving God, who not only welcomes them but was with them even during the gathering of the weights and burdens acquired on the journey.

The pragmatism of worship must acknowledge and affirm the variety of mind-sets with which the people present themselves before God. Does the worship leader try to get the worshipers' minds and eyes off the problems and negative baggage brought into the worship setting? Or does the leader try to get their eyes and minds on God? The answer is yes! The answer is no! Let me explain.

One of the tragedies of the last twenty-five or thirty years has been the proliferation of exegetical and hermeneutical extremism, particularly in the area of extreme doctrines of confession and faith, which often results in an unrealistic escape and/or denial of the reality of existential struggles, problems, and challenges. My colleague Robert Johnston has cautioned against this avoidance (Abernethy: chapter 6). The camp that declares it a negative confession to acknowledge one's struggles puts worshipers in a paradoxical dilemma: If they come to the Lord and ignore the reality of their pain or problems, they are not, and cannot, worship God in truth (John 4:24), and therefore their worship is unacceptable. Yet if they come before the Lord, bare their souls, and acknowledge and name their problems before the Lord, they are in some way making a negative confession.

Another side of this dilemma is one that few pastors and worship leaders want to recognize or wrestle with. Although many would agree that the goal is to refocus the attention of the worshipers, little spiritual value is achieved if the attention is taken off the problems and put solely on the pastor or leader. In a star-struck, celebrity-celebrated society where charismatic characters abound in the pulpit, consideration must be given to the question "Where is the attention of the people? On the living God, or on the preacher/pastor/leader?" Too often we forget the model and message of John the Baptist, who said, "He must increase, but I must decrease" (John 3:30). That is often easier said than done. The people come to hear a man or woman who they look up to, hopefully respect, and whose office they honor. It is the responsibility and challenge of the pastor and/or worship leader to point them to the Lord. The man or woman of God leading the people must walk in the reality of being taken from among the people (Exod. 28:1). The pastor struggles with the same challenges as the people from among whom he or she was taken.

One of the most dangerous like-passions is an expandable ego. If the pastor allows the people to focus on him or her, the people will do so! If the ego and character of the leader are so vulnerable or needy that the pastor feeds on the attention, power, and influence he or she has over the congregation, God will be moved farther and farther into the background. The next challenge: revelation. . .

Revelation

The journey into the presence of God anticipates a revelation of God. The question to the prophet, "Is there any word from the LORD?" (Jer. 37:17), and the request to the disciples, "Sir, we wish to see Jesus" (John 12:21), converge in the revelation of the presence of God. The Magi came to Bethlehem for one purpose: to see Jesus in order to worship him (Matt. 2:1–2).

I recall the story of a young preacher who had been at his small congregation for only a short time. Each Sunday he noticed, over in a corner, an old mother of the church who would shout and praise God. In the tradition of the African American church, she would unashamedly and unapologetically lift her voice in praise and shouts of "Thank you, Jesus! Thank you, Lord. Hallelujah."

The young preacher was fascinated by the elderly lady's exuberant praise. He finally approached her one Sunday following the service and said, "Mother, I notice you have a shout every Sunday. How is it that you can come here each week and no matter what's happening, you shout and praise God? When the choir sings well, you shout. When I preach, you shout. But sometimes the choir doesn't do so well—yet you still shout. And there are some Sundays when I've had a hard week and didn't really get to study like I would have liked to, and I didn't really do so well when I preached. But I notice, you still shout. Mother, tell me, how is it that you can shout and praise God every single Sunday?"

The old mother slowly lifted her eye to look at the much-taller young preacher and said,

> Well, son, mother has been on the road for a long time. And when I come in here, I come with one thing on my mind. I come to see Jesus. And when I see Jesus, I think about the goodness of the Lord and all he has done for me, I can't help but shout. And when the choir is singing under the anointing, I look at the choir and I see Jesus. And when I see Jesus, I think about the goodness of the Lord and I can't help but shout. And when the power of the Lord is on you when you preach, I look at you and I see Jesus, and I think about the goodness of the Lord and I can't help but shout. But when I come in here and the choir is singing a little off, and they forget the words and sing off key, and when I look at you and you ain't got no anointing, I look *around* the choir and I look *around* you and I still see Jesus. And when I see Jesus and I think about the goodness of the Lord and all he has done for me, I can't help but shout because I came to see Jesus!

The journey of worship should always culminate with the revelation of the presence of the living God. It is there in God's presence that God speaks and heals and saves and delivers. It is there that the heavy baggage of burdens is lifted. Every element of the service must have the motive of moving the people of God into the presence of God.

Another word needs to be said about the atmosphere of worship. As stated earlier, the focus and object of worship should be our almighty God. The psalmist says, "Exalt ye the LORD our God, and worship at his footstool; for he is holy" (Ps. 99:5 KJV). Jesus exhorted the woman at the well with the declaration that would change her life. In essence, Jesus told her that God was on a search. God is seeking worshipers. More particularly, God is seeking worshipers who will worship the Father "in spirit and truth" (John 4:23–24). "God wants worshipers first," A. W. Tozer wrote. "Jesus did not redeem us to make us workers; he redeemed us to make us worshipers. And then, out of the blazing worship of our hearts springs our work."[11] However, one of the ongoing challenges of the worship leader is to distinguish between an atmosphere of worship and an atmosphere of entertainment.

Almost half a century ago, Tozer gazed down the corridors of time in anticipation of the trappings of the then-future church. He said, "Ever since the New Testament writers used 'play actors' for the word that is translated hypocrites, there has been a tension between every form of drama and the Christ message. Through the centuries the struggle has been ongoing between the Christian church and the passions of weaker believers for pageants and spectacles."[12]

There are some undeniable contextual similarities. The entertainment stage is similar to the raised pulpit. In both settings there are lights, and in many there are cameras. The well-scripted show of the entertainment industry is not very far from the structured liturgical format of some high church traditions and even some predictable morning bulletins of the evangelical persuasion. The pastor takes "center stage" at the pulpit (or off-center, in some mainline churches), much as the "star" of the show moves to his mark and light on the stage of a play. Even in sanctuaries of only a few hundred congregants, large video screens cover walls to enhance and enlarge the religious activities of the eleven o'clock production/show/service. Tozer scorns all of this and would say such integration of these worldly devices verifies his observation that "entertainment is a symptom" and it is "the cause of a very serious breakdown in modern evangelicalism." Tozer goes on to say, "We now demand glamour and fast flowing dramatic action. A generation of Christians, reared among push buttons and automatic machines, is impatient of slower and less direct methods of reaching their goals. We have been trying to apply machine-age methods to our relations with God."[13] He saw it as a symptom of the spiritual anemia of such a time as this.

By contrast, I suggest that a so-called atmosphere of entertainment is both a positive accommodation and practical utilization of the technology of this age. Many ecclesiastical techies would say that the devil does not have a corner on such technology and that our God deserves the best available means of presenting the kingdom to a dark but information-driven, visually oriented culture. To some, it is part of a commitment to excellence. One can argue that such incorporation of the dramatic is an extension both of Paul and Malcolm X. Paul said it spiritually, Malcolm pragmatically. Paul's evangelistic motive broke through when he said, "To the weak became I as weak, that I might gain the weak: I am made all things to all men, that I might by all means save some" (1 Cor. 9:22 KJV). If applied to the freedom of the proclamation of the gospel, the justice in sharing it with those walking in darkness, and the equality of having the opportunity to stand toe to toe with the competing elements of our contemporary culture—Malcolm would say, "Our objective is complete freedom, justice, and equality by any means necessary."[14] What would appear to Tozer as carnal religious entertainment is in fact preaching the gospel to the whole world (this present world) by any means necessary.

Although the idea of worship being entertainment carries an unattractive innuendo, the introduction and affirmation of drama to ministry and worship as a dramatic presentation is not only more palatable but also has biblical precedence in Paul's letter to the Corinthians. Todd Farley describes the power of dramatic presentation more extensively (Abernethy: chapter 3). Although it is certainly not a universal call to start a service with "lights, camera, action," Paul does give a unique description of true ministry: "For I think that God has displayed us, the apostles, last, as men condemned to death; for we have been made a spectacle to the world, both to angels and to men" (1 Cor. 4:9 NKJV).

Paul says that we are a "spectacle" to the world. The word he uses is *theatron,* from which we get our word *theater;* it speaks of a spectacle or play[15] and gives vision into the stage production dynamic of Rome's Colosseum, where saints were sentenced to die on the stage, humiliated before the crowd. The sense of this is captured in Eugene Peterson's refreshing contemporary rendering of this verse: "It seems to me that God has put us who bear his Message on stage in a theater in which no one wants to buy a ticket" (Message). Coupled with the prophetic utterance of the psalmist, the dramatic dimension of the gospel becomes more of a possibility. God wants to put his glory on display in the world (Ps. 72:19). The constant challenge of the worship leader is to remember that the leader's function is to display the glory of God before the world by allowing the Holy Spirit to direct the holy production, with Jesus Christ as the star and God the Father as the producer, who has honored us by allowing us to be part of the supporting cast following the script of his Word.

The goal of worship is the glory of God. Although God desires to display his glory on the stage of the world (Ps. 72:19), it is also the glory of God that is released and revealed in the immediate context of the local church worship. The sincere seeker comes to the worship experience with the heart and desire of Moses desiring to see the glory of God (Exod. 33:18).

Participation

Worship involves a vertical fellowship between God and the worshiper, and a horizontal fellowship between worshipers. Worship is not a spectator sport. Worship is first and foremost a verb, an action. It is motivated by a desire to honor another. The Bible includes a wide range of physical movement and expression in its images of worship, such as bowing down, lifting hands, clapping hands, dancing, processions, and singing.[16] It involves both the presentation and the participation of the worshiper.

Worship that is truly "in spirit" (John 4:24) is worship in the power, authority, and control of the Spirit. It is allowing the Spirit of God to be in charge. Our primary participation in worship should be submission to the presence, direction, and control of the Spirit of God in the worship assembly. An anonymous sage has well and sadly said, "If the Holy Spirit were not present on Sunday mornings, most churches would not miss Him."

The corresponding dimension of interaction with the Holy Spirit in worship is interaction between the worshipers themselves. Paul speaks of over twenty-seven "one anothers." These are mandates that exhort interactive ministry between believers as demonstration of the dependency dynamic of the body of Christ. One such "one another" from James is the command "Pray for one another" (5:16).

I believe that at least two major elements of biblical worship are missing in contemporary worship. One is spontaneous flexibility; the other is corporate prayer. I am gripped by the dramatic scene at the dedication of the temple. This house of worship had been constructed in every detail according to the blueprint given by God (1 Chron. 28:11–21; 2 Chron. 3–4). The stage was set for the great dedication service of worship. And then it happened! As the choir sang, as the musicians played, as the instruments were blasting, as the people were praising and worshiping the God of their salvation—the glory of God filled the place of worship. The glory cloud of the presence of God filled the room to such an extent that "the priests could not continue ministering because of the cloud; for the glory of the LORD filled the house of God" (2 Chron. 5:13–14 NKJV).

At Faithful Central Bible Church, we have a worship meeting every Sunday morning before the service. It is an update and time for final instructions for the service that has been developing all week. Praise team, choir, offering, announcements, invitation to discipleship, guests, special ministries such as dancers or children's ministry, special periodic additions such as baptism or communion—are all itemized and put in a sequential order and time line. We then pray and move into the service. However, we have learned that whatever we have decided in that meeting must be written down in *pencil.* Then we leave, allowing (and most often expecting) the Holy Spirit to edit at will.

Some of the most powerful experiences of the glory cloud have been when we extended the invitation to accept Christ at the top of the service just after (or even in the middle of) the praise team's ministry. We have had many unplanned and unscheduled altar calls prompted by the Holy Spirit as he highlighted some point in the message, or commented on a particular lyric or passage of scripture. When the cloud moves, we try to be ready to move as God leads.

This past Father's Day was supposed to have been a rather short message (so I could make it to the family dinner planned by my children). However, in an unexpected revelation of the Holy Spirit on the point of the message where I emphasized men growing up without the blessing of a father, the cloud filled the room! I never finished my well planned, diligently prepared, and prayed-over Father's Day message. The congregation ended up praying for over a hundred men who came to the altar to receive prayer. I laid hands on every one who came and prayed for him as the father of the house and gave him the father blessing—something these men had never had. We could not have planned for the service to flow that way. We simply yielded to the editing of the script by the director, the Holy Spirit.

The final missing—or at best, least emphasized—element of worship is corporate prayer. By the grace of God, I spend a lot of my time traveling on and off airplanes. I have learned that these frequent absences from the home base of the ministry the Lord has given me are often not only ministerial but also therapeutic. Some of my most intimate moments with God have been in the middle of the night during a long flight, when seemingly the pilot and I are the only ones awake. These are moments of prayer and meditation, and often revelation.

Recently I was convinced and convicted of an alarming truth: the weakest area of our church's ministry is prayer! Prayer is the area most neglected, minimized, de-emphasized, and *especially*, least practiced. The only consolation, carnal though it may be, to such a revelation is that my church is not alone. I believe prayer is the missing ingredient in the worship of most twenty-first century churches. In fact, the dedicatory prayer in 2 Chronicles 6 is listed in *The New Study Open Bible* as "The Sermon of Solomon—1 Kings 8:12–21," but verse 12 is highlighted as "The Prayer of Solomon," indicating that part of the sermon was in fact a prayer.[17] It is very clear from scripture that at the dedication of the temple, when the glory cloud of the presence of God affirmed and blessed that holy place, Solomon dedicated it as a house of prayer.

Careful examination of the gatherings of the New Testament church reveal not only that the Holy Spirit knit them together in the spiritual bond of *koinonia* but also that corporate prayer was a prominent part of their agenda. The life of the church was a life of worship, and the life of worship was a life of prayer. If you follow the life of believers in the first church, you discover that prayer was not their last resort but their first response. The church was a church under persecution. Leaders such as Peter and John were detained, intimidated, arrested, beaten, and killed by the sword and by stoning. There was sin from within and false doctrinal attacks from without. However, through it all they remained a church of prayer.

When the Lord convicted me of my dereliction in the ministry of prayer, I was drawn to, and have been challenged by, Acts 4:31, wherein the church responded to persecution with a corporate prayer meeting. When they prayed by raising their voices to God in unity, acknowledging God's sovereignty and faithfulness in the past, and making a plea for protection and the favor and power to declare the gospel with boldness, God moved! In a unique manifestation similar to that at the dedication of the temple and the tabernacle, God responded in a marvelous and miraculous way: "And when they had prayed, the place where they were assembled together was shaken; and they were all filled with the Holy Spirit, and they spoke the word of God with boldness" (NKJV). God again showed up with a unique manifestation of his glory, approval, and affirmation. The glory of the Lord again filled the place—in fact, the glory of the Lord *shook* the place!

We are trying to incorporate deliberate, focused prayer times into all of our worship experiences. We have prayed for fathers, for forgiveness, for marriages, for loved ones serving in the armed forces, for favor in careers and jobs, for relationships, for financial favor, and for wisdom and discernment. We are trying to reestablish God's house as a house of prayer. It is much easier to get people to talk about prayer, read about prayer, and even study about prayer—yet, never pray! I can go over several sermon series that I have preached in the past that displayed exhaustive exegetical and hermeneutical disciplines; and yet as I look back on them, these series of messages about prayer *never led to prayer!* We never prayed more. We had tapes, notes, and sermons on prayer, but we were not praying. I pray that now the Lord would look at our house and see a house of prayer.

God is searching for worshipers. My prayer for you is that you will become the object of God's search. I pray that you will become a worshiper. If you are a ministry leader, I pray that above all you are developing and growing and leading your ministry into the life-changing, consistent dynamic of *worship*. Our pedagogy (sermonic, catechistic, formal, informal) should be aggressively expanded to include the presentation of worship as a lifestyle. The academic podium of the seminary and the ecclesiastical pulpit of the local church are challenged to produce scholars and servants whose lives are ordered around the practical, participatory search of the Father for worshipers. Worshipers whose lives are transformed by the power of the living God are empowered to transform neighborhoods and communities, cities and culture.

I pray that you would become hungry for God, thirsty for God, desperate for God. He is seeking worshipers. I pray you will seek him and allow him to find you as you worship him in spirit and in truth.

Notes

1. Buddy Owens, gen. ed., *The NIV Worship Bible* (Grand Rapids: Zondervan, 2000), vi.
2. Robert E. Webber, *Worship Is a Verb* (Nashville: Abbott Martyn, 1992), 2.
3. David Ritz, *Messengers: Portraits of African American Ministers, Evangelists, Gospel Singers, and Other Messengers of the Word* (New York: Doubleday, 2006), 199.
4. *Biblesoft's New Exhaustive Strong's Numbers and Concordance with Expanded Greek-Hebrew Dictionary* (Seattle: Biblesoft and International Bible Translators, 1994, 2003).
5. Kenneth S. Wuest, *Wuest's Word Studies from the Greek New Testament* (1940–55; Grand Rapids: Eerdmans, 1968–73).
6. Spiros Zodhiates, *The Hebrew–Greek Key Study Bible* (Chattanooga, TN: AMG Publishers, 1984), 1732.
7. Dallas Willard, *Renovation of the Heart: Putting on the Character of Christ* (Colorado Springs: NavPress, 2002), 58.

8. Bill Hull, *The Disciple-Making Church* (Old Tappan, NJ: Revell, 1990), 73.
9. Susan E. Gillingham, *The Poems and Psalms of the Hebrew Bible* (Oxford: Oxford University Press, 1994), 212.
10. Ibid.
11. A. W. Tozer, *Tozer on Worship and Entertainment*, compiled by James L. Snyder (Mumbai, India: GLS, 2001), 19.
12. Ibid., viii.
13. Ibid., 100.
14. From the Web site Malcolm-X.org.
15. Fritz Rienecker and Cleon Rogers, *Linguistic Key to the Greek New Testament* (Grand Rapids: Regency Reference Library, Zondervan, 1976), 397.
16. Leland Ryken et al., eds., *Dictionary of Biblical Imagery* (Downers Grove: InterVarsity, 1998).
17. *The New Study Open Bible Study Edition* (Nashville: Nelson, 1990), 507.

11
"I'm Going to Live the Life I Sing about in My Song"

Michael Joseph Brown

I. A Vision of Ministry

I could rant against the perceived excesses or deficiencies of contemporary music in the African American religious community, but since others have already sought to do this, I shall largely refrain and trust that their criticisms have been well received. I am not a musicologist, nor am I attempting to "play" one in this essay. What I am attempting to provide, however, is some meager input and reflection from a participant-observer on the experience of music and worship in the contemporary black church. I chose the title for this essay from a song [composed by Thomas A. Dorsey] made famous by Mahalia Jackson. I did so because it struck me that what the song pointed to resonated deeply with my own experience and expectation of worship in the African American church. Music, as a cultural expression, should deepen and provide greater texture to our experience of the world. Music, as an artistic expression, should provide us with insights we might not normally come across—insights that make us more complex and, arguably, better human beings.

I am not suggesting that there is or should be some simplistic direct relationship between what we sing in church and the lives we live outside the confines of the sanctuary. Clearly, language, especially in its artistic expression, can never quite capture the totality of our yearnings as beings desiring a deeper relationship with our Creator. And yet, such poetic expressions may be better vehicles for our desires than any supposedly straightforward theological tome. In other words, through expressions like sacred music we may better express the complexity of our theological concepts than the most straightforward line in a creed or textbook. It is reported that the influential twentieth-century theologian, Karl Barth, was once asked what he considered to be the most profound theological expression ever made. He responded, "Jesus loves me! This I know, for the Bible tells me so." What sacred music does for us is cast visions and fashion metaphors whose depth can never be exhausted through analytical investigation. As Gerald Janzen ably noted, "we experience more than we know, and we know more than we can think; and we think more than we can say; and language therefore lags behind the intuitions of immediate experience."[1]

In the Sermon on the Mount, Jesus says, "Beware of practicing your piety before others in order to be seen by them; for then you have no reward from your Father in heaven" (Matthew 6:1 NRSV). What Jesus says here supports what I believe to be an important standard by which a ministry of music should be judged. Jesus tells his disciples that they must "beware" of how they practice their faith. Actually, the Greek word here can also be translated as "be very careful" or "be on your guard." Thus, an alternate translation would be, "Be on guard concerning your righteousness." As the construction implies, there is a potential danger present when we do things like give money, fast, and pray (the actual practices discussed in Matthew 6). What Jesus is saying, then, is that special attention is needed when we do these things, because if we do them without concern for their righteousness, then we do them illegitimately. When we approach the things of God, Jesus says, we must be careful that the deep spiritual dimension of the practice not be lost in the process.

Many people, even some biblical scholars, misunderstand what Jesus means here because they seem to forget that what he is expressing is a Jewish understanding of how we practice our faith. Almsgiving, fasting, and prayer are expressions of our worship of God. Unfortunately, far too many Christians see something like almsgiving as a moral issue, somewhat removed from what we consider to be worship. In truth, I think the same is true when it comes to the worship of God through song. We do not take the act to be as serious as it really is. So, what is the danger present when we consider sacred music in light of our worship of God?

The danger has to do with the fact that acts of worship, like singing, are matters of performance. They have to be done by someone. They take place before an audience. As Jesus explains it, there are two possible audiences available: (1) human beings or (2) God. What is clear from Jesus' statement is that any performance before a human audience is potentially dangerous—"before others in order to be seen by them." To avoid this danger, Jesus instructs us not to perform them before others. This is difficult, of course, when it comes to the function of sacred music. If anything, singing is a matter of "doing" or "performing," so doing this before other human beings is almost always "for the purpose of being seen by them." The distinction Jesus wants to invoke is that between "theater" and "worship." The idea of confining the worship of God through song to God alone is impossible to do in a worship environment. The point in the Sermon on the Mount is not really whether other human beings will be present when we perform these acts, but whether the intention of the performer is to be seen by those present or by God.

If the intention of our singing is to be seen by the human audience, then the rules and expectations of the theater apply; that is, impressive scenery, individuals playing scripted parts, applause, emotional outbursts, and so on. Worship can degenerate into a mere public spectacle. By contrast, if the intended audience is God, then such considerations play only a secondary role. I have walked out of many worship services where I was uncertain about whether I had been in worship or at a Broadway show. This is precisely the point behind Jesus' statement: there is a thin line between worship and theater, and we must be careful to avoid crossing it.

When we worship, we glorify God and demonstrate our allegiance to God's vision for the world. Worship is a way of acknowledging the worthiness of God and God's vision for the world. This understanding, I think, brings us closer to what Jesus says in the Sermon and the standards by which I believe we should judge a ministry of sacred music. The significance resides in the purpose for which the task is undertaken. Singing is not just a performance. It is recognizing and endorsing God's vision for the world. Through our singing we paint a picture of what the world can be, not just a vision of what we want and do not want in our immediate circumstances. It is a world where God's will would be done. This is aptly illustrated in the hymn "How Great the Mystery of Faith," which says:

> The best that we can do and say,
> the utmost care of skill and art,
> are sweepers of the Spirit's way
> to reach the depths of every heart.

—*Brian Wren*
© 1989 Hope Publishing Company, Carol Stream, IL 60188

In short, through our ministry of music we worship God by recognizing and committing ourselves to God's vision of what life on earth can be.

Through our singing we also demonstrate that something is wrong with the world. God's vision for our lives and the lives of others has not been realized, and so we cast visions through song as a way of transforming the world into what God wants it to be. In short, it is fully an act of worship. Through our ministry of sacred music we participate in creating a world where God's love and will reign. We should judge our music ministry not only by what it does on Sunday mornings in service, but also in the way it commits us to the transformation of the earth into the Kingdom of God.

II. Singing About A New Jerusalem: Claiming the Prophetic Voice

It is difficult for a biblical scholar like myself to comment with any authority on the trends in African American sacred music. Certainly a shift of some sort has occurred. This may be coincident with a change in the social standing of many African Americans. It is probably premature to say that African Americans as a whole are wealthier, better-educated, savvier consumers, etc. However, this is certainly true for some. Could this perceptible shift in African American sacred music be the result of targeting an audience that is more affluent? Could the concerns of past generations of African American mothers and fathers no longer apply to this emerging group? Yes and no. While some concerns are not as central to the church-going African American community, others remain. To put it another way, while the spiritual that says, "I got shoes. You got shoes. All of God's children got shoes" or Shirley Caesar's assurance that "He's working it out for you" may be a less central concern for those with greater access to capital and credit, others, like the hymn which guarantees "we will understand it better by and by," still resonate in a community that struggles with ongoing issues of theodicy and ambiguity.

Many have pointed out that early African American sacred music was permeated with a prophetic consciousness. For example, Obery Hendricks underscores the central sensibilities of this music as "the prophetic functions of naming the oppressive reality and exhorting resistance to it, and the eschatological expectation of justice in this world."[2] A fundamental change in this early consciousness came at the beginning of the last century with the move from a largely agrarian African American population to a largely urban and industrial one. In many respects, this shift from Mississippi to Chicago was appropriate to Christianity, which was more of an urban movement than an agrarian one. The early church flourished not in the fields of villages like Nazareth but in the dense urban environments of Corinth, Ephesus, Alexandria, Carthage, and Rome. In fact, one of the most powerful symbols of the Christian vision of a transformed world was a city (Greek *polis*)—the New Jerusalem (Revelation 21:2).

Some have argued for a distinct difference between prophetic critique and an apocalyptic worldview, but the distinction may not be as clear as we might think. The central motivating question for apocalyptic thought appears to be: is God faithful? It is an effort to make theological sense of a world that does not correspond to the promises God made to bless the faithful (e.g., Deuteronomy 28:1–4) and through them, the world (e.g., Genesis 12:1–3; Isaiah 42:1–4). The dissonance between the vision and reality then prompts a crisis. How can the God we worship be a God worthy of worship, when those faithful to God find themselves in such oppressive circumstances? As Eugene Boring once wrote, "It was the honor and integrity of God that was at stake, not just human selfish longing for golden streets and pearly gates" that gave rise to apocalyptic thought and literature.[3]

By contrast, the central motivating question for prophetic thought is not the faithfulness of God, but the faithfulness of human beings. Along with "thus says the Lord," the central characteristic of prophetic speech is the contingent construction of "if. . . then." Speaking on behalf of God, the prophet points to something gone wrong with the world, something that disturbs God and initiates God's response. Humans are given the option to transform their practices before final divine judgment is unleashed. Although in many respects these perspectives are intimately related, the question of God's faithfulness is not a central concern of prophetic critique.

These two perspectives—the prophetic and the apocalyptic—are merged in Revelation. The author does not call himself a prophet, but he claims this book to be a prophecy (Revelation 1:3; 19:20; 22:7, 10, 18–19). The entire document is understood as the address of the risen Lord through his spokesman John. Although this work is saturated with apocalyptic images and content, it is probably safe to say that it is a fine example of early Christian prophecy. Thus, in truth, "prophetic" and "apocalyptic" are not alternatives when it comes to understanding Revelation, but a merged form of utterance that poses two questions not often put together in biblical literature.

This is where I would disagree with the analysis of the change in consciousness Hendricks advances. He says, "At its core, then, gospel music embodies the classic apocalyptic feeling of powerlessness to forestall the oppressive forces of this world which, in turn, is accompanied by a sense of resignation to ongoing social misery at the hands of oppressors until the apocalyptic 'day of the Lord.'"[4] The New Jerusalem, as envisioned in Revelation, is not something otherworldly but "this-worldly." The New Jerusalem comes down from heaven, we do not ascend to it (see Revelation 21:2).

The development of African American sacred music from spirituals to gospel may reflect a shift in venue from farm to factory, but the introduction of more apocalyptic elements into this musical expression did not, by necessity, mean that it had to lose its prophetic critique. Another way to frame the issue may be to say that, instead of simply naming the evil in this world for which human beings are responsible (the typical prophetic move), the development of gospel music highlights the disaffection experienced by African Americans who moved to the "promised land" and found no promise readily available. It is the introduction of the additional question "Is God faithful?" or more poignantly "Why, Lord?"

The rise of the soloist in gospel music may reflect the stark sense of individualism many felt in the teeming urban environments of Detroit, Cleveland, and Chicago. Instead of the creativity of community, the creativity of the gospel singer is found in the modernist sensibility of living a largely solitary and commodified existence even in the packed neighborhoods of the industrial North. This "solitary" turn is also reflected in the types of subjects addressed by these songs. While daily concerns were still paramount in many expressions of gospel music, their impact was clothed in a more subjective form. Personal testimony, personal crisis, and personal decision became the keystones of such artistic expression. Did this new expression of religious creativity express a profound sense of hopelessness? Maybe. Absolute resignation? No. Despite the abject conditions of an unrealized New Jerusalem, gospel music still spoke to a sense of hope in a transformed future. The central question is: what kind of transformed future does the singer or songwriter envision?

To the casual observer, like myself, it appears clear that there is little of the "prophetic" to be found in gospel music. There is a sense of something wrong in the world, but that wrong is not articulated explicitly as a critique of social systems that can and should be changed by active agents in the present. In fact, one may characterize the latest trend in gospel music to be one bordering on narcissism. Hope has been replaced by unabashed praise. Yet, is such praise really warranted given the continuing social, economic, and environmental problems that confront us? Such a question is taken up in the hymn "Woe to the Prophets." As this hymn proclaims:

> Woe to the prophets,
> who God's blood-bought people deceive,
> who teach them to trust in their idols of dust,
> and falsehood, not truth, to believe;
> who preach but for pay, and who lead men astray,
> and daily God's Spirit do grieve.
>
> —*Charles P. Jones, 1865–1949*

Still, hope as well as praise can be incorporated into prophetic critique, as they are in Revelation.

In Brian Blount's book *Can I Get a Witness?*—in a chapter aptly titled "The Rap against Rome"—he points out that the hymnic language of Revelation is filled with critique of the Roman social order. What is more interesting for this investigation, however, is that he identifies its analogue in African American culture as rap music rather than sacred music. He says, "Rap expresses its painful view of the world through traditional and historical images that are particularly meaningful for the audience it hopes to energize and that it intends to critique."[5] If energy and critique are the hallmarks of (at least some forms of) rap music, then it is possible to fashion metaphors in music that speak to the complexity of modern life with both comfort and challenge.

The worship of God through song is never just a matter of casting a vision of plenty for all. Essential to that vision must be the recognition that there is something wrong with the present state of affairs. If "we're marching to Zion," it is only because we presently do not find ourselves living in the "beautiful city of God." African American sacred music should be an ecstatic expression of the fullness of God's vision for the world. Still, this should be a carefully nuanced articulation that recognizes this vision to be an ideal toward which we work. In this sense, language—and specifically metaphor—serves an asymptotic function by luring us closer and closer to the vision without fully exhausting it or collapsing it into a caricature of itself. To accomplish this, we need both praise and critique.

III. Singing as a Conversation with God: Enriching the Tapestry of our Religious Experience

Life is not simply about problems. If we reduce life down to the challenges we face, whether internally or in the environment that surrounds us, then we overlook a large measure of what makes our lives liveable. Beauty, joy, happiness, sorrow, relatedness, solitude, love, and a host of other experiences repeatedly influence our lives from moment to moment. If we were to focus solely on those aspects of our experience that constitute specific, although repeated, instances of infelicity, then we overlook and fail to cultivate the richness of our overall journey in time. The ideal of human life, as well as that of civilization generally, is to experience as completely as possible the qualities of truth, beauty, creativity, adventure, and peace; at least according to Alfred North Whitehead.[6]

If we accept this understanding as true in the sense of our aim to conform appearance to reality, then much of our experience is lost if we focus on some experiences to the neglect (and sometimes denial) of others. Reclaiming these experiences means carrying on a larger conversation with each other and our Creator. Who cannot be affected deeply by the majesty of a hymn like "How Great Thou Art"? The "awesome wonder" expressed in this stirring musical expression inspires us to feel the grandeur of the universe we inhabit. Experiencing the tragic and the awesome wonder is what makes life a rewarding mystery; some would say that it is the very definition of beauty itself.[7] Yes, life is far too often plagued with tragedy, but it is also punctuated with experiences of joy, love, and awe.

My claim that sacred music should enrich the entire tapestry of our lives may sound to some as a contradiction of my previous assertion that African Americans should express a prophetic consciousness. I do not see them as contradictory but as complementary. In fact, such an approach would better reflect the range of material and perspectives we find in the biblical texts themselves. Joy sits alongside sorrow in our sacred text. In an interesting fashion, to say the least, they are often intertwined. Take, for example, Mary's hymnic outburst in Luke. She sings, "My soul magnifies the Lord, and my spirit rejoices in God my Savior" (Luke 1:46). This effusive expression of joy comes from a young maiden who has just found out that she is pregnant, though unmarried. This could hardly be conceived of as a moment of joy, especially in the period of the first century CE. Under normal circumstances, she could have been killed. Even in our own day, we rarely see the experience of unwed pregnancy as a reason for rejoicing, but more often as one for expressing our disappointment and pity. Of course, someone would respond that she has just found out that she is to be the mother of the Savior of the world. True. In my estimation, however, this does not cancel entirely a sense of dread that would have accompanied such a situation for a young woman living in a patriarchal society that often judged her value on the basis of her conformity to ideal virtues—one of which would be the maintenance of her sexual virtue. The rhetorical power of the Magnificat lies in the intertwining of a situation of tragedy and an expression of joy.

What gives the prophetic critique its power in many respects is that it casts a vision of a society that could be different. When the prophet articulates the "something" that is wrong with the world she does so by comparing it, even if implicitly, to an imagined world that would eradicate the "something" that is not an expression of the divine will. Again, rap music may be more helpful than contemporary gospel music in illustrating this idea. Tupac Shakur, for example, in his song "Unconditional Love," raps:

> How many caskets can we witness
> before we see it's hard to live

> life without God
> so we must ask forgiveness?[8]

This is a biting social critique. Its implication appears to be that violence, especially in its most tragic form, is emblematic of a society operating in opposition to the divine aim. Shakur's lyrics at once reveal ugly, brutal truths, and at the same time point us to pictures of a caring God. I believe it is still possible for sacred music to do the same. Take, for example, the hymn "Help Us Accept Each Other," which says:

> Teach us, O Lord, your lessons,
> as in our daily life
> we struggle to be human
> and search for hope and faith.
> Teach us to care for people,
> for all—not just for some;
> to love them as we find them,
> or as they may become.

—Fred Kaan
© 1975 Hope Publishing Company, Carol Stream, IL 60188

It at once recognizes the tragedy that pervades our world, but offers the possibility that such a situation can be redeemed.

Worship should be a far richer experience than a two-hour ego boost or a repeated recitation of a laundry list of unresolved problems. It, in fact, shapes us to be the human beings God sees in us. Along with its various components, worship is an ongoing practice of communication with God. It is sharing ourselves with our Creator and receiving into our lives what our Creator desires most for us. I say this because worship is more than simply expressing, "God, I want this," or, "Deliver me from that." When we worship, particularly in song, we are entering into a deeper relationship with the God who made us. This is what Abba Poemen, one of the desert fathers, meant when he said, "Teach your mouth to say what is in your heart."[9] As anyone who is in a long-term relationship knows, the relationship will not last long unless you find a way to explore all of those things that are in the depths of your heart. Simply telling God what we want—or praising God while neglecting concerns that are also God's concerns—is not fully participating in worship. Real worship is a dialogue, a two-way conversation between God and us, through proclamation, scripture reading, prayer, and song. As the hymn "God of Wisdom, Truth, and Beauty" proclaims:

> Grant us visions ever growing,
> breath of life, eternal strength,
> mystic spirit, moving, flowing,
> filling height and depth and length.

—Jane Parker Huber
© 1984, admin. Westminster John Knox Press

We worship because we desire to see and participate in the vision our Creator has for us and for the world. Of course, we will always have our own immediate requests and concerns. These we communicate to God in our worship as well. But this is not the end of it. Through worship we also listen attentively to God's voice as it tells us God's vision for our lives as individuals, as well as God's vision for the world we inhabit. Our experience of music in worship should assist us in seeing that vision in all of its complexity. The writer of Ephesians says, "I pray that you may have the power to comprehend, with all the saints, what is the breadth and length and height and depth, and to know the love of Christ that surpasses knowledge, so that you may be filled with all the fullness of God" (Ephesians 3:18–19). This, I believe, is what is meant by living the life we sing about, and what a creative and rich expression of sacred music can provide. Reflecting upon the collection of hymns in this volume, I believe deeply that it is still possible for such music to find its place among us, and to lure and challenge us to see the vision God still has for God's people.

Notes

1. Gerald Janzen, "The Old Testament in 'Process' Perspective: Proposal for a Way Forward in Biblical Theology," in *MAGNALIA DEI: The Mighty Acts of God. Essays on the Bible and Archaeology in Memory of G. Ernest Wright* (eds. Frank Moore Cross, Werner E. Lemke, and Patrick D. Miller Jr.; Garden City: Doubleday, 1976), 492.
2. Obery M. Hendricks Jr., "'I Am the Holy Dope Dealer': The Problem with Gospel Music Today," in *Readings in African American Church Music and Worship* (ed. James Abbington; Chicago: GIA, 2001), 564.
3. M. Eugene Boring, *Revelation*, (Louisville: Westminster John Knox, 1989) 40.
4. Hendricks, "I Am the Holy Dope Dealer," 576.
5. Brian K. Blount, *Can I Get a Witness? Reading Revelation through African American Culture* (Louisville: Westminster John Knox, 2005), 100.
6. See Alfred North Whitehead, *Adventures of Ideas* (New York: Free Press, 1933), 241–296.
7. Ibid., 252–264.
8. Quoted in Blount, *Can I Get a Witness?*, 113.
9. *The Sayings of the Desert Fathers: The Alphabetical Collection* (trans. Benedicta Ward; Kalamazoo: Cistercian, 1984), 189.

12

The Lyrical Theology of Charles Albert Tindley: Justice Come of Age

S T Kimbrough, Jr.

Charles Albert Tindley is considered to be one of the founders of urban black gospel music. His hymns appear in the hymn books of some mainline denominations[1] and his hymn "I'll Overcome Someday" is thought to be the basis for the famous song, "We Shall Overcome," of the civil-rights movement. With one exception, the songbook *Beams of Heaven: Hymns of Charles Albert Tindley* (2006),[2] the Methodist Episcopal Church, which he served, and its successor denominations (The Methodist Church and The United Methodist Church) have provided only token appreciation of his work. Without question the few Tindley hymns in surviving major hymn collections do not do justice to the full spectrum of the lyrical theology of this poet-pastor-theologian-musician.

In this chapter the author explores the breadth of major ideas in Tindley's lyrical theology expressed in his published hymns.[3]

Before addressing the theology of his hymns, however, it is important to set him in the historical context of the Delaware-Maryland-Pennsylvania region in which he grew up and served many years as a minister of the Methodist Episcopal Church. He was born to a former-slave father and a free mother in Berlin, Maryland, on July 7, 1851(?). In some of his own autobiographical comments he describes how he taught himself to read. Though he was born a free child, life was not that easy for African American children and their parents in the late nineteenth century, even in the so-called "free north." Many whites thought it best to keep African Americans illiterate.

After he married Daisy Henry, they moved to Philadelphia where Tindley hoped to find work. They located lodging in a house rented by a gentleman who was from an area of Maryland not far from where Tindley had lived. The house was on Redmon Street in the Negro/Italian ghetto of southeastern Philadelphia, where he found employment as a hod carrier.[4] He also became the janitor at John Wesley Methodist Episcopal Church, during which time he began to experience a call to ministry.

Primarily a self-educated man, Tindley completed correspondence courses of Boston University School of Theology, and pursued private tutoring in Greek and Hebrew in Philadelphia. In 1885 he was recommended for ordination in the Delaware Annual Conference of the Methodist Episcopal Church and was assigned to a parish in Cape May, NJ. In 1887 he was ordained deacon and became pastor of South Wilmington in Delaware. In 1889 he was ordained elder and appointed to Odessa, Delaware. After additional appointments in Pocomoke and Fairmont, Maryland, he returned to Wilmington to serve Ezion Methodist Episcopal Church. Then in 1900 he became Presiding Elder of the Wilmington District, a position he held until 1902 when he was assigned to East Calvary Methodist Episcopal Church (whose name would later be changed to Tindley Temple Methodist Episcopal Church) in Philadelphia where he would remain for thirty years, the most productive years of his hymn writing.

In order to understand much of the imagery and language of his hymns it is important to review some of the history of African Americans in Philadelphia and Pennsylvania, the constituency Tindley served, and the social context in which the ministries under his leadership emerged. Of equal importance are some remarks about the Delaware Annual Conference. It was created following the 1864 General Conference of the Methodist Episcopal Church, which authorized the organization of Negro Annual Conferences. The Delaware Annual Conference covered a broad geographical area with thirty-four African American churches in New York City, New Jersey, Philadelphia, Chester, Delaware, and the Eastern Shore areas of Maryland and Virginia. Of course, along side these churches there were many "Anglo" Methodist Episcopal Churches.

As one reviews Tindley's life, ministry, and literature, one sees how they reflect primary emphases of the Delaware Annual Conference: theological education, religious education of congregations, spiritual growth, stalwart character of clergy and parishioners, faithful stewardship, and an understanding and a realization of the social implications of the gospel as personified in Christ. Nevertheless, the members of the Delaware Annual Conference did not enjoy the privileges of the Anglo clergy of the Methodist Episcopal Church. Many were forced to live at a poverty level with inadequate salaries, little or no medical coverage, and no general pension plan. Parsonages, if they existed, often had no plumbing. Tindley and the fellow members of the Delaware Annual Conference understood the human condition from a different perspective than Anglo clergy, for they recognized that the church itself practiced segregation, racism, oppression, discrimination, and did not live by God's law of justice.

Into what kind of a world did Tindley and his new wife come in the 1880s? The Civil War had ended just a few short years before. From 1820 onward there was no more slavery in Philadelphia, and African Americans flocked to the city. At that time the city's population was over 100,000 and at least 12,000 were free African Americans. However, those who came from the south had experience mainly in farm labor and were not equipped or trained for the new jobs of an industrial economy. Therefore, it is not surprising that poverty increased rapidly among them. White opposition over the competition for jobs grew steadily and there were mob attacks on many African American homes in the 1840s.

Pennsylvania struggled with the civil rights of African Americans. In 1790 freemen (black and white) received the right to vote under the state constitution, but in 1838 a new state constitution took away that right and awarded it only to "white freemen." By the time Tindley was nineteen years old (1870) the Fifteenth Amendment of the U.S. Constitution was passed. It prohibited any government in the United States from denying a citizen the right to vote based on one's "race, color, or previous condition of servitude." The amendment received ratification on February 3, 1870. Nevertheless, tensions mounted, and during an election of 1871, Octavius Catto, a leading Philadelphia African American, was murdered.

During the years of Tindley's ministry at East Calvary Methodist Episcopal Church there were numerous acts of violence against African Americans in Philadelphia and its environs. In 1911 there occurred the horrific lynching of Zachariah Walker of Coatesville, PA, which precipitated the NAACP's launching of a nationwide protest against lynching.

Though thousands of African Americans migrated to Philadelphia toward the end of the nineteenth century and early twentieth century with the hope of a new beginning, they faced racial discrimination in many facets of society, particularly in education, employment, and housing. Nevertheless, this served as an impetus for the establishment of African American initiated businesses and institutions that provided much-needed infrastructure for the community. Religious institutions played a significant role in this development, as well as the emergence of fraternal and beneficent organizations and activities in the arts and sports.

During the years (1902–1932) of Tindley's ministry at East Calvary Methodist Episcopal Church he was actively engaged in a variety of social outreach ministries. The congregation served thousands of warm meals to Philadelphia residents who were poor and often unemployed. He advocated for financing options to enable African Americans to make loans and purchase their own homes. He also spent many hours on the streets in the neighborhood of the church and sought to minister to the souls and bodies of the poor and needy.

In the early years of Tindley's ministry in Philadelphia many of the members of his congregation were domestic servants and lived in the homes of their employers or in close proximity to them. Therefore, there was fraternization between African Americans and whites, though clearly differentiated by social status. This kind of interaction was very distinct from residential segregation that would come later.

There was much charitable work in Philadelphia for the depressed African Americans, but in many ways this simply reinforced the prejudices of whites. As W. E. B. Du Bois maintained in his ground breaking sociological study *The Philadelphia Negro*, published just three years before Tindley returned to Philadelphia to become the minister of East Calvary Methodist Episcopal Church: "for them there is succor and sympathy; for them Philadelphians are thinking and planning; but for the educated and industrious young colored man who wants work and not platitudes, wages and not alms, just rewards and not sermons—for such colored men Philadelphia apparently has no use."[5] Tindley definitely wanted to see this situation changed.

African American veterans returning from World War I had grave difficulties finding employment and the depression years imposed extreme hardships on the African American population. The veterans and hosts of migrants would find friendship, food, clothing, and even shelter, when Tindley's congregation decided to provide assistance and sleeping facilities for the needy and homeless. However, the steady stream of African American migration greatly threatened the white community. The result was segregation in the schools, eating establishments, theaters and other entertainment centers. Even attendance at some white churches by African Americans diminished, for they felt unwanted.[6]

Tindley's ministry in Philadelphia was conducted against a background of a city that harbored one of the first expressions of slave trade in the United States. Nevertheless, in this city there were important early benchmarks of civil rights: the first organization for the abolition of slavery, the first legislative enactments for the abolition of slavery, the first attempt at African American education, and the first African American convention.

Even so, in the introduction to the 1967 edition of *The Philadelphia Negro*, E. Digby Baltzell penned a paragraph that is important for understanding the Philadelphia in which Tindley lived toward the end of his life and ministry.

> As of the 1930s, for instance, one rarely saw a Negro in the major downtown department and clothing stores, in banks, moving-picture houses, theaters, or other public places. No major department store or bank had Negroes in white-collar positions dealing directly with the public. No Negro lawyer could obtain office space in the center city business district. Negroes sat in the balconies of the big movie palaces. Hotels and restaurants were strictly segregated. Most of these strict taboos came in during and immediately after World War I.[7]

One wonders whether Tindley studied W. E. B. Du Bois' *The Philadelphia Negro,* for in some ways his approach to the improvement of African Americans individually and collectively bears some similarities to Du Bois who wrote: "there is far mightier influence to mold and make the citizen, and that is the social atmosphere which surrounds him; first his daily companionship, the thoughts and whims of his class; then his recreation and amusements; finally the surrounding world of American civilization."[8]

In his vision for the African Americans, as individuals and as a community, Tindley adhered to a similar view that the forces of one's socialization mold character and personality. To Du Bois' vision Tindley, of course, added the importance of the gospel message and the Christian community in molding the person. Drake and Cayton in *Black Metropolis* included the church in their list of social forces that shape personality: the "emphasis upon the social relations—in family, clique, church, voluntary associations, school, and job as the decisive elements in personality formation is generally accepted."[9] As did Du Bois, Tindley believed strongly that education was a key element in this process.

It is important to add that Tindley reached out to the growing middle-class of African Americans and was respected far beyond the reaches of his own community. The well known Philadelphia entrepreneur and philanthropist John Wannamaker supported some aspects of his ministry and the owner of Horn and Hardart restaurants also supplied food for meals served at the church for the poor.

Even with the increasing intensity of segregation in Philadelphia and throughout Pennsylvania, The East Calvary Methodist Episcopal Church became the leading congregation of the annual conference and Tindley was elected six times a delegate to the General Conference of the Methodist Episcopal Church and twice was nominated for bishop. Throughout his ministry he was a highly desired speaker by white pastors and congregations.

Tindley's Lyrical Theology

Though very cursorily summarized, this background aids in understanding the imagery, figures of speech, and vocabulary in Tindley's hymns with which the poor and marginalized[10] could readily identify: justice, beggars, the poor, distress, destitute, trials, tribulation, storms of life, fears, persecution, forsaken, oppressed, burdens, misery, troubles, disappointments, despised, prisoners, bond-men, starvation, victims, the world as a battlefield, and comforts denied.

By Tindley's lyrical theology is meant the theology expressed in the poetry of his hymns. A brief look at the themes of some of his hymns underscores the double entendres of language that would have resonated with the African American community:

Pilgrim Stranger:[11] The way is dark and lonely and courage fails—even so, one must help others.

The Storm Is Passing Over:[12] Soul, take courage, for the dark night and the storm will pass.

Some Day:[13] Life is filled with burdens, disappointments, troubles, and sorrow, but there is hope.

I'll Overcome Someday:[14] The world is one great battlefield—one is faced with unseen powers and snares.

We'll Understand It Better By and By:[15] One is tossed and driven on the restless sea of time; one may be destitute of things and face trials on every hand; there will be temptations.

I Will Go, If My Father Holds My Hand:[16] One's path is filled with dangers—lack of money, poor health, the onslaught of enemies, and old age.

Just Today:[17] There will be failed plans, threats from the hosts of hell, the denial of comforts, the presence of woes, many crosses to bear, bitter grief, and losses.

The Pilgrim's Song:[18] One is a poor pilgrim of sorrow.

God Will Provide for Me:[19] One may be poor and weak, but God will provide.

Though such words, phrases, and sentences primarily may have had spiritual meaning when Tindley used them in his hymns, they unquestionably had double meaning for the struggling African Americans to whom he ministered.

The following discussion explores a variety of Tindley's views: God, grace, the Bible, witness and mission, the world, nature, saints, life's challenges, and social justice.

God

Tindley's view of God is Trinitarian, though his hymn texts are devoid of the doxological formulation "Father, Son, and Holy Spirit." Nevertheless, he speaks expressly of the persons of the Trinity and their active role in creation and human life.

In three of his hymns he speaks of *God the Father.* The hymn "I Will Go, If My Father holds My Hand" is a call to Christian duty in following Christ and being an obedient servant. Tindley repeats the following line in each stanza, "I will go, if my Father holds my hand," except in stanzas 3 and 4, where he says, "I can go, if my Father holds my hand." He is confident that he can confront all obstacles if accompanied by God the Father.

In another hymn, "I Have Found at Last a Savior," Tindley interestingly writes of the relationship of the faithful to Jesus, the second person of the Trinity.

5. By and by when the war is over,
    And the saints are gathering home,
In the presence of Jehovah,
    Where the pilgrim ne'er shall roam:
My Jesus will be there,
    His glory I shall share,
He will introduce my spirit,
    To his Father as an heir.[20]

In this hymn it is Jesus, the second person of the Trinity, who introduces the spirit of the faithful to God the Father as an heir, and for eternity one is a child of the Father. This involves the dynamic, relational activity of the Godhead.

In the hymn "In Me" there is an eloquent summary of Tindley's understanding of the second person of the Trinity *Jesus Christ*.

1.   Thou, O Christ, my Lord and King
      Grant, in Thine own name my plea;
   Take the sacrifice I bring,
      Be Thou, "All Thou art" in me.

2.   Thou, a wonder working God,
      Dwelling in eternity,
   As in flesh our planet trod
      Work Thy mighty work in me.

3.   Prince of peace beyond compare,
      Thou whose power still'd the sea
   Chief among ten thousand—fair,
      Speak Thy word of peace in me.

4.   O Thou mighty God of love,
      Died Thyself to set us free,
   Holy Spirit, heav'nly dove,
      Magnify Thy love in me.

5.   Jesus, Thou the life, the way
      In Thine image let me be;
   Keep my heart from day to day,
      Live Thy holy life in me.

6.   Jesus, Thou the joy untold,
      Like a river flowing free,
   Be Thou ever in my soul,
      Let Thy joy abound in me.[21]

While Christ is hailed in this poem as Lord, King, Prince of Peace, the way, the life, and untold joy, it is in stanza two that pastor-poet captures the wonder of the Incarnation. Just as God has worked the wonder of taking on the form of human flesh, Tindley desires that God will work in him the incarnation of love, peace, freedom, holiness, and joy, all of which issue from Christ.

Stanzas four and five resonate with emphases in the poetry of Charles Wesley: the death of the God of love for all humankind, the power of the Holy Spirit to instill love, Christ as the way, truth, and life, and the divine image within that initiates and sustains a holy life.

Tindley	Charles Wesley
4. O Thou mighty God of love,	O Love Divine what hast thou done,[22]
Died Thyself to set us free.	The immortal God hath died for thee.
Holy Spirit, heav'nly dove,	Expand thy wings, celestial Dove, [23]/...
Magnify Thy love in me.	Call forth the ray of heavenly love.
5. Jesus, Thou the life, the way	To Thee, the Way, the Truth, the Life[24]
In Thine image let me be;	Whose love my simple heart inflames. . . 6,71
Keep my heart from day to day,	Lord, thine image here restore,[25]
Live Thy holy life in me.	Fully in thy members live.

The third person of the Trinity, *the Holy Spirit*, is also present in Tindley's hymns. In the introspective "In Me," the refrain to stanza 4 reads,

> Magnify thy love in me,
> Magnify thy love in me.
> Holy Spirit, heavenly dove,
> Magnify thy love in me.[26]

This is part of a prayerful plea that the Holy Spirit will increase love within the believer. The use of the word "magnify" indicates much more than a desire to be a loving person. Rather Tindley prays for the Holy Spirit to make love larger and larger in one's life, to intensify and increase it. It is through the power of the Holy Spirit that this transpires.

In the following lines Tindley emphasizes the inner action of the Trinity. The Father's promise is realized through the indwelling Christ ("the Lord" in line 3) by the power of the Holy Spirit. This unified action of the Trinity evokes joy in the believer.

> 1. I have found the peace of heaven,
>   'Tis the Father's promise given,
>   I am happy in the Lord today,
>   It's the Holy Spirit power,
>   In my soul this very hour,
>   And I'm happy in the Lord today.[27]

A couplet from stanza 5 of "Have You Crossed the Line" states:

> But the Holy Spirit still,
> Waits believing souls to fill.[28]

The hymn corpus of Tindley is strongly Christocentric. He does not perceive that any part of life can be fulfilled without an intimate relationship to Jesus Christ. Nothing must come between the faithful and the Christ who redeems them and whom they seek to follow throughout their life journey. In his hymn "Nothing Between" he enumerates many things which can potentially separate believers from their Redeemer: "this world's delusive dream," "worldly pleasure," "habits of life," "pride or station," "self or friends," "hard trials," and the opposition of the world. Those who follow Christ must "Keep the way clear! Let nothing between."

In other hymns Tindley focuses on Christ as the giver of joy ("My Secret Joy"), the source of pleasure ("I Have Found at Last a Savior"), the way ("Christ Is the Way"), guide and leader ("A Better Home"), the source of salvation ("I Believe It"), and the only source of satisfaction ("I'll Be Satisfied").

While Tindley's view of the Trinity is not worked through cohesively in his hymns, the above evidence unquestionably points to a Trinitarian understanding of God.

Grace

Another dimension of Tindley's lyrical theology is his view of grace. Here, however, the emphasis does not resonate with the fullness of the Wesleyan concept of grace that unites the community of faith, as in Charles Wesley's hymn "Jesus, united by thy grace, / and each to each endeared."[29] Tindley's hymns stress the personal aspect of God's grace that saves from sin and sustains one along the dreary journey of life and gives strength to endure. Such a theme is certainly found in the corpus of John Wesley's sermons and Charles Wesley's hymns, but the cohesive communal emphasis of the Wesleys is missing.

In "The Pilgrim's Song" Tindley affirms God's sustaining grace in the words:

5.   My lot among men may be dreary,
        My station quite poor and despised;
     By grace I will run and not weary,
        Till called up with Jesus on high.[30]

In this same vein, in the hymn "I Will Go, If My Father Holds My Hand" he speaks of the strength that God's grace gives him when he is weak:

3.   Though my strength is weak, by his grace I will seek
     To repose like Mary at the Savior's feet;
     Then to climb to the heights of the pure delight,
     I can go, if my Father holds my hand.[31]

Tindley also links humility and the awareness of what God's grace has done for him. This is beautifully articulated in stanza one of the hymn "Here Am I, Send Me."

1.   If the Savior wants somebody just to fill a humble place,
        And to show that to the lowly God will give sufficient grace,
     I am ready now to offer all I am, whate'er it be,
        And to say to him this moment, "Here am I, send me."[32]

In "Mountain Top Dwelling" Tindley describes the encounter with saving grace "at the foot of the cross" of Christ.

2.   At the foot of the cross where I knelt confessing,
    I beheld his shining face,
And then there came the blessing,
    'Twas the light of saving grace.[33]

The grace of God, however, is not merely an abstract experience of light from the cross. It cleanses from sin. The hymn "Saved and Satisfied" expresses the confidence that one is not only cleansed from sin by God's grace, it keeps one pure within. Indeed, Tindley affirms that the grace of God enables "new creation."

3.   Promises of full salvation, from all sin and sinning too,
Making me a new creation saved completely through and through:
That the grace of God would cleanse me, from the state of inbred sin,
And each moment guide and keep me, safe without and pure within.[34]

Tindley has no static understanding of grace, for one must respond to it. Furthermore, it is to bear fruit in one's life. In the hymn "Have You Crossed the Line" through two questions he seeks to evoke a response to God's grace:

Have you crossed over the line,
Have you left the carnal mind,
    Where the works of the flesh are found?
Have you moved to the place,
Of the fruits of grace.
    Are you standing on Holy ground?[35]

Tindley's emphases on God's grace as the enabler of salvation and on the "fruits of grace" are indeed strong Wesleyan perspectives. However, missing from his hymns are emphases on the communal power of grace and on the means of grace (sacraments) one finds so prevalent in Wesleyan theology.

The Bible

The perspective of his poetry and his sermons seems to be that he received and accepted the Bible as the authoritative and inspired word of God containing all that was necessary for human salvation. He also received the Bible as great sacred literature, which he appropriated throughout his poetry for its imagery, figures of speech, and spiritual insight—a thoroughly Wesleyan view of scripture.[36]

One finds echoes of the Bible throughout his hymns, as seen in the following examples. There is a direct quotation of Matthew 14:27, "Be ye not afraid" in the second half of stanza 2 of "Pilgrim Stranger."

When the storms of life are beating,
    Hard upon your head.
God will hide you, he is pleading,
    "Be ye not afraid."[37]

In "I'm Going There" he bemoans with St. Paul, "For the good that I would I do not; but the evil which I would not, that I do" (Romans 7:19).

And often when I would do good,
And keep the promise as I should,
I miss the way, and coming short,
It makes me mourn and grieves my heart.[38]

In the fourth stanza the hymn "Today" he quotes directly from Luke 23:42, the words of the thief on the cross, "Remember me."

I hear that Thou saved a thief on the cross,
    When he turned and looked on Thee;
If Thou, as of old, art saving the lost,
    I pray Thee, "Remember me."[39]

"Christ Is the Way" focuses on the Transfiguration of Christ in Matthew 17, followed by references to other events in the life of Christ, e.g., fasting in the wilderness, Judas' betrayal, persecution, and false accusations in Pilate's hall.

Christ the way, in exaltation;
    Though he stands on heights aflame,
Glorious in transfiguration,
    He is always meek the same.[40]

The familiar "Leave It There" includes the admonition of Matthew 6:26, "Just remember, in his word, how he feeds the little bird."

The chorus of "Your Faith Has Saved You" resonates with the story of the crippled man at the Pool of Bethesda in John 5, who had been there for thirty-eight years and was finally healed by Jesus.

Your faith has made you whole
    'Tis music in my soul,
Arise and go, the Lord said so,
    Your faith has made you whole.[41]

A marvelous hymn of Christian vocation is based on "Here am I, send me" of Isaiah 6:8 (the biblical reference appears in the subtitle). Another hymn, "After Awhile," recalls the deliverance of the children of Israel at the "mighty sea" (Exodus 14) and the manna in the wilderness (Exodus 16).

And the God who gives so plentiful and free,
    Sent the precious manna down,
    Israel saw it on the ground;
'Twas the God who now provides for me.[42]

"Go Wash in the Beautiful Stream" is unique among Tindley's sacred poems, for it is the only lyrical narrative of a Bible story that he published. In four eloquent stanzas he relates Naaman's encounter with the prophet Elisha (2 Kings), and then he applies the story to the lives of Christians in his own time.

O, sinner, O, sinner, are you not the same
    As Naaman that noted Syrian?
Your sickness injures both body and soul,
    And makes you feel loathsome and mean.
If you feel you are lost, just shoulder the cross,
    And Jesus will then make you clean.
If you feel you are sick, just come along quick,
    And get into the beautiful stream.[43]

These are but a few of numerous examples of how the Bible, its stories, language, metaphors, images, and verses are integrated into Tindley's poetry and shape his thought. For him the scriptures are the source of strength of sustenance for all circumstances of life.

View of Witness and Mission

In the hymn "Heavenly Union" Tindley addresses the proclamation of the gospel. Once he had experienced the "heavenly union," namely, unity with God through salvation in Christ, he was filled with the desire to witness. Inspired by the realization that he had been redeemed through Christ's sacrifice, he proclaims in eloquent rhyming couplets:

4.   I praised the Lord both night and day,
    I went from house to house to pray,
    And if I met one on the way,
    I always found something to say,
    About the heavenly union.[44]

He concludes this poem with an interesting reflection.

5.   I wonder why the saints don't sing,
    And make the heavenly arches ring,
    And spread the news from pole to pole
    Till every nation has been told,
    About the heavenly union.

The pilgrims on earth can do something that the saints in heaven apparently cannot do, namely, "spread the news from pole to pole." While personal and social holiness are a vital part of the gospel Tindley proclaims, he also is faithful to the admonition of the New Testament to proclaim the gospel to the ends of the earth.

If one feels called to Christian vocation and mission, to share the good news of Jesus Christ, there are a number of realizations to which one must come, if one is to respond with the words, "Here am I, send me," the concluding line to all stanzas of Tindley's hymn of that name. It is a powerful mission hymn.

1. If the Savior wants somebody just to fill a humble place,
   And to show that to the lowly God will give sufficient grace,
   I am ready now to offer all I am, whate'er it be,
   And to say to him this moment,
   "Here am I, send me."

   Chorus
   "Here am I, send me,"
   "Here am I, send me,"
   If the Master wants somebody,
   "Here am I, send me."

2. If it is to bear the crosses with a heart resigned and true,
   Just to testify to others what the grace of God can do,
   I will gladly undertake it, though the way I cannot see,
   And will answer, blessed Master,
   "Here am I, send me."

3. If it is to bear afflictions so that earthly joys depart,
   With a weak and painful body and a sad and downcast heart,
   Just to show that God is with us when our health and all else flee,
   If it be Thy will, my Savior,
   "Here am I, send me."

4. If he wants someone to travel in the byways and the lanes,
   And to try and save the outcast, those whom sin has almost slain,
   In his name I make the promise, I will go where'er it be,
   If the Master wants somebody,
   "Here am I, send me."

(1) The mission vocation requires above all else humility and commitment—"I am ready now to offer all I am, whate'er it be." (2) The mission vocation often requires bearing crosses with a resigned and true heart. This is in itself a testimony to others of what the grace of God can do. One may not be able to see the way forward to do this, but one goes faithfully forward. (3) The mission vocation often mandates bearing afflictions, which create the absence of earthly joy. One may be weak, in pain, downcast, and in ill health. Yet, in the midst of all this, others can see that "God is with us." (4) The mission vocation may send one to try to save the outcast.

If one is willing to accept all of these realities and face them openly and honestly, then one can make the promise, "I will go where'er it be, / Here am I, send me."

The World

Charles Albert Tindley speaks throughout his sacred poetry as a self-educated African American out of the black experience of prejudice and oppression in the late nineteenth century and early twentieth century, and yet, his analysis of the ills of society transcends ethnic and cultural backgrounds with a universal eloquence. The opening couplets to stanzas 1, 2, and 3 of "I'll Overcome Someday" suggest perhaps the pastor-poet's grasp not only situation of pre-civil rights America, but also of the world in any age.

1. This world is one great battlefield,
   With forces all arrayed.

2. Both seen and unseen powers join
   To drive my soul astray.

3. A thousand snares are set for me,
   And mountains in my way.[45]

War is being waged in this world and set before each human being are conflicts, snares, and obstacles. Though Tindley speaks here in the first person, it is as though he speaks collectively for all persons.

He refers to this world as a "vale of tears" through which pilgrims are traveling on a perilous journey: "Ye pilgrims through this vale of tears." The word "pilgrim" appears in the New Testament (Hebrews 11:13 and 1 Peter 2:11), where in the KJV the Greek word parĕpidĕm ŏs is translated "pilgrim." While Tindley does not specifically refer to these passages in the writing of his hymns, his use of the word "pilgrim" resonates with the spirit of the reference to "strangers and pilgrims on earth," which the writer of Hebrews applies to important figures of faith in the Hebrew scriptures (Abel, Enoch, Noah, Abraham, Isaac, Jacob, and Sarah), who overcame numerous obstacles and difficulties, and all of whom sought a "better country, a heavenly one." Like these saints of scripture, Tindley saw the people of faith of his day overcoming obstacles and difficulties of the world and also seeking a "home in heaven above."

1. Ye pilgrims through this vale of tears,
   Come let us cheer each other,
   Amid the danger's doubts and fears,
   Let each console his brother.
   Our way is often dark and hard,
   Temptations all around us,
   Unless we pray with one accord,
   They surely will confound us.[46]

Another hymn speaks of "this world of woe" and opens with the expression "pilgrim stranger"—

1.   Go, ye humble pilgrim stranger,
       Through this world of woe,
   You may meet with many a danger,
       Everywhere you go.[47]

In the hymn "I'm Going There" each chorus repeats this quatrain:

Although a pilgrim here below,
Where dangers are and sorrows grow,
I have a home in heaven above,
I'm going there, I'm going there.[48]

One of Tindley's most powerful uses of the image of the pilgrim is in one of his more familiar hymns, "The Pilgrim's Song." It also resonates with the views of the writer of Hebrews. The "pilgrim of sorrow" is cast into the "wide world" which is a "waste-howling desert" and a "land of danger."

1.   I am a poor pilgrim of sorrow,
       Cast out in this wide world to roam,
   Uncertain of life for tomorrow,
       I want to make heaven my home.

3.   I'm now in a waste-howling desert,
       Not a foot of its land to call mine,
   No cottage nor tent for a shelter,
       Though storms are descending sometimes.

4.   I'm wandering in this land of danger,
       No comfort or peace do I find;
   I am a poor wayfaring stranger,
       To troubles and trials confined.

5.   My lot among men may be dreary,
       My station quite poor and despised;
   By grace I will run and not weary,
       Till called up with Jesus on high.[49]

In addition to the image of the pilgrim, Tindley sees life through the eyes of the poor and dispossessed. In a poem of cascading, rhyming triplets the climax comes in the use of the image of the poor, who suffer in this world.

1.   I am thinking of friends whom I used to know,
   Who lived and suffered in this world below;
   They've gone up to heaven; but I want to know
   What are they doing now.

2. There were some whose hearts were burdened with cares,
    They passed their moments in sighing and tears,
    They clung to the cross with trembling and fears,
    But what are they doing now?

3. There were some whose bodies were full of disease,
    Medicine nor doctor could give them much ease;
    They suffered till death brought a final release,
    But what are they doing now?

4. There were some who were poor and often despised;
    They looked to heaven through tear-blinded eyes,
    While people were heedless and deaf to their cries,
    But what are they doing now?[50]

The friends in heaven of whom Tindley is speaking are those who in this life suffered, were burdened with cares, trembled and feared as they bore the cross, were "full of disease" and "suffered till death," and some were poor and despised. Furthermore, no one paid any attention to their cries for aid.

It is not surprising that Tindley's view of heaven is a place where there are "No beggars on that golden street" (from the hymn "I'm on My Way to Heaven Above" or "Joyous Anticipation"). In that haven of the faithful "No poor are begging on the street" and "No homeless wandering soul to meet" (from the hymn "There Is a Land That Is Free" or "Will You Be There?").

2. No poor are begging on the street,
       The blind are made to see.
    No homeless wandering soul to meet,
       Through all eternity.[51]

3. No beggars on that golden street,
       No blind to lead about,
    No funeral train we there shall meet,
       For death is there cast out.[52]

Tindley's view of the world is relatively devoid of optimism, rather it is a place of hardship, snares, woe, and suffering.

Nature

In two of Tindley's hymns one encounters his interest in the beauty of nature. The first bears the title "Spiritual Springtime." He compares the cycle of the year, especially the change from the darkness and cold of winter to the light and warmth of spring and summer, with the change from a dreary sinful life to the light of salvation. Just as the warmth of the sun melts the ice and snow of winter, so the light of Christ's redemption melts the cold, sinful heart. The recurring refrain in this hymn asks:

Chorus:

> Has the sun crossed the line, do you know?
> Has he melted all the ice and snow?
> Have the birds begun to sing, do you feel the joy of spring?
> Has the sun crossed the line, do you know?

2. Winter time when earth is here, lifeless, dreary ev'rywhere,
   Winds are high, and all about is hard and cold;
   So a life's that's full of sin, where no light has entered in,
   And the peace of God has never filled the soul.

3. When the sun has crossed the line, and the earth has left behind
   Ice and snow and stormy wintering high;
   It is like a weary soul, turning from the world so cold,
   To the bosom of the Lord, a ransomed child,

4. When the earth has turned around, and the sun has warmed the ground,
   Then the ice will melt and swollen rivers flow;
   So when one has found the Lord, and received his gracious word,
   All the filthiness of sin will have to go.

5. Have you seen the pretty flowers, blessed with evening dew and showers?
   Fragrant language, happy fields and woods employ;
   Do you wonder at a soul when the Lord has made him whole,
   If he shouts when he is filled with heaven's joy.

6. Earth in summer time produces fruit for ev'ry creature's use,
   Not a bit is over kept for selfish greed;
   So a soul that's saved indeed, grows his fruit from righteous seed,
   Not for self but all is for another's need.[53]

In another hymn entitled "From Youth to Old Age" he compares the cycle of the year's seasons to those from youth to old age. In the first three stanzas Tindley eloquently describes the transitions from youthful springtime to the years when "summer was yielding to fall."

1. My life, as a year, had a bright springtime,
   > With summer and autumn to come,
   And afterward the winter with its dim sunshine
   > When springtime and summer had gone,
   The spring of my life was the joyful days,
   > When care had not entered my breast,
   When the fields and the woods were the choice of my ways,
   > And my life was all happiness.

2. It was when I was young and the world to me was new,
   > The stings and the thorns were not known,
   When wiser heads guided in all I had to do,
   > My heaven was parents and home.
   The birds gave [their] music, the flow'rs gave me joy,

>   And the world was an Eden to me,
>   The skies were my pictures, the earth was my joy,
>   I was happy as mortal could be.
>
>   3. The days shorter grew and the nights grew long,
>   And the earth brown and dreary did appall,
>   In the shedding of the leaves and the silence of song,
>   The summer was yielding to fall.
>   In the western skies where the clouds were gray,
>   The cool autumn winds then did blow.
>   And the signs were declaring in no distant day,
>   The ground would be covered with snow.[54]

Lines 5 through 8 of stanza 2 illustrate a youthful vision of "the world as an Eden"—an idyllic state, perhaps as God intended. Tindley effervesces with the beauty of nature, with awe and wonder at what God has created.

These two poems are unique in his poetical corpus, for in most of his other sacred poetry he does not return to the theme of nature.

There is one other poem, "He'll Take You Through," which uses an interesting and related metaphor, the "nature-train."

>   3. On sweetly speeds this nature-train,
>   Through tunnels dark, o'er desert plain,
>   Where trestles span the deep ravine;
>   Where towering mountain peaks are seen.
>
>   4. When through the gloom you have to go,
>   A howling wilderness of woe,
>   Where demons lurk and dangers roar,
>   And threatening clouds above you soar.
>
>   5. No accident has been his fate,
>   His train has never come in late,
>   All signals show the track is clear,
>   The passengers have naught to fear.
>
>   6. A few more stations, and we'll be
>   From toil and care and danger free.
>   O could we render praises due,
>   To Christ, the one who takes us through.

Every person is speeding through life on the "nature-train." It is an unavoidable journey, which begins with birth. The "nature-train" takes us through dark tunnels, deserts, across deep ravines and high mountains, through a "wilderness of woe" with lurking demons, roaring dangers, and threatening clouds. Nevertheless, one need not fear for Christ will take one through.

Saints

One encounters the word "saints" a number of times in Tindley's sacred poetry. He does not speak of them in terms of those who have been awarded the name "saint" by the church. While he does not make it explicit, one has the impression that for Tindley the saints are often those who have gone on to full union with God beyond this life. In "Will You Be There?" he says:

> The saints from sin are free;
> They shout the glorious harvest home,
> The year of Jubilee.[55]

The reference to "the year of Jubilee" is most interesting, since in the Old Testament it is a year in which slaves are to be freed.[56] In the hymn "Ever Since I Have Been Living" ("A Better Home") Tindley speaks of the elation after redemption that evokes the thought that his life might be "One continuous Jubilee," but he concludes by saying, "But I found out my trials had just begun."[57]

Three stanzas (3, 4, 5) of "The Home of the Soul" address the lives of the saints in heaven, who never die, who do not weep or have to say mournful goodbyes to their loved ones, and who behold the face of God.

> 3. No sickness is there and the saints never die,
>   They are happy forever in the city on high,
>   Through ages eternal they never grow old,
>   That city is heaven, the house of the soul.
>
> 4. The saints up in heaven, they weep not or sigh,
>   Or say to their loved ones the mournful goodbye,
>   But happy forever in the city of gold,
>   The city is heaven, the home of the soul.
>
> 5. No sin is in heaven, no uncleanness there,
>   For Satan can't enter that city so fair,
>   The King in his beauty the saints shall behold,
>   In the city of heaven, the home of the soul.[58]

Life's Challenges

Time and again Tindley articulates the challenges one faces in life and how the faithful should respond.

(1) *Mutual support of the community of the faithful.*

In stanza one of "Ye Pilgrims through This Vale of Tears" he underscores the importance of supporting one another in the challenges of sorrows, doubts, fears, and temptations that confront the faithful.

> Ye pilgrims through this vale of tears,
>> Come let us cheer each other,
> Amid the danger's doubts and fears,
>> Let each console his brother.
> Our way is often dark and hard,
>> Temptations all around us,
> Unless we pray with one accord,
>> They surely will confound us.[59]

(2) *Pray in the face of all obstacles.*

Tindley's prayer amid the raging storms of life is "Stand By Me."[60] In one of his most familiar hymns, "Leave It There,"[61] when facing poverty, disease, foes, and old age, he pleads: "Take your burden to the Lord and leave it there." The second line of stanza three of that hymn declares: "Don't forget that God in heaven answers prayer." Tindley firmly believed that if you pray, God "will make a way for you and will lead you safely through" adversities.

In the spirit of Isaiah's words, "They that wait upon the Lord shall renew their strength" (40:31), Tindley wrote, "And then I wait, it is not long / Before he comes in prayer and song."

There is also the corporate and communal strength of prayer. "Unless we pray with one accord, / They [temptations] surely will confound us." No matter how rough the path, "if you watch and prayer. . . / The Lord will make the way."[62]

(3) *Rely on the testimony of scripture.*

No matter the context in which one is found, paramount for Tindley is that one relies on the testimony of the Bible. He strongly believes, as he says in the hymn "A Better Home," "the word of God is true."[63] When you confront sadness and the cares of the world, his counsel is: "Go and read the Bible story."[64] Why? To learn "What Christ on earth could do." Those who do this will learn that Christ can do the same for them.

He speaks of the comfort he receives in the face of fears from the words of Christ in Mark 6:50: "I hear the Master cry, 'Be not afraid 'tis I,' / And the storm will soon be over, Hallelujah."[65] When confined to troubles and trials and "friends and relations forsake me," again he turns to the scriptures and remembers "the kind words of Jesus / Which say, 'Weary child, I am nigh."[66]

Tindley's hymns are filled with images of scripture from which the faithful may draw inspiration. He writes, "Though my strength is weak, by his grace I will seek / To repose like Mary at the Savior's feet."[67] This image of nearness to Christ in scripture shapes his life posture for addressing weakness and adversity.

(4) *Follow the "pathway of duty."*

One of Tindley's hymns, "I Will Go, If My Father Holds My Hand," opens with the line "When the pathway of duty seems with danger filled." He expands this further in another hymn, "The Lord Will Make the Way."

> To do your duty here below,
>   And be just what you say,
> May not be easy, but you know,
>   The Lord will make the way.[68]

One is to articulate with one's life what one says with words. In other words, faith or belief equals "being." One is to become a personification of what one says. "Be just what you say"!

This means, of course, being an obedient follower of Christ. "Do the things he [Christ] bids you do."[69] Practice self-denial[70] and "walk the narrow way,"[71] of which Tindley says,

> It is tedious, I admit,
>   But I am not weary yet;
> I shall travel on until the perfect day.[72]

The trials of life have taught him, "unless I lived upright I would be lost."[73]

Mutual support, prayer, scripture, and duty are hallmarks of Tindley's theology and ethic and his approach to life's challenges.

View of Social Justice

Resonating with the Wesleyan tradition within which Tindley stood, the first two lines of one hymn pleads: "Come, everyone that loves the Lord, / Let us act the part of justice, Hallelujah." This reminds one of Charles Wesley's tribute to Mary Naylor:

> The golden rule she has pursued,
> and did to others as she would
>   others should do to her:
> justice composed her upright soul,
> justice did all her thoughts control,
>   and formed her character.[74]

Wesley affirms in this poem that Mary Naylor indeed acted the part of justice.

One may not read into Tindley's words "Let us act the part of justice," however, more than he may have intended. He follows it with the lines "Let us walk the self-denial road, / In the way of suffering Jesus, Hallelujah." The emphasis is more personal than communal. Nevertheless, it is clear that a follower of Jesus is to act with justice in all things. The larger context of the Christian's life and action is unquestionably communal. Just as Tindley declares in a previously cited hymn: "Unless we pray with one accord, / They [temptations of the world] surely will confound us."[75]

In the spirit of the scriptures, Tindley anticipates a heaven where the injustices of this world have been obliterated. In the hymn "I'm on My Way to Heaven Above" ("Joyous Anticipation") he emphasizes that earth's injustices will be rectified. He describes heaven with a Wesleyan emphasis—"A land of rest and perfect love."

> I'm on my way to heaven above
> Where are free from care;
> A land of rest and perfect love
> And joy without a tear.

This is a place where there are "no beggars," "and no children there with parents dead,"—i.e., no children are without parents—and no one is denied freedom.

> No one in heaven is denied,
> The freedom of that land.

In "Will You Be There?" he adds that in heaven there is—

> no homeless wandering soul to meet.[76]

The hymn "The Home of the Soul" expands Tindley's list of heaven-rectified injustices, when he says:

> There prisoners and bond-men forever are free.[77]

One might think at first reading that Tindley is merely projecting all hope beyond this world into the future, because he sees no possibility of change in the here and now. his hope, however, for a heavenly existence absent of injustice underscores what is presently wrong in society and the need for justice now. He articulates the tension between justice in the present and future in his poem "After Awhile." He anticipates a changed nation.

> 1.   The world of forms and changes
>   Is just now so confused,
>   That there is found some danger
>   In everything you use;
>   But this is consolation
>   To every bloodwashed child:
>   The Lord will change our nation
>   After awhile.
>
> 6.   Our boasted land and nation,
>   Are plunging in disgrace;
>   With pictures of starvation
>   Almost in every place;
>   While loads of needed money,
>   Remain in hoarded piles;
>   But God will rule this country,
>   After awhile.[78]

Indeed Tindley emphasizes that it is God who will rule "after awhile" and enable the necessary changes. To aver, however, that Tindley sees such action to be devoid of human participation would be to misunderstand the totality of his poetical corpus.

Tindley emphasizes the tension between the injustices of the present world with the reign of justice that God will establish, as expressed in the hymn "A Better Day Is Coming." The eschatology expressed is one of hope. This is not an expression, however, of a realized eschatology, rather one beyond the grave.

> When Christ our Lord shall listen
>   To every plaintive sigh,
> And stretch his hand o'er every land
>   In justice by and by.[79]

Conclusion

While Tindley's hymns beyond his lifetime have enriched the life of the church and individual Christians on a somewhat limited basis, perhaps because of the delimited Tindley repertory that has survived in hymnals, and, while the published corpus is confined to ca. forty-six hymns, it is vitally important to study them against the background of the social context of African Americans in early twentieth-century Philadelphia. When read through the lens of this context, they take on much deeper meaning.

While he sometimes speaks in his hymns from the perspectives of his youth, the context out of which he most often speaks is that of the persecution and oppression of African Americans, though he lived his life primarily in the so-called "free" north of the United States. His language is eloquent and perceptive and is laced with scripture. His imagery is vivid and often his lines of poetry are terse and economical. He is Christocentric through and through, and he places less emphasis on the Holy Trinity than one might expect, though the persons of the Trinity are present in his poetry.

On the whole Tindley's lyrical theology does not embody the fullness of a Wesleyan theology of grace, but emphasizes the importance of grace for individual salvation, though there may be subtle undertones of its social implications. Nonetheless, he does emphasize the importance of the mutual support of the faithful. One does wonder, however, why there is no mention in his hymns of an important aspect of Wesleyan theology, namely, the role of baptism and the Lord's Supper in the life of the believer, for both sacraments were an integral part of the life of Tindley Temple Methodist Episcopal Church in Philadelphia, where he was pastor and administered the sacraments.

His social critique is powerful, but may have been overlooked, because the hymns that contain this dimension of his thought have not been very familiar or popular. More probably, however, this is because his social critique is encoded in a description of what heaven should be like, though this writer suspects he is also describing what the world in Tindley's own time should be like. While it would be easy to draw the conclusion that he was simply looking beyond this world for the fulfillment of all that could not be realized in this life, that would be a gross error. Tindley clearly hoped for a better day when justice would be established throughout the earth and everyone would have what he or she needed. This is evident in the social outreach ministries in which he was engaged and often initiated.

He was writing at the beginning of the twentieth century when African Americans endured immense prejudice and oppression. The world Tindley describes is seen through African American eyes. It is a great battlefield with a thousand snares. The dispossessed have no land to call their own and are confined to troubles and trials. The poor are marginalized and despised. Tindley is perhaps one of the first hymn writers in the early twentieth century to use the word "homeless" in his poetry. In his view of heaven there will be no homeless, no prisoners, and no bondsmen. If "a better day is coming," Tindley's plea to "act the part of justice" cannot mean simply "justice" beyond death, rather in the present moment. The rectification of injustices, which he sees beyond the grave, ultimately should be realized in this world. In this sense Tindley's message of justice has come of age and needs to be heard anew.

While he spoke in language that readily resonated with African Americans, the inclusion of some of his hymns today in a number of hymnbooks of people of diverse ethnic and cultural backgrounds indicates that much of what he penned articulates a universal message of redemption and hope for the present.

Selected Bibliography

Abrahams, Roger D. *Deep Down in the Jungle: Negro Narrative Folklore from the Streets of Philadelphia.* Hatboro, PA: Folklore Associates, 1964.

Blockson, Charles L. *African Americans in Pennsylvania: A History and Guide.* Baltimore: Black Classic, 1994.

———. *African Americans in Pennsylvania: Above Ground and Underground, an Illustrated Guide.* Harrisburg: RB Books, 2001.

Bowser, Charles W. *Let the Bunker Burn.* Philadelphia: Camino Books, 1989.

Brown, G. Gordon. *Law Administration and Negro-White Relations in Philadelphia: A Study in Race Relations.* Philadelphia: Bureau of Municipal Research, 1947.

Du Bois, W. E. B. *The Black North: A Social Study.* 1901. Reprint, New York: Arno, 1969.

———. *The Philadelphia Negro: A Social Study.* Philadelphia: University of Pennsylvania Press, 1899.

Fauset, Arthur Huff. *Black Gods of the Metropolis: Negro Religious Cults of the Urban North.* Philadelphia: University of Pennsylvania Press, 1944.

Jones, Ralph H. *Charles Albert Tindley: Prince of Preachers.* Nashville: Abingdon, 1982.

Lane, Roger. *Roots of Violence in Black Philadelphia, 1860–1900.* Cambridge: Harvard University Press, 1986.

———. *William Dorsey's Philadelphia and Ours: On the Past and Future of the Black City in America.* New York: Oxford University Press, 1991.

McBride, David. *Integrating the City of Medicine: Blacks in Philadelphia Health Care, 1910–1965.* Philadelphia: Temple University Press, 1989.

Nash, Gary B. *Forging Freedom: The Formation of Philadelphia's Black Community, 1720–1840.* Cambridge: Harvard University Press, 1988.

Nelson, H. Viscount. *Black Leadership's Response to the Great Depression in Philadelphia.* Lewiston, NY: Edwin Mellen, 2006.

Rose, Dan. *Black American Street Life: South Philadelphia, 1969–1971.* Philadelphia: University of PA, 1987.

Saunders, John A. *100 Years after Emancipation: History of the Philadelphia Negro, 1787 to 1963.* Philadelphia: Free African Society, 1964.

Trotter, Joe William, Jr., and Eric Ledell Smith, eds. *African Americans in Pennsylvania: Shifting Historical Perspectives.* University Park: Pennsylvania Historical and Museum Commission and the Pennsylvania State University Press, 1997.

Willis, Arthur C. Cecil. *City: A History of Blacks in Philadelphia, 1638–1979*. New York: Carlton, 1990.

Willson, Joseph. *The Elite of Our People: Joseph Willson's Sketches of Black Upper-Class Life in Antebellum Philadelphia*. University Park: Pennsylvania State University Press, 2000.

Winch, Julie. *Philadelphia's Black Elite: Activism, Accommodation, and the Struggle for Autonomy, 1787–1848*. Philadelphia: Temple University Press, 1988.

Wolfinger, James. *Philadelphia Divided: Race and Politics in the City of Brotherly Love*. Chapel Hill, 2007.

Notes

1. *The United Methodist Hymnal* (Nashville: United Methodist, 1989); *African American Heritage Hymnal* (Chicago: GIA, 2001); *African Methodist Episcopal Church Bicentennial Hymnal* (Nashville: AME, 1984); *Lift Every Voice and Sing II: An African American Hymnal*, (New York: Church Publishing, 1993); *The Baptist Hymnal* (Nashville: Convention Press, 1991); *Songs of Zion* (Nashville: Abingdon, 1981); *Zion Still Sings* (Nashville: Abingdon, 2007); *The New Century Hymnal* (Cleveland: Pilgrim, 1996). The most popular hymns appearing in these hymnals and a few other collections are: "Beams of Heaven as I Go" (Some Day), "I Am Thinking of Friends" (What Are They Doing in Heaven), "If the World from You Withhold of Its Silver and Its Gold" (Leave It There), "Nothing between My Soul and the Savior," "We Are Often Tossed and Driven" (We'll Understand It Better By and By), and "When the Storms of Life Are Raging" (Stand by Me).

2. Published by GBGMusik of the General Board of Global Ministries of the United Methodist Church.

3. The sources available to this author are as follows: *Soul Echoes: A Collection of Songs for Religious Meetings*, Nr. 2 (Philadelphia: Soul Echoes, 1909), henceforth cited as *SE*. *New Songs of Paradise* (Philadelphia: Prof. E. T. Tindley, 1941), henceforth cited as *NSP*. *Beams of Heaven: Hymns of Charles Albert Tindley*, eds., S T Kimbrough, Jr. and Carlton R. Young (New York, GBGMusik, 2006), henceforth cited as *BH*.

4. See Ralph H. Jones, *Charles Albert Tindley: Prince of Preachers* (Nashville: Abingdon, 1982), 21.

5. Du Bois, W. E. B. Du Bois, *The Philadelphia Negro: A Social Study* (Philadelphia: University of Pennsylvania Press, 1899), 352.

6. See Sadie Tanner Mossell, "The Standard of Living Among One Hundred Negro Migrant Families in Philadelphia," *The Annals of the American Academy of Social and Political Science*, XCVIII, 1921.

7. First Schocken edition, (New York: Schocken Books, Inc., 1967), xxxix–xl.

8. Ibid., 309.

9. St. Clair Drake and Horace R. Cayton. *Black Metropolis: A Study of Negro Life in a Northern City* (New York: Harcourt, Brace, 1945). 787.

10. It is important to remember that "marginalized" can be applied to anyone of color, not merely the poor.

11. *SE*, Nr. 1; *NSP*, Nr. 1; *BH*, Nr. 2.

12. *SE*, Nr. 4; *NSP*, Nr. 4; *BH*, Nr. 4.

13. *SE*, Nr. 24; *NSP*, Nr. 14; *BH*, Nr. 11.

14. *NSP*, 42; *BH*, Nr. 14.

15. *SE*, Nr. 30; *NSP*, Nr. 26; *BH*, Nr. 18.

16. *SE*, Nr. 12; *NSP*, Nr. 28; *BH*, Nr. 19.

17. *NSP*, Nr. 44; *BH*, Nr. 29.

18. *SE*, Nr. 40; *NSP*, Nr. 48; *BH*, Nr. 33.

19. *SE*, Nr. 3; *NSP*, Nr. 3; *BH*, Nr. 34.

20. *SE*, Nr. 41; *BH*, Nr. 13.

21. *NSP*, Nr. 47; *BH*, Nr. 31.

22. John and Charles Wesley, *Hymns and Sacred Poems* (Bristol: Farley, 1742), 26.

23. Charles Wesley, *Short Hymns on Select Passages of the Holy Scriptures*, 2 vols. (Bristol: Farley, 1762), 1:3.

24. Charles Wesley, "Catholic Love." Appended to John Wesley, *Catholic Spirit* (London: Cock, 1755), 29.

25. John and Charles Wesley, *Hymns and Sacred Poems* (Bristol: Farley, 1740), 166.

26. *NSP*, Nr. 47; *BH*, Nr. 31.

27. *NSP*, Nr. 44; *BH*, Nr. 29.

28. *NSP*, Nr. 53; *BH*, Nr. 46.

29. *Hymns and Sacred Poems* (1742), 86.

30. *SE*, Nr. 40; *NSP*, Nr. 48; *BH*, Nr. 33.
31. *SE*, Nr. 12; *NSP*, Nr. 28; *BH*, Nr. 19.
32. *NSP*, Nr. 37; *BH*, Nr. 25.
33. *NSP*, Nr. 32; *BH*, Nr. 37.
34. *NSP*, Nr. 41; *BH*, Nr. 41.
35. *NSP*, Nr. 53; *BH*, Nr. 46.
36. In the "Preface" to his *Book of Sermons* Tindley says that they are published "to confirm and strengthen, if not to inform, all who believe in God and in the inerrancy of the Holy Bible" (p. viii). It is difficult to know the intent of this comment by Tindley, since neither his hymns nor his sermons elaborate this position sufficiently.
37. *SE*, Nr. 1; *NSP*, Nr. 1; *BH*, Nr. 2.
38. *SE*, Nr. 44; *NSP*, Nr. 17; *BH*, Nr. 6.
39. Ibid., Nr. 8.
40. *NSP*, 20; *BH*, Nr. 16.
41. *NSP*, Nr. 33; *BH*, 22.
42. *NSP*, Nr. 37; *BH*, 35.
43. *SE*, *Nr. 13*; *SP 8*; *BH*, 22.
44. *SE*, Nr. 21; *NSP*, Nr. 52; *BH*, Nr. 32.
45. *SE*, Nr. 42; *NSP*, Nr. 18; *BH*, Nr. 14.
46. *SE*, Nr. 7; *NSP*, Nr. 5; *BH*, Nr. 1.
47. *SE*, Nr. 1; *NSP*, Nr. 1; *BH*, Nr. 2.
48. *SE*, Nr. 44; *NSP*, Nr. 17; *BH*, Nr. 6.
49. *SE*, Nr. 40; *NSP*, Nr. 48; *BH*, Nr. 33.
50. *NSP*, Nr. 19; *BH*, Nr. 15.
51. *NSP*, 36; *BH*, Nr. 24, stanza 2 of "There Is a Land That Is Free" (or "Will You Be There?")
52. *NSP*, 35; *BH*, Nr. 23, stanza 3 of "I'm on My Way to Heaven Above" (or "Joyous Anticipation").
53. *NSP*, Nr. 38; *BH*, Nr. 39.
54. *SE*, Nr. 42; *NSP*, Nr. 18; *BH*, Nr. 14.
55. *NSP*, Nr. 36; *BH*, Nr. 24.
56. See Leviticus 25:8–55.
57. *NSP*, Nr. 22; *BH*, Nr. 17, stanza 3 of "Ever Since I Have Been Living" ("A Better Home").
58. *NSP*, Nr. 41; *BH*, Nr. 26.
59. *NSP*, Nr. 7; *BH*, Nr. 1.
60. *NSP*, Nr. 2; *BH*, Nr. 3.
61. *NSP*, Nr. 30; *BH*, Nr. 20.
62. *NSP*, Nr. 16; *BH*, Nr. 12, stanza 2 of "The Hills of Life" ("The Lord Will Make the Way").
63. *NSP*, 22; *BH*, Nr. 17, stanza 5 of "Ever Since I Have Been Living" ("A Better Home").
64. *NSP*, 51; *BH*, Nr. 43, stanza 2 of "If Some Disease Has Robbed You" ("Go Talk with Jesus about It").
65. *NSP*, 4; *BH*, Nr. 4, stanza 3 of "The Storm Is Passing Over" ("Courage My Soul").
66. *NSP*, 48; *BH*, Nr. 33, stanza 4 of "I Am a Poor Pilgrim of Sorrow" ("The Pilgrim's Song").
67. *NSP*, 28; *BH*, Nr. 19, stanza 3 of "When the Pathway of Duty" ("I Will Go, If My Father Holds My Hand).
68. *NSP*, 16; *BH*, Nr. 12, stanza 3 of "The Hills of Life" ("The Lord Will Make the Way").
69. *NSP*, 43; *BH*, Nr. 28, chorus of "Lifetime Is Like a Single Day" ("He'll Take You Through").
70. *NSP*, 21; *BH*, Nr. 35, stanza 7 of "The World of Forms and Changes" ("After Awhile").
71. *NSP*, 18; *BH*, Nr. 14, stanza 5 of "This World Is One Great Battlefield" ("I'll Overcome Someday).
72. *NSP*, 22; *BH*, Nr. 17, stanza 6 of "Ever Since I Have Been Living" ("A Better Home").
73. Ibid., stanza 5.
74. Charles Wesley, *Funeral Hymns* (1759), stanza 1 of the poem "On the Death of Mary Naylor, March 21st, 1757," 49.
75. *SE*, Nr. 7; *NSP*, Nr. 5; *BH*, Nr. 1.
76. *NSP*, Nr. 36; *BH*, Nr. 24.
77. *NSP*, Nr. 41; *BH*, Nr. 35.
78. *SE*, Nr. 29; *NSP*, Nr. 21; *BH*, Nr. 35.
79. *NSP*, Nr. 40; *BH*, Nr. 40.

13
Black Megachurches in the Internet Age: Exploring Theological Teachings and Social Outreach Efforts

Pamela P. Martin, Tuere A. Bowles,
LaTrese Adkins, and Monica T. Leach

Abstract: *The research on black megachurches has been limited at best. To date, little is known about theological teachings of black megachurches. Other primary characteristics of black megachurches are even less understood, e.g., how these institutions promote their theological teachings online. Consequently, in this study, black megachurch websites constitute a data source for examining links between theological teachings and community needs. Specifically, this qualitative study of Internet-mediated research examines the websites of 12 black megachurches via content analyses of sermons and information regarding various outreach programs found on their web pages. Results indicate four broad theological themes: honoring the Holy Spirit, heavenly minded, biblical principles, and social legacy. The findings reveal that these themes were related to the social outreach efforts of the 12 black megachurches. Research implications for future studies of black megachurches are discussed.*

Understood via their historical role, black churches have emerged and matured from the "invisible institution" to its current dynamism within communities across the USA. That is to say, both historically and currently, black churches have assumed diverse responsibilities beyond spreading the gospel to save souls. While the function of black churches provides some clues about this religious institution, those clues also reveal that black churches provided more than traditional religious instruction. Consequently, a fundamental understanding of the functions of black churches requires some knowledge about how race, racism, and racial discrimination have impacted the spiritual needs of African American people. Therefore, some social scientists often study black churches to explain the achievements, cultures, and politics among African Americans (Billingsley 1999; June 2008; Lincoln and Mamiya 1990; West and Glaude 2003). For example, black churches have had to help their members overcome societal barriers by providing educational and employment opportunities (Billingsley and Caldwell 1994; Billingsley and Morrison-Rodriguez 2007; Kunjufu 1994; Lincoln and Mamiya 1990), maintaining support networks (Brown and Gary 1991; Chatters et al. 2002; Krause 2010; Mattis et al. 2007), engaging in political participation (Brown 2006; Brown and Brown 2003; Harris-Lacewell 2007; Reese et al. 2007), and increasing psychosocial well-being (Ellison 1997; McAdoo 1995; Taylor et al. 2004). Such diverse functions distinguish black churches as a metaphor of African American life itself.

However, despite the ubiquitous resourcefulness of black churches concerning African American life, neither black churches nor African Americans have remained static across time or place. Black churches, like African Americans, do not constitute a monolith (Lincoln and Mamiya 1990; Taylor 2002). The emergence, growth, and influence of black megachurches entail one of the most significant developments regarding how black churches have responded to changes over time in African American communities. Therefore, the primary purpose of the present study is to examine diverse theological teachings among a purposeful sample of black megachurches. Such an examination seems particularly salient, given the increased number of these types of churches over the past three decades. Concomitantly, this study also substantiates associations between theological teachings and social outreach efforts. By establishing those connections, this qualitative investigation essentially sketches variations of black theological teachings in relation to ministerial programs of black megachurches; by focusing on the social outreach efforts evidenced by those ministries, this study examines first-order and second-order social change as one way to document how black megachurches engage their congregations in activism.

The Emergence of Black Megachurches and Their Presence in the Online Community

Beginning in the 1970s, some black congregants abandoned smaller, more intimate, family-oriented, neighborhood churches to attend megachurches. Primary characteristics of megachurches include the following: (1) 2,000 or more people who attend the church on a weekly basis (Goh 2008; Priest et al. 2010; Warf and Winsberg 2010); (2) lively, exuberant worship services including specific instrumentation, i.e., electronic instruments and drums (Goh 2008; Hall-Russell 2005); (3) two or more Sunday worship services; and (4) integration of technology such as a church website, texting, digital multimedia, and blogging (Elligson 2009; June 2008; Patterson 2007; Pinn 2002;

Smith 2006; Warf and Winsberg 2010). Towards the goal of increasing church attendance and reaching larger and larger audiences, pastors of black megachurches purposefully have invested in online outreach to bring the gospel message to individuals beyond the confines of local geography. These churches have utilized digital resources such as websites, texting, and blogging to reach individuals beyond the physical locations of their congregations (Elligson 2009; June 2008; Pinn 2002; Warf and Winsberg 2010). Furthermore, the Christian commitment to evangelist outreach has been impacted by the 24-hour, immediate access of the Internet. In particular, Lee (2005 as cited in Hinton 2007) contends that the use of the Internet in the propagation of the Christian faith is a "drive to produce spiritual commodities for mass consumption in an ever-expanding market (p. 5)." Simply stated, black megachurches have been able to use their websites to offer all the benefits from their conventional atmosphere of religious worship and spiritual enlightenment to the rest of the world because of "the flexibility, sophistication, and ingenuity" of twenty-first century online technology (Hinton 2007). As a result, the visibility of megachurches online can disconnect individuals from their worship experience so that they can resume their participation at will while those persons attending in live time are more restricted by etiquette, rules, and protocol (Patterson 2007). With the convenience and control of being a part of a virtual, churchgoing community, people seeking religious experiences via black megachurch websites have access to the same information, services, entertainment, products, and theological teachings.

Doctrinal Differences among Black Megachurches

To date, little is known about doctrinal diversity as communicated online by pastors of black megachurches. Consequently, in this study, the content of black megachurch websites constitute a qualitative data source for examining links between theological teachings and community needs as identified by online, black megachurches. The theological teachings of black megachurches comprise guiding principles or foundations regarding the religious behaviors of individuals who practice their faith. Theological teachings of black megachurches differ, however. According to several theologians and scholars (Andrews 2002; Lincoln and Mamiya 1990; Singleton 2002; West and Glaude 2003), black churches reflect various interpretations of the Christian faith. These studies reveal two broad categories of theological teachings among African American Christians: (1) other-worldliness and (2) this-worldliness. Other-worldliness theology imparts a "race-less" spiritual orientation, emphasizing preparation to enter heaven with minimal attention to liberating African American communities from social injustices (Lincoln 1999). On the contrary, this-worldliness theology stresses the importance of focusing on the here and now, especially individual engagement in societal challenges that impact African American communities (Lincoln and Mamiya 1990). New research as well as emergent studies of doctrinal differences in black churches has to contend with how the twenty-first century online community complicates the integrity of this traditional theological continuum. Hinton (2007) asserts that the twenty-first century, soul-winning mission of the new, black church reveals its "genius" in its use of the Internet. Therefore, the distinctions in black megachurches' theological teachings can be explored from Pentecostalism to prosperity gospel to black theology by observing real-time sermons via access to the Internet.

Pentecostalism:
The Complex Tension between Other-Worldliness and This-Worldliness

Pentecostalism among black people emerged from the religious experiences of Reverend William Seymour and Bishop Charles Harrison Mason, founder of the Church of God in Christ. Pentecostalism within black churches incorporates worship experiences that characteristically include passionate preaching, inspirational music, and manifestations of the Holy Spirit such as clapping, dancing, speaking in tongues, and so forth (Pinn 2002). Lively, spirited worship is a well-known hallmark of most Pentecostal churches. This type of worship experience is also emblematic of many black megachurches. Hence, this aspect of Pentecostalism has influenced both traditional black churches and the evolution of the widely popular non-denominational megachurches (Gilkes 1998; Smith 2006).

Previous research studies have oversimplified black Pentecostalism as an entirely other-worldly theology that overlooks the influences of the Civil Rights and Black Power movements, primarily because these faith communities were understood as extreme or fanatical Christians whose primary efforts were dedicated to their preparations for the afterlife (McRoberts 1999; Turner 2006). Thus, such influences and pressures addressing human conditions on earth in the here-and-now could have some effect in encouraging Pentecostal churches to become involved with social outreach efforts. In notable contrast to the sole focus on spiritual concerns, the governing organization of the Church of God in Christ recently instituted the Urban Initiative, Inc. to strengthen communities. This initiative addresses five areas: education, economic development, crime, family relationships, and financial literacy. Examples of black megachurches influenced by Pentecostal doctrine include the Greater Emmanuel Institutional Church of God in Christ in Detroit, Michigan; the Temple of Deliverance Church of God in Christ, Memphis, Tennessee; and the West Angeles Church of God in Christ, Los Angles, California.

Prosperity Gospel:
Promoting Worship as Well as Wealth with This-Worldliness

Predating the emergence of prosperity gospel, several well-known, twentieth-century black preachers emphasized the pursuit of material wealth in the here and now rather than waiting for riches in Heaven in their theological teachings. For example, Bishop Daddy Grace, Father Devine, and Reverend Ike were leaders of ministries that highlighted this message of earthly gratification in contrast to traditional teachings of the historic black denominations (Dallam 2007; Johnson 2010). Their theology now recognized as a prosperity gospel also is accredited to Kenneth Hagin Senior, Neo-Pentecostal faith movement, which is also known as Word of Faith. According to Lee (2007), a prosperity gospel provides congregants with an energizing, exuberant other-worldly worship plus a this-worldliness message of wealth and consumerism. The prosperity gospel movement among black megachurches represents an emerging area of religious research (Elligson 2009; June 2008; Lee 2007; Pinn 2002). Much of this research has revealed that some black megachurches stress individual financial empowerment, which is much different from the historical, social gospel movement as exemplified by Reverend Dr. Martin Luther King and others as an advocate for change (Barris-Lacewell 2007; June 2008; Lee 2007). Research has suggested that in most cases, these prosperity gospel megachurches stymie progressive political involvement (Pinn 2002). In these churches, theological teachings avoid critiques of societal inequalities in education, health care, the judicial system, etc., resulting in a conservative embrace of God's power that applies spiritual prowess to helping believers overcome more personal challenges (e.g., poverty and sickness) and structural barriers such as discrimination (Smith 2006). Prosperity gospel megachurches include World Changers Church International in Atlanta, Georgia and The Potter's House in Dallas, Texas.

Black Liberation:
This-Worldliness among African Americans

Some black megachurches stress not only the spiritual growth of congregants but also the important roles of faith communities in transforming oppressive systems within the USA. Specifically, black liberation addresses challenges to transform racially polarized societies. Given this purpose, black liberation has historical roots in African Americans experiences with racial oppression in the USA (West and Glaude 2003). During times of tumultuous societal transformations, to be more precise, black liberation contributed to an understanding of biblical text as a symbolic, prophetic call for the mental, physical, and spiritual liberations of oppressed black people in the USA (Cone 1997; West and Glaude 2003). Religious scholars contend that embracing a black liberation is not confined to specific denominations (Hopkins 1998; Turner 2006). Churches with memberships larger than 2,000 that promote black liberation include Friendship West Baptist Church in Dallas, Texas and Trinity United Church of Christ in Chicago, Illinois.

Pamela P. Martin, Tuere A. Bowles, LaTrese Adkins, Monica T. Leach

The Internet and Evangelism:
Social Outreach in the Online Community

Lewis and Trulear (2008) contend that African American faith communities, especially larger congregations such as black megachurches, are situated to utilize the Internet to reach local congregations and broader consistencies (e.g., government agencies, industries, and nonprofit organizations). The websites of black megachurches permit local congregations and others to explore the different types of sponsored ministry social outreach efforts. Pargament and Maton (2000) describe six pathways through which faith communities engage in social outreach efforts. The six pathways include social action, social avoidance, social conservatism, social conversion, social sanctuary, and social service. These scholars contend that each social outreach pathway has implications for how individuals within churches conceptualize societal change.

Thus, the website descriptions of social outreach efforts convey whether black megachurches participate in either first-order change, second-order change, or both. First-order change refers to strategies to ameliorate social problems by emphasizing how individuals and specific groups effectively traverse and function within social institutions such as educational, governmental, and political (Lewis and Lambert 2006). First-order change also perpetuates existing social structures. Conversely, second-order change implements strategies to transform oppressive social structures by organizing individuals and specific groups to create more equitable, effective social structures or simply new ones.

Four social outreach efforts seem particularly relevant for this study: social conservatism, social service, social conversion, and social action. Social conservatism strives to engage individuals in benevolent institutions that maintain existing societal structures, while remaining silent regarding perpetual, social inequalities. Social service concentrates on assisting underserved individuals or populations across the developmental life span, sponsoring programs in areas such as homelessness, hunger, mentoring, parenting, etc., that support individuals or populations. Next, social conversion focuses on evangelistic missions; thus, local, state, national, and international missions characterize these churches' stance regarding societal challenges. Each of these three social outreach efforts underscores first-order strategies. In contrast, social action refers to churches that seek to transform societal inequalities through their participation in activities such as civil disobedience, community organizing, political involvement, public policy engagement, and organized protest. These outreach efforts strive to transform oppressive systems, which is characteristic of second-order change.

In this study, the influence of the Internet is a major consideration for analyzing black megachurches. Based on this electronic medium, this study explores how religious messages influenced by the theological teachings communicated at black megachurches transcend local congregations to enter the virtual community via their websites. Even more specifically, three questions focus attention on prospective ways to inform and advance religious literature regarding African American faith communities: (a) what are the theological teachings among black megachurches? (b) how are the diverse theological teachings among black megachurches linked to their social outreach efforts? and, (c) how do the diverse theological and social outreach efforts of black megachurches encourage first-order and second-order changes in the virtual community?

Method

The broad discipline and practice of qualitative research (Berg 2007; Denzin and Lincoln 2008; Schwandt 2007) permits the investigation of the online content and theological teachings of black megachurches. The traditional understanding of qualitative inquiry is that of the anthropologist, sociologist, or evaluator participating in the natural setting of a phenomenon under investigation. That is to say, researchers went into real-world settings and provided first-hand accounts of events unfolding naturally (Patton 2002). The rapid evolution of electronic information and communication technologies has significantly expanded opportunities for qualitative researchers to serve as eyewitnesses to whatever surfaces in an online environment. In a groundbreaking handbook of emergent methods (Hesse-Biber and Leavy 2008), one third of the volume is devoted to exploring how emergent technologies are impacting qualitative research. Thus, Internet qualitative research is becoming more prevalent, especially given how individuals, groups, and organizations are using technology as a communications and delivery tool. Black megachurches have capitalized on technological advances in this digital age and thus serve as a fertile ground for an online investigation of their theological teachings and social outreach efforts.

Black Megachurch Sample

Accessible 24 h/day, the researchers used an Internet-based Christian broadcasting portal, StreamingFaith.com, to identify black megachurches with a significant online presence. A directory search of all ministries yielded 355 religious broadcasts. These religious broadcasts were from churches, radio, and television programming. From the directory search, a total of 189 African American churches provided online broadcasts of entire worship services. Drawing upon the criteria for what constitutes a megachurch (Elligson 2009; Goh 2008; June 2008; Priest et al. 2010; Warf and Winsberg 2010) and the continuum of Lincoln and Mamiya (1990) from other-worldliness to this-worldliness, the senior researcher, along with another member of the research team, identified and selected 12 black megachurches. The research team purposely selected 12 exemplary black megachurches from the online portal. Purposeful sampling permits researchers to make quality selections based on their prior knowledge and expertise about the population (Berg 2007). Thus, black churches in the sample had to meet the requirements of a megachurch, which were the following: (1) 2,000 or more people who attend the church on a weekly basis; (2) lively, exuberant worship services including specific instrumentation, i.e., electronic instruments and drums; (3) two or more Sunday worship services; and (4) integration of technology such as a church website, texting, digital multimedia, and blogging.

To ensure the anonymity of the purposeful sample, a pseudonym was given to each church using the names of the Twelve Tribes of Israel. Table 1 presents the demographics of the black megachurches constituting this study. Using Lincoln and Mamiya's denomination descriptions (1990), six black megachurches in this sample represented denominations comprising the Historic Black Church Denominations (HBCD) such as African Methodist Episcopal Church, Church of God in Christ, the Baptist Convention, USA, Incorporated, and the Progressive National Baptist Convention. The remaining churches include predominantly African American congregations ($n=4$) at Non-denominational Churches, and African American congregants who attend Predominately White Churches (PWC; $n=2$). The PWC churches represent the Episcopal Church, the Presbyterian Church, and the United Methodist Church.

Procedure

For all black megachurches selected in the sample, two primary data collection methods were utilized: (1) extensive online observations of worship services with aligning field notes; and (2) archival data review of content on websites. Observations, a major source of qualitative data, entail watching and listening to what is transpiring in any given setting (Berg 2007; Patton 2002). A qualitative researcher can be a participant or a nonparticipant in a face-to-face or online setting. Given the online conduct of this study, research team members engaged in nonparticipant observations in order to understand the complexity of theological teachings in black megachurches. Overall, members of the research team engaged in more than 150 contact hours of online observations of black megachurch worship services and took aligning field notes. For each church, two sermons were audio-taped and transcribed. To ensure adequate training for transcribing sermons, the research team participated in a workshop regarding transcription and verification of qualitative data.

Archival documents were the second primary source of qualitative data utilized in this study. Patton (2002) defines documents to include "written materials and other documents from organizational, clinical, or program records; memoranda and correspondence; official publications and reports (p. 4)" and so forth. Social scientists have long drawn upon public records to define and explore social phenomena. Hence, black megachurches maintain rich and robust websites as a running archival record of their vision, mission, ministries, activities, announcements, and so on, which were helpful in understanding theological teachings and social outreach efforts.

Data Analysis

To identify codes, categories, and themes, content analysis was used in this study (Berg 2007; Patton 2002). First, the online observational data of the worship services and sermon transcriptions were transcribed and assessed. Two members of the research team listened to the sermons, read, and reread the transcripts. Team members proceeded to code the sermons in order to inductively identify emergent themes. The two researchers individually identified codes and developed code definitions. These researchers developed their codes and themes privately prior to each research meeting. The two researchers initially coded, discussed, and evaluated the sermon data, after which they read through the transcribed sermons making slight modifications to the codes and code definitions. This iterative coding process continued until researchers created themes and established consensus regarding inter-rater reliability.

Each website for the 12 black megachurches was coded on its motto and description of ministries. Each motto was coded to determine the extent to which it addressed individual, community, or societal factors. Individual factors referred to statements related to personal salvation, personal relationship with God, and embodying characteristics of God. Community factors addressed improving conditions in the local community and creating a positive sense of community among congregants and their surrounding community. Societal factors addressed macro level concerns focusing on evangelism and stewardship in the USA and other countries. The ministries listed on each church's website were coded using the social outreach efforts descriptions of Pargament and Maton (2000). Those social outreach efforts descriptions included: social action, social service, social conservatism, and social conversion.

Results

Overall, the results of this study are organized around three questions. For the primary research question, the sermon content analysis yielded the following themes: biblical principles, honoring the Holy Spirit, heavenly minded, and social legacy. For the second research question, the research explored potential links between diverse theological teachings and social outreach efforts among black megachurches. The third and final question, regarding first-order and second-order change, revealed social conversion and social services as the most prevalent outreach efforts among black megachurches. A description of each theme is presented below.

Biblical Principles

The theme of biblical principles underscores the significance of spiritual maturation as an individual develops his/her personal relationship with God. Two types of relationships (i.e., an individual's relationship with God and parents' personal accountability for their children) yielded to be the most salient dimensions within the biblical principles theme. Such spiritual maturation, whether evidenced at the personal level or in parenting practices, requires congregants to make positive lifestyle choices that are consistent with biblical teachings. All of the sermon content at the black megachurches in this study included biblical principles. A sermon from the Reuben Church illustrated the biblical principles theme in the following excerpt:

> Commitment is not popular these days. No one wants to be obligated to anything or anyone. We prefer to be fun, foot loose, and fancy free. So we do common law instead of covenant relationships to keep our options open in case we see something else we want. We do that with everything, our job, our careers, church, and even our relationship with Christ. We hang out with him until we see something better we want. Wholehearted commitment is what pleases God. Some wholehearted commitment is about love. Jesus said in Matthew 22:37, it is loving God with all one's heart and soul and mind, and loving your neighbor as you love yourself When you love God whole heartily, you don't hold back.

The theme of biblical principles, in advocating an intimate relationship with God, also requires some reflection and assessment of an individual's personal journeys in his/her encounters with the Divine. Sermons that advocate biblical principles let congregations know that "getting right with God" is very important by emphasizing the fact that, in any meaningful relationship, only commitment will provide the wherewithal to overcome negative encounters. A sermon from the Issachar Church illustrated this thematic understanding about how committed God is to those who believe.

> We don't teach people how to deal with the mess ups in life because we, we try to hold on to this thing that the church is perfect or sinlessly perfect and that nothing ever happens and the only reason other folk look good when *you* [emphasis added] mess up is not because they haven't messed up but because they haven't been exposed or caught. And so, we [then] lose a lot of people [from the church because] when they mess up,. . . they have a hard time walking back in church; [and] so, they [then] try to find another church where nobody knows them or they won't go [at all], or if they messed up actually [with]in church then they won't go to church at all because [of] the guilt and [feeling] overwhelm[ed] [by] everything [where] the mess up [has] take[n] place. But understand something, even though the church doesn't begin to teach you how to fall and get back up again [after you] mess up, believe me that God teaches you.

Parental accountability for their children also added another dimension to sermons that emphasized the biblical principles theme. Parental accountability refers to parents and other adults becoming more positively engaged in the lives of African American children and youth. Sermon content with parental accountability messages pointed to how previous generations had successfully parented children and youth in regards to how young people needed to navigate societal challenges. Further, black megachurches in this sample emphasized that God expects parents, extended family, and other adults to instill values that align with biblical teachings. Thus, some black megachurches purposefully endorse parental accountability as an extension of their theological teachings regarding biblical principles. These megachurches underscored differences between effective parenting practices and the misguided attempts of parents who want to befriend their children instead of raising them. A sermon at the Simeon Church illustrated:

> First, my father was the head of his house, and there were certain things that were not allowed or tolerated in the house. . . The discipline that we receive was an important part in shaping our character and personality, instilling positive core values and influencing a positive outlook on life. It is precisely a lack of discipline and focus today that precipitates much of the social problems that we have. . . When you have a rule less society, you have chaos and anarchy and you have the making of that society's downfall and ruin. Fathers play a key role in dispensing and modeling discipline. American society and popular culture give license and permission to all types of behavior. . . My father's house is a metaphor for a place for discipline and stability and security and honor and dignity and respect were taught and handed down. My father's house was a place where you got some learning like the old folks would say. And you got some training on how to be a decent human being.

Another example of parental accountability is a sermon at the Joseph Church, which emphasized:

> I don't know if you do this, but the success of motherhood, the success of parenting, is that every mamma, every daddy has to talk to God about their children. See Hanna prayed to God, she didn't first go to fertility doctor, she didn't first do this. It says Hanna prayed to God. . . I have to ask you how are you training your child? If your kid goes home and watches all kinds of stuff on TY, and has all kinds of stuff on their walls and listening to all kinds of stuff on their iPods and all that, you are [parent(s)] letting them do whatever they want to do and say whatever they want to say, and then [you] bring them here, and want us to fix them in 20 min. Please understand this; if you are not talking to your child about God, then your child won't know who they are. And when your child doesn't know who they are that's a problem. Then they devalue life.

Honoring the Holy Spirit

Honoring the Holy Spirit theme refers to the acknowledgment of God's indwelling within the lives of congregation members. Regardless of the theological orientation, all of the sermons mentioned the significance of the Holy Spirit in the lives of believers. For example, a sermon at the Judah Church explains the role of the Holy Spirit in empowering one to prepare for a special task. This sermon stressed the following:

> You know it, but something makes you do it anyhow because there is always a tug of war inside of us, between our deformed self and our reformed self But, the Holy Spirit was given to us so that we could be transformed; so, when you receive the Holy Spirit, the struggle between your reformed self and your deformed self is over. Because when the Holy Spirit comes on the inside, it transforms or gives you an entirely new form. And now, for every person that is in the process of being transformed, it is my assignment to tell you, "You're a champion!" And for the last four weeks, everywhere I have gone to preach or

teach, I've been teaching the people that God has called you, God has chosen you to be a champion. Touch your neighbor and say,. . . "[Y]ou're sitting next to a champion."

A sermon delivered at the Issachar Church affirms the importance of the Holy Spirit in a person's religious and spiritual maturation. This sermon illustrated the honoring of Holy Spirit theme in the following excerpt:

> Very, very important that I want to make to each of you to be filled with Holy Spirit is because the doctrine has been attached to this dwelling of the Holy Spirit. All of my life growing up, people had tried to introduce me to drugs, tried to get me to come to the altar, to pray, and I came out of the seventh and evangelist background and put my presence in the power of God was always on my right when other kids were playing with other things, I was taking cardboard boxes and cutting them up and making them into a pulpit in my room and going behind them and preaching. By having a pulpit, no one was preaching to me. The hand of God was on my life. The Holy Spirit was designated and ascribed to my life so that I could preach this message to you today. When I was a little child, before I went through drugs, before I went through prison, God had his hands on my life and God has his hands on your life, and false doctrines will alienate you from God and have you thinking something false. Bible says bless be the God who has blessed us with all spiritual blessing in heavenly places in Christ Jesus according to his chosen before the foundation of the world.

Heavenly Minded

The heavenly minded theme teaches congregants to focus on the after-life and the expectations of residing in heaven. Therefore, congregants receive messages that direct their involvement on spiritual development efforts that will benefit them in heaven and neglect searching for solutions to personal or societal challenges. This theme is consistent with the other-worldliness theological orientation. A sermon at the Levi Church illustrated:

> This is exactly where [state's name] is right now and unemployment is over 20% highest in the nation. Is there anything good in [state's name] right now? Listening to the media, they're talking about [this industry] and what they're doing to people. This [industry] is not your source. They're just a mean for God to bless you. God is your source. It is he who sustains us in the time of famine. I'll say that again, it is God who sustains us in the time of famine. We don't live by this world system. We don't care if the stock market goes down three or four times. We don't care. Why, God says, I'll always make sure you have more than enough.

Another example of the heavenly minded theme is a sermon delivered at the Dan Church. The sermon underscored:

> Have you paid attention to the oil spill in the gulf over yonder? Have you paid attention to floods in diverse places? Have you paid attention to wars and rumors of wars in diverse places? Whenever you hear of these things, I didn't say it. The Bible said it. Child of God, get ready because He's soon to come. I'm scared. Nowadays, we're still so caught up with

trying to get a shout on from down here, we've forgotten how to get our shout on to get ready for over yonder. This is what I'm trying to tell you child of God. Don't spend most of your energy and your time just celebrating the stuff of what you can have in this life. Rather you got to get ready to get ready to shout about the life to come.

Social Legacy

Social legacy, as defined by black theology literature, reveals the historic, prophetic call of black churches across three historical eras (i.e., chattel slavery, racial segregation or Jim Crow, and the modern Civil Rights Movement). The social legacy theme reflects the findings of Lincoln and Mamiya (1990) that some African American clergy accentuate African American pride messages in their sermons as one way to underscore the unique functions of black churches as bulwarks against injustices within US society. Knowledge of African American history and the plights of American Americans signify dimensions of the social legacy theme. For example, a sermon of the Judah Church centered upon:

> We are the last revolutionaries in America. If we fail to leave a legacy of revolution for our children, we have failed our mission and should be dismissed. Those of us that are 40 and over, that remember the Civil Rights struggle, marched, and were part of the [B]lack [P]ower [M]ovement. Marched and remember the March on Washington and the Million Man March. When look where we were in '67, look where we were in '87, and see where we are now. I thank God for the Will Smiths. I thank God he can make 50 million dollars a movie. I thank God for Oprah. I thank God for Barack Obama.

Furthermore, African American theologians and other religious scholars discussed the tendencies of African American Christians to view themselves in the likeness of God. Therefore, some African Americans recognize God and Jesus as the source of not only sanctifying transformation but also a source of liberation that counters oppressive societal structures (Calhoun-Brown 1998; Cone 1997; Mattis and Jagers 2001). Mattis and colleagues (2003) posit that African Americans historically have drawn upon biblical narratives as well as specific figures as metaphors for living and thriving in hostile, social environments like the story about Abraham's life; the trials of Moses, how Jesus Christ transformed various individuals, or Saul's conversion experience on the road to Damascus. These metaphors in some applications of faith are linked to famous figures in African American history such as Nat Turner, Sojourner Truth, or Martin Luther King Jr. Therefore, black megachurches facilitate a social gospel that builds upon the social justice, which defined the Civil Rights Movement by cementing the personal responsibility to raise children who understand their legacies as both heirs of God and the beneficiaries of African American struggles within US society. The sermon at the Naphtali Church described to the membership the links between African American history and a personal relationship with God. The sermon highlighted:

> See if you don't know your history, you don't know God, and if you know God that means you know your history... You have got to know what the Lord has already done for your ancestors because if you don't know what the Lord has done for your ancestors, you will pop up and say that you did this all by yourself I pulled myself up by my boot straps, I made it to Harvard and Yale all by myself I got to Dartmouth all by myself I got this job all by myself. If you look at my resume, it doesn't say anything about the Civil Rights Movement, it doesn't say anything about Malcolm X; it doesn't say anything about Martin Luther King, I did this resume all by myself Yes, you probably wrote the resume all by yourself, but if it wasn't for other people, nobody would have read your resume in the first place. If it had not been for your ancestors you got to know in order for you to be where you are right now it is because somebody else went before you and I don't know if they are sitting right here. Can you give thanks for those who have paved the way so we are where we are right now?

Social legacy also encourages congregants to critically ponder challenges facing African American communities, especially the challenges that black children must overcome. For example, social legacy sermons at black megachurches challenged members to become actively involved in social change efforts within their local communities. This call to direct action is reminiscent of how traditional black churches in earlier periods of time prepared their members to engage in social justice efforts. For those megachurch preachers who address the racial and structural inequalities experienced by many African American male children and youth, a sermon at the Asher Church, as simply one example of the continuity in social legacy messages explained:

> ... Here it is they categorize you because they want to control you. And then my brothers and sisters they define you because they want to confine you. That's what it means to be black and male in this country. Institutions are guilty in a real sense in terms of making it hard for a black man. Y'all not feeling this, but if you don't believe institutions participate in this, then Indiana will give you the word. Indiana is not the only state, but they are one state that admits that they governor determine the number of prison cells that they are going to build by the test scores of 3rd and 4th graders in the urban cities of the state of Indiana. I did not say the suburbs, I did not say the rural areas, I said the urban areas. Urban is a code word for black and Latino. And all I'm trying to say is instead of correcting the educational system that is leaving our kids behind they build more prisons because they believe in investing in incarceration as opposed to education.

The sermon of the Gad Church highlighted the following:

> What would happen if our children would see men fighting for them? It is unnerving for me to go through public schools and see that the only man in the building is teaching Gym or the janitor. Are there not any men who will take time to educate our children so that their first encounter with a man is not the police, a lawyer, or a parole officer? If we can just get men in the church to understand that I got a responsibility because someone made an investment in me and if these men would have enough focus and discipline to help the child without trying to holla at the momma then the children would understand that you ain't got to be no pretend uncle, you ain't got to be Mr. So-and-So, but you could just be a

brother from the church who is concerned about our children and making a difference. I wish we had some real men in the building who understand that if men are [to] assume their responsibility children would be at a better place.

The second research question explored the link between religious messages and theological teachings among black megachurches. The qualitative findings indicate that black megachurches vary on the degree to which they represent a particular theological teaching. The findings corroborate prevailing research that black megachurches reflect the diversity of theological teachings (Hopkins 1998). These results also qualitatively document Lincoln and Mamiya's conceptualization of other-worldliness and this-worldliness (Lincoln and Mamiya 1990). Table 2 presents the four themes in relation to Pentecostalism, prosperity gospel, and black liberation theology. For example, Levi and Zebulun represented black megachurches that endorsed other-worldliness theology along with emphasizing teachings of biblical principles and honoring the Holy Spirit. Another significant result of this study suggests that some megachurches embrace a black theology orientation such as Asher, Judah, and Naphtali. These megachurches emphasize God's transformative power to remove not only personal but societal challenges. Thus, African American history provides ample examples of God's power, love, and grace in liberating African Americans from enslavement, segregation, and current inequalities. Therefore, religious teachings in the Bible align with the struggle of African Americans. Similar to Levi and Zebulun, these black megachurches underscore biblical principles and honoring the Holy Spirit.

Two megachurches emphasizing biblical principles and honoring the Holy Spirit represented a prosperity gospel theology. At these black megachurches, sermon content implied that aspiring to and having wealth were an indication of God's blessing. These financial blessings indicate individuals' faithfulness to rely and trust God in all endeavors (e.g., economic, education, health, and social). Four megachurches were identified as biblical principles and honoring the Holy Spirit with Pentecostal leanings. These churches embrace an arousing, invigorating worship experience. Among these churches, slight distinctions exist concerning the black theology. In particular, the sermons at Reuben and Simeon incorporate black theology messages by highlighting accomplishments as well as interpreting scripture through the lens of the African American experience.

The third research question investigated the extent to which theological teachings and social outreach efforts are related to first- and second-order change in black megachurches. The research team reviewed and qualitatively assessed each megachurch's website. Specifically, we examined the motto to explore the extent to which it addressed individual, community, and societal factors. The results on the black megachurches' motto revealed 16.7% individual, 25% community, and 58.3% focused on individual to societal factors. Table 3 displays the ecological factors (i.e., individual, community, and societal) and social outreach efforts of the participating black megachurches.

The findings indicate social conversion and social service as the most prevalent outreach efforts among this sample of megachurches. Social conversion outreach programs tend to concentrate on proselytizing individuals to Christianity and to strengthen the relationship with God among congregants. Examples of these outreach programs include visiting sick and elderly congregants, visiting incarcerated individuals, participating in domestic and foreign missions, and proselytizing street ministries. Social conversion also encompasses spiritual growth of church attendees through the use of artistic expression through ministries such as choir, dance, and dramatic arts. In addition, social service programs are dedicated to efforts that benefit the underserved and disadvantaged individuals in the local community. Those ministries may include outreach at prisons, homeless shelters, substance abuse centers, domestic violence organizations, and after-school programs. Outreach at these sites conforms to the scriptural injunction to minister to society's most vulnerable members. These outreach efforts are beneficial by providing resources and support to individuals, local organizations, and communities. These ministries primarily concentrate on empowering and collaborating with existing organizations to perpetuate existing social structures.

Only a small number of black megachurches participated in social action outreach efforts. These efforts represented encouraging and participating in local, national, and global social issues campaign rallies on topics such as education, civil rights, and human rights. These same churches also participated in letter petitioning campaigns targeting local, state, and national elected officials. Another aspect of these churches' engagements is a ministry centered on addressing societal issues through examining outreach linked to policy. These black megachurches engage in outreach efforts attempting to negate oppressive systems not only in the US but also in other countries.

In this sample, only one church participated in social conservatism, and this megachurch primarily focused on two social issues. These social issues were related to definition of marriage and human sexuality. Congregants at this black megachurch were encouraged to contact their local and state representatives about objecting to either new state or federal laws on these issues. The participation in these outreach efforts embodies first-order social change efforts.

Discussion

The purpose of this study examined the theological teachings and social outreach efforts among black megachurches. The four themes identified in the study highlight the similarities and differences among black megachurches. All sermons from the black megachurches emphasized the need of congregants to have a strong biblical foundation and an understanding of the Holy Spirit. The need to establish a relationship with God in addition to relying on the Holy Spirit represents foundational teachings in Christianity. Furthermore, such teachings in black megachurches, especially how the use of the Internet allows theological teachings to transcend local congregations and to engage in an online presence, suggest a foundational application of theology that bridges the other-worldliness or this-worldliness continuum.

The heavenly minded and social legacy themes represent the differences among the black megachurches. These themes illustrate the extreme ends of the conceptualization of Lincoln and Mamiya (1990) of other-worldliness and this-worldliness. The heavenly minded theme encompasses other-worldliness, which in this study provides details about particular black megachurches. For instance, Dan, Levi, and Zebulun exemplify black megachurches that endorse theological teachings of a conservative theology of some Pentecostal churches. These black megachurches participate in primarily social service and social conversion outreach efforts. On the other hand, social legacy theme represents this-worldliness by centering on the transformation of societal norms. Black Liberation Theology underscores this-worldliness continuum. The black megachurches of Asher, Judah, and Naphtali emphasize in their theological teachings the significance of African American culture plus social action and social service outreach efforts. From the qualitative assessment of the 12 websites, all of the black megachurches identified social service ministries as part of their outreach efforts. Thus, social service outreach represents an integral part of black megachurches' outreach efforts.

As highlighted on the black megachurches' websites through live sermon broadcasts and descriptions of ministries, the utilization of Internet technology provides congregants and others about outreach efforts at these particular places of worship. The observational and archival data reveal how the use of the Internet by some black megachurches depicts these churches engagement in first- and second-order change. For example, if Black Liberation Theology predominates at some black megachurches (e.g., Asher, Judah, and Naphtali), then these churches participate in social action outreach efforts focusing on first- and second-order change. Black megachurches endorsing these theological teaching are consistent with some of the HBCDs' doctrinal understandings to promote issues around inequality and reform oppressive systems. If Pentecostalism is at the center of the theological teachings, then the church's foci are both other-worldliness and this-worldliness. Pentecostal teachings at some black megachurches encourage congregants to participate in ministries that primarily focus solely on first-order change (e.g., Issachar and Levi). In this study, the results could not distinguish among Pentecostal black megachurches ranging across the doctrinal teachings influencing social outreach efforts. The findings did not corroborate religious scholars' contention about Pentecostal churches engaging in social outreach efforts targeting second-order change. Similarly, if the prosperity gospel is at the epicenter of the theological teachings, then the church is also a combination of other-worldliness and this-worldliness wherein the primary messages conveyed rest on the individual's acquisition of wealth (e.g., Gad and Joseph). These black megachurches neglect to participate in social justices related to challenges experienced by African Americans. The outreach efforts of these black megachurches concentrate on first-order change. Hence, the examination of sermons and ministry descriptions of black megachurches via the Internet provides a particular theological orientation that is a foundation for the ministries at these churches.

Another archival data source in this study was the use of published mottos from the black megachurches' websites. The qualitative investigation revealed a consistency with the mottos and descriptions of ministries on the websites of the black megachurches. The mottos emphasized the need to engage congregants in transforming individuals and the larger society for the greater good of human kind. An inconsistency emerged concerning the examination of the mottos and ministries. In particular, the mottos indicated an outreach mission of evangelism beyond the confines of the church. However, a great deal of the ministries of these black megachurches centered upon ministries at their churches (e.g., choir, dance, Christian education classes, financial workshops, couple retreats, gender-specific retreats). Thus, the mottos used to convey what black megachurches value and espouse are not substantiated in the descriptions of the ministries at these churches. Argyris and Schon (1974) were among the early scholars to identify that there are typically two theories of action involved in institutions espoused theory and theories-in-use. In black megachurches, espoused values are often found in official literature and resources such as mottos, mission statements, strategic plans, annual reports, and so forth. Enacted values explain what black megachurches have done or currently do in their outreach, and these social outreach efforts are typically supported by how resources are allocated.

Future Research

Research on the black megachurch is emerging, and there is valued work to be accomplished. It is important that researchers engage in additional studies about this topic. Additional research also needs to be conducted on black megachurches to explore the relationship between theological teachings and social outreach efforts. Although this study attempts to begin to explore this relationship, a case study as well as ethnography can potentially provide additional insights regarding the role of theological teachings in shaping social outreach efforts among black megachurches. To illustrate, case study research would be ideal in determining the planning and programming of megachurches that espouse black theology, given that these churches engage in both first- and second-order change. Further, phenomenological studies can explore the "lived experiences" of pastors as they manage these large congregations. For example, in a cursory gendered review of the leadership roles in black megachurches, the role of women needs to be explored. Questions emerge such as: (1) how does being a female pastor influence leadership styles of women who pastor black megachurches; and (2) does Womanist or black Feminist Thought predominate in female pastors' theological understandings? In addition, a questionnaire recruiting church leadership including the pastor can also contribute to the small body of research specifically focusing on black megachurches. This type of survey research could include items focusing on pastoral characteristics such as educational training, years in the ministries, etc., to organizational characteristics of black megachurches including land ownership, membership size, and social outreach efforts. Since this study did not include black megachurches from the far western states, more research on regional differences among black megachurches are warranted. Lastly, expanded quantitative and qualitative research on the participation and engagement of megachurch members in social action activities and social movements is vital.

Additionally, researchers need to explore black megachurches at the individual, community, and societal levels. At the micro-level, research is needed on the motivation of individuals and families of smaller churches to move their membership to megachurches. The expansive opportunities for networking and professional advancement appear as alluring qualities of black megachurch (Pinn 2002; Smith 2006). Hence, future studies should investigate the degree to which churchgoers increase their social capital. Furthermore, typologies should be developed to explore the shifting roles and responsibilities of black megachurch pastors. For example, recent research points to the danger of celebrity for megachurch pastors (Twitchell 2007). With the sheer number of parishioners at black megachurches, studies are needed on the responsiveness of leaders in adjusting to the demands of membership and communities.

At the community level, in traditional mainline denominations, churches must send an apportionment or their earnings to conference and denomination-wide initiatives (e.g., educational systems, missions, and evangelism). Thus, at the community level, quantitative research is needed on the assessment of stewardship and budgets of megachurches to explore corresponding resource allocation toward social outreach. Community-based participatory action research should be conducted with the megachurch and local communities as equal co-investigators to identify new forms of partnerships that bring a synergy in solving social problems. Theoretical research on how black megachurches form a community of practice would be valuable.

To date, little is known about the extent to which societal factors such as education, economics, and politics influence black megachurches. Recently, these churches have begun to develop their own K–5 and, in some cases, K–12 schools. A dearth of research exists about how these institutions, if any, are influencing educational policy. From the pulpit, members of megachurches are often encouraged to participate in a host of campaigns, marches, and rallies; yet, no empirical evidence exists as to the rate and types of participation in which members may engage. Additional studies are needed on how a nonprofit status may facilitate or hinder the extent that the megachurch engages in social outreach. Black megachurches typically have robust television presence. Additional research is warranted on how the cost of television may hinder outreach opportunities.

Table 1 Description of Megachurches

Church name[*]	Affiliation	Membership size	Region	Number of ministries
Asher	HBCD	12,000	Southwest	45
Benjamin	ND	6,000	Southwest	13
Dan	HBCD	2,000	South	12
Gad	HBCD	6,000	Mid-Atlantic	20
Issachar	ND	2,000	South	17
Joseph	HBCD	25,000	South	40
Judah	HBCD	10,000	Mid-Atlantic	35
Levi	ND	6,000	Midwest	18
Naphtali	PWD	8,500	Midwest	41
Reuben	ND	5,000	South	71
Simeon	PWD	6,500	Midwest	130
Zebulun	HBCD	6,000	Midwest	250

[*] A pseudonym was used to protect the anonymity of the participating churches

Table 2 Doctrinal Teachings and Black Megachurches Theme

Doctrinal teachings	Black megachurches theme			
Black theology	Heavenly bound[a]	Biblical principles[b] Holy spirit[c]		Social legacy[d] Asher[b,c] Judah[b,c] Naphtali[b,c]
Pentecostalism	Dan[b,c] Levi[b,c] Zebulun[b,c]	Issachar[c] Benjamin[c] Simeon[c,d]		
Prosperity gospel		Reuben[c,d] Gad[c,d] Joseph[c]		

It is also important to note that the Holy Spirit theme was prevalent in all of the churches

a Heavenly bound
b Biblical principles
c Holy spirit
d Social legacy

Table 3 Megachurch Social Outreach Efforts and Social Change

	Affiliation	Motto	Social action	Social service	Social conversion	Social conservatism	Social change
Asher[a,e,f,g]	HBCD	Individual/ societal	X	X	X		1st & 2nd order
Benjamin[b,e,f]	ND	Individual/ societal			X		1st order
Dan[b,d,e,f]	HBCD	Community			X		1st order
Gad[c,e,f,g]	HBCD	Individual/ societal		X	X		1st order
Issachar[b,e,f]	HBCD	Individual			X		1st order
Joseph[c,e,f]	HBCD	Individual		X	X	X	1st order
Judah[a,e,f,g]	HBCD	Individual/ community/ societal	X	X	X		1st & 2nd order
Levi[b,d,e,f]	ND	Individual/ community		X	X		1st order
Naphtali[a,e,f,g]	PWD	Individual/ community/ societal	X	X	X		1st & 2nd order
Reuben[b,e,f]	ND	Community/ societal		X	X		1st order
Simeon[b,e,f]	PWD	Community	X	X	X		1st & 2nd order
Zebulun[b,d,e,f]	HBCD	Community		X	X		1st order

a Black theology
b Pentecostalism
c Prosperity gospel
d Heavenly bound
e Biblical principles
f Honoring Holy Spirit
g Social legacy

References

Andrews, D. P. *Practical Theology for Black Churches: Bridging Black Theology and African American Folk Religion.* Louisville: Westminster John Knox, 2002.

Argyris, C., and D. Schon. *Theology in Practice: Increasing Professional Effectiveness.* San Francisco: Jossey-Bass, 1974.

Berg, B. L. *Qualitative Research Methods for the Social Sciences.* 6th ed. Boston: Pearson, 2007.

Billingsley, A. *Mighty Like a River: The Black Church and Social Reform.* New York: Oxford University Press, 1999.

———, and C. H. Caldwell. "The Church, the Family, and the School in the African American Community." *Journal of Negro Education* 60, no. 3 (1994): 427–440.

———, and B. Morrison-Rodriguez. "The Black Family in the Twenty-First Century and the Church as an Action System: A Macro Perspective." In *Human Behavior in the Social Environment from an African American Perspective.* 2nd ed. Edited by Letha A. (Lee) See, 57–74. New York: Haworth, 2007.

Brown, D. R., & L. E. Gary (1991). "Religious Socialization and Educational Attainment among African Americans: Empirical Assessment." *Journal of Negro Education* 60, no. 3 (1991): 411–426.

Brown, R. "Racial Differences in Congregation-based Political Activism." *Social Forces* 84, no. 3 (2006): 1581–1604.

———, and R. Brown. "Faith and Works: Church-based Social Capital Resources and African American Political Activism." *Social Forces* 82, no. 2 (2003): 617–641.

Calhoun-Brown, A. "While Marching to Zion: Other-worldliness and Racial Empowerment in the Black Community." *Journal of Scientific Study of Religion* 37, no. 3 (1998): 427–439.

Chatters, L., R. Taylor, K. Lincoln, and T. Schroepfer. "Patterns of Informal Support from Family and Church Members among African Americans." *Journal of Black Studies* 33, no. 1 (2002): 66–85.

Cone, J. H. *Black Theology & Black Power.* Maryknoll: Orbis, 1997.

Dallam, M. W. *Daddy Grace: A Celebrity Preacher and His House of Prayer.* New York: New York University Press, 2007.

Denzin, N. K., and Y. S. Lincoln, eds. *Collecting and Interpreting Qualitative Materials.* Los Angeles: Sage, 2008.

Elligson, S. "The Rise of the Megachurches and Changes in Religious Culture: Review Article." *Sociology Compass* 3, no. 1 (2009): 16–30.

Ellison, C. G. "Religious Involvement and the Subjective Quality of Family Life among African Americans." In *Family Life in Black America.* Edited by R. T. Taylor, J. S. Jackson, and L. M. Chatters, 117–131. Newbury Park: Sage, 1997.

Gilkes, C. T. "Plenty Good Room: Adaptation in a Changing Black Church." *Annals of the American Academy of Political and Social Science* 588 (1998): 101–121.

Goh, R. B. H. "Hilsong and 'Megachurch' Practice: Semiotics Spatial Logic and the Embodiment of Contemporary Evangelical Protestantism." *Material Religion* 4, no. 3 (2008): 284–304.

Hall-Russell, C. "The African American Megachurch: Giving and Receiving." *New Directions for Philanthropic Fundraising* 48 (2005): 21–29.

Harris-Lacewell, M. V. Righteous Politics: "The Role of the Black Church in Contemporary Politics." *Cross Currents* 50, no. 2 (2007): 80–196.

Hesse-Biber, S. N., and P. Leavy, eds. *Handbook of Emergent Methods.* New York: Guilford, 2008.

Hinton, M. A. "The Visible Institution Theology and Religious Education in Two Black Megachurch Ministries." Retrieved from ProQuest Dissertations and Theses Database (2007). (304873863). http://search. proquest.com.www.lib.ncsu.edu:2048/docview/304873863?accountid=12725

Hopkins, D. "Black Theology on Theological Education." *Theological Education* 34, no. 2 (1998): 73–84.

Johnson, S. "The Black Church." In *Blackwell Companion to Religion in America.* Edited by P. Goff, 446–467. London: Wiley, 2010.

June, L. *Yet with a Steady Beat: The Black Church through a Psychological and Biblical Lens.* Chicago: Moody Publishers, 2008.

Krause, N. "The Social Milieu of the Church and Religious Coping Responses: A Longitudinal Investigation of Older Whites and Older Blacks." *International Journal for the Psychology of Religion* 20, no. 2 (2010): 109–129.

Kunjufu, J. *Adam! Where Are You? Why Most Black Men Don't Go to Church.* Chicago: African American Images, 1994.

Lee, S. *T. D. Jakes: America's New Preacher.* New York: New York University, 2005.

———. "Prosperity Theology: T. D. Jakes and the Gospel of the Almighty Dollar." *Cross Currents* 57, no. 2 (2007): 227–236.

Lewis, C. E., Jr., and H. D. Trulear. "Rethinking the Role of African American Churches as Social Service Providers." *Black Theology: An International Journal* 6, no. 3 (2008): 343–365.

Lewis, K., and M. Lambert. "Measuring Social Change Preferences in African American Adolescents: Development of the Measure of Social Change for Adolescents (MOSC-A)." *Assessment* 13, no. 4 (2006): 406–416.

Lincoln, C. E. *Race, Religion & the Continuing American Dilemma.* New York: Hill & Wayne, 1999.

Lincoln, C. E., and Mamiya, L. H. *The Black Church in the African American Experience.* Durham: Duke University Press, 1990.

Mattis, J. S., and R. J. Jagers. "A Relational Framework for the Study of Religiosity and Spirituality in the Lives of African Americans." *Journal of Community Psychology* 29, no. 5 (2001): 519–539.

———, D. L. Fontenot, and C. A. Hatcher-Kay. "Religiosity, Racism, and Dispositional Optimism among African Americans." *Personality and Individual Differences* 34, no. 6 (2003): 1025–1038.

———, N. Mitchell, A. Zapata, N. Grayman, R. Taylor, L. Chatters, et al. "Uses of Ministerial Support by African Americans: A Focus Group Study." *American Journal of Orthopsychiatry*, 77, no. 2 (2007): 249–258.

McAdoo, H. P. "Stress Levels, Family Help Patterns, & Religiosity in Middle- and Working-Class African American Single Mothers." *Journal of Black Psychology* 21, no. 4 (1995): 424–449.

McRoberts, O. "Understanding the 'New' Black Pentecostal Activism: Lessons from Ecumenical Urban Ministries in Boston." *Sociology of Religion* 60, no. 1 (1999): 47–70.

Pargament, K. I., and K. I. Maton. "Religion in American Life: A Community Psychology Perspective." In *Handbook of Community Psychology.* Edited by J. Rappaport and E. Seidman, 495–522. Dordrecht: Kluwer, 2000.

Patterson, C. E. "Give Us This Day Our Daily Bread: The African American Megachurch and Prosperity Theology." Retrieved from ProQuest Dissertations and Theses Database (2007). (30487606). http://search.proquest.com.wwvi.lib.ncsu.edu:2048/docview/304876065?accountid=12725

Patton, M. Q. *Qualitative Research and Evaluation Methods.* 3rd ed. Thousand Oaks: Sage, 2002.

Pinn, A. *The Black Church in the Post-Civil Rights Era.* Maryknoll: Orbis, 2002.

Priest, R. J., D. Wilson, and A. Johnson. "U.S. Megachurches and New Patterns of Global Mission." *International Bulletin of Missionary Research* 34, no. 2 (2010): 97–104.

Reese, L., R. Brown, and J. Ivers. "Some Children See Him. . . : Political Participation and the Black Christ." *Political Behavior* 29, no. 4 (2007): 517–537.

Schwandt, T. A. *The Sage Dictionary of Qualitative Inquiry.* 3rd ed. Los Angeles: Sage, 2007.

Singleton, H. H. *Black Theology and Ideology: Deideological Dimensions in the Theology of James H. Cone.* Collegeville: Liturgical, 2002.

Smith, V. E. "Where Do We Go from Here?" *The Crisis* (2006): 31–35.

Taylor, C. *Black Religious Intellectuals.* New York: Routledge, 2002.

Taylor, R., L. Chatters, and J. Levin. *Religion in the Lives of African Americans: Social, Psychological, and Health Perspectives.* Newbury Park: Sage, 2004.

Turner, W. *The United Holy Church of America: A Study in Black Holiness-Pentecostalism.* Piscataway: Gorgias, 2006.

Twitchell, J. B. *Shopping for God: How Christianity Went from In Your Heart to In Your Face.* New York: Simon & Schuster, 2007.

Warf, B., and M. Winsberg. "Geographies of Megachurches in the United States." *Journal of Cultural Geography* 27, no. 1 (2010): 33–51.

West, C., and E. S. Glaude. *African American Religious Thought.* Louisville: Westminster John Knox, 2003.

Section Three

Proclamation of the Word

14

Introduction to Preaching with Sacred Fire: An Anthology of African American Sermons, 1750 to the Present

Martha Simmons and Frank Thomas

This anthology [*Preaching with Sacred Fire: An Anthology of African American Sermons, 1750 to the Present*] rests first upon the premise that the main initiators of freedom and emancipation for black people have been their religious faith, the religious communities and institutions, and the souls that house that faith. The second premise is that the role of preaching to that religious faith and those religious communities, institutions, and souls has been paramount. Black preaching has sustained and liberated black people in the sweltering heat of servitude and American oppression. This anthology seeks to delineate the liberating, transformative, and celebratory role of preaching. But before we further expand upon black preaching's role, we turn to the significant connection between black preaching and Africa.

The African Roots of Black Preaching

The black preaching tradition is rooted in the religions of the foreparents of the Africans who were forcefully brought to the Americas. From the moment they were removed from their home village and tribal lands and chained in ships' holds, their traditional belief systems and rituals of communication were all they had to depend on. After they arrived in North America, they did not know how to make sense of life once separated from their tribal religions' supreme being. For instance, the Yorubas of Nigeria came here believing in a high god named Olodumare, the Yoruba term for omnipotent.[1] While they originally turned to their god for meaning and comfort, life in the Americas was so cruel and chaotic that they searched for the reigning local deity and sought to learn how that deity operated. Out of this spiritual necessity grew the slow and tedious process of creating black North American religions out of the common practices of many African belief systems. Because they were seeking to meet real needs the enslaved created a spiritual orientation and functional faith on their own terms, as opposed to what their enslavers tried to each.

The process of establishing the religions of black folk on North American shores was slow, in part, because there were Africans from many tribes, with different languages, belief systems, and worship practices. It took time to develop makeshift languages in which they could communicate with one another. Yet, the enslaved used their last drop of energy to satisfy the universal human hunger for dignity and honor, including through religious expression. They had enough commonality among their various tribal traditions to extract core beliefs and develop "one Neo-African consciousness—basically similar yet already significantly different from West African understandings of traditional African religion."[2]

There were many aspects of Traditional African Religion that were easily adaptable into the Christian-based North American cosmology; there were major overlaps between Traditional African Religion and the Old Testament. As historian Carter G. Woodson wrote, "it was easy for the Negro to accept a faith which differed little from the one he had in Africa."[3] Examples of the similarity between the two include the African concept of the "living dead" and the Christian concept of the afterlife; the African Law of Identical Harvest and the Bible's "you reap what you sow" (Galatians 6:8); the prayer offered to the Supreme Being as the creator spirit with access to extraordinary power and as the giver of health and medicine, and the Christian concept of God's ability to heal through prayer.[4] Also, the water rites of religious rebirth in African religious practices were similar to Christian baptism.[5]

Even more to our purpose in this anthology, Traditional African Religion had a great respect for the power of words, illustrated by certain folktales and myths. The Bible in Western culture was held in much this same esteem, though in Africa oral telling held sway over written text. African religion contributed to black preaching the necessity of a serious verbal engagement with the audience in order to pass on holy wisdom (proverbs and other forms) and, most importantly, the presence of the unspeakable Presence.

In fact, black religion in North America began with combinations of Bible stories told in English mixed with African retellings and interpretations, primarily in African folk styles. The most important elements were vivid narration and call-and-response. The indigenous renditions in the motherland had been at once entertaining and spiritually instructive, essentially intended to inform and teach the young in the traditions of African society. All of this served well the goals of preaching on North American shores.

Eventually, perhaps around the mid-eighteenth century, the English Bible replaced much of the indigenous wisdom tradition of the enslaved. It was chosen primarily for content, to fill the role of the holy wisdom once couched in the African languages; by this time English had become the only commonly understood language. But the Bible was also seen as a means of access to the power wielded by the deity worshiped by the masters. It was natural, after that, to add African culture's emphasis on oratory, imagery, drama, and tonality to what became black preaching in America. This was especially true after the Africans saw and heard white preachers like George Whitefield use such strategies during the First Great Awakening, a colonies-wide revival in the mid-eighteenth century.

It is not known precisely when authentic black preaching of the Christian faith began to take shape, but it is likely that the tradition formally surfaced toward the end of the First Great Awakening. Very few written records of preaching by enslaved Africans exist prior to that time. Preaching from the outset was done without notes, often without the ability to read. It is tragic that we have no record of how it sounded or what preachers said when black preaching began in what became America.

Faiths beyond Christianity

While the majority of blacks in America are part of the Christian church, from the time that Africans were first brought to the Americas and the Caribbean during the transatlantic slave trade until the present, blacks have embraced religious traditions other than Christianity.

The practice of these observances is, in large part, a reaction to social and political issues, particularly racism, that have confronted blacks over the past four hundred years, but most especially from the eighteenth to the twentieth century. The most notable and oldest of these traditions have been various forms of Islam. Finding the exact number of Muslims who landed in North America as captives is an extremely difficult task. There are no precision documents relative to the religion of human cargo noted by slave traders and slave dealers. Therefore, suggesting numbers and figures is highly problematic and risky. Allan Austin asserts that between 5 and 10 percent of all slaves from ports between Senegal and the Bight of Benin (from which half of all Africans were sent to North America) were Muslims. If the total number of enslaved was twelve million and roughly 6 or 7 percent arrived in North America, then there may have been forty thousand Muslims in colonial and pre–Civil War America. Austin admits that future systematic gathering of records on slave trading ports on both sides of the Atlantic as well as other scholarly studies will lead to "better figures and descriptions."[6] Though many African slaves were Muslim, and a number of them continued to practice Islam once in North America, African Muslim captives never formed into a sizeable American community of faith that passed on its traditions from one generation to the next.[7] The Muslim community diminishes until what Edward E. Curtis calls "the English speaking black theorists of Islam," especially Noble Drew Ali and Elijah Muhammad, define Islam in America.[8] However, blacks have also embraced other non-Christian religions, such as Judaism and Buddhism, and created Santeria, Vodun, and Rastafarianism using West African and other principles.

It is important to note that in most of these religions, there is nothing that compares exactly to the form of the sermon or the homiletical techniques and traditions of preaching discussed most often in this anthology. The Bible is not an authoritative text in most of these non-Christian traditions. Rituals, dietary customs, distinctive forms of worship, special readings, and prayers have often taken the place of preaching or made it secondary, though not unimportant.

Many significant non-Christian leaders have emerged within the black community during the years considered in this anthology, but few if any have ever enjoyed the reputation of being a "great preacher." They have been compelling orators on matters of social policy, race relations, and moral conduct. They have been masterful teachers and interpreters of the texts of their religions. However, because they did not base their speech or orations on texts taken from the Bible, which many blacks continue to view as the normative text for religious worship, the ability of these non-Christian leaders to appeal to a large cross-section of the black community has been limited. Also, because the numbers of such persons have remained relatively small in comparison to the number of Christian clergy, there are many within the Christian community who still do not have an awareness of or an appreciation for the non-Christian religious traditions and religious leaders that emerged around them. For example, though there is a tradition of at least three hundred years of Muslim preaching in North America, little is known about the continent's Muslim faith community prior to Elijah Muhammad's ascendency as the leader of the most well-known black Muslim group (the Nation of Islam) in the 1950s.

Given the general absence of the sermon in most non-Christian traditions, the entire approach to worship, and for ocher reasons, the work of spiritual formation, is quite different from those that are employed by most black Christians. Most black Christians are familiar with observing such occasions as Christmas and Easter, but they are less familiar with Ramadan and other Islamic festivals and holy days. They are generally familiar with the Bible as a book of religious instruction, but less familiar with how parts of that book are interpreted by black Jews.

Jesus Christ as the perfect sacrifice that takes away the sins of the world is a well-known doctrine among African American Christians, but animal sacrifice as practiced by the devotees of Santeria or Vodun is much less understood or appreciated. Similarly, spirit possession is frequently seen and experienced in many African American Christian settings, most notably among many of the Holiness-Pentecostal, Apostolic, and Baptist groups. However, the actions that can result in spirit possession and the reasons for seeking spiritual possession in the first place are very different among some of the black non-Christian and African-based religious groups.

Given the dominance of Christianity within the United States from the country's inception, and given the central role that the African American church has played within the lives of so many within the African American community, the question must be asked: Why or how do African Americans come to the decision to practice faiths other than Christianity? The first answer, as briefly mentioned earlier, is that the Africans who were brought to this country during the slave trade brought much of their cultural heritage with them during the Middle Passage journey from Senegal, Ghana, Angola, and other places in Africa to Brazil, Haiti, Cuba, the United States, and settlements in the Americas and Caribbean. As early as the 1730s, observers of Islam were among those from throughout West Africa who were captured and brought as slaves to North America. Islam, along with various aspects of the Yoruba religion from West Africa, was among those cultural mementos that survived the journey and continued to survive in the spirit and behavior of African people in the diaspora.

Second, African captives continued earlier African practices under the guise of Christianity, what Elizabeth McAlister calls "a creolized system" of religion or "code-switching" between some form of Christianity, usually Roman Catholicism, and traditional African religions.[9] New religions such as Santeria, in Cuba, Vodun, in Haiti, and Candomble, in Brazil, took root as a result of that process of creolization. Leonard Barrett refers to the newer religious traditions as "black redemption cults," inferring that African people turned to these created religious practices as a way to cope with and in some ways to actually resist their lives as slaves.[10] Over time, the practitioners of Santeria and Vodun, in particular, made permanent homes in the United States, especially in cities such as Miami, New Orleans, and New York.

Third, African captives practiced non-Christian religions as a protest against Christianity and white society. Some of the most charismatic and controversial figures to emerge from within the African American faith community were those who urged their followers to reject Christianity and embrace other religious traditions. They largely based their argument on the facts that Christianity had been imposed upon black people, and, to make matters worse, leaders within the white Christian church continued to support the oppression and second-class status of their black Christian brothers and sisters. The non-Christian leaders believed that the black community needed to reclaim their original, authentic, African faith and identity. This approach would include such men and movements as Noble Drew Ali and the Moorish Science Temple, Rabbi Wentworth A. Matthew and the Black Jews of Harlem, and W. D. Fard, who was followed by Elijah Muhammad and the Nation of Islam.[11]

Any discussion of the practice of non-Christian traditions in black religion would have to include the personality movements that emerged in urban centers during the Great Migration, when millions of blacks moved from the rural South to the cities of the North during World War I and into the 1920s, which was followed by the cataclysmic Depression of the 1930s. Social dislocation and harsh economic forces made the messages of some groups very appealing.

George "Father Divine" Baker of the Peace Mission Movement and Charles Manuel "Sweet Daddy" Grace of the United House of Prayer for All People founded the most prominent of these movements. In addition to religious identity, these groups also provided people with a social community and even basic needs, such as food, clothing, and minimal employment during the hard times of the Great Depression. They were providing a level of service that most Christian churches, with a few exceptions, could not or would not provide. Seiger and Singer describe these urban movements as "a variant of African American nationalism that combines religious belief with the ultimate objective of achieving some degree of political, social, cultural and/or economic autonomy."[12]

Lastly, blacks adopt non-Christian traditions of religious observance because they find those traditions fulfilling in their search for spiritual identity. As the twenty-first century dawns, there are many within the African American community who have voluntarily turned to a wide variety of non-Christian religions. In many cases, their search for spiritual identity is unrelated to any of the protest issues or the inclusion of African rituals that may have been the impetus to join or create earlier non-Christian religions. With the resurgence of African pride and the phenomenal popularity of the Jamaican singer Bob Marley, some African Americans have embraced Rastafarianism, and others, such as R&B singer Tina Turner, have turned to Buddhism in one of its many forms. Some adhere to the Baha'i faith or to another of the world's religions as a way to embrace what they view as their relevant messages and worldviews. Having briefly noted the role and nature of the main non-Christian sectors of the African American faith community, we now turn to the principles that underline African American Christian preaching.

Principles of Black Christian Preaching

When we consider the black (primarily Christian) preaching tradition, several principles emerge. The first is the centrality of the Bible. This is not to be mistaken for rigid literalism; the Bible is seen as an inspired and dynamic source for understanding the world and as a wise guide for life's decisions. Homiletician Cleophus J. LaRue has stated it thus: "Indeed, it is no secret that the Bible occupies a central place in the religious life of black Americans. More than a mere source for texts, in black preaching the Bible is the single most important source of language, imagery, and story for the sermon."[13]

The second principle of black preaching is that the Bible is made to come literally alive by means of an eyewitness style of picture painting and narration. The preacher has studied and meditated on the Bible to a point where the Bible is not only ideas, but also visual images. These images can be easily remembered and delivered, without notes, to an audience, which then shares in the preacher's experience. Faith is transmitted holistically, viscerally rather than only intellectually, as art rather than as argument. The preachers strive for sincere faith based upon religious experience, moving hearers to a relationship with the Divine.

Third, a reason for such profound sermonic insights is the cultural habit of the close observation of life, which yields a rich storehouse of interesting, true stories illustrative of biblical precepts with which the hearer may identify. This method could be termed *existential exegesis*. It was practiced by the best slave preachers and continues to this day.

Not to be overlooked is the preacher's desire for relevance. The preacher prays that his or her sermons will help the hearer at points of need, not just reach them as abstract doctrine. The Western notion held by many of sermons as primarily offered to God is supplemented by a traditional African notion of sermons as a vehicle to give useful instruction. If it glorified God, then it had to help people. Even the sermon's eloquence was not for mere decoration, but was and is seen as lending power to the Word, and fostering its purposes.

Black preaching fosters an aptitude of thinking deeply and learning wherever possible, in formal academic settings and in the classroom of life. This is in relation to all of life, not just for preaching purposes and shapes the "cultural habit of the perceptive observation of life" as expressed in principle three. This explains why the homiletical quality of sermons by the best of the self-educated preachers have not been in the least inferior to those by preachers with formal training. Indeed, it is likely that the response of the hearers to the self-educated is often better because there is a strong suspicion they have not been educated away from their own culture.

Next, the black preaching tradition is aware of dependence on a power beyond the preacher's power. It can be called transcendence, divine beneficence, the Holy Spirit, the Holy Ghost, or the Spirit. Preachers believe that beyond their best abilities and preparation, their sermons are controlled, enriched, and guided by the Spirit. Preachers believe that their words ultimately come from the Creator and Sustainer of the Universe, who has shaped them and delivers messages through the preacher's careful and thorough discipline. The glory then belongs to the Divine and not to the preacher.

A final underlying principle of much of black preaching is the use of suspense followed by a powerful and uplifting conclusion (also known as the sermon celebration or close). The timing within the art of preaching is like the timing of a great drama or symphony. Suspense is built in stages, resolved, and then concluded in a focused, emotionally powerful ending. The typical black sermon ends in a joyful celebration, not a challenge for hearers to do this or that. The admonition to do, to change, to serve, and so forth is reserved for the body of the message. The close is reserved for pure celebration. The conclusion gives reinforcement to the text and primary purpose of the sermon, or message in the case of the Koran. The weight that the black faith community places upon a good conclusion to a message or sermon is unparalleled. It is not marched by other faith communities, though there is evidence that this is slowly changing with the increase of "praise and worship" and neo-Pentecostal-styled worship services.

The Divisions of This Anthology

This anthology [*Preaching with Sacred Fire*] is divided into six periods or eras:

THE BEGINNINGS OF AFRICAN AMERICAN PREACHING: 1750–1789
SOCIAL AND RELIGIOUS EMANCIPATION: 1790–1865
FROM RECONSTRUCTION TO DECONSTRUCTION: 1866–1917
WORLD WARS, FREEDOM STRUGGLES, AND RENAISSANCE: 1918–1950
CIVIL RIGHTS AND DIRECT ACTION: 1951–1968
FROM BLACK TO AFRICAN AMERICAN AND BEYOND: 1969 TO THE PRESENT

Each section begins with a brief historical overview of the period, followed by a discussion of the preaching and then brief biographies of some of the distinguished personalities whose preaching and methods made significant impacts upon the period. Their sermons follow. Sermons have not been placed in periods using a scientific method. Rather, their placement is most often an attempt to place a preacher with his or her contemporaries and within the period in which they were most active.

Categories of Black Preaching

Detailed and careful attention to the powerful and liberating black preaching tradition reveals four classifications that serve as a homiletical umbrella: *social activist preaching*, which provides the spiritual, moral, and cultural underpinnings for liberation struggles; *black identity preaching*, which seeks to reconstruct blacks' humanity, dignity, and self-esteem; *cultural survival preaching*, which constructs and maintains black culture; and *empowerment preaching*, which provides an unequivocal message of wealth and success through change in consciousness as a liberation strategy. All black preaching falls within at least one of these classifications; some overlaps into one or more categories.

Social activist preaching aims to induce social activism by providing the spiritual, political, and cultural underpinnings for liberation struggles, including the prophetic voice of social critique and redress. It is principally projected to a wider American culture and world, but also serve as an inner critique of the black church and black culture. The social activist preaching agenda includes poverty alleviation, racial and gender equality, and all peace, justice, and economic struggles.

Preaching for black identity is preaching to construct and reconstruct humanity and dignity, and to enhance the self-esteem of blacks. The experience of slavery and its ideological justifications functioned to assault black identity and personhood. This category encompasses so much black preaching that an eminent authority on preaching, Gardner C. Taylor, has stated that the essence of *all* black preaching is raising the self-esteem of black people.[14] Though we can agree with Taylor, there are important, obvious distinctions that are blurred if we subsume all other black preaching classifications under this heading. For example, preaching for black identity is closely related to social activist preaching, in that the social activist sermon attempts to raise the esteem of hearers in order to encourage them to act. But the critical difference is that preaching for black identity usually does not feature a political program.

Preaching for cultural survival is preaching for the construction and maintenance of black culture that helps blacks endure in their average, day-to-day, week-to-week living. In addition to systemic oppression, blacks still contend with the nodal events of human life-birth, death, sickness, disease, marriage, school, financial crisis, birthdays, job loss, and so forth. The experience of oppression has often been writ so large that we can forget that much of black preaching concerned the maintenance and development of everyday survival skills. This culture of survival was forged Sunday after Sunday, prayer meeting after prayer meeting, even funeral after funeral, in the lives of religious adherents. Preaching for cultural survival often resembles preaching for black identity. It too encourages persons to endure for another week, despite the highs and lows of life. Preaching for cultural survival is the largest area of black preaching; in all of its manifestations it seeks to give stability to hearers and order to their everyday lives. It contains four subareas: the regular Sunday-morning sermon (typically concerning biblical and theological doctrines, denomination polity, local issues, and in-house church issues), the revival sermon, the funeral sermon, and the annual-day sermon (for occasions such as Men's Day, Mother's Day, Choir Anniversary, Usher's Day, and so forth).

Empowerment preaching provides an unequivocal message of black power, a belief in entrepreneurism, wealth, and success where individuals primarily find liberation through changing their consciousness and through hard work, and less through social reform movements. Empowerment preaching is a liberation strategy. For most empowerment sermons the homiletical focus is not social protest, but individual initiative buttressed by one's familial, and in some instances community, unit. For some in the black community, it is only acceptable to combine individual achievements with social movements that aid the entire black race. Empowerment preaching asserts that the American Dream is real—everyone has the opportunity to move up if they work hard and are talented. While empowerment preaching acknowledges structural barriers that limit individual wealth and success, it does not view them as forces that cannot be overcome. The message of empowerment preaching not only includes financial well-being, it also stresses the need for blacks to be political leaders and controllers of their own destiny. Being empowered to control one's destiny is the overriding concern of empowerment preaching.

Although it gained prominence among blacks in the late 1900s, by the 1930s some advocates of empowerment preaching, through white preachers who taught that faith was rewarded with wealth and health, shifted its focus to individual wealth, as opposed to communal wealth. The focus was no longer the advancement of persons so that they and their communities would thrive, nor was the focus tied to increasing appreciation of one's ethnic heritage. The focus shifted so sharply to individual wealth that it became clear by the 1980s that a segment of black preaching had adopted *prosperity preaching*. Prosperity preaching places its greatest emphasis on the achievement of financial wealth by individuals. While it may purport to have other concerns, they are all treated as secondary or insignificant. The most important thing is that individuals prosper financially. Often, such prospering occurs after preachers ask hearers to sow seeds that will result in the hearer achieving a financial and physical blessing (or healing).

With the strands of black preaching now presented, we begin the journey through the liberating, salvific, and celebratory messages of centuries of black preaching in North America. While blacks were the direct beneficiaries of this preaching, all of America and indeed the world benefited greatly from it. From]arena Lee to John Jasper to Noble Drew Ali and Vernon Johns, the African American preaching tradition has at its highest and best always had as its ultimate concern the spiritual and social liberation of all persons. This anthology salutes those

> whose words and deeds
> the Spirit called forth
> out of mourning
> the dawning of this morning.

Notes

1. E. Bolaji Idowu, *Olodumare: God in Yoruba Belief* (London: Longman Group, 1962), 30–37.
2. Mechal Sobel, *Trabelin' On: The Slave Journey to an Afro-Baptist Faith* (Westport, CT: Greenwood, 1979), xvii.
3. Carter G. Woodson, *African Background Outlined* (New York: Negro University Press, 1936), 359.
4. Kofi Asare Opoku, *West African Traditional Religion* (Accra, Ghana: FEP International Private, 1979), 137–39.
5. Ibid., 60ff.
6. Allan Austin, *African Muslims in Antebellum America: Transatlantic Stories and Spiritual Struggles* (New York: Routledge, 1997), 22, 23.
7. Edward E. Curtis IV, *Islam in Black America: Identity, Liberation, and Difference in African American Islamic Thought* (Albany: State University of New York Press, 2002), 7.
8. Ibid., 7.
9. Elizabeth McAlister, "The Madonna of 115th Street Revisited: Vodou and Haitian Catholicism in the Age of Transnationalism," in *African American Religious Thought*, ed. Cornel West and Eddie Glaude Jr. (Louisville: Westminster John Knox, 2003), 942–77.
10. Leonard Barrett, *Soul Force: African Heritage in Afro-American Religion* (Garden City, NY: Anchor Books, 1974), 96.

11. Entries on each of these men can be found in Marvin A. McMickle's *An Encyclopedia of African American Christian Heritage* (Valley Forge: Judson, 2002), as well as in the *Encyclopedia of African American Religions,* ed. Larry Murphy, Gordon Melton, and Gary L. Ward (New York: Garland, 1993).

12. Hans Seiger and Merrill Singer, "Religious Diversification During the Era of Advanced Industrial Capitalism," in *African American Religious Thought,* 525.

13. Cleophus J. LaRue, *The Heart of Black Preaching* (Louisville: Westminster John Knox, 2000), 10.

14. An informal 2003 conversation between Martha Simmons and Gardner C. Taylor at the Hampton University Ministers' Conference.

15
Preaching in the Black Church

Ruthlyn Bradshaw

God's *ecclesia* does not come in colors and tribes. However, for analytical purposes, it is necessary that one recognize the role of culture and ethnicity and their impact on certain activities—in this case preaching.

In addressing Muslims in Egypt recently (June 2009), US President Barack Obama drew on his Muslim connections and African American heritage to more effectively connect with his audience. His use of phrases in the language of the people added authenticity and richness to his speech. Ethnicity and culture help to define us and what we do and how we do it.

Africans, for instance, have an innate love of rhythm, and this is evident in their worship style, which is a dramatic contrast to the style in an Anglo-Saxon congregation. Thus preaching style and content cannot be separated from the culture of a people. While there is no inherent difference in the essence of Christianity there is a difference in how it is expressed.

The Black Church Defined

Definition is one of the main difficulties when talking about the black church, as there is no simple undisputed definition for this term. Definitions vary depending on the context. Formulating a term acceptable to all that captures the full meaning and essence of the black church is nigh impossible. Over the years several labels have been used to define or describe churches with a black majority following and just as many objections have been lodged to disqualify using them. At present, the term "black majority churches" originating in the UK seems to have superseded all other terminologies and is widely used as an acceptable description.[1]

The term black church, as used in this chapter, refers to those churches in the UK that are led by black leaders, with a majority of the congregation being Africans, African Caribbean and people from other countries who define themselves as being black.

History of the Black Church in the UK

The history and uniqueness of the black church in the UK and the associated black preaching emanated from the predicament in which post-World War II African migrants found themselves. Many of them encountered imperialism, colonialism and racism. Blacks were dehumanized and excluded from meaningful participation in British society. The development of the black church could be summarized thus: enslavement in the Caribbean to emancipation; post-Second World War mass migration and the current migration trends; permanent residence in the UK, with the task to craft a livelihood in a country established on the premise that "all men are equal until they are seen to be darker than me."

The first stage began with the Africans enslaved in the Caribbean up until emancipation. In this context the Anglo-Saxon church fully supported plantation slavery. Preaching was geared towards maintenance of the status quo despite the obvious inconsistency with the Christian message represented in the brutal dehumanization of the African. The church actively engaged in teaching the enslaved to be good servants, obedient and submissive, in spite of the inhumane treatment being meted out to them.

Although forced to worship in the church of their masters, amid grave contradictions and a theology of oppression, being deeply religious the Africans did not relinquish their religiosity. "To be without religion amounts to a self excommunication from the entire life of society and African peoples do not know how to exist without religion" (Mbiti 1989: 2). Recognizing the futility of the situation, the Africans voted with their feet and, notwithstanding the inevitable consequences, established their own brand of churches, similar to those established by their brothers and sisters in North America.[2] Their actions in defying their oppressors and establishing ecclesiastical spaces demonstrated the extent to which they esteemed religion and the role it played in shaping and defining their lives.

In addressing the overwhelming challenges facing them at the time, the church became the vehicle for their total expression and development. It functioned as a one-stop shop focusing on the "whole person" and served as their school, parliament, hospital, place of refuge and solace. The church also became their economic and spiritual warehouse and inevitably propelled their emancipation as it became the forum for plotting escape and political uprising in the name of equality.

The second stage of development of the black church in the UK concerns the post-Second World War mass migration from the Caribbean in response to the call from the colonial power for assistance in rebuilding a devastated Britain. The arrival of hundreds of descendants of enslaved Africans from the Caribbean on the SS *Empire Windrush* in 1948 has been referenced and acknowledged by historians and theologians as a focal point in the emergence of the black church in Britain (Phillips and Phillips 1998; Sturge 2005: 82).

The African migrants from the Caribbean were treated in ways not dissimilar to the treatment that they received when enslaved. Alongside this was the brutally cold climate and the hostile welcome. Confronted with the harsh realities of colonial racism, they turned to the church in hopes of finding spiritual refuge, consolation and support. In the absence of black churches in the UK, they initially attended the same denominations as the ones transplanted by Britain to their home country. Their hopes quickly dissipated as they discovered that the hostile climate, permeating the society, was equally present in many of the churches. Instead of receiving a Christian welcome they were rejected and dissuaded from attending church. One of the many disheartening reports is that of a man being told by the vicar following a church service, "Thank you for coming, but I would be delighted if you didn't come back. . . my congregation is uncomfortable in the company of black people" (Phillips and Phillips 1998: 149). Judging from the treatment received, they came to realize that the oneness and inclusiveness expressed in the church's liturgy did not include blacks in many of the main churches in the UK.

It is noteworthy to mention that not all the churches in Britain responded in this way. Some black Christians found a degree of acceptance in churches and, regardless of the shortcomings, defied the odds and remained. Their presence in these churches eventually helped to transform them. However, for the majority, racism, coupled with rejection and the absence of their familiar brand of churches, forced them to resort to the methods of their forefathers. Borrowing from the traditions of the black churches established in the Caribbean and in Africa, they initiated churches in Britain that were nonexistent before. In recent times it has been argued that it was not solely as a result of racism that black churches came into existence in Britain, but they were raised up to fulfill spiritual, social and cultural needs which would otherwise have been left unmet (Sturge 2005: 87). The church was at that stage primarily a spiritual warehouse and the preaching was similarly crafted.

The third stage of development is characterized by the black migrants permanently remaining in the UK, striving to obtain a livelihood as independent men and women. The migrants at first had no intention of permanently residing in the UK. Intending their stay in Britain to be temporary, they busied themselves with becoming economically secure, hoping to return home in better financial positions. In their quest for survival, accommodation and employment, church attendance was jeopardized and in some cases completely sacrificed. When dreams of returning home did not materialize, many reconnected with the church. With the influx of new attendees, the emerging churches quickly outgrew the bedrooms and sitting rooms in which they had begun, so it became necessary to hire halls and acquire buildings in which to accommodate the fast-growing congregations. "These are the independent 'black-majority' churches which have become such a marking feature of present-day British Christianity" (Wilkinson 1993: vi).

Emerging Black Churches and Leaders

Faced with the complex and compelling needs of their main constituents, the emerging black churches became centers of social significance, implementing various strategies and techniques for survival. In the early beginnings, the church was the only place where the suppressed emotions of black people could have been released. Subsequently the churches in this dispensation continued to provide non-threatening safe environments in which to meet, worship, share and deal with their problems together. It appears that if black people in the African diaspora were not clever enough to have formed churches and made spaces for themselves, they would not have survived (Reddie 2008: 115).

Early pioneer leaders in the black churches served as bedrocks to the new settlers. They were highly respected, admired and accepted as the instruments and oracles of God. These leaders, as representatives in a common struggle and carrying the burden of the slavery experience, understood the plight of the people they shepherded. They "lived their skin"; hence they faced the same predicaments, trying to exist in an environment that was not conducive to their survival. Nevertheless, they managed to offer a quality of pastoral care that was adequate for the spiritual, social and emotional needs of their congregants. Functioning as advocates, confidants and advisors they represented the claims and frustrations of blacks.

Most black preachers in the earlier years were limited in education and training. Yet, they preached sermons that uplifted and inspired people who were beaten down and dealing with life's contradictions and challenges. Conscious that social context plays an important part in shaping one's biblical understanding, these preachers crafted sermons that were instrumental in helping powerless people connect with a powerful God. Generally speaking, it was in a sociocultural context of marginalization and injustice that black people's understanding of God was forged. Through theologies expressed and messages preached black churchgoers saw that the God of the Bible was not indifferent to their sufferings. Aided by the scriptures they comprehended that God was not their enemy but, instead, their ally.

Preaching in the Black Church

It is not trite to say that the black church and its preaching have kept black folks going. Church services are times of retreat from the surrounding pressures. Whatever else happens in the worship service, embedded deeply in the hearts of many is the question, "Is there a word from the Lord?" In the black church, preaching is taken very seriously and is the focal point in the service. As a matter of fact, preaching is considered to be much more than an act of worship. It is an event integral to worship and not merely adjunct to it. There is a eucharistic aspect about the sermon. Unlike the more traditional churches where all aspects of the worship, including the preaching, lead up to the Eucharist, in the black church, every activity in the worship is geared towards the sermon; feasting on and embedding something of the Living Word.[3]

The sermon, usually 40 to 60 minutes long, is often introduced as being "the most important part of the service" or "the moment which we have all been waiting for." "Thus saith the Lord" and "I have a word from the Lord" are statements used to indicate that the text was provided by divine inspiration. The congregation, having a vested interest in the delivery of the word, helps the preachers by urging, groaning, praying and encouraging them.

Drawing on inherent ability and acquired skills, black preachers have developed an idiosyncratic approach to preaching. There are several distinctive qualities, which, although not exclusive to blacks, undergird and make black preaching unique.[4]

To begin with, black preaching is rooted in scripture. The Bible is key in black people's struggle for freedom and is unquestionably the main source for preaching and teaching in the black church. Unlike today, where consulting various resources in sermon preparation is not only acceptable but also encouraged, years ago the Bible was the only book black preachers used in preparing sermons. It would have been inconceivable or even deemed sacrilegious in the past for the black preacher to have consulted any other source.

The scriptures helped black people affirm a view of God that differed radically from the distorted version offered them by their white slave masters (Cone 1997: 29). Reading scripture through the lens of their experiences of powerlessness and struggle, they came to understand God to be almighty, all-powerful and forever championing the cause of the oppressed. The awareness of God being actively involved with them in their struggles, and engaged in facilitating their liberation, intuitively caused them to realize they were much more than what the white society had defined them to be. They learned from scripture that they too were made in the image of God, and this knowledge enabled them to interpret their condition from a different perspective.

It was also through the scriptures that black people learned to assimilate the truths of Jesus Christ. The "Jesus of the black experience is the Jesus of scripture" (Cone 1997: 103). He came into human existence, in human flesh and dwelt among the poor and downtrodden of earth. He was rejected, scorned, despised, ridiculed and crucified, yet he rose from the dead to a position of exaltation, high above everyone else. The unwanted Stone, cast aside by the builders, became the head of the corner, the liberator of captive humanity and the helper of people struggling with the inconsistencies of life. Black people, living in the context of discrimination, injustice and deprivation, identify with Jesus and see in his experiences similarities to their own. His final victory gives rise to hope and the possibility of a new way of living. In black churches, as well as in Christianity in general, Jesus is recognized as the central figure and hope of humanity.

Second, coming from an oral culture, many black preachers have maintained the traditional spontaneous style of delivery, which incidentally appears to have been the style practiced by Jesus. The black church tends to be characterized by spontaneity in both worship and preaching, but perhaps less so now as training including homiletics has brought changes. There is still a certain amount of seemingly extemporary preaching, but this is often underpinned by preparation. Even so, perhaps in the black church more than in others, preachers often feel "led" to depart from their elaborate notes and take direction in their sermon "as the Spirit leads." Typically, in the black church, there is stated openness to the intervention of the Holy Spirit in preaching. Allowance is always made for divine intervention.

However, this discussion about spontaneity, flexibility and prepared sermons is not meant to be dichotomous. Preparation is perhaps the best grounding for inspiration and oracular utterances. It is accepted that preparation is the best guarantee against foolish preaching.

Third, storytelling is linked to a rich African heritage that has translated over into black preaching. The preacher's skillful and creative usage of words invokes the listeners' imagination to the point where they not only understand the story but also live the story. Although entertaining, the goal is not to entertain. The preacher seeks to engage effectively and connect the hearers with the story and make the Bible story become their story. The story speaks to the hearers about what God has done in the past and also speaks of what God is doing for them in the here and now. By aligning themselves with the heroes in the story, victims envision themselves becoming victors, disinherited people see themselves reinstated and the downtrodden see themselves rising up. Simply stated, the Word of God, made current, allows for a creative encounter with God to take place.

Fourth, preaching in the black church is mostly dialogical. Preaching is never the sole right of the clergy. Provision is made in the black worship service to facilitate interaction between the listeners and the preacher. The use of repetition, prevalent in black preaching, is not a time-filler, rather it is a technique used to ensure assimilation and to elicit response. Indeed repetition is used to generate an atmosphere for congregants to experience the word.

The call-and-response interaction is an integral part of the black preaching style. Phrases such as "Do I have a witness," "Can I get an amen," "Are you with me" and "You're coming through, preacher" lace black preaching. Defining statements, assertions, affirmation and encouragement, punctuated by a chorus of response, are also associated. This kind of interaction is beneficial to both preacher and listeners. It connects and narrows the distance between the pulpit and the pew. Preaching is made a corporate event and at the same time encourages and inspires the preacher.

While there is much value in this interactive event between preacher and listeners, there is merit in the arguments put forward against it. For instance: the congregation could overly participate; listeners at times do make automatic non-thinking responses no matter what is being said; other listeners may have difficulty hearing and miss central points in the sermon. Besides, visitors not accustomed to this "freestyle" preaching may become confused by or uncomfortable with it. Preachers also, rightly or wrongly, may evaluate their performance on the basis of the listeners' responses. Nonetheless, call-and-response interaction, ingrained in the black church, plays an integral part in the preaching event.

Fifth, combining other characteristics, black preaching is prophetic, passionate, enthusiastic, energetic and expressive. Preachers in the black church feel free to be themselves, bringing to the pulpit a variety of personal styles, mannerisms and gestures, which contributes to the effectiveness of the preaching. The black congregation celebrates the preacher's ability and uniqueness and is often tolerant of his or her expressions, as long as they are not overbearing. In addition, black preaching is rhythmic, poetic, marked with linguistic flexibility and rhetorical embellishment. The musical tones, modulation of the voice, the hum, the moan, the stammering are all mechanisms used by the black preacher in conveying a message that is both emotive and cerebral.

On the subject of emotions, black preaching is sometimes described as appealing more to the emotion than to the intellect. There is no antithesis between a more emotive sermon and one that is delivered more calmly with less feeling as far as intellectual content is concerned. Black preachers who deliver dramatic and emotion-packed sermons are also mindful of intellectual and theological content. Black preaching is geared to stirring the mind as well as the emotions.

Finally, black preaching is a journey towards celebration, often culminating in a celebratory tone. Celebration is a response to the sermon. As the preaching progresses and increases in volume and intensity, the worshippers are jubilant, uplifted, encouraged and rejuvenated. "The remembrance of a redemptive past and/or the conviction of a liberated future transform the events immediately experienced" (Thomas 1997: 52). Worshippers, accepting the prophetic word preached as being already fulfilled, celebrate and rejoice. A good example of this is Dr. Martin Luther King Jr. who ended his *I Have a Dream* speech with the glorious celebration, "Free at last, free at last, thank God Almighty, I am free at last."

Black preaching encompasses a wide variety of styles. Therefore, this is not an exhaustive list of its distinctive features. The diversities and uniqueness of this tradition are much broader than what have been implied or conveyed here. Further, there are different styles and characteristics of black preaching manifested in differing denominations as well as in individual churches. Despite its diversities, black preaching is always an expression of hope, survival and liberation.

Growth of Black Churches in the UK

Black churches in the UK are growing at phenomenal rates. It is estimated that there are over 500,000 black Christians in over 4000 local congregations in the United Kingdom.[5] Furthermore, church plants from Africa are ongoing and occurring rapidly. Judging from these figures and the rising trend, it is apparent that church remains an integral part of the life of black people in the UK. Today's black generation is in need of a word from God as were their black ancestors decades ago. Every generation has their battles to fight and issues with which to contend. Undoubtedly, some of the issues have changed in appearances and positions, but the essence of them remains the same. No generation has yet emerged that is not affected by the experience of transatlantic slavery or by the color of their skin (Bailey and Wiersbe 2003: 11).

In contradiction, the dreams and hopes of the black community and individuals are gradually gaining visibility. Africans are rising in prominence all over the world and in all segments of society. In the United States of America, the highest elected position is currently held by a black man. Notable social, economic and political improvements are seen in the UK. There are now policies and legislation that support ideas of a more tolerant UK, which is now considered a multicultural society. However, old racist habits still abound, and so too does discrimination. Black people within UK society are seen and treated in ways that still present major obstacles to their livelihoods. In the light of ongoing pressure and discrimination, church intervention and preaching "suited to black temperaments and culture" (Mitchell 1990: 24) remain vital as a way of maintaining their roots and cultural identity in their quest to achieve equity in British society.

New Challenges

History has proven that black churches "are enormously resourceful and potent agents of social reform" (Billingsley 2003: 185). Surprisingly today, it appears as if the black church has lost its zest and has become passively subdued in dealing with certain issues and making representation. There are numerous compounding and demoralizing issues plaguing, crippling and oppressing humankind, which the black church cannot afford to ignore—issues such as poverty, homelessness, hunger, injustice, racism, immigration laws, human trafficking, unequal distribution of wealth, mental health, drug abuse, sexual issues, crime, unemployment and gang violence.

Of equal importance are incarceration and HIV/AIDS. A significant number of the black community, particularly men, is represented in the prison population. This holds significance for the stability of families and the vulnerability of children. HIV/AIDS is a menace to the black population worldwide with the highest prevalence in Sub-Saharan Africa. Alongside these issues are existing laws and policies in the UK, and those currently being debated, which have direct bearing on the fundamentals of the Christian faith. Churches and ministers may well be called upon to obey laws that are against conscience and the adherence to scripture. The black church, arguably one of the most dominant forces in the black community, must find intelligent and creative ways to tackle these realities.

In response to some of the challenges facing black people in the UK, some black churches have formulated strategies for social intervention. Drawing from within the churches themselves, they have initiated and developed projects such as: Families for Peace,[6] RAFFA International Development Agency, [7] Street Pastors UK[8] and The Family & Relationship Crises Centre.[9] Also, after-school programs, Saturday schools to help under-achievers, elderly day care centers, mentors and a variety of other initiatives. As trendsetters, these churches have given an indication as to where the black church is going.

Crucial to the Future of Preaching in the Black Church

In recent conversations with black religious leaders,[10] relevance, being prophetic, training and eschatology are some of the elements identified as being crucial to the future of preaching in the black churches in the UK.

Remaining relevant and consistent with its tradition of being at the forefront of the struggle for human rights is essential. It is a matter of concern that black preachers are apt when addressing spiritual matters but seem not as effective when addressing social ones. They appear at times to be out of date with the issues that the congregation and community are facing. Being attuned to social, economic and political issues is a must. The church again has to champion the cause of its constituents and rise to current challenges that pose as hindrances to people attaining their God-given potential. The context in which the church operates as well as the circumstances confronting black people and the society as a whole are factors that gave and should continue to give direction to preaching. Both the biblical text and the contemporary context have to contribute to the theological and sociological elements of sermons aiming to speak relevantly to the needs of oppressed people. Culturally relevant sermons rise out of the totality of people's existence and address all aspects of the person, spiritually, socially, intellectually, psychologically and economically.

Conscious effort to embrace change should be a critical part of black preaching. Change should be embraced strategically to preserve its uniqueness and identity. The black church must never think that there is no need for its preaching to be updated and kept in touch with reality. It is vital that preaching steps up and moves with the times, not reverting to the sixties. Its preachers and pastors must connect with lived experiences of all ages, sorts and conditions of men, women and children, if they are to inspire, challenge and hold their interest.

Prophetic preaching is also indispensable. It was the prophetic preaching of black ministers, denouncing sin, speaking up against the wrongs in society and the awful predicaments in which humans found themselves, that helped to revitalize the ailing church in Britain. Preachers speaking out on God's behalf instructed the church on issues of righteousness, justice and mercy. At present, fundamental secularism seems to be successfully displacing Christian influence. Preaching in the black church cannot be neutral. Its position must be clearly stated as it addresses the moral and spiritual values influencing the life of the UK, bringing Christianity back from the margins to the center of public life. Prophetic preaching is important in restoring Christians as believing groups possessing the power to impact society at large. The power of the gospel and a transforming encounter with Jesus Christ will save individuals and eventually the society. Prophetically, the black church has always proclaimed that Jesus Christ's death, resurrection and ultimate authority generate hope and salvation.

It is a misconception to think that prophetic preaching always means foretelling future events. Prophetic preaching tells forth more than it foretells. It speaks for God, providing guidance, direction and vision of a better world and hopeful possibilities for the future. As long as people are struggling for life and wholeness, there is need for a voice with a prophetic word to emancipate, uplift and equip. "Thus saith the Lord," proclaimed with conviction under the inspiration of the Holy Spirit, will touch people's lives, articulate their concerns and liberate the oppressed.

Additionally, training is paramount. Unfortunately, some have held and still hold the notion that training robs preachers of the anointing and the ability to deliver relevant heart-reaching sermons. This thinking is perhaps due to the fact that in early years black preachers were trained in white theological institutions that neither catered for nor celebrated black culture. This resulted in black preachers losing some of their identity; the loss came across to the black congregation as loss of anointing rather than loss of self-identity. However, black preachers who have been professionally trained admit that training, rather than taking away from, adds richness to what they present and communicate. An elderly black minister I know, in counseling the young ministers he mentored, often said to them, "a dull axe with the anointing will cut, but a sharp axe with the anointing will give the cut a cleaner finish."

The wave of modernization has brought about an enhanced intelligence that has increased both the complexity and complications of today's life. The makeup of the congregations in black churches has changed remarkably over the years and people ranging from the top to the bottom of the academic and professional ladder are occupying the pews. Sermons need to be better structured and more methodological in their presentation as this affects how they are listened to and viewed. Regrettably, lack of structure has made it difficult to keep up with the preacher's thoughts and has turned off congregations and other people seeking to learn from black preaching.

As one generation of preachers succeeds the other, training at different levels has been introduced and black preachers are becoming increasingly better equipped. Pulpits today are being filled by highly educated black preachers, many of whom, especially in the USA, have earned doctorates and other academic achievements. Black leaders who still oppose training are failing to realize the large intellectual gaps that are being created between the pulpit and pew, as well as the importance of being trained and equipped to speak skillfully into contemporary society.

Finally, in dealing with the here and now, black preaching cannot afford to lose the eschatological aspect of the message. Earlier preaching focused greatly on the hereafter and the imminent return of the Lord Jesus. The black congregation expects to be given something to look forward to that would transform their despair into hope. In the modern church, the Lord's return must still be preached with conviction and urgency. Also, the unity of the Christian faith and church must remain the central thrust in its eschatological message.

Lessons to Be Learned

Black preaching is inadvertently influencing culture and the perception of the black church and preaching, as black televangelists, radio preachers and literature expose the black preaching style and methodology to the world. There is no particular reason why black preaching, however defined, should remain the preserve of black pulpits. Black preaching has principles that can be generalized to all preaching to good effect. For instance, it can help more effectively to engage congregations, increase church attendance and enhance church growth. If this propagation of principles is to happen, literature should play a part. Black preachers and others can reflect on, analyze and write about black preaching. In other words, a body of theory emanating from practice can be built up to inform both scholarship and preaching.

Knowledge of the context from which black preaching comes will hopefully lessen the misunderstanding and misconceptions that have overshadowed the black preaching tradition for decades. Anyone wanting to gain an understanding of this unique style of preaching has to familiarize him- or herself with black culture and the concerns of black people. Dialoguing, discussing and genuine listening are all steps in the right direction in dismissing the myths and biases that people of different cultures hold regarding each other.

Pulpit swapping could be an enriching and enlightening experience for all. There are white ministers who have never listened to a black preacher. Black and white preachers need to learn to read and understand scripture from each other's point of view. It is to their credit that some religious training institutes in the UK are now introducing black preaching to students doing preaching modules. Others need to take this on board, as there are students being trained who might eventually be called to lead black majority congregations or congregations with black members.

Unfortunately the standard of preaching in the UK has not quite reached that of its American counterpart in its breadth and scope. Unlike in the UK, the black American preachers are given the necessary setting, training and exposure, and these have allowed them to excel tremendously. In the beginning the black church in the USA served as inspiration for the development of the black church in the Caribbean and now the UK. Once again an analysis of the practices and institutions that have developed as part of the black church in the USA could be used to good effect to inform and enhance the role of the black preacher and in turn broaden the scope of the black church in the UK in attending to the contemporary challenges of their constituents.

Sermon Forms and Delivery Styles in the Future

Preaching is an intensely creative event. To avoid the possibility of it becoming stale, predictable and stereotypical, new and fresh approaches are necessary. Openness to new ideas could enhance the form and delivery of sermons. New approaches might challenge both the preacher's and the listener's comfort zones. The following ideas are intended to provoke thought or simply speculate about sermon forms and deliveries in the future.

Multimedia and a vast range of technological aids offer numerous and creative approaches to preaching. Sermons could be projected or animated and can incorporate snippets from movies or songs. The hustle and bustle of life, along with the iPod and mp3 era, would mean that the parishioners would be able to download the sermons they have missed or would like to hear again while they are on the move. Virtual preaching through web links allows ill parishioners to be in the service without leaving their houses.

We must become eleventh-hour harvesters and capture the hearts of the youth. Interjecting a bit of rapping or rock into the sermon would surely delight the youth. They would be impressed with the preacher's effort in trying to engage with their culture and be more apt to listen to the sermon.

People like stories. The story in the sermon could be dramatized by a drama group while being preached. Whatever method or technique is used to package the sermon, every effort must be made to ensure that the content remains the same. The central message of liberation and salvation procured by Jesus Christ must always be kept intact.

Conclusion

"The days of coming to church for personal salvation alone are over, the time has come, or come again, for changing the community" (Billingsley 2003: 186). Jesus did not only come to save souls, he came to give life a more abundant dimension. Black preachers and black majority churches are positioned in the UK to make a difference. The black pulpit is strongly influential and is a great place from which to initiate action. Preaching must reflect that while it is imperative that black churches look after their own needs, they are engaging with the broader issues and not remaining internalized or focusing only on institutional maintenance and organizational concerns. The churches' programs may need to be re-examined. If the church is inundated with activities and not engaging with the issues of human need, then it is a far cry from its mandate and call to serve Christ's interest.

People are driven to the UK for many reasons, but they have the same spiritual and social needs. Black people ought to remember that they too were strangers in the UK and offer worship spaces and preaching that are inclusive. The lessons learnt from the past should elicit an empathic response. Diversities are to be respected, celebrated and affirmed and every human given the opportunity to fulfill his or her God-given destiny.

The future of black preaching depends on it retaining its ethos, essence and role. Black preaching, born in the context of struggle and marginalization, must seek to be relevant in the same context today. The black church and its preaching helped black people to survive the vicissitudes of dehumanization and the many attempts at breaking their body, mind and soul. People in the pews, whose circumstances and experiences daily militate against them, want to know that the preacher has heard from God and will deliver a life-changing word. Black preaching, fearlessly proclaiming the liberating truths of God to a sinful and unjust world, will efficiently serve the future.

Notes

1. The use of this term was instigated by the African Caribbean Evangelical Association (ACEA). See Sturge, 2005, p. 29.
2. The black churches referred to are those that were transplanted from America, started by slaves in response to oppression, and resonated with the Africans in the Caribbean whose circumstances were near identical to their brothers and sisters in America.
3. A conversation with Dr. Joe Aldred, pastor and published theologian, on the role of preaching in the black church.
4. See LaRue, 2000, p. 14.
5. See online Directory of Black Majority Churches UK, http://www.bmcdirectory.co.uk/, welcome page. Available also is the listing of Black Majority Churches.
6. Families for Peace is an organization campaigning against gun crime and gang violence. It was started in Birmingham in 2001 by founder and director Gleen Reid, whose son was a victim of a gun crime. She is a member of the Church of God of Prophecy, which offers support.
7. Launched by the Church of God of Prophecy, London, November 2006. Primary interests are in development research, environmental sustainability, community health and social care, social enterprise development and learning and skills.
8. Pioneered in London in January 2003 by Les Isaac, Director of the Ascension Trust. Results include drops in crime in areas where teams have been working. There are now over 100 teams around the United Kingdom.
9. Located in Luton and part of the Church of God of Prophecy, founded 12 years ago and providing intervention activities that target domestic abuse within the community, as well as other activities.

10. Lovel Bent, senior pastor at New Life Assembly Fellowship of Churches; Bishop Wilton Powell, Church of God of Prophecy; Dr. Joe Aldred, pastor and published theologian; Lloyd Crossfield, pastor of Church of God Pentecostal.

References

Bailey, E. K., and Warren W. Wiersbe. *Preaching in Black and White: What We Can Learn from Each Other*. Grand Rapids: Zondervan, 2003.

Billingsley, Andrew. *Mighty like a River: The Black Church and Social Reform*. Oxford: Oxford University Press, 2003.

Cone, James H. *God of the Oppressed*. Maryknoll: Orbis, 1997.

LaRue, Cleophus J. *The Heart of Black Preaching*. Louisville: Westminster John Knox, 2000.

Mbiti, John. *African Religions and Philosophy*. London: Heinemann, 1989.

Mitchell, Henry H. *Black Preaching: The Recovery of a Powerful Art*. Nashville: Abingdon, 1990.

Phillips, M., and T. Phillips. *Windrush: The Irresistible Rise of Multi-Racial Britain*. London: HarperCollins, 1998.

Reddie, Anthony G. *Working against the Grain: Re-imaging Black Theology in the 21st Century*. London: Equinox, 2008.

Sturge, Mark. *Look What the Lord Has Done: An Exploration of Black Christian Faith in Britain*. Milton Keynes: Scripture Union, 2005.

Thomas, Frank A. *They Like to Never Quit Praisin' God: The Role of Celebration in Preaching*. Cleveland: Pilgrim, 1997.

Wilkinson, John L. *Church in Black and White*. Edinburgh: Saint Andrew Press, 1993.

16
Prosperity Preaching in Black Communities

Stephanie Y. Mitchem

There are different ways to think about prosperity preaching in black communities. One way is to consider particular kinds of self-identified prosperity churches. This consideration will be the focus of the next three chapters—I identify three strains of prosperity churches, each of which is powerful. This chapter looks more widely at prosperity preaching in black communities. While the first chapter weighed the historic aspects of the black church that shape black prosperity preaching today, the second chapter reflected on the concrete realities of a black spirituality of longing. Both sets of considerations influence black religious life. Both sets need to be placed in the wide frame of the black community, not reduced to one particular type of prosperity church. The connections between the past and the present, concrete realities, unsatisfied longing, and the black church became clear for me through stories.

Looking for a Church Home

The first story was told by my friend Delores, about herself and her family's search for a church home. Delores has an adult daughter who invited both Delores and Delores' mother to attend the church where she was a member. The daughter had been a member for some months and both her mother and grandmother were impressed by the positive influence the church community was having on her life. With such lived witness, both older women agreed to attend. The church had two hundred members. It was a vibrant community that seemed to be growing. Eventually both the mother and grandmother became members as well as the daughter.

But many things began to bother Delores. She was putting over one hundred dollars into her weekly collection envelope, volunteering, and attending church functions, but the pastor could never remember her name. Every event in the church cost additional fees, including Bible study. Delores became aware that the pastor could not pronounce many of the words in the Bible. At one time, he gave a sermon and challenged the community in ways that stand out in Delores' memory: "If you have to shop at KMart, you are not blessed. If you do not own your own home, you are not blessed. If you can't go out shopping whenever you want, you are not blessed. If you can't wear designer clothes, you are not blessed. And then you need to find out what sins you have committed." This idea was offensive to Delores.

Her offense at this sermon is a reminder about the importance of culture and of religious education. The pastor's words are nearly verbatim from the religious group Word of Faith, which is discussed in chapter 5 [of *Name It and Claim It?*]. But the people who accept the teachings of those leaders have experienced a culture where the ideas are practiced and reinforced, unlike Delores' group. That pastor mistakenly thought that it is possible to start a group from that point—Do you have your designer clothes as a sign of personal salvation? A person in community must be educated, slowly, in different aspects of religious teaching. In religious education terms, this is called formation, and it's a process that begins when a person is attracted to some aspect of a religious group, whether it is the vibrancy of the service or the living witness of current members. Drawing a group together and trying to get them to swallow the religious teachings whole, without the support of a religious community that has its own culture, is not possible. Some of Delores' other experiences are evidences of the need to educate and build a religious community's faith lives.

Delores went to one of the church outings. The transportation was by carpooled volunteers and no food was served. She realized that the amount of money charged each person was roughly four times more than the actual cost of admittance. At another time, the pastor announced that all the tithes belonged to him. Delores' breaking point came when she realized that the pastor and staff were unwilling to financially help poor people in general or the members specifically. One of the very active church members announced that she needed four hundred dollars to get home for a family funeral. The pastor said, "I've got ten dollars on it. Anybody else?"

After that, Delores went to church in anger, watching for the fall of the pastor. In a thoroughly black cultural style, Delores also helped to expose the pastor. Her actions have cultural meaning in black communities: the pastor made a black woman angry. One man expressed the impact of dealing with a black woman's anger: "If a black woman is mad at you, you might as well be dead." The situation of anger and instigation escalated over time, and Delores was willing to help it along. For instance, in one sermon, the pastor made a comment that "All the women in the church want to have sex with the pastor;" at which point, Delores said, "I burst out laughing, so hard tears were running down my face." After a few such exchanges, the pastor finally knew her name and asked if she wanted to talk to him. Her response to that invitation was cutting: "I'm not talking to Satan. I can get to hell on my own." Delores reported on the departure of the membership: "The church mothers left. Then the Christians left. There are maybe twenty-five people still there." Delores' story reveals dimensions of ways that prosperity preaching impacts black communities and ministerial realities.

What attracts most people to any church community? In Delores' case, a person who is significant to her—her daughter—invited her. The invitation was enhanced because of the positive influence the church community had on the daughter's life. Meeting a vibrant and growing church community led both Delores and her mother to join. The invitation, the positive influence, and the church community become ministerial credentials in themselves. This is an important facet of black church life: all ministers are not seminary educated. Sometimes, a person might perceive a vocational call to ministry in a particular place for a particular community. This charismatic dimension of ministry is acceptable in many black communities. Charisma is often a more important personality trait in a minister than is education. Education itself sometimes gets a bad reputation in some Christian circles, regardless of race, because it is seen as weakening the message of God through human meddling. A deacon in one church summed up the attitude: "God save me from educated Christians!"

At a time when families want to find time for each other in their busy schedules, a family membership also enhanced the attractiveness of that particular church for Delores. She may have been drawn to this church by the circumstances and connections with her family. But what other aspects draw ministers or communities to prosperity preaching?

Prosperity preachers, as will be seen in the following chapters, are models of financially successful ministers. A model wherein the minister must work a nine-to-five job to support his or her ministry habit is historic in black communities but not attractive today, especially when one or another wealthy prosperity pastor is televised several times each week. A prosperous view of ministry is certainly more tantalizing than the overworked model. In the case of Delores' ex-pastor, prosperity preaching must have seemed easy and popular enough that he tried it. But his failure with this style of preaching indicates that it is not as easy as it might appear.

For poor black people who are frustrated by their economic realities in the United States, prosperity preaching may seem a natural and obvious way to address their longings. One author contends that one of the strains of prosperity preaching that he terms "Word of Faith"...

> ... might be seen (at least in part) as a type of "poor people's movement." The people who are its followers are primarily those whose experience has produced the desire for, if not the actualization of, upward socioeconomic mobility. This "faith formula for success" is a way of using religious doctrine to symbolically and supernaturally level the playing field with respect to access to society's resources.[1]

However, I contend that middle-class black people are also drawn to prosperity preaching, as was Delores, who is educated and not poor. There is another drawing power based on the search for a religious home. Beverly Hall Lawrence is a journalist who has noted the return of middle-class African Americans, herself included, to church participation. Her generation was the first to reap the financial benefits of the Civil Rights Movement and the self-esteem of the "black is beautiful" consciousness era. Churches seemed in opposition to new black thinking.

> My generation was one that fled churches filled with those who appeared to us to be helpless, sitting and waiting for (a white) God to intervene and settle problems for them. Many of my friends and I admit now that the idea of going to church was simply too embarrassing, because it taught people to wait for change to come and because of its reliance on European Christian symbols.[2]

While better jobs brought financial rewards, the black middle class was isolated in "a kind of limbo world—not really black or white—rather a super-black but lonely physical state of being." Security was still missing: "with the statistical failure of integration, the idea of assimilating had lost its luster for many."[3] The luster was further reduced by awareness of continued and entrenched poverty in other black sectors. Lawrence states that the need to address this was diagnosed as spiritual; church became the necessary antidote.

> Nobody really wants to see going back to church as a symbol of defeat, even if we may feel personally defeated at the time. But it is in our defeated state that we seek out a place to feel comforted. It is a closing of the circle. A beacon that we finally see. A Morse code we can decipher. A common tongue. Ties that bind.[4]

Prosperity churches provide answers for black middle-class social anguish about solidifying and growing personal assets, while justifying an often new social position. These answers become enticements to participate in prosperity churches. Middle-class money is also necessary for prosperity churches to continue their own growth.

Regardless of the changes between the past and the present moments, black churches lay claim to emotional memories. The reality is that some of the churches succeed at being a comforting presence for the community while others, like the church Delores attended, do not. These images of black churches emphasize what Woodson referred to as the *socialized* church.

Yet when most black people think about church, the words of Woodson or Lincoln are not the first or fifteenth thing that comes to mind. Religion has primal emotional content for most who have been involved; that emotional content is based on cultural understandings. Identification of sacred space is part of our socialization from childhood, and so our religious memories are personal. As one example, for many African Americans sensual and strong memories of chicken dinners and hugs or preaching and praise can influence how church is viewed in the present moment. Nostalgic images of the black church include that of a bulwark against hard times, a source of inspiration and guidance, and a center for a given community.

The history of the black church ties in with current economic conditions of black Americans who carry a spirituality of longing, and these are given expression in stories like Delores'. These ideas lead to consideration of the overlapping dynamics of culture and religion in black communities that will give shape to understanding prosperity preaching and its draw for African Americans, beyond the issues of class and income: Delores was drawn to a congregation that she defined as vibrant.

In chapter 1, I stated that there are three categories of black religious life that come into sharp focus when considering prosperity preaching: shared meaning that shapes communal identity, social constructions that help shape the black community's moral values, and worship and prayer. In Delores' story, communal identity (as the pastor tried to shape meaning) and moral values (a base on which the congregation rejected the pastor) were in greater evidence. The third category requires a closer look because worship and communal prayer are critical for creating the church community that is centered on prosperity.

Most black Christian worship services include powerful preaching, culturally specific use of scripture, and strong music ministries. African American preaching styles have moved congregations to tears or fired up community activism. Sermons are presented in a distinctive style that uses pauses and certain utterances while engaging the listeners in call-and-response dialogue. The messages of skillful black preachers are simultaneously intellectual and emotional, evoking strong responses from the listener. Martin Luther King's sermons exemplify this complexity.[5] The delivery of these messages is a form of art that is applied to political speech. The passionate declarative form has had the effect of raising the general American public's expectations of preachers and of politicians.

The Bible is used in some culturally specific ways that are only beginning to be verbalized by African American religion scholars. A collection of essays gathered by black theologian Vincent Wimbush is an example of this work that considers black cultural constructions and uses them in relation to the Bible. Wimbush asks two complex questions in the introduction to these essays that have far-reaching implications for black religious scholarship today.

> How could the formation of African America, as an example of a sociocultural formation in the West, be understood without heightened attention to the Bible, specifically, the manner in which the Bible was used as language world within which those violently cut off from their home could speak again? How African America be explained except by reference to their decidedly political, self-defensive, and offensive use of the Bible in opposition to the uses to which white Protestants put it in the construction and confirmation of their world?[6]

Studies of African Americans and the Bible must incorporate cultural dynamics and the results will not look the same as those of white Protestants.

Music, especially gospel, is the most easily identified component of black Protestant worship services. More charismatic churches, depending on the Spirit-given gifts of members, will be more expressive and, therefore, music has an especially critical role in leading the congregation to prayer. But gospel music is also commercially popular today, becoming one of the ways that many black Americans, even if they do not regularly attend church, express and respond to life's situations. Gospel artists such as Yolanda Adams, BeBe and CeCe Winans are so popular that their recordings are often played on black, secular radio stations. The success in marketing black gospel brings other problems. Religious historian Jerma Jackson states the main benefit and problem in gospel marketing:

> As gospel music gained greater exposure to the public, radio broadcasts and recordings made it available to audiences far removed from the black religious communities where the music had taken shape. Yet the exposure gospel gained also removed it from local control. For many who had come to regard gospel as a vital source of race pride and identity, this way of removing racial boundaries undermined black cultural autonomy and felt more intrusive than liberating.[7]

At its traditional best, black worship moves the participants to action. While this could be said of any culture's worship, there are particular aspects and expectations that are unique to black communities. Barbara Holmes, who gave definition to our understanding of the black church, also describes the power of worship that is specific to the black community. She names the meaning behind the worship experience as a contemplative practice.

> The spirit descends and the community is lifted. These practices are not unknown to researchers and church folks, but what makes these experiences also contemplative? I am suggesting that Africana worship experiences are contemplative because they create an atmosphere for communal listening and responsiveness to the manifestations of God, they impact the ethos and value system of a community, and they heal infected social and psychic wounds.[8]

Delores' story opens to discussion of some of the hidden aspects of prosperity preaching in black communities. The preaching might impact the shape of black church communities; it might become a badly delivered message, as Delores experienced. However, consideration of this preaching cannot be separated from aspects of black church life and expression. Prosperity preachers in black communities study these aspects and apply them to their congregations along with providing other answers that African Americans may feel they do not receive in other churches. Delores' story is one derived from one woman's personal experiences of church life. There are many Delores stories, but there are also many stories of satisfaction in prosperity churches. If there were not, the churches would not remain open and the church mothers and other Christians would leave. While these personal stories can be interesting, stories also happen in public view that have prosperity themes. One of these happened in Atlanta.

Black Church, Disrupted and Divided

If Delores' story is that of a single woman's journey into and away from one church community, prosperity preaching has created greater, and very public, rifts in what is known as the black church. In May 2006, the seminary community of the Interdenominational Theological Center (ITC) was divided over the invitation of Eddie Long to speak at the commencement, and the rift was publicized in the pages of the *Atlanta Journal-Constitution*. The ITC is a prominent consortium of six black seminaries, whose mission includes preparation of ministers for the black community. Some students sent a letter of protest to the president of the school questioning Long's ethics, citing his three-million-dollar income from a charity and his disdain for women and pastors of smaller churches. The three-million-dollar salary was investigated, as reported in *Black Enterprise* magazine, because its pastor. . .

> . . . may have violated Internal Revenue Service regulations by accepting compensation totaling $3.07 million in the use of property and salary from a charity he helped oversee. During a four-year period, he reportedly received a 20-acre, six-bedroom home estimated at $1.4 million; use of a $350,000 luxury Bentley; and more than $1 million in salary, including $494,000 in 2000. J. David Epstein, Long's tax attorney, denies any improprieties on the part of his client, insisting that the church and the charities have come to the aid of millions.[9]

In protest, several members of the board of trustees of ITC refused to participate in the graduation. Preeminent black theologian James Cone, who was to have received an honorary degree at the commencement, boycotted the ceremony when he learned of Long's engagement. The problem with Long, as reported in the *Journal-Constitution*, is that

> Long preaches what is known as prosperity gospel, that God rewards the faithful with financial success. He declared in a 2005 interview that Jesus wasn't poor. In 2003 Long told a meeting of civil rights veterans in Atlanta that blacks must "forget racism" because they had already reached the promised land. In 2004 Long led a march—while carrying a torch lit at [Martin Luther] King's crypt—where he called for a constitutional ban on gay marriage.[10]

Long, a graduate of ITC, is pastor of the largest black church in Georgia, the New Birth Missionary Baptist Church. New Birth, located on twenty-five acres and boasting a membership of more than twenty-five thousand, is a megachurch, one among many that has an impact on black religious life. The Hartford Institute for Religious Research, in a 2005 report, identifies that a megachurch has at least two thousand members. A megachurch is not necessarily a prosperity church but may be affiliated with any denomination, though the majority (56 percent) of all megachurches are evangelical.[11] While the report has some other important points, more study is needed to identify aspects of megachurches in black communities. For instance, the New Birth website includes a statement "Seven Reasons Why I Love a Big Church" that aims to dispel myths and explain the reasons and benefits for membership in a megachurch.

As I have visited many churches, I have begun to suspect that part of African Americans' attraction to large churches is the desire to be part of a successful enterprise. Large churches telegraph self-importance when a person arrives for a service: parking is acres away from the church; uniformed local law enforcement officers assist churchgoers crossing roads; and shuttles are available for the disabled. In black megachurches, the congregation becomes a self-enclosed, self-supporting community. I have wondered if recreating a sense of a village" part of the draw. Each megachurch member with whom I have spoken has a clear sense of identity with something larger than her- or himself, even if they are at the low end of the hierarchy of the church. And the megachurches do have a clear sense of hierarchy, wherein the pastor and his or her circle are often surrounded by bodyguards and not accessible by most of the congregation. Most megachurches, and this is affirmed by the Hartford study, are structured so that members are part of smaller cells, able to relate to each other as members in this way. (One wonders: If smaller cells are needed for one to feel a sense of church, why not just be part of a smaller church?)

But the glamour provided in megachurch services, beginning with arrival at the parking lot, is part of the personal affirmation of success and security experienced by black Americans in the involvement with megachurches. In one megachurch, the elderly founding pastor died. His wake and funeral became part of the show, and so his clothes were changed every hour during the body's viewing. At the time of the actual funeral service, with an open casket, members bragged that he was in brand new suit that they had never seen. Yet this excitement has an impersonal edge: how many of the five thousand other members can one member *really* get to know? A stronger question for consideration is how has membership in black churches been changed by these distant, impersonal kinds of relationships? Does the role of the pastor become more that of a CEO, less able to minister, and ultimately more liable?

> According to John Walker, chief creative officer of Chitwood and Chitwood, a Tennessee-based accounting and financial company that represents more than 4,000 churches, many large churches now have net incomes in the hundreds of millions of dollars. Although some compare pastors of today's megachurches with Fortune 500 CEOs, pastors are not held to the same level of regulatory standards and financial accountability.[12]

Some megachurch members have spoken with me about how a pastoral service, such as a funeral, is seldom performed by the head pastor. Co-pastors or others are appointed for those day-to-day pastoral functions. Even leadership becomes impersonal in such a congregation.

Megachurches also emphasize the business side of religion, as maintaining the huge properties requires steady infusions of cash. Tithing has taken on new intensity. One woman told me how she had been dropped from church rolls after missing two tithing payments. This woman's story of missing tithing payments was not rejection of her Christian duty; one of her children was dying, and church members knew it. However, processes of tailoring megachurches to black communities have been adapted for prosperity churches' growth.

New Birth's vision is stated on the website, including the following:

> God's vision is to see us prosper and be in good health even as our soul prospers. . . We believe that these are extraordinary times that call for an extraordinary people with an extraordinary anointing. . . This is the year of ruling, subduing, and taking dominion. . . Nothing shall be impossible for us. God said it, we believe it, and that settles it.[13]

In contrast, ITC has a mission statement that calls for its students to "commit to and practice a liberating and transforming spirituality; academic discipline; religious, gender, and cultural diversity; and justice and peace." The ITC vision statement states that the institution "is dedicated to producing public theologians—men and women who are intellectually keen, politically sophisticated, economically savvy, culturally sensitive, family friendly, technologically literate, and spiritually astute."[14]

Rev. Long did give the commencement address at ITC and the *Atlanta Journal-Constitution* followed up the first story. During his address, Long portrayed himself as a persecuted prophet. "Long's message—like his ministry—divided the crowd anyway. While plenty of people in the chapel bolted from their seats to cheer him, others sat stoically in their seats rolling their eyes." One of the students, Victor Cyrus-Franklin, was quoted in the article: "He said at the very beginning of his message that this ceremony was about us but he spent the majority of the time talking about himself."[15]

The Long-ITC fiasco highlights how prosperity preaching is becoming a dividing factor in black church life. The anger experienced by the ministers and students from ITC seems to reflect a sense of betrayal: Long's ministry is a denial of well-developed black community and cultural identities, the very identities that the students at ITC spend years studying and learning. That Long is himself a graduate of the school is another level of betrayal for the students, because he appears to be rejecting all that they hope to achieve. Long's work denies social memories that inform black American identity. Prosperity preaching in black communities brings all these tensions into play. While Delores and her family may have rejected the clumsy attempts of one pastor who preached prosperity, would they be drawn into the web of another, especially if their hope is to find a vibrant community? Or is talk of prosperity and religion so pervasive in black communities that there is really no way to avoid it? Before moving into descriptions of three types of prosperity churches, making connections between some of the ideas from the first and second chapters will be helpful.

Prosperity and Black Religion

In chapter 1, some thoughts of historical scholars about the black church shed light on our discussion of prosperity preaching. Carter Woodson defined a "conservative" strain of the black church, a strain with which prosperity churches have more in common than they do with Woodson's "progressive" churches. E. Franklin Frazier talked about business as a way to insure social acceptance of black Americans; in like manner, prosperity preaching offers a corporatized model that promotes financial success as a component of Christianity. C. Eric Lincoln called for a black church with a "mature religious posture." Perhaps today's prosperity churches will claim they have reached that place.

Most significantly, today's prosperity preachers reach out to provide answers to the black community's spirituality of longing, suggesting that emptiness can be filled with steady incoming cash flows. The Urban League's *2005* equality index lays out the dimensions of socially constructed black economic woes. Tavis Smiley's *The Covenant with Black America* encourages discussion in order to actively address social inequalities. But religions that emphasize prosperity as realized spirituality move the discussions from the intellectual to the emotional realm. They direct black folks' attention toward a superficial materialism, as does Reginald Lewis' title *Why Should White Guys Have All the Fun?* The unquestioning approach of prosperity preaching implies that patriarchal imperialism is "fun," not admitting its good times are restricted to only very few. With this focus, prosperity churches trump wider concerns for social justice with an extended meditation on acquired money and goods as a spiritual right. This focus is reminiscent of a 1903 warning from W. E. B. Du Bois: "What if the Negro people be wooed from a strife for righteousness, from a love of knowing, to regard dollars as the be-all and end-all of life?"[16] Du Bois warned that there is more to life than money; prosperity preaching may bring more of the "black nihilism" of which Cornel West warned. He defines nihilism as "the lived experience of coping with a life of horrifying meaninglessness, hopelessness, and (most important) lovelessness. The frightening result is a numbing detachment from others and a self-destructive disposition toward the world."[17]

I imagine that a challenge would come from those who are involved African Americans, building self-esteem and a deeper sense of American citizenship, in ways that many black churches have not been able to in recent times. Is that such a bad thing? The theologies that drive these churches of prosperity do indeed give folks fast access to a sense of personal power and self-esteem. The lessons taught in these churches imbue the listeners with hope. But is this really hope? I heard the story of a pastor in a well-established black prosperity church who has heads of big game from various spots in the world that he has hunted and killed hanging on the wall of his office. Is knowing that the pastor draws enough salary (from tithes) that he can trek the globe and kill animals a sign of black progress? Is this economic progress? If so, what is the measure of that progress? Animal trophies as indicator of black economic achievement cannot be found in scripture, in the Urban League's documents, or in the *The Covenant with Black America*. Du Bois' question holds up the traditional African American striving for justice combined with a desire for education as values that should be held dearly. How does prosperity preaching work toward the greater good while standing on the shoulders of those who came before and sacrificed for our benefit today?

But Du Bois is not as well publicized today as are prosperity preachers and their ideas. Prosperity ideas are reported in black media sources other than the recordings, books, frequently televised programs, and well-developed websites of different churches that be discussed in chapters 5 and 6. *Essence* magazine published an article on one prosperity church: "A Dollar and A Dream: Pastors Creflo and Taffi Dollar have built a multimillion-dollar megachurch empire by practicing what they preach."[18]

Prosperity theology ideas are so pervasive today that black communities are influenced, consciously or not. For instance, the language of "blessing" has become so common as to be almost meaningless among African Americans. The greeting, "Have a nice day," has been supplanted by the phrase "Have a blessed day." A person may respond to the question "How are you?" with "I'm blessed." These kinds of statements are common among young black people; rappers outfitted in tight clothing and dripping with gold accessories are quick to talk in terms of blessings. Blessing is a concept that ignores a person's talents or effort, and personal achievement is downplayed with a false humility.

The rise of new prosperity churches in the last fourth of the twentieth century did not raise warning flags among existing black churches. Their existence was just one more form of black religious creativity. But as these prosperity churches have extended their influence in black communities, they can no longer be dismissed. Prosperity churches signal changes in black religious life, ministry, and the meaning of "the" black church. They intersect with political and social life in new ways, creating new and often uncomfortable meanings that counter the status quo that exists in black communities. Most importantly, these churches are changing the constructions of black theology. These ideas will be explored in more detail in the last two chapters, after looking at three expressions of formalized prosperity preaching, beginning with the ways that theologies of prosperity historically were shaped in African American Christian religious life.

Notes

1. Milmon F. Harrison, *Righteous Riches: The Word of Faith Movement in Contemporary African American Religion* (New York: Oxford University Press 2005), 148–49.
2. Beverly Hall Lawrence, *Reviving the Spirit: A Generation of African Americans Goes Home to Church* (New York: Grove, 1996), 15–16.
3. Ibid., 17.

4. Ibid., 46.
5. There are four published volumes of these sermons, beginning with Martin Luther King, *Strength to Love* (New York: Harper and Row, 1963).
6. Vincent Wimbush, "Introduction: Reading Darkness, Reading Scriptures," in *African Americans and the Bible: Sacred Texts and Social Textures*, ed. V. Wimbush (New York, Continuum, 2001), 15.
7. Jerma A. Jackson, *Singing in My Soul: Black Gospel Music in a Secular Age* (Chapel Hill: University of North Carolina Press, 2004), 131.
8. Barbara A. Holmes, *Joy Unspeakable: Contemplative Practices of the Black Church* (Minneapolis: Fortress, 2004), 91.
9. Nicole Marie Richardson, Krissah William, and Hamil R. Harris, "The Business of Faith," www.black-enterprise.com, May 2006, accessed December 2006.
10. John Blake, "Not all seminary welcome bishop, graduation invite provokes protests," *Atlanta Journal-Constitution*, May 11, 2006, A1.
11. Scott Thumma, Dave Travis, and Warren Bird, "Megachurches Today 2005, Summary of Research Findings," http://hirr.hartsem.edu/megachurch/megastoday2005, accessed December 2006.
12. Richardson et al., "Business of Faith."
13. http://www.newbirth.org, accessed December 2006.
14. http://www.itc.edu/, accessed December 2006.
15. John Blake, "Long rebuts criticism at graduation," *Atlanta Journal-Constitution*, May 14, 2006, C1.
16. W. E. B. Du Bois, *The Souls of Black Folk* (New York: Bantam Books, 1989), 57.
17. Cornel West, *Race Matters* (Boston: Beacon, 1993), 14.
18. Isabel Wilkerson, "A Dollar and a Dream," *Essence* vol. 36, no. 5 (December 2005), 166–70.

17

Making the Unseen Seen: Pedagogy and Aesthetics in African American Prophetic Preaching[1]

Kenyatta R. Gilbert

Abstract: *This essay investigates the idea of African American prophetic preaching as a derivative of the message and agenda of the Hebrew prophet.[2] The essay demonstrates how critical consideration of the relationships between basic criteria of biblical prophetic speech, pedagogy (communal praxis), and cultural aesthetics (artistic beauty and power of Black oral expression), reveals a composite picture of the nature and function of African American prophetic preaching, and makes evident the need for a roadmap to rehabilitate the prophetic voice in America's Black pulpits. The fundamental premise is that African American preaching can become more communally constructive and consequential for our times when the African American preacher reclaims in spoken Word the voice of the prophet that speaks justice, divine intentionality and hope.*

To say all that might be said about African American prophetic preaching is not the intent of this essay. However, serious treatment must be given to this important subject if preachers are to become better informed and equipped to preach justice and hope. It is also important for homileticians to better understand the complexities within the African American preaching tradition in general, and the distinctive nature, character and function of prophetic Black preaching specifically. Few scholars have examined African American prophetic preaching, and fewer still have attempted to define its principle characteristics. In this essay, I draw attention to two conceptual features of this discourse, *conscientization* and *aesthetics,* in order to open up a way for us to think about African American prophetic preaching.

For our purposes, the basic features of prophetic speech outlined by Walter Brueggemann in his widely influential volume *The Prophetic Imagination* (2001) and his brief essay on prophetic speech in ancient Israel, "The Prophetic Word of God and History,"[3] provide us an important starting place. In his short essay "The Prophetic Word of God and History," Brueggemann identifies *five* discrete characteristic themes of prophetic speech. This speech opposes idolatry, particularly self-serving and self-deceiving ideologies. It refuses the temptation to absolutize the present; it drives toward a new unsettling, unsettled future. It is a word that speaks to the predicament of human suffering from the perspective of God's justice. This speech at all times assumes a critical posture over against established power. Lastly, the prophetic Word is a word of relentless hope.[4]

Identifying these constitutive biblical marks of prophetic speech provides us a way to take up the more fundamental matter of how one may make determinations about the theo-rhetorical character of African American prophetic preaching. While Brueggemann's scholarship on prophetic speech furnishes us with initial insight into the nature and function of prophetic Black preaching, there are important shortcomings to notice concerning its practical theological usefulness when translating Old Testament critical insight into the particular storied communities of American life. Brueggemann has not specifically tied his scholarship to a concrete people or era; he is principally concerned about the biblical prophet's social world. We cannot understand the composite nature of prophetic Black preaching from only this vantage point. Brueggemann's scholarship on the prophets needs to be set within a larger framework of specific religious histories to test his more universal claims. While Brueggemann's characteristics are generative for analytic purposes, devoid of serious attention to "the rhetorical situation,"[5] his scholarship can only convey a partial picture of African American prophetic preaching.

Another major limitation must be acknowledged. Despite using liberation hermeneutics alongside the stated declaration that prophecy tends to emerge in sub-communities, Brueggemann's principal audience in *The Prophetic Imagination* appears to be white Protestant mainline church communities.[6] His work only makes a formal theological place to demonstrate the relationship between the speech of the biblical prophet and the prophetic sermons of Black clerics in various periods of American religious history. Because his contemporary examples almost completely overlook the distinctive role and character of African American religion, and how scripture and culture have been central to naming and interpreting existential events of ultimate significance in the African American experience, his work leaves open a new avenue of possibilities for scholarship regarding prophetic preaching.

Notwithstanding these limitations, drawing on Brueggemann's general understanding of biblical prophetic speech can become a heuristic device that allows me to relate specific discourse characteristics of the ancients to the prophetic preaching that took place in the early part of the twentieth-century, during the social justice movements of the nineteen-fifties and sixties, and, in rare instances, is taking place today. By focusing in this way, it becomes clear how a distinctive prophetic discourse arose out of specific situations, echoing an outlook of divine intentionality to numerous exigencies in poetic fashion.

The African American prophet has traditionally had a certain disposition toward rhetoric and poetic imagination in the American context. There is a creative element here. Beginning in slavery Black churches have institutionalized the prophetic principle in many distinctive ways, recognizing injustice far and wide. Brueggemann's five prophetic speech characteristics are manifest in prophetic Black preaching. These characteristic themes of the prophetic Word establish basic criteria for drawing ancient and contemporary parallels. Nonetheless, it does appear that the prophetic principle has been masked in much of African American preaching today. This is where the work of Paulo Freire illuminates Brueggemann, turning our attention to the pedagogical dimension of prophetic speech. Freire's stronger emphasis on context and praxis brings lucidity and strengthens Brueggemann's claim that prophetic speech is always "concrete talk in particular circumstances where the larger purposes of God for the human enterprise come down to the particulars of hurt and healing, of despair and hope."[7]

Naming Reality

Freire says it is extremely important for oppressed people to find their own voice in order to name their own reality. Otherwise they may name the oppressor's reality as their own, and therefore contribute to their own oppression. Specific to this concern is Freire's principle of *conscientization*—from the Portuguese term *conscientizacao*, which refers to the process in which people develop a deepening awareness (consciousness) of the contradictions of the sociocultural reality shaping their lives and their capacity to transform that reality.[8] *Conscientization* joints to the significance of dialogue and critical reflection on concrete historical reality.[9] Freire's pedagogical theory originates from his own experience as a political exile from his native Brazil living in Chile, during a military coup in 1964. In his major work *Pedagogy of the Oppressed,* first published in 1970, he advances a critique of education born out of his concern for poor illiterate migrant workers. Freire's relevance to our subject matter, however, lies not in the formal tenets he proposes in his educational philosophy, but rather in his theorizing about "critical dialogical reflection on concrete historical realities and action for humanization."[10]

Theologies reflecting on African American contexts share themes with Latin American philosophies and theologies of liberation. Both are concerned with justice issues pertaining to oppression and liberation. Yet, these contexts have different socio-historical questions and concerns. African Americans, for example, have remained particularly conscious of the long history of slavery in this country and its repercussive effects.[11] In spite of differences, Freire is useful here because he connects speech with prophetic actions as concrete praxis. Praxis, defined as "reflection and action upon the world in order to transform it" is a dialogical activity.[12] In the process of *conscientization,* praxis opens up possibilities for oppressed people to combat their own "cultures of silence" (dehumanization). According to Richard Schall, such praxis "is set in thoroughly historical context, which is carried on in the midst of struggle to create a new social order."[13] To the disheartened migrant masses flooding into northern cities in the first half of the twentieth century the prophetic preaching that took place in northern Black congregations literally spoke into existence a new way of being in the world.

According to Freire, dialogue acts as an essential prerequisite to the creation of a new social order. Dialogue can only make a difference in the world if (1) love is its foundation; (2) it is an act of humility; (3) it possesses intense faith in humankind to become more fully human; (4) it takes place in a context where hope is present; and (5) it promotes critical thinking—thinking that is at once inseparable from action and constantly immersed in temporality without fear of risks.[14] The upshot of this critical dialogical reflection is that it not only affirms dialogue as an existential necessity, but also implies from the standpoint of praxis that, in order for people "to exist humanly," they must be free to participate in naming reality so that they can change it. The freedom to speak "is not the privilege of some few persons, but the right of everyone."[15]

Through dialogical action, Freire rightly observes that the dehumanized can begin to commit themselves socioculturally to the work of conscientization, "by means of which the people, through praxis, leave behind the status of *objects* to assume the status of historical *Subjects.*"[16]

The praxis of naming reality in order to transform it is what prophetic Black preaching carries out in the Great Migration and during the Civil Rights Movement of the nineteen-fifties and sixties. For the interwar period, a few Black preachers named the power of God to overcome dehumanizing political, economic, and social forces in their prophetic sermons. These preachers were guided by a vital hermeneutic of God's good intention for creation and the resolute conviction that listeners in their northern Black congregations needed a way to articulate their misery and be freed from America's making of "cultures of silence." A few representative Black preachers such as Adam Clayton Powell Sr., Reverdy C. Ransom and Florence S. Randolph, rose up to name the dehumanizing political and socioeconomic realities (e.g., substandard housing, racial and gender discrimination, unstable employment) stirred by the Great Migration, and simultaneously offered a word of hope which possessed the power to topple despair. Similarly, Martin Luther King Jr.'s prophetic message, "I've Been to the Mountaintop," delivered before a gathering of Memphis sanitation workers and supporters, named the power of God's justice in a southern city because of unjust social arrangements which circumscribed poor and working-class Blacks to menial wages. In specific terms, King took a critical stance against Memphis' powerbrokers. Criticizing the city's unfair hiring practices, King urged Blacks to commit themselves to putting pressure on the city establishment through economic withdrawal from Memphis' banks, merchants, and retailers on the one hand. On the other, he insisted that Blacks take measures to pool their resources in the quest for economic salvation. King reminded his audience to embrace the fact that they are God's people, and that the God of scripture stands against injustice and struggles alongside those in pursuit of human dignity.

Naming one's own reality to transform it happens when speech-acts are linked with prophetic actions as concrete praxis to open up possibilities for voiceless oppressed people. When oppressed people do not find their own voice to name their own reality, they may instead name the oppressor's reality as their own and therefore contribute to and redouble their own oppression. Although Freire sculpted his pedagogy in Brazil, a similar pedagogy issued forth in the prophetic voice of the African American preacher in the United States, who, in the prophetic proclamation of the Word, dared to connect that Word to the concrete social conditions of the listener. In the way that slaves sang spirituals in the cotton fields or exhorted the courageous in the "invisible church" to evoke an alternative reality in order to keep hope alive, hope was rooted in an eschatological vision that linked song and spoken Word to circumstance. This is what a few African American preachers during the Migration and Civil Rights Movement were doing in their prophetic sermons.

Great Migration preacher Florence Spearing Randolph preached a sermon entitled "If I Were White" on Race Relations Sunday before her Wallace Chapel AME Zion congregation. Based on Matthew 7:3–5 and 1 John 4:20, she interrogates the promises of American democracy, the deceptive ideology of black inferiority, and other chronic injustices on the eve of US entry into World War II. Randolph reminds her listeners of their self-worth, and reminded America's whites, claiming to be defending democracy, about their obligation to all American citizens. In the sermon, she disputes the offhanded idolatrous notion that God has created whites superior to blacks. The refusal of whites to act justly toward blacks, domestically and abroad, Randolph contends, is not only to embrace sin rather than Christ, but it is also to grasp a realistic picture of the suffering present. Her Christocentric focus is obvious. "If I were white," she says, and acted justly "I would be conscience free before him with whom I have to do." And yet more revealing are her next few lines:

> I slept, I dreamed, I seemed to climb a hard, ascending track, and just behind me labored one whose face was black. I pitied him, but hour by hour he gained upon my path. He stood beside me, stood upright, and then I turned in wrath. Go back, I cried, what right have you to stand beside me here? I paused, struck dumb with fear. For lo, the black man was not there, but Christ stood in his place. And Oh! The pain, the pain, that looked from that dear face.[17]

At this place in the sermon, when Randolph calls attention to the plight of Black human suffering, she does so only after her careful theological reflection on God's activity in the person of Jesus Christ, one who himself was degraded and misunderstood in the ancient world. There is, then, a push for her Black listeners, and overhearing whites, to see a patent connection in the life of Jesus and that of Black human suffering in America.

Accordingly, her hermeneutic of suspicion inquires: "Are whites adequately conceiving who Jesus really is?" Christ stands in the place of the rejected ones. Finally, in "If I Were White," Randolph makes a bold and vitalizing hermeneutical step to tell her congregation what to say on Race Relations Sunday reciting the captivating verse of scripture found in Matthew 7:3–5. "And why beholdest thou the mote that is in thy brother's eye, and considereth not the beam that is in thy own eye? Or how wilt thou say to thy brother, let me pull out the mote out of thine eye; and behold, a beam is in mine own? First, cast out the beam out of thine own eye and then thou shalt see clearly to cast out the mote out of thy brother's eye."

It is this determination to transcend oppression in thought and imagination, as the biblical prophets had done in the past that exemplifies prophetic Black preaching. In Freire, a key characteristic trait of African American prophetic preaching is discovered. *Prophetic Black preaching connects the speech act with prophetic actions as concrete praxis to help people freely participate in naming their reality.*

The Will to Adorn

Brueggemann's 1989 publication *Finally Comes the Poet: Daring Speech for Proclamation* focuses on the poetic character of prophetic speech. Not only does he reiterate the notion that prophetic speech evokes an alternative world or perception of reality, he also claims that the practice of preaching itself must be "subversive fiction"—a poetic construal of a world beyond the one taken for granted. This poetic speech is not about romantic caressing, moral instruction or problem solving, but the intense, unsettling proposal that the real world in which God dwells, and where God invites us to, is not the one overcome by worldly powers.[18]

Brueggemann invokes biblical authority for this aesthetic dimension of prophetic preaching, and one would not expect him to ground his discussion of this dimension in an awareness of the particular issues of social and ecclesial injustices in African American contexts. For this reason, I turn to Zora Neale Hurston's observation of the aesthetics of Black church worship as a way of talking about the poetic side of prophetic Black preaching.

The aesthetic quality of African American prophetic preaching is often perceived through contrasting lenses, in which both "the awesomely beautiful and the tragically ugly"[19] are held together. The homiletic upshot to this union is that hope and promise bear its fruit, and from this a new order for the people is established by God. Cultural aesthetics is the basis of the imaginative genius and furtive power of the prophetic preaching of legendary preachers such as Samuel Proctor, Prathia Hall, and J. Alfred Smith, who take scripture and cull out a hope-filled discourse about God's will to transform church and society, and, for the individual, "make a way out of no way."

African American prophetic preaching is not only concrete and particular speech but is also daringly poetic. At the heart of prophetic sermons is the African American preachers' ability to draw on cultural-aesthetic principles to communicate the gospel. These preachers are creative poets who possess the "will to adorn." This aesthetic impulse runs counter to preaching cultivated by contemplative, inner pietistic styles of worship. The aesthetic impulse is what furnishes the preacher's imagination and speech with subversive power, which is a valuable asset to the preacher because it allows the preacher to make lateral leaps linguistically where linear, flattened prose cannot.[20]

The speech-act inclination to adorn speech is well illustrated by African American novelist and folklorist Zora Neale Hurston in her essay, "Characteristics of Negro Expression," written ca. 1930, and published in *The Sanctified Church*. With metaphor and simile, double descriptive words, and verbal nouns, Hurston says, "the American Negro has done wonders to the English language. But it is equally true that he has made over a great part of the tongue to his liking and has his revision accepted by the ruling class."[21] The great use of metaphoric language in Hurston's portrayal seems more notable among the rare company of Black preachers afforded the opportunity of a formal education. Hurston is rightly convinced that to seek beauty is to realize that human beings have different standards of art, having different interests in art. Most are thus incapable to pass judgment on the art concepts of others?[22] The aesthetic impulse to create is always at work in the African American speech-act.

> The stark, trimmed phrases of the Occident seem too bare for the voluptuous child of the sun, hence the adornment. It arises out of the same impulse as the wearing of jewelry and the making of sculpture—the urge to adorn.[23]

Fundamentally, what Hurston shows is that the will to adorn in the speech-act is "a desire for beauty."[24] Insofar as prophetic Black preaching makes use of language and culture and carries this impulse for beauty, aesthetics holds potential as a way of talking about this tendency in the rare soundings of prophetic preaching in African America. Hurston enables us to see the evocative power of language and rhetoric, and how particular cultural-aesthetic principles that convey artistic beauty emerge as a result of the intermingling between African and American culture. Hurston accurately picks up on the power and beauty of Black oral expression; she sees that through symbolism, the use of "extended metaphors," and verbal nouns, Blacks creatively adorned their speech in attempts to recreate their lives. In prophetic Black preaching "language becomes a vehicle

Kenyatta R. Gilbert

for transforming meaning, for translating behavior into words and converting every-day life drama into written texts which are also performances."[25] Instead of singular reliance on expository prose, the preacher-poet communicates in signs and symbols that "extend the spatial and temporal boundaries of prose" to multiply the dimensions through which a listener may encounter God in the preached Word.[26]

King's aesthetic impulse is consistently evident throughout his homiletical corpus. King's sermon "Remaining Awake through a Great Revolution" exemplifies prophetic hope. King envisions a world where poverty is eradicated. Using mental pictures he finds a pathway into listener consciousness. One segment of his sermon reflects on poverty in India. From his critical attention to poverty in India he closes the gap by juxtaposing poverty there with the perplexing forces of poverty in United States. King questions why a nation of such extreme wealth and power fails to sufficiently address the issue of poverty, and by implication, human suffering. His adorned speech, noticed throughout the sermon, is clearly speech in search of an alternative to the present reality. We can get a sense of King's impulse for the beauty of speech in his creative use language and cultural symbols in the following:

"dwarf distance and place time in chains"

"Like a monstrous octopus, poverty spreads its nagging, reprehensible tentacles into hamlets and villages all over the world."

"I know where we can store food free of charge—in the wrinkled stomachs of millions of God's children all over the world who go to bed hungry at night."

The sermon reader or textual literalist insensitive to the ways scripture and experience/situation must be read dialectically in preaching will miss the beauty and power of Black oral expression. The prophetic Word comes to public expression through the creative impulse, often through the subversive and the ironic idiom. What one finds in King is an aggregate portrait of the Black preacher-poet—one situated in a once venerable but now vanishing part of the Black preaching traditions.

Like King, Gardner C. Taylor's use of language, culture, and imagination is an example of preaching displaying this same poetic impulse. In his 1964 message as president of the Progressive National Baptist Convention, Inc. in Washington DC, Taylor liberates, in voice, the evocative power and beauty of prophetic preaching. Urging his convention toward a new and unsettled future, Taylor, with metaphoric expression and eschatological imagery, points Black listeners to a hopeful reality in an unjust and collapsing American society.

There is much that is wrong, distorted, disfigured, crippled about us [Blacks] but there are gifts and powers in the very limp which is our history here. There is a quality of rapture among [B]lack people which is authentically Christian. There is a sense of optimism which sees the threatening clouds of life but sees them shot through with the light of God. "Over my head I see trouble in the air, there must be a God somewhere. Black people have been forced to be three-world people, inhabitants of white America, inhabitants of [B]lack America, inhabitants of their strange land of the amalgam of their racial dreams and what was beheld in the haunting report: 'Looked over Jordan, and what did I see? A band of angels coming after me.' There is a gift and power of [B]lack people as members of the disestablishment to see the society in its splendor and in its shame."27

Inspired by Hurston's idea about poetic language carrying an impulse for beauty, we discover in Gardner Taylor's adorned speech a creative impulse to light the way for hearers to see anew their lives in the light of a God who affirms their authentic Christian witness in a broken society. *Prophetic Black preaching carries an impulse for beauty in its use of language and culture.*

I have given consideration to two new constitutive characteristics of prophetic Black preaching. It may now be helpful to gather together the many strands that together establish a paradigmatic model of prophetic Black preaching that is both biblical and contextual. Representing this paradigm, prophetic Black preaching:

1. opposes idolatry, particularly self-serving and self-deceiving ideologies;
2. drives toward a new and unsettling future in its refusal to absolutize the present;
3. speaks to the predicament of human suffering from the perspective of God's justice;
4. assumes a critical stance over against established power;
5. refuses to relinquish hope when confronted by collective misery and despair;28
6. connects speech-act with prophetic actions as concrete praxis to help people freely participate in naming their reality;29 and
7. carries an impulse for beauty in its use of language and culture.30

A Message to Today's Black Preacher

Since Reconstruction, a call has gone out for prophetic preaching in the African American *village*.31 The once typically asset-rich Black pulpit is in deep crisis because it has become confused about its mission to the African American community. Black preachers and their congregations32 Obviously, there are myriad issues having negative impact on Black life in America. But the prosperity movement seems to be the ideological root cause of many of the distorted views about health and material success, which have long been a preoccupation of historically disenfranchised Black people. The prosperity gospel often veils itself as priestly in nature, i.e., it speaks concern about spiritual renewal. While emptying the cross of its meaning, prosperity preachers use the language of "prophecy" to motivate people in support of materialistic agendas that little serve the faithful.

According to the prosperity message the "blessed life" is the divine right of every Christian, the believer's reward for her or his unshakable faith and positive thinking.33 While it is obvious that the economic recession experienced nationwide has affected nearly all Americans, it has dealt a more devastating blow to Black communities (e.g., high foreclosure rates, credit card debt, rising crime rates). By promoting the worldview that gave us this economic crisis, prosperity theologians are partly to blame. Preaching centered on obtaining wealth based on one's positive confession and faith has had great appeal to Blacks of every social class. But it is this message of false hope that continues to lead many astray. Prophetic preaching is diametrically opposed to the prosperity message; the prophetic message's agenda is not manipulation. Instead, prophetic preaching names God at work in God's created world, and it names self-serving, self-deceiving ideological practices sin.

Facing the Hour

Religious scholars have begun to raise serious questions about the efficacy of the Black pulpit. They surmise that the general stream of Black preaching today does not address the multiple contradictions afflicting Black life in America, but rather extols the prosperity god, with focus almost entirely on interior or spiritual concerns. Unlike the slave preachers who transformed "themselves into teachers and moral guides with a responsibility to keep the people together with faith in themselves,"[34] several Black preachers today may be rightly branded double-dealing politicos, whose tamed voices are unable to speak out for justice-bearing change. African American prophetic preaching is fundamentally theo-rhetorical discourse that is grounded in hope and responsive to injustice.

Tavis Smiley's edited volume *The Covenant with Black America* (2005), reports a range of distressing statistics of exigent issues within African American communities in the United States:

- African Americans are 13 percent of the nation's population and account for 56 percent annually of new HIV infections. A quarter of these new infections are among people under 25 years of age.[35]
- Nearly one-third—32 percent—of African Americans do not have a regular doctor. By contrast, only 20 percent of white Americans do not have a regular doctor.[36]
- One of every three black males born today can expect to go to prison in his lifetime.[37]
- Forty-nine percent of the nation's homeless population is African American.[38]

These statistics provide a glimpse at only a few important concerns that militate against the health of African American villages. Who will speak legitimately on behalf of the village's weak and most vulnerable citizens if not the leaders within Black churches? These findings confirm the reality that African American communities are in crisis.

So, what, then, is the answer? What must be the contemporary Black preacher's rejoinder on the community's behalf? The answer, I think, lies in bringing these issues to the local and national community's level of consciousness where they can be dealt with. We must, as Martin Luther King once advised those fighting for freedom and justice during the Civil Rights era, name these crisis issues as finite disappointment even as we adhere to infinite hope. King once preached that the answer to the blighting of hope is to confront one's shattered dreams and to ask oneself: "How may I transform this liability into an asset... transform this dungeon of shame into a haven of redemptive suffering?"[39]

What is the Black preacher's message about God's self-disclosure in scripture and concern for transforming human action for today's Black Church contexts? Regrettably, it is not always clear what the role of the Black Church is today, especially given our society's growing pluralism and the world-shaping historical phenomena of racial, economic and cultural diversity. Perhaps the most constructive counsel for contemporary Black preachers is to urge the development of empathetic listening and dialogue with the culture, especially the voiceless and victimized residents of the village who cry out for an alternative voice, new beginnings—hope.

A Hopeful Sign

A new generation of African American preachers is emerging and making important strides to overcome the blighting of hope in Black churches and communities today. To name a few, Ray A. Owens, Leslie Callahan, and Raphael Warnock lead congregations in Tulsa, Philadelphia, and Atlanta, respectively, and have earned PhD's in the areas of Christian social ethics, religion, and theology. Alongside their obvious commitment to the agenda of African American community restoration are bold and thoughtful sermons that reveal their prophetic consciousness. Patrick Clayborn's doctoral dissertation situates the theologian and mystic Howard Thurman's preaching within the prophetic Black rhetorical tradition. Clayborn awakens the field to a reconsideration of Thurman's homiletical dexterity and poetic vision relative to his uncommon commitment to bridge the racial divide.

Emma Jordan-Simpson and Eboni Marshall stand in historic urban pulpits in New York City—churches with longstanding commitments to the work of social justice and community renewal. They proclaim the justice of God in spoken Word, and seek to call their listeners to pragmatic tasks in the *village.* The strident voice of Toby Sanders is one seldom noticed and appreciated. Sanders pastors the Beloved Community Church in Trenton, New Jersey, where his preaching seeks alignment with the teachings of Jesus in the spirit of Martin L. King's love ethic. Although these emerging clerics are less known to the general public, they are at the forefront, shaping the discourse for future generations, speaking truth to power, to provide new insights about what it means to preach prophetically in postmodern African America.

With new insights, current preaching trends, and supposed worship enhancing technology, come numerous challenges. Because the aforementioned clerics are adept readers of worship and culture trends, they have not lost appreciation for the heritage and multiple dimensions of African

American preaching, especially with the recent Black preaching trend to present didactic sermons in disregard of other preaching approaches. Owens, Callahan, Warnock, et al. might rightly be called technologians. That is to say, they are theologically astute and information-age savvy twenty-first century clerics. In their use of technology and media they well understand the times. More importantly, they know that they must not only use technology in for worship purposes; but they also must be technology critics,[40] when technology stifles the listener's reception of the Word.

The Preacher's Authorization

There is, of course, an important caveat for preachers who would proclaim a prophetic witness and speak truth on behalf of the village. Authorization to preach prophetically is reliant upon at least *three holy effects:* (1) access to God for revelation through prayer and scripture; (2) ability to hear God's voice distinct from one's own; and (3) conviction to speak about the dignity of persons as people of God.[41] The prophetic sermon is always a summoned word. Therefore, the place to begin prophetic proclamation is inquiry after God. The genesis and terminus of proclamation is God; and preaching as proclamation is theologically authorized speech (rhetoric) having concern about what is fitting to its receptor's context.[42] The messages heard across many African American pulpits are wholly suspect when they seem to say to adherents that if they do not receive God's material and spiritual blessings the problem falls under the strict province of that individual's faith, while the community of faith bears no responsibility. Consequently, the preacher must have a prophetic Word that not only takes a critical stance against the social ills of the community, but also offers rebuke to the false religion of the church.[43]

Consistent with the most basic task of the prophets of old who first retrieved God's instruction and then disseminated that instruction in the context of human affairs, the preacher who hopes to sound a prophetic note mediates for a lost people a way back to identity recognition. That is to say, the prophetic Word reminds people about who they are as people of God. Only in standing under the Word and community is the preacher truly able to discover the community's state of health and, correspondingly, is able to help that community claim its true identity.[44] God and the people have a significant role in testing the authority of the preacher. Although it does appear that the prophetic voice in African American church contexts today has been cloaked, the preacher can realize an opportunity to reclaim prophetic authority amid the complex social and ecclesial problems that dehumanize persons.

Beyond the African American Village

What might a context-specific proposal of the sort I have made here mean for preachers in other racial/ethnic communities? Part of the goal of this essay was to make clear the fact that the prophetic Word cannot be frozen into static categories or limited to any one justice-seeking, hopeful community. Prophetic preaching arises in response to rhetorical situations that need and invite it. African Americans do not have a monopoly on matters concerning community distress, human suffering, and other forms of injustice and oppression. Despite racial/ethnic classification the same abiding commitments to Christ's church in the will for justice and peace, I believe, apply to all who seek God's self-disclosure in their lived experiences.

Thus one is hardly prophetic in one's own context if indifferent to how the prophetic witness is actualized in other faith communities. Accordingly, the clothes of culture always shape meaning in the task of prophetic preaching. If naming one's own historical reality is significant in preaching a prophetic Word, then we are never permitted to say that we understand the meaning of preaching of this kind without becoming part of the arrived at meaning itself. Whether first, second, or third generation Irish, Italian, German, or Latin American, all must do the arduous work of naming their own storied reality, assessing their community's rhetorical situations, and addressing that community after hearing from God. If a particular community's concern is the gospel, this can only mean that that community must bear the responsibility of uncovering their own particular identity as journeying people in a strange new land.

Notes

1. I am cognizant of the obvious heterogeneity within Black religious life in America. However, there persists a historically constructed African American community in the U.S.—a critical mass of people of African descent, especially in heavily populated urban areas—whose shared history, cultural memory and distinctive sociocultural interests are self-evident. Readers will note that the use of the following terms *Black* and *African American* and *African American prophetic preaching* and *prophetic Black preaching* are descriptive labels used interchangeably in this essay. The interchangeable use of these terms is standard parlance today in Black studies, African American studies, and increasingly in Black homiletics. Also, my decision to capitalize the term *Black* is in recognition of the fact that recent scholarship is moving away from the term *black* in lowercase, which primarily suggests an ontological description of identity formation solely based on race. The capitalization of the term *Black* and not *white* is a way to signal "a rhetorical disruption of domination and white supremacy" and to honor, in a broader fashion, the particular historical and cultural legacy of people of African descent in this country. Frequently used as an alternate expression to the term *African American,* my decision to capitalize the term *Black* also comes from respect for the politics of its fluid and intergenerational usage in the vernacular of persons in communities of African descent. (Cf. Ronald Walters and Robert C. Smith. *African American Leadership* (NY: SUNY Press, 1999, 21); Nancy Lynn Westfield, ed. *Being Black, Teaching Black,* ed. (Nashville: Abingdon, 2008, xvi–ii).
2. Though it seems obvious that the prophetic principle is virtually institutionalized in African American churches due to racism, all Black preaching is not prophetic. Viewing African American preaching traditions through the scriptural images *prophet, priest and sage,* I think, provides a more useful conceptual framework for describing the tri-dimensional ministerial character of African American preaching.

Essentially, the *prophetic voice* mediates God's activity to transform church and society in a present-future sense based on the principle of justice. The mediating voice of Christian spiritual formation that encourages listeners to contemplate their personal relationship with their Creator and to enhance themselves morally and ethically by integrating elements of personal piety, spiritual discipline and church stewardship, characterizes the *priestly voice*. Finally, the *sagely voice* carries an eldering function. It is distinguished by its focus on wisdom, biblical faith, and realistic hope for future generations (For a more extensive treatment on this subject matter, see my forthcoming publication *The Journey and Promise of African American Preaching: The Threefold Cord*, Minneapolis: Fortress, 2011).

3. Walter Brueggemann, "The Prophetic Word of God and History" in *Texts that Linger, Words that Explode: Listening to Prophetic Voices* (Minneapolis: Augsburg Fortress, 2000), 35–44.

4. Walter Brueggemann illustrates his line of reasoning through an expository analysis of the conversation of Abraham, Sarah, and the three messengers in Gen 18:1–15. Brueggemann, "The Prophetic Word of God and History," 39–41.

5. Lloyd F. Bitzer defines this term as a complex of persons, events, objects, and relations presenting an actual or potential *exigence* (an imperfection marked by urgency; a problem, something waiting to be done) which can be completely or partially removed if discourse, introduced into the situation, can so constrain human decision and action as to bring about the significant modification of the exigence. In the way that audience, speaker, subject, occasion, and speech are standard constitutive elements of rhetorical discourse, the situation, maintains Bitzer, is likewise indispensable since it seeks to know the nature of those contexts in which speakers create discourse. "The Rhetorical Situation" in *Philosophy and Rhetoric*, 1–14, reprinted in John Louis Lucasites, Celeste Michelle Condit, Sally Caudill, eds. *Contemporary Rhetorical Theory: A Reader* (New York: The Guilford, 1999), 217, 220.

6. In his postscript on practice in *The Prophetic Imagination*, he only cites examples representative of churches and organizations to which he has had some affiliation.

7. Brueggemann, "The Prophetic Word of God and History," 44.

8. Paulo Freire, *Pedagogy of the Oppressed*, trans. Myra Bergman Ramos (New York: Continuum, 1993), 17–18. Daniel S. Schipani, *Conscientization and Creativity: Paulo Freire and Christian Education* (Lanham: University Press of America, 1984), 10.

9. Ibid.

10. Freire, *Pedagogy of the Oppressed*, 67.

11. Donald McKim, *The Bible in Theology and Preaching* (Nashville: Abingdon, 1985), 150.

12. Freire, *Pedagogy of the Oppressed*, 33.

13. Quoted in Ibid., 13–14.

14. Ibid., 68–73.

15. Quoted by Freire, Ibid., 69.

16. Ibid., 69–70.

17. Florence S. Randolph, "If I Were White," in Bettye Collier-Thomas, *Daughters of Thunder* (San Francisco, CA: Jossey-Bass, 2001), 216.

18. Walter Brueggemann, *Finally Comes the Poet: Daring Speech for Proclamation* (Minneapolis: Fortress, 1989), 4.

19. John W. de Gruchy, Christianity, *Art and Transformation: Theological Aesthetics in the Struggle for Justice*, *reprinted* (Cambridge: Cambridge University, 2003 reprinted), 171.

20. Cf. Paul Scott Wilson, *Imagination of the Heart: New Understandings in Preaching* (Nashville: Abingdon, 1988), 32–39; Wilson, "Imagination" in *Concise Encyclopedia of Preaching*, eds. William H. Willimon and Richard Lischer (Louisville: Westminster John Knox, 1995), 266–67.

21. Zora Neale Hurston, *The Sanctified Church* (Berkeley: Turtle Island, 1983), 51.

22. Hurston, *The Sanctified Church*, 54.

23. Ibid.

24. Ibid.

25. Linda Marion Hill, *Social Rituals and the Verbal Art of Zora Neale Hurston* (Washington DC: Howard University, 1996), 9.

26. Ibid.

27. Gardner C. Taylor, *The Words of Gardner Taylor: V. 4, Special Occasion and Expository Sermons*, comp. Edward L. Taylor (Valley Forge: Judson, 2001), 21–22.

28. Brueggemann, "The Prophetic Word of God in History," 39–41.

29. Cf. Freire, *Pedagogy of the Oppressed,* 69; Brueggemann, "The Prophetic Word of God and History," 36.
30. Cf. Walter Brueggemann, *Finally Comes the Poet,* (Minneapolis: Fortress, 1989), 6; Alkebulan, "The Spiritual Essence of African American Rhetoric," 34–35; Zora Neale Hurston., *The Sanctified Church,* 53.
31. This metaphor is another way of characterizing local neighborhoods and community where persons of African descent are predominant.
32. Robert M. Franklin, *Crisis in the Village: Restoring Hope in African American Communities* (Minneapolis: Fortress, 2007), 112.
33. Milmon Harrison, *Righteous Riches: The Word of Faith Movement in Contemporary African American Religion* (Oxford: Oxford University, 2005), 8.
34. Eugene Genovese, *Roll, Jordan, Roll: The World the Slaves Made.* (New York: Vintage, 1976), 272–73.
35. K. Wright, "Time Is Now! The State of AIDS in Black America," Black AIDS Institute, Los Angeles, February 2005, pp. 5, 8, quoted in Tavis Smiley, ed. *The Covenant with Black America* (Chicago: Third World, 2006), 9.
36. "2001 Health Care Quality Survey," The Commonwealth Fund, New York, November 2001, chart 37, quoted in Tavis Smiley, ed. *The Covenant with Black America,* 9.
37. Marc Mauer and Ryan Scott King, "Schools and Prisons: 50 Years After Brown vs. Board of Education," http://www.sentencingproject.org/pdfs/brownboard.pdf, The Sentencing Project, quoted in Tavis Smiley, ed. *The Covenant with Black America,* 53.
38. U.S. Bureau of the Census, "Census 2000," available at http://www.census.gov/Press, quoted in Tavis Smiley, ed. *The Covenant with Black America,* I 05.
39. Martin Luther King Jr. *Strength to Love* (Philadelphia: Fortress, 1963), 91.
40. Quentin J. Schultze, "Technology" in *The New Interpreter's Handbook of Preaching* (Nashville: Abingdon, 2008), 334–35.
41. Jeremiah 23:21–22, 28, 32.
42. James F. Kay, "Reorientation: Homiletics as Theologically Authorized Rhetoric," *The Princeton Seminary Bulletin,* Vol. XXIV, Number I, 33.
43. Russell Moldovan, *Martin Luther King Jr.: An Oral History,* 1999, 15.
44. D. Stephen Long, "Prophetic Preaching" in *Concise Encyclopedia of Preaching,* ed. William H. Willimon and Richard Lischer (Louisville: Westminster John Knox, 1995) 388.

18
Lament:
Homiletical Groans in the Spirit[1]

Luke A. Powery

Abstract: *The expression of celebration has been the normative discussion point in African American homiletical theory to the neglect of the expression of lament. This is not to say lament has not been practiced in the pulpit or beyond, but it is to claim that lament has not been named as a viable sermonic expression as has been done with celebration; thus, lament has been silenced in homiletical discussions. In light of this, this article aims to highlight lament and argue that it is a critical manifestation of the Spirit in preaching and should be voiced alongside celebration.*

Introduction

In *On Christian Doctrine*, Augustine teaches about three styles of speaking—subdued, moderate, and grand—which correlatively teach, delight, and move audiences. Being taught and delighted spark applause, but Augustine claims that the grand style persuades audiences to such an extent that there is a possibility of moving them to tears. He writes, "There are many other experiences through which we have learned what effect the grand style of a wise speaker may have on men. They do not show it through applause but rather through their groans, sometimes even through tears, and finally through a change of their way of life."[2] As a homiletician, Augustine is a forerunner in teaching preachers about lament, though he did not use that term but rather speaks of groans and tears. By speaking of such, he invites groans and tears to be a part of the Christian practice of preaching. In this particular statement, Augustine focuses his attention on the hearers' response of groans not necessarily the groans or laments of the preacher. Yet, it is important to see how Augustine allows for the full expression of worship in the event of preaching, whether it is applause and celebration or groans, tears, and lament. Augustine, as homiletician, is one of the historical precedents for speaking about lament in the preaching event. Some contemporary preaching theorists also bring lament to the fore, such as Mary Catherine Hilkert and Sally Brown;[3] but, this focus has not been developed substantially in homiletics in general and African American homiletics in particular.

The expression of celebration is usually the normative discussion point in African American homiletical theory to the neglect of the expression of lament. This is not to say that lament has not been practiced in the pulpit or beyond but it is to claim that lament has not been named as a viable "theo-rhetorical" expression in preaching as has been done with celebration. Worship or preaching is not limited to celebration nor "spoiled by tears."[4] The biblical witness demonstrates individuals and communities approaching God, not only in joy, but also in sorrow. Celebration, therefore, needs to be paired with lament, another faithful response of worship to God who should be praised in the midst of both joyful and sorrowful occasions. Lament can be an appropriate way of addressing human failure or loss before God, and celebration is an appropriate way of acknowledging God's ongoing care. In fact, just as celebration has been called a "nonmaterial African cultural survival,"[5] it has been noted that "for African peoples everywhere the experience of lamentation is as ancient as their days of existence";[6] thus, the counterparts of lamentation and celebration are embedded in the cultural fabric of African Americans. Because lament is usually silenced in conversations about African American preaching, this article highlights the importance of lament as a Christian expression and particularly as a manifestation of the Spirit in preaching. I will first explore some biblical and theological perspectives which link lament to the groans of the Spirit and all of creation, scripture, particularly the psalms, and Christ; this will ground lament as a viable theological language and expression of the Spirit in preaching. Then I will discuss what lament might mean more specifically for preaching, speaking further about its nature and its relationship to celebration as doxology. The final segment will conclude with some reflections about lament's relationship to a suffering world. Through this article, it will become clear that lament is an essential and significant expression in sermons for preaching that aims to be rooted in the Spirit.

The Spirit, Groans, and Lament

If preaching is a gift of the Spirit, and if the Spirit groans, should not Christian preaching also groan, that is, lament? To begin reclaiming lament as an expression in preaching, it is necessary to explore the Spirit's relationship to groans as a way of thinking about lament theologically. The eighth chapter of Romans presents a compelling portrait of how the Spirit is linked to hope-filled suffering through the groans of creation. The Spirit does not avoid suffering or pain but actually causes a believer to suffer with Christ in anticipation of eventually being glorified with him (Rom. 8:17). In his Romans commentary in *True to Our Native Land*, Thomas Hoyt writes,

The Spirit does not bring release from present suffering but propels believers into it. Present suffering prevents confidence for the future from becoming triumphalistic. But if the Spirit does not nullify suffering, neither does suffering nullify the confidence that the community may have for the future. In Paul's mind the Spirit is connected with a universal yearning to experience the fulfillment of God's purposes.[7]

The Christian community yearns for God's future but they are not alone "for the creation waits with eager longing for the revealing of the sons of God" (Rom. 8:19). The creation is in a "bondage to decay" and the whole created order groans in labor pains (Rom. 8:22), indicating the presence of pain in the present even while it longs for a brighter future from God. But the creation is not alone in its groaning because Paul writes, "and not only the creation, but we ourselves, who have the first fruits of the Spirit, groan inwardly while we wait for adoption" (Rom. 8:23). The Spirit engages believers, preachers, in honest groans. Gordon Fee argues that "inwardly" may mean "within ourselves" but he questions the use of the word "inwardly" as if the groans are not expressed outwardly.[8] What is important here is the possibility that these groans are voiced and expressed. One cannot endure suffering and always be silent because even the Spirit speaks through Christians, those who have the first fruits of the Spirit.

Yet, creation's groans and human groans are not enough. There is a clear sense that the Spirit, too, groans because of the travail of the world. Paul says that the Spirit "intercedes with sighs too deep for words"(Rom. 8:26). Once again, the work of Gordon Fee is insightful because he translates "sighs too deep for words" to "inarticulate groanings," not "silent" or "inexpressible" sounds but more to do with words that we cannot understand with our own minds.[9] This translation provides the opportunity to speak of the Spirit's sighs also as groanings, joining the whole creation, including human beings, in yearning for the full redemption of God. *Lament connects us to the Spirit and all of creation.* It is important to realize that the Spirit articulates groans of suffering and "the Spirit participates in the yearning by assisting the believer who hardly knows how to prepare in anticipation of the future restoration. The Spirit puts a meaning into human sighs that they would themselves not have. Thus, God, too, participates in the yearning for renewal that God is now accomplishing."[10] Creation and humanity are not isolated from God during these groans of suffering but God actually fosters such truthful groaning as part of what it means to be God's creation. This truthful groaning is an aspect of what it means to be a faithful preacher of the gospel. New Testament scholar Emerson Powery says, "groans are enlivened by the Spirit (of God) who groans through humans. Such groans recognize, by the Spirit, the incompleteness of justice and righteousness in the land."[11] For my purposes, this Spirit language of groans opens an avenue for viewing the Spirit's speech in preaching as lament.

Lament Psalms as Voice of the Spirit

To talk about lament, one should deal with the lament psalms in some fashion especially if one holds to the opinion of Hughes Oliphant Old who calls the psalms "the songs of the Holy Spirit."[12] *Lament is a way the Spirit connects us to scripture.* The truthfulness, honesty, and faithfulness of even the lament psalms are the "voice of the Spirit" crying out of humanity before God. There is precedence for this posture of lament and it is part of the language of the Spirit. Walter Brueggemann observes the full gamut of human life before God in what he calls the psalms of orientation (descriptive hymns), disorientation (laments), and reorientation (declarative hymns). Lament, psalms of disorientation, is a stance before God.[13] They comprise one third of the Psalter, which demonstrates that lament is one valid way through which humans and the divine interrelate. It is a position that one may take before God thus it is a possibility in preaching. Some scholars define lament as "that unsettling biblical tradition of prayer that includes expressions of complaint, anger, grief, despair, and protest to God."[14] The biblical tradition invites us to deal with our suffering openly before God without timidity. Why then is it that some preachers struggle to lament in preaching? Or, do preachers express it, but do not know what to call it? There is a full range of possible human situations, individually and corporately, out of which lament arises, but most importantly, they state that life is not right![15] Brueggemann says that these lament psalms say things are not the way they should be in the present arrangement and they need not stay this way and can be changed; the speaker will not accept the present arrangement, because it is intolerable; and, it is God's obligation to change things.[16] Lament in the Spirit gives voice to the suffering and indicates that suffering is not satisfactory, and it does so in the face of God.

These lament psalms, these songs of the Spirit, acknowledge that pain is present and it can be articulated with candor but it must be addressed to God even in the imperative because God cannot be protected from trouble. Lament psalms imply that dysfunction is God's proper business.[17] For instance, in Psalm 39:1–12, the psalmist can no longer keep silent because his "distress grew worse" and "heart became hot within" him. This internal burning leads him to cry out to God, "And now, O Lord, what do I wait for? My hope is in you. Deliver me from all my transgressions. Do not make me the scorn of the fool. I am silent; I do not open my mouth, for it is you who have done it. Remove your stroke from me; I am worn down by the blows of your hand. . . Hear my prayer, O Lord, and give ear to my cry, do not hold your peace at my tears." In another instance, Psalm 74 says,

> O God, why do you cast us off forever? Why does your anger smoke against the sheep of your pasture? Remember your congregation, which you acquired long ago. . . Direct your steps to the perpetual ruins; the enemy has destroyed everything in the sanctuary. . . How long, O God, is the foe to scoff? Is the enemy to revile your name forever? Why do you hold back your hand; why do you keep your hand in your bosom?

In this kind of truthful speech, Israel's discernment of God and experience of human reality converge, causing them to ask God such questions as, "How long?"(Ps. 79, 82), "Will you?" (Ps. 85), and "Why?" (Ps. 2, 43). We hear the "why?" most poignantly in Jesus' cry of dereliction, "My God, my God, why have you forsaken me?" (Ps. 22, Matt. 27:46) God is interrogated and indicted in these prayers of the Spirit but the psalmist never breaks off the relationship with God. When Jesus cries out in deep despair, he still says "my God." In fact, the laments glorify God because the psalmist turns to God with his or her pain. Even in anger and accusation the relationship is never severed, confirming what Mary Catherine Hilkert says: "anger is a mode of relatedness" to God.[18]

Furthermore, Patrick Miller notes that in these psalms or songs of the Spirit, question and trust, protest and acceptance, fear and confidence are conjoined.[19] God may be angrily questioned but God is also trusted to deliver from harsh circumstances. Womanist scholar Emilie Townes notes that lament appeals are "always to God for deliverance."[20] This trust in God leads to the hope found in most lament psalms. As many people have observed, laments have a dialectical movement from plea *almost* always to praise.[21] For example, Psalm 22 begins with "My God, my God, why have you forsaken me? Why are you so far from helping me, from the words of my groaning?" but shifts to "You who fear the Lord, praise him! All you offspring of Jacob, glorify him; stand in awe of him all you offspring of Israel. . . before him shall bow all who go down to the dust, and I shall live for him" (Ps. 22:23, 29). The one who laments is not satisfied with living in lament forever. There is hope that "trouble don't last always" because there is a God who can do something about the trouble. These psalms are a "scandal in the church, because they cannot be prayed to a god who does nothing. . ."[22] When the cry rings out to God in Psalm 85, "Will you be angry with us forever? Will you prolong your anger to all generations?" the speaker concludes with "The Lord will give what is good and our land will yield its increase."[23] In the midst of hellish situations, hope arises due to faith in a God who can help. Lamentation is thus faithful speech because it is pronounced with faith in God. Biblical lament requires the presence of God thus to lament is to embrace this God's reality. Moreover, lament cannot be resolved and answered by God unless it is first spoken. Thus, it is a theological act and because it is theological it not only has to do with our human laments, but also with God's lament and groans in the Spirit. These lament psalms, these songs of the Spirit, can also be heard resonating through the lament of God in Christ.

Lament of Christ in the Spirit

Lament is a way the Spirit connects us to God's own lament in Christ. Lament has to do with God not only because it is a posture taken before God, but also because God is one who in Christ laments and suffers in the Spirit. Though as Moltmann says, "There was no time and no period of his life when Jesus was not filled with the Holy Spirit,"[24] the Spirit does not make Jesus Christ a "superman."[25] Jesus endures the shame of the cross and laments, "My God, my God, why have you forsaken me?" Jesus weeps. Jesus sheds tears of blood. Jesus suffers. Jesus dies. The crucifixion is not a figment of the Christian imagination thus in the full expression of what it means to be a Christian preacher empowered by the Spirit, there is room to suffer and lament. The Spirit is there in death. The cross keeps our lives in the Spirit connected to the real suffering of God's creation and to the suffering experienced within the very being of the triune God. The suffering of the cross gives us sufficient reason to lament.

It is at the cross where we remember God's passionate love as suffering love and voluntary fellow-suffering which suffers in solidarity with the suffering, groaning creation, even the groaning Spirit.[26] The suffering love of the passion flows through the Spirit and continues in the sighs of the Spirit, yet, the Spirit also opens up a hope for new life through the future of the coming of God to the world. This love of the Spirit allows creation, us, to fellowship with the sufferings of Christ as well as experience the new life to come. The lament and the pain of the cross are in the Spirit but so is the joy of new life through the resurrection. Though this article just focuses on the lament, it is important to stress that the lament of Christ in the Spirit does not end in despair but is very much like the songs of the Spirit, the biblical genre of lament, in moving towards praise and hope and celebration; but, this hope is grounded in lament, pain, and suffering. As Amy Plantinga Pauw has said, "the resurrection does not erase from Christ's hands and feet the wounds of the crucifixion."[27] The marks of suffering are always present and lament acknowledges this. Lament embraces who God is, even in divine suffering.

Thus far, it has been noted that lament has to do with humanity and also divinity, not just in terms of God being the object of our lament but God as One who in Christ actually laments—lament *before* God and the lament *of* God, all expressing the groans and laments of the Spirit. Lament embraces God and human suffering *simultaneously,* which captures the divine-human communication that is worship and preaching. Christ's life is the "epitome of liturgy," according to Melva Costen in *African American Christian Worship,* thus any liturgical act, e.g., preaching, must embrace lament if it is to be truly Christological, pneumatological, and doxological.[28] If there is space for lament in creation, scripture, and God, our sermons should also make space for this posture of worship. These biblical and theological musings lead to further exploration of the nature of lament as a manifestation of the Spirit in preaching.

Lament of the Spirit in Preaching

In African American preaching, lament is one specific manifestation of the Spirit that has not been treated adequately in the academic study of homiletics, though it is fruitful as an avenue for speaking about the Spirit in relation to preaching. Homiletical lament is an expression of the Spirit who groans and sighs through humanity as indicated above.[29] Sermonic lament of the Spirit takes its cues from the insights of biblical lament in that it too not only directly and concretely names life's harsh realities (plea), but also anticipates God's intervention in faith and hope (praise) because of the belief in the reign of God. Direct speech in preaching lament is necessary as a means to exposing life's harsh realities as the psalms indicate. This approach assures that lament is linked to real life issues and experience and is not a figment of one's own imagination. This idea of the importance of direct speech for lament parallels Charles Campbell's advocacy for direct speech in exposing the deathly powers present in the world.[30] Being explicit and direct about hope in God is also vital for as noted, lament appeals are "always to God for deliverance."[31] Homiletical lament is no different; it is a sermon form that begins with the truthful declaration of human pain but moves towards hope because of a firm belief in the presence and power of God. At times, the anticipation of hope is evident through the interjection of statements of good news while painting the picture of bad news. Lament is faith speech, implying that all preaching assumes a measure of faith in God; thus, one should not preach against God in a sermon. One may be angry with God but even this implies a relationship with God that does not seek the demise of God. If one preaches against God, then one can necessarily presume that what occurs is not in fact Christian preaching nor the lament of the Spirit which one finds in the suffering Christ's cry of dereliction, "My God, my God, why have you forsaken me? (Ps. 22)

In addition, lament is important for all homiletical cultures because of the travail of the world in which we live. War, genocide, famine, and child trafficking are just a few of the serious problems pervading the global society, and African American communities in particular are burdened with issues, such as the high rate of imprisonment for black males, a high percentage of people with AIDS, and the ongoing struggle against racism. The language of lament is vital for African American preaching communities, because it links to the particular reality of pain and suffering experienced by African Americans in the past and present. A denial of lament is a denial of African American history, the Holy Spirit, and the history of Christ. I would even assert that a denial of lament is a denial of what it means to be human; but, the embrace of lament is an embrace of the Spirit of Christ and historical memory. In many ways, the concept of "trouble" articulated in the work of Paul Scott Wilson is a homiletical precursor to homiletical lament. Trouble is sin or brokenness experienced by humanity, which places a burden on people; according to Wilson, this trouble serves as part of the deep grammar of sermons. Trouble is the existential context for the response of lament.[32] However, trouble does not necessarily link to the work of the Spirit explicitly nor does it point to human expressions of the Spirit, e.g., lament in preaching. Lament implies human activity, not passivity, before God in the Spirit during the preaching event. Lament is something one does in preaching and not about which one simply speaks. Moreover, lament anticipates the eventual overcoming of vast trouble. Lament echoes Samuel Proctor's "antithesis" in his sermon method. Antithesis is the "woe is me" sermon section that is not the final answer of hope, though it anticipates it. Proctor describes antithesis as the following:

> It could be an error that must be corrected, a condition that must be altered, a mood that must be dispelled, a sin that cries out for confession and forgiveness, some ignorance that needs to be illumined, a direction that has to be reversed, an idolatry of worshiping things that are corruptible that should cease in favor of praising an incorruptible God, some pain and hurt that await the balm of Gilead, or some lethargy that needs to be replaced.[33]

Antithesis raises the need as does lament, but lament also actively longs for God's answer to the particular struggles. Lament has a Godward direction and it is important for preaching because it keeps God in focus, not to the neglect of humanity. Lament coincides with the "hermeneutic of God" discussed by Cleo LaRue in his approach to black preaching in that lament can function as a hermeneutical approach to scripture that implies faith in a powerful God while simultaneously naming difficult circumstances. LaRue says that the "hermeneutic of God, the mighty sovereign who acts mightily on behalf of the powerless and oppressed, is the longstanding template blacks place on the scriptures as they begin the interpretive process... blacks historically and to this present day believe God is proactively at work on their behalf. This is what they bring to scripture, see in scripture, and preach from scripture."[34] Furthermore, lament, in its naming of reality, nurtures truthfulness and anger, two key virtues of any preacher, according to some homileticians.[35]

As mentioned in the earlier statement by Peter Paris, lament as an expression of African Americans is not novel because it is embedded in black cultures and has been a part of the experience of oppressed black people across the world. In particular, studies on the Spirituals have been performed, stressing the struggle and lament of African Americans.[36] However, lament in sermons has not been discussed in-depth within African American homiletics or within Euro-American perspectives, as cited earlier. Barbara Holmes, in her work, *Joy Unspeakable: Contemplative Practices of the Black Church*, shares a concern that people in general, but African Americans in particular, "have forgotten how to lament"[37] though she realizes that some churches engage in this practice, even if they do not recognize it. She attempts to reclaim lament as a viable avenue of contemplative doxology. She acknowledges that the atmosphere in most black churches are joyful but contends that even the moans on the slave ships of the Middle Passage were generative and "the precursor to joy yet unknown." She poetically writes, "On the deck after evening rations, lament danced and swayed under the watchful eyes of the crew."[38] I would assert that African Americans have not forgotten how to lament in most settings, but just have not named the phenomenon in preaching as lament as has been done with celebration. The magnification of homiletical lament as a manifestation of the Spirit in this essay is not only to reveal its significance in and of itself for preaching in the Spirit, but also to realize its vital and necessary partnership with homiletical celebration. To speak of lament as manifestation of the Spirit apart from celebration would be insufficient and inadequate to a discussion about the full breadth and depth of expression in African American preaching traditions.

Albert Raboteau, religious historian at Princeton University, notes that African American Spirituality intones a "sad joyfulness"[39] and it is this mixed texture that represents the relationship of lament and celebration in preaching. This mixture of sorrow and joy is already emphasized in the singing of African Americans. William McClain writes,

> In our melancholy, our songs are not always mournful songs. Most often, they are joyous, lifting the Spirit above despair. Yet, our sad songs sometimes come in the midst of our joy, in moments of jubilation and celebration. Without warning caution emerges to remind us that songs of joy must be tempered by the stark realities of the plight of our people. In the midst of our joyful singing the soul has not forgotten depression, pain, and expressions of hopelessness on the faces of our young. Laughter turns to tears and our glad songs into laments. But, we refuse to give up or give in. There is a God sense that has become a part of the fabric of the race. We refuse to let God alone, and we know God has never let us alone! At the moment of our deepest despair we sing, "sometimes I feel like a motherless child a long way from home." Then, in the midst of our sadness, we sing with assurance, "I'm so glad that trouble don't last always!"[40]

This same pattern is present in much African American preaching. Though it has not been emphasized in homiletics, it has been recognized. James Cone says the word "arises out of the totality of the people's existence—their pain and joy, trouble and ecstasy."[41] James Earl Massey recognizes there is a "trouble-glory" mixture in black praise, even though he emphasizes the festive nature of black preaching. He says black preaching "majors in the celebrative aspects of faith even as it sings of the troubles nobody knows."[42] James Harris notes, "Black preaching is indeed exciting and jubilant, but it is also sad and reflective. It represents the ebb and flow of the Holy Spirit that correlates with the ups and downs of life. It reflects the reality of context and experience. Additionally, it is a creative interplay between joy and sorrow, freedom and oppression, justice and injustice. . . It reflects the power of the church in the presence of the Holy Spirit."[43] Harris is important because he makes an explicit pneumatological link to the "sorrowful joy" of preaching. Moreover, Evans Crawford in his book, *The Hum,* says the sermon pitch and voice of the preacher "can sound life's laments and its laughter, its grief, and its glory."[44]

Even Teresa Fry Brown captures this relationship between lament and celebration in the experience of black preaching with her notions of "weary throats" and "new songs." In her work, *Weary Throats and New Songs: Black Women Proclaiming God's Word,* Fry Brown hints at the dialectic of lament and celebration undergirding the preaching of African American women in particular. She refers to the resistance to the call of women to pulpit ministry as the "weary throats," indicating the weariness of women due to their struggle for full access to the pulpit; the weary throat is reason

Luke A. Powery

for lament. The "new song" is the support given to black women preachers, even if the support is only from God; the new song is reason for celebration. She says of her own homiletical history,

> My throat was sometimes parched due to human machinations, but I was able to sing a new song when God's word coursed through my marrow. There was life on the other side of the church restrictions. There was a light in the tunnel of discrimination. There was energy in the midst of fatigue. There was an "anyhow" in the gift of preaching. There was a dialectic balancing of the weary throat and the new song.[45]

Brown's work is not only significant because of her recognition of the close relationship between lament and celebration, but because she reclaims women's voices as potential conduits of the Spirit in the pulpit and not solely on the main floor of churches when testifying, as has traditionally been the case in many black churches. This homiletical balancing act of lament and celebration permeates the preaching of men and women in African American traditions, though lament is not the coined term for this homiletical stance embedded in many sermons. Furthermore, Harold Dean Trulear argues that the preacher "fashions that trouble into a litany in which every sentence of sorrow is punctuated with an exclamation point of God's care," sorrow balanced with joy. He notes that the "drama" of black preaching moves from crucifixion (sorrow, lament) to resurrection Goy, celebration), rehearsing the crucifixion-resurrection motif rooted in Jesus Christ.[46] Trulear's perspective on African American sermon movement coincides with Paul Wilson's understanding that the sermon should move "*from* trouble *to* grace. . .*from* the exodus *to* the promised land, *from* the crucifixion *to* the resurrection and glory."[47] One does not have to agree with the idea that all African American sermons move from crucifixion to resurrection in order to embrace the observation that both lament (crucifixion) and celebration (resurrection) are present within the preaching discourse of many African Americans. In one sense, lament and celebration may be viewed as a grammar of the Spirit underlying preaching.

If sermons do move from lament to celebration, this homiletical movement of the Spirit echoes the lament psalms. As indicated earlier, lament psalms generally move from plea or cry to praise or celebration because of hope in God for present and future deliverance and intervention. The linking of lament to celebration and viewing it as a sermon movement, parallels law/gospel, trouble/grace, antithesis/thesis, exposing/envisioning sermon patterns propagated by others.[48] Also, uniting lament and celebration is similar to the stereoscopic apocalyptic homiletic espoused by my colleague James Kay who suggests that from the vantage point of the cross, preachers should proclaim the gospel through a "bifocal" lens of Paul's "old creation" (reason for lament) and Paul's "new creation" (reason for celebration).[49]

Moreover, the juxtaposition and unity of lament and celebration in preaching may be called doxology because as a unified tensive pairing these linguistic traces of the Spirit in preaching represent the full glorification of God during times of joy and sorrow. If expressing lament and celebration, preachers are at "full stretch" as *homo adorans* before God, capturing the breadth of worship stances before God. "Full stretch" is an idea liturgical theologian Don Saliers propagates when speaking about humanity coming before God in times of joy and sorrow, in the entire scope of human pathos. He writes, "Christian liturgy without the full range of the Psalms becomes anorexic—starving for honest emotional range."[50] Speaking in the Spirit requires a full range of expression that will keep our preaching honest. Gordon Lathrop believes that the juxtaposition of lament and celebration, or what he calls beseeching and praise, along with other biblical juxtapositions, compose the heart of the liturgical *ordo*, grammar or pattern of Christian liturgy. Thus, what is presented here about preaching is also present in liturgies.[51]

This is to say that doxology implies neither the negation of lament or celebration but the unified balanced linking of the two. As noted earlier, preaching is not limited to celebration nor "spoiled by tears."[52] Weeping and rejoicing unto God are both acts of worship in the Spirit. Lament cannot be omitted from the homiletical toolbox nor can celebration. If either language of the Spirit is missing, then a sermon performance loses its Christological grounding by neglecting either the crucifixion (lament) or resurrection (celebration). The challenge is to maintain a balanced relationship between these two expressions of the Spirit because the "'yes' of the gospel does not instantly make the 'no' of human doubt and struggle disappear."[53] Without lament or celebration in a sermon, the sermon loses its doxological nature because doxology, as defined here, is the juxtaposition and unity of lament and celebration. The two exist in tension and doxology is a third identity that is produced because of their union; it is what they are together, an act of fulsome praise, that puts life into perspective before God. Doxology entails both languages of the Spirit thus *lament is a way the Spirit moves us toward robust doxology*. Said another way, the juxtaposition and unity of lament and celebration as doxology functions as a sermonic metaphor in that "the tension or energy generated between the poles" of lament and celebration "produces a third identity (or spark)" which in this case is doxology.[54] This is a tensive relationship that does not diminish or erase any one of the variables or poles, but maintains the integrity and identity of each. Doxology through the Spirit upholds the truthfulness about the grace and power of God while preserving the truthfulness about human reality. To disregard the reality of human existence in its full breadth is to live a doxological lie or to be homiletically dishonest. As Sally Brown notes, "news of grace and resurrection rings hollow disconnected from daily realities of loss, dispossession, and yearning for justice. Testifying to the God of Easter requires the language of lament."[55] Doxology, as I have defined it, is non optional for preaching and life, therefore lament is essential, especially if one is serious about engaging the suffering world.[56]

Lament and Suffering's Tears

I have shown thus far that lament is an expression of the Spirit that connects us to the groans of the Spirit and all of creation, scripture, and Christ, while moving us toward doxology in preaching as a partner of celebration. As we consider the mission of the church and the role of preaching in it, it is important to also realize that *through the Spirit, lament in preaching can act as an impetus to social justice ministry which serves a suffering world.* With the proliferation of the so-called prosperity gospel churches where there is great stress on personal health, wealth, and blessings from God, this language of lament is extremely important as it has the potential of moving us out from our narcissistic selves. Nicholas Wolterstorff notes, "Liturgy and justice are joined by cords twined out of suffering's tears."[57] Liturgy, one aspect of which is preaching, has to do with the meeting of human and divine suffering. Justice has to do with aiding those who are suffering. Lament is the voice of the suffering; thus sermonic lament is a bridge from the liturgy to the liturgy after the liturgy, that is, ethical living in the world. Lament declares life is not right. It reveals dissatisfaction with the current order of social affairs. It does not sit in the pew of passivity but participates in resilient resistance that anticipates future change. It does not acquiesce to the status quo but can serve as an impetus to sociopolitical action. By giving voice to lament in our sermons, we enter solidarity with those who are suffering as we are called to suffer with those who suffer. If lament is not present in our preaching, then one is saying that life and society are fine as they are, despite the plethora of pain. But if it is present and practiced in preaching, one is saying that things must change not only in my life, but also in the world. If we create socio-theological worlds through our liturgies, including preaching, the use of lament will give us a vision of an unjust world and urge us to seek ways to act along with God on behalf of those in trouble. Through the lament of the Spirit, the present world order begins not only to be challenged, but also to crumble in the face of doxological opposition. Our preaching is only authenticated by living out God's justice in the world—all of life is a liturgy, all of life is a sermon. As Elsie McKee says about Reformed worship, "In some instances, love of neighbor may be better evidence for the actual faithful worship of God than are liturgical or devotional practices."[58] Sermonic lament can help move us in that direction of concrete loving action towards our neighbor.

There is much fruit to be born from the practice of lament as a manifestation of the Spirit in preaching. Not only does lament keep preaching pointing in a Godward direction but also it leads the church to embrace this God who is present in all circumstances of life and ministry. It gives depth to our preaching, liturgies, and lives before God and allows us to voice our tears, moans, and groans, so that they are no longer silent. We do not need to be afraid of lamenting because God can handle it; in fact, God desires it because God is welcomed and worshipped by it. Some have tried to kill it. Others have attempted to muzzle it. But lament is a love-song in the Spirit that will continue to live, if not in our sermons or congregations, then on the streets of groaning inner cities for what Justo and Catherine Gonzalez say is right: "The word of the gospel today, as in the times of Jesus,...comes to us most clearly in the painful groans of the oppressed. We must listen to those groans. We must join the struggle to the point where we too must groan. Or we may choose the other alternative, which is not to hear the gospel at all.[59]

Notes

1. Adapted from *Spirit* Speech, copyright © 2009 by Abingdon. Used by permission of the publisher.
2. See Saint Augustine, *On Christian Doctrine* Book 4, XXIV (ca. 396–427; reprint, trans. D. W. Robertson Jr., New Jersey: Prentice Hall, 1958), 160–161.
3. See Mary Catherine Hilkert, *Naming Grace: Preaching and the Sacramental Imagination* (New York: Continuum, 1997) and Sally A. Brown, "When Lament Shapes the Sermon," in *Lament: Reclaiming Practices in Pulpit, Pew, and Public Square*, eds. Sally A. Brown and Patrick D. Miller (Louisville: Westminster John Knox, 2005).
4. Hughes Oliphant Old, *Themes & Variations tor a Christian Doxology: Some Thoughts on the Theology of Worship* (Grand Rapids: Eerdmans, 1992), 17–21. Lament would exist under the rubric of epicletic doxology, but Old also insightfully names four other senses of doxology: kerygmatic, wisdom, prophetic, and covenantal.
5. Olin Moyd, *The Sacred Art: Preaching and Theology in the African American Tradition* (Valley Forge: Judson, 1995), 101.
6. Peter Paris, "When Feeling like a Motherless Child," in *Lament: Reclaiming Practices in Pulpit, Pew, and Public Square*, eds. Sally Brown and Patrick Miller (Louisville: Westminster John Knox, 2005), 111.
7. Thomas L. Hoyt Jr., "Romans," *True to Our Native Land: An African American New Testament Commentary*, eds. Brian K. Blount, Cain Hope Felder, Clarice J. Martin, and Emerson B. Powery (Minneapolis: Fortress, 2007), 262.
8. He says, "the phrase does not ordinarily function as a mere synonym for inaudible, as over against aloud. When used with verbs of speaking it generally means "to oneself," as over against "to others" which may be audible or not. The phrase therefore probably does not refer to whether or not such groaning is expressed, but that it is not expressed in the context of others." See Gordon D. Fee, *God's Empowering Presence: The Holy Spirit in the Letters of Paul* (Peabody, MS: Hendrickson Publishers, 1994), 574–575.
9. Fee, *God's Empowering Presence*, 582–583.
10. Hoyt, 263.
11. Emerson B. Powery, "The Groans of Brother Saul': An Exploratory Reading of Romans 8 for 'Survival," *Word and World 24:* 3 (Summer 2004), 321.
12. Hughes Oliphant Old, *Worship That Is Reformed According to Scripture* (Atlanta: John Knox, 1984), 43. Old also says, "When they sang the Psalms the Holy Spirit was praising the Father within their hearts." See p. 44.
13. For more about this movement, see Walter Brueggemann, *The Psalms and the Life of Faith*, ed. Patrick D. Miller (Minneapolis: Fortress, 1995), 8–16, 24.
14. Kathleen Billman and Daniel Migliore, *Rachel's Cry: Prayer of Lament and Rebirth of Hope* (Cleveland: United Church, 1999), 6.
15. For instance, there are laments about public national disasters. See Psalms 44, 58, 74, 79, 80, 83, 89:38ff, 106, 123.
16. Brueggemann, *The Psalms and the Life of Faith*, 105. This section is just a brief overview of the lament biblical genre as a viable option for doxological speech in preaching. I do not aim to be exhaustive about the lament psalm but suggestive enough to indicate that lament is nothing new for followers of God but has always been a part of the Judeo-Christian tradition. For further study about lament, particularly in the Psalms, please see Claus Westermann, *Praise and Lament in the Psalms* (John Knox,

1981), Patrick Miller, *Interpreting the Psalms* (Fortress, 1986), 48–63, Brueggemann, *Message of the Psalms* (Augsburg, 1984), 51–77.

17. Walter Brueggemann, *Israel's Praise: Doxology against Idolatry and Ideology* (Philadelphia: Fortress, 1988), 141.

18. Mary Catherine Hilkert, *Naming Grace: Preaching and the Sacramental Imagination* (New York: Continuum, 1997), 117.

19. See Patrick Miller, "Heaven's Prisoners: The Lament as Christian Prayer," *Lament: Reclaiming Practices in Pulpit, Pew, and Public Square,* eds. Sally Brown and Patrick Miller (Louisville: Westminster John Knox, 2005), 19.

20. Townes, *Breaking the Fine Rain of Death: African American Health Issues and a Womanist Ethic of Care* (New York: Continuum, 1998), 23.

21. I say "almost always" because there are some Psalms such as Psalm 39 and 88, which seemingly do not resolve in praise. Despite this fact, the very turning to God in lament glorifies God because even in lament humanity does what it was created to do—turn to God (i.e., conversion in its literal sense). For more about the dialectical movement of hurt to joy, death to life in the Psalms, see Brueggemann, *The Psalms and the Life of Faith,* 67–83.

22. Brueggemann, *Israel's Praise,* 140.

23. I am also fully aware that praise may be in the form of what Brueggemann calls "glad self abandonment" as seen in Psalm 100 and 150. These psalms do not necessarily explicitly or implicitly name troubled times like "the Pit" but are just a glad praise for being alive. In this article, I am particularly interested in seeing the places where lament and praise are tightly interwoven, thus this does not encompass all praise psalms. However, these psalms of glad self abandonment also give the church reason to praise in an abandoned way so when speaking about doxology, which consists of lament and praise, these "exuberant" praise psalms reveal the doxological possibilities for humanity. In *The Psalms and the Life of Faith,* Brueggemann lists eleven theses about the nature of praise. He says praise is a liturgical, poetic, audacious, "basic trust," knowing, doxological, polemical, political, subversive, evangelical, and useless act. See his explanation of all of these points on pp. 113–123.

24. Jürgen Moltmann, *The Way of Jesus Christ: Christology in Messianic Dimensions* (Minneapolis: Fortress, 1993), 81.

25. *Ibid.,* 93.

26. Jürgen Moltmann, *The Crucified God: The Cross of Christ as the Foundation and Criticism of Christian Theology* (Minneapolis: Fortress, 1993), 50–51.

27. Amy Plantinga Pauw, "Dying Well," *Practicing our Faith,* eds. Craig Dykstra and Dorothy Bass (San Francisco: Jossey-Bass, 1997), 170.

28. Melva Costen, *African American Christian Worship* (Nashville: Abingdon, 1993), 127.

29. For a Spirit who groans and sighs, see Romans 8:22–23, 26. Romans 8:22–23 says, "We know that the whole creation has been groaning in labor pains until now; and not only the creation, but also we ourselves, who have the first fruits of the Spirit, groan inwardly while we wait for adoption, the redemption of our bodies." Romans 8:26 says, "Likewise the Spirit helps us in our weakness; for we do not know how to pray as we ought, but that very Spirit intercedes with sighs too deep for words."

30. See Campbell, *The Word before the Powers: An Ethic of Preaching* (Louisville: Westminster John Knox, 2002), 107–110.

31. Townes, 23.

32. For more about trouble, see Paul Wilson, *The Four Pages of a Sermon* (Nashville: Abingdon, 1999), pp.73–154, and his overview of trouble in *Preaching and Homiletical Theory* (St. Louis: Chalice, 2004), 87–100.

33. Samuel D. Proctor, *The Certain Sound of the Trumpet: Crafting a Sermon of Authority* (Valley Forge: Judson, 1994), 28.

34. LaRue, *The Heart of Black Preaching* (Louisville: Westminster John Knox, 2000), 112. Similarly, Warren Stewart says that God is the point of departure in the hermeneutical process for African American proclamation. See Stewart, *Interpreting God's Word in Black Preaching* (Valley Forge: Judson, 1984), 14–15.

35. Charles Campbell says that truthfulness, anger, patience, and hope are key virtues of any preacher. See *The Word before the Powers,* 169–188.

36. For such studies on the spirituals, see James Cone, The Spirituals and the Blues: An Interpretation (Maryknoll: Orbis, 1991), Howard Thurman, Deep River and The Negro Spiritual Speaks of Life and Death (Richmond, Indiana: Friends United, 1975), and Cheryl Kirk-Duggan, Exorcizing Evil: A Womanist Perspective on the Spirituals (Maryknoll: Orbis, 1997).

37. Barbara A. Holmes, *Joy Unspeakable: Contemplative Practices of the Black Church* (Minneapolis: Fortress, 2004), 95.

38. *Ibid.*, 75.

39. Albert Raboteau, *A Sorrowful Joy* (New York: Paulist, 2002), 50.

40. William B. McClain, *Come Sunday The Liturgy of Zion* (Nashville: Abingdon, 1990), 13.

41. James Cone, *God of the Oppressed* (San Francisco: HarperSanFrancisco, 1975), 19. Also, see Cone, *The Spirituals and the Blues* (Maryknoll: Orbis, 1992).

42. As noted by Evans Crawford, *The Hum: Call and Response in African American Preaching* (Nashville: Abingdon, 1995), 68–69.

43. Harris, *Preaching Liberation* 52–53.

44. Crawford, 69–70.

45. Teresa Fry Brown, *Weary Throats and New Songs: Black Women Proclaiming God's Word* (Nashville: Abingdon, 2003), 16. For more about the preaching ministry of black women in the 19th and early 20th centuries see Chanta M. Haywood, *Prophesying Daughters: Black Women Preachers and the Word, 1823–1913* (Columbia: University of Missouri Press, 2003).

46. Harold Dean Trulear, "The Sacramentality of Preaching," in *Primary Sources of Liturgical Theology: A Reader,* ed. Dwight W. Vogel (Collegeville: Liturgical, 2000), 266–272.

47. See Wilson, Preaching and Homiletical Theory, 98.

48. For an overview of law/gospel perspectives and its contemporary manifestation in the trouble/grace homiletical school, see Wilson, *Preaching and Homiletical Theory*, 73–100. For antithesis and thesis as part of a sermon method, see Proctor, *The Certain Sound of a Trumpet*, 28, 53–92. For the ethical impulse of exposing and envisioning as sermon movements, see Campbell, *The Word before the Powers*, 105–127.

49. James F. Kay, "The Word of the Cross at the Turn of the Ages," *Interpretation* 53, no. 1 (1999): 51. Kay also notes that this lens of "old age" and "new age" is "perceived not simply sequentially and not simply spatially, but both at once, as if looking through two lenses *simultaneously.*"

50. Saliers, *Worship as Theology: A Foretaste of Glory Divine* (Nashville: Abingdon, 1994), 120–121.

51. For Lathrop's enlightening liturgical perspective, see his *Holy Things: A Liturgical Theology* (Minneapolis: Fortress, 1998).

52. Old, 17–21.

53. Thomas Long, *The Witness of Preaching* (Louisville: Westminster John Knox, 1989), 157. In a similar vein, Paul Wilson notes, "Grace does not cancel the reality of human sin and the need for change. Easter does not obliterate Good Friday, although it puts it in a different perspective. Both are true— they exist in a tension, the final outcome of which has been determined." See Wilson, *Four Pages of a Sermon*, 22.

54. For this understanding of metaphor as it relates to preaching, see Wilson, *Preaching and Homiletical Theory*, 92–93.

55. Sally A. Brown, "When Lament Shapes the Sermon," in *Lament: Reclaiming Practices in Pulpit, Pew, and Public Square,* eds. Sally A. Brown and Patrick D. Miller (Louisville: Westminster John Knox, 2005), 28–29. Her basic argument is that lament psalms can function as a hermeneutical lens to interpret present realities of grief, loss, and suffering. There are four ways lament can shape sermons: provide a hermeneutical "map," provide lament rhetoric in the form of pastoral lament, critical-prophetic, theological-interrogatory.

56. Sally Brown calls lament "non-optional dialogue with God." See Brown, "When Lament Shapes a Sermon," 30.

57. See Nicholas Wolterstorff, "Liturgy, Justice, and Tears," *Worship* 62/5 (1988): 386–403.

58. Elsie McKee, "Context, Contours, Contents: Towards a Description of the Classical Reformed Teaching on Worship," *Princeton Seminary Bulletin* 16/2 (1995): 182.

59. See Justo and Catherine Gonzalez, *Liberation Preaching* (Nashville: Abingdon, 1980), 65.

19
Walkin' the Talk: The Spirit and the Lived Sermon

Luke A. Powery

In *The Souls of Black Folk*, W. E. B. Du Bois proclaims that African people brought "three gifts" to America: the "gift of story and song," "the gift of sweat and brawn," and the "gift of the Spirit."[1] The first and second gifts have received extensive attention compared to the third theological gift mentioned. Traditionally, African Americans have been satisfied with experiencing the Spirit during preaching without much further reflection on that experience. Scholars note the centrality of God in the survival and liberation of African Americans, but this "turn to theology" in reflecting on African American preaching has been insufficiently performed thus far. There is a theological gift of the Spirit permeating African American homiletics that should be shared with the wider church and academy.

Through the lens of the "gift of the Spirit," there are many homiletical trajectories that could be explored, but due to the limited nature of this essay, I will explore only the relationship of the Spirit to the ethics of the preacher, such that the life of the proclaimer converges with what is proclaimed. What follows in two parts is: (1) a brief discussion of the theological understanding of the Spirit within an African American context; and (2) some thoughts on the ethical implications for the preacher based upon the previous perspectives on the Spirit. It will become clear that through the Spirit the sermon is not only what is spoken in a worship service, but also what is lived in society.

Theological Thinking about the Spirit

Preaching is an act rooted in the triune God. Because of this, the Holy Spirit is vital to the entire process of preaching. In fact, the power behind preaching is the Spirit and not human rhetoric alone. As James Forbes writes, "The preaching event itself. . . is a living, breathing, flesh-and-blood expression of the theology of the Holy Spirit."[2] The effects of this event, however, are felt long after the benediction has been declared in a service because of the sacramental presence of the Spirit. The Spirit works in all of life's domains. For many African Americans, there is no division between the sacred and secular realms. Rather, there is a belief in a "sacred cosmos" which permeates all of life such that life is viewed holistically and associated with the divine presence.[3] Thus, the work of the Spirit through the sermon continues in daily life.

Moreover, in the Spirit, the various realms merge. In an article, "The Black Christian Experience and the Holy Spirit," Edward Wimberly says, "Indeed, there is a linking of the personal, communal, and social dimensions in the conception of the work of the Holy Spirit within black church tradition."[4] This is significant because an individual cannot then prioritize one dimension of life over another because all realms are spaces of the Spirit. When Howard Thurman thinks of the movement of the Spirit, he considers "the Spirit of God Without-Within"[5] because the power of the Spirit cannot be imprisoned within any realm. In addition, this idea points to the cultural perspective that the Spirit must be embodied in word and deed, not solely internalized but truly externalized "without." As African Americans note, "If you got religion, show some sign."[6] Outward signs of the Spirit are vital for authentic spirituality to be discerned and these signs are not limited to the liturgical setting. In this way, the preacher cannot emphasize speaking the Word over living the Word because the Spirit manifests through his or her entire life. One preaches in the Spirit not only through words but deeds; therefore, preachers must show some "sign" of the Spirit through how well they conduct their lives and not solely through how well they preach.

Ethical Living in the Spirit

This understanding of the Spirit from a cultural perspective links the work of the Spirit in preaching with the work of the Spirit in daily living, enabling one to consider a preaching *life* in the Spirit, that is, a life that walks the talk of the pulpit—a lived sermon. Ideally, African American Christians strive for congruency between inner experience of the Spirit and outer expression of the Spirit in the world. Though we, as preachers, on any given Sunday, may be finished with the Word as a sermon, *the* Word is never quite finished with us as the Word preached becomes the Word lived through the Spirit. The impact of the sermon does not cease after the final "amen" has been said in a worship service because as one scholar notes, sermons "travel on in the lives of those who listen," including the preacher.[7] As the Spirit works within listening preachers through the traveling sermon, preachers are challenged ethically because the Spirit aims to match the content of the message with the character of the messenger, that is, if what one means by ethical refers to the moral character of a person at work in the world.

A preaching life in the Spirit is ethical—personally, communally, and socially—because the Spirit's influence cannot be compartmentalized and limited to the normative preaching moment. Jesus "preached not only with words, but his life was the 'amen' to the proclamation of his lips."[8] The same must be true for African American preachers, especially in light of pulpit scandals dealing with pastors who perpetuate unethical behavior. The work of the Spirit strives for a life of integrity and a life of service to others, not to the self. A "crisis in the village"[9] means that there is also a crisis in the pulpit. From a homiletical perspective, a part of the crisis is separating the spoken Word from the enacted Word, whereas the Spirit forms a continuum between the liturgy and the liturgy after the liturgy. All of life is the realm of the Spirit; thus, a preacher's whole life must be ethical, not only when one steps into the pulpit.

Furthermore, one should not be satisfied with personal pastoral ethics alone but should also yearn for a preaching life that influences the social ethical domain. The best of the African American preaching traditions emphasize the need for social justice. Authentic celebration overflows into mission and social action because the Spirit is not just ecstasy but "is always empowerment as well."[10] The *other* should matter. As Thurman boldly proclaims, "No man can be happy in Heaven if he left his brother in Hell."[11] This is not a reference merely to proselytizing individuals to reach the pearly gates but it indicates a genuine care for others' needs in society because of the interconnectedness of humanity. Preachers preach with their lives too; thus, getting involved in pressing issues are important for those who desire to really preach in the Spirit. The anointing is not primarily for personal edification but "it is to enable us to be an embodiment of divine intent," which includes acts of mercy and justice in the world.[12]

African American preaching cannot be sustained or strengthened by creative rhetoric without concrete Christ-like living in the world. A preacher's lip service should match his or her life service because as Dr. Martin Luther King Jr. prophetically pronounces, ". . . it's possible to affirm the existence of God with your lips and deny his existence with your life."[13] Experience of the Spirit in the pulpit alone is insufficient in this age of diverse pulpit spirits, but the presence of the Spirit must be evident in how one lives his or her life in order to make a substantial difference in the world. A preacher's words and actions can only become integrated with the help of the Holy Spirit who not only manifests in "preaching rhetoric"[14] but also in the preacher's ethic.

Without the Spirit, African American preachers truly lack the integrity needed to holistically embody the Word; thus, preachers will dig their own homiletical grave if they are more interested in "taking a text" before taking the time to pray "Come, Holy Spirit."

Notes

1. W. E. B. Du Bois, *The Souls of Black Folk* (1903; reprint, New York: Penguin Books, 1969), 275.
2. James Forbes, *The Holy Spirit and Preaching* (Nashville: Abingdon, 1989), 19.
3. Melva Costen, *African American Christian Worship* (Nashville: Abingdon, 1993), 13–15. Further expressions of this same sentiment can be heard in the work of Dwight Hopkins, specifically in *Being Human: Race, Culture, and Religion* (Minneapolis: Fortress, 2005) in which he teaches that Spirit inherently dwells in culture; thus, culture contains the sacred. A similar trajectory can be found in *Noise and Spirit: The Religious and Spiritual Sensibilities of Rap Music* (New York: New York University Press, 2003), edited by Anthony Pinn, who believes rap stresses the spiritual found in culture.
4. Edward Wimberly, "The Black Christian Experience and the Holy Spirit," *Quarterly Review* 8.2 (Summer 1988); 19–35.
5. Howard Thurman, *The Centering Moment* (New York: Harper & Row Publishers, 1969), 21.
6. Geneva Smitherman, *Talkin and Testifyin: The Language of Black America* (Boston: Houghton Mifflin Company, 1977), 93.
7. Arthur Van Seters, *Preaching and Ethics* (St. Louis: Chalice, 2004), 132.
8. Forbes, *The Holy Spirit and Preaching*, 43.
9. See Robert Franklin's provocative work, *Crisis in the Village: Restoring Hope in African American Communities* (Minneapolis: Fortress, 2007).
10. Henry Mitchell, "African American Preaching," *Concise Encyclopedia of Preaching*, eds. William H. Willimon and Richard Lischer (Louisville: Westminster John Knox, 1995), 7.
11. Howard Thurman, *The Inward Journey* (New York: Harper & Brothers Publishers, 1961), 138. Throughout his writings, he asserts the importance of righting relations with others. For example, see *The Centering Moment*, 35.
12. Forbes, *The Holy Spirit and Preaching*, 48. He further adds that anointed preachers expose death, reveal its structure of oppression, make truth plain, which leads to transformation of life for the oppressor and oppressed, overthrow power of death in all its forms, and cast out demons of institutions whether ecclesial, political, or social. See Forbes 43, 88, 95.
13. See the sermon by Martin Luther King Jr., "Rediscovering Lost Values,' in *A Knock at Midnight: Inspiration from the Great Sermons of Reverend Martin Luther King Jr.*, eds. Clayborne Carson and Peter Holloran (New York: Warner Books, 1998).
14. For this idea and more, see Robert E. Hood, *Must God Remain Greek? Afro Cultures and God-Talk* (Minneapolis: Fortress, 1990), 193, 204–209.

20
When Prophetic Preaching Gives Way to Praise

Marvin A. McMickle

> Take away from me the noise of your songs;
> I will not listen to the melody of your harps.
> But let justice roll down like waters, and
> righteousness like an everflowing stream.
>
> —*Amos 5:23–24*

It is the central hypothesis of this book that prophetic preaching 'in the pulpits of churches in America has been hushed, hindered, and hijacked by preachers who have gone off in service to other gods. In the previous chapter, a case was made for the negative impact of patriot pastors on the work of prophetic preaching. In that instance, attention was directed primarily, though not exclusively to white, conservative, evangelical Christians.

In this chapter, the next obstacle to be discussed will be praise and worship. There is a growing tendency to be so centered on the celebration of the faith in praise and worship that it leaves no time for and places little, if any, emphasis on the issues of justice and righteousness.

Prophetic Preaching Is Missing

The crisis is not simply in the pulpits of local churches across the country; the situation is equally dire so far as pastors' conferences, denominational conventions, and preaching journals and magazines are concerned. The burning concerns of prophetic preaching are almost entirely absent. There is a deafening silence on such matters as society's care for "the least of these"; the sovereignty of God over the whole creation and not just over America; the lingering problem of racism and the festering problem of sexism; the economic and human costs of war and the affect that it has on domestic programs; and many other moral and ethical demands that are part of the life of a disciple of Jesus Christ.

Instead, there is a constant call to "praise God" that is seldom, if ever, followed up with a challenge to serve God in tangible ways that are of benefit to our brothers and sisters, to our neighbors and friends, or to the widows, orphans, and strangers who are so constantly referenced in the Bible. If you listen to sermons on religious television channels, on station after station, day after day, on one program after another, you will hear this theme of praise severed from the prophetic message.

Whether you listen to the predominantly African American preachers on the WORD Network or the predominantly white preachers on the Trinity Broadcasting Network, the message is the same. People are being invited into a celebration of their faith during worship service without any corresponding challenge to live out their faith in the face of social injustice. It was exactly that kind of religious practice that was so strongly condemned by the prophet Amos as he confronted the people of Israel for offering God their songs but not their service, their music but not their moral outrage over needless human suffering, and their harps that lift music up to God but not their outstretched hands reaching to lift up a fallen brother or sister.

Another reason for the decline in prophetic preaching in America the emotional release that many Christians experience on Sunday morning. Regretfully, this is not the empathetic response that should come when hearts made tender by the gospel of Jesus Christ see the pain and suffering that marks our nation and our world. Shouting, "Amen!" and crying out, "Hallelujah!" does not remove the drug trafficking that plagues our society. Having a "Holy Ghost good time" does not prevent one job from being down-sized or outsourced or lost as a result of corporate corruption or mismanagement. "Praising God" as an end in itself, without political advocacy or public protest, will not bring our troops home from Afghanistan or Iraq or provide them with a rational reason for being there in the first place.

Televangelists: Part of the Problem?

One of the reasons why prophetic preaching has given way to praise may be the prominence and pervasiveness of certain televangelists a serious critique either of the church or of society as a whole. The entire nation seems to have fallen in love with Joel Osteen of Houston, Texas, who has just moved his twenty-five-thousand-member congregation into the sixteen-thousand-seat Compaq Center. This massive facility was the former home to the Houston Rockets basketball team. After $95 million in renovations, the Lakewood Church has two waterfalls but does not display a cross, the central symbol of the Christian faith.

It is little wonder that there is no cross, because in Osteen's preaching, no cross is necessary—only positive thinking. He was recently quoted as saying, "It's about giving hope, giving encouragement. . . For so long, people have been beat down, just by life in general. God is good, he's for you. You can be happy."[1] Nothing was said, however, about the conditions and circumstances that caused people to be beaten down in the first place, or about how we as followers of Jesus Christ can and should respond to those problems. All the work is left to God, and all that is required of believers is that they receive the blessings that God is waiting to give them.

Osteen's congregation is a charismatic church where worshippers are likely to be "slain in the spirit," but not at all likely to be challenged concerning any of the issues of the day. John Leland of *The New York Times* notes, "If not for the religious references, Mr. Osteen's sermons on topics like procrastination, submitting to authority, and staying positive could be secular motivational speeches."[2] Attendees may find themselves on the floor while speaking in tongues, but they are not likely to encounter any serious theological question or ethical dilemma. Osteen himself says, "I don't get deep and theological"[3] Lynn Mitchell, director of religious studies at the University of Houston says, "The idea of suffering as a Christian virtue is not a part of his worldview. Some call it Christianity Lite—you get all of the benefits but don't pay attention to the fact that Jesus called for suffering. He doesn't tackle many of the problems of the world."[4] One critic refers to Osteen's preaching as "cotton candy theology."[5]

Megachurches with a Mini Gospel?

There is nothing wrong with a megachurch so long as its foundations are not rooted in a minigospel, but that is exactly what seems to be happening. There is ample emphasis on praise and worship and celebration and feeling good; however, there is scarcely a word about duty or discipleship or self-denial for the sake of others. Such churches need an immediate and intense exposure to Amos 5:23–24 where God announces that songs of praise and shouts of celebration in worship are unacceptable if they are not accompanied by works of justice and righteousness. The same point is made in Micah 6:6–8 where God announces no interest in expensive sacrifices as signs of worship and devotion. Instead, God wants us to "do justice, and to love kindness, and to walk humbly with your God."

There is no doubt that God is deserving of praise. The point of this chapter is not to argue that people should not praise God. Psalm 150 is wholeheartedly endorsed: "Let everything that breathes praise God!" Whether praise is invited during a time of song and prayer or as a response to some part of a sermon, praise is a good thing. I concur with the verse that says, "It is good to give thanks to God, to sing praises to your name, O Most High" (Ps. 92:1). The question at hand is whether the God who is worthy of being praised is also worthy and deserving of being obeyed. Isn't this that same God who calls upon us to serve God by working for a more just and peaceful and humane social order?

Sometimes Only Praise Will Do

Praise is especially important and appropriate in those instances when God has brought people through some challenging and dangerous season in their lives. When someone has survived cancer, divorce, unemployment, or the flood waters of the Gulf Coast after Hurricane Katrina, they may want to shout out, *"Thank you, Jesus!"* When people's lives are miraculously spared following an accident of one type or another, it would not be surprising to hear them exclaim, *"God, I praise you!"* There is a song that says:

> For every mountain you brought me over,
> For every trial you brought me through. . .
> For this I give you praise.[6]

There are also seasons of joy and celebration when praise is appropriate. When a child is born, praise makes sense. When the first person in the family to graduate from college walks across the stage to receive a diploma, praise makes sense. This person carries the pride and sense of achievement of the forbearers to whom the door of higher education had been firmly closed either because of cost or color. Somebody in the audience is going to shout out, "Praise God!"

Even death can be an occasion when praise is appropriate. I can recall as a child attending a service held annually at our church on New Year's Eve. At about 11:45 p.m., the pastor would invite the congregation to form a circle along the walls of the sanctuary while the lights were dimmed. For the next few minutes, he would call off the names of people from within that congregation who died during that past year. As each name was called, someone from within that sanctuary could be heard crying out, "Thank you, Jesus!"

In my youth, I misunderstood that sequence of events and thought the person still alive was celebrating the fact that someone was dead. As I learned later on, that was precisely the wrong conclusion. Those people who were praising God were not happy because their loved ones were dead, they were rejoicing because their faith assured them that their loved ones were absent from the body and present with God (2 Cor. 5:6–8). Life on earth was over, but eternal life with God had just begun. It was that kind of faith that has allowed Christians to face death with such firm resolve for two millennia. There are many moments in the life of a Christian and in the liturgy and order of worship of a congregation when praise is the most important thing that can be done.

A Balance between Praise and Worship

What is being called for is not the elimination of praise from the life of the believer, but rather a balance in the life of every church and every believer between times of praise and worship and times when our focus is directed to the justice agenda raised by Jesus. As was the case with the issue of patriot pastors and conservative evangelical Christians who draw too close a link between the Christian faith and partisan politics, the words of Jesus in Matthew 25:31–44 also pose a challenge for those whose gospel is limited solely or even primarily to the practice of praise. Jesus says that what interests him most is that his disciples will respond to those who are hungry, thirsty, naked, sick, or imprisoned. "Giving God some praise" may make for a spirited worship service, but it does not necessarily translate into a life that is pleasing and acceptable to God. In Matthew 7:21 and Luke 6:46 Jesus warns people against saying "Lord, Lord" while not doing God's will. And Jesus indicates his will as directly as possible when he says in Matthew 22:37–40:

> "You shall love your Sovereign God with all your heart, and with all your soul, and with all your mind." This is the greatest and first commandment. And a second is like it: "You shall love your neighbor as yourself." On these two commandments hang all the law and the prophets.

Let us suppose that praise and worship can comfortably fall under the commandment to love God with all our heart, soul, and mind. Throwing our hearts and souls into acts of praise and worship may be one of the ways that we demonstrate how much we love God.

This leaves out, however, the second part of the statement to part that calls us away from praising God in the sanctuary toward caring for our neighbor as we encounter our neighbors throughout the community and the society. What Amos and Micah were calling for was not an end to acts of praise worship, but the striking of a balance so that the deeds of justice and righteousness are not overlooked or ignored while Christians are busy "having a high time in the house of God."

Enter to Worship—Depart to Serve

Many congregations use worship bulletins where this balance is reinforced in print every Sunday morning: "Enter to worship—Depart to serve." On the way in, the emphasis is on praise and worship and giving glory to God. There is time for hymns and other songs and also time for prayers and testimonies. At the end of the worship service, however, the congregation must be challenged as to how they should live their lives and how they should engage their neighbor and the wider society. In other words, the problem is not that people are praising God and lifting holy hands in the sanctuary. The problem arises when nothing in the service—especially in the sermon—challenges people to move beyond worship to service and self-sacrifice.

Prophetic preaching is designed to motivate people to move beyond lifting up holy hands and begin to extend helping hands to those Jesus describes in Matthew 25 as "the least of these." It is not a matter of one over the other, nor is it a matter of one being more important than the other. Rather, it is a matter of seeing that one is really impossible without the other. We cannot serve God in this world of evil and corruption as we should unless we have a sense of the glory and greatness of God that is perfected in times of praise and worship. Similarly, we cannot sing "What a mighty God we serve" and then fail or refuse to work to establish a more humane and just society in the name of that mighty God.

Praise Not an End In Itself

In his book *The Ministry of Music in the Black Church*, J. Wendell Mapson Jr. makes some observations about the evolution of music in the life of the black church that helps to point out the danger that arises when praise is separated from the continuing work of discipleship and service. He writes:

> Increasingly, music in the black church has been separated from its theological and historical underpinnings. Instead of serving theology as a legitimate response to God and telling the story of hardship, disappointment, and hope, music in the black church has become, in many instances, an end in itself. This often fosters the goal of entertainment rather than the goal of ushering people into the very presence of the Almighty and sending them forth to serve.[7]

The danger of praise and worship fostering a goal of entertainment is a real danger in many churches today. The theological question that needs to be engaged is whether or not praise and worship should be viewed as ends in themselves, or if they are better viewed as an inseparable component of a cycle of rituals or sacred acts that should always include some challenge to action beyond the time of praise and worship themselves. Praise and worship are useful and important acts, but what do they lead to once the worship service is over?

Praise without Prophetic Preaching Is Cheap Grace

Preachers and people who settle for a spiritual diet limited to praise and worship are offering up and operating on a gospel of cheap grace. In their theology, Jesus Christ has done all the work on the cross or will continue to provide for the needy and those who turn to him in prayer. For that provision, they give thanks to God. Such a gospel requires no sacrifice, it demands no obedience, and it calls for no engagement with what is happening in the lives of people outside the doors of the church or across the country or around the world. People may be asked to tithe a portion of their income to support the ministries of their church, but they may never be called upon to serve a hot meal to a homeless person or visit the inmates in the nearest correctional center or attend an outdoor vigil in front of the scene of yet another senseless murder in our violent and gun-crazed society.

It would make no sense to call for the elimination of praise and worship in the life of the Christian because praise and worship only involve an hour or two on those Sundays when worshippers gather in the sanctuary. The question is: "What's next during the 166 hours that will intervene until the worshippers meet together again? The answer is that worship and praise are preparation for and refreshment from the work of ministry and service that ought to follow the benediction. Enter to worship—Depart to serve.

Not a New Problem

In a biography of the renowned Baptist preacher Clarence Lavaughn (C. L.) Franklin entitled *Singing the Lord's Song*, reference is made to research that was conducted in Memphis, Tennessee, in 1940 during the time when Franklin was a pastor in that city. It was conducted by Ralph Bunche, who would later work for the United Nations and become the first African American to win the Nobel Peace Prize. Bunche noted that there were 375 churches in Memphis, and of that number 213 were African American congregations. Bunche said, "Those churches and their pastors had no voice when it came to the issues that confronted blacks in Memphis."[8] Bunche continued:

> The Negro preachers of Memphis as a whole have avoided social questions. They have preached thunder and lightning, fire and brimstone, Moses out of the bulrushes, but about the economic and political exploitation of local blacks, they have remained silent.[9]

Sadly, if Bunche were to have done similar research in any other city that houses a significant black population, in every decade since the 1940s he would probably come to the same conclusion. Far too many black churches remain mute in the face of social issues. They are inactive or unresponsive when the call to action is sounded to address or correct social ills.

Across the country during the height of the Civil Rights Movement of the 1950s and 1960s, most African American pastors and churches remained uninvolved. They continued to hold church services and prayer meetings, but they did not open their doors, their budgets, or their hearts to the protests and demonstrations that were in pursuit of a more just society. Clarence James, author of "Lost Generation or Left Generation?" offers a description of this problem that persists to the present day. He says:

> The trouble with today's clergy is there are too many priests and not enough prophets. The priests are the servants of the privileged, criticizing little crimes at the bottom while ignoring those at the top. The prophets remind the rulers they are not exempt from the laws of God, but the priests are blinded by wealth and power.[10]

Is it possible that many preachers and pastors who could speak a prophetic word in the face of all that confronts our nation and our world are really more concerned about personal comfort and the good graces of those who pay their salaries and donate toward the construction of their megachurches?

A Reminder of What Is Wrong

In my book *Preaching to the Black Middle Class*, I try to make this point through the use of Luke 16:19–31, the parable of the rich man and Lazarus. Earlier in my career, I interpreted that passage using a racial motif, identifying poor Lazarus as the impoverished and neglected black community while the rich man was, of course, white society that lived well and cared little for the black neighbor just outside its door. That was an inaccurate reading of that text because both Lazarus and the rich man were Jews. What divided them was not color or ethnicity; what divided them was class or income.[11]

There are black churches throughout America located in neighborhoods that resemble bombed-out war zones. They are infested with drugs, alcoholism, HIV/AIDS, prostitution, and domestic violence. The poverty rates among school age children approach 65 percent. More often than not there is little if any interaction between those black congregations and the people and/or the problems that reside just outside the doors of the church buildings.

Worship service occurs on Sunday morning and perhaps again on Wednesday night; but not much else takes place during the week. Many of the churches sit idle and unused. The buildings are locked most of the time. The congregation, most of whom drive to the church from outlying neighborhoods and from the surrounding suburbs, has no interest or investment in the neighborhood, its people, or their problems. They just come to church "to get their praise on" and then get back in their cars and go home.

The people in those churches do not notice Lazarus as he sits just outside the door. They do not see the bleary-eyed woman who has walked the street all night long turning tricks for a pimp who beats her if she does not bring him enough money. They do not see posted signs declaring a certain house closed because it had become a "shooting gallery" for drug users. They see but do not engage the young men with their pants sagging and their tee shirts below their knees who have no place to go and nothing to do. They do not see the teenage mother with her third child or the police brutality that so often follows an incident of "driving while black."

They go to church to praise God, but they either will not notice or will not engage the issues of justice and righteousness that exist all around them every Sunday morning. What is needed is a prophetic critique that confronts the society that allows such conditions to persist as well as a prophetic critique of any local church or any Christian denomination that knows such problems exist but says and does nothing to impact or alleviate the problems. Such a critique, however, is most unlikely in churches that are so focused on praise and worship that they give no thought to and make no provision for issues of justice and righteousness and peace. In such cases, it is the churches themselves that need the challenge of a prophetic critique.

Balancing Praise with Prophetic Preaching

One way for preachers to assist people in finding the balance between praise and the performance of justice and righteousness comes from a homiletic principle dealing with sermon outcomes. In his book *The Making of the Sermon*, Robert McCracken, who followed Harry Emerson Fosdick as pastor of Riverside Church in New York City, made reference to four possible outcomes from a sermon, which he called "kindling the mind, energizing the will, disturbing the conscience, and stirring the heart."[12] The balance between praise and worship on the one hand and prophetic preaching on the other hand involves the principles of disturbing the conscience and stirring the heart. The first two principles, however, should first be reviewed.

Kindle the Mind

To kindle the mind should be viewed as an approach to a controversial sermon on a complex topic or text. The primary goal of a sermon using this principle is to encourage people to think about that topic for the first time or to challenge them to rethink views they had formerly held. The preacher's task is to provide the information for both sides of an issue, insert the relevant biblical background and theological focus, then leave it up to the listeners to think about what has been said and begin to make up their minds.

Energize the Will

To energize the will is to move people beyond the thinking stage and motivate them to take action in a certain arena. Whether the issue is race relations, women in ministry, issues of war and peace, an environmental concern, or some ecumenical or interfaith matter, the goal of this sermon is to persuade people to act. It is very possible that one or more sermons will previously have been preached that allowed for some kindling of the mind. Now the preacher's job is to energize the will and give people the motivation and the methodology to take the necessary action.

Disturb the Conscience

So far as prophetic preaching in balance with praise and worship is concerned, the last two principles offer the most guidance. To disturb the conscience is to intentionally set before the people the issues of sin, confession, repentance, and restoration. Romans 3:23 remains true: "All have sinned and fall short of the glory of God." Romans 7:18b–19 remains true: "I can will what is right but I cannot do it. For I do not do the good I want, but the evil I do not want is what I do." The task of prophetic preaching, whether it is done in the context of a local church or in a farther reaching format, is to set before people those ways in which we/they are not doing the good they should be doing. Just as importantly, prophetic preaching must seek to name the evils we/they are doing and call people to repentance.

It is impossible to avoid this third principle of disturbing the conscience if you take seriously the lessons of scripture. When Nathan confronted David concerning the king's sins in the Bathsheba episode, the prophet's intention was to disturb the conscience of the king. When Hosea confronted Israel about that nation's "adulterous affair" with idols and false gods, the prophet's goal was to disturb the conscience. When both John the Baptist in Mark 1:4 and Jesus in Mark 1:15 preached their first sermons, both of them preached about the need for repentance. Their goal was to disturb the conscience.

It is imperative that preachers learn this lesson if we are to be faithful to God and useful to those to whom we preach. In Acts 20:27, as his ministry is coming to an end, Paul says, "I have not hesitated to proclaim to you the whole will of God" (NIV). This cannot be done unless and until some of our sermons have disturbing the conscience as their intended goal. As the prophet Ezekiel was told both in 3:18–19 and again in 33:7–9, there is a consequence that falls to the preacher who does not speak truth to people who could end up saving their lives and securing their souls. People may not listen to us when we preach such sermons, and they may choose to hear us and then simply ignore everything they heard. Their decision is between them and God. If, however, we fail to say something simply because it is unpleasant or unpopular, then both the people and the preacher will face God's judgment together.

In Ezekiel 18, attention is given to the justice issues that should concern us when we preach a prophetic critique. The prophet says:

> If a man is righteous and does what is lawful and right—if he does not eat upon the mountains or lift up his eyes to the idols of the house of Israel, does not defile his neighbor's wife or approach a woman during her menstrual period, does not oppress anyone, but restores to the debtor his pledge, commits no robbery, gives his bread to the hungry and covers the naked with a garment, does not take advance or accrued interest, withholds his hand from iniquity, executes true justice between contending parties, follows my statues, and is careful to observe my ordinances, acting faithfully—such a one is righteous; he shall surely live, says your Sovereign God. (Ezek. 18:5–9)

If at any point the people to whom we preach are falling short of this standard of justice and righteousness, it is our responsibility to disturb the conscience and say, "This is what God says." If we fail to do so, the people will still face the consequences of their unjust and unrighteous behavior, but God will hold us responsible for their blood (Ezek. 3:18).

Stir the Heart

Having given equal and adequate attention to a sermon schedule that rotates between the first three principles, including disturbing the conscience, there is still ample opportunity for sermons designed to lead people in praise and thanksgiving. This is the primary goal of sermons designed to stir the heart. Here is where such themes as the love, grace, mercy, and glory of God can be addressed. Here is where assurance can be given to people in times of sickness or distress or in the face of death: "Even though I walk through the darkest valley, I fear no evil; for you are with me. . ." (Ps. 23:4a).

It is appropriate to design worship services and the sermons that will be preached at those services around themes that generate shouts of "Glory, hallelujah!" "For the one who is in you is greater than the one who is in the world" (1 John 4:4). Glory, hallelujah! "The steadfast love of God never ceases, his mercies never come to an end. They are new every morning" (Lam. 3:22–23). Praise God! "For I am convinced. . . nor anything else in all creation will be able to separate us from the love of God in Chris Jesus our Sovereign" (Rom. 8:38–9). Thank you, Jesus!

Balance and Rotation of Themes

The goal of this chapter is not to eliminate praise and worship from the life of the Christian or the life of the congregation. To the contrary, those are precious and sacred moments when believers stand in the presence of "the only God our savior," to whom "through Jesus Christ our Sovereign, be glory, majesty, power, and authority. . ." (Jude 25). What is being sought is a balance that is missing from so many churches and from so many pulpits across America. Simply by moving from kindling the mind to energizing the will to disturbing the conscience to stirring the heart, a preacher can be sure that God is being praised on the one hand and is also being served and obeyed on the other hand.

The system is proven and tested and is now awaiting any and all preachers who have the courage, the convictions, and the compassion to call the church's attention to the "least of these" in our society. The rotation is reliable and will eventually bring the preacher to the moment when truth must be spoken to power about the policies and practices that continue to result in an unjust social order where the rich get richer and the poor get poorer. Stirring the heart is a good thing to do, but never to the exclusion of those texts and topics that result in disturbing the conscience.

Protest and Praise in the Civil Rights Era

There is no better example of the balance between prophetic preaching and praise and worship than what was widely experienced during the Civil Rights Movement of the 1950s and 1960s. Those who shared in that movement can still feel the power and energy of the worship services that were held in hot and crowded churches. People prayed and sang and preached with a fervor unmatched by any Pentecostal or charismatic assembly.

The worship service, however, was never viewed as an end in itself. Rather, it was viewed as a bridge over troubled waters as the people were returning from or heading toward an encounter with racism, segregation, hatred, and violence. There was no doubt that the people "entered to worship." It was equally clear, however, that they would soon "depart to serve." The energy of the worship made the times of service possible, and the rigors and risks of the service made the worship necessary. Neither of those two aspects of the Civil Rights Movement would have made any sense without the other. Protest and praise, "Thank you, Jesus" and "Freedom now," were inseparably tied together.

Those who remember that era feel more intensely the absence of any such balance in church life today. When a passionate time of praise and worship is disconnected from a disciplined and determined time of service and even sacrifice in the name of God, the worship itself becomes invalid and inauthentic. People enter to worship but they depart to brunch or a round of golf or an afternoon in front of the television with the NFL or NBA or their favorite movie. The remainder of the week is occupied with the regular routines of life. At no point do people feel the need to speak up about war and peace, bias and discrimination, the increase in such pain indices as poverty, incarceration, teen and out-of-wedlock birth, HIV/AIDS infection rates, drug and alcohol abuse, failing public schools in inner cities, unemployment and the outsourcing of jobs, and/or domestic violence and divorce.

Praise and Justice in the Biblical Prophets

All of the above listed topics deserve and demand a prophetic critique from the believing community. Rarely, if ever, does such a critique occur because too many people—and the preachers who speak to them—have little interest in doing anything faith-related beyond lifting up holy hands and "getting their praise on." The believing community, therefore, is deserving of a prophetic critique for its unwillingness to maintain the balance between personal piety and personal responsibility for performing works of justice and righteousness.

It really is no different than it was in the days of Amos, Micah, Hosea, and Isaiah. In the eighth century B.C.E., prophets of the Old Testament voiced God's displeasure with people who disconnected their personal piety from any personal responsibility for giving voice and shape to a more just social order.

For I desire steadfast love and not sacrifice,
the knowledge of God rather than burnt offerings.
(Hos. 6:6)

I hate, I despise your festivals. . .
Take away from me the noise of your songs;. . .
But let justice roll down like waters,
and righteousness like an everflowing stream.
(Amos 5:21–24)

He has told you, O mortal, what is good;
And what does the LORD require of you
but to do justice, and to love kindness,
and to walk humbly with your God?
(Mic. 6:8)

Is not this the fast that I choose:
to loose the bonds of injustice, to undo the thongs of the yoke,
to let the oppressed go free, and to break every yoke?
It is not to share your bread with the hungry,
and bring the homeless poor into your house;
when you see the naked, to cover them,
and not to hide yourself from your own kin?
(Isa. 58:6–7)

Awaken Passive Christians

In a generation when more and more believers seem to be content with praise and worship to the exclusion of justice and righteousness, the task of the preacher is to awaken the church. It must be awakened to its role and responsibility as a herald of the justice agenda of the realm of God. The problem that must be overcome to establish the needed balance is quoted by James Cone in an essay entitled "The Pastor as Servant." This well-stated document was circulated at a poor people's rally in Albuquerque, New Mexico. It states:

I was hungry
And you formed a humanities club
And you discussed my hunger.
Thank you.

I was imprisoned
And you crept off quietly
To your chapel in the cellar
And prayed for my release.

I was sick
And you knelt and thanked God
For your health.

I was homeless
And you preached to me
Of the spiritual shelter of the love of God.

I was lonely
And you left me alone
To pray for me.
You seem so holy;
So close to God.

But I'm still very hungry
And lonely
And cold.

So where have your prayers gone?
What have they done?
What does it profit a man
To page through his book of prayers
When the rest of the world is crying for his help?[13]

Notes

1. John LeLand, "A Church That Packs Them in, 16,000 at a Time," *New York Times*, July 18, 2005, A1.
2. Ibid.
3. Ibid.
4. Ibid.
5. Jason Byasse, "Be Happy: The Health and Wealth Gospel," *Christian Century* (July 12, 2005), 20–21.
6. From "For Every Mountain" by Kurt Carr, released in 1997 on *No One Else*, the Kurt Carr Singers.
7. J. Wendell Mapson, *The Ministry of Music in the Black Church* (Valley Forge: Judson, 1984), 17.
8. Nick Salvatore, *Singing in a Strange Land: C. L. Franklin, the Black Church, and the Transformation of America* (New York: Little & Brown, 2005), 56.
9. Ibid.
10. Clarence James, "Lost Generation or Left Generation?" quoted in "Preachers Would Leave Us at the Back of the Bus," by Barbara Reynolds, *City News*, February 24–March 2, 2005, 19.
11. Marvin A. McMickle, *Preaching to the Black Middle Class* (Valley Forge: Judson, 2000), 99–101.
12. Robert McCracken, *The Making of the Sermon* (New York: Harper & Row, 1956).
13. James H. Cone, "The Servant Church," *The Pastor as Servant*, ed. Earl E. Shelp and Ronald H. Sunderland (New York: Pilgrim, 1986), 63–64.

21

Introduction to Power in the Pulpit: How America's Most Effective Black Preachers Prepare Their Sermons

Cleophus J. LaRue

Black preaching is regarded in many quarters as one of the strongest preaching traditions developed on American soil. Though hard to define because of the many dynamics that come to play in this oral/aural word event, it is not now, nor has it ever been, univocal in form, substance, or mode of presentation. Characteristics purporting to shape its parameters abound, and yet none completely capture its depth and essence. Many things are happening in the black preaching moment, but exactly how, when, and where they come together, and to what effect and why, is most difficult to establish with consistency. The difficulty in grasping what is at the heart of black preaching is equally voiced by those who are considered to have achieved some mastery and adeptness in the field.

Even while we acknowledge its non-monolithic status, it is also true that the common threads of the oral tradition, black lived experience, and a shared history of subjugation undergird and sustain this tradition. Something in the black historical journey, something at once wistful and plaintive, finds expression in the black worship experience and flows freely in the black preaching event. It is most difficult to define for it is not something blacks deliberately add to their preaching; it is simply a part of who they are as a people of faith and what they are becoming in response to their lived situation in America.

Long recognized for its emotive power, rhetorical flair, and its uncanny ability to communicate the Holy to the least in society, the black preaching moment continues to be a much anticipated event in the black worship experience. The black church with its unquenchable thirst for the preached word has never forgotten what others are apparently struggling, even now, to remember: the church lives in her preaching—always has and always will. It is the church's preaching that defines its message and mission. It is what is preached that determines what is important.[1]

Educational, denominational, geographical, and gender backgrounds notwithstanding, those in the black religious experience who have been most effective in the creation and delivery of the sermon have been those most adept at wedding the sad lyrics of black humanity to the invigorating and transformative melody of the gospel of Jesus Christ. In black churches preaching continues to be a high calling to that sacred desk—the Christian pulpit.

While it is hard to state with accuracy the exact date of the black preachers' beginning in America, the historical development of their roles and responsibilities can shed some light on the manner in which preachers came to such a place of prominence and esteem in black religious life. Historians Milton Semett, Mechal Sobel, and Eugene Genovese in their historical works on the slave preachers give us some sense of who they were and how their leadership roles developed over time. Semett's arrangement listed *ministers, exhorters, self-appointed preachers,* and *cult leaders.*[2]

Ministers were described as those who were principally active in the period when evangelical Protestantism was still seeking to win the South, and had yet to retreat from its earlier antislavery position. Preachers on the order of Harry Hosier, Henry Evans, and Lott Carey are listed in this group. They accompanied white clergy on preaching tours, preached to mixed audiences, and on the whole were well received by Southern Christians in the early days of evangelical revivalism. *Exhorters* were usually unordained and therefore unable to exercise all of the privileges of the ministerial office. They could not exercise their franchise in associational meetings, nor could they choose their own text on which to preach. They more often than not served as assistants to the white minister or "boss preachers" on the plantation.

The *self-appointed preacher* felt no compulsion to conform to the expectations of white society. God, they felt, had called them and no one but God could revoke that call. Self-appointed preachers, according to Semett, were a continual threat to the police order of the South. Nat Turner would be the best example of this third kind of preacher. No church authorized him to preach. He felt that his call to deliver his people from slavery had come directly from God. He put together a message of religion and resistance that struck a responsive chord in his fellow slaves.

Semett's last classification of religious leaders among the slaves is the *cult leader.* The voodoo cult was practiced especially in those areas where the slaves were most concentrated or most influenced by recent arrivals from the West Indies. While missionaries and Christian churches frowned upon these individuals, their influence was widespread and their abilities greatly feared by many slaves. Gullah Jack, who conspired with Denmark Vesey in his slave insurrection plot of 1822, was a native-born Angolan who brought to America practices he had known in Africa.[3]

While Sobel's classifications refer primarily to Baptists and thus have more to do with ecclesiastical designations as opposed to the manner in which slaves viewed themselves, they can still be helpful in providing some insight into the development of the black preacher on American soil. According to Sobel, the formal church organization recognized *floor, licensed,* and *ordained preachers.* In order to be an official preacher, a person needed a license from a church, which could be given for a limited time and specific area, or for a far more extensive outreach.[4] For such work, black preachers were licensed all over the South.

Moreover, if called by a church to be its presiding elder or minister, a preacher, upon examination by a board of ordained preachers, could be ordained in that church, a status he then gained for life. At least 106 black Baptist preachers were ordained prior to the Civil War.[5] Owing to the fact that the floor preacher was a category officially recognized by the formal church, preachers in such categories were probably new initiates into the ministry who hoped one day to be licensed and/or ordained by a church.

Included in the category of preachers not recognized by the formal church were *holders of papers, chairbackers,* and *exhorters. Privilege papers* were legal documents drawn up by a slave owner giving his slave preacher the privilege to preach and marry, and also to baptize anyone who made a profession of faith.[6] A *chairbacker* was a preacher whose pulpit was a common chair in a slave cabin. The *exhorter,* who in many instances had broader appeal than either the chairbacker or the holder of privilege papers, was a lay preacher who had not been licensed and had not been called by any congregation. Though never allowed in the pulpit, black exhorters were reputed to be very emotional, often even warmer than licensed preachers, and they were known to have moved many to accept salvation.[7]

Genovese's categories for the early black preachers include basically the same subdivisions as those listed by Semett and Sobel—*conjurer, exhorter, plantation, regular,* and *denominational preachers.* Genovese does point out, however, that in the cities, slaves and free blacks heard black denominational ministers who were at least as well trained as their white counterparts, and innumerable class leaders or assistants or prayer leaders, who ostensibly assisted a white minister but who, more often than not, did most of the effective preaching to the blacks.[8] Early on the slaves heard their own black preachers, if not regularly, at least frequently enough to make a difference in their lives and to establish the black preacher as a central figure in black religious life. While one can be relatively certain that such designations were not strictly observed by the people of that day, the different categories give us some sense of the origin and development of the modern-day black preacher.[9]

As important a figure as the black preacher has been historically, preachers alone can in no way take credit for the continued strength of this tradition. Without question, the vibrancy and vitality of the entire black worship experience has in large part helped to shape, fashion, and uphold black preaching through the last four hundred years of black existence in America. Move the black preacher out of the vocal, participatory groundswell of a typical black church service and what you will hear more often than not is one struggling to find his or her way, or at least acknowledging that the preaching moment was made more difficult because of the absence of a full-fledged black worshiping community.

Unless one has broad exposure to cross-cultural preaching, often it is the case that the black preacher has become so accustomed to the immediate reaction and vocal encouragement of black worship that one's rhythm, cadence, voice, and celebratory close are all negatively impacted when the preacher is removed from that setting. There can be no black preaching in the truest sense of the tradition without a black worshiping community.

The preachers who grace this present volume with their sermon-preparation methods and their model sermons were shaped, nurtured, and matured in the traditional black worship experience. They are indeed worthy witnesses to black life and to life as it is to be lived in the presence of the triune God. *As* only a true witness can, they rise from among the people to whom they preach that they might give effective voice and an eyewitness account to the "life situations" of those from whence they have come.[10] They go to the text on behalf of the people to watch and see what the text will say. They carry to the text the burdens and blessings, hopes and heartbreaks, joys and sorrows of a people who have known life in its extremes. They go faithfully week in and week out in search of an answer to the age-old question: Is there any word from the Lord and is it true?[11]

But they are also expert witnesses from the other side, for only those who have spent time in the presence of the Holy can mount the pulpit Sunday in and Sunday out and testify "effectively" as to those things they have seen and heard from the God who is made known to us in the revelation of Jesus Christ. There is yet in black churches an air of expectancy on Sunday mornings regarding the preached word. However, even with its awe-inspired expectations, participatory proclamation, and celebratory flair, the black church continues to demand of its preachers what the Greeks of old demanded of the disciples—"We would see Jesus."

Considered to be among the most effective preachers on the scene today, the preachers in this volume come from different parts of the country and different denominations. Some are pastors, some are teachers, and some are both. From church to chapel they bring their own special gifts to the preaching moment and are heard by thousands in churches, schools, conferences, and conventions throughout America. The writers were encouraged to pursue their own unique method of preparation. They were asked to reflect on and bring to conscious formation the methodological process they engage in each week. They were not privy to one another's work and were given the freedom to pursue their own particular take on the process. Though distinctive in their own right, there are at least eleven characteristics in their methodologies that many of the writers share with one another:

1. *A skillful articulation of the living voice*—In black preaching, the sermon from beginning to end is viewed as an oral/aural exercise. It is to be spoken and heard. The sermon manuscript is never regarded as an end in itself. What is written is but an "arrested performance" lying dormant on the page that can only be brought to life through the skillful articulation and mastery of the preacher's *viva vox* (living voice).[12]

   People who come from cultures with a high oral residue consider the spoken word to have great power. All oral utterance that comes from inside living organisms is "dynamic."[13] Many black preachers rely on the power of the living voice to bring to full expression what they hope to accomplish in the preaching event. Ultimately, their ability to evoke, empower, challenge, and change comes not through that which they have written, but through their spoken word-articulated sound. An awareness of the oral nature of the finished product is a key element in the composition of the sermon.

2. *A sense of divine encounter*—Each preacher speaks in some manner of being encountered by God at the outset of the initial stages of sermon development. For some it involves a sitting silent before God, while for others it is a "tarrying" for the Spirit. Something comes from without and buoys the spirit and sparks the creativity of the preacher as he or she embarks upon the sermon creation process. All attribute this creative spark to something beyond their own subconscious mindset. They refuse to advance the preparation process until they have some sense that a power from beyond them is at work in and through them. Without this inbreaking activity, any number felt that the sermon would focus too much on process and not enough on purpose.

3. *The importance of wrestling with the text*—To a person, the writers speak of a serious, personal engagement with the text. While certainly referencing the commentaries before the end of the process, they all discourage a quick end run to the commentaries. In the minds of most, an overreliance on commentaries and the scholarship of others hinders the development of the creative process in the preacher. One writer speaks of walking up and down the street on which the scripture lives in order to get one's own feel for the text. An ongoing invitation to the listening congregation to enter into the world of the text is a defining feature of traditional black preaching.

4. *The significance of the waiting congregation*—The people for whom the sermon is being prepared are never far from the thoughts of the preachers at the time of preparation. In fact, many speak of their need to maintain a constant focus on those who will hear the message. In a strange way, the preachers seem to anticipate the anticipation of the waiting congregation. Thus, every effort is made to say *for* them and *to* them what they (the congregation) would say if they had the chance. Participatory proclamation not only impacts the rhythm and cadence of their delivery, it also affects the interaction of scripture and context.

5. *An astute awareness of the culture*—There was a time in black religious life when some people believed that the truly "spiritual" preachers shut themselves away from the world and descended from the mountaintop of their studies on Sunday morning to deliver a word from on high. Today's preachers warn against such aloofness and detachment from the world. The preachers in this volume are in tune and in touch with the world around them. They sharpen their powers of observation by constantly seeking to name God's presence in every aspect of human existence. They encourage preachers to be mindful of the happenings in their social, political, educational, and economic surroundings. Many argue, in fact, that such an awareness actually strengthens one's preaching. The best of black preaching seriously engages 'the whole of God's created order in its beauty and splendor, its disorder and unruliness.

6. *The importance of a manuscript*—While many of the writers do not carry a manuscript into the pulpit, they were in agreement that to preach without a manuscript does not mean to preach unprepared. A manuscript should be written even though one does not intend to preach from it in the pulpit. Writing the sermon out helps to bring focus and clarity to the sermon, prevents one from rambling, and firms up language written for the ear. A tightly worded manuscript, where each phrase has been carefully considered, helps the preacher to paint the mental picture more effectively.

   Moreover, a manuscript allows the preacher to get comfortable with the flow and contours of the sermon and thus serves to strengthen the rhythm and cadence of the oral delivery. To have the language of the sermon set down in writing and subsequently clearly set down in one's mind sharpens the oratorical thrust and limits unintended pauses and dead air in the preaching event.

   However, those in this volume who do choose to use a manuscript in the pulpit do so with great effect because the oral nature of the event is never far from their minds even when reading from a prepared text. In black preaching the style of delivery determines, in large part, the success of the oral performer.[14] Verbal essays that sound like a lecture in the pulpit are a no-no in many black churches.[15] The oral delivery must be dynamic and invigorating. Spontaneity that allows for improvisation and digression even when using a manuscript is not only acceptable, in black preaching it's expected. Senior ministers from a generation past urged their younger cohorts to use double-spaced type when preparing their manuscripts in order to allow room for the Holy Spirit to add a line here and there.

7. *A fitting close to the sermon*—Many expressed the importance of closing the sermon in a proper manner. For some the sermon should always end in a joyful celebration, while for others the most important thing Is that the sermon end in a manner that is logically consistent with the controlling thought. On some occasions the close should cause one to reflect on faith and life. At other times it should move one to repent and to think more deeply on the mercies of God. At other times the close should call us to some specific action in the larger world in service to others. Sometimes the close should simply issue forth in ceaseless praise to the wonders of a God who is for us. The closing of the sermon should not be a disjointed distraction or some tacked-on ornamental rhetorical flourish intended to whip the congregation into a fevered pitch; rather it should send the listeners away with a clear sense of what the preacher was attempting to convey throughout the entire message. The writers were in agreement that the preacher should be clear in his or her mind how the sermon would open, where it would go, and how it would fittingly end.

8. *The sermon as continuous creation*—Our writers also spoke of continuous reflection on the sermon. For most, the sermon is never a finished product. After the sermon had been prepared and readied for Sunday service, they tell of how ideas and new ways of thinking about it continue to come. Many say even while preaching the sermon, new thoughts and ideas come pouring out and thus become unexpected additions to the sermon. Some spoke of editing the sermon soon after it had been preached in order to take advantage of fresh insights that came to them during its delivery or immediately thereafter. For some, the unplanned additions turned out to be some of the more creative parts of the sermon.

9. *Hymnody*—Preachers use the poetics of hymnody to express what mere words simply cannot say. Many of the preachers in this book sprinkled their sermons with familiar hymns. Some closed their sermons citing the cherished phrases of a well-known song. The use of hymns reaffirmed, in a way, the vital importance of the "sung word" in black religion. A recitation of the familiar—such as a hymn or some other well-known spiritual or gospel tune—encourages the congregation to join in the celebratory moment being called forth by the preacher.

One of the best ways to move a congregation to embrace the message as a word fittingly spoken to them is through the lyrics of some well-worn, beloved hymn. It is as if the congregation is saying in its audible response to the hymn, "Yes, preacher, this song helps us to drink from the fountain of the familiar. Our testimonies are wrapped up in the words of that hymn. We have been this way before and we know exactly where you are going. Yes, Lord."

10. *Discipline and perspective*—Great preaching requires great discipline and sustained study. The preachers in this volume exhibited a healthy amount of both. Some are morning people. They study in the calm and quiet of a brand-new day. Others are night hawks. Their powers of retention are keenest when burning the midnight oil. They study with great profit when their home is undisturbed, their world is quiet, and the only noise about them is the rush of their own creative process.

Still others study "on the fly." They grab a read here and there—between meetings at the church, or when they have a little downtime in the afternoon, or on the road during revivals, or during some unexpected free time made possible through a cancellation in their schedule. "While their reading requires more of a hustle, the realization that their time is limited seems to help them absorb more on the fly. All recognized that they had to study in order to remain fresh, vibrant, interesting, creative, and faithful.

The most effective preachers also bring a sense of proportion to their work. Preaching is not something they do every waking moment of their lives. "While they take their vocation seriously, they also take their avocation seriously. When asked what they did when the preaching event was done, most said they rested. They took downtime seriously, and many engaged in some type of hobby that called them away from the rigors of sermon preparation.

11. *Preaching out of the overflow*—Each of the preachers in this volume gives evidence of preaching from an overflow of gathered materials. Most acknowledge that they will never be able to preach all they have studied and set aside in the week leading up to the sermon. One never has the feeling that they scrape the bottom of the barrel for something to say. William Stidger in *Preaching out of the Overflow* used an oil well metaphor to denote three types of preaching done by most preachers: dry holes, wells that have to be pumped, and wells that overflow.[16]

> Those who preach out of the overflow preach from a wealth of materials, knowledge, disciplined insight, and experiences gained from a lifetime of diligent study and conscious reflection on God's presence in the world. Effective preachers preach from a full fountain. Or, to mix metaphors, they skim the cream from the top of their seasoned, disciplined study. When they are done with the preaching assignment, the waiting congregation is often left desiring more.

Such are the common characteristics that many of the preachers in this volume share in their sermon-preparation methods. Each pursues his or her own distinctive approach, but the paths whereby they reach the goal of the finished sermon are in a sense well-worn and familiar to all.

A book on African American sermon-preparation methods is long overdue simply because most blacks continue to learn to preach through imitation of the masters. The oral learning process of observation, participation, and subsequent mastery is the method many blacks continue to employ in their efforts to attain a higher level of proficiency in preaching. In their ground-breaking study *The Black Church in the African American Experience*, C. Eric Lincoln and Lawrence Mamiya estimated that approximately four-fifths of black ministers currently in the field were without formal training of any kind.[17]

The Association of Theological Schools' *Fact Book on Theological Education 2000–2001 listed* just over seven thousand African American men and women in all of the degree programs associated with the ATS.[18] This is an unbelievably small number of students currently enrolled in ministerial training when one considers the thousands of churches in the two-hundred-plus denominations to which blacks belong in this country.[19] It is, however, a rather pointed reminder that most blacks continue to learn to preach by observing and then imitating the styles of preachers they have come to admire.

It is not in the formal setting of the divinity school or seminary that blacks first gain exposure to the crafting of the sermon. Most have had some experience in preaching before they reach the classroom. Rather it is on the "church circuit"—local and national gatherings, and television and tape ministries—that their favorite preachers teach them how to preach through the visible/audible enactment of the preached word.

Consequently, this project serves a threefold purpose: (1) it provides in-depth reflection on the sermon-preparation methods of some of America's most effective preachers; (2) it gives pastors and students a how-to manual directly from the hands of those who are most likely to influence their preaching; and (3) it makes available to the broader culture the distinctive sermon-crafting abilities of some of the most able and celebrated black preachers on the contemporary scene.

Thomas Long notes that the preachers people seem most to admire often appear to have a certain innate flair and knack for preaching that seems more like a gift than a set of skills. They seem more born to the task than instructed in the craft. According to Long, while the church is blessed by the occasional preacher of exceptional ability, the church is nourished most by the kind of careful, responsible, and faithful preaching that falls within the range of most of us.[20] This volume is presented in hopes of broadening the preaching abilities of all preachers who take their craft seriously.

Notes

1. James M. Childs Jr., *Preaching Justice: The Ethical Vocation of Word and Sacrament Ministry* (Harrisburg: Trinity, 2000), x.
2. Milton C. Semett, *Black Religion and American Evangelicalism: White Protestants, Plantation Missions, and the Flowering of Negro Christianity, 1785–1865* (Metuchen: Scarecrow, 1975), 95.
3. Ibid., 95–100.
4. Mechal Sobel, *Trabelin' On: The Slave Journey to an Afro-Baptist Faith* (Princeton: Princeton University Press, 1980), 159–160.
5. Ibid. The earliest known ordination of a black took place in 1788 when Andrew Bryan of Savannah, Georgia, was ordained by white Abraham Marshall. White Baptists generally held that slaves should not be ordained, but whenever the question was formally raised they decided that free blacks had every right to ordination.
6. Ibid. Sobel lists this particular category in a footnote to her chapter on "The New Afro-Baptist Sacred Cosmos." See footnote 31 on p. 278.
7. Ibid., 160.
8. Eugene D. Genovese, *Roll, Jordan, Roll: The World the Slaves Made* (New York: Vintage Books, 1976), 255–79.
9. "Watchman" was another category found in some of the literature. His duties included advising on spiritual matters, opening and leading prayer meetings, counseling mourners, helping sinners seeking conversion, and generally setting a Christian example for the slaves. While many were exhorters and preachers on the plantation, after emancipation they became regular preachers. See Nancy Bullock Woolridge, "The Slave Preacher-Portrait of a Leader," The *Journal of Negro Education* 14 (winter 1945): 29; and Albert Raboteau, *Slave Religion: The "Invisible Institution" in the Antebellum South* (New York: Oxford University Press, 1978), 238.
10. Thomas G. Long, *The Witness of Preaching* (Louisville: Westminster John Knox, 1989), 42–47.
11. Karl Barth, *The Word of God and the Word of Man* (Gloucester, MA: Peter Smith, 1978), 107–12.
12. Charles Bartow, *God's Human Speech: A Practical Theology of Proclamation* (Grand Rapids: Eerdmans, 1997), 64.
13. Walter J. Ong, *Orality and Literacy: The Technologizing of the Word* (London: Taylor and Francis Group, 1982), 38.
14. Albert J. Raboteau, *A Fire in the Bones: Reflections on African American Religious History* (Boston: Beacon, 1995), 142.
15. Henry Mitchell argues that any preaching which is devoid of life and beholden to a homiletical model based on argument can be characterized as white preaching, even when it's done by black preachers in predominantly black churches. See Mitchell's essay in Richard L. Eslinger, ed., *A New Hearing: Living Options in Homiletic Method* (Nashville: Abingdon, 1987), 39–40.
16. William L. Stidger, *Preaching out of the Overflow* (Nashville: Cokesbury, 1930), 13.
17. C. Eric Lincoln and Lawrence W. Mamiya, *The Black Church in the African American Experience* (Durham: Duke University Press, 1990).
18. Louis Charles Willard, ed., *Fact Book on Theological Education, 2000–2001* (Pittsburgh: The Association of Theological Schools, 2000), 41.
19. Wardell M. Payne, ed., *Directory of African American Religious Bodies* (Washington DC: Howard University Press, 1991), 21–147, 199–216.
20. Long, *The Witness of Preaching*, 21.

Section Four

Hymnody: Sound and Sense

22

"Gotta Moan Sometime": A Sonic Exploration of Earwitnesses to Early Pentecostal Sound in North America

David Douglas Daniels III

Abstract: *Sound as a historical frame provides a new historiographic turn for Pentecostal studies and a complement to spatial and temporal studies of the Pentecostal past. This article explores how sound serves as a primary marker of early Pentecostal indentity, as sound blended the sound of prayer, preaching, testifying, singing, music-making, and silence. Embedded in early Pentecostal sound are primal cries, speech, music, and ambient sound which, for early Pentecostals, functioned as a circular continuum that Pentecostal soundways traveled. Encompassing more than orality, early Pentecostal sound generated a way of knowing that challenged the orality-literacy binary, the hierarchy of senses that privileged sight, and the hierarchy of the races.*

Prelude

The opening phrase of the title of this presidential address comes from the lyrics of an African American chorus that exclaims:

> Trouble in my way (Trouble in my way)
> You gotta cry sometime (You gotta cry sometime)

The song continues by noting that "I lay awake at night" and "That's alright." It concludes by testifying: "Jesus, he will fix after while." Then the song goes on to repeat that "you gotta moan sometime" and later "you gotta pray sometime." This song encapsulates the three frames of history: the temporal, the spatial, and the sonic.[1]

The temporal, or the duration of time or change over time, is registered by the lyrics referring to lying awake at night and the "after while" when Jesus will fix it. The change over time, a historical transition, encompasses sleepless nights to Jesus fixing it (the situation) and the return of sleep-filled nights. Within the song, time is structured by now and later, present and future. Historians have been especially preoccupied with the change over time, the duration of time, the transition from past to present as well as the change over time within the past itself. History is an eyewitness to the past, observing the past with an historical eye.

While space may be measured through time, in this song the spatial frame is highlighted by the description of trouble as an object that blocks my path and that can be fixed or removed. Can't you visualize it: "Trouble in my way." The imaginative flair of the lyrics nearly paints the picture of trouble as an obstacle or barrier that restricts movement down a path; this is spatial or geographical. The focus is on what a person can see with his or her eyes. For a while, historians have engaged spatiality or space; historians must train their visual abilities. History becomes an eyewitness to the past; it entails seeing the past through an historical eye.

The third frame is sonic. It involves sound or sounds: the sound of crying and moaning; the sound of praying. Whether the cries are whimpers or shrieks, whether the moans are melodic or ached, whether the praying is silent or shouted, what is heard is what is central. The focus is on what can be heard. Recently, historians have begun to fine-tune their listening skills to differentiate the audible sounds. In the words of Elias Canetti, history becomes an "earwitness," an earwitness to the Pentecostal past, listening for echoes from that past with an historical ear.[2]

For centuries historical writing has employed the temporal frame: history as chronology; history as the interpretation of time-space events with its segments of periodization and kronos as the substance of history. Historians of Pentecostalism have debated the changes over time within the Pentecostal past: the origins of Pentecostalism in the late nineteenth-century revival movement, or the white Holiness movement, or the black Holiness movement. Changes over time within the Pentecostal past can be observed in the development of Pentecostalism as a movement to tradition, the process in which certain Pentecostal denominations became fundamentalist, and the shift(s) in the Pentecostal Movement from being racially mixed to racially segregated or from being gender inclusive to being patriarchal.

Now switch to history as an earwitness to the Pentecostal past; listen for echoes from that past with an historical ear. What does Pentecostalism sound like? What was the sound of William Seymour's Apostolic Faith Mission? Or Abundio de Lopez's Apostolic Faith Mission in Los Angeles? Of William Durham's North Avenue mission in Chicago? Or Sturdevant's Full Gospel of Holiness Mission in New York City? Or Charles Mason's Saints Home in Memphis? Or Marie Burgess' Glad Tidings Hall in New York City?

Earwitnesses to the Azusa Street Revival Era

The various earwitnesses to the Azusa Street Revival recollect different sounds as a dimension of the Pentecostal sensorium. Sound, along with the senses of sight, taste, touch, and smell, produces the sensory experience. These early Pentecostals recalled the "sweet anthems" and "sweet Jesus," the "laying on of hands" and being washed and cleansed, and seeing visions and having dreams. Metaphors of sight, taste, and touch shaped their experience and defined their reality, just as did the acts of seeing, tasting, touching, and smelling. The early Pentecostals also heard sounds: the sounds of speaking in unknown tongues, different languages, shouts, praises, singing in English, singing in tongues, gospel hymns, "heavenly anthems," as well as laughter, shrieks, cries, moans, groans, and silence, along with the music of various instruments.

According to various authors who attended the Revival at the beginning, there were no instruments, only *a cappella* singing, because "no instruments of music are used, none are needed." Many especially remembered the singing in the spirit. William Manley recalled:[3]

> There was a most remarkable incident of the sweetest singing I ever heard by about a half a dozen women, all in unknown tongues, in which at intervals one voice would die away in very plaintive strains, while the others carried the song. Then the former would break out in rapid strong language, filled with unction, and others would give tones as of singing in the distance. This was most enchanting, and filled with tender love.

Others, such as Carley, commented that the revival was noisy and mentioned the use of "cow bone, etc." A. C. Valdez Sr. remembered one brother who "would boom a 'Hallelujah' that rattled the windows," although, according to Valdez, the "old-line churches frowned on the Azusa Street Mission's. . . 'noisy meeting.'" He recalled that there were regular moments when silence was interrupted with a cacophony of sounds. He spoke of his first time visiting the Revival in 1906 when, amidst the silence, he felt that "[s]omething unusual was happening" and he recognized that "the Spirit of God was there." "Suddenly," he recalled, "people rose to their feet," and then "[b]ig, strong men began to cry out loud, then women. . . It was as if ocean waves were moving from one end of the congregation to the other."

> Wave after wave of the Spirit went through the hall, like a breeze over a cornfield. Again the crowd settled back into their seats. And prayers began to buzz through the hall. . . a black man with a shining face leaped to his feet. Out of his mouth poured words in some language I had never heard before. . .
>
> Just when quiet settled over the hall, a white woman came off the bench like a jack-in-the-box. "Oh, My blessed Jesus," she cried in excitement.[4]

For the next three years, Valdez attended the Revival. He noted, "Sometimes after a wave of glory, a lot of people would speak in tongues. Then a holy quietness would come over the place, followed by a chorus of prayer in languages we had never before heard." This wave of the Spirit, according to one author, occurred sometimes when the Holy Spirit came as "a rushing wind and everybody may speak that has the power." Valdez testified, "How I enjoyed shouting and praising God. During the tarrying, we used to break out in songs about Jesus and the Holy Spirit, 'Fill Me Now,' 'Joy Unspeakable,' and 'Love Lifted Me.'" He reported:[5]

> Praise about the cleansing and precious blood of Jesus would just spring from our mouths. In between choruses, heavenly music would fill the hall, and we would break into tears. Suddenly the crowd seemed to forget how to sing in English. Out of their mouths would come new languages and lovely harmony that no human being could have learned.

Silence and noise, chants and shouts, singing in the vernacular and in the spirit, instrumental and non-instrumental music, all were soundmarks of the Azusa Street Revival.

A journalist captured the theme of this presidential address in an account of the Pentecostal revival in Memphis, Tennessee during May of 1907 at Saints Home Church of God in Christ. In describing and interpreting Pentecostal exchanges between Charles Harrison Mason and his congregation, the journalist wrote that Mason "would exclaim, 'Hicks, hicks,' and the congregation would answer back, 'Sycamore, Sycamore, Sycamore,' and such insignificant words, which lifted the congregation to the highest point of ecstasy, showing what has been contended for years that the Negro religion is sound instead of sense." Other contemporaries of this journalist would have contended that early Pentecostalism like "Negro religion is sound instead of sense." Scholarly interpretations would possibly describe early Pentecostalism (African American Christianity) as religion that blends sound and sense.[6]

Sound as a Historical Frame

This presidential address proposes that historical writing on Pentecostalism should focus on the "sound and sense" that constitute early Pentecostalism between 1906 and 1932. Such a focus would supplement the attention given to time and space with sound. The history of time, space, and sound are complementary, for the most part. They each open up new sectors for inquiry. The historical writing on Pentecostalism and sound tends to be underdeveloped. This is remarkable, since throughout most of the twentieth century sound has been one of the factors distinguishing between Pentecostal churches and the others—the Baptists, Methodists, Presbyterians, Episcopalians, Catholics, and Quakers. In the past, you could definitely identify Pentecostalism by its sound, a sound that encompasses singing, music-making, praying, preaching, and testifying in many quarters. As Daniel Albrecht contends, a "cacophony of sound" constitutes Pentecostal sound, a sound that includes musical and verbal "sounds that surround."[7]

Historically, Pentecostalism was more often heard than experienced by people. The neighbors would hear Pentecostal voices and music; the radio listeners would have heard Pentecostal worship services and sermons; TV viewers would hear Pentecostal songs, sermons, and prayers. Even for some Pentecostal converts, the sound of Pentecostalism is what initially captured their attention. The early Pentecostal soundscape incorporated Protestant sounds from the nineteenth century.

Attuning oneself to the cacophony of Pentecostal sound in the past becomes the task for the historian, who must attempt to sense the sound and detect the sounds. Maybe one can color sounds or soundways to differentiate them. People say that sound can sound cold or hot. Music critics classify some sound as hot or cool. Sound has been noted for its texture. One could try to touch sound, feel its texture, or decide whether a particular sound is silky or gritty. Perhaps the temperature of a sound can be taken in order to determine whether a sound is feverish or not. Mixing metaphors, early Pentecostal sound would be probably colored red as a flame of fire, experienced as hot or cold, and textured gritty; Pentecostal sound is a red, hot, gritty sound.[8]

Terminologies of Sound

Throughout this address, five terms will be used to pursue the history of sound: Sonic, soundscape, sound, soundways, and syntax. Barry Traux states that "'sonic environment' can be regarded as the aggregate of all sound energy in any given context," while 'soundscape' is used "to put the emphasis on how that environment is understood by those living within it—the people who are in fact creating it." 'Sound' in the singular refers to the ensemble of sounds, 'soundways' to the sonic paths. 'Syntax' refers to the ordering of sounds.[9]

Historians of sound study the whole sonic world; they attempt to "'un-air' sounds that have faded into the air's atmosphere and catalogue them." The historian would un-air Pentecostal sound by analyzing the sound: Musicologists would speak of instrumentation, form, rhythms, vocalization, melody, and harmony. To un-air Pentecostal sound the historian would also catalogue these sounds. For Pentecostalism, that would encompass all kinds of sound: musical sound, prayer sound, sermonic sound, praise sound, and worship sound. In studying Pentecostal sound the scholar is attuned to the intonation, the accent, and the melody along with the texture of the music, prayers, sermons, praise, and worship as a whole. The historian's task is to identify and interpret which sounds "existed when and how they were produced and heard at certain moments in time." The historicity of early Pentecostal sound requires investigation.[10]

A Pentecostal Syntax of Sound: Primal Cries and Other Initiatives

Early Pentecostals ordered "the sounds that they" made in particular ways and used "those sounds to position themselves in the world." Establishing a syntax of sound became a primary way for early Pentecostals to order their sound. What was the syntax of early Pentecostal sound? Within the early Pentecostal soundscape, soundways traveled along a circular, not linear, continuum that began and ended with primal cries with the movement of speech-music-ambient sound in between: primal cries as eruptions from deep recesses; speech as vocalizations in words; ambient sound as the "human exclamations of 'oh', 'ah', 'mmm', and the like that take their place in the ambient sound of nature in the wind, thunder, and rushing water."[11]

Rather than reducing Pentecostal sound to emotional outbursts or liminal experiences, a sonic interpretation provides an alternative explanation: Pentecostal sound as cultural borrowing from primal cries as well as ambient sounds drawn from nature along with speech. Resonating with the multidimensionality of early Pentecostalism, sonic discourse complements other forms of discourse drawn from psychology, sociology, anthropology, and economics. The sonic discourse supplies an explanation of cultural borrowings that eludes dependence on functionalist theories of social deprivation, psychological disorder, secularization, or globalization; Pentecostal religious activity as related to sound became more than reactive response. Sonic discourse emphasizes the agency of Pentecostals in participating in the production of their respective soundways and the construction of their soundscape.[12]

Early Pentecostals participated in a "riot of sound" through their syntax. Early Pentecostal sound in many ways was subversive; it undermined the dominant sound of Protestantism. The syntax of early Pentecostal sound was challenged by the majority of their Protestant counterparts on the larger American religious soundscape. While Pentecostal soundways traveled along a circular continuum, most Protestant soundways travel along a linear continuum. Afterward the Protestant majority migrated from the use of primal cries within religious settings at least corporately during the Reformation; they never returned to primal cries within North America. The so-called First and Second Great Awakenings could be described as moments of return to primal cries and ambient sound. Most U.S. Protestants stopped along the continuum at speech and music, declining even to travel further to where ambient sounds could be utilized within worship. The Protestant majority sought a predictable and ordered sound with opportunities for silence and sounds conducive to contemplation and reflection.

The syntax of early Pentecostal sound contained "more non-verbal sounds" than its Protestant counterparts on the American religious soundscape. There was a place for "sporadic, unpredictable" sounds. The sound of glossolalia found a place in this syntax. The early Pentecostal syntax of sound disrupted the Protestant soundscape. Volume, a lot of it, was valued. Particular religious noise became acceptable as part of the early Pentecostal sound within the Pentecostal syntax. The syntax of early Pentecostal sound identified and rejected other sounds such as "demonic sounds," however; these sounds signaled the need to exorcize the demons.

According to Grant Wacker, a key word used by contemporaries to describe early Pentecostal worship was "deafening." External accounts from Kansas to California to Oregon to Alabama to

Iowa to Connecticut identified the early Pentecostal sounds as "jabbering in a strange gibberish," "howlings of worshippers," "the rapid chattering of a frightened simian," "hideous noise," "moan, scream and speak unintelligible words," "chatter, scream, gnash their teeth," "laughing, high-trebled, piercing exclamations," "barking like dogs, hooting like owls," and "unearthly shrieks and groans." Primal cries and ambient sounds found a place within Pentecostal worship in North America and on various other continents.[13]

Europeans and Asians also drew from the Pentecostal repertoire of sounds. In Britain, according to Wacker, they made "sounds like ducks quacking, lambs bleating, and dogs barking"; newspaper accounts reported "'sobs, sighs, groans, and table-thumping' that resembled the 'mourning chants' of an Irish wake." In Germany in 1907, Pentecostals ranked among the "manifestations of the Spirit" of 1 Corinthians 12. Further, "[s]ome cried with loud voice, others shouted Hallelujah!, clapped their hands, jumped or laughed with joy." In India, adolescent women were described as "crying at the top of their lungs" and other people loudly confessed their sins. These Pentecostals exhibited "joy unspeakable" through "singing, clapping the hands, [and] shouting praises." A sonic interpretation would catalogue these Pentecostal sounds as primal cries or ambient sounds.[14]

Among early Pentecostals, there were those who believe that the sound of the saints was interpretable. Interpretation was possible not just for unknown tongues and spiritual writing and drawing, but also for all spiritual utterances. Charles Harrison Mason reported that in early 1907 he left the Azusa Street Revival and returned to Memphis, where the Holy Spirit began to teach him "how and what to sing and all his songs were new." He began to pray for the Holy Spirit to give him the gift of interpretation. Mason later testified that the Holy Spirit gave him "the gift of interpretation, that is, he would interpret sounds, groans and any kind of spiritual utterance."[15]

The Pentecostal repertoire of sounds was reportedly drawn from various soundways. To dismiss the Azusa Street Revival, Charles Parham in his *Apostolic Faith* compiled the list of sounds associated with it—"jabbering, chattering, wind-sucking and giving vent to meaningless sounds and noises"—and attributed the sounds to southern black religious culture. Others associated a range of these sounds with the Shouting Methodist among Euro-Americans. As noted above, some British journalists associated certain sounds with an Irish wake.[16]

The syntax of early Pentecostalism was an inversion of the syntax of the Protestant majority. This was recognized by the society. Various local governments would group certain Pentecostal sounds as noise and deem them a public nuisance if they were heard after a designated time in the evening. Noise abatement or prohibition campaigns in a sense included certain Pentecostal sounds. The Pentecostal syntax of sound established its own rules.

The Generating Soundways:
Shouting Methodist and Other Trajectories

Myriad soundways generated the early Pentecostal soundscape. As a collection of various soundways that paralleled, countered, and overlapped each other as well as produced new soundways, the early Pentecostal soundscape was multivocal and polysonic. On the Pentecostal soundscape there are different soundways constituted by a duster of certain primal cries, words and phrases, and ambient sounds from nature and humans along with styles of music-making. Among the soundways that constituted the Pentecostal soundscape were sonic trajectories that flowed out of the black and white Holiness movements of the late nineteenth century.

The late nineteenth-century Holiness soundscape was produced by various soundways with their respective cluster of certain primal cries, words and phrases, ambient sounds from humans but not nature, and music-making in various styles. These soundways flowed out of white and African American Holiness streams and drew from various currents, such as the white centrist Wesleyan Holiness, the baptistic Holiness/the Keswickians, Shouting Methodist, Burning Bush, Fire-Baptized, Salvation Army, black Holiness Baptist, and black Union Holiness and Holy Churches. While each soundway had its own particular sound, many, if not all, of these soundways shared a common hymnody. Consequently, the Shouting Methodist, Burning Bush, and Fire Baptized introduced more primal cries and ambient sounds than the white centrist Wesleyan Holiness.

Within the early Pentecostal soundscape, some of these sonic traditions remained distinct or embodied within individuals or groups while others over lapped and engaged in cultural exchanges. The Shouting Methodist tradition, especially as promulgated by the Burning Bush enthusiasts, resonated with the African American camp meeting tradition while it would have clashed with the urban African Methodist Episcopal tradition. According to Robeck, the heavenly chorus or singing in the spiritual performed at the Azusa Street Revival possibly echoed the "Negro chant" of the prays/praise houses, although the shout songs and jubilees associated with African American religious folk music were absent; they would become a part of the certain currents within Afro-Pentecostalism.[17]

Within the Azusa Street Revival, there appears to have been times when different soundways overlapped with the African-based and African American-defined sonic world of the Revival. Yet even this sonic world had various trajectories, differing according to instruments, clapping, and tunes. Possibly a distinction needs to be made either among sonic periods within the Revival or, simply, developments that occurred during the Revival era although not necessarily at Seymour's Apostolic Faith Mission.

Various accounts by Rachel Sizelove, Ernest S. Williams, and Alexander Boddy note the absence of instruments. Non-instrumental music-making became the norm at the Revival during some periods, while other periods were marked by instrumental music-making. In describing the lively music heard during the Revival in 1907, Lawrence Catley recalled that there was musical "accompaniment with bones ('cow ribs') and a washboard and thimbles. Later a piano was added—then a violin."[18]

Silence played a critical role in the Revival. Catley remembered that Seymour would intervene "when he thought the service was getting too loud or out of order."

Rachel Sizelove recalled that during the first nine months of the Revival the role of silence, especially tarrying, was evident in the worship:[19]

> We felt all flesh should keep silent before the Lord... when someone would begin to pound the seat with their hand or fist while they were praying, Brother Seymour would go to them gently and tap them on the shoulder, and say, "Brother that is the flesh," and a holy hush and quietness would settled upon those tarrying for the Holy Ghost.

According to some accounts the camp meeting tradition was missing from or evident at different periods during the Revival. An early earwitness to the Revival described the first four of months of the Revival as lacking in "shouting, clapping or jumping so often seen in camp meetings," although "shaking" occurred. By the summer of 1906, more sounds were introduced; a journalist wrote: "Another Negro started 'I am washed in the blood,' and a genuine camp-meeting time followed, with clapping of hands and stomping of feet." At the Azusa Street Revival, different soundways apparently overlapped others at different times.[20]

Joyful Noise and the Early Pentecostal Identity

Soundscapes embody history and shape identity. Difference, for instance, "embodies history in sound." Although early Pentecostal sound differed from Presbyterian sound, each sound embodied and expressed a sonic "histories—that is, histories lived" sonically and produced a different identity. Sound enlarges the scale of expression and allows for broader emotional ranges, more textured vocabulary, tonal diction, affective commitment, and fuller embodiment.

Sound serves as a "symbolic signifier" of identity. There is a symbiotic relationship between how "voice authorizes identities as identities authorize voice." One way of identifying a Presbyterian or Pentecostal during the early twentieth century was through their sound. Early Pentecostals knew that "some sounds connote one's own people and some connote the 'other.'" You had an inkling of who was among the saints by the way they sounded. In certain ways, Pentecostals used "sound to make meaning of the world around" them.[21]

Noise, music, and silence as construed by early Pentecostals shaped their identity and had a place on the Pentecostal soundscape. Pentecostals defined for themselves sounds that were noise or "sweet" rather than adopting uncritically classifications from the middle class or some other group. Noise related to volume (decibel level), dissonance, being off-key musically, or atonality became for

Pentecostals a matter of context. For Pentecostals, what outsiders called noise, even "unusual noise," was simply the activity of "praising God and speaking in tongues." Some noise is deemed inappropriate; other noise, catalogued as making a joyful noise, is deemed appropriate.[22]

Pentecostals operated in a religious soundscape in which the "meaning of religious sounds" was contested: the anthems of classical music versus the anthems of the heavenly chorus, the pipe organ versus the guitar, affective speech versus rapid-fire speech, solemn silence versus joyful noise. Regarding noise, Schmidt, registering a shift in the "threshold of hearing" during the late eighteen and nineteenth centuries, concluded:[23]

> Noise was the category for sounds that the trained ear could not discriminate or appreciate, the sounds that caused it pain instead of pleasure, that disrupted hearing's delicate harmonial balance. Noise very much acted as a social category as much as an aesthetic one. The evangelicals were not only defined by their noises; they *were* noise.

Like their evangelical forbears, early Pentecostals were probably noise, too. Many Pentecostals employed "making a joyful noise" to mark religious boundaries and construct their identity. In 1930 Elder Curry of Jackson, Mississippi, a pastor in the Church of God in Christ, offered a biblical support for "making a joyful noise," taking his text from "the 149th Division of the Psalms" and the sixteenth chapter of the Gospel of Mark. He recited the key verse of that psalm, "Make a joyful noise unto the Lord," acknowledging, "now some people they don't like that noise." Whereas the elites, the literati, might use noise to construct otherness—the African, feminine, infantile, uncivilized, or insane—Pentecostals challenge these racialized and gendered constructions. Certain noises were deemed Christian; other noises were deemed demonic.[24]

Music and music-making become a serious task in the production of early Pentecostal sound, which ranged from sounds described as heavenly to those described as lively. Music-making became a debated topic as Pentecostals explored music-making with and without instruments; with sacred, homemade, and worldly instruments; with religious and worldly sounds. Sacred instruments included the piano and organ; homemade instruments included washboards, bones, jugs, and kazoos; and "worldly" or "the devil's" instruments included the violin (fiddle), banjo, guitar, and drums. The religious sounds included tunes from Protestant hymnody as well as camp meeting songs and spirituals; the worldly sounds included certain kinds rhythms as well as chord progressions and notes associated with the nascent ragtime, honky-tonk, blues, and jazz idioms. According to various accounts the early Pentecostal soundscape privileged silence, especially in tarrying and other forms of prayer. Silence was more than a gap in worship; silence played a liturgical role.

Musicality provided another language and a means of shaping Pentecostal sound and identity. Many scholars have noted the chanting style and "sing song" texture of early Pentecostal speech. Whether in preaching, praying, testifying, or public scripture reading, various Pentecostals chanted their words, interjecting a musicality to their speech with a tune and melody.

At early Pentecostal prayer meetings and other occasions of communal prayers within the Pentecostal soundscape, primal cries and ambient sounds rang out. During prayer, one could hear whispers, cries, moanings, groanings, wailing, weeping, shrieks, and hollers. It was a setting in which a wide range of sounds was permitted rather than policed. Sounds of gratitude and desperation could be heard. This was one of the few spaces in which every voice could be raised simultaneously in praise or petition. Prayer meetings were one of the few places within early Pentecostalism in which the shunning of silence rarely occurred. Silence, even stretches of silence, was welcomed.

The sounds heard in early Pentecostal prayer could be heard in preaching: these included whispers, cries, moans, weeping, and hollers, along with squalls, yelling, and whooping. In various early Pentecostal settings, preaching, like praying, permitted a wider range of sounds to be employed. In some settings, the preacher, in shifting registers, would commence "tuning-up."

At the core of Pentecostal musicality was the song. The sound of congregational singing reverberated throughout most early Pentecostal sanctuaries. At the Azusa Street Revival, they sang songs such as "The Comforter Has Come," "Are You Washed in the Blood," "This Is Like Heaven to Me," "'Tis Heaven There," "All I Need Is Jesus," "Where the Healing Waters Flow," and "The Blood Done Signed My Name." The sound of Pentecostal songs, with their origins in the gospel hymn of the nineteenth century and the African American sound, included up-beat rhythmic sounds, hard-beat intoxicating sounds, mournful, dirge-like sounds, and soothing, mellow sounds. Hand-clapping, foot-stomping, and tambourine playing with an occasional horn or piano created this sonic world of early Pentecostalism. Early Pentecostals were known for rapid or fast-tempo music. Grant quotes Howard Goss to contrast, in Goss' words, the "slow, dragging and listless" tunes preferred by mainline Protestants with the Pentecostals' "fast music" and songs performed "at almost break-neck speed." Many, with their rousing choruses, brought the leader and congregation into a sonic embrace.[25]

The rhythmic pulse of Pentecostal musicality was sustained by clapping. For some early Pentecostals the sound of clapping communicated praise to God. Sometimes this is called praising God with Psalm 47 (O clap your hands together), a doxological form of clapping. For some early Pentecostals, clapping was a form of invocation; often accompanied with phrases such as "Thank you, Jesus," clapping was a way of "calling on the Lord." In a sense, for these Pentecostals certain clapping was also annunciatory; as they sensed the in-breaking or overflowing of God's presence they began clapping, combining an annunciatory act with an anticipatory awareness.

Seymour participated in the construction of an alternative soundscape to segregation and institutional racism through the formation of the Apostolic Faith Mission (Los Angeles) as an interzone in which interracial and multiracial sounds and interactions directly attacked white supremacy as a cultural phenomenon through its sound, space, and witness, thus undermining racial prejudice. An analysis of the racial rhetoric within the *Apostolic Faith* papers points to the construction of a Pentecostal sonic identity. There is the syntax. There is also the fact that while the concept of race informs the *Apostolic Faith* papers, the language of race escapes it. While nationalities, a key term of the early twentieth century, functioned as the term of choice, spoken sounds or language were pivotal.[26]

Within the *Apostolic Faith* papers, the world was organized sonically or linguistically. The Revival offered an alternative to the trilogy of races (Caucasoid, Mongoloid, Negroid), to the four European races (Alpine, Mediterranean, Nordic, Semitic), and to the four others (Ethiopian, Mongolian, Malay, American). It also countered the competing categorization of nationalities grouped into forty races (Irish, Italians, Syrians, Greeks, Hungarians, Poles, Serbo-Croatians, Japanese, Filipinos, Mexicans, Negroes, and so forth). The Revival focused on organizing the people of the world around the primary languages that they spoke. These languages included the languages of "India, China, Africa, Asia, Europe, and islands of the Sea as well as the learned languages of Greek, Latin, Hebrew, French, German, Italian, Chinese, Japanese, Hindu and Bengali. . . Chippewa. . ." Among the languages of Africa, they cited Cru (Kru), Zulu, and Ugandan. These languages were listed on a par with the languages of the world. The linguistic framework or the languages of the world provided a lens through which to view humanity in terms other than race.[27]

Possibly, the Azusa Street Revival under Seymour, through its sonic or linguistic organization of humanity, advanced nonracialism. The Revival downplayed race as a marker of identity and stressed language. Nonracialism, then, would avow human commonality and "equality" and would serve as a new basis for Christian unity that bridges the racial divide and zones demarcated by the color line.

Early Pentecostals employed noise, silence, music-making, musicality, and the sonic organization of humanity to construct their Christian identity, locate themselves in the society, engage in culture-crossing, and advance a nonracialism that countered the hierarchies of race advanced by the government and the majority society. Early Pentecostal sound became a means of constructing an alternative soundscape, social space, and religious culture.

Early Pentecostal Sound in the Post-Azusa Street Revival Era

Following the Azusa Street Revival Era in 1911, the syntax of Pentecostal sound changed. Here is where it might be important to acknowledge the multiple syntaxes within early Pentecostalism. We might become more attuned to how different syntaxes become dominant within sectors or maybe even across sectors within Pentecostalism.

Historians of sound are regularly in search of the demarcating lines at which major transitions in sound occur, noting previous eras or lost eras in sound or lost sounds. For Pentecostalism, there is the era before the electrical amplification of sound when naked voices or the accompaniment of hand-clapping and foot-stomping prevailed, or the parallel era in which an ensemble of scrub boards, tambourines, and perhaps a guitar would accompany the voices, clapping, and stomping, or the subsequent era in which a band with the piano, drum, guitar, and horns would blast its sound.

Pentecostal sound, in general, possesses a certain kind of historicity. I am not arguing for either a monolithic Pentecostal sound or an ahistorical sound. Pentecostal sound is made complex by the influence of region, generation, race, ethnicity, gender, class, culture, and Christian heritage. The historicity of Pentecostal sound demands a high level of specificity in exploring sound. The regionalization of early Pentecostal sound might expose an urban Northeast sound, Midwestern sound, rural Southern sound, and within the rural Southern sound, an Appalachian sound. Possibly crossing regions, there exist the distinct Pentecostal sounds of Italian Americans, Mexican Americans, and African Americans; the racialization or ethnicization of Pentecostal sound is pivotal. To engage in a comparative study of the soundways along the Pentecostal soundscape could demonstrate the mixing between the various soundways. This may even give voice to different sectors within Pentecostalism, especially marginalized voices within Pentecostalism, as they shouted, hollered, screamed, moaned, and sang.

Within early Pentecostalism, especially black and Latino/a Pentecostalism, a sonic trajectory arose within the Protestant music. These soundways charted their own sonic paths. Among Latino/a Pentecostals, Antonio Castaneda Nava translated into Spanish the lyrics of some songs from Garfield T. Haywood's *The Bridegroom's Songs* and rearranged the tunes by slowing down the quick 4/4 tempo. Among African American Pentecostals, there existed a trajectory that shaped the gospel music movement.[28]

In 1917, Aimee Semple McPherson recalled the Salvation Army Corps in St. Petersburg, Florida "bringing their drum and musical instruments" to the revival she held in that city. Later that year, African American Pentecostals in Miami, Florida "played their instruments" in a march through the city and "sang as only colored folk can" to advertise her revival meetings. Robert Clarence Lawson's congregation in the Harlem community of New York City during 1919 was noted for making "sounds like a jazz orchestra." The congregation's neighbors "complained that the church people act like 'holy rollers,' judging from the weird sounds coming from the edifice," and the church music was "rendered with organs, drums, and tambourines, and sounds like a jazz orchestra."[29]

According to historian Gayle Wald, "Sunday morning services at Fortieth Street [later Robert's Temple COGIC, Chicago] in the mid-1920s featured loud voices singing to the raucous accompaniment of tambourines, drums, triangles, a piano, guitars, and even brass, if a trumpet or trombone was available." The musicologist George Pullen Jackson in *White Spirituals in the Southern uplands* described a biracial Pentecostal convention in Cleveland, Tennessee, during September 1929 as producing a "steady and almost terrifying rhythmic noise." This noise was created by instrument strummers, a tambourine whacker, and a piano player along with those who "clapped hands to the time of the music" and those whose who shouted and spoke in unknown tongues.[30]

Arizona Dranes was a central figure in the production of this soundway during the late 1920s. Dranes was born in Austin, Texas around 1891; she was either born blind or became blind during her toddler years. From 1896 to 1910, she attended the Institute for Deaf, Dumb and Blind Colored Youths, where she studied music, and graduated in 1910. At some point prior to 1920 she joined the Church of God in Christ.[31]

The soundway that Dranes constructs circulates through the airways by radio and by records, gaining hearers and singers. The elements of this particular Pentecostal soundway are the vocalization, piano sound, and the rhythm, producing a Pentecostal gospel voice, piano sound, and gospel beat. "Located in range between a soprano and an alto, [Dranes'] voice was marked by nasality, but with clarity of pitch, and was treated like a drum when, with emotion and fervor, she shouted out the lyrics of songs." The shouting of the lyrics produced "a speech-like, sermonic delivery." She overlapped this with the call and response technique. Her piano sound blended ragtime, barrelhouse techniques, and a bluesy quality. Her piano sound had "a somewhat raucous barrelhouse or honky-tonk quality with the highly rhythmic and rapidly repeated percussive chords." Her gospel rhythm "rendered songs in 3/4 time" with a walking melodic bass line, anticipating the "boogie-woogie bass style" that would come later. Dranes utilized the syntax of Pentecostal sound with her chanting and shouting.[32]

Sound as More Than Orality: Investigating the Racial and Class Politics of Sound

During the emergence of Pentecostalism, different cultural contexts thrived. In some cultural quarters, contesting modernity, the binary opposition of orality/aurality and literacy still existed; in other quarters, heralding modernity, orality/aurality was eclipsed by literacy; and, yet, in others, heralding folk sensibility, the binary failed to exist: sight complements sound.

Engaging the historical study of sound, Pentecostal studies could go beyond the employment of the binary of orality and literacy to explain Pentecostal difference. Studies of orality based on Walter Ong and Marshall McLuhan fail to exhaust the study of sound. Focusing on orality alone misconstrues the past by characterizing premodern cultures as oral and juxtaposing them with modern cultures which are characterized as literate/print-based because premoderns experienced a wider range of sounds than speech. The narrow focus on orality is tied to a grand narrative in which, during the advent of modernity, literacy triumphs over orality, privileging sight over sound, producing the "devocalization of the universe."[33]

The triumph of literacy over orality occurred in the West during the transition between the sixteenth and seventeenth centuries. "The sixteenth did not see first," observed Lucien Febvre, "it heard and smelled, it sniffed the air and caught sound." In this ocularcentric narrative, the Enlightenment in its attack on sound as a source of religious authority sought to displace it with reason through the Enlightenment's disenchantment with the world, especially by demystifying sound; sound, being a form of immediate revelation, was proven to be an untrustworthy sense or source of knowledge.[34]

The ocularcentric narrative is challenged by scholars such as Leigh Eric Schmidt and Richard Cullen Rath, who seek to complicate rather than reproduce the "ocularcentric narrative about the Enlightenment and modernity." For them, this grand narrative misses the complexity of the relationship between orality and literacy, sight and sound. Countering the "hierarchic, oppositional convention" of orality and literacy, Schmidt argues that sight and sound remained contestants during the Enlightenment and its aftermath; sound was reshaped through its response to modernity as it functioned in a counter-hegemonic manner in various quarters. Consequently, for Schmidt, sound has a history during modernity that should be excavated.[35]

Schmidt contends that the orality-literacy binary not only loses its explanatory value, but it also relies heavily on "racialized constructions of Western rationality and ecstatic primitivism." The orality-literacy binary plots the story of the triumph of literacy on "a hierarchy of the senses, with sight vastly ennobled and hearing sharply diminished." It also sets up "a marked dichotomy between eye and ear cultures" wherein "'the African' lived in 'the magical world of the ear,' while modern Western 'typographic man' lives in 'the neutral visual world' of the eye." The world of vision produced historical progress while the world of sound was marked by magic. The historical challenge between the world of vision and the world of sound has been, as McLuhan puts it, "the inability of oral and intuitive oriental culture to meet with the rational, visual European patterns of experience." What Schmidt deemed as "a larger racialized frame of comparison" would be a major problematic in the use of the orality-literacy binary in Pentecostal studies, especially the historiography that recognizes the multicultural, multi-racial, and multi-national character of Pentecostalism as a movement.[36]

A comparative study will resist the temptation to write Pentecostal history in one voice; rather, it will be open to multiple voices and to the full range of those voices. This has been a perennial concern within the Pentecostal community. A study of the Pentecostal soundscape reveals the lost soundways in such a way that the scholar is attuned to the dissonance between them and the present: they sound alien and clash with current Pentecostal sonic sensibilities. It helps the scholar to appreciate that certain past soundways may be unretrievable because they are embedded in a different syntax of Pentecostal sound. A sonic barrier condoned these soundways in the past. While earlier soundways might have traveled certain routes, the loss of their adjacent and intersecting soundways leads to their being remixed.

Comparing Shifts in Sound to Shifts in Early Pentecostal Practice

What are the developments in Pentecostal sound? What are the transitions in the history of Pentecostal sound? Early Pentecostalism constructed a soundscape characterized by the "interpenetration" of European, African, and Hispanic soundways. The early Pentecostal soundscape really was constructed out of the "interplay" of these various soundways in which each soundway shaped and was shaped by the other. The early Pentecostal soundscape was the overlapping over sonic vibes. The sonic changes in the mid- and late-twentieth century set up new sonic barriers; while the elements of the early soundways persisted, the coherence of this soundway and the past sonic world itself was lost. Pressing to hear this lost soundway opens space for us to the dissonances, exposing the ways in which elements of this lost sonic world have been absorbed into our contemporary Pentecostal soundways.

If Cecil M. Robeck Jr. is correct, at the core of this lost sonic world of the Azusa Street Revival, and perhaps of Pentecostalism, is an African sound. "Many of the expressions approved at Azusa Street could also be found within traditional African American centers of folk worship," Robeck contends. He approvingly quotes historian Eileen Southern in claiming that "all Pentecostal worship in the United States is in some sense the direct" heir to the religious culture of the enslaved Africans. Pentecostal sound is "heir to the shouts, hand-clapping and foot-stomping, jubilee songs, and ecstatic seizures of the plantation 'praise houses.'" The African sound was later suppressed or minimized or expunged. Interestingly, James Goff contends that the African sound would re-enter white Pentecostal sound in the 1950s through the quartets of the southern gospel movement.[37]

The early Pentecostal soundscape was initially constructed with porous sonic borders. Yet, the ecclesial borders became less porous due to the denominationalization campaigns of the second generation. Did the sonic borders remain porous? Maybe some sectors had less porous ecclesial and sonic borders. The fundamentalization or evangelicalization of certain forms of Pentecostalism introduced new soundways and theologies, producing modifications in doctrine, ecclesiology, and liturgy.

Which came first? One could argue that the adoption of fundamentalist soundways preceded the theological and ecclesial fundamentalization or evangelicalization of certain Pentecostal sectors. By their sound, did these Pentecostal sectors switch from a Pentecostal to an evangelical soundscape between the 1940s and 1960s? Perhaps some Pentecostal soundways migrated to other soundscapes.

This transformation within certain sectors within Pentecostalism led to a change in the syntax of Pentecostal sound and possibly a rupture with the past. Was this change really an inversion? Recalling the circular continuum of sound discussed earlier, have various sectors of Pentecostalism adopted a more linear continuum? In contrast to other Protestants, they encompass speech, music, and ambient sound, yet discard primal cries. The more evangelicalized Pentecostal sectors might limit the embrace of ambient sound. Does the move of these Pentecostal sectors widen the sonic gulf between the various Pentecostal soundways because of differences in syntax, sensibilities, and perhaps even soundscape? Nowadays, different Pentecostal sectors do not even travel in the same sonic world.

The shift in some Pentecostal sectors from a circular to a more linear continuum transfers primal cries from the public to private soundways, stripping primal cries of their liturgical context. Overall Pentecostal soundways are modulated. This again impacts the range of Pentecostal sound: praying, preaching, singing, testifying, music-making, and other sonic activities.

Investigating the Pentecostal soundscape exposes certain deserted regions, power struggles in specific sectors between the circular and the linear continuums, but other issues are muted, such as women's ordination, women's access to the bishopric or the superintendency, as well as the access of racial or ethnic minorities within various denominations to the chambers of power.

We often attribute the differences between racialized forms of Pentecostalism to their respective origins. If African sounds have profoundly shaped the Pentecostal soundscape, the difference in racialized forms of Pentecostalism may be due less to their origins than to the sonic and ecclesial segregation that occurred later; this was further complicated by the denominationalization that isolated even these racialized forms within their racial groups. Yet, it appears that the sonic separation along racial lines possibly occurred decades after the ecclesial segregation of the races in most Pentecostal sectors.

On the other hand, is there a way of identifying the points at which racialization takes place on the Pentecostal soundscape and equally those aspects of the soundscape that are open to cultural difference and diversity? Do melodies of inclusion or harmony exist?

Sound as a Way of Knowing

Sound functions as a way of knowing, hearing, experiencing, and being in the world. Sound becomes a medium for expressing theology in song, speech, primal cries, ambient sounds, and music-making. Through the choreography of sound, meaning is internalized. Sound becomes a hermeneutic and its generation of knowledge supplements epistemology with acoustemology as a sonic way of knowing. Michael Bull ponders:[38]

If the world is for hearing, as Attali suggests, then there exists an unexplored gulf between the world according to sound and the world according to sight. Sound has its own distinctive relational qualities; as Berkeley observed, "sounds are as close to us as our thoughts". . . Sound is essentially non-spatial in character, or rather sound engulfs the spatial, thus making the relation between subject and object problematic. Sound inhabits the subject just as the subject might be said to inhabit sound, whereas vision, in contrast to sound, represents distance, the singular, the objectifying. . . Therefore aural relational experience might well differ from a more visually orientated one. This is not to suggest that they are mutually exclusive but merely to suggest that the relational nature of a technologically auditory experience differs epistemologically from an explanation that prioritizes the visual.

"Hearing has its own relation to truth: to testimony, to spoken evidence, to placing trust in words rather than in images, to accepting things that are promised, even if they cannot be shown. Hearing likewise involves a special relationship to remembering. And also knowing; admitting that something sounds credible." Pentecostals engage in "acts of making and hearing sounds" that make a world. This "world of local knowledge" "is articulated as vocal knowledge." For Pentecostals hearing is believing and seeing is believing; as Paul's letter to the Romans says, "Faith comes by hearing, and hearing by the word of God."[39]

Early Pentecostals, like eighteenth-century evangelicals, adopted "religious ways of knowing that emphasize the aliveness of sounds, the power of scriptures to speak, the capacity of music to heal or inspire ecstasy." Like their evangelical predecessors, they "cultivated an especially fine-tuned ear for the voices, sounds and noises of the divine world" as well as the created order. Being called by God to perform certain activities and to prophesy became a soundmark on the Pentecostal soundscape. For early Pentecostals, the divine sound opened itself to the Pentecostal soundscape.[40]

According to some early Pentecostals, the Holy Spirit let them eavesdrop on divine sound: "bands of angels have been heard by some in the spirit." Pentecostal soundways occasionally echoed biblical and heavenly soundscapes. Pentecostals referred to a certain form of singing in the spirit as a heavenly choir or chorus. References to an ensemble singing in the spirit as a "heavenly chorus" occurs in accounts written by Rachel Sizelove, William Durham, A. W. Orwing, and A. W. Frodsham. They called singing in the spirit the singing of heavenly anthems. These anthems were considered to be "music that is being sung by angels": the "heavenly choir" at the Azusa Street Revival sang simultaneously with the band of angels so that both were "singing the same heavenly song in harmony."[41]

These observers classified certain sounds as sounds associated with the Pentecost event. In 1908 Charles Harrison Mason recalled his Spirit baptism a year earlier: "I sat there a while and I heard a sound just like the sound of wind, a great wind. I heard the sound like in the Pentecost. I heard it just as real. . . The anthem of Heaven seemed to rise then." Mason also recalled the sound of the Crucifixion event. In the *Apostolic Faith* paper, he reported that at one moment it seemed as if he "was standing at the cross and heard him as he groaned, the dying groans of Jesus, and I groaned." Early Pentecostal sound became a way to voice moans of sorrows, groans of agony, and the cries of pain—in other words, a way for letting suffering speak.[42]

As Samuel Solivan proposes in the pneumatology of his Hispanic Pentecostal Theology project, "It is the Holy Spirit who is the transformer of the sufferer and the sufferer's circumstances into liberating *orthopathos*." He adds that "the Holy Spirit can liberate one's life, can turn one's suffering and oppression into hope and faith in spite of the evil social structures and, at times, even in spite of us." Solivan argues that *orthopathos* resonates with the pathos of God wherein *ortho-* refers to the liberating, redemptive, empowering character of *pathos* (as suffering). One might also describe it as a redemptive capacity of suffering enabled by the Holy Spirit. Consequently, Pentecostal soundings—primal cries, speech, ambient sounds, music-making—comes a way to sound out suffering in the community whereby the Holy Spirit redeems the suffering by transforming the sufferers and their circumstances.[43]

In this sonic orbit, doctrines were deemed sound or unsound; they either sounded right or wrong. The task of discernment entailed sounding out the truth. Knowledge of silence in Pentecostal sound equally produces knowledge. Walter Benjamin stated: "all sounds and things still have their silences." How "do we hear silence" in Pentecostal sound? Is silence heard differently within Pentecostal sound over against Quaker sound? Somehow it differs from the deep soundlessness of the Quaker meeting. What does it mean or what are the implications that in Pentecostal sound silence is rarely broken? Is silence in Pentecostal sound not fragile enough to break?[44]

Early Pentecostal soundscape was shaped by and reshaped the Pentecostal sensorium. The sense of touch was redefined by the advent of "the gift of playing on instruments" without instruction on playing an instrument or practicing on it; the Holy Spirit gifts with the right touch in playing an instrument. The sense of sight was refocused through the gift of drawing in the Spirit, reordering the relationship between sight and touch, as well as through the seeing of visions. The sound of speaking and singing in unknown tongues found its "literary" equivalent in the "gift of writing in unknown languages." Certain Pentecostals were given the "literary" gift of reading these "writings." Included among these "writings" were poetry and scripture. Within the Pentecostal sensorium, the orality-literacy binary of the Enlightenment was recast in ways that challenged the coupling of reason and literacy and the hierarchy of the senses that privilege sight. Early Pentecostals produced new ways of knowing about God and reality.[45]

To explore the early Pentecostal ways of knowing, a theological method focusing on orality would have to expand to focus on sound or the total sensory experience of early Pentecostals. These studies would complement the theological analysis of Pentecostal literary production such as tracts, lyrics, prayers, testimonies, biographies and autobiographies, sermons, religious curricula, doctrinal statements, theological essays, and theology books. Early Pentecostal ways of knowing challenge the Enlightenment preoccupation with the intellectual production of the elite and elite literary texts.

Postlude

In the writing of Pentecostal history, those who complement the history of time and space with the history of sound may well illumine the inability of most Pentecostal historians to reconstruct Pentecostal origins in such a way that the white religious experience, specifically the Holiness and baptistic experience, loses its normative status within early Pentecostalism and its place as the context from which the Pentecostal soundscape emerges. Since most narratives still introduce African Americans or Latino/as as individuals, often isolated individuals, a narrative that focuses on the emerging Pentecostal soundscape might provide a communal framework in which to discuss African American and Latino/a religious movements. When they are included they become a minority in the mix with the white Pentecostal majority or they are segregated into a separate chapter. Others provide discussions of the black church in general or they present portraits of African American religious culture, especially its orality, spontaneity, and bodily involvement. Will a study of Pentecostal sound produce a paradigm shift in Pentecostal historiography where the history of time and space failed? I await the results with interest.

First, perhaps a study of early Pentecostal sound will result in a reinvestigation of the relationship between Pentecostalism on one hand and other Protestant movements and modernity on the other. Early Pentecostal sound uncovers ways of knowing, acoustemology, that counters the trajectory of the Enlightenment with its orality-literacy binary, its hierarchy of the senses that privileges sight, and its hierarchy of the races that privileges Europeans.

Second, perhaps a study of early Pentecostal sound will expose multiple soundways that constructed the Pentecostal soundscape. Since the racial and gender composition of the early Pentecostal Movement is so pivotal in mounting the movement and constructing the Pentecostal phenomenon, a racialized and gendered examination of Pentecostal sound would be essential.

Third, it may be necessary for the historian of Pentecostal sound to investigate the various soundways that were present in the study of early Pentecostalism as a movement. Before investigating these soundways, the historian must learn how the study of Latino/a Pentecostal sound as a topic is lodged within Latino religious studies; how the study of African American Pentecostal sound as a topic is lodged within black religious studies; and how the study of white Pentecostal sound could be a topic within evangelical, Wesleyan, or American folk studies. After these discourses are mastered, then the investigation can begin, as the historian combs these multiple and possibly contradictory studies for angles from which to explore the construction of the early Pentecostal soundscape.

I decline to offer any guarantees as to whether a study of early Pentecostal sound can produce a conceptual framework that will steer us away from our current conceptual restrictions, but I contend that such a study, as a complement to history of time and space, offers an opportunity to make new historiographic advances.

Bibliography

Albrecht, Daniel E. *Rites in the Spirit: A Ritual Approach to Pentecostal/Charismatic Spirituality.* Sheffield: Sheffield Academic, 1999.

Boyer, Horace. *How Sweet the Song: The Golden Age of Gospel.* Washington DC: Elliot & Clark, 1995.

Brown, Uzee, Jr. "Musical Comparisons of Five Gospel Songs." Unpublished paper, 2006.

Bull, Michael. "Soundscapes of the Car: A Critical Study of Automobile Habitation." In *The Auditory Culture Reader.* Edited by Michael Bull and Les Back, 357–74. Oxford and New York: Berg, 2003.

Canetti, Elias. *Earwitness: Fifty Characters.* New York: Seabury, 1979.

Chandler, Russell. "Pasadena Cleric Recalls Mission." In *Holy Ghost Revival on Azusa Street: The True Believers.* Vol. 2. Edited by Larry Martin, 133–35. Joplin: Christian Life Books, 1998.

Cochran, Michael. "First Recorded Gospel Pianist Got Her Start in Austin: A Recent Discovery Rewrites What We Know about Arizona Dranes." *Austin American-Statesman,* March 1, 2007. http://www.austin360.com/blogs/content/music/stories/2007/02/3dranes.html

"Complain of Church Noise: Pentecostal Pastor, Colored, Summoned on Complaint of Neighbors." *The New York Times,* September 24, 1919.

Cone, James Hal. "'Let Suffering Speak': The Vocation of a Black Intellectual." In *Cornel West: A Critical Reader.* Edited by George Yancy, 105–14. Oxford: Blackwell, 2001.

Daniels, David D., III. "God Makes No Differences in Nationality: The Fashioning of a New Racial/Nonracial Identity at the Azusa Street Revival." *Enrichment Journal: A Journal for Pentecostal Ministry* (Spring 2006).

Deposition of Defendant, C. H. Mason, taken on April 27, 1908, case number 14770, Chancery Court of Shelby County, Tennessee, *Frank Avant v. C. H. Mason,* 99–101.

"Fanatical Worship of Negroes Going on at Sanctified Church." *Commercial Appeal* (Memphis), May 22, 1907.

Goff, James R. *Close Harmony: A History of Southern Gospel.* Chapel Hill: University of North Carolina, 2002.

Jackson, George Pullen. *White Spirituals in the Southern Uplands.* n.p. 1933, Reprint, 1965.

Kalu, Ogbu. *African Pentecostalism: An Introduction.* New York: Oxford University Press, 2008.

Corum, Fred T., and Rachel A. Harper Sizelove, colls. *Like as of Fire.* Republished by E. Myron Noble. Washington DC: Middle Atlantic Regional, 2001.

Mason, Mary, recompiler. *The History and Life Work of Elder C. H. Mason, Chief Apostle, and His Co-Laborers.* n.p., 1924.

McLuhan, Marshall. *Understanding Media: The Extensions of Man.* New York: McGraw-Hill, 1964.

McPherson, Aimee Semple. *This Is That.* New York: Garland, Reprint, 1985.

Moore, Paul. "Sectarian Sound and Cultural Identity in Northern Ireland." In *The Auditory Culture Reader.* Edited by Michael Bull and Les Back, 265–79. Oxford and New York: Berg, 2003.

Oliver, Paul. *Songsters and Saints: Vocal Traditions on Race Records.* Cambridge: Cambridge University Press, 1984.

Ong, Walter J. *Orality and Literacy: Technologizing of the Word.* London: Routledge, 1982.

Ramirez, Daniel. "Antonio Castaneda Nava: Charisma, Culture, and *Caudillismo.*" In *Portraits of a Generation: Early Pentecostal Leaders.* Edited by James R. Goff Jr. and Grant Wacker, 289–307. Fayetteville: University of Arkansas Press, 2002.

Robeck, Cecil M. *Azusa Street Mission and Revival. The Birth of the Global Pentecostal Movement.* Nashville: Nelson Reference & Electronic, 2006.

Roediger, David R. *Working Toward Whiteness: How America's Immigrants Became White.* New York: Basic Books, 2005.

Schafer, R. Murray. *The Tuning of the World*. London: Random House, 1977.

Schmidt, Leigh Eric. *Hearing Things, Religion, Illusion, and the American Enlightenment*. Cambridge: Harvard University Press, 2000.

Sizelove, Rachel A. "Pentecost Has Come!" In *Holy Ghost Revival on Azusa Street: The True Believers, Part 2*. Edited by Larry Martin, 75–84. Joplin: Christian Life Books, 1999.

Smith, Bruce R. "Listening to the Wild Blue Yonder: The Challenges of Acoustic Ecology." In *Hearing Cultures: Essays on Sound, Listening and Modernity*. Edited by Veit Erlmann. Oxford and New York: Berg, 2004.

———. "Tuning into London c. 1600." In *The Auditory Culture Reader*. Edited by Michael Bull and Les Back, 127–35. Oxford and New York: Berg, 2003.

Smith, Mark M. "Producing Sense, Consuming Sense, Making Sense: Perils and Prospects for Sensory History." *Journal of Social History* 40, no. 4 (Summer 2007): 841–58.

———. "Making Sense of Social History." *Journal of Social History* 37, no. 1 (2003): 165–86.

Solivan, Samuel. *The Spirit, Pathos and Liberation: Toward an Hispanic Pentecostal Theology*. Sheffield: Sheffield Academic, 1998.

Tonkiss, Fran. "Aural Postcards: Sound, Memory and the City." In *The Auditory Culture Reader*. Edited by Michael Bull and Les Back, 303–9. Oxford and New York: Berg, 2003.

Trouble in My Way. http://www.joyfulvoices.org.

Truax, Barry. *Acoustic Communication*, 2nd ed. Westport, CT: Ablex, 2001.

Valdez, A. C., Sr. "Fire on Azusa Street." In *Azusa Street: The True Believers, Part 2: More Eyewitnesses Accounts*. Edited by Larry Martin, 47–56. Joplin: Christian Life Books, 1999.

Wacker, Grant. *Heaven Below: Early Pentecostals and American Culture*. Cambridge and London: Harvard University Press, 2001.

Wald, Gayle F. *Shout, Sister, Shout!: The Untold Story of Rock-and-Roll Trailblazer Sister Rosetta Tharpe*. Boston: Beacon, 2007.

Notes

1. http://www.joyfulvoices.org
2. Elias Canetti, *Earwitness: Fifty Characters* (New York: Seabury, 1979).
3. Cecil M. Robeck, *Azusa Street Mission and Revival: The Birth of the Global Pentecostal Movement* (Nashville: Nelson Reference & Electronic, 2006), 144–49.
4. A. C. Valdez Sr., "Fire on Azusa Street," in *Azusa Street: The True Believers Part 2: More Eyewitnesses Accounts*, ed. Larry Martin (Joplin: Christian Life Books, 1999), 55, 53, 49, 50.
5. Ibid., 51–52; *Apostolic Faith* (Los Angeles), vol. 1, no. 11, October to January 1908, 2:2.
6. "Fanatical Worship of Negroes Going on at Sanctified Church," *Commercial Appeal* (Memphis) May 22, 1907, 5.
7. Daniel E. Albrecht, *Rites in the Spirit: A Ritual Approach to Pentecostal/Charismatic Spirituality* (Sheffield: Sheffield Academic, 1999), 143.
8. For the studies in the history of sound see: Mark M. Smith, "Producing Sense, Consuming Sense, Making Sense: Perils and Prospects For Sensory History," *Journal of Social History* 40, no. 4 (Summer 2007): 841–58; R. Murray Schafer, *The Tuning of the World* (London: Random House, 1977); Leigh Eric Schmidt, *Hearing Things, Religion, Illusion, and the American Enlightenment* (Cambridge: Harvard University Press, 2000).
9. Barry Truax, *Acoustic Communication*, 2d ed. (Westport, CT: Ablex, 2001), 11.
10. Bruce R. Smith, "Listening to the Wild Blue Yonder: The Challenges of Acoustic Ecology," in *Hearing Cultures: Essays on Sound, Listening and Modernity*, ed. Veit Erlmann (Oxford and New York: Berg, 2004), 22; Mark M. Smith, "Making Sense of Social History," *journal of Social History* 37, no. 1 (2003): 171; Mark M. Smith draws from Alain Corbin, *Time, Desire and Horror: Toward a History of the Senses*, trans. Jean Birrell (Cambridge, UK: Polity, 1995), 181–82, 183.
11. Bruce R. Smith, "Tuning into London c. 1600," in *The Auditory Culture Reader*, ed. Michael Bull and Les Back (Oxford and New York: Berg, 2003), 131–32.
12. On various forms of discourse used to interpret Pentecostalism see the forthcoming book by Ogbu Kalu, *African Pentecostalism: An Introduction* (New York: Oxford University Press, 2008).

13. Grant Wacker, *Heaven Below: Early Pentecostals and American Culture* (Cambridge and London: Harvard University Press, 2001), 100–102, 187.

14. Ibid., 102; *Apostolic Faith* (Los Angeles), vol. 1, no. 11 (October to January 1908), 1:2; vol. 1, no. 9 June to September 1907), 4:2.

15. Mary Mason, recompiler, *The History and Life Work of Elder C. H. Mason, Chief Apostle, and His Co-Laborers* (n.p., 1924), 30.

16. Wacker, *Heaven Below*, 235, 102.

17. Robeck, *Azusa Street Mission and Revival*, 150.

18. Russell Chandler, "Pasadena Cleric Recalls Mission," in Larry Martin, *Holy Ghost Revival on Azusa Street: The True Believers, Part 2* (Joplin: Christian Life Books, 1999), 135.

19. Rachel A. Sizelove, "Pentecost Has Come!" In Larry Martin, *Holy Ghost Revival on Azusa Street: The True Believers, Part 2* (Joplin: Christian Life Books, 1999), 79.

20. *Apostolic Faith* (Los Angeles), vol. 1, no. 3, November 1906; Robeck, *Azusa Street Mission and Revival*, 148.

21. Paul Moore, "Sectarian Sound and Cultural Identity in Northern Ireland," in *The Auditory Culture Reader*, ed. Michael Bull and Les Back (Oxford and New York: Berg, 2003), 266–67.

22. *Apostolic Faith* (Los Angeles), vol. 1, no. 3, November 1906, 1:4.

23. Schmidt, *Hearing Things*, 67.

24. Paul Oliver, *Songsters and Saint: Vocal Traditions on Race Records* (Cambridge: Cambridge University Press, 1984), 174.

25. Wacker, *Heaven Below*, 135; Robeck, *Azusa Street Mission and Revival*, 144–49.

26. *Apostolic Faith* (Los Angeles), vol. 1, no. 5, 1, in *Like as of Fire*, collected by Fred T. Corum and Rachel A. Harper Sizelove, republished by E. Myron Noble (Washington DC: Middle Atlantic Regional Press, 2001), 17; see also David D. Daniels III, "God Makes No Differences In Nationality: The Fashioning Of A New Racial/Nonracial Identity At The Azusa Street Revival," *Enrichment journal: A journal for Pentecostal Ministry* (Spring 2006).

27. David R. Roediger, *Working Toward Whiteness: How Americas Immigrants Became White* (New York: Basic Books, 2005), 50; *Apostolic Faith* (Los Angeles), vol. 1, no. 4, 1; vol. 1, no. 1, 1; vol. 1, no. 6, 1, 3, in *Like As of Fire*, 13, 1, 21, 23.

28. Daniel Ramirez, "Antonio Castaneda Nava: Charisma, Culture, and *Caudillismo*," in *Portraits of a Generation: Early Pentecostal Leaders*, ed. James R. Goff Jr. and Grant Wacker (Fayetteville: University of Arkansas Press, 2002), 299–300.

29. Aimee Semple McPherson, *This Is That* (1919, repr. New York: Garland, 1985), 137; "Complain of Church Noise: Pentecostal Pastor, Colored, Summoned on Complaint of Neighbors," *The New York Times*, September 24, 1919.

30. Gayle F. Wald, *Shout, Sister, Shout! The Untold Story of Rock-and-Roll Trailblazer Sister Rosetta Tharpe* (Boston: Beacon, 2007), 18; George Pullen Jackson, *White Spirituals in the Southern Uplands* (1933, repr. 1965).

31. Michael Cochran, "First recorded gospel pianist got her start in Austin: A recent discovery rewrites what we know about Arizona Dranes," *American-Statesman Staff*, March 1, 2007. http://www.austin360.com/blogs/content/music/stories/2007/02/3dranes.html

32. Horace Boyer, *How Sweet the Song: The Golden Age of Gospel* (Washington DC: Elliot & Clark, 1995), 38; Uzee Brown Jr. "Musical Comparisons of Five Gospel Songs." Unpublished paper, 2006.

33. Schmidt, *Hearing Things*, 7; Walter J. Ong, *Orality and Literacy: Technologizing of the Word* (London: Routledge, 1982); Marshall McLuhan, *Understanding Media: The Extensions of Man* (New York: McGraw-Hill, 1964).

34. Schmidt, *Hearing Things*, 18.

35. Ibid., 259, 22, 11, 8.

36. Mark M. Smith, "Making Sense of Social History," *journal of Social History* 37, no. 1 (2003): 169, 171; Schmidt, *Hearing Things*, 21–22, 20, 21.

37. Robeck, *Azusa Street Mission and Revival*, 137; James R. Goff, *Close Harmony: A History of Southern Gospel* (Chapel Hill, NC: University of North Carolina, 2002).

38. Michael Bull, "Soundscapes of the Car: A Critical Study of Automobile Habitation" in *The Auditory Culture Reader*, ed. Michael Bull and Les Back (Oxford and New York: Berg, 2003), 361.

39. Fran Tonkiss, "Aural Postcards: Sound, Memory and the City," in *The Auditory Culture Reader*, ed. Michael Bull and Les Back (Oxford and New York: Berg, 2003), 307.

40. Schmidt, *Hearing Things*, 35, 5.

41. *Apostolic Faith* (Los Angeles), vol. 1, no. 1, September 1906, 1:4.

42. Deposition of Defendant, C. H. Mason, taken on April 27, 1908, case number 14770, Chancery Court of Shelby County, Tennessee, *Frank Avant v. C. H. Mason*, 99–101; Apostolic Faith paper, February–March, 1907 in *Holy Ghost Revival on Azusa Street: The True Believers, Part 2*, ed. Larry Martin (Joplin, MO: Christian Life Books, 1999), 29; James Hal Cone, "'Let Suffering Speak:' The Vocation of a Black Intellectual," in *Cornel West: A Critical Reader*, ed. George Yancy (Oxford: Blackwell, 2001), 105–14.

43. Samuel Solivan, *The Spirit, Pathos and Liberation: Toward an Hispanic Pentecostal Theology* (Sheffield: Sheffield Academic, 1998), 62, 148, 61.

44. Tonkiss, "Aural Postcards," 308.

45. *Apostolic Faith* (Los Angeles), vol. 1, no. 1, September 1906, 1:3; *Apostolic Faith*, vol. 1, no. 3, November 1906, 4:4.

23
Don't Nobody Know My Troubles but God: Discursive, Social, and Aesthetic Connections and Distinctives in "Sacred" and "Secular" Black Music

Michael Fox

People are always pestering me about becoming a blues singer. They'd tell me, "Girl, you could become a great blues singer." I'd answer, "What Negro couldn't become a great blues singer!" I'll never give up my gospel songs for the blues. Blues are the songs of despair, but gospel songs the songs of hope. When you sing them, you are delivered of your burden... [but] when you get through with the blues you've got nothing to lean on.

—*Mahalia Jackson*

I call my music "Electric Church Music." The word "church" is too identified with religion, and music is my religion... I can't express myself easy in conversation—the words just don't come out right. But when I get up on stage—well, that's my whole life. That's my religion.

—*Jimi Hendrix*

On Friday night at 11:30 p.m., I was at Legends, a bar on a nondescript, poorly lit corner in downtown Chicago. The small nightclub was announced with a flamboyant neon sign, shining a glow over the almost shack-like structure that has been threatened to be bought and torn down several times, only to be saved each time by Buddy Guy, a well known blues guitarist who owns the club and uses it to promote his music and other artists within Chicago's electric urban blues scene. Tonight's show featured Carlos Johnson, a guitarist from Mississippi and one of the few musicians I've ever seen able to command silence and absolute attention merely by his presence. Dressed in a black cowboy hat and sleeveless black tank-top that clearly displays his developed muscles, he strutted on stage, sang with a growl-scream tone, threw his guitar around in an almost violent manner channeling Muddy Waters and Jimi Hendrix, and left the mostly white audience speechless. According to the stereotype, most people who patronize these types of clubs are "tourists" who possess very little cultural capital, but simply want to come to Chicago expecting to hear an elderly black man play "Sweet Home Chicago" on harmonica in a dark, smoke filled room while drinking stale beer. Carlos Johnson's ferocious display of musical virtuosity and hyper-masculinity was not exactly what they had in mind, and they reacted by starring at him in silence as one might a lion tearing through the flesh of a zebra on a safari. On the other hand, the African American patrons, and the younger, informally dressed whites who possessed enough cultural capital to understand the music (and I like to flatter myself thinking I'm in the latter category) were enraptured, yelling, applauding, and dancing in their seats to the beat with each vocal melisma, each display of guitar pyrotechnics, and each clever expression of (mostly sexual) humor in the lyrics. The only person in the club who seemed to not be reacting at all was Buddy Guy himself. A member of the Rock and Roll Hall of Fame, a man Eric Clapton calls the greatest living guitar player today, and a man who plays to sold-out areas all over the world, was nonchalantly sitting at the bar, drinking, laughing with friends, indulging in an occasional autograph, watching the baseball game on the television, and only passively paying attention to the music that has the rest of us in either bewilderment or ecstasy. After concluding a more soulful ballad that gets a uncharacteristically lukewarm response, without waiting to receive our applause, Carlos Johnson suddenly goes into "I'll Play the Blues for You," a minor-blues that has become one of the standards of the Chicago-blues art world. In fact, it's one of the songs that constitutes what some musicians refer to as the "Set-list from Hell," of songs that everyone expects to hear, and often bores those who have to perform it. Even as energetic a performer as Carlos seemed to go into this song half-heartily, as he sighs and begins to sing:

> If you're down and out and you feel real hurt
> Come on over to the place where I live
> And all your loneliness I'll try to soothe
> I'll play the blues for you

Without any exterior invitation from the band, Buddy suddenly got up and walked toward the stage, took the microphone off its stand and started an uninvited duet with Carlos on the second verse. The effect on the audience was mesmerizing. Everyone's reacts to Guy's presence on stage, making cheers, laughter, and applause that almost drowned out the music. The man sitting next to me, a 30-something male from Sweden in Chicago for his vacation, who reacted to Carlos with little more then polite applause, turned to me and starts laughing and yelling. After singing a verse by himself, Buddy Guy announces "This band is sounding so good, and since I own this joint, I have the right to come up here when I want to and just fuck things up. So, just let me get my guitar, and then I'll play the blues." Carlos Johnson reacted to this by immediately playing his most aggressive solo of the night, with rapid tremolo strums that slide to the upper limits of his instrument, even lifting his guitar above his head to play behind his back. After the solo, Buddy Guy reemerged from a backstage room, and played an equally blistering solo that concluded with him playing with his teeth. Then, the two stood, facing each other, and traded off four bar solos, with one creating a lick, and the other "answering" it with something related but more virtuosic. Each guitarist attempted to outdo each other, creating a drama of a recurring rhythmic pattern played faster and higher each time. After four choruses, and numerous shouts of "Yeah!", whistles, claps, and enraptured closed-eyes and bodies swaying to the rhythm from the audience, Buddy Guy took the microphone, and improvises one chorus with a voice that uses shouts, moans, flamboyant, gospel-like melismas, and high screeching notes. The song then concluded with both guitarists releasing a flurry of notes from their instruments. As everyone in the house started to applaud and cheer wildly, Buddy Guy simply walked off, shoved himself through the mob of people now wanting to bestow affirmation, and sat back down on his space in the bar, as Carlos Johnson diffused what felt like a near-riot by saying "Whoo! That's what I love about playing at Legends, and what I love about the blues in general. You never know what's going to happen. Well, that just about wore me out, so we're gonna take a break, but please don't go away, we'll be right back, and I have CDs, if anyone wants them, but let me warn you, I never play the same song the same way twice, so it's gonna be a little different."

A few days later, on Sunday morning, a very different, but equally energetic crowd gathered in the St. Sabina Faith Community, an elegant neo-gothic Catholic church visually modified with artwork suggestive of Africa, and a huge mural of Jesus Christ as a black African being delivered into the hands of God the Father. The church's visual aesthetic came out of an attempt to reinterpret an ancient religious heritage within an African American cultural context. In a similar way, the church reinterpreted the Mass as an extended, revival-like time of praise and worship. Unlike the blues club, the people, regardless of skin color, seemed to react in more homogeneous ways. While the majority of worshipers are African American, there is a highly visible minority of whites and Latino/as, who adapted to the encultured service, and reacted in similar ways as the black members. After several other, more fast and celebratory songs, the choir and musicians started to sing a song that was originally a folk-rock worship chorus, but that music leader Michael Drayton has readapted, arranged, and reharmonized into a blues song that can be performed by the church's Levites, the choir that leads the service:

> There is no one else for me
> None but Jesus

> Crucified to set me free
> Now I live to bring him praise.

Almost immediately as the song starts, nearly everyone sang along, in harmony and confidently. This indicates that most of the people attending the service possessed a knowledge of this song (unlike many other churches, St. Sabina does not usually use hymnals or lyric sheets during the time of singing), and an understanding that it is appropriate to sing along with the choir, showing a mostly homogeneous and high level of cultural capital among those attending the service. This chorus was repeated several times, with the congregation getting louder each time. Some people start to stand up and wave their hands with the song's beat. As the choir and congregation continued singing this song, Father Michael Pflager, the white priest who leads the services with a style highly suggestive of African American preaching, began to emotionally reflect on the meaning of this song, and chastised the congregation for not responding enough:

> Oh, yes! Lord, you have been crucified to set us free, and we worship you. You know that Jesus has been good to you, but do you really believe that there is nothing else but him for you? Do you really want to worship him, not for his stuff, but because he is God. I need some worshipers right now. Where are my worshipers? Come on worship him, worship him, worship him, open up your mouth and worship him, worship him! Come on, speak to the Lord, and lavish love on him, tell Jesus, "Even if you never did another thing for me, I will keep worshiping you, because you are worthy, and I long to be in your presence." Oh, please won't *somebody* just worship him, worship him!

As Pastor Pflager continued, some of the Spirit of David dancers, who are also a part of the church's worship team, began to express their worship by standing in the aisle or around the altar, and swaying their entire bodies back and forth and lifting their arms up and down rapidly. Pflager took notice of their movements, and then asked "Can we have some other people, not in Spirit of David to dance in the aisle and around the holy altar, and really usher in the presence of God?" Four black women, and one white man moved to the aisle and started imitating the dancer's motions. At this, people all over the sanctuary began to sing louder, nearly everyone stood up and raised their arms, and a few started shouting "Woo!" or "Oh yes Lord! We worship and adore you! You are holy! Hallelujah!" The instruments then stopped playing, and the chorus was repeated a cappella a few times. The choir got softer and then stopped, but the congregation kept singing and "worshiping" through their outstretched arms and loud shouts. Although a few people kept shouting "Give him the glory! Hallelujah! Yes Lord!" most everyone erupted into applause, and then sat down as an assistant minister walked to the podium to begin reading the first liturgical scripture passage for the Mass. This reading served as a reminder that in spite of, or perhaps because of, the unique, highly encultured celebration of praise of this church, it was still strongly rooted in a church and religious tradition that it shares with millions of believers worldwide.

These two experiences in some ways could not have been more different from each other. The party atmosphere of the blues bar and the reverent ceremonies of the black Catholic Church may at first appear to have very little in common with each other. However, both were contemporary manifestations of a common aesthetic tradition that goes back to the moans, spirituals, and work songs born of transplanted Africans forced into slave labor in the United States. Shaped by the life experiences of a common people grappling with an unequal status as non-citizens in America, the rival art communities of sacred and secular music shared both common origins and a common concern for using emotion to build a sense of community among musicians and listeners, that can be seen through the history of the rich contributions people of African decent have made to the music of the United States. Even though the social setting of the church and the urban nightclub may be very different, these connections and interactions between the categories of "sacred" and "secular" continue to the present day. The purpose of this paper is to investigate how these historical connections and common social goals play out in contemporary settings, and will use participant-observation among different churches and music clubs in Chicago to explore the connections and conflicts between Sunday morning and Saturday night.

My interest in this topic came out of my status as a Christian and musician who is strongly drawn to the contributions African Americans have made to both religion and music. As a violinist who felt deeply restricted by classical styles of performance, the emotionally-free and improvisational-based blues and blues styles of performance offered opportunities for emotional release and an expression of my individual creativity. In a similar way, my spiritual explorations into black styles of worship have altered my perspectives on what true Christian worship is, as well as helped me acquire a deeper understanding of the role Jesus' teachings play in efforts to reorganize society. For me, I have found that white American aesthetic culture, both "sacred" and "secular" is too often sheltered from real emotional experience, and I have found many examples of African American music, from spirituals and gospel to blues, jazz, soul and hip hop that have, in their attempt to grapple with oppressive social conditions and fight against a larger culture context that denied them human dignity, given solace and release to all people, and shown a way for me to honestly confront my emotional experiences. For this reason, it was frequently tempting for me to romanticize the musical and religious events I researched in this paper. Even though my ethnic background marked me as somewhat of an outsider, I still often felt deeply interpersonally connected with the performers, and may have never succeeded in fully detaching myself and my responses to the music from the impact the music is designed to have on its community.

For this reason, I was deeply indebted to many of the countless Musicologists, Sociologists, Anthropologists, Theologians, Historians, Cultural Theorists, and others who have written on related topics. Because of the overwhelming influence that African American music has had on popular music in the U.S., and therefore on musical discourse all over the world, it was easy to get lost in the countless examinations, histories, and ethnographies that have been done on African American music, both within and apart from the culture's deep rooted-ness in its particular form of Christianity. Partially helpful was Paul Berliner's examination of the process of jazz improvisation (1994), David Grazin's study of contemporary blues clubs and suggestion that attempts to appreciate blues were tempered within a "quest for authenticity" (2003), Glenn Hanson's look at how ideas about "the spirit" affected African American Christian worship services (2000), and the attempts of LeRoi Jones/Amiri Baraka (1963), Charles Keil (1963), and above all Jon Michael Spenser (1990 and 1993), to demonstrate how these musical forms were deeply tied to the larger political, social, and religious context that produced them.

Geertz suggested that both a society's collective behaviors and people's response to artistic works are a cultural creation, and that work within "his audience's capacities" to appropriately interpret the art object (Geertz 1983: 116). Art should not be studied merely as objects in and of themselves, but as social events that interact within a society and reveal that community's deep structure. Ethnomusicologist Christopher Small applied Geertz's reasoning to the study of the musical creation in the African Diaspora by introducing the concept of "to music" as a verb, because "Music is not primarily a thing or a collection of things, but an activity in which we engage." He used the term *musicking*, meaning "the art of taking part in a musical performance" (Small 1987: 50), as either "performer" or member of an "audience." Traditional discourse on musical performance has suggested a strong divide between the "composer/performer" who creates music, and the "listener" who passively accepts the artistic creation. However, according to Small's definitions, both those creating the music and those participating in it can be said to be *musicking*; that is, fully participating in the musical process. In African American musical performance especially, lines between performer and listener are frequently blurred. If Western "classical" music (and, to somewhat of a lesser extent, the traditional liturgical structure of the Latin Mass) can be considered a monologue, in which participants create an aesthetic experience which is silently received and appreciated by others, blues, and other forms of African American popular music (and most dramatically within a Sanctified/Pentecostal worship service), is much more of a dialogue in which those creating music and those appreciating are expected to interact with each other.

Durkheim theorized that, "All known religious beliefs, whether simple or complex, present one common characteristic: they presuppose a classification of all the things, real, and ideal, of which men think, into two classes or opposed groups, generally designated by two distinct term... *profane* and *sacred*" (1915: 52). Certainly, in much of African American music, this dynamic and tension between sacred and profane is seen very explicitly. In particular, blues and gospel music, although musically very similar, were frequently described as being morally opposed. The use of call-and-response, the pentatonic scale, driving shuffle rhythms, and highly emotional styles of vocal embellishment that both styles of music share have not stopped many musicians and theologians in the black community from believing that one musical style came from God, and the other came from the Devil. Blues musician Son House used to also work as a preacher, but felt he could not be both a minister and a musician, because "I can't hold God in one hand and the Devil in the other" (quoted in Spenser 1990: 119). The church and the juke joint formed two separate spaces, one sacred and one profane, and even though both became centers of musical production in the black community, it was assumed that art coming out of the later was sinful, while the former was God-honoring. Some blues musicians, such as Robert Johnson or Bessie Smith, even had mythologies built around them as being "lowdown" or demonic.

However, a more in depth look at African American music can be used to critique Durkheim's universalizing theory, because the categories of sacred "gospel music" and "sinful blues" are really not that clean-cut, but form two art worlds that frequently intersect and influence each other. Some researchers even claim that, in the West African context from which African slaves came, Durkheim's idea of religion as *inevitably* producing a sacred/profane dichotomy does not apply. Among such groups as the Ashanti, Yorba, or Dogon, the idea of a dichotomy between religious and secular music would have been absurd. For them, "all of life is manifestly religious. . . Birth, death, puberty, fertility, harvest, famine, marriage, and tragedy all have religious rites to give expression to the event" (Walker 1979: 28). Religion was not disconnected from the rest of society, but consisted of rituals inherently connected to all areas of life. Music, in turn, served the function of facilitating these rituals, making it easier for the rites to be remembered and properly passed down through the oral traditions. This made for a society in which "music is intrinsically spiritual, the sacred is intrinsically musical, and both music and the divine permeate every imaginable part of life" (Reed 2003: 5).

There is some debate about how much traditional African culture influenced the emerging slave culture. Sidney Mintz and Richard Price made the argument that the new context of American slavery caused dramatic culture changes among slaves, since "They were not able to transfer the human complement of their traditional institutions" (Mintz-Price 1976: 18–19). On the other hand, LeRoi Jones claimed that the American slaves maintained very strong cultural ties to their African cultural symbols. "Just as some of the African customs survived in American in their totality, although usually given just a thin veneer of Euro-American camouflage, so pure African songs, dances and instruments showed up on this side of the water" (Jones 1963: 27). Regardless, the Africans forced into slavery did maintain call-and-response patterns, syncopated polyrhythm, and the minor pentatonic scale, among other musical elements. They also kept their rejection of a sacred/secular dichotomy, until further engagement with European-American culture caused them to allow conflicting ideas about the nature of music in society.

In a new cultural context, the African slaves were introduced to many other new concepts and ideas, one of the more influential of which was Christianity. However, for the most part, slaves were officially given a very watered-down form of theology. Forbidden to read for themselves, the form of Christianity declared to slaves in official, segregated churches amounted to little more than a support of the slavery system that emphasized verses such as "slaves, obey your masters" (Ephesians 6:5), but had little to say about "The spirit of the Lord is upon me. . . to proclaim liberty to the captives." (Isaiah 61:1). In response to this, the slaves risked punishment to gather in the backwoods for "underground churches" in which "the slaves formulated new ideas and practices on their own and specifically colored religious principles with a pronounced longing for freedom" (Walker 1979: 30). Out of these gatherings, the spiritual, in which the universal concepts of biblical truth fit into the difficulty of the localized community developed (Walker 1979: 51). These spirituals fulfilled many different roles in the slave community, expressing longings for both for the release of heaven, and uniting the community in a desire for freedom in this life as well:

> Oh freedom, oh freedom
> Oh freedom over me
> Before I'd be a slave
> I'll be buried in my grave
> And go home to my Lord and be free.
> —*African American Heritage Hymnal*, #545

Some scholars make a distinction between the "spiritual" which used religious imagery, and "sorrow songs" that were more directly related to the cruel conditions of slavery. For Wyatt Tee Walker, such a distinction is not appropriate, since "the social context of both. . . created generally a parallel development of both strains" with a "similarity of form and rhythm. It is not uncommon to find religious songs with touches of humor and work or play songs with religious references" (1979: 40).

The strong dichotomy between sacred and secular one finds in current African American musical discourse did not really emerge until after the Civil War led to emancipation for African slaves. The establishment of independent black churches, in both Baptist forms and Richard Allen's African Methodist Episcopal Church, often had the counterintuitive effect of making African American worship styles more similar to those of other American Protestant churches. In an attempt to give dignity to black Christianity (in the eyes of Euro-American Christians), hymnals were composed and worship services were controlled and using more elements from the Wesleyan hymn tradition.

At the same time that worship services were becoming more structured, the mobility given to people at the end of slavery allowed the production of new social roles—the musician as entertainer. For people who felt trapped within the sharecropping system, which was really slavery under slightly different economic terms, becoming a musician and traveling offered economic intendance. In the words of jazz musician Nicole Mitchell:

> There was a rift, [between "gospel" and "jazz."] And it was really a generational rift—It wasn't so much a rift between "church folk" and jazz musicians, but it was really a rift between parents and kids. . . You have to think about the society during the time, post-slavery where there were not that many opportunities for black men to make a living. And this was an opportunity, you know, if you had a guitar, and you could sing, you could be your own boss. . . and get yourself around. . . so it was something that was very attractive to people—I can make a living, I can be my own boss. (interview)

Even when, through the emergence of Pentecostal/Sanctified churches, the musical gap between sacred and secular music was narrowed, this only caused the social stigma between the two worlds to grow stronger. Pierre Bourdieu suggested that different social structures, such as the conflicting ones presented by the church and the localized black entertainment industry, created a playing field for power relationships which can "shape the practical representation of one's social person, the self-image which governs the behaviors of sociability. . . and more generally, one's whole manner of conducting oneself in the social world" (1976). The church in particular, offers many opportunities for people growing up in it to learn about music and have opportunities to perform, and receive affirmation for every attempt to dedicate their music to the Lord (Priest 1998 and Reed 2003). One observer noted a time when,

> Before the service began, a frail boy of seven years propped himself up amid the components of an enormous drum set. . . The child thrashed about on the drum skins, attempting to maintain a steady beat and to perform rhythms that fit the changing musical parts around him. Every eye was upon the young drummer who beamed with tremendous pride as he performed (Berliner 1994: 25).

Conversely, the blues and blues world also offered many opportunities to perform, but within the different social settings of performance that in turn control the way the music would be created, and the way the music is understood in the outside world. Ms. Mitchell claims that,

> I think the reason why jazz kind of has had a stain on its reputation in terms of respect. . . part of it is because of Prohibition. When this country had Prohibition, it became a counter-cultural expression to have these clubs, these holes-in-the-wall, that was, it was against the law. . . African American culture, and the expression of jazz was the "cool" thing to use as the atmosphere for this type of environment, because that was seen as counter-cultural, for white Americans to partake in this life. . . The two became connected, and this became an avenue for musicians to exploit. But, with the earliest forms, there were a lot of other venues for the music. . . They had lawn parties, all types of dance halls, it was really a part of everybody's life. So, this whole thing about it starting up in the red-light district—I think that's kind of exaggerated. (interview)

As these two art worlds became more and more distinct, people wanting to be involved in music had to make a choice of which artistic community they would be a part of, a choice that might radically alter what kind of art they produced. This is demonstrated vividly though a comparison of two different autobiographies of prominent musicians. Mahalia Jackson talks about how her cousin, after seeing Mahalia sing in church, encouraged her to get into show business, but "I stayed home, and it changed my whole life" (1966: 17). Even though she privately enjoyed listening to Bessie Smith, Jackson refused to become a part of the blues art world, and remained loyal to the church and to creating explicitly Christian music her entire life. By contrast, David "Honeyboy" Edwards did not believe it was necessary to become part of the church, even after he "got saved," since "Once you got it... God don't give you nothing and take it back. You have [your religion] until you die because that's what he gives to you in your younger days. You've prayed enough and he forgives you" (1997: 12). By refusing to become a more active part of the church, Honeyboy's musical talent was utilized in other settings, often informal gatherings through an entertainment-based network with limited possibilities, in which he hitchhiked as "a musician on the road with a guitar, cars would stop and pick [me] up. 'Where y'all going? Play me some music, y'all!' We'd fall in the back and play the blues. Sometimes they'd stop and get us a drink, buy us a sandwich" (1997: 41).

However, in spite of all of these stated differences, there were many times in which these moral-social categories interceded with and influenced each other. According to Teresa Reed, many secular artists were influenced profoundly and, in turn they influenced the way "improvisation, emotional intensity, dramatic physical expression, and community interaction" played out in African American Christian worship (2003: 16). The interaction can be seen clearly even in the part of the music that is frequently the most distinct—the lyrics. "A blues verse can be changed into a religious one. We can take a line like 'Lord, I ain't seen my baby since she been gone,'... and modify it to 'Lord, come see about me.' Whether petitioned by the church folks in their spirituals or by 'juke' folks in their blues, God was the reference source in times of trouble" (Spenser 1993: 38), because the moral framework of Protestant and Holiness Christianity had an impact on every section of African American culture, not only those who chose to use the institutional church for all their musical expression.

One person who did more than anyone else to bring these seemingly conflicting worlds together was Thomas Dorsey, a blues musician who joined the church and applied the knowledge of music he gained as a pianist, arranger, and sideman for Bessie Smith to create "gospel songs" that worked (some might say reworked) blues sounds into African American worship. "As a performer he noted often that people responded similarly to blues whether heard in the theater or at an intimate gathering. Their responses, moreover, were virtually identical to moments of similar emotional appeal in churches" (Harris 1992: 96). In a sense, one could say that Dorsey "baptized" blues musical techniques by altering the discourse under which performance took place. In particular, the blues musician's talent for improvisation was altered, not in practice but in the way it was communicated. "Blues was a conduit for feeling, but the particular feeling at a given performance and the embellishments and other performance techniques used to express or evoke it were options exercised solely by the performer. Particularly for gospel blues this freedom of choice was important, for in the matter of religion. . . one had to surrender oneself to the inspiration of God" (Harris 1992: 100). A more common event for black musicians was the reverse movement from the church into the entertainment industry, particularly beginning in the 1950s, when record companies began to increase dramatically the impact and availability African American popular music on the larger U.S. musical framework. Teresa Reed provides a short list of "secular" performance artists who grew up and learned music primarily from the church, including "James Brown, Ruth Brown, Sam Cooke, DeBarge, Roberta Flack, Aretha Franklin, Marvin Gaye, Whitney Houston, Louis Jordan, B. B. King, Gladys Knight, Tina Turner, Dinah Washington, and Stevie Wonder" (Reed 2003: 12). In fact, Aretha's father was the Rev. C. L. Franklin, a very prominent minister in Detroit who pioneered the idea of recording his sermons and selling them commercially and hence became known worldwide as a model of African American preaching styles. (Some have suggested that it was influence and power in the recording industry that was a strong factor in creating Aretha Franklin's worldwide success.) In an invocation that opens for Aretha's "gospel album" (*One Lord, One Faith, One Baptism*) C. L.'s son, Rev. Cecil Franklin, who took the pulpit from his father, praised Aretha's musical career and called it a "unique advantage of preaching the gospel into the world through song" (Franklin 2003), thus implied at least a limited sanction for church musicians performing "in the world."

However, according to my interviewed subjects, this tension and stigma between performing both within and apart from the church still exists. Michael Drayton, who leads and directs the music for St. Sabina's services stated that he was "[kicked] out of [the Holiness/Apostolic] church at 16, and my music was called devil music," out of what he calls "ignorance" of pastors to fully appreciate the good that can come out of supposedly "secular" music. In his view, "we are all secular until the Blood of Jesus washes us," and it is frivolous to "delineate between good music and bad, most of the musicians I know tend to focus more on sounds and instrumentation not necessarily lyrical content" (Drayton, e-mail correspondence 2007). Likewise, Miles Tate, who plays piano in both a church and jazz setting, even said that "some people in the church think I'm going to hell because I play jazz" (Tate, personal interview 2007).

As part of this project, I attended Sunday morning worship services and weekend evening concerts at multiple churches and music clubs. Legends, a blues club in the South Loop of Chicago, had become a central tourist attraction due to its ownership by Buddy Guy, indeed, it acts as a virtual shrine to blues music, with walls covered with instruments, photographs, autographs, and other paraphernalia commemorating great musicians who have either inspired or had a relationship with Buddy Guy. One of the most prominent of these include a painting of a "Mount Rushmore" with the labeled faces of Muddy Waters, Sonny Boy Williamson, Howlin' Wolf, and Willie Dixon, carved into stone. As a performance space, Legends features two distinct spaces of listening, which, for the most part, seem to accommodate two types of listeners and fit them within either sectioned space:

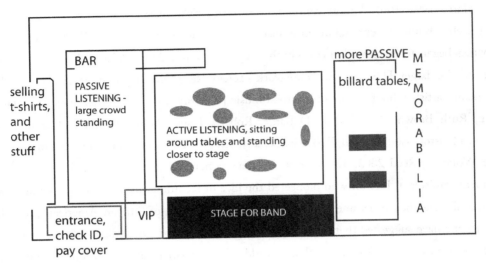

Buddy Guy's Legends, September 2007

Those engaged in passive listening, and sitting or standing farther away from the stage were not really outwardly acknowledging the music. Instead, they seemed to treat the music as background for talking with other people. They sometimes stopped for applause (but not necessarily even after every song), and don't really respond outwardly at any other time. On the other hand, those listening actively, and trying to get closer to the stage, looked at the band performing, danced or moved to the beat in their chair. During particularly engaging times, these types of listeners would lean forward "into" the performer, sometimes closing eyes, laughing at the jokes between songs and sexual innuendo of the songs, and sometimes yelling or cheering during a solo.

The Velvet Lounge is a blues club in Chicago's South Side, on East Cermak. It is also owned by a noted Chicago musician, Fred Anderson, a saxophonist very influential in the more avant-garde forms of Chicago jazz. It is interesting to note the recent emergence of clubs built around certain well-known musicians; this may reflect a certain level of dissatisfaction performers have with the nightclub atmosphere, and a desire to create spaces that allow for more experimentation and are more hospitable to creators of music. This is clearly evident in the atmosphere of the "Velvet"; the very small seating space discouraged any forms of passive listening, and so nearly everyone listens very in depth, and is forced to concentrate on the music only. In this diagram, in a performance from September 22, I have distinguished the race and gender of each person and performer:

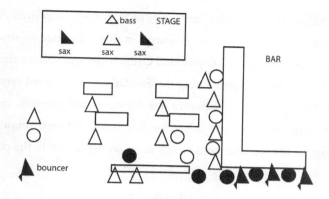

Velvet Lounge, September 22, 2007

The comparison within these two clubs indicates how, even within this common art world of African American "secular" music, there were some social difference and divisions based on genre of music. Even though the electric blues and the modernist jazz of the Artists' Association for Creative Musicians were both considered pivotal in Chicago's black music "scene," and are often distributed through similar channels (most notably through the music store Jazz Record Mart), there are many differences on how musicking takes place in both stylistic frameworks. At Velvet concerts, people's reactions were quieter and more internal: tapping feet instead of dancing, clapping quietly after solos instead of cheering, and closing eyes and leaning back instead of laughing and nodding heads to the rhythm.

One characteristic that distinguishes both clubs from both churches rather dramatically is that people sat by themselves, and generally avoided interaction with other people experiencing the musical creations. On the other hand, both churches I looked at considered the Sunday morning service a social time, both formally (through the sharing of prayer requests and recognizing of members who had a birthday or succeeded in getting a scholarship) and informally (through countless waves, smiles, and hand shakes before, during, and after the service). Many people came as families, or husband and wife, but the people who came alone were encouraged by the ushers to sit together; having empty pews was considered preferable to letting people sit by themselves. This physical closeness even becomes used multiple times in the service, when both preacher frequently stressed theological messages by saying something such as, "Turn to the person next to you and say 'Neighbor!—Do you know how much Jesus loves you?'" and people would turn towards each other, making eye-contact and repeating what the pastor told them to repeat to each other at the same time.

The two churches I looked at were Second Baptist, a small independent Baptist church in a western suburb of Chicago and the Faith Community of St. Sabina, an African American Catholic parish located in Chicago's South Side, in Auburn-Gresham. In spite of dramatic theological differences that might exist between the Baptist and Catholic denominations, the *practiced theology*, as was demonstrated and communicated during the Sunday service, differed very little. There was, however, a dramatic difference in how the space was decorated and prepared. Second Baptist was designed in a mostly functional way, to allow for interaction between musicians, singers, and ministries in directing the service, and focusing attention on the person in the pulpit:

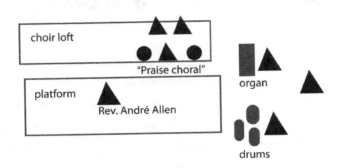

Second Baptist Church, October 2007

There were no overly religious symbols, except for a wooden cross above the choir section. On the other hand, St. Sabina, in keeping both with its visually-orientated style of Catholic worship, and its efforts to integrate African culture into its worship style, utilized art work extensively in the sanctuary.

In addition, Second Baptist used organ and drums for all of its accompaniment, while Sabina uses a fuller band featuring piano, congas and percussion, saxophone, and trumpet. The music covered in both locations is of a wide variety, including hymns, gospel songs, and CCM/Christian rock praise choruses, but all of it is rearranged, with new rhythms and harmonies to fit within the framework of the black gospel tradition. Both services open with an extended time of singing that begins at a slow level, and then begins to pick up in emotional intensity, interrupted at times when ministers will pray or exhort the congregation to worship further. Sermons follow the worship segment; these are usually preceded through improvised talking that connects the time of worship with the sermon about to be delivered, giving the entire service a feeling of flow and cognitive unity. In Sabina, this was followed by a more liturgical portion of the service that concluded with the Eucharist. According to Minister Drayton, the church has received some criticism for "not being Catholic enough," and allowing black Baptist and Pentecostal styles of worship to overwhelm traditional Catholic worship styles. However, speaking of a similar black Catholic church in San Francisco, Mary McGain says, "it's a question of rhythm, I've discovered... It requires the tension of two divergent impulses. One is stable and recurring. . . The other impulse is improvised, syncopated, unpredictable, ever unfolding, and constantly reconfigured by those making the music" (McGain 2004: 19). Sabina's unique worship came about through a blend, and negotiation of the tension of "Catholic," highly regulated worship styles with "African American" free-flowing ideas of improvisation. They did not approach the liturgy as a classical musician does, following each word in the missal directly as written down. Rather, they looked to the liturgy as a jazz musician looks at a song and its chord changes, allowing the sub-structure and basic framework to provide a guideline under which the musician/priest adapted based on personal reflections and perceived needs of the moment.

Indeed, the dynamic of improvisation was seen through the way *all* African American music that I've looked at was performed, in the contexts of both the church and the nightclub. In fact, "Both jazz and sermonic compositions tend to have supersaturate, instead of which intermediary for is created by the antistructural means of improvisation" (Spenser 1990: 243). Improvisation does not mean, as some people think, that the artist or preacher simply makes things up randomly or loses control of the creative processes. On the contrary, the antistructure of improvisation is in fact carefully crafted to fit into an aural and performed schema that creates an emotional effect on the listener. The goal of this schema is to start out at a low level of tension, frequently with a lot of negative space/silence, and then through increasing the level of notes, increasing the volume, and allowing for repetition of themes in a circular pattern, raising the tension up to a climax, and then letting the listener down to a quick release. A saying they have in the church is "Go slow, rise high, catch on fire, and then sit down" (Hinson 2000: 275). Jazz musician Kenny Barrons explains it as "You start off just playing very simply. . . and as the intensity builds, if it does, your ideas can become a little more complicated" (Berliner 1994: 201). Even though the terms of the discourse may be slightly distinct, in praxis the performance of a sermon and a good improvised solo are very similar, as I will hope to demonstrate through extended analysis of both. Because I was not permitted to make recordings in any of the nightclubs I went to, I'm going to be using a live recording of Big Mama Thornton's performance of "Ball and Chain" from a concert in New York, but I heard similar ways of building up the emotional energy of a performance during my research. I then will compare that with a sermon given by Second Baptist's Pastor André Allen during an 11 a.m. service.

"Big Mama's" song began very quietly, with the instruments very deliberately trying to keep things down and remain in the background, with the guitar and piano largely playing chords and perfect fifths against Thornton's rather straightforward vocal style:

> Sitting by my window, looking out at the rain
> Sitting by my window, looking out at the rain
> You know, something struck me, clapped on, like a ball
> and chain.

In the second stanza, everything got noticeably louder. Thornton's voice moves away from the smooth sound of the beginning into a growl:

> Hey Baby! Why you wanna do these mean things to me?
> Hey Baby! Why you wanna do these mean things to me?
> Because you know I love you, and I'm so sick and tired of being in
> misery.

On the repetition of the first line, she repeats the word "Hey" two times, hitting the note quickly and then trailing off into a moan, increasing the level of emotional urgency, and the guitar and piano respond by becoming more flamboyant in the licks they insert between lines. The chorus ("Hey Baby") is repeated again, and this time she holds the word "Hey" on a very high note and high volume for several beats, causing some people in the audience to shout encouragement. After this verse, the drummer made several hits concluding with a cymbal crash, Thornton shouted the encouragement "I want you to play your soul, now," and the guitarist began to solo. The guitar solo began with only a few licks, of a single rhythm on different notes with a lot of silence in between. (S)He then slid up to a high note, and then back down, and created a lick that gets repeated several times, raising the emotional intensity noticeably. (S)He repeated a note in eighth notes, then in sixteenth notes, and finally in thirty-second notes. By the time a second chorus rolled around, the guitarist was strumming a single chord in a rapid tremolo pattern, which gets moved up the instrument, until (s)he started "screeching" on an extremely high note. Then, silence. The crowd erupted into applause and cheering, thinking the solo was over, but then the guitar kept playing, first at a low volume, and then crescendoing to a higher dynamic level than before. In order to keep the sense of tension building, the piano came in and started a "rocking" syncopated triplet rhythm. Because the solo had already explored the high limits of the instrument, it went into the lower register, sliding on the lowest string to create a rumbling effect. As the solo drew to a close, a saxophone section, which was not audible on the recording before, hit a single chord and then slid down in pitch. Thornton began to sing again, and when she got to the chorus again, the band changed the rhythm, playing on every swung eighth notes at a louder volume. The piece then draws to a close, in a way that resolved the melody, without in any way decreasing the emotional intensity, as follows:

BIG MAMA: Why do everything have to happen to me?

GUITAR, PIANO, HORNS: *Four swung eighth-notes rhythm*

BIG MAMA: Because I know my love gonna last forever

GUITAR, PIANO, HORNS: *Four swung eighth-notes rhythm*

BIG MAMA: It's gonna last

GUITAR: *Hits chord single time*

BIG MAMA: I said it's got to last (*louder*)

GUITAR, DRUMS: *Hit chord single time together*

BIG MAMA: I know it's gonna la:::st (*embellishes with melisma*)

GUITAR, PIANO, HORNS, DRUMS: *Hit chord single time together*

BIG MAMA: [*spoken*] Woooh! Great God 'dmighty

BIG MAMA: For all etern:::ity

GUITAR: *Sliding lick to down motion*

BIG MAMA: Ball and Cha-:::::in

GUITAR, DRUMS, HORNS, PIANO: *Improvises at the same time, randomly*

BIG MAMA: [*hums/moans on blues scale*]

Rev. Allen began his sermon on October 14, 2007 by validating the children's choir performance that had preceded him:

PASTOR A. A.: Anybody been blessed already?

CROWD: Amen (*clapping*)

PASTOR A. A.: Anybody been encouraged already?

(*clapping gets louder*)

PASTOR A. A.: Let's give God a hand-clap of praise.

CROWD: (*clapping gets louder*) Amen! Thank you, Lord!

Following a prayer, he went straight into the scripture reading, which he directed the congregation to "stand for the reading of God's word," out of a reverent recognition that the words of the Bible are a pivotal part of the church's beliefs. He announced the three passages he's going to be preaching from, and reads them all at the beginning of the service. People are encouraged to have their own Bibles with them, and the pastor waited for people to find the passage in their own Bibles before he started reading. Concluding the reading, he announces the title of his sermon:

PASTOR A. A.: For a few minutes I want to speak on "Good News for Hurting People."

CROWD: (*softly, together*) hmm. . .

PASTOR A. A.: Good news for hurting people.

He then proceeds to build on the two themes laid out, the first one of the reality of human pain, and the second on how God offers good news. The bulk of the beginning of his sermon consisted of him talking about different forms of pain, suffering, and disappointment with God that some people in his church were experiencing. To compliment the strong sense of his words, he inflected and emphasized certain words, and spoke very slowly, holding certain words out in an attempt to emphasize his sympathy, causing people to respond in empathy to show they related to what the pastor described:

PASTOR A. A.. . . umm. . . Reading in the Bible and going to church and reading that God is a healer, and yet you've had (*getting louder*) this physical ailment for a l:::::::ong time. You've heard the testimonies of others, you've seen testimonies on television about how God is healing them, and yet you wonder: Why not me God? How—how come I have not experienced a miracle? Why do I seem to keep being passed by? Why don't you come see about your child?

When the response he's getting was not enough to continue the conversation between him and his church, Pastor Allen said certain stock phrases to encourage people to vocally respond more:

CROWD: (*a few voices*) Amen

PASTOR A. A.: Are there any witnesses in the house?

CROWD: (*many more people, louder*) Amen. Yes, yes.

He then shifted from expressing the "reality" that life is full of pain and hurt, to the "hope" of the good news that Jesus offers. To compliment the strong level of rejoicing that should complement this new focus, he started speaking faster and at a higher pitch, using repetition of phrases to both mentally and emotionally emphasis his point:

PASTOR A. A.:. . . I'm here today to tell you that (*voice higher and faster*) there's good news for the poor. Amen. Even when others have looked down on you, even if you're a have-not, in God's eyes, you are somebody.

CROWD: Amen. That's Right.

PASTOR A. A.: Hello, somebody. You count with God no matter how much money you have, no matter what's in your bank account (*voice gets faster and higher, tone rising and falling on each phrase*), no matter how many pairs of jeans, or how many pairs of shoes, or how many toys you have, no matter what kind of house, or apartment, you live in, you matter to God. Are there any witnesses in the house?

CROWD: Amen!

As the pastor continued raising his voice, and creating repeated phrases, people's responses became more unified. What began as scattered responses, of different words at different times throughout the congregation becomes much more of unified response of shouting, clapping, or saying "Yes" or "Amen" in rhythmic unity.

PASTOR A. A.:. . . I've got some good news for somebody: You don't have to wait till the deacons show up

CROWD: (*starts applauding over pastor*) "Yes. Amen! Come on!"

PASTOR A. A.: You don't have to wait till the preacher shows up, you don't have to wait till the preacher shows up. But YOU can ask him, YOU can seek, YOU can knock. Oh hallelujah!

As the pastor continues to "build up" and "catch a fire," he begins to make his sermon even more musical, as he allows the repetition of a phrase to take on a rhythmic quality, and he will even start chanting on a single note or phrase built on one or two pentatonic scale degrees.

PASTOR A. A.: O::::h Hallelujah! I'm so glad that when **you got faith in Christ** (ugh) (*chanted on the same pitch*) Hallelujah! You're name is written in the Lamb's book of life. (ugh) And even without **faith in Christ** (ugh) you're still God's child, you still *matter* (*voice raises up*), because God is no respecter of persons (ugh).

CROWD: (*applauding over pastor, shouting*) "Amen! Come on!"

PASTOR A. A.: It doesn't matter what nationality you have.

ORGAN: *plays V–I chord pattern in between phrase*

CROWD: (*applauding over pastor, shouting*) "Amen! Come on!"

PASTOR A. A.: It doesn't matter about the color of your skin.

ORGAN: *plays V–I chord pattern in between phrase*

CROWD: (*applauding over pastor, shouting*) "Amen! Come on!"

PASTOR A. A.: It doesn't matter what side of the tracks you grew up on.

ORGAN: *plays V–I chord pattern in between phrase*

CROWD: (*applauding over pastor, shouting*) "Amen! Come on!"

PASTOR A. A.: You matter to God (ugh)

ORGAN: *plays V–I chord pattern in between phrase*

CROWD: (*applauding over pastor, shouting*) "Amen! Come on!"

PASTOR A. A.: You are somebody. (ugh)

ORGAN: *plays V–I chord pattern in between phrase*

CROWD: (*applauding over pastor, shouting*) "Amen! Come on!"

PASTOR A. A.: Are there any witnesses in the house?

ORGAN: *elaborate minor pentatonic pattern*

CROWD: (*louder, pplauding over pastor, shouting*) "Amen! Come on!"

PASTOR A. A.: O::::::h I've got some **good news for the poor** (*sung on one pitch, descending on "-or"*) (uh) Oh, Hallelujah! There's (*raises pitch and volume*) **a GOD**.

One other way that both preachers and musicians frequently build emotional feeling is through their body language. Typically, the person "performing" began within a set space, and then proceeded to move out of it, and either lean or even walk out into the audience/congregation to emphasis particular points.

Thus, in a blues performance, as compared with a gospel song or sermon, there is any number of elements that are very similar, but yet there are some differences. One of the most notable distinctions was with the way people physically respond to the performer. In a club, people's physical reactions were often highly individualized; except for a date or friends already known to the audience member, there is very little interaction with other listeners. By contrast, members of a church congregation do interact with each other very openly, and are more willing to accept the pastor's or singer's efforts to reach out to them. When a pastor went out into the pews and started shaking hands or otherwise encouraging church members in a certain, direct way, certain people leaned towards him and her, ready to fully receive what the minister has to offer. By contrast, when a blues musician went out into the audience, people tended to laugh and cheer, demonstrating that they find this entertaining, but also stiffed up and leaned back slightly, to suggest they are somewhat fearful or intimidated. This could be an indication of how, while a church service does have a recognizable goal of leading people somewhere, and plays into deeper issues related to religious faith, most people who go to blues clubs go simply to have a good time and to be entertained. If people believed the minister or musician is going to dramatically change their life, and bring them closer to God, they will be far more receptive and less likely to feel intruded, than if they simply regard the performance as an entertaining diversion.

On the basis of the observable similarities between blues and gospel performance styles, Charles Keil has suggested, for a blues performance:

> The world ritual seems more appropriate than performance when the audience is committed rather than appreciative. . . Blues singing is more a belief role than a creative role—more priestly than artistic. . . Bluesmen and preachers both provide models and orientations, both give public expression to deeply felt private emotions, both promote catharsis. . . both increase feelings of solidarity, boost morale, strengthen the consensus (Keil 1966: 143).

The members of the church Glen Hinson looked at would sharply disagree with Keil's analysis, and argue that their worship experience has a unique feature not found in a nightclub, "This is not enjoyment one finds in worldly engagement, not the 'good time' one experiences when being entertained. Instead these are good times, 'in the name of the Lord,' where pleasure arises. . . from the joyous communion of worship" (Hinson 2000: 127). Certainly, my respect for the people I have analyzed, and my own Christian beliefs, forces me to reject the notion that the religious ceremonies are "merely emotional experiences," that are not also building community and reinforcing deeply held beliefs in an "anointing" of the Holy Spirit, and in this way they are distinct from simply another good "concert" or "performance." However, neither can I fully deny that much of blues and blues music, although not explicitly built around religious themes, does have a deeply spiritual quality. This is reflective of the common origins of these different forms of music, and the discourse of a sympathetic God who desires to bring all people to him, and to resolve the sufferings of a people who have, through America's history, suffered deeply. As an honest expression of suffering and of people's real experiences in an unforgiving world, nearly *all* black music, from the heavenly-minded and hope filled "I don't believe he's brought me this far to leave me now," to the most "earthy" and scandalous "squeeze my lemon," is built around the tension, in the words of the traditional spiritual, between the honest reflection that "My troubles [are] so hard," but the hopefulness that "my troubles" are known by God, and by the suffering community that holds us together. And when the African American musician tries to express this tension, he or she is going to do it whole-heartily, because, in the words of the jazz standard "'Tain't just what you say, it's how you say it."

Bibliography

African American Heritage Hymnal. Chicago: GIA, 2001.

Allen, André. "Good News for Hurting People." Sermon given at 11 a.m. service at Second Baptist Church. October 14, 2007.

Berliner, Paul F. *Thinking in Jazz: The Infinite Art of Improvisation.* Chicago: University of Chicago Press, 1994.

Bourdieu, Pierre. "The Economics of Linguistic Exchanges." 1976.

Drayton, Michael (Music leader for St. Sabina Sunday services). 2007 interview.

Durkheim, Emile. *The Elementary Forms of the Religious Life.* New York: Free Press, 1915.

Edwards, David [Honeyboy], Janis Martinson, and Michael R. Frank. *The World Don't Owe Me Nothing.* Chicago: Chicago Review, 1997.

Franklin, Aretha. *One Faith, One Lord, One Baptism.* Irvine: Phantom Sound & Vision, 2003.

Geertz, Clifford. "Art as a Cultural System." In *Local Knowledge: Further Essays in Interpretive Anthropology.* New York: Basic Books, 1983.

Grazian, David. *Blue Chicago: The Search for Authenticity in Urban Blues Clubs.* Chicago: University of Chicago Press, 2003.

Harris, Michael W. *The Rise of Gospel Blues: The Music of Thomas Andrew Dorsey in the Urban Church.* New York: Oxford University Press, 1992.

Hinson, Glenn. *Fire in My Bones: Transcendence and the Holy Spirit in African American Gospel.* Philadelphia: University of Pennsylvania Press, 2000.

Jackson, Mahalia, and Evan McLeod Wylie. *Movin' On Up.* New York: Avon Books, 1966.

Jones, LeRoi. *Blues People.* New York: Morrow Quill, 1963.

Keil, Charles. *Urban Blues.* Chicago: University of Chicago Press, 1966.

LaRue, Cleophus J., et al. *Power in the Pulpit: How America's Most Effective Black Preachers Prepare Their Sermons.* Louisville: Westminster John Knox, 2002.

McGain, Mary E. *A Precious Fountain: Music in the Worship of an African American Catholic Community.* Collegeville: Liturgical Press, 2004.

Mintz, Sidney W., and Richard Price. *The Birth of African American Culture.* Boston: Beacon, 1976.

Mitchell, Nicole (Jazz flutist, leader of the Black Earth Ensemble, and director of Wheaton College Jazz Ensemble). 2007 interview.

Munroe, Myles. *The Purpose and Power of Praise and Worship.* Shippensburg, PA: Destiny Image, 2000.

Nelson, Timothy J. "Sacrifice of Praise: Emotion and Collective Participation in an African American Worship Service" *Sociology of Religion* 57, no. 4 (1996): 379–396.

Pflager, Michael L. "Due Season!" Sermon given at 11 a.m. service at The Faith Community of St. Sabina. September 16, 2007.

Priest, Kersten B. *Disharmony in the 11:00 a.m. Worship Hour: A Case Study of an Abandoned Interethnic Church Merger.* MA thesis, Department of Anthropology, University of South Carolina, 1998.

Reed, Teresa L. *The Holy Profane: Religion in Black Popular Music.* Lexington: University Press of Kentucky, 2003.

Simmons, Al. *King Blue–Boogie Till the Roof Caves In: A Kingston Mines Journal.* Chicago: Stone Wind, 1992.

Small, Christopher. *Music of the Common Tongue: Survival and Celebration in African American Music.* Hanover: Wesleyan University Press, 1987.

Spenser, Jon Michael. *Protest and Praise: Sacred Music of Black Religion.* Minneapolis: Fortress, 1990.

———. *Blues and Evil.* Knoxville: University of Tennessee Press, 1993.

Tail Dragger. "Tend to Your Business." In *My Head is Bald: Live at Vern's Friendly Lounge.* Chicago: Delmark Records, 2004.

Tate, Miles (Pianist who plays both jazz and gospel). 2007 interview.

Thornton, Willie Mae [Big Mama]. "Ball and Chain." Recording from *The Best of the Blues, Live in New York.* Los Angeles: Musiccom, Inc., 2000.

Walker, Wyatt Tee. *Somebody's Calling My Name: Black Sacred Music and Social Change.* Valley Forge: Judson, 1979.

24

Gospel Goes to Church (Again): Smallwood's Hybridity as Liturgical Compromise

Braxton D. Shelley

Introduction

A preacher and musician of Richard Smallwood's stature, talent, and training could likely find a role in the music and preaching ministries of any number of churches. For the past 26 years, he has served at Washington D.C.'s Metropolitan Baptist Church. His commitment to that ministry is partially explained by Smallwood's profession of his pride with the nature of the church's department. Smallwood remarked that "I pride myself in terms of Metropolitan's musical divers[ity]. I love anthems; I love hymns; I love gospel. . . you should be able to do it all." The quote is a succinct statement of Richard Smallwood's liturgical philosophy, a term I use to refer to Smallwood's ideas about the use of various sacred music forms in the context of Christian worship. Moreover, it provides a useful approach to analyzing the composer's music. Inasmuch as Guthrie Ramsey's theory of interpretation for African American music is based upon the idea that any appropriate criticism "of black music explains the cultural work that music performs in the social world,"[1] Smallwood's celebration of his church's musical diversity is also instructive. This diversity is particularly true in light of another critical approach that Ramsey has proposed: the need to understand African American popular music through the community theaters, churches, homes, and nightclubs, among others, wherein they are performed. These theories underpin this chapter as we seek to understand Smallwood's hybridity not as a synthesis of gospel and classical music, but as an oeuvre filled with liturgical compromise, which manifests itself in genre synthesis. Following Ingrid Monson's argument that "musicians articulate cultural commentary with sound itself," this chapter will explore how Smallwood uses sound (music and lyrics) to articulate the aforementioned philosophy.

In the previous chapter [of *All Things to All Men: Richard Smallwood's Gospel Music*], I discussed the musical changes that occurred during Smallwood's undergraduate career at Howard University. The department's reluctant inclusion of gospel and other popular music in the department's curriculum and performing ensembles represented the victory of the students against the original, negative disposition of the faculty toward music from outside the European art music tradition. The resistance of the music department is only one symptom of a wider worldview that characterized antebellum African American middle-class culture. Because this worldview was also at work in the black church, and because that is the space where gospel music had its most profound early impact, I will now devote some attention to the evolution of the black church and the closely associated musical forms.

The Black Church and Its Music

African American gospel music, hymns, and anthems have been the three primary liturgical resources for the black church throughout most of its history. The black church is the collective, and in some ways idealized designation, which refers to African American Christians. Most of these individuals are members of one of the following seven denominations: "three Methodist churches (African Methodist Episcopal Church, African Methodist Episcopal Zion Church, and Christian Methodist Episcopal Church), three Baptist conventions (National Baptist Convention USA, National Baptist Convention America, and the Progressive National Baptist Convention), and one Pentecostal church (Church of God in Christ [COGIC])."[2] That gospel music would stand alongside hymns and anthems as a primary liturgical resource for the black church was not a foregone conclusion, despite what the genre's present popularity might suggest. The genre's present prominence is the result of a century-long evolution.

African American gospel music's origin can be traced back to the slave spiritual that was created in the "invisible" churches on Southern plantations. The spirituals were an organic creation that came to be during spiritual interactions between the preacher and the other congregants in these plantation meetings: Scholars think that African melodies collided with modified Christian narratives giving birth to the spirituals. They were improvisatory, highly emotional, and communal in nature. These attributes would also come to characterize African American gospel music as it became a liturgical resource for more churches.

African American gospel music began to emerge as a liturgical resource for the independent black congregations and denominations that existed before and after the abolition of slavery. Early, congregational gospel music consisted of more structured congregational spirituals, which were accompanied by tambourines, drums, horns, piano, guitar, and, eventually, the (Hammond) organ.[3] Emotional singing, hand clapping, and foot stomping characterized services in the "gospel" churches. This expressive worship style was not accepted in the traditional, middle-class black denominations but rather in the "independent" or "folk" churches of the Holiness, Pentecostal, and Sanctified sects. The music was popular because it connected with their "African and African American cultural sensibilities in a way that the white Protestant liturgical tradition did not."[4]

The creation of gospel hymns represented a more mainline denominational approach to maintaining the aesthetics of the antebellum spiritual while respecting the existing tradition of hymnody. One of the most important writers of gospel hymns was Charles Albert Tindley (1851–1933), who was a Methodist pastor and musician. He wrote gospel hymns, which combined traditional ideas of hymnody with more African aesthetics to complement his sermons.[5] One of his most famous compositions is, "We'll Understand It Better (By and By)." Tindley's hymns left space for improvisation, "interpolation of the so-called 'blue thirds and sevenths,'"[6] and thus were palatable to individuals who enjoyed the tradition of the antebellum spiritual. This first iteration of gospel hymnody can be seen as an antecedent to Smallwood's hybridity.

The rural gospel, which was the primary musical resource for classes from those of lower socioeconomic status, was an important staple of Pentecostal churches. The rural gospel was created by individuals who sang sacred lyrics, but borrowed musical techniques from the blues idiom for melody and accompaniment. Reverend Thomas A. Dorsey who spent much of his life as a blues musician is known as the "Father of Gospel Music" because of his role in creating a new genre called "the gospel blues".[7] He took the musical techniques and language with which he was conversant and created music that would come to be known as gospel. For Dorsey, gospel music was distinguished from other genres by the lyrics, not necessarily the sonic materials. Dorsey's partnerships with Sallie Martin and later with Mahalia Jackson, one of the best-known African American singers, were very fruitful in advancing the genre and his music. The genre would continue to evolve with singers and composers like James Cleveland, Albertina Walker, and Rosetta Tharpe adding their own musical ideas to the gospel blues that Dorsey had pioneered.

The persistent resistance to African American gospel music among traditionalist and more-educated segments of the black church is a symptom of certain ideological differences that contributed to the different liturgical practices of various African American denominations. Free or enslaved African Americans in the North's urban areas settled into denominations like the African Methodist Episcopal (AME) church, the Christian Methodist Episcopal (CME) church, and other white mainline Protestant denominations like the Presbyterian and Episcopal churches. The worship philosophies of many members and leaders of these more traditional denominations can be seen in the comments of 19th century AME Bishop, Daniel Payne, who wrote disparagingly about the "ring shout," a worship ritual which epitomized the worship of the plantation's "invisible institution." Payne wrote that "after the sermon, they formed a ring and, with coats of song, clap[ped] their hands and stamp their feet in a most ridiculous and heathenish way. I requested the pastor to go and stop their dancing."[8] This quote came from Payne's autobiography, wherein he wrote about his efforts aimed at cultivating a more "refined" worship practice; he thought that this would help to distinguish the race. Payne's sentiments were echoed by other church leaders who formed similar denominations with the goal of having worship practices that were less akin to those of slaves than to those of Euro-American Christian worshippers. These sentiments manifested themselves in opposition to African American gospel music, a genre that was clearly influenced by the aesthetics that governed the plantation worship.

At every stage of this evolution, including Dorsey's initial introduction of the gospel blues, traditional forces in the black church responded negatively to these new musical stylings. Dorsey's music was called "the Devil's music"; obviously, it was not well received in many African American churches. But, in a historical pattern that is outlined in Raymond Wise's dissertation, "Defining African American Gospel Music by Tracing Its Historical and Musical Development from 1900–2000" each new iteration of gospel music would be accepted, commercially, and then for use in liturgical settings.[9] Dorsey's example is important because it shows that gospel has always been a hybrid music form in which the composer's myriad musical influences, both sacred and secular, were integrated in gospel compositions that would stretch the tradition, increasing its possible reach, while being careful to maintain the genre's aesthetic values.

Throughout the 20th century, African American gospel music grew in popularity within and without the black church. This has happened to such an extent that gospel music is now the primary liturgical resource for the black church. In fact, Mellonee Burnim argues that, "in the same way that the Negro spiritual was fundamental to the religion of the black slave, so is gospel music the backbone of contemporary black religion."[10] In spite of this, the traditionalist urge of many aspects of the black church and the varied musical tastes of many congregants demand that many churches offer a wider assortment of musical selections. As a result of this, a growing number of African American churches are becoming sites of liturgical compromise. It is also important to note that this balancing act is not limited to African American churches as the concept of blended worship has become important in many of the United States' mainline denominations. This liturgical phenomenon, which some refer to as the cosmopolitan character of the contemporary church, is what Smallwood was referring to when he declared his love for hymns, anthems, and gospel, and his pride about the ways in which his church's music program is diverse.

A Close Look

A close look at many of Smallwood's pieces reveals the degree to which the philosophy projected by the quote that began this chapter is evident in his body of work. In the next section of this paper, three of Smallwood's signature pieces will be used to demonstrate the ways in which he uses text and music to synthesize liturgical forms in his oeuvre.

"I Love the Lord (He Heard My Cry)"

Smallwood's "I Love the Lord (He Heard My Cry)" was made famous by Whitney Houston in the motion picture *The Preacher's Wife*. The piece is a particularly illustrative example of Smallwood's compositional approach. The text is drawn from a source nearly as venerated as the biblical canon—the hymns of the Englishman Isaac Watts. Watts' paraphrase of Psalm 116:1 reads "I love the lord; he heard my cries, and pitied every groan; long as I live, when troubles rise, I'll hasten to his throne." This hymn appeared in a collection, "The Psalms of David," which was published in 1719. This text was also important to the black church as it was frequently used as the basis for a lined hymn. (See Appendix 2 for one possible lined hymn presentation of that text.)

Figure 1: " I Love the Lord (He Heard My Cry)" Richard Smallwood (1976)

Formal Outline:
A. Embellished version of chorale-like tune in C major
B. After a modulation upward by semitone, a harmonized version of chorale tune appears; with melody distinct from two accompanimental voices. This section is intensified by the *ad libs* of the soloist.
C. Repetitions of "I'll hasten to his throne" intensified by "inversions" and *ad libs*.

Smallwood's paraphrase of the text is divided into three sections, which will be referred to as ABC. That Figure 1 details only the piece's melody is illustrative of the fact that the piece's voice leading departs from gospel conventions, by treating the melody like a chorale tune that is joined to two other, moving voices. While the soprano's melody lingers on the pitches at the ends of most phrases, the alto and tenor voices join the instruments to propel the piece forward harmonically. The distinction between the soprano voice and the other two voices is made more distinct by the fact that the piece begins with a soprano solo, most famously done by Ms. Houston, which contains an embellished version of the melody. After a modulation by semitone the choir enters and begins the B section. The voice leading of the first two sections suggest that these portions of the piece be seen as a setting of an original *cantus firmus*, in a manner similar to the *Choralbearbeitung*, which has long been an important part of sacred music.

In the piece's last section, Smallwood uses modal mixture to provide a more chromatic support for his repetition of "I'll hasten to his throne." The section is typically presented *ad libitum* with the soloist creating a kind of call-and-response cycle, which is intensified by the use of "inversions" a revoicing technique that will be explained in more detail during the discussion of Smallwood's "Total Praise."

"Anthem of Praise"

Smallwood's "Anthem of Praise" is another stellar example of the composer's genre synthesis. "Anthem of Praise" is clearly a gospel piece; it was the first vocal track on Smallwood's 2001 recording *Persuaded: Live in Washington DC*. However, the piece's name suggests the synthesis of genres inasmuch as anthems are an autonomous genre of sacred music, which, frequently compete with gospel music for performance time during worship. They tend to make use of more Euro-American approaches to the musical materials. The clearest explanation for the piece's title is the degree to which Smallwood uses scriptural texts in the piece.

Psalm 150 (King James Version)

1Praise ye the LORD. Praise God in his sanctuary: praise him in the firmament of his power.
2Praise him for his mighty acts: praise him according to his excellent greatness.
3**Praise him with the sound of the trumpet: praise him with the psaltery and harp.**
4**Praise him with the timbrel and dance: praise him with stringed instruments** and organs.
5Praise him upon the loud cymbals: **praise him upon the high sounding cymbals.**
6**Let everything that hath breath praise the LORD.** Praise ye the LORD.

Above I have placed the King James Version of Psalm 150. It is the last book of the Psalter, which is found in the Old Testament of the Christian Bible. In the example, the bolded passages correspond to phrases that appear in "Anthem of Praise." In the piece Smallwood also makes reference to Psalm 34:3. These direct quotations of thematically appropriate verses lend the piece an anthemic quality because anthems are typically characterized by the same textual strategy. Towards the end of the piece, Smallwood departs from the quotations to pen the words "oh, praise him" and "lift him up." The change represents a shift in focus and style, which can also be ascertained through other aspects of the music.

The piece's form can be described as ABABCDEF(coda). Throughout the piece, Smallwood's approach to voice leading is fairly unconventional in that, during the piece's first three sections, the choral voices are treated with a remarkable amount of independence. Figure 2 shows the C section of the song: it is apparent how Smallwood takes care to inject a bit of textual and rhythmic difference between the soprano, alto, and tenor parts. (The staves correspond to that order.) At the end of each sub-phrase, the choir is united in harmony to sing "and clap your hands." Those moments of unity foreshadow the voice leading which will characterize the E section. Before moving to that part of the discussion, it is vital to note that Smallwood further departs from gospel's convention by including a *divisi* in the tenor part, thereby creating a four-voice texture. This gesture can be seen as a reference to the SATB choral framework which typically characterizes hymns and anthems.

Figure 2: "Anthem of Praise" Richard Smallwood (1999) C Section

Figure 3: "Anthem of Praise" Richard Smallwood (1999) E Section

In the piece's E section, Smallwood's lyrics, voice leading, and harmony move in a more contemporary direction. As I mentioned in a previous paragraph, this section's central lyric is "lift him up." The choir sings this lyric in the homophonic style using similar and oblique motion; this is conventional in gospel. The section, which occurs over a tonic pedal, makes frequent use of the subtonic harmony. The first iteration of "lift him up" features a pedal six-four over the tonic; this creates a plagal progression. The second iteration of "lift him up" features a progression from the subtonic to the tonic; both harmonies appear over the aforementioned tonic pedal. This is reminiscent of double plagality, which is a function of subdominant and subtonic harmony. The section is intensified by three upward modulations by semitone and the presence of *ad libs* from four singers, including Smallwood himself. Their method of interaction is reminiscent of a "COGIC mic toss." The "COGIC mic toss" is a term that refers to the times when, during intense portions of songs, the Church of God in Christ's (COGIC) music leaders pass the microphone to several soloists to help lead a single song. Smallwood's use of this technique connected the piece, and his oeuvre, to a rich tradition in African American gospel music.

"Total Praise"

(see the appendix for the score and linear analysis of "Total Praise.")

The sacred influence and purpose of "Total Praise" is clear from its lyrics. The piece's opening section contains lyrics that are very similar to Psalm 121:1–2 in the Christian Bible. This psalm text reads, "I will lift up mine eyes unto the hills from whence cometh my help, my help cometh from the Lord. . . ," but Smallwood renders the text as "Lord, I will lift mine eyes to the hills, knowing my help is coming from you." In so doing, Smallwood makes his lyrics better fit with the traditional lyrical methods of contemporary gospel's praise-and-worship style, a sub-genre which is focused on creating reverential communication from the worshipper to God.[11,12] After the near-quotation from the scripture, Smallwood's original lyrics continue the praise-and-worship aesthetic as his choir declares "your peace, you give me in time of the storm," to lead to the climax at "You are the source of my strength. You are the strength of my life. I lift my hands in total praise to you." Notice the subjects in this are "I" and "You," which again serve the purpose of gospel's praise-and-worship style: worshipful communication between individuals and divinity.

Smallwood's setting of the lyrics provides a valuable window into his compositional technique. The form of "Total Praise" can be described as ABC, with each letter referring to one of the piece's three sections: verse, chorus and coda. This general form is prominent through Smallwood's body of work and is significant as it is also the basic form of hymns—another musical staple of the black church. The piece's form is exceptional when compared to other hymns because of its single verse and extended coda. The use of the choral voices and the instrumental accompaniment varies between sections. In order to appreciate these variations, one must understand an important convention of gospel composition.

The traditional choral framework in African American gospel music is the three-part, Soprano, Alto, and Tenor chorus. There is also frequent use of unison singing. When in harmony, or, in the vernacular of many genre practitioners, "in parts," the chorus most frequently sings in close harmony, moving in the same direction. This convention can be traced back to what some musicologists identify as an African preference for the use of parallel intervals and chords.[13] Gospel's conventional choral framework presents special constraints for the composer, as the choruses are typically limited to parallel and similar motion. This choral texture differs from the classical approach to choral writing, which, in many early periods, included four choral parts (soprano, alto, tenor, bass) and often stressed avoiding parallel octaves and fifths. In gospel choral writing, parallel fifths abound. Smallwood's negotiation of these different approaches provides a helpful window into his compositional aesthetic.

The A section is characterized by melodically dominated homophony, a texture that is characteristic of many chorales. In this section the three choral parts plus the instrumental bass, which is played by the keyboard instruments and the bass, comprise the chorale's four parts. This section generally conforms to gospel's choral convention with a few notable exceptions. In the reduction of "Total Praise," one can see how, in measure 3, Smallwood's tenor line descends to a lower neighbor before returning to the D♭ on the next lyric. Smallwood included similar tenor-lower-neighbors in measures 7 and 19. With these brief deviations from the convention, Smallwood creates oblique motion, which will allow the parts to resolve in contrary motion for the next chord in three of the four examples. Smallwood also departs from the convention in measure 4, where the tenors descend a minor third from D♭ to B♭, while the sopranos and altos remain on the same pitch, leaving the interval of a perfect fifth between the lowest two choral voices. This oblique motion also sets up additional oblique motion as the soprano and alto parts resolve the upper member of the V 6-5 /ii harmony to the supertonic section of "Total Praise" ends with a dominant substitution of ♭VII7 for V, a kind of harmonic substitution that is characteristic of popular music idioms including Rock. The Aeolian progression, ♭VI - ♭VII - I, is a particularly compelling example of dominant substitution; it can be found in pieces like Led Zeppelin's "Custard Pie" (1975) and Bruce Springsteen's "Cover Me" (1984).

Two four-measure phrases comprise the B section of "Total Praise". Though the second of these phrases is very similar to the A section, the first differs in several important ways. This section, which contains the piece's climax and hook, makes use of more syncopated rhythms than in the piece's other two sections. Another important difference is that, unlike in the other sections where the instrumental bass functioned as a part of a four-part chorale, in measures 13–16 Smallwood's instrumental accompaniment engages in clearly accompanimental gestures with the other instruments. First, the bass acts as a pedal in measure 13, while the three choral voices rhythmically restate the cadential six-four harmony. In measure 14, the bass descends a perfect fourth to the supertonic while the three choral voices are holding their chord from the previous measure. In measures 15–16 new lyrics are set to harmonies that are nearly identical to those in the previous two measures. Under this choral repetition, the bass and instruments execute a descending fifths sequence of the following harmonies: B♭ minor 7, E♭ dominant 9, A♭ minor 7, D♭ dominant 9, G♭ major 9, C♭ dominant 7. This sequence ends in measure 16, when the bass is reunited with the choral voices to form the second iteration of the ♭VII7 harmony. The three-part choral harmonies of the section between the two ♭VII7 chords in measures 13 and 16 are possible because only three voices are needed to create the cadential six-four harmony and supertonic harmonies which characterize this section. Unlike in other sections of the piece, there are no seventh chords, thus, the instrumental bass and the choral voices are free to diverge for this brief section.

The final section of "Total Praise," Section C's coda is another very well known part of the piece. It is, in essence, an altered and extended "amen" cadence. Smallwood's inclusion of the coda is significant, as amen cadences, often manifested as plagal cadences, are frequently found at the end of hymns. The typical harmonic progression of a plagal cadence is a IV-I or iv-I progression. Smallwood's coda represents a combination of ideas from a plagal cadence, a gospel convention, which is referred to as "inverting," and four-part writing. Smallwood's modified plagal cadence makes use of inversions of the following harmonies: ♭VII9, VI-iv, iv, a passing six-four, and I. This section features 2 active vocal parts and one that serves as a tonic pedal point. This progression occurs four times, with the three choral parts being re-voiced between sopranos, altos, and tenors each time. This re-voicing technique, which causes the sopranos to take the previous tenor part in a higher octave, the altos to assume the previous soprano part, and the tenors to adopt the previous alto part in each successive iteration of the progression, is referred to as "inverting" in the African

American gospel genre. This differs from the conventional use of the harmonic term "inversion," which refers to movements of the bass. In gospel music, however, the term "inversion" is used to describe musical situations when the bass stays constant and the choral voices are re-voiced in the manner described above. The use of this technique in the piece allows for the repetition of the plagal cadence, which typically occurs only occurs once in hymns. The repetitions provide space for increasing intensity as the piece nears its end.

In each of the preceding examples, Smallwood's hybridity has been mediated by a number of contrasting sections. That is to say that, in general, Smallwood's approaches to harmony, lyrics, and voice leading are similar within a section of a piece. The differences come between the sections. These differences, and the formal design, which govern them are not merely surface events as if evinced by my linear analysis of "Total Praise," which reveals that the formal divisions in one of Smallwood's best-known pieces can be perceived at a deep, structural level. The piece's 3 sections correspond very closely to the structure of the *Ursatz*. The initial ascent is set over the entirety of the A section. The fundamental line's descent lasts throughout the entire B section. The final section, which contains the coda, is the place for the concluding ascent to the higher 1 in the obligatory register. This last observation is especially significant because the plagal cadence, which typically is found at this point in hymns, does not typically serve an important structural harmonic role; that the coda of Smallwood's piece coheres with this tendency demonstrates a connection between this piece's Ursatz, formal design, and the archetypal form of hymns.

Intertextuality and Intermusicality

The concept of intertextuality provides a useful way to understand Smallwood's hybridity. Robert Hatten's 1985 article "The Place of Intertextuality in Music Studies" applies "the concept of intertextuality, [which is] derive[d] from the view of a literary work as a text whose richness of meaning results from its location in a potentially infinite network of other texts" to music studies by differentiating between strategic and stylistic intertextuality.[14] Stylistic intertextuality refers to the use of periods from a broader music tradition without regard to a particular work, while strategic intertextuality refers to the use of an excerpt from a particular piece. Of the greatest relevance to Smallwood's work is Hatten's argument that "earlier *styles*. . . may be exploited strategically without regard for any particular work in those earlier styles, and the results are clearly an intertextual concern."[15]

Ingrid Monson argues that, "while it is possible to call [certain] references the 'intertextual' aspect of music, I prefer to call them 'intermusical' relationships to draw attention to a communication process that occurs primarily through musical sound itself rather than through words."[16] She continued by saying that "the word intermusical is best reserved for aurally perceptible musical relationships that are heard in the context of particular musical traditions." In Smallwood's body of work both intertextual and intermusical references abound. The degree to which Smallwood is invested in using lyrics from a venerated canon like the Bible or the oeuvre of Isaac Watts should be apparent from the preceding analysis. This intertextual positing is central to his compositional character inasmuch as it situates many of his "gospel" songs in the liturgical space of hymns and anthems. This characteristic, which is consistent throughout Smallwood's body of work, is no accident; when the composer writes lyrics he typically does so with the aid of several translations of the Christian bible, a thesaurus, and a rhyming dictionary. He does this out of a frustration with composers who "put their own theology or their own personal opinions in their lyrics." He continued, "I think that it's important that we put what the word of God says, so that when people hear it they'll hear what God says."[17]

Smallwood's consistent use of different patterns of harmony and voice leading, often with an eye, or should I say ear, toward a previous period, is also quite striking. In the three pieces that were afforded close analysis for this chapter we saw Smallwood make use of gospel's conventional close harmony, three relatively independent voices, and a four-voice texture, which was created by inserting a divisi into the tenor part. The pieces also contain several chorale-based settings, and Smallwood's signature polyphonic "amens" from "Total Praise." In an interview, I asked the composer which of his musical influences help to explain that "amen" section and other pieces which make use of similar voice leading patterns. He replied that this "idiosyncrasy of his most likely has its origins in the Baroque period." Later in the interview, Smallwood testified of his love for the music of the Baroque period, specifically for that of J. S. Bach, who is one of his favorite composers; this too is evident in his musical practice.

In addition to the aforementioned examples of stylistic intertextuality, there are examples of strategic intertextuality in Smallwood's body of work. His piece "Standing," which can be found on his CD *Promises* (2011), makes use of a quotation of the refrain of the hymn "Standing on the Promises." The form of "Standing" can be described as AA'BB'CB'. The hymn quotation constitutes the C section. Not surprisingly, "Standing on the Promises" and Smallwood's "Standing" are very similar in terms of their lyrical content; this explains Smallwood's decision to quote the hymn. The piece provides an example of Smallwood's consistency with other liturgical music forms.

Figure 4: "Standing" Richard Smallwood (2011) mm. 56–67

Smallwood's hybridity is so audacious because of his willingness to stylistically refer to the baroque period in one section of a song, and then proceed to compose a troping cycle based on subtonic harmony, which is inflected by semitone modulations and other characteristic techniques of African American gospel music making, in the same song. If, as Ingrid Monson, suggests, "musicians articulate cultural commentary with sound itself,"[18] what is Smallwood saying through his hybridity? I argue that, in a very fundamental way, Smallwood, who knows that intertextuality and intermusicality are not just issues for the composer, but also for the hearer who interprets Smallwood's music based on its proximity to other genres, offers comfort to those who demand the maintenance of hymns, anthems, and gospel, because he shows that they are compatible through his synthesis of the genres in his signature pieces. If, indeed, he is saying something, it is "you CAN do it all."

Figure 5: R. Kelso Carter "Standing on the Promises" 1886

Hybridity, which underlies Smallwood's urge to "do it all," is consonant with the work of generations of gospel composers. His work in the genre is significant because African American gospel music exists at the intersection of Popular Culture and sacred music, as it is a popular music genre that most often resides in the sacred space of the black church. The occasionally competitive influences of the black church, its other liturgical music forms, and popular culture make gospel a hybrid musical genre. Meeting the demands of this hybrid musical genre has been a task with which composers have wrestled throughout the idiom's history. Fortunately for them, gospel is not the only hybrid genre or institution in the constellation of African American cultural practices. Guthrie Ramsey, a musicologist whose work was referenced earlier in this chapter, contends that "a self-conscious hybridity has marked the development of African American religious practices since their appearance in the New World."[19] That is to say that gospel's hybridity is in many ways a reflection of the black church's own complexity. The diversity of perspectives that can be found in the church has frequently caused controversy for gospel composers who have sought to negotiate their popular and sacred influences. By now we know that the music Rev. Thomas Dorsey composed was not well received by traditional forces in the black church that referred to these new musical offerings as "the Devil's music." The reception of Dorsey's gospel blues foreshadowed the response to "Rosetta Tharpe's blend of jazz and gospel during the 1940s; Edwin Hawkins' and Andraé Crouch's pop-gospel of the late 1960s; and the Winanses' smooth-soul gospel of the 1980s, [which] were all seen as hybrid—and quite controversial—expressions in their day."[20] Ramsey reasons that the tension between innovative composers and conservative church leaders, when combined with the commercial success of gospel, has raised questions about the genre's ability to function as both an entertaining cultural symbol and a liturgical resource. He then translates the previous question into language that is immediately relevant to this discussion: he asks if gospel can be "art and folk at the same time?"[21]

Richard Smallwood, who notes that he has never experienced any appreciable resistance to his music from the church, is a model of a different kind of hybridity: Instead of bringing other popular music forms into the church through gospel, Smallwood's work can be understood as infusing gospel with musical and textual materials that have already been canonized for use in the church. In this, Smallwood's music asserts that a piece can be a hymn, an anthem, and a gospel at the same time. In this he caters to a wide range of congregants, offering a brand of liturgical compromise which helps to explain the place of his oeuvre in the musical canon of the black church.

Appendix 1

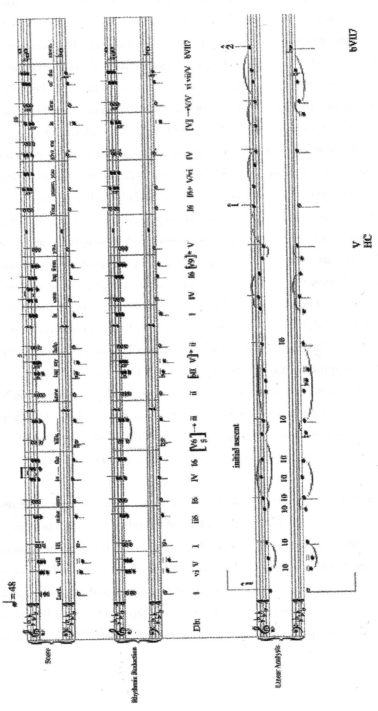

"Total Praise" Linear Analysis—Braxton Shelley

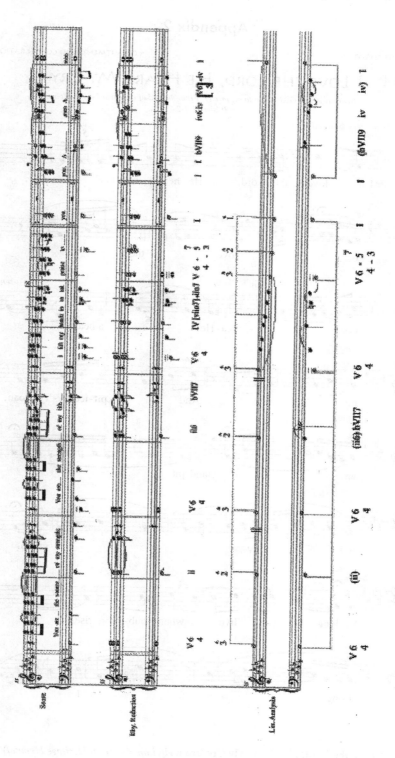

Appendix 2

394 I Love the Lord, He Heard My Cry

Hear my cry, O God; listen to my prayer. From the end of the earth I call to You...
Psalm 61:1-2

I Love the Lord, He Heard My Cry (from *African American Heritage Hymnal*)

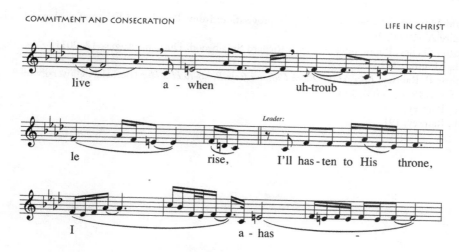

COMMITMENT AND CONSECRATION

LIFE IN CHRIST

live a - when uh-troub - le rise, I'll has-ten to His throne, I a - has - ten to His, His throne.

Text: African-American traditional
Tune: Meter hymn, anonymous; lined out by M. Adams and Louis Sykes, © 2000, GIA Publications, Inc.

I Love the Lord, He Heard My Cry (cont.)

Notes

1. Guthrie Ramsey, "The Pot Liquor Principle: Developing a Black Music Criticism in American Studies," *American Music* 22, no. 2 (Summer 2004): 288.
2. Melinda Weekes, "This House, This Music: Exploring the Interdependent Interpretive Relationship between the Contemporary Black Church and Contemporary Gospel Music," *Black Music Research Journal* 25, no. 1 (Spring/Fall 2005): 45.
3. Mellonee Burnim. "Religious Music" in *African American Music: An Introduction,* New ed., ed. Mellonee V. Burnim and Portia K. Maultsby (New York: Routledge, 2005), 68.
4. Ibid., Weekes, 46
5. Ibid., Burnim, 68
6. Ibid., Burnim, 68.
7. Anthony Heilbut, *The Gospel Sound: Good News and Bad Times—25th Anniversary Edition (Hal Leonard Reference Books),* Anniversary ed. (New York: Limelight Editions, 1997), 63.
8. Eileen Southern, ed., *Readings in Black American Music—Second Edition* (New York: W. W. Norton, 1983), 69.
9. Raymond Wise, "Defining African American Gospel Music by Tracing Its Historical and Musical Development from 1900 to 2000" (PhD diss., Ohio State University, 2001), 245–277.
10. Mellonee Burnim, "The Black Gospel Music Tradition: Symbol of Ethnicity," (thesis, Indiana University, 1980), pp. 3–4.
11. Ibid., Wise, 270.
12. Other gospel styles include the contemporary style that began with Edwin Hawkins' "Oh Happy Day." See Wise for more.
13. David Brackett, *Interpreting Popular Music* (Los Angeles: University of California Press, 2000), 116.
14. Robert S. Hatten, "The Place of Intertextuality in Music Studies, American Journal of Semiotics, vol. 3, no. 4 (185):69.
15. Ibid., Hatten, 71.

16. Ingrid Monson, "Doubleness and Jazz Improvisation: Irony, Parody and Ethnomusicology," *Critical Inquiry* 20 (1994): 307.
17. Braxton Shelley. Phone interview with Richard Smallwood. Durham, August 12, 2011.
18. Ibid., Monson, 313.
19. Guthrie P. Ramsey, *Race Music: Black Cultures from Bebop to Hip Hop* (Berkeley: University of California Press, 2003), 190.
20. Ibid., Ramsey, 191.
21. Ibid., Ramsey, 191.

25

Modes of Ritual Performance in African American Pentecostalism

Thomasina Neely-Chandler

A dynamic social institution based on traditional African and Christian religious practices constituted the core of slave culture (Blassingame 1979). In plantation "praise houses" slaves had the ability to creatively merge their traditional African concepts, beliefs and rituals with those of white America. *Africanisms*, which are not fully comprehended by scholars who approach them through mere trait listing, provided slaves the conceptual framework for ritual performance as process based on an African cultural aesthetic.[1] Old beliefs and actions were not necessarily replaced or destroyed by new ones, but were reinterpreted and absorbed within modified versions of performance. In slave communities, these processes of retention and adaptation resulted in an evolution of distinctive African-derived performance traditions still practiced in many African American churches today.[2] These traditions, include culture-specific speech, vocal, instrumental, compositional, improvisational, rhythmic and timbral styles of praying, singing, preaching; these examples also integrate movement, intense spiritual ecstasy, and communal participation. Although these practices are exemplified in varying degrees by many African American churches, Africanisms in ritual performance often appear in more extended and elaborated forms in black Pentecostal churches.

Belief as a system of knowledge, ideas, values, or impressions pertains to a group's shared experience of God. Integral to African traditional and Pentecostal belief is the reverence for a phenomenal quality or sacred power that becomes infused with music and ritual, transcending norms of social action.[3] This essay will, therefore, focus on

African-derived ritual performances of music and related behavior and action as a product of belief and aesthetic ideation in a black Pentecostal church. The denomination chosen as the focus of observation is the Church of God in Christ (COGIC), founded in 1895 by the late Bishop Charles H. Mason. With over six million members, the Church of God in Christ is the largest and oldest black Pentecostal group in America and abroad. In addition to its considerable size, longevity, and historical legacy, the Church of God in Christ contains many salient cultural features. Its diversified musical tradition can be categorized into specific ritual modes that function as symbols of faith. For the purpose of study, these modes are identified as prayer, shout, sermon, devotional, testimony, pneumatic and gospel music modes.[4] Each ritual mode contains varied stylistic features and an African-derived cultural aesthetic that give rise to distinctive performance practices.

Slave Worship

After scores of slaves were converted to Christianity, their religious services exhibited "Christian" concepts and practices through the filter of an African past, transforming the liturgy into an African ritual (Maultsby 1990: 197). The cultural attributes of interactive participation and freedom of artistic expression flowed from African values that instituted a frame of reference for meaningful performance. European and American missionaries encouraged public worship with reverence and stillness on the part of the congregation, and with uniformity in the musical textures of hymn and psalm singing. The slaves, however, deviated from these norms in their own ritual practices.

J. H. Kwabena Nketia explained that, "new ideas were created in the style of tradition, using its vocabulary and idiom, or in an alternative style which combined African and non-African resources" (Maultsby 1990: 205). Missionaries were especially critical of the slaves' musical interpretations, which they described as "short scraps of disjointed affirmations. . . lengthened out with long repetitious choruses" (Maultsby 1990: 197). The call-and-response styles of singing, unconventional chanted sermons, improvisatory styles and enraptured dance unique to the music of slaves did not conform to European-American aesthetic values. Psalms and hymn singing were enforced on slaves in a failed attempt to, "lay aside the extravagant and nonsensical chants, catches and hallelujah songs of their own composing" (Maultsby 1990: 197). Many historical accounts confirm the slaves' musical reinterpretations of Christian song forms according to African aesthetic principles.[5] Evidence from the Church of God in Christ will further support the fact that the African cultural roots of black culture reinterpreted in the religious and musical practices of slaves paved the way for a diversity of African American performance traditions.

Research Problem

The aesthetic appeal of black "folk" styles of worship, as typified in the Church of God in Christ, can be easily distorted as impulsive, aggressive, or repulsive to those unaccustomed to African traditional religions. Consequently, Pentecostals have been commonly depicted as "holy rollers" and extremists in their approach to emotionalism, trance, dance, and other physical demonstrations of ritual liminality. Fortunately, many writers and historians have brought theological, cultural, sociological, and political validation to Pentecostalism, challenging the early historical misconceptions of Pentecostalism as "primitive," or as the "religion of the poor and dispossessed" (Hollenweger 1970, 1972; McRoberts 1988; Tinney 1977). Albert Raboteau and Eileen Southern document historical accounts of African-derived musical and religious practices such as the ring shout and folk spirituals of slaves after their conversion to Christianity (Raboteau 1978: 4–5; Southern 1972: 162; 1983: 156). In her article, "West African Influences on U. S. Black Music," Portia Maultsby reported that the slaves "interpreted Christian concepts and practices in an African context, adding an emotional component and unconventional musical expression to their practice of Christianity" (Maultsby 1979: 31–32). Various scholars in Joseph Holloway's *Africanisms in American Culture* (1990) present detailed analyses of specific African conceptual approaches retained in black speech, folk belief, religion, art, folklore, and music. Other researchers in religious studies trace the African origins of American Pentecostal practices confirming that black Pentecostalism is "truly African in its origins, worship styles, philosophy of faith, and spiritual practices" (Lovett 1973; Synan 1975: 137; Tinney 1977: 135; 1979; McRoberts 1988).

Field studies of African-derived folk styles of ritual continue to examine symbolic behaviors in liminal states such as "getting happy," or "dancing in the spirit" without reference to the belief and cultural context (Cutten 1908; Ludwig 1969; Rouget 1986; Baklanoff 1987; et al.). When extracted from the underlying cultural aesthetic that binds belief, ritual, and performance into a coherent whole, many black ritual and musical responses, such as those found in the Church of God in Christ, would be inaccurately interpreted as nonsensical, cataleptic, or orgiastic (Baklanoff 1987). Insufficient field methods perpetuated by stereotyped and fabricated data would cause authentic forms of black folk worship to be misinterpreted. It seems plausible that the key to understanding the roots of Pentecostal culture lies in examining the properties of its religious symbols and symbolic behavior, the relationship between symbols and belief, what they represent to their interpreters, and how they are culturally organized through sacred time. A detailed analysis of the interrelated, interacting, and interdependent constituents of ritual in the COGIC would demonstrate the continuity of an African cultural and spiritual heritage that give rise to creative styles in black folk worship.

COGIC Belief

The relationships between belief and faith have been a pervasive theme in theological and religious studies. Theologians explain that belief belongs to religious doctrine or (dogmatism) and scripture (biblicalism), while faith belongs to the "context of encounter" (Brunner 1962: 32). Some scholars define faith in the context of an event that moves beyond the dimension of knowledge and belief (Bultmann 1967: 75). Others have distinguished belief as "intellectual assent" and faith as a "living relationship," or belief as philosophical and faith as revelational (Grant 1977: 21–22). This basic distinction is evident in traditional African and black Pentecostal religions where emphasis is placed on one's personal encounter with God (faith) as something that completes or brings to perfection one's knowledge of God (belief). In the COGIC, religion is built upon faith as a matter of inner experience that involves persons in a relationship to that which is sacred. Faith in this church is a personal commitment to belief and involves the performance or acting out of belief through ritual practices. Victor Turner expressed it this way:

> Religion like art, lives in so far as it is performed... religion is not a cognitive system, a set of dogmas, alone. It is meaningful experience and experienced meaning. In ritual one lives through events, or through the alchemy of its framings and symbolings, relives semiogenetic events, the deeds and words of prophets and saints (Turner 1982: 86).

On the basis of these distinctions, ritual in traditional African and Pentecostal religions can be described as "complex, involving beliefs, contingent behaviors or practices, some kind of experience, and 'faith' or commitment to the truth of a belief system" (Brown 1966: 259).

An integral component of traditional African and Pentecostal belief systems is the recognition of a spiritual presence or power experienced by worshipers. The sacred as an aspect of religious experience involves belief in and reverence for a holy power. In *The Idea of the Holy*, Rudolf Otto (1950) refers to the "holy" as the "real innermost core" of all religion. He coined the term "numinous" to describe something beyond rational and ethical conceptions:

> The holy is a preeminently living force. What is involved is a mystery and above all creatures, something hidden and esoteric which we can experience in feelings. It is wholly other, that which is quite beyond the sphere of the usual, the intelligible, and the familiar (Otto, 1950 quoted in O'dea 1983: 23).

Corresponding to the qualities of extraordinary power in the sacred and holy is the nature of charisma. According to Max Weber in *The Theory of Social and Economic Organization*, charisma is:

> A certain quality of an individual personality by virtue of which he is set apart from ordinary men and treated as endowed with supernatural, superhuman, or at least specifically exceptional powers or qualities... These are regarded as of divine origin or as exemplary Unusual, radically different from the routine and the everyday; it is spontaneous in contrast

to stable, established social forms; and it is a source of new forms and new movements (Weber 1947: 358–359).

In the Pentecostal religious experience, qualities of the unusual, of power, of spontaneity, and of creativity are attributed to the presence of the "anointing" in the Church of God in Christ. This acknowledged sacred power is believed to be the "living force" that sets the foundation for music and ritual performance. The spiritual source or anointing is identified as the power of the Holy Spirit commonly referred to as the Holy Ghost, or the "Holy Ghost and fire." In the context of Pentecostal ritual, worshipers may become immersed in the Holy Ghost witnessed through extraordinary physical gestures such as waving the hands, lifting the arms, clapping, dancing, running or falling prostrate. COGIC people use their own verbal expressions such as, "being caught up in," "being slain in," or "being empowered by" the spirit as a way to characterize these religious experiences.

Other verbal expressions such as "signs and wonders" and "God's moving," are used to describe the evidence of the presence of the sacred. "Signs and wonders" are believed to be special spiritual gifts, revelations, or miracles given by the Holy Spirit to edify the church body. The biblical reference on the gifts of the Holy Spirit is found in, for example, I Corinthian 12; it describes the Pentecostal practice of speaking in tongues (spiritual language uttered through the anointing also called the Holy Spirit or Holy Ghost), interpretation of tongues, prophecy, discernment, or healing. It is due to the unusual and radically different nature of a spiritual encounter with the holy that the term charisma is applied to the worldwide Charismatic Movement. The Charismatic Movement describes all manifestations of Pentecostal ritual behaviors that later emerged in other non-Pentecostal denominations such as Baptist or Catholic. Thus, the anointing as an icon of the sacred or the holy, becomes the primary participant in the religious event as conductor, motivator, and strengthener. It is within this sacred milieu that diverse ritual modes evolve and operate in the Church of God in Christ.

COGIC Ritual as Cultural Performance

Belief in the Church of God in Christ is expressed through cultural symbols, or through what I designate as ritual modes that have evolved largely from African-derived religious traditions. In the article "Culture and Religious Belief," Langdon Gilkey explained that, "[c]reative cultural forces shape and even direct forms of religious belief. Without influence from culture, religious belief has little to say to the world about the world" (Harrison 1986: 79). As early as 1955, anthropologist Milton Singer expanded the definition of cultural performance by adding such genres as prayers, ritual recitations, ceremonies, and festivals (McLeod 1980: 26; Behague 1984: 4). According to

Singer, cultural performances are encapsulations of a culture bounded within a limited time span and not exclusive to Western European classical forms such as symphony, ballet, aria, concerto or art song. In ritual, cultural performances are composed of "cultural media" or modes of communication which include not only spoken language, but such non-linguistic medias as song, dance, acting out, art, body gestures or facial expression, combined in many ways to communicate the worldview of a particular sociocultural group (Singer 1972: 76; Turner 1987: 23). These performances constitute a "cultural focusing" of highly formalized behavior that is symbolic and meaningful (Behague 1984: 4).

In the Church of God in Christ the most visible manifestations of belief in action is stylized cultural performance. Based on field research and analysis, several ritual modes have been identified in the Church of God in Christ that contain symbolic reenactment of belief. These include the prayer, dance, sermon, pneumatic, testimony, devotional arid gospel ritual modes. The COGIC liturgy is formed by a flow of African-derived cultural performances structured by symbols (modes) that pertain to religious belief. Each has a definite time span or beginning and an end, an organized program of activity, a set of performers, an audience, and a place and occasion of performance. Intrinsic to each mode are musical qualities based on scale, melody, rhythm, tonality, harmony, text, verbal art, and style of delivery. The identifiable sound characteristics of each mode are determined by combinations of these musical qualities, as well as by contextual and spiritual parameters. While a mode is the smallest unit of ritual, a performance genre is an artistic arrangement that combines one or two modes into distinctive composition styles such as gospel, folk spiritual or hymn.

Modes are categorized further as either primary or secondary in this study according to its degree of dominance in the ritual. The dominance of a symbol may be observed from the frequency of its appearance and duration in the ritual system, from the constancy of its meaning, and from its performative structure (Geertz 1973; Moore and Reynolds 1984; Morris 1987; Turner 1967, 1969, 1974). The level of dominance is also determined from observing these actions from ritual to ritual, and from one service to another. A dominant symbol may be used throughout a particular ritual in its entirety, or it may manifest in only one particular phase of the ritual. Traditional religious and musical practices that serve as the foundation of ritual and belief in the Church of God in Christ are classified as *primary* modes. Traditional performance practices are more commonly found in the prayer, shout, devotional, sermon, testimony, praise, and glossolalia/pneumatic modes.

Secondary modes have a more limited reference to the core of *COGIC* ritual and belief. Musical practices that are influenced by secular and modernistic trends that are also popular outside of the church setting are categorized as *secondary* modes. The secondary ritual mode incorporates the gospel modes, which include traditional, praise, inspirational, or what I classify as newly composed gospel styles. While the gospel mode is an important segment of ritual in the Church of God in Christ, its styles and performance practices often depend upon popular secular trends, which may be incompatible with the spiritual needs of the ordinary church liturgy. The primary modes are, therefore, the actual indicators of COGIC religious values and possess an inherent continuity of meaning and purpose in the liturgy.

Liminality

In the anthropology of performance three theoretical concepts, reflexivity, framing and liminality were applied to understand symbols as social experience in theatre and ritual. The manipulation of symbols in the Church of God in Christ coincides with Turner's concept of "performative reflexivity" where members of a sociocultural group distinctively turn, bend, or reflect back upon themselves, and upon their relations, actions, symbols, meanings, and codes as a way of obtaining an ultimate reality (Turner 1986: 24). Ritual as a process can also be characterized as a cultural mode of framing.

> To frame is to discriminate a sector of sociocultural action from the general on-going process of a community's life. It is often reflexive in that, to "frame," a group must cut out a piece of itself for inspection and retrospection. To do this it must create—by rules of exclusion and inclusion—a bordered space and a privileged time within which images and symbols of what has been sectioned off can be relived, scrutinized, assessed, revalued (Turner 1986: 140).

In deep phases of ritual liminality, the manipulation of symbols is "designed to influence preternatural entities or forces on behalf of the goals and interests of the participants" (Deflem 1991: 5). Arnold Van Gennep demonstrated the existence of reflexivity, framing and liminality in a "tripartite movement in space-time" showing that rites of passage "accompany transitions from one situation to another and from one cosmic or social world to another" (Van Gennep 1960: 13). A common processual form of ritual was subdivided into what he called the separation (preliminal), margin (liminal), and reincorporation (post-liminal) phases. As reviewed by Avorgbedor, Richard Schechner's modifications of Turner's stages include not only *separation* and *incorporation*, but also *transformation* (Avorgbedor 1999; Schechner 1986).

Separation is the phase in ritual that draws a distinction between sacred space and time and profane or ordinary space and time. During this process there are rites that influence the quality of time and construct *a cultural realm*, which is defined as "out of time;" beyond or outside the time that measures secular processes and routines. It includes also symbolic behavior (Turner 1982: 24; Van Gennep 1960: 13). In the COGIC these rites would include the kneeling prayer chant vigils, periods of fasting and consecration held prior to the official start of the service. It is the second phase of liminality that is believed to be central to the ritual process since it is the scene for cultural framing, reflexivity, and innovation. Liminal behaviors during this phase may include dancing in the spirit, prolonged prayer, speaking in tongues with interpretation, prophecy through music, or singing spontaneously composed melodies in tongues. The final phase of *incorporation* is where ritual actions such as the final altar call, or benediction prayer, return the participants to ordinary space and time prepared for the new demands of a different cultural location.

The cultural realm of African-derived ritual created within sacred space and time becomes the locus of activities in the transition or *liminal* phase. One important component of liminality in African and Pentecost ritual is the fostering of community participation that is direct, interactive, and spontaneous. People's social statuses and previous attributes are stripped temporarily, and the participants change into a bonding "communitas." Communitas is the relationship between those jointly undergoing ritual transitions; it liberates persons from conformity to general social norms (Turner 1974: 274). In liminality the social order and the cognitive schemata that give sense and order to everyday life no longer apply, but are suspended in ritual symbolism (Turner 1982: 84). Communitas in the Church of God in Christ is achieved when all are "on one accord," of equal mind and spirit for the indwelling of the Holy Ghost or anointing.

A second component of liminality manifested in traditional African and Pentecostal ritual practices involves the communication of the sacred, which involves sacred symbols, actions, or beliefs. Liminality is characterized by a high degree of symbolic elaboration as a way of approaching transcendent beings or powers. During this phase of ritual, people are considered to be more open to the influence of the supernatural (Grimes 1976: 20; Pentikainen 1978: 161; Turner 1982: 201). This is evident in the COGIC where Pentecostal behaviors such as spoken or sung glossolalia, composing songs in the spirit, healing rituals, dancing, and shouting or getting happy (emic terms used interchangeably) escalate during periods of liminality. Consequently, the presence or "moving" of the anointing belongs to the normal picture of the liminal phase. The anointing is considered quite high during the liminal phases of prayer, praise, or preaching and can interact communally or personally within ritual. While in the presence of the anointing, COGIC faithfuls believe that they are renewed in a state of wholeness. It is during these states of deep awareness that the intensity of music making and performance builds and draws the church in. The ritual modes in the Church of God in Christ are, therefore, musical conduits for the power of the anointing to act upon and change the persons involved in ritual performance.

A third component of liminality is creativity, which serves as the basis for "the emergence of a society's deepest values in the form of sacred dramas and objects" (Turner 1986: 102):

> New meanings and symbols may be introduced—or new ways of portraying or embellishing old models for living. . . Ritual liminality contains the potentiality for cultural innovation and the means of effecting structural transformations within a relatively stable sociocultural system (Turner 1982: 85).

There are also scenes of play, improvisation, and experimentation in liminal states of cultural creativity, which all lead to a fourth component of ritual liminality; ludic recombination is an important element in this component. Ludic recombination is permeated by the elements of more play, masking, imagery, costume, or cultural reenactment that may appear unusual or unknown to secular experience (Van Gennep 1960: 15). In *Yoruba Ritual*, Margaret Drewal stated that improvisation as a performative strategy in ritual, places ritual within the domain of play:

> It is indeed the playing, the improvising, that engages people, drawing them into the action, constructing their relationships, thereby generating multiple and simultaneous discourses. . . both signifying and improvisation among Afro-Americans are formal manifestations of African traditions, and more specifically of a self-reflexive tradition or rhetorical play in cultural and performance practices (Drewal 1992: 8).

In the Church of God in Christ, there is a constant play of symbolic religious behavior that evolves into unusual performance styles such as the stylized dance patterns, gospel choir rocks or choreographed choral movements, rhythmic clapping, call-and-response patterns, vocal timbral embellishments, or sermon organ accompaniments. There is often a play of verbal art skills in the "signifying" games inspired by the preacher. During sections of the sermon while the congregation is already actively participating with gestural and auditory responses, the preacher playfully draws the listeners into more spiritual ecstasy when he hints, "Oh, I wish someone here would say amen," or "You all don't know what I'm talking about." Impromptu ritual play is also created by the organist, who punctuates the sermon with harmonic, melodic and rhythmic improvisation. The organ's motifs intensify the sermon, soliciting an array of symbolic verbal, nonverbal and gestural affirmations of belief from the congregation. Other forms of ritual play such as improvisation and experimentation may also incorporate various literary devices such as rhyme, onomatopoeia, meter, rhythm, metaphor, or personal narrative as a means of creating dramatic exchanges between the pulpit, congregation, and musicians.

The ritual transitions of separation, liminality, and incorporation continually overlap and reoccur in varying degrees in the Church of God in Christ. Prayer and testifying accompanied by music as a ritual of separation may contain levels of liminality and incorporation. This may be followed later in the liturgy by even more heightened episodes of liminality in the preaching, dancing, or singing activities when the "anointing is high" and spontaneous.

Cultural Foundation of COGIC

The Church of God in Christ is a cultural storehouse of a large number of African retentions. Many traditional features of African-derived performance—including scale patterns, rhythmic agility, improvisation, melodic and textual ornamentation, movement and dance, spirit possession, and communal participation—are retained within the framework of COGIC ritual. These cultural retentions are observable in the following:

1. scale structures produced by blues notes (lowered third, fifth, and seventh scale pitches) commonly heard in chanted prayers, melismatic moans, and sermons;
2. jubilant celebration of the spirit's presence through a dance often called the "shout" or "holy dance" and historically described as ring shouts or possession dances;
3. preaching styles that are chanted with melodic, rhythmic, and textual improvisations;
4. chanted prayers with moans that also incorporate melodic, rhythmic, and textual improvisation;
5. verbal art skills similar to West African griots/*jaliya* or storytelling bards with rhythm:, metaphor, or formulaic expressions commonly used in testimonies, sermon texts, prayers, and even improvised gospel lyrics;
6. rhythmic complexity and syncopation characteristic of polyrhythmic textures, drumming, handclapping, and other percussive instruments;
7. timbral manipulation or the use of instrumental and vocal sound effects that produce a myriad of tone qualities such as the falsetto, shrill, groan, slide, bend, or grunt commonly heard in songs, prayers, sermons and organ styles;
8. song forms such as the folk spirituals that evolved into gospel with repetitive call-and-response patterns, spirited dance, percussive accompaniments, emotional intensity, and collective improvisation; communal participation and freedom of expression; and
9. multiple contexts and functions for music making.

These traits demonstrate the continuity of an African cultural and spiritual heritage, which nurtures creative styles of black folk worship in the Church of God in Christ.

Historical Foundation of COGIC

William J. Seymour was a black religious leader considered the "Apostle and Pioneer" of the Pentecostal movement that originated at the Azusa Street Revival in Los Angeles at the turn of the twentieth century. Seymour attracted the publicity of the daily papers during the revival meetings when Africanisms, supernatural gifts such as speaking in tongues, and miracles transformed the Christian liturgy. Seymour, the son of slaves, influenced black folk practices in Christianity by incorporating black religious songs into the Azusa worship experience. According Jon Spencer, "Seymour affirmed his black heritage by introducing Negro spirituals and Negro music into his liturgy at a time when this music was considered inferior and unfit for Christian worship" (1992: 141).

Charles H. Mason was a Baptist preacher who traveled to attend the Azusa revival meetings and who later founded the Church of God in Christ. After Mason experienced Seymour's leadership and the spiritual activities of the Azusa revival, he converted to Pentecostalism. During his new spiritual awakening at Azusa, Mason described tongues as sounding sweet and as something he knew was right:

> The sound of a mighty wind was in me and my soul cried and soon I began to die. It seemed that I heard the groaning of Christ on the cross dying for me. . . Then I felt something raising me out of my seat without any effort of my own. It must have been my imagination. Then I looked down to see and I saw that I was rising. Then I gave up for the

Lord to have his way within me... So when I gotten myself straight on my feet there came a light which enveloped my entire being above the brightness of the sun. When I opened up my mouth to say glory, a flame touched my tongue which ran down to me. My language changed and no word could I speak in my own tongue. I was filled with the glory of my Lord. My soul was then satisfied. I rejoiced in Jesus my Savior, whom I love so dearly (Mason 1979: 19).

The Church of God in Christ reflects the faith, spiritual qualities, mannerisms, religious practices, verbal expressions, and songs of their founder. Throughout the United Sates, religious men and women were inspired by the spiritual discipline and charismatic legacy of Mason, who became the first ordained presiding Bishop of the Church of God in Christ. He directed the church's growth from ten congregations in 1907 to the largest and oldest black Pentecostal group in America. Each established church originating from Mason served as a launching ground for new churches. Bishop Mason also made a significant contribution to music in the Church of God in Christ.

Born in 1866 in Tennessee, Bishop Mason was believed to have been enriched by a life filled with supernatural gifts. Many personal narratives regarding the spiritual astuteness of Bishop Mason describe his ministry of healing, command in rites of exorcism, gifts of the Spirit (as outlined in the Bible), and Spirit-induced song style. His ritual techniques of "laying on of hands" and anointing with oil were a customary practice throughout his lifetime. During these healing rites, anointed or blessed hands (with holy oil) are placed on the infirmity of those seeking prayer for healing, or on individuals in need. COGIC pioneers often boast about the effectiveness of Mason's prayers on the blind, the crippled, or the sick, as evidenced in reports of immediate healing and physical wholeness.

Spontaneous singing under the anointing is one of the most consecrated forms of musical expression in the Church of God in Christ. This method of singing and composing is attributed to Mason's relentless practice of praying and singing in the spirit. Mason explained his experience and personal relationship with the Holy through new songs, tongues, and prayer:

I was full of the power when I reached home. The Spirit had taken full control of me and everything was new to me and all the saints. The way that he [Holy Spirit] did things was all new. He could and was teaching me all things and showing the things of the Lord. He taught me how and what to sing, and all his songs were new... I wanted the church to understand what the Spirit was saying through me, so that they might be edified. My prayers were not in vain. I began to speak in tongues and interpret the same. He soon gave me the gift of interpretation-that is, he would interpret sounds, groans and any kind of spiritual utterance (Mason 1979: 19–20).

Azusa Street revival ushered in its own hymnody based on African-derived Pentecostal religious experiences. The style of composition and dependency on the anointing were embraced by Mason and considered the basis for COGIC's sacred music traditions.

The charismatic appeal of Pentecostal worship continues to motivate and revitalize several mainline denominations across the United States (for example, Baptist, Catholic, Episcopal, and Jewish). *The Dictionary of Pentecostal and Charismatic Movements* concluded that there is an underlying thread that ties these denominations together:

> The Pentecostal and charismatics have come to be identified with exuberant worship; an emphasis on subjective religious experience and spiritual gifts; claims of spirituality, rather than theology; and a mystical "life in the spirit" by which they daily live out the will of God (Burgess 1988: 5)

Yet, the concept of increased communal interaction, freedom in the spirit, personalized worship, dance, improvised song, and spiritual gifts associated with charismatics existed as part of the African heritage, which was integrated later into the Azusa Street phenomenon. The Azusa Street revival was unusual, not only because it served as an international shrine for more potent experiences of God with an emphasis on spiritual gifts, but also because it attracted many people from across the world. Azusa was most unusual in that it was thrived under black leadership, spirituality, and musicality. These characteristics fostered the creative integration of African traditional spiritual practices in the context of a new Pentecostal awakening. During the height of racism and segregation in America, people of many ethnic nationalities were drawn to the Azusa Street Revival under Seymour's leadership. After the emancipation of slavery, blacks were permitted to express their religious and cultural traditions across a wider spectrum of race, class, and denomination.

Pentecostal-charismatic music and worship styles of whites were also influenced by African-derived performance during the revival movements and camp meetings of the eighteenth and nineteenth centuries. As stated by one observer,

> Black music and spirituals were a major part of these revivals and camp meetings, creating a repertory and tradition that not only influenced white Pentecostals from traditional denominations but also provided the basis for much of the rich music expressions of American black Pentecostals today. Churches like the COGIC are renowned for their great choirs, soloists, impressive congregational singing, and upbeat instrumental music, all of which have become a major part of the music scene in the 20th century (Alford 1988: 691).

Pentecostalism in America was thus a new force that provided continuity of belief and practice in black, folk Christianity; it encouraged also the development of a musically diverse denomination. African roots, as exemplified in the primary ritual modes, will be examined further as a product of particular belief and practices in the Church of God in Christ. The analysis will highlight African concepts of spiritual power and ritual and the ways in which they illuminate the modes in COGIC.

Cultural Continuity:
African Roots of COGIC Religious Practices

Diaries and recorded accounts of missionaries, revivalists, foreigners, slaveholders, and slaves themselves reported performance practices that differentiated black religious traditions of slaves—and later emancipated blacks—from those of other American cultural groups. Various scholars have also documented the historical roots of black folk religion:

> Where enthusiastic and ecstatic religious behavior was encouraged, presented a congenial setting for slaves to merge African patterns of response with Christian interpretations of the experience of spirit possession, and experience shared by both blacks and whites. . . While the American slaves danced under the impulses of the spirit of the "new" god, they danced in ways their fathers in Africa would have recognized (Raboteau 1978: 72).

In *Soul Force: African Heritage in Afro American* Religion, Leonard Barrett described the syncretism of Africanisms in African American Christianity and its role in shaping Pentecostalism in America:

> Being filled with the spirit in African religion is known as possession. When evangelical Christianity and American religion met in the New World, there was a unique marriage that took place, a marriage that helped produce what we now call Pentecostalism, with its shouting, dancing, speaking in tongues and receiving the spirit. . . in these meetings Christianity rarely overcame the African element, but rather the reverse was usually the case: Christianity generally became Africanized (Barrett 1974: 85).

Concerning the black origins of the Pentecostal movement, Leonard Lovett wrote, "as with black spirituals, the Africanisms such as spirit possession, the dance, and shout songs are related to the functional character of West African religion" (Synan 1975: 137–139). Other historical accounts report that many black Pentecostal pioneers including William Seymour and Bishop Charles H. Mason were the sons of emancipated slaves whose "holistic view of religion had it roots in African religion" (Synan 1975: 138). James Tinney emphasized that, "if Pentecostalism deserves to be called a genuinely black religion because of its origins, the same holds true because of its distinctly African forms of worship" (Tinney 1977: 144). He noted further that,

> Nowhere outside of the Apostolic, Holiness Sanctified Pentecostal or Spiritualist churches (terms often used interchangeably, although doctrinal differences exist) can one find a religion which is truly black or African in its origins, worship styles, philosophy of faith, and practices (Tinney 1977: 135).

Maultsby further clarifies the historical development of the black folk church:

> For about three quarters of a century after the emancipation of slaves, freed blacks continued to engage in black religious practices that had characterized "praise house" meetings of slaves. The 20th century form of the plantation "praise house" is known as the black folk church. This church, associated with Holiness, Pentecostal, and such

independent black denominations was distinguished by practices of spirit possessions, shouts, chanted sermons, the feeling of familiarity with God. . . and the communal setting in which some songs were created and recreated (Maultsby 1981: 12).

More significant than cultural trait lists are the processes involved in the evolution of African-derived culture which, according to Lawrence Levine, continued "not as mere vestiges, but as dynamic, living, and creative parts" of black religious life in the United States.

In the Americas the religions of Africa have not been merely preserved as static "Africanisms" or as archaic retentions. . . African styles of worship, forms of ritual, systems of belief, and fundamental perspectives have remained vital on this side of the Atlantic, not because they were preserved in a "pure" orthodoxy but because they were transformed. Adaptability, based upon respect for spiritual power wherever it originated, accounted for the openness of African religions to syncretism with other religious traditions and for the continuity of a distinctively African religious consciousness (Raboteau 1978: 4–5).

Pentecostalism, as practiced in the Church of God in Christ, is undeniably colored by distinctive antebellum religious practices rooted in African cultural traditions and Judeo-Christian sources.

African Concept of Spiritual Power

A pervasive theme in many traditions throughout the world focuses on the attributes of spiritual power and its ability to change circumstances. Yet, based on many historical accounts, the concepts and daily uses of spiritual power in African and slave communities were too often described as pagan, animistic, or uncivilized. Similarly, African American folk styles of worship common in Pentecostal churches have been described in pejorative languages, based on misunderstandings of the belief in good and evil spirits, belief in the power to control evil spirits, and belief in being filled or possessed by spirits.

The African idea of God and religion is a broad and intricate subject and religion is undoubtedly of the most vital social institutions in Africa Scholars have identified a common cultural substructure for the general religious beliefs and practices associated with traditional African religions (King 1986; Mbiti 1969 and 1975; Idowu 1973). This common core includes the concept of one supreme God and lesser gods, good and evil spirits, tutelary spirits, ancestor deities, divination, spirit possession, exorcism, and the use of healing and ritual specialists who are indispensable in African religious life. Basic to many African traditional religions is the belief in God, the Creator, the highest spiritual being in the hierarchy. The supreme God is followed by lesser gods or deities whose purpose is to carry out the will of the Creator. There is also a hierarchical order of lesser deities who serve a myriad of functions related to ritual, nature, health, prosperity, or everyday domestic affairs (Mbiti 1969; Barrett 1974).

Another common aspect of African traditional religions is the belief in spirits and powers associated with God, deceased ancestors, and the human soul; they actively participate in daily among the living. Spirits are believed to be real beings that can communicate with man, appear in various forms during dreams or visions; they appear also as animate or inanimate objects. The belief that the spirits can possess those whom they favor is also prevalent. In many African ritual contexts, a devotee under possession is a transformed being that becomes a spirit, an ancestor, or just a medium that enables a spirit to make its will known. A priest or (priestess) can become possessed by a spirit for the purposes of curing or healing. (See examples in Friedson, Thompson, Emoff, Thram, and Malamusi in this volume [*The Interrelatedness of Music, Religion, and Ritual in African Performance Practice*]). Magic, divination, and forms of witchcraft or sorcery are also derived from indigenous beliefs and systems of thought. These beliefs are normally grounded in fundamental ideas about "good" and "evil" forces that can be controlled or unleashed through the ritual manipulation of materials by the experts. Music, drumming, chanted prayer, and incantation are also very important features of rites and ceremonies in which God, divinities, and spirit possessions are encountered.

In summary, many African traditional religions invoke the power of one supreme God as the provider, while others depend on spiritual mediators in their attempt to find physical and spiritual wholesomeness in life. These attributes of a spiritual power (i.e., both as a companion and a guide in daily life) are also central to COGIC belief and practices. COGIC people believe in one God, the Supreme Being and depend upon the anointing of God (and/or the Holy Spirit) for daily empowerment. While COGIC people do not worship deceased ancestors, they often describe dreams or visions of deceased family members. As documented in COGIC songs, this relationship with the deceased is a constant reminder of the spiritual world hereafter. For example, a traditional gospel song contains these words:

> One of these mornings, won't be very long,
> You're gonna look for me and I'll be gone,
> My mother will be waiting and my father too,
> And we'll just walk around, walk around heaven all day.

In *Black Sects and Cults*, Joseph Washington described many Africans as "power worshipers who seek power in all things and respect power potential wherever it is made manifest" (1972: 20–21). Gayraud Wilmore explains also the manner in which the spirit and secular worlds interconnect, based on African concepts: "The native religions of West and Central Africa had a single dominating characteristic. . . a profound belief that both the individual and the community had a continuous involvement with the spirit world in the practical affairs of daily life" (1972: 19–20). This religious perspective, which defines the reality of God as the experience of divine power manifested in everyday life, is also embedded in COGIC belief. Tinney described black Pentecostals as:

The modern day Africanists in their insistence upon the active role of both the Holy Ghost—the ultimate divine spirit, the angels—as lesser spirits of good will in God's creation, and evil spirits. Almost every event is seen as involving these principalities and powers (Tinney 1977: 149).

Many African traditional religions emphasize the role of spirits and human agents such as diviners or healers in maintaining balance, order, and control in sacred and secular affairs. While specific spiritualist practitioners such as diviners are not customary in COGIC practices, there is the use of spiritual practitioners in similar roles based on biblical methods for effecting spiritual power or presence. For example, COGIC believes that all Christians have access to spiritual gifts (such as healing, tongues, prophecy, or discernment) given by God, as described in I Corinthians 12. Members of the church, especially the elders and older "church mothers" who are considered endowed with a special anointing, are regularly sought after to minister to the church through their spiritual gifts.

The church believes that one of the most essential attributes of the gifts of the spirit is its potential as an artillery against principalities. Scripturally, principalities are associated with "powers and rulers of darkness in high places, or Satan, demonic forces, etc.: "For we wrestle not against flesh and blood, but against principalities, against powers, against the rulers of darkness in high places" (Ephesians 6:12, KJV). Again, the COGIC liturgy, founded on prayer, praise, and preaching through the anointing or the Holy Spirit, is designed for "spiritual warfare." In other words, songs, prayers, praise, and other performance traditions in the Church of God in Christ are ritually used to do battle against the "wiles of the Devil" as well as to render devotion and honor to God. An understanding of COGIC's view of Satanic forces and the ritual methods employed to subdue these evil forces is an important key in understanding why they continuously invoke the anointing of God through song, dance, prayer, or praise.

The biblical paradigm used by the church for recognizing the existence of satanic forces and the practice of exorcism called "casting out" or "loosening the hold" of Satan is the ministry of Jesus, as seen in the Gospels. The New Testament serves as the basis for the church's beliefs, since it contains several accounts of the power of Jesus over the lives of demonically influenced (i.e., possessed by evil spirits) persons:

1. The Gerasene demoniac (Matthew 8:28–34; Mark 5:1–20; Luke 8:26–39).
2. The Syrophoenician woman's daughter (Matthew 15:21–28; Mark 7:24–30).
3. The man with the unclean spirit (Mark 1:21–28; Luke 4:31–37).
4. The blind and mute demoniac (Matthew 12:22–29; Mark 3:22–27; Luke 11:14–22).
5. The epileptic boy (Matthew 17:14–21; Mark 9:14–29; Luke 9:37–43).
6. The woman with a spirit of infirmity (Luke 13:10–17).

These biblical case stories of demonic spirit possession confirm to the church the existence of these forces through their physical forms, names, ability to speak, their fear of God, and immediate obedience to God's power. The formula, "in the name of Jesus," is used in this church when casting out ungodly spirits to indicate that the ritual of "casting out" is being done under Jesus' authority and power. Other verbal commands during exorcisms still used by COGIC people include "Satan, the Lord rebuke you" "cast the devil out of the minds," and "Satan, I command you to flee." Persons in the church—including the late founder—who are considered specially endowed with spiritual gifts such as the spiritual gift of discernment, may identify the spirit by what it does or by the effects it has over a person. "Spirit of death," "spirit of lying," or "spirit of sickness" are phrases used to identify Satan's wiles. While praying for others in need, Bishop Mason identified and openly rebuked ungodly spirits:

> This is a time that we need Jesus. We need the word of his wonders. We need the wisdom of the blood. We need the coming of the coming, Jesus the Savior. Satan, the Lord rebuke you. Death, the Lord rebuke you. An enemy, the Lord rebuke you. A liar, the Lord rebuke you. Ashamed, the Lord rebuke you. The blood, the blood, the blood of Jesus Christ, God's anointing giving unto all (Mason 1988).

Another verbal command as illustrated in the above example is "blood of Jesus." The "blood of Jesus" symbolizes power and authority in the believer over Satan when exorcising spirits from persons, or when casting their presence out of a place. It is important to note that whether or not the source of a person's sickness, misfortune, or psychological problem is due to Satanic forces is not as important to COGIC people as the faith in their authority over any adversity, demon, or unclean spirit through God's anointing power.

The African's close relationship with God and interaction with supernatural spirits in controlling life circumstances remained vibrant when transported to the Americas. After conversion to Christianity, slaves retained much of their African religious practices in new forms and reinterpreting them in biblical contexts. The belief in one supreme God, the roles and influences identified with good and evil spirits, spirit possession, the ritual use of music, song, dance and other affective responses have continued in African American folk religious traditions. The spiritual practitioner rather than the folk doctor or medicine person in the Church of God in Christ assumed the role of a preacher and anointed individuals with the gift of healing. The African's belief in tutelary spirits or lesser gods thus shifted to a belief in angels and the anointing of the Holy Spirit. The practice of divination using ritual objects, potions, and the use of magic formulas in African ritual settings were substituted with the spiritual gifts referred to in I Corinthians 12 (such as the gift of discernment, or the gift of prophecy). Ritual objects and special techniques such as the healing cloth anointed with holy oil and placed on the ailing body became the Christian custom.

"Prayed-over" or anointed healing cloths, handkerchiefs, and other consecrated materials function as points of contact to heighten one's faith and expectation of healing. Trance (or altered state of consciousness) was supplanted by the holy dance or "shout." Ultimately, for scores of Africans reduced to slaves—who in turn influenced black Pentecostal traditions—the religious aesthetic of worship meant spiritual power to balance good and evil, and to liberate one from social, psychological, and spiritual bondage:

> For the African, the black slave and the black American Pentecostal, religion is primarily about experiencing the power of God. God's presence and power must be felt or revealed in a pragmatic, personal, subjective, and even exciting way. . . The God they served in their secret meetings was a God who possessed them with his spirit and liberated them in ecstatic worship. . . Feelings were to be experienced to the full, and were expressed in the melancholy and pathos of spirituals, and in the shout, the song and the dance of excited worship and the celebration of life (McRoberts 1988: 14).

This outline of continuity and change in African American religious practices highlights an important research orientation often ignored among pioneer scholars of the African Diaspora: that it is primarily the methods and forms that have changed while the African concepts and belief about the spirit world and the influential, communicative powers of the performance (i.e., music, chant, dance, and prayer) have continue to shape COGIC ritual performance. I have identified the most frequent performance frames that appear within the COGIC liturgical setting as ritual modes. These modes symbolize components of COGIC belief and are associated with distinct ritual, cultural, and musical practices. A mode is classified as either primary or secondary, based on its spiritual core, ritual context, performance frequency, and on its African cultural connections. Ritual dimensions of music that represent the spiritual foundation of belief in the Church of God in Christ are categorized as primary ritual modes. Musical practices derived from written art forms such as European classical and African American secular styles are categorized as secondary ritual modes. The following section will examine the primary ritual modes in COGIC that incorporate specific forms of dancing, singing, praying, and preaching.

Shout Mode

Sterling Stuckey researched the origins of the ring shout, which is considered one of the most spectacular slave ritual events. "Shouting," a gestural, musical, dance or verbal response to the spirit, is still preserved today in certain regions of the south, such as the island of St. Helena off the coast of South Carolina. A modified version of the shout called the holy dance in African American Pentecostal churches is often a climactic stage of ritual liminality. According to Stuckey,

> While the ring shout was endemic to both West and Central Africa, the powerful circle ritual imported from Angola-Congo region was elaborate in its religious vision that it

exerted the central influence on slaves in Carolina. Today on the island of St. Helena church elders still employ circle formations in singing spirituals (Holloway 1990: xiii).

Shouting is more spontaneously personalized in Pentecostal churches, rather than the ring or circular formation practiced in the early church. Historical accounts and eyewitness descriptions of the shout are varied, but most have looked upon the practice pejoratively. James Weldon Johnson gave this description:

> The ring shout, in truth, is nothing more or less than the survival of a primitive African dance, which in quite an understandable way attached itself in the early days to Negro's Christian worship. I can remember seeing this dance many times when I was a boy. . . A man and women arrange themselves, generally alternately, in a ring, their bodies quite close. The music starts and the ring begins to move. . . Around and around it moves on shuffling feet that do not leave the floor, one foot beating with the heel a decided accent in strict two-four time. The music is supplemented by the clapping of hands. . . The music, starting, perhaps, with a spiritual, becomes a wild, monotonous chant. . . The very monotony of sound and motion produces an ecstatic state (Johnson 1926: 33).

Eileen Southern also considered the shout to be "purely African in form and tradition" (Southern 1971: 162). Southern later compiled a number of historical sources illustrating the musical practice of the singing and shouting of slaves.

Today, there are various ritual contexts for stylized dancing or shouting in the Church of God in Christ. The shout/dance mode flows out of jubilant celebration during a climactic phase of the Pentecostal event. It is usually performed in a free style to the accompaniment of song, polyrhythmic drumming, clapping, and others. The shout mode is constructed primarily through verbal rejoicing, singing and dancing as the congregation receives blessings or spiritual confirmations through a song, prophesy, testimony or the preached Word. COGIC saints do not shout and dance to induce the Holy Spirit, but shout in celebration of the Spirit, who is considered already present.

The distinct musical idiom of the shout mode is a specialty of African American Pentecostal praise; it is also a dominant feature in COGIC dance music. A most prominent stylistic feature of the shout mode is its fast, driving beat and intricate polyrhythms. The quarter note can equal a tempo marking of MM 150–170, with the foot pattern on beats one and three, and hand clapping on beats two and four (Appendix C-2). Liminal phases of COGIC ritual increase as dancing becomes "endowed" with the Holy Spirit. Dancing during ritual celebration can be associated with ludic ritual responses since it includes joyous play and dramatic reenactment of faith through movement, gestures, and highly creative footstepping. One author explains the shout this way:

> Shouting may, at times, be put on or manipulated. But at its best it teaches. . . that the presence of God is pure ecstasy—that before God we can be absolutely free and uninhibited—that God freely accepts and loves the real person that we have to hide almost everywhere else (Henry Mitchell, quoted in Clemmons 1975: 77).

Shouting or dancing is a common encounter in COGIC worship. According to Joseph Clemmons (minister, scholar and lifelong member of COGIC), ritual dance and spiritual ecstasy "frees the people's spirit enabling them to respond to their deepest anxieties in their own particular and creative ways" (Clemmons 1975: 77).

Sermon Mode

In the Church of God in Christ one mark of an outstanding preacher is the ability to combine scriptural content and performance style with the anointing. In addition to a sermon's spiritual nucleus, there are varied storytelling techniques that incorporate verbal skills, drama, and musical devices. These devices, combined with elements of play and improvisation, shape the persuasive power of the preacher and intensify the total ritual atmosphere. Some performance practices that are central to COGIC preaching include:

A   Verbal art skills: incorporate rhyme, word ornamentation, phrase sequencing, simile, metaphor, text painting, word repetition, allusion, allegory, thematic development, reinterpreted biblical themes, formulaic expressions, hymn interpolation, and verbal play involving signifying and instigation.

B   Dramatic techniques: involve role playing, plot development (with participation and feedback from music specialists and general audience), action, gestures, facial expressions, mood painting, signifying, and instigating as play.

C   Musical devices: incorporate rhythmic timing, stall techniques used to delay time in order to heighten anticipation, melodic improvisation, timbral manipulation, pitch bending, ornamentation, vocal flexibility, harmony, and organ, piano, bass, or drum accompaniment.

Dancing, singing, testifying, and praying in the Church of God in Christ are preparatory for effective preaching. Extended narratives in the form of parables, anecdotes, personal biographical material, and traditional stories are also used to illustrate important lessons in the sermon. The full command of preaching as a composite art form is accomplished primarily through musical and paramusical resources.

In African traditional religions, including many independent or "spiritual" churches, participation in music and dance often encourages social and spiritual bonding, as well as communal interaction. These functions and attributes of music and dance in African religious contexts are increased by the inherent therapeutic and transcendent effects or benefits commonly identified with ritual music and dance. The sermon styles of slave preachers were multidimensional and were characterized by improvised chanting, singing, moaning, shouting, and dancing. This highly inventive mode of preaching is also typical of COGIC preaching, which not only dramatizes the Bible, but also prompts spirited audience participation:

Music brought everybody into the worship experience as participants. No one was to be separated as a spectator or stranger, an observer or on-looker. Everyone was invited to become a part of the free flow of spirit-empowered feelings, enhancing supernatural energies. All were in worship harmony with that spiritual energy generating from the conduit of the high office (Ofori-atta-Thomas 1986: 58).

Prayer Mode

Sung prayers, praises, and chants are directed to various deities in many traditional African religions. Petitioning God through chanted prayers is another common ritual practice in the Church of God in Christ that emphasizes one's relationship to God. A familiar sound that permeates various points of the COGIC liturgy is the heterophonic moaning of prayer chants. The moaning qualities of the prayer mode can be described as a song without words, a soulful lament, or an intoned cry of supplication. With the lowered third, perfect fourth, perfect or lowered fifth, and seventh degrees typical of blues-based scales, the moaning mode emphasizes the minor scale. Chanted prayer is similar to singing in the spirit and often punctuated by improvisatory groans, wails, crying, varieties of sonic or timbral gestures, and by other forms of verbal utterance. Heterophonic textures are produced as individually chanted lines, especially when the congregation interweave along the central melodic theme chanted by the prayer leader. On other occasions, the prayer chant may be collectively improvised without a leader.

A portion of three prayers chanted during different ritual events is transcribed in Appendix C-1. Prayer #1 was chanted during a collective prayer vigil held daily in a secluded prayer chapel located at the Mason Temple Church of God in Christ, Memphis. Prayer #2 *was* chanted by a minister who was leading the prayer or invocation during a night service. One of the more elaborate chanted prayers was Prayer #3 by the gospel singer Evangelist Dorinda Clark-Cole before her sermon, which *was* delivered at a youth revival. While there are ordinary spoken prayers and emotionally heightened or intensely charged spoken prayers, the chanted prayer is more representative of culturally patterned music behavior based on African traditional performance practices. The sounds of "blackness" embedded within COGIC chanted prayers richly illustrate blues patterns, melodic and rhythmic improvisation, spontaneity, collective interaction, extemporaneous composition, and spiritual empowerment.

Devotional Mode

The devotional mode in the Church of God in Christ involves congregational singing, testifying and the playing of instruments to enhance group interaction and freedom to verbally express faith in God. The devotional mode consists of a diverse group of song types in the style of folk spirituals, "songs of the Lord," Mason song types, lined-out hymns, charismatic praise and worship songs, and testimony songs.

Folk spiritual song types are perhaps one of the most distinct musical forms in the African American Pentecostal song service or devotional mode. Originating in slave praise houses during the antebellum period, folk spirituals have been historically associated with the African forms of celebration, festival, dance or ring shout, and spiritual possession or spiritual ecstasy. In the Church of God in Christ, songs derived from folk spirituals retain these traditional African performance practices and are ritually ordered around dancing or shouting. Folk spirituals have textually short verses, lively call-and-response melodies, varied textual themes, and *ad lib* solo lines antiphonal to the repetitive chorus. Many COGIC traditional songs such as, "If You Call on Jesus," "Have You Tried Jesus, He's All Right," "I'm a Soldier in the Army of the Lord," or "Just Like Fire Shut Up in My Bones," are popular devotional or testimony songs that incorporate the rhythmic drive of drumming appropriate for celebrating and dancing out one's faith.

A special section in the Church of God in Christ *Yes Lord Hymnal* provides a skeletal notation of the form and shout piano accompaniments of call-and-response songs as a frame of reference for musicians not trained in the oral tradition (Appendix C-2). COGIC call-and-response (i.e., folk-type spirituals) and shout accompaniments, which are free variants of the formulaic "i7-IV" chordal pattern and the minor blues scale (superimposed upon the major scale), are faster versions of the prayer and sermon chant music. In addition to drumming, COGIC folk spirituals often include a "walking bass line" on organ bass, piano or guitar, handclapping, and tambourine patterns. A dominant feature of 'jubilee" folk spiritual is the rhythmic beat of the COGIC shout mode: each block of sound creates a syncopated, polyrhythmic and heterophonic texture stressing beats two and four.

Pneumatic Mode

Another dominant musical feature of this black Pentecostal church is the emphasis on "singing in the spirit." The legacy of COGIC song expressions, including the Mason traditional songs, has been built on the belief that the Holy Spirit is a singing spirit." An observable demonstration of a spiritual intervention in this type of ritual performance is analytically classified in this study as pneumatic. Musical genres that emerge out of the pneumatic mode consist of impromptu songs believed to be composed under the influence of the Holy Ghost. These impromptu songs do not function as performance pieces but as meditative exercises of sacred devotion. The *pneuma* in Christian belief is interpreted as the breath of God:

The Greek phrase is *ode pneumatikos,* meaning songs of the pneuma—the breath of God. It could be said that God exhales songs through the yielded singer. God inspires and writes songs; he is the great author and composer. He gives spontaneous songs of praise and exhortation. These are songs of the Spirit of God (Boschman 1986: 3).

It appears that there are spiritual practitioners in the Church of God in Christ who speak and interpret tongues, while others sing and interpret tongues. According to COGIC belief, glossolalia or spoken tongues is a religious phenomenon that may be prompted abruptly without previous planning and can emerge at any time during worship, praise, and praying rituals.

Musical genres within the pneumatic mode that incorporate the practice of singing in the spirit, or singing in tongues are also called songs of the Lord, spiritual songs, prophetic songs, or sung glossolalia (Blomgren 1978; Sorge 1984; Boschman 1986). A believer considered to have the gift of interpretation may interpret the text of a song uttered in tongues. Thus, the primary function of this type of pneumatic song is to deliver a spiritual message for the edification of the entire church. Singing in the Spirit may also emerge in ordinary language using biblical texts, verses from hymns, or newly composed lyrics. In private meditative settings, singing in the spirit or singing in tongues is a high form of personal expression to God that enables believers to "make melody in their hearts to the Lord" (Ephesians 5:19; Colossians 3:16). Singing in tongues is frequently observed during an intense, liminal stage of the service and is considered by the saints the physical evidence that God is directly communicating to the church through individuals. The greatest influence on the pneumatic tradition indigenous to COGIC is the Mason spiritual songs believed to be born out of the Holy Ghost. Mason songs, which have been transcribed in the COGIC *Yes Lord Hymnal,* are still performed in Pentecostal and non-Pentecostal denominations throughout the United States.

In sum, Pentecostalism in America represents a significant African American religious and cultural initiative and elaboration, drawing primarily on African religious and ritual concepts and practices. Within the twin framework of Judeo-Christian and African heritage, African American folk Christianity engages also—albeit creatively—contemporary popular culture, including music. Slave religion and its later manifestations in COGIC (and beyond) stimulated both religious revival and musical diversity in America. The African background is essential in researching and appreciating the music and culture of African American Pentecostalism.

The arguments and evidence presented in this essay confirm that it is primarily the methods and forms of African-derived traditions that have changed while African concepts and practices about the spirit world and the power to control them through music, chant, dance and prayer have continued to shape COGIC ritual performance. I have identified the most frequent performance frames that appear within the COGIC liturgical setting as ritual modes. These modes symbolize components of COGIC belief and are associated with distinct ritual, cultural, and musical practices.

The different modes, primary and secondary, illuminate the notions of liminality and ritual/social drama; they overlap also in many specific contexts and in their performance arrangements.

Notes

1. The term "African" is employed here to designate the basic or core values that are characteristic of African philosophical, religious, ethic, social, artistic, and musical expressions. These core values are often identified with black African peoples and cultures of the various geographic regions of Africa (e.g., Mbiti 1975; Hountonji 1983; Nketia 1974; Thompson 1983).

2. The general discourse on retentions has evolved from the classic works of Melville Herskovits (1956, 1958) and comprise processes distinguished variously such as *syncretism, acculturation, reinterpretation, autonomous invention, cultural focus, revival,* etc. (see Holloway 1990 for a review of some of these concepts; for music, see for example Oliver 1970, Evans 1981, 54–66; and Kubik 1999).

3. As summed up in his title, *African Gods and Music,* the integrity of music and ritual is a popular encounter in the African context of belief, spirituality, and ritual performance (Nketia 1975).

4. These modes are not strictly exclusive; they overlap and interact in performance in various ways.

5. Some of the African ideals regarding the aesthetic include scope for individual expression, audience input, musical elaboration, emphasis on contrastive timbres, percussive sound, asymmetrical and non-linear structures, polyrhythm, allusion, irony, etc.

26
Preservation and Dissemination: The Black Gospel Music Restoration Project

Robert Darden

From the standpoint of information sharing, we are in the midst of a time of great change. The rise of the Virtual Library—the Internet—has meant that books, old and new, are becoming more available to the general public. Today, most academic journals are published online. Some are published only online. Even back issues of those journals are also available to scholars online. Back issues of many newspapers and magazines are slowly being scanned and digitized as well.

But, if a scholar or a fan wants to hear what something sounded like, the options are limited. If that scholar or fan wants to hear what African American sacred music of the past sounded like, those options are even more limited. In far too many cases, that music in any format—those arrangements and that sheet music—simply do not exist. No one thought to preserve it until it was (in many cases) too late.

The Black Gospel Music Restoration Project (BGMRP) at Baylor University Libraries was founded as a result of that stark realization. The music I loved was not available for love or money.

I am a lifelong lover of gospel music and former Gospel Music Editor for *Billboard Magazine*. As an Associate Professor of Journalism, Public Relations & New Media for Baylor University, I wrote the book *People Get Ready: A New History of Black Gospel Music* for Continuum Press in 2005. During the course of my research, I discovered that much of the seminal music I was writing about—the music that is at the foundation of virtually all American popular music—was lost. After consulting with the keepers of several major collections, we came up with the figure that seventy-five percent of all vinyl from gospel's Golden Age (a nebulously defined era that we have chosen to indicate as 1945 to 1970) is unavailable to either academic or casual collector.

Frustrated and a little angry, I wrote an editorial, titled "Gospel's Got the Blues," that appeared on the op-ed page of *The New York Times* on February 15, 2005. (http://www.nytimes.com/2005/02/15/opinion/15darden.html?_r=0) In the editorial, I lamented this irreplaceable loss and closed with the statement, "It would be more than a cultural disaster to forever lose this music. It would be a sin."

The following morning, I received a call from the office of Charles M. Royce, a well-known New York area businessman and philanthropist. Though Mr. Royce knew little about gospel music or me, he suggested that if I could devise a plan to preserve gospel's fast-disappearing vinyl legacy, he would donate the initial grant to that end.

I immediately went to the Baylor University libraries, where I met with Interim Director Bill Hair, the Assistant Vice President of the Electronic Library Tim Logan, the Director of the Electronic Library Billie Peterson-Lugo, and Unit Leader Darryl Stuhr. All four were immediately supportive. Using the Royce grant, I visited Arhoolie Records in El Cerrito, California where the Chris Strachwitz Collection of Mexican and Mexican American Recordings had begun a similar campaign to identify, digitize, and catalogue that music, establishing the Frontera Collection in conjunction with UCLA. On that trip, my wife, Dr. Mary Darden, and Lance Ledbetter, founder of the acclaimed digital reissue label, Dust to Digital, accompanied me. The initiative received an additional boost with the arrival of the new Dean of the University Libraries Vice President for Information Technologies, Pattie Orr, who immediately grasped the importance of a one-of-a-kind historic audio collection.

Over the next few years, working with the library's technical staff and the first audio engineer, Tony Tadey, the BGMRP was completed in the basement of Moody Library http://www.baylor.edu/lib/gospel/.

Today, the state-of-the-art studio is the center of preservation and restoration efforts in the library. Gospel recordings on vinyl (as well as on cassettes, eight-tracks, and reel-to-reel recordings) arrive on a daily basis, where they are cleaned, digitized, scanned (the jacket, sleeve, and even the disk itself are all scanned and logged) catalogued, and made available for scholarly and casual listeners. Although the BGMRP will accept donated materials, the preferred practice is to accept the original materials on loan, digitally record them, and then return them along with a CD or MP3 of the music, should the lender request them. The BGMRP will pay all shipping and insurance for any loaned or donated materials.

The BGMRP's mandate, from the beginning, was to include vinyl featuring African American preaching, gospel sheet music, uniquely African American choral arrangements, photographs, and other ephemera.

In its first few years, the project was featured on national radio programs, in magazines, in newspapers and on television (including, respectively, NPR's *Fresh Air* with Terri Gross, *The Texas Observer*, *The Dallas Morning News*, and HD Net [now the AXS Network]). The BGMRP is now believed to house the largest collection of digitized gospel vinyl in the United States. For copyright reasons, casual listeners who log on to the site can listen to thirty seconds of each digitized song. Off-campus scholars and academicians can request distance access to the entire collection. Students and academicians on the Baylor University campus may listen to entire songs via the campus server.

Since Mr. Royce's initial grant, other groups, including the Prichard Family Foundation, which established the Lev H. Prichard III Traditional Black Music Restoration Endowed Fund, have supported the efforts of the BGMRP.

The Black Gospel Music Restoration Project's goal is to digitize, catalogue, and make available every piece of gospel vinyl ever released, no matter how rare or obscure. Additionally, they seek to supplement that collection with an equally definitive collection of sermons by African American preachers, sheet and print music, photographs, and related ephemera. Ultimately, the BGMRP would like to create a portable studio/museum that could stop in America's historically black neighborhoods and continue the preservation process on site.

27

Pentecostalism and Black Secular Music

Teresa L. Reed

In their book *Stairway to Heaven: The Spiritual Roots of Rock 'n' Roll*, Davin Seay and Mary Neely wrote, ". . . by the mid fifties, currents of showmanship and sanctification in black American culture were rapidly converging. Whether the glory-bound black Pentecostal preacher was an archetype for James Brown (and every other conked and sweating rhythm and blues hero), or whether it was. . . the other way around hardly seems to matter. They were two sides to the same Janus-faced coin."[1] Indeed, the similarities between rhythm and blues and black Pentecostalism have been well documented. In his performances, James Brown captures the soulful spontaneity of the Sanctified church and the animated exhortation of the Sanctified preacher. He also emulates and incites an emotional intensity parallel to the Holy Spirit possession that is a trademark of the Sanctified worship service. The sounds and gestures common to both Pentecostalism and black secular music, however, result from historical conditions forged well before the 1950s.

The Pentecostal religious tradition is now embraced by many different cultures and Christian denominations. Dating from first century Christianity and transcending national, cultural, and ethnic boundaries, twentieth-century Pentecostalism has been called one of the watershed phenomena of recent times. In 1995, Pentecostals worldwide were numbered at 410 million.[2] The central tenet of this religious persuasion first appears in the Bible in the second chapter of the Acts of the Apostles: "And when the day of Pentecost was fully come, they were all gathered in one place, in one accord. And there appeared unto them cloven tongues of fire and lighted on each one of them. And they began to speak with tongues, as the Spirit gave them utterance" (Acts 2:1–4). Technically, the practice of "speaking in tongues" or *glossolalia*, is the defining characteristic of Pentecostalism. The term *Pentecostal*, however, has also been used in a broader sense to describe an approach to Christian worship characterized by emotional freedom, intensity, spontaneity, and physical expressivity. In addition to these worship practices, Pentecostals also exhibit the influence of Wesleyan Holiness, the lifestyle patterns of which reflect a more or less literal interpretation of the Bible. For this reason, although they are not synonymous, the terms *Holiness, Sanctified,* and *Pentecostal* are often used interchangeably or in conjunction with each other in many African American circles.[3]

In the United States, the father of modern-day Pentecostalism is Charles F. Parham, a Bible teacher from Topeka, Kansas. The first and most significant Pentecostal revival of this century was sparked in 1906 by Parham's student William J. Seymour, the son of former slaves. Long before Seymour's Azusa Street revival, however, the worship aesthetic of Pentecostalism was present in the bush meetings and praise houses of the black slaves.

Eyewitness accounts of slave worship practice suggest that these services were characterized by musical improvisation, emotional intensity, dramatic physical expression, and community interaction. Henry Russell's nineteenth-century account of an African American religious service cites the interplay between minister and congregation, the Africanization of an old psalm tune, and the rhythmic nature of the music. He writes: "When the minister gave out his own version of the Psalm, the choir commenced singing so rapidly that the original tune absolutely ceased to exist—in fact, the fine old psalm tune became thoroughly transformed into a kind of Negro melody; and so sudden was the transformation, by accelerating the time, that for a moment, I fancied that not only the choir but the little congregation intended to get up a dance as part of the service."[4] Another description was recorded by John Watson, the nineteenth-century Methodist clergyman who lived in Philadelphia in the early 1800s and reported his observations of African American religious practices in a work called *Methodist Error or Friendly Christian Advice to Those Methodists Who Indulge in Extravagant Religious Emotions and Bodily Exercises* (Trenton: D. and E. Fenton, 1819). In it, he rebukes African American Methodists for extravagant worship practices and, in the process, vividly describes their approach to religious singing:

> In the blacks' quarter, the colored people get together, and sing for hours together, short scraps of disjointed affirmations, pledges, or prayers, lengthened out with long repetition choruses. These are all sung in the merry chorus manner of the southern harvest field, or husking-frolic method, of the slave blacks... With every word so sung, they have a sinking of one or other leg of the body alternately; producing an audible sound of the feet at every step, and as manifest as the steps of actual Negro dancing in Virginia... If some, in the meantime sit, they strike the sounds alternately on each thigh. What in the name of religion, can countenance or tolerate such gross perversions of true religion!... I have known in some camp meetings, from 50 to 60 people crowded into one tent, after the public devotions had closed, and there continue the whole night, singing tune after tune... Some of these... are actually composed as sung, and are indeed almost endless.[5]

Fredrika Bremer, a nineteenth-century novelist, visited the United States from 1849 to 1850 and recorded her observations of a Southern camp meeting in *Homes of the New World: Impressions of America* (New York: Harper and Brothers, 1853). Her account of the tent service includes the following description of black worship style: "In the camp of the blacks is heard a great tumult and a loud cry. Men roar and bawl out; women screech like pigs about to be killed; many, having fallen into convulsions, leap and strike about them, so that they are obliged to be held down. It looks here and there like a regular fight... During all this tumult, the singing continues loud and beautiful, and the thunder joins in with its pealing kettle-drum."[6] In addition to the highly improvisatory singing, a central feature of the African American worship of the nineteenth century was the shout. A vivid description of the ring shout appears in the 1867 collection *Slave Songs of the United States*. The editor notes:

> The true "shout" takes place on Sundays or on "praise" nights through the week, or either in the praise-house or in some cabin in which a regular religious meeting has been held. Very likely more than half the population of the plantation is gathered together... The benches are pushed back to the wall when the formal meeting is over, and old and young, men and women... all stand up in the middle of the floor, and when the [spiritual] is struck up, begin first walking and by-and-by shuffling round, one after the other, in a ring. The foot is hardly taken from the floor, and the progression is mainly due to a jerking, hitching motion, which agitates the entire shouter, and soon brings out streams of perspiration.[7]

Slave narratives are full of anecdotes of the lengths to which slaves went in order to conceal the sound of their late-night worship. According to many narratives, a common practice was to place an upside-down kettle near the door of the cabin to absorb the sound of singing, clapping, and shouting.[8]

While the African worship aesthetic was pervasive in the antebellum "invisible" black church, approaches to worship would gradually change as African Americans increasingly assumed denominational identities. Some black denominations, particularly in the North, would seek to suppress the dramatic emotional displays so as to achieve a more structured church service and a more refined image; other denominations, particularly in the South, would continue to encourage physical expressions of religious ecstasy.

The intensity of the slaves' worship can be attributed, to a great extent, to their West-African spiritual heritage. Improvisatory singing, energetic dancing, and spirit possession are all part of West African religious practice. For white Americans, however, such behaviors were considered excessive and bizarre. Physical expressions of religious fervor among whites were commonly reported in the accounts of several small revivals in the United States that are viewed as significant precursors of twentieth-century Pentecostalism. In 1801, a camp meeting in Cane Ridge, Kentucky, reached its climax with the gathering of twenty-five thousand in search of religious renewal. According to eyewitnesses, the scene was one of "godly hysteria" and included such phenomena as falling, jerking, barking like dogs, falling into trances, the "holy laugh" and "such wild dances as David performed before the Ark of the Lord."[9] Evidence suggests that many whites that engaged in such practices may have been influenced by the African American example of expressive freedom. In his reprimand of the "chaotic" worship style of black Methodists, John Watson states that their example had "visibly affected the religious manner of some whites."[10]

In addition to the Cane Ridge Revival, a similar revival in 1801 swept the University of Georgia, and students who were eyewitnesses to the revival noted that they heard some of the faithful talk "in unknown tongues."[11] Theirs was one of the earliest reports of glossolalic experience in the United States. In Charles W. Conn's account of an 1896 revival in Cherokee County, North Carolina, he notes that some of the faithful were "curiously exercised by the Holy Spirit" to the extent that they were speaking in unknown languages.[12] A subsequent and much more widely publicized glossolalic manifestation occurred in 1901 in Topeka, Kansas, in a church meeting conducted by Charles F. Parham, who was then director of the Bethel Bible College.

Because he was the first to preach that glossolalia was the only evidence of Holy Spirit baptism, Parham is considered the principal pioneer of modern Pentecostalism. The events of Parham's Topeka revival, however, were but preludes to a much more significant occurrence six years later. It was the revival at the Apostolic Faith Mission on 312 Azusa Street in Los Angeles, California, that generated the Pentecostal explosion whose repercussions are still felt today.

The Apostolic Faith Mission on Azusa Street was the former Stevens African Methodist Episcopal Church, a historical connection that seems symbolic of the centrality of African Americans to the modern Pentecostal movement. The founder and leader of the revival was William Joseph Seymour, a Louisiana native and the son of former slaves.[13] Seymour enrolled in Charles Parham's Bible School, which by 1905 had moved its location to Houston, Texas. After having embraced Parham's teachings, Seymour left Texas for a preaching engagement in Los Angeles, California, where his first sermon was on Acts 2:4 and the necessity of the glossolalic experience. Although his message was opposed by the Southern California Holiness Association, which had sponsored his Los Angeles visit, Seymour continued to preach from porches to an ever-increasing crowd of people gathered in the streets. To accommodate the crowds, he began to hold services in the old Stevens AME Church building, which by that time was being used as a stable and warehouse. Seymour held his first service there on April 14, 1906, and, for three years following, services were held there three times daily, seven days a week. Aside from the unusual phenomenon of glossolalia at Azusa Street, a noteworthy feature of the revival was the racial integration and cultural diversity represented in its following. As with many smaller revivals of the nineteenth-century camp-meeting tradition, the Azusa revival was racially integrated in an otherwise segregated America. The interracial nature of the revival, however, was viewed with suspicion and disapproval by the larger society, and these sentiments were voiced in the press.

H. V. Synan comments that during the revival, it was "reported that. . . 'all the stunts common in old camp meetings among colored folks' were being performed in the services" and that "white people [were] imitating [the] unintelligent, crude negroisms of the Southland."[14] Nonetheless, by the end of 1906, Seymour incorporated his ministry as the Pacific Apostolic Faith Movement and started publication of a periodical, the *Apostolic Faith*, which was circulated to approximately 50,000 subscribers.

The Azusa revival attracted believers from all across the nation and even from overseas, but Seymour's leadership was challenged in 1908 by two of his white office workers, Clara Lum and Florence Crawford. After Seymour rejected Lum's romantic advances, these women stole the mailing list of the *Apostolic Faith* to protest his 1908 marriage to Jenny Moore. In so doing, they destroyed Seymour's ability to communicate with the thousands who considered him their leader. Struggles with other whites reduced Seymour's influence to the point that by 1914 the Azusa Street Mission was a local black church. Seymour died on September 28, 1922.

According to Synan, "Practically every early Pentecostal movement in the world can trace its origins directly or indirectly to Seymour's Azusa Street Mission."[15] Black Americans were particularly affected by the Azusa Street revival, and several founders of the first black Pentecostal denominations were in attendance at the services conducted by Seymour. Charles Harrison Mason, founder of the Church of God in Christ, received his own glossolalic experience during his five-week visit to the Azusa Street Mission.

Just as Seymour's work attracted many blacks to the experience of speaking in tongues, it created a division between blacks who embraced the practice and those who did not. One example of this tension resulted in the formation of the Church of Christ (Holiness) after Charles H. Mason's return from Azusa Street. Mason and Charles Price Jones had both been Holiness preachers and very close friends before the Azusa Revival and had cofounded the Church of God in Christ together in 1896. After Mason embraced glossolalia, however, the two parted ways. Mason's ministry retained the name Church of God in Christ and became the largest African American Pentecostal denomination in the world; Charles Price Jones founded the non-Pentecostal Church of Christ (Holiness).

Of importance here is that except for the issue of speaking in tongues, many black Holiness denominations founded around the turn of the century are identical in every other way—doctrinally, aesthetically, structurally, and socially—to the black churches that identify themselves as Pentecostal. For this reason, the term *Pentecostal* is often applied to some black churches that don't practice glossolalia, but nevertheless retain the most dramatic elements of the African aesthetic. The term *Holiness/Pentecostal* perhaps more accurately denotes the energetic worship style and Holiness-based moral codes that are common to both groups.

The revivals of the nineteenth century and the Azusa revival of the early 1900s were attractive to African Americans because they institutionalized a concept of spirituality with which blacks had long been familiar. The notion that a divine presence could engender physical responses in human beings was a core component of the West African belief system, one that persisted in the consciousness of the blacks brought to America. In West Africa, a central component of religious experience is that of spirit possession. It was believed that through ritualistic dancing, the divinities, or the *orisha*, could be summoned to literally enter the physical body of the celebrant. The divinity once "mounted" would then make its presence known by altering the dance with its characteristic gestures. With the goal of spirit possession achieved, the celebrant's intimacy with the Divine is confirmed.[16] Because spirit possession was already a familiar concept to them, blacks could easily accept the notion of possession by the Holy Spirit found in Christianity. Furthermore, they accepted that a natural result of being possessed or filled with the Holy Spirit was some type of physical manifestation, be it shouting, screaming, or speaking in tongues. Thus, for African Americans, the physical dramatics of worship associated with these revivals were not just accepted— they were expected, appreciated, and viewed as evidence of God's proximity.

Charles Harrison Mason was deliberate in his effort to retain the flavor of African slave religion in the worship style of the Church of God in Christ. In the formative years of the denomination, however, black Pentecostals were in conflict about whether to retain or to dispense with traditional slave religious practices such as the shout. This controversy resulted from the desire some blacks had to distance themselves from the stigma and stereotypes of slavery. Mason, however, taught his followers to embrace and celebrate the African expression of their faith, and in his sermons and writings he supported his position with scriptural evidence describing dance as an acceptable form of praise to God.[17]

Generally speaking, black Holiness/Pentecostal churches became easily distinguishable by their successful preservation of several elements of what Ithiel C. Clemmons calls the "African spirit cosmology."[18] These elements include devotional spontaneity, an energetic and improvisatory musical style, a communal, interactive setting, and a Spirit-led approach to temporality. Devotional spontaneity is manifest in the extemporaneous hollers, cries, and handclaps of the faithful. In some cases, individuals may spontaneously speak in tongues. In a black Holiness/Pentecostal church, it is not at all unusual to find the entire congregation—old and young alike—overtaken in the "holy dance" and speaking in tongues. These impromptu expressions are welcome features of the worship experience.

The musicians in these churches are often expert improvisers. They usually play by ear rather than by written music, and their accompaniment of the intensely animated singing, preaching, and shouting is skillfully rendered. Because they must be able to accompany any worshipper singing in any key, the musicians are flexible and creative and may even be described as virtuosic. These churches also incorporate a variety of instruments in their ensembles, the most common of which are piano, Hammond organ, drums, bass and lead guitars, saxophones, and tambourines.

Congregations usually constitute close-knit communities. They address each other as Brother, Sister, and Mother, and they participate collectively in many aspects of the service. Much of the singing is in call-and-response format, and the individual singing as well as the preaching is invariably punctuated with claps, shouts, and other gestures of encouragement from the congregation. Many black Holiness/Pentecostal churches have "nursing guilds" which function specifically to assist, comfort, and, in some cases, help control those overcome with religious ecstasy. For many years, these church nurses have worn the traditional white uniform and cap seen in hospitals. The closeness of these communities results from their frequent church attendance (several times, as opposed to once weekly) and the lifestyle disciplines that set them apart from non-members.

Finally, because the Pentecostal church service is a spirit-led event, beginning and ending times are approximate at best. While there is a loose sense of structure, in general, the preaching starts and ends as the Spirit leads, singing begins and ends as the Spirit leads, and prayer begins and ends as the Spirit leads. A black Pentecostal church service is considered successful and effective only to the extent that the dictates of the Spirit have been observed.

In the years following the Azusa revival, African Americans migrated from the rural South to the urban North in massive numbers. In 1915, many were attracted to northern cities to become part of the wartime labor force.[19] By 1930, 1.2 million blacks had left the South in search of better jobs and living conditions in the industrialized North.[20] The growth of the black church in northern cities during this period reflected these migratory patterns. In particular, Holiness/Pentecostal denominations flourished as they quickly established to meet the social and spiritual needs of the growing urban black population. Thus, church growth was not only seen in the expanding membership of existing churches but also in the establishment of many new congregations in homes, rented halls, storefronts, and wherever meetings could be held.

Today, people representing many different nationalities, ethnic backgrounds, and socioeconomic classes embrace Pentecostalism. But its first adherents—both in early Christianity and in its twentieth-century form—were drawn from society's underclass. In many ways, William Seymour himself was a prototype of the typical Holiness/Pentecostal believer at the turn of the twentieth century. Like Seymour, most had prior roots in the Holiness movement, and those who embraced glossolalia generally retained their Holiness convictions. Like Seymour, many of those attracted to the revival were either poor or, at most, from the working class. Like Seymour, they were either poorly educated, marginally educated, or, at best, self-taught. Like Seymour, they were predisposed, perhaps due to their common class identity, to more interracial tolerance than the larger society. Similar demographics apply to the developers of jazz and blues at the beginning of the twentieth century.

The flowering of American Pentecostalism around the turn of the century coincides with the most important early developments in black secular music. Although African Americans sang secular tunes during antebellum times, this discussion begins with the styles of the late 1800s and the very beginning of the 1900s, because it was during this era that the precursors of twentieth-century, black popular music emerged.[21] By the late 1800s, a distinctive type of rhythmic syncopation was widely recognized as a defining characteristic of African American music. Early on, minstrel performers included this syncopation in their caricatured portrayals of black music. In fact, Ernest Hogan, a black minstrel and vaudeville entertainer, published the first piece of sheet music with the label "ragtime." By the time Hogan published "All Coons Look Alike to Me" in 1896, the terms "ragtime" and "ragging" were common descriptors for the distinctive rhythms of black-American secular music and dance. While ragtime is perhaps most widely associated with the piano compositions of Scott Joplin, this style originated in the improvisatory devices of illiterate, black musicians who performed entirely by ear. Additionally, many composers, including Hogan, Bob Cole and J. Rosamond and James Weldon Johnson, and Thomas Turpin, wrote music in the ragtime genre for various vocal and instrumental media in the 1890s and early 1900s.

Along with ragtime, the blues started to gain recognition around the turn of the century. As is the case with ragtime, the exact originator of the blues is unknown. The genre has been described, however, as the postbellum, secular counterpart of the antebellum Negro spiritual. After the Civil War, African Americans throughout the South commonly sang of their daily life struggles and accompanied their singing on harmonicas, guitars, and other homemade musical instruments. Although the blues had undoubtedly been around for quite some time, the earliest documented case of blues singing was in 1901. Ma Rainey, the first to develop a stage career from the genre, reports having first heard the blues sung in 1902.[22]

By the 1910s, the syncopated rhythms of ragtime were incorporated into the highly popular syncopated dance ensemble, one of the most famous of which was James Reese Europe's Clef Club Orchestra. At about the same time that syncopated orchestras introduced the sound of what would be called first "jass" and later "jazz," the first generation of black blues divas was coming of age. These included Ma Rainey, who was most active in the 1910s and 1920s; Mamie Smith, the first black female to be recorded; Ma Rainey's protégé, Bessie Smith, who achieved fame in the 1920s and early 1930s, and several others.

The advent of regular radio programming and the birth of the commercial recording industry in the 1920s brought the first national exposure of black popular music in both its syncopated instrumental form and in its vocal blues form. By the mid-1920s, black-American vernacular music, while immensely popular among the grass roots, was denounced by the conservative element of society as primitive, decadent, and second-rate. The popular magazines and periodicals of the day often featured articles which attempted to critically evaluate and define the role of this new musical craze. One example of such an effort appeared in the August 1924 issue of *Etude* magazine. In it, an article entitled "Where Is Jazz Leading America?" presents a compilation of opinions about the societal role of jazz. (At the time the article was written, it was common to use the terms *jazz* and *ragtime* interchangeably.) Those polled include classically trained American composers, music professors, and orchestral conductors. The opinion of Frank Damrosch, then director of the Institute of Musical Art, encapsulates the sentiments of many in the upper class:

> Jazz is to real music what the caricature is to the portrait. The caricature may be clever, but it aims at distortion of line and feature in order to make its point; similarly, jazz may be clever but its effects are made by exaggeration, distortion and vulgarisms. If jazz originated in the dance rhythms of the Negro, it was at least interesting as the self-expression of a primitive race. When jazz was adopted by the "highly civilized" white race, it tended to degenerate it towards primitivity. When a savage distorts his features and paints his face so as to produce startling effects, we smile at his childishness; but when a civilized man imitates him, not as a joke but in all seriousness, we turn away in disgust. Attempts have been made to "elevate" jazz by stealing phrases from the classic composers and vulgarizing them by the rhythms and devices used in jazz. This is not only an outrage on beautiful music, but also a confession of poverty, of inability to compose music of any value on the part of jazz writers. We are living in a state of unrest, of social evolution, of transition from a condition of established order to a new objective as yet but dimly visualized. This is reflected in the jazz fad.[23]

The elite's disdain for jazz, ragtime, and the blues is well documented in this and other articles of the period. In denouncing these popular forms, they typically express two kinds of prejudices: (1) a general bias against the "lower" class of people responsible for generating the music; and (2) a general bias against music in improvisatory rather than notated form. Because the music required none of the literacy valued by the European tradition, the elite were ever suspicious of its authenticity as art.

Ironically, however, by the 1930s, the syncopated dance orchestra of the 1910s and 1920s had evolved into an ensemble that required of its players both musical literacy and improvisational skills. Duke Ellington, Count Basie, and other champions of the big band sound were all trained in music theory and composition and, unlike many of their predecessors who had played entirely by ear, were immortalizing their music in written form. Ellington and other educated jazz musicians were able to gain membership in the American Society of Composers, Authors, and Publishers (ASCAP) and to access its established networks and copyright protection. Thus, they secured the place of jazz as a successful crossover genre with a stable white following.

While jazz players of the 1930s and afterward relied increasingly upon the ability to read music, the typical blues singer neither required nor desired such training. Blues vocalists like Bessie Smith and Charlie Patton retained the pathos of the black rural South and the working class, and by the 1930s Thomas Dorsey's introduction of the blues sound into the religious circuit gave rise to urban gospel, another grassroots form. Dorsey's innovation would make the link between the sound of Bessie Smith's blues and the sound of Mahalia Jackson's gospel undeniable.

Despite their common roots in the vernacular forms of the early 1900s, after the 1930s, jazz and blues would develop separately in terms of performance medium and class association. Jazz would be considered highbrow, primarily instrumental, and crossover; blues, on the other hand, would be considered lowbrow, primarily vocal, and avowedly black. Rhythm and blues would successfully combine elements of both.

In 1949, *Billboard* used the term *rhythm and blues* for the first time to label what had formerly been the race record category. The music to which the term referred, however, had already been popular before it was officially named rhythm and blues. Technically, rhythm and blues is the secular music of black Americans popular from the 1940s to the 1960s. This term, however, can also apply to all of the forms of African American popular music that since the 1940s have resulted from a synthesis of genres including gospel, big-band, swing, and the blues. Nelson George notes that although it was called "rock & roll" in the 1950s, "soul" in the 1960s, and "funk," "disco," and "rap" in the 1970s, 1980s, and 1990s, respectively, the crucial elements that underscore the identity of the music have never changed.[24] Since its inception, one of those crucial elements has been its association with black-American secular dance.

An important development in the formative years of rhythm and blues came with the solo career of Louis Jordan. Jordan was a singer and tenor saxophonist who had formerly played in Chick Webb's big band. In 1938, following Webb's death, Jordan formed his own band, the Tympani Five, which included a guitar and fewer horns than the typical big band ensemble. Perhaps the most significant innovation of Jordan's band was the practice of playing the blues at an accelerated tempo. This practice was nicknamed "jumpin' the blues" and the upbeat sound itself was called "jump blues."

Evidence that Jordan was directly influenced by the Pentecostal tradition is very difficult to locate. Whether he intended it to or not, the accelerated tempo of Jordan's jump blues conveyed the energy of Pentecostalism and inspired a host of imitators, including Little Richard and Chuck Berry. Since Little Richard hailed from a Pentecostal background, however, his supposed imitation of Louis Jordan may have been more directly related to his intimate familiarity with the upbeat musical style of the Sanctified church.

Seay and Neely argue convincingly that Pentecostalism was the primary spiritual influence upon the pop music of the 1950s.[25] To support their position, they cite white artists like Elvis Presley and Jerry Lee Lewis and black artists like Little Richard, Sam Cooke, James Brown, and Marvin Gaye, all of whom were reared in the Pentecostal tradition. To this list, one could add B. B. King, whose earliest musical influence was Archie Fair, an older relative who was a guitar-playing, Sanctified preacher, and Tina Turner, who attended the Pentecostal church of a family friend during her childhood. Turner's autobiography contains a description of her childhood involvement with black Pentecostalism. Her sister, Alline, gives the following account of young Anna Mae's behavior at the Sanctified services: "You'd get the Holy Ghost in those services and you'd dance around faster and faster, and the music got louder and louder. One time Ann's underpants fell down around he ankles, she was dancing so hard. But she didn't let up."26 The hard-driving dance of Tina Turner's stage act is, at times, remarkably similar to what would be seen during a Sanctified service.

The influence of Pentecostalism is particularly salient in secular releases like "Shout!" by the Isley Brothers and "Holy Ghost" by the Bar-Kays. When the Isley Brothers released "Shout!" in 1959, it became a national hit. This song, which is still popular enough to be heard in television jingles some forty years later, does more than mimic Pentecostalism; it *is* Pentecostalism! The performance begins in true "black preacher" fashion, with the lead Isley sermonizing about his woman. Overcome with joy, he starts several lines that he can't quite seem to finish: "Now that I got my woman.../Been so good to me, better than I been to myself.../Every time I think about you..." Each phrase prompts an enthusiastic response from the audience until a rhythmic, preacher/ congregation call-and-response ensues. After several repetitions of "I gotta get myself ready," the audience is more than primed for the sudden tempo change that comes quickly on the heels of "You know it makes me wanna SHOUT!" At a lightning fast cut time (half note equals about 176), "SHOUT!" is repeated (call-and-response style, of course) atop a harmony oscillating between the I and vi chords, and to the accompaniment of handclaps, screams, and hollers. That the shouting is about a woman and not about the Lord hardly detracts from the distinctively Pentecostal emotionalism.

The continued influence of Pentecostalism in the funk era can be seen in "Holy Ghost" by the Bar-Kays. Released in 1975 (one of the last recordings issued by Stax), this cut was successful on both the pop and rhythm-and-blues charts:

"Holy Ghost" by the Bar-Kays

Holy, Yeah, Yeah, Holy Ghost (Refrain, repeated 4
    times)

Girl, your love is like the Holy Ghost
Shakin' all in my bones
I've never felt such a feelin'
In all the days I've been born
Whenever I feel your presence, child
You seem to hypnotize my mind, well
Girl, your love is like the Holy Ghost
I feel like I've been born a second time

(Refrain)

> Girl, your love is like the Holy Ghost
> The antidote that frees my soul
> And no cyclone could ever describe
> this feelin' that sets my soul on fire
> You put a runnin' in my walk
> and you put a tremble in my talk
> And this feelin' that I have within
> Said it makes me feel like I've been born again.
> Feel it, feel it,
> feel the spirit
> (repeats to fade)

The Isley's "Shout!" shows that in the 1950s and 1960s, the up-tempo sound of Pentecostal "shouting" music was so pervasive in rhythm and blues that very often the only way to distinguish between sacred and secular songs was the lyrics. By the early 1970s, however, the sound of the Holiness shout in secular music was supplanted by the hard driving feel of funk. In fact, "Holy Ghost" sounds nothing like the Pentecostal church, except perhaps at the very beginning of the track when the pitches of a vibrating rubber band evoke the image of an old, country church. In some very poor Holiness congregations, musical instruments were fashioned out of whatever materials were available. One such instrument was made my stretching a string or rubber band over a stick and plucking the "chord" at various points to produce a vibrating pitch. This primitive instrument is an Americanized version of the musical bow, a common instrument in West Africa. The Bar-Kays include the sound of the musical bow at the start of the track, but it quickly fades into the characteristic funk groove provided by horns, vocals, synthesizer, and drums.

In comparing his woman's love to the Holy Ghost, the singer gives a vivid, albeit sacrilegious, description of the Pentecostal experience. Phrases like "shakin' all in my bones," and "sets my soul on fire" are the same ones Pentecostals use to describe their religious ecstasy; "runnin' in my walk," is a direct reference to the holy dance, and "tremble in my talk," refers specifically to glossolalia. The lead singer punctuates each line with phrases typical of charismatic, black preaching ("Oh, yeah!" "Well!") with all the conviction of a fresh convert. In "Holy Ghost," the description of the Pentecostal experience is so detailed that one wonders whether the Bar-Kays were themselves backslidden members of some Holiness church.

Instrumentalists also incorporated the sound of the Sanctified church into rhythm and blues. Studio drummer David "Panama" Francis, for example, played in a rhythmic style associated with that of the Pentecostal church on several rhythm-and-blues recordings. Francis used the Church of God in Christ's "common meter" (12/8 and the triplet pattern associated with it) in Screaming Jay Hawkins' "I Put a Spell on You" (1956) and LaVern Baker's "See See Rider" (1962).[27] Many other artists who had intimate familiarity with the ethos of the Pentecostal worship style were inclined to incorporate, to varying degrees, that ethos into their secular artistry.

Later generations of black secular artists would also include several who had been reared in the Holiness/Pentecostal tradition. Deniece Williams, for example, grew up in her uncle's Faith Temple Church of God in Christ in East Chicago, Indiana, and the DeBarge family grew up singing in the Bethel Pentecostal Church in Grand Rapids, Michigan, where their uncle was pastor.[28]

Black secular music has incorporated sounds from many sectors of the black church, and the contributions of artists from other denominations figure significantly into its aesthetic. Baptist artists Aretha Franklin, Gladys Knight, and Patti LaBelle, for example, are noted for their secular presentations of the gospel sound. The specific contribution of black Pentecostalism, however, was that it specialized in preserving the ritual of spirit possession and the whole collection of African rhythms, sounds, and gestures associated with it. In addition, black Holiness/Pentecostal churches, to a greater degree than others, also approached music not simply as an avenue for devotional expression, but also as a means for inciting spirit possession. In particular, the shout was accompanied by a feel and style of music that marked rhythm and blues and its descendant forms. While many black churches actively sought to quench fiery emotionalism, Holiness/Pentecostal groups actively sought the exact opposite. Rhythm-and-blues artists adapted this approach to secular music, and, as the stage became an analog of the pulpit and the audience an analog of the congregation, these artists measured their effectiveness in direct proportion to the degree of emotional abandon they could incite. It is no wonder then that the culmination of a James Brown performance is that point at which both he and his audience are completely overwhelmed with emotion.

The salience of Pentecostal features in black secular music as well as the number of major artists with Pentecostal roots may seem to suggest that Sanctified singers, musicians, and preachers provided an archetype for rhythm and blues. To some extent, this may be the case. It is equally true, however, that the black Pentecostal church was receptive to secular musical influences. Jazz and the blues both emerged as popular forms just on the heels of the Azusa revival. It is reasonable to assume, therefore, that some of the converts to Pentecostalism had been singers and musicians in these secular venues before joining the Sanctified church. Unlike the Baptists and Methodists who had an older and more established musical tradition, the black Pentecostals had no such tradition and were thus more open to including a variety of instruments in their worship service. Explaining that this attitude continues to be prevalent in Pentecostal thinking, Harvey Cox notes that "most Pentecostals gladly welcome any instrument you can blow, pluck, bow, bang, scrape, or rattle in the praise of God." Cox claims to have seen photos of saxophones being played at Pentecostal revivals as early as 1910.[29] In her dissertation, "Testifying at the Cross: Thomas Andrew Dorsey, Sister Rosetta Tharpe, and the Politics of African American Sacred and Secular Music," Jerma Jackson also notes that while other denominations considered the guitar a sinful, decadent instrument, "members of the Church of God in Christ, along with other Holiness and Pentecostal denominations, rejected the middle class perception that religion was synonymous with restraint. These mostly working class men and women insisted that religion was a corporeal and emotional experience. They stressed that music was a way of giving praise and, as a result, assigned a religious meaning to upbeat rhythms whether generated from guitars, pianos, or tambourines."[30] The singer/guitarist Rosetta Tharpe was one of several artists who enjoyed crossover success at both the Harlem Church of God in Christ and the Cotton Club. Other artists had secular careers in jazz and blues before devoting their musical talents to the Holiness/Pentecostal church. Robert "Keghouse" Wilkins (b. 1896) was a blues guitarist whose career went as far back as the days of minstrelsy and vaudeville before becoming an ordained minister of the Church of God in Christ in 1950. Arnold "Gatemouth" Moore (b. 1913) was a blues singer with numerous minstrel troupes, carnivals, and big bands before becoming an ordained minister of the Church of God in Christ in 1948. Guitarist/pianist Blind James Brewer (b. 1921) vacillated between music ministry with the Church of God in Christ and Chicago nightclub gigs throughout his life. The Pentecostal church was perhaps as receptive to the influence of secular musical styles as rhythm and blues and other genres were to the influence of the Pentecostal worship aesthetic.

A chronology of the years surrounding the turn of the century reveals that some of the most pivotal events in the black Holiness/Pentecostal tradition and in the black secular music industry occurred almost simultaneously. In 1899, for example, Scott Joplin published his first rag compositions; also in 1899, Charles Harrison Mason and Charles Price Jones were expelled from the Baptist church for their Holiness stance and defense of slave worship practice.[31] In 1909, the Azusa revival ended and W. C. Handy composed "Memphis Blues." In 1914, ASCAP was founded, Handy published "St. Louis Blues," and white ministers withdrew from the formerly interracial Church of God in Christ to form a separate Pentecostal organization, the Assemblies of God.[32] In 1922, the first recordings of a black jazz band as an instrumental ensemble were made in Los Angeles.[33] Also in 1922, William J. Seymour died.

The development and expansion of both black Pentecostalism and rhythm and blues depended largely upon the migration of blacks from the South to the North and from the country to the city. As black Southerners reached the North, so did the Pentecostal church, in order to provide spiritual and social assistance. By the time of Charles Harrison Mason's death in 1961, the Church of God in Christ had evolved into a primarily urban church. As early as 1912, Mason had already begun to send preachers and missionaries to Kansas City, St. Louis, Chicago, New York, Los Angeles, and San Francisco. He also sent workers to establish churches to serve blacks who had left rural areas for urban areas in the South.[34] Meanwhile, wartime migration of black GIs, as well as the mass migration of blacks in search of better living conditions, exposed the larger society to the regional sounds that made up rhythm and blues. This exposure helped to create a national appetite for the music that was both satisfied and reinforced by radio and the record industry.

Because of its youth and relatively liberal climate, Los Angeles provided a mecca common to both rhythm and blues and black Pentecostalism. It was not only the site of the Azusa revival, but also the place where the first jazz band recordings were made and where the majority of the first rhythm-and-blues labels were established. Both William Seymour and Louis Jordan died and were buried in Los Angeles.

The attitudinal climate of Los Angeles was—and is—perhaps more conducive than other places to social "experiments" like the multiracial makeup of the original Azusa Street devotees. Even after the integrated congregations dispersed and reverted to segregated worship, however, Azusa would continue to have far-reaching implications for interracial and intercultural contact and exposure in the United States. First, the Azusa revival provided documentable proof that there could be a peaceful, meaningful, and egalitarian coexistence between blacks and whites. However short-lived, their interracial experience at Azusa left many blacks with the indelible persuasion that divine intervention should and could effect the social changes that were the objects of later civil rights movements. Although many segments of the black church contributed to the success of the Civil Rights Movement of the 1950s and 1960s, the fact that Martin Luther King Jr. gave his last speech at the Mason Temple Church of God in Christ seems to bring the Pentecostal example of racial harmony full circle. Secondly, Azusa exposed thousands of white Americans to the expressive freedom and African aesthetic of black worship and religious music. Because many white believers received this exposure within the context of an event that they believed to be divinely orchestrated, they were not only receptive to these elements of black culture, but they also emulated them and helped to disseminate them throughout the United States.

The interracial contact between lower- and working-class blacks and whites in both the nineteenth-century camp-meeting tradition and at the Azusa Street revival of 1906 may be said to foreshadow the interracial contact between lower- and working-class blacks and whites in the music that came to be called rhythm and blues. On one hand, this contact can be described in terms of profit-driven whites exploiting gullible black artists; on the other hand, however, both the earlier black secular styles and the development of rhythm and blues created a genuine desire in both blacks and whites for a cooperative cultural/recreational experience in a way seldom seen before. Early white jazz and blues artists received harsh criticism and scathing rebuke for singing and playing "the music of the Negro" in much the same way that white worshippers were ostracized for incorporating blatant Africanisms into their religion. Louis Jordan, described by Nelson George as "a natural crossover artist," claimed to have profited as much from white audiences as from black audiences.[35] And Johnny Otis, born in 1921, is the quintessential example of a white rhythm-and-blues artist completely absorbed in African American culture.

Each in its own way, both black Pentecostalism and the secular music industry offered a haven of self-respect and an avenue for transcendence. In the close-knit community of the Holiness/Pentecostal church, otherwise down-and-out blacks could find meaning and significance. They were free to let loose and they could count on the encouragement of others to do so. And Holy Spirit possession offered them an ecstasy that could be neither orchestrated nor controlled by societal conditions.

In the secular music arena, however, the transcendence was more tangible. However perilous and corrupt it may have been, the recording industry was, to many blacks, an invitation to an unprecedented upward mobility. While the industry produced more casualties than successes, black-American contributions and achievements—both economically and artistically—were still groundbreaking by mid-century standards. In 1957, for example, of all the artists on the year-end pop charts, 29 percent were black.[36]

The aesthetic similarities between black Pentecostalism and black secular music should be understood not in terms of a simple archetype/copy model but in terms of mutual exchange. The secular sound of jazz influenced the music of the Pentecostal church long before the sounds and gestures of the church emerged in rhythm and blues. Although it seems impossible to determine whether the influence of one outweighed the other, the fact remains that the lines between sacred and secular were permanently blurred.

In addition to their aesthetic similarities, the historical, geographical, and social parallels between Pentecostalism and black secular music suggest that these two cultural expressions were both outgrowths of a larger phenomenon. That phenomenon may be characterized, in a very broad sense, as the emergence of African American cultural identity. The turn of the twentieth century was significant for African Americans because it marked the generational divider between black former slaves and their adult children. Unfamiliar with the constraints of their parents' generation, these adults could assert and celebrate aspects of their culture with an authenticity whose appeal transcended the traditional societal norms. While this discussion cites a particular connection between the Pentecostal movement and the black secular music industry, the years framing the turn of the century and the First World War also contain the seeds of the Harlem Renaissance and the modern Civil Rights Movement. It seems reasonable to suggest, then, that black Pentecostalism and black secular music were more than two sides to the same coin, as Seay and Neely argue. Instead, they were two utterances of a fresh and multifaceted African American voice.

Notes

1. Davin Seay and Mary Neely, *Spiritual Roots of Rock and Roll*, 73.
2. See Dan Wakefield, "Speaking in Tongues," 98.
3. In this discussion, the terms *Holiness, Pentecostal, Sanctified,* and *Holiness/Pentecostal* are used interchangeably.
4. Quoted in Maultsby, "Africanisms in African American Music," 198.
5. See Southern, ed., *Readings in Black American Music*, 63–64.
6. Ibid., 105.
7. Quoted in Southern, *Music of Black Americans*, 182.
8. Ibid. 179.
9. Vinson Synan, *Holiness Pentecostal Tradition*, 12.
10. Southern, ed, *Readings in Black American Music*, 63–64.
11. Synan, *Holiness Pentecostal Tradition*, 13.
12. John Thomas Nichol, *Pentecostalism*, 18.
13. C. M. Robeck, "Azusa Street Revival."
14. Synan, *Holiness Pentecostal Tradition*, 100.
15. H. V. Synan, "William Joseph Seymour."
16. See Samuel Floyd, *Power of Black Music*, 20.
17. See Ithiel C. Clemmons, *Bishop C. H. Mason*, 31–32.
18. Clemmons, *Bishop C. H. Mason*, 31.
19. See Alton Hornsby, *Chronology of African American History*.
20. See Lincoln and Mamiya, *Black Church in the African American Experience*, 116.
21. See Southern, *Music of Black Americans*, 313–64.
22. Ibid., 332–34.
23. Dr. Frank Damrosch quoted in "Where Is Jazz Leading America," 518.
24. See Nelson George, *Death of Rhythm and Blues*, x.
25. Seay and Neely, *Spiritual Roots of Rock and Roll*, 140.
26. Tina Turner with Kurt Loder, *I, Tina*, 21.
27. Portia Maultsby, "Impact of Gospel Music," 30.
28. The religious upbringing of the DeBarge family is referenced in Michael Goldberg, "DeBarge's Family Affair," 41. I am personally acquainted with Deniece Williams' religious roots. My mother attended Faith Temple Church of God in Christ where Williams was reared.
29. Harvey Cox, *Rise of Pentecostal Spirituality*, 142.
30. Jerma Jackson, "Politics of African American Sacred and Secular Music," 153.
31. Clemmons, *Bishop C. H. Mason*, 21.
32. Ibid., 41–42.
33. Southern, *Music of Black Americans*, 378.
34. Clemmons, *Bishop C. H. Mason*, 84–100.
35. George, *Death of Rhythm and Blues*, 20.
36. Jannette L. Dates and William Barlow, eds. *African Americans in the Mass Media*, 81.

Section Five

Perspectives on Praise and Worship

28

Back to the Heart of Worship: Praise and Worship Music in a Los Angeles African American Megachurch

Birgitta J. Johnson

It is five minutes after ten o'clock on a Sunday morning, and half the Great Western Forum's parking lot is full. As one approaches the fabled sports arena's doors, the faint sound of a live band playing a mix of gospel, jazz, and funk seeps out into the parking lot to meet people hurriedly trying to get inside. With Bibles in hand (or in uniquely designed carrying cases), they quickly greet each other, barely taking their eyes off which of the large doors they can enter the quickest. Upon entering the building's inner corridors, the groove-based rhythms are even louder, but are joined by the sounds of an audience of thousands singing along with a small vocal ensemble. The call-and-response style of music is evident as people in the hall begin singing along with those in the main room before they enter a series of openings adorned with deep-blue curtains. They've been welcomed by a half dozen greeters on their way in and are now seeking the assistance of one of the legion of ushers, quickly finding empty seats among the standing, swaying, singing, dancing, and clapping thousands who've been in the 17,000-seat arena since ten o'clock.

The atmosphere inside the arena is electric and rivals anything that occurred during the building's heyday during the 1980s, hosting the Los Angeles Lakers or the Rolling Stones. One could assume this gathering in Inglewood, California, was some type of religious crusade, complete with spirited group singing, pleading to convert as many lost souls at one time as possible. However, the mood of the room is celebratory in a markedly different way. Less like a crusade, it is more like a big party after a family reunion; the people high-five and hug each other at the mere suggestion of the lead singer, who, with his small group of nine singers, are standing over twenty feet away from the nearest audience member. From the vantage point of midlevel loge seats, which are over thirty feet from the main floor, one sees a large rectangular platform where a fifty-voiced choir stands, rocking in rhythm with the small vocal ensemble and a quintet of head-bobbing musicians.

Hanging from the ceiling on both sides of the large platform are two projection screens, which show the lead singer and the lyrics to the song that have the attention of nearly every person in the room. Had one not noticed the lyrics on the screen or dozens of people bringing Bibles into the arena, this event could easily be mistaken for a rhythm-and-blues review or soul music concert. The people singing to each other and lifting their hands acknowledging a deity greater than themselves are not a group of pop music fans. Rather, they are members of the Faithful Central Bible Church and the high-spirited, Jesus-centered praise they are taking part in is only the beginning of their weekly church services. The congregation will continue in this mood of reverence and celebration for at least twenty more minutes before sitting.

This narrative represents some of my first impressions attending Faithful Central Bible Church in 2001, after the predominantly African American congregation made history by purchasing a sports arena to accommodate its rapidly growing Sunday morning service. At the time, I was unaware that the church and its contemporary style of music and worship would be the subject of a project for one of my graduate seminars at the University of California, Los Angeles (UCLA), and the subject of my doctoral research, conducted between May 2003 and September 2006, on music in Los Angeles African American megachurches (Johnson 2008).

Located in the city of Inglewood in the southwest corner of Greater Los Angeles, Faithful Central's congregation experienced the exponential growth associated with the megachurch phenomenon in the United States, growing from about two hundred members in 1984 to approximately thirteen thousand in 2001. After purchasing the Great Western Forum in late 2000, the church began holding Sunday morning services in the former sports and entertainment arena in 2001, where the average weekly attendance was between 6,500 and 7,000 congregants. In addition to the dynamic preaching of its head pastor, Bishop Kenneth C. Ulmer, the church's use of praise and worship and gospel music was also a key feature of its Sunday services. My research included participant observation of church services and special programs; interviews with church members, musicians, and staff; audio and video analysis of church services and special programs; and archival research of local newspapers, magazines, and oral histories. I also documented musical performance (i.e., congregational music, choir selections, and instrumental music) at each service to determine which sacred music genres were performed and the total time spent on musical expression.

While church growth scholars define a *megachurch* as a congregation whose Sunday morning services have at least two thousand people in attendance, African American lifestyle magazines such as *Ebony* and *Jet*, among other publications, often describe a megachurch as a congregation that has at least three thousand members in attendance ("Megachurches" 2004; "New Black Spirituality" 2004; "What Is the Future" 2004; "Where We Stand" 2005). These large churches and their supersize ministries are a relatively recent phenomenon among Christians in the United States. Furthermore, the growing presence of black megachurches in both urban and suburban communities over the last thirty years, as well as the social and political influence they have gained in cities such as Los Angeles, Atlanta, New York, and Dallas, reflect an important period in the history of the black church in the United States. Although music and its role in these churches constitute an important key to church growth, little ethnographic research has been conducted on megachurches in the United Sates and even less on music in African American megachurches (Wooley 1999; Wong 2006). Just as compelling as gifted preachers and multi-million dollar sanctuaries, music is an element that has significantly contributed to the expansion and popularity of black megachurches.

This essay has two goals: (1) to examine the way in which praise and worship music has become an integral part of the worship services at Faithful Central; and (2) to demonstrate how Faithful Central uses praise and worship music to achieve efficacy in its weekly worship. The essay is divided into four sections. First, I provide a general description of praise and worship music. Next, I present a concise overview of megachurches, including a discussion of their distinguishing characteristics and functions. Third, I present a history of African American megachurches in Los Angeles. Lastly, I focus on the factors that led to the adoption and adaptation of praise and worship music in worship services at Faithful Central.

Scholars have demonstrated that ethnic identity and the social realities of African Americans are often expressed in their music (Ricks 1960; Burnim 1980; DjeDje 1986; Maultsby 1990; Neal 1999). As the conditions of black life in the United States change, so does the music produced by African Americans, causing stylistic changes to be inevitable. However, there are times, as J. H. Kwabena Nketia (1978: 4–5) and John Blacking (1986: 3) note, when stylistic changes are deliberately adopted to create an ideal environment or familiar atmosphere in a new context. The emergence of African American megachurches has provided new contexts for African American Christian worship. Whether services are held in a modern cathedral, a traditional sanctuary, a converted warehouse, a renovated theater, a climate-controlled tent, or a sports arena, the role of music in the weekly worship services of black megachurches is just as important and culturally vital as it is in average-size black congregations.

Music has always been central in black Christian worship practices. As early as the nineteenth-century slave period, the transmission of biblical teachings in preaching and song was closely linked when people extemporaneously composed songs to emphasize and affirm aspects of sermons, especially in the secret gatherings of the invisible church. These songs were maintained as the folk spirituals and hymns that formed the roots of black sacred music in independent churches and denominations that flourished after Emancipation (Walker 1979: 182). But while spirituals, anthems, and hymns are still being sung in black churches across the country today, the many styles of gospel music have made it the dominant musical expression in most congregations. Gospel music, lyrically and stylistically, reflects the urbanization of the African American community in the twentieth century. In addition to attracting members with traditional and contemporary sounds, gospel music's ability to speak to day-to-day issues as well as spiritual concerns has kept it at the forefront of musical expression in the church.

Recently, however, even greater musical diversity has been incorporated into the weekly worship services of many churches. Originally a product of the predominantly white contemporary Christian music (CCM) industry of the 1960s and 1970s, praise and worship music has become popular in black churches across America, and particularly in Los Angeles. Praise and worship's prominence in Los Angeles African American churches began in the 1980s, and its incorporation into the gospel music tradition reflects a reaffirmation of traditional African American Christian worship practices such as congregational singing and emotive worship. The rise of praise and worship also demonstrates a desire to appeal to the diversity within today's megachurch congregations. Stylistically, praise and worship music, like contemporary gospel, incorporates a variety of secular music styles and is highly participatory.

The large gathering spaces where megachurches tend to meet can pose challenges to the sense of community that is quintessential to the black church worship experience. Since many megachurch congregations use converted structures or multiuse venues and do not always hold services in traditional sanctuary spaces (Steensland et al. 2000; Libaw 2001a, 2001b; Mostyn 2002), the structures often do not look or feel like "church." Through the use of space and interior design, megachurches contest the layers of meaning linked to iconic images and symbols identified with sacred spaces (e.g., tall steeples, stained glass windows, altars, crosses, religious portraiture, and neatly lined pews). Thus, for some church leaders, praise and worship music establishes order, encourages intimacy, and musically reinforces a sense of community and the sacred among the thousands of congregants who attend weekly services.

Praise and Worship Music

Based on my observations of praise and worship music in a variety of contexts (i.e., church services, religious conferences, and concert performances) and listening to Christian-themed music on radio, television, and Internet broadcasts, I have identified several features that characterize this genre. Praise and worship songs tend to be:

- Highly and intentionally participatory with an emphasis on call-and-response and unison singing (even during verses).
- Lyrically driven, with special emphasis on personal as well as corporate praise, adoration, reverence, and worship of God.
- Stylistically diverse, incorporating musical characteristics identified with rock, folk, gospel (southern and black traditions), Latin, world music, rap, country, and pop genres.
- Melodically uncomplicated for easy retention and execution.

- Generally groove-oriented, regardless of style, for easy accessibility in congregations or group gatherings.
- Highly repetitive lyrics with spiritual messages that encourage ecstatic or highly personal encounters with God. (Johnson 2006)

A select list of internationally known praise and worship artists and songwriters across various styles and genres includes Paul Baloche, Andraé Crouch, Rick Founds, Israel Houghton, Ron Kenoly, Robin Mark, Tim Hughes, Judith Christie McAllister, Don Moen, Matt Redman, Alvin Slaughter, Michael W. Smith, Sonicflood, Chris Tomlin, Karen Wheaton, and Darlene Zschech. Many of their songs have been rerecorded often and are sung in churches worldwide. (For a list of praise and worship recordings, go to http://musicofblacklosangeles.blogspot.com.)

Coined by the CCM industry in the mid-1970s, praise and worship generally is regarded as a subgenre of Christian and black gospel music. In the United States, CCM and gospel music describe genres based largely on the stylistic preferences and racial background of the audience: "'Gospel' music in many cases has become a term designating the religious music of African Americans. . . while 'Christian' is the term for religious pop music for predominantly white audiences, generally called contemporary Christian music" (Cusic 2002: viii). *Southern gospel*, an older term used to differentiate white southern-based gospel from black gospel, usually falls under the umbrella of Christian music. Today, the industries and local business networks for black and white gospel are still primarily separate even though the songs of individual artists may cross over.

Other labels for praise and worship music include *vertical music, worship music, praise music*, and *worship and praise.* Most praise and worship music is stylistically indistinguishable from many forms of secular music (e.g., pop, rock, soul, and rhythm and blues). Unlike inspirational music, praise and worship lyrics are explicitly God- and Christ-centered ("Praise and Worship" 2004). Don Cusic (2002: 383) describes praise and worship as "music in the church for the churched[;]. . . music sung to God by believers." While this may be true today, praise and worship's popularity began thirty years ago outside the church often among "un-churched," young Christians, and new believers. Had young Charismatic and Pentecostal Christians not been allowed to take more active roles in their churches during the 1970s and 1980s, praise and worship would have not grown within congregations in the United States to the extent that it has. Cusic explains: "Both white and black churches increasingly used contemporary music in their services during the late 1980s and throughout the 1990s until it was difficult to find vibrant, growing churches that sang old hymns. The music of Isaac Watts, the Wesleys, and others has been replaced by songs from the albums of contemporary artists, both black and white" (383).

Church leaders have found that congregants are more inspired by the lyrics and the straightforward language of praise and worship music than by the texts of traditional church hymns and anthems. In a special feature, titled "Praise and Worship," in *The Gospel Music Industry Round-*

Up (2003, 87), praise and worship is described as "a means to usher congregations into the spirit of praise and the intimate presence of God—laying the foundation for the rest of the church service—worship and praise evolved out of participatory nature of choir music." Unlike other forms of contemporary Christian and gospel music, praise and worship not only stimulates corporate participation but also encourages collective worship, which seeks to make a spiritual impact on participants that lasts throughout the church service.

In church settings, a praise (or worship) team, a vocal ensemble of six to twelve singers (two per vocal part), usually leads praise and worship music. A praise team consists of a lead singer (sometimes referred to as a worship leader) and a group of background singers. In contexts where CCM predominates, the ensemble may be referred to as a *worship band*, which usually includes singing instrumentalists who lead praise and worship.

The worship leader, in addition to singing the lead part of the songs and leading short congregational prayers, encourages congregants to sing along and outwardly express praise and adoration to God. An important aspect of praise and worship music in church settings is to involve the congregation in the act of musical worship instead of allowing them to be inactive spectators or passive listeners (Johnson 2006). Thus, many churches use praise teams and praise and worship periods at the beginning of a church service not as musical preludes but as the opening event of the church service. These periods can last anywhere from eight to ten to more than thirty minutes.

The accompaniment for the praise team usually reflects the preferred instrumentation of the congregation. In some churches, amplified acoustic guitars, keyboards, and drums accompany the praise team. In others, especially in churches where gospel music is dominant, electric keyboards, the Hammond organ, electric guitar, electric bass, and drums accompany the praise team. If budgetary limitations do not allow a large number of instrumentalists, a basic rhythm section is used (e.g., a keyboard/piano, organ, electric bass, and drums).

The type of songs performed is what distinguishes a praise team from a choir. Ideally, praise teams perform songs that are easy to learn, highly participatory (e.g., unison singing and call-and-response), reverential, and have lyrics that communicate vertically to God (either from the individual's or group's perspective). Although choirs may sing praise and worship songs, they generally perform other types of religious songs—songs that may not be as participatory as praise and worship music and include nonstrophic or through-composed arrangements. The popularity of praise and worship music has been a key element to increased participation in weekly worship and church growth commonly experienced in megachurch contexts over the last thirty years (for additional definitions and history, see Johnson 2008).

The Megachurch Phenomenon in the United States

Despite its widespread use among church growth scholars and modern theologians, and its links to high-profile televangelists in the U.S. media, many individuals are unfamiliar with the term *megachurch* (or *mega-church*). Even members of congregations with thousands of members often do not view themselves as being a part of a megachurch. The Willow Creek Community Church of South Barrington, Illinois, coined the term megachurch in the mid-1980s. Located in a suburb of Chicago, Willow Creek's Sunday services regularly drew seventeen thousand members. Until the late 1990s, there was no definitive explanation or criteria for determining what is or is not a megachurch.

Since 2000, however, several scholars have conducted research on megachurches in the United States. Led by Scott Thumma and other researchers at the Institute for Religion Research in Hartford, Connecticut, and the Leadership Network in Dallas, Texas, most studies have focused on delineating the characteristics of megachurches, describing their organizational structures, and statistically tracking their growth in the United States (see Thumma 1996, 2006; Thumma, Travis, and Bird 2005; Thumma and Bird 2008). (For statistical data on megachurches, go to http://musicofblacklosangeles.blogspot.com.) The researchers also sought to expose common myths and misperceptions that pervade the popular media's coverage of megachurches. They and other observers of culture see the increase in the number of megachurches and their exponential growth as not only a postmodern return to spirituality and religious institutions but also a reflection of the changing religious attitudes and preferences among Christians in the United States.

Regardless of the number of members a church may count on its rolls, attendance at a church's main weekly worship service is the numerical criterion that distinguishes a megachurch church from small and average-sized churches. Thumma (1996) believes that megachurches share five characteristics: a massive number of people in attendance; a charismatic, authoritative senior minister; a very active seven-days-a-week congregational community; a multitude of social and outreach ministries; and a complex organizational structure. Contrary to initial predictions in the media, the megachurch phenomenon is not declining but expanding among various denominations and Christians of all cultural and ethnic backgrounds (Thumma and Bird 2008). According to the *Megachurches Today* 2005 survey, "There are 1,210 Protestant churches in the United States with weekly attendance over 2,000, nearly double the number that existed five years ago" (Thumma, Travis, and Bird)[2].

Beyond the weekly activities of most churches (e.g., Bible study, Sunday school, and midweek prayer), megachurches provide a wide range of services for their members. From couples' counseling, singles ministries, Christian-based business management, addiction counseling, and youth ministries, to art classes, movie nights, concerts, senior aerobics, and camping groups, megachurches offer Christian alternatives to almost every aspect of a person's social life. However, such activities and programs are but a by-product of megachurches' fast and sustained growth, and not the key. Researchers and individuals who attend megachurches believe that growth is due to the power of word of mouth and "excited attendees" who tell their friends, families, and coworkers about their church (Thumma 2006: 6).

The largest numbers of megachurches are in California (178), Texas (157), Florida (85), and Georgia (73). The regional distribution of megachurches reveals that they are found primarily in the South (48 percent) and the West (25 percent). The overwhelming majority of megachurches in the Pacific region (i.e., California, Oregon, Washington, Alaska, and Hawaii) are located in the state of California, at a rate of almost four to one *(Database* 2004; Vaughan 2005). Over 80 percent of the 190 megachurches reported in California in 2005 were located near urban centers in Southern California.

Scholars believe several factors have affected the rise of large congregations: (1) the "back to church" and "born again" movements of the 1970s; (2) the increase in nondenominational and independent churches; (3) decreasing denominational differences; and (4) a conservative backlash against the cultural and political movements of the 1960s and 1970s. The growing number of young adult and middle-aged Christians who are demanding more spirituality and less religious bureaucracy from their churches is another factor for the growth in megachurches (Wooley 1999: 144; Johnson 2008: 152).

Black Megachurches in Greater Los Angeles

Researchers believe African American megachurches comprise 8 percent of the total number of megachurches in the United States—nearly one hundred congregations (Thumma, Travis, and Bird 2005). Due to problems in collection methods and the infrequency of large-scale church growth studies that include large black church congregations, this figure could be an underestimate of the actual number of African American megachurches (Johnson 2008: 56–58, 182). Typically, when one thinks of successful and affluent black megachurches, cities in the Bible Belt (e.g., Atlanta, Dallas, and Memphis) and historic urban centers of the North and Midwest (e.g., New York City, Baltimore, Chicago, and Detroit) readily come to mind. However, Los Angeles has the largest number and some of the oldest black megachurch congregations in the country. Even in the midst of the religious plurality, multiculturalism, and a geographically dispersed black population, the role of the church in the African American community of Los Angeles still resonates among many black Angelinos.

During the early 1980s, one African American megachurch congregation was located in Los Angeles. When Fredrick K. C. Price founded the Crenshaw Christian Center in 1973, the

300-member church grew rapidly, in part because of the national television ministry Price had established as part of the church's missionary outreach in 1978. The church grew to 5,500 members in two years, and, in 1981, it purchased thirty-two acres of land previously occupied by Pepperdine University to construct a 10,000-seat facility. Completed in three years, the Faith Dome was opened in 1989. Instead of a location in some distant suburb, the very large geodesic dome, one of the largest in the world, is located on Vermont Avenue in South Los Angeles. In addition to housing its eighteen thousand members each week, the building also hosts conferences, crusades, and citywide memorials. Between the widely expanding Ever Increasing Faith television ministry, the construction of the Faith Dome, and the establishment of a ministry training institute, Price and the Crenshaw Christian Center became nationally known among black and white faith communities. African Americans in particular were exposed to broader outreach possibilities available to urban churches.

By the late 1990s, at least thirteen other black congregations in Greater Los Angeles had grown to megachurch size. (For information on the thirteen megachurches, go to http://musicofblacklosangeles.blogspot.com.) Their sizes varied from an average membership of three thousand to very large megachurches of twenty-thousand to twenty-five-thousand members. Some congregations had smaller facilities and held from three to four services per Sunday to accommodate their congregation, whereas others owned or rented larger buildings and held only one or two services per Sunday. Although thousands of church members commuted long distances to some of these churches from around the metropolitan area every week, none of the largest congregations relocated to the more prosperous suburban areas surrounding Los Angeles as has been the case with other African American congregations across the country that reached megachurch operational levels. African American megachurches in Los Angeles today represent a cross section of Christian denominational organizations, although seven of the thirteen are Pentecostal or nondenominational.

The establishment of many of these churches predates the church growth movement of the 1960s and emergence of megachurches in 1980s. The oldest congregation is the First African Methodist Episcopal Church. Founded in 1872 by Bridget "Biddy" Mason, an ex-slave, cattle herder, and entrepreneur, historians refer to First AME as "the mother church for all other black churches subsequently established in the city" (Grenier, Bruce, and Nunis 1978: 85). The youngest congregation, Life Church of God in Christ, was organized in 1987 and represents one of only two black megachurches in suburban areas.

Another characteristic of African American megachurches in Los Angeles is their proximity to the entertainment industry. Famous black actors, singers, comedians, athletes, and industry power players (producers, directors, and writers) regularly attend area megachurches.[1] In addition to their presence, celebrity congregants bring economic and professional resources. During the construction of West Angeles Church of God in Christ's cathedral and worship-center complex, longtime celebrity members Stevie Wonder and Ervin "Magic" Johnson each donated several million dollars to the building fund ("LA's West Angeles Cathedral" 2001). Because of the size and impact of the entertainment industry on employment in the city (e.g., catering, production, accounting, and administrative staff, as well as writers and production assistants), some megachurches have spiritual support ministries and Bible study groups for those who work in the industry; many of these ministries also help members develop ways to maintain their integrity in an environment often antithetical to Christian beliefs.

The congregations of megachurches have become attractive to the gospel music industry as promotional, retail, live-recording, and concert venues. Instead of visiting several average-sized churches or trying to sell out a huge arena for a performance, a gospel artist can sing at one megachurch on a Sunday evening and instantly have an audience of thousands willing to buy his/her CD immediately afterward. In Los Angeles, black megachurches have become a source for recruiting skilled singers, musicians, dancers, and actors for the entertainment industry. During my research, it was not uncommon to see musicians and/or singers from local megachurches playing or providing backup vocals for secular music and gospel artists on televised shows such as those for the Grammy Awards, the Emmy Awards, and the BET (Black Entertainment Television) Awards, as well as *Good Morning America*.

The film industry also recognizes the advantages of promoting faith-based and family-oriented films directly to megachurch congregations. Films such as Mel Gibson's *The Passion of the Christ* (2004), Bishop T. D. Jakes' *Woman, Thou Art Loosed* (2004), Will Smith's *Pursuit of Happyness* (2006), and the box office success of Tyler Perry's gospel stage plays adapted for film (e.g., *The Diary of a Mad Black Woman* [2005] and *Madea's Family Reunion* [2006]) were heavily marketed and promoted in black megachurches nationwide but particularly in the Los Angeles area (Marr 2004: B1; Johnson 2008: 178). Just as white Evangelical Christians actively support efforts to increase family-oriented products in the entertainment industry, many black megachurches lend their organized support and commercial dollars to effect more positive images of African American life in film, television, and radio.

While representing several denominational traditions and serving communities across the sprawling city of Los Angeles, the thirteen congregations all have active and large music ministries. In many cases, each church's music ministry enlists over two hundred volunteers to sing in multiple choirs. In addition to providing music for weekly worship services and special programs, some participate outside the church in community service events and fundraising concerts. Just as a preacher serves as the face of a church's ministry in the community, the choir is often the sound of a church's ministry.

Faithful Central:
History, Growth, and Praise and Worship Music

Reverend A. C. Capers and eighteen charter members founded Faithful Central Bible Church in 1936. Originally named Faithful Central Missionary Baptist Church, the small group met in the home of one of its members over a small storefront on South Central Avenue in the heart of black Los Angeles. In 1938, the members moved into its first church building on Paloma Street. After Capers retired in 1953, W. L. Robinson was appointed as the new pastor and led Faithful Central for the next twenty-seven years. The church continued to grow and in 1960 moved to a 450-person-capacity sanctuary on Hoover Street and 61st Street, near downtown Los Angeles. By the time Robinson died in 1980, Faithful Central had grown to approximately 250 members. After a two-year search for a new pastor, church leaders invited Kenneth C. Ulmer to pastor Faithful Central. (For a full description of the church's history and music ministry, see Johnson 2008: 385–480.)

An East St. Louis native, Ulmer was well known in Los Angeles' gospel music circles as an organist and choir director. As a young man, he played for singing preacher Cleophus Robinson and, after moving to Los Angeles in 1970, he became the music minister at the famed Mount Moriah Missionary Baptist Church, succeeding the legendary Thurston G. Frazier. Ulmer was also active in the Gospel Music Workshop of America and appointed as a lifetime board member by its founder, James Cleveland. (For a discussion of Mount Moriah's role in the development of gospel in Los Angeles, see DjeDje 1989.)

At the time of his appointment to Faithful Central in 1982, Ulmer had left the music ministry at Mount Moriah and begun a full-time preaching ministry at the Macedonia Bible Baptist Church in San Pedro, California. In addition to bringing members from his San Pedro church, Ulmer attracted members who had known him from Los Angeles' gospel music community, as well as his work in local church youth revivals and area schools such as the University of Southern California (Allen 2003a; Watson-Blake 2005; Tramble 2006; Johnson 2008: 387–388).

Approximately six years after Ulmer's arrival at Faithful Central, the church had grown to approximately eight hundred members and was holding two Sunday services in the sanctuary and overflow rooms. Ulmer's preaching style and approach to contemporary issues (e.g., depression, celibacy, addiction, and secularism) attracted many people. Ulmer blended a theologically centered teaching style with the storytelling and preaching style of the black Baptist tradition. Sermon series such as "How to Live Holy in a Hollywood World" and "Holding Pattern" drew dozens of educated, lower-middle-class to upper-middle-class black Angelinos, most of whom were between the ages of twenty and forty.

After he became pastor, Ulmer did not abandon his musical roots: he often directed the church choir at the beginning of service or played the organ in impromptu moments during the service.

The church also hosted sacred music workshops featuring scholars such as Wyatt Tee Walker and local composers such as Diane L. White and Calvin Bernard Rhone. During the late 1980s and early 1990s, Ulmer gradually modified the choir's participation in the order of service and the role of the congregation in the musical worship. Instead of the church's deacons or elders beginning the service with devotional prayers and the singing of *a cappella*-lined hymns, as was typical in many traditional black Baptist churches, Ulmer and the church's music minister, Barbara Allen, opened Sunday services with congregational singing led by the choir. Songs included updated versions of popular hymns and gospel songs that could be sung by the whole church, setting the tone for the rest of the service. The choir sang one or two selections later in the service, but, at the time, it was unusual to start a church service with a choir singing worship music rather than the standard opening hymn or anthem from the Baptist hymnal (Byous 2005; Ulmer 2006).

Influenced by the gospel-styled praise and worship music of Patrick Henderson, Judith McAllister, and the praise team at Los Angeles' West Angeles Church of God in Christ, Faithful Central, in 1988, began experimenting with the worship leader-praise team format during Wednesday night services (Elmore 2006b). Led by singer-musician Aladrian Elmore, the praise team commenced the devotional period of church services, blending congregational gospel songs popular at Faithful Central with praise and worship songs from CCM and West Angeles' *Saints in Praise* album (1989) (Byous 2005; Fisher 2005; Elmore 2006a, 2006b). (For discussion of the pioneering role of the music ministry of West Angeles Church of God in Christ in the spread of praise and worship in black churches in Los Angeles, see Johnson 2008, 296–302.) By 1989, the praise team at Faithful Central led the beginning of each Sunday church service with about twenty to thirty minutes of congregational singing and prayer. This is also the year the church started holding Sunday morning services in the 1,700-seat auditorium of Washington High School, four miles south of the Hoover Street sanctuary. However, Faithful Central's membership continued to grow.

Between 1993 and 1998, the church purchased, converted, and outgrew several buildings and properties on Florence and Eucalyptus Avenues in Inglewood: a two-story building, a four-story office complex, a warehouse, and a seven-level parking structure. The two-story building was converted into a 1,100-seat sanctuary named the Living Room. Later, the warehouse was converted into a 2,500-seat sanctuary named the Tabernacle. (For a photo and diagram of the Tabernacle, go to http://musicofblacklosangeles.blogspot.com.)

While a small number of Faithful Central members could not adjust to the constant growth and movement of the church and subsequently left, the number of new members surpassed them as membership approached six and seven thousand. It was apparent to Faithful Central's leaders that it was time to build a larger and more permanent facility to house the congregation at one service, instead of holding four services each Sunday (all of which Ulmer preached) in the Tabernacle. Faithful Central hired an architectural firm to design a building that would seat five thousand people. Church members were excited about the building plans and pulled together resources to start construction of an $18.5 million facility to be called the Family Room. For its 1998 Watch Night Service, Faithful Central rented the Great Western Forum sports arena on New Year's Eve. It would be the first time since the Hoover Street period of the mid-1980s that the entire congregation had met together at one time. When over eight thousand members attended the New Year's Eve service, Ulmer and the members quickly realized that they had underestimated the size of Faithful Central's congregation. After adding more seats to the proposed building plans, the cost of the new sanctuary was in excess of $26 million. Faithful Central's membership roster had grown to eleven thousand members by the year 2000. That was also when the church officially changed its name from Faithful Central Missionary Baptist Church to Faithful Central Bible Church. (For information on Faithful Central's affiliation changes, go to http://musicofblacklosangeles.blogspot.com.)

By 2000, the sports teams that called the Great Western Forum home had moved to the newly built Staples Center in downtown Los Angeles. For over thirty years, the 17,500-seat arena had been the home of Los Angeles' professional sports teams, as well as the area's first premier multipurpose entertainment venue, hosting legends of popular music artists (e.g., Elton John, Stevie Wonder, and Madonna). One of the city's easily recognizable landmarks, merely blocks from the Los Angeles International Airport, the Forum was an iconic edifice symbolizing the perfect marriage between Hollywood star power and professional competitive sports. The Great Western Forum was put up for sale, and the city of Inglewood braced for the loss of revenues if the Forum was sold to owners who did not want to develop the property (J. White 2001; Baade 2003).

The sale price of the Forum and the surrounding twenty-nine acres was $22.5 million. When Ulmer announced to members that they would be buying the Forum, the congregation pulled together and braced for months of criticism in the local media, as well as repeated rejection from banks and financing companies that doubted a church (especially a predominantly African American church) could buy and/or keep a facility as big as the Great Western Forum (P. White 2001). (For a photo of the exterior of the Forum, go to http://musicofblacklosangeles.blogspot.com.)

The fact that Faithful Central was not planning to convert the Great Western Forum into a full-time, traditional pew-filled worship space was also a source of uncertainty for the business community. Faithful Central was interested in hosting conferences and crusades, as well as concerts and sporting events, much like a "family entertainment venue" (Keough 2001). No church in the United States had ventured into the entertainment realm of economic development *and* evangelism on this scale before.

After a year of raising over $2 million, many prayers, much ridicule from those in the secular *and* faith-based communities (see Johnson 2008: 414–419), and eleventh hour financial assistance from the Evangelical Christian Credit Union of Anaheim, California, the purchase of the Forum was finalized in December 2000, and the church held its first services in the building in January

2001. Faithful Central's historic purchase made it the first faith-based organization to own a major entertainment arena, the first owned by African Americans, and the largest house of worship in the United States (Keough 2001). In addition to the obvious physical challenges of moving from a converted warehouse to a 17,500-seat arena, there were psychological challenges for members who were used to the smaller and more intimate settings of the Living Room, the Tabernacle, and even the Washington High School auditorium. Because worship in a building as large and nontraditional as the Forum would probably be alienating for some churchgoers, the leaders of Faithful Central made conscious efforts to create a setting on Sunday mornings that encouraged physical interaction and connectedness during church services but also accommodated the growing congregation. They also counteracted these challenges by organizing smaller gatherings designed to bring members together at social events in addition to regular Sunday and Wednesday services (Johnson 2008: 413–414).

Transforming the Forum facility into a worship space each week involved using a 30 x 50 foot collapsible stage as a pulpit platform, state-of-the-art lighting and sound systems, and video projection technology to accommodate the large room. The weekly production crew from the Tabernacle, which consisted of volunteers from the sound and media ministries, now had to include union-affiliated technical staff employed by Forum Enterprises and worldwide entertainment venue management company SMG.

Setting up the room for Sunday services took at least three hours. Church planners decreased the amount of space congregants had to fill by moving the pulpit platform closer to the middle of the room, which resulted in "half house" seating. Not only did this create a more intimate, theater-styled seating configuration, church workers and the Forum staff could better manage the space because only about half of the seats were available for seating. This also brought the six to seven thousand regularly attending church members physically closer, making the space not appear as cavernous as it had once been. (For a diagram of the Sunday morning seating configuration of the Forum, go to http://musicofblacklosangeles.blogspot.com.)

Music at Faithful Central

As Faithful Central grew during the 1990s, so did its music ministry. The choirs and music performed reflected the social demographics (age, gender, race, etc.) and the musical preferences of the congregation. During my research (May 2003 to September 2006), the music ministry included six choirs, a praise team, a band, and a dance company (see Table 1). While the choirs were assigned to specific Sundays during the month, the praise team performed at all weekly services (Wednesday night service, Sunday morning services, and Sunday evening service). Even though the praise team usually led most of the congregational singing, the choirs were also active in encouraging musical participation.

480

Typically, choirs in Baptist churches sing at least 2–3 songs during a regular order of service, which does not include the moments when the choir *leads* music for the altar call, offering, or invitation to discipleship. Significantly fewer songs were performed or led by Faithful Central choirs during the order of service. Each Sunday, the choir sang only one selection before the sermon. The only exception would be during the annual Easter service, when the songs performed by the choir considerably outnumbered the selections sung by the praise team (Johnson 2008).

On the few occasions when Faithful Central choir sang a second (impromptu) song at the conclusion of a sermon, Bishop Ulmer continued preaching between the song's phrases, using the lyrics to emphasize his closing points. Often Ulmer conducted the choir or turned to the congregation and directed them in singing between his comments. Although the choirs typically sang with the congregation, Jimmy Fisher (the worship leader) and the praise team provided the vocal musical accompaniment for the offering, communion, baptisms, invitation to discipleship, and baby dedications.

While the types of songs performed during Faithful Central's worship services were similar to the songs performed in other black churches, Faithful Central's choirs performed significantly fewer selections in weekly church services than did choirs in traditional Baptist churches (see Table 2).

Due to congregational singing, communal participation, and few regularly occurring liturgical elements in Faithful Central's order of service, the praise team dominated the vocal music contributions each week Although, due to repetition, variation, and reprise, the one selection performed by the choir was longer (approximately 10–12 minutes) than a typical rendition, the large number of songs the praise team sang at weekly services reflects the importance and preference of praise and worship music in weekly services at the church.

Faithful Central's main Sunday service was normally held at the Forum, while the Living Room building was used for small funerals, smaller ministry events, and dance rehearsals. Faithful Central's Sunday morning service typically lasted two hours and twenty minutes, but on several occasions it extended to three hours. Average attendance at the morning service during the period of my fieldwork was between six and seven thousand congregants. In the half-house or theater-style seating configuration, people gathered into one end of the arena, but ushers made sure that seats of the loge level and the floor were filled before directing individuals to the upper sections above the loge seating in the higher colonnade level. Church bulletins were dispersed by a legion of ushers and greeters as people entered the church. Though filled with information about church activities and ministry phone numbers, only four times during the course of my fieldwork was an order of service featured in the printed bulletin. (For further discussion, go to http://musicofblacklosangeles. blogspot.com.) Not only was the order of service not included, the liturgical events that traditionally occur in churches from the Missionary Baptist Church tradition were not included. A typical Missionary Baptist order of service includes the following elements:

> Devotional
> Call to Worship
> Opening Hymn (or Congregational Song)
> Responsive Reading (or Scripture Reading)
> Altar Call
> Musical Selection
> Welcome to Visitors and Announcements
> Offering
> Musical Selection
> Sermon
> Invitation to Discipleship
> Closing Prayer
> Benediction

Instead of following a set pattern of liturgical events passed down from previous generations of church and/or denominational tradition (Ulmer 2006), Faithful Central developed a freer organic approach to weekly worship services. However, after observing worship services for nearly three years, I did note reoccurring events, which illustrate a loosely organized but regular order of service. Although not always followed in sequence, worship services at Faithful Central usually included the following:

> Musical Prelude
> Praise and Worship
> Prayer and Announcements
> (Communion on first Sundays; once a quarter: Baby Dedications or Baptisms on third and
>   fourth Sundays)
> Offering (Dance piece on third Sundays)
> Musical Selection by the Choir
> Sermon
> Invitation to Discipleship
> Benediction and Dismissal

During my fieldwork, traditional elements (e.g., devotion, altar call, responsive reading, and a formal reading of announcements) were not included in the order of service, a trend that is occurring in other black churches.[2] While some announcements were made during services and altar calls did occur, they were not scheduled during a particular point in the church service or on a regular monthly schedule.

Worship services at Faithful Central were celebratory and moderately paced. Interviews with the head pastor and presbytery staff (i.e., minister of music, pastor of worship, and the music director) revealed there was a desire to have a worship service that flowed seamlessly from one element to the next by connecting each component through music, prayer, scripture, or the spiritual mood of the moment (Allen 2003b; Carter 2005; Fisher 2005; Ulmer 2006). While the idea of an order of worship was discussed in a "worship meeting" with the presbytery staff before each Sunday morning service (or possibly during the week if more technical coordination was needed), the order of events was often changed spontaneously to complement the flow of the service. To maintain a continuous flow *throughout* the church service, the head pastor, pastoral staff, ushers, and the music ministry not only had to be flexible, but the pastor of worship, choir directors, and the musicians needed to listen closely to what was occurring during the service so adjustments could be made when necessary. In an interview, Bishop Ulmer (2006) addressed the matter of flow of worship and how he wanted to move away from a church service in which elements were grouped together in a series of unrelated parts or events:

> I don't approach service as a composite of mini-elements that may be unconnected but rather a continuum... all for the purpose of creating an atmosphere that accommodates the release of the Word and the freedom of the Holy Spirit. And for me, that means that there's great energy, there's great intentionality in this continuity between sermon and song. . .To produce that continuity really means even more flexibility and spontaneity, so that it is not so much [that]. . . the choir's on one end doing their thing and the pulpit is doing something else. But that there's. . . most often. . . this flexibility that [if] the Spirit of the Lord, the presence of God, leads the service in a different direction, that not only. . . calls for alterations in the way or what is being presented sermonically, but oftentimes. . . calls for an intentional shifting and a willingness to be flexible on the part of the music ministry.

Not only was the order sometimes adjusted, the duration of the elements was occasionally lengthened to coincide with the movement of the spirit or emotional involvement of congregants in the service. Although the invitation to discipleship (when people are invited to convert to Christianity and/or become members of Faithful Central) usually lasted five to ten minutes, it occasionally would last longer (anywhere from fifteen to twenty minutes) as Ulmer continuously exhorted individuals to come to the altar area in front of the pulpit platform. During these times, the praise and team and band closely followed what Ulmer was saying to the congregation by singing a song or a specific part of a song to complement the tone of his supplications to potential new members and believers. When necessary, the praise team also stopped singing if instrumental music became more appropriate. The elasticity of these moments created improvisatory opportunities for the church's band. To stave off monotonous repetitions of the same chord progressions, often the musicians (keyboardist, organist, bass, and lead guitarist) took turns adding variations to the chord progressions or voicings in the song. Ulmer often commented on how he and the presbytery staff (e.g., worship leader Jimmy Fisher and music director Tracey Carter) were "linked" during services, which prevented disruption to the spiritual climate and climax of the moment (Carter 2005; Fisher 2005; Ulmer 2006).

From my observations, two distinct but interrelated characteristics typify Faithful Central's weekly services: (1) the predominance of praise and worship music, which began in 1988; and (2) the malleable order of worship, which started in 1983, a year after Ulmer became pastor. Although older music genres such as arranged spirituals, hymns, anthems, and traditional gospel were included at specific times (for special holidays and through the repertoire of the Sacred Praise Chorale), Table 2 illustrates how praise and worship music was the most frequently performed; not contemporary gospel, the most popular and commercially successful genre in the black church today. In addition to using the songs of gospel artists who began writing praise and worship music in the late 1990s (e.g., Fred Hammond, Marvin Sapp, John P. Kee, and Judith McAllister), Faithful Central's worship leaders also composed songs for weekly services (Johnson 2008).

The emphasis on "the flow" and keeping an atmosphere of continuous praise, worship, and reverence greatly influenced Faithful Central's weekly services. Their nontraditional style of church worship not only attracted younger members and new converts, but also Christians who may have grown up in a more conservative environment (e.g., Episcopalian, Presbyterian, Catholic, and African Methodist Episcopal) and desired a different worship experience. Members with backgrounds in the Pentecostal denominations attended Faithful Central because of the blending of familiar black Pentecostal worship practices with Charismatic theological elements.

Summary and Conclusions

In this essay, I have demonstrated how the use of praise and worship music became both an *integral* and *effective* aspect of worship at Faithful Central. In adopting praise and worship music and blending it with gospel music performance aesthetics, Faithful Central leaders revived older patterns of communal worship to deal with challenges (e.g., nontraditional church buildings, lack of intimacy, and detached sense of community) facing megachurches today.

The early black folk church thrived on communal singing and full participation in unrestrained worship and praise. One of the reasons church services lasted part or all of a Sabbath was because of the primary role of music in congregations large and small, rural and urban. With the emergence of gospel and sacred music written for church choirs and solo singers around the mid-twentieth century, singing shifted from a united congregational effort to a smaller, increasingly more rehearsed few. The complexity of modern and contemporary gospel songs after the 1960s further shifted full congregational participation in worship to a few appointed times within a church service—during hymn singing, altar calls, and meditative prayer. As some of these genres and elements of church worship faded out of widespread use, the communal expression of many African American churches was reduced. Noticing this decrease in communal participation, some pastors and church-music leaders decided to bring congregational singing back to the heart of worship. During the 1980s, church leaders such as Bishop Charles Blake of West Angeles Church of God in Christ took steps to "give the music back to the people" (Cox 1988: 23–28).

Kenneth Ulmer's arrival at Faithful Central in the early 1980s marked a preference for group participation in weekly worship. Ulmer adopted praise and worship in the late 1980s because it offered a more focused, vertically directed praise, meditation, and devotion, and he used the praise team to encourage corporate musical participation and spiritual engagement. As several choir members and leaders at Faithful Central have stated, "We were doing praise and worship before it had a name" (Byous 2005; Ulmer 2006).

Meeting in a sanctuary space as large as the Great Western Forum, with the building being used for worship only part of the time, forced Faithful Central leaders to be proactive in creating a spiritually stimulating and personally affirming worship experience. Praise and worship music not only encouraged active and interactive participation during the musical portions of the church service; it united the nearly seven thousand people attending morning worship service. Fisher and other worship leaders at Faithful Central understood the importance of the congregation being interactive in the megachurch environment. In between phrases or verses of songs, they motivated congregants with such phrases as "High-five someone if you've been blessed this week" and "Sing this part to your neighbor." Kenneth Ulmer's previous experiences as a professional musician, radio disk jockey, choir director, and minister of music also influenced the church's music ministry, particularly in using music to facilitate the flow of weekly worship services.

The relationship between music and preaching in many churches is manifested hierarchically in which preaching is placed above music making. Lincoln and Mamiya (1990: 346) explain: "In most black churches music, or more precisely *singing*, is second only to preaching as the magnet of attraction and the primary vehicle of spiritual transport for the worshiping congregation. In the black church, good preaching and good singing are almost invariably the minimum conditions for a successful ministry." At Faithful Central, the theological view that scripturally sound and spiritually meaningful lessons can be siphoned from the singing of music is rigorously promoted. Ulmer's theological beliefs regarding the unity of preaching and music in worship affected his affinity for praise and worship styles and congregational singing. Moreover, the belief that the act of praise and worship through singing is just as effective and religiously germane as prayer and preaching is part of church's identity. In an interview with Gospelcity.com in September 2005, Ulmer discussed the unity in Faithful Central's church services:

> There's an interesting unity between the praise team leading worship through song and the preacher leading worship through the word. . . We believe that it shouldn't be one and then the other, but a united effort. We are partners in ministry, so the Word goes forth in song and sermon. . . At Faithful Central, God has created and affirmed a team ministry. . . We don't see a dichotomy or a separation between the song selection and the teaching of the Word. We are one. ("Zion Rejoice" 2005)

Viewing music as a tool of theological pragmatism and a vehicle for corporate worship was often communicated to members of the congregation who in turn began to value the deeper spiritual connections made during worship services. The congregation's understanding of these connections and their impact on their lives outside church was manifested in several ways: their active participation in all musical elements of the church; their willingness to follow the flow of the service regardless of the time spent on singing versus preaching; their efforts to arrive at church before 10 a.m. every week; and the purchase of audio and video discs of church services, which included a great deal of musical worship and prayer. Members who invited their friends, family, and/or coworkers to the church often cited the praise and worship atmosphere, along with Ulmer's progressive preaching, as major reasons to visit if the person was not very religious or if the person was looking for a church that blended traditional worship with very contemporary worship styles. Since church growth has not been negatively impacted, and the church's weekday as well as weekend ministries continue to have a positive impact in the lives of its congregants, Faithful Central demonstrates how praise and worship music can be effective in bringing music back to the heart of worship.

Notes

1. Although several well-known black entertainers are members of some high-profile black megachurches, it would be an overstatement to suggest that all black celebrities attend megachurches and every black church of megachurch size in Los Angeles has well-known entertainers attending every Sunday.
2. Today, even traditional Baptist churches are phasing out the devotional period, which is one of the oldest and most common elements in the order of service across many African American church traditions (i.e., Baptist, Pentecostal, Holiness, and rural southern Methodist).

References

Allen, Barbara. Interview with the author. Inglewood, CA, October 30, 2003.
———. Interview with the author. Inglewood, CA, November 13, 2003.
Baade, Robert. *Los Angeles City Controllers Report on Economic Impact: Staples Center*. Los Angeles: Laura Chick, City Controller and the Office of the Controller, City of Los Angeles, July 21, 2003.
Blacking, John. "Identifying Processes of Musical Change." *World of Music* 28, no. 1 (1986):3–15.
Burnim, Mellonee. "The Black Gospel Music Tradition: Symbol of Ethnicity." PhD diss., Indiana University, 1980.
Byous, Sonya. Interview with the author. Los Angeles, July 6, 2005.
Carter, Tracey. Interview with the author. Inglewood, CA, October 8, 2005.
Cox, Donna Marie McNeil. "Contemporary Trends in the Music of the Church of God in Christ." *Journal of Black Sacred Music* 2, no. 2 (1988):23–28.
Cusic, Don. *The Sound of Light: A History of Gospel and Christian Music*. Milwaukee: Hal Leonard, 2002.
Database of megachurches in the U.S. Hartford: Hartford Institute for Religion Research. http://hirr.hartsem.edu/megachurch/database.html. Accessed January 22, 2004.
DjeDje, Jacqueline Cogdell. "Change and Differentiation: The Adoption of Black American Gospel Music in the Catholic Church." *Ethnomusicology* 30 no. 2 (1986): 223–252.
———. "Gospel Music in the Los Angeles Black Community: A Historical Overview." *Black Music Research Journal* 9, no. 1 (1989): 35–79.

Elmore, Aladrian. Phone interview with the author. August 22, 2006.

———. Phone interview with the author. August 23, 2006.

Fisher, Jimmy. Interview with the author. Inglewood, CA, August 18, 2005.

Grenier, Judson, Jean Bruce, and Doyce B. Nunis Jr., eds. *A Guide to Historic Places in Los Angeles County.* Dubuque: Kendall/Hunt, 1978.

Johnson, Birgitta. "When We All Get Together: Praise and Worship Music as a Unifying Element in an African American Megachurch." Paper presented at the Annual Meeting of the Society for Ethnomusicology, Honolulu, November 18, 2006.

———. "'Oh, for a Thousand Tongues to Sing': Music and Worship in Black Megachurches of Los Angeles, California." PhD diss., University of California-Los Angeles, 2008.

Keough, Christopher. "Fabulous Forum Revival Due in Church-led purchase." *Los Angeles Business Journal.* Posted by BNET Business Network. http://findarticles.com/p/articles/mi_m5072/is_1_23/ai_69259320. Accessed January 1, 2001.

"LA's West Angeles Cathedral Dedicated: Stunning Edifice Exemplifies What Happens When a Community Comes Together." *Sacramento Observer* 38 (May 2, 2001): C3.

Libaw, Oliver. "God on a Grand Scale: Megachurches Grow Bigger and Bigger. http://abcnews.go.com/sections/us/DailyNews/megachurches010613.html. Accessed June 18, 2001.

———. More Americans Flock to Megachurches. http://abcnews.go.com/US/story?id=93111&page=1. Accessed June 13, 2001.

Lincoln, C. Eric, and Lawrence H. Mamiya. 1990. *The Black Church in the African American Experience.* Durham: Duke University Press.

Marr, Merissa. "Publicity, PR and 'Passion': Thanks to Astute Marketing, Mel Gibson's film about Jesus Is Headed for a Strong Debut." *Wall Street Journal* (February 20, 2004): B1.

Maultsby, Portia K. "Africanisms in African American Music." In *Africanisms in American culture.* Edited by Joseph E. Holloway, 185–210. Bloomington: Indiana University Press, 1990.

"The Megachurches." *Ebony* 60 (December 2004): 156–8.

Mostyn, Carolynn. "Who Are Local Churches Building For? *Connection Magazine: The Good News Magazine* November 2002. http://www.connectionmagazine.org/2002_11/ts_local_churches.htm. Accessed January 22, 2004.

Neal, Mark Anthony. *What the Music Said: Black Popular Music and Black Public Culture.* New York: Routledge, 1999.

"The New Black Spirituality." *Ebony* 60 (December 2004): 136–66.

Nketia, J. H. Kwabena. "Tradition and Innovation in African Music." *Jamaica Journal* 11, no. 3 (1978): 3–9.

"Praise and Worship." *The Gospel Music Industry Round-Up 2004* (2003): 87.

"Praise and Worship: A Primer." http://www.billboard.biz/bbbiz/search/article_display.jsp?vnu_content_id=10004 89721. April 24, 2004. Accessed June 18, 2007.

Ricks, George Robinson. "Some Aspects of the Religious Music of the United States Negro: An Ethnomusicological Study with Special Emphasis on the Gospel Tradition." PhD diss., Northwestern University, 1960.

Steensland, Brian, Jerry Z. Park, Mark D. Regnerus, Lynn D. Robinson, W. Bradford Wilcox, and Robert D. Woodberry. "The Measure of American Religion: Toward Improving the State of the Art." *Social Forces* 79, no. 1 (2000): 291–318.

Thumma, Scott. "Exploring the Megachurch Phenomena: Their Characteristics and Cultural Context." Hartford Seminary-Hartford Institute for Religion Research. http://hirr.hartsem.edu/bookshelf/thumma_article2.html. 1996. Accessed March 1, 2007.

———. Slide #6 in "Outreach Lessons from the Fastest Growing Megachurches." PowerPoint presentation at the National Outreach Conference in San Diego, November 2006. http://hirr.hartsem.edu/megachurch/MegachurchOutreach&Growth.ppt. Accessed March 1, 2007.

———, and Warren Bird. "Changes in American Megachurches: Tracing Eight Years of Growth and Innovation in the Nation's Largest-Attendance Congregations." Hartford Seminary-Hartford Institute for Religion Research. http://hirr.hartsem.edu/megachurch/mega2008_summaryreport.html. Accessed March 27, 2007.

———, Dave Travis, and Warren Bird. "Megachurches Today 2005: Summary of Research Findings." Hartford Seminary-Hartford Institute of Religion Research. http://hirr.hartsem.edu/megachurch/research.html. 2005. Accessed March 1, 2007.

Tramble, Gina Y. Interview with the author. Inglewood, CA, August 3, 2006.

Ulmer, Bishop Kenneth C. Interview with the author. Inglewood, CA, August 30, 2006.

Vaughan, John N. "America's Megachurch Attendance by State." http://www.churchgrowthtoday.org/Default.aspx?tabid=1926. January 2005. Accessed March 1, 2007.

Walker, Wyatt Tee. *"Somebody's Calling My Name": Black Sacred Music and Social Change.* Valley Forge: Judson, 1979.

Watson-Blake, Clarissa. Interview with the author. Los Angeles, July 9, 2005.

"What Is the Future of the Black Church?" *Ebony* 60 (2004): 160, 163–5.

"Where We Stand on Faith." *Newsweek* 146 (August 29–September 5, 2005): 48–9.

White, John. "House Churches and Megachurches?" http://rememberchrist.com/articles/John%20White%202.html. July 30, 2001. Accessed January 2, 2009.

White, Paula M. "New Player at the Forum: Forum Enterprise Inc., on Behalf of the Faithful Central Bible Church, Buys the Great Western Forum in Los Angeles, California." *Black Enterprise* 31, no. 9 (2001): 18.

Wong, Connie Oi-Yan. "Singing the Gospel Chinese Style: 'Praise and Worship' Music in the Asian Pacific." PhD diss., University of California-Los Angeles, 2006.

Wooley, Amy. "Music at AGAPE, Church of Religious Science: The Role and Power of Song and Chant at a Los Angeles Megachurch." Master's thesis, University of California-Los Angeles, 1999.

"Zion Rejoice: Live from Faithful Central." GospelCity.com. Posted on September 13, 2005, at http://www.gospelcity.com/news/headlines/1052. Accessed September 13, 2005.

Table 1. Faithful Central Music Ministry Groups

Choir or Group	Demographic	Director	Musical Style
One Voice (OV)	Initially an adult singles choir	Donald Taylor	Multiple sacred styles, mostly contemporary gospel
Men of Faith (MOF)	Men's choir	Byron Pope/ Donald Taylor	Traditional and contemporary gospel
Mustard Seeds of Faith (MSOF)	Children's choir (ages 5–14)	Paula Boger and Sandra Flewelen	Contemporary gospel, children's hymns
Sacred Praise Choral (SPC)	Adult choir	Diane White-Clayton	Anthems, arranged spirituals, and mixed arrangements of sacred styles
Voices of Faith (VOF)	Adult choir	Barbara Allen	Multiple sacred styles, mostly contemporary gospel
Praise Teams	Adults	Jimmy Fisher and Kurt Lykes	Praise and worship
Mass Choir	Adults	Barbara Allen, Donald Taylor, and Diane White-Clayton	Multiple sacred styles
Faithful Dance Company	Children–Adults	Ariyan Johnson	Modern, jazz, African, ballet, and hip hop
Youth Choir (hiatus since 2004)	Ages 14–21	Fred Martin	Multiple styles

Table 2. Song Types and Frequency of Music Performed at Faithful Central between December 2005 and September 2006

Arranged spirituals and choral songs	8
Anthems	4
Hymns or responsorial chants	30
Traditional gospel	18
Contemporary gospel	72
Praise and worship	172
Praise break/shout music	2
Miscellaneous ("Happy Birthday" and improvised melodies)	24

29

"Praise Is What We Do": The Rise of Praise and Worship Music in the Urban Church

Deborah S. Pollard

If the young people were allowed to. . . take over the church, we would lose Devotion. They think Devotion is a waste of time.
—*Sister Rosie Sims, in Walter F. Pitts* Old Ship of Zion

Judith Christie McAllister is great. . . because she is tied to her past. If you listen to what she does, incorporated in her new stuff, you can hear the sound of old gospel.

—*Pastor Marvin L. Winans, January 14, 2004*

They can be found standing before a few or before thousands in churches and auditoriums across the country. With microphones in hand, they speak and sing words of praise with musical accompaniment provided by a commercially produced music track, a single keyboardist, or an eight-piece band. Their lyrics are given to the congregation in call-and-response style, projected on a screen, or printed in the church bulletin. Individually, they are called praise and worship leaders, while collectively—as few as two or as many as a dozen in number—they are referred to as praise teams. Their mission: through example and exhortation, to move congregants from passive observation to active participation in the worship experience so that they might usher in and experience the presence of God.

The label "praise and worship" is used within the Christian church in reference to a particular musical repertoire and mode of performance that emerged during the last decades of the twentieth century. Generally, praise and worship music is used during the opening period of a worship service, gospel musical, or concert; however, its rising popularity has led to its use at other times as well. In some instances, entire services and events are built around praise and worship music.

While it would seem to be a benign set of rituals, especially since it is a church-oriented musical form, praise and worship has created its share of controversies. Many of its supporters view it as a "move of God" as well as a welcome break from the traditional devotional service that preceded it, thanks in large measure to its perceived and actual innovations. Others ask whether the rise of praise and worship is a case of "bandwagoning," or possibly a situation in which an older tradition that was never fully understood is being replaced by "a phenomenon that has been copied without spiritual insight."[1] Some charge that praise and worship has sidelined age-old musical repertoires and, in some denominations, middle-aged and elderly deacons. These have been replaced, the critics argue, by the under-forty praise team with its new sounds and terminology.

In reality praise and worship is neither as completely new as some would suggest nor as destructive to traditions as others assert. An examination of the music presented and the intentions expressed by those involved in praise and worship in Detroit's black churches as well as within the national gospel industry reveals that the perception that there has been a complete generational shift is incorrect. As this study reveals, praise and worship leaders and teams frequently incorporate this genre as a "new layer" that enhances rather than replaces the African, African American, and mainstream Christian rituals that already exist within the black church.[2] The result is a devotional mode that meets the spiritual demands and musical needs of many contemporary black congregations.

Praise and Worship: Definitions, Form, and Function

Although the individual words "praise" and "worship" are often spoken as if they are interchangeable, many who teach the concepts of praise and worship or who are acknowledged worship leaders differentiate between the two. Pastor and author Myles Munroe writes that praise means commending, glorifying, and otherwise "putting God in first place"; however, he writes later that "worship is what praise is all about: seeking God until he graces us with his presence."[3] The act of praise can include speaking of God's attributes in a loud voice, singing, dancing, waving the hands, or clapping.[4] Marcus Jennings, minister of praise and worship at Detroit's St. James Baptist Church as well as a minister of the gospel, explains that praise is offered to God "for what he's done, for how he's blessed us. . . He woke you up this morning. He's given you life." In contrast, he explains, worship is offered "just because he's God."[5]

Many pastors and praise leaders describe praise as a pathway to worship. Author Terry Law outlines the progression: "First we will to praise God, then we sanctify our minds through the power of the Spirit, then our emotions take over and bring us through the veil into the presence of God in worship."[6] Munroe writes that the purpose of worship is to render adoration and devotion to God because of who he is and is the sole domain of those who have a personal relationship with him.[7]

492

As for the function of praise and worship music, Consuella Smith, an evangelist and a praise and worship leader at Greater Christ Temple Church in Detroit, explains that this particular music form is usually found at the start of the worship service so that the spirit of the Lord can be ushered in. At the same time, worshippers can prepare themselves to experience the presence of God.[8] Despite its association with the opening segment of the worship service, praise and worship can occur whenever and wherever believers seek to reach beyond their current situation. Byron Cage, a native Detroiter who has become an award-winning praise and worship leader and recording artist, views praise and worship as an experience that benefits the congregants while it simultaneously glorifies God: "In order to maximize who we are and our potential we have to maximize who God is. The only way we can really do that is to get into his presence. We need to allow his presence to saturate us. The Bible says that he dwells in the midst of our praise. Where he dwells there is freedom and liberation to do whatever it is that we need to do."[9]

Ancient and Biblical Antecedents

While the contemporary Christian church has applied the inclusive label "praise and worship" to a specific set of devotional rituals, the Old and New Testaments are filled with instances of God's people performing acts of praise and worship.[10] There are a number of other words from the Old Testament/Hebrew Bible that have also found their way into the vocabulary of those involved in praise and worship, such as *barak, halal, shabach, tehillah, towdah, yadah,* and *zamar.*[11]

These terms, which Munroe calls "the seven dimensions or portraits of praise," are often alluded to in the instructions the praise and worship leader gives to the congregation ("Let's bless the Lord with a sacrifice of praise").[12] But almost as frequently, the Hebrew words themselves are included ("Now, let's *shabach* the Lord!"). Some of the most popular praise and worship songs, such as the one titled "Shabach," include several Hebrew terms, including *shabach, barak, yadah,* and others.[13]

The hyphenated names of Jehovah found in the Bible as God revealed himself to his people, including Jehovah-Jireh (provider), Jehovah-Shalom (peace and unity), and Jehovah-Nissi (banner), can also be found in praise and worship songs, such as "Because of Who You Are" composed by Martha Munizzi.[14] They are also used during the worship service to remind participants of the various attributes believers ascribe to God.

The use of these ancient terms from the Old Testament/Hebrew Bible means, among other things, that this movement within the Christian church, thought by some practitioners to be the domain of those rebels perceived as bringing something brand new to the worship experience, has in reality pulled terminology to the forefront that is older than Christianity itself.[15]

The Traditional Devotional Service

We cannot look at how praise and worship is practiced within the contemporary black church without examining its African and African American predecessors.[16] Multiple generations of Africans had been sold and born into slavery before large numbers of slave owners decided to introduce them to Christianity in North America. It was also well into the 1700s before the enslaved Africans embraced Christianity in significant numbers. This slow acceptance was due in part to the fact that many practiced the beliefs and rituals that had made the journey with them or their ancestors through the Middle Passage, much to the consternation of the missionaries and evangelists who had tried to lure them with the gospel for decades. The ring shout, spirit possession, and ecstatic/religious dance, rituals that existed before the founding of the black church, were valued links to a West African heritage that placed these expressive cultural elements at the very center of life.[17]

Once Africans in America began to accept Christianity, they adapted the religion using their own spiritual and cultural values. This adaptation included giving birth to new musical forms, such as the Negro spiritual, through which they addressed a range of earthly and heavenly concerns while praising God. While some might have difficulty connecting this part of black America's past to today's contemporary sacred music practices, there are others who see linkages between these periods. Jackie Patillo, Zomba Gospel's vice president of A&R and artist development, an industry leader in gospel music, says the roots of the genre were within the enslaved Africans: "Though we have contemporary choruses that people define as praise and worship, I would say that our ancestors had praise and worship in the fields; we call that music 'spirituals.' Some were prayers asking for help. Some were moans. And some were songs worshipping God and acknowledging his greatness."[18]

The cultural and religious rituals of these Africans in America persisted, not only during slavery, but long after, as they were carried into the establishment of the black church, a term which, according to C. Eric Lincoln and Lawrence Mamiya, is sociological and theological shorthand regarding the pluralism of black Christian churches in the United States.[19] While the line is blurry that separates some of the practices of the white church from that of the black church, certain behaviors and performances are widely viewed as synonymous with the traditional black worship experience, even if not all branches of the black church practice them. Among them is the devotional service, sometimes called "devotion," which has been the opening segment of the traditional worship in several denominations of the black church.

Arthur Paris categorizes the major sub-segments of the typical opening service he observed for his study of the black Pentecostal worship as opening song(s), scripture reading, requests for prayer, prayer, song service, and testimony service.[20] Similarly, Walter F. Pitts Jr. writes that within the

Afro-Baptist church tradition there are two ritual "frames," or segments, the first of which is the devotional service; it consists of prayers, lined hymns, congregational songs, and spirituals that precede the main frame of the service, in which the preaching and ecstatic elements of the black church ritual are to be found. He has identified these components throughout the African diaspora and views them as tying disparate black cultures to the African continent.[21] No matter which combination of building blocks is included, devotion not only signals the start of the service in the churches that practice these rituals but it also prepares the worshippers for the apex of the experience: the sermon, or "The Service of the Word," as Paris has labeled it.[22]

Among the opening music generally found within the devotional service can be congregational songs ("I'm a Soldier in the Army of the Lord" or "Woke Up This Morning with My Mind Stayed on Jesus," e.g.), well known, easily sung gospel songs ("He's Sweet I Know"), and centuries-old hymns led, or "lined out," in a call-and-response mode ("A Charge to Keep I Have" or "I Love the Lord"). This service within the Baptist Church has traditionally been conducted by the all-male or predominately male board of deacons. They lead the songs, read the scripture, offer the prayers, as well as solicit prayer requests and testimonies; within a number of progressive churches, however, women have been added to this auxiliary and also lead these services. Within Apostolic/Pentecostal churches, these services are often conducted by the ministers or evangelists. The devotional service is not, however, part of the regular worship structure of the Methodist Church.

Congregants are expected to participate by singing, listening, testifying, and praying silently along with the individuals leading the devotional service. At certain times, the congregation is directed to stand, sit, or kneel, and they may be told to perform two or more of these actions during a single song. For example, the congregation may begin singing while seated, but after a verse or two, the person leading the song can signal them to stand. If that individual segues from a song to a prayer, he or she may direct those standing to sit or may gesture for them to kneel; either position is acceptable at that point.[23]

Though the gospel and congregational songs that are performed during devotional service can be spirited and fast-paced, the lined hymns, part of the Baptist tradition, are generally sung in a manner that is anything but jubilant-sounding.[24] Lining out involves one individual, usually a deacon during a regular service or perhaps a layperson during a testimonial meeting, chanting a line or two of a hymn and ending on a specific pitch. The congregation follows by singing that same passage with some variation on the tune. Practiced in North America by early colonists, lining out later became a hallmark of hymn singing in black churches, perhaps because of its similarities to call-and-response found throughout the African Diaspora.[25] Pitts describes the practice as he observed it in the Afro-Baptist churches he documented:

> "I love the Lord, he heard my cry," Deacon cries out. The newly gathered congregation, now seated in their pews, echoes his words in a plaintive tune. They do this without the support

of piano, organ or hymnal. . . "And pitied every groan!" The deacon, not waiting for his chorus to finish the first line, bellows the second from a hymn composed by Dr. Isaac Watts at the beginning of the eighteenth century. Again the congregation resumes their mournful melody, overlapping the deacon's last verse with their chorus. . . As the interaction between deacon and congregation unfolds, mothers wrestle with their smaller children to sit still while beckoning to their older ones to come into the sanctuary.[26]

While such singing resonates with many older congregants, and with younger ones who have come to appreciate the tradition, it is usually not the music of choice for many under a certain age, as Pitts indicates. This is probably due to the tempo, the fluctuations between major and minor keys, and the unaccompanied nature of the singing. Marcus Jennings shared what he saw as the signs that the older devotional form was passing in many contemporary churches: "In the traditional devotion, people would almost purposely come late, just to avoid it, and quite frankly, it became really boring. People didn't enjoy it. They would sit there and you could just see on their face, 'As soon as this is over, the better it would be.'"[27]

Another reason many of a certain group may have not gravitated toward these songs is offered by Dorgan Needom, minister of music at Detroit's Unity Baptist Church: "Today's twenty-first-century churchgoer doesn't understand its relevance. Deacons don't take time to explain it; they just [start singing] and expect people to join in."[28] Not only were many ignorant of the significance of the rituals, there were probably as many who could not understand the actual lyrics as they were being sung. The melismatic, elongated vowels couched in often somber tones ("I-I lo-ove the Lo-o-ord, he heard my cry-e-y-ee") for years have been fodder for Christian comedians, who have commented on being amused and puzzled by much of the devotional ritual.[29]

Ironically, the old devotional service and the contemporary praise and worship service parallel one another in this area. For just as there were those younger congregants who felt left out of devotion because they did not understand the words being spoken and sung and were not drawn to the traditional music, today there are congregants who have not been schooled in the Hebrew terms or the new lyrics and music and thus may not be fully engaged by the contemporary praise and worship songs and behaviors. Fortunately, the most skillful and sensitive praise and worship leaders have learned to accommodate these congregants, as will be discussed later in this chapter.

The Emergence of Praise and Worship Music

In the 1970s, a time during which many younger black church members were not actively involved in the traditional devotional service, a similar level of disengagement was running through the white Protestant church. For many on each side of the Christian church's racial divide, the praise and worship movement would be the sound that drew them back.

Praise and worship music arose within the white Evangelical church because of a unique set of circumstances. According to Robert L. Redman, two major influences shaped what he calls the "sweeping changes in Christian worship" during the latter part of the twentieth century. The first, the evangelical seeker service movement, was launched by those who, after reviewing research on the habits of the baby boomer generation, "set to create a 'nonreligious' environment for services, an alternative setting for presenting the gospel that suggests church without its supposedly negative connotations."[30] What resulted were services that included sermons with themes about domestic life and personal development, multimedia presentations, dramatic skits that set the stage for the message, and inspirational, sometimes secular, songs whose text matched the sermon's theme.[31]

The second influence Redman names is the charismatic praise and worship movement. He outlines the worship experience: "A typical service begins with twenty to thirty minutes or more of congregational singing, led by a worship leader, a band with a small ensemble of singers, and often a choir as well, modeled on the gospel choir in African American churches. Leaders encourage a wide range of physical expressions through clapping, raising hands, swaying and even dancing."[32] The praise and worship services include "participatory" sermons and contemporary worship music, which is a considerable departure from traditional multiverse hymns in that the songs are shorter and more focused on single themes or images. This allows the congregation to create a spiritual and emotional bond with God. Another feature of this service may be "singing in the spirit," which the leader may encourage at the end of a quiet song if he or she wishes the congregation to focus on God's presence.[33]

From these seeker service and praise and worship service movements emerged the popular praise and worship musical genre that not only reflects these influences but also mirrors the fact that a generation that defined itself in its youth by music—rock and roll and Motown—seeks to do so during its religious life as well.[34] As a result, Michael S. Hamilton writes, thousands of individuals select their churches, or at least the services they attend within a given church, not on the doctrine preached, but on the music that is performed.[35] Such is the case with praise and worship music; many are drawn to those churches that offer it as a contemporary prelude to the sermon, which is still considered by most to be the high point of the worship experience.

Before the phrase "praise and worship" became widely used within the Christian church, contemporary Christian recording artists such as Twila Paris ("Lamb of God") and Keith Green ("Rushing Wind") performed songs that could be easily categorized within that genre today. Gospel singer and composer Pastor Marvin Winans also names music recorded in the late 1960s and early 1970s by Andraé Crouch, the 2nd Chapter of Acts, and Danny Lee and the Children of Truth as having opened the door for today's praise and worship explosion.[36] By 1981 there was a large enough pool of recording artists producing praise and worship music that the Gospel Music

Association (GMA), whose artists primarily sing contemporary Christian music (CCM), presented its first Dove Awards in that category.[37]

Praise and Worship Movement Grows

At the time the GMA initially created this category, most "of those who were being nominated were white artists who performed for white congregations and consumers. Eventually there would be black singers, such as Alvin Slaughter, Ron Kenoly, Bob Bailey, and Larnelle Harris, who would also perform in that style for predominately white audiences. But it would take a merging of several different factors for most black audiences to be exposed to praise and worship music.

Broadcast television and cable television outlets and programs that regularly allowed artists to interact with and be exposed to audiences who were not from their own racial or ethnic community included Black Entertainment Television (BET), Trinity Broadcast Network (TBN), and, much later, the Word Network; shows like *PTL* before the Jim Bakker scandal; and music award shows, including, the GMA (Dove), Stellar, American Music, and Grammy award programs. As for radio, the AM and FM bands have been a meeting place for racially mixed gospel music loving audiences since the advent of the medium. Because of these outlets, what was a tiny number in the late 1970s is today an impressive and growing roster of black and white artists with multicultural audiences.[38]

Also priming the black community for praise and worship were several black artists who performed and recorded praise and worship music before most members of their core audience were familiar with that designation. That list includes the late minister Thomas Whitfield, whose commercial recordings for the Sound of Gospel, Onyx, and Benson labels beginning in the 1970s included a number of songs, such as "We Need a Word from the Lord" and "Lift Those Hands," that were performed in the praise and worship style. For that reason, several of today's most prominent worship leaders and composers, among them Byron Cage, cite him as a forerunner in the genre for the black community.[39]

Another name on that list of black artists recording praise and worship for black audiences is the West Angeles Church of God in Christ, which recorded a series called Saints in Praise beginning in the late 1980s. Volume 1 of the series was an early, if not the first, praise and worship project purchased by a large segment of the black gospel music community, thus opening the door for the platinum sales of Fred Hammond, often called the "architect of urban praise and worship," at the turn of the twenty-first century to that same constituency. Judith Christie McAllister, one of the praise leaders for that series and congregation, remains one of the premier female voices of the genre today. Composer, arranger, and singer Richard Smallwood has recorded songs since the early 1980s that are now considered classics of the genre, including "Total Praise" and "Anthem of Praise."

Another catalyst for the overall expansion of praise and worship music was the emergence of several record labels whose sole or primary interest is praise and worship music, including Maranatha! Music, Integrity, Vineyard Music, Hillsong, and Hosanna! Two of the best known are Maranatha! Music and Integrity. Maranatha! Music emerged during the "Jesus movement" of the early 1970s, which found thousands of young people converting to Christianity and enjoying what was being called "Jesus music." The company flourished. Today Maranatha is an award-winning company that focuses exclusively on worship music including special series.[40]

Emerging approximately fifteen years after the founding of Maranatha was Integrity Media, known as "the largest company in the Christian music industry that specializes exclusively in the praise and worship genre." Integrity produces, publishes, and distributes praise and worship recordings, books, including Bibles and related materials.[41] Initially Integrity was to be a Christian magazine, but a plan to send an audiocassette of music to subscribers brought an avalanche of requests from recipients for more music. The company now exists to fill that need, according to Jackie Patillo, who was Integrity's general manager before moving to Zomba Gospel. Integrity has promoted and recorded some of the most recognized and respected names in that genre, among them Ron Kenoly, Joe Pace, Don Moen, and Israel and New Breed.[42]

Today, praise and worship recordings are available worldwide and are produced by artists of every ethnic and racial background, who perform in virtually every gospel subgenre, from traditional to holy hip hop. Among the recordings are individual praise and worship songs, whole CDs devoted to praise and worship, and repackaged songs from previous projects, either from one artist's catalog or from the repertoires of many.[43]

The consumer response to praise and worship—whether it is a trend, a move of God, or a combination of the two—has been noteworthy. The *New York Times* reported in 2004 that the sales of praise and worship albums had doubled between 2000 and 2003 to about twelve million units. While *music* sales overall had slumped in 2003, including that of other Christian music, worship music sales were up by 5 percent the following year.[44] And sales are not all that attest to the genre's popularity. Howard Rachinski, president of Christian Copyright Licensing International (CCLI), which tracks the music sung by congregations in 137,000 churches across America, estimated in 2004 that praise and worship music made up 75 percent of the repertoire in half of the churches in the United States. In 2006 Paul Herman, marketing manager for CCLI, updated the company's coverage to 138,000 churches in the United States and estimated that 15 to 20 percent of that number are African American Baptist or Church of God in Christ congregations.[45]

One possible key to understanding why this musical genre has found such broad acceptance in a relatively short period is to view it as another example of the complex generational behavioral transformations that have occurred throughout history. Using that perspective calls to mind a familiar interpretation of] Judaism that centers on the Bible verse "I am the God of Abraham, the God of Isaac, and the God of Jacob" (Exodus 3:6). Many understand this to mean that God remained the same over time, but each of the patriarchs saw, experienced, and responded to God uniquely and therefore loved and showed reverenced for God in his own way.[46]

The same could be said of praise and worship music: several key national performers and scores of black congregations in the metropolitan Detroit area praise God in a way that seems appropriate to them for today using praise and worship music that is reflective of this generation's aesthetics, language, and viewpoints. What their detractors may find surprising, however, is that a great deal of room and respect is still being given to older musical forms within the black church. A majority of the artists and churches reviewed for this study use an inclusive model. They combine the traditional devotional songs with the contemporary praise and worship music, as I have documented after observing several Detroit area praise and worship services, analyzing the responses to a praise and worship survey, and listening to recordings by key artists of the genre.

Bridging the Cultural Divide

One question loomed as I was conducting my research: why do the detractors of praise and worship see it as having decimated earlier devotional forms? The answer may lie in the fact that some praise and worship music, despite often presenting lyrics taken straight from the Bible, is markedly different from its predecessors in sound and instrumentation. Exposure to the forms that fall outside of the black church tradition can be troubling to some musicians. As one younger musician, who asked for anonymity, explained, "It's just too hard to play because it's not the music I know. "There are actually sub-subgenres within the subgenre, that is, different forms of praise and worship music. Artists and composers such as Shekinah Glory Ministry (Kingdom Records) and Joe Pace II (Integrity Gospel Records) produce what Patillo describes as "more gospel influenced praise and worship." Paul Allen of PAJAM explains how that combination occurs: "We make it our own by changing a little bit here, making it a little bit more soulful there, so it's praise and worship with a little black church soul. . . You add a little extra drums here when they [in the white church] just have strings and piano. We add some drums, and we add some bass and some guitar, and we add some climaxes, some key changes."[47]

In contrast to the "gospel influenced" style, there are also artists whose approach is more eclectic. The songs these musicians create can combine world music, rhythm and praise, hip hop, rock, and other contemporary styles.[48] Composer and producer Kurt Carr's 2005 release *One Church* contains several songs that could easily place the CD in the eclectic category, including the infectious "If I Tell God" with its South African influences. He explains to Rene Williams that after his composition "In the Sanctuary" from his *Awesome Wonder* collection (2000) was translated into nine languages, he felt led to reach out to a global community:

Though I never want to forsake my base—which is the black church, the Pentecostal movement, the Charismatic movement—this time, it's time for Kurt Carr to reach out to the world. Whether or not they embrace it, it's my mandate to present music and a sound that would appeal to people around the world. That's what I've done on this project. I've always tried to be broad, but this time I went further. I got African drummers and percussionists; I have an accordion player from Armenia; I have a violinist from China; I have a bagpiper from Scotland; I have a sitar on the album. So I have lots of different sounds and lots of different influences from around the world with the same message. It still has the Kurt Carr production style, but I've made it more world-appealing.[49]

The music of singer, composer, and producer Israel Houghton's music is described by one publication as "an eclectic, almost unclassifiable blend of Christian pop, gospel, worship, and other influences."[50] Similarly, Christie McAllister's CD *In His Presence Live* is characterized this way: "One of the album's unquestionable highlights is the 'Expressions From My Soul' mini-mix (Bless Thou the Lord Oh My Soul). Leading it off is an anthem of high worship, transitioning into a moment of contemporary call and response, soaring with harmonic modulations and ending with a 'Praise Jam'—an all out jamboree of dancing, shouting and high praise."[51] Carr, Christie McAllister, and Houghton are just a few on a long list who have included the sounds of the Caribbean and the African and Asian continents within their repertoires.[52] The resulting songs are an attraction for some but can be a repellent for others, especially those for whom Sunday morning connotes a very specific "black church" sound.

There are at least two observations to be made regarding this musical form, particularly the kind that steps beyond the borders of the black church sound. First, this sonic fusion has become welcoming to fans of various ethnic and racial backgrounds and thus has expanded the range of musical forms and artists many are willing to accept and enjoy. So while black artists still perform primarily for black audiences and white artists for white audiences, unprecedented numbers of black consumers are buying music recorded by white praise and worship leaders, such as Vicki Yohe, Judy Jacobs, Mary Alessi, and Martha Munizzi, each of whom has a soulful style of delivery, much like the so-called blue-eyed soul singers of a generation ago, such as Hall and Oates and the Righteous Brothers, who found themselves embraced by black audiences.[53]

That style of delivery, along with the praise and worship songs they perform and compose, makes Yohe and Munizzi bestselling favorites among thousands of consumers, black and white. Munizzi is the first white artist to win a Stellar Award (2005), widely heralded as the "Grammy of gospel" for performers of black gospel music. Her 2003 CD, *The Best Is Yet to Come*, remained on the *Billboard* magazine Top Gospel Chart—where the sales of black gospel artists are normally tracked—for seventy-two straight weeks and reached the number 2 slot on the chart. A frequent collaborator of Israel Houghton, she has written songs that are considered classics of the praise and worship genre, including "Glorious," also recorded by Karen Clark Sheard, and the previously mentioned "Because of Who You Are." Munizzi explains one of these motivators behind her music ministry: "My deepest desire is to transcend cultural, generational, and denominational boundaries, and to bring all people together through worship."[54] Her twin sister, Mary Alessi, has more recently been embraced by the same audiences.

Before Yohe signed with Pure Springs Records, owned by Detroit-born CeCe Winans, her music had not been marketed to black audiences. Still, they had embraced her after hearing and seeing her presented in huge auditoriums by such black church favorites as Bishop T. D. Jakes and Prophetess Juanita Bynum. Known for her sense of humor, Yohe has been heard to say, "I just feel like I should be on gospel radio even though I'm a white girl."[55] Apparently, a number of others agree with her. *I Just Want You* (2004), Yohe's first CD for Winans' label, enjoyed popularity on black radio and was on the gospel chart for more than eighteen months, achieving the number 7 slot at its height. The composer of such notable songs as "Mercy Seat," "Comforter," and "Under the Blood," Yohe has been described as "powerful, passionate, sincere and, above all, anointed."[56] Her second CD, *He's Been Faithful* (2005) has also found wide acceptance; the song "Deliverance Is Available" was listed as one of the ten most frequently played singles in gospel radio during the week of March 31, 2006.[57]

The second observation is that whether or not one is a devotee of praise and worship music, this genre with its world music sounds and accompanying "vertical texts," that is, lyrics that are directed to God and not to other human beings, is helping to replicate the multi-ethnic listening and, to some extent, the mingling that occurred in the worship practices during the Second Great Awakening and the Azusa Street movement that occurred at the turn of the nineteenth and twentieth centuries, respectively. While Anthony Heilbut writes that throughout the twentieth century there were white religious songs that became staples in the black church and vice versa, during the Second Great Awakening and Azusa Street movement something different occurred in that thousands of worshippers stepped beyond their natural boundaries to experience God with individuals from other cultural backgrounds.[58] Not only are today's praise and worship artists crossing the boundaries to perform, but audiences are crossing boundaries to experience this music together, sometimes in performance settings, sometimes in church settings and arenas, but more frequently in virtual togetherness as they buy the same music and then listen to it in their individual cars, homes, or on their desktops and iPods.[59]

Straight Gate International Church exemplifies black churches that have welcomed a full array of multicultural artists who perform praise and worship and that have made a name for themselves by inviting others to do the same. Founded in a storefront in 1978 by Bishop Andrew Merritt, Straight Gate, with a reported five thousand members, has incorporated praise and worship in its own services for years. Some of the best-known praise and worship artists, including

Fred Hammond and Richard Smallwood, have performed and recorded in the church's west side Detroit edifice.

But it is the event called One in Worship, also billed as "the Spiritual Super Bowl," that represents Straight Gate's most expansive efforts to bring praise and worship to the world. In 2004 and 2005 the church rented Ford Field, home of the Detroit Lions, with a seating capacity of seventy thousand, to accommodate the tens of thousands the pastor and membership invited to hear a roster of black and white praise leaders and ministers, such as Houghton, Hammond, Yohe, Jacobs, Munizzi, Phil Driscoll, David and Nicole Binion, and Morris Chapman.[60]

Certainly, many churches around the city and country host events at which dynamic praise leaders are presented. What sets One in Worship apart from most is that Bishop Merritt and Straight Gate have agreements with Total Christian Television, Christian Television Network, Daystar, the Miracle Network, and Trinity Broadcasting, which means that there is a potential international television audience of four hundred million people. Bishop Merritt explained the reasons behind the event to the *Detroit Free Press:* "Diversity is a reflection of the core of Christ, out of one blood made he all nations," Merritt said. "Arabs will participate, Greek, French, Hispanics. But no cultural names, no denomination will get in the way of what people are coming here to do, and that is to worship as one body."[61]

The Sound of a New Breed of Worshipper

Israel and New Breed are among those whose music and lyrics embody the multicultural mission expressed by Bishop Merritt and others of like mind. They were recipients of many awards in 2005, including two Stellar Awards (CD of the Year and Male Vocalist of the Year) and two Dove Awards (Contemporary Gospel Album of the Year and Contemporary Gospel Recorded Song of the Year), as well as a Soul Train Award. A worship leader at the Lakewood Church in Houston, Texas, Israel Houghton, is a self-described "black kid who grew up in a white family in a Hispanic church."[62] He writes and produces in a way that reflects his upbringing as well as the existence of a growing multicultural audience that is accepting of sounds beyond those traditionally found in their own communities. He explains: "As far as leading worship goes (which is my passion and calling), I now realize that there have been demands put on me from every part of my experience since day one— culturally, emotionally, musically, and more. So things tend to sound cross-cultural, cross-denominational, and cross-generational. I like to call it, 'The Sound of New Breed Worship.'"[63] Veteran music director and producer Aaron Lindsey discussed in a 2003 interview why he and Houghton used multicultural influences on two of their projects, *Kids Praise* and *Kids Praise 2:*

> Our kids aren't really listening to very much other than secular music most of the time. They're not listening to older versions of gospel stuff; they're listening to the new stuff, which is not that cultural.

> When you think of producers like the Neptunes, one guy is black and one guy Asian.
> . . they're very successful in getting our kids' ears. So our objective is to make sure that what
> we did is relevant. . . The way we do that is include basically every generation, every culture
> and every tribe.[64]

Though their music is culturally expansive, Israel and New Breed point out in the song called "I Hear the Sound" that trying to categorize what they do is difficult since it goes beyond racial musical profiling:

> It ain't a black thing
> It ain't a white thing
> It ain't a colored thing
> It's a kingdom thing.

Here, they sing, is music that is so reflective of diverse cultural influences that it defies easy classification.

While Israel and New Breed and many of their contemporaries create and present music through which they do not consciously strive to reflect racial aesthetics, they clearly project their desire to focus on "kingdom business" in a way that they believe separates them from earlier generations:

> I hear the sound of a new breed
> Marching toward the gates of the enemy
> We're armed and dangerous
> Strong and serious
> Clothed in righteousness
> It's a new breed, a new breed.[65]

They declare themselves to be "a new breed" of worshipper and Christian warrior, thus invoking the Abraham/Isaac/Jacob distinction mentioned earlier. The Reverend Edgar L. Vann Jr., pastor of Detroit's Second Ebenezer Church, summarized the reason he had embraced praise and worship music so readily: "Some of us have always been the 'uncola'" [a reference to a past commercial for 7Up that emphasized its distinctive place among other soft drinks].[66] Israel and New Breed project a similar message that defines their identity in the chant found in "Come in from the Outside":

> We're the generation
> That will give you praise and adoration
> Let your kingdom come
> Let your will be done
> Establish now your throne, oh my Lord.

With these lyrics, they appear to draw a generational line in the proverbial sand—"We're going to praise God in a way our forefathers did not." That is what they appear to do, until we listen and look carefully at the refrain that follows:

O my Lord
Lord, Lord, Lord
Praise you Lord
Lord, Lord, Lord

We love you Lord
Lord, Lord, Lord
O my Lord.

The refrain "Oh my Lord, Lord, Lord," one of thousands of communally created phrases and refrains within the black sacred repertoire, came to the attention of movie fans in the 1989 release *Glory*, which is set in the 1860s during the Civil War. The scene in which the refrain is heard features the soldiers enlisted in one of the country's first all-black regiments singing together the night before going into one of the bloodiest battles of the war, one in which many of them lost their lives. In the film, the refrain serves as a bridge between spoken testimonies. However, it can also be viewed as a plea to the Almighty as the men willingly face possible annihilation to be seen by society as black men fighting for their own freedom.

As Israel and New Breed repeat the refrain, its melody, which they initially sing as simply as the black soldiers perform it in the movie, takes on the complexity that is a hallmark of their contemporary sound. But their stacked, intricate harmonies in no way negate the fact that a centuries-old refrain is embedded within it. On the same CD, the infectious "Friend of God" praise and worship song and chant leads to a "Friend" medley that includes two of the venerable hymns of Christianity, "No Not One" and "What a Friend We Have in Jesus." That medley flows into several minutes of singing in the spirit, in which audience and artists eventually move into spontaneous sounds of adoration that can often arise during a successful praise and worship experience. Equally noteworthy is the combination of the so-called old school and new school that brings this audience to a moment of high worship.

Fred Hammond, the acclaimed Detroit-based composer, musician, singer, and producer, does something similar as he juxtaposes traditional devotional songs and contemporary praise and worship music on CDs and in live performance settings. One of his most popular recordings of the last decade is "Jesus Be a Fence," a traditional gospel song composed and performed by Sam Cooke in the days when he was with the gospel quartet the Soul Stirrers. Hammond first recorded it on Bishop Carlton Pearson's *Live at Azusa III*, which was released in 1999, though relatively few took note of it at the time. He rerecorded it for Verity Records in 2000 on his own CD titled *Purpose by Design*, where it is listed among songs more readily placed within the praise and worship category, such as "When You Praise" and "You Are the Living Word."

A similar mix of the traditional gospel and the contemporary praise and worship forms reportedly moved the audience that attended Hammond's performance October 4, 2004. In a review of that evening, Dwayne Lacy comments on how seamlessly and effectively Hammond brought together the past and the present:

> Fred called on guitarist Joey Woolfalk to kick some old school riffs, and then he sang a variety of old church songs such as "God Is a Good God," "I'm a Soldier in the Army of the Lord," and "I Know It Was the Blood." As he slowed things down, he sang some old COGIC favorites (such as "Yes Lord") and the Baptist devotion song "I Love the Lord, He Heard My Cry.". . . Hammond then went into a worship set with such songs as "Give Me a Clean Heart," "Please Don't Pass Me By". . . [and] into an acoustic version of "I Will Find a Way". . . People were worshipping and singing along. . . What a night! Fred Hammond was the worship leader, and we were the worshippers.[67]

Lacy acknowledges Hammond's deft interweaving of both devotional songs and praise and worship tunes during that evening; presented together by Hammond, they equaled a memorable worship experience for those involved in the service.

As Pastor Winans mentions in the epigraph to this chapter, Judith Christie McAllister incorporates "the sound of old gospel" during her live and recorded performances. The CD titled *Raise the Praise*, for example, includes her popular praise and worship songs "Hallelujah, You're Worthy" and "Lift Him High," but it also features a medley called "Jubilation" with such traditional congregational songs and hymns as "Praise Him," "Let All the People Praise Thee," and "Glory to His Name."

Similar descriptions of inclusiveness have been made about Detroit native Byron Cage. Reviewer LaTonya Taylor applauds him for including a full-out traditional gospel song, "Still Say Yes," on his award-winning self-titled CD for GospoCentric Records. She writes, "That participatory, 'inclusive' element—and the fact that there's just a touch of 'old time' church in this sound—will aid this genre's entree into churches where older members are more likely to listen to traditional gospel than CCM."[68]

Praise and Worship in Detroit's Churches

That "old time" touch is being incorporated in a number of Detroit's black churches that use praise and worship music, based on what I have witnessed personally and have documented for this study. That the traditional devotional and congregational music is usually intertwined with the contemporary sounds of praise and worship is also reflected in the responses provided by thirty-seven Detroit-area church musicians and ministers of music who completed my informal survey.[69] Almost eighty-six percent of those reported that praise and worship music is performed during their worship services; seventy percent use it during all their worship services, and sixteen percent use it during most of them. That is close to the percentage (eighty-seven percent) that reported that traditional music is used at every service (seventy-two percent) or at most services (fifteen percent).

This combination of the old and the new is also being duplicated in the churches specifically monitored for this research, Greater Christ Temple, St. James Missionary Baptist Church, and Perfecting Church.[70]

Praise and Worship at Greater Christ Temple Church

Greater Christ Temple Church, located on Hilton in Ferndale, Michigan, is led by Bishop Carl E. Holland, who became the congregation's pastor in 1969, five years after it was founded. For most of its existence, the church had been affiliated with the Pentecostal Assemblies of the World (PAW). However, in 2000 Bishop Holland founded the Pentecostal Assembly of Believers, Inc. The organization consists of churches in Michigan, Alabama, Georgia, and Tennessee, with others scheduled to be added soon in Texas and California.

Greater Christ Temple's reported current membership is three hundred. Its core congregation, with a median age between thirty and forty, comprises those with high school diplomas, those who have had some college course, and those with college degrees. Their occupations are split between blue-collar work and various professional fields.

Carl B. Phillips, the church's minister of music, has been involved in music since he was twelve and a member of the Baptist Church. His background also includes participation in high school and community gospel choirs, including singing with Savoy recording artists the Reverend Donald Vails and the Voices of Deliverance. He joined Christ Temple in 1976 and was director of the Christ Temple Inspirational Choir before assuming his current duties. His activities in the Detroit gospel music community also include serving as coordinator of local artists for the Motor City PraiseFest and as a gospel radio announcer. He served as co-host of DetroitGospel.com on the Air, heard for two years on 1340 WEXL AM, and is an international minister of music for the Pentecostal Assembly of Believers.[71]

Phillips brought the idea of praise and worship to Bishop Holland around 1998. He describes the moment that gave him the impetus to approach his pastor: "The choir was singing Kirk Franklin's 'Now Behold the Lamb' and a spirit of praise and worship was created."[72] Phillips wanted to see that spirit envelop the church regularly, so he asked the pastor's permission to slowly bring praise and worship to the church. He began with gospel songs, such as "God Is" and "Can't Stop Praising His Name," as well as the music of Fred Hammond and Thomas Whitfield.

Today, the church has five praise and worship leaders, each assigned to a different Sunday. According to Phillips, the two female worship leaders, who are also ministers, use more hymns and gospel songs; he and evangelist Consuella Smith use a combination of contemporary praise and worship songs and traditional gospel music on their respective Sundays; while the fifth and youngest leader uses almost all contemporary praise and worship songs.

The church holds Sunday morning worship at 11:30 a.m. and Bible study Wednesday at 7:30 p.m., as well as choir rehearsals on Tuesday and Thursday evenings. The praise and worship team rehearses monthly. The Sunday morning and evening services begin with praise and worship, as do revival services. Sunday night differs slightly, however, in that the opening period includes testimony service as well. All other church meetings and rehearsals begin with prayer.[73]

To ensure that the entire membership understands praise and worship, its concepts and terminology are taught to the new converts who join Greater Christ Temple by Evangelist Smith; she is, besides being one of the praise and worship leaders and an ordained evangelist, the administrative assistant to the bishop within the church and within the Pentecostal Assembly of Believers.

The Sunday, December 12, 2002, morning worship I documented is an excellent example of how praise and worship is conducted at Greater Christ Temple.[74] The service began at 11:30 a.m. with prayer by one of the church's ministers; it has been the custom at Greater Christ for the ministers, not the deacons, to handle the opening devotional services. This particular prayer included petitions for the worship service, the congregation, and the pastor. The five-person praise and worship team for that Sunday began their portion of the service at 11:42. The worship leader, Evangelist Smith, began with an adapted Christmas carol, "O Come All Ye Faithful," with additional verses that have been sung in the black church for decades ("For He alone is worthy," "O come and lift Him higher").

This seasonal song was followed by several praise and worship songs—"With My Hands Lifted Up (and My Mouth Filled with Praise)," "None Like You," and "Lord, I Lift Your Name on High," one of the most popular songs of the genre—along with the devotional songs "Jesus, I'll Never Forget" and "There's a Storm Out on the Ocean" and the traditional gospel song "Can't (Cain't) Nobody Do Me Like Jesus."

Evangelist Smith selected music that conveyed a sense of the holiday season while simultaneously involving the congregation in the worship experience by including something for the varied musical tastes represented within the congregation: praise and worship music, traditional devotional music, and gospel songs. She explains, "Our congregation is in transition. Therefore your praise and worship has to be inclusive of music for a variety of ages and tastes."[75] Her selections also coincide with the desires of Bishop Holland that the congregation maintain the hymns and apostolic music traditions.[76] Consequently, not only are they interwoven into most of the praise and worship segments, but they constitute most what the congregation sings during the balance of the service.

Praise and Worship at Saint James Missionary Baptist Church

The St. James Baptist Church was officially incorporated in 1921, but it was under the leadership of their third pastor, the Reverend W. C. Barnett (1938–72), that the church, then located at the intersection of Mt. Elliott and Pulford Streets, earned its national reputation as its St. James Young Adult Choir (later the St. James Adult Choir) released recordings that captured the sound and feel of the black Baptist gospel choir.

The church's organist at that time, Charles H. Nicks Jr., later became its fifth pastor (1972–89). He and minister of music Jimmy "J. D." Dowell led the choir through their popular "O Give Thanks" Thanksgiving week concerts, standing-room-only Sunday night musicals, appearances before and with national and international figures, and recordings that were embraced throughout the gospel music community.[77] The current pastor, the Reverend Dr. James A. Jennings Jr., who was installed in 1990, moved the church to its present location on Van Dyke in Detroit. The reported membership at the time of my fieldwork was three thousand.

Marcus Jennings, the son of Reverend Jennings, introduced the praise and worship concept to St. James Baptist around 1999. He holds the positions of minister of praise and worship and director of the young adult choir. Minister Jennings is part of a family of preachers and pastors that stretches back to his paternal great-grandfather and includes five uncles, several cousins, and his late brother. The singing tradition comes from both sides of his family but more strongly from his mother, maternal grandparents, and siblings. A former youth drummer, he has been a singer since he was fourteen.

Jennings first heard praise and worship in a local Detroit church in the late 1990s, and he talked with both Pastor Jennings and Dowell, then minister of music, about bringing it to St. James. They gave their blessing without hesitation. In fact, Dowell initially worked with him to pick out sixteen vocalists they felt would serve well as praise and worship team members. Within three months, the number was ten and remained there through the time of our interview. The team often performed songs Jennings had composed, but they also sang music from many of his favorite praise and worship artists, including Kurt Carr, Judith Christie McAllister, Richard Smallwood, and Israel and New Breed.

He summarized his views on the differences between praise and worship and the traditional devotional service this way:

> I believe the focus [of devotional service] is getting to the emotions of the people, whereas praise and worship, to me, is and should be, not about people's emotions, but [about] how can we get the people into God's presence? How can we get God to come where we are? How can we set the atmosphere to where the Holy Spirit feels welcome, to where he feels at home, where he can manifest himself and he won't have to feel awkward when he's there? . . . So he wants to be where his praise is. So, if you want to pursue his presence, you're going to have to pursue it through praise.[78]

The service I analyzed at the St. James Missionary Baptist Church was their annual Watch Night service of December 31, 2002 through January 1, 2003.[79] That evening was filled with a mix of traditional gospel, congregational songs, and contemporary praise and worship music. The praise and worship service, which began at 9:07 p.m., was led by praise and worship leader Marcus Jennings and a praise team of six. Two musicians, an organist and a drummer, provided accompaniment for the three praise and worship songs that followed: "He Is Good," "Let Jesus Fill This Place," and "Wonderful/Yes He Is)."

Next, the minister of music greeted the audience and introduced a children's liturgical dance troupe of six that performed to Fred Hammond's version of the traditional gospel song "Jesus Be a Fence." Two adult liturgical dancers followed the children and used a gospel-influenced version of the hymn "O to Be Kept" for their performance. The praise and worship segment ended with an upbeat congregational song, "This Morning When I Rose," introduced and directed by the minister of music.

As was the case with the other two spotlighted churches, both long-standing traditional songs and praise and worship songs were performed; the congregation was exhorted to offer praises to God orally and physically, regardless of the type of music being introduced at the time. The combination reflects the church's historic musical roots, the contemporary leanings of its young minister of praise, the support he has received in launching praise and worship at St. James, and, perhaps most important, his willingness to accommodate various segments of his congregation.

Minister Jennings recalls that in his early days of introducing the form, there were senior members of the congregation who asked him to teach the praise and worship team specific traditional devotional songs they loved and missed. He admits that his first response was a silent but emphatic "no." But after listening to pastor and recording artist Bishop Carlton Pearson explain that some of the older saints will never become fans of praise and worship and that they need to be reached where they are, he began to include more traditional songs.[80]

Praise and Worship at Perfecting Church

Perfecting Church is perhaps the best known of the three churches in the study because of the fame and popularity of its founder and pastor, Marvin L. Winans. The fourth of ten children born to David Sr. ("Pop") and Delores ("Mom") of the internationally acclaimed Winans family of Detroit, he was raised within the preaching and musical traditions of the Church of God in Christ. He and his family members have collected many awards, including Grammys, Stellars, and Doves, and he and three of his brothers, Ronald, Michael, and twin Carvin, known collectively as the Winans, were pacesetters in urban contemporary gospel music.[81] Pastor Winans, who has recorded two projects with his church choir, *Marvin L. Winans Presents Perfected Praise and Friends*, is still actively involved in recording as a guest with many of his colleagues and released his own solo project, *Alone but Not Alone*, in September 2007 on the Pure Springs label. His weekly activities also include hosting *Rhythm and Praise,* a Sunday morning gospel music program on Detroit's 92.3 FM WMXD.

Pastor Winans held the initial meeting for Perfecting Church in the basement of his home with eight individuals, but the first official service for the church occurred at the Michigan Inn in Southfield, Michigan, on May 27, 1989. Because of the church's rapid growth, the congregation moved several times before settling into their present edifice on East Nevada Street in Detroit in March of 1996. Under the Perfecting Community Development Corporation, the church in 2003 began a $100 million building project to create an expansive church and business complex that will better house its members, ministries, and activities.

The congregation's reported membership is four thousand, a sizeable percentage of whom have taken some college courses or have earned college degrees. Like Greater Christ, theirs too is a fairly young membership with a median age falling between thirty and forty. Perfecting Church is nondenominational.[82]

Praise and worship was instituted at Perfecting Church by Pastor Winans after a trip he took to Holland in 1990. There he heard a multicultural, multiracial congregation perform "Lord, I Lift Your Name on High," a popular praise and worship song, for the first time. He knew immediately upon hearing it that he was going to bring it to Perfecting Church.

Although pastoral duties are his primary focus, Pastor Winans continues not only to set policy for what music will be sung, but he participates in praise and worship, often playing the electric piano and introducing a variety of songs during that part of the service just as he does throughout the rest of the worship experience. Perfecting Church has embraced praise and worship extensively as exemplified by the fact that virtually every church service, as well as the Bible studies, begins with it. The church has also devoted entire weekends to exploring praise and worship and related topics, with invited speakers, classes on praise and worship, and a master songwriting course taught by Pastor Winans.[83]

Randy Short is the director of the Department of Praise and Worship; she oversees fifty individuals whose backgrounds range from having traveled the world as professional gospel singers to having served solely in the local church. There are two praise and worship leaders; the rest of the singers serve on six teams consisting of three sopranos, three altos, and three tenors. The six-piece band that accompanies them includes an organist, a keyboardist, a drummer, a percussionist, and bass and lead guitarists.

Short, who hails from a family of singers, is the niece of a former New York City district choir director for the Church of Our Lord Jesus Christ. Classically trained in elementary and middle school, Short remembers hearing praise and worship music for the first time in the 1980s: "I was a new mom, at home, and would listen to a radio program that played Hosanna! and Integrity music all through the night. Waking up to it at 3:00 a.m. is an incredible experience. Your sleep is broken by your own voice saying, 'Hallelujah!'" Her attendance at a praise and worship conference in Houston during that same time period completely transformed her into a worshipper: "I went home and got on my face, determined to get in God's presence. . . My job as the director of Praise and Worship is to lead the congregation into the presence of God, show them how to linger in his presence until he blesses them, and how to worship him for who he is, not what they can get from him."[84]

Perfecting Church's Tuesday evening Bible study is conducted with virtually the same elements as their Sunday morning worship, which is why a description of the Bible study held on Tuesday, August 12, 2003, is indicative of how praise and worship music is used there. A praise and worship team of nine opens the service, Pastor Winans delivers the lesson-sermon, an invitation is made to Christian discipleship, tithes and offerings are received, and announcements are made before the benediction. Before the music from the praise and worship team begins, the members of the congregation meditate or pray individually. That night, Pastor Winans came to the podium at 8 p.m. and led the congregation in the praise and worship song "I Love You Lord," after which the praise team and leader took over with two more praise and worship songs, "Hallelujah You're Worthy" and "Shout unto God with the Voices of Triumph (Clap Those Hands, O Ye People)." The exhortations from the praise and worship leader were placed between songs, just as they would be during the traditional devotional service.

Just before Pastor Winans began the lesson for the evening, he led the congregation in the hymn "Great Is Thy Faithfulness." Because it contains lyrics that are as reverential as those of the more contemporary songs that came before it ("Thou changest not, Thy compassions, they fail not"), the placement of this hymn at the beginning of the most sacred moment of the worship experience is testament to the pastor's knowledge of and appreciation for a wide range of musical genres, from the traditional to the contemporary, and his determination to make that eclectic mix a hallmark of the church he pastors. Short elaborates: "Pastor Winans has set an order for worship service. Our worship leaders incorporate hymns, praise and worship music in our services. We know what is expected in terms of musical content, so we choose music that edifies, speaks the truth, exhorts, and worships God."[85] Pastor Winans summarized the inclusive nature of the music that is offered: "Again Perfecting is different in that we'll go from 'The Lord Is My Light' to 'Halle, halle, hallelou.' I mean, we'll go from the islands to slavery to Holland without missing a beat."[86]

Closing Comments on Praise and Worship in the Black Church

Clearly, this model in which praise and worship music is intertwined with traditional songs can be found in a growing number of contemporary urban churches. The reasons offered by the praise and worship leaders at Greater Christ Temple, Perfecting Church, and St. James Baptist Church—a pastor's insistence that the traditional songs not be discarded, another pastor's penchant for mixing a variety of genres, and a praise and worship leader's sensitivity to the requests of the older members—provide insights into why the inclusive model is used in many congregations. Randy Short offers another explanation: "The Bible speaks of not destroying the old landmarks. I don't believe you can just remove traditional music from worship service. Modernize it, update it, whatever, but don't get rid of it. . . Revelation of praise and worship gives a better understanding of traditional music. I know why my mother and grandmother sang [those songs]. It gave them hope!"[87]

There are, of course, other models for the use of praise and worship music. Some churches, such as Detroit's Dunamis Outreach Ministries, use praise and worship music almost exclusively. Dunamis' pastor, Reginald Lane, writes many of the songs that are a part of their services. In fact, it is reportedly the central music form used by that congregation. In contrast, other churches, such as Unity Baptist Church, have no plans to incorporate praise and worship music, at least not in the foreseeable future. Unity's minister of music, Dorgan Needom, shares why he and Pastor Valmon Stotts have been reluctant to follow other churches, including their peers at St. James Baptist Church, into the trend. First, there are what he refers to as "too many gymnastics. . . the 'stand up, sit down, touch your neighbor,' which seems to be the standard thing I've seen. I think there is a difference between coercion and sincerely motivating people to come into the presence of the Lord."[88]

Needom also raises questions about the ramifications of designating a solitary part of the service as "praise and worship": "The whole 11:00 service was [once] entitled 'worship service.' Then why do we have a period defined as praise and worship? Is the rest of the service something else? The word 'praise' was not included in that, but that was what it was supposed to be." He and Pastor Stotts have not ruled out praise and worship forever. Needom concludes, "There needs to be greater understanding regarding praise and worship. I have not had the opportunity to take advantage of any seminars. If we [at Unity Baptist] were going to do it, it would be where we would sing the hymns from the hymn book, sing some of the praise and worship. . . and leave out the gymnastics."[89] The pattern he describes sounds much like the inclusive one being used in many churches already.

As thousands of churches have incorporated praise and worship music into their services, challenges have arisen that some congregations have already handled and others are still trying to resolve. Among the more common problems I have heard named are arrogant praise team members, songs that are too complex for the congregation to sing, and praise and worship that is "practiced" rather than spontaneous. Judith Christie McAllister offers this cogent analysis of what has led to the first problem, arrogance: "that ['see me'] spirit has somehow crept into the church and has set up residence in many ministries, particularly the music and or the arts ministries. Hidden agendas, secret motives have been fed by the desire to be up front."[90]

Carolyn Cole, a nationally recognized organist, singer, and choir director employed by the Hope United Methodist and Hartford Memorial churches in Detroit, believes that arrogance can set in because the praise team members are usually handpicked and, therefore, not open to "whosoever will." For that reason, she states, "Pastors have to be careful not to allow the praise team to act as if they are a step above other singers, since that can lead to divisions and resentment."[91] EMI recording artist and praise and worship leader Darwin Hobbs offers these thoughts on the phenomenon: "To say that the worship team is such a focal point is a fact. . . but the TRUTH is that it shouldn't be!. . . This is serious business. We need to change the name from 'worship team' to 'team of worshippers'. . . . Maybe this will focus the attention more on the real reason for such a component in our corporate worship experiences."[92]

A second problem many have noted is the selection of songs that are not conducive to audience participation. Cole explains: "If the praise team brings music that has two verses, a chorus, a bridge, and a special chorus, that's a choir song and too difficult for the average church member to follow easily. That can be seen as just another segment of entertainment with the members in the pews serving as mere observers in their own church."[93] In effect, then, the praise team becomes just another choir, not the group that leads the congregation into corporate worship.[94]

Finally, Cole believes there is a problem of praise and worship music and behaviors becoming so rehearsed that the very thing the praise team is there to implement cannot be achieved. She recalls being "completely turned off" at a major local church as she witnessed what appeared to be rote participation in the praise and worship part of the service, including the entire congregation speaking in tongues as soon as the pastor started and stopping as soon as he stopped. "With that kind of predictability from the church, the choir, and the band," she explains, "there is no room for the Holy Spirit to come in."[95]

With a growing number of workshops, including the Gospel Heritage Foundation's praise and worship conference and the I Hear Music in the Air conference, addressing these and other related topics, there are various opportunities for churches to identify ways to have their praise and worship teams enhance rather than detract from the worship experience, which many of them may have to do in the near future for the sake of peace and harmony in the sanctuary.

Two decades after some black churches began incorporating praise and worship music into their services, it is safe to characterize this new element within the community as something more than a "fad," if, what is meant is something that comes in and leaves quickly. Gospel record stores have sections devoted to this music form, and in many, such as Detroit's God's World Records, it has been the best selling form since 2002, according to storeowner Larry Robinson. But since "rhythm and praise," urban influenced gospel will usually do better at the cash register, there is clearly more to be considered in assessing the acceptance of praise and worship music.

Pastor William Murphy III, the native Detroiter who is both composer and lead singer of the hit recording "Praise Is What I Do," views the rise of praise and worship in the black church as a reflection of a specific need among and within worshippers:

Everybody wants to go to the next level. Everybody wants the "better." Praise and worship is taking people to that next place in God. That's why it's become so popular because there's a release. . . for instance, on the song that God gave me "Praise Is What I Do," there's a release on that song. The song releases a glory that "I Don't Feel No Ways Tired" didn't release. So as people began to grow in God and as churches began to grow and as people became tired of religion, they discerned that worship—not just praise—but worship releases "the more."[96]

Those who would comprehend the success of the genre might want to turn their gaze to the church itself, which is where the phenomenon began and where it is practiced widely. There they will find praise teams and congregations engaged in worship using music from top-selling recordings such as *Throne Room,* by CeCe Winans, *Pages of Life Chapters I and II*, by Fred Hammond, and *The Next Level,* by Israel and New Breed. But they are also likely to hear refrains that have been part of the black church experience for generations, evidence that despite the presence of innovation, there remains a place for "the sound of old gospel," at least for now.[97] Where praise and worship music will be in a quarter century, to what extent it will be practiced and in what configurations, will certainly be worth tracking.

Notes

1. Dorgan Needom, telephone interview, August 25, 2004. Paul Allen raised the question of whether the spate of praise and worship projects might be a case of "bandwagoning." PAJAM, personal interview, January 21, 2004.
2. Carl B. Phillips, telephone interview, February 16, 2005.
3. Munroe, *Purpose and Power,* 62, 145.
4. See appendix A for a list of some of the terminology and behaviors associated with praise and worship.
5. Marcus Jennings, personal interview, January 2, 2003.
6. Law, *Power of Praise and Worship,* 140.
7. Munroe, *Purpose and Power,* 61. For extensive discussions of praise and worship from a religious rather than academic standpoint, see Law, *Power of Praise and Worship,* and Munroe, *Purpose and Power.*
8. Consuella Smith, personal interview, January 6, 2003.
9. A. Williams, "Byron Cage Interview."
10. e.g., Leah praises God when she gives birth to a third son, Judah, whom she can present to her husband, Jacob (Genesis 29:35). The Psalms contain examples of the praises offered to God by David (Psalm 30), the descendants of Korah (Psalm 47), and even anonymous individuals (Psalm 92). And in the New Testament book of Luke, the crowds praise God for the miracles they had seen Jesus perform on the day of his triumphal entry into Jerusalem (Luke 19:36).
    The point at which Abraham prepares to sacrifice his son Isaac is one of the earliest mentions of the word "worship" in the Old Testament (Genesis 22:5). That act was, for the patriarch, a moment of worship in that he willingly submitted to what he believed was the will of God (Kenoly and Bernal 88). The three young men who refused to bow down to the golden image made by King Nebuchadnezzar, usually called the Hebrew Boys within the Christian church, demonstrated their unwillingness to worship anything or anyone other than their own God despite the threat of being thrown into a fiery furnace (Daniel 3). In the New Testament, the references to worship include the description of the twenty-four elders who were seated on the throne and then fell on their faces and worshipped God during John's revelation (Revelation 11:16).
11. See appendix A for a list of Hebrew words associated with contemporary praise and worship.
12. Munroe, *Purpose and Power,* 114.

13. "Shabach," written by Tobias Fox, was recorded by the Full Gospel Baptist Fellowship (*A New Thing*, 1995). It has also been recorded by Walt Whitman and the Soul Children of Chicago (*Growing Up*, 1996) and Byron Cage (*Prince of Praise*, 2003).
14. Blue Letter Bible, "The Names of God in the Old Testament," April 1, 2002, http://www.blueletterbible.org/study/misc/name_god.html (accessed May 30, 2006). Besides Munizzi, others who have recorded this praise and worship classic include Vicki Yohe, Judy Jacobs, and Juanita Bynum.
15. Certainly, the religions practiced by people of African descent throughout the diaspora are vast and encompass a variety of praise and worship rituals as well. Those, however, are outside of the focus of this chapter.
16. Among the many and varied scholarly arguments concerning the existence of African retentions within black American culture is the well-known "debate" between Melville Herskovits and E. Franklin Frazier. A concise summary of the two sides is provided by Albert J. Raboteau in *Slave Religion*, 48–55. Pearl Williams-Jones provides a list of African characteristics within gospel music in "Afro-American Gospel Music."
17. Hall, "African Religious Retentions."
18. Jackie Patillo, telephone interview, June 14, 2004.
19. Lincoln and Mamiya, *Black Church*, 1.
20. Paris, *Black Pentecostalism*, 54.
21. Pitts, *Old Ship of Zion*, 91–131.
22. Paris, *Black Pentecostalism*, 51.
23. Much of Pitts' research, especially the early chapters of his book, covers the devotional services he witnessed. For a detailed accounting of how these devotional services flow, see *Old Ship of Zion*.
24. An individual metered hymn that is performed in this style is also referred to as a "Dr. Watts," even if it was not written by Dr. Isaac Watts, the prolific English hymn writer of the eighteenth century. The label came to refer to the style, not the composer. See http://www.negrospirituals.com/song.htm.
25. Southern, *Music of Black Americans*, 29.
26. Pitts, *Old Ship of Zion*, 11.
27. Jennings, personal interview.
28. Needom, telephone interview.
29. For one example, listen to Rice, "The Deacon's Prayer."
30. Redman, "Worship Awakening," 369–70.
31. Redman explains that while the seeker service is marked by technological advances, the term goes back to the camp meetings of the early 1800s, revivalists such as Charles G. Finney, and the early Methodists, who used the label "seeker" to describe anyone interested in joining their ranks and becoming converted. He cites Aimee Semple McPherson and Robert Schuller, who used "illustrated sermons" and "star-studded musical entertainment," respectively, as twentieth-century forerunners of the current seeker service proponents (ibid., 376–77).
32. Ibid., 376.
33. Redman describes singing in the spirit this way: "The last phrase or line of the song may be repeated several times as a way of setting up what follows, then one musician (often the keyboardist) will repeat a two or three chord progression, creating a drone-like musical effect. The congregation takes over singing freely either in tongues or repeating a phrase in English. This can last for a few minutes or until the worship leaders feel led to end it" (ibid., 376–77).
34. Hamilton, "Triumph," 29.
35. Ibid., 31. This tendency to select a place of worship because of the music has been documented by other researchers who discuss various periods in U.S. church history. For example, Portia Maultsby notes that the black church of the nineteenth century pulled congregants in at least two different directions, one with services and music shaped by an African-centered aesthetic, the other with a European mode of worship. Maultsby, "Afro-American Religious Music."
36. Marvin L. Winans, personal interview, January 14, 2004.
37. The list of the artists who have won the Dove (now GMA) Award for Praise and Worship Album of the Year can be found on the GMA website: http://www.gmamusicawards.com.
38. Among them are the Winans family, Kirk Franklin, Yolanda Adams, Donnie McClurkin, Nicole C. Mullen, Martha Munizzi, and Vicki Yohe, all of whom have styles that have allowed them to reach beyond their expected constituencies with new musical sounds.

39. Taylor, "Breaking Barriers."
40. Maranatha! Music's history comes from the company's website: http://www.maranathamusic.com.
41. Promotional materials for Integrity Media, 2003–4.
42. Patillo, telephone interview, June 14, 2004. Also see the biographies section of the Integrity Music website, http://www.integritymusic.com/artists/index.html?target=/worship/artist/archives.html.
43. "We Worship You," released by holy hip hop artist the Ambassador on the CD *The Thesis*, would exemplify a praise and worship song recorded by an artist some might not readily associate with that specific genre. The Verity Records-issued, Grammy-nominated title *The Praise and Worship Songs of Richard Smallwood* contains all previously recorded songs by the acclaimed composer and singer.
44. John Leland, "Christian Music's New Wave Caters to an Audience of One," *New York Times*, April 17, 2004, late edition, A8.
45. Rachinski qtd. in ibid.; Paul Herman, personal interview, June 12, 2006.
46. I extend my gratitude to Larry Berkove, a long-time mentor and colleague, who explained this interpretation of Judaism to me and first suggested it as a way of viewing the shifts within gospel music.
47. Paul Allen, personal interview, January 21, 2004.
48. "Rhythm and praise" is a term attributed to urban contemporary gospel composers and performers Anson and Eric Dawkins, known to fans as Dawkins and Dawkins. They explain the need for the label: "Gospel rhythm and blues is an oxymoron. To say that you have good news and then you're going to sing the blues about it makes no sense. So we wanted to have rhythm and praise. It fits our music, and it fits a lot of things that folks like Jimmy (J. Moss), Kirk (Franklin), Trin-i-tee 5:7 and other groups with a hip hop, R&B, urban flavor are doing." R&P integrates urban musical influences and yet can be used for worship within and beyond the walls of the traditional church. Dawkins and Dawkins, interview.
49. Carr, "Kurt Carr's One Church."
50. Taylor, "Breaking Barriers."
51. Gospelflava.com, review of *In His Presence—Live*, by Judith Christie McAllister, http://www.gospelflava.com/articles/judithchristiemcallisterpresenceaudio.html.
52. See also Taylor, review of *Live from Another Level*.
53. In fact, when asked about the number of white artists being supported by black consumers, gospel music veteran and Music World Entertainment Vice President Telisa Stinson responded by email: It's the most EVER! I think it has a lot to do with certain white artists having a real gospel sound and the popularity of praise and worship. However, black gospel artists that sing praise and worship don't sell nearly as well. My theory is [that it is] because the gospel community actually purchases praise and worship music by those from the Christian market, but that the Christian market doesn't buy praise and worship by gospel artists to the same extent. A second industry professional concurred with her assessment. As a research topic, this is an area ripe for future inquiry.
54. Alliance Agency, Martha Munizzi biography, http://www.theallianceagency.com/artists/martha.htm.
55. Capital Entertainment, Vicki Yohe biography, http://www.capitalentertainment.com (accessed September 19, 2005).
56. Qtd. in Lockett, review of *I Just Want You*.
57. Radio and Records, "Gospel National Airplay," March 29, 2006, http://www.radioandrecords.com.
58. See Heilbut, "Secularization," 106.
59. While most Americans still worship among those who look like them, a number of churches, including such megachurches as Church without Walls (Tampa, FL), pastured by Paula White; Solid Rock (Monroe, OH), where Darlene Bishop is pastor; World Harvest Church (Columbus, OH), headed by Rod Parsley; and Lakewood Church (Houston, TX), led by Joel Osteen, have huge multicultural congregations. Praise and worship music and charismatic preaching are just two of the elements these churches have in common.
60. In 2006 One in Worship was held in Greensboro, North Carolina.
61. Qtd. in Nichole M. Christian, "'Spiritual Super Bowl' Puts Faith and Detroit in Spotlight," *Detroit Free Press*, June 6, 2005, available online at http://www.freep.com/voices/columnists/echristian6e_20050606.htm. Visit the One in Worship website, http://www.oneinworship.com, to read more about the event and its history.
62. Cummings, "Cross-Cultural Worship."
63. Ibid.

64. Lindsey, interview.
65. Israel and New Breed, "I Hear the Sound" (*Live from Another Level*, 2004).
66. The Reverend Edgar L. Vann Jr. telephone conversation with the author, December 31, 2002.
67. Lacy, "Fred Hammond Concert Recap."
68. Taylor, review of *Byron Cage*.
69. The Detroit Musicians' Fellowship Dinner is held annually in the fall. On September 10, 2004, the cofounder, Carolyn Cole, allowed me to distribute my survey on the use of praise and worship music. Although almost half of those who completed my survey were serving at Baptist churches, the balance represented a range of churches—Apostolic, Church of God in Christ, Disciples of Christ, Methodist (African Methodist Episcopal and United Methodist), Pentecostal, United Church of Christ, Spiritual, and nondenominational. Because of that diversity and the age range of those present (early twenties to over seventy), the results are another means of assessing the extent to which praise and worship music is used in Detroit's black churches. Appendix E presents the numbers and percentages for each of the questions the survey posed.
70. Appendices B, C, and D provide a chronological timeline for the praise and worship services observed for this study at Greater Christ Temple Church, St. James Baptist Church (aka Shield of Faith Ministries), and Perfecting Church, respectively.
71. More about Phillips and his gospel music-related service is on the Detroit Gospel.com website: http://www.detroitgospel.com.
72. Phillips, personal interview.
73. Smith, telephone interview.
74. Though one specific service is discussed for each of these churches. I have attended other services and events at these churches and at many others in the area that mirror what is reported here.
75. Smith, telephone interview.
76. Phillips, personal interview.
77. Read more about Reverend Nicks, St. James Baptist Church, and their contributions to gospel music at the Michigan State Museum's Lest We Forget: Legends of Detroit Gospel virtual exhibit, http://www.museum.msu.edu/museum/tes/gospel/nicks.htm.
78. Jennings, personal interview.
79. Watch Night services are held in black churches across the country on December 31, as believers praise God for seeing them through the year and ask for protection in the new one. The United Methodist Church traces the roots of Watch Night services to John Wesley, whom they believe held the first service in 1755 to encourage Christians to "reaffirm their covenant with God." See Waltz, *Dictionary for United Methodists*, s.v. "Watch Night Service." Snopes.com, a website dedicated to investigating urban legends, old wives tales, etc., places the start of these services in North America in 1750 but situates the earliest Watch Night services in 1733 in what is now the Czech Republic. Snopes also debunks the legend that had been circulating since 2001 that Watch Night began in 1862 with black slaves awaiting the enactment of the Emancipation Proclamation in 1863: http.www.snopes.com/holidays/newyears/watchnight.asp (accessed June 28, 2007).
80. Jennings, personal interview.
81. A biography of the Winans with recommended songs can be found at SoulTracks.com: http://www.soultracks.com/the_winans.htm.
82. M. Winans, personal interview. The Perfecting Church's website with more information on the church is http://www.perfectingchurch.org.
83. Beverly Ferguson (aka "Squeeze"), telephone interview, March 9, 2005. As the member auxiliary coordinator for Perfecting Church, Ferguson's duties include coordinating the annual Praise and Worship Weekend.
84. Randy Short, email message to the author, May 5, 2004.
85. Ibid.
86. M. Winans, personal interview.
87. Short, email message.
88. Needom, telephone interview.
89. Ibid.
90. Heron, "Call to Worship."
91. Carolyn Cole, telephone interview, June 18, 2007.

92. Heron, "Call to Worship."
93. Carolyn Cole, telephone interview, June 18, 2007.
94. Dorgan Needom also raised this point in a telephone interview, August 25, 2004.
95. Carolyn Cole, telephone interview, June 18, 2007.
96. Murphy, interview.
97. Marvin L. Winans, personal interview, January 14, 2004.

30

This House, This Music: Exploring the Interdependent Interpretive Relationship between the Contemporary Black Church and Contemporary Gospel Music

Melinda E. Weekes

In his groundbreaking work *Somebody's Calling My Name: Black Sacred Music and Social Change*, the Rev. Dr. Wyatt Tee Walker (1979: 17) sets forth the thesis that "what black people are singing religiously will provide a clue to what is happening to them sociologically."[1] Tracing the African and European cultural influences in slave songs, spirituals, and traditional gospel favorites, Walker establishes a clear correlation between lyrical content in black sacred music and the social circumstances of black life. In the same way this was true of the African American spiritual, for example, Walker concludes that it is no less true of gospel music. Furthermore, in the case of gospel music, he attributes certain socio-historical factors—the Great Depression, the post-World War II migration of blacks from the South to northern cities, the landmark U.S. Supreme Court desegregation case of Brown v. Board of Education, and the Civil Rights Movement—as influential to the rise of the genre (132–141). Walker's work demonstrates how, as in the case with vernacular music generally, the content and structure of early gospel music directly reflects a specific social context.

Twenty-four years and several social contexts later, ethnomusicologist and musician Guthrie P. Ramsey Jr. (2003) embraces a comparable interpretive framework wherein he advocates "attending to the specific historical moment" surrounding a particular black musical expression. But he further calls for an examination of the particular social setting that gives rise to that expression. For Ramsey, these settings are community theaters, cultural spaces, or sites of cultural memory, which "provide a window of interpretation that allows [us] to enter into some important ideas about the cultural work performed by music in the processes of African American identity making" (21). Community theaters include "cinema, family narratives, and histories, the church, the social dance, the nightclub, the skating rink, even literature" (21). Intrinsic to this "process of identity making" is the meaning making that transpires within these spaces, for in the community theaters, "real people negotiate and eventually agree on what cultural expressions such as a musical gesture mean. They collectively decide what associations are conjured by a well-placed blue note, a familiar harmonic pattern, the soulful, virtuoso sweep of a jazz run, a social dancer's imaginative twist on an old dance step, or the raspy grain of a church mother's vocal declamation on Sunday morning" (25–26; see also Walser 1993; Floyd 1991).

From these starting points, and to enhance our understanding of the theological, cultural, and musical significance of the latest installation of black sacred music—contemporary gospel music—I explore here how recent sociological phenomena have affected this genre's development. My thesis is that sociological factors that affect the contemporary black church are largely reflected in various aspects of contemporary gospel music. In the less than forty years that this form of black sacred music has emerged, the community theater that gave it birth and provided the creative, cultural, and spiritual resources for its vitality—the black church—has been undergoing its own transformation. I consider the impact of two social factors that have contributed to this transformation—integration and secularization—and examine their impact on the emergence, development, and proliferation of contemporary gospel music. By considering how these social realities have affected the black community in a broad sense and the contemporary black church in particular, we can transform our interpretive window into a lens through which understanding is magnified.

The Contemporary Black Church and Contemporary Gospel Music

According to the U.S. Census Bureau (1998), there were approximately thirty-four million black Americans in the United States in 1998. Compared with 66 percent of whites, 83 percent of blacks reported that their religious faith was "very important in their lives." Seventy-five percent of blacks agreed with the statement "God is the all-powerful, all-knowing, perfect creator who rules the world today." In 1999, about 49 percent of blacks labeled themselves "spiritual," and 61 percent labeled themselves "committed born-again Christians" (Barna Research Group). The large majority, roughly 80 percent, of these "committed born-again Christians" belong to the seven historically black denominations: three Methodist churches (African Methodist Episcopal Church, African Methodist Episcopal Zion Church, and Christian Methodist Episcopal Church), three Baptist conventions (National Baptist Convention, U.S.A., National Baptist Convention, America, and the Progressive National Baptist Convention), and one Pentecostal church (Church of God in Christ). With the exception of the Church of God in Christ (COGIC), these institutions were founded in the eighteenth and nineteenth centuries in response to the racism and rejection faced by blacks within white Christian churches.[2] These seven denominations, along with smaller denominations and predominantly black congregations generally, constitute the larger black church in the United States.

As a sociological reference, my use of the term black church refers to the diversity of a shared tradition of Christian commitment that has shaped the collective black community. Theologically speaking:

> Black religion has always concerned itself with the fascination of an incorrigibly religious people with the mystery of God, but it has been equally concerned with they earning of a despised and subjugated people for freedom—freedom from the religious, economic, social, and political domination that whites have exercised over blacks since the beginning of the African slave trade. It is this radical thrust of blacks for human liberation expressed in theological terms and *religious institutions* that is the defining characteristic of black Christianity and black religion in the United States. (Wilmore 1983: x, italics added)

Decades before the founding of these religious institutions, however, the black church was preceded by what sociologist E. Franklin Frazier (1957) has referred to as "the invisible church."[3] Groups of enslaved Africans gathered in secret meetings on Southern plantations out of view and against the wishes of their owners to engage in worship and socialization in a form very different from that of their European-American slave masters. In a time when slave literacy was prohibited, musical expression reinforced by the indomitable African oral and musical traditions emerged as the lifeblood for faith in the slave community. While the scriptures and the preached word increased in centrality after emancipation, black sacred music has always played a primary role in the religious tradition of black Americans since the time of its origins in the Africa-influenced slave culture of the antebellum period (Walker 1979: 29–30).

From the rich musical lineage of slave hollers, work songs, spirituals, anthems, the hymn-lining tradition, the meter music of Watts-style hymn singing, and Charles A. Tindley-influenced improvisational hymn-singing, gospel music surfaced in early twentieth century as the latest in the progeny of black sacred musical expression (Walker 1979: 129; Southern 1997: 461–474). It was the addition of instrumentation—tambourines, drums, horns, piano, guitar, and eventually, the organ—to the voices, hand clapping, and foot stomping that distinguished gospel music. This performance style, with an emphasis on free expression and group participation, was first experienced in the "independent" or "folk" churches of the Holiness, Pentecostal, and Sanctified sects. In later years, the music spread to other parts of the black religious community. It was attractive because it deeply resonated with their African and African American cultural sensibilities in a way that the white Protestant liturgical tradition did not (Maultsby 2001: 91–93).

A Georgia-born preacher's son who migrated to Chicago and became a bluesman, Thomas A. Dorsey is credited as the "Father of Gospel Music." By wedding a secular blues aesthetic to sacred text, Dorsey and others (e.g., Lucie Campbell, Roberta Martin, and Mahalia Jackson) pioneered a new way of singing. Heavily influenced by the "folk"-style musicianship of Methodist minister Charles Albert Tindley, Dorsey authored more than four hundred songs, the most popular of which is the legendary "Precious Lord, Take My Hand." A skilled pianist, composer, and arranger, Dorsey, like Tindley before him, captured the current socio-religious mood of blacks of the early twentieth century by fusing the hard-times sensibilities of the Great Depression with an otherworldly assurance of hope for better days.

Gospel has thus always been a hybrid musical form, incorporating improvisation, rhythmic patterns, and tonal variations of African music present in the blues with European-influenced hymnody. Its blending of sacred (text) with secular (music) attests to its African cultural inheritance; conceptual distinctions between "sacred" and "secular" had no place in the worldview of Africans. Both religion and music were integrated within the whole of African life and served a variety of practical purposes. As the history of black music demonstrates, and particularly in the case of gospel music, this framework carried over into an emerging African American community that exhibited a similar ambivalence toward separating sacred and secular musical conceptions. Since the 1960s, the idiom has been grouped into two broad categories: traditional and contemporary.

Contemporary gospel music differs from traditional gospel music in both form and scope. While Dorsey's "gospel blues" was indeed contemporary music in its time, by the 1960s and 1970s, technology had changed considerably. With the advent of new popular styles and technology, the sound of gospel became modernized. During the late 1960s, gospel musicians began using synthesizers, strings, brass, and the electronic musical styles of the burgeoning funk, rock and roll, and soul music. With this more contemporary sound, gospel music reached beyond the church into traditionally secular venues such as concert halls and recording studios. While this was not the first instance of black religious music performed outside of the church setting, it was the first significant, wide-scale introduction of black sacred music into the mainstream consciousness.[4]

A number of socio-historical factors contributed to the rise of this contemporary musical form. Two in particular, integration and secularization, operated in tandem to bring about key changes in the black church experience of the post-Civil Rights era.[5] I believe that the political quest for social integration spurred secularization in the black church as well as black life generally. It is no wonder that the development of contemporary gospel music is marked by "musical integration," or "crossover," themes of its own: appropriating secular means toward spiritual ends (e.g., in the marketing of gospel music), fusing black and white musical aesthetics and worshiping communities (e.g., in the music of Andraé Crouch), and singing sacred songs in secular arenas (e.g., protest rallies, college campuses, and television programs).

Integration: Setting the Stage

The political movement for social integration produced a musical integration as well. This sacred musical genre, born and thriving within a Christian subculture of black American spirituality, was now being fused with a decidedly public, and secular, end. The musical result was freedom songs—spirituals or hymns with lyrics espousing resistance to segregation and perseverance during the movement for racial equality of the 1950s and 1960s (Floyd 1991: 200; Reagon 1990: 4–7) These songs became one of the central icons of the Civil Rights Movement and boosted the morale of people from various racial, religious, and national backgrounds who identified with the movement's social and political goals. One of the most popular freedom songs, "We Shall Overcome," is an adaptation of C. A. Tindley's 1901 gospel hymn "I'll Overcome Someday." As the rallying cry of black and white demonstrators and movement sympathizers, these songs, in "gospelized" form, were reclaimed, popularized, and reappropriated for secular, and public, use. This music of the civil rights protesters, exposed largely via television news coverage, greatly affected mainstream white America. As a result, white churches supportive of the Civil Rights Movement incorporated gospel songs into their worship services (Walker 1979: 153–155). This music, which emphasized personal spiritual transformation, was helping to catalyze group cultural and social transformation in both black and white communities (Sellman 2004).

In addition, the struggle for social integration and political equality led to strengthened group solidarity and the reclaiming of African heritage.[6] As a result, many African Americans developed a heightened race consciousness, which during this period eventually led to "a new sense of acceptance and pride [regarding what had been considered] black sacred music's earlier stepchild, gospel" (Walker 1979: 155). Before the Civil Rights Movement, for example, the repertoire of black university choirs consisted predominantly of classical music, with a few spirituals included to conclude their concerts. As the Civil Rights Movement organized politically, this changed. According to theologian Cheryl J. Sanders (1996: 202, 206–207), "To designate the proliferation of collegiate gospel choirs as a movement seems appropriate, since they emerged as student-initiated organizations during the peak period of black student involvement in public protests, political organizations, and demands for black studies programs, outlasting many other institutionalized expressions of black awareness among colleges students. . . The push for gospel choirs. . . represented black students' desire to identify with the 'subject race' in the struggle for liberation and justice."

This embrace of gospel music among black students in both black and predominantly white campus settings—both secular—reflected a general mood change among the standard-bearers of black propriety. That which some black folks had discarded on theological grounds was now recovered on the basis of political ones. By the end of the civil rights era, these socio-historical realities aligned to create a receptive environment—within both black and white communities—for a new kind of sound in gospel.

Crossing Over: Music and People

In 1968, a West Coast community choir (the Northern California State Youth Choir) consisting of young people from throughout the Bay Area produced an album for local consumption titled, *Let Us Go into the House of the Lord*. One of the songs from that live recording, "Oh Happy Day," is a soulful, rhythmic reworking of an eighteenth-century hymn arranged by choir cofounder Edwin Hawkins (biography of Edwin Hawkins). Quite unexpectedly, the song found a home on underground FM-radio playlists across San Francisco and soon began earning airplay on mainstream R&B and pop stations across the country and around the globe. That year, the song earned the later renamed and reconstituted group—the Edwin Hawkins Singers—a Grammy Award for Best Gospel/Soul Performance (King; MSN.com; Heilbut 1997: 248). This was far beyond the expectations of a modest California youth choir, which had produced only five hundred copies for a small fund-raising campaign.

Hawkins' eclectic music influences—pop, classical, jazz, R&B, and the Holiness Pentecostal Church—all appear in the vocal and instrumental arrangements on the fund-raiser album. It was unlike anything heard in gospel recordings of the time. Gospel music scholar Horace Clarence Boyer (2000: 5) described it as a fusion of "the harmonic variety of a Duke Ellington and the soulful accentuation of a Ray Charles." It was this sound that resonated with a restlessness of a generation yearning for modernity. In spring 1969, "Oh Happy Day" reached the top 5 on the *Billboard* charts, eventually selling an astounding seven million copies (King).

When "Oh Happy Day" hit the airwaves in the spring of 1969, Dr. Martin Luther King Jr.'s assassination just one year earlier was still a fresh memory. Despite the victories of the Civil Rights Movement in raising the national consciousness around issues of racial injustice, and the passage of historic civil rights legislation,[7] King's death deflated the church-based political movement. The black church declined in significance in the lives of African Americans, and the Black Power message of a secular black nationalism gained ground in portions of the black community (Pinn 1992: 18). By the 1970s, the black church had lost its preeminent status as the lead institution championing the plight of African Americans.

In an effort to partake of opportunities previously denied them in the fields of education, employment, housing, and public accommodations, sizable numbers of African Americans began to enter formerly all-white arenas. The Christian church in America, however, was beyond the scope of the civil rights agenda, and integrating black and white churches was neither desired nor attained. In a sermon preached at the National Cathedral in Washington DC, just four days before he was assassinated, Dr. Martin Luther King Jr. observed, "We must face the sad fact that at eleven o'clock on Sunday morning when we stand to sing 'In Christ there is no East or West,' we stand in the most segregated hour of America." (King and Washington 1986: 270). It is my observation that little has changed in this regard since that Sunday morning in 1968. Given this reality, it is useful to place the career of contemporary gospel pioneer Andraé Crouch in this context. His ministry and recording career touched both white and black worshiping communities while at the same time laying important groundwork in the development of the modern gospel genre.

In 1968, Los Angeles born and COGIC bred Andraé Crouch was signed to a white gospel-oriented label, Light Records. With his group, The Disciples, Crouch recorded some of the best-known and loved songs in American congregational music: "Through It All," "My Tribute (To God Be The Glory)," "Soon and Very Soon," and "Take Me Back." His appeal to both black and white audiences, both religious and secular, sustained his continued recording success throughout the 1970s. His unique sound—part balladeer, part "Sunday morning," highly produced and very pop—gained him entree into an eclectic mix of musical circles. From collaborations with Elvis Presley to traditional black church worship settings (despite criticism he faced from gospel purists for his rock and roll-influenced lyrics, music and image) and the "Jesus Music" of the white hippie counterculture of the 1960s, Crouch unapologetically pioneered a new wave of religious music (Heilbut 1997: 247–248). Andraé Crouch and the Disciples achieved a series of "firsts" for gospel artists: they were the first to perform at Radio City Music Hall and in Australia's Sydney Opera House, and in 1980, the first to appear on the television program Saturday Night Live. He also experienced international acclaim, with sold-out concerts in Europe, Africa, the Far East, and the Americas. In many instances, Crouch's music brought blacks and whites of his generation together in worship—albeit in concert halls—for the first time. In these ways, Crouch's career embodies the musical, social, and cultural "integration" of modern gospel music reflective of the social realities of the 1960s and 1970s.

Social Integration, Social Separation

The aspiration of many African Americans in the early post-Civil Rights era went well beyond integration, toward assimilation, into white America. As these blacks attained educational, social, and economic status through their participation in mainstream institutional life, there emerged what sociologists Lincoln and Mamiya (1990: 384) describe as "two nations within a nation": a "coping sector" of middle-income working-class and middle-class blacks and a "crisis sector" of low-income blacks, who made up the working poor and the dependent poor.[8] For the first time, class became a basis of segmentation within the African American community (Powers 1998: 33, 43).[9]

Tyrone Powers (1998: 43, 44) argues: "The blinders that middle-class blacks had to put on to focus on integration caused them to ignore and abandon urban blacks." He further states: "Although a middle class existed in pre-integration black America, the divisiveness inherent in class division was subjugated by the collective conscience, which was a result of the commonality of the black experience... As middle class blacks assimilated into white America post-integration, the collective conscience of black America dissipated or was subjugated to class status. A state of anomie filled the void" (320–321).[10] The implications for the black church were profound. For example, while many middle-class blacks physically and emotionally left urban neighborhoods (what Powers describes as black flight or out migration), as well as the churches in those neighborhoods, in pursuit of the American dream, others kept their membership in black churches, commuting every Sunday into the city from the suburbs. However, the focus of the black church began to change. Whereas most black churches were previously concerned with empowerment for the entire black community, Powers contends that these churches during the 1970s began to specialize in middle-class concerns, leaving out the concerns of the urban poor. As a result, many lower-income blacks, young people, and young black men in particular fled from the black church (Lincoln and Mamiya 1990; Powers 1998: 47, 49, 133–134). Others left for ideological reasons based on what they perceived as the black church's failure to articulate and implement a nationalistic agenda for black advancement, particularly in light of the demise of the Civil Rights Movement. For these reasons, by the 1980s, there was born a second generation of blacks, of both classes, who had no direct personal relationship to the spirituality, values, or culture of the black church (Pinn 1992: 20).

The low numbers of African American urban poor, particularly young men, in the contemporary black church continues to the present day. Lincoln and Mamiya (1990: 322–324) report that a major challenge to the contemporary black church is the unchurched, urban, black teenagers and young adults, ages seventeen to thirty-five. In the decade immediately following the "black flight" of the middle class—the 1980s—black youth suffered: this group experienced unemployment rates of over 50 percent, black males were incarcerated on average at a rate of 47 percent, and teenage pregnancy rates grew to crisis proportions. While most black churches did not aggressively address these issues, some efforts were made to reach this constituency. In 1990, a survey of 2,150 urban and rural black churches included the question, "What special techniques and programs have you found to be successful in attracting young people?" The program/technique reported to have the most success was "music and choir" at 19.2 percent, with "allow greater participation and involvement in the leadership and decision-making of the church" as the second most successful, at

13.2 percent (330). For those who were serious about intervening in the lives of youth, the methodology was clear: fuse the sound, look, and feel of the hip hop culture that had so captivated the hearts and minds of urban youth with the timeless message of the gospel.

Such was the rationale of gospel artists who pioneered hip hop gospel in the 1980s and 1990s. Even without the aid of Lincoln and Mamiya's sociological research, church-based music ministers such as John P. Kee intuitively knew what it would take to reach a generation of youth who were alienated from the black church:

> Though John P. Kee was known as a composer of traditional gospel music, his concern over the nation's youth caused him to change the focus of his music to become more appealing to the younger generation. Kee picked up the hip hop culture and perfected a combination of traditional, contemporary and hip hop music that would start a trend within gospel choir singing... Because of his own experience on the streets, Kee turned his focus and thrust on street ministry. One of Kee's special missions was to reach out to hard-core drug traffickers and other troubled youth in his community to try to dissuade them from such a lifestyle. Consequently, Kee chose to perform music that combined hip hop and urban sounds with a gospel message. (Wise 2002: 183–185)

This formula proved successful in attracting teens steeped in this emerging urban youth culture.

Another case study illustrating the success of modernized gospel music in attracting young people to the gospel message came in the summer of 1993, which was arguably the key defining moment for contemporary gospel music since "Oh Happy Day." Kirk Franklin, a young unknown gospel musician from Fort Worth, Texas, released a self-titled debut album, *Kirk Franklin and The Family*. Its hit song, "The Reason Why We Sing," led the album to one hundred weeks atop *Billboard* magazine's gospel charts. It crossed over to the R&B charts and became the first gospel album ever to sell over a million units (Nu Nation).

While his inaugural album could be categorized as new traditional, Franklin's subsequent albums were mainly urban contemporary selections with a heavy hip hop influence.[11] For example, in 1997, Franklin teamed up with a youth ensemble from his native Texas, God's Property, and their album entered the pop chart at number three. The hit song from that album, "Stomp," featured a duet with hip hop veteran Cheryl James ("Salt") from the rap group Salt-n-Pepa. "Stomp" made musical history in two ways: (1) it reached number-one status on R&B, gospel, and contemporary Christian charts for several weeks that year; and (2) MTV played its video in heavy rotation. Many young people (churched and unchurched), representing a diverse demographic, became Kirk Franklin fans. Through his dress, dance moves, and lyrics, Franklin became the poster boy for crossover gospel, receiving accolades for his trailblazing but also caustic criticism from those who believed he had transgressed the line of what was proper for a gospel artist.

During the 1980s and 1990s, the music of Kee, Franklin, Brooklyn's Hezekiah Walker, and others like them attracted many to the Christian lifestyle and to church membership. Incorporating contemporary musical sounds proved to be a successful means by which to convey the Christian messages of hope, encouragement, and salvation in a way that was compelling to this hard-to-reach demographic. Church youth choirs across the country took hold of this new artistic flair, emulating these choirs and including their songs in their Sunday morning repertoires as much as the church members would allow. Although it was met with some resistance, churches could not deny that hip hop gospel produced results at a time when little else was working. Religious studies professor Anthony Pinn (1992: 54–55) writes:

> Churches have recognized contemporary gospel and are using it as a tool for evangelizing communities. During the 1980s, many churches nurtured choirs for more than the music they provided... Many churches in fact experienced growth based on the popularity of their choirs. Hence, excellent choir directors were in as much demand as charismatic preachers, and most churches now make it their business to nurture at least one choir with an understanding that there is a direct relationship between good music and full pews.

In this way, the urban sector of the black community, especially young people, who had been left out of the post-integration black church agenda, were now intentionally recruited via this new form of music ministry.

The "hip hop gospel" innovation illustrates how the black church, as a community theater that gives music its meaning and function, reinvented itself through reimagining music in a way that would capture the hearts and souls of a languishing younger generation. As the music's effectiveness for reaching young people became clear, groups on each side of the church doors experienced a conversion. Hence, Ramsey's (2003: 193) pronouncement, that "hip hop music... has transformed the community theatre that is the black church" rings true.

Another group, however, was absent and unaccounted for: those middle-class blacks who had retreated to suburbia or who had left the black church for ideological reasons. Whether it was to the doors of the seven historic black denominational churches or to the new megachurches, waves of middle-class African Americans found their way back to the church of their mothers and fathers during the 1990s.

> The black middle class expressed a feeling of living between two worlds, one generated by economic success and the other premised upon racial classification... Yet despite gains, middle-class blacks found themselves in search of a stabilizing force, a community. For those who followed their dreams out of cities, life in the suburbs proved troubling; racial discrimination could make property difficult to secure and, even when housing was found, fires and other forms of violence were often used to protest their presence... Accompanying these difficulties was a cultural uncertainty, a shaky and often changing meaning of what it was to be "black." Many middle-class black Americans found themselves "outside the loop," considered foreigners by both less well-off blacks and whites. To combat this, many returned to their religious roots. (Pinn 1992: 28–29)

It is no wonder that gospel music—in its modernized form—was an integral part of this spiritual and cultural rejourneying. It is well settled that gospel music has come to represent the essence of a distinctly African American culture (Williams-Jones 1975). For Ramsey (2003: 193–194), "gospel music reigns as a powerful sign of ethnicity among African Americans. Faithful Christian believers and nonbelievers alike have long recognized the genre as an important cultural symbol, loaded with both social and eschatological meaning." As seen in the black collegiate gospel choir movement of the 1970s, contemporary gospel music had already once served the purpose of being a source of spiritual sustenance, group solidarity, and racial pride for these affirmative-action-babies-turned-Buppies.[12] Despite any physical or political distance from the black church over the years, gospel music had been an accessible means of connection to the culture and spirituality of the church. In this way, the songs of Andraé Crouch, Edwin Hawkins, and others served as familiar and comforting passageways for liturgical re-entry. What they had enjoyed in secular venues such as the college campus, music festivals, and even on mainstream radio now resonated in even sweeter tones when enjoyed in its natural habitat: Sunday morning in a black church worship experience.

Moreover, as many in this group were wrestling with their Du Boisian "two-ness"[13]—trying to make sense of their relationship with a white America that both *beckoned* and *rejected* (Powers 1998: 43) them, as well as struggling with identity insecurities surrounding their own blackness highlighted by a similar beckoning and rejection from the black urban poor—they were attracted to contemporary gospel music. It modeled, in aesthetic form, a solution to their existential dilemma. Ethnographer and gospel singer Pearl Williams-Jones (1973: 373) argues: "Black gospel music is one of the new seminal genres of contemporary black culture which continually *maintains its self-identity* while it nourishes and *enriches the mainstream* of the world's cultural sources" (italics added). This theme resonated with a post-integration, middle-class, African American sensibility: to maintain one's self-identity while engaging fully and productively in the mainstream (i.e., white) society.[14]

Theologically, this challenge harkens back to the Christian admonition to "be ye in the world, but not of it."[15] It is the question one asks oneself after the quest for assimilation and acceptance within white America has been met with hostile demands for accommodation.[16] It is the rhetorical question posed by Jesus centuries earlier, with now perhaps a deeper and double meaning for this group of striving African Americans: "For what does it profit a man, that he shall gain the whole world, but lose his soul?"[17] At its cultural best, contemporary gospel typifies how one can incorporate the "the things of this world" without forfeiting that most prized currency of blackness—soul. This, according to jazz scholar and anthropology professor John Szwed (1970: 220), is what music is expected to do: "Song forms and performances are themselves models of social behavior that reflect strategies of adaptation to human and natural environments." Hence, contemporary gospel music appeals to both churched and unchurched sectors of the African American middle class because of all of these messages in the music—both stated and implied.

In these ways, contemporary gospel music has achieved what the traditional black church as a whole has failed to accomplish in the post-Civil Rights era: a mechanism for spiritual and cultural sustenance for both ends of its bifurcated community—the African American middle class and the African American underclass. Not only does it accomplish this, but also it does so in a way that ushers both sectors back into the pews of the waning post-Civil Rights black church. During a period in which both groups are experiencing their respective versions of anomie caused by alienation, contemporary gospel music offered itself as a channel towards the recovery of collective consciousness lost in the post-Civil Rights era.

Integrating the Music Industry

By the late 1970s, a small cadre of blacks was working professionally in the business of gospel music, particularly as white-owned Christian music labels started their black-music divisions and hired African Americans to be involved in marketing, promotions, and decisions of artists and repertoire (A&R). By the early to mid-1980s, these record labels[18] introduced the largest numbers of contemporary gospel artists to national audiences (Wise 2002: 159). In the early 1990s, several independent black-owned labels came into being, as industry veterans who had worked for these Christian labels, or in the secondary market generated by them as independent contractors, struck out on their own to establish gospel music-related ventures of national scope.

Vicki Mack-Lataillade and husband Claude are perhaps the most notable examples of this phenomenon. In 1993, Mack-Lataillade ceased operations as an independent marketer and founded a label with $6,000 from her father's postal pension fund. Gospocentric became the label behind Kirk Franklin's debut album with its historic crossover sales. The label now dominates the gospel music marketplace through its A-list roster, which includes artists such as Kurt Carr, Byron Cage, and Tramaine Hawkins.

The marketplace for entrepreneurial activity in the gospel industry continued to expand. In July 1998, Black Enterprise magazine published an article titled "Resources for Gospel Entrepreneurs," which gave advice to members of its predominantly African American readership who might have interest in launching gospel music-related businesses: "Do your homework and be as well versed in the culture and grassroots network of the black church and the gospel community as you are in the workings of the music industry. Ministers, church musical directors, church bookstores and annual conferences represent some of the support systems, informational sources and marketing opportunities for gospel music entrepreneurs" (Rhea 1998). Whether for entrepreneurs or corporate executives, the cultural capital of the black church was an important asset in the design of marketing plans and promotional campaigns, resulting in unprecedented sales, increased visibility, and greater accessibility for contemporary gospel music. Simply put, when these professionals entered the mainstream, they brought their unique understanding of the gospel market with them. In this, we notice a direct relationship between the inclusion of blacks into the mainstream of American corporate and entrepreneurial life, as a direct by-product of the Civil Rights Movement, and the commercial explosion of gospel music.

Secularization

The issue of secularization in the black church and within contemporary gospel music is a negotiated, fluid, and dynamic one. In its barely forty years of existence, a body of tensions and controversies have erupted that, in my view, are rooted in and complicated by the fact that the gospel music idiom is itself a hybrid musical form blending sacred and secular musics. As the following discussion demonstrates, these tensions and controversies were as alive at the turn of the twenty-first century as they were when Dorsey was kicked out of the black churches for playing what was viewed as "the devil's music" in the 1930s (Harris 1992).[19]

Thus, as it had in the 1960s, gospel music again experienced innovations and controversies in the 1980s. When up-and-coming musicians employed the same methods used by Dorsey, Hawkins, and Crouch by incorporating the most contemporary musical styles of their day—now, R&B, rap, and hip hop—they met resistance from all but the church teenagers and R&B fans in the pews. Perhaps the most successful progenitors of the gospel sound of the 1980s were The Winans, a quartet of brothers from a musical family in Detroit. They were the protégés of Crouch, who produced their first album, *Introducing the Winans*, in 1981 (Wise 2002: 179–180). The Winans dominated the gospel and R&B charts throughout the 1980s in part due to mainstream marketing efforts that included recording with secular artists such as Anita Baker, Teddy Riley, Stevie Wonder, and Kenny G. In the face of more secular-sounding tracks like these, mainstream radio DJs discovered that their listeners were not offended by hearing a gospel song in an otherwise secular music lineup. In fact, DJs and program directors began playing selected gospel songs during prime radio airtime periods (196). However, this use of secular musical styles, coupled with bold musical associations with secular recording artists, made this new strand of gospel unwelcome in the typical black church. According to musicologist Guthrie Ramsey (2003: 191–192): "While church leadership has generally guarded and cherished the notions of tradition and convention, forces from within the church (more often than not the younger generation) have defied the older heads. . . and claimed stylistic change as an artistic priority. The interaction of these two impulses (tradition and innovation) has provided a creative framework through which musicians have continually pursued new musical directions, despite the inevitable controversies that these innovations are sure to inspire."

A classic example of the controversies that erupted amid the impulses of tradition and innovation came as a reaction to Tramaine Hawkins' 1985 techno-funk hit "Fall Down." The song topped the dance charts despite its explicitly religious content, sending Hawkins into dance clubs to perform, much to the chagrin of many of her fans in the church community. According to one biographer, "After the uproar, Hawkins felt that everyone but her family and her church family had turned their backs on her" (Richard De La Font Agency). Years later, Hawkins returned to the music industry after taking a break to care for her ailing mother; she also returned to a more traditional style. She is heralded today as one of gospel music's "divas."

Another illustration of the tradition-innovation tension surfaced through what many considered a watering down of the gospel message in contemporary gospel songs. This was especially notable as major secular labels signed certain artists to their roster with an eye toward crossover sales. The brother and sister duo BeBe and CeCe Winans, the younger siblings of The Winans, were at the epicenter of this controversy. In the late 1980s, BeBe and CeCe's "I.O.U. Me" (1987) and "Lost without You" (1988) scored high on the R&B and Adult Contemporary *Billboard* charts but offended many in the gospel music and church community because the songs seemed to "treat spiritual love in fuzzy terms just as conducive to the physical" (Bush). It was even part of the lore of the time that when they left their Christian-owned label and signed with secular recording giant Capitol Records, their new recording contract explicitly prohibited them from using traditional religious words like "God" or "Jesus" in their songs. In his history of gospel music, Raymond Wise (2002: 181, 199) supports this suspicion with the observation that "as secular record companies began to enter the gospel market, many gospel artists were told to compromise their gospel message or omit the altar calls from their concerts." BeBe and CeCe's practice of using ambiguous terms such as "love," "light," and "him" contributed to some sectors of the Christian community questioning whether the duo had "sold out" their ministry-minded motives in exchange for acceptance in the secular marketplace (Southern 1997: 608).

As a result of these tensions and controversies, definitions of subgenres emerged to help supporters and critics alike distinguish between these new breeds of gospel music and the (now-standard) contemporary gospel music they were likely to encounter on a Sunday morning. The Gospel Music Industry Roundup, dubbed "the bible of the gospel music industry," sets forth some important distinctions that emerged as a by-product of these concerns (Collins 2001: 7):

> *Contemporary Gospel:* "Good news" music using secular influences but designed for worship both within and beyond the walls of the traditional church.
> *Urban Contemporary Gospel:* Incorporating street beats and urban influences, this may have a place in people's spiritual lives but not in the traditional church worship experience.
> *Inspirational:* Songs that are spiritually uplifting but do not necessarily convey the Gospel.
> *Praise and Worship:* Participatory call-and-response music designed to provide worshipers with a mechanism for praise within the church experience.

While such industry-driven definitions helped consumers, critics, and industry personnel comprehend the new musical landscape that was becoming contemporary gospel, new vocabulary alone could not bring consensus around the vastly different theological, musical, and business approaches these categories represented. Herein lay the subject matter for examining issues of secularization in the contemporary gospel music period.

Sociologist Mark Chaves (1994: 757) offers a conceptual framework that can be useful in interpreting issues of secularization:

> Secularization at the societal level may be understood as the declining capacity of religious elites to exercise authority over other institutional spheres. Secularization at the organizational level may be understood as religious authority's declining control over the organizational resources within the religious sphere. And secularization at the individual level may be understood as the decrease in the extent to which individual actors are subject to religious control. The unifying theme is that *secularization refers to declining religious authority* at all three levels of analysis. (italics added)

This theory opens the door to a new approach to secularization, one that situates religion and religious change in a concrete historical context. Secularization occurs, or does not occur, as the result of social and political conflicts between those social actors who would enhance or maintain religion's social significance and those who would reduce it (750–752).

In this way, Chaves' approach evokes the primary thesis of this study, forwarded by Walker and reinforced by Ramsey: that any interpretation of black sacred music necessitates socio-historical contextualization. However, Chaves' view of secularization mirrors the conceptual framework of this study even more precisely, with his hypothesis that secularization is a function of the outcome of negotiations between "social actors"—akin to what Ramsey believes transpires within the community theater.

How, then, are we to understand secularization in the case of contemporary gospel music? The tussle across shifting sacred and secular definitions appears to be its only constant. How do we assess gospel music ministers' innovative use of secular means (e.g., hip hop) to achieve the most sacred of ends (the spiritual and social reclamation of its young people)? Has the church now become more secular for having reached its young, or has it affirmed its sacredness by enacting the Great Commission in contemporary times? Both Chaves' and Ramsey's frameworks suggest close examination of the actions, motivations, and negotiations between the social actors involved in the contemporary gospel music genre. For this reason, I look at the three main groups of social actors as they relate to the music and the church: the recording industry and other corporate actors, gospel musicians and recording artists, and leaders of the black church.

The Recording Industry and Other Corporate Actors

The creative innovation, heated controversies, and high visibility of gospel music in just the last decade have made it unmistakably clear—from the pulpit to the door, from Main Street to Madison Avenue—that gospel music is hot (Jeffers 2002). Moreover, for better or for worse, gospel has become a hot commodity. Former Payne Theological Seminary president and novelist Obery M. Hendricks (2000) suggests that this "process of gospel songs being sold as commodities" began when Thomas Dorsey sold his first piece of sheet music in 1926. This commodification has continued and expanded to the point where, some sixty years later in 1996, the Gospel Music Association declared gospel "the fastest-growing musical genre in America, ranking only behind rock, country, urban contemporary, pop, and rap" (Buckles 1998). That same year, a New York-based market research firm reported that 50 percent of gospel music listeners were between ages twenty-five and forty-four, the age group that accounts for more than 59 percent of all record sales in the music industry (Rhea 1998).

Such sales prompted unprecedented involvement from the American corporate sector in the business of gospel music, as major secular labels entered into distribution deals with several independent labels in the 1990s. These arrangements afforded the product of independent labels the same prominent placement within mainstream retail chains as those of secular artists (Rhea 1998). In the 1980s, major corporations interested in strengthening their African American consumer base (such as McDonald's, Kentucky Fried Chicken, Quaker Oats, and Wrigley's Chewing Gum) sponsored gospel choir competitions and other gospel-oriented events.[20] In addition, with the aid of corporate sponsorship, local civic, art, and community organizations across the country began to produce outdoor gospel music concerts (Wise 2002: 166). In the 1990s, even Hollywood took notice: several major studios produced theatrical films incorporating contemporary gospel music or gospel music-centered story lines.[21]

Thus, as the participation of big business (representing "corporate actors") brought a level of commercialization and involvement heretofore unseen in gospel (and perhaps in any other sacred musical genre), secularization in the making and distribution of gospel music has certainly occurred. In the language of Chaves' framework, societal secularization is evidenced in the "declining capacity of religious elites to exercise authority over other institutional spheres" (Chaves 1994: 757). In this sense, much of that which had been self-contained in the churches was now at best a shared endeavor with entertainment and consumer-goods corporations.

Recording Artists

When questions concerning gospel's secular sound were raised at the height of the contemporary gospel music controversies of the 1980s, some leading artists explained the rationale behind their musical and marketing choices. Andraé Crouch stated, "We are to reach people where they are, therefore our music must be appealing" (Wise 2002: 19). Marvin Winans explained: "When you need to get a certain group to hear your music then you've got to go get that certain group. If we just wanted gospel people to hear the music, we would have gotten [other] gospel artists [to appear on our albums]... We recognize the fact that because we are gospel artists, we're only going to be played on so many stations. In order to change that we needed to get some people to help change that circumstance, not change our music, but [to] make sure other people hear us" (Smith 1988: 27–32). The previous discussion of John P. Kee's intentionality in using hip hop to reach unchurched youth also applies here.

Even at the beginning of a new century, gospel artists' motives are still the subject of inquiry. As Ramsey (2003: 212) reminds us, "[T]he appropriateness of certain musical gestures for worship, the secular nature of a song's subject matter, dress, body language, and the proper venue of presentation have become lightening rods for controversy." Enter Tonéx. Introduced to gospel audiences in 2000, he has been described as "one of gospel's most perplexing and creative talents," "gospel's avant-garde," "a twenty four year old musical prodigy" (Collins 2002: 67), and "the mad scientist," due to his "busy" musical style (Mission Productions). He is often compared to recording artist Prince, not only for his musical virtuosity but also for his salacious stage presentation. Gospelflava.com, a leading gospel website, describes the reasons for the uproar created by Tonéx:

> While the artist's music is definitely on the cutting edge, it is his appearance that has birthed a tremendous amount of heat from within the gospel community. For most of his performances or appearances, it is not uncommon to find Tonéx clad in his trademark top hat and boa, along with assorted body piercing and other retro apparel. In addition, his performances are usually heightened by a stage filled with incense and candles. His stage presence is certainly a far cry from his Apostolic upbringing. (Gospelflava.com "The World According to Tonéx, Part II: The Future")

Defending himself, Tonéx contends:

> I've made it a point to be as extreme with my appearance as possible for a reason. *It's time for the church world to understand that they must not limit God and put him in a box.* The problem with the church is that they want to look the part but not act the part. David was anointed of God but he didn't look like it... The church has made it so that they want people to be fixed up before they get cleaned up and that's not right. It is my mission to educate the church world that it's not about how you look but about the anointing. (Gospelflava.com "The World According to Tonéx, Part II: The Future" [italics added])

The "box" Tonéx refers to is the invisible line that delineates the sacred from the secular. Perhaps more consciously than his predecessors, Tonéx wants to expose and step over these lines. Toward that end, he has coined a name for a new category of gospel music, *nureau*. He explains: "It means 'new row'... as in new row in a church pew, new row in a retail shelf, etc. It's a category of music all by itself" (Gospelflava.com "Tonéx: A Chatterview"). In this, nureau marks the next wave of modernity to disrupt the contemporary gospel music status quo. While Crouch and Winans seemed fixed on "how to reach the masses," Tonéx's self-appointed mission is also to revolutionize the way that Christian insiders perceive God. In this, he claims that his futuristic sound, edgy presentation, and even his shock appeal are merely tools used for spiritual objectives.

Lincoln and Mamiya, however, would likely view such independent, nonconformist stances as squarely in tension with the dictates of the prevailing religious leadership, as a sure sign of secularization in the contemporary black church, notwithstanding the spiritualized claims of these artists. Lincoln and Mamiya (1990: 13) determine secularization in terms of the "dialectic between the communal and the privatistic": "The communal orientation refers to the historic tradition of black churches being involved in all aspects of the lives of their members, including political, economic, educational and social concerns. . . This dialectic is also useful in assessing the degree to which the process of secularization has affected black churches. In sociological theory the effects of secularization are to push towards privatism, a more personal and individualistic sense of religiousness." These artists' defiance of the norms of the "communal orientation" would seem then to constitute secularization. Tonéx's "individual sense of religiousness," Lincoln and Mamiya might argue, empowers his oppositional stance against the status quo. Yet, even Lincoln and Mamiya acknowledge that their communal-privatistic understanding of relations within the black church sits within the context of a dialectical framework—and one, they maintain, that is not resolved in a Hegelian synthesis but which remains in tension. Furthermore, as noted earlier, both Chaves and Ramsey recommend that attention be paid to the dynamic, multifaceted layers of meanings embodied in the social actors and factors of a particular historical moment.

In this way, Chaves' analysis of "individual secularization" seems most fitting. In evaluating the relationship of church musicians and gospel recording artists who embrace modernity against the preferences of church leaders, Chaves (1994) calls for a second step in the secularization analysis. First, consistent with Lincoln and Mamiya's communal-privatistic framework, Chaves recommends examining "the decrease in the extent to which individual actors are subject to religious control." Then, Chaves directs us to analyze the extent to which any loss of that religious authority has been a loss to "social actors whose agenda is to reduce the social significance of religion" (752). Evaluated against this standard, it appears that the clearly stated evangelistic goals of artists such as Crouch, Winans, and Tonéx, for example, are those that are directed to promote Christianity, not reduce its influence. As long as the gospel message is presented, according to this view, any musical style may be employed (Wise 2002: 172). While this viewpoint has traditionally stood in tension with the more conservative elements of the black church-going community, it should not be discarded outright as any less a religious stance. More than an "end-justifies-the-means" analysis is necessary.

With this more comprehensive layer of analysis suggested by Chaves' framework, we may conclude that what is taking place in this instance is not secularization after all. Simply: it is singing a new song for a new day.[22] Each generation of devotees will express religious faith through its own culturally relevant expressions borrowed from the secular society and "gospelized."[23]

Black Religious Leadership

Any consumer of American pop culture knows that gospel music is "not just for Sunday anymore." The corollary of this is also true: gospel music is no longer exclusively the province of the religious community of its origins. One leading gospel music journalist even referred to the church as merely "the incubator" for the music (Petrie 2004).

Given this reality, the recent launches of gospel music labels by several black megachurches may represent more than ministerial or even entrepreneurial objectives.[24] Apparently, these pastors believe that their extensive church networks contain the business, marketing, and creative resources to compete with mainstream and seasoned independent record labels. Perhaps these megachurches, with anywhere from 2,000 to 25,000 members (Tucker-Works 2001: 179) took note of their courting by gospel labels and reasoned that, in an industry where artists need only between five hundred and one thousand units in a given week in order to rate on the *Billboard* gospel charts (Jessen 2004), their multimillion dollar enterprises could also be major players in the gospel "mode of production."

In Chaves' scheme, organizational secularization refers to "religious authority's declining control over the organizational resources within the religious sphere" (Chaves 1994: 750–752). If music is considered as an organizational resource, the recent launching of full-service record companies by black megachurches might also be understood as an act of territorial recovery. In the perennial struggle between commerce and culture as it applies to black culture and black music in particular, such initiative on the part of several of the nation's most influential black clergy to control the gospel music mode of production is perhaps an attempt to desecularize this music.

Conclusion

In their preface to *The Black Church in the African American Experience*, C. Eric Lincoln and Lawrence H. Mamiya (1990: xii) write: "Because there has been such a dearth of serious research on black churches up to very recent times, the black church has often experienced difficulty in conceptualizing or knowing itself except as an amorphous, lusterless detail on some larger canvas devoted to other interests. In consequence the black church has often found itself repeating history it had already experienced, and relearning the black church lessons it had long since forgotten." This is especially true in the case of the black church and its relationship to the contemporary forms of gospel music. In direct response to Lincoln and Mamiya's lament, I offer the following as lessons to remember.

First, from a historical perspective, gospel music seems almost destined to cross over. In her seminal work The Music of Black Americans, Eileen Southern (1997: 609) writes: "Again and again black musical styles have passed over into American music, there to be diluted and altered in other ways to appeal to a wider public or to be used as the basis for development of new styles." History has demonstrated that once certain aspects of black culture gain popularity in the black community, mainstream market forces (i.e., "corporate America") "discover" that culture, then commodify and reappropriate it into the mainstream as popular culture (Ramsey 2003: 168). Given this historical reality, the black church should not be surprised by the crossover market appeal of gospel music; rather, it should expect it. Despite the music's explicitly religious content, I believe this country's legacy of economic exploitation of black culture will continue to support the transmission of gospel music from the sacred space of the black church community theater into the secular mainstream. Aside from the economic and cultural injustices involved when black artists and communities do not reap the financial rewards of their cultural contributions,[25] some positive ramifications do emanate from this unfortunate reality. One example is in the furtherance of the gospel message; another is in the furtherance of the gospel music genre.

It should hardly be necessary in the context of a missionary religion such as Christianity to remind any portion of the church that it is a good thing when their message is presented to groups beyond the church's ordinary reach. Yet this seems to be forgotten in the case of the black church and the use of secular music styles with sacred text. Instead, the music is often rejected as "worldly" (church lingo for "secularization") and without any spiritual merit. If the black church would only recall the recent history of this nascent genre, it would not be surprised or offended by such innovations. I am not suggesting that the church abandon all sense of propriety for what is suitable for the Sunday worship service, but I am calling for a more informed response to contemporary trends in gospel music, based on an acknowledgment that, indeed, there would be no gospel music as we know it—traditional or contemporary—if in each instance the religious traditionalists of the day had prevailed.

Second, gospel music was designed with crossover attributes. Because of its hybrid musical nature, modern gospel music will naturally appeal to listeners of contemporary secular musical styles. In this, an expanded base of musical listening communities is nearly guaranteed. That gospel music was both destined and designed to cross over underscores this simple truth: neither the Gospel nor gospel music was meant for the exclusive enjoyment of the community of its social origin.

Third, the black church itself has a number of unique roles and responsibilities regarding gospel music artists and the genre's propagation. For example, Max Siegel (2002), President of Verity

Records, the world's largest gospel music label, comments on what a professional gospel music recording artist needs to "make it" in the Christian music business:

> You've got to understand that there are tensions involved in being in that realm. . . [T]here's always a tension between creativity and ministry and business. . . [I]t really gets complicated when some of the things [the record company] may ask you to do to market your record may be compromising to your ministry. . . [F]irst and foremost,. . . you need to be under a pastor where you can learn, you can be covered, and you can be spiritually fed. That's critical. The one thing is to have someone who's going to give you some guidance and advice spiritually. (Siegel 2002)

In this way, pastors and ministers of music have unique opportunities to minister to the spiritual and vocational needs of those who earn their living as professional recording artists. While this article has focused on the communal ramifications of tensions between sacred versus secular definitions, and ministry versus business objectives, these pastoral-care, church-based issues are ones of deep personal consequence for many gospel recording artists. This is also the case for many Christians who work in high levels of the entertainment industry generally. Instead of church environments that alienate and criticize people for having "worldly" occupations, or that are ignorant of the issues faced by these individuals, more black churches can be, and many are, sources of counsel, refuge, and emotional support for these high-profile individuals.

As an institutional community theater affiliated with a black musical genre, the black church also stands in a unique position to mitigate against undesirable sociological factors associated with gospel music. For example, with Dorsey's transformation of congregational hymns into songs for church choirs, soloists, and ensembles, a unique and powerful dimension of the worship experience in the black church was altered. Lincoln and Mamiya (1990: 361–362) note: "While [congregational hymns] united worshippers through the collective activity of singing and declaring theological and doctrinal commonalities, the new style required the congregation to assume the role of audience. In essence, worshippers became bystanders who witnessed the preaching and personal testimonies of singers. . . [B]lack worshippers and concertgoers often became the audience to a new homiletical gospel experience."

The implications of this changed dynamic are most starkly felt in the case of highly stylized gospel music. The impersonal nature of American society often leaves parishioners desirous of the "temporary reduction of social alienation and. . . an interim sense of community" afforded by congregational singing (347). I believe this is in part responsible for the rise of praise and worship music as the fastest growing subgenre in Christian music today. Praise and worship is participatory music that downplays the performance tendency in the worship setting and fosters a sense of unity and equality within the congregation. Ministers of music can address the potential limitations and barriers presented by gospel music by incorporating different worship styles, including those from other aspects of the black sacred musical tradition.

The black church can also act as an advocate and guardian of the music in the larger society. Many of the sociological factors affecting the development of the genre (e.g., secularization, dilution of the music, compromising the message, inappropriate marketing strategies, harnessing black buying power and ownership opportunities in the recording industry, inadequate knowledge of music history, etc.) are ripe for the informed leadership and initiative of churches who care about the music's preservation, integrity, and proliferation. In this, the black church's credibility and leverage with respect to the recording industry would be enhanced. More important, however, the black church would then rise to the occasion of its own stewardship of its own natural resource, no small feat in these postmodern (and some say post-black and post-Christian) times in which we live.

Finally, the black churches are more than a market base for this music, but principally, they serve as spiritual and cultural institutions with unique missions, socio-historical contexts, and operational cultures. Record companies in particular would do well to remember and respect this important truth. Often, the lines between the goals of the recording studio and the choir loft seem opposed and confusing to the persons operating in these two distinct contexts. And that is as it should be. Most churches, for example, focus on ministry objectives and spiritual outcomes; record companies focus on recouping their recording and marketing funds and on making a profit by exceeding what they spend in these areas. Yet, as churches become more business minded, and as record companies appreciate that the heart of gospel music is ministry, a maturing trust and a comfort is growing between these two communities. Gospel record company executives who understand their market realize that black churchgoers are the core consumer base for black sacred music in all of its forms. They can articulate to their record industry colleagues how understanding and respecting the culture of the church is good for business objectives. In addition, organizations such as the Gospel Music Workshop of America and the Gospel Music Heritage Foundation have helped to strengthen the communication and working relationships between these groups. This serves as a model for the existing and potential collaborative work between black churches and the American private sector in other socially beneficial areas, such as economic development, education, and philanthropy. It would not be the first time that significant social change in the United States was inspired and sustained through the songs of black folk.

This article was written in fulfillment of the senior essay requirement for the master's of divinity degree at Harvard Divinity School. I wish to thank The Reverend Professor Peter J. Gomes, Plummer Professor of Christian Morals, Professor Ingrid Monson, Quincy Jones Professor of Music, and Professor Wallace Best, Associate Professor of African American Religious Studies, all of Harvard University, for their enthusiastic support of this work. Thanks to my mother, Eleanor Weekes, who filled our home with the love of God and the love of song.

Discography

Crouch, Andraé, and the Disciples. "My Tribute (To God Be the Glory)." *Andraé Crouch and the Disciples.* CGI Records 51416 1177 2.

———. "Soon and Very Soon (We Are Going to See the King)." *Songs of Andraé Crouch and the Disciples*. CGI Records 51416 1090 2.

———. "Take Me Back." *The Best of Andraé*. CGI Records 51416 1135 2.

———. "Through It All." *Andraé Crouch*. Light Records 7-115-74060-7.

Edwin Hawkins Singers. *Let Us Go into the House of the Lord*. Pavilion Records BPS 10001.

Franklin, Kirk. *Kirk Franklin and the Family*. Gospocentric GCD 2119 (1993).

———. "God's Property." *From Kirk Franklin's nu nation*. B-Rite Music TD-90093.

Hawkins, Tramaine. "Falldown." *Spirit of Love*. A&M Records SP-12146(1985).

Winans, The. *Introducing the Winans*. Light LS-5792 (1981).

Winans, BeBe, and CeCe Winans. "I.O.U. Me." *BeBe and CeCe Winans*. EMI Records 1108566 (1987).

———. "Lost without You." *Heaven*. Capitol Records CDP 7 90959 2 (1988).

References

Barna Research Group. Research archives: African Americans. http://www.barna.org/cgibin/PageCategory.asp?CategoryID=l. Accessed February 3, 2004.

———. Research archives: African Americans. http://www.barna.org/cgibin/MainArchives.asp. Accessed March 10, 2004.

Biography of Edwin Hawkins. http://208.56.4.166/Bio.pdf. Accessed January 21, 2004.

Boyer, Horace C. *The Golden Age of Gospel*. Urbana and Chicago: University of Illinois Press, 2000.

Buckles, Julie. "Gospel Music: Coming Out of Church, into the Streets." Ashland [Wisconsin] Daily Press, October 7, 1998.

Bush, John. *Biography: CeCe Winans*. http://www.allmusic.com/cg/amg.dll?p=amg&uid=UIDMISS70401171310041305&sql=Bsflgtq7zbu42. Accessed January 21, 2004.

Chapman, Brenda, Stephen Hincker, and Simon Wells, directors. *The Prince of Egypt*. Universal City, CA: DreamWorks, 1998.

Chaves, Mark. "Secularization as Declining Religious Authority." *Social Forces* 72 (1994): 749–74.

Collins, Lisa. *The Gospel Music Industry Round-Up 2002*. Culver City: Eye on Gospel, 2001.

———. *The Gospel Music Industry Round-Up 2003*. Culver City: Eye on Gospel, 2002.

———. "In the Spirit: CCC Sets the Pace for Church Labels." *Billboard Magazine* August 23, 2003.

Davis, John A., director. *Jimmy Neutron: Boy Genius*. Hollywood: Paramount Pictures, 2001.

Du Bois, W. E. B. [1903]. *The Souls of Black Folk*. New York and Ontario: New American Library, 1982.

Floyd, Samuel. A., Jr. "Ring Shout! Literary Studies, Historical Studies, and Black Music Inquiry." *Black Music Research Journal* 11, no. 2 (1991): 265–87.

Frazier, E. Franklin. *Black Bourgeoisie*. New York: Free Press, 1957.

Gospelflava.com. "Tonéx: A Chatterview." http://www.gospelflava.com/articles/tonex-chat.html. Accessed January 30, 2004.

———. "The World According to Tonéx, Part II: The Future." http://www.gospelflava.com/articles/tonex.html. Accessed January 30, 2004.

Hairston, Teresa. "Quaker Oats Company Planting Seeds in African American Youth." *Gospel Today* March/April (1995): 17.

———. "Wrigley Company Doubles Its Dedication with Gospel Choir Competition." *Gospel Today* November/December (1996): 2.

Harris, Michael W. *The Rise of the Gospel Blues: The Music of Thomas Andrew Dorsey in the Urban Church*. New York: Oxford University Press, 1992.

Heilbut, Anthony. *The Good News in Bad Times*. New York: Limelight Editions, 1997.

Hendricks, Obery M. "I Am the Holy Dope Dealer: The Problem with Gospel Music Today." *Journal of the Interdenominational Theological Center* 45 (2000): 7–59.

Hullum, Janice R. "Robert E. Park's Theory of Race Relations." Master's thesis, University of Texas, 1973.

Jeffers, Glenn. Why Gospel Music Is So Hot. *Ebony Magazine* 17 (2002): 114.

Jessen, W. Telephone interview with the author, May 5, 2004.

Jones, LeRoi. *Blues People: Negro Music in White America*. New York: William Morrow, 1963.

Kelly, Robin D. G. *Yo' Mama's Disfunktional! Fighting the Culture Wars in Urban America*. Boston: Beacon, 1997.

Kentucky Fried Chicken competition advertisement. *Totally Gospel* November (1987): 5.

King, David A. "Gospel Music: A Brief History." http://www.rskstudio.freeserve.co.uk/timelywords/2003/gmhistory.htm. Accessed January 16, 2004.

King, Coretta Scott, and James Melvin Washington, eds. 1986. *Testament of Hope: The Essential Writings and Speeches of Martin Luther King Jr.* New York: Harper Collins, 1986.

Lincoln, C. Eric, and Lawrence H. Mamiya. *The Black Church and the African American Experience.* Durham: Duke University Press, 1990.

Luketic, Robert, director. *Legally Blonde.* MGM Home Entertainment, 2001.

Lynn, Jonathan, director. *The Fighting Temptations.* Hollywood: Paramount, 2003.

Marshall, Penny. *The Preacher's Wife.* Burbank: Touchstone Home Entertainment, 1996.

Maultsby, Portia K. "The Use and Performance of Hymnody, Spirituals, and Gospels in the Black Church." In *Readings in African American Church Music and Worship.* Compiled and edited by James Abbington. Chicago: GIA, 2001.

McHenry, Doug, director. *Kingdom Come.* Beverly Hills: 20th Century Fox Home Entertainment, 2001.

Mission Productions. Reviews: Tonéx. http://www.missionpromotions.co.uk/index.htm. Accessed January 29, 2004.

MSN.com. Artist information: Edwin Hawkins. http://entertainment.msn.com/artist/?artist=141342. Accessed January 16, 2004.

NuNation. Kirk Franklin biography. http://www.nunation.com/bio.html. Accessed March 17, 2004.

Park, Robert E. *Introduction to the Science of Society.* Chicago: University of Chicago Press, 1924.

Petrie, Phil. *The History of Gospel Music.* http://www.afgen.com/gospel1.html. Accessed January 19, 2004.

Pinn, Anthony B. *The Black Church in the Post-Civil Rights Era.* New York: Orbis Books, 1992.

Powers, Tyrone. "The Decline of Black Institutions and the Rise of Violent Crime in Urban Black America Post-Integration." PhD diss., American University, 1998.

Raboteau, Albert J. *Slave Religion: The Invisible Institution in the Antebellum South.* New York: Oxford University Press, 1978.

Ramsey, Guthrie P. *Race Music: Black Cultures from Bebop to Hip Hop.* Berkeley and Los Angeles: University of California Press, 2003.

Reagon, Bernice J. "The Lined Hymn as a Song of Freedom." *Black Music Research Bulletin* 12, no. 1 (1990): 4–7.

——. *We'll Understand It Better By and By: Pioneering African American Gospel Composers.* Washington DC: Smithsonian Institution, 1992.

Rhea, Shawn E. "Gospel Rises Again: Success of Gospel Music in the Sound Recording Industry." *Black Enterprise* July 1 (1998): 17.

Richard De La Font Agency. Tramaine Hawkins. http://www.delafont.com/music_acts/tramaine-hawkins.htm. Accessed January 21, 2004.

Sanders, Cheryl J. *Saints in Exile: The Holiness Pentecostal Experience in African American Religion and Culture.* New York: Oxford University Press, 1996.

Sellman, James Clyde. Gospel Music. http://www.africana.com/research/encarta/tt_653.asp. Accessed September 3, 2004.

Siegel, Max. *Establishing Your Vision.* Gospel Music Heritage Foundation Conference. Atlanta. Audiocassette.

Smith, T. "Marvin and Vickie Winans: Top Songwriters Establishing New Trails in Gospel Music." *Totally Gospel* March (1988): 27–32.

Southern, Eileen. *The Music of Black Americans: A History.* New York: W. W. Norton, 1997.

Szwed, John F. "Afro-American Musical Adaptation." In *Afro-American Anthropology.* Edited by N. E. Whitten, 219–230. New York: Free Press, 1970.

Trousdale, Gary, and Kirk Wise. *Beauty and the Beast.* Walt Disney Studios, 1991.

Tucker-Worgs, Tamley. "Get on Board, Little Children: There's Room for Many More: The Black Megachurch Phenomenon." *Journal of the Interdenominational Theological Center* 29, nos. 1/2 (2001): 177–203.

U.S. Bureau of the Census. "Selected Social Characteristics of the Population by Sex, Region, and Race." http://www.census.gov/population/socdemo/race/blac/tabs98/tab011.txt. 1998.

Walker, Wyatt Tee. *Somebody's Calling My Name: Black Sacred Music and Social Change.* Valley Forge: Judson, 1979.

Walser, Robert. *Running with the Devil: Power, Gender and Madness in Heavy Metal Music*. Hanover, NH: University Press of New England, 1993.

Williams-Jones, Pearl. "Afro-American Gospel Music: A Crystallization of the Black Aesthetic." *Ethnomusicology* 19 (1975): 373–85.

Wilmore, Gayraud S. *Black Religion and Black Radicalism: An Interpretation of the Religious History of Afro-American People*. 2nd ed. Maryknoll: Orbis, 1983.

Wilson, William. Julius. *The Truly Disadvantaged: The Inner City, the Underclass and Public Policy*. Chicago: University of Chicago Press, 1987.

Wise, Raymond. "Defining African American Gospel Music by Tracing Its Historical and Musical Development from 1900 to 2000." PhD diss., Ohio State University, 2002.

Notes

1. Amiri Baraka, formerly known as LeRoi Jones, was the first black author to theorize extensively about the relationship between black music's development and the historical trajectory of African American social progress. See Jones (1963).

2. The Church of God in Christ was formed in 1907 by Bishop Charles H. Mason, one of the leaders of the interracial Azusa Street Revival movement, credited for the spread of Pentecostalism in the United States.

3. Religious historian Albert J. Raboteau (1978) further developed this idea in his work *Slave Religion: The Invisible Institution in the Antebellum South*.

4. For example, the Fisk Jubilee Singers had been performing spirituals in concert halls throughout the nation and the world since the 1890s.

5. See Pinn (1992) and Lincoln and Mamiya (1990, 382–404) for an examination of several theological, social, and political factors that have shaped and are shaping the contemporary black church, including the challenge of black theology, the decline of denominationalism, the rise of neo-Pentecostalism, high incarceration rates among black men, the rise of religious diversity within the black community, political passivity, and the rise of communal leadership structures.

6. For example, the Black Panthers and the Nation of Islam were influential nationalistic movements during the 1960s and early 1970s.

7. The Civil Rights Act of 1964 provided enforcement mechanisms by which the government could ensure that African Americans would be treated equal to whites in all spheres of American life; the Voting Rights Act of 1965 outlawed literacy tests, poll taxes, and other Jim Crow barriers to black voting that were prevalent in the South.

8. Lincoln and Mamiya credit their formulation of "coping" and "crisis" sectors to Professor Martin Kilson, who gave a presentation of black clientage politics in the working group of Afro-American Religion and Politics at the W. E. B. Du Bois Institute, Harvard University, October 29, 1988.

9. Also see Wilson (1987). The point is not that class was an entirely new phenomenon in American black life (see Frazier [1957]) but that in light of affirmative action and other modes of equal opportunity for blacks, class emerged as a point of social differentiation within black America with a significance and scope not before experienced in American history.

10. In essence, *anomie* is a state in which norms and expectations on behaviors are confused, unclear, or not present, causing deviant behavior among the groups involved.

11. Collins (2001, 7) defines new traditional gospel music as "Gospel music utilizing today's technology for its updated rhythms, but rooted in the vocal and lyrical execution of traditional gospel music." She defines urban contemporary gospel as "music incorporating street beats and urban influences; it may have a place in our spiritual lives, but not in the traditional church worship experience."

12. *Buppies*, an acronym for black urban professionals, is a colloquial term for the new black middle class that surfaced in the 1980s.

13. In his classic *Souls of Black Folk*, W. E. B. Du Bois ([1903] 1982, 45) likens the situation of being black in the United States to a state of perpetual duplicity: "One ever feels his two-ness—an American, a Negro; two souls, two thoughts, two unreconciled strivings; two warring ideals in one dark body, whose dogged strength alone keeps it from being torn asunder."

14. Also see Harris' (1992, 207–208) discussion of this similar attraction to "the gospel blues" of Dorsey's day.

15. Based on biblical passages such as John 17:16–18.

16. Relying on studies of sociologist Robert E. Park's (1924) work on European out-migration across the globe, Powers (1998, 39) distinguishes between *assimilation*, "a process of interpretation and fusion in which persons and groups acquire the memories, sentiments and attitudes of other persons or groups, and by sharing their experience and history are incorporated with them in a common cultural life," and *accommodation*, "the migrating group's forced adjustment to a new social situation." Also see Hullum (1973).

17. Mark 8:36; Luke 9:25.

18. For example, Benson's black-music division was Onyx; Word's black-music division was called Rejoice. Sparrow, Myrrh and Light Records, which became the number-one record company of contemporary gospel music during the 1980s, also started black-music divisions during this time.

19. What I call "the Dorsey-Hawkins-Franklin breakthroughs" represent a recurring cycle intrinsic to the identity, style, and development of gospel. It reveals a socio-historical pattern worth detailing:

    (1) A young, church-based musician or choir director integrates contemporary "secular" musical sounds and sensibilities with the existing standard black sacred musical form.

    (2) The leadership and other conservative elements of the black church resist and reject the innovation, usually highly critical of both the innovator and music itself.

    (3) Sectors of the black church community that are more accepting of charismatic, celebratory worship styles and/or secular audiences welcome the new musical innovation.

    (4) Considerable market demand for this new music propels its commercialization and popularity within mainstream, that is, "white" America.

    (5) The conservative church leadership that once rejected the music becomes accepting of the innovation; later, the church wholly embraces it.

    (6) The musical innovation is marketed to those expanded audiences via traditional and nontraditional venues and mechanisms.

    (7) The innovation becomes a standard or accepted part of black church worship, liturgical practices, and/or culture.

    (8) A generation or two later, the cycle is repeated.

20. Also see Hairston (1995, 1996) and Kentucky Fried Chicken advertisement (1987).

21. For example, *Beauty and the Beast* (Trousdale and Wise 1991), *The Preacher's Wife* (Marshall 1996), *The Fighting Temptations* (Lynn 2003), *Kingdom Come* (McHenry 2001), *The Prince of Egypt* (Chapman, Hincker, and Wells 1998), *Legally Blonde* (Luketic 1001), and *Jimmy Neutron: Boy Genius* (Davis 2001) all used gospel music.

22. This relates closely to the historical development of other aspects of modern black sacred music. Migration of blacks from southern rural communities to northern urban centers from 1900 to the 1930s influenced the way that blacks sang hymns and spirituals; once they established themselves in the North, blacks again changed the way that they sang religiously from the 1930 through the 1960s. As gospel musicologist Bernice Johnson Reagon (1992, 4–5) put it: "New situations fostered new sounds."

23. There is much cross-fertilization between church musicians and secular musicians; often, they are one and the same. In this way, it is not always evident who is borrowing from whom.

24. The Potter's House in Dallas has established Dexterity Records (Bishop T. D. Jakes), World Changers Ministries has formed Arrow Records in Atlanta (Creflo Dollar), Christian Cultural Center in New York has launched CCC Music Group (Dr. A. R. Bernard), New Covenant Christian Center has started Axiom Records in Boston (Bishop Gilbert Thompson), and Greater St. Stephen's Full Gospel Baptist Church owns Delilah Records in New Orleans (Bishop Paul S. Morton). Also see Collins (2003).

25. In this case, the record companies, distributors, publishing houses, concert promoters, and so on, that service the gospel music industry are largely not owned or operated by blacks.

31

Reflections on Praise and Worship from a Biblical Perspective: Background, Definitions, Concepts and Constructions

Rodney A. Teal

Reflections on Praise & Worship from a Biblical Perspective

The hardest part of addressing this complex subject of "praise & worship" is deciding where to begin. In order to get us on the "same page," let us begin with a brief background, where we examine some basic definitions, discuss related concepts, and explore some constructs that will buoy our study...

I. Background: Definitions, Concepts and Constructs

Praise means "to commend; to express approval or admiration; to extol in word or song or deed." It is the way in which one demonstrates, through activity that is readily observable by third parties, one's thankfulness to God. Praise may be "direct" or "indirect."

Direct praise occurs when one commends, expresses approval or admiration, or extols God to God. The Bible says we should do this "continually" (Hebrews 13:15). *Indirect praise* occurs when one commends, expresses approval or admiration, or extols God in the presence of others.

Indirect praise is a by-product of direct praise and may be termed *witness*. Allow me to clarify. Because God is omniscient and omnipresent, we can't praise God without him being aware of it. In other words, there can be no indirect praise, unless there is direct praise. Thus, when we speak of indirect praise, we use the word "indirect" as a descriptor of the word "praise" from the vantage of those ("eavesdroppers") who witness our witness.

Let's explore the concept of witness further. We may witness *intentionally* or *unintentionally*. For example, we may intentionally witness to someone by telling them about God's goodness. This is our responsibility as Christians (The Great Commission, Matthew 28:19). We may also intentionally witness by lifting our hands (or shouting unto the Lord, etc.) in front of—and for the purpose of showing—others that we are grateful to God.

Further, we may give an unintentional witness by our demeanor, our speech, our lifestyle, etc. This "unintentional, indirect praise" is our *walk*. We are, after all, God's ambassadors in all that we do (II Corinthians 5:20). We are charged with the responsibility to invite others to become "reconciled to God." How can we do that effectively when our walk does not demonstrate that have drawn water from the wells of salvation and have done so with joy? (Isaiah 12:3)

How Do We Praise?

In Providential wisdom and for divine purposes, God has ordained that praise be demonstrative. Praise is always visible and/or audible. It must be expressed physically. You may have a thankful heart (which is where praise and worship must begin), but unless you give expression to the thanksgiving in your heart, you have not praised God.

"But," you say, "God knows my heart. All that noise and all those gyrations aren't necessary. It doesn't take all of that. I'm praising God in my own way." Wrong!

God's Word tells us how to praise God. God expects us to follow biblical instruction.

Praise is an offering that is tendered by the "praiser" to God (Psalm 27:6; Amos 5:23). Leviticus 10 reminds us of the danger of rendering an unauthorized offering. God sees it as "strange fire" and will not honor it. Two of Aaron's sons offered "strange fire" to the Lord and paid for it with their lives (Leviticus 10:2). How many spiritual casualties have been suffered in the body of Christ for this same reason?

The Bible is a veritable "praise manual." Here is the top-ten list, with selected (but by no means exhaustive) scriptural references:

1. clapping hands/Psalm 47:1
2. dancing/Exodus 15:20–21; Psalm 30:11; Acts 3:8
3. kneeling/Psalm 95:6
4. lifting hands/Psalm 28:2; Timothy 2:8

5. playing musical instruments/Psalm 150

6. prostration/Revelation 19:4

7. shouting/Psalm 47:1 (also, "Make a joyful noise" can be more literally translated "Shout for joy"; see Psalm 66:1)

8. singing/Book of Psalms

9. standing/Psalm 135:2; Revelation 4:9–11

10. testifying/Psalm 26:7; Psalm 22:22

Any one of these methods can be used to praise God—to publish the thankfulness that is in our heart (e.g., Psalm 66:8). All of these praises have this in common: they require overt action on the part of the one giving praise.

Still not convinced that praise must be visible and/or audible? Remember Jesus' ride into Jerusalem on that first Palm Sunday? The Bible says in Luke 19:37: "the whole multitude of the disciples began to rejoice and praise God with a loud voice for all the mighty works that they had seen." The Bible further relates that the Pharisees got upset about all the commotion. Jesus told them this: ". . . if these should hold their peace, the stones would immediately cry out" (Luke 19:40). As the Psalmist says, we are to make the voice of his praise to be heard (Psalm 66:8).

God rightfully demands praise (Psalm 150). The Bible tells us how to praise God. We are free to choose the method of praise that we will use, but we must choose among the alternatives that God has given. You can't praise God "your own way." And you can't praise God anybody else's way, for that matter. You must praise God God's way.

What Is Worship?

Before continuing, let's make it clear that "worship" eludes precise definition. In truth, "worship" must be experienced. For purposes of our discussion, I have chosen a comprehensive definition that is loosely based on one of a list of definitions posited by Bob Sorge in *Exploring Worship* (1987). I have modified the language in light of my personal experience and Bible study, as well as several sermons that I have heard over the years. I am particularly fond of this definition because it highlights both the sacrificial and the intimately personal nature of the phenomenon we call "worship" and because it clearly demonstrates that Man's purpose is discovered, reclaimed and fulfilled through worship. All this having been said, here is our working definition:

> *Worship*—an act by a redeemed man or woman (the creature) toward God (the Creator) whereby his/her will, intellect and emotions gratefully respond in reverence, honor and devotion to the continuing revelation by God of God's person and will.

This definition highlights several important aspects about the experience we call "worship." Let's look at some of them:

1. Worship is a deliberate act directed to God. We are able to choose to worship or to choose not to do so. The response is ours to make. As God reveals the divine self and the divine will to us, we can choose to acknowledge God or not.

2. Worship is the grateful surrender of "self" (will, intellect and emotions). The "will" directs our actions. The "will" is influenced by the "intellect" (i.e., what we comprehend through cognitive processes) and the "emotions" (i.e., what we feel). Let's make our working definition of "worship" a little less theoretical (see Genesis 3). It was Man's will (as influenced by his/her intellect and emotions) that led to Man's demise in the Garden of Eden. The bottom line is this: Man made the conscious decision (i.e., "willed") to disobey God's command. Man's intellect told him/her that the serpent's reasoning was correct. Man's emotions told him/her that the fruit of the Tree of the Knowledge of Good and Evil was "pleasing to the eye" and "good for food." You might say that Man fell when he/she stopped worshiping God—when Man exalted him/her "self" above God's "Self." Worship simply puts us back where we started—in tune with God, in fellowship with the divine! Through worship, we discover, reclaim and fulfill our divine purpose! Our intellect tells us what we "ought" to do, in the normative sense. But our intellect is limited. We don't know everything. When we surrender our "intellect" in worship, we acknowledge that God is omniscient. An important element of worship is to rely on God's knowledge. Even when God asks us to do things that don't make sense to us, we must be willing to accept the fact that God's thoughts are higher than ours (Isaiah 55:9) and deeper than ours (Psalms 92:5). Our emotions tell us what we "feel like" doing. Most of us are familiar with how unreliable our emotions can be as a barometer for decision-making. What we feel like doing is not necessarily the right thing for us to do. The obverse is true, as well. Finally, we should note that the surrender of will, intellect and emotion, through worship, necessarily includes surrender of the "body" because, ultimately, the body does what we "will" it to do. When we surrender in worship, our bodies do as God instructs, for through worship we put God in the driver's seat.

3. Worship is a response to the "God-hood" of God. In worship, we acknowledge the divine just because God is "The Great 'I Am.'" *Worship* is a complex word composed of the root "worth" (meaning "value") and the suffix "-ship" (meaning "the state of"). In worship we acknowledge "the state of God's value." Through worship, we ascribe worth to God. As we worship, we definitively answer this most personal of questions: How much is God worth to you? As John reminds us in relating the story of the man blind from birth, when we understand *Who* God is, we are compelled to worship (John 9:38). Remember the wise men who came to see the Christ-child? When they found Jesus, they fell down and worshiped him (Matthew 2:11).

4. Worship necessarily involves sacrifice. The first time that the word "worship" appears in the Bible (whether the King James, New International, Revised Standard, or New American Standard translations) is in Genesis 22:5, when Abraham is going to the mountain to sacrifice Isaac. In that verse, Abraham tells his servant to wait, while he and Isaac go to the mountain to "worship." Thus, the concept of "worship" has been inexorably intertwined with the concept of "sacrifice" *ab initio.* There never has been (and there never can be) legitimate worship without sacrifice.

The Relationship Between Worship & Sacrifice

I think it is important that we take this detour through "sacrifice" because this concept is crucial to developing a fuller understanding of praise and worship. Simply defined, *sacrifice* means to surrender that which is valuable to God. There are several principles inherent in the concept of sacrifice that should be addressed in the context of praise and worship:

A. There is no sacrifice, unless that which is offered is given up. Under the Mosaic Law, burnt offerings were burned completely; nothing was left (Leviticus 1).

B. Only that which is valuable to the person making the offering is an acceptable sacrifice from God's perspective. The first sacrifice mentioned in the Bible is found in Genesis 4, in the story of Cain and Abel. Cain and Abel both presented sacrifices to God. God respected Abel and his offering; however, God did not respect Cain or his offering. What was the difference between the two offerings? The answer lies in the difference between verse 3 (Cain offered the unmodified fruit of the ground) and verse 4 (Abel offered the firstlings of his flock)—Abel offered his very best, but Cain just offered what was at hand. And notice, God's reaction to the offering and the "offerer" was the same (Genesis 4:3–5)! How tragic to be "dissed" by the God of the Cosmos! How many of us have missed out on the favor of God because we have offered a paltry sacrifice when it comes to praise and/or worship? God does not respect a sacrifice that is not valuable to the person giving it, and he does not respect the person who offers a cheap sacrifice. What was David's response to Arunah's generous offer of free oxen and a free altar (II Samuel 24)? A sacrifice that isn't valuable to the person doing the offering isn't valuable to God. When God gave instructions on sacrifices under the Mosaic Law, he made it clear that he would accept no less than the very best (e.g., Leviticus 1:3).

C. "Worship" always involves "sacrifice." I mentioned this briefly before, and we will return to this truth in a more in-depth fashion later. The surrender of will, intellect and emotion in worship is, itself, a sacrifice.

Comparing/Contrasting Praise and Worship

Based on the material that we have already covered, we can begin to see similarities and differences between the concepts of "praise" and "worship." Here is a list:

1. Praise may be direct or indirect; worship is always direct. Worship is intensely personal and self-reflective, only and always involving two parties: the giver (you or me) and the object of worship (God).

2. Praise can always be sensed by others; worship may not be so readily identifiable. For example, "fasting" is worship because it involves the surrender of "self." However, "fasting" is neither audible nor visible; thus, it is not praise.

3. Only human and angelic beings—who have will, intellect and emotion—can worship God. The whole of creation offers praise. The psalmist tells us that even nature praises God (Psalm 19:1–5).

4. Generally speaking, praise requires less of us than worship. It is easier to clap my hands than to surrender my "self" (will, intellect, and emotions). Perhaps this is why God seeks worshipers: because they are harder to find (John 4:23).

5. A person who is inhibited in praise will likely be inhibited in worship. Those same inhibitions that hinder us from praising freely, may stand in the way of the surrender of will, intellect and emotions that is essential to worship. If, for example, I am so concerned about what others may think that I cannot stand in praise, how will I ever be able to surrender my "self" in worship?

6. Praise *may* serve as a prelude to worship, but this is not necessarily so. (In a later example, I Kings 17:8–16, we will see that worship may serve as a prelude to praise) A brief digression is in order. . .

   All too often we treat praise as a pregame show, while we wait for worship. As a result, we find ourselves at the benediction, wondering why God didn't show up. However, worship does not always follow praise. In fact, it is possible to worship (through prayer and fasting, for example) without passing through praise. We must be careful not to limit worship to an "afterglow" that follows praise. Properly understood, "worship" is much more than an appendix to praise. Worship is a worthy enterprise all its own. Sometimes, it is possible and desirable to praise God without getting into the "worship mode." While using the "Outer Court (singing)-Inner Court (praise)-Holy of Holies (worship)" paradigm may be helpful in exploring praise and worship in some instances, it can lead to the fictitious belief that [a] worship is superior to praise and/or [b] worship must follow praise.

7. Neither praise nor worship is more important than the other in the life of the Christian. The Word demands that we offer God praise (Psalm 150). God doesn't need our praise. If we are obedient, we will praise God. God wants us to worship (John 4:23). In fact, God is "seeking" worshipers. The Greek word (*zeteo*, pronounced "dzay-TEH-o") that is translated "seek" in John 4:23 is the same as that used in the Parable of the Lost Sheep (Matthew 18:12) and the Parable of the Lost Coin (Luke 15:8). God is on the lookout for worshipers!

8. Praise and worship are both volitional acts. They are voluntary. God does not force them on us; we can decide to praise and/or worship him or not to do so. In Isaiah 61:3, the prophet refers to "praise" as a garment. This tells us that "praise" can be put on and it can be taken off, just like any other garment. We can choose to wear "praise." Even when we don't feel like wearing "praise" we can go to our spiritual wardrobe and pull it out. I have found this to be a true: when I feel least like praising God is really the time that I ought to praise God the most. The prophet Isaiah reminds us that "praise" is a divine remedy for the spirit of heaviness (i.e., depression). In the midst of our lowest-valley experience, we should consciously put on praise. The Enemy knows that the spirit of depression can't stand up to praise. Why? Because God is enthroned in our praise (Psalm 22:3). When we praise God, God comes and sits down in the midst of the praise. When God shows up, everything that is not like God must leave! How do you put on the garment of praise in the midst of your depression? David shows us how in Psalm 103. Read it! Remember Who God is. Magnify him. Your problems will seem insignificant. Worship is volitional, too. Why? Because we must consciously surrender our "self." Worship does not happen accidentally. It is a purposeful act, whereby we acknowledge God's "worthy-ship." You can't surrender your will, your intellect, or your emotions inadvertently.

9. We must be careful not to make two mistakes that frequently occur in the praise & worship arena: [1] artificially creating a "praise box" and a "worship box," then trying to force things into one box or the other and [2] being so concerned about getting to the worship "feeling" that we do not worship God. I call this second phenomenon "worshiping worship" because our concern is not so much with God as it is with how we feel. We want a cheap spiritual "high," rather than God's presence.

10. Finally, we should note that none of these expressions (praise, worship, praise & worship) are *feelings*; rather, they are *acts*. Certainly these acts must be rooted in and flow from the right "attitude"; in other words, thankfulness (Psalm 100:4). However, the way you feel when you praise and/or worship God is unimportant. "Praise" and "worship" are simple expressions. If you lift your hands to God, you have praised God. If you acknowledge God's worth, you have worshiped God. It's as simple as that. "Goosebumps do not praise or worship make." Too often we come to church looking for a "feeling" and leave feeling empty. It's not that God's presence wasn't in the building, and it's not that God did not want to bless us. Rather, it's that we were not in the posture to receive the blessing that God had for us. God had a Word for us, but we didn't hear it. We were too busy looking for a "feeling." God had a healing for us, but we couldn't receive it. We were too busy looking for a "feeling." Had we stopped "feeling" and started "acting we would have been postured to receive God's blessing. But we were too busy "feeling."

So, why talk about "praise" and "worship" as separate entities? Because, even though the nuances of difference between the two are shades of gray, a clearer understanding of each of the expressions helps one better understand the other.

It is interesting to note that there are some people (and some churches) that have a wonderfully full understanding of "praise," but a very skewed concept of "worship." They'll "dance, dance, dance, dance, dance, dance, dance, all night," but they don't understand (or perhaps don't want to be inconvenienced by) the surrender of self that it takes to "worship." (You know: shout all service long and put $1 in the offering plate.) "Praisers" (and "praising churches") who don't grasp the concept of worship are like those people who are in love, but can't find it in themselves to make the surrender (i.e., commitment) necessary for marriage. How much more full would the expression of praise (e.g., the lifting of hands, the dance) be if it were directed by God, not because the lifter/dancer, etc., who was lifting/dancing, etc., had chosen to do so, but rather s/he had surrendered his/her "self" in worship?

On the other side of the coin, there are some people (and some churches) that are great worshipers, but poor praisers. We usually call those people "dry" and refer to the churches that they usually attend "dead" because we don't usually see or hear any praise. Yet, in some instances, those people (and their churches) know how to worship. They regularly surrender their will, intellect and emotion—often through giving liberally. How much more meaningful would their worship be if it were fueled by the passion of praise?

Perhaps it may be helpful to use "love & marriage" as an analogy to help us better understand the relationship between "praise" and "worship." In both couplets, it is possible to do one without doing the other, but in concert, the whole is greater than the sum of the parts. Love is given fuller expression in marriage, and marriage is made more meaningful because of the passion of love. Similarly, praise is given fuller expression in worship, and worship is made more meaningful because of the passion of praise.

Thus, the phrase "praise & worship" is not completely redundant. The differences between "praise" and "worship" are slight and for the most part hypothetical and academic. It is important to remember that neither is superior to the other and both are ordained of God. From this point, I will try to be consistent in using the phrase *praise & worship*, knowing that it is the sum of these "parts" that makes the whole of the "praise & worship" experience we are studying.

II. Corporate Praise & Worship

Thus far in our study, our primary focus has been on individual praise & worship, and, quite truthfully, individual praise & worship is important to effective corporate praise & worship. In fact, I believe it is safe to say that, particularly for praise & worship leaders (including "praise team members"), individual praise & worship is essential to effective corporate praise & worship: How can you lead others to a place you have never been? We will return to a more detailed study of individual praise & worship, but for a moment, let's turn to corporate praise & worship. . .

The "Cloud Experience": Paradigm & Pitfall

When looking for models of corporate praise & worship, we often focus on the chronicler's account of the dedication of Solomon's Temple (II Chronicles 5:12–14). While that passage is a powerful account of what can happen when the people of God come together "as one" in praise & worship, that account is often a fountain of frustration for the New Testament church because we think that unless we have the "cloud experience" every Sunday, we have not worshiped successfully.

A proper, contextual understanding of II Chronicles 5 can help [a] ease our anxiety over trying to recreate the cloud experience *and* [b] foster the "atmospheric conditions" conducive to the formation of the cloud. In worship, God is in the driver's seat and, no matter what happens, we flow right along with the divine, instead of trying to direct the course of worship.

In order to better understand II Chronicles 5:1–14, we must view the Dedication of the Temple in context. Solomon had finished building the Temple, and the Ark was being brought in and set in place. Prior to this time, God's presence resided in the Tent of Meeting. When God manifested the divine presence there, God did so as a cloud, or as a pillar of fire at night (Exodus 40:34;

Numbers 9:15; Deuteronomy 31:15). A review of the previously cited scriptures makes it clear that the manifestation was not an everyday occurrence. When God did show up as the cloud, it may have lasted for days, or months at a time, or even for a year (Numbers 9:21). But it is clear that the cloud was not permanent. Moreover, God's presence was always in the Tent (because the Ark of the Covenant was there); however, the cloud was an extraordinary manifestation visible to all (i.e., not just to the high priest on the Day of Atonement) for so long as the cloud remained.

When we consider the number of times that the cloud was present in the Tent and the Temple (vis-à-vis the number of worship services held in the Tent and the Temple), it becomes clear that it is unrealistic to expect the "cloud experience" every time the church doors swing open. (It is interesting to note what Moses recorded in Numbers 9:17–22. We should be mindful that when we *do* have that cloud experience, God may be telling the church, "Hold it. I need to give you some instructions for the journey." But I digress...)

The cloud experience was, and is, relatively rare. To expect it every Sunday is unrealistic and, I submit, is a trick of the Enemy designed to divert our focus from the essence of worship: surrender of self. The Enemy would have us searching for a cloud, rather than surrendering our will, intellect and emotions in reverence to God.

One more point to put the cloud experience in context: As it is related in II Chronicles 5, the cloud was a special Sabbath dispensation. God's presence in the cloud on the day that the Temple was dedicated was an assurance to Israel that God would dwell in the Temple just as God had dwelt in the Tent (cf. Exodus 40:34; Number 9:15; II Chronicles 5:13–14). Sometimes when the Lord shows up in an unusual way during a worship service, God is reminding us that the divine presence is with us at that time just as in times past.

All of this is not to say we should not expect the cloud experience and should not savor it when it occurs, but, whether God manifests as the cloud in our service or not, God demands praise and seeks worship. We are to offer them.

Before we leave our study of II Chronicles 5, take note of the "when" factor in the passage: God's presence filled the Temple *when* the singers and musicians (the musical Levites) lifted up praises unto God by singing and playing "as one." The importance of "praise" cannot be understated. If God decides to show up in an unusual way, God will do so in the midst of praise (Psalm 22:3; cf. II Chronicles 20). Let there be praise!

Just praise God, and let God take care of filling the temple, if that is the divine will. Often, instead of praising/worshiping God, we praise/worship a "feeling"—the feeling we had three Sundays ago when "the spirit was high." Don't worship "worship." Worship God! The truth of the matter is that God manifests the divine presence in accordance with the divine will.

It is worth repeating: Praise & Worship is not a feeling; it is an act. Do your part; let God take care of the manifestation.

While we are on the subject of God's presence in the Temple, let us take a moment for internal reflection. Why? Because the presence of God, in the person of the Holy Spirit, now resides within each believer. The Bible makes it clear that the (individual) believer is the temple of the Holy Spirit (I Corinthians 6:19).

Let's back up, before we move forward: What happened when the Temple was filled with the cloud in II Chronicles 5? Right, the priests could not continue to minister. Have you ever been so "full" that you couldn't finish that song you were singing? You just had to stop playing the "shouting music" and dance yourself? That is what happens when his cloud fills your temple!

Read I Peter 2:9. Read it again. Not only are you a temple, you are a priest! God can fill your temple at any time and while you are in any place. You don't have to wait until Sunday morning service. You can have a cloud experience in the grocery store. When you choose to think of the goodness of God (how the Lord has blessed you, made a way for you, kept you), when you surrender your "self" to God, you become a priest worshiping in your own temple.

On Sunday morning, you are a temple with a priest coming to a temple with a priest! Even when you are in the midst of a worship service with other saints, whether the cloud is manifested in the service or not, the cloud can fill your temple. You don't have to wait for the church to get "pumped up." You don't need permission from Brother Hammond or Sister Leslie to offer up praise & worship in your temple!

It is worth reemphasizing, however, that whether or not you have a cloud experience in your own temple is God's sovereign decision. God may not move you that way every time. Don't get hooked on the "feeling," get hooked on the "act." God is not seeking the "feeler," he is seeking the "act-er" (John 4:23).

Singing Soldiers: The Battle Is Not Yours

Another favorite reference for corporate praise & worship is found in II Chronicles 20, where King Jehosaphat sends the singers out to the battlefield, ahead of the soldiers. Here's the passage in a nutshell: The kingdom of Judah ("Judah" means "praise") was facing three enemies. Jehosaphat knew that Judah was outnumbered and would be decimated unless God intervened. Jehosaphat called for fasting, prayer and praise. As the people praised God, one of the singers, Jahaziel, was moved by the spirit of God to prophesy that God would fight the battle on behalf of Judah and that all Judah had to do was to "stand still and see the salvation of the Lord." Trusting this prophetic word, Jehosaphat sent the praise team toward the battlefield in front of the army. As the praise team began to praise & worship, the Lord caused the enemies to destroy each other. Judah won the battle through praise & worship, without drawing a weapon. God "dropped the bomb" on the enemy, while Judah was doing what it had been called to do—praise and worship God.

Judah's praise is obvious from the text: they sang and shouted unto the Lord. But what was their worship? Remember our working definition of "worship"?

Imagine you are part of Judah's praise team, ordered by King Jehosaphat to head toward the battlefield, in *front* of the army. Think of the surrender of self (will, intellect and emotions) that it took to follow those orders. No sane person wants to be on the front lines of a battle; every intelligent person is aware of the danger of being on the front line; no sensible person "feels" like being on the front line. Yet that is exactly what these people did, and they did so without weapons and without armor.

The Word makes it clear that praise & worship is a weapon in the arsenal of the people of God. When the people praised God in II Chronicles 20, God moved on their behalf against the enemies. This brings us to the popular question: Why do we need praise leaders and teams in our churches? Answer: The same reason that Jehosaphat appointed them in II Chronicles 20: corporate praise & worship is a weapon to be used in fighting our enemies. Those fighting the battle must be led by skilled warriors.

The "praise team" leads the people in praise & worship; that's all. In some churches the deacons fulfill this role; in others there is a song leader. It's not so much what you call the people who lead praise & worship. It's just important that there be an anointed, sanctified leader. When David created the music ministry, he set certain Levites aside for this specific purpose. All the Levites were to lead the praise, but the musical Levites were specifically called to lead it through singing and playing musical instruments (II Chronicles 8:14; I Chronicles 15:16).

Returning to the *feeling v. acting* motif, notice that the chronicler does not talk about how the praise team "felt" as they went out to face the vast army without conventional weapons or armor, but he does tell us how they "acted."

Praising Prisoners: Morning at Midnight

What does the New Testament say about praise & worship? Glad you asked! Let's look at Acts 16. Paul and Silas "prayed and sang praises unto God" in jail. They had been jailed by the enemies of the church. In the middle of the jailhouse, they started praise & worship. Look what happened: Not only did their praise and worship free them, it freed those around them! Moreover, their praise and worship—remember our definition of "witness"—inspired a former enemy to accept Christ. This enemy even bandaged the wounds that he had inflicted upon Paul and Silas, took them home, and fed them. How's that for praise & worship results?!

Paul and Silas didn't call for a praise team. They were the praise team. Does the Enemy have you in chains? Do you want to break them? Do you want to be delivered from the Enemy? Learn to praise God at our midnight!

The Rev. Dr. Carolyn Showell preaches a life-changing sermon wherein she unveils the Jewish tradition of crying to God during the night watches. In biblical times, the night was divided into three watches. Dr. Showell explains that Psalm 30:5 ("joy comes in the morning") is a reflection of the Jewish custom, in which the people lamented their situations during the first watch, read the Word of God during the second watch, and rejoiced over the promises found in the Word of God during the third watch. She goes on to relate that the people became so enraptured in their joyous praise (which began during the third watch) that they were still praising God when the sun rose. Thus joy—their praise—came with the morning! Practical application: "morning" begins when we, standing on the promises of God, offer praise. No matter what time of day, no matter what the situation, morning is just a praise away. Paul and Silas knew this. We should remember it, too.

Again, it is worth noting that the Bible doesn't discuss how Paul and Silas felt while engaged in praise & worship. (You can imagine how they felt: beaten, thrown in jail. . . but that is not the point.) They offered sacrificial praise & worship and God responded. Again, "praise & worship" is *not* a feeling; it is an act.

More Than a Song: Praying for Peter

For more New Testament praise & worship, read Acts 12. Peter was thrown in jail. The church called a prayer lock-in. The Bible doesn't mention anything about a song being sung, but it does talk about worship. This time worship took the form of prayer. (Study check: Did you catch the worship through fasting in II Chronicles 20?) The prayer in Acts 12 was an "unceasing" prayer. Talk about a grateful surrender of the will, intellect and emotions. . . unceasing prayer on the behalf of a jailed brother!

Now this may be disappointing to those of you who believe that the success or failure of the worship experience is inextricably tied to your vocal ability or your talent on an instrument: the harsh truth of the matter is that the use of your talent is not a necessary prerequisite for worship. More important is the spirit in which the offering is made. Most of us have seen a "rag-tag" looking group of singers with mediocre ability "wreck" a church by offering honest, sincere praise to God. I'll say it again: "praise & worship" is *not* an enterprise based on how we *feel*; praise and/or worship is/are, purely and simply, *acts*.

In Acts 12, the church was engaged in worship. And they weren't getting together in a church building either. The church—the Body of Believers—was meeting at Mary's house. The individual believers surrendered their (individual) "self" to God—will, intellect and emotions—and allowed the divine presence to fill their individual temples, so that Mary's house was full of filled "temples." As they worshiped, God sent an angel to free Peter. Let's stay with this thought for a moment. Do you know someone who is saved, yet bound by the enemy? What kind of miracles would God do on behalf of bound Christians if we brought filled "temples" to the house of worship?

We are talking about praise & worship. Not just about singing or playing an instrument; we are talking about the effect of individuals surrendering "self" to God in worship. In Acts 12 it was worship in prayer, but it was worship, nonetheless.

Section Six

Hip Hop and/
in the Church

32
Religion and Rap Music: An Analysis of Black Church Usage

Sandra L. Barnes

Gospel rap is becoming an increasingly popular musical form and a method to evangelize to younger audiences. However, to some, its secular roots make this expression inappropriate for the Christian arena. Given their continued efforts to attract young blacks in general and males in particular; some black churches are including gospel rap in their musical repertoire. This project examines black Church usage of gospel rap music and indicators that explain its inclusion. Clergy, church, and member profiles Factor 2000 Project data for seven denominations. Findings suggest the importance of denomination and church environment in engendering use of gospel rap music. Results also show a direct relationship between increases in new members and use of gospel rap. Implications for religion, popular culture, and race in general, as well as for black Church evangelism in particular, are provided.

The contemporary black Church is challenged to provide diverse religious experiences that resonate with varied backgrounds, ages, and classes, and to strengthen evangelical efforts among younger persons (Cook 2000; Lincoln and Mamiya 1990; West 1993). Gospel rap music may represent a potential mechanism to achieve these ends.

Although studies have considered the history of secular rap music and its influence in shaping popular culture (Dent 1983; Henderson 1996; Kopana 2002; Powell 1991), fewer studies have empirically assessed its spiritual counterpart in the black religious experience. To my knowledge, no scholar has examined gospel rap music usage and its implications in the black Church[1] tradition based on a national sample. This study seeks to address this research limitation by examining the inclusion of gospel rap music during black Church Sunday services, and the demographic and religious indicators that potentially explain its usage, based on a sample of 1,863 black churches across seven denominations. This endeavor informs current research by: (1) empirically studying this musical expression based on a nationally selected sample; (2) identifying possible denominational differences; and (3) determining whether usage is influenced by church environments considered more prophetic or priestly in nature, or by other factors such as clergy or church profile. The study is also important given increased competition among black churches for congregants (Ellison and Sherkat 1995; Sherkat and Ellison 1991); disillusionment with Christianity among some black youth, especially males (West 1993); and the changing spiritual needs in the black community (Lincoln and Mamiya 1990), because it considers contemporary efforts to respond to religious heterogeneity and the role of popular culture in informing and influencing the definition of authentic Christian worship (Howard and Streck 1999). Lastly, findings may more broadly advance the literature regarding contemporary correlates between religion, race, and popular culture outside the black experience.

The Dialectic Model of the Black Church

Although the black Church has historically met temporal needs in the black community and continues to do so today (Barnes 2004, 2005; Du Bois 1903), its primary purposes are grounded in religious/spiritual dictates and include creating a worship environment considered more germane to the black experience (Billingsley 1999; Frazier 1964; Lincoln and Mamiya 1990; West 1982; Wilmore 1994, 1995). Although studies illustrate collective efforts among black churches, like any religious body, to respond to pressing needs (Morris 1984), issues that are considered contradictory to the church's sacredness or that are understood from varied theological perspectives can result in debate, conflict, and division (Barnes 2006; Fears 2004; Grant 1989; Higginbotham 1993; Konieczny and Chaves 2000; Paulson 2004; Reeves 2004; Townsend-Gilkes 2001). Such debates are generally precipitated by differences in views about the church's appropriate stance. Per Lincoln and Mamiya (1990), priestly and prophetic functions represent a common dialectic in the black Church tradition that guides congregational stance.

Priestly and Prophetic Functions

According to Lincoln and Mamiya (1990), "priestly functions involve only those activities concerned with worship and maintaining the spiritual life of members" (12). Black churches considered to be more priestly in nature provide religious symbols, worship, and activities focused on strengthening relationships with the Deity, anticipation of a more promising afterlife, and survival in an often unfriendly society. Based on this function, scripture, songs, and church events are used to strengthen congregants to live lives distinguishable from secular dictates. A priestly function is not typically associated with social or community action; instead, adherents are encouraged to establish *personal* religious traits as suggested in scripture. Although recent studies correlate certain priestly dictates with collective action (Barnes 2004; Cavendish 2001), they are more usually associated with personal introspection and growth. Priestly characteristics include scriptural study as well as personal reflection and meditation, the importance of spiritual growth, religious hygiene suggested by the model of Christ as an exemplar of commitment to the Deity, and sponsoring activities that encourage religious learning (Lincoln and Mamiya 1990; Wilmore 1994).

In contrast, the prophetic black Church is more focused on societal problems and considers Christianity a mechanism for social, economic, and political liberation. Lincoln and Mamiya state that "prophetic functions refer to involvement in political concerns and activities in the wider community. . . priestly churches are bastions of survival and prophetic churches are networks of liberation" (1990: 12). For such congregations, religion is appropriated to address societal ills. Prophetic churches challenge the status quo and often use temporal standards to determine religious conviction. Such churches tend to be more intentional and proactive and to address social problems in practical ways. Research has linked a prophetic function to activism, community involvement, the introduction of black liberation theology, and use of the pulpit as a political platform (Calhoun-Brown 1999; Cone 1995; Harris 1987; Morris 1984; Taylor 1994). A prophetic stance often suggests that one's personal religious conversion should be questioned if it is not accompanied by the desire and willingness to mobilize collectively to combat social concerns (Cavendish 2001; Day 2001; Lincoln and Mamiya 1990; Wilmore 1994). This study considers the effects of priestly and/ or prophetic functions on gospel rap music usage during black Church worship services.

Contemporary Christian Music

The topic of gospel rap music is informed by the large literature on Contemporary Christian Music (henceforth referred to as CCM). A review of the history, challenges, and milestones of CCM provides a context to better understand one of its genres—gospel rap. CCM is said to have emerged during the turbulent 1960s, as Christians, especially the young, attempted to make sense of societal changes while older adults strove to maintain social control and churches strained to respond to a growing Rock and Roll sentiment (Thompson 2000). According to Howard and Streck (1999), CCM is defined by the faith experience of its artists, lyrics that reflect Christian themes, and a collective of corporations, ideas, and audiences grounded in a shared, yet diverse, understanding of the gospel message. The CCM industry, which sells about fifty million albums annually, has its origins in a fusion of Rock and Roll music and evangelical Protestantism and exerts a special attraction for Christian adolescents (Peacock 2004). Scholars differ in their accounts of its origins, but agree that the music form has evolved over time and contains elements of pop, Rock and Roll, country, folk, black gospel, white gospel, Rhythm & Blues, and jazz music (Cusic 1990; Howard and Streck 1999). Thus this multi-genre music form developed as a result of a complex series of religious, political, social, and cultural changes. According to Peacock, CCM artists "know and understand that they have been set apart to do a unique work specific to their musical calling" (2004: 6).

Howard and Streck (1999) describe three CCM camps: separational, integrational, and transformational. Separationalists consider the music a form of ministry and are willing to incorporate elements from secular culture to make the message most relevant. Thus the attire, mannerisms, and sound of such artists are not dramatically different from their secular counterparts. For this group, song lyrics became the distinguishing factor. According to Separational proponents, CCM is important for evangelism (i.e., convincing non-believers to accept Christ), for worship facilitation (i.e., enabling adherents to communicate with the Deity), and for exhortation (i.e., encouraging believers in their daily lives). Because many listeners are already Christian, this three-part rationale also serves to justify the existence of CCM (Cusic 1990; Peacock 2004). Themes that exhort believers toward triumphant spiritual war fare from groups such as Petra, Gideon's Army ("Warriors of Love"), and more recently, Carmen and gospel gangsta-rapper T-Bone ("The Hoodlum's Testimony") resonate with younger audiences.

In contrast, Integrational proponents believe CCM represents a wholesome alternative to pop music. Often accused of compromising Christian dictates to "crossover," Integrationalists disagree with the Separationalist stance and believe their music reflects a Christian worldview, despite the absence of "Jesus-specific" lyrics. They contend that their music proselytizes based on the universal appeal of its lyrics. For them, music should be judged based on onto logical rather than utilitarian standards. Artists Amy Grant, Jars of Clay, and Michael W. Smith have experienced mainstream acclaim as members of this camp. Lastly, Transformational CCM advocates such as the late Mark Heard and Charlie Peacock believe that Christian music is valuable based on its artistic dimensions. And as an art form, it can bring about liberation and transcendence.

Although popular, especially among youth culture, CCM has had (and continues to have) its share of detractors. Churches as well as members of the music industry have considered it immoral, often referring to it as "devil's music." Other critiques considered CCM inferior as compared to hymns and anthems—with its banal lyrics and mediocre attempts to emulate mainstream popular music (Howard and Streck 1999). Still others were suspicious of its crossover appeal (Cusic 1990). The vilification of Christian rock by ministers and conservative distributors, and its simultaneous acceptance by a growing underground fan base in the late 1970s, echoed the societal response to CCM in general (Thompson 2000). Howard and Streck provide the following summary of CCM and reference gospel rap:

> CCM offers evangelical Christians who cannot identify with that they see on MTV their own set of alter egos. With its angelic waifs, strutting arena rockers, choreographed girl groups, guitar-strumming folkies, flannel-encased grunge acts, posturing rappers, and wordy singer-songwriters, CCM provides the evangelical audience with the same ethereal

voices, the same driving guitars, and the same chunky rhythms that can be found anywhere on the radio dial—but with one important difference: rather than challenging predominant evangelical values, this music affirms it. (1999: 5)

CCM's history is also connected to other artists, events, and organizations. It includes artists such as Thomas Dorsey, Larry Norman, Mahalia Jackson, Randy Stonehill, Keith Green, Sam Cooke, Sandy Patti, and MercyMe. This music form was shaped during the Jesus Movement of the 60s and 70s with its emphasis on the rapture, creative worship, youth evangel ism through music, and personal renewal. Lastly, denominations such as Baptists and various Holiness traditions helped usher in CCM (Cusic 1990; Peacock 2004). The impetus, challenges, and outcomes of CCM provide the context to better understand the emergence of gospel rap music.

Rap Music and the Black Religious Experience

Christian hip hop or holy hip hop, originally called gospel rap, is a derivative of hip hop music that includes Christian/biblical themes to convey one's faith experience. Although this music form is gaining popularity, especially among younger audiences, it has generally had limited appeal. Just as some Christians have questioned its religious or spiritual authenticity, secular rap enthusiasts have questioned its cultural authenticity. Artists such as Stephen Wiley, Sons of Jacob, GRITS, Verbs, Sev Statik, KJ-52, 2Five, R-Swift, J. Johnson, Redeemed Thought, and shia linne are popular members of this musical genre. Gospel rap songwriters and singers are from varied backgrounds and use diverse musical instrumentation, but they generally develop music to express their beliefs and to evangelize. Although gospel rap usage became more popular in the 1990s, for some, its history can be traced to CCM and secular hip hop culture and rap music (Thompson 2000) and reflects key dimensions of Howard and Streck's (1999) Separational CCM. For others, rap music in its variations can be traced to Africa and early African American music forms such as gospel and jazz (Jackson 1995; Maultsby 1995; Smitherman 1977).

According to Kopano (2002), rap music in general is an extension of the black rhetorical tradition and is a form of cultural resistance. The author provides a socio-historical examination of the music form that links it to African music and black expressions found in spirituals, blues, gospel, jazz, and Rhythm and Blues. Scholars contend that rap music emerges from the experiences of oppressed people, provides a commentary of their daily lives, and attempts to combat disenfranchisement, marginalization, and hegemony to create a black aesthetic that can be both personally and politically empowering (Henderson 1996; Powell 1991; Rose 1991; Smitherman 1977). Kopano notes that "today, rap stands as an international musical and cultural force that has redefined American and international music and culture" (2002: 211). Rap music has also been correlated with the black oral tradition and the ability of individuals to use music to determine and articulate their own identity and comment on social conditions (Dyson 1993, 1996). Other writers reference the emergence of gospel gangsta rappers such as DC Talk from the Christian rock tradition. Thompson writes:

> While fellow Christian artists were diluting their spiritual content so as not to offend mainstream ears, DC Talk decided to call the album *Jesus Freak*. Its title cut was a brazen statement of faith. (2000: 197)

Although often more marginalized than other forms of alternative music, artists such as Pete McSweet, PID (Preachers in Disguise), D-Boy, SFC (Soldiers for Christ) and Gospel Gangstaz created, "music to reach the young people" (Thompson 2000: 219). Secular rap music is often critiqued for being misogynistic, stereotypical, and hegemonic in its portrayal of blacks; scholars challenge both artists to consider their thematic choices and the larger society to consider how systemic forces influence the lived experiences being portrayed (Dyson 1993, 1996; Morgan 1995). Although Christian rappers attempt to create music based in scripture and without such negative themes (LeBlanc 2001), detractors question its basis in a secular form they often consider problematic, blasphemous, and counter to biblical tenets. Although few academic studies examine gospel rap directly, it has been the subject of numerous mainstream articles that focus on its proponents, appeal, and evangelical efforts and effects.

Several secular rappers have transitioned into the Christian hip hop arena.[2] Rapper "Kurtis Blow" is now a minister of the Hip Hop Church in Harlem that he describes as follows: "it's like a traditional church service; we have a processional, we have scripture readings, responsive reading, sermons, altar calls, offerings, benediction. . . and a whole lot of gospel rap" (Ballard and Stewart 2006: 30). He suggests a sacred element in the music form; "I've always noticed there is spirituality in hip hop" (2006: 31). Similarly, the former M. C. Hammer now raps as a minister (Jet 1998) and Run DMC and T-Bone focus their attention on gospel rap, videos, and outlets comparable to their secular counterparts (Collier 2006; LeBlanc 2001; Simmons, McDaniels, and Linden 1993). Other rappers such as Chris Martin, formerly "Play" of the rap duo "Kid-N-Play," have crossed over to the gospel genre. Reverend Phil Jackson, author of the book, *The Hip Hop Church*, and pastor of "Tha House" congregation and Danny Wilson, chairman and CEO of holyhiphop.com, position the hip hop culture in general and gospel rap in particular as godly mediums with mass appeal. The latter entrepreneur contends, ". . . the ministry of Jesus Christ is first and the music is second" (Ballard and Stewart 2006: 32). For these artists, rap music represents a tool to present the gospel message to a contemporary audience (Thompson 2000).

Quite possibly the black artist most noted for his fusion of gospel, rap, and soul, Kirk Franklin has weathered initial critiques from black religious leaders for his music. However, Franklin's cross-over appeal and his ability to attract young Christians appear to have placated some detractors and illustrate the ability of non-traditional worship forms to resonate with adherents (Ehrlich 1997; Morthland 1997) and teach them biblical tenets needed to engender godly living (Simmons, McDaniels, and Linden 1993). According to one artist:

> Holy hip hop is a tool to help our youth understand the language of Jesus Christ, who used parables to break down the gospels for people to understand. Holy hip hop is the language of this generation. . . to filter the gospel in a form of parable to music. Isaiah said God was going to do a new thing. . . the people preaching aren't the messengers your parents listened to, the message—living a positive life, being a man for God or a virtuous woman—is the same. (Ballard and Stewart 2006: 32)

These gospel rap artists use this music medium to evangelize to young audiences who are interested in both Christianity and the hip hop culture and contend that gospel rap is a viable, valid, and effective Christian expression on par with spirituals, gospels, and hymns. Furthermore, they challenge detractors who suggest that the Deity cannot employ a myriad of methods to reach potential adherents (Ballard and Stewart 2006; Ehrlich 1997; LeBlanc 2001; Morthland 1997; Simmons, McDaniels, and Linden 1993). Ironically, similar controversy followed the emergence of CCM (Howard and Streck 1999).

Kopano notes that "rap music was created primarily as means for young African Americans (predominately males) to speak their minds" (2002: 213). This author's assessments regarding the scope and purpose of rap music can possibly inform our understanding of its manifestation in some Christian churches. His observations also suggest the potential for gospel rap to transform dimensions of the black Church worship experience, to speak to the experiences of impoverished and male black youth, and to expand its proselytizing efforts. Gospel rap music in the black Church tradition may reflect new appropriations of black Church culture (Barnes 2006) for contemporary times and contemporary challenges. Henderson suggests that secular rap music that is nationalistic in origin contains, "political, cultural, psychic, and economic elements" (1996: 312) that are potentially transformative in nature. If secular rap music has such powerful potential, it would also stand to reason that gospel rap music could have similar potential as well as transformative *religious* elements.

Research Relationships

In many ways, the emergence of gospel rap parallels the growth of CCM in general. Like CCM, gospel rap is a response to the constraints of existing music forms, provides voice to an ambivalent, young Christian sub-group, has supporters and detractors, has been questioned based on issues of validity, and reflects influences of religion and popular culture. And just as it did when Christian rock, Christian pop, gospel, and CCM in general were introduced, the "sacred vs. secular" debate exists when gospel rap is considered (Cusic 1990; Howard and Streck 1999; Peacock 2004; Thompson 2000). Historically, proponents of black gospel were divided into two camps—traditional and contemporary. The former was influenced by church choir music, blues, and traditional R&B, while the latter was shaped by modern R&B, Motown, jazz, and disco (Cusic 1990). For some traditionalists, change was unnecessary and spiritually dangerous—they saw no need to alter an accepted music form. Contemporary supporters considered the new music progressive. Similar sentiments parallel the priestly verses prophetic debate where the former function tends to maintain the status quo and the latter is associated with change (Lincoln and Mamiya 1990).

Because a more prophetic function challenges the status quo and emphasizes social justice issues, it, like some forms of rap music, can provide a response to negative images and beliefs about blacks and call for redress (Henderson 1996; Kopano 2002). Thus a prophetic stance would be expected to fuel gospel rap usage. In contrast, churches that espouse a priestly stance would be expected to be somewhat reticent about gospel rap music. However, priestly dictates can be collectively transformative and, like certain rap lyrics, can instruct and provide strategies to "survive" in an uncaring world (Barnes 2004; Cavendish 2001). Thus the priestly function may also foster use of this often controversial music form. History shows that current elements of black Church culture such as gospel music were originally considered vulgar (Costen 1993; Cusic 1990) but are now part of the majority of worship services (Lincoln and Mamiya 1990). A similar response may be evident for gospel rap usage.

Studies also posit that the prevailing attitudes and programs sponsored by most black congregations are correlated with the following: church stance, ideology, or theology; pas tor's views and educational level; membership size and profile; and church's financial status (Barnes 2004; Billingsley 1999; Cavendish 2001; McRoberts 1999; Wilmore 1994). These factors may also influence usage of gospel rap music. Furthermore, LeBlanc (2001) suggests a direct relationship between contemporary music usage and church attendance a finding that will inform an analysis of church profiles here. Denominational differences in response to CCM were also evident—Baptist, Pentecostal, and Holiness followers were often more accepting of CCM (Cusic 1990; Peacock 2004). Similarly, members of these same traditions more readily embraced gospel music (Costen 1993). Thus denominational differences are predicted here. Based on the importance of denominational support in successfully championing social action and controversial causes among blacks (Lincoln and Mamiya 1990), it is important to consider their possible influence in the proliferation of gospel rap music. As noted earlier, very few academic studies have been performed on this subject. Given the popularity of rap music and the inroads being made by gospel rap, this is an important area of inquiry with potentially broad implications for religion and popular culture. Rather than debate the origins or merits of gospel rap music, the objective here is to empirically consider denominational usage patterns as well as priestly, prophetic, and other indicators and their *relative influence* on inclusion of this often-controversial music form.

Research Question

Studies suggest that the black Church has endeavored to meet needs in the black community according to biblical dictates; contemporary challenges to attract younger blacks are also apparent (Billingsley 1999; Lincoln and Mamiya 1990). I examine whether, after controlling for the influence of denomination and church and clergy profile, congregations with more priestly characteristics will be more or less likely to use gospel rap music than churches considered more prophetic in nature (Billingsley 1992, 1999; Lincoln and Mamiya 1990; Marx 1971; Morris 1984; Taylor 1994; Wilmore 1994).

Data and Methodology

The study is based on a national secondary database of black churches from the Faith Factor 2000 Project, a joint venture between the Lilly Foundation and the Interdenominational Theological Center (ITC) in Atlanta, Georgia instituted to provide a profile of such churches in the United States. The data collection process was spearheaded by the ITC with assistance from the Gallup Foundation. A total of 1,863 black churches from the following five black denominations were included; Baptist [502 churches], Church of God in Christ (COGIC) [503], Christian Methodist Episcopal (CME) [295], African Methodist Episcopal (AME) [257], and African Methodist Episcopal Zion (AMEZ) [110]. Predominately black churches from the historically white United Methodist and Presbyterian denominations—United Methodist (UM) [95] and black Presbyterian [101]—were also included, for a total of seven denominations.

Identifying the sampling frame and selecting the sample occurred in several phases. First, lists of all the congregations in the AME, AMEZ, CME, COGIC, UM, and Presbyterian denominations were provided by denominational heads or deans from the various schools at the ITC. The decentralized nature of the Baptist tradition precluded such a list. In order to develop the sampling frame for Baptists, ITC solicited information from Tri-Media, an organization that retains lists of all churches nationwide that purchase Sunday school material and supplies. Tri-Media data were used to identify the population of Baptist congregations affiliated with the three largest historically black Baptist denominations.[3] Unlike the six other denominations, the sampling frame for Baptist churches is an approximation with several clear limitations,[4] but it represents a systematic attempt to identify such churches given a lack of national hierarchy. After the seven lists were compiled, Gallup selected a random sample from each denomination to meet the desired sub-sample sizes.[5]

Telephone surveys of clergy and senior lay leaders were conducted by Gallup from February 22, 2000 through May 11, 2000. Each interview averaged approximately 16 minutes in length and 37 questions were posed. The church leaders were asked to provide aggregate demographic data on their churches as well as answering a variety of attitudinal and behavioral questions on topics such as worship and identity, missions, church demographics and financial health, spirituality, leadership and organizational dynamics, church climate, and community involvement.[6] Initial screening was used to gain cooperation from the pastor and to confirm denomination. If the pastor was unavailable, a senior lay leader or assistant pastor was interviewed. Of the 1,863 interviews, 77% (1,482) were conducted with pastors and 23% (381) were conducted with an assistant pastor or senior lay leader. Senior staff was used because they would be expected to be the most knowledgeable about their respective churches.[7]

Dependent and Independent Variables

In order to determine the extent of gospel rap music usage, I examine responses to the following question; "During your congregation's regular worship services, how often is rap music included as part of the service?" For each option, values of "0" were coded to represent "never" and "1" corresponds to "all else." There are strengths as well as limitations of use of a single-item question. Although the question cannot assess the specific ways in which gospel rap music is included (i.e., as a standard part of the liturgy or once monthly during "Youth Sunday"), its strength lies in its ability to clearly and directly identify *whether* this music form is being used at all (i.e., responses of "never") and *when* its usage occurs (i.e., during Sunday worship services). Additionally, usage during Sunday worship services, quite possibly the most important collective black Church experience, implies a certain degree of acceptance of this music form.

Three groups of independent variables are tested. Research contends that the following indicators influence black church attitudes and actions: denomination, size, financial health, member profile, the existence of paid clergy, and pastor's education (Billingsley 1992, 1999; Lincoln and Mamiya 1990). Studies identify priestly factors such as congregational emphasis on spirituality, religious programs, worship, and church religious life (Harris 1987; Lincoln and Mamiya 1990; Marx 1971) and prophetic functions as associated with emphasis on racial issues, social justice, liberation theology, political/civic and community concerns, and activism (Lincoln and Mamiya 1990; Morris 1984; Taylor 1994; West 1982; Wilmore 1994). The eleven variables selected here capture dimensions of priestly and prophetic functions as described by these scholars. The variable groupings are as follows: (1) church and membership demographics; (2) priestly functions; and (3) prophetic functions.[8] A total of twenty-eight indicators measure dimensions of religious life and church demographics as understood by the respondent. Each variable's operationalization and corresponding survey questions is provided in the appendix.

Methodology

In the first phase of the analysis, bivariate cross-tabulations of mean responses or percentages and X^2 or t-tests are used to compare the independent variables across the seven denominations (bivariate correlations provided upon request). Percentages by denomination are also provided for the dependent variable to illustrate gospel rap music usage by denomination. Next, gospel rap usage is examined using binary logistic regression analysis because the dependent variable considers two distinct 0–1 outcomes. In each analysis phase, the dependent variable is regressed on church and membership demographic variables (Model 1), in models controlling for priestly functions (Model 2), prophetic functions (Model 3), and all variables simultaneously (Model 4). Lastly, Table 3 contains membership profiles that provide additional implications for potential evangelism n the black Church tradition.

Table 1
Gospel Rap Music Usage and Independent Variables by Denomination (N = 1,863)

	Total	B	COGIC	AME	CME	AMEZ	UM	Presb.	X^2-t
Gospel Rap Music Usage (% never)	46.5	47.8	54.4	37.0	47.4	36.4	32.6	45.5	34.3***
Church and Member Demographics									
Financial Health (% good)	63.8	71.9	58.0	60.4	63.5	68.8	62.0	58.3	24.3***
% Paid Pastors	78.5	80.5	50.4	97.5	88.3	92.8	97.0	96.9	348.8***
% Pastors W/Post Dr.	31.7	33.4	14.4	46.2	24.3	42.6	54.6	61.1	412.6***
Sunday Attendance (Mean)	221	373	135	231	148	154	219	135	t***
Attending Children (Mean)	73.6	122.3	52.0	84.3	42.4	49.0	73.0	36.1	t***
% College Graduates	31.5	30.2	20.0	39.3	31.4	34.8	46.6	54.9	633.1***
% Male	24.4	25.7	21.2	25.3	23.9	26.1	25.4	29.8	467.8***
% Members 18-35 years old	32.1	35.2	33.6	32.2	27.8	30.6	29.1	26.4	395.6***
% Members 60+ years old	26.2	25.3	16.0	33.9	28.4	32.7	34.3	39.2	611.2***
% New Members	20.4	23.1	21.1	22.0	15.6	19.5	19.0	15.8	370.0***
Priestly Functions									
Spiritually Alive (% very well)	64.8	68.5	79.2	62.5	54.1	58.7	46.0	38.0	141.5***
Deepen Rel. w/ God (% v. well)	63.3	66.3	75.6	60.5	52.2	59.5	50.0	45.0	105.3***
God's Love & Care (% always)	83.1	84.1	84.5	81.3	84.7	87.3	80.0	69.0	28.3
Spiritual Growth (% always)	72.9	73.1	76.1	74.6	72.9	75.4	65.0	56.0	31.0**
Religious Programs (Mean)	3.3	3.4	3.3	3.2	3.2	3.4	3.1	3.1	
Prophetic Functions									
Social.: Env. (% very well)	42.6	41.5	46.5	49.4	37.6	43.7	32.3	35.0	39.2*
Social: Sermons (% always)	26.1	23.3	27.9	25.9	32.8	23.0	27.0	14.0	67.0***
Racial Issues (% always)	17.8	16.0	17.2	18.5	23.9	21.4	14.0	8.1	86.2***
Lib. Theologies (% always)	13.1	9.9	11.7	15.0	19.8	16.9	12.0	8.0	84.4***
Clergy: Marches (% approve)	89.9	89.2	78.5	96.1	92.7	98.4	94.9	94.9	195.4***
Church Views (% approve)	94.0	93.9	89.47	97.44	97.2	94.4	95.0	98.0	75.8***

Note: * p<0.05, ** p<0.01, ***p<0.001: B=Baptist, COGIC=Church of God in Christ, UM=United Methodist, CME=Christian Methodist Episcopal, AME=African Methodist Episcopal, AMEZ=African Methodist Episcopal Zion, Presb=Black Presbyterian: Significance tests are X^2 or t-tests: t*** means at least 4 combinations are significantly differences at p<.001. Source: ITC Faith Factor 2000 Project.

Findings
Church Views and Demographic Profile

Table 1 includes a demographic profile of the sample by denomination. When the dependent variable (gospel rap music usage) is considered, findings show that 46.5% of the sample churches never include this music form during Sunday worship services. However, statistically significant differences are apparent based on denomination. United Methodist, followed by AMEZ and AME, churches are most likely to include gospel rap music and COGIC congregations are the least likely to do so (54.4% "never"). When congregational profiles are examined, the majority are financially stable with the highest representation for Baptist (71.9%) followed by AMEZ (68.8%). Church attendance averages at least 135 each Sunday; Baptists, followed by AMEs, have the greatest mean attendance. Churches average about 74 children that attend regularly; Baptist note the most with a mean of 122.3 children and Presbyterians the least with 36.1 children. Results also show that the majority of persons from the Presbyterian tradition are college educated (54.9%), while only one-fifth of COGIC churches are similarly educated. AMEZ, UM, and Presbyterian churches are most likely to have paid pastors and COGIC churches are least likely to do so. Furthermore, the majority of Presbyterians and UMs have highly educated pastors; rates are less than 15% for COGICs. Although each denomination has similar male (about 25%) and young adult representation (about 30%), Presbyterian and AME churches have somewhat higher percentages of members 60 or more years old and Baptists tend to have more new members (23.1 %).

When indicators linked to a priestly function are considered, regardless of denomination, the majority of churches have environments that can be considered spiritually alive and that encourage persons to have deepened relationships with the Deity. Save Presbyterians, over 80% of the remaining six denominations are exposed to frequent sermonic references to God's love and care. At least 50% of churches from each denomination are also exposed to sermonic references about growing spiritually. The number of religious programs is examined next and findings show a mean of three programs and no significant difference across denominations. When variables associated with a prophetic function are assessed, Jess than 50% of congregations have environments that encourage social justice and less than 33% frequently hear sermons on the subject. While slightly more than 20% of AMEZ and CME churches are frequently exposed to sermonic references to racial issues, rates are substantially lower for the other five denominations. Fewer than 20% of churches have frequent exposure to sermons about liberation/womanist theology; representation is greatest among CMEs (19.8%) and least among Presbyterians (8.0%) and Baptists (9.9%). Regardless of denomination, the majority of respondents suggest that their congregations condone clergy involvement in protest marches and church expressions of views on political and social issues. These zero-order results suggest considerably greater emphasis of variables that connote a priestly rather than a prophetic function. The next phase of the analysis assesses whether and how the two functions will influence gospel rap music use when indicators are considered simultaneously.

Table 2
Logistic Regression Analysis for Gospel Rap Music Usage (N=1,863)

Independent Variables	Model 1 Church Demo.	Model 2 Priestly Functions	Model 3 Prophetic Functions	Model 4 All Variables
Church Demographics				
AME (1=yes)	.56(1.75)**	.62(1.86)**	.48(1.62)*	.53(1.70)**
AMEZ (1=yes)	.63(1.88)**	.67(1.95)**	.50(1.66)*	.53(1.71)*
CME (1=yes)	.21(1.23)	.23(1.26)	.14(1.15)	.14(1.14)
COGIC (1=yes)	-.18(0.84)	-.21(0.81)	-.17(0.85)	-.18(0.83)
Presbyterian (1=yes)	.29(1.34)	.48(1.62)†	.22(1.24)	.35(1.42)
UM (1=yes)	.57(1.77)*	.70(2.02)**	.63(1.88)*	.73(2.07)**
Financial Health (1=good)	-.13(0.88)	-.17(0.85)	-.19(0.82)	-.20(0.82)
Paid Pastor (1=yes)	.38(1.47)*	.36(1.44)*	.42(1.52)*	.39(1.48)*
Pastor's Educ. (1=none, 6=Post Dr.)	-.06(0.94)	-.06(0.94)	-.08(0.92)†	-.09(0.92)†
Sunday Attendance (1-6000)	.00(1.00)	-.00(1.00)	-.00(1.00)	-.00(1.00)
Attending Children (0-6700)	.00(1.00)†	.00(1.00)†	.00(1.00)†	.00(1.00)†
College Graduates (0-100%)	-.01(1.00)	-.00(1.00)	.00(1.00)	-.00(1.00)
% Male	.00(1.00)	.00(1.00)	.00(1.00)	.01(1.01)
% Ages 18-35 Years	.00(1.00)	.00(1.00)	.00(1.00)	.00(1.00)
% Over 60 Years	-.00(1.00)	-.00(1.00)	-.00(1.00)	-.00(1.00)
% New to Church	.02(1.02)***	.02(1.02)***	.02(1.02)***	.02(1.02)***
Church Demographics				
Church Environment:				
Spiritually Alive (1=not at all, 5=very well)		.17(1.18)		.15(1.16)
Deepens Rel. w/ God (1=not at all, 5=very well)		-.00(1.00)		-.07(0.93)
Sermon Focus:				
God's Love and Care (1=never, 5=always)		.11(1.12)		.00(1.00)
Spiritual Growth (1=never, 5=always)		-.17(0.84)		-.17(0.85)
Number of Religious Programs (0-4)		.23(1.26)**		.20(1.22)*
Church Demographics				
Church Environment:				
Social Justice (1=not at all, 5=very well)			.18(1.20)**	.16(1.17)*
Sermon Focus:				
Social Justice (1=never, 5=always)			-.07(0.94)	-.05(0.95)
Racial Issues (1=never, 5=always)			.02(1.02)	.01(1.01)
Liberation/Womanist Theology (1=never, 5=always)			.20(1.22)**	.19(1.21)**
Clergy in Protest Marches (1= strongly disapprove, 4 = strongly approve)			-.02(0.98)	.00(1.00)
Church Soc./Pol. Views (1= strongly disapprove, 4 = strongly approve)			.23(1.26)†	.22(1.24)†
X²	67.24	79.47	86.14	93.62
N	1486	1472	1436	1423

Note: Log odd presented first: odds in parentheses
***p <.001, **p <.01, *p<.05, †p<.10
Source: ITC Faith Factor 2000 Project.

Modeling Gospel Rap Music Usage

A series of logistic regression models are used to explain gospel rap music usage (Table 2). When church and membership demographic indicators are considered in Model I, denominational differences in usage are apparent. Findings show that AME (odds = 1.75, p<.01), AMEZ (odds = 1.88, p<.01), and UM congregations (odds = 1.77, p<.05) are significantly more likely to include gospel rap music during Sunday worship services than their Baptist counterparts. Significant differences in usage of this musical expression are not evident between Baptist and COGIC, CME, and Presbyterian churches, respectively. Congregations that have paid pastors are 1.5 times more likely to include such music than churches with non-paid pastors. Although most of the membership profile variables are not predictive, a direct, albeit minimal, relationship exists between the number of children that regularly attend church and use of gospel rap music. Thus, churches with more regularly attending children are more likely to use gospel rap music than their counterparts with fewer children. Lastly, results show that churches with more new members are also more likely to use gospel rap music.

When variables related to priestly functions are considered in Model 2, significant, positive differences continue between gospel rap music usage for AME and Baptist (odds = 1.86, p<.01), AMEZ and Baptist (odds = 1.95, p<.01), UM and Baptist (odds = 2.02, p<.01), as well as now between Presbyterian and Baptist (odds = 1.62, p<.10) congregations, respectively. The indicators that identify paid clergy, number of children in regular attendance, and the percentage of new members continue to be important and increase the likelihood of gospel rap music usage. When specific priestly indicators are assessed, only one of the five indicators is important. Findings show that churches that tend to sponsor more religious programs are more likely to also include gospel rap music during Sunday worship services than congregations that sponsor fewer religious programs (odds = 1.26, p<.01).

Model 3 considers the effects of indicators that connote a prophetic function. First, denominational affiliation continues to be important and AME, AMEZ, and UM churches are more likely to use gospel rap music than are Baptists. Variables that identify paid clergy and number of regularly attending children continue to increase chances of gospel rap music usage. Another clergy profile variable becomes significant and churches with pastors with more formal education are slightly *less likely* to use gospel rap music than their counterparts with less formal education. As was the case in the first two models, congregations with greater percentages of new members are more apt to include this musical expression than churches with fewer new members. Three of the five prophetic variables are predictive. Churches with overall environments that emphasize social justice, those with more frequent sermonic references to liberation and womanist theologies, and those that have clergy who approve of informing congregants about day-to-day social and political issues are at least 1.2 times more likely to include gospel rap music during Sunday worship services than their counterparts.

All of the indicators are examined simultaneously in Model 4. As was the case in prior models, AME, AMEZ, and UM churches and congregations with paid clergy continue to be more likely to be use gospel rap music. Pastor's education and number of regularly attending children continue to influence such usage, but in opposite directions. And the variable that indicates percentage of new members continues to be directly related to gospel rap music usage. One priestly indicator, religious program sponsorship, continues to increase the likelihood of gospel rap music inclusion. The three prophetic indicators that were important in Model 3 remain so here. Thus churches that encourage exposure to social and political issues, those with an overall social justice environment, and those exposed to liberation sermons are more likely to use gospel rap music than their counterparts. These final results, when considered within the overall model context suggests that, when priestly and prophetic indicators are considered simultaneously, the latter measures provide a stronger motivation for gospel rap music usage, but do not diminish denominational effects.

Table 3
New Member Profiles by Denomination (N=1,863)

	Total	Bap.	COGIC	AME	CME	AMEZ	UM	Presb.
% College Grad.	31.7(.7)	30.3(1.1)	20.2(1.0)	39.6(1.7)	32.3(1.8)	35.3(2.7)	47.7(2.3)	54.8(2.7)
% Male	24.5(.3)	25.7(.6)	1.2(.7)	25.5(.9)	24.1(1.0)	6.5(1.5)	25.7(1.3)	30.5(1.1)
% Low income	30.2(.7)	29.3(1.2)	35.0(1.5)	32.4(1.3)	34.8(1.9)	28.6(2.4)	21.1(2.2)	18.2(2.3)
%18-35 Years	32.5(.5)	35.0(1.0)	34.2(1.1)	32.3(1.2)	28.8(1.3)	30.8(2.0)	29.7(2.2)	26.7(2.1)
% +60 Years	26.3(.5)	25.1(.9)	16.3(.8)	34.2(1.3)	28.7(1.4)	33.2(2.1)	34.3(2.2)	40.3(2.2)
% LT HS	15.5(.5)	17.6(.9)	17.3(1.0)	11.5(1.1)	16.2(1.4)	5.2(1.8)	11.1(1.4)	9.7(1.5)
% Tithers	44.2(.7)	44.5(1.3)	56.0(1.5)	36.8(1.5)	36.5(1.7)	46.1(2.7)	34.5(2.4)	29.4(2.8)

Bap.=Baptist, COGIC=Church of God in Christ, UM=United Methodist, CME=Christian Methodist Episcopal, AME=African Methodist Episcopal, AMEZ=African Methodist Episcopal Zion, Presb=Black Presbyterian. Low income=households with annual incomes below $20,000. LT HS = Persons without a high school diploma. Source: ITC Faith Factor 2000 Project.

New Member Profiles by Denomination

One finding from this study begs further inquiry. As was determined here, one would expect the prevalence of children and early adolescents to encourage gospel rap music usage. However, the modeling results also show a clear relationship between increases in new membership (i.e., persons who have become affiliated with a church in the last five years) and usage of gospel rap music. Regarding this finding, one can debate causal ordering (i.e., increases in new members may encourage usage of gospel rap music or gospel rap usage may result in more new members). Yet, given noted contemporary challenges in attracting some blacks to church (Lincoln and Mamiya 1990; West 1993), it is important to consider the profiles of new members (Table 3). Although varied factors influence membership decisions (for example, church location, theology, history, and age), these results provide insight regarding who is "joining" contemporary black congregations. Regardless of denomination, at least one-half of new members are college graduates; rates are the greatest for Presbyterian churches (55%). Likewise, denomination not withstanding, about 25% of new members are male and about 33% can be considered low-income. Between 25–35% of new members were young adults ages 18–35 years old. Representation among the elderly is noted and at least 15% of new persons were over the age of 60 years. Fewer than 20% of new members had not received a high school diploma. When church economic support is considered, at least 35% of new members were tithers. An overall review of the new member profiles suggests that some black churches are attracting a cross-section of new members whose profiles make them valuable for individual church and collective efforts.

Discussion

This research examines whether black churches include gospel rap music in their worship services and the indicators that influence this decision. Although the research question is relatively straightforward, implications are important in terms of better assessing both the more contemporary dimensions of black Church worship services and their strategies for more effective evangelistic efforts. The findings can be broadly generalized (refer to endnotes 4 and 7 for data constraints), but do not propose to represent all black churches. However, these findings inform our understanding about whether a pervasive musical form in popular culture is being appropriated in the contemporary black Church and some of the dynamics that influence its use.

First, results suggest that, regardless of denomination, gospel rap music is being included in Sunday musical repertoires of the majority of the sample churches. The results suggest a direct relationship between churches that have: (1) paid clergy; (2) regularly attending children; (3) new members; (4) religious program sponsorship; and (5) pastors who emphasize social justice and political issues and who preach based on liberation themes, and the tendency to include gospel rap music during Sunday services. Overall, churches considered more prophetic in nature are more likely to include gospel rap music than their priestly counterparts. Just as prophetic churches have been at the forefront of economic, political, and social change in the black Church tradition (Lincoln and Mamiya 1990), they are more likely to appropriate this often-controversial music form in worship. This finding suggests the importance of church ideological environment in influencing the use of non-traditional, seemingly controversial strategies and approaches to worship the Deity and broaden church service experiences (Costen 1993; Peacock 2004).

Two additional findings should be noted. First, denominational differences in usage exist. Some of the denominations that have been at the forefront of other controversial church decisions (for example, AME and AMEZ histories of ordaining female clergy) were also more likely to use this controversial musical form. Gospel rap was also consistently important among the UM. This finding illustrates the potential importance of denomination over other church- and membership-related indicators in shaping the scope and tenor of worship experience. This result also illustrates the possible influence of denominations in fostering acceptance of gospel rap music usage. Secondly, the correlation between increases in new membership and gospel rap music usage is noteworthy and informs LaRue's (2004) findings about the direct relationship between contemporary music usage and church attendance. It is likely that feedback effects occur between the two indictors. However, the finding suggests that congregations are attracting diverse new members that include males, college graduates, young adults, and persons who financially support their respective congregations— and that such persons are receptive to non-traditional ways of worship. This result is worthy of further study and has applied implications relative to evangelizing black youth in general and black young males in particular (Lincoln and Mamiya 1990; West 1993).

Conclusion

The contemporary black Church is challenged to examine the influence of the hip hop culture for the attention of black youth—especially the poor and marginalized (Cusic 1990; Dent 1983; Howard and Streck 1999; Powell 1991). Some black Church leaders and members may consider gospel rap too secular. Others may consider it a non-traditional expression for a more heterogeneous black populace. Future academic and applied studies should consider the views of adolescents, new church members, and youth who are uninterested in the black Church to assess their experiences and determine how best to respond to their spiritual and secular needs (Ballard and Stewart 2006; Cook 2000). Studies of the hip hop culture and gospel rap as possible extensions of black Church culture are also important and needed (Barnes 2006).

More generally, these results inform our knowledge about the influence of popular culture on religion in general and Christianity in particular. Just as Christian rock was a response to the ambivalence and needs of predominately white Christian youth (Thompson 2000), gospel rap usage reflects a complex genre influenced by race (often black), religion (Christian), locale (often urban), class (often poor or working class), age (youth), and popular culture. Proponents of gospel rap do not reject Christianity, but seek religious expression they consider more authentic to their experiences (Howard and Streck 1999). I contend that the bravado, empowered personas, and often rags-to-riches tales of many contemporary rappers provide a powerful model to draw youth followers and emulators. Beliefs that these types of benefits (economic, personal, and social) can be gained with the support of the Deity may be enticing for some Christians. It will be interesting to assess whether and how similar attraction will occur as a result of popular cultural influence among post-9/11 Christian youth in general, Hispanic immigrant populations, or Catholic adolescents. Based on the proliferation of hip hop in Asian spaces (Mai 2003; *Taipei Times* 2004), these potential topics bode well for future research.

Kopano suggests that, "by holding a mirror to society, rap stands as a rhetoric of resistance primarily to issues of race but also to issues of class and sex (gender)" (2002: 213). Gospel rap may have a similar purpose. For younger audiences, gospel rap may provide a vehicle to both voice their unique faith experience and to critique older Christians (Ballard and Stewart 2006; Ehrlich 1997; Howard and Streck 1999; LeBlanc 2001). For others, the music form may provide an avenue to dialogue with the largely "religious" society regarding continued social, economic, cultural, and political divisiveness (Morthland 1997; Simmons et al 1993). And for others, gospel rap may represent an alternative to traditional Christian music. Central to the debate over use of gospel rap is one of religious legitimacy that hearkens back to dialogues about the authenticity of CCM (Howard and Streck 1999), gospel music (Costen 1993), and some secular rap music. Legitimate hip hop is said to emerge from the "black cultural context and its conceptual and geographical landscape" (Henderson 1996: 317). Thus authenticity is linked to ideology, place, and culture. Black Church leaders must grapple with whether gospel rap music represents an authentic expression of Christian faith: Is the ideology worthy of inclusion, does it have a tangible place of origin according to scripture? Is it indicative of black Church culture (Barnes 2006)? Answers to these types of questions will influence whether and how gospel rap music continues to be incorporated in the black religious tradition and can have implications for the larger Christian community as well. According to these findings, whether and how Christian institutions respond will be influenced by prophetic rather than priestly tenets.

Cusic (1990) suggests a process by which new CCM waves are embraced—initially rejected, reluctantly accepted, and once accepted, then used to stifle subsequent new waves. A variation of this pattern seems evident for gospel rap. However, the purchasing power of youth culture and influence of the media may provide an impetus for the growth of this music form yet to be witnessed. Lastly, these results also suggest some relevance in Peacock's (2004) "comprehensive kingdom perspective" that moves Christian music outside traditional theological boundaries to transform adherents, in part, through the message. Using Howard and Streck's (1999) typology, this perspective reflects separational (i.e., the utility of Christian music), integrational (i.e., its importance for its own sake), and transformational (i.e., its ability to transcend nonnative bounds) dimensions. If, as Peacock notes, "everything under God's view and care is worthy subject matter for songwriting" (2004: 148), the experiences depicted in gospel rap, no matter how sobering or disturbing, would have purpose and should be given voice.

Acknowledgments

This research is funded by a 2005 Louisville Institute Grant and through the support of the ITC Faith Factor Project sponsored by The Lily Foundation and the Interdenominational Theological Center. Direct all correspondence to Sandra L. Barnes, Department of Sociology, Case Western Reserve University, Cleveland, OH 44106; e-mail: sbarnes@case.edu.

Notes

1. Throughout the document, the term "the black Church" is used to represent the institution as a collective and "black church" when individual congregations are referenced.
2. Although they are sometimes used interchangeably, the term "hip hop" is usually used to describe the broader culture from which "rap" music, as a specific expression, emerged (Dent 1983; Kopano 2002).
3. They are the National Baptist Convention, U.S.A., National Baptist Convention of America, and the Progressive National Baptist Convention. Tri-Media data were also used to augment the lists from the six other denominations; churches found on either source were included on the composite list for that perspective denomination and duplicate churches were identified and only included once.
4. For example, Baptist churches that purchase Sunday school materials and supplies at venues not listed with Tri-Media or those that do but that are not affiliated with any of the three conferences would not be included in the sampling frame. Thus the Baptist list can be considered a lower bound of the number of black Baptist churches nationwide.
5. The UM and black Presbyterians, respectively. In order to take advantage of the available data for subsequent studies, the two latter groups were over-sampled relative to their presence in the overall population. During the modeling phase, the data were weighted to reflect the current estimates on denominational representation to correct for the disproportionate sub-sample sizes (Billingsley 1992; Lincoln and Mamiya 1990). The margin of error for the sample was +/- 2.3.
6. Chaves et al (1999:464) discuss the validity and reliability of relying on a single key informant to report church characteristics. Such persons are likely to over-estimate the extent to which their views correspond to their congregation's views. They note, "an informant's judgment about an organization's goals or mission is likely to represent the informant's interpretation of a complex reality rather than a more or less publicly available cultural fact about the congregation." In light of this dynamic, these data can be considered a best case scenario relative to gospel rap usage. However, the vast majority of respondents are senior pastors and because research shows that black pastors tend to have a greater degree of authority and influence over their congregants than their white counterparts, they are expected to have greater influence over the focus and activities of their churches (Billingsley 1999; McRoberts 1999; Wilmore 1994).
7. The response and cooperation rates by denomination are as follows: Baptist (.22, .49), COGIC (.19, .51), AME (.25, .52), CME (.40, .66), AMEZ (.24, .55), UM (.46, .69), and black Presbyterian (.37, .65). The overall sample rates were .24 and .54, respectively. Although the most current available lists were used, low response rates were due to situations such as disconnected telephones or relocation which counts against the response rate (referrals were used to locate many such churches). In such situations, the cooperation rate can be used as a reasonable proxy. The figures represent the CASRO Standard calculation for the response rate and the cooperation rate reflects the percent of churches that participated once contact was made.
8. I explored developing separate, single factors to capture priestly and prophetic functions (example, combining the five variables associated with a priestly function into a single factor). Each set of variables is theoretically related and statistically correlated at the bivariate level. However, multivariate tests and substantive reasons do not support their use as factors. Principle components factor analysis, provided upon request, do not support unique constructs. In addition, I wished to examine the potential effects of *each variable* separately to determine its influence on explaining. For example, do sermons help explain gospel rap music usage more than religious programs? This latter objective would not be possible using scales.

Appendix
Survey Questions and Variable Operationalizations

Church Demographics (11 variables)

1. *Denomination* (coded into seven 0–1 dummy variables, Baptist is the reference category): Q: What is your church denomination? Baptist, Church of God in Christ (COGIC), United Methodist (UM), Christian Methodist Episcopal (CME), African Methodist Episcopal (AME), African Methodist Episcopal Zion (AMEZ), Black Presbyterian.

2. *Financial Health* (coded such that 1=good, 0=tight/difficulty): Q:How would you describe your congregation's financial health: good, tight, or serious difficulty?

3. *Paid Pastor* (coded 0=volunteer, 1 =paid): Q: Are you/is your pastor paid or a volunteer?

4. *Pastor's Education* (1=none, 6=post Dr. Ministry/PhD.): Q: What is the highest level of (your/your pastor's) ministerial education? None, apprenticeship with senior pastor, certificate or correspondence program, Bible college or some seminary, seminary degree, post-Minister of Divinity Work or degree.

5. *Sunday Attendance* (continuous, 0–6,000): Q: What is the total attendance for all services on a typical Sunday?

6. *Attending Children* (continuous, 0–6,700): Q: Of those associated with your congregation, what is the number of children under 18 years of age?

7. *College Graduates* (continuous, 0–100%): Q: Of your total number of regularly participating adults, what total percent would you estimate are college graduates?

8. *Male Members* (continuous, 0–100%): Q: Of your total number of regularly participating adults, what total percent would you estimate are male?

9. *Members Ages 18–35 Years* (continuous, 0–100%): Q: Of your total number of regularly participating adults, what total percent would you estimate are ages 18–35 years old?

10. *Members Ages 60+ Years* (continuous, 0–100%): Q: Of your total number of regularly participating adults, what total percent would you estimate are over 60 years old?

11. *New Members to Church* (continuous, 0–100%): Q: Of your total number of regularly participating adults, what total percent would you estimate are new to your church (last 5 years)?

Variables that Describe a Priestly Function (5 variables)

Church Environment:

Q: How well does each of the following statements describe your congregation? Use a scale from 1 to 5 where "5" describes your congregation very well and "1" means not at all well.

12. *Spiritually vital and "alive"*

13. *Helps members deepen their relationship with God*

Sermon Focus:

Q: How well does each of the following statements describe the sermon focus? Use a scale from 1 to 5 where "5" means always and "1" means never.

14. *God's love and care*

15. *Personal spiritual growth*

Religious Programs:

Q: During the past 12 months, did your congregation participate in any of the following programs or activities in addition to your regular Sunday School?

16. *Bible study other than Sunday school, theological or doctrinal study, prayer or mediation groups, or spiritual retreats* (sums total number of programs, values 0–4)

Variables that Describe a Prophetic Function (6 variables)

Church Environment:

Q: How well does each of the following statements describe your congregation? Use a scale from 1 to 5 where "5" describes your congregation very well and "1" means not at all well.

17. *Working for social justice*

Sermon Focus:

Q: How well does each of the following statements describe the sermon focus? Use a scale from 1 to 5 where "5" means always and "1" means never.

18. *Social justice or social action*

19. *References to the racial situation in society*

20. *References to Black Liberation Theology or Womanist Theology*

Clergy/Church Activism:

For each one, please say whether you strongly disapprove, somewhat disapprove, somewhat approve, or strongly approve (coded such that "1" means strongly disapprove and "4" means strongly approve).

21. *Clergy in your own church taking part in protest marches on civil rights issues*

22. *Churches expressing their views on day-to-day social and political issues*

References

Ballard, Scotty, and Javonne Stewart. "The Ministry of Hip Hop." *Jet* 110, no. 8 (2006): 30–33.

Barnes, Sandra. "Priestly and Prophetic Influences on Black Church Social Services." *Social Problems* 51, no. 2 (2004): 202–21.

———. "Black Church Culture and Community Action." *Social Forces* 84, no. 2 (2005): 967–94.

———. "Whosoever Will Let Her Come: Gender Inclusivity in the Black Church." *Journal for the Scientific Study of Religion* 45, no. 3 (2006): 371–87.

Billingsley, Andrew. *Climbing Jacob's Ladder: The Enduring Legacy of African American Families.* New York: A Touchstone Book, 1992.

———. *Mighty Like a River: The Black Church and Social Reform.* New York: Oxford University Press, 1999.

Calhoun-Brown, Allison. "The Image of God: Black Theology and Racial Empowerment in the African American Community." *Review of Religious Research* 40, no. 3 (1999): 197–211.

Cavendish, James. "To March or Not to March: Clergy Mobilization Strategies and Grassroots Antidrug Activism." In *Christian Clergy in American Politics.* Edited by Sue S. Crawford and Laura R. Olson, 203–23. Baltimore: Johns Hopkins University Press, 2001.

Chaves, Mark. "Religious Congregations and Welfare Reform: Who Will Take Advantage of 'Charitable Choice'?" *American Sociological Review* 64 (1999): 836–46.

Chaves, Mark, Mary E. Konieczny, Kraig Beyerlein, and Emily Barman. "The National Congregations Study: Background, Methods, and Selected Results." *Journal for the Scientific Study of Religion* 38, no. 4 (1999): 458–76.

Collier, Aldore. "Run's House." *Jet* 110, no. 5 (2006): 52–6.

Cone, James H. "Black Theology as Liberation Theology." In *African American Religious Studies: An Interdisciplinary Anthology*. Edited by Gayraud Wilmore, 177–207. Durham: Duke University Press, 1995.

Cook, Kaye V. "'You Have to Have Somebody Watching Your Back, and If That's God, Then That's Mighty Big': The Church's Role in the Resilience of Inner-City Youth." *Adolescence* 35, no. 140 (2000): 717–30.

Costen, Melva Wilson. *African American Christian Worship*. Nashville: Abingdon, 1993.

Cusic, Don. *The Sound of Light: The History of Gospel Music*. Bowling Green, OH: Bowling Green State University Popular Press, 1990.

Day, Katie. "The Construction of Political Strategies Among African American Clergy." In *Christian Clergy in American Politics*. Edited by Sue S. Crawford and Laura R. Olson, 85–103. Baltimore: Johns Hopkins University Press, 2001.

Dent, Gina, ed. *Black Popular Culture*. New York: New Press, 1983.

Du Bois, W. E. B. *The Souls of Black Folk*. New York: The Modern Library, 1903.

Dyson, Michael. 1996. "Hip Hop and the Bad Rap: Hammer and Vanilla Ice." In *Between God and Gangsta Rap: Bearing Witness to Black Culture*. Edited by Michael E. Dyson, 161–4. New York: Oxford University Press, 1996.

———. "The Culture of Hip Hop." In *Reflecting Black: African American Cultural Criticism*. Edited by Michael E. Dyson, 3–15. Minneapolis: University of Minnesota Press, 1993.

Ellison, Christopher, and Darren Sherkat. "The 'Semi-Involuntary Institution' Revisited: Regional Variations in Church Participation Among Black Americans." *Social Forces* 73, no. 4 (1995): 1415–37.

Ehrlich, Dimitri. "Keeping the Faith: Interview with K. Franklin." *Interview* 27, no. 9 (1997): 144–6.

Fears, Darryl. "Gay Blacks Feeling Strained Church Ties." *Washington Post* (November 2, 2004): A03.

Frazier, E. Franklin. *The Negro Church in America*. New York: Schocken Books, 1964.

Grant, Jacqueline. *White Women's Christ and Black Women's Jesus: Feminist Christology and Womanist Response*. Atlanta: Scholars Press, 1989.

Harris, James H. *Black Ministers and Laity in the Urban Church: An Analysis of Political and Social Expectations*. New York: University Press of America, 1987.

Henderson, Errol. "Black Nationalism and Rap Music." *Journal of Black Studies* 26, no. 3 (1996): 308–39.

Higginbotham, Evelyn. *Righteous Discontent: The Women's Movement in the Black Baptist Church 1880–1920*. Cambridge: Harvard University Press, 1993.

Howard, Jay, and John Streck. *Apostles of Rock: The Splintered World of Contemporary Christian Music*. Lexington: University of Kentucky Press, 1999.

Jackson, Marie. "The Changing Nature of Gospel Music: A Southern Case Study." *African American Review* 29, no. 2 (1995): 185–200.

Jet. "MC Hammer Makes Switch to Gospel Music." 94, no. 9 (1998): 63.

Konieczny, Mary, and Mark Chaves. "Resources, Race, and Female-Headed Congregations in the United States." *Journal for the Scientific Study of Religion* 39, no. 3 (2000): 261–71.

Kopano, Baruti. "Rap Music as an Extension of the Black Rhetorical Tradition: 'Keepin' it Real.'" *The Western Journal of Black Studies* 26, no. 4 (2002): 204–13.

LeBlanc, Douglas. "T-Bone: The Last Street Preacha." *Christianity Today* 45, no. 6: 111.

Lincoln, C. Eric and Lawrence H. Mamiya. *The Black Church in the African American Experience*. Durham: Duke University Press, 1990.

Mai, Anna. "Peace, Unity, and Hope Through Hip Hop: The 2nd Annual Asian Hip Hop Summit." www.asianarts.ucla.edu/030425/music_cover.html. Accessed April 25, 2003.

Marx, Gary. "Religion: Opiate or Inspiration of Civil Rights Militancy?" In *The Black Church in America*. Edited by Hart Nelsen, Raytha Yokley, and Anne Nelsen, 150–60. New York: Basic Books, 1971.

Maultsby, Portia. "A Map of the Music." *African American Review* 29, no. 2 (1995): 183–4.

McRoberts, Omar M. "Understanding the 'New' Black Pentecostal Activism: Lessons from Ecumenical Urban Ministries in Boston." *Sociology of Religion* 60, no. 1 (1999): 47–70.

Morgan, Joan. "Fly-Girls, Bitches, and Hoes: Notes of a Hip Hop Feminist." *Social Text* 45 (1995): 151–7.

Morris, Aldon D. *The Origins of the Civil Rights Movement: Black Communities Organizing for Change.* New York: Free Press, 1984.

Morthland, John. "Heavenly: K. Franklin and God's Property." *Texas Monthly* 25 (1997): 28.

Paulson, Michael. "Black Clergy Rejection Stirs Gay Marriage Backers." *Globe.* http://www.boston.com/news/local/articles/2004/02/1 0/black_clergy_rejection_stirs_gay. Accessed February 10, 2004.

Peacock, Charlie. *At the Crossroads: Inside the Past, Present, and Future of Contemporary Christian Music.* Colorado Springs: Shaw Books, 2004.

Powell, Catherine. "Rap Music: An Education with a Neat from the Street." *The Journal of Negro Education* 60, no. 3 (1991): 245–59

Reeves, Frank. "Trouble for Gays in Black Churches." *Pittsburgh Post-Gazette.* http://www.post-gazette.com/pg/04106/301047.stm. Accessed April 15, 2004.

Rose, Tricia. "'Fear of a Black Planet:' Rap Music and Black Cultural Politics in the 1990s." *The Journal of Negro Education* 60 (1991): 276–90.

Sherkat, Darren, and Christopher Ellison. "The Politics of Black Religious Change: Disaffiliation from Black Mainline Denominations." *Social Forces* 70, no. 2 (1991): 431–54.

Simmons, Joseph, Daryl McDaniels, and Amy Linden. "Niggas with Beatitude." *Transition* 62 (1993): 176–87.

Smitherman, Geneva. *Talkin' and Testifyin': The Language of Black America.* Detroit: Wayne State University Press, 1977.

Taylor, Clarence. *The Black Churches of Brooklyn.* New York: Columbia University Press, 1994.

Taipei Times. "Asian Hip Hop Music Has Come a Long Way." (March 2004): 16, online at www.taipeitimes.com/News/feat/archives/2004/03/25/20031 07739.

Thompson, John. *Raised by Wolves: The Story of Christian Rock and Roll.* Toronto: ECW, 2000.

Townsend-Gilkes, Cheryl. *If It Wasn't for the Women: Black Women's Experience and Womanist Culture in Church and Community.* Maryknoll: Orbis, 2001.

West, Cornel. *Prophecy Deliverance! An Afro-American Revolutionary Christianity.* Philadelphia: Westminster, 1982.

———. *Race Matters.* Boston: Beacon, 1993.

Wilmore, Gayraud S., ed. *Black Religion and Black Radicalism: An Interpretation of the Religious History of Afro-American People.* New York: Orbis Books, 1994.

———. *African American Religious Studies: An Interdisciplinary Anthology.* Durham: Duke University Press, 1995.

33

In Search of
Our Daughters' Gardens:
Hip Hop as Womanist Prose

Tamura Lomax

An engagement on the intersections between hip hop and religion begins with a multitude of questions. For example: "How will I define, theorize, and approach the subject matter?" "What will be my primary categories of critical inquiry?" "How will I 'read' the data?" This essay deploys Alice Walker's seminal essay, "In Search of Our Mothers' Gardens," as a framework for thinking about some of these questions. I argue that Walker's essay offers a bridge between hip hop and womanist thought that is insightful for theorizing the "daughters'" (Generation Y) experiences. Specifically, "In Search of Our Mothers' Gardens" anticipates hip hop culture, particularly the artistic expressions of female MCs (a.k.a. the "daughters"). One such daughter is current hip hop sensation Nicki Minaj. Although a land mine of contradictions, Minaj provides a womanist prose that Walker posits the ancestors once danced to—in expectation of her artistry—in which the daughters and granddaughters find meaning. In this essay, I make the following moves. First, I briefly explore Walker's essay as a framework for screening in the artistry of daughters (in hip hop culture) in womanist thought. Second, I turn to hip hop music as a religio-cultural art form that provides entrée to a particular group of daughters. Third, I emphasize the complex artistry, discursive and non-discursive, of Nicki Minaj as a creative source of power and agency. Fourth, I conclude by exploring some of the challenges of reading Minaj's artistry, although empowering for many, uncritically.

"In Search of Our Mothers' Gardens" opens up with a vision of poet Jean Toomer walking through the South in the early 1920s, encountering the exquisite beauty, ethereal opacity, and divine artistry of our mothers and grandmothers, some of whom were driven to madness because "everyday" violence, and the continual threat of the same, asphyxiated the creativity within. However, Toomer posits that others danced to music that had not yet been written. According to Walker, this music signified an art that would one day be born, that would open the way for the creative expressions of their daughters and granddaughters who, like their mothers and grandmothers, would womanishly grasp the seeds of the creative sparks before them and turn rocky soil into imaginative conceptions of beauty. Walker adds that it is this creative spark that passes from generation to generation, which emerges from the density of individual spirituality, that enabled her to see poverty through a "screen of bloom" (Walker 1983). And, it is this spark that aided her in finding not only her own creative voice, but the joy in creating and keeping alive the notion of song, whether written or unwritten, which remembers the stories of the ancestors, builds the inner life of the creator, and makes room for the artistic revelations of those to come: the daughters.

However, it seems the daughter in Walker's text has experienced discursive erasure. Many womanist and feminist sources speak of "women," the "elders," etc., and their specific experiences. While all women are "daughters," signifiers like "woman" and "elder" [not so] implicitly screen out the particular experiences, appropriations, and interpretations of black girls and emerging women. Yet, it is their music that the mothers and grandmothers were dancing to (in addition to that of previous generations), and their artistry into which the mothers and grandmothers imprinted their signatures. Hip hop culture, which not only gives voice to the daughters and granddaughters but demands that we listen and watch, screens Walker's daughter back into womanist/feminist discourses through a range of expressions, styles, and rhythms that give rise to structures of thoughts and deeply held attitudes. In this way, hip hop functions as a quest for meaning for the daughters, granddaughters, and others. It is what religious scholar Charles H. Long articulates as an "orientation in the ultimate sense. . . how one comes to terms with the ultimate significance of one's place in the world" (Long 1995).

Hip hop is the daughters' "garden," a dominant cultural art form in which she may self-actualize as a talking subject who comes to terms with her existential conditions by speaking her own truth. Thus, hip hop is to the daughters and granddaughters what the slave tales and spirituals were to the ancestors, what the sermon was and is to our grandmothers, and what the novel continues to be to our mothers: a critical source of religio-cultural meanings that provides insight on the multiple ways that the daughters and granddaughters might navigate through life, the difficulties they may face, and the alternative systems of ethics and values they sometimes have to create.

Whether individualistic or communal, experienced or imagined, hip hop music expresses the soul of the artist. As a result, its contents are complex, multivalent, and nuanced, ranging from expressions of joy to disappointment, suffering to thriving, longing to despising, living to dying, injustice to justice, triumph to despair, and everything in between, often displaying multiple seemingly contradictory meanings, representations, and positionalities simultaneously. Thus, the artist, much like the trickster, songwriter, preacher, poet, painter, sculptor, or novelist, may sometimes express ethical, political, or cultural values that are inconsistent. Notwithstanding this challenge, hip hop music offers texts through which listeners may interface with, confront, or momentarily transcend their predicaments by way of witty refrains, catchy hooks, empowering chants, multilayered performances, and complex lyrics, sometimes providing untelevised "news" from the underside and exploitive Americanisms, concomitantly.

Yet, regardless of these complexities, hip hop is no less meaningful to its adherents. At minimum, it creates a space for the daughters and granddaughters to cultivate their own critical consciousness and articulate their own humanity, truths, and identities through unsuppressed, uninhibited, honest "talk," where one becomes known through speaking, not simply being *positioned* within discourse. As a site of unfettered expression, hip hop ignites a dramatic confrontation between the ego and life-world, where the artist becomes the primary subject of her own (inter-subjective) invention, thus realigning individual and cultural meanings at will. To this end, hip hop *is* the daughters' tale, spiritual, sermon, and novel. It answers different needs while denying others, and provides a platform for creatively speaking to a public, whether through linguistics, representation, or otherwise. Moreover, it gives us an account of how cultural phenomena construct meanings for the daughters and how they, in turn, appropriate these meanings for themselves.

One such daughter is Trinidadian-American hip hop sensation Nicki Minaj recently hailed as the "Queen of Hip Hop" by *Rolling Stone*. Minaj, born Onika Tanya Maraj on December 8, 1984, is Toomer's "butterfly" unleashed (Walker 1983), a creator in her own right who tells of her mother's and grandmothers' stories alongside her own, in a way that her daughters and granddaughters may one day hear. Thus, her colors and designs are her own conceptions, and although they may seem to diverge from those of her foremothers, they are no less brilliant with meaning and creativity. To this end, Minaj provides interesting *texts*, representational and linguistic, for exploring the daughters' appropriations and interpretations of race, gender, sex, sexuality, and experience in the new millennium. Of course she does not represent all daughters. Nevertheless, Minaj's artistry offers a glimpse of a daughter's day-to-day navigation and critical points of negotiation, which seem to resonate with many other daughters, and thus may inform womanist analyses on "black girls' experiences."

Of particular significance for examining Minaj's artistry is her representation. Minaj's trademark colorful wigs (ranging from pink to blonde to rainbow to camouflage), long, pointed, vampire-like nails, body-hugging garb—which shows off her tiny waist and protruding hips and buttocks—and six-inch stilettos, make her ripe for "Jezebelian" comparisons. However, to dismiss

Minaj's artistry on the assumption that she is uncritically reproducing racist and sexist praxis is to read Minaj through an ahistorical, transcultural, pornotropic lens, which reproduces and superimposes historical myths, such as hypersexuality, onto black women's and girls' bodies regardless of context or intentionality. Moreover, this kind of surface reading negates the dynamic power of both Minaj and the Jezebel trope, each of which has their own intrinsic logic, notwithstanding possible cross-references between them.

If examined in context, and pornotropia and respectability politics are bracketed, Minaj could be read in terms of Walker's definition of "womanish." Her artistry, which is simultaneously ambiguous and explicitly sex-positive, is "outrageous, audacious, and courageous" (Walker 1983: xi). In short, Minaj is a sex-positive subject who deploys her creative power and agency in a context that tends to regiment both race and gender toward hetero-normative and patriarchal ends. However, she both transcends and plays with hip hop's boundaried ideals, literally taking up multiple subject positions at once. For example, the name "Minaj" highlights the multiplicities of both Maraj's (Minaj's birth name) sexual and personal identities, each of which opens up to a variety of interpretations. However, neither her sexual or personal identities are unequivocally identifiable.

Two of her most prominent identities are "Harajuku Barbie," a sexualized, Asian-inspired woman who fights for what she wants, and "Roman Zolanski," a macho multi-sexed man who plays effortlessly with conventional sex and gender identities, sometimes appearing to both resist and acquiesce to them simultaneously. Although Minaj's allegiance to the "Barbie" aesthetic (and the "Orient," although it is important to note that she is part Asian) suggests that she is simply reviving age-old sex and beauty standards and ideas that define women's value in terms of male desirability, Minaj subverts this notion by marking her sexuality with obscurity. In an interview with *OUT* magazine last year, she posited that she dated neither women nor men and that people should be allowed to live comfortably in the "gray" areas of life. Minaj's "gray" areas include being a sexual subject that resists, embraces, and initiates the gaze on her own terms, sometimes reflecting a desire to be desired while at other times conveying power.

Minaj's gazes are often disruptive. That is, they disorient what her body, posture and dress might be communicating through comedic display, thus confusing the pornotropic gaze, which misrecognizes Minaj for sexual territory. To be sure, one could argue that she presents herself as such. Perhaps. Nevertheless, Minaj simultaneously demands to be seen as a subject. Her play in ambiguity and penchant for funny faces draw attention to this demand. Both represent an individual form of resistance against the dominant, operating, representational control for black woman/girl-hood in popular culture: the Jezebelian/hyper-sexual/black-female-as-whore stereotype. However, Minaj confronts the operative codifications within this trope, re-conceptualizes parts, and deploys others.

Minaj's representational strategies draw attention to the multiple subject positionalities of race, gender, sex, and sexuality that the daughters and granddaughters may take up, as well as the adaptive powers of circulating black female cultural images, which have traveled from nineteenth-century minstrelsy into twenty-first-century popular culture. Moreover, her representations suggest that black female cultural images are encountered, read, performed, experienced, deconstructed, resisted, and/or appropriated differently. This is not an attempt to negate the force and function of white ideological bias in the production of harmful homogeneous black female cultural representations, nor am I suggesting that Jezebelian/hyper-sexual/black-female-as-whore stereotypes should not be resisted—as they are encountered and interpreted. However, I am highlighting how Minaj both resists and deploys aspects of the trope to reimagine her own constitution, notwithstanding the tropes' assignment of cultural difference.

Minaj's positionality calls attention to Michel Foucault's notion of resistance, which acts out wherever power is and is thus internal to power, plural and irregular (Foucault 1978). Foucault argues that power is generated from a multiplicity of points from which it is distributed, confronted, and appropriated (Foucault 1978). Therefore, as harmful tropes of black woman/girl-hood emerge from a variety of cultural points where they produce multiple complex meanings and additional points of power, they are also challenged, redistributed, and realigned. Minaj performs each of these moves by taking the dominant Jezebelian/hyper-sexual/black-female-as-whore narrative, repositioning it and then mass-producing her creation, thus co-creating within culture. While these moves imply that she is also maintaining aspects of the historical type, parts of which are recalled by onlookers regardless of her perceived strategies of resistance, the issue is not that Minaj appropriates them but rather for what intent they are being used.

To be sure, intentionality is difficult to know. Nevertheless, Minaj's effects, which are multiple, provide insight on the internal logic of her representations, which are life-giving to many. Minaj takes what is pejorative, confuses it, and makes it appealing. If nothing more, this confusion is an emancipatory act for both Minaj and her fan base, many of whom are marginalized due to their race, sex, sexuality, gender and class. Her performance of these categories tells the daughters and granddaughters that they are okay as they are, and that they are beautiful, regardless.

Of equal importance for examining Minaj's artistry are her linguistic *texts*. Songs like "Here I Am," "Go Hard," "Autobiography," and "Moment 4 Life" provide clues to her experiences, spirituality, and interior consciousness that reveal nuance and complex inter-subjectivity. For example, in "Here I Am," Minaj establishes her personhood while confronting those who have marginalized her. She begins the song by asking, "Why is it that you could only see the worst in me?" (Minaj 2010). However, she concludes by quipping, "I got a couple of tricks up my sleeve. I no longer need your attention, at ease. I'm in pain. I'm ashamed. I am woman, hear me roar" (Minaj 2010). The push and pull between self-actualization, strength and agency, and uncertainty, distress and remorse, is consistent in Minaj's music.

This schema is opened up in her song, "Autobiography," a song about her father, mother, a lover and an unborn child. Minaj begins the song with a prayer, "May the Lord protect me as the world gets hectic, my voice projected, my life reflected" (Minaj 2008). However, she goes on to talk about her childhood, her drug addicted father, and his abuse toward her mother. She asserts,

> Daddy was a crack fiend, two in the morning has us running down the street like a track team... when he burnt the house down and my mother was in it, how could I forget it, the pain infinite. She's my Queen and I ain't even British. She's the only reason that I went to school and I finished. She told me that I had talent. Got on her knees and prayed for me when I started being violent. She saw something in me that, until this day I don't know if I could be that. But I'm a die tryin and when I'm done cryin, grab the iron (Minaj 2008).

Minaj concludes this verse by talking directly to her father. In a courageous stance of righteous indignation, she tells him, "I shoulda thrown a book at you cause I hate you so much that it burn when I look at you" (Minaj 2008). However, the song ends by shifting from a stance of rage toward Minaj's father to penitence toward a former lover and an unborn child.

"Autobiography" provides a framework for interpreting Minaj's artistry (to include her multiple personas) and experiences. Her lyrics and representations offer critical points of escape, both symbolic and material, from violence and the threat of violence while enabling her to confront her experiences on her own terms. The idea of escape also includes Minaj's liberation from poverty induced by her father's drug use and rage. This is perhaps the greatest motivation behind her art: to provide an alternative reality for herself and her mother. Thus, "Autobiography" instructs the audience to read Minaj's linguistic and representational artistry with both eyes open. Therefore, songs such as "Go Hard" and "Moment 4 Life," which on the surface appear sexist, individualistic and materialistic, require analyses that attend to what happens *between* the lines.

"Go Hard" and "Moment 4 Life" present Minaj as triumphant, self-assured, independent and playful. As she articulates in "Go Hard," "It's [her] time. The tears have dried... no weapon formed against [her] will prosper" (Minaj 2009). Most importantly, Minaj is now "alive," even if only for a moment. In "Moment 4 Life" she raps,

> I fly with the stars in the skies. I am no longer trying to survive. I believe that life is a prize. But to live doesn't mean you're alive. In this very moment I'm king. In this very moment I slay Goliath with the sling. In this very moment I bring, put it on everything. I will retire with the ring. And I will retire with the crown, yes. No, I'm not lucky I'm blessed, yes. Clap for the heavy weight champ, me. Wish that I could have this moment for life, for life, for life. Cause in this moment I just feel so alive, alive, alive (Minaj 2010).

In between the lines is a literal shift from dying to living triumphant, Minaj is conscious of the difference and distance between living and being alive. Being alive is achieved. However, even with hard work, it demands God's grace. Thus, it is not guaranteed.

Minaj's lyrics provide a context for the daughters and granddaughters to reimagine their reality. In her quest for meaning, Minaj confronts her existential conditions, speaks her truth, reveals her contradictions, displays her scars, plays with her nuances and finds a way to transcend her predicament, even if only momentarily. It is this sense of power and agency and complex ambiguity that resonates with the experiences, expectations and repertoires of the daughters and granddaughters in her audience. Moreover, it is this kind of creative opening that incited the mothers and grandmothers to dance. Minaj's music makes room for the artistic revelations of those past as well as those to come.

Nevertheless, while Minaj's artistry may be imagined as a site of power and agency as well as a clue to the daughters' experiences and articulations of race, sex, sexuality, and gender, there are several dangers in reading her representational and linguistic strategies uncritically. For example, although Minaj realigns dominant black female cultural stereotypes so that they are empowering, power is not equally aligned. It is unclear how much power Minaj has over her current representation. However, pre-signing footage of the artist suggests that some of what we see is her own inter-subjective creation, which draws from both context and internal consciousness. Nevertheless, whatever power Minaj has is likely unparalleled to the daughters and granddaughters in her audience. That is, Minaj the artist has the luxury of protected space. She has a team of people to guard her body from violence, although the threat of violence likely remains. There are different kinds of consequences for enacting Minaj's representational or linguistic liberties offstage, particularly in a patriarchal context that interprets black women and girls, especially sexual liberalists, as hypersexual or second-class.

An additional danger is Minaj's likely appeal to a growing, third-wave brand of feminism, which superficially celebrates female achievements while invalidating feminism in reality, thus keeping women, particularly the daughters, in their place. For example, this kind of feminism highlights women's right to embrace their sexual selves as powerful, deciding subjects as opposed to mere objects while simultaneously suggesting that power is gained through sex and sexual display—with and for male subjects. This is what sociologist and self-identified third-wave feminist, Shayne Lee, posits as "feminist chic" (Lee 2010). However, feminist cultural critic Susan J. Douglas interprets power gained through sex and sexual display *for* men as "enlightened sexism" because the underlying idea is that power is achieved by catering to male desire (Douglas 2010). Black feminist theorist T. Denean Sharpley-Whiting refers to this kind of power as "pseudo-power" (Sharpley-Whiting 2007). It depends on a corporate formula for attractiveness, which limits women and girls' value to depreciating assets on one hand, and assumes their accessibility on the other (Sharpley-Whiting 2007).

However, it is imperative to note that Minaj both caters to and does not cater to male desire. She caters to it to the extent that her desirability increases her market share, which enables the satisfaction of goods (i.e., taking care of her mother). However, Minaj resists catering to male desire by maintaining sexual ambiguity. This in itself is empowering. It loosens the yoke of rigid identity politics by embracing multi-positionality and exploring individual interests. These moves are critical to dialoguing with the daughters and granddaughters whose "gardens" are presently speaking. However, the question is "Are we listening?"

The search for our daughters' gardens requires that we not only listen closely to what their art conveys, but expand what we think art (the "garden") is. An engagement between hip hop and religion necessitates such a move. Moreover, the historical moment that we are in and its emphasis on popular culture, to include black American popular culture vernacular traditions, as well as womanist "aims toward the survival and wholeness of entire people" (Walker 1983), demands this move—that we allow the daughters' and granddaughters' "gardens" to expand and challenge our existing stocks of knowledge.

References

Anderson, Victor. *Beyond Ontological Blackness: An Essay on Religious and Cultural Criticism*. New York: Continuum, 1999.

Douglas, Susan. *Enlightened Sexism: The Seductive Message that Feminism's Work Is Done*. New York: Times Books, 2010.

Foucault, Michel. *The History of Sexuality: An Introduction, Vol. 1*. New York: Vintage Books, 1990.

Hall, Stuart, ed. *Representation: Cultural Representations and Signifying Practices*. London: Sage, 1997.

Lee, Shayne. *Erotic Revolutionaries: Black Women, Sexuality, and Popular Culture*. Lanham: Hamilton Books, 2010.

Long, Charles (1986). *Significations: Signs, Symbols, and Images in the Interpretation of Religion*. Aurora, CO: Davies Group Publishers, 1995.

Minaj, Nicki. "Autobiography." On *Sucka Free*. Young Money Entertainment, 2008.

———. *Barbie World*. Young Money Entertainment, 2010.

———. "Go Hard." On *Beam Me Up, Scotty*. Young Money Entertainment, 2009.

———. "Here I Am" and "Moment 4 Life." On *Pink Friday*. Cash Money Records/Motown Records, 2010.

Sharpley-Whiting, T. Denean. *Pimps Up, Ho's Down: Hip Hop's Hold on Young Black Women*. New York: New York University Press, 2007.

Spillers, Hortense. *Black, White and in Color: Essays on American Literature and Culture*. Chicago: University of Chicago Press, 2003.

Walker, Alice. *In Search of Our Mother's Gardens: A Womanist Prose*. San Diego: Harcourt Brace Jovanovich, 1983.

34

"It's Not the Beat, but It's the Word that Sets the People Free": Race, Technology, and Theology in the Emergence of Christian Rap Music

Josef Sorett

Abstract: *In an effort to address lacunae in the literature about hip hop, as well as to explore the role of new music and media in Pentecostal traditions, this essay examines rap music within the narratives of American religious history. Specifically, through an engagement with the life, ministry, and music of Stephen Wiley—who recorded the first commercially-released Christian rap song in 1985—this essay offers an account of hip hop as a window into the intersections of religion, race, and media near the end of the twentieth century. It shows that the cultural and theological traditions of Pentecostalism were central to Wiley's understanding of the significance of racial ideology and technology in his rap ministry. Additionally, Wiley's story helps to identify a theological, cultural, and technological terrain that is shared, if contested, by mainline Protestant, neo-Pentecostal, and Word of Faith Christians during a historical moment that has been described as post-denominational.*

Over the past two decades a growing body of research culture has taken shape. More often than not, the inquiries in this emerging literature have located hip hop (or rap) in the traditions of African American cultural (literary and musical) expression.[1] Within this corpus, little attention has focused on religion.[2] The few works that have directed their attention to rap music's spiritual dimensions have often opted to explore representations of religion in so-called "secular" hip hop.[3] *As* an effort to address lacunae in the literature on hip hop, as well as to explore the role of new music and media in Pentecostal traditions, this essay reexamines rap music within the narratives of American religious history. Specifically, through an engagement with the life, ministry, and music of Stephen Wiley—who recorded the first commercially released Christian rap song in 1985—this essay offers an account of hip hop as a window into the intersections of religion, race, and media near the end of the twentieth century. It shows that the cultural and theological traditions of Pentecostalism were central to Wiley's understanding of the significance of racial ideology and technology in his rap ministry. Additionally, Wiley's story helps to identify a theological, cultural, and technological terrain that is shared, if contested, by mainline Protestant, neo-Pentecostal, and Word of Faith Christians (black and white alike) during a historical moment that has been described as post-denominational.[4]

Since its inception more than twenty-five years ago, Christian rap has often "mirrored the stars and styles of its secular counterpart."[5] In fact, a number of Christian rappers have seemed to deliberately model themselves after mainstream hip hop artists. For instance, in the late 1980s, Michael Peace's raw vocals were comparable to that of a young LL Cool J. The trio PID (Preachers in Disguise) donned all black, like the much more popular group, RUN-DMC, several years before the latter released their religious record, *Down with the King*.[6] Entering the 1990s, Gospel Gangstaz became a mainstay in Christian rap shortly after NWA (Niggas with Attitude) captured national attention and made "Gangsta Rap" the most prominent genre within hip hop.[7] Finally, the smooth baritone voice of Stephen Wiley, Christian rap's original act, might be compared to Kurtis Blow, who in 1980 recorded the first rap song to sell over 500,000 records.[8] Ironically, in two rare instances in which "secular" artists followed the trajectory of their "sacred" foils, both Joseph Simmons (Run of RUN-DMC) and Kurtis Blow entered the Christian ministry after the end of their careers as rappers. The latter now pastors The Hip Hop Church in New York City, while the former is a member of Master Prophet Bishop Bernard Jordan's Zoe Ministries. In contrast, each of the above Christian rappers was simultaneously a youth minister, confirming that the lines between the sacred (churches) and the secular (hip hop) are much more fluid than is commonly assumed.

More pertinent to the aims of this essay, this list of early Christian MCs calls attention to the continued role that new media and technology play in the (re)shaping and (re)imagining of religious practice. In the case of Christian rap, one thinks not only of the efforts of youth ministers to adopt novel music to spread "The Word," but also of the very ways in which the different races/ cultures (black and white) and technologies (radio, recording studios, compact discs) associated with hip hop were fuel for their theological imaginations. A close analysis of Christian rap helps to illumine the ways in which the messages and the media involved in religious practice are often co-constitutive of one another.

In its present forms, gospel (or holy) hip hop, as it is now most commonly called, is as diverse and complex as the broader phenomenon from which it takes aesthetic cues.[9] There are regional sounds, underground purists, crossover sensations, socially conscious backpackers, Caribbean-inflected Reggae and Reggaeton artists, street storytellers, and others who simply prefer to tell "the old, old story" to a new soundtrack. In addition to the eclectic repertoire that is gospel hip hop's current scene, the story of Christian rap's emergence provides a compelling portrait of what's at stake at the intersections of race, technology, and theology in contemporary America. Novel musical forms have long been at the center of struggles within Christian churches in the United States. African Americans are certainly no exception to this fact. Rather, black sacred music has long been a site where religion and race, as well as class and gender, were simultaneously contested with great vigor. This history is one helpful trajectory in which to locate the story of Christian rap.[10] The gospel-blues was forged in Chicago during the 1920s and 1930s by such pioneers as Thomas Dorsey. In the 1960s and 1970s, several singers in the Bay area of northern California—most prominently, the Edwin Hawkins Singers—helped to define a new sacred sound, which was later termed contemporary gospel music. And six years after Sugar Hill Records released "Rapper's Delight," gospel hip hop made history when Stephen Wiley recorded his debut single, *Bible Break* (1985), the first commercially distributed Christian rap song.[11]

A far cry from the South Bronx, the site of hip hop's most familiar creation myth, Stephen L. Wiley was born in 1956 in the small southwestern town of Haskell, Oklahoma.[12] When he was a toddler, his parents moved the family to the county seat in order to secure a better education for their children. Wiley fondly recounts, "I started out a rascal from Haskell and I ended up an Okee from Muskogee."[13] Like most children in Muskogee, church attendance was a part of the regular routine during Wiley's youth. His family belonged to the local African Methodist Episcopal (AME) church.[14] Beginning with his early years in this historic black denomination, Wiley describes a gradual process of religious maturation that would culminate with his rap ministry and later pastoral responsibilities:

> I grew up going to church; but it was a denominational church. It wasn't until, I guess it was my experience with this one pastor, that I seriously began to look at spirituality, the reality of it all in my life. And I grew up in church. That's what you do; you get up, you go to church; but as far as making Jesus the Lord of my life and focusing in on the spiritual side, it wasn't until I was 13 that I really began to consider it.

While some might question the historical veracity of Wiley's childhood memories, his account of coming of age in Muskogee is nonetheless a telling entree into the religious landscape of a region of the United States often referred to as "the buckle of the bible belt." On one hand, Oklahoma has a long-standing tradition of mainline and liberal Protestantism; and it boasts one of the largest Unitarian congregations in the country, Tulsa's All Souls Unitarian Church. On the other hand, the state is home to a critical mass of conservative churches and para-church ministries connected to Pentecostal and Charismatic renewal movements that flourished during the latter half of the twentieth century.[15] Much scholarship has documented the recent turn away from institutional religion to the more open rubric of spirituality. However, this latter group calls attention to a network of churchgoers who, while critical of the former group, opted to forge their own tradition of nondenominational Christianity.[16]

Significantly, these two terrains—liberal and conservative Protestantisms—are not mutually exclusive. A most obvious example of the fluidity between the two is another Oklahoma native: Oral Roberts. One of the most popular televangelists of the twentieth century, Roberts is known for his "seed-faith" theology, for a television ministry that emphasized the miraculous, and for founding a university that bears his name.[17] For close to fifty years Oral Roberts University (ORU), located in Tulsa, has been a breeding ground for prominent evangelical, Charismatic, and Pentecostal preachers, including the likes of Ted Haggard and Carlton Pearson. Moreover, the college's chapel has hosted such figures as Claudette Copeland, T. D. Jakes, Marilyn Hickey, Benny Hinn, Paul Morton, and Harold Ray. A less familiar story line is the fact that Roberts was an ordained elder in the Methodist church, and that he remained a member of Tulsa's Boston Avenue United Methodist Church until his death in 2009.[18] Alongside of popular religious broadcasters like Pearson and Jakes, Dr. James Buskirk, Roberts' friend and the pastor of Tulsa's First United Methodist Church, was a recurring speaker at ORU's chapel services.[19] Illustrative of Roberts' mainline connections, Buskirk was also the founding dean of ORU's school of theology. Stephen Wiley, without nearly as much media fanfare, was a product of the same rich, religious milieu of Oklahoma that produced Oral Roberts. Now pastor of a nondenominational church, Wiley continues to balance the worlds of the historic black denominations in which he was raised and his associations with the contemporary Word of Faith movement.[20] He privileges the latter in his spiritual narrative, to be sure. Yet, Wiley nonetheless acknowledges the formative role of more traditional black churches in his development.[21]

Something of a musical prodigy on drums, during middle school Wiley began to perform in local nightclubs. At roughly the same time, a local Baptist preacher recruited him for the Muskogee City Wide Youth Choir. From the time he was thirteen until he entered college, Wiley maintained a close relationship with this pastor. He played drums for the choir and served as its president. At the age of nineteen this pastor licensed Wiley as a Baptist minister. Yet, it was not until his senior year of college that he "got born-again, spirit-filled, committed my life to the Lord." Wiley decided to attend college in his home state and matriculated at the University of Oklahoma (OU) in Norman, just a three-hour drive from Muskogee. At OU, he had a great time. He immersed himself in black Greek life and pledged Alpha Phi Alpha, the oldest African American fraternity. He found moderate success in a local band that opened up for big-name acts that visited the region. And he made a name for himself on campus as a disc jockey on OU's radio station. Known on air simply as "Dr. OJ," Wiley would begin each show with a poetic prelude:

> I'm the wicked doctor of soul, jester of jive, clown of sound, professor of poetic profound statements. I am a poet and I know it, not ashamed to show it. I can't lose with the stuff I use. Sugar pie guy, that's the reason why I can dim the rainbow's glow with my DJ show.

Just as rap music was gaining recognition as a distinct genre of popular music, Wiley's introduction revealed his indebtedness to black vernacular cultures. During the 1970s a number of black poets—including the likes of Gil Scot-Heron, Nikki Giovanni, and the Last Poets—experimented with music and gained national attention. Wiley's verse displayed both hyperbole and hyper-braggadocio, as well as it paired rhythm and rhyme; all characteristics of the African American tradition of signifying, a set of cultural practices commonly considered an antecedent of rap music.[22]

Despite the signs of a budding career in music and radio, Wiley quickly changed course. Recalling this transition, he explained, "It was my senior year. The Spirit of God spoke to me and said, 'Seek ye first the Kingdom of God and his righteousness, and all these things will be added unto you'. . . I left the band and I just began to pray." After graduating with a degree in broadcast journalism, Wiley took a position at a local Christian radio station owned by the Assemblies of God pastor, gospel artist, and televangelist Jimmy Swaggart. By the end of the 1980s Swaggart's name was synonymous with a sex scandal that captured headlines in 1988.[23] Earlier in the decade, however, Swaggart was at the height of his popularity after starting a television broad cast in 1975 that grew to reach an international audience. Additionally, between 1976 and 1980 he was twice nominated for a Grammy award for his work as a gospel musician. Despite Swaggart's background in southern gospel music, the shift from fraternity life and playing in a band that featured a repertoire of jazz, R&B and funk to working alongside few other African Americans proved to be a dramatic transition for Wiley. That the radio station's rotation primarily featured preachers like Kenneth Copeland, Jerry Savelle and R. W. Shambach—all white men and then prominent figures in the Word of Faith movement—only made matters more difficult. While working at the station Wiley was sorting through the tensions between Swaggart's media-savvy Pentecostalism, the prosperity theology of Word of Faith preachers, and his own roots in black churches. He marked this moment as the starting point in a process of "renewing" his mind. Sorting through the cultural dissonance caused by these new surroundings, Wiley happened upon strategic support.

Although licensed to preach at the age of nineteen, Stephen Wiley had begun to sense a call to ministry more acutely during his senior year of college. Prompted by this possibility, he began listening to sermon tapes and perusing periodicals that were lying around the apartment he shared with a college friend. These spiritual commodities were gifts sent by his roommate's girl friend, who was a student at Rhema Bible Training Center in Broken Arrow, OK. While only a couple of hours from Norman, Wiley had not heard of Rhema prior to these care packages. Nor was he familiar with its founder, Kenneth Hagin Sr. and the Word of Faith movement, of which Rhema was then the epicenter.[24] Initially Hagin's race was a turn-off for Wiley, he recalled:

> He [my roommate] would play Kenneth Hagin tapes and had *Word of Faith* magazine come in the mail and at the time I had a radical mind. I felt, here's a white guy. He can't teach me anything. I'm looking at *Word of Faith* magazine and seeing white faces. Radical mind—he can't teach me anything about preaching. I know what preaching is. They're not even preaching. They're just talking, just lecturing. Until I got a book from Fred Price. I said, "I've never heard a black man talk like this."

Although he would not meet Price in person for several years, Wiley's entrance into the Word of Faith community was mediated by the teachings of a man who was then the movement's most prominent black preacher. Price was ordained by Kenneth Hagin in 1975, just two years after founding Ever Increasing Faith Ministries in Los Angeles. Beginning in 1955 Price had held several ministerial appointments, in AME, Baptist, and Presbyterian churches. During the 1970s, however, he became one of the first African American pastors within the growing Word of Faith community. He was also one of the first black ministers to be on national television. In this prominent role, Price added an air of racial authenticity to the Word of Faith movement, helping it make inroads into thousands of black homes across the country. Wiley was but one of many African Americans for whom Price's race made the new religious ideas of the faith message more accessible.[25] Still, in other ways, Stephen Wiley's story was unique.

More than ten years later Fred Price recruited Wiley and his wife to serve as youth pastors at his Los Angeles megachurch, Crenshaw Christian Center, known more popularly as "the Faith Dome." But it was this initial encounter with Price's books and sermons, and their frequent references to Kenneth Hagin, that started Wiley on a new journey. Shortly after first hearing Price he applied and enrolled at Hagin's Rhema Bible Training Center. According to Wiley:

> From that my mind began to get renewed, not to black and white, but to the Word of God. But it still took a black man to get my attention. So I've always looked at it from the perspective that it's not a black thing or a white thing, it's all about the blood of Jesus. . . Even when I did my music I didn't try to make the music a black thing or white thing, but I always tried to put the Word in the forefront.

It is through the language of "renewal" (renew, renewing, renewed, and so forth), an appeal to a verse in the New Testament book of Romans, that Wiley frames his transition from "the black church" to the Word of Faith movement.[26] For him, this renewal required a shift in perspective from prioritizing racial identity to privileging religious commitment. Now, his aim in ministry is not to make it a "black thing or white thing," but "to put *the Word* in the forefront" (italics mine).

As Milmon Harrison has noted, treating the Bible as a "contract between the born-again believe and God" is a fundamental precept in Word of Faith theology. In this regard, "the Faith message" proved to be a perfect match for a budding preacher who rapped, as his songs provided a space to practice "positive confession" of Bible verse over trendy bass lines. Equally significant, the dominant ideology of race in Word of Faith circles is one of "racial reconciliation," wherein the word is presented as a panacea for America's painful racial history. Vis-à-vis Word of Faith theology, for Wiley this contractual understanding of the Christian Bible superseded his prior perspective's dependence upon a black/white binary, a product of the logic of white supremacy that Charles Mills has identified as *The Racial Contract* embedded in modernity.

In 1980 Stephen Wiley began a formal relationship with Kenneth Hagin Ministries, as a student at the Rhema Bible Training Center and member of Hagin's Crusade Team, which lasted until 1995. Moreover, his career as a Christian rapper was launched on resources and relationships made available by immediate access to what were three of the most influential ministries shaping contemporary Pentecostal and Charismatic communities: (1) Oral Roberts University (and Oral Roberts Ministries); (2) Rhema Bible Training Center (and Kenneth Hagin Ministries); and (3) the former Higher Dimensions Evangelistic Center (and the AZUSA conference and fellowship) led by Carlton Pearson. As has already been stated, Roberts was among the most popular, if a controversial, Protestant clergyman of the twentieth century. Hagin and Rhema provided a key institutional home for what would become known as the prosperity gospel.[27] And Carlton Pearson, whom Jonathan Walton has dubbed "the Pied Piper of Neo-Pentecostals," was the "spiritual powerbroker" who almost singlehandedly brought black Pentecostalism to the center of American religious broadcasting.[28] All three of these institutions were located within the borders of Tulsa County. Along with countless other like-minded ministries, they helped make the region a veritable ground zero for the Charismatic Christian world. It was in this context that Wiley began to "renew" his mind as well as to incubate his ministry as a Christian rap artist.

According to Stephen Wiley, his first recorded rap song, "Bible Break," began as part of a Rhema Crusade Team song that sought to infuse cultural diversity into an otherwise lily-white ministry. Remembering those earliest performances, Wiley explained:

> We did a song with the Rhema band—"Jesus Loves the Little Children"—and when it would get to "red and yellow, black and white...," when it would get to the red part we'd do a little Indian thing, put on a headdress and dance. When it got to yellow, we put on a Chinese hat. And when it got to the black, one of the guys would do a little *Soul Train* dance. So I just wrote a few phrases of rap, "Red and yellow, black and white. Everybody is a star in Jesus sight. He loves you so, he came into this world, to give his life for every boy and girl." That's where it started.

601

Although the song's content elevated familiar racial caricatures, or perhaps for this very reason, it caught on quickly. Wiley's verse became a regular routine and, with a growing repertoire of songs, he secured a place as a regular performer at Hagin's annual Campmeeting in Broken Arrow. Over the next couple of years he recorded *Bible Break* with the help of his friend Mike Barnes, an in-demand producer of Christian music who lived in Tulsa and served on the staff of Carlton Pearson's Higher Dimensions Evangelistic Center. The two took advantage of access to the recording studios at Kenneth Hagin Ministries and converted the short verse into Wiley's first full-length Christian rap song.[29] Through his relationship with Hagin, Wiley was also able to broker a relation ship with a local tape duplication business that used his single to drum up business at an annual meeting of the Christian Booksellers Association (CBA). From that one event, according to Wiley, several Christian music labels approached him with contract offers. At this point he began to believe he was on to something. As a musician, Wiley could not help but be excited by the prospect of signing a recording contract. As a minister in training, especially within the overlapping circles of Charismatic Christianity and religious broad casting, he could sense that more was at stake theologically. Significantly, the religious worlds that Wiley now called home actively cultivated "a faith in redeeming power of communications technologies."[30] As a former DJ he had a good sense of the listening tastes of the American public. Now, with his renewed mind taking form, more records sales also meant more souls saved.

A dramatically different experience helped clarify for Wiley that God was indeed calling him to a rap ministry. During the 1980s he served as youth minister at Love Center Church, an African American Pentecostal congregation on Tulsa's North Side. At the same time, he and his wife, Pamela, were volunteer chaplains at the Lloyd Rader Juvenile Detention Center, just outside of city limits in Sand Springs. Faced with the daunting task of managing one of the few times that young men and women were allowed to co-mingle—in the chapel—Wiley prayed for divine intervention. Accompanied by his classic "Jam-Box," with two new songs and a still developing lead single, he felt led to draw on his growing musical inventory. "A lot of the teenagers there had hard hearts, and I couldn't get to them with my message alone," Wiley told a reporter, "so I would do a rap song to get their attention."[31] The results proved providential. "So literally," he recalled, "before my eyes, I couldn't speak to the children unless I rapped." Wiley continued:

> So I'm writing these rap songs and the chapel service would pack out. Literally, it was standing room only. They would tell their friends, "The chaplain's rapping, you got to come hear it." So I would do a couple of rap songs and then I would preach. And that's when I noticed the power of the music and it began to evolve for me. Black, white, Hispanic, Indian kids; everybody loved it.

To Wiley, that his songs reached young people, irrespective of race, was further confirmation that Christian rap was his calling. Following the national distribution of *Bible Break* in 1985, Wiley began to receive invitations to perform beyond the familiar settings of Lloyd Rader and Rhema. His earliest invitations came from white Word of Faith churches associated with Hagin's network. Gradually, some black mainline and Pentecostal churches, as well as public and parochial schools, opened their doors to him as well. As Gangsta Rap captured national attention in the late 1980s, institutions competing for the souls and minds of young people seemed to sense that Wiley's positive lyrics might be a resource that served their varying missions well.[32] His core audience, no doubt, remained churches; especially Word of Faith congregations. However, Wiley garnered wider attention from the mainstream music press, including a feature in the November 1988 issue of *Spin* magazine, which dubbed him the "Grandmaster of God."[33]

Stephen Wiley steadily moved more fully into his ministry as a Word of Faith preacher and Christian rapper. Like Fred Price, his was another African American face that helped spread the faith message within black communities. Yet, Wiley's presence—as an African American and as a rapper—addressed several needs across the color line. Just as his initial verse with the Rhema Crusade Team provided an image of cultural diversity, his blackness offered largely white congregations confirmation of the program of racial reconciliation to which many of them aspired.[34] Still, though many whites accepted his performance as a representation of racial authenticity in the pursuit of their multi-racial commitments, they kept his body at arm's length. As white Word of Faith churches welcomed Wiley into their pulpits, racial boundaries emerged more clearly when it came to his accommodations. "I stayed in more pastors' homes," Wiley recalled, "because the pastors were pretty much the only ones open enough to let the black guy stay with them." White congregations embraced his music in public, but they rejected him as their social and intimate equal. A group of youth pastors in Louisiana stood out in Wiley's memories of the ways race constrained his interactions during this time:

> They realized they needed me to reach their kids... I got a call and went to Shreveport and I met with the youth pastors. White guys, Presbyterians, Episcopalians, Methodists, Baptist... every group you could imagine. They are having outreaches and their bringing in a lot of gang members... They say... "You're a gang specialist!" I'm not a gang specialist. I'm from L.A. I'm a black guy. [They assumed that] I must be a gang specialist. Plus I can do rap music. I must know something about gangs... Now the music is what they knew to bring me in, but once I got in I was able to help them. With what? *The Word* of God. [italics mine]

Wiley's perceived resemblance to certain stereotypes (for example, the black male as gangster) facilitated many of these invitations, even as it created expectations that he was ill-fitted to meet (such as the rapper as "gang specialist"). At least in retrospect, Wiley was aware of the irony in the racial logic attendant to his identity as an African American in largely white religious worlds. On the one hand, it was his racial difference that made him desirable. And Wiley embraced the opportunities this afforded him. Yet, on the other hand, that his body was read through familiar racial tropes colored the contours of these exchanges. Here race largely limited these encounters to public spaces (churches) and particular practices (rap), reinscribing the very fact of his otherness. Still, what mattered most for Wiley was that he was able to deliver "the word."

Indeed, Stephen Wiley's appearance as the "authentic" racial other opened doors for him in white churches. Conversely, many black churches rejected the very thing that whites appreciated: the "street sound" that rap music represented. According to Wiley, black churches were at times noticeably hostile to his music. Occasionally, church mothers spoke out—or as Wiley put it, "prophe-lied"—against his ministry. Such experiences of rejection by African Americans stood out in his memory. Once, a disagreement among the leadership of a Gary, Indiana congregation shut down his show. "I didn't get the chance to do a full concert," he explained. "I may have done two songs, because the deacons and the trustees got into a fist fight over the concept of gospel hip hop." Wiley elaborated:

> Half of them believed, "We're not bringing the world into the church. The kids are going to be breakdancing and spinning on their heads on the pulpit and the altar." The other half believed, "This is what's going to reach our young people. This is going to bring them in the church. We need this. This is youth evangelism." And they literally got into a fist-fight because of that spirit of resistance.

For Wiley, the novel aesthetics and technologies associated with hip hop were welcome resources for spreading the gospel to the next generation. So he interpreted any antagonism in theological terms. His critics, in short, were swayed by a "spirit of resistance." Clearly, part of these conflicts can be credited to media coverage that connected rap music to drugs, sex, and violence. For obvious reasons this made parents, perhaps churchgoers especially, anxious. However, the opposition he encountered from many black churches is also part of a longer history of class tensions. As far back as the late nineteenth century, black sacred music has been a site of contestation for both racial and religious identities. During the 1920s, churches in northern cities attended by the black middle class were reluctant to embrace the blues-inflected sounds that working-class blacks brought with them from the South. Thus, it was largely in storefront and spiritualist congregations, as well as mainline churches willing to experiment with "Sanctified" culture, that the gospel-blues took hold.[35] Moreover, these same churches were able to compete with the black Protestant establishment by employing the novel technologies of radio and race records.[36] Similarly, during the 1980s Word of Faith churches were quick to capitalize on the burgeoning business of televangelism. Just as Spiritualist congregations and storefronts put pressure on mainlines in the 1920s, black Word of Faith congregations created a complex of churches that competed with traditional black denominations as the twentieth century approached its end.[37] This religious network, which valorized new media and valued cultural relevance, created a space for Stephen Wiley's ministry to emerge.

Significantly, Wiley seems to have preferred the subtle insults of white congregations to the open "spirit of resistance" in black mainline churches. Surely, his spiritual analysis—that white's churches temporarily suspended their prejudices because he made the word relevant to young people—was magnified by the disparity in material resources between these two camps. While black denominational churches provided him with love offerings, at best, and "Pentecostal handshakes"[38] at worst, honorariums were the norm with white Word of Faith churches. Rather than simply rejecting one for the other, according to Wiley, the latter made it financially feasible for him to maintain relationships with the former. After all, he still felt more at home, culturally, in black churches, even as he was growing increasingly theologically estranged from them. Additionally, in Word of Faith theology, the honoraria he received confirmed that he was indeed doing God's will.[39] Reflecting on his first year as a full-time Christian rapper, Wiley shared,

> I had more income in one month from being on the road full-time than I had the entire year before. So that was [clearly], "God is in this". . . I learned; "If it was God's will, it was God's bill." . . . and it became the easiest thing and I haven't looked back.

By the time his rap ministry was taking off, Wiley was a Rhema graduate and was well versed in the prosperity gospel. Between the late 1980s and early 1990s Wiley claimed to earn an average of $12,000 per week, with a single largest check of $10,000 coming from Fred Price's Crenshaw Christian Center. As Shayne Lee has noted, prosperity teachings provided believer's license to "enjoy their wealth and consumerism as their rightful inheritance as God's faithful children."[40] It is of little surprise, then, that Wiley was persuaded to join the staff of Price's Los Angeles congregation. At the time Price was pastor of the most prestigious church in the worlds of black Word of Faith adherents. For that matter, because of his television broadcast Fred Price was one of the most visibly prominent ministers in the Word of Faith movement, without the racial qualifier. Clearly, Wiley's rap ministry had received the seal of God's blessing!

Given Wiley's affiliation with the Word of Faith movement, which views scripture as an antidote to apply literally to all earthly problems, his emphasis on the word carried added theological significance. For Wiley, most obviously, "the word" refers to the Christian Bible. For sure, his songs' lyrics included scripture. But here, "the word" also signals a particular hermeneutic inherent to the faith message, wherein words, more generally, are indicative of identity, destiny, and purpose. And it is through words—namely, "positive confession"—that such things are affirmed.[41] In this view, reciting positive lyrics over hip hop beats presented the possibility of redeeming both the generation who grew up on hip hop and the genre itself And putting biblical lyrics on a portable recording (audiocassettes) only magnified their spiritual value. Wiley, first, as a "secular" and then as a "saved" musician, understood all of this uniquely well. In his view, the "word," in the form of gospel hip hop, mediated between two radically opposed worlds; sacred and secular, good and evil, God and the Devil. And Wiley drew a wealth of meaning from the very media that facilitated such mediations.

That is, media technologies (recording studios, compact discs, and so forth) created both the needs that required, and raw materials that facilitated, theological ingenuity. Specifically, the words of his songs not only carried a religious message, but they were also indicative of a larger spiritual reality at work. According to Wiley, consumers of "secular" hip hop were subject to the spirits of MCs and producers who are "full of the devil, popping pills, smoking dope, [and had] groupies all over the place." In contrast, Christian rap albums carried the spirit of musicians who were "full of the Holy Ghost, speaking in tongues, [and] love the Lord." The recording studio was thus conceived as a sacred space wherein "the spirit of the anointing" forever altered the substance of a compact disc and influenced the destiny of its consumers. Much like prayer cloths sent home by healing evangelists, Wiley imagined his COs as physical repositories of "the word" that allowed young Christians to "take the anointing home" in the form of songs suited to their cultural tastes.

In a plastic cassette case adorned by a cartoon image of Stephen Wiley holding a boom-box on his shoulder and a Bible at this waist, *Bible Break* arrived in Christian bookstores across the country in 1985. Wiley's music entailed an extended effort to make Christianity relevant to the so-called hip hop generation. *Bible Break* began this task by teaching children to recite the books of the Bible; but Wiley's lyrics evolved beyond strategies for memorizing scripture. During a recording career that produced six albums over a period of roughly ten years, he addressed such issues as gang violence, drug abuse, and racism. For each problem, Wiley posed the same solution: "the word." On his fourth album, *Get Real*, he explicitly articulated his hermeneutic, which might be read as much as Christian apologetics as an apology for subpar musical production. That his tracks were inferior to most mainstream hip hop was justifiable because, Wiley rapped, "It's not the beat, but it's the Word that sets the people free. So, gimme the Word!" [42] And, in music and in life, it was his ability to simply put "the word" first that enabled him to succeed. His faith in the power of "the word" led him into unfamiliar and unwelcoming territory for a black man. "I'd go to all white cities," he explained, "and 100, 500 kids show up. I would rap to them. Literally, I was the only black person in town. I went there and was well received and rapped, gave an altar call and blessed the kids." Conversely, he attributed declines in royalties on later albums to the fact that he had developed more complicated business arrangements. Wiley implied that rather than relying on "the word," he had become more concerned with contracts and the money they could secure.

To be sure, Wiley's reflections on the trajectory of his ministry as a Christian rapper say as much about the politics (and pitfalls) of memory as they do as a measure of the historical record. Still, his story helps sheds light on the relationship between history and theory in the study of religion. It serves as an example of how religious practitioners theorize (or theologize) race and technology as well as their own personal histories. To borrow from Emerson, "All history becomes subjective; there is properly no history, only biography." [43] Accordingly, Wiley's recollections of the intersection of racial ideologies and media technologies in his own rap ministry (and his broader spiritual evolution) reveal much about the cultural and theological traditions of the modern Word of Faith movement. Twenty-five years after the release of *Bible Break* Stephen Wiley continues to call this religious community home. As a pastor of congregations in Tulsa and Muskogee, Oklahoma, he is a member of both Fred Price's Inner-City Word of Faith Ministries and Rhema Ministerial Alliance International. His memories, as much as these affiliations, evince a deep commitment to the faith message.

Moreover, Stephen Wiley's story captures the critical contributions of American Pentecostalism in reimagining new media technologies as novel methods for (and means of) Christian ministry. As an ardent advocate of the ability of "the word" to overcome racial and cultural differences, his language mirrors the story of racial transcendence in the emergence of Pentecostalism on Azusa Street at the dawn of the twentieth century. It was there that the spirit descended on an interracial crowd of believers, borrowing from the New Testament story in Acts and providing a creation myth for future racial reconciliation movements. In recent years, Wiley's role in the formation of Christian rap has been publicly celebrated within Christian music circles, where he is affectionately referred to as the "godfather" of gospel hip hop. In 2009 he was inducted into the Oklahoma Jazz Hall of Fame for his contributions.[44] Such occasions have provided him with a platform to share his message about the means and meaning of the music. For him it is simple: "Don't put the music first. Don't put the style first. Don't put race first. Keep the Word of God first," Wiley shares. "Because the Bible says, 'The Word will never pass away.' The style will change and we see even the name has changed from rap to hip hop. But if you put the Word first. . . " In this regard, "the Word" is imagined as the ultimate litmus test: a measure of the appropriate alignment of race, music, and technology with theology. That is to say, for Wiley, race, music, and technology must be submitted to the authority of "the word." After all, he explained, "The Word is the difference. . . whether you teach it, sing it, rap it, have it with ice cream, with whip cream and a cherry on top."

Notes

1. The two seminal works in the field of hip hop studies are Tricia Rose's *Black Noise: Rap Music and Black Culture in Contemporary America* (Middletown, CT: Wesleyan, 1993); Houston Baker's *Black Studies, Rap, and the Academy* (Chicago: University of Chicago Press, 1993).
2. Felicia Miyakawa's *Five Percenter Rap: God Hop's Music, Message and Black Muslim Mission* (Bloomington: Indiana University Press, 2005) is the only academic monograph focused solely on hip hop and religion. Perhaps indicative of this trend, Murray Forman and Mark Anthony Neal's definitive anthology, *That's the joint: The Hip Hop Studies Reader* (New York: Routledge, 2004), brilliantly maps out the contours of the field but neglects to include even one entry on religion.
3. Anthony Pinn edited the first book-length project on religion and hip hop, *Noise and Spirit: The Religious and Spiritual Sensibilities of Rap Music* (New York: New York University Press, 2003). He has also coedited, with Monica Miller, a special edition of *Culture and Religion: An Interdisciplinary Journal* 10, no. 1 (March 2009) on the subject. Of the fourteen essays in these two volumes, only one—Garth Kasimu Baker-Fletcher's "African American Christian Rap: Facing 'Truth' and Resisting It"—examines the genre of gospel hip hop.

4. Robert Wuthnow, *The Restructuring of American Religion* (Princeton: Princeton University Press, 1988). Wuthnow argues that after the culture wars of the 1960s the political/cultural divide between "right" and "left" is a more salient marker of religious identity than allegiance to any particular denominational affiliation.

5. Josef Sorett, "Bears, Rhymes and Bibles: An Introduction to Gospel Hip Hop," *The African American Pulpit* (Winter 2006–2007): 14.

6. RUN-DMC, *Down with the King* (Profile, 1993).

7. Sorett, "Beats, Rhymes and Bibles," 14.

8. Kurtis Blow, "The Breaks," *Kurtis Blow* (Mercury, 1980).

9. Even the evolution of the genre's name—from Christian rap to gospel hip hop—mirrors the trajectory of the broader phenomenon, which has evolved over time from being named as "rap" to being called "hip hop."

10. For an introduction to debates about musical innovation within African American churches, and American culture more broadly, see Jerma Jackson, *Singing in My Soul Black Gospel Music in a Secular Age* (Chapel Hill: University of North Carolina Press, 2004).

11. The Sugarhill Gang, "Rapper's Delight" (Sugar Hill Records, 1979). "Rapper's Delight" is credited as being the first commercially released rap song. For a discussion of the song's significance in hip hop history, see Jeff Chang, *Can't Stop, Won't Stop: A History of the Hip Hop Generation* (New York: St. Martin's, 2005). Stephen Wiley, *Bible Break* (Brentwood Music, 1985).

12. Chang, *Can't Stop, Won't Stop*, 7–88.

13. Stephen Wiley: Interview, August 9, 2006. Unless otherwise indicated, all Wiley quotations are taken from my interview with him on this date.

14. Susan Sawyers, "Gospel Rapper Uses Music to Reach Young Converts," source unknown (Winston-Salem, NC, 1988). Wiley provided me with a photocopy of this article. Unfortunately, the copy does not indicate the name of the publication.

15. For an introduction to charismatic renewal movements, see Vinson Synan. *The Century of the Holy Spirit: 100 Years of Pentecostal and Charismatic Renewal, 1901–2001* (Nashville: Thomas Nelson, 2001); Scott Billingsley, *It's a New Day: Race and Gender in the Modern Charismatic Movement* (Tuscaloosa: University of Alabama Press, 2008).

16. Robert Wuthnow, *After Heaven: Spirituality in American since the 1950s* (Berkeley: University of California Press, 1998).

17. Oral Roberts, *The Miracle of Seed Faith* (Grand Rapids: Fleming Revell Co., 1977).

18. Bill Sherman, "Oral Roberts Dies," *Tulsa World* (December 15, 2009).

19. Buskirk is discussed in detail in David E. Harrell's biography of Roberts, *Oral Roberts: An American Life* (Bloomington: Indiana University Press, 1985).

20. For an account of the place of black churches within the Word of Faith movement, see Milmon Harrison, *Righteous Riches: The Word of Faith Movement in Contemporary African American Religion* (New York: Oxford University Press, 2005). Wiley's church, Praise Center Family Church is an affiliate of Fred Price's Fellowship of Inner-City Word of Faith Ministries.

21. C. Eric Lincoln and Lawrence Mamiya, *The Black Church in the African American Experience* (Durham: Duke University Press, 1991). Lincoln and Mamiya use the term *the black church* to refer to seven historically black denominations: the African Methodist Episcopal Church; the African Methodist Episcopal Zion Church; the Christian Methodist Episcopal Church; the National Baptist Convention, USA, Incorporated; the National Baptist Convention of America, Unincorporated; The Progressive National Baptist Convention; and the Church of God in Christ.

22. For an introduction to "signifying," see Henry Louis Gates Jr., *The Signifying Monkey: A Theory of African American Literary Criticism* (New York: Oxford University Press, 1988); Geneva Smitherman, *Talking that Talk: Language, Culture and Education in African America* (New York: Routledge, 2000).

23. "Swaggart Is Barred from Pulpit for One Year," *Associated Press* (March 30, 1988).

24. For a discussion of the Word of Faith movement, see: D. R. McConnell, *A Different Gospel: A Historical and Biblical Analysis of the Modern Faith Movement* (Peabody, MA: Hendrickson, 1988); and Harrison, *Righteous Riches*.

25. Lee, *T. D. Jakes*, 101–4; Walton, *Watch This*, 98–99.

26. Romans 12:2a (KJV). "And be not conformed to this world: but be ye transformed by the renewing of your mind. . . ." Harrison, *Righteous Riches*, 8–9. In addition to an understanding of the Bible as contract,

Harrison identifies Word of Faith's "three core beliefs and practices": "the principle of knowing who you are in Christ; the practice of positive confession, and a worldview that emphasizes material prosperity and physical health as the divine right of every Christian." Walton also points out that Word of Faith teachings allow for racial identity to be subsumed under one's "spiritual identity as a 'child of God'" (*Watch This*, 176).

27. For a recent popular treatment of the prosperity gospel, see Hanna Rosin, "Did Christianity Cause the Crash," *The Atlantic* (December 2009).
28. Harrell, *Oral Roberts*; McConnell, *A Different Gospel*, 55–74; Walton, *Watch This*, 83–87.
29. Wiley shared that he recorded Bible Break in Hagin's studio when it wasn't being used by the ministry. In his 1988 interview with *Spin*, however, he claimed to have borrowed money to record *Bible Break*. What these stories agree upon is that it was access to Rhema's recording equipment (whether free or paid for), and its ties to the community of religious broadcasting, that gave Wiley access to such opportunity.
30. Quentin Schultze, "Defining the Electronic Church," in Robert Abelman and Stewart M. Hoover, eds., *Religious Television: Controversies and Conclusions* (Norwood, NJ: Ablex, 1990), 46.
31. Cathy Spaulding, "Gospel Put to Rap Beat," *Tulsa Tribune* (date not available). Wiley shared this newspaper clipping with me during the interview. The story indicates that Wiley was on the staff of Love Center Church, where he served from 1987 to 1991. As such, the story can be dated within this time period.
32. Wiley claims to have toured with the "Just Say No" drug prevention program made popular by Nancy Reagan, and he recorded a song with that title on his 1989 album *Get Real* (Brentwood Music).
33. Bill Francis, "Rappin' For Jesus: Steven Wiley, Grandmaster of God," *Spin* (November 1988): 22.
34. Harrison, *Righteous Riches*, 104–5.
35. Jackson, *Singing in My Soul*, 8–26.
36. David Wills, "An Enduring Distance: Black Americans and the Establishment," in William R. Hutchison, ed., *Between the Times: The Travail of the Protestant Establishment in America, 1900–1960* (Cambridge: Cambridge University Press, 1989), 168–92; Evelyn Brooks Higginbotham, "Rethinking Vernacular Culture: Black Religion and Race Records in the 1920s and 1930s," in Wahneema Lubiano, ed., *The House that Race Built* (New York: Vintage Books, 1998), 157–77.
37. Wallace D. Best, *Passionately Human, No Less Divine: Religion and Culture in Black Chicago, 1915–1952* (Princeton: Princeton University Press, 2005), 71–93; Walton, *Watch This*, 92–101.
38. "Pentecostal Handshakes" refers to a practice of rewarding a preacher by shaking his hand while at the same time exchanging a cash gift.
39. Harrison, *Righteous Riches*, 9.
40. Lee, *T. D. Jakes*, 100.
41. Ibid., 10–11.
42. Stephen Wiley, "Gimme Da' Word,' on *Get Real* (Brentwood Music, 1989).
43. Ralph Waldo Emerson, "History," in *Essays and Lectures* (Digireads.com, 2009), 123.
44. James D. Watts Sr., "Jazz Hall Honors Tisdale, Five Others," *Tulsa World* (October 22, 2009).

35

"The Promiscuous Gospel": The Religious Complexity and Theological Multiplicity of Rap Music

Monica R. Miller

Abstract: *Over the past several decades, there has been increased attention to the religious exploration of popular culture, including rap music. However, as is often the case, such attention has resulted in a narrowing of rap music's religious and theological meaning—a forcing of rap music into preconceived cartographies of life. In this article, I suggest that the slippery, messy and complex nature of the sacred dimensions of rap music can only be addressed in a rigorous way through the use of theoretical and methodological tools that are flexible. This article proposes this type of flexible framework can be achieved through combining Anthony B. Pinn's notion of* complex subjectivity *and his nitty-gritty hermeneutic with Laurel C. Schneider's theory of* multiplicity.

If you God, then save your own, don't mentally enslave your own.

—"G.O.D.," *Common*

Some say that God is black and the devil is white, then the devil is wrong and God is what's right. . . As a child given religion with no answer to why, just told believe in Jesus for my sins he did die, curiosity killed the catechism. . . Long as you know it's a bein' that's supreme to you. . . he still created with the imperfection of man. . . I just wanna be happy with being me.[1]

—"G.O.D.," *Common*

These lyrics excerpted from various parts of rap artist Common's song "G.O.D." (Gaining One's Definition) featuring Cee-Lo offer a small sample into the messy religious and theological imagination of the rap world. This song in particular stages a lyrical dialogue between rappers Common and Cee-Lo in which both rappers exchange ideas about their personal experiences and life journey with spirituality and religion. Throughout the song, Common desires to highlight the commonalities of the many religious influences throughout his life, while Cee-Lo lyrically persuades his listeners to transcend mental slavery by claiming their own divinity.[2] The song concludes by repeating, "If you God then save your own, don't mentally enslave your own."

Exploring the sacred dimensions of rap music is a slippery slope, one that is both messy and complex; a reality that necessitates fluid and complex religious and theological approaches that can affirm and come to grips with (and be gripped by) the religious density presented within the music itself. What I am suggesting here is that in order to have a fuller and more meaningful engagement with the religious imagination of rap music, such a task requires theories and frameworks (of the religious and theological) that can embrace, confront, and be changed by (in a dialectical manner), that which is already present within this cultural modality. A more supple, fluid and flexible engagement has potential to give voice to, and make sense of the religious in general.[3]

Since the early 1990s, there has been much scholarly engagement with rap music in general from varieties of disciplines, yet the religious and theological exploration of rap music has been an under-engaged project. In addition to such disciplinary under-engagement, non-academic black church-based attempts such as Watkins' (2007) and Smith and Jackson's (2005),[4] have culminated into what I believe are hegemonic projects that seek to sanitize and baptize hip hop's stylistic expressions into the mainstream institutional church. That is to say, works such as these ask questions (e.g., how do Christians "reach" the hip hop generation), which more often than not culminate into the re-appropriation of rap music and other hip hop products (style, music, language, etc.) as *tools* of Christian evangelization through a process that I refer to as "lyrical sanitization" and "institutional importation." In addition, such projects seem to collapse hip hop culture with rap music in particular, a conflation which fails to see hip hop as one of the many modes of our broader culture, and rap music as one of its many expressions.[5]

Despite scholarly and disciplinary under-engagement by scholars of religion and theology, efforts such as Pinn's (2003a) engagement with rap music in the edited volume *Noise and Spirit: The Religious and Spiritual Sensibilities of Rap Music* work to expose the variety of religious dimensions and contours of rap music. Moreover, Pinn's humanist analysis and broad theory of the religious configures the hard questions of life raised by many rap artists as religious questions that seem to express (and many times prefer) human responsibility over strict theistic options. Pinn's work is among the first, I believe, to take seriously rap music's *complex* religious dimensions as his flexible theory of the religious configured as *complex subjectivity*[6] gives expression to the profound multifarious religious movements of rap music in particular. For example, Pinn configures the *quest for complex subjectivity* as movement—an underlying impulse that gives rise to or (in Pinn's language) "…gains historical manifestations" in a plurality of religious modalities (including but not confined to institutional forms); as such, its flexibility allows for a humanist analysis as *one* possibility of rap's many religious sensibilities (Pinn 2003b: 157).

While the work of Pinn and others points in a useful direction, ongoing work must explore the vigorous theological and religious (de)construction taking place within the music itself.[7] Cultural productions such as rap music ostensibly disrupt our neat, tidy, comfortable and coherent systems of religion and theology by re-signifying traditional language and concepts, while often displaying a level of comfort with religious and theological uncertainty.

Mindful of the above, it is my argument that rap music is calling for deeper religious and theological exploration that necessitates thicker, more complicated frameworks and approaches that can assess more broadly, and embrace more fully the varied intricacies and complexities of rap's religious stylings in the broader cultural marketplace of hip hop. In this essay, I work to establish this alternate base of analysis through a "thought experiment" between Laurel C. Schneider's framework of *multiplicity* (a theological approach to divinity in *Beyond Monotheism)* in conversation with Pinn's thesis of *complex subjectivity* and *nitty-gritty-hermeneutics* as a starting point from which we can explore and analyze the religious signifiers, play and (de)construction within the cultural production of rap music. In this sense, this "thought experiment" moves beyond solely using Pinn and Schneider as helpful theoretical guides to "approach" the religious in rap, but moreover, they accompany me as dynamic "dialogue" partners in confronting, wrestling, and being gripped *by* the religious terrain of rap music. Both Pinn and Schneider point us, I believe, in helpful directions for future work at the corners of culture and religion broadly in that the movement of their projects allow for slippage, flux and tension, a few characteristics that describe the complicated terrain of rap music in specific and popular culture in general.

For the purposes of this paper, my methodological posture is one of epistemological open-endedness grounded in hermeneutical uncertainty that seeks to make room for a multi-dimensional approach that can embrace the porosity of the religious in rap music. This posture attempts to make sense of the robust religious movement within rap songs without necessarily resolving the tension and over-determining the meaning between competing religious ideas that may be both present *and* absent at the same time. I have often been struck by the competing religious signifiers and syncretic *bricolage-like* blending of the religious often present within the contours of rap music, and as such, I have on many occasions been frustrated in my attempts to explore and make sense of rap music *religiously*. Thus, here is the fundamental rub of this essay: I am interested in the manner in which we scholars of religion and theology approach the religious messiness of rap music, messiness that seemingly forces a more open-ended and complicated analysis that turns out many of our religious and theological equations. In a qualitative sense, what's the religious "math" of rap music, especially when that math defies "proper" religious and theological academic formulations? In this essay, I begin with the theoretical (Pinn and Schneider) and move into the lyrical as a way into exploring rap music's post-religious *habitus*, which invariably confronts us with the challenge of expanding and diversifying our own religious and theological constructions.

The Rap on Rap's Significance

As an artistic expression that historically emerges within and among marginalized communities within stratified urban metropolises, rap music serves as a cultural medium that sheds light on varied historical tensions and fissures that have permeated the black religious experience.[8] Using the trope of "archeology as metaphor," Pinn (2003b: 137) encourages the exploration of cultural "stuff," the material matter of human "activity" and "creativity" for the study of religion, as such, he states, "it becomes much more necessary for the study of religion to include attention to a continually unfolding array of cultural products." Important here is the recognition that the study of religion is invariably connected to and not divorced from human doing and making within the time and space of history itself. Attention to cultural production as such offers much to understanding the movement of the religious within the materiality of space and place, as Pinn notes, "that is to say, material culture points beyond itself to more fundamental modes of meaning and expression" (2003). Of interest here is the important reminder that exploring the religious topography of rap is not like picking certain lyrics and words from the tree of hip hop, rather, such a task recognizes that the quest for meaning is weaved into its syntax, language, bodily presentations and everyday practices. Rap music can be viewed and understood as valid expression(s) of religiosity because it articulates a quest for meaning and belonging that contributes towards the complex constructions of religion broadly and black religion specifically. Pinn (2003a: 2) writes, "The field of religious studies needs to get up to speed with respect to rap music and hip hop culture in more general terms... is there anything of religious significance in rap music?" Building on Pinn's challenge, I ask a question: On the level of theory, what can rap music teach about the complexity of the nature and meaning of life (the quest for life meaning), about the perceived solidity of our religious and theological suppositions and assumptions?

Much like the spirituals and the blues, rap music has served as a way to tell multiple stories about the quest for meaning within times of struggle and absurdity. Even rap artist Sean "P Diddy" Combs has noted that:

> I always relate hip hop to our old Negro spirituals... They were sung in the cotton fields to help us get by, to help us not kill ourselves by going crazy [under] the worst oppression in the world. The music, the soulfulness, the spirituality expressed in song helped us to get through another day. That's the same impact hip hop has had on this generation. People could try to undermine it, but it's honestly the truth. Hip hop has helped us make it through our life in the inner cities. (Reid)

Rap music, like the spirituals and the blues, does not boast a monolithic religious preference. Religious and theological analyses of such songs require the disruption of simple and neat binary categories traditionally used in theology such as: religious/non-religious, sacred/secular and Christian/non-Christian. Although the rapper may make use of traditional theological language in their productions, more attention is required to the ways in which such conventional language is continually being (re)signified, (re)contextualized and (de)constructed. That is to say, when exploring the religious dimensions of rap music, meanings of words are slippery and traditional values both are and are not being held in place.

Rappers are indeed clever and playful with words, often turning traditional meanings on their head. In his most recent book *Racial Paranoia: The Unintended Consequences of Political Correctness* (2008) anthropologist Jackson gives attention to the "vocabulary lessons" of rap music. He notes:

> However, fast rhyming, playing with the phonetics of language, and continually redefining words all conspire to make hip hop almost as indecipherable as a foreign language for anyone not raised on its idiomatic expressions or committed to learning them. Fully comprehending hip hop demands decoding its intricate use of language to the point where one is able to recognize relatively obscure and cloaked references to veiled philosophies found in African American versions of Islam or explicit invocations of alternate discourses on racism popularized by books such as *Isis Papers*. (Jackson 2008: 147)

What Jackson continually points out throughout his chapter on hip hop is how the language of rap music creates what he calls "useful incomprehensibility," which ultimately, as he notes, ". . . makes it much more difficult to excavate all the hidden lyrical meanings beneath its complexly textured acoustic landscape" (147). At the least, hip hop calls for us to listen more closely and astutely to the ways in which it "flips the script" and beckons for anything other than "easy listening."

Pinn and Schneider Rap the Absurd: Complex Subjectivity and Theological Multiplicity

On rap music's "humanist sensibilities" and (rap's) interrogation of the concept of god, Pinn notes that what one often hears in rap music is an "ontological stance," a specific way of being that often stands in "contradiction" to traditional ways of understanding God. Pinn (2003a: 17) continues by saying that what rings loud within the music is the question of ". . . What is God?" Pinn argues, for example that Tupac Shakur's (Pac) concept of God is a *rhetorical* one, ultimately arguing that Pac finds the answers to his "ontological concerns" on earth, and in human activity (95). Moreover, Pinn configures Pac's slippage between the ranges of his theistic constructions as linear shifts away from reliance on a god concept, opting instead for human-centered approaches to the angst of life. Pinn's humanist lens of analysis heightens and sensitizes his analysis of rap's internal critique of god as "contradiction" laced with "oppressive tendencies that harm the socially disadvantaged" (99).

Theologically speaking, Pinn feels there is an under-reliance on the traditional concept of God in some rap. He writes:

> ... they point in a direction, raise questions, advance a critique, and in the process speak a late-twentieth-century and early twenty-first-century word of appreciation to human centered accountability, responsibility, and opportunity. (100–1)

Pinn's (1996) earlier efforts set forth in *Why, Lord? Suffering and Evil in Black Theology* suggest an interpretive methodology, a *nitty-gritty-hermeneutics* that can assist in analyzing the larger meaning embedded within various cultural texts beyond dominant interpretations that often fail to acknowledge both the particularity of the black experience and the broadness of black religious thought. Moreover, his hermeneutical lens maintains a focus on the ways in which cultural materials address the nature and meaning of human suffering and evil (Pinn 1996: 116). This interpretive lens focuses on the "tell it like it is facts" characterized by black life, a "heuristic rebellion" which searches for what is "hidden, unexpressed and unspoken," beyond theological conformity and strict theistic expression (Pinn 1996: 117, 135).

Pinn's later work sets forth a unique theory of religion, one that accounts for and takes seriously the messiness that inhabits black religious life. He reconfigures the rubric of black religion as a search for *complex subjectivity* one that is best understood as a quest that troubles normative ideas of religious "certainty" and "dogmatism," and rather, addresses the complexity of "life meaning" (2003b: 173). In his continued efforts to expand black religion beyond fixity and theological certainty, Pinn writes:

> ... I would like to define the religious experiences, in the context of black America, as the recognition of and response to the elemental feeling for complex subjectivity and the accompanying transformation of consciousness that allows for the historically manifest battle against the terror and fear of fixity. (175)

Pinn's "rebellious" hermeneutical posture, fluid theory of the religious and serious descriptive analysis of cultural products (including but not restricted to rap),[9] are all contributions that provide a more adequate framework for the exploration of the religious dimensions of black culture specifically and popular culture in general. Moreover, and more importantly, Pinn understands that the religious dimensions often expressed in black cultural production are fluid, malleable, syncretic, and embody the *complexity* of black life, a complexity often expressed in music such as the blues in which "... humans are encouraged to remove psychologically comforting theological crutches and develop themselves as liberators" (1996: 121). He broadens the frames of black religious expression beyond rigid fixity by reconfiguring and rethinking black religion as a quest *against* the fixity of identity, terror and dread. As such, the movement of black bodies in time and space is not just a causal or reactionary one, rather, in the move against the fixity of subjectivity, one moves in ways that open space for creativity, agency and possibility.

This broadening makes space for the ingenuity of cultural production through hermeneutical lenses that gives critical attention to subjugated religious knowledge buried deep within the contours of black cultural expressions. This broadening allows for a more creative range of suppositions such as Pinn's (2003a) humanist analysis of rap music, and unearthing that humanism is one among many expressions of the rap world as noted in *Noise and Spirit*. Pinn's broadening of both religion and theology not only redefines traditional approaches and assumptions, but equally important offers much purchase to exploring the convoluted and contradictory nature of religion represented within the rap world.

Rap music requires more attention be given beyond its internal theological "critique" by paying close attention to its ever-changing organic theological constructions.[10] Beyond the competing religious expressions one finds within rap music, the religious incoherence of many songs represents the reality of our sense-making abilities, or as Schneider (2008: 136) puts it, the hard fact that reality does indeed ". . . shift, slip, approximate, or contradict."

Pinn takes a reminder from Lewis Gordon that bodies are "ambiguous, complex, and multidimensional" beings, and as such, *complex subjectivity* ". . . maintains this multidimensional notion of being" and does not seek to resolve the tensions with ambiguity, rather, configures the movement of ambiguity as multifarious human expressions in the quest for meaning vis-à-vis a process of becoming (2003b: 158–9). Pinn makes clear that the human search for meaning and orientation is a quest that is full of complexities and uncertainties. He notes that the "certainty" of black religious claims to theism ultimately ". . . leads to dogmatism that is counterproductive." This is a necessary posture in the exploration of rap's confusing religious contours, especially in places where we may see "contradictory" claims being made, but yet embraced by the rapper in sometimes seemingly comfortable ways.

Schneider challenges the logic of certainty by demonstrating the ways in which the "logic of the One" has produced false illusions and claims to divine "Oneness." While Pinn's work on *complex subjectivity* and *nitty-gritty-hermeneutics* assists in thinking the black religious experience beyond the theological and dogmatic confines of Christianity and unearthing subjugated religious knowledge, likewise Schneider's work on *multiplicity* offers a way to think beyond rigid ideas of divinity and monotheism, more specifically, ideas that are lodged and frozen in what she refers to as the "logic of the One." She writes, "exclusive monotheism *demands* the denial of all but the One God. There is no other God but the One God, in other words, all other appearances of or claims about divinity are deemed false" (Schneider 2008: 79). In *Beyond Monotheism: A Theology of Multiplicity* (2008), Schneider makes a compelling argument and call towards theological multiplicity, urging us to rethink stale, unchanging logics and ideas about the divine. This multiplicity brings together seemingly bifurcated opposites, "limitation and possibility," "co-constitution. . . creativity *made possible* by disability," and most importantly a defiant posture towards "either/or" thought structures

(Schneider 2008: 137). Schneider is clear that logics of certainty have constricted Christian theology for centuries, and taking a lyrical cue from poem and story, she writes that "Divine multiplicity, which requires a leap into the metaphysical, emerges for me out of poetry and story" (10). For Schneider, attention to cultural products such as poetry ". . . are ways to allow for possibilities for being that disobey the logic of the One, that exceed the demands of 'either/or' thought" (137). Schneider's theological gesture towards a theology of multiplicity, is one that is characterized by ideas of "fluidity, porosity, temporality, heterogeneity, and a centered relation," adding that, ". . . in spite of all those abstractions it [divine multiplicity] is utterly *there* and so impossible to abstract, after all. It is incarnation, again. After all" (10).

Unlike Pinn, who seeks to expand traditional definitions of theology to include constructions without divinity, Schneider (2008: 11–12) presupposes that "theology is mostly predicated on a belief in god, in the reality of the divine, in its existence interdependent on human imagining and manipulation." Throughout this text, Schneider creatively constructs new ways of seeing and thinking divinity, freeing divinity from what Pinn would call "strict theological conformity." Schneider pushes the reader to think a new logic, beyond the One, which she argues was never really "1", beyond absurd illusions and drives for certainty. Moreover, she argues that this logic is grounded and rooted in "demands for truth" that ultimately "do not change" (Schneider 2008: 73). Equally powerful is her challenge to "intellectual dilemmas" that demand and rely upon binary oppositions such as true/false, adding that, "this either/or reality structure is brittle and absolute. It requires a great deal of apology, defense, and reinforcement to survive" (2008: 79). Ultimately, binary illusions of difference do not represent the complex reality of "everyday" life. On this point she writes:

> . . . everyday experiences requires some kind of frame precisely because it is messy and complex. . . for all of reality to be "One," or subsumed in a One, however, means that *all* discontinuities, aberrations, and complexity must at some point disappear. (Schneider 2008: 80)

Schneider "flips the script" on traditional theological constructions, turning concepts like Hell on their head, to begin the story of divinity, again. In this Hell, Schneider finds the "way out." She asks, "How can the waters of Hell free divinity from our labor of illusion that it must never change?" (2008: 103). Moreover, she suggests that "Hell" is really "Heaven's closet" arguing that, "the way out of the lie of stasis may be in Hell. That is where the waters of creation are, after all" (Schneider 2008: 102–3). Similar theological suggestions and reversals are made within rap, like the one made by rapper Pac in his song "Thugz Mansion"[11] where he asks the question, "Where do niggaz go when we die?" In this song, Pac turns the traditional Christian interpretation of heaven into a "thugz mansion," where the "morally corrupt" people of the ghetto can go and be who they want to be, where "you gotta be a G to get into thugz mansion."

Both Schneider and Pinn's religious and theological constructions are important for the religious exploration of rap music in that both approaches are committed to disrupting the hegemony and domination of (religious) fixity and stasis. While Pinn configures black religion and the ingenuity of its sense making abilities against fixity and terror, Schneider likewise seeks to unfreeze stale logics that subsume and melt differences in exchange for totalizing sameness. As Schneider suggests:

> . . . stories, words, and images change with experience. Those that do not change gradually lose their grasp on meaning, as fewer and fewer experiences find expression in them. The threads of connections between words, images, stories, and meaning are therefore tangled and dense. (Schneider 2008: 107)

A close analysis of rap music will show how religious ideas, concepts, illustrations and constructs are rarely linear in their own logic. What we encounter however are positions and postures that are ever-changing, even contradictory and seemingly incoherent. Above all, the fluid like nature of these religious and theological constructions and critiques require a multiplicity of perspectives that embrace change and respect the porosity of such incoherence.

Together, Pinn and Schneider offer a more adequate frame for a critical analysis of the religious exploration of rap music for the following reasons: Pinn's theory of the religious brings attention to both black bodies and the genius of cultural productions that emerge from, are rooted in, and take seriously the material trappings and historical specificities of the experiences of marginality. He offers an understanding of religion that embraces tension, movement, is rooted in human construction, and is not determined by the forces and structures of domination that have so longed attempted to keep black bodies in place (bodies are both ambiguous and multidimensional). For the study of rap music, such an approach keeps one ever cognizant that such cultural productions have not been created in a vacuum; rather its emergence is social, cultural and historical. Schneider's project reminds us that much expressed in rap music in this current historical moment radically confronts us with postmodern expressions of the construction of "difference," comfortability with uncertainty, religious pluralism and change. Schneider offers a postmodern theology that does not shun that which seems fractured; rather, it embraces possibility, change and fluidity as its theological starting point. In this sense, she provides a frame that is not limiting and over-rationalizing, rather it is a perspective that embraces the "discontinuities, aberrations, and complexity" of everyday life (Schneider 2008: 80).

The (Un)Intelligibility and Promiscuity of Rap's Religious Expressions: Three Examples

People talk about hip hop like it's some giant, livin in the hillside, comin down to visit the townspeople/We (are) hip hop/Me, you, everybody, we are hip hop/So hip hop is goin where we goin/So the next time you ask yourself where hip hop is goin/ask yourself. . . where am I goin? How am I doin?[12]

—"Fear Not of Man," Mos Def

Any time I mention the Lord, I'm genuine about it. God is my n—a. He's my big homie. I hope I always remember that and never lose contact with what the reality is.

—Jim Jones, Co-CEO of Diplomat Records (Reid)

Many rappers seem to display a level of comfortability with the (religious) uncertainty that pervades the reality of their lives, the fact that each day is a new day with new questions, fresh answers and innovative ways to "get by." A thick exploration of rap music, I believe, requires a posture and epistemology of uncertainty, precisely because rap music is both rhetorically and experientially, certain and uncertain about religious and theological claims. While a few examples cannot lay normative claims for all of rap songs, I suspect that many rappers do not have neat systematic theologies, and linear evolutions of their religious expressions. Rather, what we encounter, I believe, is an ever-changing reality, incoherence to lives in process, a continual becoming that disrupts the reality and illusions of unchanging religious sameness, but yet offers a peak into the convoluted nature of the quest for meaning.[13]

Talib Kweli: Losing Religion

I have always been struck by the way that religious and theological signifiers have been used and configured in the work of rap artist Talib Kweli. Going back to his 2002 album *Quality*, his song "Get By"[14] explored the various ways in which [black] people have "gotten by," such as selling crack. The hook is sung by a church-like choir that sings ". . . Just to stop smoking and stop drinking / I have been thinking I've got my reasons / Just to get by / just to get by." Interestingly, in this song religion is configured as just another way to "get by" in a Feuerbachian sense as a way to cope and deal with life, the projected need for dependence, as Kweli states,

> Some people get breast enhancements and penis enlargers / Saturday sinners Sunday morning at the feet of the Father / They need somethin to rely on, we get high on all types of drug / When all you really need is love.

Kweli's 2004 album *Beautiful Struggle* boasted yet another hotchpotch combination of spirituality and in-your-face talk about life on the margins of the hip hop game. One song in particular "Around My Way"[15] chronicles the pain and grief that fills the corners and streets and opens up with the lyrical conjuring of religious tropes, as Kweli raps the negative,

> People let me paint a picture / You know I ain't a Christian / I ain't a Muslim, ain't a Jew / I'm losing my religion / I speak to God directly / I know my God respect me / Cause he let me breathe his air and he really blessed me

as he equates rhyming with spitting "the gospel / truly knowing Jesus like Apostles do" and notes that his songs are synonymous to "psalms" as he is "spiritual / when I am lyrical." Lamenting the plight of what poor black people have to go through on a daily basis, he even indicts the church in such plight when he rhymes, "feeling like you gotta sneak into heaven / when the reverend looking like the pimp and the pimp look like the reverend." The song ends by Kweli calling for the creativity and ingenuity of resilience and self-help strategies such as keeping one's money in their own neighborhood. Perhaps, here, we can feel Kweli's disdain for dominant religious options, and rather, seems more Christocentric, aligning himself more closely with the spiritual walk of Jesus, thus equating his lyrical rhyming with similar spiritual weight. The song indeed confronts the raw realities of poverty and struggle, and likewise uses religious language to get at the exploration of social ills while not conforming to or adopting any one particular religious way.

Off Kweli's 2007 album *Eardrum*, he gets more theological in the song entitled "Give 'Em Hell,"[16] Kweli asks the question, "they say Hell is underground, and heaven is in the sky, and they say that's where you go when you die, but how they know?" and while questioning religious doctrine and institutional authority, he asks:

> if we all God's children then what's the word of the reverend worth. . .? If we made in God's image then that means his face is mine / Or wait, is that blasphemy? It's logical it has to be, if I don't look like my father then the way I live is blasphemy.

After noting the many religious discourses that have influenced him over the years from Rastafarianism to various strands of Islam, Kweli states, "I learned that Heaven and Hell exist right here on earth, word." He goes on to rap about the absurdity of violence that emerges from religious competition in the world, as the chorus repeats over and over that, "It's all going to Hell, it's all going to Hell, yup we living in, yup they giving us Hell." Although it is uncertain as to what kind of religious option Kweli seems to be advocating here, one is not hard pressed to feel his challenge towards institutionalized religion and doctrinal authority. In fact, he says up front that all he encountered in the church was "gossip," "blasphemy" and "confusion" among dogmatically constructed, symbolically violent distinctions of "difference" between different strands of religion such as Islam when he raps, "religion create the vision make the Muslim hate the Christian/make the Christian hate the Jew" and even questions Jesus' Christian identity when he states that Christianity "Never question the fact that Jesus was Jewish not a Christian or that Christianity was law according to politicians." Clearly, Kweli is rapping against the destruction cause by the category of "religion," and makes a distinction between a path that is "religious" and one that lives a "spiritual" life.

I would argue that Kweli is challenging dominant religious claims to truth by positing a vision of religious inclusion, opting for a spiritual path, opposed to an institutionally confined one. Although he mocks the "blasphemy" of the institutional church, he maintains a theological certainty that God exists. Kweli is unapologetic about being a product of religious syncretism, clearly opposing religious competition and sheepish, blind following of religious leaders, which for him ultimately breeds violence. At the end of the song Kweli states:

> The Lord is my shepherd I shall not want / Just because the Lord is my shepherd don't mean I gotta be no sheep / You feel me? / More blood is spilled over religion than anything in world history / We saying the same thing.

On one hand, Kweli is critiquing religious competition, and on the other, constructs a model of religious inclusion that emphasizes and highlights religious similarities, rather than their differences (although he does seem to melt the forms of religious difference into sameness when he says "we are saying the same thing"). Kweli expresses a strong internal critique against the church, but not against spiritual and religious experiences of everyday life. What can we make of the varying degrees of religious competition represented by Kweli? Interestingly, Kweli notes that vis-à-vis studying the lessons (Five Percent Concepts of Islam) and Rastafarianism he learned that "Hell" exists on earth or configured more politically as that place Rastafarians call "Babylon." Most poignantly, at the end of the song Kweli mocks "God forbid you go to Hell / but if you walked through any ghetto then you know it well," so while he maintains his stance throughout the song that this place called hell is really the space of depravation of resources (the ghetto), the chorus interestingly invokes heaven by saying, "if we don't get to heaven it's hell," although the concept of heaven is never mentioned or addressed in a sustained way.

While Kweli wants to "Give 'Em Hell," he seems less concerned with offering a religious vision and more concerned with demonstrating the ways in which his body (comfortably) holds traces and markers of religious difference constructed through a discourse of sameness. His body is an amalgamation of the multiplicity of religious influences that have influenced him throughout his life. Kweli's religious incorporations offer interesting ways to think about a religious *habitus* and religio-cultural markers inscribed upon the materiality of the black body, and how the body works out the competition of such markers. This song contends with traditional religious and theological assumptions about concepts such as "Hell" and offers a scathing deconstruction of dogmatic and institutionalized religion. At best we can say that Kweli is honest about his dipping and dabbling in various philosophies of life, and perhaps is able to hold in tension the best of spiritual lessons he has learned from various religious modalities throughout life. Rather than allowing religion to create divisive lines of difference, he trades in religion for a spiritual walk that highlights sameness, as he states at the end, "we saying the same thing."

On the same album (*Eardrum*) in which "Give 'Em Hell" appears, another song invoking the church appears, entitled "The Hostile Gospel Part 1 (Deliver Us)."[17] The video was shot in Lagos, Nigeria and opens up with Kweli, wearing traditional African garb, looking out his window onto the busy streets, a picture of a Christ flashes, and a chorus (reminiscent of a church choir) begins singing "deliver us, deliver us, deliver us, deliver us," Kweli adding that "this is what the people want/ this is what the people need." Throughout the song, he sets forth a number of challenges to various constituencies, such as rap artists, congress and the government, and people in the rap "biz" as he states,

> you can't trust a soul in the biz, so be careful who you eatin with / and sleepin with and also who you chiefin with / You never know they might've added in secret ingredients.

Interestingly, at the end of the song in the outro, the singer states, "it's salvation that I need / so I'm reaching to the sky / Lord can you deliver me?" While the chorus' hook is captivating, the video is of equal interest as shots oscillate back and forth between spaces such as the streets, dance clubs and a sandy beach where a group of African women are dressed in white garb crying out, hands lifted to the sky. It is hard to tell what Kweli wants the listener to do with sweaty black bodies crying out, the religious iconography and church-like-chorus produced hook, but in part, I hear him saying that perhaps the "Hostile Gospel" is the real, the reality that people are in need all around the world and as such, hip hop, which he says is "not a nation" needs to recognize this and get their game right. In fact, an online hip hop web site quotes him saying (in reference to this statement he makes about hip hop) that:

> I don't think we necessarily need to be a nation. A nation is bigger than a genre of music or a lifestyle. A nation requires nation-building. It requires real structure. That's not what hip hop is about. Hip hop is about rebelling and being free—not that a nation isn't about being free, but nation-building needs leaders, and I'm not sure that hip hop needs leaders.[18]

Nas: Performing Religion

Rapper Nas has definitely been no stranger to invoking religious themes and recasting them with a thugged-out twist. Born Nasir Jones and often self-described by names such as "God's Son" or the "Streets Disciple," Nas, like Kweli, often uses religious words and ideas as ways into talking about social inequity. In a 2005 interview with Associated Press, when asked about his religious background growing up, Nas answered that he was influenced by Christians, particularly Southern Baptist, and Five Percent Islam as he got older, but now he doesn't identify with either when he states, "But (I'm not any) religion." The interviewer, pressing their question of religion further asks,

"Would you consider yourself Agnostic?" and Nas replies, "I consider myself. . . [pauses] I know there's a higher power." His 2004 album *Streets Disciple* cover is reminiscent of the Last Supper, with Nas playing different characters such as Jesus, Judas and the thugged-out street warrior; he is sitting in a chair dressed like a king in red, as the thugged-out Nas pours some liquor into his goblet. Even more interesting than the album cover, is that there are 27 songs on this album, like 27 books of the Bible [New Testament], with two divisions (disc 1 and disc 2). When asked about this coincidence in the interview, Nas responds by saying that, like the Bible, his CD tells an "imaginative" and "personal" story, and, "it represents all the sides of me as a street warrior" Associated Press 2005. The song "Disciple" opens up with "Prophecy it's 'prophecy baby'," and of particular interest is the second verse which opens up with Nas comparing himself to Jesus' disciples claiming that he is the "disciple of music," claiming to be "the righteous invitin' you haters." Nas on this song tropes religious themes to spit daggers at other rappers and the overall rap game. On his 2002 album *God's Son* the song "The Cross"[19] opens up in the sandy deserts of the Middle East with Nas carrying the cross, heading towards his crucifixion wearing a crown of thorns and lashes on his black body, hecklers on each side. The song opens up with Nas invoking the cross,

> I carry the cross, if Virgin Mary had an abortion / I'd still be carried in the chariot by stampeding horses / Had to bring it back to New York / I'm happy that the streets is back in New York / For you rappers, I carry the cross.

Using the symbolic capital and the weight associated with the oppressed Jesus, here Nas becomes the Jesus of the rap game, the one who went from being "the old king of the streets" to "N.A.S. (Niggaz Against Society)" transforming the rap game. Although one is hard pressed to make claims about what Nas is doing religiously, what we can say is that Nas makes creative use of religious concepts, stories and histories, and makes them his own, to invariably say something about his journey and struggles through his journey as a rap artist attempting to "keep it real." From his album covers to re-depicting religious stories with him as the main actor, the putting on of religion gives Nas a level of power to make his case that, as he believes, he is the "King of the Streets." Perhaps, we turn to his song "Heaven,"[20] the chorus asks, "If Heaven was a mile away / would I pack up my bags and leave this world behind? / If Heaven was a mile away / Would I fill the tank up with gas and be out the front door in a flash?" Posing this question to the listener, Nas begs the question if this *was* the case [that Heaven was a mile away], what would you do, how would this change your life? For example, some of the scenarios he gives include situations such as: "Would you try to run inside when it opens would you try to die today?"; "Would you pray louder finally believing his power?"; "Even if you couldn't see, but you could feel would you still doubt him?"; "Would a fiend even want to get high, would he stop smoking?" and "And I bet you there's a Heaven for an atheist." Interestingly, although Heaven is used as a signifier of escape out of the world, a place whereby Nas can juxtapose the craziness going on in society, one does not get the sense that Nas is advocating a

624

quick escape; rather, I believe he wants to get at the larger issue of social transformation and what would it take for one to wake up to the social sins of this world, ones Nas shouts out as, "Preachers touching on altar boys / Sodomizing not realizing God is watching before the Lord," concluding that "Hell it hurts just to fathom the thought wishing that I fled the earth."

Common: Religious Syncretism

Similar to Kweli, Common's religious, critique, syncretism and blending has always struck me as a unique and brilliant sampling, but one that likewise makes the religious and theological exploration a tedious and careful one. Common, in the lyrics noted at the start of this article, suggests a redefinition of the god concept in his song "Gaining One's Definition."[21] He frees it from more traditional theological understandings, but yet lyrically we encounter much more slippage between competing ideas of god. Common, for example, calls on the name of a supreme god and also refers to himself as God. Although he notes his "bloodline is one with the divine" he is up front with the admission that he fights with himself in the "ring of doubt and fear." I believe, Common is confessing his own religious and theological uncertainty, but also affirming the God-like nature of humanity. Common puts more emphasis on the importance on racial metaphors for God: "some say that God is black, and the devil is white," concluding that "well the devil is wrong and God is what's right." Cee-Lo answers, "I do know the devil ain't no white man, the devil is a spiritual mind that is color blind, white folks and even niggaz you surely find." The final existence and nature of god remains open to debate. Common notes, "Curiosity killed the catechism," which led him to believe that religion is a way of life, not an institutional emblem.

While Common professes his belief in a "supreme being," the latter half of the song blurs the line between humanity and divinity, with Cee-Lo asserting:

> So how can you call yourself God when you let a worldly possession
> Become an obsession and the way you write your rhymes and
> Can't follow your lesson
> If a seed's sown, you make sure it's known, you make sure it's grown
> If you God, then save your own, don't mentally enslave your own
> If you God, then save your own, don't mentally enslave your own
> If you God, then save your own, don't mentally enslave your own
> I just wanna be happy. . . bein' me
> Bein' me.

This song highlights the ambiguity of the God question/concept; yet is there a concept or understanding of god being both constructed and deconstructed at the same time? While my humanist orientation might automatically lure me to highlight and emphasize the supernatural and theistic suspicion within this song, I think the concept of God functions within both Common and Cee-Lo as a trope that metaphorically has meaning, but also assists in their own rethinking of theological anthropology by reconstructing human beings as God in a very concrete way. Rap's religio-cultural cross-pollination and play with theological concepts such as "god" at times hold in place traditional meanings of such words, yet at the same time offers up new twists on old religious constructions. Undeniably, whether or not Common or Cee-Lo in fact believe in God, of more importance here is that the *concept* of God functions in this song, whether as a hegemonic marker of definition or an assumed reality.

This small sampling of some of the more common religious tropes found in popular culture suggest that hip hop is no stranger to making use of religious themes and concepts. The creativity and ingenuity whereby hip hop "flips the script" of many traditional religious and theological meanings makes the religious exploration of hip hop culture more difficult. As we can see with each rap artist, religious ideas hardly progress in a linear and systematic sort of way from song to song; rather, the religious movement is circular, performative, chaotically creative and theologically playful from stanza to stanza. What hip hop culture brings to the table of religious studies is a gritty space, a shape-shifting cultural terrain of creativity and struggle whereby existential questions, the quest for life meaning are produced between the bringing together of religious motifs and reality of everyday life. Moreover, the postmodern edge of hip hop calls for more practice-oriented and theoretically diverse approaches to the religious exploration of popular culture. More than that, the religious imagination of rap music necessitates a reshaping, reimagining and reconstruction of the category of religion itself. As explored in culture, religion no longer becomes a static discourse to be picked from the tree or observed; rather, it becomes a lived reality, an active process embedded within everyday cultural practices. In this sense, engagement with hip hop challenges the more traditional approach of looking for expressions of dominant religions (i.e., Christian or Islamic) manifest in the cultural practices, and rather, calls for more attention towards the ways such language is used, practiced, and re-appropriated, the multifarious ways in which life experiences and cultural creativity are combined with religious and theological tropes to produce new forms of religiosity. The religious exploration of hip hop culture is invariably an examination of cultural practices, and as such, requires leaving behind the taken-for-granted regimes of truth (e.g., logics of certainty) that has dominated religious and theological studies for way too long. It calls for a more complex and multiplicative approach to that which we call the religious, it deconstructs theology as confessional and fashions and practices theology as an interpretive tool.

Riffin on Rap: Disrupting Our Drive for Certainty

I have attempted to bring Pinn and Schneider's religious and theological projects in dialogue with exploring the religious dimensions of hip hop culture as both examples and ways to think about what future engagement may necessitate. Although the expansion of black religious thought must extend beyond the rigid theological confines of dominant religious traditions, we must also keep in mind that new constructions must contend with religious plurality, syncretism and new constructions emerging from within the music itself. What do we make of the intricate lyrical combinations and creative play between say songs that express both an atheistic, agnostic and theistic posture, or a certain and uncertain disposition at once? For example, in the song, "Ghetto Gospel," Pac raps "never forget, that God isn't finished with me yet, I feel his hand on my brain when I write my rhymes, I go blind and let the Lord do his thang," while at the end screaming, "Lord can you hear me speak [where are you Lord?—wait I just felt you helping me write my rhymes—where did you go]!! We pay the price of being Hell bound. . . " While Pac's God as expressed in this song may solely be a trope, a metaphor, divorced from personal belief, we the listeners and readers are often presented with competing and contradictory suppositions and claims simultaneously. Although Pac may question God or traditional Christian theology, these lyrics suggest to me that he *experiences* what one may call divinity, embodied, at least in certain times within the song, and at others expresses uncertainty regarding the presence of the real. In other songs, Pac may express a rather different dimension and perspective of his own religious sensibilities and experiences, ones that are, as Pinn has cited elsewhere, overtly humanist in orientation. Pac's religious inconsistencies and theological slippage is representative of the messiness of everyday life, especially for cultural workers like rappers who have access to dominant capital yet maintain a desire to live, reflect, romanticize or speak truth about life on the margins. Likewise, theological and religious frameworks engaging rap music must also be dexterous enough to embrace and explore these sometimes dizzying religious realities expressed so intricately within the broader culture that often shifts and approximates quicker than we can analyze it.

Most apparent is the necessity for *suspicion, (un)certainty* and *possibility* as preconditions of any religious or theological exploration of rap music. While Schneider approaches theology from a logic of *possibility,* Pinn maintains and privileges both a necessary posture of *complexity* and theistic *suspicion* paying acute attention to the lyrical and cultural critique of religion within rap, especially the more overt supernatural and theistic challenges. The religious exploration of rap music necessitates both approaches. Suspicion and doubt must be balanced with possibility open to the unexpected, especially within rap music. Humanism as a religious mode of orientation cites as one of its five more general themes "suspicion toward or a rejection of supernatural explanation and claims" (Pinn 1996: 87). I think rap music is calling attention to the complexities of the quest for meaning in general, where ideas of the religious and theological are used from a multiplicity of vantage points, to accomplish different things, to speak different and competing truths about everyday life. In this sense, religious language at times may be codified within more humanist expressions and supernatural and theistic affirmations often times are resolved into a preference for a more humanist practice. That is to say, the rapper may not ever fully conclude or come to terms with one's own religious uncertainty, but often times claims are made cloaked in language that would point otherwise. The disjointed nature of both overt and subtle religious and theological claims within rap may not necessarily suggest a mind made up about religion, but rather, may be more consistent with the sort of complexity in which our theological concepts shift, modify, and change with life and the veracity of our everyday social situations.

The theological and religious exploration of rap music calls for a thick re-conceptualization of the struggle for meaning, especially for marginal bodies often displaced by the austere conditions of one's social and political reality. Does the quest for ultimate meaning automatically assume a thirst for divinity or spiritual presence, as Schneider seems to suggest (2008: 11)? Perhaps in rap music there are multiple quests occurring at once, a thirst for and pulling back from the real, so on this point, a constructive framework for an approach to the religious in culture must include a broader understanding of theology beyond a "predicated belief in God," within black religious scholarship. To account for the diverse ways in which life meaning is sought after, theology is in need of a broader perspective that both includes and transcends theistic assumptions. Here is where Pinn's *nitty-gritty-hermeneutics* is helpful in thinking theological epistemological limits and claims beyond traditional (theistic) conformity.

What shapes and forms does the quest for meaning take on as expressed in rap music? From a theological perspective, rap music requires a plurality of theological understanding, and a careful reinterpretation of traditional language. How are we to understand the relationship between the organic language of hip hop's cultural production and its tensions with and influence of intergenerational transmission (e.g., family, upbringing) of more traditional religious understandings? Perhaps, as Pinn suggests, there is a "linguistic playfulness" to the language of rap music, a creative play that is not always meant to be understood as literal (1996: 18). If theological projects for the future are to be understood from a posture that embraces change and rejects the over determination of religious stasis, then we must also allow for a continual process of redefining and reinterpretation of the very language we use.

Building from the work of scholars such as Long (1986) and Pinn (1996, 2003a, 2003b), the changing cartography of our cultural landscape provides much room for the continued growth and expansion of black religious thought. Continued engagement with cultural products such as rap music and their unapologetic lyrical quest for meaning challenges the rigidity of our own theological frames of analysis. Here, we must take Schneider's cue that multiplicity is about unleashing and unfreezing static certainties that, over time, become frozen in the intellectual polarity of dualism. While the quest for meaning in rap music is not always grounded in a metaphysical reality with a functioning centre called god, yet and still, it can be configured as a "religious" quest open to [divine] possibility. Building on what Schneider suggests to Christian theology, I suggest that rap music requires that we "listen again" to the ways in which these stories are "disenchanted" with polarized realities and experiences. Learning to move beyond logics of Oneness, we must remind ourselves that lyrical expressions of theistic and religious uncertainty cannot always be quantified into an "either/or" reality, but on the other hand, the lyrical ambiguity doesn't always gesture the affirmation of divine presence. Here, we are in desperate need of more approaches to multiplicity and complexity, approaches that are careful not to become theologically totalizing, ones that can reconnect to and with the complexities of life, and its creative contributions.

Rap music's religious disposition is one that seems to be quite promiscuous, tasting and sampling different ideas, conceptions and formulations in a sometimes unruly and rebellious kind of way. This looseness, openness and "wayward" reality hints at the need for a more promiscuous approach embracing and taking serious a variety of theoretical and methodological tools by which the scholar of religion and theology can sample. Rap music is calling for multiple religious and theological postures, whose theories and assumptions may contradict, yet when put together in a dialogical manner can embrace more fully the religious movement and complexity of life in general.

Hip Hop Aint Dead: Future Engagement

Hip hop culture, and rap music as one of its expressions, is not dead as rapper Nas had seemed to suggest in his 2007 album *Hip Hop Is Dead;* in fact, it's more alive than ever. New projects such as Nas' latest untitled album (originally entitled *Nigger)* remind us that rappers, like preachers and politicians, are still in business, they still have a market with high volumes of supply and demand. Unlike churches and religious institutions however, rap music offers a more expansive arena, a cultural milieu in which the nature and meaning of life has more freedom to be questioned, constructed, and played with in ever-creative and ingenious ways. Black religious discourse and theological studies must continue in its expansion of black religion beyond the confines of strict religious language, stasis of theological definition and tactics of institutional religious incarceration. Likewise, religious and theological studies must "make room" at the table for rap music, recognizing its utility as a resource for religious and theological exploration, while also taking note of the way the inner workings of rap's religious elements both challenges and enhances our often stagnant religious assumptions.

Even more challenging will be how religious institutions such as the black church deal with our ever-changing cultural landscape, and the shifting nature of religious exploration. The cultural productions of hip hop cannot be perceived as solely passive products waiting to be co-opted in the service of religious and institutional market maintenance. Rather, they call us to listen, to begin the story again, as they invite us into the messy, creative and chaotic reality of everyday life. An organic approach to rap music requires an *epistemology of uncertainty,* paying careful attention to the ways in which our traditional theological assumptions and religious language constricts the diversity of meaning present. One must not assume that the rhetorical play with religious and theological metaphors in rap music always carries a traditional meaning of religion without space for cultural contestation and resignification. Engagement with rap music calls into question our more common conceptualizations of the *quest for meaning*. The search for meaning is grittier, edgier and challenges the ways in which theistic religions have habitually reduced and exchanged ultimate concerns into quests for theistic reliance and simple solutions.

Rap music both inherits traditional theological and religious heritage, while also transcending these categories with a creative pulse. In a Derridian sense, most rappers are "faithfully unfaithful" to their religious inheritances and influences, both denying and yet affirming a move towards and away from particular familial and social traditions. Consequently, rap music, I believe, offers new ways to understand religious and theological concepts, like God, but yet seemingly pushes up against our traditional assumptions of what these concepts purport to mean. Perhaps, rap music is calling for yet another way that calls for something beyond, in between, and on the boundaries of both the absence and presence of religious reality. While all meaning-making does not necessarily infer a religious dimension, a theological approach must allow for both religious and non-religious expression. That is to say, not all ontological questions can or should be collapsed into solely religious quests; likewise, the weighty questions of life should have the ability to be envisioned as religious concerns without having to prove their religious merit.

Rap music holds much promise for the academic study of both culture and religion, not as a cultural force competing with and against the viability of faith institutions and traditional religious and theological claims, but rather, as a realization that culture is not the enemy of religion and institutional authority, rather it is both the site and production of life which gives creative expression to the many dimensions and terrains of our multifaceted lives. A sustained engagement with hip hop culture from the corners of religion and theology forces a rethinking of traditional religious and theological concepts that we bring to such a study, rap music challenges us to broaden our epistemological limits by confronting us with post-religion and postmodern questions that necessitate interdisciplinary theoretical, methodological and conceptual broadening. Lastly, rap music challenges religionists and theologians to broaden and rethink our understanding of the concept of religion itself when explored through everyday cultural practices recognizing that although traditional concepts hold much symbolic weight in this art form, their meanings and reconstructions are many times being contested and recast. As such, we cannot naively always look for the religiously obvious and explicit; the quest for meaning in rap music is much more complicated, implicit and unstructured. It is calling for, I believe, a new way to understand the process and lived reality of religion in general.

Acknowledgments

I am most grateful to Dr. Anthony B. Pinn, Dr. Mary Keller, and Dr. Laurel C. Schneider for their insightful comments, challenges, suggestions and questions related to an earlier version of this essay.

Notes

1. Common Featuring Cee-Lo. "G.O.D.," Sony BMG, 2007. Lyrics can be found at: http://www.lyricsdepot.com/common/g-o-d-gaining-ones-definition.html

2. Here, and throughout this essay, my point is not to give an assumed religious or theological analysis and explication of such lyrics, rather my intention is to demonstrate the varied religious and theological perspectives that may be both present and absent at the same time within a particular song. Such complexity challenges and disrupts perspectives on the religious whose static approaches fail to come to grips with, and be gripped by, such complexity. For the purposes of this paper, I use the rubric "religious complexity and theological multiplicity" taken from Anthony B. Pinn and Laurel C. Schneider's work, as a descriptive framing of the way in which I believe rap music confronts the religious in general. That is to say, there is something about the way in which the modality of rap music in specific and popular culture in general wrestles with the nature and meaning of life in general that poses an inherent challenge to static and inflexible approaches, definitions and frameworks of religion and theology. How does—or is—the scholar of religion and theology to grapple with what can sometimes seem like religious and theological syncretism or incoherence within cultural phenomena such as rap music?

3. Here, I am calling for not only more expansive and complex approaches to the religious exploration of rap music (which is likewise a call to expand traditional understandings of the religious and theological in general), but equally important, I am also suggesting that a fruitful religious and theological engagement with rap music is one that should be dialectical, that is, one that embraces the messiness (as expressed within the music) of life and can give articulation to its religious and theological dimensions, and likewise one that can be changed by the "religious confrontation" within rap music itself. I am most interested in expansive approaches that can give articulation to the struggle for meaning within popular culture, but likewise use such cultural production to interrogate our own ideas and assumptions of both religion and theology respectively.

4. I cite these two books as non-academic examples that continue to polarize and cheapen both the engagement and understanding of rap music in particular and hip hop in general. These two church-based examples are not presented to represent the breadth of church-based engagement and, likewise, the wider academic scholarship on rap music and hip hop, such as works by Michael Eric Dyson and Cornel West. Although these examples are not representative of the larger scholarship between hip hop and religion, what they do however represent is a growing hegemonic approach whereby theological and ideological limitations cheapen a full and meaningful engagement with rap music and hip hop.

5. This more common conflation of and collapse between "hip hop" and "rap music" become important distinctions, especially when the stigmatization and moral critiques of the cultural "products" become literal critiques representative of the broader culture itself.

6. It is important to keep in mind that what Anthony B. Pinn gives us alongside the *Noise and Spirit* (2003) volume is a theory of the religious, what he calls *complex subjectivity* most poignantly stated in his work entitled *Terror and triumph* published in 2003. I draw particular attention to this distinction because it is important to recognize that what Pinn offers religious studies in general is a theory of the religious, and although Pinn has always used and incorporated varied materials of raw data (bodies, ritual, music, etc.) his more descriptive work in *Noise and Spirit* gives attention to the religious confrontation in rap music from diverse perspectives. Although Pinn's Humanist analysis is a valid religious option in a religious exploration of rap among others, his theory of religion broadly engages, but is not limited to, particular cultural material such as rap music.

7. That is not to say that all of rap music deconstructs in general. Rather what I am suggesting here is that with regards to the struggle, search, and quest for meaning in rap music, configured as religious questions, that there is likewise both a challenge and construction taking place, a (de)construction, that is in the Derridian sense, never a destruction or full incorporation of norms, values, and ideologies, but rather, a move that both embraces and denies, challenges and constructs, absent and present, and that is "faithfully unfaithful" to tradition(s) in general.

631

8. By "historical tensions and fissures" I mean similar to the spirituals and the blues, rap music offers a lyrical window into vital questions and concerns raised within black religion in general. Such tensions, are theologically and religiously oriented, and include different approaches to theology, religion, God, and spirituality. Black religion has never been a monolithic experience, and this element, I believe is best expressed within cultural products, such as music, that arise organically, from within the communities themselves.

9. I am not suggesting that Pinn's theoretical and conceptual contribution has only been specific to rap music, although I do believe he is one of the first scholars of religion to take seriously the complex religious dimensions embedded within rap music. Pinn's theory of the religious is drawn from cultural resources and data that include rap music, but is not limited to only musical production; his work takes into account a broad array of "unfolding cultural productions." I do not want to conflate collapse nor suggest that Pinn's theory of the religious, his hermeneutical contribution and descriptive work is specific to rap music only. What I am suggesting however is that Pinn's unique theory of religion is one that is flexible and robust enough to engage cultural productions such as rap given its flexibility and comfortability with religious and theological uncertainty.

10. For example, what other (new and different) god constructions or religious realities are being constructed and played with beyond the more dominant and already legitimated forms of religious traditions? Tupac may rhetorically construct a god that looks very different from Common's human-god motif. How do we understand these competing illustrations and constructions of religious reality, especially its unstable nature?

11. 2 Pac featuring Anthony Hamilton. "Thugz Mansion," Interscope Records. Lyrics can found at: http://www.azlyrics.com/lyrics/2pac/thugzmansion.html, Video can be watched at: http://www.youtube.cornlwatch?v=dx-Vs2L7llk

12. Mos Def. "Fear Not of Man," *Black on Both Sides.* Priority Records, 1999. http://www.youtube.com/watch?v=8BEg38-bWY8

13. Throughout this paper I continually give deference to the "fluidity" and "uncertainty" of rap's many religious suppositions, questions and answers, however, I am also aware that rap music is also afflicted and overshadowed by its demands for "realness" and authenticity that certainly yearn for "truth," essentialisms, and a sort of precision that is not representative of the realities of our lives. However, while I acknowledge this thirst for authenticity (gender, sexuality, etc.) within the music, I also sense a deep comfort with regard to religious incoherence and contradiction.

14. Talib Kweli. "Get By," *Quality.* Rawkus Records, 2002. Watch video at: http://www.youtube.com/watch?v=9pUKLD_ONsE

15. Talib Kweli. "Around My Way," *Beautiful Struggle.* Rawkus/Geffen Records, 2004. Lyrics can be found at: http://www.azlyrics.com/lyrics/talibkweli/aroundmyway.html

16. Talib Kweli. "Give 'Em Hell," *Eardrum.* Blacksmith Music/Warner Bros. Records, 2007. Lyrics can be found at: http://www.azlyrics.com/lyrics/talibkweli/giveemhell.html

17. Talib Kweli. "Hostile Gospel, Part 1 (Deliver Us)," *Eardrum.* Blacksmith Music/Warner Bros. Records. 2007. Video can be seen at: http://videos.onsmash.com/v/UGnFSAj6PvlmNuuB

18. Nas. "Disciple," *Streets Disciple.* Columbia Records 2004. Lyrics can be found at: http://www.azlyrics.comllyrics/nas/disciple.html

19. Nas. "The Cross," *God's Son.* Ill Will/Columbia Records, 2002. Video can be seen at: http://www.youtube.com/watch?v= 35AQQSislvM

20. Nas. "Heaven," *God's Son.* Ill Will/Columbia Records. 2002. Lyrics can be found at: http://www.azlyrics.com/lyrics/nas/heaven.html

21. Common featuring Cee-Lo. "G.O.D." Lyrics can be found at: http://www.lyricsdepot.com/common/g-o-d-gaining-ones-definition.html

References

Jackson, J. *Racial Paranoia: The Unintended Consequences of Political Correctness.* New York: Basic Civitas Books, 2008.

Long, C. *Significations: Signs, Symbols, and Images in the Interpretation of Religion.* Aurora: Fortress, 1986.

"Nas: The Mature Voice of Hip Hop." http://www.msnbc.msn.com/id/6786474/. Associated Press, 2005.

Pinn, A. *Why, Lord?: Suffering and Evil in Black Theology.* New York: Continuum, 1996.

———. *Noise and Spirit.* New York: New York University Press, 2003.

———. *Terror and Triumph.* Minneapolis: Fortress, 2003.

Reid, Shaheem. "Finding My Religion: Hip Hop Gets the Spirit." MTV website. http://www.mtv.com/bands/h/hip_hop_religion/news_feature_071904. Accessed December 22, 2008.

Schneider, L. *Beyond Monotheism: A Theology of Multiplicity.* New York: Routledge, 2008.

Smith, E., and P. Jackson. *The Hip Hop Church: Connecting with the Movement Shaping Our Culture.* Downers Grove: InterVarsity, 2005.

Talib Kweli's "Hostile Gospel Part 1." http://www.aceshowbiz.com/news/view/0014210.html. Ace Showbiz, 2008.

Watkins, Ralph. *The Gospel Remix: Reaching the Hip Hop Generation.* Valley Forge: Judson, 2007.

36
Building "Zyon" in Babylon: Holy Hip Hop and Geographies of Conversion

Christina Zanfagna

> *Khanchuz (pronounced "conscious") locks the doors of his metallic beige Cadillac and swaggers slowly up the side street towards Los Angeles' Leimert Park Village, his faux diamond cross swinging gently across his chest. Formerly known as "Sleep" in his early days as a secular rapper, his eyes are wide and awake, drinking in the dark night's surroundings. We walk down the street and pass Sonny's Spot—a tiny cavern of a jazz club. The walls are tagged with layers of writing and papered with old posters and paintings of jazz musicians. We lean against a black-and-white photograph of King Oliver's Creole Jazz Band as the pianist solos on "Nina's Dream." Our final destination is Kaotic Sound—home to the infamous weekly underground hip hop open-mic Project Blowed. Tonight we are here for something else—a monthly Christian hip hop open-mic called Klub Zyon. Zyon, the open-mic's founders explain, is where we are going—the ultimate place, a spiritual homeland for wandering travelers. A decade earlier, Khanchuz was at Project Blowed rapping in street-corner battles about slingin' drugs, pimpin' women, and gang bangin'. Now he raps for Christ. His first God-inspired rap was delivered in a jail cell in Colorado to the rhythm of metal spoons clanking against the bars. As we approach the front door of Klub Zyon, Khanchuz steps back and reflects on the conversion of both his soul and this place.*

In this essay, I investigate how holy hip hop practitioners, through their musical practices and discourses, work with and on what I refer to as the *living architecture* of the city to create sites of gospel rap production. Specifically, I am interested in how gospel rappers perceive and perform *place* as a converting body and a site for the potential conversion of religious subjects, as well as how they undergo and enact *conversion* as both a spiritual transformation and a spatial practice. By *spatial practices*, I am referring to the manifold ways in which people move through, use, alter, and make meaning out of space.

Holy hip hop (a.k.a. gospel rap or Christian rap) represents a highly complex field of practices comprised of music labels, localized scenes, ministries, radio programs, award shows, artistic crews, and collectives that function in an astonishing variety of buildings and locations, deemed both religious and nonreligious. Sometimes considered musical mavericks in the church, corny Bible-thumpers in the streets or in hip hop clubs, and criminal youth by law enforcement in the so-called ghettos of Los Angeles, gospel rappers are often strained by accusations that their ways of being and expressing are blasphemous and/or inauthentic. These competing critiques constitute the triple bind of holy hip hop's multifronted struggle to uphold their contingent positioning and find a spiritual/musical dwelling place—to find "Zyon." In fact, holy hip hop is one of the few religio-musical movements and genres in African American culture where the church—often referred to as the Body of Christ by both Catholics and Protestants—is not the primary location of power and performance. But the early history of predominantly black religious gatherings in the "invisible churches" of brush harbors shows us that when the traditional church is not available or displaced, other possibilities are actualized—the Body of Christ refigured.

I ask, how does the space of a church, street corner, or club, reworked by the musical and lyrical practices of gospel rap, serve as a site for the creation of new kinds of places of activity and interaction, as well as new kinds of religious subjects? How do the lived and imagined geographies of holy hip hoppers in Los Angeles inform, define, and disrupt the socially constructed and policed boundaries between the sacred and the profane, Christianity and hip hop, ministry and entertainment, the church and the streets? I focus on three critical, alternative sites of gospel rap performance in Los Angeles that aim to integrate believers and nonbelievers: The Row, a street corner on L. A.'s Skid Row, *converted* into an "airborne church" (i.e., open-air) service; Klub Zyon, a hip hop-based cultural center *converted* into a place of musical worship and religious fellowship; and Club Judah, a church sanctuary *converted* into a holy hip hop "club." These geographies of conversion, as they intersect with holy hip hoppers' own biographies of conversion, point to music's role in the mutual construction of both the changing body of the city and the changing bodies inhabiting it.

Thus, I examine what holy hip hoppers do physically and performatively to their urban surroundings through the cultural production of gospel rap in relationship to the sedimented meanings and histories of specific places. Following the phenomenological orientations of Basso and Casey (Feld and Basso 1997), Jacqueline Brown writes that "places are essentially selves" (2005: 11), linking human experience to the experience of place. Inherent in this view is that places, like human selves and bodies, *act* as they are *acted* upon. In this light, the relationship between people and places can be understood as a kind of ecological practice where as one body changes, so do others around it. Therefore, the embodied musical practices, spiritual practices, and spatial practices of holy hip hoppers are deeply enmeshed, acting as allied modalities of agency fleshing out different bodies of the city.

Hip Hop Studies and Hip Hop Space

Murray Forman and Ian Condry bring a critical spatial awareness to the emergent area of hip hop studies. In *The 'Hood Comes First: Race, Space, and Place in Rap and Hip Hop* (2002), Forman argues that hip hop has been in a process of "going local" where representations of and contestations around turf, territory, and 'hood are inextricably enmeshed in the cultural production of the music. Here, the meanings people make from particular spaces are critical and contingent on a variety of linked social realities, including race, religion, class, and gender. Moving the focus from the hip hop nation as a historical construct to hip hop as a "geo-cultural amalgamation of personages and practices that are spatially dispersed" (Forman 2004: 201) allows us to interrogate the various geographies that hip hop practitioners—as "alternative cartographers" (202)—reimagine and remap.

Ian Condry's examination of key sites of hip hop performance and networking in *Hip Hop Japan* (2006) provides some useful pathways into rethinking the mutual construction and embodiment of popular music scenes by hip hop artists, audiences, and culture industries. His emphasis on "key performative locations" (88) is not just about locating the music in a specific locale or place; rather, Condry is privileging hip hop performativity as the actualizing force that converts a *space* (a general field of resources) into some *place* (a specific located product of meaning-making practices—space made meaningful) and constructs the *there* of a musical culture as both a physical destination and an aesthetic world. In this analytic conception, holy hip hop is actualized in the practices of creating and converting spaces not traditionally used for either hip hop or religious expression into locations that can house the interface of diverse social actors and sacred, secular, and profane elements. And yet, where gospel rap is performed and actualized matters. I would like to expand Condry's theorization to include the ways in which specific places (as always and already constituted by an arrangement of social relations, spatial imaginaries, and grounded, material realities) also affect the people that seek to use, shape, and inhabit them.

The Spatial Politics of the Church, the Club, and the Streets

The history of black music in Los Angeles is one charged with both race and religion, marked by extreme contrasts of both intercommunal and intracommunal integration and segregation, and inextricably embedded in the geopolitics of the ever-expanding and converting body of the city (Davis 1992; Kelley 1996; DjeDje and Meadows 1998). Scholars articulate Los Angeles as both a city of racial, class-based, and territorial divisions, on the one hand, and cultural assimilation and multiculturalism, on the other. These narratives enunciate the entanglement of both realities and myths of the city. Los Angeles nightclubs have historically been one of the battlegrounds of such enduring patterns of racial discrimination, violence, and exclusion precisely because of the possibilities for mixing they can offer and inspire. Conversely, the church continues to be romanticized as a haven of black politics and community organizing, as well as a musical resource in both everyday and scholarly discourse.

In his influential book, *What the Music Said: Black Popular Music and Black Public Culture* (1999), Mark Anthony Neal recognizes the church and the *jook joint* (i.e., club) as the two main centers of black life. During my field research, I also encountered numerous pastors, church members, community members, and hip hop artists articulating a separation between the church and the club, and, more often, between the church and the streets. While this couplet has been useful in outlining some of the oppositional, interrelated, and codependent aspects of each social context, this duality runs the risk of reifying them as distinct, autonomous spaces and their associated musics as disparate and spatially contained. It also points to the ways that discursive categories (e.g., sacred, secular, profane) are mapped onto spatial categories (e.g., church, sports arena, nightclub).

For instance, on the surfaces of Los Angeles' church-laden streets, Khanchuz maps a cityscape of separation: "There is an aura of spiritual division here. L. A. is made up of churches, motels and liquor stores. In Inglewood, you have church, motel, liquor store, church, motel, liquor store, liquor store" (2007). This topography of Inglewood, California, which is repeated in similar neighborhoods throughout Los Angeles, reveals the proximity of sacred and secular spaces but occludes certain alliances, integrations, and manipulations of space that are socially and relationally produced by gospel hip hop practitioners and that occur suddenly in unexpected places, behind walls, after hours, and therefore out of sight. The tendency of black music studies to represent the church and the club as spatial binary of black cultural life and avoid examinations of nontraditional uses of space has led to a spatial bias that excludes valuable forms of black music making. Few scholars have explored the internal pluralities, divisions, and interactions within black communities between the church and the club and, most recently, between the church and the streets (Baraka 1963; Cone 1972; Spencer 1991, 1993; Sylvan 2002; Dyson 2003; Reed 2003; Pinn 2003). While academic and practical discourses separate these sites, music *sounds* their entanglement, giving voice to lived spatial resonances.

After outlining a brief history of holy hip hop's relationship to the church, I examine how the spatial practices of holy hip hoppers challenge and diverge from the constructed order of urban edifices and literal or functional readings of urban space.

Hip Hop and the Church: Shifting Grounds

During the 1980s, postindustrial formations under the Reagan-Bush administration adversely impacted the American inner cities. The African American urban community was acutely affected by these geopolitical and economic shifts. Weakened by the black middle-class flight from urban ghettos to the suburbs and the loss of black youth to the crack cocaine epidemic, gang violence, and prison, the black urban church—long the bedrock of the African American community—suffered significantly as its membership waned. Bakari Kitwana writes, "According to the National Opinion Research Center at the University of Chicago, attendance for 18–35-year-olds dropped 5.6% from 1995 to 2000" (2002: 22). Furthermore, as unemployment soared and poverty increased, African American inner-city youth became more vulnerable to a variety of social ills, including a "generalized demoralization" and nonconformist behaviors associated with the culture of poverty (Anderson 1992: 4). In an effort to steer its young members from these vices of street culture, some church elders and clergy vilified their own offspring as "criminals."

In an interview, Christian MC and poet Compton Virtue states, "The church is dying. The congregation is forty and above. Where are the young people? It's not tangible for young people. Don't talk over them; talk to them. How do you talk to them? You have to speak their language" (2004). Or as Tupac, a Los Angeles-based MC who is known for exploring Christian themes in his unique brand of gangsta rap, states on "Black Jesuz" (1999), "Went to church but don't understand it, they underhanded." Both quotes elucidate how some African American youth felt alienated from the church because of its inability to preach uplifting messages that addressed the harsh realities of street life and practice a politics of unconditional inclusion. While some hip hop heads sought guidance and insight from a variety of religious teachings, most notably with the Nation of Islam and an Islamic sect known as the Five Percenters, a number of young people in Los Angeles and other urban areas attempted to explore Christianity and scripture through hip hop music instead of the gospel music of the church. In the 1980s, such Christian rap acts as D.C. Talk, I.D.O.L. (In Dedication of Louis) King, S.F.C. (Soldiers for Christ), and P.I.D. (Preachas in Disguise) led the way. These early gospel rap artists explain the merging of hip hop and Christianity as arising out of the need to address a spiritual crisis and to bridge a generational schism between the black church and its restless youth. Although many gospel rappers tell a gangbanger-turned-churchgoer narrative, other youth have grown up simultaneously in the church and hip hop—frequenting hip hop events and parties with their friends, but attending church with their parents on Sunday. In some cases, parents themselves are fans or practitioners of hip hop, having grown up around the sounds of early rap music.

Holy hip hop's relationship to the church continues to be inconsistent and contested despite significant efforts by some pastors and church leaders to incorporate both hip hop youth and hip hop music, language, street codes, and aesthetics into worship services and events. This presence often evokes a sense of "moral panic" among some "older heads" who view the "noise" and iconography of hip hop as an unorthodox presence in the church. For them, holy hip hop literally brings a street sensibility of the block parties and schoolyard battles associated with early hip hop into the sanctuary. This is not the first time that popular music has crossed over the threshold of

African American churches or that religiously charged music has entered so-called profane spaces. Styles such as the blues, jazz, rhythm and blues, soul, rock, and even punk music have been blended into the sounds of Christian worship, but not without a thunderous backlash of skepticism that often (re)polarized religious discourses on the permissibility of sacred/profane maneuverings.

(Re)Placing the Church, (Re)Figuring the Body of Christ

Thus, many gospel hip hop artists prefer not to perform in churches, not only because of their evangelical impulse to preach to the unsaved but also because they feel artistically limited and monitored inside the church walls. At times, the performance of gospel hip hop can be understood as a particular kind of indirect resistance to or critique of the traditional church and some of its "outdated" and exclusionary practices. Gospel rap artists also feel performatively restrained, which is ironic considering the emotive power, expressive potential, and physical intensity of many practices of African American worship. B-Love, a female gospel rapper and member of the Hip Hopposite crew, feels obliged to make a forewarning statement before performing at a church, beseeching the congregation to try to listen past their negative assumptions about rap music to hear the spiritual message within her rhymes (2007). She also grows weary of being the musical aberration or pop novelty of a given church service—the hip hop element that feels *out of place* in relationship to an overarching gospel music aesthetic.

Those who have attempted to bring hip hop into the church have encountered other institutional and aesthetic challenges. The development of hip hop ministries housed within traditional churches engenders a complex web of power relations between proponents and critics of holy hip hop. In Los Angeles, Kurtis Blow, along with Pastor Carol Scott, Sean Heads, and Sharon Collins-Heads, founded the Hip Hop Church LA—a monthly hip hop ministry on Friday nights housed within Inglewood's Holy Trinity ELCA (Evangelical Lutheran Church in America). The relationship between what I am calling the "traditional" church and the hip hop ministry was fraught with distrust, miscommunications and, ultimately, some very painful betrayals. As a result, the Hip Hop Church LA decided to transform itself into a mobile ministry that took their service to various churches and events around Greater Los Angeles. In their own words, members of the hip hop ministry felt unwelcome, monitored, and surveyed as leaders of the traditional church would often drop in (conspicuously and inconspicuously) on the Friday night services to check up on their activities (Collins-Heads 2007). At the services I attended, the leaders of the traditional church would sometimes walk in late, sit in the back pews, and often portrayed a stoicism and sternness at odds with the playful and lively nature of the hip hop service.

In one of the harsher critiques of the Christian church, Stephen "Cue" Jean-Marie, born in Barbados, raised in Texas, former member of the secular rap group College Boyz, and now a member of the L. A.-based Christian rap group Asylumz, states:

So the church has become more like a negative asylum and I wouldn't say all churches, but most of them. That's why we call our group Asylumz. So I don't feel like I'm going to church just because I went to the church building. I feel like I'm going to church when I sit down face to face with somebody in the context of where they are, wherever they are. . . So we still have to deal with the stigma that goes with hip hop. You still have to go to bat with some heads—people preaching that it's the devil's music. But I tell gospel hip hoppers, you're all so busy trying to get the church to accept you. Hip hop is made for the streets. We should be out in the streets reaching people. The church will come because the church always follows the movement. (2007)

In the spirit of this assessment, Jean-Marie and his gospel rap group, along with members of the New Song Church (of which he is also a member), started holding an outdoor church service every Friday night on the infamous streets of Skid Row in downtown Los Angeles. They call it the "airborne church." He explains:

We call it the Row. It's not a building but we call it the church without walls—the church moving. The street that we preach at on Skid Row is a major crack vein—drug vein. There's no real format to it. We preach the Word and sometimes we'll do a song or someone from the street will just sing a gospel song. After the Word, we feed the people and eat with them because we want to be a part of their community, as well. We don't just make them our project. People are not projects. If we would love people, then the church would go airborne. No matter where you are, there would be church. So that's what Asylumz is; it's a place of refuge. (2007)

The Row illustrates the way that certain gospel rappers collapse people and place. Jean-Marie's statement asserts that *people* are an embodiment of the church and that Asylumz—a group of people—is actually a *place* of refuge. Gospel hip hop artists perform a conscious expansion of the sacred beyond the church to other social arenas in both their discourses and practices; they spatialize holy hip hop in clubs, schoolyards, living rooms, street corners, cyberspace, radio airwaves, and public access TV shows. Thus, the "church" in gospel rap practice cannot be understood as a *fixed stage* but rather as a *shifting ground*. I use anthropologist Donald Moore's spatial metaphors here to understand the diverse, varying formations of hip hop ministries. He rethinks domination and resistance as interrelated spatial practices that, rather than occurring on separate and *fixed stages*, together shape the *shifting grounds* of culture, power, and space (1998: 327). Renovations and restructuring in the wake of the Watts and Rodney King riots, along with the changing nature of Los Angeles churches, specifically the rise of megachurches, further complicate and diversify the city's shape-shifting religious landscape.

Holy Hip Hop Mappings and Conversions of Urban Space

Gospel rap enables the production of certain kinds of new and alternative sites and gatherings. The Row, as a church without walls, holds specific implications for experiencing the city as a constantly converting body and the manner in which gospel hip hop artists hold out the same potential of conversion for space as they do for the conversion of souls. Based on my fieldwork experience, gospel hip hop artists generally prefer mixed events that embody heterogeneity and promote an individual's process of becoming in both a musical sense and a religious sense (although, this was not always what was actualized at these events, and sometimes the outcomes of such gatherings served to strengthen the very discursive, musical, spatial, and imagined borders they were trying to dismantle). I now turn to two ongoing holy hip hop events mentioned earlier in the introduction: Klub Zyon and Club Judah. They currently act as the main consistent loci and crossroads of holy hip hop activity in Los Angeles. They both exist at the intersections of multiple fields of power, juxtaposing and integrating hip hop space, church space, and city space in experimental, conjunctural, and ever-changing ways. Like the Row, Zyon and Judah fall between the cracks of the classic binary of the church and the streets and are an example of some of the new hybrid performance experiences that look to bring believers and nonbelievers into spatial proximity and dialogue with one another, producing a kind of sacred/secular borderlands through gospel rap. How do these two sites help us rethink power in gospel rap or local hip hop scenes? How are the temporal and the spatial interlaced in holy hip hop performances? How do the life stories of individual gospel rappers intersect with the histories and uses of particular buildings? How do holy hip hoppers perform their own religious conversions as they convert space? Through an arrangement of strategies and tactics, including musical practices, verbal messages, bodily movements, the use of material props, and the aesthetic modification of particular places, gospel rap is actualized and given form.

On another level, gospel rap serves as an arena for alternative mappings of the city as a sacred imaginary. In interviews, informal conversations, and musical lyrics, gospel rappers often use religious metaphors to refer to Los Angeles and map biblical spatial categories onto particular locations within it. Los Angeles, with Hollywood at its cultural and commercial center, is imagined as the biblical city of Babylon: a city of excessive luxury, sensuality, vice, and corruption. More specifically, the Bible portrays Babylon as a place of captivity or exile for the Jews after the ancient empire of Babylonia conquered Israel in 6th century BCE. The exilic experience of holy hip hoppers navigating and traversing religious, musical, and physical borderlands of L. A.'s Babylon parallels and remaps this ancient narrative of displacement. Klub Zyon takes on added significance in this particular geographical imagination as a place both real and imagined.

Klub Zyon

Klub Zyon, as mentioned in the initial passage of this essay, is a monthly open-mic that takes place in Kaotic Sound—a cultural center that filmmaker and activist Ben Caldwell opened in 1984 in the historic black arts district of Leimert Park often associated with L. A.'s underground hip hop movement. Jean-Marie founded the event a couple years ago through his nonprofit organization the SHAW (sports, health, arts, and well-being) Community Transformation Corporation in the Crenshaw community of Los Angeles with the mission to provide an artistic meeting ground for different bodies and beliefs in the city. This vision of encounter and integration is realized and experienced in certain moments, however brief; other times, it stands as a spatial and social metaphor of holy hip hop politics. On fliers and on their Myspace page, it reads, "Zyon is more than just an open-mic. It is a place that offers a safe place for expression to artists, to the community, to activists, to those who are ready to see things change and are ready to make that happen." Avoiding any explicit links to Christianity in marketing and promotion, Jean-Marie hopes to attract a range of diverse participants. Occasionally, some very unlikely artists take the mic. According to John (a.k.a. Johnny Cash), a white man in his twenties and current member of Asylumz who helps run the open-mic, "Zyon is an open space for free expression, all who grab the mic are entitled to spit whatever they would like. NO CENSORSHIP. Klub Zyon does not share or promote ideas expressed by those who grab the mic. Klub Zyon is an event that is open to all, regardless of race, religion, gender, sexual orientation, socioeconomical standing, style of clothing, and/or eye color" (2008). Biblically speaking, Zion is known as the historic land of Israel and as a symbol of the Jewish people. More specifically, it is the Canaanite hill fortress in Jerusalem referred to in the Bible as City of David and used to symbolize the city as a religious center. In a metaphoric light, it represents heaven as the final gathering place of true believers or any an idealized, harmonious community a utopia.

The night starts around 10 or 11 p.m. and costs five dollars. (All proceeds go to the SHAW.) People arrive early to sign up for the open-mic and then hang on the street corner right outside until they hear the thumping bass of the turntables. Once participants enter the small, intimate space, they are greeted by three large wall hangings: a painting of Fela Anikulapo Kuti (Nigerian musician, political activist, and pioneer of Afrobeat music), a poster of Charlie Parker, and the image of a sphinx-like head bordered by different hieroglyphs and figurines rendered in an Egyptian aesthetic. The interior décor paints a particular politics of diaspora that links specific places and genres—Los Angeles, hip hop, Nigeria, Afrobeat, Egypt, black America, and bebop— across both real and imagined terrains of local and transnational crossing. Nothing is physically altered inside the cultural center except the sounds and bodies that inhabit it; the social, musical, and religious dimensions of Klub Zyon are what define the event as distinct from Project Blowed. Although the majority of the performers are African American men, I am always struck by the diversity of the crowd—people hailing from different neighborhoods across Los Angeles of varying socioeconomic classes, ages, sexual orientations, and racial and ethnic backgrounds (e.g., African American, Asian, African, white, Latino, and South Asian) exhibiting a diverse array of urban apparel and fashion.

Sonically, hip hop artists subject the building to both the rhythms and dynamics of hip hop music, rapping, freestyle, testimony, and prayer. DJ Heat, also a member of Hip Hopposite who has his own Christian rap radio show on Headz Up FM, spins both secular hip hop beats and gospel rap songs throughout the evening. He has an extensive knowledge of a wide range of hip hop artists and styles, which is impressive and surprising given the choice by many gospel rap artists to avoid listening to "secular" hip hop. When playing secular hip hop, he will only play the instrumental versions. (But most crowd members are familiar with the lyrics of these tracks, as they are usually well-known hits.) DJ Heat doesn't show much emotion or energy, playing the part of the classically stoic DJ or church musician, steadily and dutifully providing music for people to catch the spirit.

Klub Zyon is divided into three distinct sections. Initially, after the host MC welcomes everybody, anyone can take the stage and freestyle (improvise rhymes) over hip hop beats of DJ Heat's choosing. Then, those who have signed up on the open-mic perform one or two *writtens* (precomposed rhymes or songs) either a cappella or over prerecorded tracks that they generally bring in on CD or their iPods. Finally, there is a featured performance set by a local gospel hip hop artist or group. On a cool November night at Klub Zyon, Johnny Cash introduces TripLL-H as the MC for the night. Khanchuz is quick to remind me that MC to him means Minister of Christ. Khanchuz and Gandhi (short in stature, of South Asian descent) take the stage and bust verses (mostly written, some freestyle) over a series of beats that DJ Heat lays down—some of them are secular beats, perhaps leaving traces of secular hip hop, its lyrics and associations, to hang in the air. Khanchuz comes with it hard, kicking his leg up in the air, getting his tough muzzle on. His whole body compresses with conviction, his stomach becoming the fulcrum from which his chest and legs contract. His flow is clear and well annunciated. Gandhi's flow is sporadic, sometimes right on the beat, other times falling off it. He eventually loses his voice while rapping. TripLL-H confirms that this is how we do it for Jesus—we lose our voices for Jesus (Zanfagna 2007).

Statements like this are part of a larger effort to inscribe a sacred meaning on the activities that shape Klub Zyon, however secular they appear. They also undergird the desire and willingness to offer up one's body for the glorification of Jesus and the edification of the Body of Christ, even if one is ultimately rendered voiceless. In a similar manner, Young Chozen, a young black MC in his late teens, shouts into the mic, "How many of you glad you got butts to shake? God is good." In one verbal move, he celebrates both body and spirit, calling for butt-shaking as praise as he praises God for butts that shake. These are the body politics of Klub Zyon. Young Chozen, in particular, has an ability to intertwine religious and secular themes, thus appealing to both religious and secular audiences. His friendship with Wes Nile, another young male MC who frequents Klub Zyon, resulted in Wes Nile's eventual conversion to Christianity.

Later in the evening, as it approaches the midnight hour, Asylumz—the featured performers—take to the small stage. The group consists of six men of varying ethnicities, all of them in their twenties and thirties. They dance and bounce around on stage, bumping into each other, bringing a contagious, spirited, and raucous energy with a hard, masculine edge that matches the earsplitting volume of the music. At one point in the performance, they jump down into the crowd almost forming a mosh pit, clearing space on the floor as they collide into audience members' bodies and chant, "This ain't your daddy's music. This ain't your mama's music. This is how we praise. This is how we praise." As these lyrics and bodily movements suggest, the members of Asylumz refer to their particular brand of gospel hip hop "worsh-hop."

After the performance, Khanchuz explains to me that he wasn't particularly "feeling them" that night because he could not hear what they were saying: "I'm not gonna lie, it was entertaining, but I couldn't hear a word they were saying. For all I know, it could have been secular rap" (2007). For many gospel rappers, the message is the main element that distinguishes holy hip hop from secular hip hop. Thus, sound level as it relates to the respective volumes of the lyrics and beats is a contested terrain in gospel hip hop. PK 1000's, a twenty-two-year-old African American man who frequents Klub Zyon, often tells DJ Heat before he begins rapping to turn his track down so that the audience can hear his lyrics. But after he delivers a few lines of rhyme, he has DJ Heat turn up the volume to get himself inspired and pumped up. Given these negotiations of musical dynamics, it is not surprising that an interested passerby not familiar with the mission of Klub Zyon or the religious orientation of its founders might mistake the sounds emanating from Kaotic Sound as secular, commercial, or even gangsta rap as opposed to holy hip hop. Such aural assumptions and misrecognitions are often what produce spontaneous, unexpected, and experimental moments of encounter.

One such instance took place when an Asian-American woman, Magita Passion, performed during the open-mic in 2007. Her hair is long, black, straight, and striking, streaked with bleached blond and hot pink highlights. A short tattered shirt reveals her slightly bulbous belly—smooth and unashamed—and a large Chinese character tattoo peaking up from black-and-white pin-striped pants belted by a red, dragon-print ribbon. Fuchsia patent-leather platforms and eyelids sparkling with burnt-orange shadow finish the look. The crowd is definitely not sure what to expect from her. Unaware of Klub Zyon's Christian underpinnings and familiar with the location as the home of Project Blowed, she begins a spoken-word piece that reveals herself as a sex worker and advocate of sex-worker rights (including the decriminalization of sex workers and the legalization of prostitution) to an audience comprised mainly of Christians. She further explains that, historically, people have been supporting themselves with the money they earn from sex work—in her words, "getting paid for making love"—but they have been marginalized and stigmatized by a society with double standards.

After Magita finishes her performance and proclamation, the room stands still in deafening silence. TripLL-H walks over to her, puts his arm around her shoulders, and says ruefully, "We're going to pray for you." A Christian woman approaches the stage attempting to befriend her as members of the crowd shout, "Plant that seed!" Realizing what's happening, Magita rolls her eyes in annoyance, retorting back, "I don't need your prayers." Sensing that TripLL-H's call to prayer may not have been the most sensitive or affective response, the crowd begins to encourage her to perform another song, hoping to restore the environment of openness and tolerance. Deciding that she wasn't in the mood anymore, Magita leaves with the apology "Sorry for crashing your *church*." She had just wanted to share her music and message.

Despite the appearance of failure in terms of achieving Klub Zyon's vision for an all-inclusive space, this is just the kind of interaction that Jean-Marie is attempting to instigate: a nonbeliever to walk into the mix and stir things up. After Magita Passion leaves, Jean-Marie asks Mercy, another member of Asylumz, to lead everyone in a prayer for her. Mercy says many things, but most strikingly, he prays, "We ask for forgiveness, Lord, yours and hers, if we've offended her in any way. She is one of us. We are all the same. What I like about her, Lord, is that she is bold. Jesus needs bold people in the kingdom." Through this gesture, something is restored. Although the particular methods for bridging a religious divide did not prove to be successful that night, both the real and imagined geographies of Klub Zyon were remembered and re-visioned through this collective communication.

The stories relayed here highlight some of the moments of interaction and transformation between believers and nonbelievers and expose the cross-cutting interests and investments (e.g., artistic, political, and religious) at work and at play in sites of holy hip hop. The walls of the building have less to do with the lived geography of Klub Zyon than the dynamic of musical interrelations that the event produces among diverse spatial bodies, human bodies, and anatomies of belief. (That said, the fact that Klub Zyon takes place in a well-respected location for "underground" hip hop battles gives credibility and accessibility to the event.) At Klub Zyon, unexpected brushes with the profane and brushes with the sacred suggest a contested, yet ecological, relationship among church bodies, club bodies, and the arteries of the streets. What *happens* in this time and place (which includes biblical superimpositions and literal realities), as well as the shape and character of experiences, are less defined by the event producers than they are by the participants, audience, and passersby. This broadens our conceptions of what we consider to be gospel rap and who we consider to be participants and cultural shapers of the scene. What can we draw from the relationship between the biographies and geographies of holy hip hoppers is that the very actualization of these sites is capable of diverting temporal itineraries and life courses, thus illustrating the ways that a walk *with* God is in many senses a walk *through* the city.

Club Judah

Club Judah is a weekly holy hip hop night housed at the Love and Faith Christian Center near Western Avenue and Manchester Boulevard on the outskirts of Inglewood. On Saturday nights, church members and volunteers roll out the pews, set up large circular tables with black tablecloths, dim the lights, and create a club-like atmosphere for young people to experience God in a hip, relaxed environment. Pastor Collette created Club Judah six years ago for her adolescent daughter, who is a fan of hip hop music. On the church's website, it reads, "We're Spittin' Holy Fire! Club Judah began as a club for teens, a Christian alternative to what the world offers them on the weekends. Each week now, gospel hip hop artists from all over Southern California come in to minister through heavy beats and even heavier Word-based lyrics. . . Admission: Jesus has already paid the cost" (Pastor Collette 2008).

Club Judah represents and enacts both historical and ongoing geographies of conversion. The spatial transformations that take place every Saturday night entail a literal and physical conversion of the church sanctuary into a club. While the club is in session, the room remains very dark, making it difficult to tell who is present. The stage, which serves as the pulpit area during church services, is lit with colorful lights against a maroon curtain. The interior space, like the exterior of the building, is stark, unadorned, and boxy. At the end of the night, everyone present helps to dismantle and reconvert the club back into a church space for Sunday-morning service. The fluorescent lights flicker on; those present fold up the tables and chairs and stack them neatly in rows against the walls. The youth who are invited there in the hopes of religious conversion are also a part of the spatial conversion of the evening.

Delving into a deeper layer of history, we reach other relics and traces within the space. The site was home to a Western Surplus (gun store) before the building was looted and burned during the 1992 Rodney King riots, the carcass then renovated into a place of worship. Undergoing a kind of urban alchemy, the plain, unassuming white façade of the building now reads "House of Judah." In the Bible, Judah is known as the fourth son of Jacob and Leah and the forebear of one of the tribes of Israel. The name originated in Leah's words of praise to the Lord on account of her son's birth—"Now will I praise Jehovah, and she called his name Yehudah" (Genesis 29:35)—and is now known to mean praised or praise. Therefore, Club Judah quite literally means Club Praise—a club where one praises instead of parties, and gets high on Christ instead of drugs or alcohol.

For the year and a half that I frequented Club Judah, Pastor Graham (a pastor and gospel rapper in his early thirties) of Hood Ministries and Khanchuz hosted the evening program. With tattoos and silver chains, both of these men embody an aesthetic and an intimate knowledge of the streets. On first appearance, they seem more *gangsta* than *gospel*. They lead the attendees in a hybrid church service/concert, interspersed with prayer, musical performance, a short sermon, announcements, collective dancing, and a final altar call. (I have witnessed several young people give their life over to Christ at Club Judah, performing their religious conversion in the "club.") There is no open-mic; instead, Pastor Graham and Khanchuz perform every week and other artists are invited and scheduled to perform ahead of time. In spring 2008, for undisclosed reasons, Pastor Graham decided he could no longer remain the host of Club Judah. Khanchuz has stayed on as a promise to the youth to maintain a consistent weekly space for them to congregate.

The almost all-black audience composed mainly of families with children ranging from two to eighteen years old often arrives at 7 p.m. to hang out; play monopoly, basketball, or video games; shoot pool; and offer fellowship. The building itself feels impenetrable and set apart from the streets and passerby, in contrast to the social warmth and affability experienced within the walls. On a warm summer in Los Angeles, I stroll up to the blacktop parking lot in the back of the church. Young guys are playing basketball at the far end under the florescent street lamps. A group of young gals, one of which is Khanchuz's daughter Jaysha, lock my arms with theirs, forming a line of about five or six of us. They call me Cousin, skipping a bit, talking over each other, erupting with laughter, and buzzing like butterflies. "Hey Cousin, come on, follow us. We'll take you in." They yell at the group of boys to stop playing basketball so that we can pass in peace. The ball flies by right in front of my face, but they keep escorting me through the cool light of parking lot, parting the mess of boys like the Red Sea. They leave me inside and run back out to play. I hang out in the Green Room with Khanchuz before the "show" begins. He's just awoken from a nap. I can tell that working two jobs—part time administering drug tests for people on federal probation and part time at an out-patient drug program where he does counseling on relapse prevention, anger management, and HIV/AIDS awareness—has really taken its toll on him this week. Like his name's transformation suggests (from Sleep to Khanchuz), he doesn't get much rest anymore. There is something a little depressing about his energy and the building tonight. It's the first time I've been there since Pastor Graham left, and it's hard to tell how much of the emptiness of this place is caused by the void his departure left (Zanfagna 2008).

Khanchuz said that the space was depressing that night in part because of Pastor Graham's recent departure and also because of the weight that he feels the space carries. Quite literally, the site used to "pack a lot of weight," as it is weighted by sedimentations of racial discrimination and physical violence. Hindrances to the conversion of space come in the form of unseen spiritual forces (e.g., the felt presence of the Devil), history, memory, and power. When holy hip hoppers create places of activity, those activities change buildings just as the buildings carry meanings that mold the subjects within them.

Conclusion: Born-Again Bodies of the City

The Row, Klub Zyon, and Club Judah illustrate that the key sites of gospel rap production are not always clearly defined or physically delineated places, but instead temporary, provisional, and overlapping embodiments produced through musical, verbal, and material practices at the interstices of strategic constraints. Holy hip hop provides arenas where the negotiation of what constitutes the sacred and profane gets worked out by diverse social actors using a confluence of evangelical and hip hop-related tactics, methods, and modalities. In this multiplicity of connotation, it is always possible to do something different on and with the bodies of the city than is specified by certain structures of power while, at the same time, acting as though one remains operative inevitably only within them (Simone 2004: 409). Furthermore, performance sites like Klub Zyon and Club Judah make visible certain "off the map" or "below the radar" activities and life stories of people living in predominantly black communities in Los Angeles while sounding subterranean levels of urban history, urban life, and urban space that are concealed by the current topography of "church, motel, liquor store." When refracted through holy hip hop optics and acoustics, both the city and human body are understood as *living architectures* capable of being rebuilt, renovated, and reformed. The forming of rare urban configurations exposes the unfinished business of spiritual maturation, as well as the unfinished terrain of Los Angeles—the bodies of the city "born again"—that at specific moments allows for the creation and conversion of new kinds of social arrangements, subjects, and spaces. These sites may feel fleeting and, at times, blighted by their indefinite nature but also provide the grounds for envisioning and embodying potential futures of racially, religiously, and intergenerationally integrated space.

References

Anderson, Elijah. *Streetwise: Race, Class, and Change in an Urban Community*. Chicago: University of Chicago Press, 1992.

Baraka, Amiri. *Blues People: Negro Music in White America*. New York: Quill, 1963.

B-Love. Interview with the author. Santa Monica: 2007.

Brown, Jacqueline. *Dropping Anchor, Setting Sail: Geographies of Race in Black Liverpool*. Princeton: Princeton University Press, 2005.

Collins-Heads, Sharon. Interview with the author. Inglewood, CA: 2007

Compton Virtue. Interview with the author. Los Angeles: 2004

Condry, Ian. *Hip Hop Japan: Rap and Paths of Cultural Globalization*. Durham: Duke University Press, 2006.

Cone, James. *The Spirituals and the Blues: An Interpretation*. Maryknoll: Orbis, 1972.

Davis, Mike. *City of Quartz: Excavating the Future in Los Angeles*. New York: Vintage Books, 1992.

DjeDje, Jacqueline Cogdell, and Eddie S. Meadows. "Introduction." In *California Soul: Music of African Americans in the West*, 1–19. Berkeley: University of California Press, 1998.

Dyson, Michael Eric. *Open-mic: Reflections on Philosophy, Race, Sex, Culture and Religion*. New York: Basic Civitas Books, 2003.

Feld, Steven, and Keith Basso, eds. *Senses of Place*. Santa Fe: School of American Research, 1997.

Forman, Murray. *The 'Hood Comes First: Race, Space, and Place in Rap and Hip Hop*. Wesleyan, CT: Wesleyan University Press, 2002.

———. "Represent: Race, Space and Place in Rap Music." In *That's the Joint! The Hip Hop Studies Reader*. Edited by Murray Forman and Mark Anthony Neal, 201–22. New York: Routledge, 2004.

Jean-Marie, Stephen "Cue." Interview with the author. Inglewood, CA: 2007.

John [a.k.a. Johnny Cash]. Klub Zyon (Crenshaw). http://www.theupperground.com/index.php/Find-Sessions/Community-Centers/Klub-Zyon-Crenshaw.html. Accessed December 15, 2008.

Kelley, Robin D. G. "Kickin' Reality, Kickin' Ballistics: Gangsta Rap and Postindustrial Los Angeles." In *Droppin' Science: Critical Essays on Rap Music and Hip Hop Culture*. Edited by William Eric Perkins, 117–58. Philadelphia: Temple University Press, 1996.

Khanchuz. Interview with the author. Los Angeles: 2007.

Kitwana, Bakari. *The Hip Hop Generation: Young Blacks and the Crisis in African American Culture*. New York: Basic Civitas Books, 2002.

Moore, Donald. "Subaltern Struggles and the Politics of Place: Remapping Resistance in Zimbabwe's Eastern Highlands." *Cultural Anthropology* 13, no. 3 (1998): 344–81.

Neal, Mark Anthony. *What the Music Said: Black Popular Music and Black Public Culture*. New York: Routledge, 1999.

Pastor Collette. Club Judah. http://www.loveandfaithcc.org/ministries/judah.htm. Accessed December 15, 2008.

Pinn, Anthony. "Making a World with a Beat: Musical Expression's Relationship to Religious Identity and Experience." In *Noise and Spirit: The Religious and Spiritual Sensibilities of Rap Music*. Edited by Anthony Pinn, 1–26. New York: New York University Press, 2003.

Reed, Teresa L. *The Holy Profane: Religion in Black Popular Music*. Lexington: University Press of Kentucky, 2003.

Simone, Abdou Maliqalim. "People as Infrastructure: Intersecting Fragments in Johannesburg." *Public Culture* 16, no. 3 (2004): 407–29.

Spencer, Jon Michael. *Theological Music: Introduction to Theomusicology*. New York: Greenwood, 1991.

———. *Blues and Evil*. Knoxville: University of Tennessee Press, 1993.

Sylvan, Robin. *Traces of the Spirit: The Religious Dimensions of Popular Music*. New York: New York University Press, 2002.

Tupac. "Black Jesuz." *Still I rise*. Interscope Records, 1999.

Zanfagna, Christina. Field notes from research on holy hip hop in Los Angeles, 2007.

———. Field notes from research on holy hip hop in Los Angeles, 2008.

37

From Black Theology and Black Power to Afrocentric Theology and Hip Hop Power: An Extension and Socio-Re-Theological Conceptualization of Cone's Theology in Conversation with the Hip Hop Generation

Ralph C. Watkins[1]

Abstract: *In this paper Dr. James H. Cone's* Black Theology and Black Power *is put in conversation with two hip hop socio-theologians, Lauryn Hill and Talib Kweli. The next move in black theology will be led by the hip hop generation and this move will be towards an Afrocentric/African-centered theology. The method and socio-theological conditions that surrounded Dr. Cone's work are compared and contrasted with the present state of affairs in the African American community. Dr. Cone was writing after the assassinations of Malcolm X and Dr. Martin L. King Jr. Hip hop is writing after the election of President Barack Obama. Hip hop is raising theological questions. As one generation celebrates the realization of a dream, hip hop is rapping about a nightmare. The theological tension between Cone's generation, my generation, and hip hop are also explored.*

Introduction

I philosophize
Possibly speak tongues
Beat drum, Abyssinian, street Baptist
Rap this in fine linen, from the beginning
My practice extending across the atlas
I begat this

—Lauryn Hill, "The Miseducation of Lauryn Hill"

Religion, you learn Jesus
Turn the other check
Inherit the Earth, just stay meek
Fuck the way you speak
Try to run, we chop off your feet
Fast forward to 2004 we selling
Yo this ain't what I'm settling for
I want more, yo

I got a part to play, we going hard these days
Fuck the harder way, we doing it the smarter way
To my God I pray, that's how I start my day
The bullets start to spray the revolution starts today
I say the shit these people ain't got the heart to say
Fuck the harder way, we doing it the smarter way
To my God I pray, that's how I start my day
The bullets starts to spray the revolution starts today

—Talib Kweli, "The Beautiful Struggle"

The present work seeks to be revolutionary in the sense that it attempts to bring to theology a special attitude permeated with black consciousness Unless theology can become "ghetto theology," a theology which speaks to black people, the gospel message has no promise of life for the black man—it is a lifeless message

—James Cone, Black Theology and Black Power, *32*

Toward the Identification of the Hip Hop Theologian

These three opening quotes establish the existing tension by putting James H. Cone in dialogue With Lauryn Hill and Talib Kweli. Lauryn Hill steps up to the microphone and she says "I begat this." As an African American woman she begins to philosophize and theologize. Her speech is God-speak as she hints at speaking in tongues, interrogates the role of the church, while reaching back to an African center for her socio-theological starting point. She extends her words across the atlas as she points her followers back home to Mother Africa and introduces the Afrocentric frame.

Talib Kweli steps up to the microphone and he, like Dr. Cone, is critiquing the passivity of the African American church. The church, as Talib understands it, encourages you to turn the other cheek, not be critical and engaged in society; and this is not a stance with which Talib can agree. It is as if what Cone wrote in *Black Theology and Black Power* is in direct dialogue with Talib Kweli as he says, "religion you learn Jesus, turn the other cheek. . . Fuck the way you speak." Talib is critiquing institutionalized religion and what they are saying. He is effectively dismissing their message. Talib's dismissal of their message is based on its irrelevance to what young, inner city African Americans face every day. As bullets spray in the 'hood there has to be another way, and that way is the smarter way that calls for a revolution, according to Talib.

Talib sides with Cone when Cone says, "Unless theology can become 'ghetto theology,' a theology which speaks to black people, the gospel message has no promise of life for the black man [woman]—it is a lifeless message."2

Cone appears to be calling black theology back to the people. When we say Cone is calling black theology back to the people we mean the masses, the African American masses, "the lower classes the ones you left out." The question this paper raises is, did black theology become a ghetto theology? Did black theology migrate to the academy and away from the 'hood? When Cone wrote in 1968, a shift was occurring in the African American community: the doors of the academy were propped open for the professionalization and institutionalization of black theology. Was the professionalization of theologians as academicians versus leaders of embodied, religious communities indigenous to the African American community a symbolic and literal removal of black theology from the ghetto?

Has a chasm developed between the larger, grass-roots African American community, the institutionalized African American church and the black theologian? Did the theologian of the 'hood become the voice of the hip hop theologian? I was on Facebook the other day, Status Update; a young brother just put this on the wall: "Hip hop is a religion." I replied, and suddenly we are in the midst of a discussion. This young man and many like him are looking to hip hop theologians as conversational partners and not the institutionalized African American church or the theologian. The theologians to the ghetto are not us, professionally trained, institutionalized theologians, but rather those who come out of the ghetto and/or those who speak back to the ghetto.

These "hip hop 'hood theologians" are the ones who are making black theology a "ghetto theology." It is a theology that is contextualized in the African American community and conscious of the class divide within that community. As bell hooks says,

> More and more, our nation is becoming class-segregated. The poor live with and among the poor—confined in gated communities without adequate shelter, food, or health care— the victims of predatory greed. More and more poor communities all over the country look like war zones, with boarded-up bombed-out buildings, with either the evidence of gunfire everywhere or the vacant silence of unsatisfied hunger.3

What theology speaks of and into the class reality that bell hooks describes? Is it the hip hop 'hood theologians who speak of and back into the working class, working poor, and non-working poor in the communities that bell hooks describes? Talib Kweli says, "To my God I pray, that's how I start my day. The bullets start to spray the revolution starts today."[4] It is Talib Kweli, hip hop 'hood theologian, who talks back to the bullets and announces the revolution starts today. Kweli empowers the 'hood to act as he says; it is to God they pray, as they start their day. To go directly to God and bypass the traditional institutionalized forms of religion is the order of the day for the hip hop theologian.

It is clear that Talib places himself and hip hop in the middle of the religious/theological discourse when he says in the second verse, "In the battle between God and the devil, I lay claim to your spirit, your religion, your belief system." This is the root of his work. He is not hedging his bets on where he stands in the dialogue. He is right there in the middle, intentionally, laying claim to the belief system of his devotees and informing their spirituality and religiosity. This is not incidental or accidental, but as Talib claims, he is in the middle of this dialogue as an active participant, making claims, taking a stand, and sharing a hip hop theology and worldview informed by their understanding of God that informs their faith. Hip hop sees God as the creative power as they co-create with God. This co-creative theological principle is central to hip hop theology. God is using hip hop to speak to the people as they take their gifts as given to them by God to write, rap, make beats, and inspire a God-conscious lifestyle for the artist and *the* artist's followers.

The lifestyle is one that is sustained by God as hip hop theology is an incarnational theology that is real-world oriented, as hip hop lives in the moment, in the harshness of the city. James Cone would call this a "worldly theology," as he says, "Theology is not, then, an intellectual exercise but a worldly risk."[5] A worldly theology is one that is in dialogue with God and real-world issues that are facing the present age; confronting this generation. This young-adult hip hop generation are developing their worldly theology, taking theological risks as they engage in theological dialogue with the issues that plague their generation.

Talib Kweli wrote in the liner notes to *Eardrum,* "I speak of God often in my music, because we all try to achieve a greater understanding." Kweli goes on to say, "Of course, first and foremost, all praises and accolades are forwarded to the Most High, our creator, the Spirit that connects us." The fact that Talib Kweli talks about God in his music is not a coincidence or secondary in his mind. He sees God as the one who inspires him and his work. God is the one who, by the power of his Spirit, connects him with his followers. As Kweli raps he engages in God-talk or what Will Coleman calls "tribal talk." According to Coleman, "tribal talk" "is committed to the future. It is a way of doing theology within a post-Christian, pluralistic, and postmodern reality... it realizes that African American spirituality, both non-Christian and Christian, is that which sustains all generations via God's life-giving spirit."[6] This is what Kweli is appealing to; namely, God's life-giving spirit, as he models for us the way in which hip hop does theology, a theology that is life-giving and which sustains his followers.

Lauryn Hill opens her liner notes, "Thank God, my salvation and inspiration." She is not making some blanket perfunctory acknowledgment of God, but she is citing God as her savior and her salvation. She is also making a theological claim that God is the inspiration and co-creator of her music. These claims by both Talib and Lauryn Hill position them as theological voices empowered by God to speak on behalf of God to the people. Equally important is how those who follow them receive their word. These artists are not simply seen as artists by their followers; rather they are respected theologians who bring weight to bear on the theological conversation or discourse.

As the pastor for young adult ministry at First African Methodist Episcopal Church in Los Angeles, I have learned from young adults the seriousness with which they take the words of their hip hop theologians. In November of 2009 we put Lauryn Hill in dialogue with the book of Philippians, and if I was not yet convinced, I was that Thursday night, as the words of Lauryn Hill became flesh in that church basement. Lauryn Hill was the theologian, helping us understand God, how God acts, how God acted, and how God will act, as we dealt with the theological textures in "The Miseducation of Lauryn Hill":

> I look at my environment
> And wonder where the fire went
> What happened to everything we used to be
> I hear so many cry for help
> Searching outside of themselves
> Now I know his strength is within me
> And deep in my heart, the answer it was in me
> And I made up my mind to define my own destiny[7]

The theological richness of this verse sparked a conversation that lasted for hours. Lauryn Hill doe not just reference the urban environment; she talks about how the urban center has redefined our people. The decay of the city has taken the hope and desire to dream out of our people. Then, she points to a theological resource of inner strength that is God. This strength is not delivered via the institutionalized church or via the words of a preacher, but rather, this resource is abundantly available to the one who looks for it. In truth, it is already inside of them. Her theology begs the point of the need for some type of "conversion experience;" or if one is "born in sin," the claim of God being in her hearers is what empowers them to uncover their own destiny as divinely designed by their creator. This is an important finding that cannot be dismissed, because one of the key developments in hip hop theology is their interrogation of ecclesiology. They raise the question of whether the institutionalized church is relevant and necessary to be in relationship with God and or to hear from God. Hip hop claims to have God, to know God, to talk directly to God, to hear from God, and therefore, can bypass institutionalized religious authority.

From Black Power and the Black Church to Hip Hop and the New Jack and New Jackie

James Cone said in *Risk of Faith: The Emergence of Black Theology of Liberation, 1968–1998*, "I did not limit my critique to white churches and their theologians. In *Black Theology and Black Power* I also leveled sharp critique against the post-Civil War black church for its other-worldliness and indifference toward the political and cultural implications of Black Power."[8]

Talib Kweli joins Cone in this critique of the post-civil-rights church; a church that Talib goes on to say is passive, irrelevant, and has failed to speak to the suffering and pain index of the African American community. Talib Kweli and Lauryn Hill are talking about a "ghetto gospel," or as Talib said on his *Eardrum* CD, "the hostile gospel":

> Every Sunday dressing up catching gossip at its worst
> Couldn't see the difference in the Baptist and the Catholic Church
> Caught up in the rapture of the first chapter and second verse
> If we all God's children then what's the word of the reverend worth[9]

What is the word of the reverend worth? The preachers are not speaking into the lives of young African Americans. There is no significant difference between churches or denominations. They are all dealing with gossip, or insignificant issues that are linked to congregational life, with little to no concern for what is happening outside the walls of the church.

Kweli goes on to spit:

> Taught early that faith is blind like justice *when* you facing time
> If we all made in God's image then that means his face is mine
> Wait or it's that blasphemy it's logical it has to be
> If I don't look like my father then the way I live is bastardly
> Naturally that's confusion to a young'n trying to follow Christ
> Taught that if you don't know Jesus then you lead a hollow life
> Never question the fact that Jesus was Jewish not a Christian
> Or that Christianity was law according to politicians
> Who was King James?
> And why did he think it was so *vital* to remove chapters and make his own
> version of the Bible
> They say Hell is underground and Heaven is in the sky
> And they say that's where you go when you die but how they know[10]

Here Kweli is willing to be blasphemous. He is willing to raise difficult, unsettling questions. He is questioning the church's role, authority, and liberative nature—or lack thereof? Where James Cone was coming from inside the church, and in many ways talking to his peers in ministry, Talib Kweli and Lauryn Hill are standing outside the institutionalized church and making their critique from that positional stance. They are questioning the power and authority of the African American preacher and the institution they represent. They are questioning the authority of scripture. The questions they are raising are more vexing than those that James Cone raised. Cone lodges his method within the context of a Christian community as he elevates the role of scripture in his socio-theological method. The move toward an Afrocentric/African-centered hip hop theology levels the scripture with the revelation of the experience of the hip hop generation. This is a critical point. Whereas Cone was raised in the church, hip hop is raised in the streets, outside of the church; looking at the institutionalized church with a hermeneutic of suspicion. The relationship between the institutionalized church and the hip hop generation is a tenuous relationship at best and antagonistic at worst.

Whereas Cone's conversational partners were ". . . Black Power. . . Christianity, the church and contemporary American theology,"[11] in hip hop theological method, the church, and Christianity are suspect partners. At best, Christianity is put on a level playing field with other religious traditions in the city. The church as an institution is talked about, not talked to. The institutional church is not invited as a partner in the conversation. The institutionalized church is an outsider within the African American community according to hip hop. When you hear the hip hop 'hood theologian talk about the African American church it sounds a lot like James Cone's critique of the white church. As Cone defines what the church is and where Christ is, in his critique of the white church, he said:

> Where there is black, there is oppression, but blacks can be assured that where there is blackness, there is Christ who has taken on blackness so that what is evil in men's eyes might become good Therefore Christ is black because he is oppressed, and oppressed because he is black And if the church is to join Christ by following his opening, it too must go where suffering is and become black also[12]

The question James Cone and the hip hop 'hood theologians are raising is how black is the black church? Is the African American church speaking to the oppression that African Americans in the inner city are facing? Are the prophetic voices that spoke truth to justice being exchanged for the new praise and prosperity gospel of Fifty-cent and Creflo Dollar? It is hip hop that is where black is. It is hip hop that is blasting from the earbuds of iPods in the 'hood. It is hip hop that encourages kids to dream, tells their story of suffering, struggle, and pain. It is hip hop that talks about "black girl pain." It is hip hop that as Lauryn Hill says, tells of every city and every ghetto.

God Has Left the Building: A Hip Hop 'Hood Theology

In the eyes of the 'hood hip hop socio-theologian, the critique of the church is more scathing than that issued by James Cone in 1968, aged thirty. Talib at age thirty-four says, "The reverend looking look a pimp and the pimp look like the reverend."[13] Not only has the church lost its authority and respect, the very leaders of that institution have been likened to pimps. As even members of the academy echo the views of Talib; as Marvin McMickle asked in his book *Where Have All the Prophets Gone? Reclaiming Prophetic Preaching in America.* This issue is being addressed by both Talib, in his rapping, and McMickle in his writing. So for those who may be struggling to hear Talib, allow me to do the remix, and put Marvin McMickle on the mic:

> prophetic preaching is absent from the scene because too many of those whose responsibility it is to raise the issues of justice and righteousness have become distracted and preoccupied with other topics and other aspects of ministry. . . Too many preachers are ignoring the issues and the urgency of prophetic preaching as they invest all of their time and energy and imagination in some of what James and Christine Ward referred to as obscuring the wider dimensions of the gospel.[14]

The absence of preachers preaching to the powers that be and dealing with the issues of poverty, the prison industrial complex, under-funded and over-crowded schools, homicide, greed, and wealth, puts the mantle on the shoulders of the hip hop 'hood theologian who is looking back at the preacher and saying, "we can't tell the difference between you and the pimp." In essence, they are saying that our black preachers have become the pimps of the community and no longer hold the hallowed office of the prophet.

The fact that the prophet does not come from the institutionalized church does not obviate the need for the prophet. The prophet is now found in the voice of the hip hop 'hood theologian. That voice is Lauryn Hill, Jill Scott, Erykah Badu, Dead Prez, Immortal Technique, Mos Def, Talib Kweli, Outkast, Goodie Mod, Cee-Lo, and other emerging prophetic voices. Hip hop is prophet to the institutionalized church and pastor-prophet to the people whom the institutionalized church has disregarded. In 1968 James Cone could talk to the church and in that venue the masses were reached, but in this world, in this age, the masses of our people are not in the church. The masses are in a virtual church that is not enclosed by walls. This is truly the church without walls. We used to talk about a "church without walls" as we spoke of its ministry outside the four walls of the church. That metaphor now speaks to the development of a church that is not thinking about coming inside.

> Rap, your daddy is the blues; your mama is gospel. That's what they didn't want you to know. They want you to think you're illegitimate but I was there. I saw them jump the broom and I know they loved each other; still do. Some people want to judge but love is love. You the love child of gospel and blues and don't let nobody take that away from you. You belong.[15]

The baby has come of age: hip hop, the baby born to blues and gospel. The baby born out of the post-civil-rights movement has grown up, the baby that James Cone saw and recognized in 1968 without calling her name. James Cone said,

> It would seem that it is time for theology to make a radical break with its identity with the world by seeking to bring to the problem of color the revolutionary implication of the gospel of Christ. It is time for theology to leave its ivory tower and join the real issues, which deal with dehumanization of blacks in America. It is time for theologians to relate their work to life-and-death issues, and in so doing to execute its function of bringing the church to recognition of its task in the world.[16]

The theologians who clearly heard his cry were the hip hop 'hood theologians—they never entered the ivory tower. They stayed in touch and in tune with the streets. These theologians were not sequestered in four-walled churches. They talk about the issues of the streets, track after track; they raise socio-theological issues in their music. Lauryn Hill said,

> I was just a little girl
> Skinny legs, a press and curl
> My mother always thought I'd be a star
> But way before the record deals
> Streets that nurtured Lauryn Hill
> made sure that I'd never go too far
>
> Every ghetto, every city
> and suburban place I been
> Make me recall my days, in New Jerusalem[17]

Lauryn Hill was mindful of not going too far. She made sure that she stayed connected by acknowledging that the streets are what nurtured her, before the record deals, and it was important to keep in touch with those streets after fame ensued. You see Lauryn Hill struggling with this even more when she does her second solo project in 2003. Lauryn Hill and the hip hop 'hood theologians are conscious and deliberate as they seek to remember the streets from whence they have come and with which they continue to represent and dialogue. As Lauryn says, these streets are the "New Jerusalem." As hellish as they are and as much as they struggle, these streets are heaven and the source for theological reflections and God-consciousness.

For the hip hop 'hood theologian, theology is not a function or property of the church. James Cone said in *Black Theology and Black Power,* "Theology functions within the Church. Its task is to make sure that the 'church' is the Church. The mission of the church is to announce and to act out the gospel it has received."[18] This theological conversation has moved outside of the church. The hip hop 'hood theologian questions if the institutionalized church is even capable of having a meaningful theological dialogue that raises serious ecclesiological issues. In an age when mega is *betta* and big is brighter and the suburbs are richer, where is the revolutionary radical African American church? In an age where the Civil Rights pastors are retiring and dying, who is replacing their voice in the pulpit?

The very goals and impetus of black theology as defined by James Cone are conspicuously absent from the majority of inner-city churches in America. Cone said, "The goal of black theology is to prepare the mind of blacks for freedom so that they will be ready to give all for it. Black theology must speak to and for black people as they seek to remove the structures of white power which hover over their being, stripping it of its blackness."[19] Is the church doing this or is it hip hop? When we listen to Talib as he spits out what he says on "Hostile Gospel Pt. 1 (Deliver Us)," what do we hear? We hear the cry of hip hop theology as a cry for deliverance. As Talib opens this track, the intro cries, "deliver us, deliver us, deliver us, deliver us."[20] This is the cry from the streets, far removed from those who have been seduced by corporate America and have bought into the shallow "American Dream."

As he moves to the first verse he refers to rappers as baby seals who have been government fed. The implication here is that commercial rap—versus conscious, theologically inspired rap—is trapped in an economic system that is intent on holding African Americans down by exploiting them. Talib Kweli targets those rappers in the rap game who are going after profits and are not prophets who speak truth. They become a target for Talib Kweli as he tries to make sense of the oppression African Americans continue to experience in the twenty-first century. As Talib moves into the chorus he says, "What the people want? Please deliver us." This cry is consistent. I would go as far as to say that those whom Talib characterizes as government pawns and tools of oppression also want to be delivered. Who, after all, enjoys being oppressed?

The "hostile gospel" is what he calls it. This is obviously a play on the word "gospel" as used by the church culture. The hostile gospel is a cry for deliverance from a people who are fed up with systems that systematically oppress them in the forms of institutional oppression. Talib puts the church among those institutions that oppress others. Therefore, his gospel is not the church's gospel because that is a gospel of oppression that calls for the oppressed to conform via socialization to their oppressor. The hostile gospel is the good news that we are to be angry and to rise up against this oppression. It is up to us to fight back via our definition and construction of a liberative gospel that is co-created with God, via hip hop culture and the hip hop 'hood theologian. Within the hip hop community there is this engagement and critique of hip hop as well, especially the commodification of the art form and how it is being used to sell-out the movement. As Lauryn Hill says,

It's funny how money change a situation
Miscommunication leads to complication
My emancipation don't fit your equation. . .
You might win some but you just lost one![21]

Hill is critiquing a system of money and profits that calls prophets to compromise. She is questioning the system of capitalism and what it does to hip hop. She and Talib call for a hostile gospel that takes into account the construct of karma. Personal responsibility is highlighted in this gospel. Systems of oppression are implicated, but this does not dismiss personal responsibility for participating in oppression or submitting to it. Kweli and Hill want to be the "lost one" as they did not buy in to a system that is inherently oppressive.

As I look back over my career in the academy and the African Methodist Episcopal Church, I have to ask myself did money change the situation, did it lead to miscommunication and complication? Did the situation lead to my and our peoples' liberation? The hip hop 'hood theologian like Hill is always raising the question that Patricia Hill Collins put before us: "Is buying in selling out?" A major enemy to the liberation struggle is the hip hop industry that has prostituted hip hop culture, according to Kweli. "The industry inside us is vipers with fangs trying to bite us."[22] This is a call for hip hop not to be seduced by the American Dream, and on the other hand, to embrace the struggle for freedom by being both a disciple and preacher of the "hostile gospel." The hostile gospel as espoused by hip hop 'hood theologians is an oppositional gospel. It is oppositional as it seeks to reclaim the good news to the poor and broken people by acknowledging their presence and struggle, while simultaneously critiquing those institutions that are supposed to be liberative but in reality are a part of the oppressive system that keeps the poor, poor and the rich, rich. As Lauryn Hill says, "I'm about to change the focus from the richest to the brokest."[23]

The hostile gospel is a bottom-up critique of capitalism as it is manifested inside and outside of the church at the expense of the poor. Lauryn Hill goes on to say, "Make a slumlord be the tenant give his money to kids to spend it. And then amend it, every law that ever prevented."[24] The hostile gospel is one that is about changing the socioeconomic arrangement. The hostile gospel is a gospel that reaches down, while pulling the African American poor up and helping them see God. Hill says, "Our survival since our arrival. Documented in the Bible, like Moses and Aaron. Things gon' change, it's apparent. And all the transparent gonna. Be seen through, let God redeem you."[25] Lauryn is reaching back to the biblical image of revolutionary leaders in Moses and Aaron. She has essentially taken the story of the exodus and re-contextualized it in the hostile gospel. The story does not need the preacher or the institutionalized church to be actualized. The story becomes incarnational in the struggle for freedom in the context of the 'hood.

The hip hop 'hood socio-theologians' view of God is not what has been defined by the African American institutionalized church, but they are reaching back to Africa, before Nicaea, and asking who is this God who comes out of Africa? Lauryn Hill says, "Still be in the church of Lalabella, singing hymns a cappella." She is going back to Ethiopia. She is reaching back to an African/Afrocentric center to begin her theological journey. The hip hop 'hood theologian will not be restricted to a Western canonized view of God or the constraints of what has been considered orthodox theology. As Hill says, "I've been here before this ain't a battle, this is war."[26]

The hip hop 'hood socio-theologian is conscious of history. They have seen how former liberative movements have been derailed and even undermined by trying to appeal to a liberal audience of whites who have not had the interests of African Americans at heart. The hip hop 'hood socio-theologian is not looking for acceptance from anybody but the 'hood. As Hill says, "I make shallot like a Sunni. Get diplomatic immunity in every ghetto community. Had opportunity went from hoodshock to hoodchic. But it ain't what you cop, it's what you keep. And even if there are leaks, you can't capsize this ship. Cause I baptize my lips every time I take a sip."[27]

The hip hop 'hood theologian is the re-embodiment of Dr. James Cone in the present-day context. They are young, as he was, back in 1968. Both Talib Kweli and Lauryn Hill were in their early thirties when they penned these works. The hip hop 'hood theologian is a prophet who speaks truth to the powers within the African American community and outside it. They have reframed the gospel, and this gospel is not limited to a Christian conversation or a church context. Rather, they are looking at and have an appreciation for the veracity of other religious traditions that live in the 'hood. They are inclusive and not exclusive when it comes to their theological dialogue. The willingness to have multiple theological conversational partners has given the hip hop 'hood theologian a broader audience that appreciates their moving beyond religious tolerance to theological inclusion. The principle of inclusion and dialogue makes for a richer, more robust conversation that is reflective of the real socio-theological-religious life that is actualized in the 'hood.

The question that remains is will we hear and respect the hip hop 'hood socio-theologian or will we condemn them? James Cone said of the white church, "we must say that when a minister condemns the rioters and blesses by silence the conditions which produce the riots, he gives up his credentials as a Christian minister and becomes inhuman. He is an animal, just like those who, backed by an ideology of racism, order the structure of society on the basis of white supremacy."[28]

While the African American institutionalized church condemns hip hop, is hip hop the rioters? Is hip hop the ones that are crying from the streets saying we are in pain! We are hurting! We feel neglected! We feel left out! We have not been fathered! We have not been mothered! We have been disowned by our own people! We have been blamed for the disarray in our communities! But it is our elders who failed to critique a system that is built on white supremacy and racism that created the 'hood, created overcrowded and under-funded schools. Why is that? In the words of The Black Eyed Peas, "Where is the love?"

Holler If Ya Hear Me!

Notes

1. Ralph Watkins is Assistant Dean of the African American Church Studies Program and Associate Professor of Society, Religion, and Africana Studies. He is the author of *I Ain't Afraid to Speak My Mind* (Augusta, GA: Unity Council, 2003), *The Gospel Remix: Reaching the Hip Hop Generation* (Valley Forge: Judson, 2007), *Jay Z to Jesus: Reaching and Teaching Young Adults in the African American Church*, which he co-authored with Benjamin Stephens (Valley Forge: Judson, 2009), and his new book, *Leading Your African American Church through Pastoral Transition* (Valley Forge: Judson, 2010). He is currently working on his next book project, *Hip Hop Redemption: Finding God in the Music and the Message*, to be released by Baker Academic in late 2011.
2. James Cone, *Black Theology and Black Power* (New York: Seabury, 1969), 32.
3. bell hooks, *Class Matters* (New York: Routledge, 2000), 2.
4. Talib Kweli, "The Beautiful Struggle," on *Going Hard* (CD) (New York: Rawkus Entertainment, 2004).
5. Cone, *Black Theology*, 84.
6. Will Coleman, *Tribal Talk: Black Theology, Hermeneutics, and African/American Ways of "Telling the Story"* (University Park: Pennsylvania State University Press, 2000), 194.
7. Lauryn Hill, "The Miseducation of Lauryn Hill," on *The Miseducation of Lauryn Hill* (CD) (New York: Ruffhouse Records, 1998).
8. James Cone, *Risk of Faith: The Emergence of Black Theology of Liberation, 1968–1998* (Boston: Beacon, 1999), xxiv.
9. Talib Kweli, "Give 'Em Hell," on *Eardrum* (CD) (Burbank: Warner Brothers Records, 2007).
10. Kweli, "Give 'Em Hell."
11. Cone, *Black Theology*, 1.
12. Cone, *Black Theology*, 69
13. Talib Kweli, "Around My Way," on *The Beautiful Struggle* (CD) (Rawkus/Umgd, 2004)
14. Marvin McMickle, *Where Have All the Prophets Gone? Reclaiming Prophetic Preaching in America* (Cleveland: Pilgrim, 2006), 8.
15. Nikki Giovanni, "Rap-Blues Child," in *Acolytes* (New York: William Morrow, 2007),
16. Cone, *Black Theology*, 83.
17. Lauryn Hill, "Every Ghetto, Every City," on *The Miseducation of Lauryn Hill*.
18. Cone, *Black Theology*, 84.
19. Cone, *Black Theology*, 118.
20. Talib Kweli, "Hostile Gospel Pt. 1 (Deliver Us)," on *Eardrum*.
21. Lauryn Hill, "Lost Ones," on *The Miseducation of Lauryn Hill*.
22. Talib Kweli, "Give 'Em Hell," on *Eardrum* (CD).
23. Lauryn Hill, "Final Hour," on *The Miseducation of Lauryn Hill*.
24. Lauryn Hill, "Final Hour," on *The Miseducation of Lauryn Hill*.
25. Lauryn Hill, "Final Hour," on *The Miseducation of Lauryn Hill*.
26. Lauryn Hill, "Final Hour," on *The Miseducation of Lauryn Hill*.
27. Lauryn Hill, "Final Hour," on *The Miseducation of Lauryn Hill*.
28. Cone, *Black Theology*, 80.

Bibliography

Coleman, W. *Tribal Talk: Black Theology, Hermeneutics, and African/American Ways of "Telling the Story."* University Park: Pennsylvania State University Press, 2000.

Cone, J. H. *Black Theology and Black Power.* New York: Seabury, 1969.

———. *Risk of Faith: The Emergence of Black Theology of Liberation, 1968–1998.* Boston: Beacon, 1999.

Giovanni, N. "Rap-Blues Child." In *Acolytes.* New York: William Morrow, 2007.

Hill, L. "The Miseducation of Lauryn Hill." On *The Miseducation of Lauryn Hill* (CD). New York: Ruffhouse Records, 1998.

hooks, b. *Class Matters.* New York: Routledge, 2000.

Kweli, T. "The Beautiful Struggle." On *Going Hard* (CD). New York: Rawkus Entertainment, 2004.

———. "Give 'Em Hell." On *Eardrum* (CD). Burbank: Warner Brothers Records, 2007.

McMickle, M. *Where Have All the Prophets Gone? Reclaiming Prophetic Preaching in America.* Cleveland: Pilgrim, 2006.

38
Baptized in Dirty Water: An Ontology of Hip Hop's Manufacturing of Socio-Religious Discourse in Tupac's "Black Jesuz"

Daniel White Hodge[1]

"Hip hop" is a voice. A voice that openly speaks for the marginalized, the poor, the downtrodden, and the oppressed (Chang; Dyson; Hodge *The Soul of Hip Hop: Rimbs, Timbs and a Cultural Theology;* Kitwana *The Hip Hop Generation: Young Blacks and the Crisis in African American Culture;* One). Hip hop is an urban sub-culture that seeks to express a life-style, attitude, and/or urban individuality. It rejects dominant culture, and seeks to increase a social consciousness along with a racial/ethnic pride. Thus, hip hop uses rap music as the vehicle to send and fund its message (Hodge *The Soul of Hip Hop;* Smith and Jackson). Tricia Rose argues in her work *Black Noise: Rap Music and Black Culture in Contemporary America* that hip hop culture emerged as a source for young people of alternative identity formation and social status in a community, to have that social status and identity within a system that had abandoned them (Rose 31–33). Moreover, hip hop and rap were, and still are in many ways, the conduit between urban-ites and pop culture for almost four decades (Asante). Hip hop culture provides an outlet and a voice for many young people in the inner city today. In addition, Angela Nelson states, "The racial oppression of black people in many ways has fueled and shaped black musical forms in America" (Nelson 51). Rap music is one of those forms; Nelson further states, "Contemporary rappers, like early blues people, are responding to the 'burden of freedom,' in part by relaying portrayals of reality to their audiences through their personal experiences" (Nelson 56). Thus, rap music is the main medium of the hip hop culture that brings definition, value, understanding and appreciation to the social isolation, economic hardships, political demoralization and cultural exploitation endured by most ghetto poor communities. Rap and hip hop captures and esteems the ghetto poor existence as valid and real to all ethnic minorities and poor whites (Hodge *The Soul of Hip Hop;* Smith and Jackson).

Within this discourse of connectivity, there is something larger at work: a fundamental attempt to make God more accessible to a people who have been, in large part, ignored by many Christian churches. The seemingly foul language, lewd sexuality, and lifestyles appearing to be "anti-god" make it difficult for many religious individuals to relate and engage. Yet, that does not make hip hop any less spiritual. In my book, *The Soul of Hip Hop,* I found that young persons ages 14–21 understood God and Christian sacred scripture with deeper meaning from artists such as Tupac, DMX, Lupe Fiasco, and Lauryn Hill because it ". . . is from their perspective and language" (Hodge *The Soul of Hip Hop* interviews). As Christina Zanfagna, an ethnomusicologist who studies hip hop and religion, exclaims in her article "Under the Blasphemous W(Rap): Locating the 'Spirit' in Hip Hop," "Mainstream hip hop percolates with unlikely and multifaceted religious inclinations. Despite its inconsistent relationship to organized religion and its infamous mug of weed smoking, drug pushing, gun slinging, and curse spewing, rap music is not without moral or spiritual content. . . religious messages have always been delivered through a vast array of sounds." (2006: 1)

Therefore, hip hop is, simply put, a contextualized form of manufacturing religious discourse, meaning, and identity from within and for the people who are its listeners. Artists such as Tupac act as a type of natural theologians who interpret scripture and comment on it no differently than, say, a T. D. Jakes or a Joel Osteen would do for their constituents. Hip hop, however, pushes past the traditionalized white, blonde, blue-eyed, social construct of Jesus and asks for a Jesus that smokes like we smoke, drinks like we drink, and acts like we act—a Jesus that "we can relate to in the 'hood." This type of Jesus also questions authority, seeks to increase social consciousness, validates and acknowledges the social isolation as valid and real to all the 'hood, and every now and then "puts a foot in someone's ass to tell a muthafucka he real" (Hodge *Heaven Has a Ghetto: The Missiological Gospel & Theology of Tupac Amaru Shakur* interview).

Therefore, in this article, I will briefly historicize the socioeconomic conditions that gave rise to hip hop's religious and spiritual discourse. Then, through a close textual analysis using Jon Michael Spencer's framework of theomusicology, I analyze Tupac Shakur's song "Black Jesuz" to argue (1) that sensationalized images of Jesus are the missing pieces that mediate the growing gulf between traditional Christianity and hip hop culture; and (2) that hip hop produces a more relevant and applicable theological mantra for Christianity.

Societal Conditions

Marcus Garvey stated that when all else fails to organize the people, if the people could not arise and create change, the conditions will. Around the late 1950s and early 1960s, the beginnings of the first wave of what was to be called de-industrialization began to occur (George *Post-Soul Nation: The Explosive, Contradictory, Triumphant, and Tragic 1980s as Experienced by African Americans (Previously Known as Blacks and before That Negroes);* Murray; Palen; Sides; Wiese). Businesses began to find it more profitable to outsource their work, pay less in benefits, use cheaper labor, and ultimately generate larger profits for the shareholders. This adversely affected black communities, which led to a fragmentation of the middle class and a growth of people in poverty (Sides; Wiese). The American economy was beginning to change; it was shifting from an industrial economy to one more focused on technology and highly skilled labor—which paid a lot more but required specialized training and education. Because of historic discrimination in colleges, many blacks found it difficult to compete with peers with specialized degrees; jobs in the aerospace industry, for example, did not typically hire blacks; moreover, if the applicant did not have the necessary training, there was no point in applying. Todd Boyd notes, "We're not talking about people who had careers. We're talking about people who had jobs. If you have a job you are dependent on *that job*. So when that factory closes, you are in essence assed out" (Peralta interview on DVD). By the late 1960s, most of those thriving factories have disappeared. In the wake of this loss, leaders put nothing into place for the thousands of workers now out of a *job*.

By 1968, you have full de-industrialization with many of these corporations leaving the U.S. to go to Mexico, India, and China (Paris; Peralta; Sides; Wiese). The once-hopeful and almost cheerful black middle class was dismantled and beginning to crumble. The black generation born during the mid- to late-1960s were in worse financial and social shape than their predecessor's generations—moreover, these new generations were growing up without black leaders and visionaries such as Martin Luther King, Bobby Seal, and Malcolm X. What was worse was there were very few programs that could handle and deal with the significant rise in black families who were jobless.

On Thursday March 10, 1975—eleven years after the Civil Rights Movement, an entire section of the Los Angeles Times entitled "A Ghetto Is Slow to Die" engaged this very real phenomena in the black community. John Kendall researched families and the economic structures from 1963–1975 and stated that, "The fearful live behind protective bars and double locks. High schools are graduating functional illiterates." He also asserted, "Little has changed in the basic conditions of the black ghetto in 10 years since the Watts riots erupted. . ." The article was a sobering reality that did not give a very promising future for anyone living in ghetto-like conditions, but principally for blacks. Kendall continued, "Some black people have got businesses; some professionals have gotten into significant jobs. But if you talk about the masses or that guy who was in trouble in '65, it is more difficult now." The social manifest that so many black churches fought to create and instill was surmised in one word for life: survival (Kendall).

Charles Murray, an urban ethnographer recorded that, in essence, once de-industrialization began, large swatches of the black community—particularly the young under the age of twenty—laid in financial ruin in its wake (Wiese 2004). What little capital and access to education blacks had, by the early 1960s, begun to wither away and created a distinct ghetto that was ripe with anger, filled with those searching for answers, and experiencing a disenfranchisement from the rest of American society.

There was a distinct shift in social, theological, philosophical, and even Christological ontology during the late 1960s and early 1970s; this shift was partly a result from the ensuing economical change for blacks, but also the reality that such societal mantras like "Work hard, and your dreams will come true" were shattered.[2] For blacks, a type of "Great Depression" set in and a new generation of youth was raised in this ethos of shattered dreams and hopes. They saw that the old way of life was not working for the old and this new world they found themselves in was one riddled with double standards, failed promises, destroyed social structures, and a government that seemed almost obtuse and belligerent towards them (Hodge *The Soul of Hip Hop*; Moss; Watkins). An angry generation of black and brown youth were now culcuminating within the ghettos around the U.S. and in the mid- to late-1970s; a new shift was taking place for black and brown youth's social and cultural expressions; in the womb of this shift, hip hop was forming within the theological void and vacuum of the 'hood (Rose 34–40).

By the time the 1980s arrived an entire section of America's cites lay in ruin by the degenerate destruction of the crack era (Hodge *Heaven Has a Ghetto*; Neal; One; Peralta; Quinn; Ruskin). Moreover, most affluent churches had left the ghetto for a safer, cleaner, suburban area. Black and brown youth had little to no recourse and faced a society that viewed them at thugs, pimps, and ho's. Hip hop stood up and artists such as Melly Mel told us "The Message"; Run DMC reminded us of "Hard Times"; NWA told us to "F... the Police" in response to police brutality; and Tupac prompted us to "Keep Our Heads Up."

Black Jesuz

Thus, the need for a contextual, relevant, and appropriate Christ was—and still is—needed to interpret deity and spirituality for the 'hood. In the song "Black Jesuz" by Tupac and The Outlawz, there is an attempt to make a God—which appeared too perfect, too nice, and too white on a social level—more accessible to the 'hood. Understanding the theological message, tone, structure, and discourse in music is what Jon Michael Spencer calls *theomusicology*. Spencer states, "Theomusicology is a theologically informed musicological study of how music is created, shared, and encountered. . . it is how a particular peoples perceive the universal mysteries that circumscribe their mortal existence and how the ethics, theologies, and mythologies to which they subscribe shape their worlds and THE world."[3] In their article "Theomusicology and Christian Education: Spirituality and The Ethics of Control in the Rap of MC Hammer," N. Lynne Westfield and Harold Dean Trulear state:

> Theomusicology treats black music in a holistic manner and secularity as a context for the sacred and profane, rather than as the antithesis of the sacred. . . As such, theomusicology is a tool for us to move beyond the simplistic notions of "good" and "bad" that are uncritically used to characterize black secular music and especially rap music, and to help us develop an understanding of the meaning system under construction by African American youths (219–220).

Therefore, within the song "Black Jesuz," an attempt to make hell on earth—life in the 'hood—more understandable; to create a space for the thug, the nigga, and the pimp to find God; and a space for some sort of reconciliation to the social environment are at work. The intersection of Spencer's trinary construct is at work: where the sacred and the profane both reveal themselves in secular contexts—in this case, hip hop artists. Tupac reverses the hermeneutical flow[4] and uses culture—in this case hip hop—to interpret God in a context which is hostile.

The song is in three parts: (1) the Doxology—giving respect and acknowledgment; (2) the Lament—how is life and love done in this ghetto hell; and (3) the Benediction to Black Jesuz—we are searching for a Jesus *for* us.

Tupac opens with a call out to a Jesus who can relate, the Doxology:

> Searching for Black Jesus
> Oh yeah, sportin jewels and s. . . , yaknahmean?

A God whose religious affiliation does not matter:

> (Black Jesus, you can be Christian
> Baptist, Jehovah Witness)
> Straight tatted up, no doubt, no doubt
> (Islamic, won't matter to me
> I'm a thug; thugs, we praise Black Jesus, all day)
> Young Kadafi in this b. . . , set it off nigga. . . What?

Once again, Christina Zanfagna reminds us, "Hip hop wrestles with the ways in which the hedonistic body and the seeking soul can be fed and elevated in dynamic tension. This wrestling is often expressed through a dialectic of pleasure and pain or recreation and suffering" (5). Here, the search is clear; a Jesus who is "blinging," without denominational affiliation, and one who can relate. The "thug Jesus" is someone to be praised and a deity figure needed from the Outlawz stance.

Kadafi from the Outlawz exegetes his environment with laments to Jesus: (1) it is a nightmare; (2) times are desperate; (3) the form of religion does not relate; and (4) questions if God can relate.

> Stuck in a nightmare, hopin he might care
> Though times is hard, up against all odds, I play my cards
> like I'm jailin, shots hittin up my spot like midnight rains hailin
> Got me bailin to stacks more green

The visibility of pain and suffering is evident while the assertion to "survive" and make money is also evident. Can a God who "loves" everyone conjure up a resolution within a "nightmare" situation? The ageless theological inquiry of doubt begins to manifest itself:

> Gods ain't tryin to be trapped
> on no block slangin no rocks like bean pies
> Brainstorm on the beginnin
> Wonder how s... like the Qur'an and the Bible was written
> What is religion?
> Gods words all cursed like crack
> Shai-tan's way of gettin us back
> Or just another one of my Black Jesus traps

Storm follows and essentially proposes three questions: (1) Who has the guts to stand beside him in hell? (2) Can we meet at the intersections of the profane and sacred? (3) Is heaven a possibility or even a reality?

> Who's got the heart to stand beside me?
> I feel my enemies creepin up in silence
> Dark prayer, scream violence—demons all around me
> Can't even bend my knees just a lost cloud; Black Jesus
> give me a reason to survive, in this earthly hell
> Cause I swear, they tryin to break my well
> I'm on the edge lookin down at this volatile pit
> Will it matter if I cease to exist? Black Jesus.

Tupac, allowing members of the Outlawz to go first, then enters and creates a relatable Jesus— one who can affirm the social isolation and disinherited:

> In times of war we need somebody raw, rally the troops
> like a Saint that we can trust to help to carry us through
> Black Jesus, hahahahaha
> He's like a Saint that we can trust to help to carry us through
> Black Jesus

Tupac reminds Storm that surroundings in the 'hood are similar to war-like conditions but that there is a saint who can "carry us through."

Young Noble begins the Benediction—the fourth verse—affirming that race, culture, and religion are different in the 'hood.

> Outlawz we got our own race, culture, religion
> Rebellin against the system

Noble keeps the lament tension intact while still begging Black Jesus to "please watch over my brother." This delicate treading with the sacred and the profane is similar to what Spencer refers to as "unreligious people's quest for the sacred" (*Theological Music: Introduction to Theomusicology,* 7–8). Spencer argues that this is a way to understand the nature of irreligious music and the community therein which produces it.

Thus Young Noble, in an irreligious way, is in search of a God who does not flinch in the face of crap. He is engaging in a conversation with Black Jesuz in which the answers of his pain are still yet to be revealed. This is similar to David's prayers in the Psalms. "Keep me safe, O God, for I have come to you for refuge" (Psalm 16:1 NLT), "My God, my God! Why have you forsaken me? Why do you remain so distant? Why do you ignore my cries for help? Every day I call to you, my God, but you do not answer. Every night you hear my voice, but I find no relief" (Psalm 22:1–2 NLT). These passages are similar to Noble's own apprehension that he is laying before Black Jesuz:

> The President ain't even listenin to the pain of the youth
> We make music for eternity, forever the truth
> Political prisoner, the two choices that they givin us
> Ride or die, for life they sentence us
> Oh Black Jesus, please watch over my brother Shawn
> Soon as the sky get bright, it's just another storm
> Brothers gone, now labeled a statistic
> Ain't no love for us ghetto kids, they call us nigglets
> History repeats itself, nuttin new
> In school I knew, e'rything I read wasn't true
> Black Jesus

In the fifth verse, Tupac discusses the ill effects of a life within nefarious conditions:

> To this click I'm dedicated, criminal orientated
> An Outlaw initiated, blazed and faded
> Made for terror, major league niggaz pray together
> Bitches in they grave while my real niggaz play together
> We die clutchin glasses, filled with liquor bomblastic
> Creamated, last wishes nigga smoke my ashes
> High sigh why die wishin, hopin for possibilities
> I'll mob on, why they copy me sloppily
> Cops patrol projects, hatin the people livin in them
> I was born an inmate, waitin to escape the prison

In this verse, he exegetes the life of the thug, the pimp, and the pusher; moreover, he asserts what those types of lifestyles produce: drug abuse, hate, and distrust of systems. Church, for Tupac and the Outlawz, is no different. If, in their estimation, the cops beat you, schools lie to you, systems fail you, why would the "church" be any different? Tupac ends the verse:

> Went to church but don't understand it, they underhanded
> God gave me these commandments, the world is scandalous
> Blast til they holy high; baptize they evil minds
> Wise, no longer blinded, watch me shine trick
> Which one of y'all wanna feel the degrees?
> Bitches freeze facin, Black Jesus

Michael Eric Dyson asserts, "Tupac was the secular external articulation of an ongoing religious debate about the possibility of identifying with a God who became what we are" (Peters DVD interview). In other words, Tupac is surmising that within the fallout of failed systems, promises, and theologies, there is a need for a Black Jesuz; one in which "bitches freeze" when standing in his manifestation.

Kastro finishes the last verse with a declaration to Jesus: we are hurting, please help. Kastro shows a Jesus who "walks through the valley." Once again, a Jesus who can identify with hunger; a Jesus who realizes that this is not the intended mode of life for humans; a Jesus who, as Ebony Utley asserts, was gangsta, hung out with thieves, prostitutes, beat down some fools, used foul language to castoff religious pastors and rejected the religiosity of his day:

> Jesus is the transitional God figure because, according to the Bible, God "out there" sent Jesus "down here" to sacrifice himself via death, burial, and resurrection to redeem humanity. The physical experience of walking the earth anchors Jesus to the human experience. . . only a God who walked among humans could truly redeem them. This perspective is not lost on gangstas who connect with Jesus' experience with haters (persecutors), murder (crucifixion), and resurrection (redemption). Jesus is familiar with suffering because he suffered. Jesus is familiar with victory because his resurrection conquered death (Utley 8).

Kastro wants to see something better than the life he has now and has experienced thus far.

> And it ain't hard to tell, we dwell in hell
> Trapped, black, scarred and barred
> Searching for truth, where it's hard to find God
> I play the Pied Piper, and to this Thug Life, I'm a lifer
> Proceed, to turn up the speed, just for stripes
> My Black Jesus, walk through this valley with me
> Where we, so used to hard times and casualties
> Indeed, it hurt me deep to have to sleep on the streets
> And haven't eaten in weeks, so save a prayer for me
> And all the young thugs, raised on drugs and guns
> Blazed out and numb, slaves to this slums
> This ain't livin. . . Jesus

Kastro wants a deity that is "down here" and can redeem the mounting negative experiences within the 'hood.

Lastly, Tupac, in the last call of the song, exhorts to us that they are in search for Jesus that hurts like we hurt, smokes like we smoke, drinks like we drink, and understands where we coming from—a basic ontological hermeneutic for us all:

> Searchin for Black Jesus
> It's hard, it's hard
> We need help out here
> So we searchin for Black Jesus
> It's like a Saint, that we pray to in the ghetto, to get us through
> Somebody that understand our pain
> You know maybe not too perfect, you know
> Somebody that hurt like we hurt
> Somebody that smoke like we smoke
> Drink like we drink
> That understand where we coming from
> That's who we pray to
> We need help y'all

Dyson states, "Black Jesus for Tupac meant for him that figure that identities with the hurt, the downtrodden, and the downfallen. The Black Jesus is a new figure; both literally within the literary traditions of black response to suffering, but also religious responses to suffering. If this is the Black Jesus of history, it is the Jesus that has never been talked about and most people who talk about Jesus would never recognize" (Peters DVD interview). Tupac not only knew this, but also embodied this within his body of work, which is one of the many reasons he argued in so many songs for the contextualization of the gospel for the 'hood. Tupac blurred the lines between the sacred and the profane. Tupac entered into blasphemous zones and waded into deep heretical waters while searching for this Black Jesuz who could redeem his context. "Black Jesuz" is a song made in an attempt to bring a type of 'hood redemption to non-traditional church members living within the postindustrial urban enclave called the ghetto.

Conclusions

Jesus was, and still is in many ways, a controversial persona. He was not one to mince words no miss an opportunity to connect with the disinherited. Utley writes:

> Jesus fraternized with sexually licentious women, cavorted with sinners, worked on the Sabbath, had a temper, used profane language with religious people, praised faithfulness over stilted forms of religious piety, and honored God more than the government. Gangstas respect Jesus because they see the parallels between his life and theirs (49).

However, most of the critical, radical, and post-soul images of Jesus have been lost and too often domesticated for either political or racial reasons.

Is it possible that seemingly blasphemous images of the sacred Christ create spiritual awareness? Theologian Tom Beaudoin has told us, "Offensive images or practices may indicate a familiarity with deep religious truths" (Beaudoin 123). One must understand the authority of "official" sacraments to forcefully de-valorize them. Likewise, it takes a true believer in the power of worship to turn curses into praise, the word "nigga" into a nomination of the highest respect. The point here is not to allow degrading terms, but to acknowledge that such rhetorical devices are making a serious theological attempt at grasping a practice of inequality that is *very* real (c.f. Cupitt).

Tupac and The Outlawz present a Jesus that is not only relatable, but one who is able to connect with the inequalities of life. While most of the song is questioning if a Jesus is able to connect, the subtext of the song is about a Jesus who can—moreover, a Jesus who can relieve the burden of ghetto life; a Jesus who, in the Psalmist's terms, is a shepherd and causes those in dire straits to lie down in green pastures; a Jesus who is able to blow through the blunt-smoking persona and redeem back to him those who are hurting.

These sensationalized images of Jesus are needed. More importantly, they are needed in the discourse of Christian theology as many of these personas of Jesus get lost within the dominant Western Eurocentric Roman Catholic model of Christianity (e.g., George *Post-Soul Nation*; Taylor; West; Yinger; Zizek). Suffering in context is nothing new. The search for meaning within that suffering is nothing new. Neither is the rejection of dominant models of deity.

Sensationalized images of Jesus such as Aaron McGruder's Black Jesus, Lil Wayne's Trap Jesus, and Tupac's Black Jesuz represent a fundamental attempt to make deity, the divine, and the sacred more accessible to those who typically do not grace the sanctuaries of Christian churches. They represent the fusing of the sacred and profane—a space that Spencer argues is vastly misunderstood. They use culture to help interpret the sacred scriptures while utilizing humor to break away some of the seriousness characteristically associated with Jesus.

Finally, they are more relevant and applicable to those seeking Jesus from the post-soul, hip hop, and urban generation. This generation is not interested in a God that sits in multi-million dollar churches. They reject pastors who net more than their congregations make in a year combined; despise the double standards of the church; and they do not want a Jesus "too perfect." What Tupac and the Outlawz do well is present a Jesus in human form for this current time and generation. I hope we can listen to this message and move beyond the shallow analysis of pop culture to which so many Christian churches have fallen prey. It is time for Black Jesus!

Notes

1. Daniel White Hodge PhD, Director of Center for Youth Ministry Studies, Assistant Professor of Youth Ministry, North Park University. Author of *The Soul Of Hip Hop: Rimbs, Timbs and A Cultural Theology* (InterVarsity, 2010). Currently investigating the religious identification of urban & hip hop youth in Chicago. dwhodge@northpark.edu

2. For more on this see Boyd *Am I Black Enough for You? Popular Culture from the 'Hood and Beyond* and *The H.N.I.C.: The Death of Civil Rights and the Reign of Hip Hop*; Cox; Cupitt; George *Buppies, B-Boys, Baps & Bohos: Notes on Post-Soul Black Culture* and *Post-Soul Nation: The Explosive, Contradictory, Triumphant, and Tragic 1980s as Experienced by African Americans (Previously Known as Blacks and before That Negroes)*; Hodge *The Soul of Hip Hop: Rimbs, Timbs and a Cultural Theology*; Kitwana *Why White Kids Love Hip Hop: Wankstas, Wiggers, Wannabes, and the New Reality of Race in America*.

3. See Spencer's works *Protest and Praise: Sacred Music of Black Religion* and *The Emergency of Black and the Emergence of Rap* and *Theological Music: Introduction to Theomusicology*" and "The Mythology of the Blues."

4. I draw from Kreitzer's use of the phrase from the "The New Testament in Fiction and Film: On Reversing the Hermeneutical Flow."

Works Cited

Asante, Molefi K. *It's Bigger Than Hip Hop: The Rise of the Post-Hip Hop Generation*. New York: St. Martin's, 2008.

Beaudoin, Tom. *Virtual Faith: The Irreverent Spiritual Quest of Generation X*. San Francisco: Jossey Bass, 1998.

Bennett, Lerone. *The Shaping of Black America*. New York: Penguin Books, 1993.

Boyd, Todd. *Am I Black Enough for You? Popular Culture from the 'Hood and Beyond*. Bloomington & Indianapolis: Indiana University Press, 1997.

———. *The H.N.I.C.: The Death of Civil Rights and the Reign of Hip Hop*. New York: New York University Press, 2002.

Chang, Jeff. *Can't Stop Won't Stop: A History of the Hip Hop Generation*. New York: St. Martin's, 2005.

Cox, Harvey. *Religion in the Secular City: Toward a Postmodern Theology*. New York: Simon & Schuster, 1984.

Cupitt, Don. "Post-Christianity." In *Religion, Modernity, and Postmodernity*. Edited by Paul Heelas, 218–32. Oxford, UK and Malden, MA: Blackwell, 1998.

Dyson, Michael Eric. *Holler If You Hear Me: Searching for Tupac Shakur*. New York: Basic Civitas, 2001.

George, Nelson. *Buppies, B-Boys, Baps & Bohos: Notes on Post-Soul Black Culture*. 1st ed. New York: HarperCollins, 1992.

———. *Post-Soul Nation: The Explosive, Contradictory, Triumphant, and Tragic 1980s as Experienced by African Americans (Previously Known as Blacks and before That Negroes)*. New York: Viking, 2004.

Hodge, Daniel White. *Heaven Has a Ghetto: The Missiological Gospel & Theology of Tupac Amaru Shakur*. Saarbrucken, Germany: VDM Verlag Dr. Muller Academic, 2009.

———. *The Soul of Hip Hop: Rimbs Timbs & a Cultural Theology*. Downers Grove: InterVarsity, 2010.

Kendall, John. "A Ghetto Is Slow to Die." *Los Angeles Times*. 1975.

Kitwana, Bakari. *The Hip Hop Generation: Young Blacks and the Crisis in African American Culture*. New York: Basic Civitas, 2003.

———. *Why White Kids Love Hip Hop: Wankstas, Wiggers, Wannabes, and the New Reality of Race in America*. New York: Basic Civitas, 2005.

Kreitzer, L. Joseph. "The New Testament in Fiction and Film: On Reversing the Hermeneutical Flow." In *Variation: The Biblical Seminar*. Sheffield: JSOT, 1993.

———. "The Old Testament in Fiction and Film: On Reversing the Hermeneutical Flow." In *The Biblical Seminar*. Sheffield: Sheffield Academic, 1994.

Moss, Otis. "Real Big: The Hip Hop Pastor as Postmodern Prophet." In *The Gospel Remix: Reaching the Hip Hop Generation*. Edited by Ralph Watkins, 110–38. Valley Forge: Judson, 2007.

Murray, Charles. *Losing Ground: American Social Policy, 1950–1980*. New York: Basic Books, 1984.

Neal, Mark Anthony. *Soul Babies: Black Popular Culture and the Post-Soul Aesthetic*. New York: Routledge, 2002.

Nelson, Angela S. "Theology in the Hip Hop of Public Enemy and Kool Moe Dee." *The Emergency of Black and the Emergence of Rap*. Vol. 5. Edited by Jon Michael Spencer, 51–59. Durham: Duke University Press, 1991.

One, KRS. *Ruminations*. New York: Welcome Rain Publishers, 2003.

Palen, J. John. *The Urban World*. 2nd ed. New York: McGraw-Hill, 1981.

Paris, Peter J. *The Social Teaching of the Black Churches*. Philadelphia: Fortress, 1985.

Peralta, Stacy. *Crips and Bloods: Made in America*. 2008. DVD.

Peters, Ken. *Tupac vs.* 2001. DVD.

Pinn, Anthony. *The Black Church in the Post-Civil Rights Era*. Maryknoll: Orbis, 2002.

Quinn, Eithne. "Popular Cultures, Everyday Lives." In *Nuthin' but a "G" Thang: The Culture and Commerce of Gangsta Rap*. New York: Columbia University Press, 2005.

Rose, Tricia. *Black Noise: Rap Music and Black Culture in Contemporary America*. Middletown, CT: Wesleyan University Press, 1994.

Rosenberg, Scott K., Queen Latifah, and Bruce Willis. *The Hip Hop Project*. 2009. DVD.

Sides, Josh. *L. A. City Limits: African American Los Angeles from the Great Depression to the Present*. Berkeley and Los Angeles: University of California Press, 2003.

Smith, Efrem, and Phil Jackson. *The Hip Hop Church: Connecting with the Movement Shaping Our Culture*. Downers Grove: InterVarsity, 2005.

Spencer, Jon Michael, ed. *The Emergency of Black and the Emergence of Rap*. Vol. 5. Durham: Duke University Press, 1991.

———. "The Mythology of the Blues." *Sacred Music of the Secular City: From Blues to Rap*. Vol. 6. Edited by Jon Michael Spencer, 98–140. Durham: Duke University Press, 1992.

———. *Protest and Praise: Sacred Music of Black Religion*. Minneapolis: Fortress, 1990.

———. *Theological Music: Introduction to Theomusicology*. New York: Greenwood, 1991.

Taylor, Paul C. "Post-Black, Old Black." *African American Review* 41.4 (2007): 625–40.

Trulear, Harold Dean, and N. Lynne Westfield. "Theomusicology and Christian Education: Spirituality and the Ethics of Control in the Rap of MC Hammer." *Theomusicology: A Special Issue of Black Sacred Music: A Journal of Theomusicology* 8.1 (1994): 218–38.

Tupac, and Outlawz. "Black Jesuz." Transcr. Fatal, Fula, Kastro, Noble. *Still I Rise*: Interscope Records, 1999.

Utley, Ebony A. *Rap and Religion: Understanding the Gangsta's God*. Santa Barbara: Praeger, 2012.

Watkins, Ralph Basui. "Engaging Culture." *Hip Hop Redemption: Finding God in the Rhythm and the Rhyme*. Grand Rapids: Baker Academic, 2011.

West, Cornel. *Prophetic Thought in Postmodern Times: Beyond Eurocentrism and Multiculturalism*. Vol. 1. Monroe, ME: Common Courage, 1993.

Wiese, Andrew. "Historical Studies of Urban America." In *Places of Their Own: African American Suburbanization in the Twentieth Century*. Chicago: University of Chicago, 2004.

Yinger, J. Milton. *Religion, Society, and the Individual; an Introduction to the Sociology of Religion*. New York: Macmillan, 1957.

Zanfagna, Christina. "Under the Blasphemous W(Rap): Locating the 'Spirit' in Hip Hop." *Pacific Review of Ethnomusicology* 12 (2006): 1–12.

Zizek, Slavoj. *In Defense of Lost Causes*. New York: Verso, 2008.

Section Seven

Perspectives on Women and Gender

39
Playin' Church:
Remembering Mama and
Questioning Authenticity
in Black Gospel Performance

Alisha Jones

"That don't make any sense—that don't make any sense!!!" exclaimed Grammy, Stellar, and GMA award winning gospel artist and producer Kirk Franklin (1970) who was hosting BET's gospel competition Sunday Best. Y'Anna Crawley's (1977) soul stirring gospel cover of "Grandma's Hands" from Bill Wither's *Just As I Am* album (1971) was a game changing performance in. After she initially sang the song and received feedback from the judges, Franklin demanded that she sing a reprise, without any accompaniment. He was sure that Crawley didn't need any musical cues to respond. She immediately obliged and squalled her response, "When I get to heaven, I'll be looking foooor grand-ma's hands." Then Crawley firmly walked off stage left, shaking her head, waving her fists inwardly toward her body, and speaking without the mic. Indeed, with her musical response, Y'anna proverbially dropped the mic.

It wasn't just the high caliber of Crawley performance that stunned the judges.[1] But for those who are familiar with the song's original secular context, they know that "Grandma's Hands" is not a gospel selection. However it was seamlessly executed as though it was. Crawley illustrated a typical church experience, where an iconic Pentecostal grandma is portrayed as enthusiastically playing the tambourine, clapping her hands in church and then issuing out warnings. Crawley progressively used a range of vocal technique, from singing to growls to squawking, to convey Grandma's impact. According to one of the judges BeBe Winans (1962), her performance of "Grandma's

Hands" was undoubtedly the pivotal moment in the competition in which she reverently played with the symbolic meaning of grandmother. On May 10, 2009, Crawley won the coveted title of Sunday Best. She was groomed in the famously versatile Eastern High School choir of Washington DC. Under the direction of Joyce Garrett, she learned jazz, classical, and gospel repertoire. Prior to her win, Crawley was best known as a lead vocalist with DC go-go bands. Then a single mother of two, she is similar to many artists who return to gospel, after making a living in secular venues. Yet she re-emerged into a gospel competition and deployed particular skills that demonstrated her ability to be a bona fide gospel artist.

What are ways in which musicians can verify their authentic connection to the gospel tradition? African American popular artists are often scrutinized when they reach outside the Christian church to sign with secular music labels in order to make a living. Musicians who do not proclaim their Christian conversion or relationship in their music are thought to be merely "playin' church" or just claiming connection to the church but are not spiritually connected to the "body of Christ." Comedians, gospel showcase hosts, and other observers jest that acknowledging God has become convenient for performers when they accept a coveted award. Like many "saints," they wonder whether the offstage lives of popular musicians are compatible with their supposedly sincere conversions or relationships with God. Gospel musicians such as Tye Tribett have gone on record accusing popular artists of squandering their musical gifts for the entertainment of people, rather than using them properly, as an offering for the glory of God. In the *saints'* perception, musicians who have made it big in the *world* and return to the church to make music, risk contaminating the sacred atmosphere if they do so without a consistent value of their conversion experience in their daily lives.

How do these musicians make a distinction between performance (secular) and demonstration (Christian sacred) in their presentation of sacred music? In this chapter, we examine the gospel music showcase performance culture, a presentation by an emerging African American popular musician's return to the "church," during a gospel music showcase and the skills that she demonstrates to exhibit *competence* in leading the worship of the "saints."

The *playin' church* concern has gone viral. Video clips of artists who have returned to the church and performed lackluster hymns or gospel songs are now cropping up on YouTube, Facebook and other Internet sites. Viewers often draw comparisons between successful presentations versus unsuccessful ones, as a reflection on the musician's relationship with God. Like any other organized musical training, there is a set of performance practices that are learned, studied and practiced in African American gospel music. This skill set must be demonstrated to the "church" and the musicians are not permitted to let these skills expire. They also must be intentional about their song selection. For it must display their musical facility and sensitivity to the move of the spirit in the worship context.

For example, Keyshia Cole's (1981) rendition of "His Eye Is on the Sparrow" at City of Refuge in Gardena, CA has received over 110,000 "hits." It is a standard hymn that was revived when Lauryn Hill covered it in the movie *Sister Act* (1992). Cole's performance revealed her uncomfortability with the song selection and her inability to adjust to mistakes on the spot. Because of Cole's non-traditional performance viewers have expressed disappointment about her presentation, even though her personal narrative is not centered on an upbringing in the church. Such gospel audience disappointment indicates the ways in which firm connection to the church plays a role in popular black artists' reception. Many artists rely on skills cultivated in the church to demonstrate their musical versatility in live performance for their record labels. This YouTube footage and viewer commentary damages the popular artists' personal folklore, the viewers' opinion of their overall musicianship and thus, the musician's worthiness of churchgoers' patronage.[2]

On the other hand, there are popular musicians who were raised in and reiterate their connection to the church. They demonstrate this connection when they are called upon to return to the "saints" to make music. Fantasia Barrino's childhood footage is linked as a related video to Keyshia's performance. The person who posted the footage writes in the description, "Take note Keyshia Cole."[3] Commentary on the video expresses jubilation, deducing that Fantasia is from the church and has continued in her competence as a gospel trained performer.

Competence in performances is treated in Richard Bauman's concept of *verbal art as performance.* It is a notion derived from a synthesis of verbal art scholarship in folklore, the ethnography of speaking, sociolinguistics and literary stylistics. *Verbal art as performance* theory proposes an exploration of performance as a mode of speaking. I am concerned with two components of performance: artistic *action* or the doing of folklore and the artistic *event* or what Bauman refers to as "the performance situation, involving performer, art form, audience, and setting." Continuing this inquiry, he conceives the terms for a performer's communicative *competence.* The performer must assume accountability to the audience and in turn the audience is permitted to evaluate the performance.[4] The discourse of performance *competence* moves "beyond the boundaries of separate academic disciplines" and offers fruitful considerations that can expand verbal art findings to vocal music (Bauman: 290). Once the authenticity codification is established, there can be a rubric, by which gospel audiences assess the gospel music performances of secular musicians.

Many artists perform in televised gospel showcases and tributes, as a means to connect or reconnect to their church community and solidify their fan base. One of the most popular ways to signify a consistent connection to the church is to sing about the impact of one's mother or grandmother on their life. Crawley acknowledged that she did not select "Grandma's Hands." Yet she tapped into expertise that is transmitted through black live performance traditions, in a manner that delivered the Wither's cover as a widely acclaimed gospel moment.[5]

In particular she wielded grandmother imagery and memory, which has particular saliency for the majority of churchgoers. Many of whom are single mothers like Y'anna Crawley. I contend that it was the grandmother remembrance that she displayed, which allowed her to best convey her connection to the church. Her presentation utilized conventions such as mother and grandmother imagery that have been championed by gospel great Rev. Shirley Caesar in songs such as "I Remember Mama" (1992).[6] With regard to mother remembrance practice, in what ways are grandmother and mother images incorporated into gospel to convey a performer's competency?

Grammy, Dove, and Stellar award-winning gospel soloist, Rev. Shirley Caesar (b. 1938) entered into gospel music history, as a member of the popular 1950s Chicago-based group, The Caravans.[7] Throughout Caesar's career she attests to the influence of two women who have guided her throughout her life: Albertina Walker, who is her musical mentor; and her mama, who is a persistent spiritual influence and whose memory is evoked regularly throughout her original music and performances.[8] In fact, she has carved out a repertoire niche that highlights the role of mothers in embodying God's characteristics in the lives of their children. This narrative contributes to her competence because she reiterates her female spiritual pedigree and esteem of the authentic tradition. With popular songs such as "No Charge (1983)," "I Love You, Mama (1980)," and "Don't Drive Your Mama Away (1992)," she offers a more inclusive female imagery in gospel performance that caters to its largely female patron demographic. She sings of church mothers constructed as advocates who sacrifice and fervently pray for their families. In her presentations, mothers demonstrate righteous lives that are worthy of praise.

The title track to her 1992 sophomore solo album, "I Remember Mama," recounts her childhood conversion experience, while "playin' church" in the backyard with her family members, in Durham, NC. It begins with her kneeling at her ailing mother's bedside. The song is in a walking tempo, with piano, drum set, and electric bass accompaniment. She has both a choir and background vocalists with whom she does call and response. During the verses, she has a select group sing the cut time refrain "I re-mem-ber Ma-ma," while she sings her narrative.

This song positions Shirley Caesar to the gospel music public as a critic of authenticity. Within in this song, we find Caesar's call narrative, as prophesied by her mother. Caesar's mother exhorted her, "The people are depending on you, Shirley. Don't you let 'em down." This call narrative resists popular male dominated black church theology of the time that prohibited women in ministry. It proposes subversive sources of authority for confirming one's calling who are spiritual, familial, and women. Her mother's caution to live right remains in Caesar's horizon throughout her ministry. In the song, she recalls all the ways in which her family struggled and was able to stay together. Caesar sings further,

> Now mama is sleeping in the bosom of Jesus Christ. Yeah.
> Somehow I know she's smiling, she's smiling on us right now.

One day I'll see her again, how happy we will be. Yeah, yeah.
I remember Mama in a happy way.
I remember Mama in a happy way.

For Caesar, her mother's approval of her spiritual well-being is important to maintain, even after her mother has passed away. "Somehow I know she's smiling, she's smiling on us right now." Since her mother's passing, her family has scattered. Yet, her mother's influence remains in their memory. "We're all gonna pull together and stay in the holy place." With every performance as remembrance, she joins ongoing spiritual devotion to a continued tribute to her mother's presence in her spiritual formation. She concludes, "I remember mama in a happy way."

Caesar's signature song encompasses her style of singing-preaching that was pioneered by gospel foremothers such as Mother Willie Mae Ford Smith (1904–1994) and Madam Edna Gallmon Cooke (1918–1967). She interweaves her guttural and visceral gospel vocals with her preaching of sermonettes, during her presentations. Following the "I Remember Mama" sung section, there emerges her famous sermonette, where Caesar shares the precise moment when her mother witnessed and endorsed her conversion experience. After her mother chastised Caesar about "playin' church," Caesar learned that "once you meet Jesus, you will never be the same."

Mama said, "I'm sick of you going down to that church playin' with God." Then and there, we went outdoors, we started playin' church. Sat down on the bottom step. My brother was the preacher and we were the members of the church. And he put some old glasses and put 'em right here on his nose. And he said, he said, "I, I want you to shout 'Jesus' three times." And I jumped up and I shouted "Jesus" two times. But when I jumped up the third time, something got a hold of me. Aha, I could not sit back down.

Anne ran in the house. She said, "Mama, Shirley Anne is out there playin' with the Lord." Mama came to the door. She looked out there and saw me shouting and dancing all over the back yard, tears running down my face.

It's just like fire!!!

Mama looked out there and she said, "She ain't playin' this time!"

Hallelujah!!

And I remember Mama, aw Lord, in a happy way.

Caesar continues to howl repeatedly, "I remember mama in a happy way," until the song ends. Her impassioned repetition of that phrase echoes the transformation she felt when, as a child, she shouted, danced and cried in the backyard. That day she ceased "playin' church" and started her journey to preserving the church. Now, she embodies an authentic gospel tradition gauge and assumed the mantel that her late mother bequeathed to her.

While Rev. Caesar is known for performing gospel songs about mothers, this imagery and remembrance had already been deployed in traditional black sacred repertoire. Black sacred songs about mother cannot be exhausted in this chapter but I will briefly review some major themes.

Negro spirituals such as "It's Me Lord" refer to mother and other family members as intercessor. "Sometimes I Feel Like A Motherless Child" expresses one's since of longing and yearning as signified by motherly absence. Heaven is imagined as a teleological vision in which mama will greet her children in "Walk Around Heaven," as performed by the Might Clouds of Joy, Cassietta George and Patti LaBelle. The Winans "Special Lady" (1985) and R. Kelly's "Sadie" (1993) is a song in remembrance of their late churchgoing grandmother and mother. Dorothy Norwood's "A Denied Mother" (1966) likens a mother to a denied Christ, when her daughter exhibits shame about her disfigurement. Unbeknownst to the child, her mother's scars are a remnant from her mother's early valiant rescue of her from a fire. Finally, like "I Remember Mama," many gospel style songs have also been recorded as odes to mother's role in one's conversion experience. There are songs often referring to mama or grandma as a praying woman who saved them physically and spiritually. Eventually the narrator became a believer due to mama's fervent prayer such as recorded in Mary Mary's "Believer," (2005) R. Kelly's "U Saved Me," (2004) and "Helen's Testimony" (1999) by Helen Baylor. Theses songs are not only remember mamas, but also are instructive about the motherhood to which one should aspire.

I am curious about the ways in which maternal imagery about natural mothers intersects with a more consideration of inclusive divine feminine imagery from the Bible. While "Mother God" language is not interchanged with Father God language in gospel music, such gender inclusive imagery harmonizes with God's biblical traits. Maternal language and imagery of God is pervasive throughout the text. God is described as many-breasted, a midwife (Psalm 22:9–10a; 71:6; Isaiah 66:9), suckling (Numbers 11:12), birthing or with a womb (Isaiah 46:3–4).[9] The Holy Spirit has been associated with female imagery as one who births (John 3:5; cf. John 1:13; I John 4:7b; 5:1, 4, 18) or one who groans in travail for us (Romans 8:25–27).

The divine feminine as manifested in the lives of natural mothers becomes a symbol for performers to provide as evidence of God enfleshed. Utilizing female-gendered attributes, the aforementioned repertoire builds a persuasive argument for existing gender inclusivity in black church imagery and language. To explore the possibilities, womanist theological writer RevSisRaedorah has mused, for example, about the god nature of mothers in her poem "When Mama was God."[10] Feminist theologians such as Virginia Ramey Mollenkott have asserted that such inclusive language eschews the exploitation of women and fosters mutuality between men and women.[11]

> If we go further and recognize the biblical images that say God is womanlike and motherlike, so that women and mother are in turn godlike. The type of relationship that suggests itself when only one partner is godlike is a dominance-submission relationship. The type of relationship that suggests itself when both partners are godlike is mutuality (Mollenkott: 5).

A shift toward inclusivity in divine feminine language can also be instructive for men to explore the nurturant aspects of the Godhead. Mother language can provide possibilities for men's intimacy with God as well. In exploring the divine female attributes, women can identify a reflection of their godlikeness in the imagery and language. Especially men for whom the homoeroticism of Father language and imagery is a challenge to engage.

Since the 1980s, Rev. Caesar has become a fixture and motherly figure in many gospel showcases. Her presence in these forums as a soloist serves as an endorsement of authenticity for Christian musicians in gospel music and Christian musicians in secular music who participate in gospel tributes. The mixture of these two groups, often opens up a conversation about "playin' church" that occurs in both groups but is evaluated intensely in this mixed setting. During these events, performers are expected to display skills of competency in and shared knowledge of gospel performance. Her presence is also evoked, like her mother's presence, through allusions to the musical conventions that she has established in gospel venues.

Central to Rev. Caesar's precaution against "playin' church" is the presence of the *anointing* in her music, which was felt in her conversion, is felt in her life and is welcomed in every musical presentation. While observing the sanctified communities of Long Branch, NC, anthropologist Glenn Hinson explained that he had to expand his definition of what the term *anointing* encompasses, to move beyond what was perceived to be a spontaneous touch in the worship experience.[12]

> What moves me is the transformative power of the holy touch, a power felt both physically (the "feeling" that penetrates from head to foot) and emotionally (the rapturous infusion of joy). More important than its impact in either of these realms, however, is the Spirit's power to move the soul, to touch that mysterious wellspring that grants being its experiential essence. The saints of the African American sanctified community say that the soul is the domain not of body or mind, but of spirit. And when the Spirit touches the spirit, the soul rejoices in an epiphany of truth and knowledge. (Hinson: 2)

In musicological inquiry, soul, spirit, and experience language are used rarely or it is used with apprehension. Because these terms are however in common parlance, within the worship of sanctified communities of the "saints" or "believers" scholars must attend to the significance of these components in gospel performance. "To ignore these matters is to deny the saints experiential world, and thus craft a portrait that speaks more to academic understandings than to the lived reality of believers." (Hinson: 2) The reality of the "believers" view is that singing is not entertainment but rather, singing is unequivocally worship. "Saints" of sanctified communities define *worship* as "an outward demonstration of an inward attitude." In addition to regular worship services, they attend, celebrations, anniversaries, showcases and concerts, which are also referred to as "services," as opposed to entertainment. The classification of these musical presentations as "services," instead of as a form of entertainment, suggests a revision of performance terminology to worship language. It is also an indication of the posture and approach to which artists should aspire in these spheres.

To what extent do gendered symbols and imagery play a part in secular artists transitional performance back into gospel sphere as "services"? Let us briefly consider the contour of Fantasia's secular career and her re-emergence into a major gospel showcase.

Fantasia Monique Barrino's (b. 1984) journey to *American Idol* and *Broadway*, as a star in the hit musical *The Color Purple,* is a quintessential rags-to-riches story of a single, impoverished and illiterate teenage mother, who risks everything and won big in a reality music competition. Unbeknownst to the *American Idol* voting viewers, she has a strong musical pedigree. She boasts kinship to secular recording artists Dave Hollister (b. 1971) and first cousin duo, K-Ci and Jo-Jo (Cedric Hailey, b. 1969 and Joel Hailey, b. 1971). All of whom have infused their gospel roots with their popular styles.

While Fantasia vied for the title of American Idol, her unique vocal sound and style attracts attention because of the fiery sanctified church heritage evoked in her performances. When asked about her early musical influences, Fantasia immediately responds that the music of the greats Aretha Franklin, Patti LaBelle, the Clark Sisters and fellow North Carolinian Shirley Caesar have impacted her. I would like to note that Fantasia's verbal response constitutes a Baumanian performance in itself—one that goes hand in hand with her evocative musical delivery to (re) construct her image as "competent" and as an authentically black, sacred, American, traditional, performer. Although as of this publication, Fantasia is signed to RCA records as a secular artist, her gospel tradition is a key ingredient in Fantasia's vocal style and reception in gospel performance circles. Let's turn to Fantasia debut on *Bobby Jones Gospel* during the 2008 Thanksgiving special, to study her approach to gospel music performance.

As Fantasia begins the first song selection aired in the taped broadcast, she instructs the *Bobby Jones Gospel* audience, "Everybody get up on your feet, come on. Now we gon' keep it movin' on this one, so if you gotta take your shoes off, take your shoes off!" And with a distinct howl she sings, "Ay, yeah, yeah, yeah, yeah, yeah, yeah, aw Lord! Aw Lord!" Fantasia shares and practices the same song and sermonette gospel music tradition as Shirley Caesar. These verbal cues are signals for "keying a performance," which utilizes an opening or closing statement that proclaims performance. Bauman explains that when a performer *keys a performance* "all communication that takes place within that frame is to be understood as performance within that community." (Bauman: 295) The studio and viewing audiences know that she is taking authority in worship or performance, in a manner that simulates a worship leader capacity.

"Here we go Calvary!" Fantasia says. *Calvary* is a double entendre referring to the name of the choir and a cue to "saints" witnessing her performance. She demands, "Listen!" Then she begins to sing the verse, "If the Lord, never does anything else for me, I want you to know, He's done enough." She *ad libs* using paralinguistic reiteration patterns of vocalization for emphasis ("If the, If the, If the, If the"), continues to sing the verse of the song, "If the Lord, never does anything else for me," and commands the audience "look at your neighbor and tell your neighbor," then growls, "He's done enough. He's blessed me once and blessed me twice, every, every, every, every, every day of my life. Calvary, help me sing. If the Lord, never does anything else for me, He's done enough." Within the first verse of the song, Fantasia takes authority of the performance by instructing the audience *qua* choir to start singing and engaging in a "collaborative expectancy" of her as a performer to lead them into worship (Bauman: 295). She is aware of the musical contour of the song, so she can *ad lib* melodically and verbally. The audience is alerted to her potential preparedness to lead the audience in worship. Her repetitive emphasis on the conditional word "If" and qualifying word "every" also provide what Bauman calls a sort of *prosodic pattern* of tempo, stress and pitch that keys the performance. She incorporates a variation of these tools throughout the performance but the most traditional trope that proposes her competence to lead worship was an extra-musical move that follows.

After the first verse, she calls to stage right. "Come here mama, I want you to help sing this." Her mother Diane Barrino, who is a second-generation preacher, enters stage right. She starts to sing with the vocal style of Pastor Beverly Crawford. Fantasia's stance is turned toward her mother and enacts a humble deference to her, as she moves her mic away. And then, visibly away from the mic, she encourages her mother to minister as she sings her solo. Fantasia wraps her right arm around her mother. Television viewers can observe her communication. Fantasia accepts her mother's musical partnership, and then improvises a testimony over the refrain about the ways in which "He's done enough!" Visibly away from the mic her mother intermittently affirms her testifying with "Yes" and a melodic echo or response to Fantasia's call.

Just as the song was planned to finish, the choir, instrumentalists, and director noticeably derailed and lost their musical places. They missed Fantasia's cue. She does not flinch, keeps the pulse, and sings in the mic, "He's done enough!" Speaking into the mike, Fantasia admonishes the instrumentalists and sharply says, "I told y'all we weren't gonna break no more," then she sings, "He's done enough!" She says, "Y'all know how we do it on Sundays," then she sings a cadence in the melody of the refrain, "You keep on going." And in the frame, the TV viewers can see her mother in the background smiling, clapping, saying "yes," and nodding to suggest agreement that this is "how we do it on Sundays." Fantasia sings, "See it ain't got to be perfect for Jesus. Aw, it ain't got to be perfect for him." And as she proclaims about the idiosyncrasies of Sunday worship, the director, choir and instrumentalist collect themselves and await her cue to end the song. "I told my mama sometimes I have to give God an ugly praise. I'll take my shoes off in a minute and give God praise."

She proceeds to take off her shoes. "You see just like he blessed me with them, I want me some more. So I am going to dance everyday, every time I get a chance to."

With her verbal cue of "one more time," the musicians launch into another cycle of the refrain. She descends from the stage, as she continues to express gratitude to God, while erasing the spatial barriers between her and the audience. She stops in front of the host, who is observing on the front row and high fives him, as she speaks of God's goodness. And then just before the refrain cycle cadences, Fantasia turns from the audience toward the platform and signals the director, choir and musicians, with stock African American gospel music choir director gestures to conclude the song. Everyone in the audience and on stage finished the song. Unlike Cole's City of Refuge presentation, Fantasia firmly establishes her authenticity as the performer or worship leader because of her competence in adjusting to a musical derailment in a church music ministry fashion. What could have been a fiasco, turned into verification that Fantasia was not "playin' church" but rather is a full-fledged member of the church who knows how to handle worship leadership.

The incorporation of Fantasia's mother's presence in the background and her vocal style, while in her performance frame were familiar imagery and sound qualities of the gospel tradition. The audience's familiarity with the repertoire is important for successful reception as well. Fantasia did not perform original music but rather covered current gospel repertoire. For example, those familiar with the tradition recognize that Beverly Crawford (b. 1963) recorded the original song "He's Done Enough" on her album *Live from Los Angeles, CA* (2007) and performed it at the 2008 Dove Awards. Dr. Jones mentioned later that he saw Fantasia when she met Crawford at the BET Awards for the first time. She replied that she is a huge fan of Pastor Crawford.

This performance could have stood alone as evidence of her competence as a performer in black gospel music but at the request of Dr. Bobby Jones (b. 1939) she decided to sing another song. Like Franklin, Dr. Jones' explicit request for another selection communicates confidence in her competence. In regular worship services, pastors or music ministers may make a similar request. We should note that *Bobby Jones Gospel* is a peculiar gateway to the church because presenters must interact with the host Dr. Bobby Jones. Dr. Jones often provides commentary about the popular artists. He may comment on how they have "never left the church," when he speaks about prior conversations or observations of the artists in tough times. Sometimes he questions the artist publicly about how they have demonstrated their faith. At the end of her first song, he interviewed Fantasia about growing up and "catching the Holy Ghost in the living room," as she watched his program. Dr. Jones stated, "She's not one of those people that the Lord has blessed, that have shown favor to, that don't have sense enough to say 'thank you...'"

Dr. Jones begins the second segment saying, "And all of you at home, I know you're in the blessing spirit! Let me tell ya' you are just gonna have to be late for church because we are going to bring you church, right in your house, today!" Such a statement likens the showcase to a service, thus setting up the audience's expectations to assume the posture of a congregation. The *Bobby Jones Gospel* show is taped at the Black Entertainment Television Headquarters in Washington DC. The second song selection was entitled "Total Praise" and is a popular composition by Washingtonian Richard Smallwood. She was very intentional about the context in which she performed. As Dr. Jones points out, the audience was familiar with this selection because it is a favorite congregational song turned hymn. As a sign of her competence, Fantasia appeals to the gospel tradition, by singing her rendition in a call and response with the choir. Fantasia then varies the performance. She adds a solo verse to this choral song and uses this opportunity to demonstrate performative competence fluently signifying on the gospel riffs of well-established gospel artists such as CeCe Winans, Kiki Sheard, and Yolanda Adams. Fantasia thus shows that she has maintained a connection, practices the tradition, and values the worship music.

At the culmination of Smallwood's four-fold "Amen" doxology, Fantasia testifies about recent health challenges that jeopardized her voice. She illustrates the significance of "Total Praise," preaching that in spite of the doctor's diagnosis that she would never sing again, she is singing praise to God. She extends the song and descends into the audience, as she tells her story. Then she turns, faces the stage, bows, and weeps as she sings, "Thank you, thank you, thank you." These gestures are interpreted as a manifestation of the anointing in her presentation, which exemplifies a connection to God. She not only says "thank you" but also presents an outward showing of her inward attitude in the manner of a worship leader. She signals the musicians on the stage to end the song and the riffs on the final "(asé), amen" akin to the contrasting light style of CeCe Winans.

The transformational power of African American gospel music is a guarded and coveted resource. Insiders scrutinize musicians who were formed in the tradition but who decided to make their living outside of the church. The training that musicians receive inside the church is a valuable marketing tool because the skills provide insight on engaging an audience. To be received in churchgoer settings, performers learn, study and practice their training in order to maintain performance competence. As I have shown artists use a variety of gospel tropes to establish their competence as performers of the sacred. These tropes include, the presence and/or endorsement of a mother figure, signifying on traditional riffs, testifying, sensitivity to the anointing, instructing attendees in the performance and seamless adjustment to any mistakes. Traditional gospel music is an instrument to prepare the congregation to receive what "saints" say is a "word from the Lord" or the minister's delivery of a life changing message. A musician's improper preparation of the atmosphere can be detrimental to the climax and *telos* of the worship, which is the altar call, conversion experience or a divine encounter. To prevent a fiasco in gospel performance, artists are expected to employ these skills so that they can perform with fluency, sincerity and authority, otherwise they can be dismissed as just "playin' church."

Notes

1. "BET's 'Sunday Best' Winner Y'Anna Crawley Savors a Heavenly Opportunity" by Deneen L. Brown http://www.washingtonpost.com/wp-dyn/content/article/2009/06/04/AR2009060404820.html, last accessed December 13, 2012.
2. A visitor named COGICSTICKS on March 2, 2009 wrote, "WOW!!! This is shocking,people you gotta pray and ask the Lord to help you with everything you do.she change key i dont know how many times i stop counting after five.I like keyshia cole but this one she really messed up.with respect i would take this down,i fill sorry for her." http://www.youtube.com/watch?v=0a8guHJm704, accessed on December 14, 2012.
3. Fantasia—His Eye Is on the Sparrow http://www.youtube.com/watch?v=pU08ncg7U6w&feature=related, accessed on December 13, 2012.
4. "This *competence* rests on the knowledge and ability to speak in socially appropriate ways. Performance involves on the part of the performer an assumption of accountability to an audience for the way in which communication is carried out, above and beyond its referential point. From the point of view of the audience, the act of expression on the part of the performer is thus marked as subject to evaluation for the way it is done, for the relative skill and effectiveness of the performer's display of competence. Additionally, it is the intrinsic qualities of the act of expression itself. Performance thus calls forth special attention to and heightened awareness of the act of expression, and gives license to the audience to regard the act of expression and the performer with special intensity." Richard Bauman. 1975. "Verbal Art as Performance," from *American Anthropologist*. New Series, Vol. 77, No. 2, 293.
5. Y'Anna Crawley a former vocalist with Go-Go bands Lissen and Heaven Sent Bands. Crawley is also an expert in the Go-Go tradition, which primarily requires performance of cover songs, while placing one's musical signature on them. For the first time we see a woman representing the entrance of the male-dominated Go-Go music into a national gospel forum.
6. It is interesting that viewer made a comparison between the two artists because they have differing narratives about their relationships with their mother. Keyshia Cole has been open about her estrangement from her mother who has had challenges with substance abuse. Fantasia's mother and grandmother have been her spiritual leaders.
7. The Caravans was comprised of gospel heavy hitters including the legendary founder and "Queen of Gospel Music" Albertina Walker (1929–2010), Inez Andrews (b. 1929), Cassietta George (1929–1995), Dorothy Norwood (b. 1935), and the late James Cleveland (1931–1991). Their fame grew as they toured and appeared on "Gospel Time" and the "Jubilee Showcase." The Caravans impact on gospel and popular music has reached artists such as Ray Charles (1930–2004). It must be noted that their level of notoriety poised Caesar for a career as a stalwart in gospel music circles. When Shirley Caesar left the group in 1966, she became a solo artist and continued to grow in visibility, through regular appearances on showcases like the *Bobby Jones Gospel* show.
8. In addition to mother evocation throughout her music, she has starred in three gospel musicals with the same theme: *Mama I want to Sing, Sing: Mama 2* and *Born to Sing: Mama 3*.
9. African American composer, conductor, and musical innovator Bobby McFerrin has used gender inclusive language in the "The 23rd Psalm" (1990). He revises the Trinitarian names of God and replaces them with "mother, daughter and holy of holies."
10. RevSisRaedorah. 2006. "When Mama was God," from *Deeper Shades of Purple: Womanism in Religion and Society*. New York: New York University Press.
11. Virginia Ramey Mollenkott. 1983. *The Divine Feminine: The Biblical Imagery of God as Female*. New York: Crossroad.
12. Glenn Hinson. 2000. *Fire in My Bones: Transcendence and the Holy Spirit in African American Gospel*. Philadelphia: University of Pennsylvania Press.

40

From Spirituals to Swing: Sister Rosetta Tharpe and Gospel Crossover

Gayle Wald

Jazz aficionados will recognize the title of this essay as the name of the famous 1938 concert featuring an eclectic line-up of African American popular musicians in no less venerable and commanding an art institution than New York's Carnegie Hall. The brainchild of white music impresario John Hammond, "From Spirituals to Swing" was a cultural event with a social mission: to transform attitudes about race by displaying exemplars of black musical achievement to an urban white audience. In particular, Hammond hoped that by booking an array of top-notch African American acts, many of them newcomers to New York, and showcasing them at a high-culture venue typically unwelcoming of black artists, he could use music as a medium of social change.

As its name promised, "From Spirituals to Swing" offered listeners a from-soup-to-nuts sampling of African American sounds. Included on the roster were blues shouters Jimmy Rushing and Joe Turner, the North Carolina-based quartet Mitchell's Christian Singers, boogie-woogie pianist Albert Ammons, jazz soloist Sidney Bechet, and star-studded swing bands led by Count Basie and Benny Goodman. Diversity wasn't Hammond's only goal, however; "From Spirituals to Swing" also enshrined his idea of African American social development expressed in musical form: from spirituals sung by "unlettered" musicians to the swinging rhythms of "sophisticated" dance bands, from South to North, from folk functionalism to mass entertainment from the sounds of slavery to the music of modernity. In the audible transition from sacred to secular lay nothing less, or so Hammond imagined, than the sounds of African American progress.

Among the musicians to play to the sold-out crowd that December 23 was a young "gospel" singer (the term had only recently begun to circulate as the name of a genre) with a clear, ringing voice, a big, vivacious stage presence, and an uncanny talent on guitar. Rosetta Tharpe (1915–1973)—or "Sister" Rosetta Tharpe, as she was better known in the church—fit neatly into Hammond's vision. Born Rosetta Nubin in Cotton Plant, Arkansas, but raised for a time in Chicago, Tharpe was only six when she gave her first public performance at the city's 40th Street Church of God in Christ (later Roberts Temple), where, so the story goes, she was so small she had to be hoisted atop a piano so congregants could get a view of Little Sister Nubin, the "singing and guitar-playing miracle." During her childhood and adolescence Tharpe traveled the southern "gospel highway" with her mother Katie Bell Nubin, a mandolin player and COGIC evangelist who enlisted her daughter's musical gifts to attract converts. For a time the two toured with F. W. McGee, a COGIC bishop and faith healer; later, along with Tharpe's first husband, COGIC preacher Thomas J. Thorpe (whose name Tharpe later adapted as her stage name), they established themselves as a popular draw at Florida storefront churches.[1]

By 1938, however, the twenty-three-year-old's growing professional ambitions had expanded beyond the bounds of the tent-meeting circuit and, ultimately, the church itself.[2] Following the trajectory of musical migration established by blues and later jazz musicians, Tharpe moved to New York, where she secured gigs at Cafe Society Downtown, the city's first major racially integrated nightspot, and the prestigious (and whites only) Cotton Club on Broadway, where she appeared on a program with Cab Calloway and His Orchestra. She also signed a recording contract, a first for a gospel performer, and on October 31 cut four sides for Decca Records, including "Rock Me" and "That's All," songs she performed (backed by Albert Ammons) less than two months later at "From Spirituals to Swing." There, according to Hammond, she was "a surprise smash," a performer whose singing "showed an affinity between gospel and jazz that all fans could recognize and appreciate."[3] Count Basie recalled how Tharpe tore up Carnegie Hall, inspiring the crowd of "cool New Yorkers" to the point where they were "almost shouting in the aisles."[4]

In adapting the music and performance style of African American Pentecostal churches for the purpose of secular entertainment, Tharpe exemplified the irreverent hybridity that made "From Spirituals to Swing" a landmark event. Although Hammond, pitching the concert in The New York Times, depicted it as racially groundbreaking, a show that would introduce whites to "the authentic music of the American Negro," the historical significance of "From Spirituals to Swing" sprang as much from its determined confusion of sacred and secular music styles as from its liberal political agenda.[5] In presenting performers such as the Golden Gate Quartet and bluesman Big Bill Broonzy on a single program, that is, "From Spirituals to Swing" ventured to breach African American cultural conventions that made such a pairing not merely unlikely but also anathema. In COGIC as in other black Pentecostal denominations, blues (as both a distinct form and a catch-all for secular dance styles) was the "devil's music," and steering clear of it was an important aspect of sanctified living, like avoiding alcohol and attending Sunday service.

In the late 1930s, however, members of Holiness sects were not the only ones to regard blues as an affront to the very principles spirituals stood for; African American Christians generally speaking, as well as (or including) proponents of "Negro uplift," voiced similar discomfort with the mixing of functionally distinct styles, one keyed to the spirit and the other to the flesh. Likewise, gospel had its own detractors, especially among members of Protestant denominations who found the spirited sounds emanating from urban "Holy Roller" churches (so called because of styles of worship that emphasized the expression of faith in movement) dubious as religious music. In fact, by 1939 gospel was arguably the more pressing threat, for whereas blues was at least theoretically relegated to speakeasies, nightclubs, and the like, gospel insinuated blues directly into the rhythms, melodies, and vocal styles of worship music, troubling the fragile boundary between the church and the "world."

Beginning with her commercial recording and performance debuts in 1938, Tharpe would be at the forefront of these and other controversies over the distinction of sacred and secular music and thus at the forefront of a larger struggle over African American cultural identity at mid-century. The terms of this larger struggle were spelled out, albeit in a somewhat rudimentary fashion, as early as 1940 by writer Arna Bontemps in one of the first published analyses of gospel, "Rock, Church, Rock!"[6] In the article, Bontemps actually sketches two dilemmas: the first a generational battle being waged in northern, urban churches between traditionalists who looked askance at the "swinging" of spirituals and "younger elements" who didn't mind a little backbeat in their worship services; the second was a brewing resentment among "church folks" over the dissemination of gospel as secular entertainment music. Bontemps spends the majority of his time in the article on the first dilemma, offering an appreciative overview of the career of gospel composer and entrepreneur Thomas A. Dorsey, a man who, in an earlier incarnation as Georgia Tom, had played piano for Ma Rainey and penned the lyrics of the decidedly un-spiritual ditty "It's Tight Like That."

Yet "Rock, Church, Rock!" also concedes that by 1940 the music of Dorsey and others had become an ineluctable element of the Afro-Christian soundscape: "the seasoning is there now," Bontemps writes, using a gumbo metaphor, "and like it or not, it may be hard to get out. Indeed, some churchgoers [and implicitly Bontemps himself] are bold enough to ask, 'Why shouldn't church songs be lively?'"[7] That, however, still left the second issue of what would happen when these gospel sounds, themselves an amalgamation of "old tabernacle songs, the Negro spirituals, and the blues," found their way out of the church and onto the Hit Parade. Should African American sacred music be shared with non-churchgoing and/or white audiences? Was gospel music in fact sacred if it was performed in a nightclub? Should sanctified musicians use their talents for purposes other than the glorification of God? With regard to these and other concerns it was Tharpe, the rising female crossover star, rather than Dorsey, the already established "father of gospel," who would come to occupy center stage.

This essay examines how Tharpe negotiated the process of "crossing over" and the impact of the sacred/secular division on her musical development from the late 1930s through the early 1950s. By looking closely at several key performances from this period—also that of Tharpe's greatest commercial visibility—I show how she made gospel music "popular" through a complex process of cultural re-signification that held special significance for her as a female singer-instrumentalist. She did so at a time marked musically by the rise and decline of big-band swing and the emergence of new styles such as jump and bebop and socially and culturally by the advent of wartime and postwartime upheavals that manifested themselves domestically in new imaginings of women's "roles," of black civil rights struggles, and of femininity, race, and citizenship themselves. Tharpe's development over the period in question is, of course, embedded in these larger historical narratives, in particular the decline of swing, the genre that most facilitated her popularity in the world of secular entertainment. At the same time her omission from so many historical fields leads me to focus on her refusal of neat categorization (in terms of identity, musical genre, and the like) and the implicit deconstructive potential of her cultural practice as a pioneering crossover artist.

This article is admittedly invested in the historical resuscitation of Tharpe, one of the most significant and yet egregiously overlooked performers of the era. Tharpe was an important influence on later generations of singer-guitarists from Chuck Berry, Little Richard, and Elvis Presley to contemporary artists such as Bonnie Raitt and Eric Clapton. Moreover, just as she made music that resisted conventional categorization, so her influence spans geography and time: in addition to being a favorite of legendary Memphis disc jockey Dewey Phillips, she has been cited as an important force in the development of Chicago blues and is an inspiration for performance artist/ singer Robert Lopez, who channels her spirit in his work as El Vez, the Mexican American Elvis. Tharpe was, in the words of jazz historian Rosetta Reitz, one of the gospel women "underneath it all," a musician whose charismatic guitar playing and extroverted stage persona helped to establish what today we take for granted as "rock" convention.[8]

The point, however, is not simply to add Tharpe to the existing canon but to use her to reimagine American cultural history. Centering gospel, among the most under-studied of U. S. musical genres, allows us to center African American women as agents of musical history and cultural change: to ask not merely how they "fit in" to existing narratives but how and why they don't fit and how we might subsequently revise received models. More particularly, examining Tharpe's reputation as a popularizer of gospel enables us to develop strategies to understand the figure of the crossover musician as other than a sellout. Unlike Bontemps in 1940, cultural critics today take gospel's hybridity for granted, linking it to a long and productive tradition of sonic boundary-crossing and confusion that lies at the root of all African American music.[9] The testimony of innumerable African American musicians, meanwhile, reveals a certain blending of sacred and secular influence as the very precondition of postwar blues, soul, and rhythm 'n' blues.[10]

Nevertheless, the sacred/secular division has continued to loom large in contemporary gospel scholarship—albeit as a social rather than a strictly sonic concern. For example, in a major 1979 article that set the terms for subsequent debate, musicologist Horace Clarence Boyer, an authority on gospel, concluded that gospel singers jeopardized African American musical tradition when they facilitated gospel's entrance into the commercial "mainstream."[11] Widespread enthusiasm for gospel in the 1970s, Boyer writes, led gradually to church members' realization that "gospel music was the one remaining pure Afro-American music expression to which the Afro-American could lay claim."[12] As this last phrase (with its particular emphases) reveals, Boyer framed the issue of gospel's secular dissemination in terms of cultural ownership; according to his logic gospel music ceased to "belong" to the church once it crossed the race and class boundary dividing sacred and secular.

Yet to pin the question of gospel's popularization to the "loss" of cultural heritage is inevitably to become ensnarled in the very "authenticity" debates that Bontemps first encountered when he explored controversies over church music that "rocked." Moreover, it puts the question of how precisely gospel gets re-signified as "popular" music—not to mention the question of the significance of the term "popular" itself—outside of cultural analysis. A focus on cultural practices, however, gets us out of such quagmires of authenticity. Indeed, it not only recognizes the fluidity and arbitrariness of cultural categorization but also foregrounds the agency of the crossover musician herself as a shaper of musical meaning.

As the word "herself" implies, a related claim of this essay is that "sacred" and "secular" designate gendered modes of representation and as such cannot be accurately understood in narrowly racial terms. Indeed, although the canonical literature on gospel commonly celebrates the achievements of a cadre of highly visible women stars, including Tharpe, Mahalia Jackson, Marion Anderson, and Clara Ward, it seldom takes gender seriously as what Joan Scott, in a brilliant understatement, once called "a useful category of historical analysis."[13] Rather, because of gospel's longstanding ambivalent relationship to the market, the interests of which are seen as conflicting with the interests of the music's communities of origin, debate in the field of gospel studies has focused on secularization and commercialization as racial and economic but not gendered processes. No matter whether they performed in COGIC churches or New York nightclubs, however, female gospel musicians at mid-century (the period sometimes called gospel's "Golden Age") wore their social identities as women every time they worked to move an audience or, like Tharpe, ventured to make a recording. Their gender extracted additional "dues" from these women gospel musicians, who like all such women performers had to negotiate their publicity as professional entertainers in the context of ongoing and sometimes ruthless sexualization and constant pressures to display normative femininity.[14] Their performances therefore have much to teach us, not only about gospel but also about gender as it is represented and produced in African American popular music.

In what follows, I analyze Tharpe's negotiation of the "line" between sacred and secular spheres as a musical negotiation of femininity. In asking what the sacred/secular divide meant for Tharpe, who was gospel's first bona fide hit-maker and thus the first national gospel musician, I inquire into how she performed her cultural publicity as a gospel musician who was also a woman. I do this not to suggest that women gospel musicians are somehow "different" because they are women, or that gender is the only lens through which to examine Tharpe's cultural practice, but because such analysis sheds light on the larger question of the cultural production of femininity through music. How are ideas about what it means to be a woman shaped in popular music culture? How and under what conditions are notions of femininity reworked in cultural performance? Gospel is a particularly important place to pose such questions, I believe, because of the uniquely prominent place it historically has accorded women as both producers and consumers, despite its emergence in the context of patriarchal religious institutions and ideologies. In fact, this paradox of the music suggests that the contradictions of femininity may be more than ordinarily audible in gospel sounds.

For answers to these questions, I turn to three of Tharpe's performances drawn from different moments between 1938 and 1951. The first such performance "text" I examine actually consists of two separate versions of the song "Rock Me," a Dorsey composition that Tharpe first recorded in the October 1938 session that preceded "From Spirituals to Swing" and later rerecorded in a "swing" version with Lucky Millinder and His Orchestra in November 1941.[15] I also look at a 1941 soundie, or proto-music video, of the song "The Lonesome Road," in which Tharpe again fronts Millinder's band. My third example is a live show—Tharpe's elaborately staged 1951 wedding concert in Washington DC, attended by tens of thousands of "guests" who were actually paying fans. For this performance, Tharpe turned the occasion of her marriage to Russell Morrison into a multimedia extravaganza marked by over-the-top pageantry and riotous self-promotion, all for the pleasure of an audience of mostly African American women.

The evidence I gather in analyzing these texts varies; indeed, the question of evidence is at the forefront of my discussion of the wedding concert, which was widely reported in the African American press and yet absent from "mainstream," white media. My analysis of the concert is thus inseparable from the question of its representation in print media addressed to racially specific readers. Tharpe's records and soundie, meanwhile, raise different questions of representation linked to their circulation via technologies of recorded sound and video. Where the concert was a one-time affair, existing in a particular place and time, as reified commodities (i.e., performances rendered "things") the 78 rpm records (78s) and soundie were widely available for consumption at a distance from the time and place of their production. While mass reproduction facilitated Tharpe's cultural visibility outside of the church, it thus implied new circumstances and challenges. In her recordings of "Rock Me" for Decca, Tharpe repackaged a song from her tent-meeting repertoire for distribution as a domestically consumed "race record"—meaning, among other things, that she performed it without a live audience (indeed, to use a distinction Boyer makes she performs to rather than with an audience[16]) and within the time restraints dictated by the recording capacity of 78s. The 1941 soundie, which was produced for viewing in African American bars or night-clubs on coin-operated machines akin to jukeboxes, finds Tharpe ditching her trademark guitar to act the girl singer in a performance keyed to visual display.

In turning to these performances, I'm also tacitly arguing that culture is a "performative" realm in its own right. Culture, that is to say, is not merely where social struggles are symbolized or reflected—these terms suggesting a hierarchical, mimetic relation between "society" and "culture"— but, more importantly, where new possibilities and desires also actively tested, defined, and worked out.[17] In addition to inquiring into what kinds of crossovers were available to Tharpe, I focus therefore on how she used these possibilities, moving constantly between the sacred and secular rather than sticking, more conventionally, to one side of the divide. Gender becomes especially important to understanding this process of crossover insofar as Tharpe's negotiation of sacred and secular is both audible and visible in her performance of femininity. Moreover, although pressures to demarcate the sacred and secular impose limitations on the imagination of gender, their fluidity is ultimately discernible in Tharpe's appropriation of sacred styles as a means of constructing an identity as a popular entertainer. What's at stake here is the way secularization occurs: not as a one-way process, but as a series of cultural "moves" as complex and shifting as the categories sacred and secular themselves.[18]

Within months of "From Spirituals to Swing" Tharpe was already being incorporated into an emerging mythology of gospel crossover, one that would blossom more fully in the 1940s along with the growth of commercial interest in religious music as a mainstay of the race record industry.[19] This "crossover mythology," as I will call it, was the product of contradictory narratives: one that insisted on identifying Tharpe as a folk musician whose art was indissolubly linked to the traditions of African American Pentecostalism and another that celebrated the capacity of gospel song to transcend socially bounded categories of identity. Both of these narratives were, in fact, necessary to authenticating Tharpe's modest commercial success. In August of 1939, for example, life magazine did a short feature piece on Tharpe, noting with enthusiasm her talent for making church music into "swing hits" that set off jitterbugging crowds at New York nightclubs.[20] As illustration, the article contains two photographs, one depicting Tharpe singing and playing guitar for an African American audience at a Sunday COGIC service and a second showing her performing on a

Monday night at the all-white Cotton Club on Broadway. The accompanying text makes no explicit mention of race or segregation, although the photographs clearly imply the power of the charismatic Christian performer to conquer social dividing lines of race, religion, and class.

Months earlier, the New York Amsterdam News, an African American newspaper, similarly trumpeted Tharpe as a "Holy Roller singer" who had, in the course of a few short months, become the "toast of Broadway."[21] Nevertheless, even as it lauded Tharpe's achievements the article made a point of noting her modest origin, lack of formal education (Tharpe never attended high school), and, through quotations, her use of southern dialect. Indeed, it resorts to embarrassing stereotype in portraying Tharpe as a seemingly "completely happy person. . . almost always smiling, dimples rippling in and out of her deep brown cheeks."[22] Even though it qualifies this image in the next sentence, assuring the reader that "Sister Tharpe has not always been happy and her life has not always been easy," the article assumes that Tharpe's charisma as a performer (even at this early point in her career, Tharpe was well known for her exciting stage presence) stems from her identity as a southern Pentecostal, not her skill in projecting "personality."

What these disparate articles are so quick to naturalize—Tharpe's blurring of boundaries between church and nightclub, Sunday morning and Monday night—was in reality the result of complex representational practices. We can begin to discern these practices in Tharpe's ground breaking recordings of "Rock Me," a Dorsey composition better known to the churchgoing faithful under its original title "Hide Me in Thou Bosom." "Rock Me" not only mediates Tharpe's entrance into the realm of commercial recording, thereby constituting an important text in the history of gospel's migration out of the church and into the secular public sphere, but it also illustrates how the categories of sacred and secular could entail what might be called distinct "soundings" of femininity. Typically lyrics are taken as the measure of the translation of church songs into popular songs. A good example would be Ray Charles' "This Little Girl of Mine," in which the lyrical substitution of "girl" for "light" changes the song from a joyous celebration of self into a joyous celebration of young love. At the same time, the shift to "girl" requires a radical and, I would argue, more significant shift in the gendering of voice: whereas "This Little Light of Mine" can be sung by anyone (and can signify a communal "I" if sung collectively, as Bernice Johnson Reagon has argued[23]), "This Little Girl of Mine" projects an individualized male speaker, a guy addressing his girl. (Presumably, too, of course, there could be a "This Little Boy of Mine" that would effect the complementary change in gendered address.)

There are three points I wish to make here. The first is that the secularization of religious songs is never an isolated process in the sense that a secular song is not merely a sacred song stripped of overt religious reference. Sacred and secular, in other words, are categories whose meaning is not simply a function of musical or lyrical" content." That said, romantic love is nevertheless the abiding signifier of the secular, although sacred songs are often infused in complicated ways with sexual desire. At a practical level, this means that changes in lyrics (e.g., from "light" to "girl") are seldom, if ever, innocent of questions of gender and sexuality.[24] Finally, although secularization is often associated with the freeing of a song from narrow, religious signification, it inevitably imposes new and no less powerful limitations on meaning. A secular song in which the singer-persona praises the virtues of a particular girlfriend is in this sense no less constrained in its significance than a sacred song praising the virtues of the Lord.

Since it circulated as a race record absent any significant change in lyrics, "Rock Me" provides an interesting counterpoint to "This Little Light of Mine." In Dorsey's original lyric, the phrase "rock me" appears in the chorus, which portrays God as a loving, protective, and ambiguously gendered parent—the father-deity of Pentecostal tradition who offers the speaker-child a maternal, sheltering "bosom." Tharpe's energetic delivery of the phrase "Rock Me" in both versions of the song underscores this lyrical ambiguity consistent with Pentecostal worship traditions that yoke together the corporal and the spiritual, the human body and the Holy Ghost.[25] Trilling the "r" and warbling the vowel in "me" so that "rock me" comes out as a juicy growl (as "rrRock Me"), Tharpe produces a sound that calls forth the spirit even as it calls to mind the pleasures of the flesh:

> You hold [hide] me in thou bosom
> 'Til the storm of life is over
> Oh, rock me in the cradle of thou love;
> Only feed me 'til I want no more
> Then you take me to your blessed home above.[26]

Where the two versions of "Rock Me" differ significantly, and where the sounding of gender enters the mix, is in their different arrangements and Tharpe's correspondingly disparate vocal performances. Where the 1941 "Rock Me" features the lush sounds of a fully orchestrated swing band, the 1938 "Rock Me" is spare, with Tharpe accompanying herself on guitar, mostly strumming chords but occasionally plucking melodic embellishments. In this version the emotion of the song is conveyed almost entirely through Tharpe's voice: through precise, sometimes "talky-y" elocution, subtle changes in pitch, volume, and tempo, unfussy melismatic flourishes, and a bouncy but controlled energy. There are also preacherly touches—in Tharpe's intonation and her pronunciation of "the" as "thee," for example—and a "country," barrelhouse quality of her guitar playing that makes plain her southern musical roots. In both her vocal and instrumental performances, Tharpe's musical choices are shaped by an African American Pentecostal aesthetic that elevates "authenticity" over polish, "realness" over refinement. This is not to say that Pentecostal audiences of the era didn't place a premium on virtuosity but rather that they defined virtuosity according to a performer's ability to tap into, and give meaning to, collective emotion through the performance of a personal relation to the music. The measure of a performer's value lay less in her mastery of skills associated with European art music (e.g., "chest" singing over "head" singing), than in whether her particular musical choices—in singing, of intonation, tone, timbre, pitch, phrasing, elocution, and soon—could induce an audience to collective joy or sorrow, awe or celebration.

Although Tharpe arrived in New York already highly credentialed in Pentecostal terms, Sammy Price, Decca's house pianist and recording supervisor at the time Tharpe recorded "Rock Me," apparently wasn't feeling any of this joy. Tharpe, he recalled in his 1990 autobiography, "tuned her guitar funny and sang in the wrong key." In all likelihood Price was referring to Tharpe's use of Vestapol (sometimes called "open D") tuning popular among blues musicians in the Mississippi Delta region. (Muddy Waters is among the many blues guitarists, for example, who learned Vestapol technique in the 1930s, when he was growing up in Clarksdale, Mississippi.) As common as it was in the South, however, Vestapol tuning could sound distinctly crude and out-of-place in the context of northern jazz bands. By his own account, Price, who later went on to record several hits with Tharpe, refused to play with her until she used a capo, the bar that sits across the fingerboard and changes the pitch of the instrument. "With a capo on the fret," he explained, "it would be a better key to play along with, a normal jazz key."[27]

Price's brief story of the capo as a normalizing technology is rich with implications for the discussion of what "crossing over" to the realm of popular entertainment might have meant for Tharpe. Resonant of southern black communities and of musicians who honed their craft in churches as well as on back porches—musicians Hammond quite un-self-consciously called "unlettered"—Tharpe's "funny" guitar playing introduced, to Price's ear, an apparently inassimilable element into the prevailing sounds of urban jazz. It's also possible that Price was demanding that Tharpe sing at a higher pitch, to conform with popular as well as commercial expectations that high pitch evidences a correspondingly "high" degree of femininity. In any case, and as Price suggests, Tharpe quite literally had to adjust her guitar and singing techniques to make commercially popular, "secular" records that would earn her an audience beyond the relatively small market of consumers of "religious music."[28] The "makeover" of Tharpe's sound also has important gender and class implications less obvious from Price's comment. In bringing her sound more into line with the sounds of commercial jazz, Tharpe would not only have to change her tuning, but also "change her tune" as far as her performance of femininity was concerned.

This change is audible in the transition from the 1938 to the 1941 "Rock Me." In part because it is a solo performance, in which Tharpe provides her own accompaniment, the 1938 "Rock Me" conveys a quality of self-sufficient femininity that evokes the singing of a Ma Rainey or a Bessie Smith, female performers who profoundly shaped gospel through their respective influences on Dorsey and Mahalia Jackson. What's more, because the address of "Rock Me" is explicitly to God,

Tharpe isn't beholden in her performance to 1940s-era gendered protocols of the popular romantic ballad, in which the female speaker's expression of desire is circumscribed by bourgeois ideals of female virginity and passivity. Here Tharpe differs radically, however, from the sexually frank blues women who appropriated the blues tradition of lyrical double-entendre to give voice to a variety of socially insubordinate sexual identities: the bisexual, the woman in search of sexual pleasure outside of marriage, the female paramour of younger men. Unlike her secular sisters, Tharpe fashioned a popular voice by adapting the hallmark energy of Pentecostal worship services and the tradition of women's centrality in COGIC. In "Rock Me," she projects a supremely confident female musical persona who derives strength from the certainty of her faith in God's abiding love. When she sings "Oh, if you leave me, I will die"—words one might well imagine being addressed to a lover in a secular ballad or blues song—at the end of the first verse of the 1938 "Rock Me," the phrase conveys a desire unburdened of the necessity of a mitigating sexual coyness or pathos.

The 1941 "Rock Me" sounds femininity quite differently. On this slowed down version, which, despite being a full verse shorter is fifteen seconds longer than the 1938 "Rock Me," Tharpe performed only vocals, Trevor Bacon having taken over on guitar. She thus is cast, at least superficially, in the more conventional role of the girl singer fronting an all-male swing band. And this version does swing, with a smooth horn section and an easy, bouncy rhythm. Tharpe imparts swing in her vocal performance as well, hovering playfully around the beat, extending the length of vowels, using more vibrato, and abandoning the preacherly locution of the earlier recording for a smoother, more evened-out sound. From the viewpoint of a secular, commercial swing aesthetic, these changes would almost certainly have been regarded as marked improvements on the 1938 version. Whereas that "Rock Me" possesses an undeniable intimacy, this big-band version is undeniably catchy and, in its syncopated rhythms, highly danceable. Yet just as secular styles do not afford higher level of expressive possibility at the level of lyrics, in this instance the "secularization" of singing technique audibly circumscribes the range of vocal choices available to Tharpe. In particular, the norms of commercial swing require Tharpe to produce a certain vocal cheer, although the lyrics of the song are more supplicating than (merely) happy. In so doing, Tharpe replaces the 1938 recording's more idiosyncratic performance with a performance emphasizing commercial "personality."

The shift in orchestration is significant in other ways, as well. In the 1938 "Rock Me," the simple arrangement serves as a musical complement to the lyrics, which emphasize a lone speaker's celebration of the power of God's company through the "storms of life"; God's presence shines through even in moments of human desertion. In the 1941 version, lyrics such as those beseeching God to "hold me in the hollow of thou hand" pack a very different punch precisely because Tharpe is so obviously not alone; rather, her voice is buoyed by the lush sounds produced by three trumpets, three trombones, two alto saxophones, a tenor and a baritone saxophone, a piano, a guitar, a bass, and a drum kit.

Finally, there's a glossiness to Tharpe's 1941 vocal performance, a quality that I'd venture to dub (turning around Price's earlier, negative assessment) "singing in the 'right' key." By "right" I don't mean to imply that this sleeker, more professionalized version of "Rock Me"—not surprisingly, the more popular of the two—is necessarily more musical than the 1938 version or, conversely, that the earlier, more intimate "Rock Me" is necessarily more authentic in its rawness and immediacy. Nor am I suggesting that the difference between these two versions be interpreted as the measure of Tharpe's capitulation to market interests, a claim that would only deprive her of agency in her professional self-fashioning. Rather, borrowing again from Price, "wrong" and "right" here reference degrees of proximity to secular norms with distinct implications for the musical representation of femininity. In their different stylings, that is, the two recorded versions of "Rock Me" allow us to hear what different modes of femininity sound like: one "funny" and idiosyncratic, the other squarely within the boundaries of the "normal."

When these two versions of "Rock Me" were brought together, in a January 1943 Jubilee Broadcast Recording taped before a live Hollywood audience, the differences in their respective sounds becomes glaringly obvious. This live "Rock Me" starts out where the 1938 record begins—with Tharpe plucking a few bars on Vestapol guitar to introduce the musical themes. Once these opening flourishes end, Lucky Millinder's orchestra comes in and Tharpe lays aside her guitar to take the role of lead vocal, as she did in the 1941 record that helped launch her national career. Presumably the organizers of the broadcast thought to arrange the song this way because even by 1943 Tharpe was thoroughly associated with her resonating National guitar, and the introductory riffs gave her the opportunity to show off her considerable talents. But the overall effect is lopsided and jarring, with Tharpe introducing the theme of the song in one key, and Lucky Millinder's band picking up the opening phrases in another. Until the awkward transition has passed, it's unclear where the song is headed, or even whether it's part of a medley or a single composition.

In their variety and dissimilarity, the various versions of "Rock Me" Tharpe recorded raise the question of how femininity is not only represented, but also articulated (i.e., produced and worked out, as well as symbolized) in sound. Scholars of popular music, like their counterparts in musicology, typically have considered the gendering of sound in the context of embodied musical performance, presumably because bodies bear the visible social inscription of gender and sexuality. Yet as the two versions of "Rock Me" attest, gender also maybe inscribed in the ensemble of sounds—not only the voice, that seemingly most embodied of instruments—that constitute a given musical "text." It seems obvious that Tharpe's negotiation of the sacred/secular divide was not only a matter of technology (i.e., sound recording) and marketing (i.e., the commercialization of gospel) but that gender is equally important as a means of signifying the "transition" from spirituals to swing. In particular, the two versions of "Rock Me" sound this transition in the audible re-articulation of femininity.

The 1941 soundie of "The Lonesome Road" manifests Tharpe's musical negotiation of femininity through sound as well as visual display.[29] Briefly, soundies were three-minute, black-and-white "juke-box" musical films that had a fleeting existence between 1941 and 1947, the year the Soundies Distributing Corporation stopped servicing soundie juke boxes or Panorams. These were large wooden machines fitted with colorful lights and 16mm projectors that displayed the films to viewers gathered around them in pubs, nightclubs, cabarets and the like. Soundie reels usually contained eight films, each of which could be viewed for ten cents, although users who wanted to watch the fifth soundie in a single reel would have to fork over fifty cents. Like phonograph recordings of the era, soundies were marketed and distributed according to a strict racial protocol; hence soundies featuring African American performers circulated in venues that catered to African American audiences. Unlike 78s, however, soundies took two recording sessions to make—one to produce the film, another to produce the optical soundtrack. The predictable result consisted of sounds and images that sometimes didn't match, despite the best lip-synching that vocalists could muster. No one knows for sure what spelled the demise of soundies, although it's speculated that wartime shortages in industrial materials, competition with television, the high cost of Panorams relative to jukeboxes, and difficulties in using Panorams, whose television-sized screens were visible to a limited number of patron sat a time, all contributed.[30]

As is the case with other now-obsolete technologies of recorded sound, the history of soundies has to date been told as such a history of technological innovation and of marketing success and subsequent failure. What's left out of such tellings, however, is an attempt to ascertain how users interacted with the technology and how it, in turn, shaped their patterns of use. As Lisa Gitelman has shown, bringing users into the picture invariably introduces gender as an explicit analytical concern.[31] The Panoram, for example, was a new device for projecting musical short films but it was also a new technology for the eroticized display of women's bodies. From the beginning of their manufacture, the makers of soundies—in this case those aimed at African American audiences—presumed African American women's sexuality as an available commodity, a source of visual pleasure, and a marketing device. Because most of the musicians in soundies were men, black women frequently appeared in supporting roles as dancing chorus girls, thus translating the conventions of musical spectacle in places like the Cotton Club, with its famous line-up of light-skinned chorines. Female musicians were hardly exempt from this imperative; they, too, were expected to market their music through sexual display. One such soundie, of Dorothy Dandridge performing "Zoot Suit," has her singing and dancing in a sequined bikini! Needless to say, male performers were encouraged to perform masculinity in very different terms, mainly by effecting dapper displays of musical prowess visually highlighted by close-up images of their piano or horn performances. Images of women emphasized, in contrast, sexualized body parts and facial expressions signifying feminine charm.

Tharpe's 1941 "Lonesome Road" soundie similarly centers its visual narrative on the display of women's sexuality, although such a focus is not suggested by the song's simple two-bar form or its lyric, which reminds the mortal listener to think of her Maker as she travels the "lonesome road" of life. Tharpe recorded a gospel-toned solo version of "The Lonesome Road" in the same 1938 session that produced "Rock Me"; but here, in the soundtrack for the 1941 soundie, she sings along with Millinder's band, in an arrangement that emphasizes swing over spirit.

Where the visual representation of femininity is concerned, however, the "message" of the soundie is decidedly mixed. The first segment is focused entirely on Tharpe. As the music begins, she appears standing in front of the piano, dressed in an unassuming dark skirt and jacket and a high-necked white lace blouse. Although her hair is neatly pressed and curled and her eyebrows carefully shaped, she wears no conspicuous jewelry and doesn't appear highly made up; in fact, the only glamorous touch comes in the form of a lace handkerchief peeking out of the corner of her jacket pocket. Her body language, meanwhile, reads like an amalgamation of the Holiness church and Hollywood. During close-ups she flashes the camera exaggerated smiles that have showbiz, not sanctified joy, written all over them. But the movements she makes—the snapping of fingers, clapping of hands, head bobbing, and gentle rocking back and forth from hips to shoulders—come straight from the Pentecostal church. She also performs familiar theatrical gestures, motioning to an imaginary audience—arms spread wide, palms turned upward, and head thrust back slightly—to punctuate the end of musical phrases. Occasionally she mimics lyrics, as when she raises her eyes heavenward while intoning, "Look up, look up and see your maker / Before Gabriel blows his horn."

After the first verse, when the song moves into a piano interlude, a group of four light-complexioned chorines moves in, standing directly in front of the bandstand. In contrast to Tharpe, they're dressed for maximum skin exposure, in white feathered and sequined bikinis, high heels, and matching feather headpieces. Smiling madly as they execute frenetic dance moves, they're the embodiment of commercial swing: a choreographed vision of lively, "crazy" fun. They're also the signifiers of swing's sensuality. While in the vocal segment Tharpe appears primarily in medium-view or close-ups that showcase her singing, here the camera trains itself on the women's whirling, kicking bodies, closing in for shots of gyrating hips and thighs. In this capacity the chorus girls are eventually joined by a jitterbugging couple dressed like a busboy and cocktail waitress.

What's remarkable about the "Lonesome Road" soundie is how precisely it displays the tensions between sacred and secular in gendered, specifically feminized terms. Although all of the instrumentalists and the bandleader in the soundie are men, they are only fleetingly visible in occasional close-ups. Otherwise, their role is to serves an appreciative, smiling and clapping audience for the dancers—in other words, to model a privileged mode of (male) spectatorship of the soundie itself. (In one awkward moment of the soundie, some of this initial footage of the dancers is recycled during a second instrumental interlude, but the effect is jarring because we see the musicians looking at the dancers, their instruments at rest, although we hear them playing.) Very little of this erotic attention is focused on Tharpe, meanwhile, although as vocalist she occupies a privileged position of visibility relative to the other band members. The presence of the dancers mitigates this role considerably, however. In particular, their presence "liberates" Tharpe from the need to act as a focal point of female eroticism, as women fronting all-male bands often are called upon to do. The shifting of erotic energy from Tharpe to the dancers is abetted, moreover, by Tharpe's professional identity as "Sister" Rosetta Tharpe—that is to say, as a singer who brings a "gospel" sound to secular songs.

The tensions between sacred and secular in the "Lonesome Road" soundie are anticipated lyrically in Tharpe's original 1938 recording of the song, in the same Decca session that produced the earliest version of "Rock Me." On the 78 Tharpe sings "The Lonesome Road" with two verses: a more traditionally gospel "A" verse that reminds the listener to "look up" to the Lord on the "lonesome road" of life, and a distinctly bluesy "B" verse that rehearses a familiar "Lover-what-have-I-done?" lament, infusing the phrase "lonesome road" with an alternative set of secular meanings. The overall effect of the 1938 "Lonesome Road" is plaintive and introspective, portraying a desire for companionship that attaches itself to both sacred and secular objects. The blurring of the sacred/secular boundary is reflected in one set of liner notes, which refers to "The Lonesome Road" as a song "with secular lyrics that sound uncannily like [Tharpe's] gospel numbers."[32]

In omitting the "B" verse, the "Lonesome Road" soundie erases the song's explicitly secular lyrical references. Musically and visually, however, "The Lonesome Road" is reinterpreted in the soundie as an overwhelmingly secular dance song. What's illustrated is, in effect, analogous to the musical "translation" of "Rock Me" as a swing number. Only here, supplementing and transforming the soundtrack is the visual representation of Millinder's swinging band, not to mention a line-up of smiling, jiggling chorus girls who remind the viewer that the correct means of consuming the song is to "get happy" to it. In fact, as Sherrie Tucker points out, camera work depicting women's legs and crotches lend the singer's lyrical exhortation to "look up and see your Maker" an alternative set of meanings referencing simultaneously African American women's sexuality, their sexualization in popular culture, and their power as creative forces in Afro-Christian churches.[33] Although perhaps unintended, the combination of sacred (lyrics) and secular (images) is ironically apropos as a commentary on musical crossover as a treacherous minefield for Tharpe and other African American women.

Thus far I've been analyzing Tharpe's negotiation of categories of sacred and secular as a musical negotiation of femininity. I began by tracing how Tharpe's two versions of "Rock Me" indexed the tensions she confronted in "crossing over" into secular entertainment culture via the medium of recorded sound. Here I was interested in explicating the processor secularization as a series of normalizing pressures brought to bear on Tharpe's performance of gender and sexuality. In contrast, the "Lonesome Road" soundie illustrates how Tharpe appropriated the fiction of the opposition of sacred and secular to secure a mode of "secular" visibility that did not depend on her hypersexualization. Whereas the two versions of "Rock Me" sounded out the sacred/secular distinction in the form of a musical imperative (rich with implications for gender and sexuality) that Tharpe "change her tune," "The Lonesome Road" shows that Tharpe was also able to use this distinction to advance her own interests, even if the gender identities it made available still hinged on an analogous division of women according to their perceived sexual availability. In short, these performances suggest that gender is not merely where the imaginary line between sacred and secular is reflected, but that it is also, more importantly, where this line is actively constructed, and hence where it becomes available for appropriation.

Tharpe's 1951 wedding extravaganza is a good place to follow through on this point about appropriation because it's finally where categories of sacred and secular collided and recombined in unexpected ways. That the occasion for these collisions was a wedding is ironic but also fitting. Weddings, after all, are social rites rigged to display the binary logic of gender in a ceremonial context that conjoins the authority of church and state. They're where the sacrament of secular union is made official and public and where class rituals of heterosexuality receive divine blessing. Perhaps above all, they are where normative gender identities are displayed and reinforced through the choreographed exhibition of female virginity: from the appearance of the bride in her white dress to the moment of her being "given away" by her father to the sexual protocols of bridesmaids and honeymoons. In short, weddings are events of ideological enclosure, where otherwise muddled categories (of gender, sexuality, class, and the like) are temporarily brought to order.

Tharpe's wedding to Russell Morrison staged a train wreck between these rituals of ideological enclosure and Tharpe's crossing of boundaries, marrying solemnity with humor, the sacrosanct with the carnivalesque. Staged in Griffith Stadium, long since defunct but for fifty-nine years Washington's major baseball stadium and one of its few unsegregated venues (located, it should be noted, in the environs of Howard University and the historically African American Shaw neighborhood), the wedding doubled as a stop on a ninety-seven-city, eighteen-state tour organized by Decca, which required Tharpe to be on the road for one hundred fifteen days straight. The Super Music chain of record stores, which sponsored the wedding concert locally, turned the unusual aspects of the event into a marketing strategy. "WITNESS THE MOST ELABORATE WEDDING EVER STAGED! EVERYBODY IS WELCOME!" a print advertisement in the city's leading Negro newspaper, the Washington Afro-American, beckoned, adding, almost as an afterthought, "PLUS WORLD'S GREATEST SPIRITUAL CONCERT!" Unlike most weddings, this one charged admission of between 90 cents and $2.50—about as much as spectators had to pay to see a Washington Senators baseball game.[34] It also was the basis of a live album, simultaneously released in 78 and 45 rpm formats by Decca, featuring concert excerpts and the exchange of wedding vows in their entirety.

The spectacle of holy matrimony in a baseball stadium on July 3, the day before the annual celebration of national independence, playfully and unabashedly merged church and state, secular and spiritual, service and spectacle. It also amusingly tweaked ceremonial conventions: Tharpe, the undisputed star of the evening, was given away by her mother, and fellow musicians played the roles of maid of honor (Marie Knight), bridesmaids (The Rosettes), and best man (Lucky Millinder). The bride walked down an improvised "aisle" leading from the dugout to a platform at second base, and she regaled the crowd by playing a steel-bodied guitar in her wedding gown. Elder Samuel Kelsey, a popular local radio evangelist, presided in the crowd-massaging manner of a master of ceremonies, spicing up the exchange of vows with irreverent quips about the fragility of the marriage bond. "I sure know how to put folks together," he riffed. "If they don't stay together, it isn't my fault." Ever respectful of her audience, Tharpe stuck to a gospel repertoire, performing "I Shall Know Him," "My Journey to the Sky," a popular duet with Marie Knight, and "God Don't Like It," an original composition about the evils of moonshine. In keeping with the spirit of July Fourth, the wedding concert concluded with a massive fireworks display featuring "a 20-foot, animated, lifelike reproduction of the famed Sister Tharpe, rhythmically strumming her guitar," "a huge display of Cupid's hearts pierced with arrows," and simulations of Niagara Falls and a duck laying eggs.[35]

Janice Joplin's biographers typically cite her as the first woman to achieve prominence as a stadium rocker. The phenomenal success of Tharpe's affair—which drew an audience of between fifteen and twenty-seven thousand people, despite the holiday and a transit strike that suspended much of the city's trolley and bus service—not only complicates this claim, but also hints at the limitations of the crossover model. For although Tharpe was "big" enough, in market terms, to outdraw the Senators in their regular season, the concert failed to secure her the publicity conferred on a typical mid-season baseball game. (Decca speculated, "Had traffic conditions been normal, the stadium would have been filled far beyond its capacity of 30,000."[36]) Or rather, it was unsuccessful in earning her publicity where it most "counted"—that is, where official musical memory is concerned. Although it made front-page news in the Afro-American and was featured in African American newspapers as far away as Los Angeles via the ANP (American Negro Press) wire service, to readers of the city's prominent white newspapers, the Washington Post and the Evening Star, it was as though the concert had never happened.

This absence is noteworthy because Tharpe's concert attracted a distinctly gendered audience— one that, like COGIC, comprised disproportionate numbers of African American women. Like African American churches, that is to say, the concert constituted a specifically black female public sphere where women's voices were particularly audible, notwithstanding that fact that institutional control remained largely in the hands of men. (In COGIC churches, women such as Tharpe's mother were permitted to evangelize but couldn't be called "Reverend" or "Elder.") Tellingly, this aspect of the concert entered public discourse via the charge that Tharpe's nuptials had shortchanged the groom! In a feature story replete with photos of the happy couple, Ebony announced: "Groom Almost Forgotten in Advertising For Wedding"—a formulation that constructs Tharpe as a threat for placing commercial interests, and by implication her own ambitions, above patriarchal interests that define women as subordinate to their husbands.[37] It didn't help that Morrison was Tharpe's third husband and seven years her junior. The bride and groom's professional inequity, which flew in the face of conventions of the male breadwinner, was also painfully evident in the headline in the Afro-American. "Spiritual Singer Bride of Pa. Man," the paper proclaimed, elevating Tharpe's professional identity while relegating Morrison to the geographical and professional hinterlands of Pennsylvania.

The structural similarities between the wedding concert and COGIC go much deeper than audience composition alone would suggest. Like COGIC services, which threatened not merely the black Protestant establishment but the calculated reserve and propriety of the African American middle class, Tharpe's nuptials flew in the face of black bourgeois sensibilities. Just as Baptist leaders resisted the seeming abandon of Holiness worship as unbefitting a community bent on "uplift" instead encouraging their flocks to adopt a "concert demeanor" for musical performances, so middle-class observers of Tharpe's wedding were quick to point to its excesses. Even apparently fawning reports of the wedding's material opulence—a testament to Tharpe's commercial success and, by extension, to the promise of "Negro" achievement in segregated America—were double-edged. While there were varying reports of the cost of Tharpe's ensemble—Ebony claimed her to be wearing an $800 dress and a $350 corsage composed of twenty-eight white orchids; the ANP reported a gown that cost an even grand—it is indisputable that the dress cost a fortune by 1950s standards.[38] Yet in such reporting hovered the insinuation that Tharpe's money had not bought her purchase over bourgeois tastes. More than one article in the African American press found the wedding's apparent lack of gravity, no less than its freewheeling embraceor commercialized spectacle, disturbing. Even a British jazz journalist, upon listening to the Decca recording of the wedding, complained that it took on "the atmosphere of a cheap, phony publicity stunt," admitting in the next breath (more than once, in fact) that he had not seen "a genuine Negro wedding service (nor any other religious ceremony)."[39] In short, for these observers the wedding concert failed as both a wedding (sacred ritual) and a concert (secular spectacle). Indeed, it offended precisely to the degree that it was both and neither at the same time.

In magnitude and scope the 1951 wedding concert was a daring leap even for Tharpe, a notorious cut-up who turned in enthusiastic performances wherever an audience could be found, in a storefront church or a glitzy cabaret. After all, Tharpe was the same woman whose first husband, less than fifteen years earlier, had publicly scolded her for violating church decorum by appearing hatless at the Cotton Club. (So vociferous were these objections, meanwhile, that they made headlines in the Baltimore Sun.[40] In so doing, the Rev. Thorpe, of course, was not merely exercising his "rights" and "obligations" as her husband, but voicing the interests of COGIC as an institution. Discussions of African American Holiness sects in relation to mainstream Protestant denominations often convey the impression that as the former were more spontaneous and corporal in their style of worship, so they exercised correspondingly less restraint on women members of the church. Yet in practice Holiness sects could be as doctrinaire as Baptists and Methodists in matters pertaining to gender. In COGIC, regulating women's bodies was a primary means of securing and representing the identity of collective body; in this way, both the righteousness of COGIC religious beliefs and the value of African American cultural practices *vis à vis* those of the dominant (white) culture found their most convenient metaphor in the sexual modesty of COGIC women.

Cloaked in the garments of religious pageantry and state authority, Tharpe's wedding concert undermined such a patriarchal monopoly over black Christian women's bodies, and it did so in spectacular fashion and in defiance of taboos on tarnishing the public (racial) image of African American churches. To do so, moreover, Tharpe had availed herself of an iconic American civic space—the sole baseball stadium in the nation's capital—as "her" church, reversing the logic of male control over religious practice while simultaneously giving reign to entrepreneurial, spiritual, and artistic ambitions. A public relations *coup de grâce* despite the inevitable criticisms, the wedding concert additionally and perhaps most importantly celebrated Tharpe's clout as an African American female singer and instrumentalist who could command a mass audience. Race and gender notwithstanding, there were few performers—in gospel or in other idioms—who could draw such a crowd in the early 1950s. If the wedding was dubious as a display of religious faith and of the gendered order of things, its success in this one respect was irrefutable.

The 1951 Wedding Concert, even more than the recordings of "Rock Me" or the "Lonesome Road" soundie, concisely illustrates the crossover options Tharpe availed herself of as a sanctified musician of modest origin and stadium-sized ambition. Its brilliance lay in making it impossible to know where the sacred ended and the secular began. Such blurring of boundaries enabled Tharpe simultaneously to inhabit apparently contradictory gendered positions: to play the modest bride and, without even a change of costume, to slip into the role of guitar goddess, tearing it up on her solid-body National for tens of thousands of fans. Both of these positions were, in fact, instrumental to Tharpe's musical "moves" as a female gospel-blues-rock pioneer. Although Tharpe would suffer greatly in later years, when church audiences rejected her for having cut blues sides, she was also empowered by her constant shuttling between the church and entertainment worlds, capitalizing on the possibilities for musical self-expression in each realm.

Two photographs offer a final means of tracking Tharpe's negotiation of the sacred/secular division. One is a well known early publicity shot of Tharpe that illustrated the 1939 Amsterdam News article trumpeting her as the "toast of Broadway"; the other is a photo of Tharpe singing and playing guitar during the 1951 wedding concert at Griffith Stadium. The first is a carefully composed and retouched studio shot by James Kriegsmann, a New York photographer, taken around the time of Tharpe's first Decca recordings.[41] It shows Tharpe attired in a floor-length gown, her cheerfully smiling face tilted slightly to the side, her eyes gazing ardently upward, as though to symbolize her status as a singer of "spiritual" songs. Notably, the photograph pictures Tharpe playing her guitar (at least, her hands are carefully positioned on the strings), not holding it like an ornament, as was sometimes the case, as Sherrie Tucker has documented, with "girl" musicians of the era.[42] Yet although the photograph secures competent musicianship as an aspect of Tharpe's commercial image, it conveys nothing of what Sammy Price found to be the disruptive, discordant sound of her Vestapol tuning or "off-key" voice. Instead, slender and poised, resplendent in satin brocade, Tharpe is the picture of feminine refinement, a figure who calls to mind sounds that are by analogy tuneful, sweet, and melodious.

The second image is a "candid" shot by an Ebony freelancer, and it is replete with the authenticity and immediacy that the term implies. Whereas the studio shot is a soft-focus, full-length portrait taken at a carefully calibrated distance from Tharpe (the better to display a high-heeled foot peeking out from below the hem of her dress), this photo looks up at Tharpe from a slightly skewed position at the base of the stage set up in the middle of Griffith Stadium. Buzzing with kinetic energy, it depicts Tharpe strumming her guitar and singing, her mouth open in mid-syllable (revealing her tongue and teeth), her eyes gazing away from the camera in obvious concentration. It's hard to tell exactly, but in this picture Tharpe seems to have changed out of her wedding gown and veil into a reception outfit, a white short-sleeved gown with a lace bodice and a beaded necklace supporting what appears to be a feathery brooch. In contrast to the earlier photo, which concealed the apparatus of the studio, this image is rough around the edges: a spotlight illuminating the stage is visible in the background, as is the figure of an unidentified man. Similarly, the image itself primarily represents the labor of music-making, not the glamour of celebrity: it is an image of "liveness" itself. In fact, were a viewer not to know that this was a wedding, she might associate the intensity of the image with the carefully choreographed abandon of a rock concert or, perhaps, Sunday service at a COGIC church. Particularly in this last point, my descriptions of these photographs of Tharpe beg the following questions: Which image is sacred, which secular? Which pictures "saintly" femininity; which commodified female charm? Which are spirituals; which swing?

The photographs reiterate an early point of this essay—namely that gender is a privileged (if overlooked) site where the sacred/secular division is worked out, especially for women artists. Yet the arguments they illustrate have several wider implications for the study of women musicians working with African American vernacular traditions. For one, it's insufficient merely to note the fluidity of sacred and secular, to argue that the line between the two spheres is more porous and more mobile than it might at first seem. While this is true, it's only a useful observation if we inquire into the agency behind the binary organization of sacred and secular—which is to say, not only "who" decides where the line is drawn, but also what the effects of a particular demarcation will be. In reading various texts from a thirteen-year period in Tharpe's career, I've argued that as is the case with the nineteenth-century division of public and private, the "separation of spheres" into sacred and secular is an area of feminist concern. How women musicians negotiated these categories, what they meant for their performance of gender, and the degree to which women musicians were able to use and appropriate them are part and parcel of this concern.

It's also important that we not draw conclusions about the relative value of sacred and secular musical spheres for women based on evidence drawn from stereotype or assumption. While it may have seemed to "free" sanctified women musicians like Tharpe from certain restraints on their sexual and/or gender identity, the process of secularization was no less fraught by such restraint; if anything, it brought new challenges related to the negotiation of cultural visibility outside of the space of racial and class intimacy that the church itself represented. On the other hand, it would be misleading to assume that Pentecostal institutions were necessarily preferable performance spaces for African American women musicians, insofar as they eschewed the blatant sexual commodification and sexual definition that were part and parcel of the secular public sphere. Sequined bikinis are not the only symbols of patriarchal power over women's bodies and sexuality, although they are an obvious and visible one. Religious discourses advocating the "protection" of women and the circumscription of their movement within the secular public sphere could be no less restrictive for claiming to represent women's best interests (recall the Rev. Thorpe's outrage over Tharpe's lack of a hat at the Cotton Club). Likewise, the sacred sphere was far from a de-sexualized sphere for women performers. Rather women gospel musicians negotiated sexuality in the context of sacred performance, on pulpits, at southern tent-meetings, and at urban revivals.

In short, neither sphere, however constituted, afforded women musicians freedom from gender definition, although neither shut down women's ability to define gender, either. Such a conclusion would keep us open to signs of possibility and change in both spheres. It would also encourage us to reject narratives that either conflate women's liberty, as gendered subjects, with their geographical and creative movement beyond the church or equate their secular success with "selling out." "From Spirituals to Swing" may be a catchy title, but it does not capture the musical development of gospel musicians like Rosetta Tharpe—women who could alternately rock the congregations and raise the spirit from second base.

Acknowledgments

I am indebted to Sherrie Tucker and David W. Stowe, whose astute comments on an earlier draft of this essay I eagerly incorporated in this version. Carolyn Betensky, Keith Leonard, and Melani McAlister graciously offered their suggestions on an earlier draft.

Notes

1. On Tharpe's musical development, see Horace Clarence Boyer, The Golden Age of Gospel (Urbana: University of Illinois Press, 2000); and Anthony Heilbut, The Gospel Sound: Good News and Bad Times (New York: Simon and Schuster, 1971). The most reliable single source of historical evidence on Tharpe is an unpublished work, Jerma Jackson's valuable dissertation, "Testifying at the Cross: Thomas Andrew Dorsey, Sister Rosetta Tharpe and the Politics of African American Sacred and Secular Music," (PhD diss., Rutgers University, 1995). I should note at the outset various discrepancies in accounts of Tharpe's early life. Some sources, for example, give her date of birth as 1921, whereas Jackson cites Social Security records to support the date of 1915; it's clear, in any case, that Tharpe was often deliberately cagey about her age. Names, spellings, and chronologies vary as well (for example, Boyer writes that Tharpe's first husband was Wilbur Thorpe and refers to evangelist P. W. McGhee, not McGee). In every case I have tried to present facts that seem reliable or that I have been able to confirm independently, although some errors may be inevitable.

2. There is some dispute about when, exactly, Tharpe moved to New York. Boyer writes that Tharpe moved to Harlem in he mid-1930s; Jackson (167) discusses the uncertainty about this date.

3. John Hammond with Irving Townsend, John Hammond on Record: An Autobiography (New York: Penguin, 1981), 203.

4. Count Basie, as told to Albert Murray, good Morning Blues: The Autobiography of Count Basie (New York: Random House, 1985), 221.

5. John Hammond, "From Spirituals to Swing," New York Times, Dec. 18, 1938, Sec. 9, p. 4.

6. Arna Bontemps, "Rock, church, rock!" Common Ground (Autumn 1942): 75–80.

7. Ibid., 80.

8. Rosetta Reitz, "Sister Rosetta," Hotwire (May 1991): 16–20. Reitz also put together one of the first compilations of Tharpe's music on her independent label Rosetta Records. See Sincerely Sister Rosetta Tharpe (Rosetta Records no. 1317, 1988).

9. On gospel's hybridity, see LeRoi Jones, "The Changing Same" in Black Music (New York: Da Capo, 1998); John F. Szwed, "Negro Music: Urban Renewal" in Our Living Traditions: An Introduction to American Folklore, ed. Tristram Potter Coffin (New York: Basic Books, 1968), 272–282; and Portia K. Maultsby, "The Impact of Gospel Music on the Secular Music Industry" in We'll Understand It Better By and By: Pioneering African American Gospel Composers, ed. Bernice Johnson Reagon (Washington DC: Smithsonian Institution, 1992), 19–33.

10. T-Bone Walker, for example, told interviewers in the 1950s of getting his first taste of boogie-woogie piano at Dallas' Holy Ghost Church, and Muddy Waters has described how he learned to sing blues attending Sunday service at his local Pentecostal congregation. On Walker, see "Hear Me Talkin' to Ya'": The Story of Jazz as Told by the Men Who Made It, ed. Nat Shapiro and Nat Hentoff (New York: Dover, 1955), 250–51; on Muddy Waters, see Pete Welding, "An Interview with Muddy Waters" in The American Folk Music Occasional (1970): 5.

11. Horace Clarence Boyer, "Contemporary Gospel Music," The Black Perspective in Music 7 (Spring 1979): 5–34.

12. Ibid., 6. The sections I quote are from the first part of the article, which Boyer reprinted from First World (Jan.–Feb. 1977): 46–49.

13. Joan Scott, "Gender: A Useful Category of Historical Analysis," American Historical Review 91 (Dec., 1986): 1053–1075.

14. Sherrie Tucker's book Swing Shift (Durham: Duke University Press, 2000) provides an excellent discussion of these pressures in the context of "all-girl" swing bands of the 1940s.

15. "Rock Me" (Decca no. 2243) and "Rock Me" (Decca no. 18353).

16. Boyer, "Contemporary Gospel Music," 8.

17. Here I am particularly influenced by the work of Stuart Hall. See his "What Is This 'Black' in Black Popular Culture?" in Stuart Hall: Critical Dialogues in Cultural Studies, ed. David Morley and Kuan-Hsing Chen (New York: Routledge, 1996).

18. My notion of cultural "moves" is influenced by personal conversations with Herman Gray.

19. According to Eileen Southern, the turning-point in the professionalization of gospel was the 1936 "Battle of Song" in Chicago. Spectators paid fifteen cents admission to hear a singing contest between Roberta Martin and Sallie Martin, two of the music's early standouts. See Eileen Southern, the Music of Black Americans: A History, 3rd ed. (New York: W. W. Norton, 1997), 464–65.

20. "Singer Swings Same Songs in Church and Night Club," Life 7 (Aug. 28, 1939): 37.

21. See Marvel Cooke, "Holy Roller Singer Toast of Broadway: Sister Rosetta Tharpe Swings Spirituals for Sophisticated Cotton Club Clientele," Amsterdam News [New York], Mar. 4, 1939 p. 16–17. Thanks to Judith Jackson Fossett for pointing out the significance of the phrase "Holy Roller" to me.

22. Ibid., 16.

23. Johnson Reagon makes this point in a video interview with Bill Moyers released as The Songs are Free (Mystic Fire Video, 1991). Thanks to Kyra Gaunt for bringing the video and Johnson Reagon's comments to my attention.

24. This point has important methodological implications for popular music studies. A recurring critique of certain work in the field, especially from trained musicologists, is the tendency of scholars with backgrounds in literary or historical studies to privilege lyrics (linguistic text) over sounds (musical text). And yet both lyrics and sounds may be constitutive of a song's meaning. My claim here about the secularization of gospel indeed brings lyrics to the forefront, not because I wish to ignore sound but because lyrics are a place where secularization often gets "worked out" in the music.

25. See Boyer's The Golden Age of Gospel for a lengthier discussion of Holiness worship practices, especially as they compare to Baptist worship practices.

26. This is a composite transcription of the chorus from the 1938 and 1941 versions. I have omitted minor differences, such as the addition of the word "just" in the phrase "You [just] hide me in thou bosom" in the 1938 version, or the elimination of the last words of the phrase "Only feed [me 'til I want no more] in the second chorus of the 1941 version.

27. Sammy Price, What Do They Want?: A Jazz Autobiography, ed. Caroline Richmond (Urbana: University of Illinois Press, 1990), and 52.

28. Commentators of Tharpe's day, like listeners today, have a hard time coming to any sort of consensus about the tuning Tharpe used: B♭? C? D?

29. My source for the soundie is Jivin' Time: Harlem Roots, vol. 4 (Storyville Films no. 6003), a 1988 compilation of soundies put out by Storyville Films, the longtime European distributor of soundies.

30. The best source for information on soundies is Maurice Terenzio, Scott MacGillivray, and Ted Okuda, the Soundies Distributing Corporation of America: A History and Filmography of Their "Jukebox" Music Films of the 1940s (Jefferson, NC: McFarland & Company, 1991).

31. Lisa Gitelman, "How Users Define New Media: A History of the Amusement Phonograph," available online at <http://media-in-transition.mit.edu/articles/index_gitelmanh.tml>.

32. Ken Romanowski, liner notes to Sister Rosetta Tharpe: Complete Recorded Works 1938–1944 in Chronological Order, vol. 1 1938–1941 (Document Records, 1995; DOCD no. 5334).

33. From personal correspondence with Sherrie Tucker.

34. "20,000 Watch Wedding of Sister Rosetta Tharpe," Ebony 6 (Oct. 1951): 27–30, esp. 27.

35. "Sister Rosetta Tharpe to Wed Russell Morrison: Costly Gowns, Fireworks, Concert Added Features," Washington Afro-American, June 30, 1951, p. 13.

36. Liner notes, The Wedding Ceremony of Sister Rosetta Tharpe (Decca DL 5382, 1951).

37. "20,000 Watch," Ebony, 30.

38. "Sister Rosetta Tharpe Weds," Sentinel [Los Angeles], July 19, 1951, sec. A, p. 6.

39. Derrick Stewart-Baxter, "Preachin' the Blues," Jazz Journal International 17 (July 1952): 17.

40. Malcolm Johnson, "Sister Tharpe Gets Reprimand From Her Husband for Not Wearing Hat," in his "Café Life in New York" column, the Sun [Baltimore], Sept. 5, 1939.

41. The Kriegsmann photograph is the most frequently reproduced image of Tharpe. A print of this and other Kriegsmann publicity shots are available at the Photographs and Prints Division of the Schomburg Center for Research in Black Culture, at the New York Public Library.

42. See Tucker, Swing Shift.

41

Singing Like David Sang: Queerness and Masculinity in Black Gospel Performance

Melvin L. Butler

Writers in a variety of academic disciplines have long explored the cross-cultural dimensions of masculinity and expressions of queer identity. However, research on performances of gender and sexuality in gospel music remains sorely underrepresented in scholarly literature. In 2006, at the annual conference of the Society for Ethnomusicology, I presented a paper exploring this issue. I grappled, in my usual reflexive fashion, with a number of concerns, not the least of which was how my identity as a heterosexual African American Pentecostal scholar and musician would shape the research questions I asked and chose not to ask. The paper was received well enough, but I have not, until now, returned to it. My apprehension stemmed, I think, from a sense that the topic was simply too complicated and that my own theological understandings were too fragile for me to tackle with confidence a critical discussion of the gender ambiguities and contradictions I have been noticing in black churches I have attended since the late 1980s.

A number of questions sparked my initial broaching of the subject: (1) How might I understand the tension between homophobic church discourses about sexuality and bodily performances of queerness in gospel music making? This question still strikes me as fundamental, perhaps because gospel artists and audiences seem more attuned than in previous decades to the ways in which certain sounds and gestures index (for churchgoers and the wider public) orientations that threaten the perceived stability of a strict gender binary. (2) How does the implicit acceptance of "effeminate" male gospel artists relate to church demographics, namely, the high percentage of women in black congregations? (3) What socio-musical factors account for churchgoers' apparent appreciation for male gospel singers who are thought to be secretly gay—despite these singers' supposed sexual "shortcomings"?

Over four years have passed since my conference presentation. I have since relocated from Charlottesville, Virginia to Chicago, Illinois, where the "black church" in all of its inescapable complexity shouts even more enthusiastically for ethnomusicological attention. I cannot pretend to be any surer of myself than in previous years, and I will not succeed in addressing all of my aforementioned questions in this short piece. However, I do sense—perhaps also because of current events drawing attention to gender and sexuality in African American churches—that the time has come for me to revisit this topic.

Major media outlets have certainly not been shy about publicizing any news of same-sex "improprieties" among those who profess to preach the gospel.[1] More importantly, I note the recent emergence of some highly relevant work in religious and performance studies (e.g., Griffin 2006, Finley 2007, and Johnson 2008), which delves boldly and critically into issues of queer performance and theology. This fascinating body of scholarship has no doubt jump-started my interest while bringing into stronger relief the nagging scarcity of ethnomusicological writing in this vital area. And so having outlined the context of my concerns, I offer this brief work-in-progress, starting with an ethnographic vignette describing an event that took place near the end of my decade (1994–2004) in New York City—an event like many others that prompts me to re-ponder negotiations of faith and musical masculinity in black gospel performance.

> It's mid-April 2004, and my wife and I have just left our apartment on the Upper West Side in Manhattan to begin a ten-minute walk to the closest subway station, located on 125th Street in Harlem. As usual, we don't have much time to spare, because in order to be on time to Friday night service at our Pentecostal church, we can't afford to miss the A Train, which runs express all the way into the Crown Heights section of Brooklyn. Having set out a couple of minutes behind schedule, we walk briskly and with a sense of purpose. But we start to slow our pace when we notice an unusually large number of Harlemites assembled in front of an outdoor stage just down the street. Curiosity gets the best of us, and we decide to investigate. It turns out that there's a live concert that evening: Gospel songwriter/producer/bassist/and vocalist Fred Hammond, sometimes referred to as the "architect" of urban praise and worship,[2] is promoting his latest CD and treating a growing crowd of men and women to an energetic sampling of some of his new recording's most promising pieces. Heading back toward the subway, we discuss how one of the consistent attributes of Fred Hammond's performance style is that he embodies what many African American Pentecostals perceive to be definitive "masculine" characteristics.

Masculinity is, as Jason King asserts, "deeply encoded into the way we understand the aesthetics of the voice" (445: n. 21). Likewise, I contend that the voice, along with the ways in which we perceive the body itself, informs our understanding of gender identity. This is certainly the case with

Fred Hammond. I have had numerous conversations with black churchgoers who insist that "Fred," as he is affectionately called, exemplifies a "manly" gospel singer—one who stands in contradistinction to any number of other(ed) artists whose sexual orientations instill less confidence in those who prefer their gospel music "straight, not gay." It seems as though Hammond's thick vocal timbre and controlled delivery, together with his heavy-set body type, fuel a stereotypical perception of him as a quintessential male gospel performer—able to sing uncompromisingly about his love for Jesus Christ while employing performative codes that register as unambiguously masculine.

It is interesting—and particularly germane to the goals of this essay—that lyrical allusions to biblical narratives about King David abound in Fred Hammond's compositions. In fact, one of his most successful albums of the 1990s is entitled *The Spirit of David*, in reference to David's character, his commitment to praise and worship, and repentant heart. This recording, the title of which has inspired the title of this essay, features the song, "When the Spirit of the Lord."

> When the spirit of the Lord comes upon my heart
> I will dance like David danced.
> . . .
> When the spirit of the Lord comes upon my heart
> I will pray like David prayed.
> . . .
> When the spirit of the Lord comes upon my heart
> I will sing like David sang.

The lyrics "I will sing like David sang" are perhaps an obvious point of departure for an article by a music scholar. I note, however, that they are preceded by references to prayer and to an even more demonstrative form of praise—namely, dance—which David, like Fred Hammond, feels compelled to do. Highlighting the embodied nature of black Christian worship is one way to reveal the irony of church discourses that privilege highly demonstrative forms of expression while also carefully demarcating the boundaries of how the body is adorned, presented, and pleasured in public and private spaces. Dancing, in particular, could create something of a dilemma for those men who understand it to be most characteristic of an "open" body—a vulnerable body that is penetrable by a Holy Spirit typically referred to as a "he," albeit one without flesh and bones (Gordon 2000: 118–119). Stephen Finley elaborates on this point, going so far as to argue that "the impervious, fully armored, black male body is an impediment to finding meaning in the black church in that worship of God is a homoerotic entry into the body" (2007: 18). Fred Hammond's recorded performance (or perhaps his performed recording) can be read as a means of reasserting a heteronormative style of praise and worship, recouping a musical "posture of masculinity," and rising up to meet the challenge and to solve the existential crisis posited Lewis Gordon, who rhetorically asks, "Can one worship God and remain masculine too?" (2000: 119).

The words "When the spirit of the Lord comes upon my heart, I will dance like David danced" are sung against the boisterous background voices of Hammond's group, Radical for Christ. The group's members repeatedly chant, "Let's celebrate, let's celebrate," sonically suggesting both a battle cry and a party-like atmosphere of joyous resistance to pretension and sanctimony. The track begins with Hammond *commanding* listeners to "put those hands to together all over this place," and then he grunts an exclamation as if to underscore the physicality of his praise. Verbal punctuations of "Come on! Come on!" intersperse with Hammond's smooth singing delivery. His performance suggests that we dare not mistake his Christian expression for the half-hearted hummings of one who is weak in body and mind. Rather, this is to be understood as the musical praise of a muscular man—a fully *masculine* man, trained and equipped, as it were, for musical battle—a man, who like King David, is not the least bit ashamed to praise God with everything he has.

I mention Fred Hammond's evocation of David because I believe an understanding of this biblical figure is critical to grasping how black masculinities are constructed and contested in church services and gospel concerts. An important aspect of what we might refer to as "Davidian masculinity" is revealed in Hammond's response to the question of why he chose *The Spirit of David* as the title of his album. He explains: "Well I think we understand that David was a worshiper. He was a *true* worshiper. He had the heart of God. And that is what this kinda displays. Plus, you know, it kinda goes through things that believers have to go through—the same thing David had to go through. You know, praise and thanksgiving, adversity and triumph, and restoration and justification, and I think that's what we gon' talk about and get into with all of these songs right here" (*The Spirit of David*, Track 1). The notion that David was a "true worshiper" who "danced before the Lord with all his might" so much so that his clothing fell off (2 Sam. 6:14) is often articulated in Pentecostal churches. King David's unabashed celebratory praise embarrasses his wife, who scolds him for his lack of restraint and is subsequently shown to be punished through her inability to bear children. David's enthusiasm, manifested in bodily danced praise and worship, often serves as a biblical call for *true* men in the church to do likewise.

One minister I spoke to, a man in his mid-40s, told me, "It's backwards today. Instead of standing back all serious and reserved, we are really the ones who are supposed to set the example— we should out-praise the women in the church. . . Oh yes! We should be showing *them* how to praise God!" I've attended more services than I can remember in which a praise and worship leader put forth a call for men in the congregation to break free of their social restraints, to "let go and let God" animate their bodies. During one service I attended, where many of the women were quite obviously feeling the move of the Holy Spirit, a male minister took the microphone and exclaimed, "The presence of the Lord is in this place! I need a *man* who isn't afraid to worship God. Come on! Are there any *worshippers* in the house? Where are the men who aren't ashamed to worship?" This semi-rhetorical question challenged each man in the congregation to prove his openness to the spirit's touch, to show that no matter what his "neighbor"—that is, the person standing next to him—thinks of him, he is willing to let his love for God manifest itself physically in a way that has been socially constructed as feminine (cf. Finley 2007: 17). Holy dancing, dancing in the spirit, "shouting": These are all terms used to describe the kinds of bodily movement many congregants—both men and women—engage in during praise and worship services. It is understood that the Holy Spirit touches the minds, bodies, and souls of believers who may earnestly seek to be touched, or in some cases, may be caught off guard by a bit of spiritually inspired music making, preaching, testifying, or praying such that their bodies become animated by what anthropologist Glenn Hinson refers to simply as "the holy touch" of transcendence (3).

Given that women outnumber men so dramatically in many churches, it is not surprising that praise and worship activities are often experienced as the specialty of women and girls. Yet scholars have pointed out that black church worship may also provide a safe haven of sorts for expressions of queer sexuality among black men and boys. In *Sweet Tea: Black Gay Men of the South*, E. Patrick Johnson devotes an entire chapter to discussion of black gay Christians and their relation to practices and discourses of the churches in which they have held membership. His interviewees' narratives are eye-opening. They are also significantly varied in terms of the degree to which the narrators reconcile their faith and their sexuality. Nevertheless, many of their stories resonate strongly with Johnson's personal account of growing up in the church and participating in the choir:

> Grown folks marveled at, and some of my peers envied my soaring melismas and general vocal theatrics. What I realize now, but didn't back then, was that I was a budding diva who was using the medium of gospel music to express not only my spirituality, but also my sexual and gender identity. I would catch the spirit at times, especially during my solos, and step down out of the choir stand and twirl down the aisle while my robe ballooned around [my] pudgy body—all the while holding a note and making sure that no one took the microphone out of my hand. The little queen in me was begging to show out, and I had a captive audience. (2008: 185)

Johnson's childhood experiences thus shed light on an experiential overlap between spirit-influenced musical praise and expressive performances of queer identity. The choir, he notes, was his "saving grace" because it allowed him to express himself freely—to "flame as bright as [he] wanted" (185). Along with several other "budding queens in the church," he took advantage of "the theatricality already built into the church service" and "learned very quickly. . . how express and affirm [his] queerness without ever naming [his] sexuality" (184). At the same time, Johnson's account reminds me of the tension many heterosexual men feel when observing and participating in gospel choirs and demonstrative forms of bodily worship. Does "catching the spirit," as Johnson describes it, require losing one's masculinity, or at least a portion of it? Is it possible to go too far in one's worship—to "let oneself go" or "open oneself up" to the point of crossing over into a less "masculine" form of expression? Indeed, these are questions I have often found myself pondering, not only in the cool contexts of academia, but also in the heated spaces of charismatic worship.

I have often heard Pentecostal preachers present David as ideal man of God: He catches the spirit and keeps his masculinity. He is a worshipping warrior who, despite his position of authority, possesses a heart that is malleable and attuned to divine will. As a musician and composer of many psalms, David stands out as one who "blesses" or gives praise "at all times" to a Jehovah whom he describes as abundantly merciful and able to deliver or save from the hand of the enemy. Yet David is also not perfect—and this is *also* stressed among Pentecostals in sermonic recitations of David's character traits. He commits the biblical sin of fornication by sleeping with Bathsheba, the wife of Uriah, one of David's soldiers. Then, in an attempt to cover up his dishonorable deed, he positions the noble Uriah to be killed in battle and thus becomes guilty (indirectly) of murder as well.

The fact that David succumbed to this temptation, along with the fact that his "natural" attraction to the opposite sex is what *led* to his transgression, serves as an often-repeated reminder that men—even, or especially, spirit-filled Pentecostal men—can be lured down the wrong path if they yield to their carnal desires. A key point in this narrative is that David, being the *man* who he was, eventually seeks God's forgiveness, thus securing his bibliohistorical legacy as a prime exemplar of Godly reconciliation. It is understood that this worshipping warrior David is a man to whom "good" Christian men—which is to say *heterosexual* Christian men—should be able to relate. His character flaws and (hetero)sexual sins—damnable as they may be—are of the *understandable* sort, and he ultimately succeeds in spite of them. One *Newsweek* writer makes precisely this point in a recent article entitled "The Black Church, Homophobia, and Pastor Eddie Long":

> If Long's accuser were a woman, even if her allegations were found to be true, I think he could weather the storm—everyone loves a story of a man's redemption after a moment of relaxed vigilance allows Satan to find a toehold. (Alston 2010)

It hardly seems accidental that in his much anticipated speech to his Baptist congregation—his first public remarks since being accused of using his pastoral influence to coerce young male church members into sexual acts—Long compared himself to David: "I feel like David against Goliath," he declared, "but I got five rocks, and I haven't thrown one yet."

It is easy to recognize that Johnson is on to something when he asserts, in an earlier piece, "a certain amount of heterosexual loose play is accepted as a normal part of the church community—even or especially among its anointed" (1998: 401). The "black church," he claims, "tolerates the obvious paradox of [ministers'] behavior in a way that. . . makes heterosexuality [and heterosexual offenses] normal" (402) and much less problematic than same-sex relationships, even when the latter consist of monogamous unions. Although I am a bit uncomfortable with the generalization implied by Johnson's critique, a considerable amount of my own experience would seem to corroborate his assertions.

Many of the instrumentalists I have encountered in black churches do present particular challenges for pastors and laity. Instrumentalists have a tendency to appear almost apathetic during church meetings, having grown accustomed to the ritualized aspects of Sunday morning services: prayer, scripture readings, testimonies, slow songs, fast songs, the sermon with its high points, low points, offertories, the altar call, and so on and forth. . . The "musicians," as they are called, appear to have seen and heard it all, and not unlike instrumentalists in a variety of African and African diasporic ritual traditions (Marks 1982), they have come to accept emotional-spiritual detachment as a requisite quality of effective church musicianship. To be sure, there are lots of exceptions, yet the fact that most black church instrumentalists are men seems to reinforce the stereotype of the male musician who remains staid and steady—unfazed even amidst the most "heated" segments of praise and worship. As a church musician myself, I have found myself striving not to embody the character of the stereotypical instrumentalist.

Church members sometimes complain about organists and keyboardists who act as though by playing in church they are doing members of the congregation, if not the Lord Almighty himself, a favor. But more often, these instrumentalists appear to get a pass. Because of the musical service they render, it seems they are allowed to be slothful and slack in their obligation to walk the Christian walk. My sense is that many church musicians feel exempt and immune from pastoral calls to spiritual devotion. These feelings are often reinforced, in my view, by the extreme gratification they receive as a result of congregational responses to their musical talents. Certainly, a significant amount of bodily movement that is portrayed as "holy dancing" might simply be a willed response to a musically induced emotional high. But if not careful, musicians can start to feel that they are somehow indispensable to the move of the spirit, and this feeling leads, in turn, to a decrease in the amount of effort they put forth toward sincere praise and worship on a personal level. And there is no shortage of rumors about ministers of music who engage in sexual behavior that is "outside the bounds" of accepted Christian practice.

Historically speaking, a view of music as a potential source of moral decay is nothing new. As Philip Brett reminds us in a chapter from the influential edited volume, *Queering the Pitch*, "[M]usic has often been considered a dangerous substance, an agent of moral ambiguity always in danger of bestowing deviant status upon its practitioners" (1994: 11). He continues, "Nonverbal even when linked to words, physically arousing in its function as initiator of dance, and resisting attempts to endow it with, or discern in it precise meaning, it represents that part of our culture which is constructed as feminine and therefore dangerous" (12).

I think issues of gender and sexual identity are still underdiscussed in most African American Pentecostal churches, particularly the apostolic Pentecostal churches I know best. But thanks to the work done by prominent ministers such as T. D. Jakes and others, these issues have started to come up much more frequently in men's retreats. Retreats are occasions in which the men of a particular congregation or church district spend a weekend—generally out of town—by themselves to fellowship with one another, share testimonies of "deliverance," hear sermons and Bible classes geared towards the emotional challenges men face, and engage in friendly competitive events, such as basketball and chess. During praise and worship services, King David, the worshipping warrior, is often mentioned. However, there is a tender side to David that is less frequently emphasized among Pentecostal men. As a very young man, David develops an intimate bond with King Saul's son Jonathan. The hearts of David and Jonathan are said to have been "knit together" and my sense is that the obvious love that existed between them is a perennial source of discomfort for some Pentecostal men, many of whom preach defensively against any speculation that their relationship was predicated on feelings of romantic attraction. As one preacher I know explained during a Sunday morning sermon, "David and Jonathan were very close friends. And yes, they had an intimate relationship. *But wadn't no funny stuff goin' on!*" Funny stuff, in this context, refers of course to the homoerotic tension that many scholars of religion such as John Boswell (1980) have long detected in some biblical pairs—including also Ruth and Naomi, and Jesus and his "beloved disciple" John.

Over the past fifteen years, I have heard countless references to male gospel artists, church singers and instrumentalists that include the words, "He just has feminine ways." Such words have most often been spoken by women who are responding to a not-so-subtle suggestion that some gospel musician whose music they admire might be involved in queer sexual behavior of some sort. The list of male gospel artists who have been the subject of such rumors is quite long and includes such generally beloved figures as Richard Smallwood, Daryl Coley, Hezekiah Walker, and James Cleveland to name just a few. According to Michael Eric Dyson (2003), the black church has yet to deal openly with Cleveland's sexual identity or the rumors that he died from AIDS. I must state, as does Jason King in his 2000 article on Luther Vandross, that I can claim no insider knowledge of the sexual identities and orientations of various gospel artists. What I do claim to know is that the *discourses* surrounding these artists are informed by their visual and aural performances. And these musical performances have a profound impact on the ongoing constructions of gender that are negotiated among African American Pentecostals.

So what does it mean, exactly, when Pentecostal churchgoers insist that a male gospel artist has "feminine ways"? There are several ways in which musical performances often register as feminine or perhaps "queer" to church audiences. Video footage from a live concert in Los Angeles commercially released in 1991 by Keith Pringle and the Pentecostal Community Choir provides a case in point. It features soloist Brother Marshall Petty leading the song "Jesus Saves." Almost two decades have passed since this concert took place, and the perceptions of queerness have not remained static over the past two decades, but Petty's performance is indicative of the kind that many African American Pentecostals would now find problematic. Most disturbing for some is that Petty epitomizes what Johnson refers to as "one of the most enduring stereotypes in the black church. . . that of the flamboyant choir director, musician, or soloist" (2008: 184).

Petty's physical appearance adds to this perception. His eyebrows are thinly arched, his hair is "permed" (i.e., chemically straightened) and flattened against his head with what appear to be finger waves, and his extra-long fingernails are flawlessly manicured. After a couple of bars, the soloist begins—not by singing the lyrics, but, rather, with a bluesy close-lipped moan of pitches acclimating the listener to the minor tonality of the piece. Petty deliberately teases his audience, using a vocal style that is much different from the full-throated delivery of Fred Hammond. As Petty descends the minor scale, his mouth opens and he reveals the breathy timbre he will employ, sometimes with a sensuous growl, throughout the song. He begins, "We have heard the joyful sound. Spread the tidings all around," placing just such a growl on the phrase "all around" and on non-referential vowel sounds he intones between the first and second verses.

By the song's halfway point, Petty has deployed an arsenal of melismatic runs, soaring to the upper extremities of a vocal range that seems to match his arched eyebrows, long fingernails, and processed hair. At times, he parachutes downward in virtuosic fashion to reintroduce the husky baritone timbre with which he began. His vocal stylings register for me as sexually ambiguous on a sonic level; they contrast quite remarkably with Fred Hammond's rendition of "When the Spirit of the Lord," in which sensuality and theatricality take a beat seat to an aesthetic of musical muscularity. It is when the sonic aspects of Petty's presentation are combined with the visual appearance of his performance that an interpretation of it as something other than "straight" becomes seemingly unavoidable. The soloist's use of flowing hands and arms are what some heterosexual male and female viewers referred to as a "dead giveaway," as is a moment in the song when Petty twirls his index finger high above his head to dramatize the lyrics, "He'll pick you up and turn you around."

When I played the video of Petty's rendition for my 24-year-old niece, a recent convert to Pentecostal Christianity, she exclaimed, "You'd have to be crazy not to know that that person is gay!" She clearly saw his gayness as a negative attribute, especially for a *gospel* singer; and her reaction is similar to others I have received from Pentecostal women: "He can sing, but I don't *know*. . . Something ain't right. . ." An interesting variation on this sometimes comes from women who make halting comments such as, "I don't know. . . I think he might be. . . you know. . . But he sure can sing!" The verbs "play" or "direct" (as in direct choirs) are often substituted for sing, but the point remains the same: There is a certain tolerance of male musicians perceived to be effeminate or gay within many Pentecostal congregations.

Michael Eric Dyson laments what he sees as the exploitation of gay musicians in African American churches: "One of the most painful scenarios of black church life is repeated Sunday after

Sunday with little notice or collective outrage. A black minister will preach a sermon railing against sexual ills, especially homosexuality. At the close of the sermon, a soloist, who everybody knows is gay, will rise to perform a moving number, as the preacher extends an invitation to visitors to join the church. The soloist is, in effect, being asked to sing, and to sign, his theological death sentence" (2009: 244).[3] Dyson's notion that "*everybody knows*" the soloist is gay is remarkable to me. It reminds me of Philip Brett's discussion of the "open secret": "We know perfectly well that the secret is known, but nonetheless we must persist however ineptly in guarding it" (2009: 12).

Perhaps certain gospel artists remain popular due to an ethic of empathy that allows or even encourages the expression of queer identities that disrupt a strict masculine-feminine binary. However, this ethic stands to lose its sociopolitical efficacy if or when audiences and congregants are confronted with undesired and unequivocal proof that what has been suspected is indeed the truth. Indeed, that "certain tolerance" to which I referred has strings attached. As Horace Griffin reminds us, "While black church leaders and congregants tolerate a gay presence in choirs, congregations, and even the pulpit as long as gays cooperate and stay 'in their closeted place,' gays quickly experience the limits of this tolerance if they request the same recognition as their heterosexual counterparts" (2006: 20–21).

African American churchgoers often retain a sense of togetherness because their unity as brothers and sisters in Christ so often depends on a refusal to pass judgment. "If you can't say something nice, don't say anything at all." In this context, of course, "nice" is almost always taken to mean "unambiguously heterosexual." Indeed, what is understood is that "accusing" one's brother in the Lord of being gay would most certainly *not* be a nice thing to do. Instead of *affirming* the contributory presence of queer individuals in the church, and instead of risking the need to wrestle with the theological chaos that might result should such affirmation become contagious, Pentecostal men and women most often opt to be silent. I wonder, though, whether there is any silver lining to this silence—whether silence in these contexts may even be powerful. Rather than creating emotional or spiritual distance among black churchgoers, perhaps it creates what Jason King calls a "space of inclusion rather than exclusion in between contradictory interpretations of cultural texts" (430).

Sources

Alston, Joshua. "The Black Church, Homophobia, and Pastor Eddie Long." *Newsweek*. September 23, 2010. http://www.newsweek.com/2010/09/23/the-black-church-homophobia-and-pastor-eddie-long. html

Boswell, John. *Christianity, Social Tolerance, and Homosexuality: Gay People in Western Europe from the Beginning of the Christian Era to the Fourteenth Century.* Chicago: University of Chicago Press, 1980.

Brett, Philip. "Musicality, Essentialism, and the Closet." In *Queering the Pitch: The New Gay and Lesbian Musicology.* Edited by Philip Brett, Elizabeth Wood, and Gary C. Thomas. New York: Routledge, 1994.

Butler, Melvin L. "'I Will Sing like David Sang': Negotiating Gender, Faith, and Performance in African American Pentecostal Churches." Paper presented at the Annual Meeting of the Society for Ethnomusicology. Honolulu: November 16, 2006.

Dyson, Michael Eric. "Homotextualities: The Bible, Sexual Ethics, and the Theology of Homoeroticism." In *Open Mike: Reflections on Philosophy, Race, Sex, Culture, and Religion*. New York: Basic Books, 2003.

———. *Can You Hear Me Now?: The Inspiration, Wisdom, and Insight of Michael Eric Dyson*. New York: Basic Civitas Books, 2009.

Finley, Stephen C. "'Real Men Love Jesus?': Homoeroticism and the Absence of Black Heterosexual Male Participation in African American Churches." *CSSR Bulletin* 36, no.1 (February 2007): 16–19.

Gordon, Lewis R. *Existentia Africana: Understanding Africana Existential Thought*. New York: Routledge, 2000.

Griffin, Horace. *Their Own Receive Them Not: African American Lesbians and Gays in Black Churches*. Cleveland: Pilgrim, 2006.

Hinson, Glenn. *Fire in My Bones: Transcendence and the Holy Spirit in African American Gospel*. Philadelphia: University of Pennsylvania Press, 2000.

Johnson, E. Patrick. "Feeling the Spirit in the Dark: Expanding Notions of the Sacred in the African American Gay Community." *Callaloo* 21, no. 2 (Spring 1998) 399–416.

———. *Sweet Tea: Black Gay Men of The South*. Chapel Hill: University of North Carolina, 2008.

King, Jason. "Any Love: Silence, Theft, and Rumor in the Work of Luther Vandross." *Callaloo* 23, no. 1 (Winter 2000) 422–47.

Marks, Morton. "'You Can't Sing Unless You're Saved': Reliving the Call in Gospel Music." In *African Religious Groups and Beliefs: Papers in Honor of William R. Bascom*. Edited by Simon Ottenberg, 305–31. Meerut, India: Archana, 1982.

Audio and Video Recordings

Hammond, Fred and Radical for Christ. *The Spirit of David*. Audio CD. Verity Records, 1996.

Keith Pringle and the Pentecostal Community Choir. Video Recording. VHS. Savoy Records, 1991.

Notes

1. An obvious case in point is the well-publicized scandal involving Atlanta-based televangelist Bishop Eddie Long and his alleged same-sex relations with teens under his pastoral care. Also, the cover of a recent *Newsweek* declares, "Man Up! The Traditional Male Is an Endangered Species. It's Time to Rethink Masculinity" (September 27, 2010).
2. See, for example, http://www.cbn.com/cbnmusic/artists/Hammond_Fred.aspx.
3. E. Patrick Johnson also comments on this contradictory attitude toward gay musicians, noting that the black church "exploits the creative talents of its gay members even as it condemns their gayness, while also providing a nurturing space to hone those same talents" (2008: 183).

42
Work the Works: The Role of African American Women in the Development of Contemporary Gospel

Tammy L. Kernodle

I must work the works of him who sent me while it's day, for when the night is come the time for work will be done away. Would you be willing to work for Jesus any time and every day? He'll reward you when he comes to take his bride away.

—*Danniebelle Hall, "Work the Works"*

The popularity of black gospel music has expanded beyond the grass roots network of churches and small concert venues that powered the genre to new heights in the 1950s and early 1960s. Today, gospel has earned a distinct place on mainstream black radio, and gospel videos have moved from being shown on Sunday mornings between 11 a.m. and noon and are now played in rotation with Missy Elliott, Tupac Shakur, and Mariah Carey on BET and VH1. Recent marketing strategies that include concert tours, music videos, e-mail listservs, downloadable ring tones, concert DVDs, and movies have placed the genre's profits well above other forms of popular music. At the center of this popularity is a creative community of singers, composers, producers, instrumentalists, and independent and major records companies that have drawn from myriad musical styles and production methods.

More important is gospel's meteoric evolution to a form that today is emblematic of the social, economic, and musical beliefs of the urban identities and theological perspectives that developed in the generations that followed the Civil Rights Movement. The term *contemporary gospel*, much like its counterpart *traditional gospel*, has served as an umbrella term that represents the stylistic characteristics and production methods that have defined gospel music from circa 1968 forward. Turn on gospel radio today or download the newest gospel single, and you will hear a complex arrangement of sampled bass lines, explosive rhythms, and intricate vocal interactions that are more reflective of the sound identities that each performer, production team, and record company has created than one singular sound. With the growing influence that R&B, jazz, Western art music, and hip hop have had on contemporary gospel, producers such as Donald Lawrence, Kevin Bond, Kurt Carr, and J. Moss have become as notable if not as popular as the performers.

While the criticism against "secular-sounding" gospel music has grown, and fears that the church has "lost" gospel to the world are nurtured in many traditional circles, the influence of the music—and its accompanying images of dancing choirs, glamorized and highly coiffed purveyors in the newest and hippest fashions—on younger and secular audiences has not lessened.

Central to understanding the history and development of contemporary gospel is the role that gender has played in its basic practice and conceptualization. While black men have continued to hold important roles as composers, producers, instrumentalists, and CEOs in gospel music, women have shaped the performance aesthetic of the genre. It was, after all, the creative textural interpretation and vocal dexterity of female vocalists that gave Edwin Hawkins, Walter Hawkins, and Andraé Crouch their signature sounds. Today, artists such as Yolanda Adams, CeCe Winans, Shirley Caesar, and the Clark Sisters have defined and in some cases redefined the sound and image of contemporary gospel and placed it in the realm of mainstream popularity that continues in the vein of singers Mahalia Jackson, Sister Rosetta Tharpe, and Clara Ward, who spread gospel beyond the boundaries of black churches and popularized it on concert stages and in nightclubs during the 1940s and 1950s.

Framing the present discussion around the post-Civil Rights generations (1969–present), specific performers, and the performance approaches each has introduced or popularized, I consider the contributions of African American women to the development of contemporary gospel music.[1] In an effort to bring clearer understanding to the ever-evolving concept of "contemporary," this discussion extends beyond the work of previous scholars, which has focused on the contemporary gospel sound of the late 1960s and early 1970s. For this purpose, I examine the years 1969 through 2005 as three stylistic periods: (1) 1969–1985; (2) 1985–1994; and (3) 1994–2005. These years are, of course, approximations, representing dramatic stylistic shifts in gospel music and building on previous scholars' definition of contemporary gospel.[2]

The First Era (1969-1985)

It is a commonly held notion among scholars, critics, and performers that the transition to the contemporary gospel era began in 1969 with the recording of a revamped version of the Baptist hymn "Oh Happy Day" by the Northern California State Youth Choir.[3] What began as a fund raising initiative for the regional choir soon became a hit on radio stations in the Bay Area and a musical landmark. The initial goal was to make five hundred copies for the group to sell on the streets. But when a disc jockey at KSAN in the Bay Area began playing "Oh Happy Day" during his midday show, it became one of the most requested songs. The recording earned a listing on *Billboard's* pop charts, reaching the top five, and in time sold an unprecedented one million copies.

The visionary who had conceived of the fund-raising idea and who had crafted the sound of the song was pianist Edwin Hawkins. He and his younger brother Walter had become staples in the Bay Area's gospel scene. But neither had predicted that their grassroots effort would propel them to overnight stardom and a five-thousand-dollar recording contract. The song opens with electric bass and piano establishing the simple, but rhythmic vamp that returns several times throughout the performance. Then a husky, alto voice enters with the first lines of text, "Oh, happy day." The choir's subsequent response and the building antiphony between lead, choir, and instruments, which climaxes at the bridge, "He taught me how to watch, fight, and pray," foreshadows the younger generation's reconceptualization of gospel. The song rose to number four on *Billboard's* pop charts and number two in England (Harris 1999).

Gospel's crossover to mainstream audiences, which had begun years earlier with Mahalia Jackson and Clara Ward's appearances at the Newport Jazz Festival, gained momentum with "Oh Happy Day." While the preceding generation of gospel performers had created a number of stylistic approaches that in time had come to define the sound of 1960s soul music, especially the music of Aretha Franklin, Ray Charles, and Sam Cooke, "Oh Happy Day" reflected the complete opposite. Hawkins' arrangement was a combination of Sly Stone, James Brown, and the saintly voices and rhythms of his Pentecostal upbringing. But the revolutionary nature of the Northern California State Youth Choir was not simply in the sound but also in the group's attire, which included bell-bottoms and Afros. The group's members, female and male, exchanged the clean-cut popadours and press and curls of the previous generation for that which was defining the younger mainstream black culture and the Black Power movement's "black is beautiful" rhetoric.

Despite criticism from traditionally minded church folks, "Oh Happy Day" proved to be only the beginning of a stronger, more audible marriage of the secular and the sacred, delineating a new style of gospel. Although many such performances concentrated on the funk-inspired bass line and instrumentation, the soul-inspired vocals were the biggest draw. One of the first voices of contemporary gospel was not Edwin Hawkins, although he is often thought to have been the architect of the sound, but Dorothy Combs Morrison, the soloist on "Oh Happy Day." Her earthy vocals were more in the vein of Mavis Staples and Aretha Franklin than Mahalia Jackson, and her exclamations of "Good God, my Lord," spoke more to the rich emotional energy of soul music than the sanctified shouts of the previous artists.

"Oh Happy Day" inspired a number of debates concerning the direction in which gospel was going. Despite often spirited conversations about too much of the "world" showing up in the music, the record resonated strongly with younger audiences, who in the wake of the Black Power movement had become more disapproving of what many deemed outdated theological perspectives and practices. Edwin Hawkins' success birthed a number of new voices in gospel music, most notably, his brother Walter and peer Andraé Crouch. Coming from similar Holiness/Pentecostal backgrounds, these two composers expanded the concept of gospel hymns beyond those written by Charles Tindley, Lucie Campbell, Thomas Dorsey, and others.

Crouch, in particular, went beyond the funk influences that Edwin Hawkins had introduced and infused rock elements into his gospel compositions. Many mainstream black churches rejected the contemporary gospel sound, but Crouch and Walter Hawkins managed to cultivate a black church audience. Both attracted black and white sacred and secular audiences, and Crouch even found acceptance in white rock and jazz circles. According to gospel scholar Horace Boyer (1985: 128), Crouch attracted a large following in part because he created a "split-compositional" personality. Crouch's compositions included "The Blood Will Never Lose Its Power" and "Soon and Very Soon," modernized hymns that served as extensions of the works of previous schools of gospel songwriters, with lyrics that preach transcendence over everyday problems and issues through faith in God. But he also wrote contemporary compositions, such as "I Got the Best," that reflected the fusion of disco, rock, and gospel. Crouch served as composer, pianist, and oftentimes, lead vocalist, employing a number of musicians and singers who helped bring to life his complex and sometimes controversial compositions. His most notable group was called The Disciples, founded in 1965, which aided in Crouch's global gospel takeover during the 1970s. One of the prominent female voices of the group was pianist and composer Danniebelle Hall.

Born in 1938 in Pittsburgh, Pennsylvania, Hall established a formidable career as a singer, pianist, and composer. Critics often compared her to Roberta Flack because of the intimate way in which she sang and accompanied herself, but in the gospel community, she had few peers. She learned to play the piano at age three and as an adolescent formed the group The Jones Sisters with her two younger sisters. She came to national attention in 1969 when she formed The Danniebelles. The group toured internationally during the early 1970s and eventually recorded an album. The Danniebelles achieved international fame when they toured with the World Crusade Ministries, but the group disbanded a few years later, and Hall joined Andraé Crouch and The Disciples. Danniebelle was the featured soloist on a number of Crouch's classic hits, including "Take Me Back" and "Soon and Very Soon."

Although her stint with The Disciples brought her to more prominence, it was Hall's solo work that made her a favorite of gospel performers and audiences. She composed or arranged most of the music found on the nine albums she would produce over the next twenty years. Her music contributed considerably to the Sunday morning repertoire of black and white churches. Songs like "Ordinary People" and her arrangement of Dottie Rambo's "I Go to the Rock" from a 1977 live album remain gospel standards. Her repertoire ranged from blues-tinged traditional songs to pop-influenced tunes. Hall was also admired in gospel circles for her musical settings of biblical passages. Her 1975 album *This Moment* features several such works. She remained active in gospel music, mentoring younger artists and performing until 1995. Stricken with breast cancer and complications from diabetes, Hall stopped performing and concentrated on recovery. Despite all efforts, Hall died in 2000.

After Dorothy Combs Morrison left the Northern California State Youth Choir shortly after the success of "Oh Happy Day" to pursue a solo career, Edwin Hawkins found other voices to fill the void. Renamed the Edwin Hawkins Singers, the group began using Lynnette Hawkins, Edwin's sister, as a soloist, in addition to a young soprano named Tramaine Davis. Despite his efforts, Edwin never recreated the success he had had with "Oh Happy Day." His brother, Walter, however, would become one of the most important gospel composers of the late twentieth century. His songs were modern hymns, or as Boyer (1985) suggests, "gospel ballads," with memorable melodies and lyrics of praise and supplication that focus on the everyday experiences of Christians. Walter's importance as a song writer was solidified with songs such as "Be Grateful," "Goin' Up Yonder," and "Jesus Christ Is the Way." His compositions, popular with audiences, have also found their way into church services across the country. He found a muse in Tramaine Davis, and over the next twenty years, the two collaborated on and produced some of gospel's most notable and memorable songs.

Tramaine Davis (b. 1951) developed musically in the gospel music community of the San Francisco Bay Area. Her mother, the late Lois Davis, was a gospel singer, and her grandfather, the Bishop E. E. Cleveland, was pastor at the Ephesians Church of God in Christ, where Tramaine reportedly began singing at age four. She was greatly influenced by Mahalia Jackson and often cites a 1961 concert of the famed singer as a major source of early inspiration. On that night at the Oakland Auditorium, "Mahalia wore this glorious, white choir robe, and she put everything into each word she'd sing," she recalled. "When she got down on her knees to sing 'The Lord's Prayer,' we were all crying. I just can't tell you how beautiful and inspirational it truly was" (Roos 1997). In addition to Jackson, Davis also cited Dionne Warwick, Gladys Knight, and the Staple Singers as influences.

While a member of the gospel group The Heavenly Tones, ten-year-old Davis recorded her first single, "He's All Right." Two years later, the group came to the attention of the Rev. James Cleveland, who produced their next recording. When the Heavenly Tones accepted an offer to tour with Sly and the Family Stone in 1965, Davis remained behind, deciding that finishing her education was more important. She later joined Andraé Crouch and the Disciples, with whom she sang for eleven months. In 1969, shortly after her high school graduation, she joined the Edwin Hawkins Singers (then the Northern California State Youth Choir) and participated in the historic recording of "Oh Happy Day." In 1970, she traveled all over the world with the group and became close friends with Walter Hawkins, who served as the group's pianist. Hawkins and Davis developed a close relationaship and were married in 1970.

In 1973, Walter Hawkins, following in his brother's steps, entered ministry and started the Love Center Church in Oakland, California. Davis (now Hawkins) became one of the leading vocalists at the church, where the congregation was treated to her husband's newest compositions each week. In 1975, with an eighteen-hundred-dollar loan from his mother-in-law, Walter and Tramaine Hawkins returned to her home church, Ephesians, where they recorded the live album *Love Alive* with the Love Center Choir. The album spent several months on *Billboard*'s Top 40 gospel chart and yielded the single "Goin' Up Yonder." The album also became a mainstay on *Billboard*'s Gospel Top 40 for three consecutive years, and it was one of the decade's biggest-selling gospel albums ("Veteran Gospel Singer" 1998). "Goin' Up Yonder" remains one of Tramaine Hawkins' signature songs and a Sunday morning standard in both black and white churches. The *Love Alive* album was followed by *Jesus Christ Is the Way* (1977) and *Love Alive II* (1978), which sold more than three hundred thousand copies.

Tramaine Hawkins' elastic mezzo-soprano voice, coupled with Walter's strong writing, galvanized the gospel music industry throughout the late 1970s and early 1980s. Her clear voice was unlike that of any vocalist who had preceded her. While many gospel performers used vibrato and other guttural effects to create a signature sound, Hawkins used hardly any vibrato. She also could move without much effort from the warm tones of her lower register to the brilliant notes of the high. Like Ward, Jackson, and many of the great gospel women, Hawkins' interpretation of the lyrics and her ability to elevate the simplest phrase to a higher level drew audiences to her performances. Her phrasing was such that with a small melisma or unique combination of notes, she could highlight words that the listener may have ignored. For example, in her performance of the gospel ballad "Changed," from the album *Love Alive*, accompanied by Hammond B3, piano, drums, and a small ensemble of solo voices and a larger choir, Hawkins begins subtly with the text, "a change, a change has come over me." Each phrase is separated by the small ensemble's completion of the statement in close harmonies, reminiscent of more traditional gospel groups. The emotional energy increases with each verse and reaches a crescendo when Hawkins gets to the chorus that begins, "He changed my life complete. And now I sit at my Savior's feet." As she begins to interpolate the text and melody, the background voices push the emotional level further with the response of "changed." As the antiphony continues, the dynamics, level of improvisation, and text interpolation grow, and the audience and choir begin to clap. The climax occurs as she proclaims, "I'm not what I want to be, I'm not what I used to be."

In the early 1980s, Tramaine Hawkins launched a solo career with a lucrative recording contract with Light Records, but she wanted to take her music in a different direction than her previous work on the *Love Alive* albums. Her 1980 solo debut, *Tramaine Hawkins*, stayed on *Billboard*'s Gospel Top 10 throughout the year and into 1981. But despite a series of successful recordings with Light, Hawkins and the company had different expectations for her music and parted amicably. She sought out record companies that would embrace her evolving musical personality and message. Although she had served primarily as a purveyor of her husband's compositions, Hawkins believed that they were still not reaching a segment of the population that she felt desperately needed to be reached. She recounts the experience as follows:

> I did some seeking out of record companies. I leaned toward going some place where my desire to make gospel music that could reach the masses could be realized. I don't like the term "crossover," it paints a picture that you're leaving something to do another kind of music. No matter what I sing, or what the accompaniment is, I always sing about the Lord, about what I believe, about what I live for. I'd gone to a number of record companies because I had a desire to try and create gospel music that could reach young people but, more often than not, they didn't include any young people. The record labels just assumed that the secular audience didn't want what we were offering—that it wouldn't appeal to them. ("Tramaine Hawkins" 1989)

In 1984, Hawkins signed with A&M Records, which brought her the mainstream exposure she desired. However, in 1985, her successful standing with gospel audiences was compromised when A&M released the single "Fall Down." This dance-friendly single intensified the debate regarding the sacredness of contemporary gospel. Immediately, the gospel community split over the issues of its appropriateness as the record climbed its way to the top of *Billboard*'s dance music chart and was featured regularly in dance clubs. Some critics argued that the song was "just too secular" to be considered gospel and blamed A&M's marketing strategy for the reaction it received from some within the gospel community. Others felt that the song took gospel to audiences who would not have otherwise readily embraced it.

Hawkins found herself in a precarious situation and has often recounted the instance as being one of the most painful moments in her life. "With the right moves and care," she recalled, "they [A&M] could have had the best of both worlds. Instead they targeted it for the dance clubs with no interest in embracing the gospel market. They loved the song's beat, but they didn't even consider things—like the lyrics—from a spiritual side. So it never got the exposure it deserved" (Roos 1997). In the months following the single's initial release, Hawkins felt that she had been abandoned by most within the gospel community, which only a decade earlier had heralded her as the heir to Mahalia Jackson's throne. "There were few, if any, other artists who were mixing an inspirational message with a dance beat," she recalled. "It felt like I was totally alone" ("Tramaine Hawkins" 1989). But in time, the combination of dance rhythms, infectious melodies, and inspirational lyrics would become the formula for contemporary gospel.

Although their marriage dissolved in the late 1980s, Tramaine and Walter Hawkins still worked together well into the early twenty-first century.

In the tradition of the Caravans, the Sallie Martin Singers, and the Barrett Sisters, the Detroit-born Clark Sisters also contributed to the shifting sound of gospel music. Reared in the city that had given birth to a strong jazz and blues scene and the musical dynasty of Motown, sisters Jacky, Denise, Elbernita ("Twinkie"), Dorinda, and Karen came to prominence during the Midnight Musicales at the Church of God in Christ (COGIC) conventions. Their mother, Dr. Mattie Moss Clark, molded the young women musically and spiritually and helped them become one of contemporary gospel's most influential groups.

By the 1970s, Mattie Moss Clark had already earned a place of distinction in gospel music circles. In similar fashion to Lucie Campbell and Thomas Dorsey in the 1920s, she had redefined gospel through denominational musical circles. Born in 1928, Clark was raised in the Methodist Church and began piano lessons at age six. She attended Selma University for one year before relocating to Detroit to live with a sister. Within a year of her arrival, she discovered COGIC, joined the church, and became director of the choir at Bailey Temple COGIC (Boyer 1985: 126). Her compositional and musical abilities led to her appointment as the music director of the Southwest Jurisdiction of COGIC. She later became the international president of the denomination's music department. In this role, she directly mentored a number of talented singers and musicians, including Walter Hawkins, Ranee Allen, and Vanessa Bell Armstrong. "She was tough," recalls gospel singer LaShun Pace-Rhodes. "Once as a girl, she called me up to do a solo. I was so nervous and shy, I couldn't get the words out. After a few minutes, she took the mike, handed it to my sister, and told me to sit down. The next time I was up to do a solo, I sang that song" ("In the Spirit" 1994: 52).

Clark became a dominant force behind the choir movement in the COGIC denomination and is credited with introducing three-part harmony to the gospel arrangement. In 1958, she became the first person to record a gospel choir, and in her lifetime, she penned more than seven hundred songs, including "Climbing Up the Mountain," "Salvation Is Free," and "Foot Stomping." Frequently asked to train choirs, soloists, and musicians, she founded the Detroit-based Clark Conservatory of

Music in 1979. The conservatory, which is still functioning, offers vocal and instrumental lessons, as well as music theory. Despite Clark's twenty albums and numerous accolades, perhaps her greatest contribution and lasting legacy to gospel was her work grooming The Clark Sisters. From an early age, Clark instructed her daughters not only musically, but also in the proper way in which to conduct themselves on and off stage. "Mama would wake us up in the middle of the night and tell us, 'I've got a song! Come on and help me sing it,'" recalls Dorinda. "She'd be taping it on an old reel-to-reel recorder and she was serious about it. She'd say 'Girl, wake up now. Here's your part and you better get it right.' That's the reason our harmonies are so close, because of all that singing in the middle of the night. And because we're sisters, of course" ("Clark Kin's" 1990; Clark-Cole).

By the late 1960s, the sisters were appearing at area churches and the COGIC annual convention. In 1973, the group recorded its first album, *Jesus Has a Lot to Give*, on a local label owned by their uncle, Bill Moss. The record had some regional success but went virtually unnoticed nationally. The following year, the recording *Mattie Moss Clark Presents the Clark Sisters* also created much interest in the Detroit area. The two albums produced the classic songs "Something Worth Living For," "If You Can't Take It," and the group's signature song, "Hallelujah," which they frequently performed at the COGIC Midnight Musicales. In 1976, the group came to national prominence when they signed to the Sound of Gospel label, founded by fellow Detroiter Thomas Whitfield. Clark subsequently turned the creative and musical control of the group over to Elbernita, commonly known as "Twinkie" and also known as the "Queen of the Hammond B-3." Twinkie's songwriting and playing abilities came to define the group's sound. The combination of innovative instrumental vamps and vocal harmonies propelled the group to national success.

Between 1976 and 1977, the group released four albums on the Sound of Gospel label, but widespread acclaim in both sacred and secular circles did not come until 1981, when the group released *Is My Living in Vain?* The live album remained on *Billboard*'s gospel charts for over a year and peaked at number one in October 1981. It produced hits such as "Pure Gold," "Expect Your Miracle," and the title song, "Is My Living in Vain?" which was so popular that it was covered years later by the R&B girl group Xscape. The Clark Sisters' follow-up recording, *You Brought the Sunshine*, was equally as popular. In 1981, the title tune became the first contemporary gospel song to be played on mainstream radio.[4] According to Dorinda Clark-Cole, Frankie Crocker, a disc jockey on WBLS in New York, "heard the song and put it on the turntable and people just kept calling in. We got a lot of flak from the church because people felt we shouldn't reach that audience. They felt we were church girls and should have stayed in church" (Collins and Harris 2002).

The Clark Sisters provided a blueprint for both sacred and secular vocalists with their intricate harmonies, swinging leads, melismatic melodies, and infectious accompaniment.[5] Today, a range of artists, from Mariah Carey to Faith Evans, have credited members of the group, especially Karen Clark (Sheard), with inspiring their style and sound. While the 1980s proved to be a decade of success for the Clark Sisters, the next decade would bring significant changes but continued success.

Second Phase (1985–1994)

When Tramaine Hawkins released "Fall Down" in 1985, she had no idea that she was aiding contemporary gospel in its transition from the funk- and soul-influenced styles of the previous era to a more dance-oriented and hip hop-inflected sound that would define the late 1980s and early 1990s gospel sound. The eight-minute song featured techno-influenced beats and used a number of production techniques that at the time were associated with the post-disco dance culture. Hawkins' gospel-laced vocals remained unaffected by the song's accompaniment, but the infectious nature of the beat was unlike anything previously heard on gospel or secular radio. While the gospel music of Walter Hawkins and Andraé Crouch had alluded to funk, jazz, and rock, "Fall Down" was essentially soul and techno, funk, and disco blended with gospel lyrics. Although some within the gospel music industry accused Tramaine Hawkins of further obscuring the already-blurred lines between the sacred and the secular, she stated that her "primary thought . . . was to get gospel music mainstreamed and have that kind of music being played on secular stations that you could hear around the clock, not only at 6 o'clock in the morning, where gospel usually is in this country" (Willman 1986: 5).

Tramaine Hawkins' successful crossover hit was followed with the album *The Search Is Over*. Working extensively with producer Robert Byron Wright, Hawkins perfected gospel's new crossover, dance-oriented sound. The second single, "In the Morning Time," not only appealed to black secular audiences but also found a home on white Christian radio stations. The criticism leveled at Hawkins was extensive but limited to traditional gospel circles. Despite the criticism, she viewed "Fall Down" and "In the Morning Time" as the embodiment of her desire to create music that would appeal to diverse audiences. They also were not the end of Hawkins' experimentation. In 1992, she collaborated with West Coast rapper MC Hammer, singing lead on his revamped version of "Do Not Pass Me By," from his *Too Legit to Quit* album.

After a short hiatus, Hawkins signed in 1994 with Columbia Records and released the album *To a Higher Place*. The label called the album its most significant debut by a gospel artist since Mahalia Jackson was signed in 1954. The album's sound was semiclassical with pop overtones. A full orchestra accompanied Hawkins on a number of tracks, and she explored the limits of digital technology when she sang "I Found the Answer" with Mahalia Jackson, who recorded the song in 1959. It marked the first time in gospel that such a feat was attempted. Hawkins explains how the recording came to be:

It was quite amazing to put that piece together. My manager and I spent a long time looking for a song of Mahalia's that was conducive to us singing as a duet,... one with the proper tempo and melody. "I Found the Answer" was just the right one. Then we had to avoid the strong temptation to try and update it, because to mess with her extraordinary, magical voice would be a tragedy. So we stayed as true as we possibly could to the spirit and timbre of the original. During the actual recording, everything just clicked, and I felt something down in the pit of my stomach. Let me tell you, we all got goose bumps. It was such a spiritual experience. (Roos 1997)

Throughout the 1990s, Hawkins continued to produce noteworthy recordings. Today, she is affectionately known as "Mother" because she more than any other artist served as the midwife to the contemporary gospel movement. Artists such as The Winans and their siblings Benjamin (BeBe) and Priscilla (CeCe) took this marriage of secular and sacred, gospel and dance music, even further.

CeCe Winans emerged on the Detroit music scene in the 1970s when she participated in the family's annual Christmas concerts. Although not considered a standout talent at the time, she would prove to be one of the central voices of the second and third periods of the contemporary gospel movement. She and brother BeBe came to national prominence in 1981 when they joined the PTL Singers, which was associated with the megaministry of Jim and Tammy Faye Bakker. During her three-year experience with the television ministry, the teenaged CeCe developed as a singer. She and BeBe became the highlight of the weekly television show with their rendition of "Lord Lift Us Up." The highly requested song became the basis of their first album, *Lord Lift Us Up*, which was recorded independently with PTL Ministries in 1984 (Winans 1999). CeCe left PTL soon afterward and returned to Detroit to marry Alvin Love.

Months after the birth of her first child, she and BeBe signed with Sparrow Records and recorded the single "I.O.U. Me." Defined by synthesized beats and accompaniment, the song features ambiguous lyrics that make no reference to God but discuss a deep love between two entities. With lyrics that state, "When I saw you / I knew it was me you came to find / By the smile that was on your face," listeners were hard-pressed to believe that it was a gospel song and not an R&B love song. But it garnered considerable attention and proved to be one of the many popular songs on their debut album, *Introducing BeBe and CeCe Winans* (1987). CeCe earned a Grammy Award for Best Soul Gospel Performance Female for her performance on "For Always," and "I.O.U. Me" became a hit with R&B audiences.

A year later, the duo released *Heaven*, which became the first gospel record to reach the Top 10 on *Billboard*'s "Hot R&B" chart since 1972, when Aretha Franklin's *Amazing Grace* achieved the same distinction (Dyson 1992). The album, which featured then pop superstar Whitney Houston on "Hold Up the Light," received wide acclaim. BeBe and CeCe received Grammy Awards for Best

Gospel Vocal Performance, as well as an NAACP Image Award, six Stellar Awards, a Soul Train Music Award, and four Dove Awards. Their 1991 release *Different Lifestyles* was the first album to reach number 1 on the *Billboard* R&B charts. It was also number 1 on the gospel charts, rated platinum by the Recording Industry Association of America, and awarded a Grammy for Best Contemporary Soul Gospel Album.

Despite these accolades, many critics and traditionally minded church folk took issue with the duo's sound, with their booming bass lines and synthesized riffs, which the critics felt catered to the tastes of secular listeners. They interpreted the duo's use of ambiguous pronouns not as blatant references to divinity, but as a dilution of the gospel, bringing into question the duo's real motives. As a Chicago-based disc jockey argued: "[T]he horns and the synthesizers override the message, and because of the instrumentation the message is vague and void. It gets lost in the beat and you end up having a shindig on Sunday morning. Whereas traditional gospel talks about the love of God, contemporary gospel music wants to make love to God" (Dyson 1992). CeCe Winans (1999: 172) wrote in her autobiography that when the duo started singing, they anticipated the enthusiastic support of the church.

> We thought the church would be happy that we were spreading the gospel message with a sound with which youth could identify, but we were wrong. We were accused of selling out gospel, of not being Christian enough, of not loving God, and of just being after the money. Those were really hard. Some of our worst criticism has come from those in the church. All we have ever wanted to do was to sing songs that were in our hearts, songs that ministered to and encouraged people, and songs that glorified the power and presence of the Lord.

While the debate as to whether contemporary gospel was too jazzy or secular to be called gospel raged within music circles, BeBe and CeCe continued to experiment with the newest innovations in production and music videos. The popularity of their music with secular audiences spawned the term *inspirational* to denote what some viewed as a new subgenre of contemporary gospel, one that crossed over to secular audiences with a message of hope but without scriptural and divinity references. The duo toured throughout the early 1990s and appeared on a range of television shows, from *The Tonight Show with Jay Leno* to *Sesame Street*. But they, as well as their siblings who made up The Winans, were criticized continually for their musical experimentation.

Vickie Winans, sister-in-law of BeBe and CeCe, also contributed to the development of contemporary gospel and experienced the full wrath of traditional gospel circles. Born Vickie Bowman in Detroit, Winans began singing gospel in the church choir at age eight. She came to national prominence while hosting *Singsation*, a syndicated gospel television show. In 1977, she met Marvin Winans, then a member of the Testimonial Singers (later known as The Winans) at a church concert. Within six months, the two were married (Davis 1992).

Vickie Winans became more involved in the gospel music industry in the early 1980s, when she sang with BeBe and CeCe Winans in a group called Winans II. Vickie launched her solo career in 1985 with the album *Be Encouraged*. At first, some thought that she was relying on the Winans name, but her signature song from the album, "We Shall Behold Him," changed those opinions. "[It] was the very first song that really got me out, helped me stand on my own two feet," she recalls (Davis 1992).

With subsequent albums, *Total Victory* (1989), *The Lady* (1991), and *Vickie Winans* (1994), she established herself as one of the powerhouse female vocalists in gospel. But all of her success would be tarnished when in 1994, she performed at the Tenth Annual Gospel Music Stellar Awards. Winans took to the stage with modern dancers to accompany her then-current single, "Don't Throw Your Life Away," from the album *The Lady*. While the inclusion of the dancers was intended to be an artistic addition to her vocalizations, the gospel community interpreted it quite differently. For some, this was the proverbial "last straw" in the steady move to further secularize gospel. Winans recalled later that the moment she walked off stage, she knew she had committed the biggest mistake of her career:

> I remember CeCe coming over to me and saying something to the effect of, Oh, Lord, they're going to put us all out of the church. . . After it aired I started hearing everybody calling what I'd done a shame before God and that people were offended. They say that controversy sells. Well, mine didn't. Not only was I hurt, but after hearing so much flac, I went in the studio and recorded a tape—apologizing. I made 1,500 copies and sent them to radio stations and sent them to radio stations. I was criticized for asking people to forgive me. (Collins 2000: 26)

Despite the controversy, Winans recouped her career and became one of the busiest gospel performers throughout the 1990s. As the decade progressed, it became increasingly clear that the developments in style, sound, and production used by Tramaine Hawkins, BeBe and CeCe Winans, and Vickie Winans were only the beginning of a new period of experimentation in gospel. Indeed, contemporary gospel in the second half of the 1990s would prove to be much more controversial with the gospel community and popular with secular audiences.

Third Phase (ca. 1995–2005)

By 1994, it was evident that gospel music's influence was growing. It was registered as the sixth most popular form of music, beating out jazz and classical, and by 1995, it had reported revenues that amounted to $381 million (Rhea 1998: 94). A number of factors contributed to such growth, including advances in the production quality of the music, more favorable demographic and sales research, more upscale marketing and packaging of the artists and their albums, and better record distribution. With the success of artists such as BeBe and CeCe Winans, Kirk Franklin and the Family, and Yolanda Adams, production budgets for gospel albums increased from the average of forty thousand dollars to well over one hundred thousand. As a duo, BeBe and CeCe Winans helped redefine gospel music in the late 1980s and early 1990s. Their adaptation of slick production approaches, associated mainly with secular music, and collaborations with a host of secular artists including Luther Vandross, MC Hammer, Whitney Houston, and Mavis Staples, helped make their albums some of the biggest selling gospel albums in the history of the genre. With the successful recordings of Kirk Franklin in 1995 (*Whatcha Looking 4*) and 1997 (*God's Property*), gospel's revenues increased even more. Gospel not only came to a more prominent place on secular mainstream radio, but gospel videos found their way into rotation on BET and MTV.

Although contemporary gospel was becoming decidedly male and more hip hop-influenced, female performers still maintain a dominant place in the genre. A newly revamped version of the Clark Sisters, consisting of Karen, Dorinda, and Jackie, released the much-acclaimed album *Miracles*, which took on a very different sound from their previous work. Vickie Winans, who had suffered emotionally and professionally from the fallout over her controversial Stellar Awards performance, remade herself with the album *Live in Detroit* and overnight became the newly crowned "Queen of Traditional Gospel."

CeCe and BeBe Winans decided to split temporarily to pursue other musical interests. The release of CeCe's first solo album *Alone in His Presence* in 1995 presented listeners with a side of the singer not heard on the previous recordings. It featured a blend of contemporary Christian songs and traditional hymns arranged in a number of different ways, including "Blessed Assurance" as a big band tune. The album earned a Grammy for the Best Soul/Gospel Album, and CeCe Winans became the first African American woman to win a Dove Award for Female Vocalist of the Year (Gillespie 1997).

The following year, CeCe Winans joined the cast of the popular off Broadway musical *Born to Sing, Mama, I Want to Sing, Part 3* and recorded the highly acclaimed single "Count on Me" with Whitney Houston for the *Waiting to Exhale* soundtrack. Winans' popularity soared, and she became one of the most visible and marketable gospel performers of the year. She sold her CD on QVC's shopping network, pitched Crest toothpaste, had her own television show called *CeCe's Place* on the Odyssey network, and was featured in print ads and television commercials for Revlon products.

CeCe Winans has continued to be as successful with her subsequent albums, including *Everlasting Love* (1998), which moved away from the more traditional gospel sound of the previous album to feature a more hip hop and R&B feel. The transition in sound was deliberate, Winans citing that she "wanted to get a message out to the world and that is about God's everlasting love and when you want to do that, you kind of want to package it in away that can be played on any (radio) format" (Banez 1998: 5).

In 1999, CeCe Winans formed CW Wellspring Entertainment, which features the Wellspring Gospel recording label as well as management, consulting, and marketing services. She released her first album on the imprint the same year (*Alabaster Box*), which was certified gold. Winans has continued to be one of the biggest and best-known names in gospel music, appearing in corporate ads (K-Mart) and at the White House on numerous occasions. Her success in gospel and secular circles has been equaled only by another equally exciting and innovative performer—Yolanda Adams.

Yolanda Adams' voice and face have become two of the prominent representations of contemporary gospel since the unprecedented success of her 1999 recording *Mountain High. . . Valley Low*. Still, her road to stardom was full of the same criticism about "selling out" gospel that her predecessors experienced. Adams was born in 1961 in Houston, Texas, and developed her voice while singing in the choir at the Berean Baptist Church. Following a successful career as a fashion model as a teen, Adams attended the University of Houston and Texas Southern University. After earning a degree in radio communications and journalism, Adams then obtained a teaching certificate. For years, she taught elementary school while singing in the Southeast Inspirational Choir on weekends.

Singing with that group brought Adams to the attention of composer and producer Thomas Whitfield. The defining moment of her career came during the summer of 1986, giving her the opportunity to record her first album (Foster 1996). In 1987, the album, *Just as I Am*, was released on Sound of Gospel Records. In 1990, she signed with the Tribute (now Verity) label and released *Through the Storm* (1991) and *Save the World* (1993). Both were highly acclaimed and featured an eclectic blend of songs that drew on her affinity for jazz and R&B. Adams' adaptation of jazz riffs and vocalizations, especially on *Save the World*, can be attributed to the musical relationship she had with gospel jazz artist and vice president of Tribute Records, Ben Tankard. With each album, both her popularity and her vocal prowess and image grew. Each record cover became glossier and more focused on highlighting Adams' beauty. In addition, her sound began to move farther away from traditional gospel to a blend of R&B-laced accompaniments and gospel vocals.

While she remained a favorite among gospel audiences, garnering a string of awards from Stellar Awards to Grammy nominations, Adams had yet in the early 1990s to reach the wider audience she was targeting. That changed when she performed at the White House Christmas Celebration for President Clinton and released *More Than a Melody* (1995). With this album, Adams' sound became what many categorized as R&B gospel. The criticism began mounting, and some claimed that Adams was creating music that was not gospel at all. While songs such as "The Battle Is Not Yours" from the album *Save the World* and "Even Me" from the album *Through the Storm* attracted the traditional black church listener, "Sailing on the Sea of Your Love" and "Open Arms" from the album *Mountain High. . . Valley Low* found a place on secular radio, and the video for "Open Arms" played on BET. But Adams was determined not to be pigeon-holed by critics and listeners. "I do traditional; I do contemporary; I do urban contemporary; I do it all," she stated in 1995:

> I don't keep anybody from hearing the word of God. What I have been able to do through the power of God is choose songs that minister to everybody. Albertina Walker told me that they had critics back in their day. People were telling them that they were singing the blues when they were singing "Precious Lord". . . So we are not concerned about the critics always talking about what gospel is or isn't. As long as it's called in the name of God—Jesus, you can't tell me that isn't gospel. (Butler 1995: 1B)

Her album *Songs from the Heart* continued to push the musical envelope, consisting of songs that ranged from the traditionally minded "Is Your All on the Altar" to the R&B ballad "Still I Rise" to "Never Alone," which featured Adams scatting á la Ella Fitzgerald.

In the mid-1990s, Adams carried on her crusade to make music that would reach all audiences. She toured with Kirk Franklin, enrolled in Howard University and earned a masters' degree in theology, expanded her ministry to include preaching, and got married. In 1997, Sylvia Rhone, president and CEO of Elektra Records, attended Adams' performance at New York's Beacon Theater and decided to sign Adams to Elektra. Adams became the first gospel artist signed to the secular label and in 2000 was the label's top-selling urban artist of the year (Robertson 2002).

Adams' first release on the Elektra label, *Mountain High. . . Valley Low*, went platinum. The album achieved unprecedented commercial success, galvanized by the Jimmy Jam and Terry Lewis song "Open My Heart." The song, with its message of hope and full submission to God, featured a sound that blended well with the secular ballads of Mary J. Blige, Patti LaBelle, and Luther Vandross, and crossover radio embraced it. Elektra's larger production budgets and strong marketing had seemingly overnight propelled Adams to a higher stratum of commercial success.

Adams was not the only woman at the end of the twentieth century to experience the success of what has been deemed "crossover gospel." Following the successful solo recordings of sister Twinkie Clark, the remaining Clark sisters released their own solo recordings. Karen Clark-Sheard was the first, with the highly acclaimed *Finally Karen*. Released in 1997, it sold more than three hundred thousand units and was nominated for a Grammy Award and nine Stellar Awards. After a five-year hiatus, Clark-Sheard returned in 2002 with her Elektra debut, *2nd Chance*, which featured R&B-influenced ballads and hip hop-laced tracks with production from Donald Lawrence and Missy Elliott. Dorinda Clark-Cole, considered the "jazziest" of the sisters because of her vocal stylings, followed with a self-titled release on Gospocentric in 2002. Groups like Mary Mary, Trin-i-tee 5:7, and Virtue have taken the Clark Sisters' formula of powerful vocals, stellar production, and glamorous stage presence to the next level and have found success with traditional, contemporary, secular, and younger audiences.

In the past thirty-plus years, gospel music has grown to a multimillion dollar industry. At the heart of the genre's growing popularity is a collective of female performers who have created a sound and message that appeal to larger and more diverse audiences. While debates still continue as to what is acceptably called gospel and what is not, gospel artists like Yolanda Adams, Karen Clark-Sheard, and CeCe Winans continue to push the musical boundaries. Their recent albums have debuted to much acclaim, and subsequent live performances have packed secular venues. While many credit male producers, songwriters, and musicians as being the architects of the contemporary gospel movement, history has shown that it has been their female counterparts who have served as its most seminal voices.

Notes

1. Scholars Mark Anthony Neal and Nelson George use the term post-soul to describe the cultural, political, and social experiences of African Americans since the end of the Civil Rights and Black Power movements (see Neal 2002).
2. Horace Clarence Boyer (1985, 1979) has contributed some of the first and landmark works on this subject. For more information on his definition and contextualization of contemporary gospel (see also Maultsby (1992).
3. "Oh Happy Day" was one of several songs recorded on the album *Let Us Go into the House of the Lord*. Selections from the album are featured on a number of recordings, including *The Best of the Edwin Hawkins Singers*.
4. Contemporary gospel was the acceptable moniker for the new R&B, jazz-influenced gospel by the early 1980s. Such terminology was not used when "Oh Happy Day" appeared in 1969.
5. Denise Clark left the group to launch her own ministry in the mid-1980s (see Morgan "Tribute and Retrospective").

Discography

Adams, Yolanda. *Just as I Am*. Sound of Gospel 3006 (1987). Compact disc.
———. *More Than a Melody*. Verity 43025 (1995). Compact disc.
———. *Mountain High. . . Valley Low*. Elektra 62439 (1999). Compact disc.
———. *Save the World*. Verity 43026 (1993). Compact disc.
———. *Songs from the Heart*. Verity 43123 (1998). Compact disc.
———. *Through the Storm*. Verity 43027 (1991). Compact disc.
The Clark Sisters. *Is My Living in Vain?* Sound of Gospel 22145 (1981). Compact disc.
———. *Jesus Has a Lot to Give*. Bilbo (1973).
———. *Mattie Moss Clark Presents the Clark Sisters*. Bilbo (1974).
———. *Miracles*. Sparrow Records/EMD 51368 (1994). Compact disc.
———. *You Brought the Sunshine*. Sound of Gospel 3000. Compact disc.
Clark-Cole, Dorinda. *Dorinda Clark-Cole*. Gospocentric 70033 (2002). Compact disc.
Clark-Sheard, Karen. *Finally Karen*. Island 524397 (1997). Compact disc.
———. *2nd Chance*. Elektra 62767 (2002). Compact disc.
Crouch, Andraé, and the Disciples. "Soon and Very Soon." *This Is Another Day*. Compendia 4875 (1976).
———. "Take Me Back." Light Records El-60051 (1975).
Edwin Hawkins Singers. "Oh Happy Day." *The Best of the Edwin Hawkins Singers*. Buddah Records BDS 69012 (1976).
Franklin, Kirk. "God's Property." *Nu Nation Project*. B-Rite Music 70007 (1997).
Franklin, Kirk, and the Family. *Whatcha Looking 4*. Gospocentric 70012 (1996).
Hall, Danniebelle. "I Go to the Rock." *Danniebelle Live in Sweden with Choralerna*. Sparrow SPR 1019 (1978).

———. "Ordinary People." *Let Me Have a Dream.* Sparrow SPR-1016 (1977).

———. *This Moment.* Light LS5675 (1975).

———. "Work the Works." *Danniebelle.* Light LS5638 (1974).

Hammer, MC. "Do Not Pass Me By." *Too Legit to Quit.* Capital C2-98151 (1991). Compact disc.

Hawkins, Tramaine. "Fall Down." (1985).

———. *The Search Is Over.* A&M Records 75021-5110-2

———. *To a Higher Place.* Sony 57876 (1994). Compact disc.

———. *Tramaine Hawkins.* Light Records A&M Records 75021-5110-2 (1983).

Hawkins, Walter. *Jesus Christ Is the Way.* Light Records 4861 (1977).

———. *Love Alive.* Platinum Ent. 161012 (1975).

———. *Love Alive II.* Platinum Ent. 161011 (1978).

Houston, Whitney, and CeCe Winans. "Count on Me." *Waiting to Exhale Soundtrack.* Arista 18796 (1995).

Northern California State Youth Choir. "Oh Happy Day." *Let Us Go into the House of the Lord.* Century Records 31016 (1969).

Winans, BeBe, and CeCe Winans. *Different Lifestyles.* Capitol 92078 (1991). Compact disc.

———. *Heaven.* Capitol 90959 (1988). Compact disc.

———. *Introducing BeBe and CeCe Winans.* Capitol C2-46883 (1987).

———. "I.O.U. Me." *Introducing BeBe and CeCe Winans.* Capitol C2-46883 (1987).

———. *Lord Lift Us Up.* PTL Ministries. PTL QQQ (1985).

Winans, CeCe. *Alabaster Box.* Sparrow Records 51711 (1999). Compact disc.

———. *Alone in His Presence.* Sparrow Records 51441 (1995). Compact disc.

———. *Everlasting Love.* PMG/Atlantic 92793 (1998).

Winans, Vickie. *Be Encouraged.* Light 72001 (1985).

———. *The Lady.* MCA 10394. (1992).

———. *Live in Detroit.* CGI Records 1279 (1997).

———. *Total Victory.* Light 72020 (1989).

———. *Vickie Winans.* Intersound 9127 (1994).

References

Banez, Cherry. "The gospel truth." *Philadelphia Tribune* (May 29, 1998): 5.

Boyer, Horace Clarence. "A Comparative Analysis of Traditional and Contemporary Gospel Music." In *More Than Dancing: Essays on Afro-American Music and Musicians.* Edited by Irene V. Jackson, 127–146. Westport, CT: Greenwood, 1985.

———. "Contemporary Gospel Music." *Black Perspective in Music* 7, no. 1 (Spring 1979): 5–58.

———. "Mattie Moss Clark." In *How Sweet the Sound: The Golden Age of Gospel.* 125–7. Urbana and Chicago: University of Illinois Press, 1995.

Butler, Tim. "Her Mission Is 'More Than a Melody'." *Tri-State Defender* (September 6, 1995): 1B.

"Clark Kin's Super Gospel." *Washington Post* (February 2, 1990): N21.

Clark-Cole, Dorinda. NuthinButGospel, http://nuthinbutgospel.com. Accessed on August 26, 2005.

Collins, Lisa. "A New Wave of Artists Gets to Church on Time." *Billboard* (January 29, 2000): 26.

———, and Ron Harris. Move On Up a Little Higher: Black Women and Gospel. *American Legacy Woman* (2002): 16–24.

Davis, Samuel. "Meet Vickie Winans." *Philadelphia Tribune* (March 24, 1992): 10-C.

Dyson, Michael Eric. "Mixed Blessing: Gospel Music's Popularity Vexes Devotees." *New York Times* (January 5, 1992): 1H.

Foster, Pamela. "Yolanda Adams Live." *Tennessee Tribune* (October 23, 1996): 4.

Gillespie, Fern. "Without Compromise: CeCe Winans' Musical Ministry." *About. . . Time* (January 31, 1997): 8.

Harris, Hamil R. "'Oh Happy Day' Still Shines—25 Years after First Hit, Hawkins Family Goes on Tour." *Washington Post* (August 4, 1999): M12.

"In the Spirit." *Billboard* (October 15, 1994): 52.

Maultsby, Portia K. "The Impact of Gospel Music on the Secular Music Industry." In *We'll Understand It Better By and By: Pioneering African American Gospel Composers.* Edited by Bernice Johnson Reagon, 19–33. Washington DC: Smithsonian Institution, 1992.

Morgan, Joe. "Tribute and Retrospective: The Clark Sisters—A Focus on Glory." Gospelflava.com. http://www.gospelflava.com/articles/clarksisterstribute.html. Accessed on August 26, 2005.

Neal, Mark Anthony. *Soul Babies: Black Popular Culture and the Post-Soul Aesthetic.* New York: Routledge Books, 2002.

Rhea, Shawn. "Gospel Rises Again." *Black Enterprise* (July 1998): 94.

Robertson, Gil. "The Robertson Treatment: Messages of Inspiration—Yolanda Adams Is Contemporary Gospel Music's Proud Ambassador." *Sacramento Observer* (February 27, 2002): E2.

Roos, John. "Gospel According to Tramaine." *Los Angeles Times* (August 30, 1997): F-2.

"Tramaine Hawkins: I Never Felt I Left Gospel." *Tri-State Defender* (July 5, 1989): 15.

"Veteran Gospel Singer Walter Hawkins Celebrates 25 Years of Love." *Sentinel* (July 29, 1998): B6.

Willman, Chris. "Tramaine Brings the Gospel to the Dance Floor." *Los Angeles Times* (April 5, 1986): 5–8.

Winans, CeCe. *On a Positive Note.* New York: Pocket Books, 1999.

43
Womanist Musings

Cheryl A. Kirk-Duggan

Oh, Black, Beautiful Woman:
Old as time
Young as the day
Cherished by some;
Thrown aside by others;
Magnificently made;
Honored by God
Elegant heart beat
Sing the pulse of life.

Spirituals are songs of motivation that champion the possibility, the process, and the product of liberation and freedom. Slaves and freedom fighters identified with Paul and Silas as they walked out of jail. They knew they had stayed in the wilderness too long. Although the search sometimes seemed as elusive as the quest for the Holy Grail, these seekers of freedom never gave up, never questioned the rightness and the goal of the quest. Womanists look at the spirituals and see the distant and recent past, the present, and the future. Each existential moment is one of cruelty yet one of hope, with opportunities for affirmation and liberation. With power and love, Womanists know that the wholeness of no person is complete until the African American woman is no longer the victim of race, gender, and class bias and prejudice.[1] Womanists hear the plea of the spirituals for freedom, justice, and personal and communal empowerment. In our search for unearthing the hidden and not-so-hidden priceless lessons in the spirituals, this chapter thematically probes the impact of Womanist thought toward understanding the message of the spirituals during slavery and the 1960s Movement, and involves a Womanist reading of black women living, singing, and arranging the spirituals.

African American women have lived, sung, or arranged the spirituals and have engaged in erasing oppression in various forms, and this chapter celebrates their contributions and the significance of their work. These women are African Americans whose lives and contributions echo the desires that undergird the spirituals, that unmask the oppression of gender, race, and class. Thus, the spirituals become a symbol of Womanist empowerment.

The spirituals symbolize the quest for justice, empowerment, and liberation now, right now, and at the same time later. They are eschatological in that whatever goals not met in immediate time will ultimately be met. While the spirituals certainly see suffering as unmerited and paradoxical, these songs do *not* see God as manipulating evil toward the Christian's advantage or toward some form of heaven or deferred well-being.[2] Spirituals tend not to ask for retribution, but they do not assume enslavement is a game wherein African Americans are pawns to be redeemed later. The spirituals want justice, oneness with God or heaven *now*. Many slaves already had a concept of God and a concept of retributive justice (i.e., "you reap what you sow") before being stolen from Africa. Their intimate notions of God with their daily life would argue that those in bondage trusted that God would deliver them. They certainly knew they had done nothing to deserve what they experienced in slavery. Deferred deliverance is not the same thing as allowing an evil to exist for the sake of a religious or faith goal. Slave owners were the oppressors, not God. Further, many of the slaves, encouraged by the call for freedom and justice, used these songs as an impetus to take action themselves. Surely countless runaway slaves and those blacks conducting the Underground Railroad did not sense a call to acquiesce or accommodate in the spirituals. This broader reading/hearing of the spirituals involves the theoretical and emphatically deals with the practical. Oppression is real.

Divine Care, Divine Love (Agape)

The spiritual "He's [God/Jesus] Got the Whole World in His Hands" reflects a foundational concern for Womanists: God cares; and, as beings created in God's image, we care. Caring requires active courage. Since arriving on these shores, black women have exercised strength and boldness in their daily acts of survival and overcoming. A Womanist reading sees and experiences as a call to be bold and to take outrageous steps to care about all babies—the babies of national political leaders, the babies of mothers on Aid to Dependent Children (ADC), the babies that die from violence, those that die a living death due to neglect; and the babies in all of us that somehow never mature. A Womanist reading looks for the many infant ideas in the spirituals yet to be unearthed and considers these songs, born in response to evil and sin, as a potential antibiotic, depressant, or stimulant. Since the spirituals can be vehicles for healing in a way as yet not fully developed, working with them from a Womanist perspective ensures the caring of others as this experience triggers the act of love and the process of identity.

Womanists love all people in all kinds of ways. The spirituals celebrate love as *agape*. *Agape* as love envisioned in the New Testament is a love that creates community and communion. This deep yet gentle transcendent feeling of affection and solicitude of lived, divine grace and charity embraces others, shares affection, and shares a meal. *Agape* love invites one to be a part of the larger body, as signified in the spirituals, "I'm Gonna Sit at the Welcome Table" and "Let Us Break Bread Together."

To break bread or sit at the welcome table means one has the opportunity to avoid hunger, false imprisonment, ignorance, brutality, and injustice. Consequently, our children will not have to fight some of the same inane battles that their parents have had to fight. We can hope, can trust, and must participate in communal and self-actualization, for God cares, and "[We can] tell God how you treat me." Spirituals that sing of inclusiveness, of being welcomed, mean individuals and societies have choices about their activities. That inclusiveness symbolizes Martin L. King's dream of people being judged by the content of their character as opposed to the color of their skin, their political connections, or their pedigrees. These spirituals announce the possibility leveling the playing field toward equality and justice for all. Womanists remind us that, globally, many have yet to receive an invitation to the table. At best, some have received nothing, some have been served scraps, some have been denied even a drink of water; others have been ridiculed or totally dismissed. The welcome table stands before us as a reality check to both the oppressor and the oppressed and asks questions of identity and visibility: who are you, where are you, where are you going?

Affirming Identity

The spirituals affirm the identity of black folks—the interconnectedness of their individual and collective human experiences of body, spirit, mind, memory, personality, and patterns of conscious acts, needs, and desires. The spirituals reflect this essence in bad times and good. "I've Been 'Buked" remembers the scorn and the troubles that most people experience during the course of life.

Nevertheless, the taunted ones vow that, no matter what, they will not "lay my 'ligion down!" They will not give up their faith in God or their hopes in new possibilities. These oppressed also realize that each individual must participate in his or her own empowerment, and consequently, they see the need for strong, faith-based community solidarity. Communal solidarity, as vital as it is, does not always protect community members from the impact of harm's way. "I've Been in the Storm" rehearses the long season of oppression and difficulty experienced by most African Americans. Even so, the devastation of the storm can be life-giving; and God's justice and mercy mean that "trouble [unwarranted, uncivilized suffering] won't last always." The singers know that they do not stand alone, and therefore they ask for prayer time:

I've been in the storm, so long
I've been in the storm, so long, children
I've been in the storm, so long
Lord, give a little time to pray.
                              —*Traditional*

Prayer acknowledges the reality of God and gives the oppressed visibility. Often the move from invisibility and silence to visibility and speaking is the first step toward being all God created one to be. Self-actualization relates to the Womanist focus of survival and wholeness.

Throughout history, black folks survived: across middle passage, in the bowels of slavery, and through the false promises of Reconstruction, the insanity of many wars, the hope of the Civil Rights Movement and the Great Society, the economic strain of Reaganomics, the conservative bent of the Bush era, and the promises and shortcomings of Clinton. This quest for survival affects all people, black and non-black, female and male. Since the spirituals are an oral documentation of the antebellum and civil rights eras and still are sung to the present day, singing these songs celebrates the survival and wholeness of all people, along with the possibility of a relationship between the community and God. Like ancient Israelites, black folk have traditionally trusted God. "My Good Lord's Done Been Here" honors a surviving people who know the reality of God:

My good Lord's done been here,
Blessed my soul, my soul and gone
My good Lord's done been here
Bless my soul and gone.

O brothers, where were you?
O sisters, where were you?
O Christians, where were you?
O mourners, where were you?
When my good Lord was here?
                              —*Traditional*

God is not an abstract, absent being. God is present, and that presence provides blessing. This spiritual also calls everyone, regardless of color, to experience conversion.

Call to Conversion, Call to Praise

Conversion, a prerequisite needed for injustice to cease and for justice to exist occurs when one adopts a new religion, faith, or belief. The conversion or transformation of people and of social and political systems revives the *imago Dei* in humanity. Divine-human encounter occurs and elevates humanity to the level of the sacred. Not only does singing the song itself transform one's spirit, but meditation on the song helps reveal that there is another way to experience life other than the present one where the cries of wrongdoing drown out those of praise.

The praise of God acknowledges that humanity recognizes its fragility, its inability to control everything, and its gratitude toward God for the blessings of life and possibilities. "Certainly, Lord" is a praise response about spiritual health and well-being. The leader asks "Have you got good religion?" And the chorus responds, "Certainly, Lord!"

> Have you got good religion? Cert'nly, Lord!
> Have you got good religion? Cert'nly, Lord!
> Have you got good religion? Cert'nly, Lord!
> Cert'nly, cert'nly, cert'nly, Lord!

This type of praise response is not about religiosity, hypocrisy, or window dressing, but values who people are and what the community can be. Participation in such praise response proclaims that "I Wanna Be Ready" to "walk in Jerusalem just like John":

> I wanna be ready,
> I wanna be ready,
> I wanna be ready,
> To walk in Jerusalem just like John.
> —*Traditional*

To walk like John gives one a sense of authority, integrity, and visibility here on earth. African Americans were active in this country before it became a republic, which justifies a Womanist reading of the spirituals because of the historical, liberating, transformational tenets and possibilities of looking at the past to learn where we must go for the future. The spirituals, indeed, are metaphors for two key movements that altered the meaning of living in these United States: slavery and the 1960s Movement.

The Search for Empowerment

Many women and men sang freedom songs in the 1960s with the intent of empowerment and creatively used their anger to protest the ravages poured out on African Americans. Too often, however, the voices of women have been silenced. In honor of theological justice or theodicy, that voice is awakened here. Black women experienced and participated in the Movement; the insight of black women as intracommunity-oriented brings a focus on the participant as protagonist; and contemporary black women's poetic abilities mirror the spirituals and honor Womanists' moral judgments and ethical choices, in life and in literature.

The redacted spirituals embrace the experience of the 1960s activists, especially the call for freedom now, for deliverance from all oppression. The Womanists who sang the spirituals expressed a desire to fight for justice as they imitated their mothers, grandmothers, and great-grandmothers, singing the spirituals as an act of storytelling, as a "habit of survival" in response to pain and suffering that lessens anger, gives a sense of self-control, and offers hope.[3] Through the spirituals and other stories, Womanists address the dynamics of the gifts of freedom: self-empowerment and intracommunal development, with implications for intercommunal relations. Singing the spirituals for a Womanist is an act of naming the violence, pain, and hope, unmasking the issues, and engaging each other and the system to create change.

A Womanist vision recalls the many times when movement was only internal for the Africans of the diaspora and celebrates the "quiet grace" reflected in the courage of those who faced death in the wake of demanding equal treatment. Womanist ideas help us to focus on issues internal to the community, to see the female and male characteristics of the spirituals and to call attention to one segment of society that symbolizes those oppressed by race, sex, and class, illuminating the complexity of justice praxis in American society:

> I think songs are both male and female. I think they are projectile. They can have a piercing, penile energy; and, they also absolutely can rock you in a womb-like way. But within the range of an African American musical experience you would have both. 'Cause that "going forward thing" has a thrusting to it. And I think what you get is both forward motion, thrusting as well as nurturing, womb, healing, taking care. . . I think you have both.
>
> Can we say that there is a sense in which the songs acted or songs could act to be a liberating force from that place of racism, sexism, or classism?. . . I'm not conscious that there was a consciousness of those things in that way. I think reading back, you can talk about that, but I think it is stretching it. . . My sense is that a song and singing in the black tradition is an instrument that is shaped by the singer so that it could actually liberate if that is the point, but it is not. It does not operate or stand outside of the intent of the singer. . . [Some] great black singers [are] despots. . . The singer is wonderful and is used in terrible ways. . . So singing does not exist outside the intent of the singer.[4]

Spirituals have been sung by men and women with the intent of empowerment. Too often, however, the voices of women have been silenced. In honor of justice or theodicy, that voice is awakened here.

Womanists knew the tensions enmeshed within the Civil Rights Movement as part of one's life cycle. A Womanist grasp of "We Shall Not Be Moved" made one accountable for movement within the community and reminded others of their need to deal with their own movement or lack thereof. Two African American women who opposed oppression, Rutha Harris and Bernice Johnson Reagon, together with two male singers, Cornell Hall Reagon and Charles Neblett, transcended the fear of death as they toured throughout the country as the Freedom Singers, singing for justice and righteousness. Womanists celebrate the authority to speak out and celebrate community, by all people, everywhere.

Honoring Empowerment and Community Building

The spirituals, born in community, are a means to get behind history and glean insight about how extended families and communities helped black people survive. The survival of all people depends largely on seeing all of humanity as human beings, not as "others" to be denied. A Womanist reading of the spirituals celebrates the power that holds the community together—the God of mercy, love, and solidarity. With the work toward solidarity comes the effort of letting people be who they are and helping them to be whole and well without hurting others. One of the best ways to help transform a moment of anxiety and to help heal the hurt is to get someone to sing. Singing brings people together as a group and provides hope; singing requires that we breathe. People in the middle of an anxiety attack forget to breathe. A sense of wholeness understands the possibility of spiritual transformation that can occur through meditative deep breathing, a by-product of certain types of singing. Just as God "breathed breath" into clay and created a human being who became a living, sentient creature, singing and breathing can help bring a sense of new life into a hurting community.

Community singing can also bring meaningfulness to empty hearts. Most professional African American entertainers, even today, got their start by performing in church. Performing helps to instill self-esteem, confidence, and a sense of belonging. The experience of belonging reinforces the ability to survive and to enjoy a supportive quality of life. The singing says "No!" to stereotypes and sinful acts and says "Yes!" to worthiness and well-being. The message of these spirituals affirms a risk-taking faith that requires one to take a stand in the church and the world. The holistic, life-giving, and relational God of the spirituals calls for us to be like-minded: to care and to be just and merciful. The prophetic voices which speak of this relational God reveal the prophetic voice of the spirituals, as in "O Daniel" and "Didn't My Lord Deliver Daniel?":

> You call yourself a church member,
> You hold your head so high,
> You praise God with your glitt'ring tongue,
> But you leave all your heart behind.
>
> Oh my Lord delivered Daniel
> O Daniel, O Daniel
> Oh my Lord delivered Daniel,
> O why not deliver me too?
>
> ——*Traditional*
>
> Didn't my Lord deliver Daniel,
> Deliver Daniel, deliver Daniel?
> Didn't my Lord deliver Daniel?
> Then why not every man?
>
> He delivered Daniel from the lions' den,
> And Jonah from the belly of the whale,
> He delivered children from the fiery furnace,
> And why not every man?

If you cannot sing like angels,
If you cannot preach like Paul,
You can tell the love of Jesus
and you can say he died for all.

——Traditional

Prophets deliver God's message. This God-message says there is a Messiah and a God who delivers. Because God delivers, we are to share that message and help empower peoples to get out of situations that oppress them.

Community Solidarity

The communal sense inherent in the spirituals signifies that it matters if our neighbors are in pain, are abused, or lack self-esteem. Singing the spirituals presses one to use God language to help people fight for themselves, not acquiesce to dominating persons, and to avoid situations or persons that can sabotage their mental, moral, and/or spiritual health. The long-dead voices of earlier composers of the spirituals faced daily destruction, exploitation, dehumanization, humiliation, and violence. Womanists help awaken these voices and help us hear them in a way that ministers to our own internal and existential brokenness. Often the first step toward healing is the recognition that the pain and brokenness exist. One can then help others by assuring them that, despite their present state, they are worthy. The first step is an invitation to celebrate themselves and to celebrate life:

Dere's a little wheel a turnin' in my heart
Dere's a little wheel a turnin' in my heart
In my heart, in my heart,
Dere's a little wheel a turnin' in my heart.

O I feel so very happy in my heart,
O I feel so very happy in my heart,
In my heart, in my heart,
Dere's a little wheel a turnin' in my heart.

O I don't feel no ways tired in my heart,
O I don't feel no ways tired in my heart,
In my heart, in my heart.
O I don't feel no ways tired in my heart.

——Traditional

Womanist theory calls us to be inclusive and to love each other well. Active love empowers and gives me an opportunity to know that because I am worthy, I am worth fighting for, and I can choose to stand up for myself or for some other worthy cause:

You got a right,
I got a right,
We all got a right
To the tree of life.

—Traditional

When we stand up for ourselves, we affirm with the community:

Done made my vow to the Lord
And I never will turn back.
I will go, I shall go
To see what the end will be.

—Traditional

Out of this lived experience, we can tell others:

Ain't gonna let nobody turn me 'round.
Turn me 'round, turn me 'round,
Turn me 'round.
Ain't gonna let nobody turn me 'round.
Keep on walkin', keep on talkin',
Marchin' to freedom's land.

—Redacted civil rights version

These spirituals afford us an ethics of resistance to all unhealthy experiences and move us to an ethics of aesthetics, a way of seeing and being in the world that brings out the best in us. The spirituals embody a form of Einstein's $E=mc^2$ where the energy of equality equals the matter of music multiplied by the creative desire for reform squared to embrace both the oppressed and the oppressor. In celebrating this energy as new possibility using old songs that remain eternal, I turn now to examine the women, past and present, who have lived, sung, and arranged the spirituals in a way that has and is having a major impact on American life and culture.

Black women signify as they wear and celebrate the garments of self-expression via living, singing, and arranging the spirituals. The spiritual "On My Journey" is a testament about the unwillingness of an individual to be downhearted, discouraged about, or deterred from his or her task or journey. No system or male human being could silence black women's signifying—the revising and renaming—of their realities. In communicating, these women used coded language, gave old ideas new names, and edited their conversations, so that those listening who were not supposed to know the full reality of what was transpiring would not understand.

On ma journey now, Mount Zion [*pronounced zine*],
Ma journey now, Mount Zion,
Well I wouldn't take nothin', Mount Zion
For my journey now, Mount Zion.

One day, one day,
I was walkin' along,
And de elements opened,
And the love come down, Mount Zion.

Well, I went to de valley,
And I didn't go to stay,
Well ma soul got happy,
An' I stayed all day, Mount Zion.

You can talk about me,
Just as much as you please
Well, I'll talk about you,
When I get on ma knees, Mount Zion.

—Traditional

These magnificent creatures of ebony, chocolate, and cocoa butter gave utterances of exultation and excitement, pleasure and pain, love and life, anxiety and anger, relief and reverence for God. With the onset of slavery, sounds of black women's daily life in the African motherland became mere echoes of the near yet distant past, as slave ships rocked midst the waves of the Atlantic during middle passage. Middle passage, the denigrating journey toward institutionalized slavery, brought African women to these shores. The stench of death and nausea, the near starvation and the angst of hopelessness dampened but did not kill their spirits. Not the intentional separation of peoples with similar language and culture, the dehumanization of bodies packed like sardines, the loss of home and country, nor the fear of what was to come could silence black female signifiers.

From the beginning of civilization to the present day, these women have signified as I now signify about them. Black women's signifying, or play on language, is part of the social, musical infrastructure of black language systems and embraces the rhythm of black life itself. The beautiful and the brusque shape these women's creative utterances as they signify via word, song, dance, politics, education, and domestic and graphic art, in praise and in protest, about their existential life rhythms. In revisiting these women's lives, we celebrate the smorgasbord of black women's signification in the areas of art, literature, music, education, social protest, and religion, by interweaving biographical commentary with the words, songs, and expressions of black women throughout history, from the antebellum period through the 1990s—protesting, signifying, testifying women symbolized through living, singing, and arranging the spirituals. History provides the categories; black women's lives provide the material.

Abolition Activists

The first signifiers via the spirituals are abolitionist activists Sojourner Truth, Maria Stewart, Harriet Ross Tubman, and Frances Watkins Harper. Sojourner Truth (c. 1799–1883) lived the spirituals as abolitionist, feminist, and religious leader, for she fearlessly signified freedom, liberation, and truth. Truth wrote orally, not with a pen. Celebrated for her 1851 "Ain't I a Woman" speech, Truth took the position made into a hallmark by Womanist scholars: she dealt with issues of race, gender, and class. (Some recent scholars claim this speech did not occur; yet the story of her audacious statements has inspired many women.) She defied those who wanted to deny black women the status of being female and the status of being black. In 1858, Truth again defied sexism and slavery by publicly baring her breasts in answer to the claim by some men who argued that such a forceful speaker could not be a woman. Between 1826 and 1827, Truth gained freedom via emancipation by New York State law; she successfully sued for the freedom of her son, who had been illegally sold into slavery in Alabama; and she had a dramatic religious conversion experience and joined the Methodist Church. The Second Great Awakening, as well as the related piety and religiosity of Methodism, had a lasting impact on her, particularly when many unlettered itinerant preachers of both sexes, often in the Quaker and Methodist traditions, began to preach and evangelize. She began to preach during the 1830s and aligned with several millenarian groups who thought judgment was imminent. In 1843, she changed her name from Isabella to Sojourner Truth (itinerant preacher) and left her home to preach Jesus to all, as commanded by the Spirit, without telling her family. In the latter 1840s and the 1850s, Truth met with Frederick Douglass and William Lloyd Garrison. She lived for a while within a utopian community, the Northampton Association, which supported abolitionist activities and feminism. Sojourner Truth preached to audiences as an antislavery feminist, basing her authority on her slave experience. She published *The Narrative of Sojourner Truth*, in 1850, which allowed her to support herself and pay off her mortgage in Massachusetts (a second edition appeared in 1875). She worked against poverty and petitioned Congress to demand that land in the western frontier be set aside for freed African Americans. Though the petition failed, many blacks began traveling toward Kansas. A feminist, Truth supported women being included in the drafting of the Fourteenth Amendment to the Constitution: in debates at an 1867 Equal Rights Convention, Truth argued that both black men *and black women* were disenfranchised. For Sojourner Truth, one must claim the spiritual "I'm a-Rollin'":

> I'm a-rollin', I'm a-rollin',
> I'm a-rollin' thro' an unfriendly world
> I'm a-rollin', I'm a-rollin',
> Thro' an unfriendly world.
>
> O sister, won't you help me,
> O sister, won't you help me to pray,
> O sister, won't you help me,
> Won't you help me in the service of the Lord?

> O brothers, won't you help me,
> O brothers, won't you help me to pray,
> O brothers, won't you help me,
> Won't you help me in the service of the Lord?
> —*Traditional*

Preacher, singer, and antislavery lecturer, Truth knew she was "a-rollin'," knew she needed to hold on to the gospel plow, and as such, she was an evangelical spokesperson for the cause of justice and humanity.[5] Like Sojourner Truth, Maria Stewart also sang the cause of freedom.

Maria Stewart (1803–1879), an orphan nurtured in a parsonage via religious rhetoric and philosophical conviction for self-help and community service, lived the spirituals as an advocate for abolition, freedom, and equality for African American slaves. She was the first woman ever to give a public lecture series before both race- *and* gender-integrated audiences. Stewart's outspokenness about major contemporary issues, from colonization and racial unity to self-determination and race pride, remained part of her teaching philosophy when she taught in New York and Washington DC. Racism and sexism hindered nineteenth-century America from embracing Stewart's public political dialogues and her published pamphlets. Because Stewart had a bold message she wanted to proclaim, the spiritual "Peter, Go Ring Dem Bells" could announce her message, for she had "heard from heaven" and wanted all to hear her words:

> Peter, go ring dem bells,
> Peter, go ring dem bells,
> Peter, go ring a dem bells,
> I heard from heaven today.
> Wonder where ma mother has gone,
> Wonder where ma mother has gone,
> Wonder where ma mother has gone,
> Heard from heaven today.
>
> Wonder where Sister Mary has gone. . .
> Wonder where Sister Martha has gone. . .
> It's good news, and I thank God. . .
> Wonder where brother Moses has gone. . .
> Wonder where brother Daniel's gone. . .
> Wonder where Elijah has gone. . .
> —*Traditional*

Abolitionist William Lloyd Garrison reported Stewart's four speeches in his abolitionist newspaper the *Liberator*.[6] Just as Stewart spoke and taught with vigor and tenacity, so did Harriet Tubman drive those in her trust through unspeakable hardships to freedom, to Canaan.

Harriet Ross Tubman (c. 1821–1913) lived the spirituals as the "Moses of her people," the best-known Underground Railroad conductor. She was a feminist, Union spy, social reformer, and provider for African American aged and indigent. Born into slavery in Maryland, Tubman escaped to Philadelphia and worked to garner contacts and resources to rescue her sister and her sister's children out of slavery. This started Tubman's mission to help runaway slaves with shelter, clothes, money, disguises, or transportation, and this earned her the epithet "Moses." The spiritual that signifies Tubman best then, is

> Go down, Moses,
> Way down in Egypt's land [*the South*].
> Tell ole Pharaoh [*slave owners; racists*]
> To let my people [*the oppressed*] go
> —*Traditional*

Tubman feared no one. Formally uneducated, she knew nature, the Bible, music, and southern contemporary folklore. She used these assets to communicate safety or danger to her hidden, waiting passengers going north. She disguised herself, used various routes, and kept a gun to discourage any runaways from leaving the freedom train; she kept paregoric to quiet any crying babies. Tubman was so successful that Maryland slave owners offered a $40,000 reward for her capture. She worked with a network of black and white abolitionists, with all people, regardless of race, gender, or socioeconomic status, including Frederick Douglass, William Lloyd Garrison, John Brown, Susan B. Anthony, and Ralph Waldo Emerson, as she testified about the horrors of slavery and continued to move runaway slaves north. Tubman operated out of Canada for a while because of the Fugitive Slave Law of 1850. This law threatened the Underground Railroad and all free northern blacks, for now the federal government could be used to arrest and return escaped slaves anywhere in the country. Tubman continued to provide safe passage for slaves until late 1860. Black leaders including Tubman, Sojourner Truth, and Frederick Douglass were upset and irate about President Abraham Lincoln's denial that the war was to abolish slavery, and about the fact that blacks were not welcome to participate in the Union Army. Lincoln did finally issue the Emancipation Proclamation announcing that slaves in rebellious states would be free on January 1, 1863, and that blacks could enlist in the army in early 1863.

Tubman, as scout, nurse, and spy, distinguished herself as the only woman to plan and execute armed warfare against the enemy in American military history. She was present at the battle of Fort Wagner, where the black Massachusetts Fifty-Fourth Regiment with Colonel Robert Gould Shaw (lionized in the recent novel and movie *Glory)* gave their lives for the Union cause. After the Civil War, Tubman did other humanitarian work. She participated in Reconstruction work, nursed the sick and wounded soldiers, and taught newly freed blacks strategies for self-sufficiency. With assistance from the Massachusetts Antislavery Society, she bought a house for herself and her parents. Tubman purchased twenty-five adjoining acres, where, with some of the military pension she had to fight the government for thirty years to receive, she built the Harriet Tubman Home for

Indigent Aged Negroes, which formally opened in 1908. With other women, Tubman helped provide social services and relief for the families of black soldiers and for recently manumitted slaves.[7] Along with Tubman, other women, like Frances Harper, worked as abolitionists.

Frances Watkins Harper (1825–1911) lived the spirituals as a member of the Underground Railroad, an abolitionist lecturer, one founder of the American Woman Suffrage Association, a member of the Women's Christian Temperance Union, an officer of the National Association of Colored Women, an officer of the Universal Peace Union, the director of the American Association of Educators of Colored Youth, a member of the National Colored Women's Congress, and a tireless worker in the African Methodist Episcopal Church. She was an internationally recognized poet, writer of essays and other fiction, and journalist who focused on women's rights, black achievement, and temperance, among other topics. Some essays were response papers to contemporary writers like Charles Dickens and Harriet Beecher Stowe. Harper took controversial stands, not as a separatist nor an assimilationist, but she preferred education to violence. Harper clarified the record about slavery and Reconstruction and about the import of Christlike humanity, and she chastised white southern women who would not work with or see the common interests they shared with black women.[8] Along with activism through writing, Harper empowered by teaching others about an ethical life through her dedication to social service, together with the place of beauty and the love of freedom. Born to free parents and orphaned at an early age, Harper lectured on equal rights and antislavery throughout New England and southern Canada. As Harper stood up and spoke out, she epitomized the spiritual "I Shall Not Be Moved": "I shall not, I shall not be moved. . . Just like a tree planted by the water, I shall not be moved." The abolitionist activist women signified through words and actions. Three other women joined their commitment to empowerment and liberation through aesthetics and art: Katherine Dunham, Faith Ringgold, and Toni Cade Bambara.

Evocative Expressionists

Katherine Dunham (1909–) lives the spirituals through the music of dance and through her accomplishments in social activism, anthropology, and education. Her work in the Caribbean with Melville Herskovits enabled her to mine African ritual, dance, and musics of the African diaspora. She expresses her political awareness and social conscience through her art of dance. For example, she created a ballet, *Southland*, which dramatized lynching during the aftermath of the 1954 Emmett Till torture/murder in Mississippi. Dunham worked with the NAACP and the Urban League to fight segregationist practices in public accommodations. This international choreographer and winner of countless awards began the Katherine Dunham School of Arts and Research in New York, where students studied dance, literature, art, and world culture. The Katherine Dunham Troupe toured internationally from 1940 to 1963. After teaching and training dancers in Africa,

Dunham returned to the United States and moved to East St. Louis to develop a performing arts and training center with a multicultural program that embraces culture and dance. Dunham's exuberance, energy, and impact on the world echo the sentiments of this spiritual:

Oh, when the saints go marching in
Oh, when the saints go marching in
Oh, Lord, I want to be in that number
When the saints go marching in.

—*Traditional*

Dunham wants everyone "to be in that number" of those who celebrate life and celebrate themselves. Dunham has also published many works, including her autobiographical *A Touch of Innocence* (1959). Her teaching and concerts use her acute understanding of people, culture, beauty, human psychology, social values, and commitment to justice and human well-being.[9] The protest and encouragement that Dunham expresses through dance, Faith Ringgold expounds with paints and cloth.

Faith Ringgold (1934–) lives the spirituals in her artwork, beginning when she decided to train herself during the 1960s. Previously, her teachers did not know how to help her mix paints to capture black skin tones. While doing French impressionist styles, she was told that a black woman was incapable of doing good Eurocentric art. After reading Amiri Baraka and James Baldwin and living through the shifting political scene from Civil Rights to black revolution, Ringgold used her artistry to evoke the dignity and pride proclaimed in the words of Adam Clayton Powell Jr. and Stokely Carmichael. Her paintings of the early 1970s period, including *The Flag Is Bleeding, U.S. Postage Stamp Commemorating the Advent of Black Power,* and *Die,* contain imagery characteristic of African art. Ringgold empowered black women by making portrait masks of Harlem women and painting a mural at the Women's House of Detention on Rikers Island, New York City, to show that women could do many different kinds of jobs. In this manner, she championed the possibility of rehabilitation. Though whites found her work too political and too Afrocentric, and black men found her work too Africanized and too soft, Ringgold continued to protest against sexism and racism in her work and in political and artistic arenas. With others, she protested the exclusion of black artists from a 1970 Whitney Museum of American Art exhibition of artists from the 1930s. After much protest, the show was opened to minority artists and women. Ringgold joined the Ad Hoc Committee on Women Artists and Students for Black Liberation, which brought pressure on museums to show the work of women artists. In 1976, Ringgold focused more attention on performance art as a vehicle for political and artistic protest and expression. Her soft sculptures and masks recounted the African American experience. She turned to quilting as a form that powerfully tells the stories and experiences of African American women's lives.[10] Her social vision for change echoes the power of this spiritual:

I'm a witness fo' ma Lawd
I'm a witness fo' ma Lawd
I'm a witness fo' ma Lawd
I'm an everyday witness fo' ma Lawd.
I'm a Monday witness fo' ma Lawd...
I'm a Wednesday witness fo' ma Lawd...
I'm a Sunday witness fo' ma Lawd...
                    —*Traditional*

What Ringgold has seen she has shared via act, paints, clay, and cloth. Ringgold paints and quilts; Toni Cade Bambara painted, wrote, and told stories.

Toni Cade Bambara (1939–1995), artist, writer, and activist, lived the spirituals in her self-proclaimed ambassadorship to tell the truth and not be compromised by prevailing stereotypes. Her stories and edited anthologies champion this social, cultural, and political commitment to African American well-being. Her work covers vast pockets of black cultural experience and exposes divisiveness between various spiritual, psychological, and political forces within the black community. Bambara studied and worked in Milan, Italy, took a master's degree, worked in many neighborhood programs, and taught in the New York City college system. She participated in the women's liberation and black nationalist movements but realized neither activity fully dealt with black women's issues. She responded to that abyss by editing *The Black Woman: An Anthology*. In her edited anthologies and collections, Bambara empowers black women, encourages young readers to learn through living history and storytelling, and inspires them to write, read, and think critically. With her travel abroad and her work in community groups, Bambara uses art to communicate social and political messages about the well-being and wholeness of the African American community.[11] Bambara's many collaborative efforts call to mind this spiritual:

Plenty good room, plenty good room
Plenty good room in my Father's kingdom
Plenty good room, plenty good room
Plenty good room, choose your seat an' sit down.

I would not be a sinner
I'll tell you the reason why
'Cause if my Lord should call on me
I wouldn't be ready to die.

I would not be a backslider
I'll tell you the reason why
'Cause if my Lord should call on me
I wouldn't be ready to die.
                    —*Traditional*

Bambara wanted all to know that there's "plenty good room" to work together to spread the message of social and political justice. The social and political messages central to the life and work of Bambara often served as catalysts for the African American women who live the spirituals through their commitment to political activism on behalf of African Americans especially as they champion the rights of women as Womanists, feminists of color. These women include Naomi Anderson, Mary Church Terrell, Nannie Burroughs, Daisy Lampkin, Pauli Murray, and Dorothy Height.

Champions of Women's Rights

Naomi Bowman Talbert Anderson (1843–) lived the spirituals' quest for justice as she supported the black women's club movement. Born of free blacks, this nineteenth-century feminist participated in and encouraged westward migration, self-help, and feminism. Though she experienced numerous hardships with family deaths and illnesses, Anderson remained fearless and supported various feminist activities, including temperance and woman suffrage; protested against sexism and racism; and worked on behalf of housing and care for black children. Her life was dedicated to the service of women and African Americans.[12] Anderson's focus on collective response underlies the spiritual "Give Me Yo' Hand":

Give me yo' hand, give me yo' hand,
all I want is the love of God.
Give me yo' hand, give me yo' hand,
You must be loving at God's command.

You say you're aimin' for the skies,
Why don't you stop your tellin' lies!. . .
You say you're glad you been set free?
Why don't you let your neighbor be?
—*Traditional*

Like Anderson, Mary Church Terrell worked on behalf of women's rights as an early precursor of the foundations of Womanist theory.

Mary Church Terrell (1863–1954) lived the spirituals as an African American female activist for more than sixty-six years. In 1890, Terrell voiced what Womanists today explore: white women have a handicap of sex; black women have a dual handicap of sex and race. This handicap is not inherent to black women but is the burden society imposes. Born into a family of African American elite, Terrell did not experience classism and, initially, was also protected from racism. Terrell's growing awareness of discrimination and oppression led her to do well academically and helped her exemplify the strengths and abilities of blacks, especially African American women. In the United States, her intellectualism was dismissed, and she was under constraints to be an ideal Victorian woman and to stay in her place. When faced with oppression because of her race and gender in the United States, Terrell went to Europe. She returned after two years and started the National Association of Colored Women (NACW) to cultivate unity through self-help and to locus on the problem of oppression due to race and sex—one problem, not two. The NACW worked on improving black living standards, set up supportive institutions (Such as day care, kindergartens, and mothers' clubs), and focused on fund-raising for schools of domestic science and homes for the sick, the aged, and girls. Terrell began to concentrate on the accomplishments of African Americans despite oppression. Through her speeches, articles, and short stories, Terrell bolstered black morale and exposed lynching, black disenfranchisement, chain gangs, classism, and the passing of mulattos. She criticized anyone, black or white, who did not have the best interests of humanity at heart. In the last twenty years of her life, Terrell became more militant. Her battle cry against oppression is the thrust of the spiritual "Joshua Fit De Battle of Jericho," for the fate of these walls was her envisioned fate for racist evil:

> Joshua fit de battle of Jericho
> Jericho, Jericho
> Joshua fit de battle of Jericho
> And de walls come a tumblin' down.
>
> You may talk about the kings of Gideon
> You may talk about the men of Saul
> But there's none like good ol' Joshua
> And de battle am in his hand.
>
> —*Traditional*

Terrell despaired the continued economic difficulties of blacks and the irony of black soldiers fighting for democracy overseas when they were denied that same democracy here. She realized that morality and interracial dialogue had not abolished and would not abolish racism. In response, she began to picket, boycott, and participate in sit-ins. She worked with others to successfully struggle against segregated eating establishments and lived to see the blow to segregated public education in 1954 with *Brown v. Board of Education*.[13] Terrell not only participated in the struggle, she nurtured and mentored others, like Nannie Burroughs, who would carry the mantle for justice.

Nannie Burroughs (1879–1961) lived the spirituals as she made an outcry against sexism and led the struggle for women's rights, desegregation laws, industrial education for girls and women, and anti-lynching laws. Her passion for courageous change echoes the sentiments within this spiritual:

> Little David, play on your harp, Hallelu, Hallelu
> Little David, play on your harp, Hallelu.

God told Moses, O Lord!
Go down into Egypt, O Lord!
Tell ol' Pharo', O Lord!
Loose my people, O Lord!

Down in de valley, O Lord!
Didn't go t' stay, O Lord!
My soul got happy, O Lord!
I stayed all day, O Lord!

Come down angels, O Lord!
With ink an' pen, O Lord!
An' write salvation, O Lord!
To dyin' men, O Lord!

—*Traditional*

Burroughs was a David who helped kill off bits of the Goliath of ignorance, helplessness, sexism, and racism. Burroughs took the helm of leadership in many areas: religion, education, women's clubs, politics, and civil rights. She was instrumental in forming the largest African American women's organization in the United States, the Woman's Convention Auxiliary of the National Baptist Convention. Mentored by Anna Julia Cooper and Mary Church Terrell, Burroughs grew in her oratorical abilities and in her commitment to empowering black Baptist Church women in the fight against injustice. Burroughs initiated National Women's Day, a day celebrated in most black Protestant churches to honor sisterhood and as a means of fund-raising. She encouraged black Baptist churches to support women's suffrage and political empowerment as a way to overcome racism and sexism. Committed to overcoming the wholly impossible, Burroughs worked to instill black pride and racial self-help; stressed the import of black women being self-sufficient employees; founded the National Training School for Women and Girls (1909), renamed the Nannie Helen Burroughs School for Elementary School Education (1964); fought for justice and equality; and demanded that blacks protest and fight injustice with dollars and ballots, and not beg whites for mercy.[14] Burroughs radiated the commitment to women and blacks that was inherent to the life and work of Daisy Lampkin.

Daisy Adams Lampkin (c. 1884–1965) lived the spirituals through her work with civil rights, the National Council of Negro Women (NCNW), and the National Association of Colored Women (NACW). Lampkin worked for the equality of women and blacks. Her humanitarian activities were vast, and she mentored numerous persons in their public careers. As the national field secretary for the NAACP, Lampkin was a fundraiser and fighter for many civil rights organizations. She worked as president of the Negro Women's Franchise League (1915), with the National Suffrage League, and in the women's division of the Republican Party. Her work with the NAACP and the *Pittsburgh Courier*, from 1912, helped Lampkin foster success, particularly in the victorious battle against the nomination of pro-segregationist Supreme Court nominee Judge John J. Parker. In an earlier gubernatorial campaign, Parker had argued that blacks should be excluded from the political process, and in 1954 he wrote the narrow lower court decision in *Brown v. Board of Education*, which held that nongovernmental segregation was lawful. Lampkin, Roy Wilkins, and Walter White together formed a powerful triumvirate whose work laid the foundation for successes in civil rights throughout the nation. The spiritual "Swing Low, Sweet Chariot" champions Lampkin's inclusive zeal to enlist and then to gather and carry all to empowerment:

> Swing low, sweet chariot
> Coming for to carry me home [justice, freedom]
> Swing low, sweet chariot
> Coming for to carry me home.
>
> I looked over Jordan, and what did I see?
> Coming for to carry me home
> A band of angels coming after me
> Coming for to carry me home.
>
> If you get there before I do
> Coming for to carry me home
> Tell all my friends I'm coming, too
> Coming for to carry me home.
>
> I'm sometimes up, I'm sometimes down
> Coming for to carry me home
> But still my soul feels heavenly bound
> Coming for to carry me home.
> —*Traditional*

Lampkin had phenomenal success in boosting funds and membership for the NAACP along with being active in the NACW, NCNW, and Delta Sigma Theta, a service sorority. After giving up her post as field secretary for the NAACP due to extreme fatigue, Lampkin continued as a member of the boar of directors. From 1930 to just months before her death, Lampkin continued to devote herself totally to "the cause" of justice and civil rights.[15] Lampkin's call to fight for justice was part of Pauli Murray's call to the law and the gospel.

Pauli Murray (1910–1985) lived the spirituals as an advocate for women's rights, as lawyer, poet, teacher, and minister, and as a founding member of the National Organization for Women (NOW) in 1966. Murray tried unsuccessfully in 1938 to thwart racism by applying for graduate school admission at the University of North Carolina at Chapel Hill. Audacious, she graduated from Howard University Law School as first in her class, and the only woman. Her 1965 doctoral dissertation from Yale University Law School was: "Roots of the Racial Crisis: Prologue to Policy."

Murray was an early activist in civil rights from the New Deal through the 1980s. She participated in freedom rides and sit-ins, crusaded as a human rights attorney, and kept the mantle for justice as a professor, a civil and women's rights activist, a poet and writer (writing the first textbook in a series on African law), and an Episcopalian priest. After receiving her call to ministry, Murray completed a Master of Divinity and was ordained as the first black female priest of the Episcopal Church in 1977 at the National Cathedral in Washington DC. Murray's call to justice included an autobiography, *Song in a Weary Throat: An American Pilgrimage* (1987), two other books, and many articles and monographs.[16] Murray's evangelical propensities reflect the impetus within the spiritual "I Wanta Live So God Can Use Me":

I wanta live so God can use me
Victorious in this lan'
I wanta live so God can use me
Victorious in this lan'.

I wanta walk so God can use me. . .
I wanta pray so God can use me. . .
I wanta sing so God can use me. . .
I wanta work so God can use me. . .
I wanta preach so God can use me. . .
Treat my sisters so God can use me. . .
Treat my brothers so God can use me. . .
Treat my children so God can use me. . .
Treat my neighbors so God can use me. . .

—*Traditional*

Murray worked tirelessly to see that "dis worl' is on fire" for truth and justice. The journey for Murray had evangelical tenets, the tenets that filtered through women's club movements in the person of Dorothy Height.

Dorothy Height (1912–) lives the spirituals via her activism and leadership toward rights and equality for all humanity. Height began her service career working against sexism and on behalf of women's rights with the National Council of Negro Women, the Young Women's Christian Association, and Delta Sigma Theta. In the 1930s, Height dealt with the Harlem riots, became one of the leaders of the National Youth Movement during the New Deal, and joined Mary McLeod Bethune in the fight for full, equal employment, equal pay, and educational opportunities. Height spearheaded Delta's activism, volunteerism, social protest, and educational interests. Her concerns for women's rights encompass international concerns. The spiritual that reflects Height's words of encouragement to countless women across the years is:

Oh, Mary, doncha weep, doncha moan
Oh, Mary, doncha weep, doncha moan

Pharaoh's army got drownded
Oh, Mary, doncha weep.

—Traditional

Height taught that there is no reason to cry and fret, for, like Pharaoh's army, oppression and remnants of sexism and racism "got drownded." All the organizations she has led have been influenced by her focus on human and international relations. Her tremendous leadership has brought about justice and empowerment in numerous arenas: women's rights; child care, education, and development; food drives; housing projects; and positive black family life celebrated in the national Black Family Reunion Celebration that Height envisioned and created in 1986.[17] Often the lives of black women working on behalf of African Americans and for African American women support, influence, and overlap activists who are more focused in the political arena, for the moment one participates in relationships and in seeking justice, one has become political. The political activists include Shirley Chisholm, Mary Frances Berry, Marian Wright Edelman, and Elaine Brown.

Political Firebrands

Shirley Chisholm (1924–) lives the spirituals as she seeks to empower African Americans and women, on a sure, independent platform stated autobiographically: *Unbought and Unbossed* (1970). Along with being the first African American woman elected to the U.S. House of Representatives (1968–1982), Chisholm has worked for civil rights and women's liberation issues. She was the first black person to run for U.S. President in the Democratic party. Disappointed by the cool response from black male- and white female-led organizations, Chisholm retired from politics and spends her time on the educational lecture circuit.[18] The response to Chisholm's efforts in national politics reflects the essence of the spiritual "I'm a Rolling":

I'm a rolling
I'm a rolling
I'm a rolling
Thro' an unfriendly world.

O brothers, won't you help me,
O brothers, won't you help me to pray?
O brothers, won't you help me,
Won't you help me in the service of the Lord?
O sisters, won't you help me. . .
O preachers, won't you help me. . .

—Traditional

Chisholm's political savvy and eloquence parallel the scholastic excellence of Mary Berry.

Mary Frances Berry (1938–) lives the spirituals through her academic distinction, political activism, and public service that authorize and ground her fight against immorality and impropriety of domestic and foreign racist policies. In addition to her many publications, Berry has excelled in educational administration and served as assistant secretary for education in the Department of Health, Education, and Welfare from 1977 to 1980. She has lived the spirituals as a member of the U.S. Commission on Civil Rights; was arrested protesting South African apartheid; and was a co-founder of the national Free South Africa movement. Berry has worked in numerous grassroots organizations and in advocacy with other scholars in filing amicus curiae (friends of the court) briefs in defending the civil rights of African Americans.[19] Because of the choices that Berry has worked to make possible in America and Africa, a spiritual that embodies where she is and what she asks is this:

> Lord, I can't stay away,
> I can't stay away.
>
> I got to go to judgment to stand my trials,
> I got to go to judgment to stand my trials.
>
> They're coming from the east, coming from the west,
> Coming from the north, coming from the south,
> Coming on the rainbow, coming on the cloud.
> —*Traditional*

Both Berry and Marian Edelman have signified in the national government arena.

Marian Wright Edelman (1939–) has lived the spirituals as a sit-in participant in Atlanta, a worker for voter registration, and an intern for the NAACP Legal Defense and Education Fund. Edelman has worked to use laws on behalf of the poor. She developed the Children's Defense Fund, begun as the Washington Research Project, to advocate for children and youth. Her work concerns teen pregnancy, child care and health, social service, youth employment, child welfare, and adoption. Edelman, an author and a 1985 MacArthur Foundation Fellow, is a skilled lobbyist on behalf of children and the poor.[20] Edelman's advocacy on behalf of children proclaims the message of this spiritual:

> Dere's a little wheel a turning in my heart,
> Dere's a little wheel a turning in my heart,
> In my heart, in my heart,
> Dere's a little wheel a turning in my heart.
>
> I feel so very happy in my heart. . .
> O I don't feel no ways tired in my heart. . .
> O I feel like shouting in my heart. . .
> —*Traditional*

Edelman's passion for the plight, care, and love of children echoes a similar concern for children and for student welfare held by Elaine Brown.

Elaine Brown (1943–), having grown up singing in church choirs in Philadelphia, first lived the spirituals by teaching piano to children in Watts. This privilege of working with and empowering others led to her participation with the Black Panther Party (BPP) during the 1960s and 1970s. Brown was a member of several black student political organizations. After moving up the ranks, she became chairperson of BPP and led it into being an important force in Oakland, California, especially concerning voter registration. Brown's work on behalf of others celebrates the spiritual "We Are Climbin' Jacob's Ladder," the ladder of success:

> We are climbin' Jacob's ladder,
> We are climbin' Jacob's ladder,
> We are climbin' Jacob's ladder,
> Soldiers of the cross.
>
> Every round goes higher, higher. . .
> Do you think I'd make a soldier. . .
> —*Traditional*

Brown has worked to establish social programs for the poor and for African Americans by forming coalitions between legal constituencies and the community. Brown released two albums that contained songs based on her BPP experience: *Until We're Free* and *Seize the Tie.*[21] Brown's work with voter registration and community uplift echoes the work of African American women who have lived the spirituals through their engagement in human uplift, especially with civil rights, including Ida Wells-Barnett, Septima Clark, Ella Baker, Rosa Parks, Fannie Lou Hamer, Daisy Bates, Constance Baker Motley, Unita Blackwell, Eleanor Norton, and Barbara Jordan.

Catalysts for Human Uplift

Ida B. Wells-Barnett (1862–1931) lived the spirituals through upholding African American civil rights, economic rights, and the rights of women. Wells-Barnett's gifts as an activist and journalist enabled her to expose race, gender, and economic oppression. Wells-Barnett did not let the threat of physical harm or social isolation dissuade her from exposing and confronting oppression through teaching, debating, and writing pamphlets and newspaper articles. Her articles appeared in local and national publications, including features in the *Memphis Free Speech and Headlight,* the newspaper in which she held part interest. Rosa Parks was not the first to not want to give up a seat. Wells-Barnett was physically removed from a train in 1884 for refusing to ride in the rear, segregated car. After three black independently successful colleagues were jailed, shot, and lynched because they refused to acquiesce to a competing white grocer, Wells-Barnett began to question and investigate lynching. Most Americans assumed that black men accused of rape were the persons who were lynched. Wells-Barnett determined that lynching was a racist tool for eradicating financially independent African Americans, designed to terrorize blacks into accepting the labels of inferior, unequal, and subordinate. In fewer than twenty years, she documented more than 10,000 lynchings of unarmed and powerless blacks. After she challenged local justice in Memphis and the notions of white female purity in an editorial, her newspaper office was destroyed and her life threatened. Wells-Barnett went to New York and continued to focus on lynching. After two tours to England, she became more controversial for exposing white so-called supporters of black causes who remained silent on the problem of lynching. Wells-Barnett and others met with President McKinley to protest the horrid injustice of lynching. After her involvement with the 1893 Chicago World's Fair, Wells-Barnett stayed in Chicago, where she supported and founded organizations that supported reform and women. Her anti-lynching activities triggered her initial involvement in the NAACP, though she left the organization later because of its timid stances and predominantly white board. Wells-Barnett worked with and successfully integrated the United States suffragette movement, for she felt the vote was the key to black empowerment and to social, political, and economic equality. For Wells, the spiritual "The Crucifixion," also known as "They Crucified My Lord," is what happened to countless blacks, as, ironically, their judges and executioners "never said a mumblin' word" of truth or justice about their victims:

> They crucified my Lord,
> And he never said a mumblin' word
> Not a word, not a word, not a word.
> They nailed him to the tree...
> They pierced him in the side...
> He bowed his head and died...
> —*Traditional*

Wells-Barnett's support of Marcus Garvey and her dislike of Booker T. Washington's accommodationism, together with her concerns about lynching, disenfranchisement, and unequal segregated public education, caused the U.S. Secret Service to dub her a dangerous individual and a radical. Valiantly, she continued to write about lynching, riots, and exploitation of African Americans in her many articles, speeches, and reports, and her autobiography, *Crusade for Justice: The Autobiography of Ida Wells* (edited by her daughter, Alfreda Duster), was published posthumously in 1970.[22] While Wells-Barnett engaged in civil rights activities as a protest journalist, Septima Clark used politics and education to make a difference.

Septima Poinsette Clark (1898–1987) lived the spirituals as a civil rights leader, educational reformer, political activist, and champion of citizenship education. Clark embraced the assertiveness, dignity, gentleness, and nonviolent temperament and importance of education from her parents. She resolved to bring health and educational reform when she worked in the economically, hygienically, and socially horrendous circumstances on John's Island, South Carolina. Inspired by studies with W. E. B. Du Bois, Clark was an advocate for equality in educational facilities and teacher salaries in South Carolina. She saw the links between protest, education, and documentation. Her work with the NAACP in protest and litigation was a fight against injustice. After teaching for forty years, Clark lost her teaching job and retirement benefits, because her work helped overturn many segregationist laws and because she refused to stop working with the NAACP. At the invitation of Myles Horton, director of the Highlander Folk School in Tennessee, Clark helped this citizenship school mobilize to support local social protest programs. Clark had studied at Highlander and was impressed by its biracial, humanist approach to working on national problems, teaching civil disobedience, democratic empowerment, and literacy empowerment. Her zealous efforts in education and protest echo the temperament in the spiritual "Sit Down, Servant":

> Sit down, servant, I can't sit down
> Sit down, servant, I can't sit down
> Sit down, servant, I can't sit down
> My soul's so happy,
> That I can't sit down.
> —*Traditional*

Clark still had too much work to do to sit down. Her work with Highlander in training settings all over the South transformed southern political systems, and she did similar work with the Southern Christian Leadership Conference. Clark noted that along with the racist harassment, beatings, murders and oppression by the KKK and the White Citizen's Council, she and women like Ella Baker and Rosa Parks had to fight sexism and were often not recognized for their contributions to the Civil Rights Movement.[23]

Ella Josephine Baker (1903–1986) lived the spirituals through her grassroots work and behind-the-scenes activity in black politics from the 1930s to her death. She was a worker and an advocate in several arenas: on behalf of civil rights in Harlem; against poverty and hunger (1930s); as an NAACP field secretary and director of local branches (1940s); and in out reach, volunteer, and voter registration work for the SCLC (1950s). Baker helped found the Student Nonviolent Coordinating Committee (SNCC), a new, independent youth organization with militant tactics and an egalitarian structure, for she did not want the movement to fizzle out or to be co-opted by more conservative and moderate African Americans. The SNCC, with Baker's leadership, helped start the grassroots Mississippi Freedom Democratic Party. Baker's legacy affected causes including the Students for a Democratic Society, the Black Panther Party, mainstream elections, and women's liberation activities (1970s). Baker built bridges between the Civil Rights activities of the 1950s and 1960s, and black resistance through the 1980s. Affiliated with more than fifty coalitions and organizations, Baker used her upbringing in southern black culture with the traditions of mutual cooperation, self-help, and extended family, which made for close-knit communities, to enrich her fight for democratic principles, cooperative leadership, inclusion of women, and grassroots participation. Personally and politically, Baker refused to accept a "woman's behavior and place."[24] Baker accomplished much because she could bring people together in the manner celebrated in the spiritual "Four and Twenty Elders":

> Dere are four and twenty elders on their knees
> Dere are four and twenty elders on their knees
> An' we'll all rise together,
> An' face the risin' sun,
> O Lord, have mercy if you please.
>
> Dey are bowin' 'round the altar on their knees. . .
> See Gideon's army bowin' on their knees. . .
> See Daniel 'mong the lions on their knees. . .
> —*Traditional*

Like Baker, one day Rosa Parks refused to accept the place society relegated to her—to sit in the "Colored" place, in the back of the bus.

Rosa McCauley Parks (1913–) lives the spirituals through her civil rights activism as she has challenged and helped transform southern racist traditions and laws. With the support of the Montgomery Improvement Association, the Montgomery NAACP, and the Women's Political Council (led by Jo Ann Gibson Robinson), Parks sat down on the bus in Montgomery, Alabama, in December 1955. Her stance was a catalyst for the historic Montgomery bus boycott that ended when the Supreme Court decreed that city bus segregation was unconstitutional. The boycott helped to usher in the 1960s Civil Rights Movement, together with organized, massive non-violent disobedience and the national leadership of Martin Luther King Jr. Both Parks and her husband, Raymond, were active in their local NAACP chapter. Parks also trained at the Highlander Folk School with others who were concerned about the struggle for justice and equality. Parks relocated to Detroit and received an appointment as staff assistant to Congressman John Conyers. In 1987, Parks was able to fulfill a longtime goal by starting the Rosa and Raymond Parks Institute of Self-Development in Detroit, which focuses on career training for African American youth and supports her commitment to human rights struggles.[25] Parks had learned that even if the progress of the Movement echoed the following spiritual, she would persevere and could say, "There I'll take my stand":

> Done made my vow to the Lord
> And I never will turn back.
> I will go, I shall go
> To see what the end will be.

Goin' to serve my Lord while I have breath
To see what the end will be.
So I can serve Him after death.
To see what the end will be.

When I was a sinner, just like you. . .
I prayed and prayed until I come through. . .
            —*Traditional*

While Parks was busy protesting in Alabama, Fannie Lou Hamer helped effect change in Mississippi.

Fannie Lou Hamer (1917–1977), who lived and sang the spirituals in protest against injustice, was a symbol of the 1960s Civil Rights Movement. Hamer was a sharecropper who shaped the Movement as one committed to voter registration, as an orator, and as a political activist with two social activist bodies: as a field worker with the Student Nonviolent Coordinating Committee (SNCC) and as one of the founders of the Mississippi Freedom Democratic Party (MFDP). In the process of overcoming the racist literacy tests to become a registered voter and a member of SNCC, Hamer became the brunt of economic intimidation and physical violence. Her life and the lives of her family were constantly threatened. Hamer captured the nation's attention with her televised objection to racism at the 1964 Democratic Convention, where the MFDP challenged the seating of the all-white Democratic delegation from Mississippi. Though the MFDP's challenge failed, the resulting action was that the national Democratic Party pledged not to seat any delegations that excluded African Americans at the 1968 convention. Until her death, Hamer fought for human rights as she sang and lived "This Little Light of Mine" and "Go Tell It on the Mountain"[26]:

This little light of mine, I'm gonna let it shine
This little light of mine, I'm gonna let it shine
This little light of mine, I'm gonna let it shine
Let it shine, let it shine, let it shine.
            —*Traditional*

Go tell it on the mountain,
Over the hills and everywhere
Go tell it on the mountain,
To let my people go.
            —*Hamer's redacted version*

Hamer's perseverance on behalf of justice shifted the politics of Mississippi and the nation, just as the protest work of Daisy Bates helped transform politics and educational discrimination in Alabama.

Daisy Gatson Bates (1920–) has lived the spirituals as a freedom fighter via journalism, as a civil rights participant, and as a catalyst for integrating the public schools of Little Rock, Arkansas.

Bates and her husband, L. C., began a weekly newspaper, the *Arkansas State Press,* an independent voice that worked toward improving the economic and social lives of blacks and that exposed brutality by the police. Bates was president of the Arkansas NAACP when the U.S. Supreme Court handed down the 1954 decision in *Brown v. Board of Education,* which overturned the legal standard for segregated public school education. In 1957, Bates, a thousand paratroopers, and the national NAACP leaders worked to get nine African American students into Little Rock's Central High. This courageous charge for justice led Bates and her students through the scenario of this spiritual:

> We will walk through the valley in peace
> We will walk through the valley in peace
> If Jesus himself be our leader
> We will walk through the valley in peace.
>
> We will walk through the valley in peace. . .
> Behold I give myself away. . .
> We will walk through the valley in peace. . .
> This track I'll see and I'll pursue. . .
>
> There will be no sorrow there
> There will be no sorrow there
> If Jesus himself will be our leader
> We will walk through the valley in peace.
> —*Traditional*

Bates remains active in African American community, social, and economic activities in Little Rock.[27] Bates worked as a citizen to effect change, while Constance Baker Motley has helped transform the reality of civil rights in America as a litigator and judge.

Constance Baker Motley (1921–) has lived the spirituals by using the U.S. courtrooms to do battle for justice, for civil rights. An activist during high school, Motley worked for the National Youth Administration. She later attended college with the help of a benefactor and got her law degree from Columbia Law School in 1946. While working with the NAACP Legal Defense and Education Fund as assistant counsel, she faced racism and sexism in the public arena. In this capacity, she tried cases and wrote briefs for Supreme Court school desegregation cases against southern universities that dealt a blow to legal institutional racism. Motley won nine out of the ten cases she argued before the Supreme Court, served in the New York State Senate, and was elected as the president of the Borough of Manhattan for four years. All along, Motley's call for justice has been the call symbolized in the spiritual "Honor, Honor":

> King Jesus lit the candle by the watuh side,
> To see the little children when dey truly baptize',
> Honor, honor unto the dying lamb.

Oh run along, children, an' be baptize',
Mighty pretty meetin' by de watuh side,
Honor, honor unto the dying lamb.

I prayed all day; I prayed all night,
My head got sprinkled wid duh midnight dew.
—Traditional

After staunch sexist- and racist-based opposition to her nomination as a U.S. district judge, Motley was confirmed in August 1966. Motley continues to uphold the fight for justice as a senior district judge in New York.[28] While Motley sits on the bench, Unita Blackwell has pursued justice through civil rights protest, in state politics, and on the local level, in city government.

Unita Blackwell (1933–), a Mississippian, became the mayor of a town where she was once forbidden to vote. Blackwell lived the spirituals during the 1960s Civil Rights Movement as a member of the Student Nonviolent Coordinating Committee. She participated in voter registration and civil nonviolent protest, and was arrested and jailed more than seventy times. A founding member of the Mississippi Freedom Democratic Party, she helped to bring suits challenging segregation. The many struggles Blackwell experienced meant that some days Blackwell would think the words of this spiritual:

Nobody knows the trouble I've seen,
Nobody knows but Jesus
Nobody knows the trouble I've seen,
Glory, hallelujah.

Sometimes I'm up, sometimes I'm down,
Oh, yes, Lawd,
Sometimes I'm almost to de groun',
Oh, yes, Lawd.

Although you see me going long so. . .
I have my trials here below. . .

One day when I was walking along. . .
De element opened, and de love came down. . .

I never shall forget the day. . .
When Jesus washed my sins away. . .

—Traditional

Blackwell's commitment to social action permeates her work involving rural development and housing, energy conservation, and support of low-income housing opportunities, as well as her work with women.[29] Like Blackwell, another Mississippian, Eleanor Norton, has also worked as activist, litigator, and educator in state government and for humanitarian rights.

Eleanor Holmes Norton (1937–) lives the spirituals through her lifelong commitment to civil rights. Her journey has included her work with the Student Nonviolent Coordinating Committee, her participation with the Mississippi Freedom Democratic Party, and her tasks as a national staff member for the 1963 March on Washington. Norton has championed civil rights and civil liberties in her work with the American Civil Liberties Union in New York City, especially when she represented former Alabama governor George Wallace, who wanted to have a political rally at Shea Stadium. She has also worked for civil rights issues with the New York City Commission on Human Rights (1970–77); as chair of the Equal Employment Opportunity Commission; as a law professor at Georgetown University; as a congressional representative for the District of Columbia; and as legal scholar and coauthor of *Sex Discrimination and the Law: Causes and Remedies* (1975).[30] Her unceasing work on behalf of humanitarian rights indicates a sense of preparation undergirding this spiritual:

> I wanna be ready, I wanna be ready,
> I wanna be ready
> to walk in Jerusalem just like John.
>
> John said that Jerusalem was four-square...
> I hope, good Lord, I'll meet you there...
> When Peter was preaching at Pentecost...
> O he was filled with the Holy Ghost...
> —*Traditional*

Like Eleanor Norton, Barbara Jordan's work blended a concern for civil rights with the law and education.

Barbara Jordan (1936–1995) lived the spirituals in her legislative work as a state senator and U.S. congresswoman on behalf of the disadvantaged, the poor, and African Americans. She tolled the bell for justice with her activities during President Nixon's impeachment hearings. As a senator, she worked for the Workman's Compensation Act; as a congresswoman, she worked to expand the 1965 Voting Rights Act. The former increased the maximum amount of benefits an injured worker could be paid; the latter covered Mexican Americans in southwestern states and in other states where minorities had their voting rights restricted via unfair registration practices, or where they had been denied the right to vote. Hers was the voice of cool disdain in evaluating the impeachment of President Nixon. The thrust of Jordan's political agendas shows that she had her ear attuned to the public, implied in this spiritual:

> Listen to the lambs, all a-cryin'
> Listen to the lambs, all a-cryin'
> Listen to the lambs, all a-cryin'
> All a-cryin', all a-cryin'.

> He shall feed his flock like a shepherd,
> And carry the young lambs in his bosom.
> Come on, sister, with you' ups an' downs,
> Listen to the lambs, all a-cryin';
> Angels waiting for to give you a crown,
> Listen to the lambs, all a-cryin'.
>
> Come on, sister, and a don't be ashamed. . .
> Angels waiting for to write your name. . .
>
> Mind out, brother, how you walk de cross. . .
> Foot might slip, an' your soul get lost. . .
> —*Traditional*

After leaving pubic political office in 1978, Jordan served as a professor at the Lyndon B. Johnson School of Public Affairs at the University of Texas at Austin, where she taught the preaching she formerly practiced.[31] Jordan used the university podium to share the cause of justice and civil rights. The classroom podium has long been the arena for many African American women, as they live the spirituals through the ministry of education, including Sister Aloysius, Anna Julia Cooper, Mary McLeod Bethune, and Marva Collins.

Talented, Transformative Teachers

Anne Marie Becroft, or Sister Aloysius (1805–1833), lived the spirituals as she gave black females education and religion in a society where slavery, racism, and sexism were rampant. Her activities helped to shape black U.S. Catholic history. Becroft, an excellent teacher, with the help of other nuns, ran an academy for students until 1831, when she left to join the Oblate Sisters of Providence in Baltimore and became Sister Aloysius. Sister Aloysius taught her students English, math, and embroidery but died just one year after taking her habit.[32] Her dedication to the ministry of education and of the church in thanksgiving parallels the focus of this spiritual:

> Oh, rise an' shine, an' give God de glory, glory
> Rise an' shine, an' give God de glory
> Rise an' shine, an' give God de glory
> In de year of Jubilee [freedom].
>
> We are climbing Jacob's ladder. . .
> Every round goes higher and higher. . .
> Rise and shine. . .

Sister Aloysius believed and lived that one could "rise and shine" to freedom from oppression, freedom to love, and freedom of knowledge. The enlightenment that Sister Aloysius accorded students in parochial schools was the goal of Anna Julia Cooper in public and private school education, in human rights activities, and in black women's organizations.

Anna Julia Cooper (1858–1964) lived the spirituals as an individual who, early on, committed to the empowerment and education of women. She exemplified this quest in her intellectual pursuits from St. Augustine's Normal School and Collegiate Institute in Raleigh, North Carolina, to the Sorbonne in Paris. In addition to being an educator, Cooper was a human rights advocate, scholar, essayist, author, lecturer, feminist, and vital participant in the black women's club movement. Throughout her life, Cooper addressed the needs and situations of the oppressed, especially the indignities and unequal treatment experienced by black women. Her evocation to black women embraces the words of this spiritual:

> March on! March on!
> Way over in de Egyp' lan'
> You shall gain de victory
> You shall gain the day.
>
> —*Traditional*

After teaching at Wilberforce and St. Augustine, Cooper was invited to teach in the public school system of Washington DC. She was active with nineteenth-century black intellectuals and was the only female member of the American Negro Academy. Cooper completed her dissertation at the Sorbonne at the age of sixty-six, which indicated her scholastic excellence and interest in pan-Africanism. It was titled "The Attitude of France toward Slavery during the Revolution." Cooper became the second president of Frelinghuysen University, a nontraditional group of schools founded to educate working African Americans in Washington DC. Though lack of funding caused the demise of this institution, Cooper's accomplishments were vast. This teacher, lecturer, poet, writer, feminist, and activist addressed many themes, gave of herself tirelessly, and did not retire until age eighty-four.[33] Cooper shares the ranks of the tireless worker in higher education with Bethune.

Mary McLeod Bethune (1875–1955) lived the spirituals as a most extraordinary public figure—educator, politician, administrator, and diplomat. She championed the well-being of African Americans, especially women and youth. Her belief in God and in herself, along with her missionary spirit and tremendous teaching ability, moved Bethune to begin a training school for girls (1904) that later merged with Cookman Institute to become Bethune-Cookman College. Bethune cared for empowerment, economic and community development, and black culture. She also trained her students to sing the spirituals. Her political and social service activities included national leadership of the National Association of Colored Women's creative and leadership interests in the National Council of Negro Women, a national umbrella organization for existing national women's organizations; and work with public housing, army desegregation, and civil rights. Along with the federal Council on Negro Affairs with the New Deal in Washington DC. Bethune was instrumental in many avenues, and this power was supported by her close liaison with President

Franklin Roosevelt, Eleanor Roosevelt, and President Harry S. Truman. Despite her sponsorship of democratic ideals and patriotism, Bethune was a victim of the House Congressional Committee on Un-American Activities. She still continued to work for justice and equality. The weight of her responsibilities and her missionary spirit probably came together prayerfully in a manner displayed by this spiritual:

> I want Jesus to walk with me
> I want Jesus to walk with me
> All along this tedious journey
> Lord, I want Jesus, to walk with me
>
> In my trials, Lord, walk with me. . .
> When I'm in trouble, Lord, walk with me. . .
>
> —*Traditional*

Bethune was instrumental in the development of the National Youth Administration (NYA) and the Civilian Conservation Corps. She facilitated employment and equitable educational opportunities for black youth through the NYA. Through more than fifty years of service, Bethune championed both accommodationism (self-help, vocational skills, and appeals to philanthropic whites) and, later, full citizenship rights, governmental assistance, and higher education.[34] Bethune's quest for expansive education for her students, including the best in the arts and sciences, was one of the major building blocks of the curriculum designed by Marva Collins.

Marva Collins (1936–) lives the spirituals by standing up to the Chicago public school system, using creative and progressive concepts to educate previously neglected children on Chicago's West Side. Collins began Westside Preparatory School as an alternative educational institution. She wanted to establish the same kind of nurturing environment she grew up in for Chicago's African American children. Collins used personal funds, dedication, confidence, a strong will, and love for young people to overcome racism, classism, low expectations, and low self-esteem that had kept many Chicago youth in bondage. Collins' success in creating excellence has been documented in two *60 Minutes* features, in invitations to be the U.S. Secretary of Education, and in the adaptation of her ideas and methods by school systems in Ohio and Oklahoma. The 1995 *60 Minutes* feature showed that twenty years later, all of the first class of Collins' Westside Preparatory were college students or graduates, and all were successful. None had succumbed to crime or failure.[35] Collins celebrates the success of her methodology with her students, as proclaimed in this spiritual:

> Glory, glory, hallelujah.'
> Since I laid my burden [*the load of inept education*] down
>
> Glory, glory, hallelujah!
> Since I laid my burden down.
>
> Friends don't treat me like they used to,

Since I laid my burden down. . .
I'm goin' home to live with Jesus
Since I laid my burden down. . .

—Traditional

Just as black women have lived the spirituals via education, others have chosen other avenues of expression. Three women who have signified via religion or social change include Jarena Lee, Josephine Allensworth, and Mother Hale.

Social Strategists

Jarena Lee (1783–?) lived the spirituals and signified despite the prejudice against a woman preacher, by proclaiming the Word of God. This antebellum feminist was the first woman to ask the African Methodist Episcopal Church for the authority to preach in 1809. Lee claimed authority to preach via an inner spiritual experience. Lee had wrestled with her conscience, and her relationship with God for many years. After several bouts with near suicide, Lee had a conversion experience. After experiencing sanctification, she knew a flush of ecstasy, of light and bliss, and received a call from God to preach the gospel. Against opposition, Lee asked why people should think it improper for a woman to preach, since the Savior died for women as well as men. Their denial did not stop Lee. After the death of her husband, Lee continued to have a commitment to preach the gospel while caring for two small children. Lee asked the then bishop Richard Allen, a second time, for the authority and freedom to hold prayer meetings and to preach in her own home. Lee made no apologies, for her life was contained in this spiritual:

I know the Lord, I know the Lord,
I know the Lord has laid His hands on me.
I know the Lord, I know the Lord,
I know the Lord has laid His hands on me.

Did you ever see the like before?
Know the Lord has laid His hands on me.
King Jesus preaching to the poor,
Know the Lord has laid His hands on me.

Oh, wasn't that a mighty day. . .
When Jesus washed my sins away. . .

—Traditional

After granting permission, Allen publicly acknowledged her ministerial and preaching gifts. Lee preached throughout the Northeast, and she likened herself to Paul of Tarsus as she traveled to deliver the Word of God. Lee recorded her experiences in two works: *Life and Religious Experience of Jarena Lee, a Colored Lady, Giving an Account of Her Call to Preach (1836)* and *Religious Experience and Journal of Mrs. Jarena Lee, Giving an Account of Her Call to Preach the Gospel* (1849). With only three months of schooling, Lee felt safe in, protected by, and led of the Lord. Just as Lee made strides for the call of women to ministry, Josephine Allensworth, the spouse of a minister, made great strides by working on behalf of black veterans and by founding a town.

Josephine Leavell Allensworth (1855–1939), born in Kentucky, lived spirituals as one of the leaders in social change and as advancement in the development of Allensworth, California, an all-black colony (1908–1950s). She and her husband, Allen (a Civil War veteran, Baptist minister, and chaplain for the U.S. Army, 24th Infantry), founded this settlement to afford a home for black soldiers, fair and equal treatment, and freedom from race restrictions. She worked with the school board, started a library, and worked with social and educational groups. Although the colony failed, Allensworth's activities provided housing, education, and political opportunities for many. The gift and beauty of the city to empower others is embodied in this spiritual:

> Oh what a beautiful City,
> Oh what a beautiful City,
> Oh what a beautiful City,
> Twelve gates unto the city, a Hallelu'.
>
> Three gates in uh de East,
> Three gates in uh de West,
> Three gates in uh de South,
> Three gates in uh de North,
> Makin' it twelve gates unto the city, a Hallelu'.
>
> My Lawd built uh dat city,
> And he said it was just a four-square,
> And he said he wanted you sinners,
> To meet Him in uh de air,
> Makin' it twelve gates unto the city, a Hallelu'.
> —*Traditional*

The care Allensworth exhibited for the masses resembles the care and compassion exhibited by Mother Hale for black babies.

Clara (Mother) McBride Hale (1904–1992) lived the spirituals as a humanitarian, homemaker, and licensed foster mother who devoted her time and life to taking care of numerous drug-addicted and unwanted black babies, when young mothers brought their babies to her. Mother Hale, so named by her charges, began Hale House in 1970. In more than twenty years, Mother Hale and her staff cared for more than eight hundred babies born either with AIDS or addicted to drugs.[36] The special, devoted attention Hale House provided for the unwanted and the displaced is the healing power of this spiritual:

> There is a balm in Gilead,
> To make the wounded whole,

There is a balm in Gilead,
To heal the sin-sick soul.

Sometimes I feel discouraged,
And think my work's in vain,
But then the Holy Spirit
Revives my soul again.

Don't ever be discouraged,
For Jesus is your friend,
And if you lack for knowledge,
He'll ne'er refuse to lend.

If you cannot preach like Peter,
If you cannot pray like Paul,
You can tell the love of Jesus,
And say he died for all.

—*Traditional*

Mother Hale wrote love and care on the hearts of her wards; many other African American women, such as Charlotte Grimké, Maya Angelou, Lorraine Hansberry, Sonia Sanchez, and Nikki Giovanni, have written words that have inspired, challenged, and entertained us.

Singing coast to coast
With words, with songs
Across the sea
In city, and in country
'Til the walls of injustice
Came tumbling down.
Inspiring thousands
Joyful noises
Your moan incarnated
The silent prayer
Of folk in bondage:
Unjust laws
The nonessentials of life;
The hopelessness beyond pain.

Witnessing Wordsmiths

Charlotte L. Forten Grimké (1837–1914) lived the spirituals in her anti-slavery crusades and her poetry. Many of her antislavery works appeared in antislavery print media such as the *Liberator*, the *National Anti-Slavery Standard*, and the *Anglo African* magazine. She empowered her students by teaching them about black leaders and liberators. Grimké wrote about the life of the Sea Islands to show the northern reading public that blacks wanted to work, learn, and be citizens. She

Cheryl A. Kirk-Duggan

continued to write and advocate for black civil rights, repeating that blacks wanted all the rights accorded all American citizens.[37] Grimké wanted her students to know the reminder in this spiritual:

> Somebody's knocking at your door
> Somebody's knocking at your door
> Oh, sinner, why don't you answer,
> Somebody's knocking at your door.
>
> Knocks like Jesus, Somebody's knocking at your door. . .
> Can't you hear him, Somebody's knocking at your door. . .
> Answer Jesus, Somebody's knocking at your door. . .
> Jesus calls you, Somebody's knocking at your door. . .
> Can't you trust him, Somebody's knocking at your door. . .
> —*Traditional*

Born more than a century after Grimké, Maya Angelou inspires all who listen to rise to the heights of human magnificence, through her words and support of protest.

Maya Angelou (1928–) lives the spirituals through the majesty, protest, and empowerment of her poetry, prose, and song. She transcended early rape by her mother's boyfriend by choosing silence and by ultimately having a perpetual love affair with libraries and books. During the 1960s, Angelou, with Godfrey Cambridge, wrote a revue to help raise funds for the Southern Christian Leadership Conference. After living and working as a journalist, editor, and professor in Africa, Angelou returned to the United States in 1966 and wrote the autobiographical *I Know Why the Caged Bird Sings* in 1970. Her autobiographical works, poetry, and other presentations are a lesson to all, celebrated in the spiritual "We Shall Overcome":

> We shall overcome, we shall overcome,
> We shall overcome, someday [today].
> Deep in my heart, I do believe,
> We shall overcome, someday.
>
> We'll walk hand in hand. . .
> The Lord will see us through. . .
> —*Traditional*

A professor at Wake Forest University, Angelou continues to inspire and call for the eradication of injustice and cruelty.[38] While Angelou evokes and proclaims in prose and poetry, Lorraine Hansberry electrified and inspired via drama, and she participated in fund-raising.

Lorraine Hansberry (1930–1965) lived the spirituals in her dynamic writings, notably *A Raisin in the Sun*, which opened in New York in 1959. The play depicts the lives of working-class black folk as they deal with overcrowded living conditions and racist, restricted housing covenants that mean that white homeowners will not sell their property to blacks. (The staged and televised versions of this play contained Hansberry's revisions that reflect the growing militant mood of African Americans in the 1960s.) Hansberry knew racism, though she grew up in a middle-class family. She knew the plight of black tenants who rented from her father. She supported the 1960s protests by raising funds to help support civil rights organizations and the southern freedom movement. Along with desire for social and political change, Hansberry helped transform American theater by shifting from characters rife with despair to characters that celebrated and affirmed life in spite of cruelty, destruction, and disappointment. Hansberry empowered blacks and women before the 1970s feminist movement began.[39] Her dramatic messages reiterated the gifts of freedom in this spiritual:

> No more auction block for me,
> No more, no more,
> No more auction block for me,
> Many thousand gone.
>
> No more peck o' corn for me...
> No more driver's lash for me...
> No more pint o' salt for me...
> No more hundred lash for me...
> No more mistress call for me...
>
> —*Traditional*

The change effected by Hansberry's plays embraces some of the revolutionary voice of Sonia Sanchez.

Sonia Sanchez (1934–) lives the spirituals in her commitment to civil rights and to improving the quality of African American life through her writings. A 1960s activist, Sanchez spoke out against poverty and substandard educational opportunities. She helped to raise the consciousness of students at several major universities and continues to teach at Temple University. Sanchez uses colloquial conversation and street language to expose the oppression of blacks, and she critiques racism, sexism, capitalism, child abuse, drug abuse, generational conflicts, initiation rituals for women, black-on-black crime, imperialism, womanizing and useless men, and the death and destruction of key black leaders. Sanchez's poetry and poem plays remind African Americans not to fall prey to valueless life trapped by materialism and the objectification of human life, and remind white America about the price of continuing black oppression. She continues to speak nationally and internationally against violence and turmoil and against the oppressions of racism, sexism, and capitalism.[40] Her writing and speaking extol the message of the spiritual "I Ain't Got Weary Yet":

> I ain't got weary yet,
> I ain't got weary yet,
> I've been in the wilderness
> A mighty long time,

> An' I ain't got weary yet.
>
> I ain't got weary yet,
> I ain't got weary yet,
> I've been on my knees...
>
> I've been praying like Silas,
> I've been preaching like Paul,
> I've been serving my Lord...
>
> I've been walkin' with the Savior,
> I've been talkin' with the Lord,
> I've been in the wilderness...
>
> —*Traditional*

As Sanchez issues warnings about being, but not getting stuck in, the wilderness, Nikki Giovanni unearths bad attitudes and aimlessness, and teaches about black ancestry.

Nikki Giovanni (1943–) lives the spirituals through her written, poetic, militant calls against American racism and injustice, and through her commitment to the Civil Rights Movement. Giovanni exposes African American notions and attitudes of inferiority as she calls for a sense of personal direction and nonviolent protest. Her work reflects her personal evolution independence, in this spiritual:

> Good news! De Chariot's coming
> Good news! De Chariot's coming
> Good news! De Chariot's coming
> And I don't want her leave a me behind.
>
> Get up in de chariot, carry me home...
> Dar's a long white robe in de heaven, I know...
> Dar's a golden harp in de heaven, I know...
>
> —*Traditional*

Giovanni celebrates and creates stories about the power of ancient black civilizations and writes for adults and children. Her work often focuses on the connections between arts and culture, and she makes casual yet insightful comments on the political and social situation in America.[41] The symbolic living of the spirituals has existed and continues to emerge in the powerful social, political, religious, educational, life-affirming signifying of many African American women. Likewise, the realm of the aesthetic, often framed by the political, social, and religious, bas been blessed and elevated by African American women who sing the spirituals, including Marian Anderson, Mahalia Jackson, Odetta, Leontyne Price, Jessye Norman, Kathleen Battle, Barbara Hendricks, Bernice Johnson Reagon and Sweet Honey in the Rock, and Sister Thea Bowman.

Womanist Creative Singing

Women who sing the spirituals sing them because they are moved to do so. Marian Anderson (1902–1993) sang the spirituals and brought them to the world in hundreds of recitals. First singing in the church choir, Anderson studied vocal technique in high school. Racism thwarted her path when the Daughters of the American Revolution refused to let Anderson perform at Constitution Hall in Washington DC. Eleanor Roosevelt helped secure her an invitation to sing at the Lincoln Memorial, where she sang before 75,000 people on Easter Sunday, April 9, 1939. Anderson served as a goodwill ambassador and as an ambassador to the United Nations. The programming of her more than fifty farewell concerts, culminating more than thirty years of performing, included the spirituals.[42] While Anderson took thousands to the heights of majestic elegance on the operatic and concert stage, Mahalia Jackson moved thousands up a little higher singing the spirituals and gospel songs.

Mahalia Jackson (1911–1972) sang and lived the spirituals. She supported and encouraged civil rights protesters as she sang the spiritual "We Shall Overcome" and the gospel "If I Could Help Somebody." Though primarily a singer of gospels who bridged the distance between secular and sacred music, Jackson sang the spirituals with a rich contralto voice, using a full range of emotions, vocal techniques, lyrical and rhythmic freedom, and an emotional power that often signified black preaching. Her singing "I Been 'Buked and I Been Scorned" at the 1963 March on Washington made Jackson a public symbol for the 1960s protest. Financially, she supported the movement and the educational opportunities of black youth. Her deep faith through song was one gift she gave internationally to millions.[43] Just as Jackson sermonized through religious songs, Odetta preaches to and about life and people through folk songs.

Odetta (1930–) has sung the spirituals and other folk songs for more than forty years. She has lectured throughout the United States, has appeared in numerous plays and films, and celebrates and captures the folk idiom, which has endeared her to the folk and to the feminist movement. This citizen of the folk and of the world honors and gives praise to the ancestors, who have shown Odetta the import of "positive energy in vanquishing the negative forces that keep the struggle from advancing."[44] While the travels of Odetta have been extensive, Leontyne Price has also traveled worldwide and has brought the folk gold through her sound.

Leontyne Price (1937–), "La Diva" of opera, has sung the spirituals all her life. Deciding to become a musician after hearing Marian Anderson, Price entered the Juilliard School with a commitment to excel. Price developed an international opera career that has taken her to all the major world opera houses. Price concluded her strenuous operatic career of more than thirty years with a performance of *Aida* at the Met in 1985. She equally excelled in the Italian operas of Puccini and Verdi and in German, Slavic, Spanish, French, and American works, including her powerful rendering of the spirituals. Price always celebrates her lush sound as dark and smoky, and as the gift of her blackness, the pigmentation of her skin. Since retiring from the opera stage, Price has continued as a recitalist.[45] Price once told Marian Anderson, "Because you were, I am." Certainly because Anderson and Price were, Jessye Norman now is.

Jessye Norman (1945–) sings the spirituals with the bravura and commitment of a consummate artist and of one who has lived them. Her mastery, musical commitment, understanding of history and texts, and impeccable scholarship make her music soar. Her vast range and bearing, apparent in her televised live recording of the spirituals with Kathleen Battle, made these powerful songs come alive once again.[46]

Kathleen Battle (1948–), a native of Ohio and product of Cincinnati College-Conservatory, made her debut at Spoleto in 1972. Battle is an international opera singer, soloist, and recitalist. Her performances of the spirituals can be intensely joyous, silvery brilliant, and filled with precious intimacy. The live recording *Spirituals in Concert,* with Battle and Jessye Norman at Carnegie Hall in March 1990, continues the recital tradition of concert artists singing arranged spirituals. Her renditions are versatile, sacred and secular, and transforming.[47] Born the same year as Battle, Barbara Hendricks also brings a distinctive, inspiring singing style to the spirituals.

Barbara Hendricks (1948–) sings the spirituals from a context of celebrating her heritage. Hendricks has an international career as an opera singer and recording artist. Her singing empowers others, and she was appointed goodwill ambassador to the United Nations. Having grown up in a Methodist parsonage where her mother sang, early in life Hendricks focused on church and on praising God. Her understanding, interpretation, and being moved by her own memories of the spirituals, merge to enrich her performances of the spirituals. Though originally intent on group singing, Hendricks renders a solo performance with rich and powerful ambiance.[48] A testament to solo and communal singing of the spirituals finds signification in Bernice Johnson Reagon and Sweet Honey in the Rock.

Bernice Johnson Reagon (1945–) signifies through weaving together her skills and experiences as a civil rights activist, singer, writer, historian, and social protester. Reagon, born in Albany, Georgia, started the Grammy-winning women's a cappella group Sweet Honey in the Rock (1973), is a former curator at the National Museum for American History at the Smithsonian Institution, and received a prestigious MacArthur fellowship. She has signified by editing the three-disk field recording collection *Voices of the Civil Rights Movement: Black American Freedom Songs, 1960–66,* a music history journal with an illustrated booklet. In 1994, Reagon helped to launch the series Wade in the Water: Black Sacred Music Tradition on National Public Radio.[49] Reagon and Sweet Honey in the Rock have performed at churches, concerts, and festivals throughout this country, and internationally they have performed in Ecuador, Mexico, Germany, Japan, England, Canada,

Australia, Africa, and the Caribbean. Sweet Honey in the Rock sings the spirituals and other songs of struggle. It builds on the black congregational church-singing style and proclaims to listeners the need for all to fight for social justice and equality. The group sings West African chants, spirituals, black gospel, field hollers, reggae, rap, and urban blues. Sweet Honey in the Rock deals with human concerns including apartheid, AIDS, economic oppression, homelessness, self-esteem, community building, civil rights, political prisoners, and global human rights.[50] A testament of Reagan's commitment, and of those similarly committed, is a song that Sweet Honey in the Rock often sings:

> We who believe in freedom cannot rest
> We who believe in freedom cannot rest until it comes.
> Until the killing of black men,
> Black mothers' sons
> Is as important as the killing of white men,
> White mothers' sons. . .[51]

Similarly, Sweet Honey in the Rock addresses the issues of women:

> WOMEN!
> Should be a priority, respected and upheld in society
> Given all the proper notoriety
> Never used or abused by authority figures
> Like the media that trashes us
> Play down the hype chat constantly bashes our image. . .
> Use women's bodies to create a sex symbol
> Too many times seen as a sex symbol
> No real intelligence, just a brainless bimbo
> Not taken seriously, for who she needs to be
> A human being with the right to be free. . .[52]

The power, passion, and presence of Sweet Honey in the Rock is magnetic; the presence of Sister Thea was prophetic and dynamic.

Sister Thea Bowman (1937–1990) sang, taught, and lived the spirituals as a prophet, evangelist, singer, dancer, liturgist, and educator. Bowman preached the good news and brought together people from various walks of life as a pilgrim on a journey. Sometimes she felt "like a motherless child," but she always knew she was God's special child, as all people are beautiful, special children of God. Sister Thea joined the order of the Franciscan Sisters of Perpetual Adoration in La Crosse, Wisconsin. After she completed her doctorate, Sister Thea's work included teaching English, including black literature at all levels, and starting and directing the Hallelujah Singers, a choir that specialized in the spirituals as sung in the African American South. Sister Thea promoted multiculturalism before it was in vogue: she built community between blacks, whites, Native Americans, Hispanics, and Asian Americans. Sister Thea was living inspiration as she used the spirituals to help people improve their quality of life and to know joy.[53] Like Sister Thea, Eva Jessye taught others and directed choirs which sing the spirituals, and, like a few other musicians, she arranged the choir's music.

> You affect sound
> Teaching, arranging
> Building on traditions
> Of unsung poets of old;
> Ancestors sharing the blood
> Sharing the creativity
> Of African soil
> Mist American ethos;
> As prelude and offering
> For a new day;
> The ritual of possibility
> A clarion call for change
> A prophetic word
> Announcing:
> Awake, Arise, Act.[54]

Womanist Creative Arranging

Eva Jessye (1895–1992) lived the spirituals through her numerous contributions to music, her directorship of the Eva Jessye Choir, which sang a variety of works, including the spirituals, and her work on American music and folklore. "I've got a song, you've got a song, all of God's children got a song" is the litany for choral directors and arrangers—there are always songs to sing, to shout "all over God's heav'n." For more than seventy-five years, Jessye was involved in acting, directing, and choral conducting. She was the musical director of *Hallelujah*, the first motion picture starring African American actors. Jessye directed major choral performances on radio and was the unofficial protector of the *Porgy and Bess* score. George Gershwin, the composer, appointed Jessye as the choral conductor for *Porgy*, and she did much to sharpen the cultural flavor of the work and to maintain its integrity for more than thirty years. Her choir toured as ambassadors of goodwill, and Jessye worked on behalf of peace, the arts, and women's progress, as poet, actress, composer, inspirational lecturer and choir director.[55] Other African American arrangers of spirituals include Margaret Bonds, Undine Moore, Rachel Eubanks, and Lena McLin.

Margaret Bonds (1913–1972) arranged the spirituals as part of her prolific repertoire of compositions. Hailing from Illinois, Bonds received numerous awards, performed with many orchestras, and worked with the Cultural Center in Los Angeles. Bonds, influenced by jazz, blues, and her interest in social themes, composed music for many genres: ballet, orchestra, art songs, popular songs, piano pieces, and arranged spirituals. Her music illumined her sense of ethnic identity. Her association with other African American artists, poets, and musicians greatly influenced her work. Leontyne Price commissioned and recorded many of Bonds' arrangement of spirituals. Some of her arrangements include "Didn't It Rain!" "Ezekiel Saw De Wheel," "Five Creek-Freedmen Spirituals," "Mary Had a Baby," and one frequently performed and recorded, "He's Got the Whole World in His Hands."[56] A composer-arranger of spirituals who hails from Virginia is Undine Moore.

Undine Smith Moore (1905–) arranges and composes, and is an organist, pianist, and educator, especially in the states of North Carolina and Virginia. She was instrumental in cofounding and co-directing the Black Music Center and in developing the Black Man in American Music Program at Virginia State College. Moore's repertoire of spirituals includes "Fare You Well," "Rise Up, Shepherd, and Follow," and "We Shall Walk through the Valley."[57]

Rachel Eubanks (1923–), educator, musician and composer, arranges spirituals for solo and choral voices. Eubanks has headed music departments at Wilberforce University and Albany State College. She began the Eubanks Conservatory of Music in 1951. Concerned with the study of diverse kinds of music and music history, Eubanks also supports African American musics and the work of women in music, and has been so honored for her participation and musical excellence. Some of the spirituals Eubanks has arranged include "Deep River," "Jesus on the Waterside," and "Let Us Break Bread Together," all for solo voice; and the following spirituals for choral ensemble: "Ezekiel Saw the Wheel," "I Want Jesus to Walk with Me," "It's a Me, O Lord," and "Let Us Break Bread Together."[58]

Lena Johnson McLin (1928–) is a composer of more than two thousand compositions that include cantatas, anthems, piano works, orchestral works, and arranged spirituals. McLin is also a singer, conductor, and educator. She founded and directed the McLin Ensemble, a small opera company. The spirituals McLin has arranged include "Cert'nly, Lord," "Done Made My Vow to the Lord," "Glory, Glory Hallelujah," "Give Me That Old Time Religion," "Gonna Rise Up in the Kingdom," "I'm So Glad Trouble Don't Last Always," and "My God Is So High."[59] Other African American female composer-arrangers of the spirituals include Jacqueline Hairston, Betty Jackson King, Eurydice Osterman, Zenobia Powell Perry, Charlene Moore Cooper, Barbara Sherrill, Patsy Ford Simms, and Jean Taylor.[60]

"I am woman, hear me roar" pealed forth in the 1960s but was sounded more than a century earlier; as black women like abolitionist Sojourner Truth said, Jesus came from "God and a woman—*man* had nothing to do with it."[61] Harriet Tubman, Union spy, freed slaves, established a home for the aged, and worked with Ida Wells-Barnett in the suffragette movement and the anti-lynching campaign which helped launch the modern Civil Rights Movement. Their politics and struggle presaged the lives of Fannie Lou Hamer, Ella Baker, Septima Clark, Rosa Parks, and the countless unnamed, outrageous black women who lived and fought and sang for twentieth-century freedom. Male privilege denied these women national leadership positions, and most black male theologians failed to address sexism. From the 1800s through the 1960s, African American women reclaimed family ties after the Civil War, worked for suffrage, founded colleges, worked for educational reform, and formed women's clubs like the National Association of Colored Women (NACW), which predates the NAACP. Those women, with outrageous courage, fortitude, and brilliance, lived the spirituals. Many have sung the spirituals, transforming lives, launching careers, and spreading the gospel of freedom, justice, life. Others have arranged the spirituals in ways that make them timeless and profound. Womanists live, sing, teach, and preach the spirituals as they defend black women against white male sexual exploitation. Womanists liberate black women from black male subjugation and transform the minuscule way in which some black women see themselves. Womanists work for justice, and labor to overcome poverty. They give support to black women individually and as a group, and criticize negative black male attitudes about black women. They work for health care and work to shatter the stereotypes about black women. Womanists inspire African American women to celebrate, appreciate, and love themselves.[62] The spirituals are metaphors for holistic health, for spiritual transformation, for creating opportunities for justice. Women have sung, marched, and conquered. Without the participation of women and Movement would not have happened, and there would be a lot less compassion in the world. Womanists call us to "be there" for the "least of these."

> Oh, Beautiful Blackness
> You sing with melodious voices
> Alto, contralto, soprano,
> Lyric, coloratura, gospel persuasion
> On stage, at church, in fields.
> You sing
> Only for the ears of God
> Other times before great halls of justice
> Broadcast before shuttering masses
> As deputized lynched mobs
> Lurked in the shadows.

Notes

1. See the work of authors Alice Walker, the late Audre Lorde, Toni Morrison; Katie Cannon in Womanist ethics; Jacqueline Grant and Delores Williams in Womanist theology; and Cheryl Gilkes in Womanist sociology of religion.
2. Anthony Pinn, *Why God? Suffering and Evil in Black Theology* (New York: Continuum, 1995), 19.
3. Kesho Yvonne Scott, *The Habit of Surviving* (New York: Ballantine Books, 1991), 3–10.
4. Bernice Johnson Reagon, Interview by author, tape recording, Washington DC, November 19, 1991.
5. Darlene Clark Hine, Elsa Barkley Brown, and Rosalyn Terborg-Penn, *Black Women in America: An Historical Encyclopedia* (Bloomington: Indiana University Press, 1993), 1174–76.
6. Ibid., 1113–14.

7. Ibid., 1176–80; and Jessie Carney Smith, ed., *Epic Lives: One Hundred Black Women Who Made a Difference* (Detroit: Visible Ink, 1993), 529–37.
8. Hine, Brown, and Terborg-Penn, *Black Women in America*, 532–36.
9. Ibid., 363–67.
10. Ibid., 982–84.
11. Ibid., 80–82.
12. Ibid., 33–34.
13. Ibid., 1157–59.
14. Ibid., 201–6.
15. Ibid., 690–93.
16. Ibid., 825–26.
17. Ibid., 552–55.
18. Ibid., 236–38.
19. Ibid., 110–12.
20. Ibid., 377–79.
21. Ibid., 175–76.
22. Ibid., 1242–46; and Smith, *Epic Lives*, 579–86.
23. Hine, Brown, and Terborg-Penn, *Black Women in America*, 248–52.
24. Ibid., 70–74.
25. Ibid., 907–9.
26. Ibid., 518–19.
27. Ibid., 94–96.
28. Ibid., 822–24.
29. Ibid., 138–39.
30. Ibid., 886–87.
31. Ibid., 658–59.
32. Ibid., 105–6.
33. Ibid., 275–81.
34. Ibid., 113–26.
35. Ibid., 260–61.
36. Ibid., 513.
37. Ibid., 505–7.
38. Ibid., 36–38.
39. Ibid., 525–27.
40. Ibid., 1003–5.
41. Ibid., 487–90.
42. Ibid., 29–33.
43. Ibid., 620–23.
44. Ibid., 901.
45. Ibid., 941–43.
46. Ibid., 881. See also Kathleen Battle and Jessye Norman, *Spirituals in Concert*, Deutsche Grammophone 429 790-2, 1991; Jessye Norman, *Spirituals*, with Dalton Baldwin and the Ambrosian Singers, Phillips 416 462-2, 1978, Jessye Norman, *Amazing Grace*, Phillips 432 546-2, 1991.
47. Hine, Brown, and Terborg-Penn, *Black Women in America*, 97; see also Battle and Norman, *Spirituals in Concert*.
48. Hine, Brown, and Terborg-Penn, *Black Women in America*, 556–57. See also Barbara Hendricks, *Negro Spirituals*, EMI 7470262, 1983; *Great American Spirituals*, vol. 9, Angel CD 7 664669, 2 1992; and *Great American Spirituals*, Musical Heritage Society CD 513725Z, 1994.
49. Smith, *Epic Lives*, 434–39.
50. Ibid., 1134.
51. Bernice Johnson Reagon and Sweet Honey in the Rock, *We Who Believe in Freedom: Sweet Honey in the Rock. . . Still on the Journey* (New York: Anchor/Doubleday, 1993), 21.
52. Sweet Honey in the Rock, "A Priority," *In This Land*, Redway, CA: EarthBeat, CA 9 42522-2, 1992.
53. Hine, Brown, and Terborg-Penn, *Black Women in America*, 156–57.

54. Title from Marcia Riggs, *Awake, Arise, and Act: A Womanist Call for Black Liberation* (Cleveland: Pilgrim, 1994).

55. Ibid., 635–36.

56. Ibid., 147–48; and Helen Walker-Hill, *Music by Black Women Composers: A Bibliography of Available Scores*, CBMR Monographs, no. 5 (Chicago: Center for Black Music Research, Columbia College, 1995), 271.

57. Hine, Brown, and Terborg-Penn, *Black Women in America*, 814; and Walker-Hill, *Music by Black Women Composers*, 56–57, 91–93.

58. Shirelle Phelps, ed., *Who's Who in Black America*, 1994–95, 8th ed. (Detroit: Gale Research, 1994), 451–52; and Walker-Hill, *Music by Black Women Composers*, 50, 81–82.

59. Hine, Brown, and Terborg-Penn, *Black Women in America*, 773; Phelps, ed., *Who's Who in Black America*, 1004; and Walker-Hill, *Music by Black Women Composers*, 89–91.

60. See Walker-Hill, *Music by Black Women Composers*, 51–54, 57–58, 80, 84–85, 94–99, 100.

61. Elizabeth Cady Stanton, Susan Anthony, and Matilda Joslyn Gage, eds., *The History of Woman Suffrage*, vol. 1 (Rochester, NY: n.p., 1881), 115–17; and Eleanor Flexner, *Century of Struggle: The Women's Rights Movement in the United States* (Cambridge and London: Belknap/Harvard University Press, 1959, 1975, 1979), 91.

62. Paula Giddings, *When and Where I Enter: The Impact of Black Women on Race and Sex in America* (New York: Bantam Books, 1984), 57, 65, 73, 85–89, 94, 102, 108, 113–17, 130, 135–44.

Acknowledgments

I. Worship and Liturgical Practices

"Twenty-One Questions Revisited" by Valerie Bridgeman Davis. In *Companion to the Africana Worship Book*. Nashville: Discipleship Resources. © 2007, Discipleship Resources. Used by permission.

"Lectio Divina: A Transforming Engagement with Sacred Scripture" by Lisa M. Weaver. Previously unpublished. © 2014, Lisa M. Weaver.

"Differences in Similarity: An Examination of the Baptismal Rite in the Apostolic Tradition and the African Methodist Episcopal Church" by Lisa M. Weaver. Previously unpublished. © 2014, Lisa M. Weaver.

"Introduction" by James Melvin Washington. In *Conversations with God: Two Centuries of Prayers by African Americans*. New York: HarperCollins. © 1994, James Melvin Washington. Reprinted by permission of HarperCollins Publishers.

"And We Shall Learn through the Dance: Exploring the Instructional Relationship between Liturgical Dance and Religious Education" by Kathleen S. Turner. In *And We Shall Learn through the Dance: Liturgical Dance as Religious Education,* a Fordham University dissertation. Previously unpublished. © 2012, Kathleen S. Turner.

"The Spiritual Arrangement since 1999 and Its Use in Contemporary Worship" by Leo H. Davis Jr., from the 2008 Hampton University Choir Directors' Organists Guild Workshop. Previously unpublished. © 2014, Leo H. Davis Jr.

"If It Had Not Been for the Lord on My Side: Hymnody in African American Churches" by James Abbington. In *New Songs of Celebration Render: Congregational Song in the Twenty-First Century*. Compiled and edited by C. Michael Hawn. Chicago: GIA. © 2013, GIA Publications, Inc.

II. Liturgical Theologies

"Black Worship: A Historical Theological Interpretation" by James H. Cone. In *Speaking the Truth: Ecumenism, Liberation, and Black Theology*, paper presented at a workshop sponsored by Black Methodists for Church Renewal, Detroit, Michigan, 1976. Grand Rapids: Eerdmans. © 1986, William B. Eerdmans Publishing Co.

"The Theological Validation of Black Worship" by Samuel D. Proctor. *Journal of the Interdenominational Theological Center* 14, nos. 1–2 (1987): 211–23. © 1987, JITC.

"Transformational Worship in the Life of a Church" by Kenneth C. Ulmer. In *Worship Narratives and Transformation in Worship that Changes Lives*. Edited by Alexis Abernethy. Grand Rapids: Baker Academic. © 2008, Baker Academic, a division of Baker Publishing Group. Used by permission.

"I'm Going to Live the Life I Sing about in My Song" by Michael Joseph Brown. In *New Wine in Old Wineskins: A Contemporary Congregational Song Supplement, Vol. 1*. Edited by James Abbington. Chicago: GIA. © 2007, GIA Publications, Inc.

"The Lyrical Theology of Charles A. Tindley: Justice Come of Age" by S T Kimbrough, Jr. Previously unpublished lecture, 2006, rev. 2013. © 2006, S T Kimbrough, Jr.

"Black Megachurches in the Internet Age: Exploring Theological Teachings and Social Outreach Efforts" by Pamela P. Martin, Tuere A. Bowles, LaTrese Adkins, and Monica T. Leach. *Journal of African American Studies* 15, no. 2 (2011): 155–76. © 2011, Springer Science + Business Media, LLC.

III. Proclamation of the Word

"Introduction" by Martha Simmons and Frank Thomas. In *Preaching with Sacred Fire: An Anthology of African American Sermons, 1750 to the Present*. New York: W. W. Norton. © 2010, W. W. Norton & Company.

"Preaching in the Black Church" by Ruthlyn Bradshaw. In *The Future of Preaching*. Norwich, England: SCM. © 2010, SCM Canterbury Press, Ltd.

"Prosperity Preaching in Black Communities" by Stephanie Y. Mitchem. In *Name It and Claim It?* Cleveland: Pilgrim. © 2007, The Pilgrim Press.

"Making the Unseen Seen: Pedagogy and Aesthetics in African American Prophetic Preaching" by Kenyatta R. Gilbert. From a Howard University School of Divinity essay. Previously unpublished © 2014, Kenyatta R. Gilbert.

"Lament: Homiletical Groans in the Spirit" by Luke A. Powery. *Homiletic* 34, no. 1 (2009): 22–34. © 2009, *Homiletic*.

"Walkin' the Talk: The Spirit and the Lived Sermon" by Luke A. Powery. *The African American Pulpit* 11, no. 4 (Fall 2008): 20–22. © 2008, *The African American Pulpit*.

IV. Hymnody: Sound and Sense

V. Perpectives on Praise and Worship

"This House, This Music: Exploring the Interdependent Interpretive Relationship between the Contemporary Black Church and Contemporary Gospel Music" by Melinda E. Weekes. *Black Music Research Journal* 25, nos. 1/2 (2005): 43–72. © 2005. Reprinted with the permission of the Center for Black Music Research at Columbia College, Chicago.

"Reflections on Praise and Worship from a Biblical Perspective: Background, Definitions, Concepts and Constructions" by Rodney A. Teal. In *Reflections on Praise and Worship from a Biblical Perspective.* Self-published. © 2000, Rodney A. Teal.

VI. Hip Hop and/in the Church

"Religion and Rap Music: An Analysis of Black Church Usage" by Sandra L. Barnes. *Review of Religious Research Review of Religious Research* 49, no. 3 (2008): 319–38. © 2008, Sandra L. Barnes.

"In Search of Our Daughters' Gardens: Hip Hop as Womanist Prose" by Tamura Lomax. *Bulletin for the Study of Religion* 40, no. 3 (2011): 15–20. © 2011, Equinox Publishing Ltd.

"It's Not the Beat, but It's the Word that Sets the People Free: Race, Technology, and Theology in the Emergence of Christian Rap Music" by Josef Sorett. From a Columbia University essay. Previously unpublished. © 2011, Josef Sorett.

"The Promiscuous Gospel: The Religious Complexity and Theological Multiplicity of Rap Music" by Monica R. Miller. *Culture and Religion: An Interdisciplinary Journal* 10, no. 1 (2009): 39–56. © 2009, Monica R. Miller.

"Building 'Zyon' in Babylon: Holy Hip Hop and Geographies of Conversion" by Christina Zanfagna. *Black Music Research Journal* 31, no. 1 (2011): 145–62. © 2011, Board of Trustees of the University of Illinois. Used with the permission of the University of Illinois Press.

"From Black Theology and Black Power to Afrocentric Theology and Hip Hop Power: An Extension and Socio-Re-Theological Conceptualization of Cone's Theology in Conversation with the Hip Hop Generation" by Ralph C. Watkins. *Black Theology: An International Journal* 8, no. 3 (2010): 327–40. © 2010, Maney Publishing.

"Baptized in Dirty Water: An Ontology of Hip Hop's Manufacturing of Socio-Religious Discourse in Tupac's 'Black Jesuz'" by Daniel White Hodge. *Memphis Theological Seminary Journal* 50, no. 11 (2012): 195–215. © 2012, Daniel White Hodge.

VII. Perspectives on Women and Gender

"Playin' Church: Remembering Mama and Questioning Authenticity in Black Gospel Performance" by Alisha Jones. Previously unpublished. © 2014, Alisha Jones.

"From Spirituals to Swing: Sister Rosetta Tharpe and Gospel Crossover" by Gayle Wald. *American Quarterly* 55, no. 3 (September 2003): 387–416. © 2003, Gayle Wald.

"Singing Like David Sang: Queerness and Masculinity in Black Gospel Performance" by Melvin L. Butler. Previously unpublished. © 2014, Melvin L. Butler.

"Work the Works: The Role of African American Women in the Development of Contemporary Gospel" by Tammy L. Kernodle. *Black Music Research Journal* 26, no. 1 (Spring 2006): 89–109. © 2006. Reprinted with the permission of the Center for Black Music Research at Columbia College, Chicago.

"Womanist Musings" by Cheryl A. Kirk-Duggan. In *Exorcizing Evil: A Womanist Perspective on the Spirituals*, Maryknoll: Orbis. © 1997, Cheryl A. Kirk-Duggan.

Appendix:
Contents of Volume One

I. Historical Perspectives

II. Surveys of Hymnals and Hymnody

V. Composers

VI. The Organ

VII. Contemporary Perspectives

Bibliography

Abbington, James. *Let Mt. Zion Rejoice! Music in the African American Church.* Valley Forge: Judson, 2001.

———. *Let the Church Sing On!: Reflections on Black Sacred Music.* Chicago: GIA, 2009.

———, ed. *Readings in African American Church Music and Worship,* Vol. 1. Chicago: GIA, 2001.

Abernathy, Alexis D., ed. *Worship That Changes Lives: Multidisciplinary and Congregational Perspectives on Spiritual Transformation.* Grand Rapids: Baker Academic, 2008.

Aghahowa, Brenda Eatman. *Praising in Black and White: Unity and Diversity in Christian Worship.* Cleveland: United Church, 1996.

Alexander, Darrell R. *Excellence in Worship: Should Church Musicians Be Paid?* Bloomington: Trafford, 2006.

Alexander, Estrelda Y. *Black Fire: One Hundred Years of African American Pentecostalism.* Downers Grove: InterVarsity, 2011.

Anderson, Leith. *A Church for the 21st Century: Bringing Change to Your Church to Meet the Challenges of a Changing Society.* Minneapolis: Bethany House, 1992.

Andrews, Dale P. *Practical Theology for Black Churches: Bridging Black Theology and African American Folk Religion.* Louisville: Westminster John Knox, 2002.

Arnold, Talitha. *Worship for Vital Congregations.* Cleveland: Pilgrim, 2007.

Bailey, E. K., and Warren Wiersbe. *Preaching in Black and White: What We Can Learn From Each Other.* Grand Rapids: Zondervan, 2003.

Ballou, Hugh. *Moving Spirits, Building Lives: The Church Musician as Transformational Leader.* Kearney: Morris, 2005.

Barna, George. *Futurecast: What Today's Trends Mean for Tomorrow's World.* Austin: Tyndale, 2011.

———, and Frank Viola. *Pagan Christianity?: Exploring the Roots of Our Church Practices.* Austin: Barna Books, 2008.

Bauer, Michael J. *Arts Ministry: Nurturing the Creative Life of God's People.* Grand Rapids: Eerdmans, 2013.

Bauerlin, Mark. *The Dumbest Generation: How the Digital Age Stupefies Young Americans and Jeopardizes Our Future (or, Don't Trust Anyone under 30)*. New York: Jeremy P. Tarcher/Penguin, 2009.

———, ed. *The Digital Age: Arguments for and Against Facebook, Google, Texting, and the Age of Social Networking*. Jeremy P. Tarcher/Penguin, 2011.

Begbie, Jeremy S. *Resounding Truth: Christian Wisdom in the World of Music*. Grand Rapids: Baker Academic, 2007.

Bell, Derrick. *Gospel Choirs: Psalms of Survival in an Alien Land Called Home*. New York: Basic Books, 1996.

Bell, Jerome. *Bridging the Gap Between the Music Department and the Pulpit*. Maitland: Xulon, 2006.

Bell, John L. *The Singing Thing: A Case for Congregational Song*. Chicago: GIA, 2000.

———. *The Singing Thing too: Enabling Congregations to Sing*. Chicago: GIA, 2007.

Berger, Teresa, and Bryan D. Spinks, eds. *The Spirit in Worship—Worship in the Spirit*. Collegeville: Liturgical Press, 2009.

Berglund, Brad. *Reinventing Sunday: Breakthrough Ideas for Transforming Worship*. Valley Forge: Judson, 2001.

Berkley, James D., ed. *Leadership Handbook of Preaching and Worship*. Grand Rapids: Baker Book, 1992.

Best, Harold M. *Music through the Eyes of Faith*. New York: HarperCollins, 1993.

Black, Kathy. *Culturally Conscience Worship*. Georgia: Chalice, 2000.

Blount, Brian K. *Can I Get a Witness? Reading Revelation through African American Culture*. Louisville: Westminster John Knox, 2005.

———, ed. *True to Our Native Land: An African American New Testament Commentary*. Minneapolis: Fortress, 2007.

Bond, Adam. *The Imposing Preacher: Samuel DeWitt Proctor and Black Public Faith*. Minneapolis: Fortress, 2013.

Borsch, Frederick Houk. *Introducing the Lessons of the Church Year: A Guide for Lay Readers and Congregations*. New York: Seabury, 1978.

Bower, Peter C., ed. *Handbook for the Revised Common Lectionary*. Louisville: Westminster John Knox, 1996.

Boyer, Horace Clarence. *How Sweet the Sound: The Golden Age of Gospel*. Washington DC: Elliott & Clark, 1995.

Bradley, C. Randall. *From Memory to Imagination: Reforming the Church's Music*. Grand Rapids: Eerdmans, 2012.

———. *From Postlude to Prelude: Music Ministry's Other Six Days.* St. Louis: MorningStar, 2004.

Bradshaw, Paul F. *Reconstructing Early Christian Worship.* Collegeville: Liturgical Press, 2010.

Bridges, Flora Wilson. *Resurrection Song: African American Spirituality.* Maryknoll: Orbis, 2001.

Brown, Frank Burch. *Inclusive Yet Discerning: Navigation Worship Artfully.* Grand Rapids: Eerdmans, 2009.

Brown, Michael Joseph. *The Lord's Prayer and God's Vision for the World: Finding Your Purpose through Prayer.* Crawfordsville, IN: Self-published, 2012.

Brueggemann, Walter. *Praying the Psalms.* Winona, MN: Saint Mary's, 1982.

———. *Praying the Psalms: Engaging Scripture and the Life of the Spirit,* 2nd ed. Eugene: Cascade Books, 2007.

———. *The Message of the Psalms: A Theological Commentary.* Minneapolis: Augsburg, 1984.

———. *The Psalms and the Life of Faith.* Edited by Patrick D. Miller. Minneapolis: Fortress, 1995.

Burnin, Mellonee, and Porita Portia, eds. *African American Music: An Introduction.* New York: Routledge, 2006.

Burroughs, Bob. *An ABC Primer for Church Musicians.* Nashville: Broadman, 1990.

Bush, Peter, and Christine O'Reilly. *Where 20 or 30 Are Gathered: Leading Worship in the Small Church.* Herndon: Alban Institute, 2006.

Butler, Anthea D. *Women in the Church of God in Christ: Making a Sanctified World.* Chapel Hill: University of North Carolina Press, 2007.

Byars, Ronald P. *Future of Protestant Worship: Beyond Worship Wars.* Louisville: Westminster John Knox, 2002

Carpenter, Bill. *Uncloudy Days: The Gospel Music Encyclopedia.* San Francisco: Backbeat, 2005.

Carr, Nicholas. *The Shallows: What the Internet Is Doing to Our Brains.* New York: W. W. Norton, 2011.

Carson, Tim and Kathy. *So You're Thinking about Contemporary Worship.* St. Louis: Chalice, 1997.

Causey, C. Harry. *Things They Didn't Tell Me about Being a Minister of Music.* Rockville: Music Revelation, 1988.

Chapman, Mark L. *Christianity on Trial: African American Religious Thought Before and After Black Power.* Maryknoll: Orbis, 1996.

Chenu, Bruno. *The Trouble I've Seen: The Big Book of Negro Spirituals.* Valley Forge: Judson, 2003

Cherry, Constance M. *The Worship Architect: A Blueprint for Designing Culturally Relevant and Biblically Faithful Services.* Grand Rapids: Baker Academic, 2010.

Cherwien, David M. *Let the People Sing!* St. Louis: Concordia, 1997.

Clark, Linda J. *Music in Churches: Nourishing Your Congregation's Musical Life.* New York: Alban Institute, 1994.

———. *How We Seek God Together: Exploring Worship Styles.* New York: Alban Institute, 2001.

Cone, James H. *The Spiritual and the Blues.* Maryknoll: Orbis, 1972.

Corbon, Jean. *The Wellspring of Worship.* San Francisco: Ignatius, 2005.

Costen, Melva W. *African American Christian Worship.* Nashville: Abingdon, 2007.

———. *In Spirit and In Truth: The Music of African American Worship.* Louisville: Westminster John Knox, 2005.

Darden, Robert. *People Get Ready! A New History of Black Gospel Music.* New York: Continuum, 2006.

Davidson, James Robert. *A Dictionary of Protestant Church Music.* Metuchen, NJ: Scarecrow, 1975.

Davies, J. G., ed. *The New Westminster Dictionary of Liturgy and Worship.* Philadelphia: Westminster, 1986.

Davis, Valerie B., and Safiya Fosua. *Companion to the Africana Worship Book: Year A.* Nashville: Discipleship Resources, 2007.

———. *The Africana Worship Book: Year A.* Nashville: Discipleship Resources, 2006.

———. *The Africana Worship Book: Year B.* Nashville: Discipleship Resources, 2007.

———. *The Africana Worship Book: Year C.* Nashville: Discipleship Resources, 2007.

Dawn, Marva J. *A Royal "Waste" of Time: The Splendor of Worshiping God and Being Church for the World.* Grand Rapids: Eerdmans, 1999.

———. *How Shall We Worship? Biblical Guidelines for the Worship Wars.* Wheaton: Tyndale, 2003.

———. *Reaching Out Without Dumbing Down: A Theology of Worship for the Turn-of-the-Century Culture.* Grand Rapids: Eerdmans, 1995.

Day-Miller, Barbara. *Encounters with the Holy: A Conversation Model for Worship Planning.* Herndon: Alban Institute, 2010.

Dean, Talmage W. *A Survey of Twentieth Century Protestant Church Music in America.* Nashville: Broadman, 1988.

de Waal Malefyt, Norma, and Howard Vanderwell. *Designing Worship Together.* Herndon: Alban Institute, 2005.

Deymaz, Mark. *Building a Healthy Multi-Ethnic Church: Mandate, Commitments, and Practices of a Diverse Congregation.* San Francisco: Jossey-Bass, 2007.

Doran, Carol, and Thomas H. Troeger. *Trouble at the Table: Gathering the Tribes for Worship.* Nashville: Abingdon, 1992.

Dozer, Dan. *Come Let Us Adore Him: Dealing with the Struggle Over Style of Worship in Christian Churches and Churches of Christ.* Joplin: College Press, 1994.

Du Bois, W. E. B. *The Souls of Black Folk.* New York: Dover, 1994.

Duck, Ruth. *Worship for the Whole People of God.* Louisville: Westminster John Knox, 2013.

Dudley, Grenae D., and Carlyle F. Stewart III. *Sanfoka: Celebrations for the African American Church.* Cleveland: United Church, 1997.

Dyrness, William A. *Poetic Theology: God and Poetics of Everyday Life.* Grand Rapids: Eerdmans, 2011.

———. *Senses of the Soul: Art and the Visual in Christian Worship.* Eugene: Cascade Books, 2008.

Dyson, Michael Eric. *Between God and Gangsta Rap: Bearing Witness to Black Culture.* New York: Oxford University Press, 1996.

Easurn, William. *Dancing with Dinosaurs: Ministry in a Hostile and Hurting World.* Nashville: Abingdon, 1993.

Ellinwood, Leonard. *The History of American Church Music.* New York: Morehouse-Gorham, 1953.

Erskine, Noel Leo. *From Garvey to Marley: Rastafari Theology.* Gainesville: University Press of Florida, 2005.

———. *Plantation Church: How African American Religion Was Born in Caribbean Slavery.* New York: Oxford University Press, 2014.

Eskew, Harry T., and Hugh T. McElrath. *Sing with Understanding: An Introduction to Christian Hymnology.* 2nd ed., rev. and exp. Nashville: Church Street, 1995.

Evans, James H., Jr. *We Have Been Believers: An African American Systematic Theology.* Minneapolis: Fortress, 1992.

———. *We Shall All Be Changed: Social Problems and Theological Renewal.* Minneapolis: Fortress, 1997.

Farhadian, Charles E. *Christian Worship Worldwide: Expanding Horizons, Deepening Practices.* Grand Rapids: Eerdmans, 2007.

Ferrone, Rita. *Liturgy: Sacrosanctum Concilium (Rediscovering Vatican II).* New York: Paulist, 2007.

Fisher, Miles Mark. *Negro Slave Songs in the United States.* New York: Citadel, 1953.

Floyd, Samuel A., Jr. *The Power of Black Music: Interpreting Its History from Africa to the United States.* New York: Oxford University Press, 1995.

Frame, John M. *Worship in Spirit and Truth: A Refreshing Study of the Principles and Practice of Biblical Worship.* Phillipsburg: P&R Publishing, 1996.

Frank, Thomas Edward. *The Soul of the Congregation: An Invitation to Congregational Reflection.* Nashville: Abingdon, 2000.

Franklin, Robert M. *Another Day's Journey: Black Churches Confronting the American Crisis.* Minneapolis: Fortress, 1997.

Gaddy, C. Welton. *The Gift of Worship.* Nashville: Broadman, 1992.

Gay, Kathlyn. *African American Holidays, Festivals, and Celebrations: The History, Customs, and Symbols Associated with Both Traditional and Contemporary Religious and Secular Events Observed by Americans of African Descent*. Detroit: Omnigraphics, 2006.

Gilbert, Kenyatta. *A Time to Preach, a Time to Cry: An Investigation into the Nature of Prophetic Preaching in Black Churches during the Great Migration Period, 1916–1940*. Princeton: Princeton Theological Seminary, 2007.

———. *Journey and Promise of African American Preaching*. Minneapolis: Fortress, 2011.

Goatley, David Emmanuel. *Were You There? Godforsakenness in Slave Religion*. Maryknoll: Orbis, 1996.

Gordon, T. David. *Why Johnny Can't Preach: The Media Have Shaped the Messengers*. Phillipsburg: P&R Publishing, 2009.

———. *Why Johnny Can't Sing Hymns: How Pop Culture Rewrote the Hymnal*. Phillipsburg: P&R Publishing, 2010.

Hackett, Charles D., and Don Saliers. *The Lord Be with You: A Visual Handbook for Presiding in Christian Worship*. Cleveland: OSL, 1990.

Hall, Christopher A. *Worshiping with the Church Fathers*. Downers Grove: InterVarsity, 2009.

Hansen, Marsha. *My Soul Is a Witness: The Message of the Spirituals in Word and Song*. Minneapolis: Augsburg, 2006.

Harris, Michael W. *The Rise of Gospel Blues: The Music of Thomas Andrew Dorsey in the Urban Church*. New York: Oxford University Press, 1992.

Hawn, C. Michael. *Gather into One: Praying and Singing Globally*. Grand Rapids: Eerdmans, 2003.

———, ed. *New Songs of Celebration Render: Congregational Song in the Twenty-First Century*. Chicago: GIA, 2013.

Hickman, Hoyt L., Don E. Saliers, Laurence Hull Stokey, and James White. *The New Handbook of the Christian Year*. Nashville: Abingdon, 1992.

Hinson, Glenn. *Fire in My Bones: Transcendence and the Holy Spirit in African American Gospel*. Philadelphia: University of Pennsylvania Press, 2000.

Hoffman, Lawrence A., and Janet R. Walton, eds. *Sacred Sound and Social Change: Liturgical Music in Jewish and Christian Experience*. Notre Dame: University of Notre Dame Press, 1992.

Holck, Manfred, Jr., comp. *Dedication Services for Every Occasion*. Valley Forge: Judson, 1984.

Hollies, Linda H. *A Trumpet for Zion: Black Church Worship Resources*. Grand Rapids: Woman to Woman Ministries, 1995.

———. *A Trumpet for Zion: Year A*. Cleveland: Pilgrim, 2001.

———. *A Trumpet for Zion: Year B*. Cleveland: Pilgrim, 2002.

———. *A Trumpet for Zion: Year C*. Cleveland: Pilgrim, 2003.

Holmes, Zan W., Jr. *Encountering Jesus*. Nashville: Abingdon, 1992.

Hood, Robert E. *Begrimed and Black: Christian Traditions on Blacks and Blackness*. Minneapolis: Fortress, 1994.

———. *Must God Remain Greek? Afro Cultures and God-talk*. Minneapolis: Fortress, 1990.

Hoon, Paul Waitman. *The Integrity of Worship*. Nashville: Abingdon, 1971.

Hooper, William L. *Ministry and Musicians: The Role of Ministry in the Work of Church Musicians*. Nashville: Broadman, 1986.

Hopkins, Dwight N. *Heart and Head: Black Theology—Past, Present and Future*. New York: Palgrave, 2002.

Hunter, James Davison. *Culture Wars: The Struggle to Define America*. New York: Basic Books, 1991.

Hurston, Zola Neale. *The Sanctified Church*. Berkeley: Turtle Island, 1981.

Hustad, Donald P. *Jubilate! Church Music in the Evangelical Tradition*. Carol Stream: Hope, 1981.

———. *Jubilate II: Church Music in Worship and Renewal*. Carol Stream: Hope, 1993.

Jackson, Irene V., ed. *Afro-American Religious Music: A Bibliography and Catalogue of Gospel Music*. Westport, CT: Greenwood, 1979.

Johansson, Calvin M. *Discipling Music Ministry: Twenty-First Century Directions*. Peabody, MA: Hendrickson, 1992.

———. *Music and Ministry: A Biblical Counterpoint*, 2nd ed. Peabody, MA: Hendrickson, 1998.

Johnson, Jason Miccolo. *Soul Sanctuary: Images of the African American Worship*. New York: Bulfinch, 2005.

Johnson, Todd E., ed. *The Conviction of Things Not Seen: Worship and Ministry in the 21st Century*. Grand Rapids: Brazos, 2002.

Jones, Arthur C. *Wade in the Water: The Wisdom on the Spirituals*. Maryknoll: Orbis, 1993.

Jones, Cheslyn, Geoffrey Wainwright, Edward Yarnold, and Paul Bradshaw, eds. *The Study of Liturgy*, rev. ed. Oxford: Oxford University Press, 1992.

Jones, Joseph. *Why We Do What We Do: Christian Worship in the African American Tradition*. Nashville: R. H. Boyd, 2006.

Jordan, James. *Evoking Sound: Fundamentals of Choral Conducting and Rehearsing*. Chicago: GIA, 1996.

———. *The Musician's Soul*. Chicago: GIA, 1999.

Keener, Craig S., and Glenn Usry. *Defending Black Faith: Answers to Tough Questions about African American Christianity*. Downers Grove: InterVarsity, 1997.

Keikert, Patrick R. *Welcoming the Stranger: A Public Theology of Worship and Evangelism*. Minneapolis: Fortress, 1992.

Kimbrough, S T, Jr. *Radical Grace: Justice for the Poor and Marginalized—Charles Wesley's View for the Twenty-First Century*. Eugene: Cascade Books, 2013.

Kinnaman, David. *You Lost Me: Why Young Christians Are Leaving the Church and Rethinking Faith*. Grand Rapids: Baker Books, 2011.

Kirk-Duggan, Cheryl A. *African American Special Days: 15 Complete Worship Services*. Nashville: Abingdon, 1996.

———. *Exorcizing Evil: A Womanist Perspective on the Spirituals*. Maryknoll: Orbis, 1997.

———. *Soul Pearls: Worship Resources for the Black Church*. Nashville: Abingdon, 2003.

Knowles, Michael P., ed. *The Folly of Preaching: Models and Methods*. Grand Rapids: Eerdmans, 2007.

Kroeker, Charlotte, ed. *Music in Christian Worship: At the Service of Liturgy*. Lanham: Rowman & Littlefield, 2009.

LaRue, Cleophus J. *I Believe I Will Testify*. Bloomington: iUniverse, 2011.

———. *The Heart of Black Preaching*. Louisville: Westminster John Knox, 2000.

Lavberton, Mark. *The Dangerous Act of Worship: Living God's Call to Justice*. Downers Grove: InterVarsity, 2007.

Lewis, Charles E., Sr. *Reconciliation of Worship in the Black Church: Spontaneous Worship*. Collegeville: Liturgical Press, 2000.

Lewis, Tamara E. *Plenty Good Room: A Bible Study Based on African American Spirituals*. Nashville: Abingdon, 2002.

Liesch, Barry. *The New Worship: Straight Talk on Music and the Church*. Grand Rapids: Baker Book, 1996.

Lincoln, Eric, and Lawrence Mamiya. *The Black Church in the African American Experience*. Durham: Duke University Press, 1990.

Long, Kimberly Bracken. *The Worshiping Body: The Art of Leading Worship*. Louisville: Westminster John Knox, 2009.

Long, Thomas. *Accompany Them with Singing: The Christian Funeral*. Louisville: Westminster John Knox, 2009.

———. *The Witness of Preaching*. Louisville: Westminster John Knox, 2005.

———. *What Shall We Say? Evil, Suffering, and the Crisis of Faith*. Grand Rapids: Eerdmans, 2011.

———, and Thomas Lynch. *The Good Funeral: Death, Grief, and the Community of Care*. Louisville: Westminster John Knox, 2013.

Lornell, Kip, ed. *From Jubilee to Hip Hop: Readings in African American Music*. Louisville: Westminster John Knox, 2004.

Lovelace, Austin C., and William C. Rice. *Music and Worship in the Church*. Nashville: Abingdon, 1976.

Lovell, John., Jr. *Black Song: The Forge and the Flame.* New York: Macmillan, 1972.

Lucarini, Dan. *It's Not about the Music: A Journey into Worship.* Carlisle, PA: EP Books USA, 2010.

Mapson, J. Wendell, Jr. *Strange Fire: A Study of Worship and Liturgy in the African American Church.* St. Louis: Hodale, 1996.

———. *The Ministry of Music in the Black Church.* Valley Forge: Judson, 1984.

Marshall, Madeleine Forell. *Common Hymnsense.* Chicago: GIA, 1995.

Marti, Gerardo. *Worship across the Racial Divide: Religious Music and the Multiracial Congregation.* New York: Oxford University Press, 2012.

Maynard-Reid, Pedrito U. *Diverse Worship: African American, Caribbean, and Hispanic Perspectives.* Downers Grove: InterVarsity, 2000.

McClain, William B. *Come Sunday: The Liturgy of Zion.* Nashville: Abingdon, 1990.

McGann, Mary E. *A Precious Fountain: Music in the Worship of an African American.* Collegeville: Liturgical Press, 2004.

———. *Let It Shine! The Emergence of African American Catholic Worship.* New York: Fordham University Press, 2008.

McGrath, Alister E. *Theology: The Basics.* Malden, MA: Blackwell, 2004.

McKinney, Lora-Ellen. *Total Praise: An Orientation to Black Baptist Belief and Worship.* Valley Forge: Judson, 2003.

Migliore, Daniel L. *Faith Seeking Understanding: An Introduction to Christian Theology.* Grand Rapids: Eerdmans, 1991.

Miller, Barbara Day. *Encounters with the Holy: A Conversational Model for Worship Planning.* Grand Rapids: Baker Academic, 2009.

———. *The New Pastor's Guide to Leading Worship.* Nashville: Abingdon, 2006.

Mitchell, Robert H. *I Don't Like That Music.* Carol Stream: Hope, 1993.

Mitchem, Stephanie. *Name It and Claim It: Prosperity Preaching in the Black Church.* Cleveland: Pilgrim, 2007.

Muchimba, Felix. *Liberating the African Soul: Comparing African and Western Christian Music and Worship Styles.* Colorado Springs: Authentic, 2007.

Music, David W., and Milburn Price. *A Survey of Christian Hymnody,* 5th ed. Carol Stream: Hope, 2011.

Myers, Kenneth A. *All God's Children and Blue Suede Shoes: Christians and Popular Culture.* Wheaton: Crossway Books, 1989.

Nelson, Timothy J. *Every Time I Feel the Spirit: Religious Experience and Ritual in African American Church.* New York: New York University Press, 2005.

Nichols, Stephen J. *Getting the Blues: What Blues Music Teaches Us about Suffering and Salvation.* Grand Rapids: Brazos, 2008.

Niebuhr, H. Richard. *Christ and Culture.* New York: Harper & Row, 1951.

Noland, Rory. *The Heart of the Artist: A Character-Building Guide for You and Your Ministry Team.* Grand Rapids: Zondervan, 1999.

Olsen, Charles M. *The Wisdom of the Seasons: How the Church Year Helps Us Understand Our Congregational Stories.* Herndon: Alban Institute, 2009.

Orr, N. Lee. *The Church Music Handbook for Pastors and Musicians.* Nashville: Abingdon, 1991.

Owens, Bill. *The Magnetic Music Ministry.* Nashville: Abingdon, 1996.

Pass, David B. *Music and the Church: A Theology of Church Music.* Nashville: Broadman, 1989.

Peretti, Burton W. *Lift Every Voice: The History of African American Music.* Lanham: Rowman & Littlefield, 2009.

Perry, Roland W., III. *The African American Church Musician's Compensation & Salary Handbook,* Eden Prairie: Ready Writer, 2004.

Pierson, Mark. *The Art of Curating Worship: Reshaping the Role of Worship Leader.* Minneapolis: Sparkhouse, 2010.

Pitts, Walter F., Jr. *Old Ship of Zion: The Afro-Baptist Ritual in the African Diaspora.* New York: Oxford University Press, 1993.

Plantinga, Cornelius, Jr. *Reading for Preaching: The Preacher in Conversation with Storytellers, Biographers, Poets, and Journalists.* Grand Rapids: Eerdmans, 2013.

———, and Sue A. Rozeboom. *Discerning the Spirits: A Guide to Thinking about Christian Worship Today.* Grand Rapids: Eerdmans, 2003.

Pollard, Deborah Smith. *When the Church Becomes Your Party: Contemporary Gospel Praise and Worship.* Detroit: Wayne State University Press, 2008.

Powery, Luke. *Dem Dry Bones: Preaching Death and Hope.* Minneapolis: Fortress, 2012.

Price, Emmett G., III, ed. *The Black Church and Hip Hop Culture: Toward Bridging the Generational Divide.* Lanham: Scarecrow, 2012.

Raboteau, Albert J. *A Fire in the Bones: Reflections on African American Religious History.* Boston: Beacon, 1995.

———. *Slave Religion: The "Invisible Institution" in the Antebellum South.* New York: Oxford University Press, 1978.

Ramshaw, Gail. *Christian Worship: 100,000 Sundays of Symbols and Rituals.* Minneapolis: Fortress, 2009.

Reagon, Bernice Johnson, ed. *We'll Understand It Better By and By: Pioneering African American Gospel Composers.* Washington DC: Smithsonian Institution, 1992.

Redman, Robb. *The Great Worship Awakening: Singing a New Song in the Postmodern Church*. San Francisco: Jossey-Bass, 2002.

Reed, Teresa L. *The Holy Profane: Religion in Black Popular Music*. Lexington: University Press of Kentucky, 2003.

Reid, Stephen Breck. *Psalms and Practice: Worship, Virtue, and Authority*. Collegeville: Liturgical Press, 2001.

Reynolds, William J., and Milburn Price. *A Survey of Christian Hymnody*. Carol Stream: Hope, 2011.

Rienstra, Debra and Ron. *Worship Words: Discipling Language for Faithful Ministry*. Grand Rapids: Baker Academic, 2009.

Roberts, William Bradley. *Music and Vital Congregations: A Practical Guide for Clergy*. New York: Church Publishing, 2009.

Routley, Erik. *A Panorama of Christian Hymnody*. Rev. and exp. Edited by Paul Richardson. Chicago: GIA, 2005.

———. *Church Music and the Christian Faith*. Carol Stream: Agape, 1978.

———. *Twentieth Century Church Music*. Carol Stream: Agape, 1964.

Ruth, Lester. *Longing for Jesus: Worship at a Black Holiness Church in Mississippi, 1895–1913*. Grand Rapids: Eerdmans, 2013.

Saliers, Don E. *Music and Theology*. Nashville: Abingdon, 2007.

———. *Worship as Theology: Foretaste of Glory Divine*. Nashville: Abingdon, 1994.

———. *Worship Come to Its Senses*. Nashville: Abingdon, 1996.

Sample, Tex. *Powerful Percussion: Multimedia Witness in Christian Worship*. Nashville: Abingdon, 2005.

Sanders, Cheryl J. *Saints in Exile: The Holiness-Pentecostal Experience in African American Religion and Culture*. New York: Oxford University Press, 1996.

Satterlee, Craig A. *When God Speaks through Worship: Stories Congregations Live By*. Herndon: Alban Institute, 2009.

Scheer, Greg. *The Art of Worship: A Musician's Guide to Leading Modern Worship*. Grand Rapids: Baker Books, 2006.

Schilling, S. Paul. *The Faith We Sing: How the Message of Hymns Can Enhance Christian Belief*. Philadelphia: Westminster, 1983.

Schmidt, Eric, and Jared Cohen. *The New Digital Age: Reshaping the Future of People, Nations and Business*. New York: Alfred A. Knopf, 2013.

Schultze, Quentin J., et al. *Dancing in the Dark: Youth, Popular Culture, and the Electronic Media*. Grand Rapids: Eerdmans, 1991.

Segler, Franklin M. *Understanding, Preparing for, and Practicing Christian Worship*, 2nd ed. Revised by Randall Bradley. Nashville: Broadman & Holman, 1996.

Senn, Frank. *Christian Liturgy: Catholic and Evangelical*. Minneapolis: Fortress, 1997.

Simmons, Martha, and Frank Thomas, eds. *Preaching with Sacred Fire: An Anthology of African American Sermons, 1750 to the Present*. New York: W. W. Norton, 2010.

Simpson, Eugene Thamon. *Hall Johnson: His Life, His Spirit and His Music*. Lanham: Scarecrow, 2008.

Smith, Efrem, and Phil Jackson. *The Hip Hop Church: Connecting with the Movement Shaping Our Culture*. Downers Grove: InterVarsity, 2005.

Smith, Kathleen S. *Stilling the Storm: Worship and Congregational Leadership in Difficult Times*. Herndon: Alban Institute, 2006.

Smith, William S. *Joyful Noise: A Guide to Music in the Church for Pastors and Musicians*. Franklin: Providence, 2007.

Southern, Eileen. *Readings in Black American Music*. New York: W. W. Norton, 1971.

———. *The Music of Black Americans: A History*, 3rd ed. New York: W. W. Norton, 1997.

Spencer, Donald A. *Hymn and Scripture Selection Guide: A Cross-Reference Tool for Worship Leaders*. Grand Rapids: Baker Book, 1993.

Spencer, Jon Michael. *Black Hymnody: A Hymnological History of the African American Church*. Knoxville: University of Tennessee Press, 1992.

———. *Protest and Praise: Sacred Music of Black Religion*. Minneapolis: Fortress, 1990.

———. *Sing a New Song: Liberating Black Hymnody*. Minneapolis: Fortress, 1995.

Spinks, Bryan D. *The Worship Mall: Contemporary Responses to Contemporary Culture*. New York: Church Publishing, 2010.

Springer, Janice. *Nurturing Spiritual Depth in Worship: Ten Practices*. San Jose: Resources Publications, 2009.

Stewart, Carlyle F., III. *African American Church Growth: 12 Principles for Prophetic Ministry*. Nashville: Abingdon, 1994.

———. *Black Spirituality and Black Consciousness: Soul Force, Culture and Freedom in the African American Experience*. Trenton: Africa World, 1999.

———. *Soul Survivors: An African American Spirituality*. Louisville: Westminster John Knox, 1997.

Synan, Vinson. *The Holiness-Pentecostal Tradition: Charismatic Movements in the Twentieth Century*. Grand Rapids: Eerdmans, 1997.

———, and Charles E. Fox, Jr. *William J. Seymour: Pioneer of the Azusa Street Revival*. Alachus, FL: Bridge-Logos, 2012.

Talbot, Frederick H. *African American Worship: New Eyes for Seeing*. Lima, OH: Fairway, 1998.

Tel, Martin, Joyce Borge, and John Witvliet. *Psalms for All Seasons: A Complete Psalter for Worship.* Grand Rapids: Faith Alive Christian Resources, 2012.

The Liturgy Documents: A Parish Resource, 3rd ed. Chicago: Liturgy Training, 1991.

The Psalms: An Inclusive Language Version Based on the Grail Translation from the Hebrew. Chicago: GIA, 2000.

The Revised Common Lectionary: The Consultation on Common Texts. Nashville: Abingdon, 1992.

Thompson, Bard. *A Bibliography of Christian Worship.* Metuchen, NJ: American Theological & Scarecrow, 1989.

Tisdale, Lenora Tubbs. *Prophetic Preaching: A Pastoral Approach.* Louisville: Westminster John Knox, 2010.

Tozer, A. W. *Tozer on Worship and Entertainment.* Compiled by James L. Snyder. Camp Hill: Christian Publications, 1997.

———. *Whatever Happened to Worship? A Call to True Worship.* Edited by Gerald B. Smith. Camp Hill, PA: WingSpread, 2006.

Twenge, Jean M., and W. Keith Campbell. *The Narcissism Epidemic: Living in the Age of Entitlement.* New York: Free Press, 2009.

Uzukwu, Elochukwu E. *Worship as Body Language: Introduction to Christian Worship: An African Orientation.* Collegeville: Liturgical Press, 1997.

Vanderwell, Howard, ed. *The Church of All Ages: Generations Worshiping Together.* Herndon: Alban Institute, 2008.

Van Dyke, Leanne. *A More Profound Alleluia: Theology and Worship in Harmony.* Grand Rapids: Eerdmans, 2004.

Vann, Jane Rogers. *Gathered Before God: Worship Center Church Renewal.* Louisville: Westminster John Knox, 2004.

Vitz, Paul C. *Psychology as Religion: The Cult of Self-Worship*, 2nd ed. Grand Rapids: Eerdmans, 1994.

Vogel, Dwight W., ed. *Primary Sources of Liturgical Theology: A Reader.* Collegeville: Liturgical Press, 2000.

Wahl, Thomas Peter. *The Lord's Song in a Foreign Land.* Collegeville: Liturgical Press, 1998.

Walker, Wyatt Tee. *Somebody's Calling My Name: Black Sacred Music and Social Change.* Valley Forge: Judson, 1979.

———. *Spirits that Dwell in Deep Woods: The Prayer and Praise Hymns of the Black Religious Experience.* Edited by James Abbington. Chicago: GIA, 2004.

Wallace, Robin Knowles. *Things They Never Tell You before You Say "Yes": The Nonmusical Tasks of the Church Musician.* Nashville: Abingdon, 1994.

Warren, Gwendolin Sims. *Ev'ry Time I Feel the Spirit: 101 Best-Loved Psalms, Gospel Hymns, and Spiritual Songs of the African American Church*. New York: Henry Holt, 1997.

Washington, James Melvin. *Conversations with God: Two Centuries of Prayers by African Americans*. New York: HarperCollins, 1994.

Watkins, Ralph C. *The Gospel Remix: Reaching the Hip Hop Generation*. Valley Forge: Judson, 2007.

Watley, William D. *Doing Church: A Practical Guide, By Those Who Do It*. Vols. 1–2. Atlanta: New Seasons, 2010.

Webber, Robert E. *Ancient-Future Time: Forming Spirituality through the Christian Year*. Grand Rapids: Baker Books, 2004.

———. *Planning Blended Worship: The Creative Mixture of Old and New*. Nashville: Abingdon, 1998.

———. *Worship Is a Verb: Eight Principles for Transforming Worship*, 2nd ed. Peabody, MA: Hendrickson, 1995.

Westermeyer, Paul. *Let Justice Sing: Hymnody and Justice*. Collegeville: Liturgical Press, 1998.

———. *Let the People Sing: Hymn Tunes in Perspective*. Chicago: GIA, 2005.

———. *Te Deum: The Church and Music*. Minneapolis: Fortress, 1998.

———. *The Church Musician*, rev. ed. Minneapolis: Augsburg Fortress, 1997.

———. *With Tongues of Fire: Profiles in 20th-Century Hymn Writing*. St. Louis: Concordia, 1995.

White, Calvin, Jr. *The Rise of Respectability: Race, Religion, and the Church of God in Christ*. Fayetteville: University of Arkansas Press, 2012.

White, Susan J. *Foundations of Christian Worship*. Louisville: Westminster John Knox, 2003.

Williams, Juan, and Quinto Dixie. *This Far by Faith: Stories from the African American Religious Experience*. New York: William Morrow, 2003.

Wilmore, Gayraud S. *Last Things First: Library of Living Faith*. Philadelphia: Westminster, 1982.

Wilson-Dickson, Andrew. *The Story of Christian Music*. Minneapolis: Fortress, 1996.

Wimberly, Anne E. Streaty. *Nurturing Faith and Hope: Black Worship as a Model for Christian Education*. Cleveland: Pilgrim, 2004.

Wimbush, Vincent L., ed. *African Americans and The Bible: Sacred Texts and Social Textures*. New York: Continuum, 2000.

Witvliet, John. *The Biblical Psalms in Christian Worship: A Brief Introduction & Guide to Resources*. Grand Rapids: Eerdmans, 2007.

———. *Worship Seeking Understanding: Window into Christian Practice*. Grand Rapids: Eerdmans, 2007.

Woods, Robert, and Brian Walrath, eds. *The Message in the Music: Studying Contemporary Worship: An African Orientation.* Collegeville: Liturgical Press, 1997.

Wren, Brian. *Praying Twice: The Music and Words of Congregational Song.* Louisville: Westminster John Knox, 2000.

Wright, Jeremiah A., Jr. *Africans Who Shaped the Faith: A Study of 10 Biblical Personalities.* Chicago: Urban Ministries, 1995.

Wuthnow, Robert. *Christianity in the 21st Century: Reflections on the Challenges Ahead.* New York: Oxford University Press, 1993.

———. *Rediscovering the Sacred: Perspectives on Religion in Contemporary Society.* Grand Rapids: Eerdmans, 1992.

Zimmerman, Joyce Ann. *Silence: Everyday Living and Praying.* Chicago: Liturgy Training, 2010.

Contributors

James Abbington
Associate Professor of Church Music and Worship, Candler School of Theology, Emory University, Atlanta, Georgia
Executive Editor, *African American Church Music Series*, GIA Publications, Inc., Chicago, Illinois

LaTrese Adkins
Adjunct Faculty, University of North Texas, Denton, Texas

Sandra L. Barnes
Professor, Department of Human and Organizational Development and the Divinity School, Vanderbilt University, Nashville, Tennessee

Tuere A. Bowles
Associate Professor,
Leadership, Policy and Adult and Higher Education Department, North Carolina State University, Raleigh, North Carolina

Ruthlyn Bradshaw
Pastor and Evangelist, Plymouth, Montserrat, West Indies

Michael Joseph Brown
Director of the Malcolm X Institute of Black Studies, Wabash College, Crawfordsville, Indiana

Melvin L. Butler
Assistant Professor, Department of Music, University of Chicago, Chicago, Illinois
Charles Augustus Briggs Distinguished Professor of Systematic Theology, Union Theological Seminary, New York, New York
David Henry Winters Luce Professor of World Christianity, McCormick Theological Seminary, Chicago, Illinois

James H. Cone
Charles Augustus Briggs Distinguished Professor of Systematic Theology, Union Theological Seminary, New York, New York

David Douglas Daniels III
David Henry Winters Luce Professor of World Christianity, McCormick Theological Seminary, Chicago, Illinois

Robert Darden
Associate Professor, Baylor University, Waco, Texas

Leo H. Davis Jr.
Director of Musical Arts, Mississippi Boulevard Christian Church, Memphis, Tennessee

Valerie Bridgeman Davis
Adjunct Professor, "Womanist Biblical Interpretation," Memphis Theological Seminary, Memphis, Tennessee
President and CEO of WomanPreach! Inc.

Michael Fox
Candidate for Master of Arts, Intercultural Studies, Worship, Theology and Arts Emphasis, Fuller Seminary, Pasadena, California

Kenyatta R. Gilbert
Associate Professor of Homiletics, Howard University School of Divinity, Washington DC

Daniel White Hodge
Director, Center for Youth Ministry Studies, Assistant Professor, North Park University, Chicago, Illinois

Birgitta J. Johnson
Assistant Professor, Ethnomusicology, School of Music & African American Studies Program, University of South Carolina, Columbia, South Carolina

Alisha Jones
PhD candidate, Ethnomusicology, Instructor in Ethnomusicology and Music History, Department of Music, University of Chicago, Chicago, Illinois

Tammy L. Kernodle
Associate Professor of Musicology, Department of Music, Miami University, Oxford, Ohio

S T Kimbrough, Jr.
Research Fellow of the Center for Studies in the Wesleyan Tradition, Duke Divinity School, Durham, North Carolina
Center of Theological Inquiry, Princeton, New Jersey

Cheryl A. Kirk-Duggan
Professor of Theology and Women's Studies, Director, Women's Studies, Shaw University Divinity School, Raleigh, North Carolina

Cleophus J. LaRue
Francis Landey Patton Professor of Homiletics, Princeton University, Princeton, New Jersey

Monica T. Leach
Associate Professor, North Carolina State University, Raleigh, North Carolina

Tamura Lomax
Assistant Chair and Assistant Professor of African American Studies, Virginia Commonwealth University, Richmond, Virginia

Contributors

Pamela P. Martin
Associate Professor and Chair, Department of Psychology, North Carolina State University, Durham, North Carolina

Marvin A. McMickle
President, Colgate Rochester Crozer Divinity School, Rochester, New York

Monica R. Miller
Postdoctoral Fellow in Religion and Popular Culture, Department of Religious Studies, Lewis and Clark College, Portland, Oregon

Stephanie Y. Mitchem
Chair, Department of Religious Studies, University of South Carolina, Columbia, South Carolina

Thomasina Neely-Chandler
Adjunct Professor, Morehouse University, Spelman College, Atlanta, Georgia

Deborah S. Pollard
Associate Professor, English Literature, University of Michigan, Dearborn, Michigan

Luke A. Powery
Dean of Duke Chapel and Associate Professor, Homiletics, Duke Divinity School, Durham, North Carolina

Samuel D. Proctor *(deceased)*
President, Virginia Union University, Richmond, Virginia
North Carolina A&T University, Greensboro, North Carolina
The Martin Luther King Jr. Professor Emeritus, Rutgers University, New Brunswick, New Jersey
Visiting Professor, Divinity School, Vanderbilt University, Nashville, Tennessee
The Samuel DeWitt Proctor School of Theology at Virginia Union University, Richmond, Virginia was named in his memory

Teresa L. Reed
Director, School of Music, Associate Professor of Music, The University of Tulsa, Tulsa, Oklahoma

Braxton D. Shelley
PhD candidate, University of Chicago, Chicago, Illinois

Martha Simmons
Associate Minister, Rush Memorial United Church of Christ, Atlanta, Georgia

Josef Sorett
Assistant Professor, Columbia University, New York, New York

Rodney A. Teal
Pastor, Jerusalem Baptist Church, Washington DC

Frank Thomas
The Nettie Sweeney and Hugh Thomas Miller Professor of Homiletics
and Director of the Academy of Preaching and Celebration,
Christian Theological Seminary, Indianapolis, Indiana

Kathleen S. Turner
PhD candidate, Religion and Religious Education, Fordham University, Bronx, New York

Kenneth C. Ulmer
Senior Pastor-Teacher, Faithful Central Bible Church, Inglewood, California
President, The King's College and Seminary, Los Angeles, California

Gayle Wald
Professor and Chair of English, George Washington University, Washington DC
Professor, Church History, Union Theological Seminary and Columbia University,
New York, New York

James Melvin Washington *(deceased)*
Professor, Church History, Union Theological Seminary and Columbia University,
New York, New York

Ralph C. Watkins
Associate Professor of Evangelism and Church Growth, Columbia Theological Seminary,
Decatur, Georgia

Lisa M. Weaver
Doctoral candidate, Liturgical Studies/Sacramental Theology, Catholic University of America,
Washington DC

Melinda E. Weekes
Managing Director, Race Forward (formerly Applied Research Center), New York, New York
Gospel Music Theorist, Weekes In Advance Enterprises, New York, New York

Christina Zanfagna
Assistant Professor, Music Department and Ethnic Studies, Santa Clara University,
Santa Clara, California